ABOUT THE COVER

The cover of this book captures the dynamic nature of retailing. Retailing is evolving into a global, high-tech industry. Customers are interacting with retailers—seeking information and buying merchandise—through multiple channels, such as PDAs, computers, web-enabled kiosks, telephone lines to call centers, and stores. Retailers are using sophisticated technologies and information systems to improve the customer's shopping experience, reduce their costs, and provide better value. This edition captures the excitement in retailing and a view of the future for students as shoppers and retail managers.

Levy Weitz

RETAILING
MANAGEMENT

THE McGRAW-HILL/IRWIN SERIES IN MARKETING

Arens
Contemporary Advertising
Ninth Edition

Arnould, Price, & Zinkhan
Consumers
Second Edition

Bearden, Ingram, & LaForge
Marketing: Principles & Perspectives
Fourth Edition

Belch & Belch
Advertising & Promotion: An Integrated
Marketing Communications Approach
Sixth Edition

Bingham & Gomes
Business Marketing Management
Second Edition

Boyd, Walker, Mullins, & Larreche
Marketing Management: A Strategic
Decision-Making Approach
Fourth Edition

Cateora & Graham
International Marketing
Eleventh Edition

Cole & Mishler
Consumer and Business Credit
Management
Eleventh Edition

Cravens & Piercy
Strategic Marketing
Seventh Edition

Cravens, Lamb, & Crittenden
Strategic Marketing Management Cases
Seventh Edition

Crawford & Di Benedetto
New Products Management
Seventh Edition

Dolan
Marketing Management: Text and Cases
First Edition

Duncan
IMC: Using Advertising and Promotion
to Build Brands
First Edition

Dwyer & Tanner
Business Marketing
Second Edition

Eisenmann
Internet Business Models: Text and Cases
First Edition

Etzel, Walker, & Stanton
Marketing
Twelfth Edition

Forrest
Internet Marketing Intelligence
First Edition

Futrell
ABC's of Relationship Selling
Eighth Edition

Futrell
Fundamentals of Selling
Seventh Edition

Hair, Bush, & Ortinau
Marketing Research
Second Edition

Hawkins, Best, & Coney
Consumer Behavior
Ninth Edition

Johansson
Global Marketing
Third Edition

Johnston & Marshall
Churchill/Ford/Walker's Sales Force
Management
Seventh Edition

Kerin, Hartley, & Rudelius
Marketing: The Core
First Edition

Kerin, Berkowitz, Hartley, & Rudelius
Marketing
Seventh Edition

Lehmann & Winer
Analysis for Marketing Planning
Fifth Edition

Lehmann & Winer
Product Management
Third Edition

Levy & Weitz
Retailing Management
Fifth Edition

Mason & Perreault
The Marketing Game!
Third Edition

McDonald
Direct Marketing: An Integrated
Approach
First Edition

Mohammed, Fisher, Jaworski, & Cahill
Internet Marketing: Building Advantage
in a Networked Economy
Second Edition

Monroe
Pricing
Third Edition

Pelton, Strutton, & Lumpkin
Marketing Channels: A Relationship
Management Approach
Second Edition

Peppers & Rogers
Managing Customer Relationships
to Build Competitive Advantage
First Edition

Perreault & McCarthy
Basic Marketing: A Global Managerial
Approach
Fourteenth Edition

Perreault & McCarthy
Essentials of Marketing: A Global
Managerial Approach
Ninth Edition

Peter & Donnelly
A Preface to Marketing Management
Ninth Edition

Peter & Donnelly
Marketing Management: Knowledge
and Skills
Seventh Edition

Peter & Olson
Consumer Behavior
Sixth Edition

Purvis & Burton
Which Ad Pulled Best?
Ninth Edition

Rayport & Jaworski
Introduction to e-Commerce
Second Edition

Rayport & Jaworski
e-Commerce
First Edition

Rayport & Jaworski
Cases in e-Commerce
First Edition

Richardson
Internet Marketing
First Edition

Roberts
Internet Marketing: Integrating Online
and Offline Strategies
First Edition

Spiro, Stanton, & Rich
Management of a Sales Force
Eleventh Edition

Stock & Lambert
Strategic Logistics Management
Fourth Edition

Ulrich & Eppinger
Product Design and Development
Second Edition

Walker, Boyd, Mullins, & Larreche
Marketing Strategy: A Decision-Focused
Approach
Fourth Edition

Weitz, Castleberry, & Tanner
Selling: Building Partnerships
Fifth Edition

Zeithaml & Bitner
Services Marketing
Third Edition

ii

RETAILING MANAGEMENT

FIFTH EDITION

Michael Levy, Ph.D.
Babson College

Barton A. Weitz, Ph.D.
University of Florida

 Irwin

Boston   Burr Ridge, IL   Dubuque, IA   Madison, WI   New York   San Francisco   St. Louis
Bangkok   Bogotá   Caracas   Kuala Lumpur   Lisbon   London   Madrid   Mexico City
Milan   Montreal   New Delhi   Santiago   Seoul   Singapore   Sydney   Taipei   Toronto

RETAILING MANAGEMENT

Published by McGraw-Hill/Irwin, a business unit of The McGraw-Hill Companies, Inc.; 1221 Avenue of the Americas, New York, NY, 10020. Copyright © 2004, 2001, 1998, 1995, 1992 by The McGraw-Hill Companies, Inc. All rights reserved. No part of this publication may be reproduced or distributed in any form or by any means, or stored in a database or retrieval system, without the prior written consent of The McGraw-Hill Companies, Inc., including, but not limited to, in any network or other electronic storage or transmission, or broadcast for distance learning.

Some ancillaries, including electronic and print components, may not be available to customers outside the United States.

This book is printed on acid-free paper.

domestic 1 2 3 4 5 6 7 8 9 0 DOW/DOW 0 9 8 7 6 5 4 3
international 1 2 3 4 5 6 7 8 9 0 DOW/DOW 0 9 8 7 6 5 4 3

ISBN 0-07-249720-3

Publisher: *John E. Biernat*
Executive editor: *Linda Schreiber*
Managing developmental editor: *Nancy Barbour*
Marketing manager: *Kimberly Kanakes*
Media producer: *Craig Atkins*
Senior project manager: *Christine A. Vaughan*
Senior production supervisor: *Rose Hepburn*
Director of design BR: *Keith J. McPherson*
Photo research coordinator: *Ira C. Roberts*
Photo researcher: *Mike Hruby*
Lead supplement producer: *Cathy L. Tepper*
Senior digital content specialist: *Brian Nacik*
Cover design: *Keith J. McPherson*
Cover and interior spot illustrations: *Doug Ross, Lori Nowicki & Associates*
Interior design: *Maureen McCutcheon*
Typeface: *10.5/12 Janson*
Compositor: *Shepherd-Imagineering Media Services Inc.*
Printer: *R. R. Donnelley*

Library of Congress Cataloging-in Publication Data

Levy, Michael.
    Retailing management / Michael Levy, Barton A. Weitz.—5th ed.
      p. cm.—(The McGraw-Hill/Irwin series in marketing)
    ISBN 0-07-249720-3 (alk. paper)—ISBN 007121481X (international : alk. paper)
      1. Retail trade—Management. I. Weitz, Barton A. II. Title. III. Series.
  HF5429.L4828 2004
  658.8'7—dc21

                                      2002044483

INTERNATIONAL EDITION ISBN 0-07-121481-X
Copyright © 2004. Exclusive rights by The McGraw-Hill Companies, Inc. for manufacture and export. This book cannot be re-exported from the country to which it is sold by McGraw-Hill. The International Edition is not available in North America.

www.mhhe.com

To George Kessler (1915–2002), loving father, whose entrepreneurial spirit and creative retailing energy has always been my inspiration.
Michael Levy

To Helen Weitz, who at 87, still knows what's a bargain and what is not.
Barton Weitz

To Eleanore Snow, our first developmental editor at Irwin, whose assistance, understanding, and patience was invaluable in creating this textbook.

ABOUT THE AUTHORS

Michael Levy, PhD
Babson College
mlevy@babson.edu

Michael Levy, PhD, is the Charles Clarke Reynolds Professor of Marketing at Babson College and co-editor of *Journal of Retailing.* He received his PhD in business administration from The Ohio State University and his undergraduate and MS degrees in business administration from the University of Colorado at Boulder. He taught at Southern Methodist University before joining the faculty as professor and chair of the marketing department at the University of Miami. He has taught retailing management for 25 years.

Professor Levy has developed a strong stream of research in retailing, business logistics, financial retailing strategy, pricing, and sales management that has been published in over 40 articles in leading marketing and logistics journals, including the *Journal of Retailing, Journal of Marketing,* and *Journal of Marketing Research.* He currently serves on the editorial review board of the *Journal of Retailing, Journal of the Academy of Marketing Science, International Journal of Logistics Management,* and the *International Journal of Logistics and Materials Management.*

Professor Levy has worked in retailing and related disciplines throughout his professional life. Prior to his academic career, he worked for several retailers and a housewares distributor in Colorado. He has performed research projects with many retailers, including Accenture, Burdines Department Stores, Mervyn's, Neiman Marcus, and Zale Corporation.

Barton A. Weitz, PhD
University of Florida
bart.weitz@cba.ufl.edu

Barton A. Weitz, PhD, received an undergraduate degree in electrical engineering from MIT and an MBA and a PhD in business administration from Stanford University. He has been a member of the faculty at the UCLA Graduate School of Business and the Wharton School at the University of Pennsylvania. He is presently the JCPenney Eminent Scholar Chair in Retail Management in the Warrington College of Business Administration at the University of Florida.

Professor Weitz is the executive director of the David F. Miller Center for Retailing Education and Research at the University of Florida. The activities of the center are supported by contributions from 30 national and regional retailers, including JCPenney, Sears, Burdines, Richs, Macy's, Wal-Mart, Famous Footwear, Helzberg Diamonds, Home Depot, and Office Depot. Each year the center places over 200 undergraduates in paid summer internships and management trainee positions with retail firms and funds research on retailing issues and problems.

Professor Weitz has won awards for teaching excellence and has made numerous presentations to industry and academic groups. He has published over 50 articles in leading academic journals on electronic retailing, salesperson effectiveness, sales force and human resource management, and channel relationships. He is on the editorial review boards of the *Journal of Retailing, Journal of Interactive Marketing, International Journal of Research in Marketing,* and *Journal of Marketing Research.* He is a former editor of the *Journal of Marketing Research* and is presently co-editor of *Marketing Letters.*

Professor Weitz is the chair of the American Marketing Association and a member of the board of directors of the National Retail Federation, the National Retail Foundation, and the American Marketing Association. In 1989 he was honored as the AMA/Irwin Educator of the Year in recognition of his contributions to the marketing discipline.

In this fifth edition of *Retailing Management*, we have responded to three important developments in retailing. First, retailers are increasing the sophistication of retail operations and decision-making tools for coordinating their supply chains, buying merchandise, and managing store operations. They are using customer databases and decision support systems to tailor assortments to local markets, schedule sales associates, set prices for merchandise, and target promotions to customers.

Second, retailers are increasingly looking to international markets for growth opportunities. For instance, Carrefour, France's hypermarket chain, is the second-largest retailer in the world and operates in 25 countries. To compete globally, retailers must be tuned to the needs of their local markets but exploit the scale economies gained through centralized purchasing and common systems.

Finally, both large and small store-based and catalog retailers are making significant investments in the Internet channel to communicate with and sell merchandise and services to their customers. Retailers are striving to provide a seamless shopping experience for their customers whether they shop in their stores, place orders from catalogs, or purchase merchandise from their websites.

Our objective in preparing this fifth edition is to capture this excitement and challenge in the retail industry as we inform students about the state-of-the-art management practices of these important institutions in our society. In preparing the fifth edition, we have made a number of changes to reflect the evolving nature of retailing.

NEW FEATURES IN THE FIFTH EDITION

New Chapter on Customer Relationship Management   The new Chapter 11 examines how retailers are using customer databases to build repeat business and realize a greater share of wallet from key customers. These customer relationship management activities exploit the 80–20 rule—20 percent of the customers account for 80 percent of the sales and profits. In this chapter, we discuss how retailers identify their best customers and target these customers with special promotions and customer services. Some topics covered in this new chapter are

- Why retailers want to provide special services for their best customers.
- How retailers use customer databases to determine who are their best customers.
- How retailers build loyalty from their best customers.
- What retailers do to increase their share of wallet.
- How retailers balance customer privacy concerns with the provision of personalized promotions and services.

New Chapter on Multichannel Retailing   The new Chapter 3 describes the opportunities and challenges retailers face interacting with customers through multiple channels—stores, catalogs, and the Internet. While the e-commerce bubble has burst for e-retailing entrepreneurs, traditional retailers are investing in using the Internet to complement their stores. In this chapter, we discuss the unique issues that store-based retailers face when communicating with and selling merchandise to customers over the Internet. This new chapter addresses issues such as

- The unique customer benefits offered to customers by the different channels—stores, catalogs, and the Internet.
- How multichannel retailers provide more value to their customers.
- Factors that will affect the growth of the Internet channel.
- Why most pure electronic retailers fail.
- The key success factors in multichannel retailing.
- How might technology affect the future shopping experience.

More Extensive Treatment of New Technologies and Methods   Retailers are using innovations to improve operating efficiencies and deliver more value to their customers. Some examples of these retail innovations reviewed in the fifth edition are

- Use of the Internet to provide information and sell products and services to customers (Chapter 3).
- Application of geographic information system (GIS) technology for store location (Chapter 8).
- Internet applications for effective human resource management (Chapter 9).
- Quick response supply chain management systems (Chapter 10).
- Analysis of customer databases to determine customer lifetime value (Chapter 11).
- Implementation of frequent shopper programs (Chapter 11).
- CPFR (collaboration, planning, forecasting and replenishment) systems (Chapter 12).
- Sophisticated inventory management systems (Chapter 13).
- Reverse auctions for buying merchandise (Chapter 14).
- Use of profit optimization decision support systems for setting prices in different markets and taking markdowns (Chapter 15).
- Development of targeted promotions using customer databases (Chapter 16).
- Decision support systems for scheduling sales associates (Chapter 17).
- Creation of planograms to optimize the sales and profits from merchandise categories (Chapter 18).
- Use of in-store kiosks and the Internet to improve customer service (Chapter 19).

Greater Emphasis on International Retailing   We examine international retailing strategies ranging from those used to enter new international markets to the global sourcing of merchandise. The expanded number of international retail examples are designated with a special global icon. As retailing evolves into a global industry, it is imperative that students understand how firms adapt their business practices to the cultural and infrastructure differences in international markets. The fifth edition includes expanded treatment of non-U.S. global retailers such as Zara, Sephora, H&M, and Carrefour as well as discussions of issues confronting U.S. retailers as they expand from their domestic base. For example,

- Cultural impacts on buying behavior (Chapter 4).
- Keys to successful entry into international markets (Chapter 5).
- Evaluation of international growth opportunities (Chapter 6).
- Global sourcing of merchandise (Chapter 14).
- Employee management issues in international markets (Chapters 9 and 17).

Expanded Treatment of Brand Development Issues   To differentiate their offering and build a competitive advantage, retailers are placing more emphasis on developing their brand image, building a strong image for their private-label merchandise, and extending their image to new retail formats. Issues related to the development of brand images and private-label merchandise are discussed in more detail from both a merchandise management and a communications perspective.

Updated Material on Legal and Ethical Issues Confronting Retailers
These issues include store design in light of the American with Disabilities Act (ADA), sexual harassment, discrimination in hiring and promotions, managing diversity, glass ceilings, and purchasing and pricing merchandise.

Go Out and Do It! Exercises   Found at the end of each chapter, these exercises suggest projects that students can undertake by either visiting local retail stores, surfing the Internet, or using the Student CD accompanying the textbook. The exercises are designed to provide a hands-on learning experience for students.

Monthly Newsletter with Short Cases   These cases are based on recent retailing articles appearing in the business and trade press. Instructors can use these short cases to stimulate class discussions on current issues confronting retailers. The newsletter is e-mailed to instructors and archived on the text's webpage.

Fifteen New Cases   These include cases on Sephora, American Eagle Outfitters, Gadzooks, Dollar General, Abercrombie & Fitch, Enterprise Rent-a-Car, Home Depot, Build-A-Bear, Nordstrom, Avon, Sears, and Toys "R" Us Online. All of the 31 cases in the textbook are either new or updated with current information. A number of the cases have 10- to 12-minute videos complementing the written case.

Completely Redesigned Student CD   The CD contains four new exercises. It now provides an opportunity for students to evaluate international markets, examine the financial performance of a retailer, edit the assortment in a merchandise category, develop a merchandise budget plan, and evaluate various markdown strategies.

READER-FRIENDLY TEXTBOOK

In the fifth edition, we continued our attempt to interest and involve students in the course and the industry by making the textbook a "good read" through the use of Refacts (retailing factoids), Retailing Views, and retail manager profiles at the beginning of each chapter.

Refacts   We have updated and added more interesting facts about retailing, called Refacts, in the margin of each chapter. Did you know that a Montgomery Ward buyer created Rudolph the Red-Nosed Reindeer as a Christmas promotion in 1939? Or that the teabag was developed by a Macy's buyer and pantyhose was developed by a JCPenney buyer?

Retailing Views   Each chapter contains new and updated vignettes called Retailing Views to relate concepts to activities and decisions made by retailers. The vignettes look at major retailers like Wal-Mart, Walgreens, Sears, JCPenney, Macy's, Neiman Marcus, and Home Depot, which interview students on campus for management training positions. They also discuss innovative retailers like REI, Starbucks, the Container Store, Sephora, Harry Rosen, Wet Seal, Chico's, and the Bass Pro Shop.

Profile of Retail Managers   To illustrate the challenges and opportunities in retailing, each chapter in the fifth edition begins with a brief profile of a manager or industry expert whose jobs or expertise is related to the material in the chapter. These profiles range from Bruce Nelson, CEO of Office Depot, to Stephanie Calhoun, a senior assistant buyer at JCPenney. They include people who have extensive experience in a specific aspect of retailing like Kevin Brailesford (vice president of store environment for Blockbuster) and Debbie Harvey (director of merchandise buying for Ron Jon Surf Shops). These profiles illustrate both how senior executives view the industry and the career opportunities for college students. They provide students with firsthand information about what people in retailing do and their rewards and challenges.

Website for Students and Instructors (www.mhhe.com/levyweitz)   Just as retailers are using the Internet to help their customers, we have developed a website to help students and instructors use the fifth edition of this textbook effectively. Some of the features on the website are

- Multiple-choice questions on the student site.
- Chapter-by-chapter Instructor Manual coverage.
- Case and video notes.
- Retailing trade publications and professional associations.
- News articles about current events in retailing.
- PowerPoint slides summarizing key issues in each chapter.
- Hot links to retailing news sites and sites associated with the Internet exercises in the textbook.
- Additional cases about retailers.

The fifth edition of *Retailing Management* maintains the basic philosophy of the previous four editions. We continue to focus on the broad spectrum of retailers, both large and small retailers selling merchandise or services. The text examines key strategic issues with an emphasis on the financial considerations and store management issues. We include descriptive, how-to, and conceptual material.

Broad Spectrum of Retailing   In this text, we define retailing as the set of business activities that add value to the products and services sold to consumers for their personal or family use. Thus, in addition to the products in stores, this text examines the issues facing service retailers like Starbucks and Ritz-Carlton Hotels and nonstore retailers like eBay, Lands' End, and Avon.

Critical Issues in Retailing   Strategic thinking and the consideration of financial implications are critical for success in the present dynamic, highly competitive retail environments. In addition, operations and store management are playing an increasingly important role.

Strategic Perspective   The entire textbook is organized around a model of strategic decision making outlined in Exhibit 1–6 in Chapter 1. Each section and chapter is related back to this overarching strategic framework. In addition, the second section of the book focuses exclusively on critical strategic decisions such as selecting target markets, developing a sustainable competitive advantage, and building an organizational structure and information and distribution systems to support the strategic direction.

Financial Analysis   The financial aspects of retailing are becoming increasingly important. The financial problems experienced by some of the largest retail firms like Kmart highlight the need for a thorough understanding of the financial implications of retail decisions. Financial analysis is emphasized in selected chapters, such as Chapter 6 on the overall strategy of the firm, Chapter 11 on the evaluation of customer lifetime value, and Chapter 13 on retail buying systems. Financial issues are also raised in the sections on negotiating leases, bargaining with suppliers, pricing merchandise, developing a communication budget, and compensating salespeople.

Operations and Store Management   Traditionally, retailers have exalted the merchant prince—the buyer who knew what the hot trends were going to be. This text, by devoting an entire chapter to information systems and supply chain management and an entire section to store management, reflects the changes that have occurred over the past 10 years—the shift in emphasis from merchandise management to the block and tackling of getting merchandise to the stores and customers and providing excellent customer services and an exciting shopping experience. Due to this shift toward store management, most students embarking on retail careers go into store management rather than merchandise buying.

BALANCED APPROACH

The fifth edition continues to offer a balanced approach for teaching an introductory retailing course by including descriptive, how-to, and conceptual information in a highly readable format.

Descriptive Information   Students can learn about the vocabulary and practice of retailing from the descriptive information throughout the text. Examples of this material are

- Leading U.S. and international retailers (Chapter 1).
- Management decisions made by retailers (Chapter 1).
- Types of store-based and nonstore retailers (Chapter 2).
- Approaches for entering international markets (Chapter 5).
- Locations (Chapter 7).
- Organization structure of typical retailers (Chapter 9).
- Flow of information and merchandise (Chapter 10).
- Branding strategies (Chapter 14).
- Methods for communicating with customers (Chapter 16).
- Store layout options and merchandise display equipment (Chapter 18).
- Career opportunities (Appendix 1A to Chapter 1).

How-to Information   *Retailing Management* goes beyond this descriptive information to illustrate how and why retailers, large and small, make decisions. Step-by-Step procedures with examples are provided for making the following decisions:

- Comparison shopping (Appendix 2A to Chapter 2).
- Managing a multichannel outreach to customers (Chapter 3).
- Scanning the environment and developing a retail strategy (Chapter 5).
- Analyzing the financial implications of retail strategy (Chapter 6).
- Evaluating location decisions (Chapter 8).
- Developing a merchandise assortment and budget plan (Chapters 12 and 13).
- Negotiating with vendors (Chapter 14).
- Pricing merchandise (Chapter 15).
- Recruiting, selecting, training, evaluating, and compensating sales associates (Chapter 17).
- Designing the layout for a store (Chapter 18).

Conceptual Information   *Retailing Management* also includes conceptual information that enables students to understand why decisions are made as outlined in the text. As Mark Twain said, "There is nothing as practical as a good theory." Students need to know these basic concepts so they can make effective decisions in new situations. Examples of this conceptual information in the fourth edition are

- Retail evolution theories (Appendix 2B to Chapter 2).

- Customers' decision-making process (Chapter 4).

- Market attractiveness/competitive position matrix for evaluating strategic alternatives (Appendix 5A to Chapter 5).

- Activity-based costing analysis of merchandise categories (Appendix 6A to Chapter 6).

- The strategic profit model (Chapter 6).

- Price theory and marginal analysis (Chapters 15 and 16).

- The gaps model for service quality management (Chapter 19).

Supplemental Materials   To improve the student learning experience, the fifth edition includes new cases and videos illustrating state-of-the-art retail practices, a computer exercise package for students, and a comprehensive instructor's manual with additional cases and teaching suggestions.

ACKNOWLEDGMENTS

Throughout the development of this text, several outstanding individuals were integrally involved and made substantial contributions. We wish to express our sincere appreciation to Ngoc-Giao Nguyen (Babson College) and Cecilia Schulz, Kathy Brown, Margaret Jones, and Betsy Trobaugh (David F. Miller Center for Retailing Education and Research, University of Florida) who provided invaluable assistance in preparing the manuscript. Gopal Iyer (Florida Atlantic University) for preparing the Instructor's Manual, and Cecelia Schult for preparing the test bank and PowerPoint slides on the Instructor's CD. Our special thanks is also extended to Ross Petty (Babson College), who made sure the legal issues sections were up to date; Kathleen Seiders (Babson College), who helped in the preparation of Appendix 6A on activity-based costing; and Andrea L. Godfrey (University of Texas at Austin), who assisted in the preparation of Chapter 6.

The support, expertise, and occasional coercion from our sponsoring editor, Linda Schreiber, and senior development editor, Nancy Barbour, are greatly appreciated. The book would also never have come together without the editorial and production staff at McGraw-Hill/Irwin: Kim Kanakes, Craig Atkins, Mike Hruby, Steve Gomes, Cathy Tepper, Ira Roberts, Keith McPherson, Rose Hepburn, and Christine Vaughan.

Retailing Management has also benefited significantly from contributions by several leading executives and scholars in retailing and related fields. We would like to thank

William Alcorn
JCPenney

Robert Beall
Beall's Inc.

Tony Burns
ESRI

Mike Buskey
Home Depot

Cynthia Cohen
Strategic Mindshare

Anne Collins
Office Depot

Bob Dietrich
BFS Retail & Commercial Operations, LLC

Scott C. Friend
ProfitLogic

Bryan Gildenberg
MVentures

Jakki Gilvicky
ProfitLogic

John Gremer
Walgreens

Dhruv Grewat
Babson College

Tom Gruen
University of Colorado at Colorado Springs

Linda Hyde
Retail Forward

George Kehl
KPMG LLP

Steven Kirn
Consultant

Steve Knopik
Beall's Inc.

Doug Koch
Famous Footwear

Mary Lwin
National University of Singapore

Bruce Mager
Macy's East

Richard A. McAllister
Florida Retail Federation

Kathleen McManus
Rich's/Lazarus/Goldsmith's

Tracey Mullins
National Retail Federation

Bruce Nelson
Office Depot

Mike Odell
Sears, Roebuck & Company

Ken Ouimet
KhiMetrics

Tim Ouimet
KhiMetrics

Jan Owens
University of Wisconsin–Parkside

Coleman Peterson
Wal-Mart

Susan Reda
Stores *Magazine*

Tom Redd
Retek

Donald Rome
Retek

Ann Rupert
Burdines

Ron Sacino
Sacino's Formalwear

Carol Sanger
Federated Department Stores

Lori Schafer
Marketmax

Bryon Schllaci
Retek

Ayal Steinberg
ProfitLogic

Armanda Thomas
Marketmax

John Thomas
Pinch-A-Penney

Suzanne Voorhees
The Grapevine Group

Mike Wilson
Marketmax

Bruce Zarkowsky
Walgreens

The fifth edition of *Retailing Management* has benefited from the reviews of several leading scholars and teachers of retailing and related disciplines. Together, these reviewers spent hundreds of hours reading and critiquing the manuscript. We gratefully acknowledge

Mark Abel
Kirkwood Community College

Jill Attaway
Illinois State University

Willard Broucek
Northern State University

Donald W. Caudill
Bluefield State College

James Clark
Northeastern State University

Drew Ehrlich
Fulton-Montgomery Community College

Susan Harmon
Middle Tennessee State University

Kae Hineline
McLennan Community College

David Horne
CSU-Long Beach

Michael Jones
Auburn University

Bryan D. Little
KY

Ann Lucht
Milwaukee Area Technical College

Tony Mayo
George Mason University

Michael McGinnis
University of South Alabama

Phyliss McGinnis
Boston University

Cheryl O'Hara
Kings College

Janis Petronis
Tarleton State University

Sue Riha
University of Texas–Austin

Steve Solesbee
Aiken Technical College

Janet Wagner
Robert H. Smith School of Business

Gary Walk
Lima Technical College

Mary Weber
University of New Mexico

Fred T. Whitman
Mary Washington College

Merv Yeagle
University of Maryland

We also thank the following reviewers for their diligence and insight in helping us prepare previous editions:

Mary Barry
Auburn University

Lance A. Bettencourt
Indiana University

Jeff Blodgett
University of Mississippi

George W. Boulware
Lipscomb University

Leroy M. Buckner
Florida Atlantic University

David J. Burns
Purdue University

Lon Camomile
Colorado State University

J. Joseph Cronin, Jr.
Florida State University

Irene J. Dickey
University of Dayton

Ann DuPont
University of Texas

Chloe I. Elmgren
Mankato State University

Richard L. Entrikin
George Mason University

Kenneth R. Evans
University of Missouri–Columbia

Richard Feinberg
Purdue University

Kevin Fertig
University of Illinois

David M. Georgoff
Florida Atlantic University

Peter Gordon
Southeast Missouri State University

Larry Gresham
Texas A&M University

Tom Gross
University of Wisconsin

Michael D. Hartline
Louisana State University

Tony L. Henthorne
University of Southern Mississippi

Eugene J. Kangas
Winona State University

Herbert Katzenstein
St. John's University

Terrence Kroeten
North Dakota State University

Elizabeth Mariotz
Philadelphia College of Textiles and Science

Harold McCoy
Virginia Commonwealth University

Kim McKeage
University of Maine

Robert Miller
Central Michigan University

Mary Anne Milward
University of Arizona

John J. Porter
West Virginia University

Nick Saratakes
Austin Community College

Laura Scroggins
California State University–Chico

Shirley M. Stretch
California State University–LA

William R. Swinyard
Brigham Young University

Janet Wagner
University of Maryland

Ron Zallocco
University of Toledo

We received cases from professors all over the world. Although we would like to have used more cases in the text and the Instructor's Manual, space was limited. We would like to thank all who contributed but are especially appreciative of the following authors whose cases were used in *Retailing Management* or in the Instructor's Manual:

Ronald Adams
University of North Florida

Laura Bliss
Stephens College

Valerie Bryan
University of Florida

James Camerius
Northern Michigan University

Sue Cullers
Tarleton State University

David Ehrlich
Marymount University

Sunil Erevelles
University of North Carolina, Charlotte

Ann Fairhurst
Indiana University

Linda F. Felicetti
Clarion University

Susan Fournier
Harvard Business School

Joseph P. Grunewald
Clarion University

K. Douglas Hoffman
University of North Carolina–Wilmington

Kirthi Kalyanam
Santa Clara University

Dilip Karer
University of North Florida

Hean Tat Keh
National University, Singapore

GUIDED TOUR

For four editions, Retailing Management has been known for its strategic focus, application orientation, decision-making emphasis, and current coverage. The authors and McGraw-Hill/Irwin are proud to introduce the fifth edition and invite you to see how this new edition has been built on the book's strong foundation.

A new chapter on **multi-channel marketing** describes the opportunities and challenges retailers face interacting with customers through multiple channels- stores, catalogs, and the Internet.

A timely and important discussion of **Customer Relationship Management** is introduced in its own chapter, new to this edition.

We have extended the coverage of **new technologies and methods** to underscore their importance and ubiquity. Featured technologies include: the Internet; Geographic Information Systems; Quick Response supply chain management; collaboration, planning, forecasting, and replenishment systems, reverse auctions, profit optimizing decision support systems, and customer databases.

In keeping with the evolution of retailing into a global industry, the fifth edition increases the emphasis on **International Retailing** through an expanded number of international retail examples and broader treatment of non-U.S. retailers such as Zara, Sephora, H&M, and Carrefour.

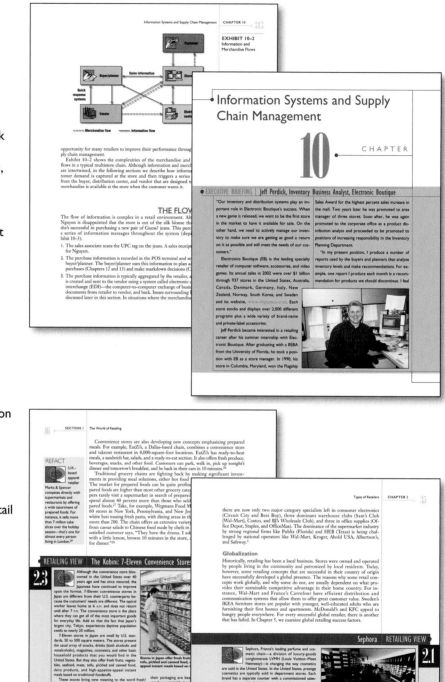

Refacts (retail factoids) are interesting facts about retailing that are found in the margins. They break up the text and provide students with an interesting break. For instance, did you know that a Montgomery Ward buyer created Rudolph, the Red-Nosed Reindeer as a Christmas promotion in 1939? Or, that the teabag was developed by a buyer for Macy's?

Retailing Views are vignettes in each chapter that relate the concepts discussed in the case to decisions made by retailers. These vignettes include major retailers like Wal-Mart, Walgreens, Sears, JCPenney, Macy's, Neiman Marcus, and Home Depot that interview students on campus for management training positions; innovative retailers like REI, Starbucks, The Container Store, Sephora, Harry Rosen, Wet Seal, Chico's, and The Bass Pro Shop.

Of the **31 cases** in the text, 15 of them are completely new and the remainder are completely updated with current information.

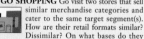

Get Out and Do It! at the end of each chapter suggest hands-on projects that students can complete either by visiting a local retailer, using the Internet, or working with the student CD-ROM.

GET OUT & DO IT!

1. **INTERNET EXERCISE** Visit the websites for Kohl's (www.kohls.com) and Restoration Hardware (www.restorationhardware.com). Do these sites reflect the retail strategies for the companies as discussed here?

2. **INTERNET EXERCISE** Go to the websites for Wal-Mart (www.walmartstores.com), Carrefour (www.carrefour.com), Royal Ahold (www.ahold.com), and Metro AG (www.metro.de). Which chain has the most global strategy? Justify your answer.

3. **INTERNET EXERCISE** Choose your favorite national retail chain. Pick a country for it to enter. Using information found on the Internet, collect information on that country and the retailer. Develop a report that analyzes whether or not the retailer should enter the country, and if so, how it should do so.

4. **GO SHOPPING** Go visit two stores that sell similar merchandise categories and cater to the same target segment(s). How are their retail formats similar? Dissimilar? On what bases do they have a sustainable competitive advantage? Explain which you believe has a stronger position.

5. **GO SHOPPING** Develop a strategic plan for your favorite retailer. Go to the store. Observe and interview the store manager. Supplement your visit with information available online through Hoovers, the store's website (which should include its annual report), and other published sources.

6. **CD EXERCISE** Go to your student CD and click on Market Position Matrix.

Exercise 1: This spread sheet reproduces the analysis of international growth opportunities discussed in the appendix to chapter 5. What numbers in the matrices would have to change to make China and France more attractive opportunities? To make Brazil and Mexico less attractive opportunities? Change the numbers in the matrices and see what effect it has on the overall position of the opportunity in the grid.

Exercise 2: The market attractiveness/competitive position matrix can also be used by a department store to evaluate merchandise categories and determine how much investment should be made in each category. Fill in the importance weights (10 = very important, 1 = not very important) and the evaluations of the merchandise categories (10 = excellent, 1 = poor) and then see what is recommended by the plot on the opportunity matrix.

Exercise 3: Think of another investment decision that a retailer might make and analyze it using the strategic analysis matrix. List the alternatives, the characteristics of the alternatives, and then put in the importance weights for the characteristics (10 = very important, 1 = not very important), and the evaluation of each alternative on each characteristic (10 = excellent, 1=poor).

The **free Student CD-ROM** packaged with each copy of the text provides students the opportunity to evaluate international markets, examine the financial performance of a retailer, edit the assortment in a merchandise category, develop a merchandise budget plan, and evaluate the desirability of various markdown strategies though interactive spreadsheets and simulations.

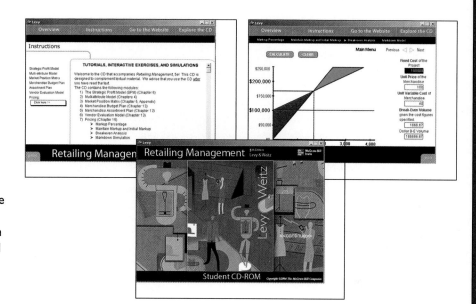

The **Online Learning Center's Instructor's Center** is a website that includes the Instructor's Manual, the PageOut course management system, PowerPoint slides, PowerWeb (an excellent research resource), and the archived Retailing Newsletter. For the student, the site offers self-quizzes, flashcards, and PowerWeb.

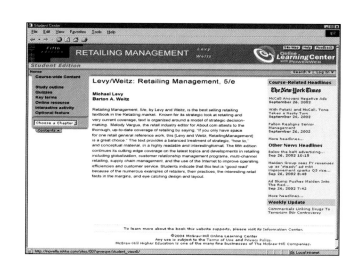

Video segments accompany many of the 31 cases in the text and treat companies like Home Depot, Burdines, and Starbucks. In addition, the video package that accompanies the fifth edition includes new segments on Build-A-Bear, RainForest Cafe, Walgreens, Wal-Mart, JCPenney, and Sears.

Each month, the authors create a **Retailing Newsletter,** that is distributed via e-mail to any retailing instructor interested in receiving it. Each newsletter includes short cases based on recent articles appearing in the business and trade press. Past issues of the newsletter are archived on the text's website.

BRIEF CONTENTS

SECTION I | THE WORLD OF RETAILING

1   Introduction to the World of Retailing,   2
2   Types of Retailers,   32
3   Multichannel Retailing—A View into the Future,   78
4   Customer Buying Behavior,   106

SECTION II | RETAILING STRATEGY

5   Retail Market Strategy,   146
6   Financial Strategy,   184
7   Retail Locations,   216
8   Site Selection,   242
9   Human Resource Management,   272
10   Information Systems and Supply Chain Management,   308
11   Customer Relationship Management,   334

SECTION III | MERCHANDISE MANAGEMENT

12   Planning Merchandise Assortments,   362
13   Buying Systems,   402
14   Buying Merchandise,   432
15   Pricing,   476
16   Retail Communication Mix,   512

SECTION IV | STORE MANAGEMENT

17   Managing the Store,   550
18   Store Layout, Design, and Visual Merchandising,   586
19   Customer Service,   618

SECTION V | CASES

CONTENTS

SECTION I THE WORLD OF RETAILING

CHAPTER 1 INTRODUCTION TO THE WORLD OF RETAILING, 2

What Is Retailing? 6
A Retailer's Role in a Distribution Channel, 6
Functions Performed by Retailers, 7
Economic Significance of Retailing, 9
Retail Sales, 9
Employment, 10
The Top 25 Global Retailers, 10
Structure of Retailing and Distribution Channels around the World, 13
Opportunities in Retailing, 14
Management Opportunities, 14
Entrepreneurial Opportunities, 15
The Retail Management Decision Process, 17
Understanding the World of Retailing—Section I, 17

Developing a Retail Strategy—Section II, 19
Implementing the Retail Strategy—Sections III and IV, 23
Summary, 24
Key Terms, 24
Get Out & Do It! 25
Discussion Questions and Problems, 25
Suggested Readings, 25
Appendix 1A: Careers in Retailing, 25
Appendix 1B: Trade Publications for Retailing, 30

CHAPTER 2 TYPES OF RETAILERS, 32

Trends in the Retail Industry, 34
Growing Diversity of Retail Formats, 34
Increasing Industry Concentration, 34
Globalization, 35
Retailer Characteristics, 36
Price–Cost Trade-Off, 36
Type of Merchandise, 37
Variety and Assortment, 38
Customer Services, 39
Cost of Offering Breadth and Depth of Merchandise and Services, 41
Food Retailers, 41
Conventional Supermarkets, 42
Big-Box Food Retailers, 42
Convenience Stores, 45
Issues in Food Retailing, 45
General Merchandise Retailers, 47
Discount Stores, 48
Specialty Stores, 48
Category Specialist, 50
Department Stores, 53
Drugstores, 54

Off-Price Retailers, 55
Value Retailers, 56
Nonstore Retail Formats, 57
Electronic Retailing, 57
Catalog and Direct-Mail Retailing, 58
Direct Selling, 60
Television Home Shopping, 60
Vending Machine Retailing, 61
Services Retailing, 62
Differences between Services and Merchandise Retailers, 64
Types of Ownership, 66
Independent, Single-Store Establishments, 66
Corporate Retail Chains, 67
Franchising, 68
Summary, 69
Key Terms, 69
Get Out & Do It! 70
Discussion Questions and Problems, 71
Suggested Readings, 71
Appendix 2A: Comparison Shopping, 72
Appendix 2B: Theories of Retail Evolution, 72

CHAPTER 3 | **MULTICHANNEL RETAILING—A VIEW INTO THE FUTURE, 78**

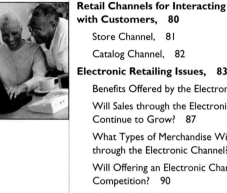

Retail Channels for Interacting with Customers, 80

Store Channel, 81

Catalog Channel, 82

Electronic Retailing Issues, 83

Benefits Offered by the Electronic Channel, 83

Will Sales through the Electronic Channel for Shopping Continue to Grow? 87

What Types of Merchandise Will Be Sold Effectively through the Electronic Channel? 89

Will Offering an Electronic Channel Lead to More Price Competition? 90

Which Channel Is the Most Profitable? 91

Why Did So Many Electronic Retailer Entrepreneurs Fail? 92

Will Manufacturers Use the Electronic Channel to Sell Their Products? 96

The Evolution toward Multichannel Retailing, 97

Reasons for Becoming a Multichannel Retailer, 97

Issues in Multichannel Retailing, 100

Shopping in the Future, 101

Shopping Experience, 101

Supporting the Shopping Experience, 102

Summary, 103

Key Terms, 103

Get Out & Do It! 104

Discussion Questions and Problems, 104

Suggested Readings, 105

CHAPTER 4 | **CUSTOMER BUYING BEHAVIOR, 106**

Types of Buying Decisions, 107

Extended Problem Solving, 108

Limited Problem Solving, 109

Habitual Decision Making, 110

The Buying Process, 110

Need Recognition, 111

Information Search, 114

Evaluation of Alternatives: The Multiattribute Model, 117

Purchasing the Merchandise, 122

Postpurchase Evaluation, 123

Social Factors Influencing Buying Decisions, 123

Family, 123

Reference Groups, 124

Culture, 125

Market Segmentation, 126

Criteria for Evaluating Market Segments, 127

Approaches for Segmenting Markets, 129

Composite Segmentation Approaches, 134

Summary, 135

Key Terms, 135

Get Out & Do It! 136

Discussion Questions and Problems, 137

Suggested Readings, 137

Appendix 4A: Consumer Behavior toward Fashion, 138

SECTION II   RETAILING STRATEGY

CHAPTER 5 | **RETAIL MARKET STRATEGY, 146**

What Is a Retail Strategy? 148

Definition of Retail Market Strategy, 148

Target Market and Retail Format, 149

Building a Sustainable Competitive Advantage, 151

Customer Loyalty, 151

Location, 155

Human Resource Management, 156

Distribution and Information Systems, 156

Unique Merchandise, 156

Vendor Relations, 157

Customer Service, 157

Multiple Sources of Advantage, 157

Growth Strategies, 158

Market Penetration, 159

Market Expansion, 160

Retail Format Development, 160

Diversification, 161

Strategic Opportunities and Competitive
Advantage, 162

Global Growth Opportunities, 162

Who Is Successful and Who Isn't, 162

Keys to Success, 164

Entry Strategies, 166

The Strategic Retail Planning Process, 167

Step 1: Define the Business Mission, 168

Step 2: Conduct a Situation Audit, 169

Step 3: Identify Strategic Opportunities, 174

Step 4: Evaluate Strategic Opportunities, 174

Step 5: Establish Specific Objectives and Allocate
Resources, 175

Step 6: Develop a Retail Mix to Implement
Strategy, 175

Step 7: Evaluate Performance and Make
Adjustments, 175

Strategic Planning in the Real World, 176

Summary, 177

Key Terms, 177

Get Out & Do It! 178

Discussion Questions and Problems, 178

Suggested Readings, 179

**Appendix 5A: Using the Market
Attractiveness/Competitive Position Matrix, 179**

CHAPTER 6   **FINANCIAL STRATEGY, 184**

The Strategic Profit Model: An Overview, 186

The Profit Path, 188

Net Sales, 190

Gross Margin, 190

Expenses, 191

Net Profit, 192

The Turnover Path, 194

Current Assets, 194

Accounts Receivable, 195

Merchandise Inventory, 196

Cash and Other Current Assets, 197

Fixed Assets, 197

Asset Turnover, 198

Liabilities and Owner's Equity, 199

The Strategic Profit Model, 200

Return on Assets, 200

**Integrating Marketing and Financial Statements
for Kelly Bradford's Gift Stores, 202**

Profit Path, 204

Turnover Path, 205

Return on Assets, 206

Recap of the Strategic Profit Model, 206

Setting Performance Objectives, 207

Top-Down versus Bottom-Up Process, 207

Accountability, 209

Performance Measures, 209

Summary, 211

Key Terms, 211

Get Out & Do It! 212

Discussion Questions and Problems, 212

Suggested Readings, 213

Appendix 6A: Activity-Based Costing, 214

CHAPTER 7   **RETAIL LOCATIONS, 216**

Shopping Centers, 218

Strip Shopping Centers, 218

Shopping Malls, 220

City or Town Locations, 228

Central Business Districts, 228

Redevelopment Efforts in City and Town
Locations, 229

Freestanding Sites, 232

Other Retail Location Opportunities, 232

Location and Retail Strategy, 234

Department Stores, 234

Specialty Apparel Stores, 235

Category Specialists, 235

Grocery Stores, 235

Optical Boutique, 236

Summary, 237

Key Terms, 237

Get Out & Do It! 238

Discussion Questions and Problems, 238

Suggested Readings, 239

Appendix 7A: Terms of Occupancy and Location Legal Issues, 239

CHAPTER 8 SITE SELECTION, 242

Factors Affecting the Demand for a Region or Trade Area, 244

Economies of Scale versus Cannibalization, 245

Demographic and Lifestyle Characteristics, 246

Business Climate, 246

Competition, 247

Span of Managerial Control, 247

Global Location Issues, 247

Factors Affecting the Attractiveness of a Site, 248

Accessibility, 248

Locational Advantages within a Center, 250

Estimating Demand for a New Location, 252

Trade Area, 252

Sources of Information, 255

Methods of Estimating Demand, 259

Summary, 269

Key Terms, 269

Get Out & Do It! 270

Discussion Questions and Problems, 270

Suggested Readings, 271

CHAPTER 9 HUMAN RESOURCE MANAGEMENT, 272

Gaining Competitive Advantage through Human Resource Management, 274

Objectives of Human Resource Management, 274

The Human Resource Triad, 276

Special HR Conditions Facing Retailers, 277

Designing the Organization Structure for a Retail Firm, 278

Organization Design Considerations, 280

Retail Organization Structures, 282

Organization of a Single-Store Retailer, 282

Organization of a Regional Department Store, 287

Corporate Organization of a Regional Department Store Chain, 287

Organization Structures of Other Types of Retailers, 289

Retail Organization Design Issues, 289

Centralization versus Decentralization, 290

Coordinating Merchandise and Store Management, 291

Motivating Retail Employees, 292

Policies and Supervision, 293

Incentives, 293

Organization Culture, 294

Building Employee Commitment, 296

Developing Skills, 297

Empowering Employees, 298

Creating Partnering Relationships, 299

Trends in Retail Human Resource Management, 300

Managing Diversity, 300

Legal and Regulatory Issues in Human Resource Management, 302

Use of Technology, 304

Summary, 305

Key Terms, 305

Get Out & Do It! 305

Discussion Questions and Problems, 306

Suggested Readings, 307

CHAPTER 10 INFORMATION SYSTEMS AND SUPPLY CHAIN MANAGEMENT, 308

Strategic Advantages Gained through Supply Chain Management, 310

Improved Product Availability, 311

Improved Return on Investment, 312

The Flow of Information, 313

Data Warehousing, 314

Electronic Data Interchange, 315

Security, 318

The Physical Flow of Merchandise—Logistics, 319

The Distribution Center, 319

Quick Response Delivery Systems, 327

The Logistics of Electronic Retailing, 329

Outsourcing, 329

Summary, 331

Key Terms, 331

Get Out & Do It! 332

Discussion Questions and Problems, 332

Suggested Readings, 332

CHAPTER 11 CUSTOMER RELATIONSHIP MANAGEMENT, 334

The CRM Process, 336

What Is Loyalty? 336

Overview of the CRM Process, 338

Collecting Customer Data, 338

Customer Database, 338

Identifying Information, 339

Privacy and CRM Programs, 342

Analyzing Customer Data and Identifying Target Customers, 344

Identifying Market Segments, 345

Identifying Best Customers, 345

Developing CRM Programs, 348

Customer Retention, 349

Converting Good Customers into Best Customers, 352

Dealing with Unprofitable Customers, 354

Implementing CRM Programs, 355

Summary, 356

Key Terms, 357

Get Out & Do It! 357

Discussion Questions and Problems, 357

Suggested Readings, 358

SECTION III MERCHANDISE MANAGEMENT

CHAPTER 12 PLANNING MERCHANDISE ASSORTMENTS, 362

Organizing the Buying Process by Categories, 365

The Category, 365

Category Management, 365

The Category Captain, 366

The Buying Organization, 367

Setting Objectives for the Merchandise Plan, 369

Putting Margin, Sales, and Turnover Together: GMROI, 370

Measuring Inventory Turnover, 372

Advantages of High Inventory Turnover, 374

Disadvantages of Too High an Inventory Turnover, 376

Sales Forecasting, 377

Category Life Cycles, 377

Developing a Sales Forecast, 382

Store-Level Forecasting, 386

CPFR, 389

The Assortment Planning Process, 390

Variety, 390

Assortment, 391

Product Availability, 391

Assortment Planning for Service Retailers, 391

Trade-Offs between Variety, Assortment, and Product Availability, 392

Determining Product Availability, 395

The Assortment Plan, 397

Summary, 399

Key Terms, 399

Get Out & Do It! 400

Discussion Questions and Problems, 400

Suggested Readings, 401

CHAPTER 13 BUYING SYSTEMS, 402

Staple Merchandise Buying Systems, 404

What the Staple Merchandise Buying System Does, 405

The Inventory Management Report, 406

Merchandise Budget Plan for Fashion Merchandise, 409

Monthly Sales Percent Distribution to Season (Line 1), 410

Monthly Sales (Line 2), 410

Monthly Reductions Percent Distribution to Season (Line 3), 411

Monthly Reductions (Line 4), 412

BOM (Beginning-of-Month) Stock-to-Sales Ratio (Line 5), 412

BOM Stock (Line 6), 414

EOM (End-of-Month) Stock (Line 7), 414

Monthly Additions to Stock (Line 8), 415

Evaluating the Merchandise Budget Plan, 415

Open-to-Buy, 415

Calculating Open-to-Buy for Past Periods, 417

Calculating Open-to-Buy for the Current Period, 417

Allocating Merchandise to Stores, 418

Analyzing Merchandise Performance, 419

ABC Analysis, 420

Sell-Through Analysis, 421

Multiattribute Method, 423

Summary, 424

Key Terms, 425

Get Out & Do It! 425

Discussion Questions and Problems, 426

Suggested Readings, 427

Appendix 13A: Retail Inventory Method, 428

CHAPTER 14 BUYING MERCHANDISE, 432

Branding Strategies, 434

Manufacturer Brands, 434

Private-Label Brands, 436

A Brand or a Store? 440

International Sourcing Decisions, 441

Costs Associated with Global Sourcing Decisions, 442

Managerial Issues Associated with Global Sourcing Decisions, 445

Source Close to Home or Buy "Made in America"? 446

Connecting with Vendors, 447

Internet Exchanges, 448

Wholesale Market Centers, 451

Trade Shows, 451

Buying on Their Own Turf, 452

Resident Buying Offices, 452

Negotiating with Vendors, 452

Guidelines for Planning Negotiations with Vendors, 453

Guidelines for Face-to-Face Negotiations, 456

Establishing and Maintaining Strategic Relationships with Vendors, 458

Defining Strategic Relationships, 458

Maintaining Strategic Relationships, 459

Building Partnering Relationships, 460

Summary, 461

Key Terms, 462

Get Out & Do It! 463

Discussion Questions and Problems, 463

Suggested Readings, 463

Appendix 14A: Ethical and Legal Issues in Purchasing Merchandise, 464

Appendix 14B: Terms of Purchase, 470

CHAPTER 15 **PRICING, 476**

Pricing Strategies, 478
  Everyday Low Pricing, 478
  High/Low Pricing, 479
  Deciding Which Strategy Is Best, 479
Approaches for Setting Prices, 480
  The Cost-Oriented Method of Setting Retail Prices, 482
  The Demand-Oriented Method of Setting Retail Prices, 486
  The Competition-Oriented Method of Setting Retail Prices, 488
  Profit Impact of Setting a Retail Price: The Use of Break-Even Analysis, 489
Price Adjustments, 491
  Markdowns, 491
  Coupons, 496

  Rebates, 497
  Price Bundling, 497
  Multiple-Unit Pricing, 497
  Variable Pricing, 498
  Pricing on the Internet, 499
Using Price to Stimulate Retail Sales, 501
  Leader Pricing, 501
  Price Lining, 501
  Odd Pricing, 502
Summary, 502
Key Terms, 503
Get Out & Do It! 503
Discussion Questions and Problems, 504
Suggested Readings, 505
Appendix 15A: Legal Issues in Retail Pricing, 506

CHAPTER 16 **RETAIL COMMUNICATION MIX, 512**

Using Communication Programs to Develop Brands and Build Customer Loyalty, 514
  Value of Brand Image, 514
  Building Brand Equity, 515
  Extending the Brand Name, 519
Methods of Communicating with Customers, 519
  Paid Impersonal Communications, 519
  Paid Personal Communications, 521
  Unpaid Impersonal Communications, 522
  Unpaid Personal Communications, 523
  Strengths and Weaknesses of Communication Methods, 523
Planning the Retail Communication Process, 525
  Setting Objectives, 525
  Setting the Communication Budget, 527

  Allocation of the Promotional Budget, 531
  Planning, Implementing, and Evaluating Communication Programs—Three Illustrations, 531
Summary, 537
Key Terms, 537
Get Out & Do It! 538
Discussion Questions and Problems, 538
Suggested Readings, 539
Appendix 16A: Implementing Retail Advertising Programs, 539

SECTION IV   **STORE MANAGEMENT**

CHAPTER 17 **MANAGING THE STORE, 550**

Store Management Responsibilities, 552
Recruiting and Selecting Store Employees, 553
  Job Analysis, 554
  Job Description, 555
  Locating Prospective Employees, 555
  Screening Applicants to Interview, 556
  Selecting Applicants, 557

  Legal Considerations in Selecting and Hiring Store Employees, 558
Socializing and Training New Store Employees, 560
  Orientation Programs, 560
  Training Store Employees, 561

Motivating and Managing Store Employees, 563

Leadership, 563

Motivating Employees, 564

Maintaining Morale, 566

Sexual Harassment, 566

Evaluating Store Employees and Providing Feedback, 567

Who Should Do the Evaluation? 567

How Often Should Evaluations Be Made? 568

Format for Evaluations, 568

Evaluation Errors, 569

Compensating and Rewarding Store Employees, 570

Extrinsic Rewards, 570

Intrinsic Rewards, 571

Compensation Programs, 572

Legal Issues in Compensation, 575

Controlling Costs, 575

Labor Scheduling, 575

Store Maintenance, 577

Energy Maintenance, 577

Reducing Inventory Loss, 577

Calculating Shrinkage, 578

Detecting and Preventing Shoplifting, 578

Reducing Employee Theft, 580

Summary, 582

Key Terms, 582

Get Out & Do It! 583

Discussion Questions and Problems, 584

Suggested Readings, 584

CHAPTER 18 STORE LAYOUT, DESIGN, AND VISUAL MERCHANDISING, 586

Objectives of a Good Store Design, 588

Design Should Be Consistent with Image and Strategy, 588

Design Should Positively Influence Consumer Behavior, 589

Design Should Consider Costs versus Value, 589

Design Should Be Flexible, 589

Design Should Recognize the Needs of the Disabled— The Americans with Disabilities Act, 590

Store Layout, 591

Types of Design, 592

Feature Areas, 595

Space Planning, 598

Location of Departments, 599

Location of Merchandise within Departments: The Use of Planograms, 602

Leveraging Space: In-Store Kiosks, 604

Merchandise Presentation Techniques, 605

Idea-Oriented Presentation, 606

Style/Idea Presentation, 607

Color Presentation, 607

Price Lining, 607

Vertical Merchandising, 607

Tonnage Merchandising, 607

Frontal Presentation, 608

Fixtures, 608

Atmospherics, 609

Visual Communications, 610

Lighting, 611

Color, 612

Music, 613

Scent, 613

Summary, 614

Key Terms, 615

Get Out & Do It! 616

Discussion Questions and Problems, 616

Suggested Readings, 617

CHAPTER 19 CUSTOMER SERVICE, 618

Strategic Advantage through Customer Service, 620

Customer Service Strategies, 621

Customer Evaluation of Service Quality, 624

Role of Expectations, 624

Perceived Service, 625

The Gaps Model for Improving Retail Service Quality, 627

Knowing What Customers Want: The Knowledge Gap, 628

Researching Customer Expectations and Perceptions, 628

Using Customer Research, 630

Setting Service Standards: The Standards Gap, 630

Commitment to Service Quality, 631

Developing Solutions to Service Problems, 631

Defining the Role of Service Providers, 633

Setting Service Goals, 633

Measuring Service Performance, 634

Meeting and Exceeding Service Standards: The Delivery Gap, 634

Giving Information and Training, 634

Providing Instrumental and Emotional Support, 636

Improving Internal Communications and Providing Support, 636

Empowering Store Employees, 637

Providing Incentives, 638

Communicating the Service Problem: The Communications Gap, 639

Realistic Commitments, 639

Managing Customer Expectations, 639

Service Recovery, 640

Listening to Customers, 640

Providing a Fair Solution, 641

Resolving Problems Quickly, 642

Summary, 643

Key Terms, 643

Get Out & Do It! 643

Discussion Questions and Problems, 644

Suggested Readings, 645

SECTION V	CASES

Case 1 — Rainforest Café: A Wild Place to Shop and Eat, 648

Case 2 — Retail Entertainment at Build-A-Bear Workshop, 649

Case 3 — Gadzooks Targets the Teen Market, 649

Case 4 — Sears Looks for a New Direction, 650

Case 5 — Toys "R" Us Online, 653

Case 6 — WeddingChannel.com, 655

Case 7 — The Chen Family Buys Bicycles, 656

Case 8 — Dollar General and Family Dollar Buy Low and Sell Low, 657

Case 9 — Ahold: The Biggest Supermarket Retail You Have Never Heard Of, 658

Case 10 — American Eagle and Abercrombie & Fitch Battle for the Teen/College Market, 660

Case 11 — Neiman Marcus and Family Dollar: Comparing Strategic Profit Models, 661

Case 12 — Stephanie's Boutique: Selecting a Store Location, 663

Case 13 — Hutch: Locating a New Store, 664

Case 14 — Home Depot: New Directions, 669

Case 15 — Avon Embraces Diversity, 671

Case 16 — Lawson Sportswear, 672

Case 17 — SaksFirst Builds with Customer Relationships, 674

Case 18 — Nolan's Finest Foods: Category Management, 675

Case 19 — Developing a Buying Plan for Hughe's, 678

Case 20 — McFadden's Department Store: Preparation of a Merchandise Budget Plan, 679

Case 21 — eBay, 680

Case 22 — Enterprise Builds on People, 682

Case 23 — Borders Bookstore: A Merchandise Display Problem, 683

Case 24 — Promoting a Sale, 683

Case 25   Picking the Best Display,   684

Case 26   Sephora,   685

Case 27   A Stockout at Discmart: Will
           Substitution Lead to
           Salvation?   686

Case 28   Customer Service and Relationship
           Management at Nordstorm,   687

Case 29   GoodLife Fitness Clubs,   689

Case 30   Lindy's Bridal Shoppe,   694

Case 31   Starbucks Coffee Company,   696

Glossary,   700

Notes,   725

Index,   751

RETAILING
MANAGEMENT

The chapters in Section I provide the background information about retail customers and competitors needed to understand retailing and develop and effectively implement a retail strategy.

Chapter I describes the functions retailers perform and the variety of decisions they make to satisfy customers' needs in a rapidly changing, highly competitive environment. The remaining chapters in this section give you background information to understand the retail environment.

Chapter 2 describes the different types of retailers.

THE WORLD OF RETAILING

CHAPTER ONE
INTRODUCTION TO THE WORLD OF RETAILING

CHAPTER TWO
TYPES OF RETAILERS

CHAPTER THREE
MULTICHANNEL RETAILING—A VIEW INTO THE FUTURE

CHAPTER FOUR
CUSTOMER BUYING BEHAVIOR

Chapter 3 examines how retailers are using multiple selling channels—stores, Internet, and catalogs to reach their customers.

Chapter 4 discusses factors consumers consider when choosing stores and buying merchandise.

Section II outlines the strategic decisions retailers make.

Sections III and IV explore tactical decisions concerning merchandise and store management.

Introduction to the World of Retailing

1

EXECUTIVE BRIEFING | Maxine Clark, Founder and Chief Executive Bear, Build-A-Bear Workshop

"I had a passion for retailing even when I was a young girl. At an early age, I recognized the importance of having exciting merchandise and providing an engaging store experience for customers. But I never realized how significant these feelings would be in my life." Maxine started her retail career, like many college graduates going into retailing, as an executive trainee at May Department Stores Company. Her skill at spotting merchandising and retail trends, and capitalizing on them, led to a series of promotions that eventually resulted in her becoming president of Payless Shoe Stores in 1992.

In 1996, she decided to devote her energies to an innovative retail concept she developed, Build-A-Bear Workshop,® "a teddy bear–themed experience retailer that combines the universal appeal of plush animals with an interactive assembly line that allows

children of all ages to create their own huggable companions." The first Build-A-Bear Workshop opened in St. Louis in the fall of 1997 to astounding success.

QUESTIONS

- What is retailing?
- What do retailers do?
- Why is retailing important in our society?
- What career and entrepreneurial opportunities does retailing offer?
- What types of decisions do retail managers make?

Build-A-Bear Workshop's innovative concept unifies "great merchandise, great people, and impeccable store execution." These three factors combine to flawlessly create an environment where families share quality time and form irreplaceable memories.

Clark's strong passion for serving her guests is emulated by the firm's dedicated associates, known as "Master Bear Builders sm," who make every effort to ensure that each visit is memorable and enjoyable. Employees are empowered to make sure that every guest feels special every time they visit their stores. Build-A-Bear Workshop has "created a company culture where great service and recognition are a daily occurrence." Maxine Clark has translated her creative vision into personal retail experiences that customers come to cherish as a part of their lives.

Five years after opening her first store in 1997, Build-A-Bear Workshop has grown into a specialty chain of more than 100 mall-based stores generating annual sales of nearly $200 million. In 2001, Maxine Clark was recognized as Retail Innovator of the Year by the National Retail Federation.

Retailing is evolving into a global, high-tech business. Wal-Mart is now the world's largest corporation and has become the largest food retailer in the United States. French-based Carrefour, the world's second-largest retailer, operates hypermarkets in 24 countries (but not in the United States.) Some of the largest retailers in the United States, such as A&P, Food Lion, Stop & Shop, and 7-Eleven, are owned by companies with headquarters in Europe and Japan.

Retailers are using sophisticated communication and information systems to manage their businesses. For example, at the 8,200 7-Eleven stores in Japan, each customer's market basket is scanned. These data are sent via satellite and the Internet to corporate headquarters. Headquarters then aggregates the data by region, product, and time and makes that information available to all stores and suppliers by the following morning. Orders for fast-food and fresh-food items are placed three times a day, magazines once a day, and processed-food items three times a week. Because of the stores' limited size, deliveries are made 10 times a day.[1]

Amazon.com maintains a data warehouse with information about what each customer has bought. With this information, customers returning to its website (www.amazon.com) are immediately recognized and suggestions based on past purchases are made. E-mails are sent to the customers when new books in their area of interest are published. Amazon.com showed its first profits in the fourth quarter of 2001. But other e-tailers were not so lucky. For instance, in 2001 alone, an estimated 384 e-tailers either filed for bankruptcy or ceased operations.[2]

Bricks-and-mortar stores are leveraging their customer base by making it easy and convenient to buy at stores, over the Internet, or by phone using a catalog. As a result, multichannel customers typically purchase more than their single-channel counterparts. REI customers, for example, may get an idea for a purchase by looking through a catalog. Going to the Internet, they can obtain more detailed information and solicit expert advise from an online representative. Then they can order either over the phone or the Internet, or they go into an REI store to pick up their purchase. Retailing View 1.1 examines multichannel retailing at REI.

To compete against nonstore retailers, stores are becoming more than just places to buy products. They are offering entertaining and educational experiences for their customers. The new Toys "R" Us in Times Square in New York City has a full-size Ferris wheel. Bass Pro Shops Outdoor World in Lawrenceville, Georgia, has a 30,000-gallon aquarium stocked with fish for casting demonstrations, an indoor archery range, and a 43-foot-high climbing wall. These features enhance customers' visual experiences, provide them with educational information, and enhance sales potential by enabling them to "try before they buy."

In this dynamic environment, entrepreneurs are launching new companies and concepts and becoming industry leaders, while traditional firms have had to rethink their business or go bankrupt. Thirty years ago, some of the largest retailers in the United States—Wal-Mart, The Gap, Home Depot, and Best Buy—either were small start-ups or did not even exist. European retailers H&M and IKEA are making their move to the United States, while the second-largest retailer in the world, Carrefour, is continuing to open its hypermarkets in Europe and South America. Unfortunately, over the past 10 years, a number of retailers with more than $1 billion in annual sales—Kmart, Revco, Zales, Service Merchandise, and Montgomery Wards—filed for bankruptcy. The late 1990s saw the demise of the majority of pure-play Internet retailers: online grocer Webvan, fashion purveyor eToys.com, Garden.com, and Pets.com, just to name a few.

Retailing is such a part of our everyday lives that it's often taken for granted. Customers often aren't aware of the sophisticated business decisions retail managers make and the technologies they use to provide goods and services. Yet most of what you learned in your basic marketing class is part of everyday life for retailers. Retail managers must make complex decisions in selecting target markets and retail locations, determining what merchandise and services to offer, negotiating with suppliers and distributing merchandise to stores, training and motivating sales associates, and deciding how to price, promote, and present merchandise. Considerable skill and knowledge are required to make these decisions effectively. Working in this highly competitive, rapidly changing environment is challenging and exciting and offers significant financial rewards.

The new Toys 'R' Us in New York City's Times Square has a full-size Ferris wheel.

A Multichannel Approach to Enjoying the Outdoors: Recreational Equipment, Inc. (REI)   RETAILING VIEW

1.1

Recreational Equipment Incorporated (REI) is one of the largest outdoor specialty retailers, with more than $600 million in annual revenues, specializing in high-performance mountain climbing and outdoor gear and clothing.

In the face of growing competition in the outdoor market, REI is transforming itself into a hipper, multichannel retailer. It currently operates 52 stores in 22 states. Its Seattle flagship store is an exciting shopping experience with a huge 65-foot-high, freestanding climbing rock; mountain-bike trails; and "rain rooms" so customers can test all their equipment before buying it. REI also sells merchandise domestically and internationally through catalogs and its three websites (www.rei.com, www.rei-outlet.com, and www.japan.rei.com). The company also operates REI Adventures, a full-service travel agency for outdoor adventures.

REI began selling merchandise over the Internet in 1996. The Internet offered a way for REI to "deliver any product, any time, any place, and answer any question."

- *Any product:* a larger selection on the Internet.

- *Any time:* 24 hours/seven days a week.

- *Any place:* Internet/stores/catalog, domestic and international.

- *Any question:* rich product information on the Web.

REI has achieved a level of integration among its channels that has eluded many clicks-and-bricks retailers. From the get-go, company managers intertwined REI's stores, telephone and catalog units, and website.

REI has integrated its multichannel strategy with surprising results. First-time REI.com customers spent 22 percent more when shopping in REI stores in 1998 than they did in 1999, and 45 percent of online customers also made store, phone, or catalog purchases. Clearly, many of REI's customers go to a store for one reason and shop online for another. Then they pick up a catalog during the holiday season and buy a couple of items over the phone.

REI.com tries to build loyalty by creating a community for outdoor enthusiasts, who, through dozens of message boards, exchange stories about their adventures, seek guidance on products, and post snapshots of their travels. The site also includes primers written by expert users, covering topics such as how to choose gear and "If You Become Lost." When REI opened its first overseas store in Tokyo this year, the company already had 80,000

REI believes in getting their customers involved.

Japanese customers, thanks to its decade-old catalog operation and a year-old Japanese website (www.rei.co.jp).

Now REI has brought the Internet into its stores by linking its point-of-sale (POS) terminals to the Internet. Through the connection, cashiers gain Internet access and additional product-search functionality. Since the kiosks are linked to the Internet, even its smallest stores are able to offer their full assortment.

Sources: Eric Chabrow, "Biz Model: Recreational Equipment Inc.— Outdoor Retailer REI Gets a Head Start in the Clicks-and-Mortar Race," *InformationWeek*, May 1, 2000, pp. 51–54; Marianne Wilson "Peak Experience," *Chain Store Age*, June 2000, pp. 144–45; and www.rei.com/reihtml/about_rei/about_rei.html?stat=side_30.

This book describes the world of retailing and gives principles for effectively managing businesses in this challenging environment. Knowledge of retailing principles and practices will help you develop management skills for many business contexts. For example, Procter & Gamble and Hewlett-Packard managers need to have a thorough understanding of how retailers operate and make money so they can get their products on retail shelves and work with retailers to sell them to consumers. Financial and health care institutions are using retail principles to develop assortments of services, improve customer service, and make their offers available at convenient locations. Thus, students interested in professional selling, advertising, and many other retail-related careers will find this book useful.

WHAT IS RETAILING?

A Bass Pro Shops sporting goods store in Gurnee Mills Mall near Chicago lets customers try out archery. Bows and arrows are on display nearby.

Retailing is the set of business activities that adds value to the products and services sold to consumers for their personal or family use. Often people think of retailing only as the sale of products in stores. But retailing also involves the sale of services: overnight lodging in a motel, a doctor's exam, a haircut, a videotape rental, or a home-delivered pizza. Not all retailing is done in stores. Examples of nonstore retailing are Internet sales of record albums by CDNOW (www.cdnow.com), the direct sales of cosmetics by Mary Kay, and catalog sales by L. L. Bean and Patagonia.

A Retailer's Role in a Distribution Channel

A **retailer** is a business that sells products or services, or both, to consumers for their personal or family use. Retailers attempt to satisfy consumer needs by having the *right* merchandise, at the *right* price, at the *right* place, when the consumer wants it. Retailers also provide markets for producers to sell their merchandise. Retailers are the final business in a distribution channel that links manufacturers to consumers. A **distribution channel** is a set of firms that facilitate the movement of products from the point of production to the point of sale to the ultimate consumer. Exhibit 1–1 shows the retailer's position within a distribution channel.[4]

Manufacturers typically make products and sell them to retailers or wholesalers. When manufacturers like Polo.com and Avon sell directly to consumers, they are performing both the production and retailing business activities. Wholesalers buy products from manufacturers and resell these products to retailers, and retailers resell products to consumers. Wholesalers and retailers may perform many of the same functions described in the next section. But wholesalers satisfy retailers' needs, whereas retailers direct their efforts to satisfying needs of ultimate consumers. Some retail chains, like Home Depot and Sam's Wholesale Club, are both retailers and wholesalers. They're performing retailing activities when they sell to consumers and wholesaling activities when they sell to other businesses like building contractors or restaurant owners.

EXHIBIT I–I
Example of a
Distribution Channel

In some distribution channels, the manufacturing, wholesaling, and retailing activities are performed by independent firms. But most distribution channels have some vertical integration.

Vertical integration means that a firm performs more than one set of activities in the channel, such as investments by retailers in wholesaling or manufacturing. For example, most large retailers—such as Safeway, Wal-Mart, and Office Depot—do both wholesaling and retailing activities. They buy directly from manufacturers, have merchandise shipped to their warehouses for storage, and then distribute the merchandise to their stores. Other retailers, such as The Gap and Victoria's Secret, are even more vertically integrated. They design the merchandise they sell and then contract with manufacturers to produce it exclusively for them.

Functions Performed by Retailers

Why bother with retailers? After all, wouldn't it be easier and cheaper to buy directly from those who produce the products? The answer is, generally no. Although there are situations where it is easier and cheaper to buy directly from manufacturers, such as at a farmer's market or from Dell Computer, retailers provide important functions that increase the value of the products and services they sell to consumers and facilitate the distribution of those products and services for those who produce them. These functions are

1. Providing an assortment of products and services.

2. Breaking bulk.

3. Holding inventory.

4. Providing services.

Providing Assortments   Supermarkets typically carry 20,000 to 30,000 different items made by over 500 companies. Offering an assortment enables their customers to choose from a wide selection of brands, designs, sizes, colors, and prices in one location. Manufacturers specialize in producing specific types of products. For example, Campbell makes soup, Kraft makes dairy products, Kellogg makes breakfast cereals, and McCormick makes spices. If each of these manufacturers had its own stores that only sold its own products, consumers would have to go to many different stores to buy groceries to prepare a single meal.

All retailers offer assortments of products, but they specialize in the assortments they offer. Supermarkets provide assortments of food, health and beauty care, and household products, while The Limited provides assortments of clothing and accessories. Most consumers are well aware of the product assortments retailers offer. Even small children know where to buy different types of products. But new types of retailers offering unique assortments appear each year, such as Play It Again Sports (used sporting goods), HotHotHot! (hot sauces at www.hothothot.com), and Mini Maid (home cleaning services).

Breaking Bulk   To reduce transportation costs, manufacturers and wholesalers typically ship cases of frozen dinners or cartons of blouses to retailers. Retailers then offer the products in smaller quantities tailored to individual consumers' and households' consumption patterns. This is called **breaking bulk.** Breaking bulk is important to both manufacturers and consumers. It is cost effective for manufacturers to package and ship merchandise in larger, rather than smaller quantities. It is also easier for consumers to purchase merchandise in smaller, more manageable quantities.

Holding Inventory   A major function of retailers is to keep inventory that is already broken into user-friendly sizes so that products will be available when consumers want them. Thus, consumers can keep a small inventory of products at home because they know the retailers will have the products available when they need more. By maintaining an inventory, retailers provide a benefit to consumers—they reduce the consumer's cost of storing products. This is particularly important to consumers with limited storage space and for purchasing perishable merchandise like meat and produce.

Providing Services   Retailers provide services that make it easier for customers to buy and use products. They offer credit so consumers can have a product now and pay for it later. They display products so consumers can see and test them before buying. Some retailers have salespeople on hand to answer questions and provide additional information about products. Multichannel retailers offer the flexibility of buying anytime, day or night. Customers can choose whether they want to pick merchandise up at a store or have it shipped to their home.

Increasing the Value of Products and Services   By providing assortments, breaking bulk, holding inventory, and providing services, retailers increase the value consumers receive from their products and services. To illustrate, consider a door in a shipping crate in an Iowa manufacturer's warehouse. The door won't satisfy the needs of a do-it-yourselfer (DIYer) who wants to replace a closet door today. For the DIYer, a conveniently located home improvement center like Home Depot or Lowe's sells one door that is available when the DIYer wants it. The home improvement center helps the customer select the door by displaying doors so they can be examined before they're purchased. An employee is available to explain which door is best for closets and how the door should be hung. The center has an assortment of hardware, paint, and tools that the DIYer will need for the job. Thus, retailers increase the value of products and services bought by their customers. Retailing View 1.2 illustrates how retailers provide value to their communities as well as their customers.

ECONOMIC SIGNIFICANCE OF RETAILING

Retail Sales

Retailing affects every facet of life. Just think of how many contacts you have with retailers when you eat meals, furnish your apartment, have your car fixed, and buy clothing for a party or job interview. U.S. retail sales in 2001 were $3 trillion.[5] These official statistics include only store and catalog sales; they don't include other types of nonstore retail sales, such as Internet sales to consumers, TV home shopping, and sales of services to consumers such as movie tickets, hotel rooms, and legal assistance. In 1997, there were 2,889,041 retail firms in the United States.[6]

Community Pride Food Stores Bring Pride Back to the Community | RETAILING VIEW

1.2

When Jonathan Johnson was growing up in Richmond, Virginia, his neighbors took great pride in their homes and community. Now the neighborhood bears the scars of economic hardship, crime, and drugs. Johnson started Community Pride Food Stores in 1992 with the objective of developing a new spirit of community in Richmond's inner city.

Community Pride has six clean, well-managed stores in urban Richmond that offer affordable, quality products. Eighty percent of its employees live within three miles of the store where they work. Each store has two vans providing rides to customers who aren't mobile. Customers can also cash checks, pay utility bills, and buy bus tickets, postage stamps, and money orders at the stores.

Johnson stresses the importance of education. Employees are encouraged to enroll in many structured training programs. Also, $5,000 scholarships are awarded to employees who pursue college education. Families of high school students who earn all As and Bs and don't miss more than one day of classes per month get a 10 percent discount on food.

After struggling over a stolen bottle of wine that cost Johnson four teeth, he gained a new perspective on shoplifters. "If they steal steaks, I'll arrest them," he says. "If they steal bologna and bread I'll give them $50 and a job application." He claims that since 1992 he's hired hundreds of shoplifters and at least 60 have stayed with the company for more than three years.

Turnover is low at Community Pride; only 2 of 47 core managers have left. Johnson actively hires from the city welfare rolls—300 employees since 1997, out of a total staff of 1,030. He has cosigned more than 100 car loans and handed out his credit card to cash strapped employees for emergencies (for which service Johnson deducts up to 5 percent from the next weekly paycheck). He once posted bail for the son of a deli manager. "The needs of

Community Pride's New Van Service Fleet

Community Pride Plus+

Jonathan Johnson of Community Pride stores is a community leader in Richmond, Virginia.

the urban employee are quite different from the typical suburban resident," says Johnson.

Sources: Tomas Kellner, "He Keeps His Ear to the Ground," *Forbes,* November 15, 1999, pp. 204–6; Derek Dingle, "Architects of the New Millennium," *Black Enterprise,* June 1998, pp. 93–98; and "Retail Entrepreneur of the Year," *Chain Store Age Executive,* December 1995, pp. 74, 78.

EXHIBIT 1–2
Employment by
Industry 2010
(estimated)

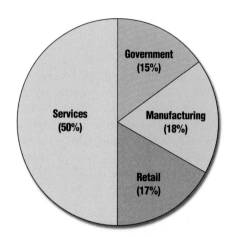

SOURCE: "BLS Releases 2000–2010 Employment Projections," Bureau of Labor Statistics, December 3, 2001, www.bls.gov/news.release/ecopro.nr0.htm.

Employment

Retailing also is one of the nation's largest industries in terms of employment. As Exhibit 1–2 shows, it is projected that by 2010, there will be 26 million people employed in retailing—approximately 17 percent of the U.S. workforce. Exhibit 1–3 illustrates the growth in employment in the major sectors of the U.S. economy. Over the next eight years, it is estimated that employment in retail trades will grow by 3 million jobs. Note that these figures understate the impact of retailing as an employer because many of the 20 million service jobs involve firms retailing services to consumers.

The Top 25 Global Retailers

 Exhibit 1–4 lists the 25 largest global retailers in 2000.[7] With world-wide retail sales estimated at $7 trillion by *Euromonitor*, the 25 largest retailers represent a 14 percent share. Combined, the 200 largest retailers capture 30 percent of worldwide sales.

Wal-Mart remains the undisputed leader in the retail world. Its sales are three times as large as those of Carrefour, the second-largest retailer. Home Depot

EXHIBIT 1–3
Projected Job Gains,
2000–2010

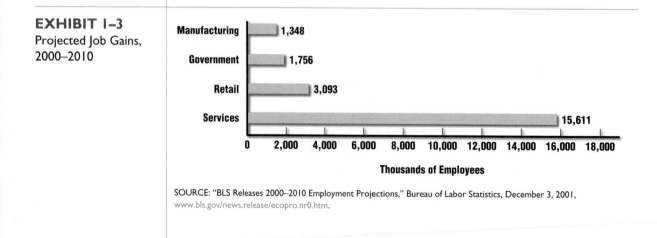

SOURCE: "BLS Releases 2000–2010 Employment Projections," Bureau of Labor Statistics, December 3, 2001, www.bls.gov/news.release/ecopro.nr0.htm.

Rank	Name of Company	Country of Origin	Formats	2000 Retail Sales (US$ millions)	Countries of Operation
1	Wal-Mart	U.S.	Discount, warehouse	191,329	Argentina, Brazil, Canada, China, Germany, South Korea, Mexico, Puerto Rico, U.K., U.S.
2	Carrefour	France	Cash and carry, convenience, discount, hypermarket, supermarket	59,703	Argentina, Belgium, Brazil, Chile, China, Colombia, Czech Rep., France, Greece, Indonesia, Italy, Japan, Malaysia, Mexico, Poland, Portugal, Singapore, Slovakia, Spain, South Korea, Switzerland, Taiwan, Thailand, Turkey
3	Kroger	U.S.	Convenience, department, drug, specialty, supermarket	49,000	U.S.
4	Home Depot	U.S.	do-it-yourself, specialty	45,738	Argentina, Canada, Chile, Puerto Rico, U.S.
5	Metro	Germany	Department, do-it-yourself, hypermarket, mail order, specialty, supermarket, warehouse	42,439e	Austria, Belgium, Bulgaria, China, Czech Rep., Denmark, France, Germany, Greece, Hungary, Italy, Luxembourg, Morocco, Netherlands, Poland, Portugal, Romania, Slovakia, Spain, Switzerland, Turkey, U.K.
6	Ahold	Netherlands	Cash and carry, convenience, discount, drug, hypermarket, specialty, supermarket	41,539	Argentina, Brazil, Chile, Czech Rep., Denmark, Ecuador, El Salvador, Estonia, Guatemala, Honduras, Indonesia, Latvia, Lithuania, Malaysia, Morocco, Netherlands, Norway, Paraguay, Peru, Poland, Portugal, Spain, Sweden, Thailand, U.S.
7	Kmart	U.S.	Discount	37,028	Guam, Puerto Rico, US, Virgin Islands
8	Albertson's	U.S.	Drug, supermarket	36,762	U.S.
9	Sears	U.S.	Department, mail order, specialty	36,548	Canada, Puerto Rico, U.S.
10	Target (Dayton Hudson)	U.S.	Department, discount	36,362	U.S.
11	Safeway	U.S.	Supermarket	31,977	Canada, U.S.
12	JCPenney	U.S.	Department, drug, mail order	31,846	Brazil, Mexico, Puerto Rico, U.S.
13	Tesco	U.K.	Convenience, hypermarket, supermarket	31,751	Czech Rep., France, Hungary, Poland, Rep. of Ireland, South Korea, Slovakia, Taiwan, Thailand, U.K.
14	Costco	U.S.	Warehouse	31,621	Canada, Japan, Korea, Mexico, Taiwan, U.K., U.S.
15	Rewe	Germany	Cash and carry, convenience, department, discount, do-it-yourself, hypermarket, specialty, supermarket	31,100e	Austria, Bulgaria, Czech Rep., France, Germany, Hungary, Italy, Poland, Romania, Slovakia, Ukraine
16	Intermarche	France	Convenience, discount, do-it-yourself, hypermarket, restaurant, specialty, supermarket	30,698e	Belgium, Bosnia, France, Germany, Italy, Poland, Portugal, Spain
17	Auchan	France	Convenience, do-it-yourself, hypermarket, restaurant, specialty, supermarket	29,134	Argentina, China, France, Hungary, Italy, Luxembourg, Mexico, Morocco, Poland, Portugal, Spain, Taiwan, Thailand, U.S.

e = estimate.

(continued)

EXHIBIT 1–4   Continued

Rank	Name of Company	Country of Origin	Formats	2000 Retail Sales (US$ millions)	Countries of Operation
18	Edeka/AVA	Germany	Convenience, discount, do-it-yourself, supermarket, hypermarket	28,782	Austria, Czech Rep., Denmark, France, Germany, Luxembourg, Poland
19	Ito-Yokado	Japan	Convenience, department, discount, hypermarket, restaurant, specialty, supermarket	25,381	Canada, China, Denmark, Japan, Malaysia, Mexico, Norway, Philippines, Singapore, South Korea, Sweden, Taiwan, Thailand, Turkey, U.S.
20	J Sainsbury	U.K.	Convenience, hypermarket, supermarket	25,266	France, U.K., U.S.
21	Tengelmann	Germany	Discount, do-it-yourself, drug, hypermarket, specialty, supermarket	25,154	Austria, Canada, China, Czech Rep., Denmark, France, Germany, Hungary, Italy, Poland Portugal, Slovakia, Slovenia, Spain, Switzerland, U.S.
22	Aeon	Japan	Convenience, drug, department, discount, hypermarket, restaurant, specialty, supermarket	22,859	Canada, China, Japan, Malaysia, Taiwan, Thailand, U.S.
23	Eleclerc	France	Hypermarket, supermarket	22,541e	France, Poland, Portugal, Slovenia, Spain
24	Daiei	Japan	Convenience, department, discount, hypermarket, specialty, supermarket	22,433	China, Japan, U.S.
25	Walgreen	U.S.	Drug	21,207	Puerto Rico, U.S.

e = estimate.

Source: "Top 200 Global Retailers," *Stores*, January 2002, www.stores.org. Reprinted by permission.

also has made significant sales gains over the last several years. Its fourth-place ranking in 2000 was up from 24 in 1996. Most of Home Depot's growth has come from store openings and new formats such as the popular Expo home furnishings stores.

Through merger and acquisition activity, many of these large retailers are diversifying their format offerings to consumers. But 47 percent of the 200 largest retailers still operate only one store type. A significant number of these large global retailers, therefore, are continuing to focus on a single business segment.

The majority of the largest global retailers remain involved in the food sector. More than half of the 200 largest retailers have supermarket, warehouse, hypermarket, or cash and carry formats, or some combination of them.

Geographically, U.S. companies dominate the 200 largest retailer list. The 78 American companies in the top 200 list represent 49 percent of the sales. Wal-Mart alone represents 9.1 percent of the top 200 sales.

Despite a decade of poor economic performance, the Japanese remain major global retailers. By country of origin, the 30 companies based in Japan are the second-largest group of the top 200.

While globalization is increasing throughout the retail world, it has become particularly pronounced for U.S. retailers. The 78 U.S. firms in the top 200 operate in an average of three countries, although this figure excludes retailers such as Avon and McDonald's, whose global or near-global coverage would skew the average.

Historically, a large consumer market and relatively abundant land have kept many U.S. retailers from seeking global expansion. But with domestic markets reaching saturation, U.S. companies are seeking opportunities abroad. Still, the American companies have not caught up to the largest European firms, which operate in an average of seven countries.

Structure of Retailing and Distribution Channels around the World

The nature of retailing and distribution channels in the United States is quite unique. Some critical differences between U.S., European, and Japanese retailing and distribution systems are summarized in Exhibit 1–5.

The U.S. distribution system has the greatest retail density and the greatest concentration of large retail firms. Some people think that the United States is overstored. Many U.S. retail firms are large enough to operate their own warehouses, eliminating the need for wholesalers. The fastest-growing types of U.S. retailers sell through large stores with over 20,000 square feet. The combination of large stores and large firms results in a very efficient distribution system.

Home Depot's EXPO Division is an upscale version of the original.

Comparison of Retailing and Distribution Channels across the World | **EXHIBIT 1–5**

Characteristic	U.S.	EUROPE								Japan
		NORTHWEST				SOUTHERN		CENTRAL		
		U.K.	Belgium	France	Germany	Spain	Italy	Hungary	Czech	
Concentration (% of retail sales in category by top three firms)	High	High				Low		Very low		Medium
Number of outlets per 1,000 people	Medium	Medium				High		Low		High
Retail density (sq. ft. of retail space per person)	High	Medium				Low		Low		Medium
Store size (% of retail sales made in stores over 10,000 sq. ft.)	High	Medium				Low		Low		Low
Role of wholesaling (wholesale sales as a % of retail sales)	Low	Medium				Medium		High		High
Distribution Inefficiency (average maintained markup—distribution costs as a % of retail price)	Low	Medium				High		High		High

In contrast, the Japanese distribution system is characterized by small stores operated by relatively small firms and a large independent wholesale industry. To efficiently make daily deliveries to these small retailers, merchandise often might pass through three distributors between the manufacturer and retailer. This difference in efficiency results in a much larger percentage of the Japanese labor force being employed in distribution and retailing than in the United States.

The European distribution system falls between the U.S. and Japanese systems on this continuum of efficiency and scale, but the northern, southern, and central parts of Europe have to be distinguished, with northern European retailing being the most similar to the U.S. system. In northern Europe, concentration levels are high—in some national markets 80 percent or more of sales in a sector such as food or home improvements are accounted for by five or fewer firms. Southern European retailing is more fragmented across all sectors. For example, traditional farmers' market retailing is still important in some sectors, operating alongside large "big-box" formats. In central Europe the privatization of retail trade has resulted in a change from a previously highly concentrated government-controlled structure to one of extreme fragmentation characterized by many small family-owned retailers.

Some factors that have created these differences in distribution systems in the major markets are (1) social and political objectives, (2) geography, and (3) market size.

First, a top priority of the Japanese economic policy is to reduce unemployment by protecting small businesses like neighborhood retailers. The Japanese Large Scale Retail Stores Law regulates the locations and openings of stores of over 5,000 square feet. Several European countries have also passed laws protecting small retailers. For example, in 1996, France tightened its existing laws to constrain the opening of stores of over 3,000 square feet. European governments have also passed strict zoning laws to preserve green spaces, protect town centers, and inhibit the development of large-scale retailing in the suburbs.

Second, the population density in the United States is much lower than in Europe and Japan. Thus, Europe and Japan have less low-cost real estate available for building large stores.

Third, the U.S. retail market is larger than Japan or any single European country. In Europe, distribution centers and retail chains typically operate within a single country and are therefore not able to achieve the scale economies of U.S. firms serving a broader customer base. Even with the euro and other initiatives designed to make trade within European countries easier and more efficient, barriers to trade still exist that are not found in the United States.

OPPORTUNITIES IN RETAILING

Management Opportunities

To cope with a highly competitive and challenging environment, retailers are hiring and promoting people with a wide range of skills and interests. Students often view retailing as a part of marketing because management of distribution channels is part of a manufacturer's marketing function. But retailers undertake most of the traditional business activities. Retailers raise capital from financial institutions; purchase goods and services; develop accounting and management information systems to control operations; manage warehouses and distribution systems; and design and develop new products as well as undertake marketing activities such as advertising, promotions, sales force management, and market research. Thus, retailers employ people with expertise and interest in finance, accounting, human resource management, logistics, and computer systems as well as marketing.

Retail managers are often given considerable responsibility early in their careers. Retail management is also financially rewarding. After completing a management trainee program in retailing, managers can double their starting salary in three to five years if they perform well. The typical buyer in a department store earns $50,000 to $60,000 per year. Store managers working for department or discount store chains often make over $100,000. (See Appendix 1A at end of this chapter.)

Entrepreneurial Opportunities

Retailing also provides opportunities for people wishing to start their own business. Some of the world's richest people are retailing entrepreneurs. Some are household names because their names appear over the stores' door; others you may not recognize.[8] Retailing View 1.3 examines the life of one of retailing's great entrepreneurs, Sam Walton.

 After his research uncovered that Internet usage was growing at a 2,300 percent annual rate in 1994, Jeffrey Bezos, the 30-year-old son of a Cuban refugee, quit his job on Wall Street, leaving behind a hefty bonus to start an Internet business.[9] While his wife MacKenzie was driving their car across country, Jeffrey pecked out his business plan on a laptop computer. By the time they reached Seattle, he had rounded up the investment capital to launch the first Internet book retailer. The company, Amazon.com, is named after the river that carries the greatest amount of water, symbolizing Bezos's objective of having the greatest volume of Internet sales. Today's Amazon.com sells more than just books and CDs. For instance, its consumer electronics business sells 25,000 items, compared to about 5,000 in a big electronics superstore. The company has also developed partnerships with Sotheby's auction house, Toys "R" Us, and Borders Group, among others.[10]

In 1945, Luciano Benetton lost his father when he was only 10 years old.[11] He had to sell newspapers to help his family make ends meet. In the sixties, he and his sister, Guiliana, started a small sweater company. One designed the sweaters and was in charge of manufacturing, while the other handled the marketing side, acting as a commercial representative. Luciano went to England to study a technique whereby one knitted in off-white yarn, only dying the wool at the last minute, thus keeping up with ever-changing fashion trends. Benetton now operates stores in 120 different countries, under the United Colors of Benetton, O12, and Sisley labels. Luciano continues to run the now $1.8 billion (2000 sales) fashion empire as well as other major businesses.

Most think of Giorgio Armani only as a fashion designer. Yet this Italian, with an estimated net worth of $1.7 billion, oversees ownership of 260 stores. After stints designing for Cerruti, Ungaro, and Zegna, he sold his Volkswagen to start his own label. In 1973–74, at a fashion show in Florence, he presented to great acclaim bomber jackets that treated leather as a regular, everyday fabric. This penchant for using materials in unexpected contexts and combinations came to be known as a defining characteristic of his genius. In 1975, Armani and partner Sergio Galeotti started their own company, Giorgio Armani S.p.A., and founded the Armani label.[12] Armani, who barely speaks English, has built his firm into a $1 billion brand (annual revenues).

RETAILING VIEW   Sam Walton, Founder of Wal-Mart (1918–1992)

1.3

"Like Henry Ford with his Model T," said a professor of rural sociology at the University of Missouri, "Sam Walton and his Wal-Marts, for better or for worse, transformed small-town America." Others think he transformed the entire nation.

After graduating from the University of Missouri in 1940, Walton began working at a JCPenney store in Des Moines, Iowa. After serving in the Army during World War II, he purchased a Ben Franklin variety store franchise in Newport, Arkansas. He boosted sales by finding offbeat suppliers who would sell to him lower than he could buy from Ben Franklin.

Walton lost his store, however, in 1950 when the landlord refused to renew the lease. He then moved to Bentonville, Arkansas, where he and a younger brother franchised another Ben Franklin store. Walton employed a new self-service system, one he had discovered at two Ben Franklin stores in Minnesota: no clerks or cash registers around the store, only checkout lanes in the front. By 1960, Walton had 15 stores in Arkansas and Missouri and had laid the foundation for his own discount chain.

By the early 1960s, retailers had developed the discount superstore concept using self-service, large inventories, and massive parking lots. Walton joined them in 1962 when he opened his first Wal-Mart Discount City in Rogers, Arkansas. At least one observer called it a mess—with donkey rides and watermelons mixed together outside under the boiling sun and merchandise haphazardly arranged inside.

But Walton quickly brought order to his enterprise and pursued an important new concept: large discount stores in small towns. Walton saw cities saturated with retailers and believed he could prosper in towns that the larger companies had written off. By the 1980s, Walton started building stores in larger suburbs. Walton then started Sam's Clubs, warehouse-style stores that sold merchandise at discount prices in bulk. Next came Wal-Mart Supercenters, ranging from 97,000 to 211,000 square feet, that featured a supermarket and a regular Wal-Mart under one roof. As a result of their success, Wal-Mart is now the largest food retailer in the United States.

Walton often visited his stores, dropping in unannounced to check the layouts and books and talk to his

Sam Walton believed in "Management by Walking Around."

"associates." He prided himself on a profit-sharing program and a friendly, open atmosphere. He often led his workers in a cheer—some called corny, others uplifting. He once described it: "Give me a W! Give me an A! Give me an L! Give me a Squiggly! (Here, everybody sort of does the twist.) Give me an M! Give me an A! Give me an R! Give me a T! What's that spell? Wal-Mart! What's that spell? Wal-Mart! Who's number one? THE CUSTOMER!"

He offered his own formula for how a large company must operate: "Think one store at a time. That sounds easy enough, but it's something we've constantly had to stay on top of. Communicate, communicate, communicate: What good is figuring out a better way to sell beach towels if you aren't going to tell everybody in your company about it? Keep your ear to the ground: A computer is not—and will never be—a substitute for getting out in your stores and learning what's going on."

In 1991, Walton reached a pinnacle as America's wealthiest person. He died of leukemia in 1992. Wal-Mart is now the world's largest corporation.

Source: "Sam Walton," *American Business Leaders*, January 1, 2001. Reprinted by permission.

There are entrepreneurial opportunities in retailing. Jeff Bezos, founder of Amazon.com, pecked out a business plan for his new company in 1994 while driving across the U.S. with his wife. Luciano Benneton and his sister Guliana started a small sweater company in Italy in 1945. Today their fashion empire sports almost $2 billion in annual sales.

THE RETAIL MANAGEMENT DECISION PROCESS

This book is organized around the management decisions retailers make to provide value to their customers and develop an advantage over their competitors. Exhibit 1–6 identifies chapters in this book associated with each type of decision.

Understanding the World of Retailing—Section I

The first step in the retail management decision process, as Exhibit 1–6 shows, is getting an understanding of the world of retailing. Retail managers need to understand their environment, especially their customers and competition, before they can develop and implement effective strategies. The first section of this book provides a general overview of the retailing industry and its customers.

The critical environmental factors in the world of retailing are (1) the macroenvironment and (2) the microenvironment. The impacts of the macroenvironment—including technological, social, and ethical/legal/political factors on retailing—are discussed throughout the book. For example, the influence of multichannel retailing is reviewed in Chapter 3; the use of new information and supply chain technologies is examined in Chapter 10; ethical, legal, and public policy issues are discussed throughout the book.

The introductory section on the world of retailing focuses on the retailer's microenvironment—the retailer's competitors and customers.

Competitors At first glance, identifying competitors appears easy. A retailer's primary competitors are those with the same format. Thus, department stores compete against other department stores and supermarkets against other supermarkets. This competition between the same type of retailers is called **intratype competition.**

To appeal to a broader group of consumers and provide one-stop shopping, many retailers are increasing their variety of merchandise. **Variety** is the number of different merchandise categories within a store or department. By offering

EXHIBIT 1–6
Retail Management
Decision Process

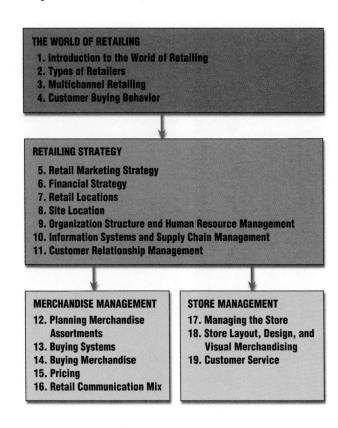

THE WORLD OF RETAILING
1. Introduction to the World of Retailing
2. Types of Retailers
3. Multichannel Retailing
4. Customer Buying Behavior

RETAILING STRATEGY
5. Retail Marketing Strategy
6. Financial Strategy
7. Retail Locations
8. Site Location
9. Organization Structure and Human Resource Management
10. Information Systems and Supply Chain Management
11. Customer Relationship Management

MERCHANDISE MANAGEMENT
12. Planning Merchandise Assortments
13. Buying Systems
14. Buying Merchandise
15. Pricing
16. Retail Communication Mix

STORE MANAGEMENT
17. Managing the Store
18. Store Layout, Design, and Visual Merchandising
19. Customer Service

greater variety in one store, retailers can offer one-stop shopping to satisfy more of the needs of their target market. For example, clothing and food are now available in grocery, department, discount, and drugstores. Fast food is available at McDonald's and 7-Eleven convenience stores. The offering of merchandise not typically associated with the store type, such as clothing in a drugstore, is called **scrambled merchandising.** Scrambled merchandising increases **intertype competition**—competition between retailers that sell similar merchandise using different formats, such as discount and department stores.

Increasing intertype competition has made it harder for retailers to identify and monitor their competition. In one sense, all retailers compete against each other for the dollars consumers spend on goods and services. But the intensity of competition is greatest among retailers located close together with retail offerings that are viewed as very similar.

Since convenience of location is important in store choice, a store's proximity to competitors is a critical factor in identifying competition. Consider two videotape rental stores, Blockbuster and Harry's Video, in two suburbs 10 miles apart. The stores are the only specialty videotape rental retailers within 50 miles, but a grocery store also rents a more limited selection of videotapes in the same strip center as Blockbuster. Due to the distance between Blockbuster and Harry's Video, they probably don't compete against each other intensely. Customers who live near Harry's Video will rent tapes there, whereas customers close to Blockbuster will rent tapes at Blockbuster or the grocery store. In this case, Harry's major competition may be movie theaters and cable TV, because it's too inconvenient for customers close to Harry's to rent videotapes elsewhere. On the other hand, Blockbuster competes most intensely with the grocery store.

Management's view of competition also can differ, depending on the manager's position within the retail firm. For example, the manager of the Saks Fifth Avenue women's sportswear department in Bergen County, New Jersey, views the women's sportswear specialty stores also in the Riverside Square mall (www.shopriverside.com) as her major competitors. But the Saks store manager views the Bloomingdale's store in a nearby mall as her strongest competitor. These differences in perspectives arise because the department sales manager is primarily concerned with customers for a specific category of merchandise, while the store manager is concerned with customers seeking the selection of all merchandise and services offered by a department store.

On the other hand, the CEO of a retail chain views competition from a much broader geographic perspective. For example, Nordstrom identifies its strongest competitor as The Bon Marche in the Northwest, Macy's in northern California, and Bloomingdale's in northern Virginia. The CEO may also take a broader strategic perspective and recognize that other activities compete for consumers' disposable income. For example, Blockbuster Video's CEO takes the consumer's perspective and recognizes that videotape rental stores are competing in the entertainment industry with other videotape rental stores, other retailers that rent videotapes (such as grocery and convenience stores), movie theaters, regular and cable TV, WebTV, theater, opera, ballet, nightclubs, and restaurants.

Retailing is intensely competitive. Understanding the different types of retailers and how they compete with each other is critical to developing and implementing a retail strategy. Chapter 2 discusses various types of retailers and retail strategies; and Chapter 3 concentrates on how many retailers have adopted multichannel strategies to give them a competitive edge.

Customers The second factor in the microenvironment is customers. Customer needs are changing at an ever-increasing rate. Retailers are responding to broad demographic and lifestyle trends in our society, such as the growth in the elderly and minority segments of the U.S. population and the importance of shopping convenience to the rising number of two-income families. To develop and implement an effective strategy, retailers need to understand why customers shop, how they select a store, and how they select among that store's merchandise—the information found in Chapter 4.

Developing a Retail Strategy—Section II

The next stages in the retail management decision-making process, formulating and implementing a retail strategy, are based on an understanding of the macro- and microenvironments developed in the first section. Section II focuses on decisions related to developing a retail strategy. Sections III and IV concern decisions surrounding the implementation of the strategy.

The **retail strategy** indicates how the firm plans to focus its resources to accomplish its objectives. It identifies (1) the target market, or markets, toward which the retailer will direct its efforts, (2) the nature of the merchandise and services the retailer will offer to satisfy needs of the target market, and (3) how the retailer will build a long-term advantage over competitors.

The nature of a retail strategy can be illustrated by comparing strategies of Wal-Mart and Toys "R" Us. Initially Wal-Mart identified its target market as small towns (under 35,000 in population) in Arkansas, Texas, and Oklahoma. It offered name-brand merchandise at low prices in a broad array of categories, ranging from laundry detergent to girls' dresses. Although Wal-Mart stores have many different categories of merchandise, selection in each category is limited. A store might have only three brands of detergents in two sizes, while a supermarket carries eight brands in five sizes.

In contrast to Wal-Mart, Toys "R" Us identified its target as consumers living in suburban areas of large cities. Rather than carrying a broad array of merchandise categories, Toys "R" Us stores specialize in toys, games, bicycles, and furniture for children. While Toys "R" Us has limited categories of merchandise, it has almost all the different types and brands of toys and games currently available in the market.

Both Wal-Mart and Toys "R" Us emphasize self-service. Customers select their merchandise, bring it to the checkout line, and then carry it to their cars. Customers may even assemble the merchandise at home.

Since Wal-Mart and Toys "R" Us emphasize low price, they've made strategic decisions to develop a cost advantage over competitors. Both firms have sophisticated distribution and management information systems to manage inventory. Their strong relationships with suppliers enable them to buy merchandise at low prices.

Strategic Decision Areas   The key strategic decision areas involve determining a market strategy, financial strategy, location strategy, organizational structure and human resource strategy, information systems and supply chain strategies, and customer relationship management strategies.

Chapter 5 discusses how selection of a retail market strategy is based on analyzing the environment and the firm's strengths and weaknesses. When major environmental changes occur, the current strategy and the reasoning behind it are reexamined. The retailer then decides what, if any, strategy changes are needed to take advantage of new opportunities or avoid new threats in the environment.

The retailer's market strategy must be consistent with the firm's financial objectives. Chapter 6 reviews how financial variables such as sales, costs, expenses, profits, assets, liabilities, and owner's equity are used to evaluate the market strategy and its implementation.

Decisions concerning location strategy (reviewed in Chapters 7 and 8) are important for both consumer and competitive reasons. First, location is typically consumers' top consideration when selecting a store. Generally consumers buy gas at the closest service station and patronize the shopping mall that's most convenient to their home or office. Second, location offers an opportunity to gain long-term advantage over competition. When a retailer has the best location, a competing retailer has to settle for the second-best location.

A retailer's organization design and human resource management strategy are intimately related to its market strategy. For example, retailers that attempt to serve national or regional markets must make trade-offs between the efficiency of centralized buying and the need to tailor merchandise and services to local needs. Retailers that focus on customer segments seeking high-quality customer service must motivate and enable sales associates to provide the expected levels of service. The organization structure and human resources policies discussed in Chapter 9 coordinate the implementation of the retailing strategy by buyers, store managers, and sales associates.

Retail information and supply chain management systems will offer a significant opportunity for retailers to gain strategic advantage in the coming decade. Chapter 10 reviews how some retailers are developing sophisticated computer and distribution systems to monitor flows of information and merchandise from vendors to retail distribution centers to retail stores. Point-of-sale (POS) terminals read price and product information that's coded into Universal Product Codes (UPCs) affixed to the merchandise. This information is then transmitted to distribution centers or directly to vendors electronically, computer to computer. These technologies are part of an overall inventory management system that enables retailers to (1) give customers a more complete selection of merchandise and (2) decrease their inventory investment.

Basic to any strategy is understanding the customers so as to provide them with the goods and services they want. And even more important is to understand and cater to the wants of the retailer's most-valued customers. After all, these customers account for the lion's share of a retailer's sales and profits. Chapter 11 examines customer relationship management from a B-to-C, or retailer to consumer, perspective. **Customer relationship management (CRM)** is a business philosophy and set of strategies, programs, and systems that focuses on identifying and building loyalty with a firm's most-valued customers. This chapter examines some of the data-analysis methods retailers use for identifying their most-valued customers. Once these customers are identified, special programs are designed to build their loyalty.

JCPenney Moves from Main Street to the Mall The interrelationships among these retail strategy decisions—market strategy, financial strategy, organization structure and human resource strategy, and location strategy—are illustrated by a major strategic change JCPenney made in the early 1960s.[14]

In the late 1950s, Penney was one of the most profitable national retailers. Its target market was small towns. In its Main Street locations, Penney sold staple soft goods—underwear, socks, basic clothing, sheets, tablecloths, and so forth—at low prices with minimal service. All sales were cash; the company didn't offer credit to its customers. Penney had considerable expertise in the design and purchase of soft goods with private labels—brands developed by the retailer and sold exclusively at its stores.

Organization structure was decentralized. Each store manager controlled the type of merchandise sold, the pricing of merchandise, and the management of store employees. Promotional efforts were limited and also controlled by store managers. Penney store managers were active participants in their community's social and political activities.

Although Penney was a highly successful retailer, there was a growing awareness among company executives that macroenvironmental trends would have a negative impact on the firm. First, as the nation's levels of education and disposable income rose, consumers grew more interested in fashionable rather than staple merchandise. Second, with the development of a national highway system, the growth of suburbs, and the rise of regional malls, small-town residents were attracted to conveniently located, large, regional shopping malls. Third, Sears (the nation's largest retailer) was beginning to locate stores and auto centers in regional malls. These trends suggested a decline in small-town markets for staple soft goods.

In the early 1960s, Penney undertook a new strategic direction that was consistent with changes it saw in the environment. All new Penney stores were located in regional malls across the United States. Penney opened several mall locations in each metropolitan area to create significant presence in each market. The firm began to offer credit to its customers and added new merchandise lines: appliances, auto supplies, paint, hardware, sporting goods, consumer electronics, and moderately priced fashionable clothing.

To effectively control its 1,150 department stores, Penney installed a sophisticated communication network. Each store manager can monitor daily sales of each type of merchandise in his or her store and every other store in the chain. Buyers at corporate headquarters in Dallas communicate daily with merchandise managers in each store over a satellite TV link.

To respond to the increased time pressure on two-income and single–head-of-household families, Penney launched its catalog operation and now is the largest catalog retailer in the United States. Penney has used its catalog distribution capability to aggressively move into selling merchandise over the Internet (www.jcpenney.com). Its multichannel strategy has been quite successful. Customers who shopped at Penney across all three of its channels—stores, catalogs, and Internet—on average spent $1,050 each in 1999, more than four times more than Penney's average single-channel customer.[15]

Now JCPenney is facing a new challenge. Middle-market department stores such as Penney are caught in the middle between higher-priced, fashion-oriented department store chains like Macy's that are lowering their prices through sales and, at the other end of the spectrum, lower-priced, stores such as Kohl's and Target that are offering more fashionable merchandise.

This illustrates how retailers must respond continually to a changing environment. These changes often result in new strategic directions that must be supported by new locations, new organization design, and new information and communication systems.

REFACT

James Cash Penney opened the first JCPenney store, called Golden Rule, in Kemmerer, Wyoming, in 1902.[16]

In the 1960s, JCPenney made a dramatic strategic change moving from Main Street (left) to malls (right) in response to changes in the macroenvironment.

Implementing the Retail Strategy—Sections III and IV

To implement a retail strategy, management develops a retail mix that satisfies the needs of its target market better than its competitors. The **retail mix** is the combination of factors retailers use to satisfy customer needs and influence their purchase decisions. Elements in the retail mix (Exhibit 1–7) include the types of merchandise and services offered, merchandise pricing, advertising and promotional programs, store design, merchandise display, assistance to customers provided by salespeople, and convenience of the store's location. Section III reviews the implementation decisions made by buyers, and Section IV focuses on decisions made by store managers.

Managers in the buying organization must decide how much and what types of merchandise to buy (Chapters 12 and 13), the vendors to use and the purchase terms (Chapter 14), the retail prices to set (Chapter 15), and how to advertise and promote merchandise (Chapter 16).

Store managers must determine how to recruit, select, and motivate sales associates (Chapter 17), where and how merchandise will be displayed (Chapter 18), and the nature of services to provide customers (Chapter 19).

Whole Foods Market: An Organic and Natural Food Supermarket Chain Whole Foods Market, one of the fastest-growing supermarket chains, illustrates the use of merchandise and store management activities to implement a retail strategy. Whole Foods owns Bread & Circus in New England, Mrs. Gooch's Natural Foods Market in Los Angeles, Fresh Fields on the East Coast and Chicago, and many others.

It is easy to mistake John Mackey for an aging hippie rather than the founder and CEO of Whole Foods Market, a retailer with over $1.8 billion in annual sales.[17] At the University of Texas in Austin, Mackey developed a passion for philosophy and religion. When he found that textbooks weren't going to provide the answers he was looking for, he dropped out of college, lived in a vegetarian housing co-op, worked in an Austin natural food store, and eventually opened his own health food store and restaurant. Unlike other veggie joints, Mackey's store catered to a broad clientele by carrying items typically not found at health food stores, such as refined sugar and eggs. Then he teamed up with a local organic grocer to open the first Whole Foods, which was an instant success.

Whole Foods stores, which average 26,000 square feet and renovated existing stores 35,000 square feet, are much larger and carry a much broader assortment

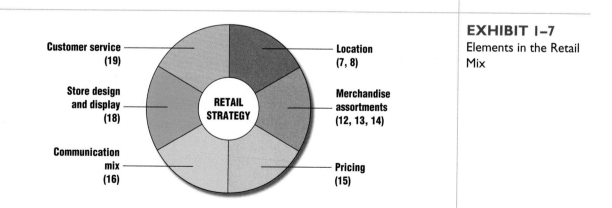

EXHIBIT 1–7
Elements in the Retail Mix

This juice counter at Whole Foods Market is part of the firm's retail mix.

than the typical natural and organic grocery store. The stores sell vegetarian no-nos, such as red meat and coffee, so that health-conscious nonvegetarians can have a one-stop shopping experience. The assortment includes two lines of private-brand products that are free of artificial sweeteners, colorings, artificial flavorings, and preservatives. Buyers work with artisan food producers and organic farmers for products sold under the Whole Foods™ premium label. The 365 Day Value™ line provides natural products at value prices. To ensure the quality of its private labels, three inspectors fly over 100,000 miles a year visiting farms and checking the crops.

The flower power of the 60s is reflected in Mackey's guiding management principles: love, trust, and employee empowerment. All employees are organized into self-managed teams. The teams meet regularly to discuss issues and solve problems. Almost all team members have stock options in the firm. To ensure that employees are compensated equitably, the company has a cap on salaries so that no employee's total compensation can be more than 10 times the average compensation of all employees.[18]

Mackey has a 60s mentality about equality, but he also has an old-fashioned competitive drive to dominate Whole Foods' segment of the supermarket industry. When Whole Foods opened a store in Boulder, Colorado (headquarters of rival Wild Oats), Mackey sent Wild Oats CEO Michael Gilliland the game Risk with a note: "Forewarned is forearmed."

SUMMARY

An important institution in our society, retailing provides considerable value to consumers while giving people opportunities for rewarding and challenging careers. Due to significant shifts in consumers' needs and technology, the retail industry too is changing. Retail formats and companies that were unknown 30 years ago are now major factors in the industry.

The key to successful retailing is offering the right product, at the right price, in the right place, at the right time, and making a profit. To accomplish all this, retailers must understand what customers want and what competitors are offering now and in the future. Retailers' wide range of decisions extends from setting a brown wool sweater's price to determining whether a new multimillion-dollar store should be built in a mall. This book is written to provide insights and directions for making such decisions. Some publications for retail managers are listed in Appendix 1B.

KEY TERMS

breaking bulk, *8*
customer relationship
    management (CRM), *21*
distribution channel, *6*
intertype competition, *18*

intratype competition, *17*
retail mix, *23*
retail strategy, *19*
retailer, *6*

retailing, *6*
scrambled merchandising, *18*
variety, *17*
vertical integration, *7*

GET OUT & DO IT!

 1. GO SHOPPING Visit your favorite multichannel retailer by going to a store, going to its Internet site, and looking at a catalog. Evaluate how well the company has integrated these three channels into one seamless strategy.

DISCUSSION QUESTIONS AND PROBLEMS

1. Choose a pure-play Internet retailer. Do you think it will be profitable in the next five years?

2. Why bother going to a retailer when you could probably purchase the same product cheaper directly from a manufacturer?

3. Does Wal-Mart contribute to or detract from the communities in which it operates stores?

4. Choose one of the top 25 retailers (Exhibit 1–4) with which you are familiar. Has it been successful expanding beyond its parent country? Why or why not?

5. From a personal perspective, how does retailing rate as a potential career compared to others you are considering?

6. How might managers at different levels of a retail organization define their competition?

7. Explain the strategy used by your favorite retailer.

SUGGESTED READINGS

Kahn, Barbara, and Leigh McAllister. *The Grocery Revolution*. Reading, MA: Addison-Wesley, 1997.

Marcus, Bernard, and Arthur Blank. *Built from Scratch: How a Couple of Regular Guys Grew the Home Depot from Nothing into $30 Billion*. New York: Random House, 1999.

Scardino, Emily. "Fashion's Future." *DSN Retailing Today*, December 10, 2001, www.dsnretailingtoday.com.

Schultz, Howard, and Dori Jones Lang. *Pour Your Heart into It: How Starbucks Built a Company One Cup at a Time*. New York: Hyperion, 1997.

Spector, Robert, and Patrick McCarthy. *The Nordstrom Way: The Inside Story of America's #1 Customer Service Company*. New York: Wiley, 1995.

Stern, Neil Z. "Tomorrow's Hot Retail Ideas." *International Trends in Retailing*, Arthur Anderson. December 2000, http://retailindustry.about.com/cs/retailtrends.

Tiernan, Bernadette. *E-Tailing*. Dearborn Financial Publishing, Inc., 1999.

APPENDIX IA   Careers in Retailing

Retailing offers exciting and challenging career opportunities. Few other industries grant as many responsibilities to young managers. When students asked Dave Fuente, former CEO of Office Depot, what they need to become a CEO someday, he responded, "You need to have profit and loss responsibility and the experience of managing people early in your career." Entry-level retail jobs for college graduates offer both of these opportunities. Most college graduates begin their retail careers as assistant buyers or department managers. In these positions, you will have responsibility for the profitability of a line of merchandise or an area of the store, and you will be managing people who work for you.

Even if you work for a large company, retailing provides an opportunity for you to do your own thing and be rewarded. You can come with an idea, execute it almost immediately, and see how well it is doing by reviewing the sales data at the end of the day.

Retailing offers a variety of career paths such as buying, store management, sales promotion and advertising, personnel, operations/distribution, loss prevention, and finance in several different corporate forms such as department stores, specialty stores, food stores, and discount stores.

In addition, retailing offers almost immediate accountability for talented people so they can reach key management positions within a decade. Starting salaries are competitive, and the compensation of top management ranks among the highest in any industry.

CAREER OPPORTUNITIES

In retail firms, career opportunities occur in the merchandising/buying, store management, and corporate staff functions. Corporate positions are found in such areas as accounting, finance, promotions and advertising, computer and distribution systems, and human resources.

The primary entry-level opportunities for a retailing career are in the areas of buying and store management. Buying positions are more numbers-oriented, while store management positions are more people-oriented. Entry-level positions on the corporate staff are limited. Retailers typically want all of their employees to understand their customers and their merchandise. Therefore, most managers on the corporate staff begin their careers in store management or buying.

Store Management

Successful store managers must have the ability to lead and motivate employees. They also need to be sensitive to the customers' needs, making sure that merchandise is available and neatly displayed. Store management involves all the discipline necessary to run a successful business: sales planning and goal setting, overall store image and merchandise presentation, budgets and expense control, customer service and sales supervision, personnel administration and development, and community relations.

Store managers work directly in the retail environment—often at quite a distance from the home office. Thus they have limited direct supervision. Their hours generally mirror their store's and can therefore include some weekends and evenings. In addition, they spend time during nonoperating hours tending to administrative responsibilities.

The typical career path begins as a department manager with responsibility for merchandise presentation, customer service, and inventory control for an area of the store. Next, you advance to a position known as area or group manager with responsibility for executing merchandising plans and achieving sales goals for several areas, as well as supervising, training, and developing department managers. After these positions, you might become a store manager and then a district manager or move into a merchandising or staff position in the corporate office.

Merchandise Management

Merchandise management attracts people with strong analytical capabilities, an ability to predict what merchandise will appeal to their target markets, and a skill to negotiate with vendors as well as store management to get things done. Many retailers have broken the merchandising/buying function into two different yet parallel career paths: buying and merchandise planning.

Buyers are responsible for knowing customers' needs and wants, monitoring competition, and working with vendors to select and purchase merchandise. They must constantly stay in contact with their stores by visiting them, by talking to sale associates and managers, and by monitoring the sales data available on their merchandise management systems.

Planners have a more analytical role than buyers do. Their primary responsibility is to determine how many styles, colors, sizes, and individual items to purchase. Planners also are responsible for allocating merchandise to stores. Once the merchandise is in the stores, planners closely monitor sales and work with buyers on decisions such as how much additional merchandise to purchase if the merchandise is doing well, or when to mark down merchandise if sales are below plan.

Corporate Staff

These areas provide opportunities for individuals with specific skills and interests. Thus career opportunities in these areas are more difficult to break into.

Computer Systems Experience with computer applications is an important plus when looking for a career in retailing. Such areas as data capture and application, quick response (QR) inventory systems to minimize inventory costs and ensure product availability, expedient point-of-sale systems, and electronic data interchange (EDI) ensure retailers of an efficient merchandise flow.

Operations/Distribution People in this area oversee the movement of merchandise in an accurate, efficient, and timely manner. They are responsible for operating and maintaining the store's physical plant, for providing various customer services, for the receipt, ticketing, warehousing, and distribution of a store's inventory, and for buying and maintaining store supplies and operating equipment.

Promotions/Advertising Promotion's many aspects include public relations, advertising, visual merchandising, and special events. The creative people in sales promotion departments try to presell the customer on the assumption that the best way to generate sales is to encourage people to want new merchandise.

Loss Prevention Loss prevention people provide asset protection for associates, facilities, and merchandise. They are responsible for developing and maintaining loss prevention systems and controlling internal and external theft.

Finance/Control Financial management specialists and top financial officers are among the most highly paid people in retailing. Many retailers have been involved in complicated corporate restructuring leading to high levels of debt. Most retailers also operate on a tight net profit margin. With such a fine line between success and failure, retailers continue to require top financial experts—and they compensate them generously.

The finance/control division is responsible for the financial soundness of the company. This involves preparing the financial reports for all aspects of the business, including long-range forecasting and planning, economic trend analysis and budgeting, shortage control and internal audit, gross and net profit, accounts payable to vendors, and accounts receivable from charge customers.

Real Estate People in the real estate division are responsible for selecting locations for stores, negotiating leases and land purchases, and managing the leasehold costs.

Store Design Retailers are finding that clearly defined, comfortable, and visually pleasing stores give them that extra edge over competition. Key elements of store design in the future include easy-to-shop, easy-to-maintain, and flexible store layouts. Talented, creative students in business, architecture, art, and other related fields will have innumerable opportunities for growth in the area of retail store design.

Human Resource Management Human resource management is responsible for the effective selection, training, placement, advancement, and welfare of employees. Because there are seasonal peaks in retailing (such as Christmas when many extra people must be hired), human resource personnel must be flexible and highly efficient.

IS RETAILING FOR ME?

One of the most important decisions a student must make is what career to pursue. In deciding on careers, you need to pick a career that involves doing things you like to do and are good at doing. Every career has its pros and cons. Finding the best fit, however, takes considerable thought and planning.

Responsibility

Retailing is for people who like responsibility. Starting management trainees are given more responsibility more quickly than in other industries. Buyers are responsible for choosing, promoting, pricing, distributing, and selling millions of dollars worth of merchandise each season. The department manager, which is generally the first position after a training program, is often responsible for merchandising one or more departments as well as for managing 10 or more full- and part-time sales associates.

Career Advancement

Many opportunities for rapid advancement exist simply because of the sheer size of the retail industry. There are millions of retail establishments, and the larger ones have many different positions and multiple managerial levels. Yet in choosing a particular retailer, take care to choose a growth firm. Firms that have recently undergone corporate restructuring may have a glut of middle-management positions. If store operations is an appealing career area, pursue chains with multiple outlets. But these stores don't present particularly good opportunities for people who seek a buying career, because they have relatively small buying staffs compared to the number of outlets. If buying is your primary career interest, choose a firm with a relatively large buying staff (e.g., a department store) or a firm with more decentralized purchasing (e.g., Nordstrom).

Compensation and Benefits

Retailing can be both financially and personally rewarding. Careers in retailing combine continuous personal development with almost immediate responsibility and new challenges. Each day is different, so sales associates and executives are rarely bored. Starting salaries are competitive, and the compensation of top management ranks with the highest in industry. For example, store managers with only a few years of experience can earn up to $100,000 or more, depending on bonuses. Top buyers, systems professionals, and other technical experts may earn just as much.

The average store manager earns a base salary of $55,770, compared to $26,000 in 1983. The latter figure equates to $44,722 in today's dollars once inflation is factored in.[19] Compensation varies by amount of responsibility. Specialty store managers are generally paid less than department store managers because their annual sales volume is lower. But advancements can be faster. Aggressive specialty store managers often are promoted to district managers and run 8 to 15 units after a few years so they quickly move into higher pay brackets. Typical compensation for management trainees ranges from $22,000 to $32,000. A senior buyer for a department store earns from $50,000 to $90,000 or more. A department store manager can earn from $50,000 to $150,000; a discount store manager makes from $70,000 to $100,000 or more; and a specialty store manager earns from $35,000 to $60,000 or more.

Because sales can be related to specific managers, retailers typically see a link between performance and compensation. As a result, in addition to salaries, retail managers are generally given strong monetary incentives based on sales. In a recent survey of store managers, 92 percent of respondents say they receive an annual bonus. The average is 20 percent of their base salary, or $11,540. In 1983, respondents reported receiving an average annual bonus of just 6 percent, or $1,560. That equates to $2,683 today. Still salary was one of the major gripes of store managers who responded to this survey. Dissatisfaction with salary, at 38.9 percent, ranked second behind long work hours.[20]

A compensation package consists of more than salary alone. In retailing, the benefits package is often substantial. It may include a profit-sharing plan; savings plan; stock option plan; medical and dental insurance; life insurance; long-term disability protection and income protection plans; and paid vacations and holidays. Two additional benefits of retailing careers are that most retailers offer employees valuable discounts on the merchandise that they sell, and some buying positions include extensive foreign travel.

Working Conditions

Retailing has an often exaggerated reputation of demanding long and odd hours. Superficially, this reputation is true. Store managers do work some evenings and weekends. But many progressive retailers have realized that if the odd hours aren't offset by time off at other periods in the week, many managers become inefficient, angry, and resentful—in a word, burned out. It's also important to put the concept of long hours into perspective. Most professional careers require more than 40 hours per week for the person to succeed. In a new job with new tasks and responsibilities, the time commitment is even greater.

People shouldn't go into retailing if they like a calm, orderly, peaceful work environment with no surprises. Retailing is for those who like having exciting days, making quick decisions, and dealing with a variety of assignments, tasks, and people—often all at once.

Job Locations

Depending on the type of retailer and the specific firm, retailing enables executives to change locations often or not at all. In general, a career path in store management has more opportunity for relocation than paths in buying/merchandising or corporate. Because buying and corporate offices are usually centrally located, these positions generally aren't subjected to frequent moves.

Women and Minorities in Retailing

Many people consider retailing to be among the most racially and gender-blind industries. Retailers typically think that their manager and executives will make better decisions if they mirror their customer. Since most purchases are made by women and because minorities are becoming an increasingly important factor in the market, most retailers have active programs designed to provide the experiences and support that will enable women and minorities to be promoted to top management positions.

GETTING READY FOR AN INTERVIEW WITH A RETAILER

Here are some things you need to do to make a good impression in an interview with a retailer:

- *Visit the retailer's stores before the interview.* Actually seeing the store can give you insight for discussing the company intelligently throughout the interview process. Well-stocked and orderly departments (with the exception of deep-discount stores that sometimes purposely maintain a disorderly look) suggest (but don't prove) that the company is in good health. Signs of decay either could mean the store is planning a relocation or a massive renovation, or could indicate poor management or financial problems.

- *Read about the retailer.* In conjunction with store visits, read the retailer's annual report to stockholders; examine reports from Value Line and other investment service firms; study trade publications such as *Discount Store News, Chain Store Age,* and *Stores;* and visit its website on the Internet.

- *Find out whether the retailer is hiring primarily for store or merchandise management positions.* For example, if you're interested in fashion, a career in a department store or national off-price chain like T. J. Maxx or Marshalls may be the way to go. Be certain that its needs coincide with your goals.

- *Determine whether there have been recent changes in ownership or top management.* A change isn't necessarily bad, but it does add some uncertainty—and therefore risk—to the decision.

- *Research the retailer's strategy and growth potential.* Has it been expanding? Is it in strong markets? How strong and innovative are its competitors? Successful retailers in the new millenium will increase their emphasis on marketing to satisfy customer needs by focusing heavily on service. Moreover, by employing creative organizational and management strategies, retailers will concentrate on giving buyers and store managers greater responsibility, while supporting them with logistics and systems specialists.

- *Determine whether the retailer is known for innovation.* An innovative retailer has a greater chance of long-term success than a stodgy one. To measure innovativeness, look at its stores and promotions. Are they modern? Do the stores and promotions reflect the times? Do they appeal to their target markets?

- *Find out about the retailer's computers and distribution systems.* Highly sophisticated retail technology symbolizes a view toward the future. Technology, if used properly, makes firms more efficient and therefore profitable. Finally, quick response inventory management systems, EDI, and sophisticated POS terminals relieve managers from much of the tedious paperwork previously associated with careers in retailing.

Exhibit 17–4 lists some questions frequently asked during interviews. Advance knowledge of some of the questions that may arise should boost your confidence, reduce your anxiety, and improve the interviewer's impression of you.

SUMMARY

Retailing isn't for everyone. This appendix has provided a framework for considering a career in retailing. A variety of careers available in the retail industry have been described. Advantages and disadvantages of a retailing career have been presented. The characteristics necessary to become a successful retail executive were examined. The appendix concluded with the answers to some commonly asked questions about a career in retailing and discussed how to get ready for an interview.

APPENDIX 1B   Trade Publications for Retailers

Apparel Merchandising Reports, forecasts, and interprets apparel merchandising trends and strategies in women's, men's, and children's wear. www.dsnretailingtoday.com

Chain Store Age Monthly magazine for retail headquarters executives and shopping center developers. Deals with management, operations, construction, modernization, store equipment, maintenance, real estate, financing, materials handling, and advertising. More oriented to operations than stores. www.chainstoreage.com

CS News Monthly magazine for convenience store and oil retailing executives, managers, and franchisees. Covers industry trends, news, and merchandising techniques. www.csnews.com

DNR (formerly *Daily News Record*) Daily newspaper on retail fashion, product, merchandising, and marketing for men's and boy's wear. Geared to retailers, wholesalers, and manufacturers. www.dnrnews.com

Dealerscope Monthly publication for retailers of consumer electronics, appliances, and computers. www.dealerscope.com

DSN Retailing Today Biweekly national newspaper describing marketing developments and productivity reports from executives in full-line discount stores, catalog showrooms, warehouse clubs, and specialty discount chains. www.dsnretailingtoday.com

Drug Store News Biweekly publication covering chain drug and combination store retailing. www.drugstorenews.com

Fairchild's Executive Technology Monthly publication with executive interviews, feature reports, show coverage, international news, and analysis. Retail classes of trade, from specialty apparel, department, and discount to supermarket, drug, and convenience. www.executivetechnology.com

Furniture/Today Weekly newspaper for retail executives in furniture and department stores and for executives in manufacturing firms. www.furnituretoday.com

Hobby Merchandiser Monthly publication for suppliers and retailers in the model hobby industry. www.hobbymerchandiser.com

Home Improvement Centers Monthly magazine for full-line and specialty retailers and wholesale distributors of home improvement products. Covers systems and products to sell to customers ranging from do-it-yourselfers to professional remodelers.

Hotel and Motel Management Bimonthly magazine reports news and trends affecting the lodging industry. www.advanstar.com

Internet Retailer Monthly magazine devoted to electronic retailing issues. www.internetretailer.com

Mass Market Retailers Biweekly newspaper for executives in supermarket, chain drug, and chain discount headquarters. Reports news and interprets its effects on mass merchandisers. www.massmarketretailers.com

Modern Grocer Weekly newspaper covers regional and national news current events relating to food retailing. http://griffcomm.net

Modern Jeweler Monthly magazine for jewelry retailers looks at trends in jewelry, gems, and watches. www.modernjeweler.com

NACS Magazine Monthly publication for convenience stores. www.cstorecentral.com

Private Label Bimonthly magazine for buyers, merchandisers, and executives involved in purchasing private, controlled packer, and generic-labeled products for chain supermarkets and drug, discount, convenience, and department stores. www.privatelabelmag.com

Progressive Grocer Monthly magazine reporting on the supermarket industry. In-depth features offer insights into trends in store development, technology, marketing, logistics, international retailing, human resources, and consumer purchasing patterns. www.grocerynetwork.com

Retail Info Systems News Monthly magazine addressing system solutions for corporate/financial, operations, MIS, and merchandising management at retail. www.risnews.com

Retail Merchandiser Published monthly for retail buyers, CEOs, financial investors, visual merchandisers, and consultants. www.retail-merchandiser.com

Retailtech Magazine Monthly magazine reporting on and interpreting technologies available for all levels of the fashion distribution chain from manufacturers to retailers. Includes computers, retail point-of-sales systems, computer-aided design and manufacturing, software, electronic retailing, credit systems, visual merchandising, and factory automation. www.retailtech.com

Shopping Center World Monthly magazine on new-center developments and leasing, redevelopments and releasing, management, operations, marketing, design, construction, and financing of shopping centers. www.intertec.com

Shopping Centers Today Monthly publication on the development of new shopping centers and the expansion of existing ones. www.icsc.org

Store Planning Design and Review Monthly publication describing new trends and techniques in store design and merchandise presentation. www.retailreporting.com

Stores Monthly magazine published by the National Retail Federation (NRF). Aimed at retail executives in department and specialty stores, it emphasizes broad trends in customer behavior, management practices, and technology. www.stores.org

VM/SD (Visual Merchandising/Store Design) Monthly magazine for people involved in merchandise display, store interior design and planning, and manufacturing of equipment used by display and store designers. www.magazinesofamerica.com

WWD (formerly *Women's Wear Daily*) Daily newspaper reports fashion and industry news on women's and children's ready-to-wear, sportswear, innerwear, accessories, and cosmetics. www.wwd.com

Types of Retailers

CHAPTER

EXECUTIVE BRIEFING | Bobby Ukrop, President and CEO, Ukrop's Super Markets, Inc.

"As a young boy, I enjoyed the grocery business. I always wanted to help my family build an even better business while living the Golden Rule by which my parents operated, served the community, and had fun. In 1963, when I was 16, my older brother, Jim, talked my Dad into opening a second store. [The first store opened in 1937.] Under Jim's leadership, we added three more stores in the 1960s. By 1972, I had become involved with the business on a day-to-day basis. I have faced various opportunities to learn from mistakes and grow as a leader through these experiences. In doing so, I was able to earn the respect of customers and associates by hard work, sincerity, and delivering on my promises. Over time, trusting relationships were built.

"We build and maintain customer loyalty by offering the products and services our customers desire, whether it is having items in stock or treating customers with warmth and respect. Beyond this, we trust our customers. For example we allow a customer to take groceries home if they have forgotten their checkbook, on the promise that they will return to pay the next time they shop. In addition, Ukrop's recognizes the value of good listening skills

and innovation in order to keep up with our customers' changing needs.

"Since 1987, we have offered a customer loyalty program, Ukrop's Valued Customer (UVC) card, which provides them with discounts on certain items in our store. Over the years, our UVC program has experienced tremendous growth; not only does it provide mass customization for Ukrop's, but it offers various discounts on events in the communities we serve. In 1989, we began offering cafés and grills in our stores as well as chilled, prepared foods in response to the on-the-go lifestyles of our customers. Most recently, we have begun to focus on increasing

Jim and Bobby Ukrop

QUESTIONS

● What trends are shaping today's retailers?

● What are the different types of retailers?

● How do retailers differ in terms of how they meet the needs of their customers?

● How do services retailers differ from merchandise retailers?

● What are the types of ownership for retail firms?

our natural and organic sections as many of our customers place a higher focus on overall health.

"Aside from our great-tasting, fresh food and signature items prepared in our facilities, as well as fair prices, customers choose to shop at Ukrop's because of the warm, caring atmosphere our associates strive to provide. Our vision is to be a world-class provider of food and services (within the context of our values based organization).

"Advice to others starting a business? Be passionate about what you are making or selling. Also, be prepared to work hard and go the extra mile. Walk your talk and be a team builder."

Ukrop's employs more than 5,600 associates in its 27 supermarkets, three food manufacturing plants, and a distribution center in Virginia. The chain is the marketshare leader in the Richmond, Virginia, market. In 2001, Ukrop's was selected by *Fortune* magazine as one of the 100 best places to work (for the third straight year) and Ukrop's was chosen as *Progressive Grocer* magazine's Supermarket Retailer of the Year and received national recognition by the Ernst and Young Entrepreneur of the Year awards program with the Principle-Centered Leadership award.

You want to have a cup of real coffee in the morning, not instant, but you don't want to bother with boiling water, pouring it through ground coffee in a filter, and waiting. You decide to buy an automatic coffeemaker with a timer so your coffee will be ready when you wake up. Think of all of the different retailers you could buy a coffeemaker from. You could buy a coffeemaker at a discount store like Wal-Mart or Target, a department store like Macy's, a drugstore like Walgreens, or a category specialist like Circuit City; you could also order a coffeemaker from the JCPenney catalog; or you could go to www.shopping.yahoo.com, search for "coffeemaker," and review the information on 270 models sold by more than 60 Internet retailers. All of these retailers are competing against each other to sell you a coffeemaker. Many of them are selling the same brands, but they offer different services, prices, atmospheres, and convenience.

To develop and implement a retail strategy, you need to understand the nature of competition in the retail marketplace. This chapter describes the different types of retailers—both store- and nonstore-based retailers. Retailers differ in terms of the types of merchandise and services they offer to customers, the nature of the retail mixes used to satisfy customer needs, the degree to which their offerings emphasize services versus merchandise, and the ownership of the firm.

TRENDS IN THE RETAIL INDUSTRY

As we discussed in the first chapter, the retail industry is changing rapidly. Some of the most important changes discussed in this section involve (1) the greater diversity of retailers, (2) increasing industry concentration, (3) globalization, and (4) the use of multiple channels to interact with customers. The first three trends are discussed below. Chapter 3 examines the development of multichannel retailing—retailing through stores, catalogs, and the Internet—to better serve their customers and compete in today's complex retail environment.

Growing Diversity of Retail Formats

Over the past 20 years, many new retail formats have been developed. Consumers now can purchase the same merchandise from a wider variety of retailers as illustrated by the coffeemaker example at the beginning of this chapter. The initial category specialists in toys, consumer electronics, and home improvement supplies have been joined by a host of new specialists including MARS (musical instruments), Bed Bath & Beyond (home furnishings), and PETs-MART (pet supplies). Wal-Mart is closing some of its traditional discount stores to open supercenters—large stores (150,000 to 200,000 square feet) combining a discount store with a supermarket. CarMax competes with automobile dealers selling used cars using traditional retailing methods. The Internet has spawned a new set of retailers offering consumers the opportunity to buy merchandise and services at fixed prices (www.amazon.com), participate in auctions (www.ebay.com), or submit "take-it-or-leave-it" bids (www.priceline.com). Retailing View 2.1 describes how a French retailer is changing the way cosmetics are sold in the United States.

 Tesco's development of new food retailing formats in the U.K. targeting different market segments illustrates the trend toward increasing diversity. The superstore, or large supermarket (20,000 to 50,000 square feet), is the main format. The other formats are Tesco Metro, smaller food stores designed for urban locations; Tesco Express, combination gasoline and convenience stores; and Tesco Extra, hypermarkets, or very large retail stores that offer low prices and combine a discount and a superstore food retailer in one warehouse-like building.[1]

These new types of retailers coexist with traditional retailers. Each type of retailer offers a different set of benefits, thus consumers patronize different retailers for different purchase occasions. For example, a consumer might purchase a pair of cargo pants from a catalog as a gift for a friend in another city and then visit a local store to try on and buy the same pants for himself. The greater diversity of retail formats increases competition in the industry and also enables consumers to buy merchandise and services from a retailer that better satisfies their needs for the specific purchase occasion.

Increasing Industry Concentration

While the number of different retail formats has grown, the number of competitors within each format is decreasing. A few national retailers dominate most formats. For example, Wal-Mart, Kmart, and Target account for over 85 percent of the sales in full-line discount stores, and Walgreens, CVS, Rite-Aid, and Eckerd (JCPenney), represent 53 percent of the drugstore sales.[2] In the United States, there are now only two major category specialists left in consumer electronics (Circuit City and Best Buy), three dominant warehouse clubs (Sam's Club [Wal-Mart], Costco, and BJ's Wholesale Club), and three in office supplies (Office Depot, Staples, and OfficeMax). The dominance of the supermarket industry by strong regional firms like Publix (Florida) and HEB (Texas) is being challenged by national operators like Wal-Mart, Kroger, Ahold USA, Albertson's, and Safeway.[3]

Globalization

Historically, retailing has been a local business. Stores were owned and operated by people living in the community and patronized by local residents. Today, however, some retailing concepts that are successful in their country of origin have successfully developed a global presence. The reasons why some retail concepts work globally, and why some do not, are usually dependent on what provides their sustainable competitive advantage in their home country. For instance, Wal-Mart and France's Carrefour have efficient distribution and communication systems that allow them to offer great customer value. Sweden's IKEA furniture stores are popular with younger, well-educated adults who are furnishing their first homes and apartments. McDonald's and KFC appeal to hungry people everywhere. For every successful global retailer, there is another that has failed. In Chapter 5, we examine global retailing success factors.

Sephora | RETAILING VIEW

2.1

Sephora, France's leading perfume and cosmetic chain—a division of luxury-goods conglomerate LVMH (Louis Vuitton–Moet Hennessy)—is changing the way cosmetics are sold in the United States. In the United States, prestige cosmetics are typically sold in department stores. Each brand has a separate counter with a commissioned salesperson stationed behind the counter to help customers.

Sephora is a cosmetic and perfume specialty store offering a deep assortment in a self-service, 9,000-square-foot format. The 70-plus U.S. stores have over 13,000 SKUs, including 365 different, private-label lipsticks. Merchandise is grouped by product category with the brands displayed alphabetically so customers can locate them easily. Video walls and interactive kiosks provide extensive product and use information.

Customers are free to shop and experiment on their own. Sampling is encouraged. Salespeople, wearing a single black glove (to better display stylish perfume boxes), are available to assist customers. However, the salespeople are paid a flat salary by Sephora, not a commission by the manufacturer. The low-key atmosphere results in customers spending more time shopping.

Sephora avoids the hard sell, encouraging shoppers to sample the makeup and fragrances.

Sources: www.hoovers.com/premium/profile/4/0,2147,41804, 00.html; "Sephora: Retail Store of the Year," *Chain Store Age*, February 1, 2001, pp. RS15 15RSOY; Barry Janoff, "Market Makeover, *Progressive Grocer*, February 2000, p. 91; and "Selling Open Sell," *Women's Wear Daily Eye on Fragrance Supplement*, June 1999, p. 4.

Some factors stimulating retail globalization are the maturation of domestic markets, the development of skills and systems to effectively manage global operations, and the removal of trade barriers.

Maturation of Domestic Markets   Most large retailers have saturated their domestic markets. For example, in the United States, many retail failures are attributed to having too many stores in a market selling the same category of merchandise. Growth-oriented retailers therefore often see greater opportunities in other countries.

Skills and Systems   Today's retailers are better prepared to effectively manage stores in nondomestic markets. Their expertise in managing information and distribution systems is easily transferable to international markets. Many have learned that global merchandise sourcing can provide their customers with a better selection and value. Global sourcing and sophisticated information and distribution systems make global expansion easier to do. Distribution and information systems are discussed in Chapter 10. Global sourcing is examined in Chapter 14.

Trade Barriers   Finally, the relaxation of trade barriers makes global expansion easier. The World Trade Organization (WTO), NAFTA (North America) countries, ASEAN (Southeast Asia) countries, and the European Union (EU) have taken significant steps to lower the barriers to international trade. These issues are discussed in Chapter 14.

While there are millions of retailers across the globe, there are a limited number of retail institutions. The following sections discuss some common types of store-based retailers, nonstore-based retailers, and service retailers. Appendix 2B, at the end of the chapter, outlines some theories about the evolution of retail institutions.

REFACT

The four largest food retailers account for 62 percent of the sales in the U.K., 78 percent in Germany, and 83 percent in France.[4]

RETAILER CHARACTERISTICS

The 1.5 million U.S. store-based retailers range from street vendors selling hot dogs to large corporations such as Sears that have become an integral part of American culture.[5] Each retailer survives and prospers by satisfying a group of consumers' needs more effectively than its competitors. Over time, different types of retailers have emerged and prospered because they have attracted and maintained a significant customer base.

The most basic characteristic of a retailer is its retail mix—the elements used by a retailer to satisfy its customers' needs (see Exhibit 1–7). Four elements of the retail mix are particularly useful for classifying retailers: the type of merchandise sold, the variety and assortment of merchandise sold, the level of customer service, and the price of the merchandise. Retailers often shop at their competitors' stores to compare their retail offering with the competition.

Price–Cost Trade-Off

As you read about the different types of retailers, notice how patterns among retail mix elements arise. For example, department stores appeal to consumers looking for fashionable apparel and home furnishings. Typically, department stores have higher prices because they have higher costs due to stocking a lot of fashionable merchandise, discounting merchandise when errors are made in forecasting consumer tastes, providing some personal sales service, and having convenient but expensive mall locations. On the other hand, discount stores appeal to customers who are looking for lower prices and are less interested in services and a wide range of merchandise sizes and colors.

This difference between the retail mix of department and discount stores illustrates the trade-off retailers make between the price and assortment of merchandise they sell and the services they offer to their customers. Offering more sizes, colors, and brands; making the store atmosphere more attractive and entertaining; and increasing the staff of knowledgeable sales associates raises the retailer's costs. To make a profit and provide these additional benefits to their customers, department stores have to increase the prices of their merchandise to cover the additional costs.

Type of Merchandise

The U.S. Bureau of the Census uses a classification scheme to collect data on business activity in the United States. As part of this overall classification scheme, it classifies all retail firms into a hierarchical set of six-digit **North American Industry Classification System (NAICS) codes** (Exhibit 2–1).[6] NAICS has replaced the U.S. Standard Industrial Classification (SIC) system that has been in effect since the 1930s. Developed jointly by the United States, Canada, and Mexico, NAICS provides comparable statistics about business activity in North America.

The classification scheme for food retailers is illustrated in Exhibit 2–1. The first two digits, 44 and 45, denote the retail sector. (Restaurants have been moved to sector 72—accommodation and food services.) The third digit denotes the subsector (this is the first column in Exhibit 2–1). The fourth digit represents the industry group. Thus, under subsector 448, clothing and clothing accessory stores, we have 4481 (clothing stores) and 4482 (shoe stores.) The fifth digit provides a further breakdown—44811 is men's clothing stores, whereas 44812 is women's clothing stores. The last digit, not illustrated in Exhibit 2–1 and not always used, may differ between the three countries. Exhibit 2–2 shows the annual sales of the larger categories as reported by the Census of Retail Trade.

While a retailer's principal competitors may be other retailers with the same NAICS code, there are many exceptions. For example, clothing's primary designation is subsector 448. But clothing can be purchased in sporting goods stores (45111), department stores (4521), warehouse clubs and superstores (45291), and electronic shopping and mail-order houses (4541). Although these stores all sell sports clothing, they satisfy different consumer needs and thus appeal to different market segments. Sporting goods stores have a large variety of sports clothing at relatively high prices and knowledgeable sales assistance. Department stores are equally expensive and service-oriented, but they don't offer the same broad assortment of sporting goods. **Warehouse clubs** may have a narrow assortment of relatively inexpensive sports clothing. Finally, a wide variety of sports clothing is available at an Internet shop like Fogdog.com; whereas NFL.com specializes in National Football League clothing and other football paraphernalia.

The degree to which retailers compete against each other isn't simply based on the similarity of their merchandise. The variety and assortment of the merchandise they offer and the services they provide must also be considered.

EXHIBIT 2–1 | NAICS Codes for Retailers

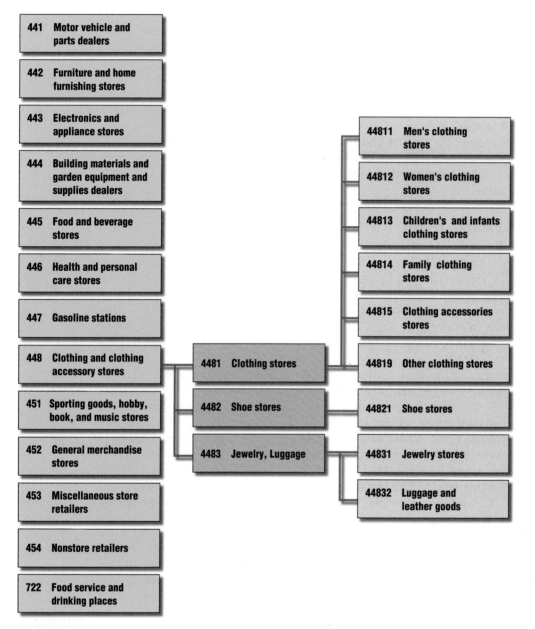

SOURCE: "1997 NAICS Matched to 1987 SIC: Sectors and Subsectors," U.S. Census Bureau, 2002, www.census.gov/epcd/www/naics.html.

Variety and Assortment

Variety is the number of merchandise categories a retailer offers. **Assortment** is the number of different items in a merchandise category. Each different item of merchandise is called a **SKU (stock keeping unit).** For example, a 32-ounce box of Tide laundry detergent and a white, long-sleeved, button-down-collar Tommy Hilfiger shirt, size 16–33, are both SKUs.

Retail Sales by NAICS Category | **EXHIBIT 2–2**

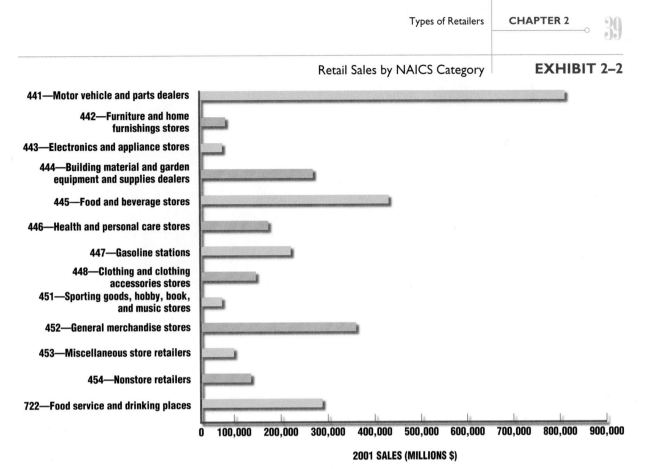

2001 SALES (MILLIONS $)

SOURCE: "2001 Monthly Retail and Food Service Sales." U.S. Census Bureau http://www.census.gov/mrts/www/data/html/nsal01.ht

Warehouse club stores, discount stores, and toy stores all sell toys. However, warehouse clubs and discount stores sell many other categories of merchandise in addition to toys. (They have greater variety.) Stores specializing in toys stock more types of toys (more SKUs). For each type of toy, such as dolls, the specialty toy retailer offers more assortment (more models, sizes, and brands, and deeper assortment) than general merchants such as warehouse clubs or discount stores.

Variety is often referred to as the **breadth of merchandise** carried by a retailer; assortment is referred to as the **depth of merchandise.** Exhibit 2–3 shows the breadth and depth of bicycles carried in a local bicycle shop in Boston called International Bicycle Centers (a specialty store), in Toys "R" Us (a category specialist), and in Wal-Mart (a discount store). Toys "R" Us carries three basic types and has a narrower variety than the International Bicycle Centers store, which carries four types; but Toys "R" Us has the greatest depth of assortment in children's bicycles. Wal-Mart has the lowest number of total SKUs (34) compared to Toys "R" Us (142) and the International Bicycle Centers (253). Note that Wal-Mart and Toys "R" Us have some of the same brands, but the International Bicycle Centers store offers a completely different set of brands.

Customer Services

Retailers also differ in the services they offer customers. For example, the bicycle shop offers assistance in selecting the appropriate bicycle, adjusting bicycles to fit

The local bike shop (left) offers the deepest assortment of bicycles. Wal-Mart (middle) has a narrow assortment of bicycles, but lots of variety overall. Toys "R" Us (right) is in the middle of the assortment/variety dimension.

EXHIBIT 2–3

Variety and Assortment of Bicycles in Different Retail Outlets

	Adult Road	Adult Hybrid	Mountain	Child
International Bicycle Centers	Trek, Bianchi, Specialized, Lemond, Klein, Litespeed, Merlin	Gary Fisher, Trek 800, Specialized, Bianchi, Lemond	Gary Fisher, Trek, Klein Attitude, Specialized	Gary Fisher, Trek, Specialized, Haro
	80 SKUs	44 SKUs	99 SKUs	30 SKUs
	$599–5,405	$239.99–1,299.99	$219–4,900	$109–349.99
Toys "R" Us	Mongoose, Huffy Bicycles, Pacific Cycle, Kent International		Pacific Cycle, Dynacraft	Mongoose, AMX/Patriot, Pacific Cycle, Gravity Games, Dynacraft, Rand International, Koncept, Hyper, Cosmic, Huffy Bicycles, Girl Power, Fisher Price, Barbie, Girls Starbright, Blossom Girls' Mountain Bike, Power Wheels, Magna, Rallye Bikes, Kent International, Murray Cycle
	16 SKUs		28 SKUs	98 SKUs
	$99.99–149.97		$59.98–399.98	$29.98–119.98
Wal-Mart	Tri-Fecta		Mongoose, RoadMaster, Next	RoadMaster, Mongoose, Next, Barbie
	13 SKUs		8 SKUs	13 SKUs
	$89.68–269.96		$89.96–149.96	$48.88–129.78

SOURCES: International Bicycle Centers, http://internationalbike.com/site/index.cfm?Loaderl; Toys "R" Us, www.toysrus.com; and Wal-Mart, www.walmart.com.

the individual, and repairing bicycles. Toys "R" Us and Wal-Mart don't provide any of these services. Customers expect retailers to provide some services: accepting personal checks, providing parking, and being open long and convenient hours. Some retailers charge customers for other services, such as home delivery and gift wrapping. Retailers that cater to service-oriented consumers offer customers most of these services at no charge.

Cost of Offering Breadth and Depth of Merchandise and Services

Stocking a deep assortment like the Toys "R" Us offering in bicycles is appealing to customers but costly for retailers. When a retailer offers customers many SKUs, inventory investment increases because the retailer must have backup stock for each SKU.

Similarly, services attract customers to the retailer, but they're also costly. More salespeople are needed to provide information and assist customers, to alter merchandise to meet customers' needs, and to demonstrate merchandise. Child care facilities, rest rooms, dressing rooms, and check rooms take up valuable store space that could be used to stock and display merchandise. Offering delayed billing, credit, and installment payments requires a financial investment that could be used to buy more merchandise.

A critical retail decision involves the trade-off between costs and benefits of maintaining additional inventory or providing additional services. Chapters 6 and 12 address the considerations in making this trade-off.

FOOD RETAILERS

What companies are food retailers? Ten years ago, this would have been a silly question. People purchased food primarily at conventional supermarkets. Today, however, discount stores and warehouse clubs are significantly changing consumers' food purchasing patterns because they too sell food. AC Nielsen Homescan Panel data indicate that 54 percent of U.S. households have done food shopping at one of the big three discounters—Wal-Mart, Kmart, or Target. Additionally, 20 percent say they are making fewer trips to the grocery.[9] At the same time, traditional food retailers carry many nonfood items, plus many have pharmacies, photo processing centers, banks, and cafés.

Surprisingly, the world's largest food retailer is Wal-Mart, with supermarket-type sales of $77 billion in 2000. Yet supermarket-type products still generate only 40 percent of its revenue.[10] The second- and fifth-largest food retailers, Kroger and Albertson's, respectively, are also U.S. based. Yet these stores are considered to be conventional supermarkets since about 90 percent of their sales come from supermarket-type products. The third-largest food retailer is France-based Carrefour, the hypermarket pioneer. With over 70 percent of its sales in supermarket-type products, it is simultaneously the largest retailer in France, Spain, Italy, Brazil, and Argentina. Finally, the fourth-largest global food retailer, Royal Ahold, is also a conventional supermarket chain with over 90 percent of its sales from supermarket-type products. This Dutch supermarket chain derives the majority of its revenue from its U.S.-based stores such as BI-LO, Stop and Shop, Giant, and Tops Market.[11]

EXHIBIT 2–4
Types of Food
Retailers

	Conventional Supermarket	Supercenter	Hypermarket	Warehouse Club	Convenience Store
Percentage food	70–90	30–40	60–70	60	90
Size (000 sq. ft.)	20–50	150–220	100–300	100–150	2–3
SKUs (000)s	20–30	100–150	40–60	20	2–3
Variety	Average	Broad	Average	Broad	Narrow
Assortment	Average	Deep	Deep	Shallow	Shallow
No. of checkout lines	6–10	20–30	40–60	10–15	1–2
Prices	Average	Low	Low	Low	High

The third largest food retailer in the world is France based Carrefour, the hypermarket pioneer.

It is now easy to see that one can't easily answer the question, When is a food retailer really not a food retailer? Nonetheless, our discussion of food and **combination stores** will include conventional supermarkets, big-box food retailers, and convenience stores. Wal-Mart and other discount stores will be examined in the following section on general merchandise retailers. Exhibit 2–4 shows the sales revenues and retail mixes for different types of food retailers.

Conventional Supermarkets

A **conventional supermarket** is a self-service food store offering groceries, meat, and produce with limited sales of nonfood items, such as health and beauty aids and general merchandise. **Superstores** are larger conventional supermarkets (20,000 to 50,000 square feet) with expanded service deli, bakery, seafood and nonfood sections.[12]

In the United States, about half of the conventional supermarkets are very promotional. One day each week, they advertise that week's sale items in local papers. These promotion-oriented supermarkets also offer their own coupons and may agree to reimburse customers double or triple the face value of manufacturer coupons. This is called a *high-low pricing strategy*.

The other half of conventional supermarkets use very few promotions and sell almost all merchandise at the same price every day. This is called an *everyday low pricing (EDLP) policy*. Typically, everyday prices in these supermarkets are lower than regular prices in promotional supermarkets. For example, Food Lion (a Salisbury, North Carolina–based chain that uses an EDLP strategy) keeps costs low by offering a "no-frills" shopping experience. By adopting everyday low pricing, Food Lion reduces advertising costs to 25 percent of typical advertising expenses for a supermarket. Cereal and pet food are sold at cost to draw people into the store.[13] High-low and EDLP strategies are discussed in detail in Chapter 15.

Big-Box Food Retailers

Over the past 25 years, supermarkets have increased in size and have begun to sell a broader variety of merchandise. In 1979, conventional supermarkets accounted for 85 percent of supermarket sales. By 1998, only 41 percent of U.S. supermarket sales were in conventional supermarkets due to the growth of big-box food retailing formats: supercenters, hypermarkets, and warehouse clubs.[15]

Supercenters are 150,000-to-220,000-square-foot stores that offer a wide variety of food (30–40 percent) and nonfood merchandise (60–70 percent).[16] They are the fastest-growing retail category. Supercenters stock between 100,000 and 150,000 individual items (SKUs). The largest supercenter chains in the United States are Wal-Mart Supercenters (2001 sales of approximately $74 billion from 1,066 stores), Meijer (2001 sales of approximately $11.5 billion, although Meijer is more like a hypermarket—see next section), Kmart (2001 estimated sales of $5.5 billion), and Fred Meyer (a division of Kroger, with 2001 estimated sales of $5 billion).[17]

By offering broad assortments of grocery and general merchandise under one roof, supercenters provide a one-stop shopping experience. Customers will typically drive farther to shop at these stores than to visit conventional supermarkets (which offer a smaller selection). General merchandise items (nonfood items) are often purchased on impulse when customers' primary reason for coming to the store is to buy groceries. The general merchandise has higher margins, enabling the supercenters to price food items more aggressively. However, since supercenters are very large, some customers find them inconvenient because it can take a long time to find the items they want.

Many supercenters in the United States also sell gasoline—over $11 billion in 2001 and expected to double by 2005. The addition of gasoline to their assortment is designed to increase traffic; add convenience for shoppers, which boosts customer loyalty; increase sales of higher-margin convenience store items to customers waiting to fill up; and increase grocery sales through affinity programs linking fuel purchases to in-store discounts, and vice versa.[18]

Hypermarkets are also large (100,000 to 300,000 square feet) combination food (60–70 percent) and general merchandise (30–40 percent) retailers. Hypermarkets typically stock less than supercenters, between 40,000 and 60,000 items ranging from groceries, hardware, and sports equipment, to furniture and appliances, to computers and electronics.[20]

Hypermarkets were created in France after World War II. By building large stores on the outskirts of metropolitan areas, French retailers could attract customers and not violate strict land-use laws. They have spread throughout Europe and are popular in some South American countries such as Argentina and Brazil.

 Consider, for instance, France-based Auchan. It is a hypermarket chain with a workforce of 145,000 operating in 14 countries, including Taiwan, China, Argentina, the United States, Mexico, and most European countries. Auchan now has two stores in Houston, Texas. Each store is 240,000 square feet and has 60 checkout counters, more than 100,000 food and nonfood items, and 2,000 shopping carts. Auchan offers everything from fresh produce to groceries to housewares to electronics.

Supercenters versus Hypermarkets Hypermarkets, per se, are not prevalent in the United States,[21] although the differences between a French hypermarket and a Wal-Mart or Target supercenter are sometimes difficult to distinguish. Both hypermarkets and supercenters are large, carry grocery and general merchandise categories, are self-service, and are located in warehouse-type structures with large parking facilities.

Hypermarkets are often larger, but they carry fewer items. The merchandise mix is different as well. Hypermarkets carry a larger proportion of food items than supercenters. Further, fresh food—produce, meat, fish, and so forth—is

REFACT

Supercenter sales are expected to exceed $166 billion by 2005.[19]

their speciality, provides a profit center, and is the primary reason why many people shop there. Supercenters, on the other hand, have a larger percentage of nonfood items. Further, on the food side, their specialty is dry grocery, such as breakfast cereal and canned goods, instead of fresh items.

Warehouse Club   A warehouse club is a retailer that offers a limited assortment of food and general merchandise with little service at low prices to ultimate consumers and small businesses. Stores are large (at least 100,000 square feet, with some over 150,000[22]) and located in low-rent districts. They have simple interiors and concrete floors. Aisles are wide so forklifts can pick up pallets of merchandise and arrange them on the selling floor. Little service is offered. Customers pick merchandise off shipping pallets, take it to checkout lines in the front of the store, and pay with cash. The largest warehouse club chains are Costco Club and Sam's Club, a division of Wal-Mart (both with 2000 sales of over $26 billion). A distant third is BJ's Wholesale Club (with 2000 sales of nearly $5 billion).[23] Retailing View 2.2 describes the battle between Sam's and Costco.

Merchandise in warehouse clubs is about half food and half general merchandise. Specific brands and items may differ from time to time because the stores buy merchandise available on special promotions from manufacturers. Ware-

RETAILNG VIEW   The Battle of the Warehouse Clubs: Sam's versus Costco

2.2

Long known for selling huge quantities of diapers, detergent, and diskettes at discounted prices, Wal-Mart's warehouse club, Sam's Club, is now using diamonds, along with luxury watches, fine wines, and even sculpture, to woo the well-to-do customers who for years have helped Costco consistently best Sam's.

Costco lures its more affluent clientele with warehouse prices for gourmet foods and upscale brands such as Waterford crystal, Raymond Weil watches, and Ralph Lauren clothing. Costco also is one of the largest purveyors in the world of Dom Perignon champagne, which it sells for about $94 a bottle.

Warehouse clubs traditionally have served small business and consumers who like to buy in bulk. But Costco devotes 25 percent of its merchandise to what it calls treasure-hunt items. Costco says its wine buyer prides himself on finding up-and-coming premium wines before they hit *Wine Spectator* magazine. And Costco has sold diamonds for years; the company promises to give members a refund plus $100 if one of its diamonds is appraised for less than double the Costco price.

Taking its cue from Costco, Sam's is making its stores brighter and adding colorful signs to spruce up its grungy girders-and-cardboard-boxes image. In 2000, Sam's unveiled a revamped jewelry division that offers a wider assortment and higher grade of diamonds, pearls, and other gems, plus watches by Ebel, Concord, and TechnoMarine that sell for little more than half of department-store prices.

Costco lures its more affluent clientele with warehouse prices for gourmet foods and upscale brands such as Waterford crystal, Raymond Weil watches and Ralph Lauren clothing.

Source: Ann Zimmerman, "Tres Cheap: Taking Aim at Costco, Sam's Club Marshals Diamonds and Pearls," *The Wall Street Journal*, August 9, 2001, p. A1. Copyright 2001 by Dow Jones & Co., Inc. Reproduced with permission of Dow Jones & Co., Inc. via Copyright Clearance Center.

house clubs reduce prices by using low-cost locations and store designs. They re-duce inventory holding costs by carrying a limited assortment of fast-selling items. Merchandise usually is sold before the clubs need to pay for it.

Most warehouse clubs have two types of members: wholesale members who own small businesses, and individual members who purchase for their own use. For example, many small restaurants are wholesale customers who buy their sup-plies, food ingredients, and desserts from a warehouse club rather than from food distributors.

Some clubs require individual members to have an affiliation with a govern-ment agency, utility, or credit union, although this is significantly less prevalent than in the past. Typically, members must pay an annual fee of $35 to $45. In some stores, individual members pay no fee but pay 5 percent over an item's tick-eted price. Wholesale members typically represent less than 30 percent of the customer base but account for over 70 percent of sales. The membership, fee-driven warehouse club is a U.S.-based phenomenon and is not prevalent worldwide.

Convenience Stores

Convenience stores provide a limited variety and assortment of merchandise at a convenient location in a 2,000-to-3,000-square-foot store with speedy check-out. They are the modern version of the neighborhood mom-and-pop grocery/general store.

Convenience stores enable consumers to make purchases quickly, without hav-ing to search through a large store and wait in a long checkout line. Over half the items bought are consumed within 30 minutes of purchase. Due to their small size and high sales, convenience stores typically receive deliveries every day.

Convenience stores only offer a limited assortment and variety, and they charge higher prices than supermarkets. Milk, eggs, and bread once represented the majority of their sales. Now almost all convenience stores in nonurban areas sell gasoline, which accounts for over 55 percent of annual sales.

Although the convenience store concept has stagnated a bit in the United States and Europe, it has been growing throughout Japan, the rest of Asia, and in parts of Latin America. The reason is that they are so convenient. In many Asian countries, consumers face space constraints at home; so they prefer buying in smaller quantities at neighborhood locations. Additionally, many e-tailers in Asia use convenience stores as distribution points. Customers buy online and pick up at the store.[24] Retailing View 2.3 illustrates how the Japanese version of 7-Eleven has little resemblance to convenience stores in the United States.

Issues in Food Retailing

The primary issue facing food retailers in general, and supermarket and conve-nience store retailers in particular, is the increasing level of competition from other types of retailers. As we mentioned earlier, supercenters in the United States and hypermarkets in the rest of the world are growing at a rapid pace. In the United States, this growth has been spurred by Wal-Mart's aggressive strat-egy, which has caused other discount store chains, notably Target and Kmart, to follow suit. Competition is coming from other sources as well. Drug chains like Walgreens and CVS carry many grocery essentials found in convenience stores, such as bread and milk. Fast-food restaurants like Subway sandwich shops have positioned themselves as a healthy food alternative.

REFACT

"Uncle Johnny" Jefferson Green, owner of Southland Ice, opened the first convenience store in 1927 on the corner of 12th and Edgefield in Dallas, Texas.[25]

Convenience stores are also developing new concepts emphasizing prepared meals. For example, EatZi's, a Dallas-based chain, combines a convenience store and takeout restaurant in 8,000-square-foot locations. EatZi's has ready-to-heat meals, a sandwich bar, salads, and a ready-to-eat section. It also offers fresh produce, beverages, snacks, and other food. Customers can park, walk in, pick up tonight's dinner and tomorrow's breakfast, and be back in their cars in 10 minutes.[26]

Traditional grocery chains are fighting back by making significant investments in providing meal solutions, either hot food or partially cooked entrées. The market for prepared foods can be quite profitable. Profit margins on prepared foods are higher than most other grocery categories. Also, although shoppers rarely visit a supermarket in search of prepared foods alone, those who do spend almost 40 percent more than those who seldom or never purchase prepared foods.[27] Take, for example, Wegmans Food Markets, which operates over 60 stores in New York, Pennsylvania, and New Jersey. Wegmans has chefs in white hats tossing fresh pasta, with dining areas in the stores offering seating for more than 200. The chain offers an extensive variety of prepared meals ranging from caesar salads to Chinese food made by chefs in full view of its customers. A satisfied customer says, "They have the drama. I ask for a fresh salmon sautéed with a little lemon, browse 10 minutes in the store, and take it home to my wife for dinner."[28]

RETAILING VIEW   The Kobini: 7-Eleven Convenience Stores Japanese Style

23

Although the convenience store blossomed in the United States over 40 years ago and has since matured, the Japanese have continued to improve upon the format. 7-Eleven convenience stores in Japan are different from their U.S. counterparts because the customers' needs are different. The typical worker leaves home at 6 A.M. and does not return until after 7 P.M. The convenience store is the place where they can get all of the most important goods for everyday life. Add to that the fact that Japan's largest city, Tokyo, experiences daytime population swells to nearly 20 million.

7-Eleven stores in Japan are small by U.S. standards, 50 to 500 square meters. The stores present the usual array of snacks, drinks (both alcoholic and nonalcoholic), magazines, cosmetics, and other basic household products that you would find in the United States. But they also offer fresh fruits, vegetables, seafood, meat, tofu, pickled and canned food, dairy products, and high-appetite-appeal instant meals based on traditional foodstuffs.

These stores bring new meaning to the word fresh! The shelves are physically rearranged four times per day, every day. Of the nearly 3,000 products that are stocked, 60 percent of the food items are perishable in one day. In Japan, neatness counts—for everything. Shelves feature clean display cartons lined up in neat rows. The goods and

Stores in Japan offer fresh fruits, vegetables and seafood, meat, tofu, pickled and canned food, dairy products, and high-appetite appeal instant meals based on traditional foodstuffs.

their packaging are beautifully presented. They are instantly recognizable branded products, offered in colorful and attractive single-serve portions.

Source: Neil J. Kozarsky, "Delivering to 'King' Consumer—Do Japan's C-Stores Have the Answers?" *BrandPackaging*, July 2000, pp. 12–17. Reprinted by permission.

GENERAL MERCHANDISE RETAILERS

The major types of general merchandise retailers are discount stores, specialty stores, category specialists, department stores, home improvement centers, off-price retailers, and value retailers. Exhibit 2–5 summarizes characteristics of general merchandise retailers that sell through stores. Many of these general merchandise retailers sell through multichannels, such as the Internet and catalogs. Multichannel retailing is discussed in the next chapter.

Characteristics of Different General Merchandise Retailers | **EXHIBIT 2–5**

Type	Variety	Assortment	Service	Prices	Size (000 sq. ft.)	SKUs (000)	Location
Discount stores	Broad	Average to shallow	Low	Low	60–80	30	Stand alone, power strip centers
Specialty stores	Narrow	Deep	High	High	4–12	5	Regional malls
Category specialists	Narrow	Very deep	Low to high	Low	50–120	20–40	Stand alone, power strip centers
Home improvement centers	Narrow	Very deep	Low to high	Low	80–120	20–40	Stand alone, power strip centers
Department stores	Broad	Deep to average	Average to high	Average to high	100–200	100	Regional malls
Drugstores	Narrow	Very deep	Average	Average to high	3–15	10–20	Stand alone, strip centers
Off-price stores	Average	Deep but varying	Low	Low	20–30	50	Outlet malls
Value retailers	Average	Average and varying	Low	Low	7–15	3–4	Urban, strip

Discount Stores

A **discount store** is a retailer that offers a broad variety of merchandise, limited service, and low prices. Discount stores offer both private labels and national brands, but these brands are typically less fashion-oriented than brands in department stores. The big three full-line discount store chains are Wal-Mart (with 2000 annual sales of $191.3 billion), Kmart ($37 billion), and Target ($36 billion).[30]

Issues in Discount Store Retailing[32]   As we noted in the previous section, the most significant trend in discount store retailing is the Wal-Mart–led push toward supercenters that carry grocery items. Additionally, discount stores face intense competition from specialty stores that focus on a single category of merchandise, such as Circuit City, Sports Authority, and Home Depot. They also compete with Old Navy and Marshall's for apparel, Tuesday Morning for home furnishings, and Walgreens and CVS for health and beauty products. (These retailers are described in a subsequent section.) To respond to this competitive environment, discount stores have created more attractive shopping environments, placed more emphasis on apparel, and developed strong private-label merchandise programs.

Unfortunately, the number two U.S. discount store, Kmart, filed for Chapter 11 bankruptcy at the beginning of 2002. Although Kmart faced competition from all sides, most believe that its poor performance in recent years has been its inability to successfully compete with Wal-Mart and Target.

Wal-Mart pioneered the everyday low price concept. And its efficient operations have allowed it to offer the lowest-priced basket of merchandise in every market in which it competes. This doesn't mean that Wal-Mart has the lowest price on every item in every market. But it tries to be the lowest across a wide variety of things. Many students of business think the Bentonville, Arkansas–based company has the best and most sophisticated supply chain and information systems in the industry.

With Wal-Mart, success has been a matter of efficiency and timing. Target, on the other hand, wins with merchandising. Opting for quality and style, Target has even developed a certain cult quality among fashion hipsters with its private labels. Target has also successfully read several important broad consumer trends: Americans are looking for a good value, but that doesn't mean the same thing as cheap. It has also realized that Americans who are farther up the economic ladder than typical discount shoppers will become customers if the merchandise is well designed and of high quality. Quality of merchandise is important, but it isn't the only place where Kmart lost its foothold. In terms of convenience and logistics, Wal-Mart's and Target's locations are at least as good as, and often newer than, Kmart's in every market in which they compete.

Specialty Stores

A **specialty store** concentrates on a limited number of complementary merchandise categories and provides a high level of service in an area typically under 8,000 square feet. Exhibit 2–6 lists some of the largest U.S. specialty store chains.

Issues in Specialty Store Retailing   In recent years, specialty apparel stores has been one of the weakest, slowest-growing areas in retailing. One reason is the aging population: Older people typically don't spend as much money on

EXHIBIT 2–6
Largest Specialty Store
Chains

Company	Sales 2000 (millions)	Earnings (millions)	No. of Stores (2001)	Affiliated Stores
APPAREL				
The Gap	13,673	877	3,676	Baby Gap, Banana Republic, Gap Kids, Old Navy
The Limited	10,104	427	5,129	Henri Bendel, Intimate Brands, Lane Bryant, Lerner New York, Limited Too, Structure, Express
Intimate Brands	5,117	432	2,390	Victoria's Secret, Bath & Body Works, White Barn Candle Company
SHOES				
Foot Locker	4,217	111	3,582	Foot Locker, Lady Foot Locker, Champs Sports, Kids Foot Locker
Payless ShoeSource	2,948	129	4,633	
AUTO PARTS				
AutoZone	4,482	267	3,000+	
Pep Boys	2,418	−51,094	628	
Advance Auto	2,200	NA	2,400	
FURNITURE				
Pier 1 Imports	1,411	95	860	
MUSIC				
Tower Records	1,079	90	173	
Hastings Entertainment	458	15	142	
FOOD SUPPLEMENTS				
General Nutrition			4,500	General Nutrition Centers, GNC Live Well, Health and Diet Centres, Value
JEWELRY				
Zales	1,793	111	2,344	Piercing Pagoda, Zales, Gordon's, Peoples, Baily Banks & Biddle, Zales Outlet
Tiffany	1,668	190	225	
OPTICAL				
Cole National	1,077	2	3,453	Sears Optical, Pearle, Things Remembered, Target Optical, BJ's Optical, Cole Vision
ACCESSORIES				
Pacific Sunwear	589	40	589	
Hot Topic Inc.	257	23	291	

Sources: "Top 100 Specialty Stores," Stores Online, 2001, www.stores.org; and "Company Profiles," Hoovers Online, 2002, www.hoovers.com.

At Zara's flagship store in Madrid, their philosophy is "fashion on demand."

clothing as teenagers.[33] A soft economy and a shift to more casual apparel in the workplace have further dampened apparel sales.

The Gap, once the darling of specialty stores, has experienced negative growth in same-store sales[34] during the first few years of the decade. Reasons for the decline are lower-priced imitators such as Target and The Gap's own Old Navy stores. Also, long known for high-quality traditional basics that appeal to multiple age groups, The Gap strayed from its roots by experimenting with higher-fashion items. Its core customers also strayed because they found little need for another pair of khakis.[35]

Europe-based apparel specialty stores Zara (Spain) and H&M (short for Hennes & Mauritz, in Sweden) are very successful on the continent and in the U.K., and they are expanding into the United States. Zara's philosophy is "fashion on demand." At the end of every day in each of the chain's more than 1,000 shops around the world, the manager goes online to company headquarters in Spain and describes which items were moving and which weren't. Using this simple method as a guide, designers can get a newly created item on the racks within little more than a week, compared to as long as six months for The Gap or The Limited. In the fickle and fast-changing world of fashion, agility means success. Zara produces more than half of its own clothes and makes 40 percent of its own fabric. H&M also responds quickly to fashion trends. In contrast, however, H&M, has 900 suppliers and no factories.[36] H&M also competes at lower price points than both Zara and The Gap. Its philosophy is "disposable chic," and its merchandise is so inexpensive that it doesn't matter if it goes out of style quickly.[37]

Category Specialist

A **category specialist** is a discount store that offers a narrow variety but deep assortment of merchandise. These retailers are basically discount specialty stores. Most category specialists use a self-service approach, but some specialists in consumer durables offer assistance to customers. For example, Office Depot stores have a warehouse atmosphere, with cartons of copying paper stacked on pallets plus equipment in boxes on shelves. However, some merchandise, such as computers, is displayed in the middle of the store, and salespeople in the display area are available to answer questions and make suggestions.

By offering a complete assortment in a category at low prices, category specialists can "kill" a category of merchandise for other retailers and thus are frequently called **category killers.** Because category specialists dominate a category of merchandise, they can use their buying power to negotiate low prices and are assured of supply when items are scarce. Department stores and full-line discount stores located near category specialists often have to reduce their offerings in the category because consumers are drawn to the deep assortment and low prices at the category killer. Exhibit 2–7 lists the largest category specialists in the United States. Retailing View 2.4 describes Bass Pro Shop, a category specialist targeting fishing and hunting enthusiasts.

One of the largest and most successful types of category specialist is the home improvement center. A **home improvement center** is a category specialist of-

EXHIBIT 2–7
Largest Category
Specialists

Company	Sales 2000 (millions)	Earnings (millions)	No. of Stores 2001
CONSUMER ELECTRONICS			
Best Buy	15,327	395	419
Circuit City	12,959	160	627
OFFICE SUPPLY			
Office Depot	11,569	49	953
Staples	10,673	597	1,307
TOYS			
Toys "R" Us	11,332	404	710
COMPUTERS			
CompUSA	6,150	NA	220
BOOKS			
Barnes & Noble	4,376	519	1,886
Borders Group	3,271	44	1,150
PET SUPPLIES			
PETsMART	2,224	31	533
Pet Valu	1,151	28	538
SPORTS EQUIPMENT			
Sports Authority	1,499	25	198
Gart Sports	751	23	120
HOME			
Bed Bath & Beyond	2,397	172	316
Williams-Sonoma	1,829	57	382
CRAFTS			
Michaels Stores	2,249	79	765
AC Moore	262	NA	56
APPAREL			
Mens Wearhouse	1,273	43	651
Kids "R" Us	620	NA	198
BABY			
Babies "R" Us	1,310	NA	145
HOME IMPROVEMENT CHAINS			
Home Depot	45,738 (2001)	2,581	1,287
Lowe's Companies	18,779	809	859
Menards	4,750	NA	160

Sources: "Top 100 Retailers," Stores Online, 2001, www.stores.org; and "Company Profiles," Hoovers Online, 2002, www.hoovers.com.

fering equipment and material used by do-it-yourselfers and contractors to make home improvements. The largest U.S. home improvement chains are Home Depot (2001 annual sales of $45.7 billion), Lowe's Companies ($18.7 billion), and Menard ($4.7 billion).[38] While merchandise in home improvement centers is displayed in a warehouse atmosphere, salespeople are available to assist customers in selecting merchandise and to tell them how to use it.

The needs for home improvement merchandise vary considerably across the country. As a result, there are opportunities for differentiating on customer service and merchandise selection. As Home Depot saturates the United States with its present format, it is launching new formats, including Expo Design and

Villager's Hardware. Expo Design targets women in higher-income families. Its stores feature low, painted ceilings and track lights, with individually designed display rooms highlighting possibilities for kitchens, baths, lighting, and appliances once available only through a decorator. Certified designers are on staff and ready to assist for a fee. Villager's Hardware is positioned as a "fill-in" store for do-it-yourselfers who normally shop at the company's large stores. The stores also target women by using improved housekeeping and signage and devoting a significant amount of selling space to merchandise similar to that in Bed Bath & Beyond or Crate and Barrel.[39]

Issues for Category Specialists   Most category specialist chains started in one region of the country and saturated that region before expanding to other regions. For example, Office Depot started in Florida and expanded through the

RETAILING VIEW   The Big Fish Story—Bass Pro Shops

2.4

The first and largest Bass Pro Shops Outdoor World Showroom, located in Springfield, Missouri, may be the most visited store in the country. Every year, the 300,000-square-foot showroom attracts more than 4 million visitors, making it the number one tourist attraction in Missouri. It has a four-story waterfall, rifle and archery ranges, four aquariums, an indoor driving range, a putting green, and a 250-seat auditorium and conference room for fish-feeding shows and workshops. Visitors can also get a haircut or dine at McDonald's or Hemingway's Blue Water Café, which has a 30,000-gallon saltwater aquarium. The company has 21 other stores that are smaller (although still over 133,000 square feet) yet also highly interactive and entertaining. They are located in Dallas, Houston, Detroit, Fort Lauderdale, Charlotte, Nashville, Atlanta, the Florida Keys, and other U.S. locations.

The store offers everything a person needs for hunting and fishing—from 27-cent plastic bait to boats and recreational vehicles costing $45,000. The merchandise and service include fishing tackle, shooting and hunting equipment, camping gear, boats and marine accessories, taxidermy studio, cutlery, rod and reel repair, gifts, outdoors-related books and videos, and sportswear and footwear.

Sales associates are knowledgeable outdoors people. Each one is hired for a particular department that matches that person's expertise. All private-branded products are field tested by Bass Pro Shops' professional teams: Redhead Pro Hunting Team and Tracker Pro Fishing Team.

The retailer and the sports are promoted through a syndicated radio show, Bass Pro Shops Outdoor World, heard on 450 radio stations in 48 states and 139 foreign countries. A magazine of the same name is available by subscription and at newsstands throughout the country.

This Bass Pro Shop in Springfield, Missouri, attracts four million visitors a year, making it the state's largest tourist attraction.

Bass Pro Shops also puts on a Fall Hunting Classic and Spring Fishing Classic. The events are essentially trade shows with manufacturer and service booths, professional sports persons, demonstrations, hot air balloon rides, NASCAR race cars, and thousands of dollars in prizes.

Sources: "Bass Pro Shops Outdoor World: Retail Store of the Year," *Chain Store Age*, February 1, 2002 pp. 24 RSOY; Bruce Adib-Yazdi, "Design Leads to Outdoor Adventure at Bass Pro Shops," *Shopping Center World*, July 1, 2001; and Edwin McDowell, "Adventures in Retailing," *New York Times*, April 3, 1999, pp. B1, B14.

Southeast and Southwest, and Staples started in Boston and expanded through New England and the Midwest. During this period of expansion, competition between specialists in a category was limited.

Now competition between specialists in each category is very intense as the firms expand into the regions originally dominated by another firm. In many merchandise categories, the major firms are now in direct competition across the nation. This direct competition focuses on price, resulting in reduced profits because the competitors have difficulty differentiating themselves on other elements of the retail mix. All the competitors in a category provide similar assortments since they have similar access to national brands. They all provide the same level of service.

In response to this increasing competitive intensity, the category killers continue to concentrate on reducing costs by increasing operating efficiency and acquiring smaller chains to gain scale economies. Where appropriate, category specialists have attempted to differentiate themselves with service. For example, both Staples and Office Depot have specialized sales associates dedicated to selling electronic office equipment.

Department Stores

Department stores are retailers that carry a broad variety and deep assortment, offer some customer services, and are organized into separate departments for displaying merchandise. The largest department store chains in the United States are Sears (2001 annual sales of $40 billion), JCPenney ($32.6 billion), Federated Department Stores ($18.4 billion), and The May Company ($14.5 billion).[41] Department store chains are very diverse. There are those that carry relatively inexpensive products and compete closely with discount stores, such as Sears, JCPenney, and Kohl's, and chains that sell expensive, exclusive merchandise that compete with high-end specialty store chains, such as Neiman Marcus, Bloomingdale's, and Saks Fifth Avenue. The chains that are part of Federated Department Stores, such as Macy's and Burdines, and those of The May Company, such as Filene's and Lord and Taylor, fit somewhere in the middle.

Each department within the store has a specific selling space allocated to it, a POS terminal to transact and record sales, and salespeople to assist customers. The department store often resembles a collection of specialty shops. The major departments are women's, men's, and children's clothing and accessories; home furnishings and furniture; and kitchenware and small appliances.

In some situations, departments in a department store or discount store are leased and operated by an independent company. A **leased department** is an area in a retail store that is leased or rented to an independent firm. The lease holder is typically responsible for all retail mix decisions involved in operating the department and pays the store a percentage of its sales as rent. Retailers lease departments when they feel they lack expertise to efficiently operate the department. Commonly leased departments in U.S. stores are beauty salons, pharmacies, shoes, jewelry, furs, photography studios, and repair services. While relatively few departments are leased in U.S. stores, most of the departments, even men's and women's apparel, are leased in Japanese department stores.

Department stores are unique in terms of the shopping experience they offer—the services they provide and the atmosphere of the store. They offer a full range of services from altering clothing to home delivery. To create excitement, apparel is displayed on mannequins; attention is drawn to displays with theatrical lighting; and sales associates are frequently stationed throughout the store demonstrating products. Department stores also emphasize special promotions such as elaborate displays during the Christmas season.

Issues in Department Store Retailing Department stores' overall sales have stagnated and market share has fallen in recent years due to increased competition from discount stores and specialty stores and a decline in perceived value for merchandise and services. Department stores, which started in the nineteenth century, attracted consumers by offering them ambience, attentive service, and a wide variety of merchandise under one roof. They still account for some of retailing's romance—its parades, its Santa Claus lands, and its holiday windows. Department stores also offer designer brands that are not available at other retailers.

Unfortunately, many consumers believe that department stores are no longer romantic or convenient. Many believe that they are difficult to get to because they are located in large malls, that it is difficult to find specific merchandise because the same category is often located in several designer departments, and that it is difficult to get professional sales assistance because of labor cutbacks. At the same time, they typically charge higher prices than their discount and specialty store competitors.

The same competitive pressures are occurring in Europe and Asia. Many of the older European department stores own their own sites, having purchased them decades ago when real estate was relatively cheap. This gives them an inherent rent subsidy that helps their bottom line, at least in the short term.[44]

How are department stores responding to their declining position?[45] Nordstrom and Saks Fifth Avenue are lowering prices on some merchandise. Saks and Federated are investing heavily in their private-label program. In addition, Federated is revamping its young women's departments with sound systems, adding Internet access, and placing the young men's department nearby, to create some excitement. The May Company is adding new emphasis to the bridal segment by increasing advertising and selection.

Department store retailers are working closely with their vendors to ensure better in-stock positions for fashion merchandise and still reduce average inventory levels. These initiatives, referred to as quick response (QR), are similar to the ECR and CPFR programs undertaken by supermarkets. For example, at the beginning of a season, a department store chain that has a QR relationship with a vendor will commit to buying 120,000 sweaters but will specify the sizes and colors for only the initial shipment of 2,500 sweaters. The vendors and retailer will closely monitor initial sales and use this information to knit and dye the sweaters in sizes and colors that will match customer demand for the rest of the season.

Drugstores

Drugstores are specialty stores that concentrate on health and personal grooming merchandise. Pharmaceuticals often represent over 50 percent of drugstore sales and an even greater percentage of their profits. The largest drugstore chains in the United States are Walgreens (2001 annual sales of $21.2 billion), CVS ($22 billion), Rite Aid ($114.5 billion), and Eckerds, a division of JCPenney ($13.1 billion).[46]

Issues in Drugstore Retailing   Drugstores, particularly the national chains, are experiencing sustained sales growth because the aging population requires more prescription drugs. Further, managed care and Medicare have expanded coverage to most Americans.[48] Although the profit margins for prescription pharmaceuticals are higher than for other drugstore merchandise, these margins are shrinking due to government health care policies, HMOs, and public outcry over lower prices in other countries, especially Canada. The nonprescription side of drugstores is also being squeezed by considerable competition from pharmacies in discount stores and supermarkets, as well as from prescription mail-order retailers.

In response, the major drugstore chains are building larger stand-alone stores offering a wider assortment of merchandise, more frequently purchased food items, and drive-through windows for picking up prescriptions.[49] To build customer loyalty, the chains are also changing the role of their pharmacists from dispensing pills (referred to as count, pour, lick, and stick) to providing health care assistance such as explaining how to use a nebulizer.

Drugstore retailers are using systems to allow pharmacists time to provide personalized service. For example, at Walgreens, customers can order prescription refills via the phone. They are automatically called when the prescription is ready. Based on the time they plan to pick up the prescription, a computer system automatically schedules the workload in the pharmacy. The systems also monitor the frequency of refilling prescriptions so the pharmacist can make phone calls or send e-mails to ensure patient drug compliance.[51]

Walgreens is building larger stand-alone stores offering more merchandise categories, more food items, and drive-through windows for picking up prescriptions.

Off-Price Retailers

Off-price retailers offer an inconsistent assortment of brand-name, fashion-oriented soft goods at low prices. America's largest off-price retail chains are TJX Companies (operates T.J. Maxx and Marshalls, with 2001 annual sales of $9.5 billion), Ross Stores ($2.7 billion), and Burlington Coat Factory ($2.2 billion).[52]

Off-price retailers can sell brand-name and even designer-label merchandise at low prices due to their unique buying and merchandising practices. Most merchandise is bought opportunistically from manufacturers or other retailers with excess inventory at the end of the season. This merchandise might be in odd sizes or unpopular colors and styles, or it may be irregulars (having minor mistakes in construction). Typically, merchandise is purchased at one-fifth to one-fourth of the original wholesale price. Off-price retailers can buy at low prices because they don't ask suppliers for advertising allowances, return privileges, markdown adjustments, or delayed payments. (Terms and conditions associated with buying merchandise are detailed in Chapter 14.)

Due to this pattern of opportunistic buying, customers can't be confident that the same type of merchandise will be in stock each time they visit the store. Different bargains will be available on each visit. To improve their offerings' consistency, some off-price retailers complement opportunistically bought merchandise with merchandise purchased at regular wholesale prices. Two special types of off-price retailers are closeout and outlet stores.

Closeout Retailers **Closeout retailers** are off-price retailers that sell a broad but inconsistent assortment of general merchandise as well as apparel and soft home goods. The largest closeout chains are Big Lots, Inc. (Big Lots, Big Lots furniture, MacFrugal's Bargains Close-outs, Odd Lots, Odd Lots furniture, Pic 'N' Save—2001 sales of $3,433 million in 13,000 stores) and Tuesday Morning (sales of $642 million in 440 stores).[54]

Outlet Stores **Outlet stores** are off-price retailers owned by manufacturers or by department or specialty store chains. Outlet stores owned by manufacturers are frequently referred to as **factory outlets.** The largest outlet chains are Dress Barn/Dress Barn Woman/Westport Ltd./Westport Woman (396 stores), Rue 21 Company Store (286), Nine West Outlet (256), Van Heusen (241), and G.H. Bass (222).[55] Outlet stores are typically found in one of the fastest-growing types of malls—the outlet mall, discussed in Chapter 8.

Manufacturers view outlet stores as an opportunity to improve their revenues from irregulars, production overruns, and merchandise returned by retailers. Outlet stores also allow manufacturers some control over where their branded merchandise is sold at discount prices.

Retailers with strong brand names such as Saks (Saks Off Fifth) and Brooks Brothers operate outlet stores too. By selling excess merchandise in outlet stores rather than selling it at markdown prices in their primary stores, these department and specialty store chains can maintain an image of offering desirable merchandise at full price.

Value Retailers

Value retailers are general merchandise discount stores that are found in either lower-income urban or rural areas and are much smaller than traditional discount stores (less than 9,000 square feet). The largest value retailers are Dollar General (2001 sales of $4,550 million in 5,500 stores) and Family Dollar Stores (2001 sales of $3,665 million in over 4,000 stores).[56] Value retailers are one of the fastest-growing segments in retailing.[57] Many value retailers, particularly Family Dollar and Dollar General, target low-income consumers, whose shopping behavior differs from typical discount store or warehouse club customers. For instance, although these consumers demand well-known national brands, they often can't afford to buy large-size packages. Since this segment of the retail industry is growing rapidly, and known to pay its bills on time, vendors are creating special smaller packages for them.

Value retailers follow a variety of business models. Although most cater to low-income groups, Dollar Tree, Greenbacks, and 99 Cents Only Stores draw from multiple income groups and are generally located in suburban strip malls. They specialize in giftware, party, and craft items rather than consumables. Despite some of these chains' names, few just sell merchandise for a dollar. In fact, the two largest—Family Dollar and Dollar General—don't employ a strict dollar limit. The $1 price is the focus for Dollar General, but the chain carries 14 different price points, all rounded off in even dollars. Prices at Family Dollar go up to $20. The names imply a *good value*, while not limiting the customer to the arbitrary dollar price point.

NONSTORE RETAIL FORMATS

In the preceeding sections, we have examined retailers whose *primary* modes of operation are bricks-and-mortar stores. In this section, we will discuss types of retailers that operate primarily in nonstore environments. The major types of nonstore retailers are electronic retailers, catalog and direct-mail retailers, direct selling, television home shopping, and vending machines.

Electronic Retailing

Electronic retailing (also called **e-tailing** and **Internet retailing**) is a retail format in which the retailers communicate with customers and offer products and services for sale over the Internet. The rapid diffusion of Internet access and usage and the perceived low cost of entry stimulated the creation of over 10,000 entrepreneurial electronic retailing ventures during the last five years of the twentieth century. These electronic retailers ranged in size from Amazon.com, with over $3 billion annual sales, to niche retailers such as Dilmah's, which sells teas from the plantations in the highlands of Ceylon (www.dilmahtea.com), and Steel of the Night, which offers a complete line of steel drums (www.steelofthenight.com).

Electronic retailing entrepreneurs such as Priceline.com and eBay developed innovative retail business models. These electronic retailing entrepreneurs were able to raise significant venture capital to support their concepts. For example, Webvan, an electronic supermarket retailer, had a market capitalization of $11 billion when it made its initial public offering (IPO) of its stock; 20 months later, after spending $1.2 billion, it declared bankruptcy.[59]

The growth and profitability expectations for electronic retail entrepreneurs diminished in 2000. When the Internet bubble burst, electronic retailers such as Garden.com, eToys, and Boo.com could no longer raise funds to support their unprofitable businesses and were forced to declare bankruptcy. Although electronic retail entrepreneurs—retailers that only offer an electronic channel for purchasing merchandise and services—have faced difficulties, consumer interest in electronic retailing continues to increase.

In 2001, $38 billion of merchandise and services were purchased electronically. Electronic retail sales were 16 percent greater than in the previous year, while the growth rate for retail sales in stores was less than 3 percent.[61] Books, CDs, DVD, videos, apparel, computer software, and toys are the best-selling merchandise online.[62] Customer satisfaction with online shopping is improving to the point were Amazon.com (American Consumer Satisfaction Index = 84) and Barnes & Noble.com (82) have higher satisfaction scores than store-based retailers (77).[63]

The continued consumer interest in buying electronically is the result of traditional store-based and catalog retailers beginning to offer merchandise through an electronic channel. While the electronic retail innovators had superior skills in using the new technology, they lacked retailing expertise and a deep understanding of customer needs.[65] Traditional retailers have incorporated an Internet channel into a multichannel offering that provides more value to customers. The

REFACT

By 2010, it is expected that 12 percent of all U.S. retail sales will be through catalogs, direct mail, interactive television, and the Internet.[58]

REFACT

In 2001, 54 percent of the U.S. population had access to the Internet, up from 44 percent in 2000.[60]

REFACT

By 2001, 39 percent of the population in the United States had purchased merchandise and services over the Internet and 67 percent had used the Internet to find information about products.[64]

success of multichannel retailing is reflected in the rating of retail websites. Each year, *Internet Retailer* selects the best Internet sites. In 2002, only 4 of the top 25 websites were pure electronic retailers, whereas in 2001, 14 were pure electronic retailers.[66]

In Chapter 3, we discuss the unique benefits offered by the three basic approaches for interacting with retail customers—stores, catalogs, and the Internet. After discussing the advantages of a multichannel approach, we examine how technology may change the nature of shopping in the future.

Catalog and Direct-Mail Retailing

Catalog retailing is a nonstore retail format in which the retail offering is communicated to a customer through a catalog, whereas **direct-mail retailers** communicate with their customers using letters and brochures. Historically, catalog and direct-mail retailing were most successful with rural consumers, who lacked ready access to retail stores. Today's customers enjoy the convenience of shopping by catalog. The major catalog retailers have embraced a multichannel strategy by integrating the Internet into their catalog operations. Customers often get a catalog in the mail, look it over, and go to the Internet for more information and to place an order.

In 2001, $120 billion of merchandise and services were sold through catalogs in the United States.[67] The typical household receives three to four catalogs per week.[68] Clothing accounts for 32 percent of all catalog sales, followed by home furnishings (9.4 percent), housewares (7 percent), and toys and games (7 percent).[69]

About half of the consumers in a recent survey made at least one catalog purchase in a year. Over half of the women surveyed made at least one catalog purchase, compared to 36 percent of the men.[70] The average U.S. household receives 1.9 catalogs and a similar number of direct-mail solicitations per week. However, households that patronize catalog retailers receive three times as many catalogs as the average household.[71]

Types of Catalog and Direct-Mail Retailers

Two types of firms selling products through the mail are (1) general merchandise and specialty catalog retailers and (2) direct-mail retailers. **General merchandise catalog retailers** offer a broad variety of merchandise in catalogs that are periodically mailed to their customers. For example, JCPenney distributes a 1,200-page catalog to over 14 million people.[73] Besides its general merchandise catalog, Penney distributes 70 specialty catalogs each year. **Specialty catalog retailers** focus on specific categories of merchandise, such as fruit (Harry and David), gardening tools (Smith & Hawken), and seeds and plants (Burpee).

Direct-mail retailers typically mail brochures and pamphlets to sell a specific product or service to customers at one point in time. For example, USAA sells a broad array of financial services targeted to the military community,[75] and a division of JCPenney sells life insurance through the mail. In addition to the focus on a specific product or service, most direct-mail retailers are primarily interested in making a single sale from a specific mailing, whereas catalog retailers typically maintain relationships with customers over time.

Exhibit 2–8 lists the nation's largest catalog and direct-mail retailers and illustrates the variety of products and services sold directly to customers through impersonal methods. About two-thirds of the sales are for merchandise; one-third are for services.

EXHIBIT 2–8
Leading U.S. Catalog
and Direct-Mail
Retailers

Company	2000 Sales ($ millions)	Offering
Dell Computer Corp.	31,890.00	Computers
Corporate Express	4,054.30	Office products
JCPenney Co.	3,823.00	General merchandise
CDW Computer Centers	3,800.00	Computers
Office Depot	3,600.00	Office supplies
MicroWarehouse	2,564.80	Computers
Federated Department Stores	1,940.00	General merchandise
Spiegel	1,711.20	General merchandise
Brylane	1,400.00	Apparel and home goods
Lands' End	1,355.00	Apparel and home goods
L. L. Bean	1,110.00	Outdoor gear, apparel, and home goods
Intimate Brands	962.00	Women's apparel
School Specialty	639.30	B-to-B school supplies
Hanover Direct	603.00	Apparel and home goods
Cabela's	583.80	Outdoor sporting goods
Blair Corp	574.60	General merchandise
ABC Distributing	410.00	General merchandise
Neiman Marcus Group	363.80	Apparel, home décor, and cookware
Mattel	358.00	Toys and collectibles

Source: "The Ninth Annual Ranking of the Top 100 U.S. Catalogers," *Catalog Age*, August 1, 2001, http://industryclick.com/magazine.asp?magazineid=153&siteid=2. Reprinted by permission.

Issues in Catalog Retailing Catalog retailing can be an attractive business opportunity because the start-up costs are relatively low. On the other hand, catalog retailing can be very challenging. First, it is difficult for smaller catalog and direct-mail retailers to compete with large, well-established firms that have embraced a multichannel strategy. The Internet has become a natural extension to most catalogers' selling strategy. Ninety-five percent of catalogers describe themselves as multichannel retailers, with 53 percent defining their companies as catalog/Internet/retail and 42 percent as catalog/Internet.[76] Second, the mailing and printing costs are high and increasing. Third, it is difficult to get consumers' attention as they are mailed so many catalogs and direct-mail promotions. Finally, the length of time required to design, develop, and distribute catalogs makes it difficult for catalog and direct-mail retailers to respond quickly to new trends and fashions. Most analysts believe that the future will bring a seamless multichannel offering that integrates catalogs, the Internet, and often bricks-and-mortar stores.

Specialty-catalog retailers focus on specific categories of merchandise such as fruit (Harry and David), sporting goods (REI and Bass Pro Shops), seeds (Burpee), and home furnishings (Restoration Hardware).

Direct Selling

Direct selling is a retail format in which a salesperson, frequently an independent businessperson, contacts a customer directly in a convenient location, either at the customer's home or at work, and demonstrates merchandise benefits, takes an order, and delivers the merchandise to the customer. Direct selling is a highly interactive form of retailing in which considerable information is conveyed to customers through face-to-face discussions with a salesperson. However, providing this high level of information, including extensive demonstrations, is costly. Retailing View 2.5 describes Avon's struggle with direct selling versus the Internet.

Annual U.S. sales for direct selling total $25.6 billion and more than $82 billion worldwide. The largest categories of merchandise sold through direct selling are home/family care (e.g., cooking and kitchenware), personal care (e.g., cosmetics and fragrances), services, wellness, and leisure/educational. About 64 percent of all direct sales are made in the home, with 9 percent in the workplace and 15 percent over the phone.[77]

Almost all of the 11 million salespeople who work in direct sales are independent agents. They aren't employed by the direct sales firm but act as independent distributors, buying merchandise from the firms and then reselling it to consumers. Eighty-three percent of the salespeople work part-time (less than 30 hours per week). In most cases, direct salespeople may sell their merchandise to anyone. But some companies, such as Avon, assign territories to salespeople who regularly contact households in their territory.

Two special types of direct selling are party plan and multilevel selling. About 28 percent of all direct sales are made using a party plan system. In a **party plan system,** salespeople encourage customers to act as hosts and invite friends or coworkers to a "party" at which the merchandise is demonstrated in a partylike atmosphere. Sales made at the party are influenced by the social relationship of the people attending with the host or hostess, who receives a gift or commission for arranging the meeting.

Almost three-quarters of all direct sales are made through multilevel sales networks. In a **multilevel network,** people serve as master distributors, recruiting other people to become distributors in their network. The master distributors either buy merchandise from the firm and resell it to their distributors or receive a commission on all merchandise purchased by the distributors in their network. In addition to selling merchandise themselves, the master distributors are involved in recruiting and training other distributors.

Some multilevel direct-selling firms are illegal pyramid schemes. A **pyramid scheme** develops when the firm and its program are designed to sell merchandise and services to other distributors rather than to end users. The founders and initial distributors in pyramid schemes profit from the inventory bought by later participants, but little merchandise is sold to consumers who use it.

Television Home Shopping

Television home shopping is a retail format in which customers watch a TV program demonstrating merchandise and then place orders for the merchandise by telephone. The three forms of electronic home shopping retailing are (1) cable channels dedicated to television shopping, (2) infomercials, and (3) direct-response advertising. **Infomercials** are TV programs, typically 30 minutes long, that mix entertainment with product demonstrations and then solicit orders placed by telephone. **Direct-response advertising** includes advertisements on TV and radio that describe products and provide an opportunity for consumers to order them.

TV home shopping is a $6 billion business in the United States.[78] The three largest home shopping networks are QVC, HSN (Home Shopping Network), and ValueVision. Although Americans with cable television have access to a television shopping channel, relatively few watch on a regular basis. Further, most of the purchases are made by a relatively small proportion of the viewers. Like catalogs, TV home shopping is embracing the Internet. The major home shopping networks all have Internet operations. Further growth in this shopping venue will depend on how quickly interactive TV becomes available and the degree to which it is adopted by consumers.

The major advantage of TV home shopping compared to catalog retailing is that customers can see the merchandise demonstrated on the TV screen. However, customers can't examine a particular type of merchandise or a specific item when they want to, as they can with catalogs. They have to wait for the time when the merchandise shows up on the screen. To address this limitation, home shopping networks schedule categories of merchandise for specific times so customers looking for specific merchandise can plan their viewing time.

TV home shopping retailers appeal primarily to lower-income consumers. Forty percent of TV home shopping sales are inexpensive jewelry. Other major categories are apparel, cosmetics, and exercise equipment.

Vending Machine Retailing

Vending machine retailing is a nonstore format in which merchandise or services are stored in a machine and dispensed to customers when they deposit cash or use a credit card. Vending machines are placed at convenient, high-traffic locations such as in the workplace or on university campuses and primarily contain snacks or drinks.

Direct Seller: Avon and the Internet | RETAILING VIEW

2.5

Avon (www.avon.com), the cosmetics company, currently employs 572,000 women in the United States, as well as 3.4 million women around the world, to produce 98 percent of its annual sales of $5.7 billion. A few years ago, Avon had considered getting rid of its Avon women representatives and selling all of its products over the Internet. In the end, however, Avon rejected the pure clicks model in favor of a "representative-centric" web-sales model. In this hybrid model, the company's representatives would sell products to their customers both face-to-face and online, while Avon would also sell its products over the Internet to those customers who did not like to purchase them from Avon ladies. In addition, the company would try other ways of selling its cosmetics, primarily through mall kiosks and retail stores.

Avon is sensitive to cannibalization issues. After all, there have been Avon ladies since 1886.* The company has been testing the mall kiosk concept and has found that 95 percent of the mall kiosk customers had never bought Avon before. The company's Internet strategy is even more Avon Lady–compatible. Rather than cannibalizing existing sales, its Internet site enables its representatives to serve customers through their own customized web pages.

Not all of Avon's markets are adopting multichannel strategies, however. In Brazil, Malaysia, and other developing countries, the traditional door-to-door sales approach is still the primary operation model.

*Prior to 1939, the company was called California Perfume Co.

Sources: Mary Jo Foley and Tom Steinart-Threlkeid, "The Ultimate CRM Machine" *Baseline*, November 14, 2001; and Jennifer Pellet, *Chief Executive*, June 2000, pp. 26–31.

REFACT

There are 5.4 million vending machines in Japan—one machine for every 23 people. Unlike the packaged-food and soft-drink offerings in the United States, products in Japan range from rice crackers and eyebrow shapers, to micro radios and condoms.[81]

While $25.6 billion in goods is sold annually through vending machines in the United States, vending machine sales growth is relatively slow, less than 5 percent, and closely mirrors the growth in the economy.[79]

Technological developments in vending machine design may result in long-term sales growth. New video kiosk vending machines enable consumers to see the merchandise in use, get information about it, and use their credit cards to make a purchase.

The new vending machine designs also enable the retailers to increase the productivity of the machines. Electronic systems in the machine keep track of inventory, cash, and other operating conditions. Then radio devices transmit data back to a host computer. These data are analyzed, and communications are sent to route drivers telling them when stockouts and malfunctions occur.[80]

SERVICES RETAILING

The retail firms discussed in the previous sections sell products to consumers. However, services retailers, firms selling primarily services rather than merchandise, are a large and growing part of the retail industry. Consider a typical Saturday. After a bagel and cup of coffee at a nearby Einstein's Bagels, you go to the laundromat to wash and dry your clothes, drop a suit off at a dry cleaner, leave film to be developed at a Walgreens drugstore, and make your way to the Jiffy Lube to have your car's oil changed. Since you are in a hurry, you drive through a Taco Bell so you can eat lunch quickly and not be late for your haircut at 1 P.M. By midafternoon, you're ready for a swim at your health club. After stopping at home for a change of clothes, you're off to dinner, a movie, and dancing with a friend. Finally, you end your day with a caffe latte at Starbucks, having interacted with 10 different services retailers during the day.

There are several trends that suggest considerable future growth in services retailing. For example, the aging of the population will increase demand for health services. Younger people too are spending increasing amounts of time and money on health and fitness. Parents in two-income families are willing to pay to

These are retailers, too. You start the day with a bagel, get your oil changed, and then burn off the calories at the fitness center.

have their homes cleaned, lawns maintained, clothes washed and pressed, and meals prepared so they can spend more time with their families.

Exhibit 2–9 shows the wide variety of services retailers along with the national companies that provide these services. These companies are retailers because they sell goods and services to consumers. However, some of these companies are not just retailers. For example, airlines, banks, hotels, and insurance and express mail companies sell their services to businesses as well as consumers. Also, a large number of services retailers such as lawyers, doctors, and dry cleaners are not in the exhibit because they focus on local markets and do not have a national presence.

Many organizations such as banks, hospitals, health spas, legal clinics, entertainment firms, and universities that offer services to consumers traditionally haven't considered themselves as retailers. Due to increased competition, these organizations are adopting retailing principles to attract customers and satisfy their needs. For example, Zoots is a new dry-cleaning chain in the Boston area. Founded by a former Staples executive, Zoots has adopted many retailing best practices. It has several convenient locations, plus it offers pickup and delivery service. Zoots stores have extended hours, are open on weekends, and offer a drop-off option for those who cannot get to the store during operating hours.

EXHIBIT 2–9
Examples of Services Retailers

Type of Service	Service Retail Firms
Airlines	American, Delta, British Airways, Singapore Airway
Automobile maintenance and repair	Jiffy Lube, Midas, AAMCO
Automobile rental	Hertz, Avis, Budget, Enterprise
Banks	Citibank, NCNB, Bank of America
Child care centers	Kindercare, Gymboree
Credit cards	American Express, VISA, MasterCard
Education	Babson College, University of Florida
Entertainment parks	Disney, Universal Studios, Six Flags
Express package delivery	Federal Express, UPS, U.S. Postal Service
Financial services	Merrill Lynch, Dean Witter
Fitness	Jazzercise, Bally's, Gold's Gym
Health care	Humana, HCA, Kaiser
Home maintenance	Chemlawn, Mini Maid, Roto-Rooter
Hotels and motels	Hyatt, Sheraton, Marriott, Days Inn
Income tax preparation	H&R Block
Insurance	Allstate, State Farm
Internet access/electronic information	America Online, Mindspring
Long-distance telephone	AT&T, MCI, Sprint
Movie theaters	AMC, Odeon/Cineplex
Real estate	Century 21, Coldwell Banker
Restaurants	TGI Friday's, Wendy's, Pizza Hut
Truck rentals	U-Haul, Ryder
Weight loss	Weight Watchers, Jenny Craig
Video rental	Blockbuster
Vision centers	Lenscrafters, Pearle

EXHIBIT 2–10 | Merchandise/Service Continuum

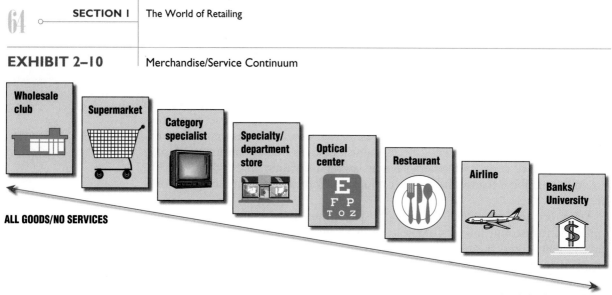

The stores are bright and clean. Clerks are taught to always welcome customers and acknowledge their presence if there is a line.[82]

All retailers provide goods and services for their customers. However, the emphasis placed on the merchandise versus the services differs across retail formats, as Exhibit 2–10 shows. On the left side of the exhibit are supermarkets and warehouse clubs. These retail formats consist of self-service stores that offer very few services. However, these formats do offer a few services such as check cashing and some assistance from store employees. Moving along the continuum from left to right, we find category specialists, which also emphasize self-service but have employees who can answer questions, demonstrate merchandise, and make recommendations. Next, department and specialty stores provide even higher levels of service. In addition to assistance from sales associates, these stores offer services such as gift wrapping, bridal registries, and alterations.

Optical centers and restaurants lie somewhere in the middle of the merchandise/service continuum. In addition to selling frames, eyeglasses, and contact lenses, optical centers also provide important services like eye examinations and eyeglasses fittings. Similarly, restaurants offer food plus a place to eat, music in the background, a pleasant ambience, and table service. As we move to the right end of the continuum, we encounter retailers whose offering is primarily services. However, even these retailers have some products associated with the services offered, such as a meal on the airplane or a check book at a bank. **Services retailers** are defined as retailers for which the major aspect of their offerings is services versus merchandise.

Differences between Services and Merchandise Retailers

As a retailer falls more to the right on the merchandise/service continuum, services become a more important aspect of the retailer's offering. Four important differences in the nature of the offering provided by services and merchandise retailers are (1) intangibility, (2) simultaneous production and consumption, (3) perishability, and (4) inconsistency of the offering to customers.[83]

Intangibility   Services are generally intangible—customers cannot see, touch, or feel them. They are performances or actions rather than objects. For example, health care services cannot be seen or touched by a patient. Even after diagnosis and treatment, the patient may not realize the full extent of the service that has been performed.

Intangibility introduces a number of challenges for services retailers. First, since customers can't touch and feel services, it's difficult for customers to evaluate services before they buy them or even after they buy and consume them. Due to the intangibility of their offering, services retailers often use tangible symbols to inform customers about the quality of their services. For example, lawyers frequently have elegant, carpeted offices with expensive antique furniture.

Services retailers also have difficulty in evaluating the quality of services they are providing. For example, it's hard for a law firm to evaluate how well its lawyers are performing their jobs. To evaluate the quality of their offering, services retailers emphasize soliciting customer evaluations and complaints.

Simultaneous Production and Consumption   Products are typically made in a factory, stored and sold by a retailer, and then used by consumers in their homes. Service providers, on the other hand, create and deliver the service as the customer is consuming it. For example, when you eat at a restaurant, the meal is prepared and consumed almost at the same time.

The simultaneity of production and consumption creates some special problems for services retailers. First, the customers are present when the service is produced, may even have an opportunity to see it produced, and in some cases may be part of the production process, as in making their own salad at a salad bar. Second, other customers consuming the service at the same time can affect the quality of the service provided. For example, an obnoxious passenger next to you on an airline can make the flight very unpleasant. Finally, the services retailer often does not get a second chance to satisfy the needs of its customers. While customers can return damaged merchandise to a store, customers that are dissatisfied with services have limited recourse. Thus, it is critical for services retailers to get it right the first time.

Because services are produced and consumed at the same time, it is difficult to reduce costs through mass production. For this reason, most services retailers are small, local firms. Large national retailers are able to reduce costs by "industrializing" the services they offer. They make substantial investments in equipment and training to provide a uniform service. For example, McDonald's has a detailed procedure for cooking french fries and hamburgers to make sure they come out the same whether cooked in Paris, France, or Paris, Illinois.

Perishability   Because the creation and consumption of services are inseparable, services are perishable. They can't be saved, stored, or resold. Once the airline takes off with an empty seat, the sale is lost forever. This is in contrast to merchandise that can be held in inventory until a customer is ready to buy it.

Due to the perishability of services, an important aspect of services retailing is matching supply and demand. Most services retailers have a capacity constraint, and the capacity cannot be changed easily. There are a fixed number of tables in a restaurant, seats in a classroom, beds in a hospital, and electricity that can be generated by a power plant. To increase capacity, services retailers need to make major investments such as buying more airplanes or building an addition to increase the size of the hospital or restaurant.

In addition, demand for service varies considerably over time. Consumers are most likely to fly on airplanes during holidays and the summer, eat in restaurants at lunch and dinner time, and use electricity in the evening rather than earlier in the day. Thus, services retailers often have times when their services are underutilized and other times when they have to turn customers away because they can't accommodate them.

Services retailers use a variety of programs to match demand and supply. For example, airlines and hotels set lower prices on weekends when they have excessive capacity because businesspeople aren't traveling. To achieve more capacity flexibility, health clinics stay open longer in the flu season, while tax preparation services are open on weekends during March and April. Restaurants increase staffing on weekends, may not open until dinner time, and use a reservation system to guarantee service delivery at a specific time. Finally, services retailers attempt to make customers' waiting time more enjoyable. For example, videos and park employees entertain customers while they wait in line in Disney theme parks.

Inconsistency Merchandise is often produced by machines with very tight quality control so customers are reasonably assured that all boxes of Cheerios will be identical. Because services are performances produced by people (employees and customers), no two services will be identical. For example, tax accountants can have different knowledge and skills for preparing tax returns. The waiter at the Olive Garden can be in a bad mood and make your dining experience a disaster.

Thus, an important challenge for services retailers is providing consistently high-quality services. Many factors determining service quality are beyond the control of the retailers; however, services retailers expend considerable time and effort selecting, training, managing, and motivating their service providers.

TYPES OF OWNERSHIP

Previous sections of this chapter discussed how retailers are classified in terms of their retail mix (the variety and depth of merchandise and services offered to customers) and the merchandise and services they sell (food, general merchandise, and services). Another way to classify retailers is by their ownership. The major classifications of retail ownership are (1) independent, single-store establishments, (2) corporate chains, and (3) franchises.

Independent, Single-Store Establishments

Retailing is one of the few sectors in our economy where entrepreneurial activity is extensive. Over 60,000 new retail businesses are started in the United States each year.[84] Many such stores are owner-managed. Thus, management has direct contact with customers and can respond quickly to their needs. Small retailers are also very flexible and can therefore react quickly to market changes and customer needs. They aren't bound by bureaucracies inherent in large retail organizations.

Approximately one-third of all U.S. retail sales are made by franchisees like these.

While single-store retailers can tailor their offerings to their customers' needs, corporate chains can more effectively negotiate lower prices for merchandise and advertising due to their larger size. In addition, corporate chains have a broader management base, with people who specialize in specific retail activities. Single-store retailers typically have to rely on owner-managers' capabilities to make the broad range of necessary retail decisions.

To better compete against corporate chains, some independent retailers join a **wholesale-sponsored voluntary cooperative group,** which is an organization operated by a wholesaler offering a merchandising program to small, independent retailers on a voluntary basis. Independent Grocers Alliance (IGA), Tru Serv (supplier to True Value Hardware), and Ace Hardware are wholesale-sponsored voluntary cooperative groups. In addition to buying, warehousing, and distribution, these groups offer members services such as store design and layout, site selection, bookkeeping and inventory management systems, and employee training programs.

Corporate Retail Chains

A **retail chain** is a company operating multiple retail units under common ownership and usually has centralized decision making for defining and implementing its strategy. Retail chains can range in size from a drugstore with two stores to retailers with over 1,000 stores such as Safeway, Wal-Mart, Target, and JCPenney. Some retail chains are divisions of larger corporations or holding companies. For example, Venator owns Foot Locker, Lady Foot Locker, Kids Foot Locker, Foot Locker International, Champs Sports, and Footlocker.com/Eastbay.Champs; Intimate Brands owns Victoria's Secret, Bath & Body Works, and The White Barn Candle Co.; and Target Corporation owns Target, Dayton's, Hudson's, Marshall Field's, and Mervyn's.

There has been considerable concern that corporate retail chains drive independent retailers out of business. For example, Wal-Mart and other discount store chains have pursued a strategy of opening full-line discount stores and supercenters on the outskirts of small towns.[85] These stores offer a

EXHIBIT 2–11   Franchise Retailers

Name	Type	Number of Outlets in U.S. (2001)	Start-Up Cost	Royalty (% of Sales)
FAST-FOOD RESTAURANTS				
Subway	Submarine sandwiches	12,682	63.4K–175K	8
Yogen Fruz Worlwide	Ice cream, frozen yogurt, and ices	1,656	25K–250K	6
McDonald's	Hamburgers	11,051	489.9K–1.5M	12.5+
KFC Corp.	Chicken, miscellaneous	3,980	1.1M–1.7M	4
Dunkin' Donuts	Donuts	3,732	242.8K–1.3M	5.9
Denny's Inc.	Family restaurants	1,065	858K–1.5M	4
Arby's	Miscellaneous sandwiches	3,175	333.7K–2.3M	4
Orion Food Systems Inc.	Miscellaneous fast food	1,047	16K–680K	0
Taco Bell Corp.	Mexican fast food	4,152	3M	5.5
MERCHANDISE RETAILERS				
7-Eleven Inc.	Convenience stores	3,539	12.5K+	Varies
AM/PM Convenience Stores	Convenience food stores	647	1M–3.2M	5
White Hen Pantry	Convenience stores	295	63.4K–205.9K	Varies
Medicap Pharmacies Inc.	Pharmacy	159	22.1K–324.7K	2.4
SERVICES RETAILERS				
Mail Boxes Etc.	Postal/business/communications services	3,489	125.9K–195.9K	5
AIM Mail Centers	Postal and business services	53	88.9K–133.9K	5
Better Homes Realty Inc.	Real estate	42	61.5K	6
Coldwell Banker Real Estate Corp.	Real estate	2,780	23K–477K	6
Results Travel	Travel services	214	10.7K	$600/yr.
Payless Car Rental System Inc.	Auto rentals/sales	73	235.9K–6.3M	5
Rent-a-Wreck	Auto rentals and leasing	491	32.8K–207K	$30/car/mo.
Lady of America	Fitness centers	293	21.4K–175.4K	10

Source: "Franchise 500," 2002, *Entrepreneur,* www.entrepreneur.com/franchisezone. Reprinted by permission.

broader selection of merchandise at much lower prices than previously available from local retailers. Due to scale economies and an efficient distribution system, corporate chains can sell at low prices. This forces some directly competing local retailers out of business and alters the community fabric.

On the other hand, local retailers offering complementary merchandise and services can prosper. When large chain stores open, more consumers are attracted to the community from surrounding areas. Thus, the market for the local stores expands. While chain stores may have cost advantages over local retailers, large retail chains can be very bureaucratic, stifling managers' creativity with excessive rules and procedures. Often, all stores in the chain have the same merchandise and services, whereas local retailers can provide merchandise compatible with local market needs. Finally, chain stores each employ 200 to 300 people from the local community.

Franchising

Franchising is a contractual agreement between a franchisor and a franchisee that allows the franchisee to operate a retail outlet using a name and format developed and supported by the franchisor. Approximately one-third of all U.S. retail sales are made by franchisees. Exhibit 2–11 lists some retailers governed by franchise agreements.

In a franchise contract, the franchisee pays a lump sum plus a royalty on all sales for the right to operate a store in a specific location. The franchisee also agrees to operate the outlet in accordance with procedures prescribed by the franchisor. The franchisor provides assistance in locating and building the store, developing the products or services sold, management training, and advertising. To maintain the franchisee's reputation, the franchisor also makes sure that all outlets provide the same quality of services and products.

The franchise ownership format attempts to combine advantages of owner-managed businesses with efficiencies of centralized decision making in chain store operations. Franchisees are motivated to make their store successful because they receive the profits (after the royalty is paid). The franchisor is motivated to develop new products and systems and to promote the franchise because it receives a royalty on all sales. Advertising, product development, and system development are efficiently done by the franchisor, with costs shared by all franchisees.

SUMMARY

This chapter explained different types of retailers and how they compete with different retail mixes to sell merchandise and services to customers. To collect statistics about retailing, the federal government classifies retailers by type of merchandise and services sold. But this classification method may not be useful in determining a retailer's major competitors. A more useful approach for understanding the retail marketplace is classifying retailers on the basis of their retail mix, the merchandise variety and assortment, services, location, pricing, and promotion decisions made to attract customers.

Over the past 30 years, U.S. retail markets have been characterized by the emergence of many new retail institutions. Traditional institutions (supermarkets, convenience, department, discount, and specialty stores) have been joined by category specialists, superstores, hypermarkets, convenience stores, warehouse clubs, off-price retailers, catalog showrooms, and hypermarkets. In addition, there has been substantial growth in services retailing. The inherent differences between services and merchandise result in services retailers emphasizing store management while merchandise retailers emphasize inventory control issues.

Traditional retail institutions have changed in response to these new retailers. For example, department stores have increased their emphasis on fashion-oriented apparel and improved the services they offer. Supermarkets are focusing more attention on meal solutions and perishables. Appendix 2B describes theories of retail change.

KEY TERMS

assortment, *38*
breadth of merchandise, *39*
catalog retailing, *58*
category killers, *50*
category specialist, *50*
closeout retailer, *56*

combination store, *42*
convenience store, *45*
conventional supermarket, *42*
department store, *53*
depth of merchandise, *39*
direct-mail retailers, *58*

direct-response
  advertising, *61*
direct selling, *60*
discount store, *48*
drugstore, *54*
electronic retailing, *57*

e-tailing, *57*

factory outlet, *56*

franchising, *68*

general merchandise catalog retailers, *58*

home improvement center, *50*

hypermarket, *43*

infomercials, *60*

Internet retailing, *57*

leased department, *53*

NAICS (North American Industry Classification System), *37*

multilevel network, *60*

off-price retailer, *55*

outlet store, *56*

party plan system, *60*

pyramid scheme, *60*

retail chain, *67*

services retailer, *64*

SKU (stock keeping unit), *38*

specialty catalog retailer, *58*

specialty store, *48*

supercenter, *43*

superstore, *42*

television home shopping, *60*

value retailers, *56*

variety, *38*

vending machine retailing, *61*

warehouse club, *37*

wholesale-sponsored voluntary cooperative group, *67*

GET OUT & DO IT!

1. **GO SHOPPING** Go to an athletic footwear specialty store such as Foot Locker, a department store, and a discount store. Analyze their variety and assortment of athletic footwear by creating a table similar to Exhibit 2–3 on page 40.

2. **GO SHOPPING** Keep a diary of where you shop, what you buy, and how much you spend for two weeks. Get your parents to do the same thing. Tabulate your results by type of retailer. Are your shopping habits significantly different from your parents? Do you and your parents' shopping habits coincide with the trends discussed in this chapter? Why or why not?

3. **GO SHOPPING** The Comparison Shopping Exercise in Appendix 2A gives you the opportunity to see a retail store from the eyes of a retailer instead of a consumer. Choose two stores and follow the format outlined in Appendix 2A.

4. **INTERNET EXERCISE** Data on U.S. retail sales are available at the U.S. Bureau of the Census Internet site at www.census.gov/mrts/www/mrts.html.

Look at the unadjusted monthly sales by NAICS. Which categories of retailers have the largest percentage of sales in the fourth quarter (the holiday season)?

5. **INTERNET EXERCISE** Four large associations of retailers are the National Retail Federation (www.nrf.org), the Food Marketing Institute (www.fmi.org), the National Association of Chain Drug Stores (www.nacds._org), and the National Association of Convenience Stores (www.nacs.org). Visit these sites and report the latest retail developments and issues confronting the industry.

6. **INTERNET EXERCISE** Go to www.wal-mart.com. Scroll to the bottom of the page and click on Wal-Mart Stores Information. Look for "About Wal-Mart," and click on "Divisons." Look for "Retail Divisons," and click on "Supercenters." Now go to www.auchanhypermarket.com. See if you can determine the differences between a Wal-Mart supercenter and an Auchan hypermarket.

DISCUSSION QUESTIONS AND PROBLEMS

1. Distinguish between variety and assortment. Why are these important elements of retail market structure?

2. How can small independent retailers compete against the large national chains?

3. What do off-price retailers need to do to compete against other formats in the future?

4. Compare and contrast the retail mixes of convenience stores, traditional supermarkets, supercenters, hypermarkets, and warehouse stores. Can all of these food retail institutions survive over the long run? Why?

5. Why haven't hypermarkets been successful in the United States? Do you believe they will be successful in the future?

6. The same brand and model personal computer is sold in specialty computer stores, discount stores, category specialists, and warehouse stores. Why would a customer choose one store over the other?

7. Choose a product category that both you and your parents purchase (e.g., clothing, CDs, electronic equipment). In which type of store do you typically purchase this merchandise? What about your parents? Explain why there is, or is not, a difference in your store choices.

8. At many optical stores you can get your eyes checked *and* purchase glasses or contact lenses. How is the shopping experience different for the service as compared to the product? Design a strategy designed to get customers to purchase both the service and the product. In so doing, delineate specific actions that should be taken to acquire and retain optical customers.

9. Which of the store-based retail formats discussed in this chapter is most vulnerable to competition from Internet retailers? Why? Which is least vulnerable? Why?

10. Many experts believe that customer service is one of retailing's most important issues in the new millennium. How can retailers that emphasize price (such as discount stores, category specialists, and off-price retailers) improve customer service without increasing costs and, thus, prices?

SUGGESTED READINGS

Bond, Ronald L. *Retail in Detail: How to Start and Manage a Small Retail Business.* 2nd ed. PSI Research/The Oasis Press, 2001.

"Food for Thought: Discount Stores Eat into Supermarket, Drug Store Sales." *Chain Store Age*, May 2000, p. 49.

Michman, Ronald, and Edward Mazze. *Specialty Stores: Marketing Triumphs and Blunders.* Westport, CT: Quorum Books, 2001.

Quinn, Bill. *How Wal-Mart Is Destroying America (and the World): And What You Can Do about It.* Ten Speed Press, 2000.

Roush, Chris. *Inside Home Depot: How One Company Revolutionized an Industry through the Relentless Pursuit of Growth.* McGraw-Hill Professional, 1999.

Schulz, David P. "*Triversity Top 100 Retailers: The Nation's Biggest Retail Companies.*" www.stores.org, 2001.

Sherman, Andrew J. *Franchising and Licensing: Two Ways to Build Your Business.* AMACOM, 1999.

Spector, Robert. *Lessons from the Nordstrom Way: How Companies Are Emulating the #1 Customer Service Company.* Wiley, John & Sons, Incorporated, 2000.

"68th Annual Report of the Grocery Industry." *Progressive Grocer*, April 2001.

"Top 100 Retailers." *Stores*, August 2001.

Taylor, Don, and Jeanne Smalling Archer. *Up against the Wal-Marts: How Your Business Can Prosper in the Shadow of the Retail Giants.* AMACOM, 1996.

Way, Bill. *Vending Success Secrets: How Anyone Can Grow Rich in America's Best Cash, Business!* Freedom Tech Press, 2001.

APPENDIX 2A   Comparison Shopping

All retailers learn about their competitors through comparison shopping. Comparison shopping might be as informal as walking through a competitor's store and looking around. But a structured analysis is more helpful in developing a retail offering that will attract consumers from a competitor's store.

The first step in the process is to define the scope of the comparison. For example, the comparison might be between two retail chains, two specific stores, two departments, or two categories of merchandise. The appropriate scope depends on the responsibilities of the person undertaking the comparison. For example, CEOs of retail chains would be interested in comparing their chain with a competitor's. Comparisons might focus on chains' financial resources, inventory levels, number of stores and employees, store locations, merchandise sold, employee compensation programs, and return policies. Thus, CEOs would examine factors for which the corporate office is responsible.

On the other hand, store managers would be interested in comparing their store with a competing store. For example, department store managers would want to know more about other department stores anchoring the mall where they're located. Buyers and department managers would focus on specific areas of merchandise for which they're responsible.

Exhibit 2–12 lists questions to consider when comparison shopping. Exhibit 2–13 suggests a format for comparing merchandise, in this case lugsole shoes in JCPenney and a men's shoe store.

APPENDIX 2B   Theories of Retail Evolution

A number of theories have been developed to explain the present structure of the retail industry and predict how the structure will change. No individual theory explains all of the changes in the retailing environment. Yet as a whole, the theories provide insights for understanding the evolution of retail institutions.[86]

Four theories of retail evolution are the wheel of retailing, accordion theory, dialectic process, and natural selection. The first two theories are cyclical theories. These theories suggest that retail institutions go through cycles, beginning with one state and then returning to that state at some time in the future. The last two theories, dialectic process and natural selection, are evolutionary theories suggesting that changes in retail institutions are similar to patterns observed in biological evolution.

THE WHEEL OF RETAILING

One of the first and most famous frameworks for explaining changes in retailing institutions is the wheel of retailing (Exhibit 2–14). The wheel represents phases through which some types of retailers pass.[87] The cycle begins with retailers attracting customers by offering low price and low service. Over time, these retailers want to expand their market and they begin to stock more expensive merchandise, provide more services, and open more convenient locations. This trading-up process increases the retailers' costs and the prices of their merchandise, creating opportunity for new low-price retailers to enter the market.

The evolution of the department store illustrates the wheel of retailing theory. In its entry phase, as Exhibit 2–14 shows, the department store was a low-cost, low-service venture. After World War II, department stores moved into the trading-up phase. They upgraded their facilities, stock selection, advertising, and service. Today, department stores are in the vulnerability phase. They're vulnerable to various types of low-cost, low-service formats such as full-line discount stores and category specialists.

The first phase of full-line discount stores was the national mass merchandise chains such as Sears and JCPenney. But over the years, these retailers have also succumbed to the turning of the wheel of retailing. Both of these retailers have made a con-

MERCHANDISE PRESENTATION

1. How is the selling floor laid out? What selling areas are devoted to specific types of merchandise? How many square feet are devoted to each area?
2. Where are the different selling areas located? Are they in heavy traffic areas? By restrooms? On the main aisle? On a secondary aisle? How does this location affect sales volume for merchandise in the area?
3. What kind of fixtures are used in each selling area (faceouts, rounders, cubes, bunkers, tables, gondolas)?
4. Are aisles, walls, and columns used to display merchandise?
5. What is the lighting for sales areas (focus, overhead, bright, toned down)?
6. How is the merchandise organized in the selling areas (by type, price point, vendor, style, color)?
7. Evaluate the housekeeping of the selling areas. Are they cluttered or messy? Are they well maintained and organized?
8. What's the overall atmosphere or image of the selling areas? What effect does the lighting, fixturing, spacing, and visual merchandising have on customers?
9. What type of customer (age, income, fashion orientation) would be attracted to the store and each selling area within it?

EXHIBIT 2–12

Examples of Issues to Address in Comparison Shopping

SALES SUPPORT/CUSTOMER SERVICES

1. How many salespeople are in each department? Is the department adequately staffed?
2. How are salespeople dressed? Do they have an appropriate appearance?
3. Do salespeople approach customers promptly? How soon after entering a selling area is a customer greeted? How do customers respond to the level of service?
4. Evaluate salespeople's product knowledge.
5. Do salespeople suggest add-on merchandise?
6. Where, if applicable, are fitting rooms in relation to the selling floor? In what condition are they? Are they supervised? Are there enough fitting rooms to meet demand?
7. How many registers are on the selling floor? Are they well staffed and well stocked with supplies?
8. What services (credit charges acceptance, gift wrapping, delivery, special ordering, bridal registry, alterations, other) does the store offer?
9. What level of customer service is provided in the selling area?

MERCHANDISE (EACH CATEGORY)

1. Who are the key vendors?
2. How deep are the assortments for each vendor?
3. What are the private labels and how important are they?
4. What are the low, average, and top prices for merchandise in the category?

SUMMARY AND CONCLUSIONS

1. Who is the store's target customer?
2. What are the competitor's strengths and weaknesses?
3. How can we capture more business from the competitor?

certed effort to upgrade their stores and merchandise. For instance, it is now hard to distinguish between a new Penney store and a department store at the same mall, so Sears and Penney became vulnerable to new forms of low-price, low-service retailers just like other department store chains.

Now these low-cost, low-service full-line discount stores such as Target and Wal-Mart stores offer credit, more fashionable merchandise than before, some carpeted departments, and limited service. One could view these discount stores as beginning to enter the trading-up phase of the wheel of retailing.

The new entry in the low-status, low-price arena is the warehouse club. These stores, such as Sam's Wholesale Club and Costco, require customers to become members and are a cross between wholesale warehouses and discount stores. The question remaining for warehouse clubs is whether they'll proceed to the trading-up phase on the wheel of retailing. This question raises a general criticism of the wheel. Some types of retailers never trade up. A corollary criticism is that some institutions don't begin as low-price, low-service entrants. Upscale fashion specialty stores,

EXHIBIT 2–13
Format for
Merchandise
Comparisons

Retailer	Factors	Lug sole casual shoes			Comments
JC Penney	Style	3 eyelet oxford			
	Brands	St. Johns Bay (private)			
	Price	$35			
	% mix	5%			
	Depth	36 pair			
	Breadth	4 colors			
Father/Son Shoes	Style	3 eyelet oxford	Tie suede	Chukka suede	
	Brands	British Knights Private	Private	Private	
	Price	$38.99– 39.99	$29.99	$37.95	
	% mix	10%	5%	5%	
	Depth	24 pairs	36 pairs	12 pairs	
	Breadth	3 colors	3 colors	2 colors	
Harwyns	Style	2 eyelet oxford	Tie suede		
	Brands	British Knights	Private		
	Price	$39.99	$29.95		
	% mix	5%	5%		
	Depth	36 pairs	36 pairs		
	Breadth	3 colors	3 colors		

Style For clothing, style might be the fabric or cut. For example, sweater styles might be split into wool, cotton, or polyblend and V-neck, crewneck, or cardigan.

Brands The identifying label. Indicate whether or not the brand is a national brand or store brand.

Price The price marked on the merchandise. If the item has been marked down, indicate the original price and the marked-down price.

Percent mix The percentage of the total assortment devoted to this style of merchandise.

Depth The amount of inventory for this style. The amount on display is one indicator of inventory depth. Another indicator is the amount of space devoted to the style.

Breadth The number of SKUs in this style.

for instance, have never fit the wheel of retailing pattern.

THE ACCORDION THEORY

The Accordion Theory, the second cyclical theory, proposes that the retail institutions fluctuate from the strategy of offering many merchandise categories with a shallow assortment to the strategy of offering a deep assortment with a limited number of categories. This expansion and contraction calls to mind an accordion. During this nation's early development, relatively small general stores succeeded by offering rural Americans many categories of merchandise under one roof. As towns grew, they were able to support retail specialists like shoe, clothing, drug, and food stores. Department stores developed during the next expansion of the accordion. Department stores, somewhat like giant general stores, again offered customers multiple merchandise categories under one roof. This time, however, the depth of selection improved as well. The next contraction of the retail accordion results from specialty stores' tendency to have become even more specialized in the past two decades. These retail formats known as category killers or category specialists (such as Toys "R" Us, Circuit City, and Sports Authority) offer consumers deep selections in a limited number of merchandise categories.[88]

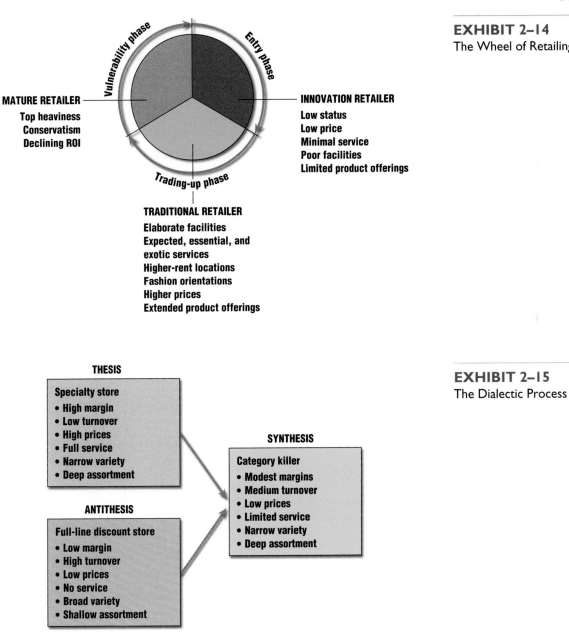

EXHIBIT 2–14
The Wheel of Retailing

Vulnerability phase

Entry phase

MATURE RETAILER
Top heaviness
Conservatism
Declining ROI

INNOVATION RETAILER
Low status
Low price
Minimal service
Poor facilities
Limited product offerings

Trading-up phase

TRADITIONAL RETAILER
Elaborate facilities
Expected, essential, and exotic services
Higher-rent locations
Fashion orientations
Higher prices
Extended product offerings

THESIS

Specialty store
- **High margin**
- **Low turnover**
- **High prices**
- **Full service**
- **Narrow variety**
- **Deep assortment**

SYNTHESIS

Category killer
- **Modest margins**
- **Medium turnover**
- **Low prices**
- **Limited service**
- **Narrow variety**
- **Deep assortment**

ANTITHESIS

Full-line discount store
- **Low margin**
- **High turnover**
- **Low prices**
- **No service**
- **Broad variety**
- **Shallow assortment**

EXHIBIT 2–15
The Dialectic Process

DIALECTIC PROCESS

The first of the two evolutionary theories of change in retail institutions is the dialectic process of thesis, antithesis, and synthesis (Exhibit 2–15). This theory implies that new retail institutions result from stores borrowing characteristics from other very different competitors, much like children are a combination of the genes of their parents. The established retail institution, known for relatively high margins, low turnover, and plush facilities, is the specialty store—the thesis. Discount stores in their early form were the antithesis of service-oriented specialty stores. That is, they were characteristically low-margin, high-turnover, Spartan operations, with broad variety. Over time, characteristics from both department stores and discount stores were synthesized to form category specialist stores like Best Buy and Sports Authority.[89]

NATURAL SELECTION

A final theory, natural selection, has the stronger intuitive appeal for explaining change in retailing institutions. It follows Charles Darwin's view that organisms evolve and change on the basis of survival of the fittest. In retailing, those institutions best able to adapt to changes in customers, technology, competition, and legal environments have the greatest chance of success. For instance, the increased number of women in the workforce and America's interest in physical fitness have made salad bars successful in some grocery stores. Video stores appeared in virtually every neighborhood in America only a few years after videocassette recorder technology was developed. Department stores have tried to battle specialty stores' competitive inroads by creating small specialty stores or boutiques within their stores.[90]

Multichannel Retailing—A View into the Future

CHAPTER

EXECUTIVE BRIEFING | Bruce Nelson, Chairman and CEO, Office Depot

"Today people can buy office supplies from a number of different places. Our goal is to impress our customers so much that they keep coming back to Office Depot because they find it a compelling place to shop, whether they shop our stores, use our catalogs, telephone our customer service centers, or visit our e-commerce sites. We find that when our customers shop more than one channel, their loyalty and spend increases three to four times the average. Some customers want to shop our stores for the broad assortment we carry, while other times they find it more convenient to place an order through our e-commerce sites. Our goal is to provide customers with fanatical customer service seamlessly across all of our channels, no matter which one they choose to order from.

"Our people play a major role in offering customers what we define as 'fanatical' customer service. Our store employees are spending more time greeting customers and helping them with their purchase decisions. Our distribution people are focused on quality of our deliveries, our merchants ensure that we have the right merchandise in stock, and our store planners layout the store to improve the shopping experience and offer point-of-purchase signage that gives customers the product information they need.

QUESTIONS

- What are the unique customer benefits offered by retailing through stores, catalogs, and the Internet?
- What factors will affect the growth of electronic retailing?
- Why did most pure electronic retailers fail?
- How do multichannel retailers provide more value to their customers?
- What are the key success factors in multichannel retailing?
- How might technology affect the future shopping experience?

"Our websites in 10 countries offer innovative features to enhance the shopping experience for e-commerce shoppers. For example, Quick Order by Stock Number lets customers enter catalog product codes directly onto an online order form and Supplies QuickFind helps customers identify the correct ink cartridges, ribbons, or toners needed for their business machines. Our sites also provide real-time stock information, keeping track of what is actually available and in stock. The sites are also a source of information for small business owners. They can download job application forms and benefit information, find out about best practices for running their business, and get all the latest business news.

"Office Depot is the world's largest seller of office products and an industry leader in every distribution channel, including retail stores, direct mail, contract delivery, and business-to-business e-commerce. By continuing to make Office Depot a compelling place to shop, we can grow this base and continue to further our industry leadership."

What a difference a few years make. In 1998, most analysts were predicting that a new breed of high-tech, web-savvy entrepreneurs would dominate the retail industry. They suggested that everyone would be doing their shopping over the Internet in the future. Stores would close due to lack of traffic and paper catalogs would become obsolete. We now realize the Internet is not a revolutionary new retail format replacing stores and catalogs. It is a tool that retailers can use to complement their store and catalog offerings to grow revenues and provide more value for their customers.

In this chapter, we take a strategic perspective in our discussion of the different channels—stores, catalogs, and the Internet—through which retailers can communicate with and sell merchandise and services to customers. After describing the unique benefits of these channels, we discuss some specific issues related to the electronic channel. Then we look at how retailers can increase revenues and improve their customers' shopping experience by using all of these channels to interact with their customers. At the end of the chapter, we illustrate how integrating these channels and using new technologies will create a compelling shopping experience in the future.

In other chapters, we examine how retailers use the Internet in specific applications, including managing employees, buying merchandise, managing customer relationships, advertising and promoting merchandise, and providing customer service.

RETAIL CHANNELS FOR INTERACTING WITH CUSTOMERS

Chapter 2 categorized retailers by the channel they used to reach their customers. Retailers were either classified as store-based or nonstore (electronic, catalog/direct mail, direct selling, TV home shopping, and vending machine) retailers. However, many retail firms use more than one channel to reach their customers. For example, Gateway started as an electronic retailer and has opened up stores; Amazon.com now distributes a catalog; Eddie Bauer and JCPenney interface with customers through their stores, catalogs, and websites.

A **multichannel retailer** is a retailer that sells merchandise or services through more than one channel. Single-channel retailers are evolving into multichannel retailers to attract and satisfy more customers. By using a combination of channels, retailers can exploit the unique benefits provided by each channel. Retailing View 3.1 describes how Lawson, a Japanese convenience store chain, provides more value to its customer by installing kiosks with Internet access in their stores.

REFACT

Of the top 50 business-to-consumer websites, 66 percent are supported by multichannel retailers.[1]

RETAILING VIEW   Using Kiosks with Internet Access in Stores

3.1

The convenience store concept started in the United States nearly 40 years ago; however, it has blossomed into the "24-hour village square" in Japan. With more than 50,000 convenience stores (*konbini*) in Japan today, there is virtually a convenience store on every block. Lawson is the second-largest chain, with over 7,000 outlets. Adults in Japan patronize a convenience store three times a week, on average.

The Japanese convenience stores project a high-quality image that invites browsing and "hanging out." The stores are restocked and reset with deliveries four times a day, every day—with a different assortment for morning, lunchtime, afternoon, and evening customers. Of the nearly 3,000 products that are stocked, 60 percent of the food items are perishable in one day.

To increase revenues and attract a young clientele, Lawson installed kiosks with broadband Internet access into its stores. The kiosks, referred to as Loppi, allow customers to sign on, browse online catalogs, and place orders. They can also order tickets for sports events, concerts, movies, or travel; popular books, music CDs, and videos; game software; cosmetics and fashion accessories; and PCs and peripherals. The biggest-selling items are tickets (about 40 percent of sales) and game software. Ticket sales sometimes surpass 100,000 per day. When a popular new computer game was released last year, the Loppi system nationwide logged nearly 3,000 orders in a minute.

After browsing through the online catalogs and reserving their desired items, shoppers take a paper receipt issued by the Loppi terminal to the store's cash register to pay for their selections. Then, depending on the item, the purchase is either shipped to the store for pickup within three to four days, delivered directly to the home, or, for some game software, downloaded directly through Loppi's network. Users who order items through Web Loppi (www.lawson.co.jp/loppi/loppi_top.html) will be able to visit Lawson's 24-hour stores to pay for and pick up their purchases.

By offering a broader assortment of products and services, Lawson has attracted a new clientele. Convenience store customers have tended to be mostly in their 20s and 30s. Since Lawson introduced the machines, with their entirely new range of products, it attracted new groups of customers—senior citizens, young mothers, and children. Makoto Tazaki, a leading expert in store solutions at IBM Japan says, "The core value of a convenience store is its proximity to a customer's home or office. Networked kiosks enable customers to [access] computer software or book a holiday as easily as [they] could pick up a carton of milk. This amounts to a revolution in retail."

Sources: Hau Lee and Seungjin Whang, "Demand Chain Excellence: A Tale of Two Retailers," *Supply Chain Management Review*, March 2001, pp. 40–51; and Penelope Ody, "Sign on to 'Clicks-and-Mortar' World," *Financial Times* (London), May 3, 2000, p. 1.

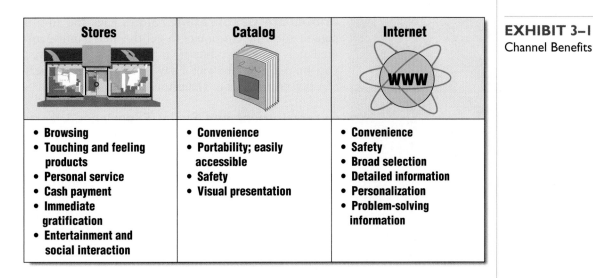

Stores	Catalog	Internet
• Browsing • Touching and feeling products • Personal service • Cash payment • Immediate gratification • Entertainment and social interaction	• Convenience • Portability; easily accessible • Safety • Visual presentation	• Convenience • Safety • Broad selection • Detailed information • Personalization • Problem-solving information

EXHIBIT 3–1
Channel Benefits

Exhibit 3–1 lists the unique benefits of stores, catalogs, and the Internet. These benefits illustrate how the channels can be used to complement each other.[2]

Store Channel

Stores offer a number of benefits to customers that they cannot get when shopping through catalogs and the Internet.

Browsing   Shoppers will often only have a general sense of what they want (such as a sweater, something for dinner, or a gift) but don't know the specific item they want. They go to a store to see what is available before they decide what to buy. While many consumers surf the Internet and look through catalogs for ideas, most consumers still prefer browsing in stores.

Touching and Feeling Products   Perhaps the greatest benefit offered by stores is the opportunity for customers to use all of their senses when examining products—touching, smelling, tasting, seeing, and hearing. While new technologies can provide 3-D representations on a CRT screen, these visual improvements will not provide the same level of information you get when actually trying on that swimsuit.

Personal Service   Although shoppers can be critical of the personal service they get in stores, sales associates still have the capability of providing meaningful, personalized information. They can tell you if a suit looks good on you, suggest a tie to go with a dress shirt, or answer questions you might have about what is appropriate to wear at a business casual event. Customers for durable goods such as appliances report that salespeople are the most useful information source, more useful than *Consumer Reports*, advertising, and friends.[3]

Cash Payment   Stores are the only channel that accepts cash payments. Many customers prefer to pay cash because it is easy, resolves the transaction immediately, and does not result in potential interest payments.

REFACT

Ninety-four percent of purchases in stores are made with cash.[4]

The climbing wall in a Galyan's store provides an exciting, entertaining experience for customers that cannot be matched by the retailer's catalog and Internet offerings.

Immediate Gratification Stores have the advantage of allowing customers to get the merchandise immediately after they buy it. If your child has a fever, you are not going to wait a day or two for the delivery of a prescription from Drugstore.com.

Entertainment and Social Experience Stores provide more benefits to consumers than simply having merchandise readily available and helping them buy it. For example, in-store shopping can be a stimulating experience for some people, providing a break in their daily routine and enabling them to interact with friends. Paco Underhill, author of *How We Shop*, points out, "Stores are a social experience. I don't care how many chat rooms there are on a site, they will never provide what the experience of brick-and-mortar shopping provides for all five senses, if not six or seven."[5]

All nonstore retail formats are limited in the degree to which they can satisfy these entertainment and social needs. Even the most attractive and inventive web pages and video clips will not be as exciting as the displays and activities in a Bass Pro Shop or Niketown store. However, some store formats are more exciting than others. For example, most people view grocery shopping as a chore to be accomplished as quickly as possible.[6]

Catalog Channel

Convenience Catalogs, like all nonstore formats, offer the convenience of looking at merchandise and placing an order any day at any time from almost anywhere. With a catalog, consumers have the added convenience of not being restricted to a place with an Internet connection and a computer. They can look through a catalog on the beach or propped up in bed. Finally, the information in a catalog is easily accessible for a long period of time. Consumers can refer to the information in a catalog anytime by simply picking it up from the coffee table. The development of "magalogs," catalogs with magazine-type editorial content, enhances the desire to keep catalogs readily available.

In some situations, catalogs are much more convenient than shopping in stores or over the Internet.

Safety Security in malls and shopping areas is becoming an important concern for many shoppers. Nonstore retail formats have an advantage over store-based retailers by enabling customers to review merchandise and place orders from a safe environment—their homes.[7]

Quality of Visual Presentation The photographs of merchandise in catalogs, while not as useful as in-store presentations, are superior to the visual information that can be displayed on a CRT screen.

Since Internet shopping is more novel than shopping in stores and using catalogs, we discuss the electronic channel in more depth in the following section.

ELECTRONIC RETAILING ISSUES

The scenario in Exhibit 3–2 illustrates the unique benefits offered by the electronic retail channel.

Benefits Offered by the Electronic Channel

The scenario in Exhibit 3–2 illustrates that, in addition to the convenience and security of shopping from home or work at any time, the electronic channel has the potential for offering a greater selection of products and more personalized information about products and services.

Broader Selection   As Exhibit 3–1 shows, a potential benefit of the electronic channel, compared to the other two channels, is the vast number of alternatives available to consumers. Judy, living in Columbus, Ohio, can shop electronically at Harrod's in London in less time than it takes her to visit the local supermarket. However, having a lot more alternatives to consider is not that much of a benefit.

Consumers rarely visit more than two outlets even when buying expensive consumer durables.[8] Consider Judy Jamison's search with FRED. Does Judy

---

Buying a Present over the Internet   **EXHIBIT 3–2**

Judy Jamison wants to buy a present for her son Dave, whose birthday is in several weeks. She goes to her home computer, accesses her personal shopper program called FRED, and has the following interactive dialog:

FRED: Do you wish to browse, go to a specific store, or buy a specific item?
JUDY: Specific item

FRED: Occasion? [Menu appears and Judy selects.]
JUDY: Gift

FRED: For whom? [Menu appears on screen.]
JUDY: Dave

FRED: Type of gift? [Menu appears.]
JUDY: Toy/Game

FRED: Price range? [Menu appears.]
JUDY: $75–$100

[Now Fred goes out and literally shops the world electronically, visiting the servers for companies selling toys and games in Europe, Asia, Africa, Australia, and North and South America.]

FRED: 121 items have been identified. How many do you want to review? [Menu appears.]
JUDY: Just five

[FRED selects the five best alternatives based on information about Dave's age and preference for toys and Judy's preference for nonviolent, educational toys. The five toys appear on the screen with the price, brand name, and the retailer listed beneath each one. Judy clicks on each toy to get more information about the toy. With another click, she sees a full-motion video of a child Dave's age playing with the toy. She selects the toy she finds most appealing.]

FRED: How would you like to pay for this? [Menu appears.]
JUDY: American Express

FRED: Toys "R" Us [the firm selling the toy Judy selected] suggests several books that appeal to children who like the toy you have selected. Do you want to review these books?
Judy: Yes

[The books are displayed on the screen. Judy reviews each of the books and decides to order one.]

Fred: Would you like this gift wrapped?
Judy: Yes

[The different designs for wrapping paper are displayed on the screen and Judy selects paper with a baseball motif.]

really care if FRED initially found 10 or 121 toys initially? Having identified 121 Internet retail sites selling a product you might like, how many sites would you take the time to visit? The advantages of having a lot of alternatives is only meaningful if you have FRED to search through them and find a few items you might like to look at in detail.

More Information to Evaluate Merchandise   An important service offered by retailers is providing information that helps customers make better purchase decisions. As indicated in Exhibit 3–1, retail channels differ in terms of how much information they provide and whether customers can format the information to easily compare different brands.

For instance, some catalogs provide only a few facts for each item, such as price, weight, and brand/model. Other catalogs offer much more detail about each item carried. For many clothing items, Lands' End not only provides color pictures but often gives extensive detail about the construction process, stitching, and materials. Stores also differ in the information they make available to consumers. Specialty and department stores typically have trained, knowledgeable sales associates, whereas most discount stores do not. However, the personal knowledge of sales associates is typically limited. The space available in self-service stores and catalogs to provide information is constrained by the size of a printed page, a sign, and a package on a shelf.

Using an electronic channel, retailers have the capability of providing as much information as each customer wants, more information than they can get through store and catalog channels.[9] The electronic channel can respond to customers' inquiries just like a sales associate would. Customers shopping electronically can drill down through web pages until they have enough information to make a purchase decision. Unlike catalogs, the information on the electronic channel database can be frequently updated and will always be available. On the other hand, retaining knowledgeable sales associates is difficult and, in many cases, not cost-effective. The cost of adding information to an electronic channel is likely to be far less than the cost of continually training thousands of sales associates.

In addition, the electronic channel can format the information so that customers can effectively use it when evaluating products. Exhibit 3–3 illustrates how Circuit City provides information in a side-by-side comparison format. In contrast, customers in stores usually have to inspect each brand, one at a time, and then remember the different attributes to make a comparison.[10]

Personalization   The most significant potential benefit of the electronic channel is the ability to economically personalize the information for each customer. Often, sales associates in service-oriented retailers like department and specialty stores can provide this benefit. They know what their preferred customers want. They can select a few outfits and arrange to show these outfits before the store opens or even take the outfits to the customer's office or home. However, an electronic agent like FRED also can search through a wide range of alternatives, select a small set for the customer to look at in detail, and provide the information that the customer typically considers. In addition, FRED never is in a bad mood, is not paid anything to do its job, and is always available—7/24 (seven days a week, 24 hours a day).

EXHIBIT 3–3
Side-by-Side Comparison Offered by an Electronic Channel

Product Name	Olympus 2.0 Megapixel 5x Digital Zoom Digital Camera	Sony 2.8 Megapixel 3x Digital Zoom Digital Camera	Sony 5.0 Megapixel 5x Optical/10x Digital Zoom Digital Camera
Price	$199.99	$429.95	$999.99
Customer Ratings	4.0	3.9	4.7
Purchase Online!	BUY	BUY	BUY
Availability	DIRECT SHIP	DIRECT SHIP	DIRECT SHIP
Model	D380L	DSCP3	DSCF707
Warranty Labor Months	12	3	3
Warranty Parts Months	12	12	12
Item Height in Inches	2.6	2.1	6.3
Item Width in Inches	4.8	4.1	4.9
Item Depth in Inches	1.8	1.5	2.6
Megapixel Gross	2.1	3.3	5.2
Megapixel Effective CCD	2.0	2.8	5.0

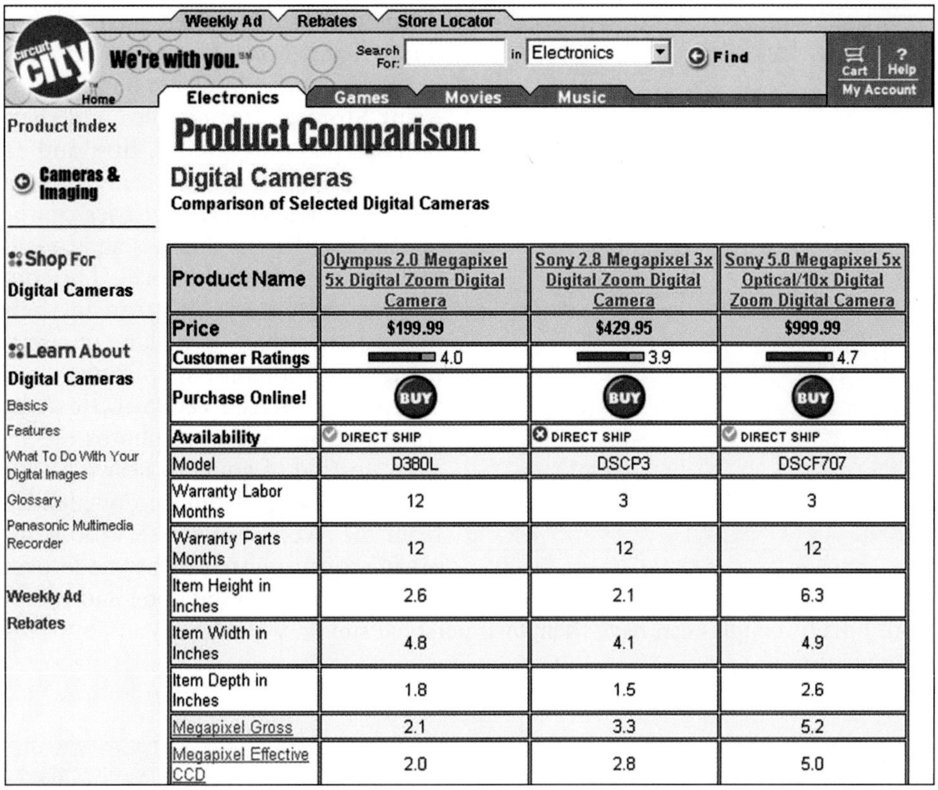

FRED is called an electronic agent. An **electronic agent** is a computer program that locates and selects alternatives based on some predetermined characteristics.[11] In the future, electronic agents may be computer software programs bought by consumers or offered as a service to their customers by retailers or third parties. The agent could learn about a consumer's tastes by asking questions when it's installed on the customer's computer or when the customer goes to the retailer's website. For example, when Judy adds the FRED software to her home electronic systems, the software asked her questions to learn about her tastes and preferences.

These agents function as a super sales associate in a department store, helping customers locate merchandise they might like. For example, Amazon.com has an electronic agent that recommends books based on the customer's previous purchases. Retailing View 3.2 illustrates how a retailer of high-fashion apparel tailors the presentation of its merchandise for each customer.

Problem-Solving Information The electronic channel also offers an opportunity to go beyond the traditional product information offered in stores to provide tools and information for solving customer problems. For example, the typical engagement/wedding planning process lasts for 14 months and costs almost $20,000. The process involves many emotionally charged decisions such as how many people and whom to invite, what print style to use on the invitations, where to hold the reception, what music to play during the ceremony, and what gifts to list in a registry.

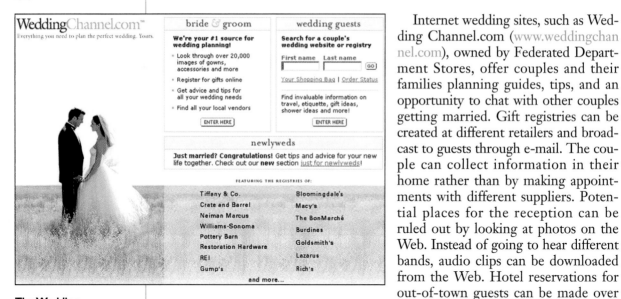

The Wedding Channel.com offers merchandise, services, and information for couples planning a wedding.

Internet wedding sites, such as Wedding Channel.com (www.weddingchannel.com), owned by Federated Department Stores, offer couples and their families planning guides, tips, and an opportunity to chat with other couples getting married. Gift registries can be created at different retailers and broadcast to guests through e-mail. The couple can collect information in their home rather than by making appointments with different suppliers. Potential places for the reception can be ruled out by looking at photos on the Web. Instead of going to hear different bands, audio clips can be downloaded from the Web. Hotel reservations for out-of-town guests can be made over the Internet, and maps can be created showing how to get to the hotel and reception. Finally, couples can have their own personal site on which they can post wedding pictures.[12]

RETAILING VIEW   Bluefly.com—Selling Designer Apparel on the Net

3.2

Not everyone will buy a $295 Gianni Versace jacket without trying it on first—even if it has been marked down from $1,400. But enough people will do so that Bluefly.com has trouble keeping them in stock.

Bluefly.com is an electronic off-price retailer selling end-of-season and excess production designer clothing from such elite design houses as Donna Karan and BCBG at discounts up to 75 percent. It uses the Net to reach a broader audience than store-based retailers. In addition to selling fashionable apparel, the site offers fashion tips and personalized "shopping carts" that make suggestions based on a customer's size, complexion, and designer preferences.

Bluefly.com exploits the ability of an electronic retailer to personalize its offering and overcome the common frustration of the size-12 off-price shopper finding a garment she really wants and then finding out it is only available in a size 3. Its "MyCatalog" service allows customers to enter their sizes and preferences. When they go to the site, the clothing they view is preselected. They don't have to look through pages of merchandise that they don't like or that isn't available in their size. The registered users are also notified by e-mail when their favorite clothing is posted on the site. In addition to providing a service to its customers, the e-mail notifications help Bluefly.com move merchandise faster.

Rather than serving as a clearinghouse for manufacturers, Bluefly.com owns its inventory. Thus, it can ensure that all orders are reliably filled. By buying the merchandise from manufacturers, consolidators, and retailers clearing

Bluefly.com personalizes its website so that customers can easily see apparel they prefer, in sizes that are available.

out end-of-season merchandise, Bluefly.com develops strong relationships with its suppliers.

Sources: www.bluefly.com; Bob Tedeschi, "Fine Tuning Customer Behavior," *New York Times,* April 1, 2002, p. C3; Jean Thilmany, "Bluefly.com: The Pains and Gains," *WWD,* July 26, 1999, p. 25; and Marcia Stepanek, "Closed, Gone to the Net," *Business Week,* June 7, 1999, p. 113.

Virtual communities, networks of people who seek information, products, and services and communicate with each other about specific issues, are examples of these problem-solving sites. For example, iVillage (www.ivillage.com) is a virtual community for women with subcommunities for pregnant women, women with babies, and working women. The site for pregnant women offers information and advice on morning sickness, birth options, and body changes; books and apparel for pregnant women; and chat rooms in which community members can express their views and ask and answer questions. Retailers are ideally suited to offer these problem-solving sites for customers. They have the skills to put together merchandise assortments, services, and information to attract members. Chat rooms are discussed in more detail in Chapter 19.[13]

Will Sales through the Electronic Channel for Shopping Continue to Grow?

The electronic channel accounts for about 1 percent of retail sales in the United States and Europe and even a smaller percentage of retail sales in Asia. However, the annual growth of U.S. electronic retail sales is four to five time greater than sales in retail stores.[15] Three critical factors affecting the adoption of a new innovation such as shopping electronically are (1) the ease with which customers can try the innovation, (2) the perceived risks in adopting the innovation, and (3) the advantages of the innovation compared to the present alternatives.[16]

Trying Out Electronic Shopping   More and more consumers are getting an opportunity to experience electronic shopping. In 2002, over 544 million people had Internet access at home or work, with 181 million in North America, 171 million in Europe, and 157 million in Asia.[17] In the United States, 66 percent of all primary household shoppers own a home computer and 63 percent have personal access to the Internet at home, school, or work. About one-quarter of the households with Internet access have a broadband, high-speed connection. Online shopping has become a common practice in the United States. Among the primary households shoppers with Internet access, 55 percent purchased a product online during the last 12 months. While the early users of the Internet were mainly male, educated, and with higher income than the general U.S. population, as this innovation diffuses, the demographics of Internet users now reflect the general population.[18]

 The substantial Internet usage by young people suggests a bright future for electronic retailing. Teenagers and children constitute one of the fastest-growing Internet populations, with 77 million people under 18 expected to be online globally by 2005. Surfing the Net is a highly regarded activity by this age group. Internet users in the U.K. are described as clever, friendly, cool, trendy, and rich by both users and nonusers. As one would expect, entertainment products such as games, music, tickets, and videos are the most common purchases by these young consumers.[19]

However, the younger brothers and sisters of these young adults often cannot shop electronically because they do not have the credit cards required for payment by electronic retailers. Several Internet shopping sites are offering a way around this problem. RocketCash (www.RocketCash.com), UcanBuy.com (www.UcanBuy.com), and DoughNET.com (www.DoughNET.com) now let parents establish an account for their children using a credit card to set the initial balance. The teenager logs onto the site using a password, browses the site's

The fastest-growing segment of Internet users is people over 50 years old.

electronic retailer partners, selects desired merchandise, and puts it in an electronic shopping cart. The shopping site takes care of the payment. Using their own passwords, parents can check up on the teen's buying habits and balance.[21]

But it's not just teenagers and young adults surfing the Web. In the United States, adults over 50 years old are the fastest-growing market going online, now comprising almost 20 percent of the Internet users. Seventy percent of Americans in this age group have home access to the Internet. Studies have found that older people are receptive to new technology and have the time, money, and enthusiasm to surf the Web regularly. They spend an average of 130 minutes a day online, almost 50 percent more than any other age group. Their primary attraction to the Internet is the use of e-mail to stay in touch with long-distance family and friends. Older people tend to buy merchandise and services online because shopping in stores can be difficult for them.[22] Some websites providing services to this market segment are ThirdAge (www.thirdage.com) and SeniorNet (www.seniornet.org).[23]

Perceived Risks in Electronic Shopping   While most consumers have the opportunity to try out electronic shopping, they also have some concerns about buying products through an electronic channel. The two critical perceived risks are (1) the security of credit card transactions on the Internet and (2) potential privacy violations. While many consumers are concerned about credit card security, security problems have not arisen in actual usage. Almost all retailers use sophisticated technologies to encrypt communications. The perception of risk also is diminishing as credit card companies promote the use of their cards on the Internet and inform customers that the customers will not be responsible for security lapses.[24]

Consumers are concerned about the ability of retailers to collect information about their purchase history, personal information, and search behavior on the Internet. Issues related to privacy, and the steps that retailers are taking to allay these concerns, are discussed in more detail in Chapter 11.

Relative Advantages of Electronic Shopping   Since many consumers have Internet access and can try out electronic shopping and technological developments are reducing security and privacy risks, the primary factor determining the growth of electronic shopping will be whether the electronic channel can provide sufficient benefits to interest customers in surfing the Net rather than going to stores.

Even though electronic retail sales are still relatively small, the electronic channel has the potential for producing significant sales in the future, because the channel can offer consumers superior benefits to those offered by present in-store and nonstore formats. Due to the interactive nature of the electronic channel, customers can have a selection of merchandise and information about the merchandise tailored to their needs. In effect, the electronic channel has the potential for preparing an individually tailored catalog for the customer each time the customer goes shopping. Using this individually tailored shopping experience, customers will be able to make more satisfying selections of merchandise using the electronic format compared to other formats. The growth of electronic shopping depends on the degree to which retailers exploit the opportunity to provide a wide variety of personalized information through the electronic channel.

What Types of Merchandise Will Be Sold Effectively through the Electronic Channel?

In addition to the amount and presentation of information, the three retail channels also differ in the type of information they can present effectively. For instance, when you purchase apparel, some critical information might be "look-and-see" attributes like color and style, as well as "touch-and-feel" attributes like how the apparel fits. It is impossible to feel the fabric in a dress, taste a sample of an ice cream flavor, or smell a perfume before buying the product through an electronic channel. Customers' ability even to assess color electronically depends on the adjustment of a computer monitor. Fit can only be predicted well, if the apparel has consistent sizing and the consumer has learned over time what size to buy for a particular brand.

The difficulty of providing touch-and-feel information electronically suggests that clothing, perfume, flowers, and food, products with important touch-and-feel attributes, will not be sold successfully through an electronic channel.[27] However, this type of merchandise is presently sold through nonstore channels, such as catalogs and TV home shopping. Branding can overcome many of the uncertainties in purchasing merchandise without touching and feeling it.

Consider branded merchandise like Nautica perfume or Levi's 501 jeans. Even though you can't smell a sample of the perfume before buying it, you know that it will smell like your last bottle when you buy it electronically because the manufacturer of Nautica makes sure each bottle smells the same. Similarly, if you wear a size 30-inch waist/32-inch inseam Levi's 501 jeans, you know it will fit when you buy it electronically.

The retailer's brand can also provide information about the consistency and quality of merchandise. For example, consumers might be reluctant to buy produce using an electronic channel because they cannot see the fruits and vegetables before purchasing. However, the same consumers would likely feel comfortable buying fruit from the Harry and David catalogs or Internet site, because Harry and David has established a reputation for selling only the highest-quality fruit.

Even though it is limited to providing "look and see" information, in some situations, the electronic channel might even be able to provide superior information compared to stores. For example, Judy, before she started to shop electronically, wanted to see toys before buying one for her son Dave. So she went to stores to look at the toys. But in the stores, the toys were not displayed, so she could only see a picture on the side of the box containing the toy. Now that Judy shops electronically, she can get superior information from the full-motion video clip showing a child playing with the toy.

Imagine being able to shop with a friend 3,000 miles away.

Only landsend.com lets you shop online with someone else, anywhere else. We call it Shop With A Friend.℠ And it lets each of you, at your own computer screen, simultaneously flip through our web site. Compare selections together, look at different colors, different outfits. Try it with a friend, or family, or anyone.

www.landsend.com

Lands' End uses its Internet channel to provide its customers benefits they cannot get using its catalogs.

The Red Envelope makes it easy to shop for gifts.

Gifts In other situations, touch-and-feel information might be important, but the information in a store is not much better than the information provided electronically. For example, suppose you're buying a bottle of perfume for your mother. Even if you go to the store and smell the samples of all the new scents, you might not get much information to help you determine which one your mother would like. In this situation, stores offer little benefit over an electronic channel in terms of useful information provided about the merchandise. But buying gifts electronically offers the benefit of saving you the time and effort in packing and sending the gift to your mother. For this reason, gifts represent a substantial portion of sales made through the electronic channel.

Services Some services retailers have been very successful over the Internet, because the look-and-see attributes in their offering can be presented very effectively online. For example, Travelocity (www.travelocity.com) is an Internet travel planning service. After you go to the Internet site and fill in an online form indicating your destination and preferred departure time, the electronic agent locates the lowest-cost fare for the flight. To purchase a ticket, you simply click on the purchase ticket icon, enter your credit card information, and get an e-ticket confirmation number. Travel service providers like Travelocity and Expedia (msn.expedia.com) provide detailed information about destinations like the locations of hotels on a map. Chat rooms provide an opportunity for travelers to share their experiences in hotels and restaurants.[29] Due to the appeal of the Internet for providing services, many banks are making major investments to provide banking services online.[30]

Thus, the critical issue determining what types of merchandise can be sold successfully by electronic retailers is whether the electronic channel can provide enough information prior to the purchase to make sure customers will be satisfied with the merchandise once they get it. There are many buying situations in which electronic channels can provide sufficient information even though the merchandise has important touch-and-feel attributes.

Will Offering an Electronic Channel Lead to More Price Competition?

Many store-based retailers offer similar assortments of branded merchandise and thus have difficulty differentiating themselves on the basis of their merchandise offering. However, price competition between these store-based retailers offering the same merchandise is reduced by geography. Consumers typically shop at the stores and malls closest to where they live and work. However, using the Internet, consumers can search for merchandise across the globe at low cost. The number of stores that a consumer can visit to compare prices is no longer limited by physical distance.[31]

Searching for the lowest prices is facilitated by shopping bots. **Shopping bots** or **search engines** are computer programs that search for and provide a list of all Internet sites selling a product category or price of specific brands offered.

To limit price comparisons, electronic retailers initially made it hard for customers to go from one Internet site to another. These electronic retailers used different interfaces so customers needed to learn how to search through the offerings at each new site they visited. In addition, some Internet retailers electronically prevented shopping bots from accessing their sites, collecting information about the products sold at the site, and using this collected data to compare the prices offered at different electronic retailing sites.[32] While these strategies made it more difficult to compare prices, they also made it more difficult to attract customers to their websites.

While consumers shopping electronically can collect price information with little effort, they can get a lot of other information about the quality and performance of products at a low cost. For instance, an electronic channel offering custom-made oriental rugs can clearly show real differences in patterns and materials used for construction. Electronic grocery services offered by Safeway (www.shop.safeway.com) and Albertson's (www.albertsons/shop) allow customers to sort cereals by nutritional content, thus making it easier to use that attribute in decision making. The additional information about product quality might lead customers to paying more for high-quality products, thus decreasing the importance of price.[33]

Retailers using an electronic channel can reduce the emphasis on price by providing better services and information. Because of these services, customers might be willing to pay higher prices for the merchandise. For example, Amazon.com provides a customer with the table of contents and synopsis of a book as well as reviews and comments by the author, or authors, and people who have read the book. When the customer finds an interesting book, Amazon's system is programmed to suggest other books by the same author or of the same genre. Finally, customers can tell Amazon about their favorite authors and subjects and then receive e-mail on new books that might be of interest. The classic response to the question, What are the three most important things in retailing? was "location, location, location." In the world of electronic retailing, the answer will be "information, information, information."[34]

Which Channel Is the Most Profitable?

Many people thought that the electronic channel would enable retailers to sell products at a lower price because they would not have to incur the costs of

PriceGrabber.com
The Smart Place to Start Your Shopping

Popular Electronics | Rebates

Home Computers Softwa

Home > Electronics > Cameras > Camera Accessories

Canon Speedlite 420EX Flash

Manufacturer: Canon
Part Number: C500781
Lowest Price: $ 179.95
Rebate: (None)

▶ Sell Yours Here!   **Description:** No Description Available

Price Comparisons

	Seller	Price
Shop	Abe's of Maine Merchant Info	$179.95
Shop	CameraClub Merchant Info	$182.99
Shop	Etronics Merchant Info	$189.00
Shop	TheNerds.net Merchant Info	$217.84
Shop	BuyMicro.com Merchant Info	$219.94
Shop	PageComputer Merchant Info	$221.54

Shopping bots make it easy for consumers to locate retailers and compare their prices for branded merchandise.

REFACT

Merchandise returns can be as high as 40 percent for sales made through an electronic channel, compared to 6 percent for catalogs and even less for store sales.[35]

It is very costly to deliver merchandise to homes, but customers typically bear most of these costs.

building and operating stores and compensating sales associates working in stores. However, the electronic channel involves significant costs to design, maintain, and refresh a website; attract customers to the sites; get merchandise to homes; and deal with the high level of returns. These costs associated with operating an electronic channel may even be greater than the costs of operating physical stores.

It is quite costly to deliver merchandise in small quantities to customers' homes. Customers presently pay for a portion of the cost of shipping and returning merchandise when they buy products through catalogs or an electronic channel. However, retailers using an electronic or catalog channel incur considerable costs in developing and operating systems and warehouses to ship small packages to homes and receive returns from individual customers. In contrast, customers using a store channel spend their own time and money going to stores to pick out and take home merchandise and then going back to the stores to return merchandise they don't want.

Why Did So Many Electronic Retailer Entrepreneurs Fail?

In light of the potential for selling merchandise and services over the Internet, one can understand the initial enthusiasm for entrepreneurial companies such eToys, RX.com, and Garden.com that have failed. The history of one of these major failures, Webvan, is described in Retailing View 3.3.

Resources Needed to Successfully Operate an Electronic Channel   To understand why so many of these entrepreneurs failed, and the reason for the evolution to multichannel retailing, you must consider the critical resources needed to profitably sell merchandise over the Internet. The resources, shown in Exhibit 3–4, are (1) well-known brand name and trustworthy image, (2) customer information, (3) complementary merchandise and services, (4) unique merchandise, (5) information systems for effectively presenting information on web pages and managing the fulfillment process, and (6) a distribution system to efficiently ship merchandise to homes and receive and process returns. Exhibit 3–4 lists

EXHIBIT 3–4 | Capabilities Needed to Successfully Sell Merchandise Electronically

Capabilities	Electronic-Only Retailers	Catalog Retailers	Store-Based Retailers	Merchandise Manufacturers
Strong brand name and image to build traffic and reduce customers' perceived risk	Low	Medium to high	High	Medium to high
Availability of customer information to tailor presentations	Medium to high	High	Medium to high	Low
Providing and managing complementary merchandise and services	High	High	High	Medium
Offering unique merchandise	Low	Medium to high	Medium to high	High
Presenting merchandise and information in electronic format	High	High	Medium to high	Medium
Efficient distribution system to deliver merchandise to homes and accept returns	Low	Medium to high	High	Low

these critical resources with an assessment of the degree to which electronic-only retailers (such as Webvan and eToys), catalog, traditional store-based retailers, and merchandise manufacturers possess them.

Well-Known Brand Name and Trustworthy Image   Brand name and image are important for two reasons. First, when operating a store channel, retailers compete against only the limited set of other retailers in the local area. However, a retailer's electronic channel competes against over 100,000 alternative URLs that consumers can visit. Thus, it is important for a retailer operating an electronic channel to be well known.

Second, a trustworthy reputation is important because buying merchandise over the Internet is risky. Customers cannot see the merchandise before they buy it. Thus, electronic shoppers need to believe the retailer will provide secure credit card transactions, deliver the quality of merchandise described on its web pages, and maintain privacy of any information revealed by the customer.

Customer Information   As mentioned previously, a unique benefit provided by the electronic channel is tailoring presentations to meet the needs of specific customers. To tailor merchandise and recommendations, retailers operating an electronic channel need information about the preferences and past purchase behavior of their customers.

REFACT

While 59 percent of U.S. Internet users trust small businesses "most of the time," only 26 percent trust websites that sell products and services.[37]

Webvan—Bankrupt after Spending $1.2 Billion   RETAILING VIEW 3.3

In 1997, Louis Borders, who also founded Borders bookstores, started Webvan. His vision was to develop a national electronic supermarket chain. By using state-of-the-art, automated warehouses and a sophisticated scheduling system for the company-owned fleet of delivery trucks, Borders felt he could home deliver groceries, charge customers the same prices they would get shopping in a local supermarket, and make a profit. To deal with the problem of delivering perishables, Webvan commited to delivering orders within the 30-minute window specified by its customers.

Four months after delivering its first order, Webvan raised $375 million in an initial public offering (IPO) and began to implement its plan to open 100,000-square-foot warehouses in 26 U.S. cities. The warehouses, costing $35 million each, were capable of processing 8,000 orders during an eight-hour shift.

However, the demand for Webvan's services grew too slowly. In its most successful region, the San Francisco Bay Area, only 6.5 percent of the households placed orders with Webvan and half of those ordered only once. The company never achieved the patronage to operate its warehouses anywhere near capacity. Thus, after an additional investment of $825 million, Webvan declared bankruptcy in July 2001. Considering all of its overhead costs, Webvan lost $132 on every order it received.

Many analysts felt that Webvan should have perfected its business model and demonstrated its profitability in one city before expanding across the United States. But David

Beirne, a venture capitalist who was Webvan's earliest financial backer, argued, "It's easy to say we could have opened a few less markets, but we had catch-22. We had a unique opportunity to raise a lot of capital and build a business faster than Sam Walton rolled out Wal-Mart. But in order to raise the money, we had to promise investors rapid growth."

Webvan's demise does not mean that operating an electronic channel for groceries is infeasible. Tesco, a $30 billion supermarket chain in the U.K., dipped its toe into e-commerce in 1995. To test whether customers would buy groceries without shopping in conventional supermarkets, it outfitted a single store in Osterley, England, to accept orders by phone, fax, and a crude website. Rather than building a special warehouse, Tesco had employees pick the orders from its store. After determining there was sufficient demand and the store-picking system was feasible, in 1999, Tesco rolled out the service to 100 of its 690 stores.

By 2001, Tesco.com was generating $500 million in annual sales and making a profit on its grocery sales through its electronic channel. It handled over 3.7 million orders a year, and half of its online customers did not patronize Tesco before buying from it online.

Sources: Saul Hansell, "Online Grocer Calls It Quits after Running out of Money," *The Wall Street Journal,* July 10, 2001, p. A1; Penelope Patsuris, "E-Groceries Still Have a Shelf Life," *Forbes.com,* August 10, 2001, and "Tesco Bets Small, Wins Big," *Business Week,* October 1, 2001, pp. E8–E9.

Providing and Managing Assortments of Complementary Merchandise and Services The opportunity to make multiple-item sales of complementary merchandise through an electronic channel is important for two reasons. First, when making multiple-item purchases through an electronic channel, customers reduce their shipping costs. Second, the electronic channel is ideally suited for making recommendations to a customer based on the customer's primary purchase by offering a set of items that solves a customer's problem. Remember how Toys "R" Us in Exhibit 3–2 suggested gift wrapping and a book to go with the toy Judy ordered.

Offering Unique Merchandise Due to the low search cost, price comparisons are made easily for merchandise sold through an electronic channel. By offering unique merchandise through an electronic channel, retailers can differentiate themselves and reduce the potential for price competition. Basically, if a firm is the only retailer selling a specific model or brand, customers cannot easily compare its price with the prices offered through other electronic channels. Three approaches for offering unique merchandise are (1) private-label merchandise, (2) branded variants or co-branded merchandise, and (3) prepackaged assortments. Retailers can differentiate themselves by developing their own private-label merchandise that they sell exclusively. For example, the merchandise sold at The Gap, Victoria's Secret, and Lands' End can be bought only from these retailers. Retailers can also work with manufacturers to provide "branded variants" that they sell exclusively.[38] For example, Sony sells VCRs at Wal-Mart and Circuit City that look the same but have different model numbers and slightly different features.

Presenting Merchandise and Information Electronically The design of websites in terms of the download time, ease of navigating through the site, and sensory experiences plays an important role in stimulating purchases, promoting multi-item purchases, and encouraging repeat visits.[39]

Efficient Fulfillment As mentioned previously, when customers shop at retail stores, they bear the cost of transporting merchandise from stores to their homes and bringing unsatisfactory merchandise back to the store. When buying through an electronic channel, the cost of home delivery can significantly increase the total cost incurred by the customer.[40]

Fulfillment costs and systems play a particularly important role in the growth of electronic grocery shopping. Since many items sold in supermarkets are perishable, deliveries must be made when someone is at home to put the perishables in a refrigerator or freezer. Some electronic supermarkets such as NetGrocer (www.netgrocer.com) avoid the problem by only selling nonperishable merchandise and shipping it via standard package delivery firms. Peapod (www.peapod) and Webvan.com committed to making deliveries within a 30-to-120-minute window and charged extra for this service. Streamline tried to address this problem by installing refrigerated storage boxes with touch-pad security, enabling deliveries to garages and other secure locations outside the home. Due to the difficulty of passing the high fulfillment costs along to customers, most of the pure electronic grocery retailers went bankrupt.

Who Has These Critical Resources? As indicated in Exhibit 3–4, catalog retailers are best positioned to exploit an electronic retail channel. They have very efficient systems for taking orders from individual customers, packaging the merchandise ordered for shipping, delivering it to homes, and handling returned merchandise. They also have extensive information about their customers and database management skills needed to effectively personalize service. For example, many catalog retailers presently have systems used by their telephone operators to search their customer databases and make suggestions of complementary merchandise. Finally, the visual merchandising skills necessary for preparing catalogs are similar to those needed in setting up an effective website.

Store-based and catalog retailers are ideally suited to offer assortment and efficiently manage merchandise inventories. Typically, they have more experience and greater skills in putting together merchandise assortments, a skill that most manufacturers and pure electronic retailers lack. In addition, store-based and catalog retailers typically have more credibility than manufacturers when suggesting merchandise, since they offer an assortment of brands from multiple suppliers. These traditional retailers also have relationships with vendors, purchasing power, and information/distribution systems in place to manage the supply chain from its vendors to the retailers' warehouses. Finally, as indicated in Exhibit 3–4, some catalog and store-based retailers presently sell unique merchandise—they have developed private-label merchandise.

However, most store-based retailers and manufacturers lack the appropriate systems for shipping individual orders to households. Their warehouse systems are designed to fill large orders from retail firms or stores and deliver truckloads of goods to retailers' warehouses or stores. However, store-based retailers with broad market coverage can use their stores as convenient places for electronic shoppers to pick up their merchandise and return unsatisfactory purchases.

While electronic-only retail entrepreneurs such as Amazon.com were highly valued by investors, Exhibit 3–4 suggests that most of them did not possess most of the resources needed for long-term success. These pure electronic retailers were immersed in Internet technology and had considerable skills in the design of websites and developing systems to manage transactions. They had the opportunity to exploit this unique interactive feature of the Internet, but they lack extensive information about their customers. They did not have the wealth of past purchase data that store-based and catalog retailers had. Since manufacturers sell to retailers, they have even less information about specific customers who buy their products.

In addition, the electronic-only retailers lacked the retailing skills necessary in building merchandise assortments, managing inventory, and fulfilling small orders to households. Over time, these electronic retail entrepreneurs have recognized the importance of these retailing skills and distribution systems. They have hired executives from traditional retailers to undertake the merchandise management tasks and build their own warehouses.[42]

Finally, large store-based retailers and national brand manufacturers have high awareness and strong reputations. On the other hand, only a few catalog and Internet-only retailers are well known and respected by consumers.

To illustrate the differences in resources possessed by pure electronic retailers and traditional bricks-and-mortar retailers, compare the electronic drugstores such as Drugstore.com, PlanetRx, Rx.com, and Soma.com that generated

REFACT

While the electronic channel only accounts for 1 percent of U.S. retail sales, 21 percent of the sales made by Lands' End and 17 percent of J. Crew's sales are made over the Internet.[41]

Clicks and mortar drugstore retailers like Walgreens can offer customers the choice of picking up merchandise at the store or having it delivered to their home.

EXHIBIT 3–5
Top 25 Website
Designs

Amazon	www.amazon.com
American Eagle	www.ae.com
Jos. A. Bank	www.josbank.com
Bluefly	www.bluefly.com
Circuit City	www.circuitcity.com
dELiAs	www.delias.com
Drugstore.com	www.drugstore.com
eBay	www.ebay.com
Eddie Bauer	www.eddiebauer.com
Hallmark	www.hallmark.com
IBM	www.ibm.com/products/us
KBToys	www.kbtoys.com
Lands' End	www.landsend.com
L.L. Bean	www.llbean.com
Office Depot	www.officedepot.com
Orvis	www.orvis.com
Overstock.com	www.overstock.com
Polo	www.polo.com
Replacements	www.replacements.com
RitzCamera	www.ritzcamera.com
Sears	www.sears.com
Uncommon Goods	www.uncommongoods.com
Vacuum Bags	www.vacuum-bags.com
Williams-Sonoma	www.william-sonoma.com
Wine.com by eVineyard	www.wine.com

Source: "Lessons from the Top 25," *Internet Retailer,* January 2002.
Reprinted by permission.

considerable investor enthusiasm and Walgreens.[43] Walgreens had the following resources to build on when it introduced an electronic channel:

- Three thousand conveniently located stores in the United States with drive-in windows for picking up prescriptions and merchandise.

- A distribution system in place for picking, packing, and shipping prescription pharmaceuticals and merchandise presently ordered by phone.

- A strong reputation for being trustworthy and helping customers on health-related decisions.

- Agreements in places with third-party payers (HMOs and insurance companies) to accept and provide pharmaceutical benefits for its customers.

Recognizing these synergies between store-based and electronic retailing, CVS acquired Soma.com and Rite-Aid bought a 25 percent interest in Drugstore.com.[44] Most of the other electronic drugstores were either acquired or went bankrupt. Electronic-only retailers that pioneered selling merchandise and service over the Internet have had a difficult time defending their initial success when store-based retailers became click-and-mortar retailers by launching an electronic channel. To illustrate this point, the top 25 retail websites designs selected by *Internet Retailer* are shown in Exhibit 3–5. In 2002, only 4 of the top 25 sites (shown in red) were operated by pure electronic retailers. The 2001 list contained 14 pure electronic retailers.

Will Manufacturers Use the Electronic Channel to Sell Their Products?

Disintermediation occurs when a manufacturer sells directly to consumers, bypassing retailers. Retailers are concerned about disintermediation because manufacturers can get direct access to consumers by establishing a retail site on the Internet. But as indicated in Exhibit 3–4, manufacturers lack some of the critical resources to sell merchandise electronically. Retailers are more efficient in dealing with customers directly than manufacturers. They have considerably more experience than manufacturers in distributing merchandise directly to customers, providing complementary assortments, and collecting and using information about customers. Retailers also have an advantage since they can provide a broader array of product and services to solve customer problems. For example, if consumers want to buy a dress shirt and tie directly from the manufacturers, they must go to two different Internet sites and still can't be sure that the shirt and tie will go together.

Finally, if manufacturers start selling direct, they risk losing the support of the retailers they bypass. For example, Macy's decided not to offer Levi's merchandise when Levi experimented with selling merchandise directly over the Internet. Home Depot issued a warning to its vendors indicating that any one attempting to sell directly to its customers would be treated as a competitor.[45]

THE EVOLUTION TOWARD MULTICHANNEL RETAILING

As we discussed in the previous section, store-based and catalog retailers have the skills and assets to effectively operate an electronic channel. However, store-based and catalog retailers with extensive market coverage initially were cautious about selling merchandise over the Internet. They were concerned that an electronic offering would cannibalize their existing sales. They viewed electronic retailing as a college football coach would view an inquiry by the NCAA Infractions Committee. It is something they prefer to avoid but find too dangerous to ignore. Thus, many large retailers just put a toe in the water, establishing Internet sites with a limited number of offerings. These sites didn't have the features and merchandise assortments to attract a large number of customers. Many of the sites were used to support their in-store business rather than develop incremental sales. For example, the sites would simply provide store locations, a general description of the merchandise available in the stores, and financial information about the firm. However, in response to the growth of Internet access and usage and the success of some Internet retailers such as Amazon.com, many store-based and catalog retailers now are aggressively selling merchandise over the Internet or at least considering it.[46]

REFACT

On average, retailers are spending 4.5 percent of revenue on e-business technologies, more than twice the expenditures of other businesses. Of 3,500 retailers surveyed, 57 percent have e-commerce servers.[47]

Reasons for Becoming a Multichannel Retailer

Traditional store-based and catalog retailers are placing more emphasis on their electronic channels and evolving into multichannel retailers for five reasons. First, the electronic channel gives them an opportunity to reach new markets. Second, they can leverage their skills and assets to grow revenues and profits. Third, an electronic channel overcomes some limitations of their traditional formats. Fourth, an electronic channel enables retailers to gain valuable insights into their customers' shopping behavior. Finally, providing a multichannel builds "share of wallet." **Share of wallet** is the percentage of total purchases made by a customer in your store.

Expanding Market Presence Adding an electronic channel is particularly attractive to firms with strong brand names but limited locations and distribution. For example, retailers such as Tiffany's, Harrod's, Saks Fifth Avenue, Bloomingdale's, and Neiman Marcus are widely known for offering unique, high-quality merchandise, but they require customers to travel to England or major U.S. cities to buy many of the items they carry. Interestingly, most of these

Gateway has opened retail stores to complement its Internet channel.

Issues in Multichannel Retailing

Customers want to be recognized by a retailer whether they interact with a sales associate or kiosk in a store, log on to the retailer's website, or contact the retailer's call center by telephone. JCPenney is providing this type of customer interface through its "threetailing" strategy: "Come in, call in, log on." In Penney's new flagship store in Frisco, Texas, shoppers can walk the aisles or browse and buy through a web kiosk, which gives them access to all the merchandise in Penney's catalog. Catalog items can be purchased in the store as well, and merchandise received at home can be returned to the store.[53]

However, to provide this same face to a customer across multiple channels, retailers need to integrate their customer databases and systems used to support each channel.[54] In addition to the information technology issues, other critical issues facing retailers that desire to provide an integrated, customer-centric offering involve (1) brand image, (2) merchandise assortment, and (3) pricing.[55]

Brand Image   Multichannel retailers need to project the same image to their customers through all channels. For example, Talbots reinforces its image of classic-style apparel and excellent customer service in its stores, catalogs, and website. Customers enter the website (www.talbots.com) through an image of the red doors used in its stores and are greeted by "Always classic, never closed." At the website, customers can consult an online style guide offering seasonal fashion tips and articles about how to buy the right size swimsuit, the art of layering, and petite sizing. Talbots' commitment to "friendly" service is reinforced by the availability of 24-hour personal service.

Merchandise Assortment   Typically, customers expect that everything they see in a retailer's store will also be available on its website. A significant product overlap across channels reinforces the one-brand image in the customer's mind. However, the product overlap across channels varies dramatically across retailers. Some retailers, like Wal-Mart, Kmart, Macy's, and Barnes & Noble, operated their electronic and catalog channels as separate businesses or independent divisions during the dot-com boom. This situation resulted in uncoordinated merchandise offerings. The trend now is to integrate the merchandise offerings across channels. Issues related to the organization of multichannel retail firms are discussed in Chapter 9.

Other multichannel retailers use their Internet channel to increase revenues by expanding the assortment they can offer to customers. For example, Gap.com sells more colors and sizes for some merchandise categories than are available in Gap stores. The implications of multichannel capability on merchandise assortments is discussed in Chapter 12.

Finally, many multichannel retailers have tailored the assortments sold on their website to only include products their customers are likely to buy over the Internet. For example, Walmart.com discontinued offering low-price cosmetics and apparel items because the shipping costs were greater than the value of the merchandise.

Pricing   Pricing is another difficult decision for a multichannel retailer. Customers expect pricing consistency across channels (excluding shipping charges and sales tax). However, in some cases, retailers need to adjust their pricing strategy because of the competition they face in different channels. For example,

Barnes & Noble.com offers lower prices over its electronic channel to compete effectively against Amazon.com.

Retailers with stores in multiple markets often set different prices for the same merchandise to deal with differences in local competition. Typical customers do not realize these price differences because they are only exposed to the prices in their local markets. Multichannel retailers may have difficulties sustaining these regional price differences, when customers can easily check prices on the Internet.

Multichannel retailers are beginning to offer new types of pricing, like auctions, that take advantage of the unique properties of the Internet. We discuss these pricing alternatives in Chapter 15.

In conclusion, there is a growing expectation among customers to interact with retailers anytime, anywhere, any place, and to have the retailer recognize them and their transaction history independent of the channel used to contact the retailer. Multichannel retailers face a difficult challenge in providing this seamless interface that their customers expect. In the next section, we illustrate the benefits to customers that multichannel retailers can provide.

SHOPPING IN THE FUTURE

The following scenario illustrates the seamless interface across channels that customers in the future may experience.

Shopping Experience

It's Tuesday morning, Judy Jamison is reviewing her calendar and notices that she will be going to a cocktail party and dinner for the Cancer Society this Friday night. The event is being held at the Ritz Carlton and will be attended by a lot of movers and shakers in town. Judy decides she needs to buy a new dress for the party. She goes to look at some dresses displayed on the websites of local department stores. She finds some dresses she likes at one of her favorite stores and decides to go to the store after work.

Shortly after Judy walks into the store, a chip on her credit card signals her presence and her status as a frequent shopper to a PDA (personal digital assistant) held by the store sales associate responsible for preferred clients. Information about items that Judy might be interested in, including the items she viewed on the website earlier in the day, is downloaded from the store server to Judy's and the sales associate's PDAs.

As Judy is looking through the dresses, she comes across some special merchandise on sale at the department store.

A sales associate approaches Judy and says, "Hello Ms. Jamison. My name is Joan Bradford. How can I help you?" Judy tells the associate she needs to buy a dress for a cocktail party. She has seen some dresses on the store's website and would like to look at them in the store. The sales associate takes Judy to a virtual dressing room.

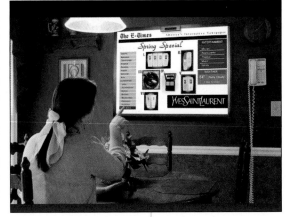

In the dressing room, Judy sits in a comfortable chair and sees the dresses displayed on her image. Judy's image is drawn from a body scan stored in Judy's customer file. Information about Judy's recent visit to the retailer's website and past purchases is used to select the dresses displayed.

Judy sits in a virtual dressing room reviewing dress selections based on her preferences shown on her virtual image.

Judy shares this shopping experience electronically with her friend using a PDA

Using her PDA, Judy is able to share this personalized viewing with her friend who is still at work in California. They discuss which dress looks best on Judy. Then using her PDA, Judy drills down more information about the dress—the fabrication, cleaning instructions, and so forth. Finally she selects a dress and purchases the dress with one click.

Using information displayed on her PDA, Joan, the sales associate helping Judy, suggests a handbag and scarf that would complement the dress. These accessories are displayed on the image of Judy in the dress. Judy decides to buy the scarf but not the handbag. Finally, Judy is told about the minor alterations needed to make the dress a perfect fit. She can check the retailer's website to find out when the alterations are completed and then indicate whether she wants the dress delivered to her home or if she will pick it up at the store.

As Judy passes through the cosmetics department on her way to her car, she sees an appealing new lipstick shade. She takes the lipstick and a three-ounce bottle of her favorite perfume and walks out of the store. The store systems sense her departure, and the merchandise she has selected is automatically charged to her account through the use of RFID (radio frequency identification).

Supporting the Shopping Experience

This scenario illustrates the advantages of having a customer database shared by all channels and integrated systems. The sales associate and the store systems are able to draw on this database for information about Judy's body scan image, her interaction with the retailer's website, and her past purchases and preferences. Judy can use the retailer's website to review the available merchandise before she goes to the store, check the status of her alterations, and decide about having the merchandise delivered to her home.

The scenario also includes some new technologies that will be in the store of the future, such as RFID, self-checkout, and personalized virtual reality displays.

SUMMARY

While the bubble burst for most pure electronic retailers, traditional store-based and catalog retailers are adding an electronic channel and evolving into being integrated, customer-centric, multichannel retailers. This evolution toward multichannel retailing is driven by the increasing desire of customers to communicate with retailers anytime, anywhere, anyplace.

Each of the channels (stores, catalogs, and websites) offers unique benefits to customers. The store channel enables customers to touch and feel merchandise and use the products shortly after they are purchased. Catalogs enable customers to browse through a retailer's offering anytime and anyplace. A unique benefit offered by the electronic channel is the opportunity for consumers to search across a broad range of alternatives, develop a smaller set of alternatives based on their needs, and get specific information about the alternatives they want.

By offering multiple channels, retailers overcome the limitations of each channel. Websites can be used to extend the geographical presence and assortment offered by the store channel. Websites also can be used to update the information provided in catalogs. Stores can be used to provide a multiple sensory experience and an economical distribution capability supporting the electronic channel.

The type of merchandise sold effectively through the electronic channel depends on delivery costs, the consumer's need for immediacy, and the degree to which electronic retailers can provide prepurchase information that helps customers determine whether they will be satisfied with the merchandise. Successful use of an electronic channel overcomes the limitations of collecting touch-and-feel data by offering testimonials from other buyers, providing video information about the experience with the merchandise, or using information about brand-size combinations that fit specific members of the household. For consumers who have previously purchased a branded product, brand name alone may be enough information to predict satisfaction with the purchase decision.

Some critical resources needed to successfully sell merchandise electronically are (1) strong brand name and image, (2) customer information, (3) skills in providing and managing complementary merchandise assortments and services, (4) unique merchandise, (5) ability to present information on web pages, and (6) a distribution system to efficiently ship merchandise to homes and receive and process returns. Traditional store-based and catalog retailers possess most of these assets and thus are better positioned to evolve into multichannel retailers than the entrepreneurial electronic retailers that first started using an electronic channel to reach customers. Disintermediation by manufacturers is unlikely because most manufacturers do not have the capability to efficiently distribute merchandise to individual consumers, provide assortments, and use information about specific consumers to develop individual catalogs for specific customers.

Providing the seamless interface across channels is very challenging for multichannel retailers. Meeting the customer expectation will require the development and use of common customer databases and integrated systems. In addition, multichannel retailers will have to make decisions on how to use the different channels to support the retailer's brand image and how to present consistent merchandise assortments and pricing across channels.

KEY TERMS

disintermediation, *96*

electronic agent, *85*

multichannel retailer, *80*

search engines, *91*

share of wallet, *97*

shopping bots, *91*

virtual communities, *87*

GET OUT & DO IT!

1. GO SHOPPING Go to a store that has a web-enabled kiosk. Use the kiosk to search for information about a product you might be interested in buying in the store. Was the information provided by the kiosk useful? How could it have been made more useful to you? Do you think the availability of the kiosk in the store would be an important service for customers? Why or why not?

2. GO SHOPPING AND INTERNET EXERCISE Compare the merchandise assortment offered and the prices in your favorite store and on the store's website. If there are differences, what is the reason for these differences?

3. INTERNET EXERCISE Go to The Gap (www.gap.com), JCPenney (www.jcpenney.com), and Lands' End (www.landsend.com) and shop for a pair of khaki pants. Evaluate your shopping experience at each site. Compare and contrast the sites and experience on characteristics you think are important to consumers.

4. INTERNET EXERCISE A listing and description of shopping bots is at www.botspot.com, and some specific sites are www.mysimon.com, www.bottomdollar.com, www.pricescan.com, and www.shopping.yahoo.com. Go to the sites and search for this textbook, a particular video, and brand of and model of athletic shoes. How useful was the information returned by the shopping bot? How could the information be improved to be more useful to you?

5. INTERNET Nua Limited (www.nua.ie/surveys) and www.e-tailing.com compile studies and information about electronic retailing. Go to the sites, read the results of some of the studies, and make a list of some critical issues affecting the growth of electronic shopping.

DISCUSSION QUESTIONS AND PROBLEMS

1. Why are store-based retailers aggressively pursuing sales through an electronic channel?

2. Why did most of the pure electronic retail entrepreneurs fail?

3. From a customer's perspective, what are the benefits and limitations of stores? Catalogs? Retail websites?

4. Do you think sales through an electronic channel will eventually have annual sales greater than catalog sales? Why or why not?

5. Why are electronic and catalog channels frequently patronized for gift giving?

6. Should a multichannel retailer offer the same assortment of merchandise for sale on its website at the same price as it sells in its stores? Why or why not?

7. Which of the following categories of merchandise do you think could be sold effectively through an electronic channel: jewelry, TV sets, computer software, high-fashion apparel, pharmaceuticals, and health care products such as toothpaste, shampoo, and cold remedies? Why?

8. What is an electronic agent? What benefit does it offer to consumers?

9. Assume you are interested in investing in a virtual community targeting people interested in active outdoor recreation such as hiking, rock climbing, and kayaking. What merchandise and information would you offer on the site? What type of a company do you think would be most effective in running the site: a well-known outdoors person, a magazine targeting outdoor activity, or a retailer selling outdoor merchandise. Why?

10. Outline a strategy for an electronic-only retail business that is involved in selling merchandise or services in your town. Outline your strategy in terms of your target market and the offering available at your Internet site. Who are your competitors in providing the merchandise or service? What advantages and disadvantages do you have over your competitors?

SUGGESTED READINGS

Barsh, Joanna; Blair Crawford; and Chris Grosso. "How E-Tailing Can Rise from the Ashes." *McKinsey Quarterly* 31 (2000), pp. 98–109.

Borzo, Jeanette. "Out of Order?" Special Report: E-Commerce. *The Wall Street Journal,* September 24, 2001, p. 3.

"A Cross-Channel Approach to Net Sales." *Chain Store Age Executive*, February 2002, pp. 8A–10A.

Dawson, John. "Successful Bricks and Clicks at JCPenney." *Retail Merchandiser,* February 2002, pp. 54–55.

De Figueiredo, John. "Finding Sustainable Profitability in Electronic Commerce." *Sloan Management Review* 41 (Spring 2000), pp. 41–52.

Grewal, Dhruv; Gopalkrishnan Iyer; and Michael Levy. "Internet Retailing: Enablers, Limiters, and Market Consequences." *Journal of Business Research* 2002, forthcoming.

Gulati, Ranjay, and Jason Garino. "Get the Right Mix of Bricks and Clicks." *Harvard Business Review*, May–June 2000, pp. 107–14.

"Grocery Manufacturers of America 2001 E-Business Report." Washington, DC: Grocery Manufacturers Association of America, 2001.

Lindstrom, Marty; Martha Rodgers; and Don Pepper. *Clicks, Bricks, and Brands.* Dover, NH: DualBook, 2001.

Mathwick, Charla; Edward Rigdon; and Naresh Malhotra. "Experiential Value: Conceptualization, Measurement and Application in the Catalog and Internet Shopping Environment." *Journal of Retailing* 77 (Spring 2001), pp. 1–39.

Porter, Michael. "Strategy and Internet." *Harvard Business Review*, March 2001, pp. 63–78.

Tang, Fang-Fang, and Xiaolin Xing. "Will the Growth of Multi-Channel Retailing Diminish the Pricing of Efficiency of the Web?" *Journal of Retailing* 77 (2001), pp. 291–305.

Weintraub, Arlene. "The Year of the E-Piggyback." *Business Week*, December 3, 2001, p. EB24.

Customer Buying Behavior

4

EXECUTIVE BRIEFING | Andrea Learned, Co-Founder, ReachWomen.com

"For a good part of my business career I worked for men. Eventually I realized that women and men approach problems and make decisions differently. Men attacked problems hierarchically, solving them from the top down, while women solved problems from the center out." Since women make most household purchases, Andrea Learned decided that she, and her partner Lisa Johnson, could make a successful business, REACHWomen, out of educating companies on how to market products and services to women.

In her regular articles for the REACHWomen e-newsletter, *Reaching Women Online,* and several Internet e-publications, Andrea has written about segmenting women by life-stage categories in addition to looking at them from the traditional demographic perspective. As Learned notes: "Single Women, Business Women and Moms cross some of the generations, but combined, they represent a large portion of the consumer attitudes of women ages 24–45."

When marketing to the single-woman segment, Andrea suggests, "Retailers must understand these women have power, money, intelligence, and are free from family commitments or anything that will tie them down." Thus, a marketer needs to REACH these women by, recognizing the new definition of family, focusing on the positives of single life, responding to their healthy lifestyles, enhancing the importance of spirituality, and acknowledging their empowered mind-set.

QUESTIONS

● What stages do customers go through when selecting a retailer and purchasing merchandise?

● What social and personal factors affect customer purchase decisions?

● How can retailers get customers to visit their stores more frequently and buy more merchandise during each visit?

● Why and how do retailers group customers into market segments?

On the other hand, mature women, never call them "seniors," are a huge market because they are very active, involving themselves in activities related to leisure and technology. With growing free time and disposable income, older consumers are looking for products to enhance their varied and active lifestyle. Retailers need to REACH these women by focusing on their lifestyles, not their age. They can do this by highlighting unrecognized contributions and accomplishments of other women in the same generation, and by focusing on luxury items such as furniture and household objects.

As discussed in Chapter 1, an effective retail strategy satisfies customer needs better than competitors' strategies. Thus, understanding customer needs and buying behavior is critical for effective retail decision making. When Dennis Pence (co-founder and CEO of Coldwater Creek, a northern Idaho catalog retailer) was asked about his company being the highest-performing retailer in a Management Horizon study, he responded, "Our success has everything to do with our intense customer focus. We have never allowed ourselves to think that we are smarter than the customer is and can anticipate what she wants. We take all our cues from her."[1]

This chapter focuses on the needs and buying behavior of customers and market segments. It describes the stages customers go through to purchase merchandise and the factors that influence the buying process. We then use the information about the buying process to discuss how consumers can be grouped into market segments.[2] The appendix to this chapter examines special aspects of consumer behavior that concern retailers selling fashion merchandise.

TYPES OF BUYING DECISIONS

Exhibit 4–1 describes how Jennifer Sanchez, a student, bought a new suit for job interviews. Such purchases typically involve several stages.

Jennifer Sanchez, at San Francisco State University, is beginning to interview for jobs. For the first interviews on campus, Jennifer had planned to wear the blue suit her parents bought her three years ago. But looking at her suit, she realizes that it's not very stylish and that the jacket is beginning to show signs of wear. Wanting to make a good first impression during her interview, she decides to buy a new suit.

Jennifer surfs the Internet for tips on dressing for interviews (www.collegegrad.com and www.careercity.com) and looks through some catalogs to see the styles being offered. But she decides to go to a retail store so she can try it on and have it for her first interview next week. She likes to shop at Abercrombie and Fitch and American Eagle Outfitter, but neither sells business suits. She remembers an ad in the *San Francisco Chronicle* for women's suits at Macy's. She decides to go to Macy's in the mall close to her apartment and asks her friend Brenda to come along. Jennifer values Brenda's opinion, because Brenda is a clothes horse and has good taste.

Walking through the store, they see some DKNY suits. Jennifer looks at them briefly and decides they're too expensive for her budget and too stylish. She wants to interview with banks and thinks she needs a more conservative suit.

Jennifer and Brenda are approached by a salesperson in the career women's department. After asking Jennifer what type of suit she wants and her size, the salesperson shows her three suits. Jennifer asks Brenda what she thinks about the suits and then selects one to try on. When Jennifer comes out of the dressing room, she feels that the shoulder pads in the suit make her look too heavy, but Brenda and the salesperson think the suit is attractive. Jennifer decides to buy the suit after another customer in the store tells her she looks very professional in the suit.

Jennifer doesn't have a Macy's charge card, so she asks if she can pay with a personal check. The salesperson says yes, but the store also takes Visa and MasterCard. Jennifer decides to pay with her Visa card.

As the salesperson walks with Jennifer and Brenda to the cash register, they pass a display of scarves. The salesperson stops, picks up a scarf, and shows Jennifer how well the scarf complements the suit. Jennifer decides to buy the scarf also.

The **buying process** begins when customers recognize an unsatisfied need. Then they seek information about how to satisfy the need: what products might be useful and how they can be bought. Customers evaluate the various alternative sources of merchandise such as stores, catalogs, and the Internet and choose a store or an Internet site to visit or a catalog to review. This encounter with a retailer provides more information and may alert customers to additional needs. After evaluating the retailer's merchandise offering, customers may make a purchase or go to another retailer to collect more information. Eventually, customers make a purchase, use the product, and then decide whether the product satisfies their needs.

In some situations, customers like Jennifer spend considerable time and effort selecting a retailer and evaluating the merchandise. In other situations, buying decisions are made automatically with little thought. Three types of customer decision-making processes are extended problem solving, limited problem solving, and habitual decision making.

Extended Problem Solving

Extended problem solving is a purchase decision process in which customers devote considerable time and effort to analyzing alternatives. Customers typically engage in extended problem solving when the purchase decision involves a lot of risk and uncertainty. There are many types of risks. Financial risks arise when customers purchase an expensive product. Physical risks are important when customers feel a product may affect their health or safety. Social risks arise when customers believe a product will affect how others view them.

Consumers engage in extended problem solving when they are making a buying decision to satisfy an important need or when they have little knowledge about the product or service. Due to high risk and uncertainty in these situations, customers go beyond their personal knowledge to consult with friends, family members, or experts. They may visit several retailers before making a purchase decision.

Retailers influence customers engaged in extended problem solving by providing the necessary information in a readily available and easily understood manner and by offering money-back guarantees. For example, retailers that sell merchandise involving extended problem solving provide brochures describing the merchandise and its specifications; have informational displays in the store (such as a sofa cut in half to show its construction); and use salespeople to make presentations and answer questions.

Limited Problem Solving

Limited problem solving is a purchase decision process involving a moderate amount of effort and time. Customers engage in this type of buying process when they have had some prior experience with the product or service and their risk is moderate. In these situations, customers tend to rely more on personal knowledge than on external information. They usually choose a retailer they have shopped at before and select merchandise they have bought in the past. The majority of customer decision making involves limited problem solving.

Retailers attempt to reinforce this buying pattern when customers are buying merchandise from them. If customers are shopping elsewhere, however, retailers need to break this buying pattern by introducing new information or offering different merchandise or services.

Jennifer Sanchez's buying process illustrates both limited and extended problem solving. Her store choice decision was based on her prior knowledge of the merchandise in various stores she had shopped in and an ad in the *San Francisco Chronicle*. Considering this information, she felt the store choice decision was not very risky, thus she engaged in limited problem solving when deciding to visit Macy's. But her buying process for the suit was extended. This decision was important to her, thus she spent time acquiring information from a friend and the salesperson to evaluate and select a suit.

One common type of limited problem solving is **impulse buying.** Impulse buying is a buying decision made by customers on the spot after seeing the merchandise.[4] Jennifer's decision to buy the scarf was an impulse purchase.

Retailers encourage impulse buying behavior by using prominent displays to attract customer attention and stimulate a purchase decision based on little analysis. For example, sales of a grocery item are greatly increased when the item is featured in an end-aisle display, when a "BEST BUY" sign is placed on the shelf with the item, when the item is placed at eye level (typically on the third shelf from the bottom), or when items are placed at the checkout counter so customers can see them as they wait in line. Supermarkets use these displays and prime locations for the profitable items that customers tend to buy on impulse, such as gourmet food, rather than commodities such as flour and sugar, which are usually planned purchases. Impulse purchases by electronic shoppers are stimulated by putting special merchandise on the retailer's home page and by suggesting complementary merchandise.[5]

REFACT

Seventy percent of all supermarket buying decisions are unplanned, impulse purchases.[6]

Supermarkets use a variety of approaches to increase impulse buying, including point-of-sale advertising, end-aisle displays, and in-store coupons.

Habitual Decision Making

Habitual decision making is a purchase decision process involving little or no conscious effort. Today's customers have many demands on their time. One way they cope with these time pressures is by simplifying their decision-making process. When a need arises, customers may automatically respond with, "I'll buy the same thing I bought last time from the same store." Typically, this habitual decision-making process is used when decisions aren't very important to customers and involve familiar merchandise they have bought in the past.

Brand loyalty and store loyalty are examples of habitual decision making. **Brand loyalty** means that customers like and consistently buy a specific brand in a product category. They are reluctant to switch to other brands if their favorite brand isn't available. Thus, retailers can only satisfy these customers' needs if they offer the specific brands desired.

Brand loyalty creates both opportunities and problems for retailers. Customers are attracted to stores carrying popular brands. But since retailers must carry the high-loyalty brands, they may not be able to negotiate favorable terms with the supplier of the popular national brands. Chapters 12 and 14 cover buying and stocking branded merchandise.

Store loyalty means that customers like and habitually visit the same store to purchase a type of merchandise. All retailers would like to increase their customers' store loyalty. Some approaches for increasing store loyalty are selecting a convenient location (see Chapters 8 and 9), offering complete assortments and reducing the number of stockouts (Chapter 13), rewarding customers for frequent purchases (Chapters 11 and 16), and providing good customer service (Chapter 19).

THE BUYING PROCESS

Exhibit 4–2 outlines the buying process—the stages in selecting a retailer and buying merchandise. Retailers attempt to influence consumers as they go through the buying process to encourage them to buy the retailer's merchan-

EXHIBIT 4–2
Stages in the Buying
Process

STAGES	SELECTING A RETAILER	SELECTING MERCHANDISE
Need recognition	Need recognition	Need recognition
Information search	Search for information about retailers	Search for information about merchandise
Evaluation	Evaluate retailers	Evaluate merchandise
Choice	Select a retailer	Select merchandise
Visit	Visit store or Internet site or look through catalog	Purchase merchandise
Loyalty	Repeat store patronage	Postpurchase evaluation

dise and services. Each stage in the buying process is addressed in the following sections.

As we discuss the stages in the buying process, you should recognize that customers may not go through the stages in the same order shown in Exhibit 4–2. For example, a person might see an ad for a Sony 3.3 digital camera, decide to buy the camera, and then search for a retailer selling the camera. Here the customer decides what product he wants and selects the specific retailer at the same time. In addition, the amount of time spent at each stage may differ depending on the type of decision being made. For example, customers engaged in habitual problem solving spend very little time searching for information and evaluating alternatives.

Need Recognition

The buying process is triggered when people recognize they have an unsatisfied need. An unsatisfied need arises when a customer's desired level of satisfaction differs from his or her present level of satisfaction. For example, Jennifer Sanchez recognized that she had a need when she was faced with interviewing for jobs in her blue suit. She needed a suit that would make a good impression and realized her worn, outdated blue suit wouldn't satisfy this need.

Need recognition can be as straightforward as discovering there's no milk in the refrigerator, or it can be as ambiguous as feeling the need for an uplifting experience after a final exam. Visiting stores, surfing the Internet, and purchasing products are approaches to satisfying different types of needs.

Types of Needs   The needs motivating customers to go shopping and purchase merchandise can be classified as functional or psychological.[9] **Functional needs** are directly related to the performance of the product. For example, people who need to style their hair might be motivated to purchase a hair dryer. This purchase is based on the expectation that the hair dryer will assist the customer in styling hair.

Psychological needs are associated with the personal gratification customers get from shopping or from purchasing and owning a product. For example, a Tommy Hilfiger shirt may not serve the function of clothing any better than a knit shirt from Kmart, but the Hilfiger shirt may also satisfy the customer's need to be perceived as a fashionable dresser. When products are purchased to satisfy psychological needs, the product's functional characteristics are typically less important.

Many products satisfy both functional and psychological needs. The principal reason for purchasing a Tommy Hilfiger shirt may be to enhance one's self-image, but the shirt also satisfies the functional need for clothing. Most Americans have more income than they require to satisfy their functional needs for food, liquid, clothing, and shelter. As disposable income rises, psychological needs become increasingly important.[10] Thus, store ambiance, service, and fashionable merchandise are more important to American retail customers than to customers in countries with less developed economies.

Functional needs are often referred to as *rational*, while psychological needs are called *emotional*. These labels suggest that visiting stores or buying products to satisfy psychological needs is irrational. But is it really irrational for people to buy designer clothing because it makes them feel more successful? Anything customers do to improve their satisfaction should be considered rational, whether the action satisfies a functional or a psychological need. Successful retailers attempt to satisfy both the functional and psychological needs of their customers. Psychological needs that can be satisfied through shopping and purchasing merchandise include stimulation, social experience, learning new trends, status and power, and self-reward.[11]

1. *Stimulation.* Retailers and mall managers use background music, visual displays, scents, and demonstrations in stores and malls to create a carnival-like, stimulating experience for their customers.[12] These environments encourage consumers to take a break in their daily environment and visit these sites. Retailers also attempt to stimulate customers with exciting graphics and photography on their websites and in their catalogs.

2. *Social experience.* Marketplaces have traditionally been centers of social activity, places where people could meet friends and develop new relationships.[13] Regional shopping malls in many communities have replaced open markets as social meeting places, especially for teenagers. Mall developers satisfy the need for social experiences by providing places for people to sit and talk in food courts. Barnes & Noble bookstores have cafés where customers can discuss novels while sipping a latte. Retailers provide similar social experiences through chat rooms for people visiting their websites. For example, visitors to the Amazon.com (www.amazon.com) can share information and opinions about books with other readers.

3. *Learning new trends.* By visiting retailers, people learn about new trends and ideas. These visits satisfy customers' needs to be informed about their

environment. For example, record stores use displays to show shoppers what new trends and artists are emerging.

4. *Status and power.* Some customers have a need for status and power that's satisfied through shopping. When shopping, a person can be waited on without having to pay for the service. For some people, a store is one of the few places where they get attention and respect. Ralph Lauren's store on Madison Avenue satisfies this need by creating an atmosphere of aristocratic gentility and the good life in a refurbished mansion in New York City. The store is furnished with expensive antiques. Cocktails and canapés are served to customers in the evening.

5. *Self-reward.* Customers frequently purchase merchandise to reward themselves when they have accomplished something or want to dispel depression. Perfume and cosmetics are common self-gifts. Retailers satisfy these needs by "treating" customers to personalized makeovers while they are in the store.[15]

Alloy.com's website sells merchandise and offers information in an exciting environment for teenagers.

Conflicting Needs Most customers have multiple needs. Moreover, these needs often conflict. For example, Jennifer Sanchez would like to wear a DKNY suit. Such a suit would enhance her self-image and earn her the admiration of her college friends. But this need conflicts with her budget and her need to get a job. Employers might feel that she's not responsible if she wears an expensive suit to an interview for an entry-level position. Typically, customers make trade-offs between their conflicting needs. Later in this chapter we will discuss a model of how customers make these trade-offs between their needs.

Because needs often cannot be satisfied in one store or by one product, consumers may appear to be inconsistent in their shopping behavior. For example, an executive might own an expensive Mercedes-Benz auto and buy gas from a discount service station. A grocery shopper might buy an inexpensive store brand of paper towels and a premium national brand of orange juice. The pattern of buying both premium and low-priced merchandise or patronizing expensive, status-oriented retailers and price-oriented retailers is called **cross-shopping.**

While cross-shoppers are seeking value, their perception of value varies across product classes. Thus, a cross-shopper might feel it is worth the money to buy an expensive sweater in a boutique but feel there is little quality difference between jeans at Kmart and designer brands at the boutique. Similarly, consumers may cut back on dining at an expensive restaurant but still want to treat themselves to expensive, high-quality jams, mustards, and olive oils in the supermarket. While retailers might think the buying patterns of cross-shoppers do not make sense to them, it makes sense to their customers.[16]

Stimulating Need Recognition   As we have said, customers must recognize unsatisfied needs before they are motivated to visit a store and buy merchandise. Sometimes these needs are stimulated by an event in a person's life. For example, Jennifer's department store visit to buy a suit was stimulated by her impending interview and her examination of her blue suit. An ad motivated her to look for the suit at Macy's. Retailers use a variety of approaches to stimulate problem recognition and motivate customers to visit their stores and buy merchandise. Advertising, direct mail, publicity, and special events communicate the availability of merchandise or special prices. Within the store, visual merchandising and salespeople can stimulate need recognition. For example, a salesperson showed Jennifer a scarf to stimulate her need for an accessory to complement her new suit.

One of the oldest methods for stimulating needs and attracting customers is still one of the most effective. The Saks Fifth Avenue store in Manhattan has 310 feet of store frontage along 49th and 50th streets and the famed Fifth Avenue. Each day at lunchtime, about 3,000 people walk by the 31 window displays. Saks has 1,200 different window displays each year, with the Fifth Avenue windows changing each week. These displays can dramatically impact sales.

Information Search

Once customers identify a need, they may seek information about retailers or products to help them satisfy the need. Jennifer's search was limited to the three suits shown her by the salesperson at Macy's. She was satisfied with this level of information search because she and her friend Brenda had confidence in Macy's merchandise and pricing, and she was pleased with the selection of suits presented to her. More extended buying processes may involve collecting a lot of information, visiting several retailers, and deliberating a long time before making a purchase.[17]

Window displays and free samples can stimulate need recognition and start the buying process.

Amount of Information Searched In general, the amount of **information search** depends on the value customers feel they'll gain from searching versus the cost of searching. The value of the search is in how it improves the customer's purchase decision. Will the search help the customer find a lower-price product or one that will give superior performance? The cost of search includes both time and money. Traveling from store to store can cost money for gas and parking, but the major cost incurred is the customer's time. The Internet can dramatically reduce the cost of information search. Information about merchandise sold across the world is just a mouse click away. Retailing View 4.1 describes how readily available information on the Web is affecting the automobile buying process.

Factors influencing the amount of information searched include (1) the nature and use of the product being purchased, (2) characteristics of the individual customer, and (3) aspects of the market and buying situation in which the purchase is made.[18] Some people search more than others. For example, customers who enjoy shopping search more than those who don't like to shop. Also, customers who are self-confident or have prior experience purchasing and using the product tend to search less.

Buying a Car in the Internet Age   RETAILING VIEW

4.1

Ten years ago, if consumers wanted to buy a car, they would visit several dealers, look at different models, test drive the cars sold by each dealer, and then negotiate price and financing with the dealer. Many consumers view this traditional process of buying a car as being about as pleasurable as going to the dentist. But now the Internet is changing this experience as well as the nature of automobile retailing.

The Internet is putting consumers in control of the car buying process. Consumers can access a wealth of information about automobile specifications plus the dealer's costs for cars and options, and reviews of the car's performance are available from websites such as Edmund's (www.edmunds.com) or Carclub (www.carclub.com). This information enables consumers to walk into a dealership knowing as much or more than the dealer's salespeople.

If consumers want to buy a car without visiting a dealer and bargaining over price, they can submit a request for the car they want through a buying service such as Autobytel (www.autobytel.com) or CarsDirect (www.carsdirect.com). Nearby dealers can respond by telephone or e-mail within 24 hours, offering a car similar to the desired model, and close the deal in a day.

Sites like www.bankrate.com and www.alg.com help consumers figure out how much they can afford to spend on a car, whether they should buy a new car or used car, and whether they should lease or buy. The sites feature calculators to walk consumers through questions like, Is it better to use a home equity loan or take the $1,500 rebate or take the 1.9 percent finance charge offered by the dealer?

Sources: "Car Buying 2001: Smart Maneuvers—How to Get the Right Car-Buying Information so You Can Take Control of the Deal," *Consumer Reports,* April 2001, p. 21; and Catherine Greenman, "Women Turn to Web to Avoid Sales Pressure," *New York Times,* January 5, 2000, p. F1.

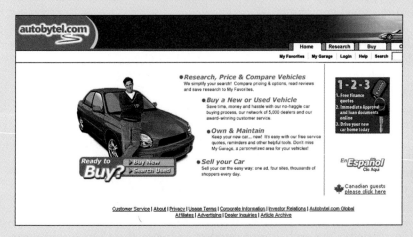

Customers can get a wide variety of useful information on the Internet from sites like Autobytel.com when they are in the buying process for a car.

Marketplace and situational factors affecting information search include (1) the number of competing brands and retail outlets and (2) the time pressure under which the purchase must be made. When competition is greater and there are more alternatives to consider, the amount of information searched increases. The amount decreases as time pressure increases.

Sources of Information Customers have two sources of information: internal and external. **Internal sources** are information in a customer's memory such as names, images, and past experiences with different stores. For example, Jennifer relied on an internal source (her memory of an ad) when choosing to visit Macy's. **External sources** are information provided by ads and other people. Customers see hundreds of ads in print and the electronic media; they notice signs for many retail outlets each day. In addition, customers get information about products and retailers from friends and family members.

The major source of internal information is the customer's past shopping experience. Even if they remember only a small fraction of the information they are exposed to, customers have an extensive internal information bank to draw upon when deciding where to shop and what to buy.[19]

When customers feel that their internal information is inadequate, they turn to external information sources. Remember how Jennifer Sanchez asked a respected friend to help her make the purchase decision. External sources of information play a major role in the acceptance of fashions, as discussed in the appendix to this chapter.

Reducing the Information Search The retailer's objective at the information search stage of the buying process is to limit the customer's search to its store or website. Each element of the retailing mix can be used to achieve this objective.

First, retailers must provide a good selection of merchandise so customers can find something to satisfy their needs within the store. Providing a wide variety of products and a broad assortment of brands, colors, and sizes increases the chances that customers will find what they want. For example, Circuit City uses in-store kiosks to increase the selection of merchandise available to customers by giving them the opportunity to purchase merchandise not available in the store such as custom-designed computers.

Services provided by retailers can also limit search to the retailer's location. The availability of credit and delivery may be important for consumers who want to purchase large durable goods such as furniture and appliances. And salespeople can provide enough information to customers so they won't feel the need to collect additional information by visiting other stores. For example, mail-order retailer of sportswear and sports equipment L.L. Bean gives employees 40 hours of training before they interact with their first customer. Due to this extensive training, people across the United States call L.L. Bean for advice on such subjects as what to wear for cross-country skiing and what to take on a trip to Alaska. If the employee answering the phone can't provide the information, the customer is switched to an expert within the company. Thanks to L.L. Bean's reputation for expertise in sportswear and sporting goods, customers feel they can collect all the information they need to make a purchase decision from this one retailer.

Everyday low pricing is another way retailers increase the chance that customers will buy in their store and not search for a better price elsewhere. Since

Wal-Mart and Best Buy have everyday-low-pricing policies, customers can feel confident that they won't find that merchandise at a lower price in the future. Many stores with everyday low pricing offer money-back guarantees if a competitor offers the same merchandise at a lower price. Chapter 15 talks about benefits and limitations of various pricing strategies.

Retailing View 4.2 describes how retailers are trying to offer enough information so that customers will feel comfortable buying apparel through their electronic channel.

Evaluation of Alternatives: The Multiattribute Model

The multiattribute attitude model provides a useful way for summarizing how customers use the information they have about alternative products, evaluate the alternatives, and select one that best satisfies their needs. We will discuss it in detail since it offers a framework for developing a retailing strategy.[20]

The **multiattribute attitude model** is based on the notion that customers see a retailer or a product as a collection of attributes or characteristics. The model is designed to predict a customer's evaluation of a product or retailer based on (1) its performance on relevant attributes and (2) the importance of those attributes to the customer. Retail buyers can also use the multiattribute model to evaluate merchandise and vendors (see Chapter 14).

Beliefs about Performance To illustrate this model, consider the store choice decision confronting a young single professional woman who needs groceries. She considers three retailers: a supercenter in the next suburb, the local supermarket, and an Internet grocery retailer such as Peapod (www.peapod.com). They're compared in Exhibit 4–3.

Trying on Clothes in Virtual Reality at the Lands' End Website   RETAILING VIEW

4.2

At the Lands' End website (www.landsend.com), women can enter information about their body types, including hair color, height, weight, and shoulder and waist descriptions, such as narrow or generous. Based on their responses, a three-dimensional model resembling their body type appears on the screen. Then customers are provided with suggestions of appropriate apparel for their body type. These suggestions are offered for four apparel styles: dressy office attire, casual office, after-work, and very casual. Using a click-and-drag interface, customers can electronically "try on" different outfits and accessories and see how they look.

In the future, this virtual shopping experience will be made even more realistic by enabling customers to see clothing on their actual body and view the fit from all angles by rotating the three-dimensional picture.

The use of virtual models at some websites lets customers "try on" the merchandise.

Sources: Jonathan Boorstein, "Online Mini-Me: 3-D Modeling Enhances E-Commerce Sites," *Direct*, June 2000, p. 101; and Mary Wagner, "Picture This: E-Retailers Aim to Zoom, Spin and Model Their Way to Higher Sales," *Internet Retailer*, May 2000, pp. 56, 58–60.

EXHIBIT 4–3
Characteristics
of Retailers

A. INFORMATION ABOUT STORES SELLING GROCERIES			
Store Characteristics	**Supercenter**	**Supermarket**	**Internet Grocer**
Grocery prices	20% below average	average	10% above average
Delivery cost ($)	0	0	10
Total travel time (minutes)	30	15	0
Typical checkout time (minutes)	10	5	2
Number of products, brands, and sizes	20,000	15,000	5,000
Fresh produce	Yes	Yes	Yes
Fresh fish	Yes	Yes	No
Ease of finding products	Difficult	Easy	Easy
Ease of collecting nutritional information about products	Difficult	Difficult	Easy
B. BELIEFS ABOUT STORES' PERFORMANCE BENEFITS*			
Performance Benefits	**Supercenter**	**Supermarket**	**Internet Grocer**
Economy	10	8	6
Convenience	3	5	10
Assortment	9	7	5
Availability of product information	4	4	8

*10 = excellent; 1 = poor.

The customer mentally processes Exhibit 4–3A's "objective" information about each grocery retailer and forms an impression of the benefits the stores provide. Exhibit 4–3B shows her beliefs about these benefits. Notice that some benefits combine several objective characteristics. For example, the convenience benefit combines travel time, checkout time, and ease of finding products. Grocery prices and delivery cost affect the customer's beliefs about the economy of shopping at the retail outlets.

The degree to which each retailer provides the benefit is represented on a 10-point scale: 10 means the retailer performs well in providing the benefit; 1 means it performs poorly. Here no retailer has superior performance on all benefits. The supercenter performs well on economy and assortment, but is low on convenience. The Internet grocer offers the best convenience but is weak on economy and assortment.

Importance Weights   The young woman in the preceding example forms an overall evaluation of each store based on the importance she places on each benefit the stores provide. The importance she places on a benefit can also be represented using a 10-point rating scale, with 10 indicating the benefit is very important and 1 indicating it's very unimportant. Using this rating scale, the importance of the store benefits for the young woman and a parent with four children are shown in Exhibit 4–4, along with the performance beliefs previously discussed. Notice that the single woman values convenience and the availability of product information much more than economy and assortment. But the par-

EXHIBIT 4–4
Evaluation of Stores

	IMPORTANCE WEIGHTS*		PERFORMANCE BELIEFS		
Characteristic	Young Single Woman	Parent with Four Children	Supercenter	Supermarket	Internet Grocer
Economy	4	10	10	8	6
Convenience	10	4	3	5	10
Assortment	5	8	9	7	5
Availability of product information	9	2	4	4	8
OVERALL EVALUATION					
Young single woman			151	153	221
Parent with four children			192	164	156

*10 = very important; 1 = very unimportant.

ent places a lot of importance on economy; assortment is moderately important; and convenience and product information aren't very important.

The importance of a store's benefits differs for each customer and may also differ for each shopping trip.[21] For example, the parent with four children may stress economy for major shopping trips, but place more importance on convenience for a fill-in trip.

In Exhibit 4–4, the single woman and parent have the same beliefs about each store's performance, but they differ in the importance they place on benefits the stores offer. In general, customers can differ on their beliefs about the stores' performance as well as on their importance weights.

Evaluating Stores   Research has shown that a customer's overall evaluation of an alternative (in this situation, a store) is closely related to the sum of the performance beliefs multiplied by the importance weights.[22] Thus, we calculate the young single woman's overall evaluation or score for the supercenter as follows:

$$
\begin{aligned}
4 \times 10 &= 40 \\
10 \times 3 &= 30 \\
5 \times 9 &= 45 \\
9 \times 4 &= \underline{36} \\
& 151
\end{aligned}
$$

Exhibit 4–4 shows the overall evaluations for the three retailers using the importance weights of the single woman and the parent. For the single woman, the Internet grocer has the highest score, 221, and thus the most favorable evaluation. She would probably select this retailer for most of her grocery shopping. On the other hand, the supercenter has the highest score, 192, for the parent, who'd probably buy the family's weekly groceries there.

When customers are about to select a store, they don't actually go through the process of listing store characteristics, evaluating stores' performance on these characteristics, determining each characteristic's importance, calculating each store's overall score, and then visiting a store with the highest score! The multi-attribute attitude model doesn't reflect customers' actual decision process, but it does predict their evaluation of alternatives and their choice.[23] In addition, the

Benefits Provided by Suits	Importance Weights	BELIEFS ABOUT PERFORMANCE		
		Suit A	Suit B	Suit C
Economy	6	6	5	5
Quality	6	10	7	8
Conservative look	8	6	6	10
Complement to wardrobe	8	7	6	9
Fashion	4	7	10	5
Fit	10	?	?	8
Overall evaluation				380

model provides useful information for designing a retail offering. For example, if the supermarket here could increase its performance rating on assortment from 7 to 10 (perhaps by adding a bakery and a wide selection of prepared meals), customers like the parent might shop at the supermarket more often than at the supercenter. Later in this chapter we'll discuss how retailers can use the multiattribute attitude model to increase their store's evaluation.

The application of the multiattribute attitude model in Exhibit 4–4 deals with a customer who's evaluating and selecting a retail store. The same model can also be used to describe how a customer evaluates and selects merchandise in a store. For example, Exhibit 4–5 shows Jennifer Sanchez's beliefs and importance weights about the three suits shown to her by the salesperson. Jennifer didn't evaluate suits A and B on fit because she didn't try them on. She bought suit C because it was good enough. Its overall evaluation passed some minimum threshold (which in terms of this multiattribute attitude model might be a score of 320).

Customers often make choices as Jennifer did. They don't thoroughly evaluate each alternative as suggested in the multiattribute attitude model. They simply buy merchandise that's good enough or very good on one particular attribute. In general, customers don't spend the time necessary to find the very best product. Once they've found a product that satisfies their need, they stop searching.[24]

Implications for Retailers   How can a retailer use the multiattribute attitude model to encourage customers to shop at its store more frequently? First, the model indicates what information customers use to decide which store to visit. Thus, to develop a program for attracting customers, the retailer must do market research to collect the following information:

1. Alternative stores that customers consider.

2. Characteristics or benefits that customers consider when evaluating and choosing a retailer.

3. Customers' ratings of each store's performance on the characteristics.

4. The importance weights that customers attach to the characteristics.

Armed with this information, the retailer can use several approaches to influence customers to select its store.

Getting into the Consideration Set   The retailer must make sure that it is included in the customer's consideration set. The **consideration set** is the set of alternatives the customer evaluates when making a selection.[25] To be included in the consideration set, the retailer must develop programs to increase the likelihood that customers will remember it when they're about to go shopping. The retailer can influence this top-of-the-mind awareness through advertising and location strategies. Heavy advertising expenditures that stress the retailer's name can increase top-of-the-mind awareness. When a retailer locates several stores in a geographic area, customers are exposed more frequently to the store name as they drive through the area.[26] A major factor contributing to the failure of many pure Internet retailers was the high cost of creating awareness and getting into consumer consideration sets.

After ensuring that its store is in the consideration set, the retailer can use four methods to increase the chances that customers will select the store for a visit:

1. Increase the belief about the store's performance.

2. Decrease the performance belief for competing stores in the consideration set.

3. Increase customers' importance weights.

4. Add a new benefit.

Changing Performance Beliefs   The first approach involves altering customers' beliefs about the retailer's performance—increasing the retailer's performance rating on a characteristic. For example, the supermarket in Exhibit 4–4 would want to increase its overall rating by improving its rating on all four benefits. The supermarket could improve its rating on economy by lowering prices and could improve its rating on assortment by stocking more gourmet and ethnic foods.[28]

It's costly for a retailer to improve its performance on all benefits. Thus, a retailer should focus efforts on improving performance on benefits that are important to customers in its target market. For example, 7-Eleven's market research found that women avoid convenience stores because they view them as dingy and unsafe. To attract more women, 7-Eleven has improved the shopping environment in a number of its stores. To create a sense of space, brighter lighting was installed and aisles were widened. Cigarette racks and other clutter were cleared off checkout counters, and colorful signage was used to designate merchandise areas.[29]

A change in the performance belief concerning an important benefit results in a large change in customers' overall evaluation. In Exhibit 4–4's situation, the supermarket should attempt to improve its convenience ratings if it wants to attract more young single women who presently shop on the Internet. If its convenience rating rose from 5 to 8, its overall evaluation for young single women would increase from 153 to 183 and thus be much higher than the young women's evaluation of supercenters. Note that an increase in rating from 7 to 10 on a less important benefit such as economy would have less effect on the store's overall evaluation. The supermarket might try to improve its rating on convenience by increasing the number of checkout stations, using customer scanning to reduce checkout time, or providing more in-store information so customers could locate merchandise more easily.

Research suggests that consumers in Germany, France, and the U.K. place different weights on three important attributes— price/value, service/quality, and relationships—considered in selecting a retailer to patronize. German consumers tend to place more weight on price/value, whereas customer service and product quality are more important for French consumers and affinity benefits such as loyalty cards and

REFACT

eToys, prior to its bankruptcy, had annual sales of $151 million and spent $120 million annually to attract customers to its website and get into their consideration sets.[27]

preferred customer programs are more important for English consumers. Thus, in general, retailers that emphasize price and good value will be more successful in Germany than France or the U.K.[30]

Another approach is to try to decrease customers' performance ratings of a competing store. This approach may be illegal and usually isn't very effective, because customers typically don't believe a firm's negative comments about its competitors.

Changing Importance Weights Altering customers' importance weights is another approach to influencing store choice. A retailer would want to increase the importance customers place on benefits for which its performance is superior and decrease the importance of benefits for which it has inferior performance.

For example, if the supermarket in Exhibit 4–4 tried to attract families who shop at supercenters, it could increase the importance of convenience. Typically, changing importance weights is harder than changing performance beliefs because importance weights reflect customers' values.[31]

JCPenney, as a national department store chain, offers a unique benefit to a gift buyer. Customers from around the U.S. can use its registry on the Internet and the gift recipients can return or exchange the gifts at their local store.

Adding a New Benefit Finally, retailers might try to add a new benefit to the set of benefits customers consider when selecting a store. Since JCPenney is a national department store, a customer can purchase a gift at a local Penney store or from its website and send it to a person in another part of the country knowing that, if necessary, the recipient can exchange it at her local Penney store. Normally, customers wouldn't consider this when selecting a retailer. This approach of adding a new benefit is often effective because it's easier to change customer evaluation of new benefits than old benefits.

Purchasing the Merchandise

Customers don't always purchase a brand or item of merchandise with the highest overall evaluation. The item offering the greatest benefits (having the highest evaluation) may not be available in the store, or the customer may feel that the risks outweigh the potential benefits. Some of the steps that retailers take to increase the chances that customers can easily convert their positive merchandise evaluations into purchases are

1. Don't stock out of popular merchandise. Have a complete assortment of sizes and colors for customer to buy.

2. Reduce the risk of purchasing merchandise by offering liberal return policies and refunds if the same merchandise is available at a lower price from another retailer.

3. Offer credit.

4. Make it easy to purchase merchandise by having convenient checkout terminals.

5. Reduce the actual and perceived waiting time in lines at checkout terminals.[32]

Postpurchase Evaluation

The buying process doesn't end when a customer purchases a product. After making a purchase, the customer uses the product and then evaluates the experience to determine whether it was satisfactory or unsatisfactory. **Satisfaction** is a postconsumption evaluation of how well a store or product meets or exceeds customer expectations. This **postpurchase evaluation** then becomes part of the customer's internal information that affects future store and product decisions. Unsatisfactory experiences can motivate customers to complain to the retailer and to patronize other stores.[34] Consistently high levels of satisfaction build store loyalty—an important source of competitive advantage for retailers. Chapters 17 and 19 discuss means to increase customer satisfaction, such as offering quality merchandise, providing accurate information about merchandise, and contacting customers after a sale.

SOCIAL FACTORS INFLUENCING BUYING DECISIONS

Exhibit 4–6 illustrates that customer buying decisions are influenced by both the customer's beliefs, attitudes, and values and factors in the customer social environment. The previous section described how personal characteristics affect store and merchandise evaluations and choices. In this section, we discuss how buying decisions are affected by the customer's social environment—the customer's family, reference groups, and culture.

Family

Many purchase decisions are made for products that the entire family will consume or use. Thus, retailers must understand how families make purchase decisions and how various family members influence these decisions.

Family Decision Making   The previous discussion of the buying decision process focused on how one person makes a decision—how Jennifer purchases a suit for herself. When families make purchase decisions, they often consider the needs of all family members.[35] In a situation such as choosing a vacation site, all family members may participate in the decision making. In other situations, one member of the family may assume the role of making the purchase decision. For

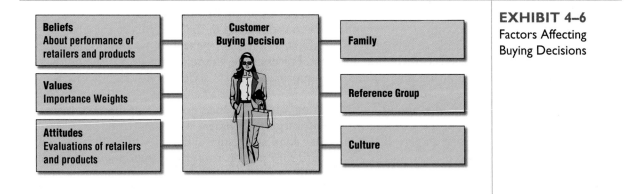

EXHIBIT 4–6
Factors Affecting Buying Decisions

Beliefs
About performance of retailers and products

Values
Importance Weights

Attitudes
Evaluations of retailers and products

Customer Buying Decision

Family

Reference Group

Culture

Many purchase decisions consider the needs of family members other than the shopper.

example, the husband might buy the groceries, the wife uses them to prepare their child's lunch, and the child consumes the lunch in school. In this situation, the store choice decision might be made by the husband, but the brand choice decision might be made by the mother, though greatly influenced by the child.

Children play an important role in family buying decisions.[36] Satisfying the needs of children is particularly important for many baby boomers who decide to have children late in life. They often have high disposable income and want to stay in luxury resorts, but they still want to take their children on vacations. Resort hotels now realize they must satisfy children's needs as well as adults. For example, Hyatt hotels greet families by offering books and games tailored to the children's ages. Parents checking in with infants receive a first-day supply of baby food or formula and diapers at no charge. Baby-sitting and escort services to attractions for children are offered.[37]

Retailers can attract consumers who shop with other family members by satisfying the needs of all family members. For example, IKEA, a Swedish furniture store chain, has a "ball pit" in which children can play while their parents shop. Nordstrom has sitting areas in its store and pubs where men can have a beer and watch a football game while their wives shop. By accommodating the needs of men and children who might not be interested in shopping, the family stays in the stores longer and buys more merchandise.[38]

Retailing View 4.3 profiles some retailers that are targeting "tween" shoppers who visit stores with their parents.

Reference Groups

A **reference group** is one or more people whom a person uses as a basis of comparison for beliefs, feelings, and behaviors. A consumer might have a number of different reference groups, although the most important reference group is the family, as we discussed in the previous section. These reference groups affect buying decisions by (1) offering information, (2) providing rewards for specific purchasing behaviors, and (3) enhancing a consumer's self-image.

Reference groups provide information to consumers directly through conversation or indirectly through observation. For example, Jennifer received valuable information from her friend about the suits she was considering. On other occasions, Jennifer might look to women like soccer player Mia Hamm and tennis player Venus Williams to guide her selection of athletic apparel. The role of reference groups in creating fashion is discussed in the appendix to this chapter.

Some reference groups influence purchase behaviors by rewarding behavior that meets with their approval. For example, the reference group of employees in a company might define the appropriate dress style and criticize fellow workers who violate this standard.

By identifying and affiliating with reference groups, consumers create, enhance, and maintain their self-image. Customers who want to be seen as members of an elite social class may shop at prestige retailers, while others who want to create an image of an outdoors person might buy merchandise from the L.L. Bean website.

Department stores use their teen boards to provide a reference group influence on teenage shoppers. The teen board members are selected because they are a group of students whom other students would like to emulate. By buying apparel worn by teen board members, other students can identify with these student leaders.

Culture

Culture is the meaning and values shared by most members of a society. For example, core values shared by most Americans include individualism, freedom, mastery and control, self-improvement, achievement and success, material comfort, and health and fitness. Retailing View 4.4 describes how the Chinese cultural value of collectivism affects their shopping behavior.

Gift giving is another example of how cultural values affect shopping behavior. Gift giving plays a much more important role in Japanese than American culture. Each Japanese person has a well-

Retailing to Tweens   RETAILING VIEW

4.3

Tween shoppers, between the ages of 8 and 12 years old, are the fastest-growing age segment in the United States. The 20 million tweens spend $14 billion annually on apparel using their own money and influence the $175 million their parents spend on them.

The tween girl may want to emulate her older sister, but sex and romance are not part of her life yet. She is still a little girl at heart. She likes fun, frilly, glittery, sensory environments that tap into the kid in her. She wants to be treated as young, but not babyish.

Limited Two is a market leader in the tween segment. It realizes that the tween girl might want to look like a 15 year old but that apparel assortments need to be fine-tuned to a younger body type and be more modest and sensible. Limited Two's stores create a mood of power and excitement for the tween girl. They include colorful storefront windows, light displays, photographic sticker booths, ear-piercing stations, and gumball machines. Special fixtures are placed at eye level for younger girls, even though the girls will be visiting the store with mom, because the tweens choose and the parents pay.

Club Libby Lu offers a more interactive format for the tween girl. "It is about the total experience, from the store design to the featured activities to the associates—we call them club directors. The customer is not just a customer at Club Libby Lu. She is a club member," says Mary C. Drolet, founder and president of the Chicago-based company.

Girls can dress up in costumes at Club Libby Lu as well as make their own jewelry and celebrate birthdays. They can create personalized T-shirts and receive a princess makeover. Or they can cover themselves in glitter and make their own lotions. However mature today's young

Tweens are an important segment targeted by retailers like Adessa.

girls may act, Drolet says, fantasy still has huge appeal to this age group. "We want the girls to feel that the store was created just for them," she adds. "We want them to hang out and play out their fantasy, not just rush in and out for a quick purchase."

The retailer also develops its own merchandise targeted to tweens, such as scented sleepwear or complete sleep-over kits.

Sources: Rachel Carlton, "A World of Her Own," *Display and Design Ideas*, November 2001, pp. 34–36; Dave Siegel, Tim Coffy, and Greg Livingstone, *The Great Tween Buying Machine. Paramount Marketing the Great Tween Buying Machine: Marketing to Today's Tweens* (Ithaca, NY: Paramount Marketing Publications, 2001); and Marianne Wilson, "Girls' Club," *Chain Store Age*, October 1, 2000, p. 62.

defined set of relatives and friends with whom they share reciprocal gift giving *(kosai)*. Most Japanese feel a need to bring gifts for family and friends when they return from a trip. In one study, about half of the Japanese tourists returning home from Los Angeles bought gifts for over 15 family members and friends. They spent as much on gifts for others as on merchandise for their own use. Gift packaging and wrapping offered by retailers is particularly important to Japanese consumers because gifts aren't opened in front of the gift giver. Thus, the gift's appearance is particularly important to the giver.[39]

Subcultures are distinctive groups of people within a culture. Members of a subculture share some customs and norms with the overall society but also have some unique perspectives.[40] Subcultures can be based on geography (southerners), age (baby boomers), ethnicity (Asian Americans), or lifestyle (punks).

MARKET SEGMENTATION

The preceding discussion focused on (1) how individual customers evaluate and select stores and merchandise and (2) factors affecting their decision making. To increase their efficiency, retailers identify groups of customers (market segments)

RETAILING VIEW   Cultural Values Affect Chinese Shopping Behavior

4.4

An important value in most Western cultures is individualism—people should only look out for themselves and their immediate family. Thus, consumers in individualistic cultures rely on their own inner standards and beliefs when making decisions. However, Eastern cultures value collectivism, emphasizing that considerations of others should guide behavior. Thus, social relationships are more important and material goods are less important to consumers in collectivist cultures.

Research has found that collectivists are more price sensitive than individualistic consumers about private goods—products and services consumed privately—but less price sensitive about public goods, those consumed in public. For example, supermarkets patronized by Chinese consumers compared to mainstream American supermarkets in southern California have 37 percent lower prices for packaged goods of the same brand and size and more than 100 percent lower for meats and seafood of the same type and description.

In addition, research reports that Chinese shoppers spend more time selecting products and make greater use of their five senses in evaluating products. For example, a sample of Chinese shoppers took four times longer to select bananas and touched four times more bunches before making a selection than consumers in an American sample in the same store. In addition, signifi-

The shopping behavior of customers in collectivistic cultures (Eastern) differs from that of people in individualistic cultures (Western).

cantly more Chinese customers smelled the fruit than American customers.

Sources: David Ackerman and Gerald Tellis, "Can Culture Affect Prices? A Cross-Cultural Study of Shopping and Retail Prices," *Journal of Retailing* 77 (Spring 2001), pp. 57–63; and Aaron Ahuvia and Nancy Wong, "The Effect of Cultural Orientation in Luxury Consumption," in *Advances in Consumer Research*, vol. 25, eds. Eric J. Arnould and Linda M. Scott (Ann Arbor MI: Association for Consumer Research, 1998), pp. 29–32.

and target their offerings to meet the needs of typical customers in that segment rather than the needs of a specific customer. A **retail market segment** is a group of customers whose needs are satisfied by the same retail mix because they have similar needs. For example, families traveling on a vacation have different needs than executives on business trips. Thus, Marriott offers hotels with different retail mixes for each of these segments.

The Internet enables retailers to efficiently target individual customers and market products to them on a one-to-one basis. This one-to-one marketing concept is discussed in Chapter 11 on customer relationship management.

REFACT

In 1994, the Swedish furniture retailer IKEA aired the first mainstream TV ad targeted toward the gay subculture by featuring a gay relationship.[41]

Criteria for Evaluating Market Segments

Customers are grouped into segments in many different ways. For example, customers can be grouped on the basis that they live in the same city, have similar incomes and education, or barbecue at their homes twice a week or more. Exhibit 4–7 shows different methods for segmenting retail markets. There's no simple way to determine which method is best. Four criteria for evaluating whether a retail segment is a viable target market are actionability, identifiability, accessibility, and size.

Actionability   The fundamental criteria for evaluating a retail market segment are (1) customers in the segment must have similar needs, seek similar benefits, and be satisfied by a similar retail offering, and (2) those customers' needs must be different from the needs of customers in other segments. **Actionability** means that the definition of a segment must clearly indicate what the retailer should do to satisfy its needs. According to this criterion, it makes sense for Lane Bryant (a division of Charming Shoppes catering to full-figure women) to segment the apparel market on the basis of the demographic characteristic physical size. Customers who wear large sizes have different needs than those who wear small sizes, so they are attracted to a store offering a unique merchandise mix. In the context of the multiattribute attitude model discussed previously, women who wear large sizes place more importance on fit and fashion because it's relatively hard for them to satisfy these needs.

On the other hand, it wouldn't make sense for a supermarket to segment its market on the basis of customer size. Large and small men and women probably have the same needs, seek the same benefits, and go through the same buying process for groceries. This segmentation approach wouldn't be actionable for a supermarket retailer because the retailer couldn't develop unique mixes for large and small customers. Thus, supermarkets usually segment markets using demographics such as income or ethnic origin to develop their retail mix.

Identifiability   Retailers must be able to identify the customers in a target segment. **Identifiability** is important because it permits the retailer to determine (1) the segment's size and (2) with whom the retailer should communicate when promoting its retail offering.

Segmentation Descriptor	Example of Categories
GEOGRAPHIC	
Region	Pacific, Mountain, Central, South, Mid-Atlantic, Northeast
Population density	Rural, suburban, urban
Climate	Cold, warm
DEMOGRAPHIC	
Age	Under 6, 6–12, 13–19, 20–29, 30–49, 50–65, over 65
Gender	Male, female
Family life cycle	Single; married with no children; married with youngest child under 6; married with youngest child over 6; married with children no longer living at home; widowed
Family income	Under $19,999; $20,000–29,999; $30,000–49,999; $50,000–$74,999; over $75,000
Occupation	Professional, clerical sales, craftsperson, retired, student, homemaker
Education	Some high school, high school graduate, some college, college graduate, graduate degree
Religion	Catholic, protestant, Jewish, Islam
Race	Caucasian, African American, Hispanic, Asian
Nationality	American, Japanese, British, French, German, Italian, Chinese
PSYCHOSOCIAL	
Social class	Lower, middle, upper
Lifestyle	Striver, driver, devote, intimate, altruist, fun seeker, creative
Personality	Aggressive, shy, emotional
FEELINGS AND BEHAVIORS	
Attitudes	Positive, neutral, negative
Benefit sought	Convenience, economy, prestige
Stage in decision process	Unaware, aware, informed, interested, intend to buy, bought previously
Perceived risk	High, medium, low
Innovativeness	Innovator, early adopter, early majority, late majority, laggard
Loyalty	None, some, completely
Usage rate	None, light, medium, heavy
Usage situation	Home, work, vacation, leisure
User status	Nonuser, ex-user, potential user, current user

Accessibility **Accessibility** is the ability of the retailer to deliver the appropriate retail mix to the customers in the segment. Customers for Marriott convention hotels and resort hotels are accessed in different ways because they use different sources to collect information about products and services. Convention hotel customers are best reached through newspapers such as *USA Today* and *The Wall Street Journal*, whereas resort hotel customers are best reached through ads on TV and in travel and leisure magazines.

Size A target segment must be large enough to support a unique retailing mix. For example, in the past, health food and vitamins were found primarily in small, owner-operated stores that catered to a relatively small market. In the wake of a higher consciousness about exercise and nutrition, health food stores like General Nutrition have flourished. Supermarkets have also expanded their offering of health foods and vitamins to meet this substantial market segment's needs.

On the other hand, the number of consumers in a target segment may not be a good indicator of potential sales. For example, international retailers are very interested in China because it has 1.2 billion consumers. Although many consumers in China's coastal cities have considerable disposable income, 70 percent of all Chinese live in rural areas with minimal incomes. Even in the urban areas, many Chinese consumers are in their twenties and live with their parents in an apartment.[42]

Approaches for Segmenting Markets

Exhibit 4–7 illustrates the wide variety of approaches for segmenting retail markets. No one approach is best for all retailers. They must explore various factors that affect customer buying behavior and determine which factors are most important. Now we'll discuss methods for segmenting retail markets.

Geographic Segmentation   **Geographic segmentation** groups customers by where they live. A retail market can be segmented by countries (Japan, Mexico) and by areas within a country such as states, cities, and neighborhoods. Since customers typically shop at stores convenient to where they live and work, individual retail outlets usually focus on the customer segment reasonably close to the outlet.

In the United States, many food retailers concentrate on regions of the country. For example, HEB concentrates on Texas, while Wegmans concentrates on Western New York. However, in the U.K., supermarket retailing is dominated by national firms such as Sainsbury and Tesco.

Even though national retailers such as The Gap and Sears have no geographic focus, they do tailor their merchandise selections to different regions of the country. Snow sleds don't sell well in Florida, and surfboards don't sell well in Colorado. Even within a metropolitan area, stores in a chain must adjust to unique needs of customers in different neighborhoods. For example, supermarkets in affluent neighborhoods typically have more gourmet foods than stores in less affluent neighborhoods.

Segments based on geography are identifiable, accessible, and substantial. It's easy to determine who lives in a geographic segment such as the Paris metropolitan area and to target communications and locate retail outlets for customers in Paris. When customers in different geographic segments have similar needs, it would be inappropriate to develop unique retail offerings by geographic markets. For example, a fast-food customer in Detroit probably seeks the same benefits as a fast-food customer in Los Angeles. Thus, it wouldn't be useful to segment the fast-food market geographically. Even though Target and The Gap vary some merchandise assortments geographically, the majority of their merchandise is identical in all of their stores because customers who buy basic clothing (underwear, slacks, shirts, and blouses) have many of the same needs in all regions of the United States. On the other hand, Home Depot and many supermarket chains have significantly different assortments in stores located in the same city.

REFACT

Across the United States, vanilla is the number one ice cream flavor and chocolate is number two; however, Häagen-Dazs coffee is most popular in New York, butter pecan elsewhere in the East, and chocolate chip in California.[43]

Demographic Segmentation   **Demographic segmentation** groups consumers on the basis of easily measured, objective characteristics such as age, gender, income, and education. Demographic variables are the most common means to define segments because consumers in these segments can be easily identified and accessed. The media used by retailers to communicate with customers are defined in terms of demographic profiles. Demographics such as gender are related to differences in shopping behavior.

Men show little ability or interest in honing their shopping skills, whereas women view the supermarket as a place where they can demonstrate their expertise in getting the most value for their money. Rather than looking for items on sale or making price comparisons, men tend to select well-known brands. They also tend to not pay attention at the checkout register, whereas women watch the cashier to be sure they're charged the right price. Men and women even buy different merchandise. Women buy more health-oriented foods (such as cottage cheese and refrigerated yogurt) and household essentials (such as cleaning and personal health products). Men's shopping baskets contain more beer, cupcakes, ice cream, and hot dogs. Men also do less planning and make numerous last-minute grocery trips. Single men visit supermarkets 99 times a year; single women make 80 trips a year. These eleventh-hour trips make men more susceptible to impulse purchases such as potato chips and cookies.[44]

However, demographics may not be useful for defining segments for some retailers. For example, demographics are poor predictors of users of active wear such as jogging suits and running shoes. At one time, retailers assumed that active wear would be purchased exclusively by young people, but the health and fitness trend has led people of all ages to buy this merchandise. Relatively inactive consumers find active wear to be comfortable. Initially, retailers felt that VCRs would be a luxury product purchased mainly by wealthy customers. But retailers found that low-income customers and families with young children were strongly attracted to VCRs because they offered low-cost, convenient entertainment.

Geodemographic Segmentation   **Geodemographic segmentation** uses both geographic and demographic characteristics to classify consumers. This segmentation scheme is based on the principle that "birds of feather flock together."[45] Consumers in the same neighborhoods tend to buy the same types of cars, appliances, and apparel and shop at the same types of retailers. The most widely used tool for geographic segmentation is **PRIZM** (Potential Rating Index by Zip Market) developed by Claritas (www.claritas.com). Claritas identified 62 geodemographic segments, called neighborhoods or clusters, by using detailed demographic and consumption information and data on media habits of the people who live in each U.S. block tract (zip code+4).

In addition to providing demographic information about each cluster, Claritas provides indexes comparing the buying behavior and media habits of consumers in the cluster to the national average. The national average is 100. Thus, an index of 155 for a cluster indicates that the cluster is 55 percent greater than the national average.

The information in the table below describes three PRIZM clusters:

Cluster name	Town & Gown	Gray Collars	Latino American
Cluster number	31	42	44
Description	College-town singles	Aging couples in near suburbs	Hispanic middle class
Lifestyle/products	Foreign videos (551)*	Lottery tickets (169)	Boxing (443)
	Online services (216)	Six-month CDs (140)	Dance music (194)
	Dogs (54)	Museums (68)	Campers (45)
	Sewing (35)	Tennis (42)	Barbecuing (57)
Food and drink	Tequila (183)	Fresh cold cuts (136)	Avocado (230)
	Coca-Cola (145)	Fast food (134)	Pita bread (115)
	Pasta salad (141)	Frozen dinners (130)	Chewing gum (105)
	Fast food (105)	Non-alcoholic beer (129)	Coca-Cola (108)
Media used	*Cosmopolitan* (183)	*Ebony* (159)	*Cosmopolitan* (228)
	Sports Illustrated (182)	*McCall's* (141)	*Touched by an Angel* (193)
	Friends (222)	*Good Morning America* (139)	*Court TV* (156)
	Face the Nation (164)	TV wrestling (137)	*Seventeen* (117)

*Index based 100 = average

These neighborhoods with similar demographics and buying behaviors can be any place in the United States. For example, Exhibit 4–8 outlines the location of Gray Collar areas in the United States.

Geodemographic segmentation is particularly appealing to store-based retailers, because customers typically patronize stores close to their neighborhood. Thus, retailers can use geodemographic segmentation to select locations for their stores and tailor assortment in the stores to the preferences of the local community. In Chapter 8, we illustrate how geodemographic segmentation is used to make store location decisions.

Lifestyle Segmentation **Lifestyle** or **psychographics** refers to how people live, how they spend their time and money, what activities they pursue, and their attitudes and opinions about the world in which they live. The segments are identified through consumer surveys that ask respondents to indicate whether they agreed or disagreed with statements such as "My idea of fun in a national park would be to stay in an expensive lodge and dress up for dinner," "I often crave excitement," and "I could not stand to skin a dead animal." Retailers today are placing more emphasis on lifestyles than on demographics to define a target segment.

The most widely used tool for **lifestyle segmentation** is the **Value and Lifestyle Survey (VALS2)**[46] conducted by SRI Consulting Business Intelligence (www.sric-bi.com/VALS). On the basis of responses to this survey, consumers are classified into eight segments shown in Exhibit 4–9.

The segments are described by two dimensions: (1) the consumers' resources, including their income, education, health, and energy level, and (2) personal orientation or what motivates them—principles, status, or actions. Principle-oriented

EXHIBIT 4–8
Location of Gray
Collar Neighborhoods

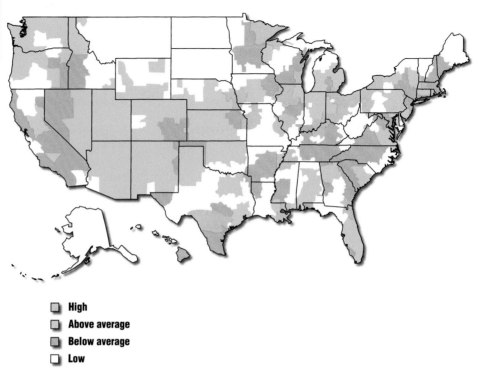

☐ **High**
☐ **Above average**
☐ **Below average**
☐ **Low**

Source: Michael J. Weiss, *The Clustered World* (Boston: Little, Brown, 2000), p. 262. Reprinted by permission.

consumers are guided by their internal values rather than the opinions of others. Status-oriented consumers strive to win the approval of others. Action-oriented people seek activity, variety, and risk in their daily lives.

Nature's Northwest focuses on a lifestyle segment of consumers interested in health and wellness. These consumers are primarily Achievers and Actualizers in the VALS2 segmentation scheme. The 42,000-square-foot Nature's Northwest combines an upscale supermarket and natural-foods store with unexpected offerings such as fitness classes and spa/salon services. Shoppers can take a yoga class, soak in a hydrotherapy tub, learn about herb gardening, or get their hair colored. An on-site interactive learning center and lending library is devoted to health and related subjects. The pharmacy offers conventional therapies as well as homeopathic remedies.[47]

Lifestyle segmentation is useful because it identifies what motivates buying behavior. On the other hand, it is difficult to identify and access consumers in specific lifestyle segments.

Buying Situation Segmentation   Buying behavior of customers with the same demographics or lifestyle can differ depending on their buying situation. Thus, retailers may use **buying situations** such as fill-in versus weekly shopping to segment a market. For example, in Exhibit 4–4, the parent with four children evaluated the supercenter higher than the Internet grocer or supermarket for weekly grocery purchases. But if the parent ran out of milk during the week, he or she would probably go to the convenience store rather than the wholesale club for this fill-in shopping. In terms of Exhibit 4–4's multiattribute attitude model, convenience would be more important than assortment in the fill-in

VALS2 American Lifestyle Segments | **EXHIBIT 4–9**

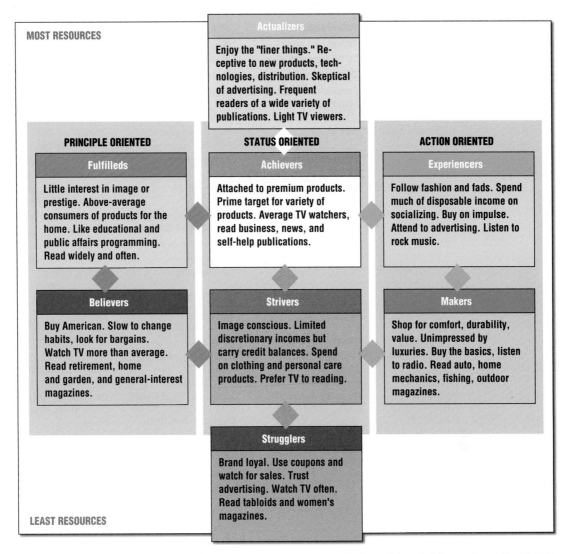

SOURCE: VALS2 SRI Consulting Business Intelligence, Menlo Park, CA; Cited in Judith Waldrop, "Markets with Attitudes," *American Demograhics*, July 1995, pp. 22–23. Reprinted by permission.

shopping situation. Similarly, an executive will stay at a convention hotel on a business trip and a resort on a family vacation.

Benefit Segmentation   Another approach for defining a target segment is to group customers seeking similar benefits; this is called **benefit segmentation.** In the multiattribute attitude model, customers in the same benefit segment would have a similar set of importance weights on the attributes of a store or a product. For example, customers who place high importance on fashion and style and low importance on price would form a fashion segment, whereas customers who place more importance on price would form a price segment.

EXHIBIT 4–10
JCPenney's Segments
for Women's Apparel

A. SEGMENT DESCRIPTION		
	Conservative	**Traditional**	**Update**

	Conservative	**Traditional**	**Update**
Size	23% of population 16% of total sales	38% of population 40% of total sales	16% of population 24% of total sales
Age	35–55 years old	25–49 years old	25–49 years old
Values	Conservative values Satisfied with present status	Traditional values Active, busy, independent, self-confident	Contemporary values Active, busy, independent, very self-confident
Employment	Has job, not career	Family- and job/career-oriented	Family- and job/career-oriented
Income	Limited disposable income	Considerable income	Considerable income
Benefits sought	Price-driven, reacts to sales Wants easy care and comfort Not interested in fashion Defines value as price, quality, fashion	Quality-driven, will pay a little more Wants traditional styling, seeks clothes that last Interested in newness Defines value as quality, fashion, price	Fashion-driven, expresses self through apparel Wants newness in color and style Shops often Defines value as fashion, quality, price

B. RETAIL OFFERING		

Retail Mix	**Conservative**	**Traditional**	**Update**
Pricing	Budget	Moderate	Moderate to better
Merchandise	Basic styles, easy-care fabrics	Traditional styling, good quality	Fashion-forward, more selection, comfortable fit, tailored look, newer colors
Brands	Alica, Cobble Lane, Motion, Cabin Creek	Joneswear, Worthington, Russ Togs, Halston, Wyndham, Hunt Club, Dockers	Claude, Mary McFadden, Counterparts, Jacqueline Ferrar
Merchandising approach	Price signing, "save stories," stack-out tables	Well-coordinated merchandise, collections, uncluttered displays, knowledgeable salespeople	Color statements, mannequins, theme areas

Benefit segments are very actionable. Benefits sought by customers in the target segment clearly indicate how retailers should design their offerings to appeal to the segment. But customers in benefit segments aren't easily identified or accessed. It's hard to look at a person and determine what benefits he or she is seeking. Typically, the audience for media used by retailers is described by demographics rather than by the benefits sought.

Composite Segmentation Approaches

As we've seen, no one approach meets all the criteria for useful customer segmentation. For example, segmenting by demographics and geography is ideal for identifying and accessing customers, but these characteristics often are unrelated to customers' needs. Thus, these approaches may not indicate the actions necessary to attract customers in these segments. On the other hand, knowing what benefits customers are seeking is useful for designing an effective retail offering; the problem is identifying which customers are seeking these benefits. For these reasons, **composite segmentation** plans use multiple variables to identify customers in the target segment. They define target customers by benefits sought, lifestyles, and demographics.

JCPenney's Segmentation of the Women's Apparel Market   The market for women's apparel is typically segmented into five categories: conservative, traditional, update, bridge, and designer or fashion-forward. The conservative segment is the most price-conscious and least fashion-oriented. The designer segment seeks just the opposite: fashion and style with little regard for price.

Penney customers are in the first three segments, but the firm is targeting its offering to customers in the traditional and updated segments. Exhibit 4–10A shows characteristics of each women's apparel segment. Note how these descriptions include segment size, customers' values, benefits they seek, and demographic information. Penney has different departments within each store and different private labels tailored to meet each segment's needs. Exhibit 4–10B lists Penney's retail offerings directed toward these segments.

SUMMARY

To satisfy customer needs, retailers must thoroughly understand how customers make store choice and purchase decisions and the factors they consider when deciding. This chapter describes the six stages in the buying process (need recognition, information search, evaluation of alternatives, choice of alternatives, purchase, and postpurchase evaluations) and how retailers can influence their customers at each stage. The importance of the stages depends on the nature of the customer's decision. When decisions are important and risky, the buying process is longer; customers spend more time and effort on information search and evaluating alternatives. When buying decisions are less important to customers, they spend little time in the buying process and their buying behavior may become habitual. The buying process of consumers is influenced by their personal beliefs, attitudes, and values and by their social environmental. The primary social influences are provided by the consumer's families, reference groups, and culture.

To develop cost-effective retail programs, retailers group customers into segments. Some approaches for segmenting markets are based on geography, demographics, geodemographics, lifestyles, usage situations, and benefits sought. Since each approach has its advantages and disadvantages, retailers typically define their target segment by several characteristics.

KEY TERMS

accessibility, *128*

actionability, *127*

benefit segmentation, *133*

brand loyalty, *110*

buying process, *108*

buying situation segmentation, *132*

buzz, *140*

compatibility, *142*

complexity, *142*

composite segmentation, *135*

consideration set, *120*

cross-shopping, *113*

culture, *125*

demographic segmentation, *130*

extended problem solving, *108*

external sources of information, *116*

fashion, *138*

functional needs, *112*

geodemographic segmentation, *130*

geographic segmentation, *129*

habitual decision making, *110*

hype, *140*

identifiability, *127*

impulse buying, *109*

information search, *115*

internal sources of information, *116*

knockoff, *140*

lifestyle, *131*

lifestyle segmentation, *131*

limited problem solving, *109*

mass-market theory, *140*

multiattribute attitude model, *117*

observability, *142*

postpurchase evaluation, *123*

psychological needs, *112*

PRIZM, *130*

psychographics, *131*

reference group, *124*

retail market segment, *127*

satisfaction, *123*

store loyalty, *110*

subculture, *126*

subculture theory, *141*

trialability, *142*

trickle-down theory, *140*

Values and Lifestyle Survey (VALS2), *131*

GET OUT & DO IT!

1. **GO SHOPPING** Go to a supermarket and watch people selecting products to put in their shopping carts. How much time do they spend selecting products? Do some people spend more time than others? Can you identify any characteristics of the people who take a while to make a decision?

2. **GO SHOPPING** Visit your favorite store to buy apparel and pretend that you are looking for some slacks to buy. Write down all of the things that the department store does to try to stimulate you to buy merchandise in addition to the slacks.

3. **CD-ROM EXERCISE** Use the CD-ROM that comes with the textbook to develop a multiattribute model describing your evaluation and decision concerning some relatively expensive product you bought recently, such as a car or consumer electronics. Open the multiattribute model exercise. List the attributes you considered in the left-hand column. List the alternatives you considered in the top row. Now fill in the importance weight for each attribute in the second column on the left (10—very important, 1—very unimportant). Now fill in your evaluation of each product on each attribute (10—excellent performance, 1—poor performance). Based on your weight and beliefs, the evaluation of each product is shown in the bottom row. Did you buy the product with the highest evaluation?

4. **INTERNET EXERCISE** Visit SRI's website at www.future.sri.com/VALS/presurvey. shtml. Click on the "Take the survey" button near the bottom of the page and answer the questions used to classify people into different VALS segments. When you have completed the survey and click on "submit," you should get a form that states your primary and secondary types. You can read descriptions of the types at www.future.sri. com/VALS/types.shtml. Type up a two-page, double-spaced report on what the survey said about you and whether you agree with it.

5. **INTERNET EXERCISE** Go to the following Internet sites offering information about the latest fashions: www.style. com *(Vogue)*, www.fashioninformation. com (U.K.), www.fashion.telegraph. co.uk (U.K.), www.t-style.com (Japan), and www. infomat.com/information/trends. Write a report describing the latest apparel fashions that are being shown by designers? Which of these fashions do you think will be popular? Why?

DISCUSSION QUESTIONS AND PROBLEMS

1. Does the customer buying process end when a customer buys some merchandise? Explain your answer.

2. What would get a consumer to switch from making a habitual choice decision to eat at Wendy's to making a limited or extended choice decision?

3. Reflect on your decision process in selecting a college. (Universities are nonprofit service retailers.) Was your decision-making process extensive, limited, or habitual? Did you go through all of the stages shown in Exhibit 4–2?

4. Why is geodemographic segmentation used by retailers to locate stores?

5. Any retailer's goal is to get a customer in its store to stop searching and buy a product at its outlet. How can a sporting goods retailer ensure that the customer buys athletic equipment at its outlet?

6. A family-owned used record store across the street from a major university campus wants to identify the various segments in its market. What approaches might the store owner use to segment its market? List two potential target market segments based on this segmentation approach. Then contrast the retail mix that would be most appropriate for two potential target segments.

7. Develop a demographic profile for two different target market segments for a hardware store. Outline the difference in the retail mixes that would be most appealing to each of these target markets.

8. How would you expect the buying decision process to differ when shopping on the Internet compared to shopping in a store?

9. Using the multiattribute attitude model, identify the probable choice of a local car dealer for a young single woman and for a retired couple with limited income (see the table that follows). What can the national retail chain do to increase the chances of the retired couple patronizing its dealership? You can use the multiattribute model template on the CD-ROM accompanying the book to analyze this information.

Performance Attributes	IMPORTANCE WEIGHTS		PERFORMANCE BELIEFS		
	Young Single Woman	Retired Couple	Local Gas Station	National Service Chain	Local Car Dealer
Price	2	10	9	10	3
Time to complete repair	8	5	5	9	7
Reliability	2	9	2	7	10
Convenience	8	3	3	6	5

SUGGESTED READINGS

Agins, Terri. *The End of Fashion: The Mass Marketing of the Clothing Business.* New York: William Morrow, 1999.

Birstwistle, Grete; Ian Clarke; and Paul Freathy. "Customer Decision Making in Fashion Retailing: A Segmentation Approach." *International Journal of Retail & Distribution Management* 26 (April–May 1998), pp. 147–55.

Hiu, Alice S. Y.; Noel Y. M. Siu; Charlie C. L. Wang; and Ludwig M. K. Chang. "An Investigation of Decision-Making Styles of Consumers in China." *Journal of Consumer Affairs* 35 (Winter 2001), pp. 326–46.

Kumar, V, and Anish Nagpal. "Segmenting Global Markets: Look before You Leap." *Marketing Research* 13 (Spring 2001), pp. 8–13.

Otnes, Cele, and Mary Ann McGrath. "Perceptions and Realities of Male Shopping Behavior." *Journal of Retailing* 77 (Spring 2001), pp. 111–37.

Sirgy, M. Joseph; Dhurv Grewal; and Tmara Mengleburg. "Retail Environment, Self-Congruity, and Retail Patronage: An Integrative Model and a Research Agenda." *Journal of Business Research* 49 (August 2000), pp. 127–38.

Sullivan, Pauline, and Ronald Savitt. "Store Patronage and Lifestyle Factors: Implications for Grocery Retailers." *International Journal of Retail & Distribution Management* 25 (August–September 1997), pp. 351–65.

Taubes, Gary. "Confessions of a Shopper." *Forbes,* April 6, 1998, pp. S66–70.

Underhill, Paco. *Why We Buy: The Science of Shopping.* New York: Simon & Schuster, 1999.

APPENDIX 4A   Consumer Behavior toward Fashion

Many retailers, particularly department and specialty stores, sell fashionable merchandise. To profitably sell this type of merchandise, retailers need to (1) understand how fashions develop and diffuse through the marketplace and (2) use operating systems that enable them to match supply and demand for this volatile merchandise. This appendix reviews the consumer behavior aspects of fashion. The operating systems for matching supply and demand for fashion merchandise are discussed in Chapter 13.

Fashion is a type of product or a way of behaving that is temporarily adopted by a large number of consumers because the product or behavior is considered to be socially appropriate for the time and place.[48] For example, in some social groups, it is or was fashionable to have brightly colored hair, play golf, wear a coat made from animal fur, have a beard, or go to an expensive health spa for a vacation. In many retail environments, however, the term *fashion* is typically associated with apparel and accessories.

CUSTOMER NEEDS SATISFIED BY FASHION

Fashion gives people an opportunity to satisfy many emotional and practical needs. Through fashions, people develop their own identity. They can use fashions to manage their appearance, express their self-image and feelings, enhance their egos, and make an impression on others. Through the years, fashions have become associated with specific lifestyles or roles people play. You wear different clothing styles when you are attending class, going out on a date, or interviewing for a job.

Fashion also can be used to communicate with others. For example, you might wear a classic business suit when interviewing for a job at Sears but more informal attire when interviewing for a job with Abercrombie & Fitch. These different dress styles would indicate your appreciation and understanding of the differences in the cultures of these firms.

People use fashions both to develop their own identity and to gain acceptance from others. These two benefits of fashion can be opposing forces. If you choose to wear something radically different, you will achieve recognition for your individuality but might not be accepted by your peers. To satisfy these conflicting needs, manufacturers and retailers offer a variety of designs and combinations of designs that are fashionable and still enable consumers to express their individuality.

WHAT CREATES FASHION?

Fashion is affected by economic, sociological, and psychological factors.

Economic Factors

Fashion merchandise is a luxury. It includes design details that go beyond satisfying basic functional needs. Thus, demand for fashion merchandise is greatest in countries with a high level of economic development and in market segments with the greatest disposable income.

Sociological Factors

Fashion changes reflect changes in our social environment, our feelings about class structure, the

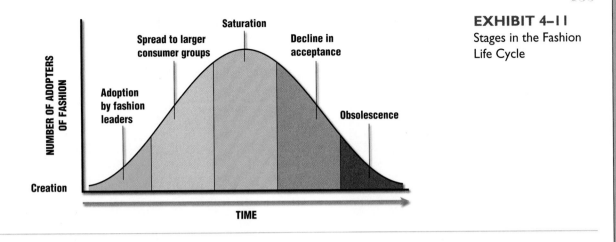

EXHIBIT 4–11
Stages in the Fashion
Life Cycle

roles of women and men, and the structure of the family. For example, time pressures arising from the increased number of women in the workforce have led to the acceptance of low-maintenance, wrinkle-resistant fabrics. Rising concern for the environment has resulted in natural fibers becoming fashionable and fur coats going out of fashion. Interest in health and fitness has made it fashionable to exercise and wear jogging clothes, leotards, and running shoes.

Psychological Factors

Consumers adopt fashions to overcome boredom. People get tired of wearing the same clothing and seeing the same furniture in their living room. They seek changes in their lifestyles by buying new clothes or redecorating their houses.

HOW DO FASHIONS DEVELOP AND SPREAD?

Fashions are not universal. A fashion can be accepted in one geographic region, country, or age group and not in another. In the 1970s, the fashion among young women was ankle-length skirts, argyle socks, and platform shoes, while older women were wearing pantsuits, double-breasted blazers, and midheeled shoes. During the 1970s, natural hairstyles were fashionable among African Americans, whereas cornrow hairstyles became fashionable in the early 1980s.

The stages in the fashion life cycle are shown in Exhibit 4–11. The cycle begins with the creation of a new design or style. Then some consumers recognized as fashion leaders or innovators adopt the fashion and start a trend in their social group. The fashion spreads from the leaders to others and is accepted widely as a fashion. Eventually, the fashion is accepted by most people in the social group and can become overused. Saturation and overuse set the stage for the decline in popularity and the creation of new fashions.

Creation

New fashions arise from a number of sources. Couture fashion designers are only one source of the creative inspirations. Fashions are also developed by creative consumers, celebrities, and even retailers. Courtney Cox and Jennifer Anniston, two actors in the TV program *Friends*, created an interest in wearing hair accessories such as banana clips and scrunchies. Britney Spears popularized low-rider jeans. The Sungil baby carrier was designed by American Ann Moore based on slings she saw African women use.[49]

REFACT

The bikini was designed by a former civil engineer, Louis Reard, in 1947.[50]

Adoption by Fashion Leaders

The fashion life cycle really starts when the fashion is adopted by leading consumers. These initial adopters of a new fashion are called *fashion leaders* or *innovators*. They are the first people to display the new fashion in their social group. If the fashion is too innovative or very different from currently accepted fashion, the style might not be

Britney Spears played a major role in creating the low-rider fashion.

The trickle-down theory suggests that new fashions start with upper-class people buying the latest fashions presented at designer shows.

accepted by the social group, thus prematurely ending the life cycle.

Three theories have been proposed to explain how fashion spreads within a society. The **trickle-down theory** suggests that the fashion leaders are consumers with the highest social status—wealthy, well-educated consumers. After they adopt a fashion, the fashion trickles down to consumers in lower social classes. When the fashion is accepted in the lowest social class, it is no longer acceptable to the fashion leaders in the highest social class.

Manufacturers and retailers stimulate this trickle-down process by copying the latest styles displayed at designer fashion shows and sold in exclusive specialty stores. These copies, referred to as **knock offs,** are sold at lower prices through retailers targeting a broader market. For example, shortly after the models walk down the runway at Prada's annual fashion show in Milan, Italy, displaying the latest designs using pajama prints and gold lamé, sewing machines are whirring 6,000 miles away in Hong Kong, churning out men's cotton "medallion" print shirts. Six month later, these shirts, which look a lot like Prada's pajama designs, appear in J. Crew's catalog and stores selling for $44.[51]

The second theory, the **mass-market theory,** suggests that fashions spread across social classes. Each social class has its own fashion leaders who play a key role in their own social networks. Fashion information "trickles across" social classes rather than down from the upper classes to the lower classes. Department stores use teen boards to stimulate diffusion of fashion across social classes. Social leaders are selected to be members of the board and promote the retailer and the merchandise sold in its stores.

However, consumers often can distinguish between hype and buzz. **Buzz** is genuine, street-level excitement about a hot new product; **hype** is artificially generated word of mouth, manufactured by public relations people. Sometimes hype and buzz converge. For example, shortly after the launch of the "Yo Quiero Taco Bell!" advertising campaign featuring the talking Latino Chihuahua, the dog started showing up on skateboards in Venice Beach, California, and on black-market T-shirts.[52]

The third theory, the **subculture theory,** is based on the development of recent fashions. Subcultures of mostly young and less affluent consumers, such as motorcycle riders and urban rappers, started fashions for such things as colorful fabrics, T-shirts, sneakers, jeans, black leather jackets, and surplus military clothing. These fashions started with people in lower-income consumer groups and "trickled up" to mainstream consumer classes. Nike employs "cool-hunters" to canvas subcultures and find out what will be the next hot sneaker.

The goth scene is an example of a subculture that has developed a unique style. It revolves around dark fashion and even darker, moody music performed by artists like Marilyn Manson. Hot Topics, a Pomona-based mall retailer, is the goth Gap, selling clothing and accessories to hip-hop kids, punks, and lounge rats. Some goth fashions are black lipstick, nail polish, and eyeliner as well as silver bracelets and earrings, black rubber pants, hooded capes, black fishnet leggings, and fitted, square-neck velvet gowns. Popular items at Hot Topics are two dolls, Misery and Tragedy, dressed in goth fashion—the Ken and Barbie dolls of goth.[54]

These theories of fashion development indicate that fashion leaders can come from many different places and social groups. In our diverse society, many types of consumers have the opportunity to be the leaders in setting fashion trends. Retailing View 4A.1 describes the challenges facing Kathy Bronstein, CEO of Wet Seal, as her company tries to predict the latest in fashion.

Predicting the Teen Trend | RETAILING VIEW

4A.1

Running an apparel specialty store chain catering to teenagers is not for the faint of heart. Teens are notoriously fickle—what's in one day is out the next. In the fashion retail business, the game is always changing. But Wet Seal has shown ability to generate sales increases and profits even in tough economic times.

Kathy Bronstein, Wet Seal's CEO, is a hands-on executive with a keen sense of fashion. She is decisive, confident, and demanding. As she looks through the collection slated for the stores in the summer, she is generally pleased with the peasant blouses, ruffled skirts, and slinky dresses on display. But a striped dress doesn't fit in. "Go away," she says, yanking the dress from the wall and tossing it on the floor.

To compete in this turbulent and competitive market, Wet Seal needs to anticipate the whims of teens and then cut its losses if it makes a bad choice. Sometimes the teen fashion apparel retailer has to back out of an order if the sales of the style start to slow down. But Bronstein says she is tough but fair. "We don't cancel orders unless the terms of the order have not been adhered to—that is delivery dates, quality, and fit."

Bronstein says her knack for knowing what will sell comes from instinct and experience. Wet Seal subscribes to at least four trend-predicting services, and she regularly visits Europe to stay in tune with global trends. Last fall, when she was walking down a street in Rome, a young Italian woman wearing a shirt crocheted at the wrist and neckline caught her eye. Six months later, sweaters with the crocheted details were selling well in Wet Seal stores.

This teenager at a Wet Seal store is looking to see if the retailer is in tune with the latest fashions.

Sources: Leslie Earnest, "Wet Seal CEO Fit for a Tough Business," *Los Angeles Times,* April 5, 2002, p. 1; and Marianne Wilson, "Wet Seal's Primo Performance," November 2001, *Chain Store Age,* p. 50.

Spread to Large Consumer Groups

During this stage, the fashion is accepted by a wider group of consumers referred to as *early adopters*. The fashion becomes increasingly visible, receives greater publicity and media attention, and is readily available in retail stores.

The relative advantage, compatibility, complexity, trialability, and observability of a fashion affect the time it takes the fashion to spread through a social group. New fashions that provide more benefits have a higher relative advantage compared to existing fashions, and these new fashions spread faster. Fashions are often adopted by consumers because they make people feel special. Thus, more exclusive fashions like expensive clothing are adopted more quickly in an affluent target market. On a more utilitarian level, clothing that is easy to maintain, such as wrinkle-free pants, will diffuse quickly in the general population.

Compatibility is the degree to which the fashion is consistent with existing norms, values, and behaviors. When new fashions aren't consistent with existing norms, the number of adopters and the speed of adoption are lower. Since the mid-1960s, the fashion industry has repeatedly attempted to revive the miniskirt. It has had only moderate success because the group of women with the most disposable income to spend on fashion are baby boomers, many of whom no longer find the miniskirt a relevant fashion for their family-oriented lifestyles.

Complexity refers to how easy it is to understand and use the new fashion. Consumers have to learn how to incorporate a new fashion into their lifestyle. For example, at times, tie manufacturers have tried to stimulate sales of bow ties but were unsuccessful because men had difficulty tying the knot.

Trialability refers to the costs and commitment required to initially adopt the fashion. For example, when consumers need to spend a lot of money buying a new type of expensive jewelry to be in fashion, the rate of adoption is slower than if the fashion simply requires wearing jewelry that the consumer already owns on a different part of the body.

Observability is the degree to which the new fashion is visible and easily communicated to others in the social group. Clothing fashions are very observable compared to fashions for the home, such as sheets and towels. It is therefore likely that a fashion in clothing will spread more quickly than a new color scheme or style for the bedroom.

Fashion retailers engage in many activities to increase the adoption and spread of a new fashion through their target market. Compatibility is increased and complexity is decreased by showing consumers how to coordinate a new article of fashion clothing with other items the consumer already owns. Trialability is increased by providing dressing rooms so customers can try on clothing and see how it looks on them. Providing opportunities for customers to return merchandise also increases trialability. Retailers increase observability by displaying fashion merchandise in their stores and advertising it in newspapers.

Saturation

In this stage, the fashion achieves its highest level of social acceptance. Almost all consumers in the target market are aware of the fashion and have decided to either accept or reject it. At this point, the fashion has become old and boring to many people.

Decline in Acceptance and Obsolescence

When fashions reach saturation, they have become less appealing to consumers. Because most people have already adopted the fashion, it no longer provides an opportunity for people to express their individuality. Fashion creators and leaders are beginning to experiment with new fashions. The introduction of a new fashion speeds the decline of the preceding fashion.

Section I describes retail management decisions; the different types of retailers, including how retailers are using multiple selling channels—stores, the Internet, and catalogs—to reach their customers; and factors that affect consumers' choice of retailers and merchandise. This broad overview of retailing provides the background information needed to develop and implement an effective retail strategy.

Section II discusses strategic decisions made by retailers.

Chapter 5 describes the development of a retail market strategy.

Chapter 6 examines the financial strategy associated with the market strategy.

Chapters 7 and 8 discuss the location strategy for retail outlets.

Chapter 9 looks at the firm's organization and human resource strategy.

●RETAILING STRATEGY

CHAPTER FIVE
RETAIL MARKET STRATEGY

CHAPTER SIX
FINANCIAL STRATEGY

CHAPTER SEVEN
RETAIL LOCATIONS

CHAPTER EIGHT
SITE SELECTION

CHAPTER NINE
HUMAN RESOURCE MANAGEMENT

CHAPTER TEN
INFORMATION SYSTEMS AND SUPPLY CHAIN MANAGEMENT

CHAPTER ELEVEN
CUSTOMER RELATIONSHIP MANAGEMENT

Chapter 10 examines systems used to control the flow of information and merchandise.

Chapter 11 details approaches that retailers take to manage relationships with their customers.

As outlined in Chapter 1, these decisions are strategic rather than tactical because they involve committing significant resources to developing long-term advantages over competition in a target market segment.

Sections III and IV review tactical decisions concerning merchandise and store management to implement the retail strategy. These implementation or tactical decisions impact a retailer's efficiency, but their impact is shorter term than the strategic decisions reviewed in Section II.

Retail Market Strategy

CHAPTER

Diann Mahood, Executive Vice President, Marketing, Rich's/Lazarus/ Goldsmith's, Division of Federated Department Stores

"Business is tough. You need have a strategy, a vision of where you want to go plus a strong organization, persistence, and patience in order to succeed." Diann has been in marketing for two years, after having grown up in the world of merchandising. She moved up through the ranks at Rich's/Lazarus/ Goldsmith's (RLG), holding positions in the stores, in the buying office, as divisional merchandise manager for several divisions, general merchandising manager, and most recently executive vice president of marketing. "RLG has a successful business strategy because it is definable and actionable, driving brand and demand simultaneously. Everyone in the division knows our strategy and can act on it.

"My consistent challenge in developing and implementing our division's strategy, is staying in touch with the customer. At RLG we really need to think like a customer and make everything simple for her. I must stay in touch with the target market (primarily college-educated females ages 25–54 in the upper-income bracket) and satisfy their particular wants and needs. By understanding who your customers are, you are able to anticipate their needs and desires. RLG must fulfill on our brand promise, 'you can trust our

QUESTIONS

● What is a retail strategy?

● How can a retailer build a sustainable competitive advantage?

● What steps do retailers go through to develop a strategy?

● What different strategic opportunities can retailers pursue?

tradition of quality, fashion and value with fast and friendly service.'

"A clearly defined brand promise and business strategy that supports the brand helps us on keeping focused on keeping and strengthening RLG's competitive niche. Since RLG has been around for over 150 years, our customers trust us and believe our products to be of superior value. Sometimes it can be difficult for well-established department stores to keep up with the trends and implement changes. However, it is highly essential to adapt to the constantly changing retail environment."

The growing intensity of retail competition due to the emergence of new formats and technology plus shifts in customer needs is forcing retailers to devote more attention to long-term strategic thinking. As the retail management decision-making process (discussed in Chapter 1) indicates, retailing strategy (Section II) is the bridge between understanding the world of retailing, that is, the analysis of the retail environment (Section I), and the more tactical merchandise management and store operations activities (Sections III and IV) undertaken to implement the retail strategy. The retail strategy provides the direction retailers need to take to deal effectively with their environment, customers, and competitors.[1]

The first part of this chapter defines the term *retail strategy* and discusses three important elements of retail strategy: the target market segment, retail format, and sustainable competitive advantage. Next, we outline approaches for building a sustainable competitive advantage. The chapter concludes with a discussion of the strategic retail planning process.

> **REFACT**
>
> The word *strategy* comes from the Greek word meaning the "art of the general."[2]

WHAT IS A RETAIL STRATEGY?

The term *strategy* is frequently used in retailing. For example, retailers talk about their merchandise strategy, promotion strategy, location strategy, and private-brand strategy. In fact, the term is used so commonly it appears that all retailing decisions are now strategic decisions. But retail strategy isn't just another expression for retail management.

Definition of Retail Market Strategy

A **retail strategy** is a statement identifying (1) the retailer's target market, (2) the format the retailer plans to use to satisfy the target market's needs, and (3) the bases upon which the retailer plans to build a sustainable competitive advantage.[3] The **target market** is the market segment(s) toward which the retailer plans to focus its resources and retail mix. A **retail format** is the retailer's mix (nature of merchandise and services offered, pricing policy, advertising and promotion program, approach to store design and visual merchandising, and typical location). A **sustainable competitive advantage** is an advantage over competition that can be maintained over a long time. Here are examples of retail strategies.

- Kohl's Corporation is an apparel powerhouse that sells midrange designer clothes and footwear in about 400 stores. Annual sales (2001) were $7,489 million.[4] The company, based in Menomonee Falls, Wisconsin, is a cross between a discount chain and chain of midlevel department stores. Kohl's offers department store brands with the conveniences typically provided by discount stores, including strip center locations, shopping carts, and centralized checkout counters. Its relatively small nonmall locations work to its advantage on several fronts. First, customers have easy access to both the store and merchandise in the store. Second, since the stores are physically separate from their mall competitors, it is more difficult for their customers to price-comparison shop. As a result, Kohl's can avoid major discounting.[5]

- Restoration Hardware targets the wealthiest 10 percent of U.S. consumers by offering high-end home furnishings in over 100 mall locations. Annual sales (2001) were $350 million.[6] What makes the stores particularly exciting is their merchandise assortment, which is peppered with whimsically nostalgic items that are sometimes risky investments. Consider, for instance, the 20,000 record players they ordered one year for the holiday season. The vintage black-and-tan apparatus, which unfolds from a 1960s-style suitcase, turned out to be the best-selling item in the company's over-20-year history. Also popular are retro cocktail shakers, shot glasses decorated with an optometrist's eye chart, and billowy "foot duvet" slippers.[7]

- Chico's, with about 300 stores and annual sales of approximately $400 million, specializes in comfortable, easy-to-wear apparel. Chico's sells casual offerings that are stylish but clearly designed with a woman aged 35 to 55, not a teenager, in mind. The company sells only its own brand and handles everything from sourcing, design, supervision of manufacturing, merchandising, and delivery. Although its loyalty program is only a few years old, it has over 1.2 million members who account for 80 percent of the company's sales. The average transaction for loyalty club members is more than $130, compared with under $90 for those not enrolled in the program. Chico's also delivers high-quality customer service. It tries to establish a person-to-person relationship with each of its customers.[8]

- Starbucks operates more than 5,000 stores and kiosks, selling gourmet coffee in Asia, Australia, Europe, and North America. Starbucks generates annual sales of over $2.6 billion (2001). The cafés provide an opportunity for people to take a break from their busy lives to savor specialty coffee drinks in a relaxing atmosphere. Friendly, knowledgeable counter servers, called *baristas* (Italian for bartenders), educate customers about Starbucks' products. The company has entered into some creative partnerships to put its cafés in Barnes & Noble stores, airports, and other nontraditional locations. It serves its coffee on United Airlines and on many college campuses. Licensing the brand name for other food products such as ice cream and soft drinks has increased its brand awareness.[9]

Want unusual home furnishings? Try Restoration Hardware.

Each of these retail strategies involves (1) selecting a target market segment and retail format and (2) developing sustainable competitive advantage that enables the retailer to reduce the level of competition it faces. Now let's examine these central concepts in a retail strategy.

TARGET MARKET AND RETAIL FORMAT

The **retailing concept** is a management orientation that focuses a retailer on determining the needs of its target market and satisfying those needs more effectively and efficiently than its competitors. Successful retailers satisfy the needs of customers in their target segment better than the competition does. The selection of a target market focuses the retailer on a group of consumers whose needs it will attempt to satisfy. The selection of a retail format outlines the retail mix to be used to satisfy needs of those customers. The retail strategy determines the markets in which a retailer will compete. Traditional markets, like a farmers' market, are places where buyers and sellers meet and make transactions—say, a consumer buys six ears of corn from a farmer. But in modern markets, potential buyers and sellers aren't necessarily located in one place. Transactions can occur without face-to-face interactions. For example, many customers contact retailers and place orders over the Internet using a computer.

We define a **retail market** not as a specific place where buyers and sellers meet but as a group of consumers with similar needs (a market segment) and a group of retailers using a similar retail format to satisfy those consumer needs.[10] Exhibit 5–1 illustrates a set of retail markets for women's clothing. A number of retail formats are listed down the left-hand column. Each format offers a different retail mix to its customers. Customer segments are listed in the exhibit's top row. As mentioned in Chapter 4, these segments can be defined in terms of the customers' geographic location, demographics, lifestyle, buying situation, or benefits sought. In this illustration, we divide the market into three fashion-related segments:

EXHIBIT 5–1 | Retail Market for Women's Apparel

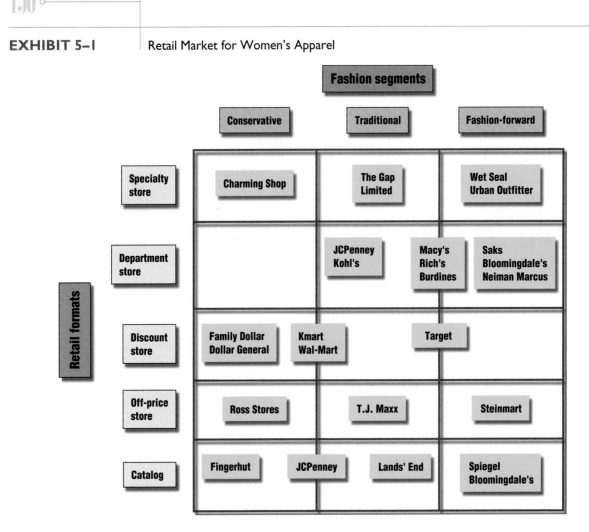

conservative, those who place little importance on fashion and are price-sensitive; traditional, those who want classic styles that are moderately priced; and fashion-forward, those who want the most fashionable merchandise. Each square of the matrix shown in Exhibit 5–1 describes a potential retail market where two or more retailers compete with each other. For example, Wal-Mart and Kmart stores in the same geographic area compete with each other using a discount store format targeting conservative customers, while Saks and Neiman Marcus compete against each other with a department store format targeting the fashion-forward segment.

The women's clothing market in Exhibit 5–1 is just one of several representations that could have been used. Retail formats could be expanded to include outlet stores and electronic retailing. Rather than being segmented by fashion orientation, the market could have been segmented using the other approaches described in Chapter 4. Although Exhibit 5–1 isn't the only way to describe the women's retail clothing market, it does illustrate how retail markets are defined in terms of retail format and customer market segment.

Basically, Exhibit 5–1's matrix describes the battlefield on which women's clothing retailers compete. The position in this battlefield indicates the first two elements of a retailer's strategy: its target market segment and retail format. Consider the situation confronting The Gap as it develops a retail strategy for the women's clothing market. Should The Gap compete in all 15 retail markets shown in Exhibit 5–1, or should it focus on a limited set of retail markets? If The Gap decides to focus on a limited set of markets, which should it pursue? The Gap's answers to these questions define its retail strategy and indicate how it plans to focus its resources.

BUILDING A SUSTAINABLE COMPETITIVE ADVANTAGE

The final element in a retail strategy is the retailer's approach to building a sustainable competitive advantage. Any business activity that a retailer engages in can be a basis for a competitive advantage; but some advantages are sustainable over a long period of time, while others can be duplicated by competitors almost immediately.[11] For example, it would be hard for Starbucks to get a long-term advantage over Seattle's Best Coffee by simply offering the same coffee specialties at lower prices. If Starbucks' lower prices were successful in attracting customers, Seattle's Best would know what Starbucks had done and would match the price reduction. Similarly, it's hard for retailers to develop a long-term advantage by offering broader or deeper merchandise assortments. If broader and deeper assortments attract a lot of customers, competitors will simply go out and buy the same merchandise for their stores.

Establishing a competitive advantage means that a retailer builds a wall around its position in a retail market. This makes it hard for competitors outside the wall to contact customers in the retailer's target market. If the retailer has built a wall around an attractive market, competitors will attempt to break down the wall. Over time, all advantages will be eroded due to these competitive forces; but by building high, thick walls, retailers can sustain their advantage, minimize competitive pressure, and boost profits for a longer time. Thus, establishing a sustainable competitive advantage is the key to long-term financial performance.

Seven important opportunities for retailers to develop sustainable competitive advantages are (1) customer loyalty, (2) location, (3) human resource management, (4) distribution and information systems (5) unique merchandise, (6) vendor relations, (7) and customer service. Exhibit 5–2 shows the aspects of these sources for competitive advantage that are more and less sustainable. Let's look at each of these approaches.

Customer Loyalty

Customer loyalty means that customers are committed to shopping at the retailer's locations. Many of the bases for maintaining a sustainable competitive advantage discussed in this section also help attract and maintain loyal customers. For instance, having dedicated employees, unique merchandise, and superior customer service all help solidify a loyal customer base. But having loyal customers is, in and of itself, an important method of sustaining an advantage over competitors.

EXHIBIT 5–2
Methods for
Developing
Competitive Advantage

	SUSTAINABILITY OF ADVANTAGE	
Sources of Advantage	**Less Sustainable**	**More Sustainable**
Customer loyalty (Chapters 11 and 16)	Habitual repeat purchasing; repeat purchases because of limited competition in the local area	Building a brand image with an emotional connection with customers; using databases to develop and utilize a deeper understanding of customers
Location (Chapters 7 and 8)		Convenient locations
Human resource management (Chapter 9)	More employees	Committed, knowledgeable employees
Distribution and information systems (Chapter 10)	Bigger warehouses; automated warehouses	Shared systems with vendors
Unique merchandise (Chapters 12 to 14)	More merchandise; greater assortment; lower price; higher advertising budgets; more sales promotions	Exclusive merchandise
Vendor relations (Chapter 14)	Repeat purchases from vendor due to limited alternatives	Coordination of procurement efforts; ability to get scarce merchandise
Customer service (Chapter 19)	Hours of operation	Knowledgeable and helpful salespeople

Loyalty is more than simply liking one retailer over another.[12] Loyalty means that customers will be reluctant to patronize competitive retailers. For example, loyal customers will continue to shop at Restoration Hardware even if Pottery Barn opens a store nearby and provides a slightly superior assortment or slightly lower prices. Some ways that retailers build loyalty are by (1) developing clear and precise positioning strategies and (2) creating an emotional attachment with customers through loyalty programs.[13]

Positioning   A retailer builds customer loyalty by developing a clear, distinctive image of its retail offering and consistently reinforcing that image through its merchandise and service. **Positioning** is the design and implementation of a retail mix to create an image of the retailer in the customer's mind relative to its competitors.[14]

Positioning emphasizes that the image in the customer's mind (not the retail manager's mind) is critical. Thus, the retailer needs to research what its image is and make sure that its image is consistent with what customers in its target market want. A perceptual map is frequently used to represent the customer's image and preference for retailers.

Exhibit 5–3 is a hypothetical perceptual map of retailers selling women's clothing in the Washington, DC, area. The two dimensions in this map, fashion/ style and service, represent the two primary characteristics that consumers in this example use in forming their impression of retail stores. Perceptual maps are developed so that the distance between two retailers' positions on the map indicates how similar the stores appear to consumers. For example, Neiman Marcus and Bloomindale's are very close to each other on the map because consumers in this illustration see them as offering similar service and fashion. On the other hand, Nordstrom and Kmart are far apart, indicating consumers think they're quite

Hypothetical Perceptual Map of Women's Apparel Market in Washington, DC | **EXHIBIT 5–3**

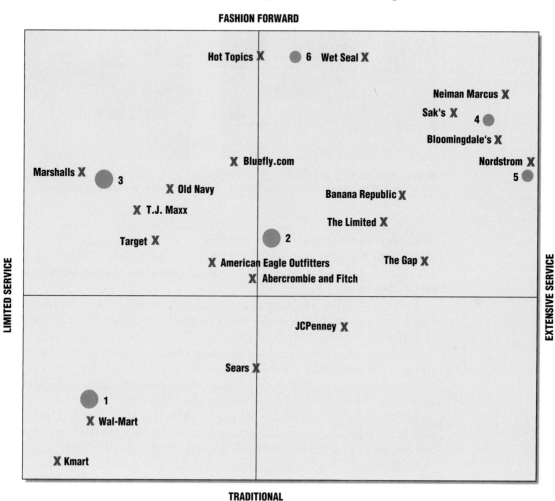

different. Note that stores close to each other compete vigorously with each other because consumers feel they provide similar benefits.

According to this example, The Limited has an image of offering moderately priced fashionable women's clothing with good service. T. J. Maxx offers more fashionable clothing with less service. Sears is viewed as a retailer offering women's clothing that's not fashionable and has relatively limited service.

The ideal points (marked by green dots on the map) indicate characteristics of an ideal retailer for consumers in different market segments. For example, consumers in segment 3 prefer a retailer that offers high-fashion merchandise with low service, whereas consumers in segment 1 want less expensive/more traditional apparel and aren't concerned about service. The ideal points are located so that the distance between the retailer's position (marked with a blue "x") and the ideal point indicates how consumers in the segment evaluate the retailer. Retailers that are closer to an ideal point are evaluated more favorably by the

Neiman Marcus (left) and Bloomingdale's (right) are close to each other on the perceptual map in Exhibit 5–3 because consumers see them as offering similar service and fashion.

consumers in the segment than retailers located farther away. Thus, consumers in segment 6 prefer Wet Seal and Hot Topics to Neiman Marcus because they are more fashion forward and their target customers do not require such high service levels.

Starting in 2000, The Gap began a streak of monthly sales declines for stores that have been open at least a year. The chief executive officer of the company at that time, Millard "Mickey" Drexler, had many explanations, including staying with outdated styles too long and then overreacting by filling the stores with too many trendy looks. Customers have since complained that they can't get the same assortment of high-quality basics—button-down shirts and khaki pants—that made The Gap famous. Probably the biggest problem is that The Gap's success spawned lower-priced imitators, including its own lower-priced chain, Old Navy, which is closer to segment 2 than The Gap. At the same time, Target has become more fashion forward. So both Target and Old Navy are vying for customers in the huge segment two in Exhibit 5–3. Additionally, The Gap is positioned too far away from segment 5 to compete successfully with Nordstrom on service. In fact, its sister chain, Banana Republic, is closer to segment 5 and is therefore also siphoning sales from The Gap.[15] Finally, The Gap has two strong competitors for segment 2 with Abercrombie and Fitch and American Eagle Outfitters.

Loyalty Programs   Loyalty programs are part of an overall customer relationship management (CRM) program that is examined in Chapter 10. These programs are prevalent in retailing, from airlines and department stores to the corner pizza shop.

Customer loyalty programs work hand-in-hand with CRM. Members of loyalty programs are identified when they buy because they use some type of loyalty card. The purchase information is stored in a huge database known as a **data warehouse.** From this data warehouse, analysts determine what types of merchandise and services certain groups of customers are buying. Using this information, retailers tailor their offerings to better meet the needs of their loyal customers. For instance, by analyzing its database, Safeway may identify customers who buy expensive wines and gourmet food. Having identified these customers, Safeway could develop a special promotion focusing on preparing a gourmet meal with recipes, a list of ingredients, and coupons offering a discount for some of the products. Retailing View 5.1 describes how a Canadian menswear chain uses customer information to build store loyalty through customer service and by targeting its promotional activities to improve customer satisfaction.

Location

The classic response to the question What are the three most important things in retailing? is "location, location, and location." Location is the critical factor in consumer selection of a store. It is also a competitive advantage that is not easily duplicated. For instance, once Walgreens has put a store at the best location of an intersection, CVS is relegated to the second best-location. Finding great locations is particularly challenging in older urban locations, where space is finite and tenant turnover is relatively slow.

Starbucks has developed a national presence and a strong competitive advantage with its location strategy. It conquers one area of the city at a time and then expands in the region, saturating a major market before entering a new market. For example, there were over 100 Starbucks outlets in the Seattle area before the company expanded to a new region. Starbucks will frequently open several stores close to one another. It has two stores on two corners of the intersection of

Harry Rosen Knows a Lot about Its Customers | RETAILING VIEW

5.1

Harry Rosen operates 18 stores in Canada, where it sells high-end clothing from Ermenegildo Zegna, Samuelsohn, Hugo Boss, and others, as well as nine Hugo Boss boutiques across the United States. This retailer with annual sales of $150 million, Canadian, uses information to improve customer service and build long-term relationships. Each Harry Rosen salesperson can access the firm's data warehouse with customer information from any POS terminal in any store. The database tells what the customer has bought in the past and also provides personal information. All sales associates are urged to contribute to the database. If a wife buys a birthday gift for her husband, salespeople are encouraged to find out his birthday and how old he is and include this information in the system rather than in their personal notebook.

The information system improves customer service and targeting of retail promotions. For example, when garments are left in the store for alterations, the system tracks their progress and electronically notifies the salesperson of any delay so the salesperson can relay this information to the customer. Heavy spenders are easily identified and invited to special promotional events. The system is also used to sell slow-moving merchandise. For example, a store may have too many size-44–short suits. A salesperson can go to a terminal, generate a list of all customers who have bought 44-short suits in the past few months, and contact them. When new merchandise arrives, the salesperson can identify customers who have bought that type of merchandise in the past and inform them of the new merchandise.

Sources: "Harry Rosen: The Company" March 25, 2002, www.harryrosen.com/company/e_index.html; Andree Conrad, "Harry Rosen Unveils IT Refit," *DNR* 31, no. 5 (January 2001), p. 10; and "State of the Industry: Customer Management," *Chain Store Age*, August 1998, pp. 20–24.

Harry Rosen operates 18 stores in Canada where it sells high-end clothing from Ermenegildo Zegna, Samuelsohn, Hugo Boss, and others.

Robson and Thurlow in Vancouver. Starbucks has such a high density of stores that it lets the storefront promote the company and does very little media advertising. In heavily trafficked downtown districts, Starbucks often operates kiosks in commercial buildings. Neighborhood locations that attract customers in the evenings and on weekends are important because they become part of the path of people's weekly shopping experience or their route to work.

By concentrating its locations, Starbucks creates a market presence that is difficult for competition to match. In addition, multiple locations facilitate scale economies that enable frequent deliveries, thereby ensuring fresh merchandise. Chapters 7 and 8 discuss this approach to developing a sustainable competitive advantage.

Human Resource Management

Retailing is a labor-intensive business. Employees play a major role in providing services for customers and building customer loyalty. Knowledgeable and skilled employees committed to the retailer's objectives are critical assets that support the success of companies such as Southwest Airlines, Whole Foods, Home Depot, and Men's Wearhouse.

Recruiting and retaining great employees does not come easy. Chapter 9 examines how retailers gain a sustainable competitive advantage by developing programs to motivate and coordinate employee efforts, by providing appropriate incentives, by fostering a strong and positive organizational culture and environment, and by managing diversity.

Distribution and Information Systems

All retailers strive for efficient operations. They want to get their customers the merchandise they want, when they want it, in the quantities that are required, at a lower delivered cost than their competitors. By so doing, they will satisfy their customers' needs and, at the same time, either provide them with lower-priced merchandise than their competition or decide to use the additional margin to attract customers from competitors by offering even better service, merchandise assortments, and visual presentations.

Retailers can achieve these efficiencies by developing sophisticated distribution and information systems. For instance, merchandise sales information flows seamlessly from Wal-Mart to its vendors like Procter & Gamble to facilitate quick and efficient merchandise replenishment. Wal-Mart has the largest data warehouse in the world, enabling the company to fine-tune merchandise assortments on a store-by-store, category-by-category basis. Wal-Mart's distribution and information systems have enabled the retailer to be the lowest-cost provider of merchandise in every market in which it competes.

Unique Merchandise

It is difficult for retailers to develop a competitive advantage through merchandise because competitors can purchase and sell the same popular national brands. But many retailers realize a sustainable competitive advantage by developing **private-label brands** (also called *store brands*), which are products developed and marketed by a retailer and available only from that retailer. For example, if you want to buy a Kenmore washer and dryer, you have to buy it from Sears. Issues concerning the development of store-branded merchandise are discussed in Chapter 14. As discussed in Chapter 3, the low search associated with electronic shopping increases the importance of unique merchandise as a source of competitive advantage.

Vendor Relations

By developing strong relations with vendors, retailers may gain exclusive rights (1) to sell merchandise in a region, (2) to obtain special terms of purchase that are not available to competitors who lack such relations, or (3) to receive popular merchandise in short supply. Relationships with vendors, like relationships with customers, are developed over a long time and may not be easily offset by a competitor.[16] For example, Ahold, the Holland-based food retailer, works very closely with Swiss food giant Nestlé to bring its customers products tailored to meet the tastes of customers in local markets.[17] Chapter 14 examines how retailers work with their vendors.

Sears has a strong private label program. If you want to buy a Kenmore washer/dryer, you have to buy it from Sears.

Customer Service

Retailers also build a sustainable competitive advantage by offering excellent customer service.[18] But offering good service consistently is difficult. Customer service is provided by retail employees—and humans are less consistent than machines. Retailers that offer good customer service instill its importance in their employees over a long period of time. It becomes part of the retailer's organizational culture, a topic examined in Chapter 9.

Some retailers offer services customers don't necessarily want, such as banking or dry cleaning, yet make customers jump through hoops to return merchandise. Most customers simply want retailers to trust them and tend to basic requests. In the past, for example, Home Depot focused primarily on offering a broad assortment and, secondarily, on offering superior service. Now the retailer dominates its industry with world-class service.[19]

It takes considerable time and effort to build a tradition and reputation for customer service, but good service is a valuable strategic asset. Once a retailer has earned a service reputation, it can sustain this advantage for a long time because it's hard for a competitor to develop a comparable reputation. Chapter 19 discusses how retailers develop a service advantage.

Multiple Sources of Advantage

To build a sustainable advantage, retailers typically don't rely on a single approach such as low cost or excellent service.[20] They need multiple approaches to build as high a wall around their position as possible. For example, McDonald's success is based on providing customers with a good value that meets their expectations, having good customer service, maintaining good vendor relations,

McDonald's has great locations all over the world, including this one in Paris, France.

and having great locations. By doing all of these things right, McDonald's has developed a huge cadre of loyal customers.

McDonald's has always positioned itself as providing fast food at a good value—customers get a lot for not much money. Its customers don't have extraordinary expectations. They don't expect a meal prepared to their specific tastes. But customers do expect and get hot, fresh food that is reasonably priced.

McDonald's customers also don't expect friendly table service with linen tablecloths and sterling silverware. Their service expectations, which are typically met, are simple. By developing a system for producing its food and using extensive training for store managers, McDonald's reduces customers' waiting time. This training also means that customers will be handled quickly and courteously.

McDonald's vendor relationships ensure that it will always have quality ingredients. Its distribution and inventory control systems enable it to make sure that the ingredients are available at each location.

Finally, McDonald's has a large number of great locations. It is important for convenience products, such as fast food, to have lots of locations. Given its market power, it has been successful in finding and opening stores in prime retail locations. In every great city in which it operates around the world, McDonald's has outstanding locations.

By developing unique capabilities in a number of areas, McDonald's has built a high wall around its position as a service retailer, using a fast-food format directed toward families with young children.

Each of the retail strategies outlined at the beginning of the chapter involves multiple sources of advantage. For example, Starbucks has developed a strong competitive position through its excellent product line with a strong brand name, high-quality service provided by committed employees and excellent and plentiful locations. Retailing View 5.2 describes the Container Store, a retail chain that built a sustainable competitive advantage through unique merchandise, excellent customer service, strong customer relations, and easily accessible locations.

GROWTH STRATEGIES

Four types of growth opportunities that retailers may pursue (market penetration, market expansion, retail format development, and diversification) are shown in Exhibit 5–4.[21] The vertical axis indicates the synergies between the retailer's present markets and growth-opportunity markets—whether the opportunity involves markets the retailer is presently pursuing or new markets. The horizontal axis indicates the synergies between the retailer's present retail mix and the growth-opportunity retail mix—whether the opportunity exploits the retailer's present format or requires a new format.

Market Penetration

A **market penetration opportunity** involves directing efforts toward existing customers by using the present retailing format. The retailer can achieve this growth strategy either by attracting consumers in its current target market who don't shop at its outlets or by devising strategies that induce current customers to visit a store more often or to buy more merchandise on each visit.

Approaches for increasing market penetration include attracting new customers by opening more stores in the target market and keeping existing stores open for longer hours. Other approaches are displaying merchandise to increase impulse purchases and training salespeople to cross-sell. **Cross-selling** means that sales associates in one department attempt to sell complementary merchandise from other departments to their customers. For example, a sales associate

REFACT

A 4 percent increase in weekly store visits by customers can result in a 58 percent increase in profits for a typical grocery store.[22]

The Container Store—Building a Competitive Advantage in Selling Products to Make Life Simpler   RETAILING VIEW

5.2

A customer enters a Container Store and is approached by a cheerful salesperson who asks if she can be of help. "My wife loves romance novels," says the customer. "She's got them scattered all over the house. I need something to keep them in." Customers come into the Container Store with problems, or challenges, as the company likes to call them. The salespeople work with them to find solutions.

The privately held, 22-unit company with annual sales of over $200 million boasts annual sales per square foot of $400, more than three times the industry average. It also operates an innovative website (www.containerstore.com) that allows customers to plan a project, organize a space, and purchase merchandise. The Container Store sells products to organize people's lives. Multipurpose shelving and garment bags are available to organize closets. Portable file cabinets and magazine holders create order in home offices. Backpacks, modular shelving, and CD holders can make dorm rooms less cluttered. Recipe holders, bottles, jars, and recycling bins bring harmony to kitchens.

How has the Container Store developed a sustainable competitive advantage over the last 25 years? The company positions its stores as being "problem solvers," not just order fillers. Although many of the stores' items are available elsewhere, few competitors offer such an extensive assortment under one roof, coupled with great customer service. The Container Store places a lot of emphasis on customer service. Considerable time is spent educating sales associates about the merchandise. Then sales associates are empowered to use their own intuition and creativity to solve customer problems.

Over the years, the company has developed strong vendor relations. Most of its vendors' primary focus has

The Container Store spends considerable time educating sales associates about its unique merchandise that simplifies its customers' lives.

been to manufacture products for industrial use. Yet, over the years, the company has worked closely with its vendors to develop products that are appropriate for the home.

Finally, with over 20 stores in the United States, its on-line store, and plans to grow at 20 percent per year, the Container Store is accessible to most Americans.

Sources: Debby Garbato Stankevich, "Finding a Place in Home Retailing," *Retail Merchandiser*, January 2002, pp. 18–21; and Keith L. Alexander, "Cultivating a Culture," *Washington Post*, April 21, 2002, p. H01.

EXHIBIT 5–4
Growth Opportunities

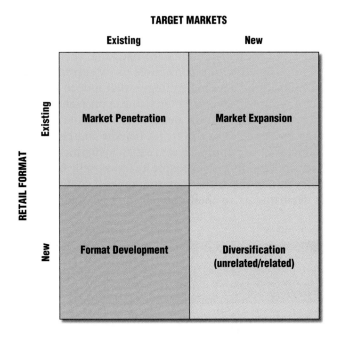

who has just sold a dress to a customer will take the customer to the accessories department to sell her a handbag or scarf that will go with the dress. More cross-selling increases sales from existing customers.

Market Expansion

A **market expansion opportunity** employs the existing retail format in new market segments. For example, Abercrombie & Fitch (A&F) Co.'s primary target market is college kids, not high-schoolers. Since college-age people don't particularly like to hang out with teens, A&F is rolling out a new, lower-priced chain called Hollister Co. Although the merchandise and ambience are slightly different than A&F, the retail format is essentially the same.[23] When the French hypermarket chain Carrefour expanded into other European and South American countries, it was also employing a market expansion growth strategy because it was entering a new geographic market segment with essentially the same retail format.[24]

Retail Format Development

A **retail format development opportunity** involves offering a new retail format—a format with a different retail mix—to the same target market. For example, Barnes & Noble, a specialty book store-based retailer, exploited a format development opportunity when it began selling books to its present target market over the Internet (www._barnesandnoble.com). Another example of a retail format development opportunity is when a retailer adds merchandise categories, such as when Amazon.com began selling CDs, videos, and electronics in addition to books. Adjusting the type of merchandise or services offered typically involves a small investment; whereas providing an entirely different format, such as a store-based retailer going into electronic retailing, requires a much larger and riskier investment.

Diversification

A **diversification opportunity** is when a retailer introduces a new retail format directed toward a market segment that's not currently served. Diversification opportunities are either related or unrelated.

Related versus Unrelated Diversification In a **related diversification opportunity,** the present target market or retail format shares something in common with the new opportunity. This commonality might entail purchasing from the same vendors, using the same distribution or management information system, or advertising in the same newspapers to similar target markets. In contrast, an **unrelated diversification** lacks any commonality between the present business and the new business.

Foot Locker, the world's largest retailer of athletic footwear and apparel (formerly known as Venator), became involved in several unrelated diversification endeavors in the 1990s.[25] For instance, it owned some Burger King franchises and Afterthoughts accessory stores. After realizing that athletic apparel and footwear was its core business, it dumped businesses that didn't fit the mold and streamlined and remodeled the remaining stores. Unrelated diversifications are considered to be very risky and often don't work, as was the case with Foot Locker. As a result, most retailers apply the old adage "stick to your knitting" and seek growth opportunities that are closer in nature to their current operations.

Foot Locker now operates Foot Locker stores, Lady Foot Locker, Kids Foot Locker, Champs Sports, and Foot Locker stores in Europe. Foot Locker is currently involved in a related diversification by opening several Nike Jordan stores in the United States. As Nike's biggest account, Foot Locker delivers 26 to 28 percent of Nike's total domestic revenue and benefits from the limited distribution of its premiere products.

After several attempts at unrelated diversification, Foot Locker decided to stick to its core business, athletic shoes.

Vertical Integration **Vertical integration** is diversification by retailers into wholesaling or manufacturing.[26] Examples of vertical integration are The Limited's acquisition of Mast Industries (a trading company that contracts for private-label manufacturing) and Zale Corporation's manufacturing of jewelry. When a retailer integrates by purchasing or otherwise partnering with distribution or manufacturing concerns, it is engaging in *backward integration* because the requisite skills are different from those usually associated with retailing. Additionally, retailers and manufacturers have different customers—the immediate customers for a manufacturer's merchandise are retailers, whereas a retailer's customers are consumers. Thus, a manufacturer's marketing activities are very different from those of a retailer. Note that some manufacturers and designers like Nike, Prada, and Ralph Lauren *forward integrate* into retailing.

REFACT

Brooks Brothers, a men's specialty store chain, sold the rights to the Polo brand name to Ralph Lauren.[27]

Strategic Opportunities and Competitive Advantage

Typically, retailers have the greatest competitive advantage in opportunities that are similar to their present retail strategy. Thus, retailers would be most successful engaging in market penetration opportunities that don't involve entering new, unfamiliar markets or operating new, unfamiliar retail formats.

When retailers pursue market expansion opportunities, they build on their strengths in operating a retail format and apply this competitive advantage in a new market. Thus, those retailers that successfully expand globally are able to translate what they do best—their core competencies—to a new culture and market. We will discuss global growth opportunities in the next section.

A retail format development opportunity builds on the retailer's reputation and success with present customers. Even if a retailer doesn't have experience and skills in operating the new format, it hopes to attract its loyal customers to it. For example, as discussed in Chapter 3, retailers that have successfully developed multichannel strategies by seamlessly integrating stores, the Internet, and catalogs provide extra convenience and multiple opportunities for their current customers to shop.

Retailers have the least competitive advantage when they pursue diversification opportunities. Thus, these opportunities are generally risky and often don't work, as was the case with Venator/Foot Locker. Vertical integration, however, albeit risky, often has overwhelming benefits for those large and sophisticated retailers that can invest heavily for the long term. By making direct investments in distribution or manufacturing facilities, these retailers have total control over the entire marketing channel.

GLOBAL GROWTH OPPORTUNITIES

REFACT

Of the largest 100 retailers worldwide, over 89 percent are from France, Germany, Japan, the United Kingdom, and the United States.[28]

International expansion is one form of a market expansion strategy. The most commonly targeted regions are Mexico, Latin America, Europe, China, and Japan. International expansion is risky because retailers using this growth strategy must deal with differences in government regulations, cultural traditions, different supply chain considerations, and language. The types of retailers that successfully compete globally are discussed first, followed by a look at some of the pitfalls of global expansion. Then the key success factors for global expansion are examined. Finally, the strategies for entering a nondomestic market are evaluated.

Who Is Successful and Who Isn't

Retailers—particularly specialty store retailers with strong brand names such as The Gap and Zara, and food and discount retailers such as Wal-Mart, Carrefour, Royal Ahold, and Metro AG—may have a strong competitive advantage when competing globally.

Some U.S. retailers have a competitive advantage in global markets because the American culture is emulated in many countries, particularly among young people. Due to the rising prosperity and rapidly increasing access to cable TV with American programming, fashion trends in the United States are spreading to young people in emerging countries. The global MTV generation prefers

Coke to tea, athletic shoes to sandals, Chicken McNuggets to rice, and credit cards to cash.[29] In the last few years, China's major cities have sprouted American stores and restaurants, including KFC, Pizza Hut, and McDonald's. Shanghai and Beijing each have more than two dozen Starbucks. Coffee was not the drink of choice until Starbucks came to town. But these Chinese urban dwellers go there to impress a friend or because it's a symbol of a new kind of lifestyle. Although Western products and stores have gained a reputation for high quality and good service in China, in some ways it is the American culture that many Chinese want.[30]

Coffee was not the drink of choice until Starbucks came to China. But now Shanghai and Beijing each have more than two dozen Starbucks.

On the other hand, some large European and Japanese retailers have considerably more experience operating retail stores in nondomestic markets. For example, France's Carrefour has been operating stores in nondomestic markets for almost 30 years. It is very good at adapting its hypermarket format to local tastes. The company buys many products locally and hires and trains local managers, passing the power and authority to them quickly. Even though Wal-Mart has a more efficient distribution system, Carrefour has competed effectively against Wal-Mart in Brazil and Argentina.[32]

Category killers and hypermarket retailers may be particularly suited to succeed internationally because of the expertise they've already developed at home. First, these retailers are leaders in the use of technology to manage inventories, control global logistical systems, and tailor merchandise assortments to local needs. For instance, firms such as Home Depot provide consumers with an assortment of brand-name merchandise procured from sources around the world. This advantage is particularly valuable if brand-name merchandise is important to consumers. Second, retailers like Wal-Mart and Carrefour have become the low-price provider in every market they enter because of their buying economies of scale and efficient distribution systems. Third, despite idiosyncrasies in the international environment, category killers and hypermarket retailers have developed unique systems and standardized formats that facilitate control over multiple stores. These systems and procedures should work well regardless of the country of operation. Fourth, because of the category killer's narrow assortment and focused strategy, communications across national boundaries and cultures are specifically focused, which improves management coordination. Finally, at one time, people felt that consumers outside the United States were used to high levels of personalized service and would not accept the self-service concept employed by category killers and hypermarket retailers. However, consumers around the globe are willing to forgo the service for lower prices.[33] Retailing View 5.3 examines Costco's strategy for success in Japan.

Global expansion is often difficult and full of pitfalls. For instance, The Gap is pulling back on some of its European store base. U.K.-based Marks & Spencer (M&S) has sold off its U.S. operations, Brooks Brothers, as part of an overall withdrawal from markets outside Britain. Its plans to close its 18 stores in France demonstrates the difficulty of operating in foreign markets. M&S found it was in violation of French labor laws when it announced the closures. The laws require prior consultation with the employees. U.K.-based J. Sainsbury, on the other hand, got caught up in a geopolitical conflict. It has abandoned expansion plans

REFACT

The world's largest retailers are likely to be global players. Thirty-eight out of the top 50 global retailers operate in more than one country. The implication: Eventually one must go global to keep growing.[31]

REFACT

Among the top 100 retailers worldwide, the average company had operations in 7.2 countries at the end of 2000, compared to 2.8 in 1986.[36]

into Egypt because of a consumer boycott and heavy losses. The Egyptians believe that the company is pro-Israel, despite Sainsbury's denials.[34]

Keys to Success

Four characteristics of retailers that have successfully exploited international growth opportunities are (1) globally sustainable competitive advantage, (2) adaptability, (3) global culture, and (4) deep pockets.[35] A hypothetical evaluation of international growth opportunities is described in the appendix to this chapter.

Globally Sustainable Competitive Advantage Entry into nondomestic markets is most successful when the expansion opportunity is consistent with the

---

RETAILING VIEW | Costco, Japanese Style

5.3

Spiraling deflation, shrinking consumer spending, and white-hot competition—that's the state of play in the Japanese retail market. So why would any U.S. company want in? For one thing, Japan's retail market is the second-largest in the world, after the United States. For another, deregulation has finally leveled the playing field for foreign companies and domestic rivals. If a company can succeed in this market, it's virtually guaranteed success anywhere else. Following are some strategies Costco is using in Japan.

- *Open multiple stores.* Costco's current two-store operation in Japan is not profitable. But six or seven stores will generate the scale economies necessary to be profitable. Real estate prices have come down, so the chain can find sites that are relatively inexpensive.

- *Learn from past experience.* Costco learned a few lessons from its earlier ventures in Asia. First, it doesn't think of Asia as one big market. Each market is quite distinct. But, second, it can learn from the similarities. For instance, a lot of its start-up experiences in Taiwan and South Korea were similar to Japan: things like real estate negotiations and supplier relations. Also, Japanese and Korean commercial and labor laws are very similar.

- *Recognize different operating cost structures.* Operating costs, such as utilities, service, and maintenance expenses are high in Japan, compared to in the United States. Therefore, sales per store need to be higher to be profitable.

- *Adjust the assortment to meet local needs.* Japanese people are very particular about food packaging. They will buy in bulk, but not in the large packages like those purchased in the United States. So Costco is experimenting with smaller multipacks.

Costco has taken the plunge by opening two stores in Japan.

- *Buy direct.* Japan's distribution channels are fraught with multiple layers of wholesalers, which can be inefficient and keep prices unnecessarily high. To avoid this problem, Costco purchases 86 percent of its merchandise directly from manufacturers. If a manufacturer won't sell directly to the company because it wants to protect its long-standing relationships with other retailers, Costco goes elsewhere.

- *Sell "Made in the U.S.A."* U.S. imports have done very well, and demand is growing. Costco's top-selling U.S. items are nonfood: clothing, sporting goods like basketball hoops, jewelry, and housewares.

Source: "Costco: Still Finding Its Way in Japan," *Businessweek Online,* March 25, 2002. www.businessweek.com

retailer's core bases of competitive advantage. Some core competitive advantages for global retailers are shown below:

Core Advantage	Global Retailer
Low cost; efficient operations	Wal-Mart, Carrefour
Strong private brands	Royal Ahold, Ikea, Starbucks
Fashion reputation	The Gap, Zara, H&M (Hennes & Mauritz)
Category dominance	Office Depot, Home Depot
Image	Disney, Warner Brothers

Thus, Wal-Mart and Carrefour are successful in international markets where price plays an important role in consumer decision making and distribution infrastructure is available to enable these firms to exploit their logistical capabilities. On the other hand, The Gap and Zara are successful in international markets that value fashionable merchandise.

Adaptability   While successful global retailers build on their core competencies, they also recognize cultural differences and adapt their core strategy to the needs of local markets.[37] Color preferences, the preferred cut of apparel, and sizes differ across cultures. For example, in China, white is the color of mourning and brides wear red dresses. Food probably has the greatest diversity of tastes. Ahold operates under nearly 20 brand names around the globe, including Superdiplo in Spain, ICA in Sweden, Albert Heijn in the Netherlands, and Stop & Shop and Giant in the United States. Ahold firmly believes that, like politics, all retailing is local, as customers develop loyalty toward a store brand they've known for decades. Ahold's mantra: "Everything the customer sees, we localize. Everything they don't see, we globalize."[38]

Selling seasons also vary across countries. The Gap's major U.S. selling season is back-to-school in August; however, this is one of the slowest sales periods in Europe because most people are on vacation. Back-to-school in Japan is in April.

Store designs need to be adjusted. In some cultures, social norms dictate that men's and women's clothing cannot be displayed next to each other. In the United States, the standard practice is to place low-priced, private-label merchandise on the shelf to the right of national brands, assuming that customers' natural eye movement is from left to right. This merchandising approach does not work in cultures where people read from right to left or up and down. IKEA initially tried to sell its Scandinavian beds in the United States before discovering they were the wrong size for American bed linens.

Government regulations and cultural values also affect store operations. Some differences such as holidays, hours of operation, and regulations governing part-time employees and terminations are easy to identify. Other factors require a deeper understanding. For example, the Latin American culture is very family oriented. Thus, U.S. work schedules need to be adjusted so that employees can have more time with their families. Boots, a U.K. drugstore chain, has the checkout clerks in its Japanese stores standing up because it discovered that Japanese shoppers found it offensive to pay money to a seated clerk. Retailers in Germany must recycle packaging materials sold in their stores.[39] Also in Germany, seasonal sales can be held only during specific weeks and apply to only specific product categories, and discounts are limited. Unlimited guarantees are generally forbidden, which is why Lands' End may not describe such a guarantee on its goods in an ad and may only talk about it if customers ask for it first.[40]

Global Culture   To be global, one has to think globally. It is not sufficient to transplant a home-country culture and infrastructure into another country. In this regard, Carrefour is truly global. In the early years of its international expansion, it started in each country slowly, which reduced the company's ethnocentrism. Further enriching its global perspective, Carrefour has always encouraged rapid development of local management and retains few expatriates in its overseas operations. Carrefour's management ranks are truly international. One is just as likely to run across a Portuguese regional manager in Hong Kong as a French or Chinese one. Finally, Carrefour discourages the classic overseas "tour of duty" mentality often found in U.S. firms. International assignments are important in themselves, not just as stepping-stones to ultimate career advancement back in France. The globalization of Carrefour's culture is perhaps most evident in the speed with which ideas flow throughout the organization. A global management structure of regional "committees," which meet regularly, advances the awareness and implementation of global best practices.

The proof of Carrefour's global commitment is in the numbers. It has had almost 30 years of international experience in 21 countries—both developed and developing.[41]

Deep Pockets   Expansion into international markets requires a long-term commitment and considerable upfront planning. Retailers find it very difficult to generate short-term profit when they make the transition to global retailing. Wal-Mart's $8.2 billion cash flow and 48 percent share of the $225 billion discount store industry in the United States provides the ability to maintain this type of staying power.[42]

Entry Strategies

Four approaches that retailers take when entering nondomestic markets are direct investment, joint venture, strategic alliance, and franchising.[43]

Direct Investment   **Direct investment** involves a retail firm investing in and owning a division or subsidiary that builds and operates stores in a foreign country. This entry strategy requires the highest level of investment and exposes the retailer to significant risks, but it has the highest potential returns. One advantage of direct investment is that the retailer has complete control of the operations. For example, McDonald's chose this entry strategy for the U.K. market, building a plant to produce buns when local suppliers could not meet its specifications.

Joint Venture   A **joint venture** is formed when the entering retailer pools its resources with a local retailer to form a new company in which ownership, control, and profits are shared. Examples of successful joint ventures are Royal Ahold (the Netherlands) and Velox Holdings (Argentina); Metro AG (Germany) and Koc Group's Migros (Turkey); Carrefour and Sabanci Holding (Turkey); Metro AG (Germany) and Marubeni (Japan); and Monsoon (United Kingdom) and Charming Shoppes (United States).[44]

A joint venture reduces the entrant's risks. Besides sharing the financial burden, the local partner understands the market and has access to resources—vendors and real estate. Many foreign countries, such as China, require joint ownership, although these restrictions may loosen as a result of World Trade Organization (WTO) negotiations.[45] Problems with this entry approach can arise if the partners disagree or the government places restrictions on the repatriation of profits.

Strategic Alliance.   A **strategic alliance** is a collaborative relationship between independent firms. For example, a foreign retailer might enter an international market through direct investment but develop an alliance with a local firm to perform logistical and warehousing activities.

Franchising   Franchising offers the lowest risk and requires the least investment. However, the entrant has limited control over the retail operations in the foreign country, potential profit is reduced, and the risk of assisting in the creation of a local domestic competitor is increased. U.K.-based Marks & Spencer, for example, has 136 franchised stores in 27 countries, including Cyprus (8), Greece (28), Indonesia (10), and Thailand (10).[46]

The rest of this chapter outlines steps in developing a retail strategy.

THE STRATEGIC RETAIL PLANNING PROCESS

The **strategic retail planning process** is the set of steps a retailer goes through to develop a strategic retail plan[47] (see Exhibit 5–5). It describes how retailers select target market segments, determine the appropriate retail format, and build sustainable competitive advantages. As indicated in Exhibit 5–5, it is not always necessary to go through the entire process each time an evaluation is performed (in step 7). For instance, a retailer could evaluate its performance and go directly to step 2, conduct a situation audit.

The planning process can be used to formulate strategic plans at different levels within a retail corporation. For example, the corporate strategic plan of American Express indicates how resources are to be allocated across the corporation's various businesses such as credit cards and travel services. Each business within American Express has its own strategic plan, and then strategies are developed for products within a business such as for the American Express Gold card.

As we discuss the steps in the retail planning process, we will apply each of them to the planning process Kelly Bradford is undertaking. Kelly owns Gifts To Go, a small, two-store chain in the Chicago area. One of her 1,000-square-foot stores is in the downtown area; the other is in an upscale suburban mall. The target market for Gifts To Go is upper-income men and women looking for gifts in the $50-to-$500 price range. The stores have an eclectic selection of merchandise, including handmade jewelry and crafts, fine china and glassware, perfume, watches, writing instruments, and a variety of one-of-a-kind items. The stores have developed a number of loyal customers who are contacted by sales associates when family anniversaries and birthdays come up. In many cases, customers have a close relationship with a sales associate and have enough confidence in the associate's judgment that they tell the associate to pick out the gift. The turnover of Gifts To Go sales associates is low for the industry, because Bradford treats

EXHIBIT 5–5
Steps in the Strategic
Retail Planning Process

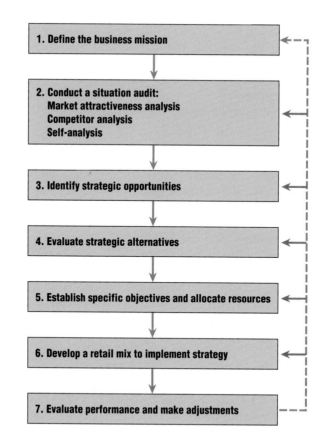

associates as part of the family. The company pays for medical and dental insurance for all associates. Sales associates share in the profits of the firm.

Step 1: Define the Business Mission

The first step in the strategic retail planning process is to define the business mission. The **mission statement** is a broad description of a retailer's objectives and the scope of activities it plans to undertake.[48] The objective of a publicly held firm is to maximize its stockholders' wealth by increasing the value of its stock and paying dividends.[49] Owners of small, privately held firms frequently have other objectives, such as achieving a specific level of income and avoiding risks rather than maximizing income.

The mission statement should define the general nature of the target segments and retail formats that the firm will consider. For example, the mission statement of an office supply category specialist, "Serve the customer, build value for shareholders, and create opportunities for associates," is too broad. It does not provide a sense of strategic direction.

In developing the mission statement, managers must answer five questions: (1) What business are we in? (2) What should be our business in the future? (3) Who are our customers? (4) What are our capabilities? (5) What do we want to accomplish? Gifts To Go's mission statement is "The mission of Gifts To Go is to be the leading retailer of higher-priced gifts in Chicago and provide a stable income of $100,000 per year for the owner."

MARKET FACTORS

Size
Growth
Seasonality
Business cycles

COMPETITIVE FACTORS

Barriers to entry
Bargaining power of vendors
Competitive rivalry

ENVIRONMENTAL FACTORS

Technology
Economic
Regulatory
Social

ANALYSIS OF STRENGTHS AND WEAKNESSES

Management capabilities
Financial resources
Locations
Operations
Merchandise
Store management
Customer loyalty

EXHIBIT 5–6
Elements in a Market Analysis

Since the mission statement defines the retailer's objectives and the scope of activities it plans to undertake, Gifts To Go's mission statement indicates its management won't consider retail opportunities outside the Chicago area, won't consider opportunities for selling low-priced gifts, and won't consider opportunities that would jeopardize its ability to generate $100,000 in annual income.[50]

Step 2: Conduct a Situation Audit

After developing a mission statement and setting objectives, the next step in the strategic planning process is to do a situation audit. A **situation audit** is an analysis of the opportunities and threats in the retail environment and the strengths and weaknesses of the retail business relative to its competitors. The elements in the situation analysis are shown in Exhibit 5–6.[51]

Market Factors   Some critical factors related to consumers and their buying patterns are market size and growth, sales cyclicality, and seasonality. These factors are also addressed in Chapter 8. Market size, typically measured in retail sales dollars, is important because it indicates a retailer's opportunity for generating revenues to cover its investment. Large markets are attractive to large retail firms. But they are also attractive to small entrepreneurs because they offer more opportunities to focus on a market segment. Some retailers, however, prefer to concentrate on smaller markets. Cato, for instance, sells value-priced women's fashion in 700 stores located in 24 southeastern U.S. states, primarily in smaller markets.[52]

Growing markets are typically more attractive than mature or declining markets. For example, retail markets for specialty stores are growing faster than those for department stores. Typically, margins and prices are higher in growing markets because competition is less intense than in mature markets. Since new customers are just beginning to patronize stores in growing markets, they may not have developed strong store loyalties and thus might be easier to attract to a new store. Some retailers, however, prefer to locate in mature markets. These locations are attractive when the customer base is stable and competition is weak. Carrefour's success can, in part, be attributed to its astute global growth strategy in which new stores were located in markets where competition was relatively weak.

Firms are often interested in minimizing the business cycle's impact on their sales. Thus, retail markets for merchandise affected by economic conditions (such as cars and major appliances) are less attractive than retail markets unaffected by economic conditions (such as food). In general, markets with highly seasonal sales are unattractive because a lot of resources are needed to accommodate the peak season, but then resources are underutilized the rest of the year. For example, to minimize these problems due to seasonality, ski resorts promote summer vacations to generate sales during all four seasons.

To do an analysis of the market factors for Gifts To Go, Kelly Bradford went to the library to get information about the size, growth, cyclicity, and seasonality of the gift market in general and, more specifically, in Chicago. Based on her analysis, she concluded that the market factors were attractive. The market for more expensive gifts was large, growing, and not vulnerable to business cycles. The only negative aspect was the high seasonality of gifts, with peaks at Valentine's Day, June (due to weddings), Christmas, and other holidays.

Competitive Factors   The nature of the competition in retail markets is affected by barriers to entry, bargaining power of vendors, and competitive rivalry.[53] Retail markets are more attractive when competitive entry is costly. **Barriers to entry** are conditions in a retail market that make it difficult for firms to enter the market. These conditions include scale economies, customer loyalty, and availability of great locations.

Scale economies are cost advantages due to a retailer's size. Markets dominated by large competitors with scale economies are typically unattractive. For example, a small entrepreneur would avoid becoming an office supply category specialist because the market is dominated by three large firms: Staples, Office Depot, and OfficeMax. These firms have a considerable cost advantage over the entrepreneur because they can buy merchandise cheaper and operate more efficiently by investing in the latest technology and spreading their overhead across more stores. Retailing View 5.4 discusses how some small retailers develop sustainable advantages over national chains with larger-scale economies.

Similarly, retail markets dominated by a well-established retailer that has developed a loyal group of customers offer limited profit potential. For example, Home Depot's high customer loyalty in Atlanta makes it hard for a competing home improvement center to enter the Atlanta market.

Finally, the availability of locations may impede competitive entry. Staples, for instance, attributes part of its success over its rivals in the northeastern United States to its first-mover advantage. Since the Northeast has a preponderance of mature but stable retail markets, finding new locations is more difficult there than it is in most of the rest of the United States. Staples started in the Northeast and was therefore able to open stores in the best available locations.

Entry barriers are a double-edged sword. A retail market with high entry barriers is very attractive for retailers presently competing in that market, because those barriers limit competition. However, markets with high entry barriers are unattractive for retailers not already in the market. For example, the lack of good retail locations in Hong Kong makes this market attractive for retailers already in the region, but less attractive for retailers desiring to enter the market.

Another competitive factor is the **bargaining power of vendors.** Markets are less attractive when a few vendors control the merchandise sold in it. In these situations, vendors have an opportunity to dictate prices and other terms (like delivery dates), reducing the retailer's profits. For example, the market for retailing fashionable cosmetics is less attractive because two suppliers, Estée Lauder (Estée Lauder, Clinique, Prescriptives, Aramis, Tommy Hilfiger, M.A.C., and Origins)[54] and L'Oréal (Maybelline, Giorgio Armani, Helena Rubinstein, Lancôme, Lanvin, and Ralph Lauren brands),[55] provide the most desired premium brands. Since department stores need these brands to support a fashionable image, these suppliers have the power to sell their products to retailers at high prices.

The final industry factor is the level of competitive rivalry in the retail market. **Competitive rivalry** is the frequency and intensity of reactions to actions undertaken by competitors. When rivalry is high, price wars erupt, employee raids occur, advertising and promotion expenses increase, and profit potential falls. Conditions that may lead to intense rivalry include (1) a large number of competitors that are all about the same size, (2) slow growth, (3) high fixed costs, and (4) the lack of perceived differences between competing retailers.

Competing against the Giants RETAILING VIEW

5.4

Small retailers can effectively compete head-to-head against industry giants like Wal-Mart and Home Depot. These large retailers with buying power can sell merchandise at lower prices than small retailers. However, small retailers can compete effectively by (1) offering unique merchandise tailored to the local community, (2) giving customers a personal touch, and (3) developing ties with the local community. For example, Toys "R" Us and Wal-Mart are primarily interested in selling well-known toys and games at low prices and letting their manufacturers advertise how the toys work. But many toys are too complicated to explain in a 30-second commercial. Playmobil construction toys are only sold through independent toy stores, because these stores are interested in setting up Playmobil playpens on their floors so parents and children can have "an out-of-box experience."

At Classic Creations (a Venice, Florida, jewelry shop) the owners of the store, rather than a commissioned salesperson, wait on customers. By offering personal attention, they build customer loyalty. For example, a man recently bought a $4,000 engagement ring because of a recommendation he received from his parents, who had their wedding bands redesigned there several years ago.

Independent fishing tackle shops compete against discount giants like Wal-Mart and Sports Authority by offering special services. In Sarasota, Florida, Mr. CB's Bait & Tackle teams up with local charter boat captains to offer seminars and discounted trips. The captains get the fishing trips and Mr. CB's sells the fishing gear. K & K True Value Hardware in Bettendorf, Iowa, focuses on fishing experts who want to make their own lures. The store stocks the raw materials: spinner blades in 14 sizes, tinsel in 40 colors, chicken feathers, deer fur, weights, and hooks.

Mr. CB's Bait and Tackle store in Sarasota, Florida competes with Wal-Mart and Sports Authority by offering superior service.

Bookseller's in Fridley, Minnesota, competes against Barnes & Noble by specializing in books on Christianity. Customers include pastors, Sunday school teachers, and people who seek spiritual guidance. For example, the owner suggested some books for a mother concerned about her son's drug problems. The son is now an honors student in college.

Sources: Ken Clark, "Hammering away at Service," *Chain Store Age* 77, no. 8 (August 2001), pp. 50–54; Scott Clark, "Yes, the Small Business Can Fight Wal-Mart," *Arizona Business Gazette,* November 9, 2000, p. 4; and Reginald A. Litz and Alice C. Stewart, "The Late Show: The Effects of After-Hours Accessibility on the Performance of Small Retailers," *Journal of Small Business Management* 38, no. 1 (January 2000), pp. 1–26.

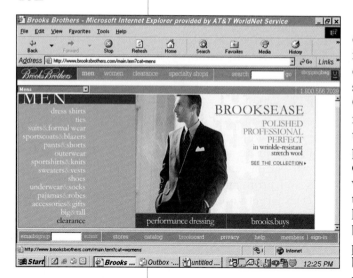

Do you buy your clothes at Brooks Brothers? Do your parents? How can they appeal to the casual dresser and keep their traditional customer base?

When Kelly Bradford started to analyze the competitive factors for Gifts To Go, she realized that identifying her competitors wasn't easy. While there were no gift stores carrying similar merchandise and price points in the Chicago area, there were a number of other retailers where a customer could buy these types of gifts. She identified her primary competitors as department stores, craft galleries, catalogs, and Internet retailers. Kelly felt there were some scale economies in developing customer databases to support gift retailing. The lack of large suppliers meant that vendors' bargaining power wasn't a problem and competitive rivalry was minimal because the gift business was not a critical part of the department store's overall business. In addition, merchandise carried by the various retailers offered considerable opportunity to differentiate the retailers.

Environmental Factors   Environmental factors that affect market attractiveness span technological, economic, regulatory, and social changes.[56] When a retail market is going through significant changes in technology, present competitors are vulnerable to new entrants that are skilled at using the new technology. For example, in the late 1990s, many traditional retailers were nervously scrambling to define their space in e-tailing. Thousands of pure-play e-tailers with technological sophistication flooded the Internet. Many of the bricks-and-mortar retailers invested heavily in Internet technology and were able to integrate the Internet with their other selling channels.

Some retailers may be more affected by economic conditions than others. Neiman Marcus and Nordstrom employ many well-paid salespeople to provide high-quality customer service. When unemployment is low, their costs may increase significantly, as salespeople's wages rise due to the difficulty in hiring qualified people. But retailers like Wal-Mart that provide little service and have much lower labor costs as a percentage of sales may be less affected by low unemployment.

Government regulations can reduce the attractiveness of a retail market. For example, it is difficult for large retailers to open new stores in France due to size restrictions placed on new stores. Also, many local governments within the United States have tried to stop Wal-Mart from entering their market in an attempt to protect locally owned retailers.[57]

Finally, trends in demographics, lifestyles, attitudes, and personal values affect retail markets' attractiveness. Brooks Brothers, for example, has been struggling with several trends simultaneously. Known for traditional suits and button-down shirts, the company has not learned how to appeal to younger customers and businesspeople who prefer to dress casually without alienating its traditional customer base.[58]

Retailers need to answer three questions about each environmental factor:

1. What new developments or changes might occur, such as new technologies and regulations or different social factors and economic conditions?

2. What is the likelihood that these environmental changes will occur? What key factors affect whether these changes will occur?

3. How will these changes impact each retail market, the firm, and its competitors?

Kelly Bradford's primary concern when she did an environmental analysis was the potential growth of bricks-and-mortar and catalog retailers into e-tailing operations. Gifts seem to be ideal for multichannel retailing. Customers can get ideas by visiting the store or browsing through a catalog. Then they can order the item over the Internet. Since many Gifts To Go customers are buying presents for other people, the convenience of placing shipping instructions on the Internet is appealing. Kelly also felt that multichannel retailers could effectively collect information about customers and then target promotions and suggestions to them when gift-giving occasions arose.

Strengths and Weaknesses Analysis   The most critical aspect of the situation audit is for a retailer to determine its unique capabilities in terms of its strengths and weaknesses relative to the competition.[59] A **strengths and weaknesses analysis** indicates how well the business can seize opportunities and avoid harm from threats in the environment. Exhibit 5–7 outlines issues to consider in performing a self-analysis.

In performing a self-analysis, the retailer considers the potential areas for developing a competitive advantage listed below and answers the following questions:

   At what is our company good?
   In which of these areas is our company better than our competitors?
   In which of these areas does our company's unique capabilities provide a sustainable competitive advantage or a basis for developing one?

EXHIBIT 5–7
Strengths and
Weaknesses Analysis

 MANAGEMENT CAPABILITY
Capabilities and experience of top
  management
Depth of management—capabilities of
  middle management
Management's commitment to firm

 MERCHANDISING CAPABILITIES
Knowledge and skills of buyers
Relationships with vendors
Capabilities in developing private brands
Advertising and promotion capabilities

FINANCIAL RESOURCES
Cash flow from existing business
Ability to raise debt or equity financing

STORE MANAGEMENT CAPABILITIES
Management capabilities
Quality of sales associates
Commitment of sales associates to firm

 OPERATIONS
Overhead cost structure
Quality of operating systems
Distribution capabilities
Management information systems
Loss prevention systems
Inventory control system

LOCATIONS

 CUSTOMERS
Loyalty of customers

Here is Kelly Bradford's analysis of Gifts To Go's strengths and weaknesses:

Management capability	Limited—Two excellent store managers and a relatively inexperienced person helped Kelly with buying merchandise. An accounting firm kept the financial records for the business but had no skills in developing and utilizing customer databases.
Financial resources	Good—Gifts To Go had no debt and a good relationship with a bank. Kelly had saved $255,000 that she had in liquid securities.
Operations	Poor—While Kelly felt Gifts To Go had relatively low overhead, the company did not have a computer-based inventory control system or management and customer information systems. Her competitors (local department stores and catalog and Internet retailers) certainly had superior systems.
Merchandise capabilities	Good—Kelly had a flair for selecting unique gifts, and she had excellent relationships with vendors providing one-of-a-kind merchandise.
Store management capabilities	Excellent—The store managers and sales associates were excellent. They were very attentive to customers and loyal to the firm. Employee and customer theft were kept to a minimum.
Locations	Excellent—Both of Gifts To Go's locations were excellent. The downtown location was convenient for office workers. The suburban mall location was at a heavily trafficked juncture.
Customers	Good—While Gifts To Go did not do the sales volume in gifts done in department stores, the company had a loyal base of customers.

Step 3: Identify Strategic Opportunities

After completing the situation audit, the next step is to identify opportunities for increasing retail sales. Kelly Bradford presently competes in gift retailing using a specialty store format. The strategic alternatives she is considering are defined in terms of the squares in the retail market matrix shown in Exhibit 5–1 and the growth strategies in Exhibit 5–4. Note that some of these growth opportunities involve a redefinition of her mission.

Market penetration	1. Increase size of present stores and amount of merchandise in stores. 2. Open additional gift stores in Chicago area.
Market expansion	1. Open gift stores outside the Chicago area (new geographic segment). 2. Sell lower-priced gifts in present stores or open new stores selling low-priced gifts (new benefit segment).
Retail format development	1. Sell apparel and other nongift merchandise to same customers in same or new stores. 2. Sell similar gift merchandise to same market segment using the Internet.
Diversification	1. Manufacture craft gifts. 2. Open apparel stores targeted at teenagers. 3. Open a category specialist selling low-priced gifts.

Step 4: Evaluate Strategic Opportunities

The fourth step in the strategic planning progress is to evaluate opportunities that have been identified in the situation audit. The evaluation determines the retailer's potential to establish a sustainable competitive advantage and reap long-term profits from the opportunities under evaluation. Thus, a retailer must focus on opportunities that utilize its strengths and its area of competitive advantage. For example, expertise in developing private-label apparel is one of The Gap's sources of competitive advantage. Thus, The Gap would positively evaluate opportunities that involve development of private-label merchandise. Some areas retailers consider when evaluating new opportunities are shown in Exhibit 5–7.

Both the market attractiveness and the strengths and weaknesses of the retailer need to be considered in evaluating strategic opportunities. The greatest investments should be made in market opportunities where the retailer has a strong competitive position. A formal method for performing such an analysis is described in the appendix to this chapter. Here's Kelly's informal analysis:

Opportunity	Market Attractiveness	Competitive Position
Increase size of present stores and amount of merchandise in stores.	Low	High
Open additional gift stores in Chicago area.	Medium	Medium
Open gift stores outside the Chicago area (new geographic segment).	Medium	Low
Sell lower-priced gifts in present stores or open new stores selling low-priced gifts (new benefit segment).	Medium	Low
Sell apparel and other nongift merchandise to same customers in same or new stores.	High	Low
Sell similar gift merchandise to same market segment using the Internet.	High	Medium
Manufacture craft gifts.	High	Low
Open apparel stores targeted at teenagers.	High	Low
Open a category specialist selling low-price gifts.	High	Low

Step 5: Establish Specific Objectives and Allocate Resources

After evaluating the strategic investment opportunities, the next step in the strategic planning process is to establish a specific objective for each opportunity. The retailer's overall objective is included in the mission statement. The specific objectives are goals against which progress toward the overall objective can be measured. Thus, these specific objectives have three components: (1) the performance sought, including a numerical index against which progress may be measured, (2) a time frame within which the goal is to be achieved, and (3) the level of investment needed to achieve the objective. Typically, the performance levels are financial criteria such as return on investment, sales, or profits.

Step 6: Develop a Retail Mix to Implement Strategy

The sixth step in the planning process is to develop a retail mix for each opportunity in which investment will be made and to control and evaluate performance. Decisions related to the elements in the retail mix are discussed in Sections III and IV.

Step 7: Evaluate Performance and Make Adjustments

The final step in the planning process is evaluating the results of the strategy and implementation program. If the retailer is meeting or exceeding its objectives, changes aren't needed. But if the retailer fails to meet its objectives, reanalysis is needed. Typically, this reanalysis starts with reviewing the implementation programs; but it may indicate that the strategy (or even the mission statement) needs to be reconsidered. This conclusion would result in starting a new planning process, including a new situation audit. Retailing View 5.5 illustrates how changes in the environment forced bowling alley operators to reevaluate their strategy, target a new market segment, and tailor their offering to meet the needs of this new segment.

Strategic Planning in the Real World

The planning process in Exhibit 5–5 indicates that strategic decisions are made in a sequential manner. After the business mission is defined, the situation audit is performed, strategic opportunities are identified, alternatives are evaluated, objectives are set, resources are allocated, the implementation plan is developed, and, finally, performance is evaluated and adjustments are made. But actual planning processes have interactions among the steps. For example, the situation

---

Cosmic Bowling   RETAILING VIEW

5.5

Those who came of age in the 40s, 50s, and 60s made recreational and competitive bowling a major part of American social life. But the prevailing image of a bowling alley for those growing up in the 70s, 80s, and 90s can be summed up in one word: B-O-R-I-N-G. Young children were hauled to the bowling alley by baby boomer parents. By the time those youngsters became teenagers, they didn't want anything more to do with an activity that seemed to them to be dominated by out-of-shape, middle-aged guys in tacky matching shirts. Without an enthusiastic new generation of bowlers to look forward to, bowling seemed ready for the history books.

In today's bowling centers, laser lights, neon, glow-in-the-dark alleys, fog machines, and a top-quality sound system are as important as bowling balls and pins. Turn down the lights, and turn on the special effects, and the center is transformed into a nightclub. DJs with portable microphones work the crowd. Video cameras are installed so customers can see all the action by watching monitors placed throughout the center, or the monitors can show music videos.

Brunswick developed the "cosmic bowling" concept to attract young people to its centers. The nightclub atmosphere draws lots of high school students who aren't old enough to attend clubs. But they also appeal to youngsters and oldsters. Theme nights are used to attract different segments by varying the type of music played such as retro, rap, and country.

The increased revenues from cosmic bowling are due to more efficient space utilization as well as attracting a new market segment. Typically, bowling centers have few customers from 10:00 P.M. to 2:00 A.M. Cosmic bowling enthusiasts fill the centers during this dead time with people who pay a premium to party.

REFACT

Bowling is the number one participant sport in the United States.[60]

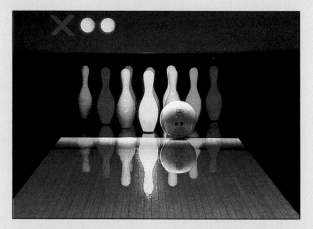

Brunswick developed cosmic bowling to attract a younger generation to bowling when its target market of league bowlers declined.

Sources: Douglas Trattner, "Late-Night Bowling That's Out of This World," *Cleveland Plain Dealer,* April 26, 2002, p. 12; and Scott Berg, "Changing Lanes Late at Night," *Washington Post,* December 14, 2001, p. T67.

audit may uncover a logical alternative for the firm to consider, even though this alternative isn't included in the mission statement. Thus, the mission statement may need to be reformulated. Development of the implementation plan might reveal that resource allocation to the opportunity is insufficient to achieve the objective. In that case, the objective would need to be changed or the resources would need to be increased, or the retailer might consider not investing in the opportunity at all.

SUMMARY

Strategic planning is an ongoing process. Every day, retailers audit their situations, examine lifestyle trends, study new technologies, and monitor competitive activities. But the retail strategy statement isn't changed every year or every six months. The strategy statement is reviewed and altered only when major changes in the retailer's environment or capabilities occur.

When a retailer undertakes a major reexamination of its strategy, the process for developing a new strategy statement may take a year or two. Potential strategic directions are generated by people at all levels of the organization. These ideas are evaluated by senior executives and operating people to ensure that the eventual strategic direction is profitable in the long run and can be implemented.

A retailer's long-term performance is largely determined by its strategy. The strategy coordinates employees' activities and communicates the direction the retailer plans to take. Retail market strategy describes both the strategic direction and the process by which the strategy is to be developed.

The strategic planning process consists of a sequence of steps, including a detailed analysis of (1) the environment in which the retailer operates and (2) the retailer's unique capabilities. Based on this analysis, the retailer can evaluate alternatives using financial theory and a market attractiveness/competitive position matrix.

The retail strategy statement includes identification of a target market and the retail offering to be directed toward the target market. The statement also needs to indicate the retailer's methods to build a sustainable competitive advantage.

KEY TERMS

bargaining power of
  vendors, *170*
barriers to entry, *170*
competitive rivalry, *171*
cross-selling, *159*
customer loyalty, *151*
data warehouse, *154*
direct investment, *166*
diversification
  opportunity, *161*
joint venture, *166*
market attractiveness/
  competitive position
  matrix, *179*

market expansion
  opportunity, *160*
market penetration
  opportunity, *159*
mission statement, *168*
positioning, *152*
private-label brands, *156*
related diversification
  opportunity, *161*
retail format, *148*
retail format development
  opportunity, *160*
retail market, *149*
retail strategy, *148*

retailing concept, *149*
scale economies, *170*
situation audit, *169*
strategic alliance, *167*
strategic retail planning
  process, *167*
strengths and weaknesses
  analysis, *173*
sustainable competitive
  advantage, *148*
target market, *148*
unrelated diversification, *161*
vertical integration, *161*

GET OUT & DO IT!

1. **INTERNET EXERCISE** Visit the websites
   for Kohl's (www.kohls.com) and Restoration Hardware (www.restorationhardware.com). Do these Internet sites reflect the retail strategies for the companies as discussed here?

2. **INTERNET EXERCISE** Go to the websites for Wal-Mart (www.walmart stores.com), Carrefour (www.carrefour.com), Royal Ahold (www.ahold.com), and Metro AG (www.metro.de). Which chain has the most global strategy? Justify your answer.

3. **INTERNET EXERCISE** Choose your favorite national retail chain. Pick a country for it to enter. Using information found on the Internet, collect information on that country and the retailer. Develop a report that analyzes whether or not the retailer should enter the country, and if so, how it should do so.

4. **GO SHOPPING** Go visit two stores that sell
   similar merchandise categories and cater to the same target segment(s). How are their retail formats similar? Dissimilar? On what bases do they have a sustainable competitive advantage? Explain which you believe has a stronger position.

5. **GO SHOPPING** Develop a strategic plan
   for your favorite retailer. Go to the store. Observe and interview the store manager. Supplement your visit with information available online through Hoovers, the store's website (which should include its annual report), and other published sources.

6. **CD EXERCISE** Go to your student CD and click on Market Position Matrix.

   Exercise 1: This spread sheet reproduces the analysis of international growth opportunities discussed in the appendix to chapter 5. What numbers in the matrices would have to change to make China and France more attractive opportunities? To make Brazil and Mexico less attractive opportunities? Change the numbers in the matrices and see what effect it has on the overall position of the opportunity in the grid.

   Exercise 2: The market attractiveness/competitive position matrix can also be used by a department store to evaluate merchandise categories and determine how much investment should be made in each category. Fill in the importance weights (10 = very important, 1 = not very important) and the evaluations of the merchandise categories (10 = excellent, 1 = poor) and then see what is recommended by the plot on the opportunity matrix.

   Exercise 3: Think of another investment decision that a retailer might make and analyze it using the strategic analysis matrix. List the alternatives, the characteristics of the alternatives, and then put in the importance weights for the characteristics (10 = very important, 1 = not very important), and the evaluation of each alternative on each characteristic (10 = excellent, 1=poor).

DISCUSSION QUESTIONS AND PROBLEMS

1. For each of the four retailers discussed at the beginning of the chapter, describe their strategy and basis of competitive advantage.

2. What approaches can a retailer use to develop a competitive advantage?

3. Give an example of a market penetration, a retail format development, a market expansion, and a diversification growth strategy for Circuit City.

4. Draw and explain a positioning map like that shown in Exhibit 5–3 for the retailers and customer segments (ideal points) for your favorite retailer.

5. Do a situation analysis for McDonald's. What is its mission? What are its strengths and weaknesses? What environmental threats might it face over the next 10 years? How could it prepare for these threats?

6. What are Neiman Marcus' and Saks Fifth Avenue's bases for sustainable competitive advantage? Are they really sustainable?

7. Assume you are interested in opening a restaurant in your town. Go through the steps in the strategic planning process shown in Exhibit 5–5. Focus on doing a situation audit of the local restaurant market, identifying alternatives, evaluating alternatives, and selecting a target market and a retail mix for the restaurant.

8. Walt Disney Co. is splitting its Disney Stores chain into two separate retail concepts. The first group, Disney Play, is aimed at kids. The second group, Disney Kids at Home, is targeted toward parents, with a greater focus on apparel and lifestyle goods like sheets, furniture, and mirrors for kids. Do you believe this is a good strategy?

9. Identify a store or service provider that you believe has an effective loyalty program. Explain why it is effective.

10. Choose a retailer that you believe would be, but is not yet, successful in other countries. Explain why you think it would be successful.

11. Amazon.com started as an Internet retailer selling books. Then it expanded to music, DVDs, electronics, software, and travel services. Evaluate these growth opportunities in terms of the probability that they will be profitable businesses for Amazon.com. What competitive advantages does Amazon.com bring to each of these businesses?

SUGGESTED READINGS

Aaker, David. *Strategic Market Management*. 6th ed. New York: Wiley, 2001.

Alexander, Nicholas. *International Retailing*. Cambridge, MA: Blackwell, 1997.

"Global Retailing: Global Uncertainties." *Chain Store Age*, December 1998, pp. 132–41.

"Global Retailing Supplement." *Chain Store Age*, December 1997.

Goldbrick, Peter, and Gary Davies. "International Retailing: Trends and Strategies." *Journal of Retailing and Consumer Services* 5 (June 1998), pp. 23–32.

Lehmann, Donald, and Russell Winer. *Analysis for Marketing Planning*. 5th ed. Burr Ridge, IL: McGraw-Hill/Irwin, 2001.

Porter, Michael. "What Is Strategy?" *Harvard Business Review*, November–December 1996, pp. 61–78.

Samli, A. Coskun. *Strategic Marketing for Success in Retailing*. New York: Quorum Books, 1998.

Sternquist, Brenda. *International Retailing*. ———. ABC Media, Inc., 1998.

Woodruff, Robert. "Customer Value: The Next Source of Competitive Advantage." *Journal of the Academy of Marketing Science* 25 (Spring 1997), pp. 139–53.

APPENDIX 5A Using the Market Attractiveness/Competitive Position Matrix

The following example illustrates an application of the **market attractiveness/competitive position matrix**.[61] The matrix (Exhibit 5–8) provides a method for analyzing opportunities that explicitly considers both the retailer's capabilities and the retail market's attractiveness. The matrix's underlying premise is that a market's attractiveness determines its long-term profit potential for the opportunity, and the retailer's competitive position indicates the profit potential for the opportunity. The matrix indicates that the greatest investments should be made in opportunities where the retailer has a strong competitive position.

EXHIBIT 5–8
Evaluation of
International Growth
Opportunities

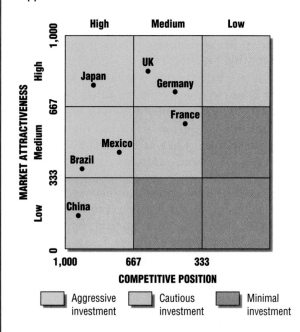

4. Rate each strategic investment opportunity on (1) the attractiveness of its market and (2) the retailer's competitive position in that market. Typically, opportunities are rated on a 1-to-10 scale, with 10 indicating a very attractive market or very strong competitive position and 1 indicating a very unattractive market or very weak competitive position.

5. Calculate each opportunity's score for market attractiveness and competitive position. Scores are calculated by (1) multiplying the weights by each factor's rating and (2) adding across the factors.

6. Plot each opportunity on the matrix in Exhibit 5–8.

In this example, a fashion-oriented U.S. women's apparel retailer is evaluating seven countries for international expansion: Mexico, Brazil, Germany, France, the U.K., Japan, and China. Some information about the markets is shown in Exhibit 5–9.

To evaluate each country's market attractiveness, management identified five market factors, assigned a weight to each factor, rated the markets on each factor, and calculated a market attractiveness score for each alternative (Exhibit 5–10). Here management assigned the highest weight to the attitude that consumers in the country have to the United States (30) and gave the lowest weight to economic stability (15). Ratings for market size and market growth are based on country data; the firm had to consider size of its target market—middle-class women between the ages of 25 and 50. For this reason, Brazil, Mexico, and China had low ratings on market size. These countries are also low on economic stability; however, the retailer did not think that factor was particularly important because the buying power of its target segment is relatively insensitive to the country's economy. The business climate factor includes an assessment of the degree to which the government supports business and foreign investment. The European countries and Japan are high on this dimension.

There are six steps in using the matrix to evaluate opportunities for strategic investments:

1. Define the strategic opportunities to be evaluated. For example, a store manager could use the matrix to evaluate departments in a store; a vice president of stores for a specialty store chain could use it to evaluate stores or potential store sites; a merchandise vice president could use it to evaluate merchandise categories sold by the retailer; or a retail holding company's CEO could use it to evaluate international growth opportunities.

2. Identify key factors determining market attractiveness and the retailer's competitive position. Factors that might be selected are discussed in the market attractiveness, competitor analysis, and self-analysis sections of the situation audit.

3. Assign weights to each factor used to determine market attractiveness and competitive position. The weights assigned to each factor indicate that factor's importance in determining the market attractiveness and competitive position. Typically, weights are selected so that they add up to 100.

Exhibit 5–11 shows the factors, weights, and ratings used to evaluate the retailer's position in each country versus the competition. In evaluating the competitive position,

Data on International Markets **EXHIBIT 5–9**

	U.S.	Mexico	Brazil	Germany	France	U.K.	Japan	China
Population, 2002 (millions)	287	103	176	83	60	60	127	1,284
Population's projected annual growth rate (%)	0.86	1.37	0.78	0.22	0.29	0.18	0.06	0.75
GDP, 2000 (billion $)	9,963	575	624	1,878	1,299	1,415	4,753	1,100
Projected GDP annual growth rate 2001–2005 (%)	2.7	4	3.7	2.2	2.5	2.3	1	7.8
Per capita GDP, 2000 ($)	35,352	5,800	3,763	22,845	21,863	23,793	37,558	869
Retail sales per capita, 2000 ($)	8,135	962	533	5,448	4,833	5,268	8,578	307
% of consumer expenditures on clothing	5	6	4	7	6	6	6	8
% of wealth in top 20% of population	42	55	67	40	42	44	38	44
Population density (per sq. km.)	30	51	20	235	107	246	336	134
% living in urban areas	75	74	81	86	74	90	78	36
Business climate index	2	31	37	11	15	3	26	41
Retail industry concentration	High	Avg.	Low	High	High	High	Avg.	Low
Logistical infrastructure	Very good	Good	Moderate	Very good	Very good	Very good	Good	Moderate
Local vendors	Exc.	Avg.	Avg.	Exc.	Exc.	Exc.	Avg.	Poor

Sources: 2001 World Population Data Sheet, www.prb.org//content/NavigationMenu/Other_reports/2000-2002/2001 world_ population_data_sheet.htm; Laura M. Beaudry, "Apparel: Statistical Overview," *Catalog Age* 17, no. 4 (March 15, 2000), pp. 52–56; and "2002 Global Powers of Retailing," Stores Online, January 2002, www.stores.org.

Market Attractiveness Ratings for International Growth Opportunities **EXHIBIT 5–10**

	Weight	Mexico	Brazil	Germany	France	U.K.	Japan	China
Market size	20	2	2	7	6	5	10	4
Market growth	10	10	7	3	3	3	2	6
Economic stability	15	2	2	10	9	9	5	2
Business climate	25	4	2	7	7	10	6	2
Attitude toward U.S.	30	7	5	8	3	10	10	2
Total	100	480	340	735	550	815	745	280

Competitive Position for International Growth Opportunities **EXHIBIT 5–11**

	Weight	Mexico	Brazil	Germany	France	U.K.	Japan	China
Cost	10	9	10	5	5	5	7	10
Brand image	30	8	10	4	3	7	9	6
Vendor relations	20	7	7	4	4	3	8	8
Locations	20	6	8	6	5	7	6	10
Marketing	20	8	8	6	3	6	8	10
Total	100	750	860	490	380	630	780	840

management felt that brand name was the most critical aspect of competitive position because image is particularly important in selling fashionable merchandise. Since cost was viewed as the least important factor in determining the competitive position of a high-fashion retailer, it received a weight of only 10.

In terms of the retailer's competitive position within each country, the firm felt its brand name was very well known in Japan and Brazil but not well known in France and Germany. Brazil, Mexico, and China offer the best opportunities to operate efficiently due to the low labor costs in these countries.

Evaluations of each of the countries are plotted on the business attractiveness/competitive position matrix shown in Exhibit 5–8. Based on the recommended investment level and objectives associated with each cell in the exhibit, the retailer should invest substantially in Japan, the U.K., Germany, Mexico, and Brazil and be cautious about investments in China and France.

Financial Strategy

6*

Rick is responsible for investor relations at this *Fortune* 100 company, ensuring the financial community has a clear picture of what's happening at Walgreens.

"Every quarter I have phone conversations with Wall Street analysts to review our financial performance. I answer their questions about our balance sheet, income and cash flow statements, and key measures like gross margin, inventory turnover, growth in same store sales, and new store openings.

"The most important aspect of my job is being honest with our investors. Our company believes in being upfront with the analysts by disclosing both good and bad news. We simply give investors and analysts the facts and let them draw the conclusions. I guess that's part of our midwestern culture."

In addition to being responsible for investor relations, Rick also manages Walgreens' banking relationships, cash management, and employee stock plans. Prior to his current position, Rick scouted for

QUESTIONS

- How is retail strategy reflected in retailers' financial objectives?
- Why do retailers need to evaluate their performance?
- What measures do retailers use to assess their performance?
- What is the strategic profit model and how is it used?

new store locations as a real estate manager. "Even though I represent our company to some very influential people in the investment community, my proudest moments are seeing how well stores are doing that I had a hand in as a real estate manager."

Rick graduated from the University of Wisconsin–Madison with a degree in geology. He received his master's degree in materials science and engineering from the University of Texas at Austin and his MBA from the University of Notre Dame. He is also a chartered financial analyst.

Financial decisions are an integral component in every aspect of a retailer's strategy. In Chapter 5, we examined how retailers develop their strategy for sustaining a competitive advantage. In this chapter, we look at financial tools retailers use to measure and evaluate their performance.

Kelly Bradford, owner of the Gifts To Go store we described in Chapter 5, needs to know how well she is doing because she wants to be successful and stay in business. She sees how many customers enter her store and counts up the receipts at the end of the day to see how much she has sold. Unfortunately, these simple measures aren't enough. For instance, sometimes she finds that sales are good, but she still can't afford to buy new merchandise. When things are good, she doesn't need to think about her strategy. But when things go bad, she thinks about nothing else.

Based on the strategies Bradford set, it is important to establish quantifiable performance objectives. If she is achieving her objectives, changes in strategy or implementation programs aren't needed. But if the performance information indicates that objectives aren't being met, she needs to reanalyze her plans and programs. For example, after reviewing her accountant's

*This chapter was prepared with the assistance of Andrea L. Godfrey, PhD student, University of Texas at Austin, while as an MBA student at Babson College.

financial report, Kelly might conclude that she's not earning a fair return on the time and money she's invested in the store. Based on this evaluation, she might consider changing her strategy by appealing to a different target market and lowering the average price point of the gifts that she carries.

We'll first show how financial information taken from standard accounting documents can be used to plan and evaluate strategies. Specifically, retailers have two paths available to achieve a high level of performance: the profit path and the turnover path. Different retailers, however, pursue different strategies, resulting in different types of financial performance. The two paths are combined into the strategic profit model to illustrate that retailers using very different strategies and financial performance characteristics can be financially successful. As a vehicle for discussion, we'll compare the financial performance of two very different retailers: Tiffany & Co. (a national jewelry store chain) and Wal-Mart (the world's largest retailer).

Then we will discuss how retailers set performance objectives and how different performance measures are used throughout the organization. The chapter concludes with an appendix that describes activity-based costing and how it is used to make retailing decisions.

We begin our examination of corporate-level performance measures by looking at the strategic profit model.

REFACT

Tiffany introduced the six-prong setting for diamond solitaires and established the traditional choice for engagement jewelry recognized to this day.

THE STRATEGIC PROFIT MODEL: AN OVERVIEW

Every retailer wants to be financially successful. One important financial goal is to achieve a high return on assets. For instance, Kelly Bradford invested $174,000 in setting up her store and buying merchandise to sell. At the end of the year, she made $33,000 in profit, a 19 percent return on her investment ($33,000 ÷ 174,000). This ratio, net profit ÷ total assets, is called return on assets. To determine whether 19 percent is a good return on her investment, Bradford compares it with what she thinks she could make on another investment with similar risk.

Return on assets can be divided into two paths: the profit path (which is measured by net profit margin) and the turnover path (which is measured by asset turnover). Net profit margin is simply how much profit (after tax) a firm makes divided by its net sales. Asset turnover is used to measure the productivity of a firm's investment in assets. It is expressed as net profit ÷ total assets. When you multiply net profit margin times asset turnover, the net sales cancels out of the equation and you get return on assets:

$$\text{Net profit} \times \text{Asset turnover} = \text{Return on assets}$$

$$\frac{\text{Net profit}}{\text{Net sales}} \times \frac{\text{Net sales}}{\text{Total assets}} = \frac{\text{Net profit}}{\text{Total assets}}$$

To illustrate how the strategic profit model works, consider the two very different hypothetical retailers in Exhibit 6–1. La Madeline Bakery has a net profit margin of 1 percent and asset turnover of 10 times, resulting in a return on assets of 10 percent. The profit margin is low due to the competitive nature of this commodity-type business. Asset turnover is relatively high, because the firm

	Net Profit Margin	×	Asset Turnover	=	Return on Assets
La Madeline Bakery	1%		10 times		10%
Kalame Jewelry	10%		1 time		10%

EXHIBIT 6–1

Return on Assets Model for a Bakery and Jewelry Store

doesn't have its own credit card system (no accounts receivable). Also, it rents its store, so fixed assets are relatively low, and it has a very fast inventory turnover—in fact, its inventory turns every day!

On the other hand, Kalame Jewelry Store has a net profit margin of 10 percent and an asset turnover of one time, again resulting in a return on assets of 10 percent. The difference is that even though the jewelry store has higher operating expenses than the bakery, its gross margin is much more—it may double the cost of jewelry to arrive at a retail price. Kalame's asset turnover is so low compared to the bakery's because Kalame has very expensive fixtures and precision jewelry-manufacturing equipment (fixed assets), offers liberal credit to customers (accounts receivable), and has very slow inventory turnover—possibly only one-half to one turn per year. In sum, these two very different types of retailers could have exactly the same return on assets.

Thus, La Madeline is achieving its 10 percent return on assets by having a relatively high asset turnover—the *turnover path*. Kalame Jewelry, on the other hand, achieves its return on assets with a relatively high net profit margin—the *profit path*.

In the next three sections we will take a close look at these three financial ratios. Specifically, we will examine the relationship between these ratios and retailing strategy and describe where the information can be found in traditional accounting records.

One way to define financial success is to provide the owners of the firm with a good return on their investment. Although retailers pursue similar financial goals, they employ different strategies. For instance, Tiffany & Co., described in Retailing View 6.1, has broad assortments of jewelry and gifts, exceptionally high levels of service, and opulent surroundings. Tiffany & Co. concentrates on the profit path. Wal-Mart, described in Retailing View 6.2, takes the opposite approach. It concentrates on the turnover path. Wal-Mart has narrow assortments, relatively little service, and functional decor. Based on this description, why

Jewelry stores typically have a higher net profit margin than bakeries, but their asset turnover is much lower. How can return on assets of a jewelry store and a bakery be the same?

would anyone shop at Wal-Mart? The answer is that Wal-Mart strives for and maintains everyday low prices. The strategic profit model is used to evaluate the performance of different retailers that, like Tiffany and Wal-Mart, may employ very different strategies.

THE PROFIT PATH

The information used to analyze a firm's profit path comes from the income statement. The income statement summarizes a firm's financial performance over a period of time. Exhibit 6–2 shows income statements adapted from corporate reports of Wal-Mart and Tiffany & Co. The profit path portion of the strategic profit model that utilizes such income statement data appears in Exhibit 6–3. Let's look at each item in the income statement.

RETAILING VIEW | Tiffany & Co.: A Great American Brand

6.1

Of all the great American brands, Tiffany, which has been around for over 160 years, is among the best known. Tiffany is more than a retailer; it's an American icon that has worked its way into movies and songs. The company's flagship location on Fifth Avenue in New York City has become a tourist attraction. Even the company's trademarked robin's egg blue boxes have become known as "Tiffany blue" and symbolize the brand's quality and craftsmanship.

Such reputations can be profitable. The company has grown aggressively—from $456 million in sales in 1990 to $1.7 billion in 2000. With the mission to be the world's most respected jewelry retailer, Tiffany plans to continue this growth. To achieve this, the store is attracting a wider clientele while preserving the company's image of elegance and exclusivity through superior customer service and product quality. Tiffany's strategy has involved expanding its advertising to promote a wider variety of price points, opening new stores every year, and broadening its reach through the Internet.

In an attempt to appeal to a wider variety of customers, the company advertises items ranging from $200 to $100,000 in daily ads in the *New York Times* as well as in upscale fashion and lifestyle magazines. The variety in the ads is designed to attract both mall habitués in Guess Jeans as well as ladies who lunch in Chanel suits. Mark Aaron, vice president of investor relations, explains: "We believe advertising a wide range of price points helps build long-term relationships with people, including those who merely aspire to be Tiffany customers."

To provide easier access for those aspirational customers, Tiffany has adopted a growth strategy that involves expanding into new markets internationally and opening three to five stores in the United States each year. To achieve this goal, the company has had to move into

less elite addresses, including shopping malls. While some critics question whether Tiffany will dilute the exclusiveness of its brand by making itself accessible to the middle-tier consumer, the broader-market strategy appears to be paying off—worldwide sales increased 13 percent in 2000.

In addition, Tiffany's retail website, www.tiffany.com, was launched in November 1999. The challenge for Tiffany's move to the Web was to come up with a strategy that provides access to a potentially huge Internet audience and yet retain the image of exclusivity. While the typical website strives to offer bells and whistles at the fastest speed possible, Tiffany took a different approach with its website. Tiffany's website is characterized by simple layouts and sparse text that highlight its exclusive items. To further preserve the cachet of Tiffany's impeccable service, the company does not sell its diamond engagement rings over the Internet. The company feels strongly that professional input and conversation are needed for such a purchase.

The website appears to be achieving its objective of helping Tiffany expand its customer base. A large percentage of the purchasers at tiffany.com are new customers. There are also many customers who live in cities where Tiffany has a regular bricks-and-mortar store, indicating the site isn't only for luxury shoppers in smaller towns or remote locations. The website can help cater to the aspirational customer who is interested in researching a couple of items but might be intimidated by going into the store.

Sources: www.tiffany.com; www.freeedgar.com; Kate Fitzgerald, "Jewelers Out to Protect Cachet," *Advertising Age,* March 11, 2002; and Lisa Vickery, "E-Commerce—Keeping the Cachet: Luxury Goods Makers Embrace the Web," *The Wall Street Journal,* April 23, 2001. www.wsj.com.

Wal-Mart: The World's Largest Retailer | RETAILING VIEW

6.2

How big is Wal-Mart? Some 100 million people a week buy into the "we're just like you" message. The company's annual sales rival the gross domestic product of Austria, the world's twenty-second largest economy. Wal-Mart topped *Forbes* magazine's list of the top 500 companies based on revenue, stealing the top spot from longtime holders General Motors and Exxon Mobil. Wal-Mart is constantly expanding its store count—the company operates close to 3,500 stores in the United States, which includes over 1,000 Supercenters and 500 Sam's Clubs. Even as discount retailers face intense competition from category specialists, like Circuit City and Home Depot, and increasingly compete against grocery and pharmacy retailers, there seems to be no end to Wal-Mart's success story.

Most experts agree that Wal-Mart's amazing results can be attributed to efficiency and innovation. Wal-Mart is an industry leader in supply chain and information systems. It was the first to use a hub-and-spoke distribution system in which the company opens stores around a central distribution facility. The company pioneered the policy of providing suppliers with access to sales and in-stock information through electronic data interchange (EDI) and has developed a process known as collaborative planning, forecasting, and replenishment (CPFR), which is quickly becoming the standard product planning procedure for retailers and their suppliers.

In addition, Wal-Mart invested in most of the waves of information technology systems earlier and more aggressively than did its competitors. This allowed Wal-Mart to reduce inventory significantly, which resulted in cost savings and higher productivity. Founder Sam Walton summed up the company's attitude toward IT: "People think we got big by putting big stores in small towns. Really we got big by replacing inventory with information." These innovations have made Wal-Mart the industry leader in buying and distribution efficiency.

Wal-Mart uses its competitive advantages in computer systems and logistics to create a "productivity loop"—a cycle of lowering prices and margins but reinvesting in the business to keep prices low and squeeze out competition. Wal-Mart was the first retailer at sustaining this pricing strategy. Because of its efficient operations, Wal-Mart can keep its prices low enough to operate the lowest-priced basket of merchandise in every market in which it competes.

Although much of its success can be attributed to its innovative use of technology, Wal-Mart's edge also stems from managerial innovations that have nothing to do with IT. For example, Wal-Mart's appeal with consumers is largely based on its promotion of small-town flavor. From

How big is Wal-Mart? The company's annual sales rival the gross domestic product of Austria, the world's twenty-second largest economy.

a people greeter in every store to in-store events, including Halloween fashion shows and Oreo stacking contests, the company's goal of spreading that hometown flavor has been a key to its success.

This distinct approach to discount retailing is imbedded in the company's corporate culture. This culture began with Sam Walton's own charismatic personality and is fostered among the company's employees, who are referred to as "associates." The company puts an almost obsessive focus on exceeding customer expectations and continuously mines the associates for fresh ideas. In return, the company receives a cultlike loyalty from its associates, some of whom have become millionaires as a result of company stock options.

To ensure continued growth and success, Wal-Mart continues to innovate its retail format. In addition to its traditional merchandise categories, Wal-Mart is the third-largest pharmacy retailer in the United States and has plans to start offering products and services as diverse as household appliances and Internet access. Wal-Mart has become the world's largest food retailer through its Supercenters—huge stores that carry groceries in addition to the usual general merchandise. By 2004, Wal-Mart plans to have approximately 1,400 Supercenters operating in the United States leading one of the most significant trends in discount store retailing.

Sources: Laurent Belsie, "Wal-Mart's Ascent to No.1 Signals Many Things," *Christian Science Monitor,* February 19, 2002; Bradford C. Johnson, "Retail: the Wal-Mart Effect," *McKinsey Quarterly,* no. 1 (2002); Michael Levy and Dhruv Grewal, "So Long Kmart Shoppers," *The Wall Street Journal,* www.wsj.com, January 28, 2002; and Barbara Thau, "Sam Walton's Wal-Mart," *HFN Visionaries Supplement,* November 27, 2001.

EXHIBIT 6–2

Income Statements for Wal-Mart Stores, Inc., and Tiffany & Co. and Subsidiaries, 2002 ($ in millions)

	Wal-Mart	Tiffany
Net sales	219,812	1,607
Less: Cost of goods sold	171,562	663
Gross margin	48,250	944
Less: Operating expense	36,173	634
Less: Interest expense	1,326	20
Total expense	37,499	653
Net profit, pretax	10,751	291
Less: Taxes*	3,897	116
Tax rate	36.25%	39.79%
Net profit after tax	6,854	175

*Effective tax rates often differ among corporations due to different tax breaks and advantages.

Source: Annual reports via Edgar SEC website.

Net Sales

The term **net sales** refers to the total number of dollars received by a retailer after all refunds have been paid to customers for returned merchandise:

Net sales = Gross amount of sales – Customer returns – Customer allowances

Customer returns represents the value of merchandise that customers return because it's damaged, doesn't fit, and so forth. Customer allowances represents any additional price reduction given to the customer. For instance, if an item at Gifts To Go regularly retails for $5 but is sold for $4.50 because it's scratched, the 50-cent difference is the customer allowance.

Sales are an important measure of performance because they indicate the activity level of the merchandising function. Retailers are particularly interested in sales growth due to its direct link to the firm's overall profitability. Chapters 12 and 13 cover sales forecasting techniques.

Gross Margin

Gross margin = Net sales – Cost of goods sold

Gross margin, also called **gross profit,** is an important measure in retailing. It gives the retailer a measure of how much profit it's making on merchandise sales without considering the expenses associated with operating the store.

Gross margin, like other performance measures, is also expressed as a percentage of net sales so retailers can compare (1) performances of various types of merchandise and (2) their own performance with other retailers.

$$\frac{\text{Gross margin}}{\text{Net sales}} = \text{Gross margin \%}$$

Wal-Mart: $\dfrac{\$48{,}250}{\$219{,}812} = 21.95\%$

Tiffany: $\dfrac{\$944}{\$1{,}607} = 58.75\%$

(Throughout this chapter, dollar figures are expressed in millions.)

Profit Margin Models for Wal-Mart Stores, Inc., and Tiffany & Co. and Subsidiaries, 2002
($ in millions)

EXHIBIT 6–3

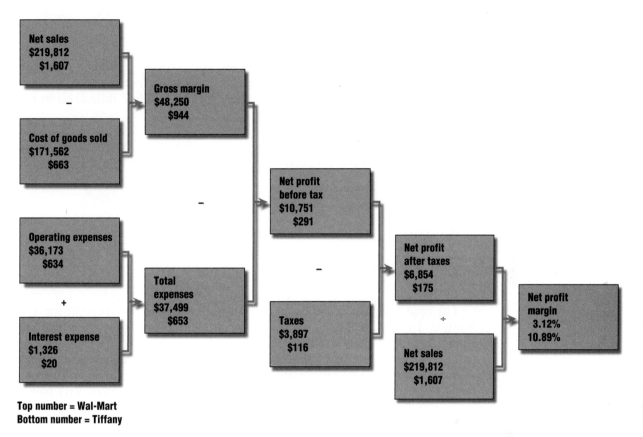

Net sales
$219,812
$1,607

−

Cost of goods sold
$171,562
$663

Gross margin
$48,250
$944

Operating expenses
$36,173
$634

+

Interest expense
$1,326
$20

Total expenses
$37,499
$653

−

Net profit before tax
$10,751
$291

−

Taxes
$3,897
$116

Net profit after taxes
$6,854
$175

÷

Net sales
$219,812
$1,607

Net profit margin
3.12%
10.89%

Top number = Wal-Mart
Bottom number = Tiffany

Superficially, Tiffany appears to outperform Wal-Mart on gross margin. However, further analysis will show that other factors interact with gross margin to determine overall performance. But first, let's consider the factors that contribute to differences in gross margin performance.

Discount stores like Wal-Mart generally have lower gross margins than jewelry stores because discount stores pursue a deliberate strategy of offering merchandise at everyday low prices with minimal service to several cost-oriented market segments. Discount stores have tried to increase their average gross margin by adding specialty products and departments like gourmet foods and jewelry. But Wal-Mart's overall average gross margin lags behind Tiffany's. Chapters 12, 13, and 15 explore the use of gross margin in merchandise and pricing decisions.

Grocery stores attempt to increase their average gross margin by emphasizing high-margin departments like produce.

Expenses

Expenses are costs incurred in the normal course of doing business to generate revenues. One expense category in Exhibit 6–3, operating expenses, is further defined in Exhibit 6–4.

EXHIBIT 6–4
Types of Retail
Operating Expenses

Selling expenses	**= Sales staff salaries + Commissions + Benefits**
General expenses	**= Rent + Utilities + Miscellaneous expenses**
Administrative expenses = Salaries of all employees other than salespeople +	
Operations of buying offices + Other administrative expenses	

Another major expense category, interest, is the cost of financing everything from inventory to the purchase of a new store location. For instance, if a bank charges Tiffany 10 percent interest, Tiffany pays $49 million in interest to borrow $490 million.

Tiffany has significantly higher total expenses as a percentage of net sales than Wal-Mart. Like gross margin, total expenses are also expressed as a percentage of net sales to facilitate comparisons across items and departments within firms.

$$\frac{\text{Total expenses}}{\text{Net sales}} = \text{Total expenses/Net sales ratio}$$

$$\text{Wal-Mart: } \frac{\$37,499}{\$219,812} = 17.06\%$$

$$\text{Tiffany: } \frac{\$653}{\$1,607} = 40.65\%$$

The total expenses/net sales ratio is only approximately 17 percent for Wal-Mart; at Tiffany, it's over 40 percent. This difference is to be expected. Discount stores have relatively low selling expenses. They're also typically located on comparatively inexpensive real estate so rent is relatively low. Finally, discount stores operate with a smaller administrative staff than a store like Tiffany's. For instance, buying expenses are much lower for discount stores. Their buyers don't have to travel very far, and much of the purchasing consists of rebuying staple merchandise that's already in the stores. On the other hand, a jewelry store's total expenses are much higher because its large, experienced sales staff requires a modest salary plus commission and benefits. Unlike Wal-Mart stores' locations that are usually suburban or in rural areas, Tiffany's stores are in some of the most expensive malls in the country, not to mention its flagship store on Fifth Avenue in New York. Tiffany's locations therefore command high rent and incur other expenses.

Net Profit

Net profit is a measure of the firm's overall performance:

Net profit = Gross margin – Expenses

Net profit can be expressed either before or after taxes. Generally, it's more useful to express net profit after taxes, since this is the amount of money left over to reinvest in the business, disburse as dividends to stockholders or owners, or repay debt.

Net profit margin, like gross margin, is often expressed as a percentage of net sales:

$$\text{Net profit margin} = \frac{\text{Net profit}}{\text{Net sales}}$$

However, net profit measures the profitability of the entire firm, whereas gross margin measures the profitability of merchandising activities. In Exhibit 6–3, the after-tax net profit margin is 3.12 percent for Wal-Mart and

REFACT

The most profitable retailers in 2000 were Wal-Mart ($6.29 billion), Home Depot ($2.32 billion), and Dell Computer ($1.67 billion).[3]

10.89 percent for Tiffany. From a profit perspective alone, Tiffany is outperforming Wal-Mart. Even though Tiffany has a higher total expenses/net sales ratio, its gross margin percentage is so large compared to Wal-Mart's that it still surpasses the discount store's profit performance. Retailing View 6.3 looks at the strategic profit model of Kohl's, which is focusing on its profit path to outperform its competition.

Kohl's Is Beating Up Its Competition — RETAILING VIEW 6.3

Kohl's, the promotional department store retailer based in Menomonee Falls, Wisconsin, has an aggressive nationwide expansion plan. They are competing head-to-head with and stealing market share from national chains like Sears and JCPenney. Kohl's success can be attributed to the strength of its business model compared to its primary competitors. Let's see how Kohl's strategy and its strategic profit model stack up against Sears and JCPenney.

Kohl's objective is to sell moderately priced, brand-name apparel, footwear, accessories, and home products to middle-income consumers shopping for their families and homes. To achieve this, the company positions itself as "your neighborhood Kohl's store" by primarily locating in strip mall and freestanding locations. The average size of a Kohl's store is less than half the size of a typical department store and has an attractive, easy to navigate layout. Kohl's carries a more edited assortment of both styles and price points than competitors, focusing on a narrow but deep assortment of key "everyday essentials" from national brands. The narrow assortment translates into a fairly narrow range of price points that is augmented with aggressive but disciplined sales promotions. Kohl's also encourages customer loyalty through its proprietary credit card Most Valued Customer (MVC) frequent shopper program.

Factors contributing to Kohl's success can be illustrated by comparing the company's profit path to that of Sears and JCPenny. Kohl's gross margin is 34.1 percent compared to 26.4 percent for Sears and 27.7 percent for JCPenney. A narrow vendor structure and concentration on fewer styles that are purchased in large quantities contribute to a lower cost of goods sold percentage. This allows Kohl's to offer lower prices than its competitors without sacrificing gross margin. In addition, the company's higher gross margin reflects a gradual shift in its merchandise mix toward higher-margin categories, such as women's and juniors' apparel.

Operating efficiencies have allowed Kohl's to improve its selling, general, and administrative expenses as a percent of sales to 23.5 percent compared to 28.3 percent at Sears and 27.6 percent at JCPenney. Lower occupancy costs, smaller management teams, and leaner store-level staffing all contribute to the lower operating expenses. As a result of its higher gross margin and lower operating expenses, Kohl's had a net profit margin of 6.04 percent

Kohl's positions itself as "your neighborhood Kohl's store." They sell moderately priced, brand-name apparel, footwear, accessories, and home products to middle-income consumers shopping for their families and homes.

compared to 3.28 percent for Sears and −2.87 percent for JCPenney in 2000.

The turnover path shows many more similarities than differences between Kohl's and its competitors. Each of the retailers has a similar number of inventory turns; Kohl's inventory turnover is 4.52 times, slightly greater than the 4.11 turns of JCPenney and slightly less than the 5.03 turns of Sears.* Kohl's and JCPenney have similar asset turnovers, 1.59 and 1.61, respectively; whereas Sears' is significantly lower at 1.11. As a result of Kohl's stronger performance on net profit margin and its edge over Sears on asset turnover, its return on asset is significantly greater than Sears and JCPenney. Kohl's had a return of assets of 9.62 percent compared to only 3.64 percent for Sears and a negative return of 2.87 percent resulting from the net loss at JCPenney in 2000.

*Inventory turnover was calculated as cost of goods sold divided by average inventory, where average inventory was assumed to be equal to ending inventory for the year 2000.

Sources: "Kohl's—Why It Works and What You Can Learn," January 2002, www.retailforward.com; and form 10-K405 for Kohl's Corporation, filed on April 17, 2001; form 10-K for Sears, Roebuck and Co., filed on March 21, 2001; form 10-K405 for JCPenney Corp. Inc., filed on April 24, 2001, www.freeedgar.com.

194

THE TURNOVER PATH

The information used to analyze a firm's turnover path primarily comes from the balance sheet. While the income statement summarizes the financial performance over a period of time, the balance sheet summarizes a retailer's financial position at a given point in time, such as the last day of the year. The balance sheet shows the following relationship:

Assets = Liabilities + Owners' equity

Assets are economic resources (such as inventory or store fixtures) owned or controlled by an enterprise as a result of past transactions or events. **Liabilities** are an enterprise's obligations (such as accounts or notes payable) to pay cash or other economic resources in return for past, current, or future benefits. **Owners' equity** (owners' investment in the business) is the difference between assets and liabilities. It represents the amount of assets belonging to the owners of the retail firm after all obligations (liabilities) have been met.

Exhibit 6–5's balance sheets for Tiffany and Wal-Mart continue the comparison between them. The turnover path portion of the strategic profit model is shown in Exhibit 6–6's asset turnover model. The remainder of this section covers elements of the balance sheet.

Current Assets

By accounting definition, **current assets** are those that can normally be converted to cash within one year. In retailing,

Accounts receivable + Merchandise inventory + Cash + Other current assets = Current assets

EXHIBIT 6–5
Balance Sheets for Wal-Mart Stores, Inc., and Tiffany & Co. and Subsidiaries ($ in millions)

	Wal-Mart (as of 1/31/02)	Tiffany (as of 1/31/02)
ASSETS		
Current assets		
Accounts receivable	$ 2,000	$ 99
Merchandise inventory	22,614	612
Cash	2,161	174
Other curent assets	1,471	71
Total current assets	28,246	955
Fixed assets		
Building, equipment, and other Fixed assets, less depreciation	55,205	675
Total assets	$83,451	$1,630
LIABILITIES		
Current liabilities	$27,282	$ 341
Long-term liabilities	18,732	221
Other liabilities	2,335	30
Total liabilities	$48,349	$ 593
OWNERS' EQUITY		
Common stock	$ 1,929	$ 332
Retained earnings	33,173	705
Total owners' equity	$35,102	$1,037
Total liabilities and owners' equity	$83,451	$1,630

Accounts Receivable

Accounts receivable are monies due to the retailer from selling merchandise on credit. This current asset is substantial for some retailers. For example, Wal-Mart's investment in accounts receivable is proportionately much smaller than Tiffany's due to Wal-Mart customers' high propensity to pay cash or use third-party credit cards like Visa or MasterCard. Here are their accounts receivable:

Wal-Mart: $2,000, or 0.9 percent of sales

Tiffany: $99, or 6.1 percent of sales

From a marketing perspective, the accounts receivable generated from credit sales may be the result of an important service provided to customers. The retailer's ability to provide credit, particularly at low interest rates, could make the difference between making or losing a sale. Paying cash for a sizable purchase like a diamond engagement ring or car may be difficult for many people!

Unfortunately, having a large amount of accounts receivable is expensive for retailers, who of course would like to sell a product for cash and immediately reinvest the cash in new merchandise. When merchandise is sold on credit, proceeds of the sale are tied up as accounts receivable until collection is made. The money invested in accounts receivable costs the retailer interest expense and keeps the retailer from investing proceeds of the sale elsewhere. To ease the financial burden of carrying accounts receivable, retailers can use third-party

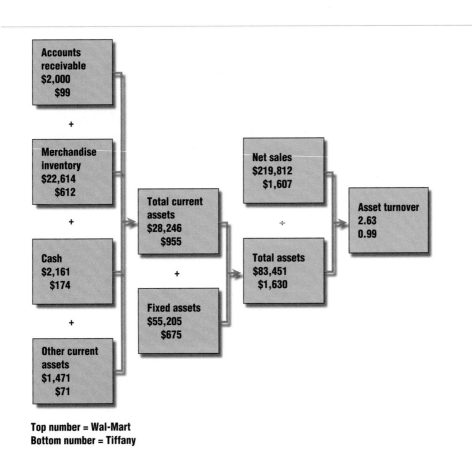

Top number = Wal-Mart
Bottom number = Tiffany

EXHIBIT 6–6
Asset Turnover Model for Wal-Mart Stores, Inc., and Tiffany & Co. and Subsidiaries ($ in millions)

credit cards such as Visa or MasterCard, give discounts to customers who pay with cash, discourage credit sales, and control delinquent accounts.

Merchandise Inventory

Merchandise inventory is a retailer's lifeblood, representing approximately 27.10 percent of total assets for Wal-Mart and 37.53 percent of total assets for Tiffany. An exception to this generalization is service retailers such as Sears Pest Control Service, Marriott Hotels, and your local barber shop/beauty salon, which carry little or no merchandise inventory.

Think of inventory as "merchandise in motion." The faster it moves through the store, the greater the inventory turnover.

$$\frac{\text{Inventory}}{\text{Total assets}}$$

Wal-Mart: $\dfrac{\$22,614}{\$83,451} = 27.10\%$

Tiffany: $\dfrac{\$612}{\$1,630} = 37.53\%$

Inventory turnover is used to evaluate how effectively managers utilize their investment in inventory. Inventory turnover is defined as follows:

$$\text{Inventory turnover} = \frac{\text{Net sales}}{\text{Average inventory}}$$

Note that average inventory is expressed at retail rather than at cost.

Think of inventory as a measure of the productivity of inventory—how many sales dollars can be generated from $1 invested in inventory. Generally, the larger the inventory turnover, the better. Exhibit 6–7 illustrates the concept of inventory turnover. Inventory is delivered to the store, spends some time in the store, and then is sold. We can think of inventory turnover as how many times, on average, the inventory cycles through the store during a specific period of time (usually a year).

EXHIBIT 6–7
Inventory Turnover

Wal-Mart's inventory turnover is about seven times Tiffany's: 7.59 compared to 1.08.[5]

$$\frac{\text{Net sales}}{\text{Average inventory}} = \text{Inventory turnover}$$

Wal-Mart: $\dfrac{\$219{,}812}{\$28{,}974} = 7.59$

Tiffany: $\dfrac{\$1{,}607}{\$1{,}484} = 1.08$

Wal-Mart's faster inventory turnover is expected due to the nature of discount and grocery stores. First, most items in Wal-Mart are commodities and staples such as batteries, housewares, and basic apparel items. Its new superstores carry grocery products such as baked goods, frozen meat, and produce. Tiffany, on the other hand, specializes in unique luxury items. Second, since Wal-Mart–type merchandise is available at other discount and grocery stores, it competes by offering lower prices, which results in rapid turnover. Third, discount stores carry a simpler stock selection than jewelry stores do. In a Wal-Mart store, for example, there may be only two brands of ketchup, each in two sizes, which represents four inventory items. Jewelry stores, on the other hand, may stock 100 distinctly different types of necklaces. Finally, due to Tiffany's unique positioning strategy, much of its inventory, particularly the jewelry, is made especially for it in other countries, requiring buyers to place orders several months in advance of delivery. Discount stores, on the other hand, order items daily or weekly. These factors, when taken together, explain why Wal-Mart has a faster inventory turnover than Tiffany.

Management of this aspect of retailing permeates most retailing decisions. Chapters 12 and 13 address the crucial subject of merchandise inventory management.

Cash and Other Current Assets

Cash = Monies on hand
+ Demand and savings accounts in banks to which a retailer has immediate access
+ Marketable securities such as Treasury bills

Other current assets = Prepaid expenses + Supplies

Wal-Mart reports cash of about 0.98 percent of sales, whereas Tiffany's cash percentage is 10.81 percent.

Fixed Assets

Fixed assets are assets that require more than a year to convert to cash. In retailing,

Fixed assets = Buildings (if store property is owned rather than leased)
+ Fixtures (such as display racks)
+ Equipment (such as computers or delivery trucks)
+ Long-term investments such as real estate or stock in other firms

These trucks belonging to 7-Eleven Stores in Japan are fixed assets.

Fixed assets represent 66.15 percent and 41.44 percent of total assets for Wal-Mart and Tiffany, respectively. Wal-Mart's fixed assets are relatively higher than Tiffany's because they have vast real estate holdings in stores and distribution centers, whereas Tiffany typically rents space in malls and has direct store delivery.

$$\text{Fixed assets} = \text{Asset cost} - \text{Depreciation}$$

Since most fixed assets have a limited useful life, those assets' value should be less over time—in other words, they're depreciated. For instance, Tiffany stores require refurbishing every few years due to general wear-and-tear. So, carpet and some fixtures are depreciated over 3 to 5 years, whereas a building may be depreciated over 25 years.

Asset Turnover

Asset turnover is an overall performance measure from the asset side of the balance sheet.

$$\text{Asset turnover} = \frac{\text{Net sales}}{\text{Total assets}}$$

Although fixed assets don't turn over as quickly as inventory, asset turnover can be used to evaluate and compare how effectively managers use their assets. When a retailer redecorates a store, for example, old fixtures, carpeting, and lights are removed and replaced with new ones. Thus, like inventory, these assets cycle through the store. The difference is that the process is a lot slower. The life of a fixture in a Tiffany's store may be five years (instead of five months, as it might be for a diamond ring in the store's inventory), yet the concept of turnover is the same. When a retailer decides to invest in a fixed asset, it should determine how many sales dollars can be generated from that asset.

Suppose that Tiffany needs to purchase a new fixture for displaying dinnerwear. It has a choice of buying an expensive antique display cabinet for $5,000 or having a simple plywood display constructed for $500. Using the expensive antique, it forecasts sales of $50,000 in the first year, whereas the plywood display is expected to generate only $40,000. Ignoring all other assets for a moment,

$$\frac{\text{Net sales}}{\text{Total assets}} = \text{Asset turnover}$$

Antique cabinet: $\dfrac{\$50,000}{\$5,000} = 10$

Plywood cabinet: $\dfrac{\$40,000}{\$500} = 80$

The antique cabinet will certainly help create an atmosphere conducive to selling expensive dinnerwear. Exclusively from a marketing perspective, the antique would thus appear appropriate. But it costs much more than the plywood shelves. From a strict financial perspective, Tiffany should examine how much additional sales can be expected to be generated from the added expenditure in assets. Clearly, by considering only asset turnover, the plywood shelves are the way to go. In the end, a combination of marketing and financial factors should be considered when making the asset purchase decision.[6]

Wal-Mart's asset turnover is 2.7 times Tiffany's. The asset turnover is 2.63 for Wal-Mart and 0.99 for Tiffany. This finding is consistent with the different strategies each firm is implementing. We saw earlier that Wal-Mart has a higher inventory turnover. Its other assets are relatively lower than Tiffany's as well. For instance, the fixed assets involved in outfitting a store (such as fixtures, lighting, and mannequins) would be relatively lower for a discount store than a jewelry store.

The other side of the balance sheet equation from assets involves liabilities and owners' equity. Now let's look at the major liabilities and components of owners' equity.

Liabilities and Owners' Equity

Current Liabilities   Like current assets, **current liabilities** are debts that are expected to be paid in less than one year. The most important current liabilities are accounts payable, notes payable, and accrued liabilities. Current liabilities as a percentage of net sales is 12.41 percent for Wal-Mart and 21.24 percent for Tiffany.

Accounts Payable   **Accounts payable** refers to the amount of money owed to vendors, primarily for merchandise inventory. Accounts payable are an important source of short-term financing. Retailers buy merchandise on credit from vendors. The longer the period of time they have to pay for that merchandise, the larger their accounts payable—and the less they need to borrow from financial institutions (notes payable), issue bonds or stock, or finance internally through retained earnings. Since retailers normally don't have to pay interest to vendors on their accounts payable, they have strong incentive to negotiate for a long time period before payment for merchandise is due (see Chapter 14).

Accounts payable management can play an important role in retailer's profit strategy. This is the case for many European hypermarkets like Carrefour. Hypermarkets are similar to U.S.-style supercenters but have some key differences. Hypermarkets are primarily food-based and emphasize fresh products to drive customer traffic, whereas supercenters are primarily nonfood retailers that focus on dry goods. Carrefour is able to negotiate extended supplier terms because, like most European food retailers, it has national scope and is able to exert significant influence over its suppliers. As a result, Carrefour manages its accounts payable as a profit center. For example, Carrefour typically has about 42 days of inventory on hand and roughly 90 days in payables. That 48-day float generates income that contributes as much as 25 to 35 percent of Carrefour's operating profit.[7]

Notes Payable   **Notes payable** under the current liabilities section of the balance sheet are the principal and interest the retailer owes to financial institutions (banks) that are due and payable in less than a year. Retailers borrow money from financial institutions to pay for current assets, such as inventory.

Accrued Liabilities   **Accrued liabilities** include taxes, salaries, rent, utilities, and other incurred obligations that haven't yet been paid. These are called accrued liabilities because they usually accumulate daily but are only paid at the end of a time period, such as a month.

Long-Term Liabilities   **Long-term liabilities** are debts that will be paid after one year. The notes payable entry in the long-term liability section of the balance sheet is similar to the one in the current liability section except that it's due to be paid in more than one year. Other long-term liabilities include bonds and mortgages on real estate.

Owners' Equity   Owners' equity, also known as **stockholders' equity,** represents the amount of assets belonging to the owners of the retail firm after all obligations (liabilities) have been met. In accounting terms, the relationship can be expressed as

Owners' equity = Total assets – Total liabilities

Although there are several entries in the owners' equity category, two of the most common are common stock and retained earnings.

Common stock is the type of stock most frequently issued by corporations.[8] Owners of common stock usually have voting rights in the retail corporation. They also have the right to share in distributed corporate earnings. If the firm is liquidated, common stock owners have the right to share in the sale of its assets. Finally, they have the right to purchase additional shares to maintain the same percentage ownership if new shares are issued.

Retained earnings refers to the portion of owners' equity that has accumulated over time through profits but hasn't been paid out in dividends to owners. The decision of how much of the retailer's earnings should be retained in the firm and how much should be returned to the owners in the form of dividends is related to the firm's growth potential. Specifically, retailers with a propensity toward and opportunities for growth will retain and reinvest their profits to fund growth opportunities. For example, a high-growth retailer such as Wal-Mart retains most of its earnings to pay for the new stores, inventory, and expenses associated with its growth.

Total owners' equity is over $35,102 million for Wal-Mart and over $1,037 million for Tiffany.

THE STRATEGIC PROFIT MODEL

REFACT

Tiffany's return on assets is much higher than that of Zale Corporation, the largest specialty retailer of fine jewelry in the United States—10.74 percent compared to 5.68 percent, respectively. Also, Wal-Mart's return on assets is much stronger than that of its largest competitor, Target Corporation— 8.21 percent compared to 5.66 percent.[9]

The previous sections defined the most important balance sheet and income statement entries as well as the most useful performance ratios. Yet many of these items are interrelated, and when examined alone they can be confusing. More important, it's hard to compare the performance of retailers with different operating characteristics, such as Tiffany and Wal-Mart. The strategic profit model (Exhibit 6–8) combines the two performance ratios from the income statement and balance sheets: net profit margin and asset turnover. By multiplying these ratios together, you get return on assets.

Return on Assets

$$\text{Return on assets} = \text{Net profit margin} \times \text{Asset turnover}$$
$$= \frac{\text{Net profit}}{\text{Net sales}} \times \frac{\text{Net sales}}{\text{Total assets}}$$
$$= \frac{\text{Net profit}}{\text{Total assets}}$$

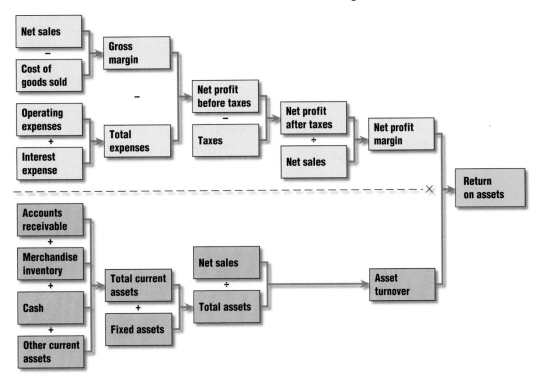

Return on assets determines how much profit can be generated from the retailer's investment in assets. (Note that when we multiply net profit margin by asset turnover, net sales drops out of the equation.)

The most important issue associated with return on assets is that the money that would be invested in retailing could also be invested in any other asset, such as a CD or Treasury bill. For instance, if a retailer can achieve 9 percent return on assets by opening a new store, and 10 percent by investing in a nearly risk-free Treasury bill, the retailer should take the higher-yield, lower-risk investment. In fact, should the return on assets of another investment with similar risk be greater, it would be the manager's fiduciary duty to invest in the other asset. In general, return on assets is effective in evaluating the profitability of individual investments in assets because it can easily be compared with yields of other investments with similar risk. It has also been shown to be an effective predictor of business failures.[10]

$$\frac{\text{Net profit}}{\text{Total assets}} = \text{Return on assets}$$

Wal-Mart: $\frac{\$6,854}{\$83,451} = 8.21\%$

Tiffany: $\frac{\$175}{\$1,630} = 10.74\%$

Return on assets for Tiffany and Wal-Mart is very similar! Tiffany generated a larger net profit margin, 10.89 percent, compared to 3.12 for Wal-Mart (Exhibit 6–3). But Wal-Mart outperformed Tiffany on asset turnover, 2.63 compared to 0.99, respectively (Exhibit 6–6).

EXHIBIT 6–9
Strategic Profit Models
for Selected Retailers

	(1) Net Profit Margin (%)	(2) Asset Turnover	(3) Return on Assets (%)
	$\dfrac{\text{net profit}}{\text{net sales}}$	$\dfrac{\text{net sales}}{\text{total assets}}$	net profit margin × asset turnover
DISCOUNT STORES			
Costco Wholesale Corporation	1.73	3.45	5.97
Family Dollar Stores, Inc.	5.17	2.62	13.54
Best Buy Co., Inc.	2.58	3.17	8.17
GROCERY STORES			
Winn-Dixie Stores, Inc.	0.35	4.24	1.48
The Kroger Company	2.08	2.62	5.46
Safeway Inc.	3.66	1.96	7.18
DEPARTMENT STORES			
The May Department Stores Company	4.96	1.19	5.90
Sears, Roebuck and Co.	1.79	1.11	1.99
Federated Department Stores, Inc.	−1.76	1.04	−1.83
SPECIALTY STORES			
Circuit City Stores, Inc.	1.24	3.35	4.15
The Limited, Inc.	5.54	1.98	10.98
The Gap, Inc.	−0.06	1.82	−0.11
Barnes & Noble, Inc.	1.31	1.86	2.44
CATALOGS			
Spiegel, Inc.	3.46	1.44	4.99
Lands' End, Inc.	4.26	2.62	11.16

Exhibit 6–9 shows strategic profit model (SPM) ratios for a variety of retailers. In the next section, we continue the strategic plan developed for Kelly Bradford in Chapter 5. Retailing View 6.4 looks at the strategic profit model of online retailer Amazon.com and compares it to traditional retailers Wal-Mart and Tiffany & Co.

INTEGRATING MARKETING AND FINANCIAL STRATEGIES FOR KELLY BRADFORD'S GIFT STORES

Recall from Chapter 5 that Kelly Bradford owns Gifts To Go, a two-store chain in the Chicago area. She's considering several growth options, one of which is to open a new Internet store called Giftstogo.com. She determined that the market for such a store is high but very competitive. Now she needs to do a financial analysis for the proposed online store and compare the projections with Gifts To Go.

We'll first look at the profit path, followed by the turnover path. Then we'll combine the two and examine the stores' return on assets. Exhibit 6–10 shows income statements for one of her Gifts To Go stores and her projections for Giftstogo.com.

Working the Ratios for an E-Retailer: Amazon.com   RETAILING VIEW

6.4

Online retailer Amazon.com opened its "virtual doors" in July 1995. The company's original mission was to be the world's largest bookseller by using the Internet "to transform book buying into the fastest, easiest, and most enjoyable experience possible." The company claims that millions of people in over 220 countries have purchased items from its site. Amazon.com's ability to attract a growing customer base has resulted, in part, through its increasing variety of merchandise. Besides offering a huge selection of books, music, and videos, Amazon.com now has added merchandise as diverse as electronics and lawnmowers. In addition to expanding its merchandise assortment, the company has expanded geographically through its British site, Amazon.com.co.uk, and German site, Amazon.com.de.

Despite its strong growth and established presence as a leader in online retailing, Amazon.com has struggled to become profitable. Amazon.com was subject to much skepticism regarding its viability as a retail channel because of its inability to make a profit. The differences between Amazon.com and traditional bricks-and-mortar retailers are reflected in the differences in the strategic profit models. In the profit path, Amazon.com's gross margin of 25.6 percent is slightly more than Wal-Mart's 21.9 percent but is significantly less than Tiffany's 58.7 percent. One would expect Amazon.com to be close to, but slightly higher than, Wal-Mart because of its overall strategy of providing a wide variety of products at low prices.

Operating expenses as a percentage of sales at Amazon.com are 38.8 percent compared to 16.5 percent at Wal-Mart and 39.4 percent at Tiffany. Although Amazon.com does not incur the expenses to operate stores, as Wal-Mart and Tiffany do, it has made massive investments in Internet technology infrastructure to fuel its aggressive expansion. Additionally, Amazon.com has one of the most sophisticated fulfillment systems in retailing. Unlike Wal-Mart and Tiffany, Amazon.com fills orders from its distribution centers one item at a time. To reduce operational costs, Amazon.com has focused on improving its distribution network, one of its biggest expenses. The company worked to improve productivity by improving inventory tracking and sorting capability and cutting costs by outsourcing some of its book fulfillment needs to distributors. With its relatively low gross margin and relatively high operating expenses, Amazon.com had a negative profit margin of 18.2 percent compared to a positive 3.1 percent for Wal-Mart and 10.9 percent for Tiffany in 2001.

The turnover path also illustrates some interesting differences between the firms. Amazon.com has no accounts receivable, in contrast to Wal-Mart with receivables of 2.4 percent of total assets and Tiffany with 6.0 percent. Amazon.com owns few fixed assets compared to traditional bricks-and-mortar retailers. Amazon.com's primary fixed assets are its distribution centers and information technology systems, whereas Wal-Mart and Tiffany have significant investments in stores and other distribution and manufacturing facilities, respectively. Amazon.com's fixed assets account for 16.6 percent of total assets, compared to Wal-Mart's 66.2 percent and Tiffany's 41.4 percent.

In addition, Amazon.com carries very little inventory compared to the other retailers. Amazon.com's inventory is only 8.8 percent of total assets, compared to 27.1 percent at Wal-Mart and 37.5 percent at Tiffany. This is because, in many cases, Amazon.com does not hold the merchandise featured on its website but rather acts as a "showroom" and distributor for other manufacturers, wholesalers, and retailers. For example, Amazon.com has developed partnerships with retailers, including Toys "R" Us, Circuit City, and Target. In exchange for featuring the retailers on its site, the retailers absolve Amazon.com of carrying inventory and pay it fees to handle distribution and customer service. As a result, Amazon.com has an inventory turnover of 16.2 times, which is more than double the 7.6 times at Wal-Mart and significantly higher than the 1.1 times at Tiffany.

Although Amazon.com's inventory turnover is quite high, its fixed assets are currently too high relative to its capacity in terms of distribution facilities and equipment. This results in a relatively low asset turnover. While Amazon.com's asset turnover of 1.9 times is higher than Tiffany's turnover of 1.0 times, it is lower than Wal-Mart's 2.6 times. To improve this situation, the company's goals are to continue increasing productivity without major capital expenses.

On January 22, 2002, Amazon.com proved its skeptics wrong and, on the same day that traditional retailer Kmart filed for bankruptcy protection, reported a net profit of $5 million for its 2001 fourth quarter. While reaching profitability in its final quarter of 2001 is an important milestone, Amazon.com still has its work cut out for it. With its negative annual profits and relatively low asset turnover, Amazon.com still has a negative return on assets relative to a return of 8.2 percent at Wal-Mart and 10.7 percent at Tiffany.

Sources: www.amazon.com; www.freeedgar.com; Robert D. Hof and Heather Green, "How Amazon Cleared That Hurdle," *Business Week*, February 4, 2002; Molly Prior, "Amazon to Open Target Tab," *DSN Retailing Today*, October 1, 2001.

EXHIBIT 6–10

Income Statements for
Gifts To Go and
Giftstogo.com

	Gifts To Go	Giftstogo.com (projected)
Net sales	$200,000	$200,000
Less: Cost of goods sold	110,000	110,000
Gross margin	90,000	90,000
Less: Total expenses	30,000	50,000
Net profit, pretax	60,000	40,000
Less: Taxes	27,000	18,000
Tax rate	45%	45%
Net profit after tax	$33,000	$22,000

Profit Path

Gross Margins   We expect Giftstogo.com to have about the same gross margin as Gifts To Go because it will carry a similar but more extensive assortment.

$$\frac{\text{Gross margin}}{\text{Net sales}} = \text{Gross margin \%}$$

Gifts To Go: $\dfrac{\$90,000}{\$200,000}$ $= 45\%$

Giftstogo.com: $\dfrac{\$90,000}{\$200,000}$ $= 45\%$

Total Expenses/Net Sales Ratio   You might think that the total expenses/net sales ratio would be lower for Giftstogo.com because it doesn't have to maintain stores with highly trained salespeople. Actually, the total expenses/net sales ratio is projected to be much higher for Giftstogo.com because it must hire people and have space to maintain the website, process orders, and get them ready for shipment. Also, Gifts To Go has an established clientele and a great location. Although the new website may attract some of their current customers, there is a lot of competition for gifts on the Internet. Kelly must invest a lot of money to establish awareness for her new brand—giftstogo.com—to people who are unfamiliar with her store.

$$\frac{\text{Total expenses}}{\text{Net sales}} = \frac{\text{Total expenses}}{\text{Net sales ratio}}$$

Gifts To Go: $\dfrac{\$30,000}{\$200,000}$ $= 15\%$

Giftstogo.com: $\dfrac{\$50,000}{\$200,000}$ $= 25\%$

Net Profit Margins   Although the gross margins for the two stores are projected to be the same, since Giftstogo.com is projected to have higher expenses than Gifts To Go is projected to have, Giftstogo.com is expected to generate a lower net profit margin, at least in the short term.

	Gifts to go	Giftstogo.com
ASSETS		
Current assets		
Merchandise inventory	$44,000	$22,000
Cash	2,000	0
Other current assets	3,000	2,500
Total current assets	49,000	24,500
Fixed assets	$125,000	$70,000
Total assets	$174,000	$94,500
LIABILITIES		
Current liabilities		
Accounts payable	$ 35,000	$30,000
Notes payable	7,000	5,000
Total current liabilities	$ 42,000	$35,000
Long-term liabilities	$ 10,000	$12,000
Total liabilities	$ 52,000	$47,000
OWNERS' EQUITY		
Owners' equity	$122,000	$47,500
Total liabilities and owners' equity	$174,000	$94,500

EXHIBIT 6–11
Balance Sheets for Gifts To Go and Giftstogo.com

$$\frac{\text{Net profit}}{\text{Net sales}} = \text{Net profit margin}$$

Gifts To Go: $\dfrac{\$33,000}{\$200,000} = 16.5\%$

Giftstogo.com: $\dfrac{\$22,000}{\$200,000} = 11\%$

Turnover Path

Now let's compare the two stores using the turnover path. Exhibit 6–11 shows balance sheets for Gifts To Go and Giftstogo.com.

Accounts Receivable and Inventory Turnover   Like Gifts To Go, Giftstogo.com would have no accounts receivable due to taking credit cards like Visa, MasterCard, and American Express.

Giftstogo.com should have a faster projected inventory turnover than Gifts To Go because it will consolidate the inventory at one centralized distribution center that services a large sales volume, as opposed to Gifts to Go that has inventory sitting in several stores with relatively lower sales volume.

$$\frac{\text{Net sales}}{\text{Average inventory}} = \text{Inventory turnover}[11]$$

Gifts To Go = $\dfrac{\$200,000}{\$80,000} = 2.5$

Giftstogo.com = $\dfrac{\$200,000}{\$40,000} = 5$

Fixed Assets Gifts To Go and Giftstogo.com rent their space. Thus, their fixed assets consist of the fixtures, lighting, and other leasehold improvements in their store as well as equipment such as point-of-sale terminals and computers. Gifts to go has more invested in assets that make their store aesthetically pleasing, whereas Giftstogo.com has its investment in computer and distribution systems.

Asset Turnover As we would expect, Giftstogo.com's projected asset turnover (2.12) is significantly higher than Gifts To Go's (1.15). Giftstogo.com is projected to have a higher inventory turnover. Its other current assets and fixed assets should be lower as well.

$$\frac{\text{Net sales}}{\text{Total assets}} = \text{Asset turnover}$$

$$\text{Gifts To Go} = \frac{\$200,000}{\$174,000} = 1.15$$

$$\text{Giftstogo.com} = \frac{\$200,000}{\$94,500} = 2.12$$

Return on Assets

$$\frac{\text{Net profit}}{\text{Total assets}} = \text{Return on assets}$$

$$\text{Gifts To Go:} \quad \frac{\$33,000}{\$174,000} = 19\%$$

$$\text{Giftstogo.com:} \quad \frac{\$22,000}{\$94,500} = 23\%$$

Although Gifts To Go's net profit margin is much higher than that projected for Giftstogo.com (16.5 percent versus 11 percent), Giftstogo.com's asset turnover should be greater than Gifts To Go's (2.12 versus 1.15). When we multiply the asset turnovers by the net profit margins, the resulting return on assets ratios are similar: 19 percent for Gifts To Go and 23 percent projected for Giftstogo.com.

If Kelly believes she's receiving an acceptable return on her investment with Gifts To Go, then based on this financial analysis alone, Giftstogo.com becomes a very viable alternative. She must, however, combine this financial analysis with her findings from the strategic audit described in Chapter 5 before determining whether to proceed.

RECAP OF THE STRATEGIC PROFIT MODEL

The strategic profit model is useful to retailers because it combines two decision-making areas—margin management and asset management—so managers can examine interrelationships among them. The strategic profit model uses return on assets as the primary criterion for planning and evaluating a firm's financial performance.

The strategic profit model can also be used to evaluate financial implications of new strategies before they're implemented. For instance, suppose Kelly Bradford wishes to increase sales by 10 percent at Gifts To Go. Using the strategic profit model, she can estimate this action's impact on other parts of the strategic profit model. For instance, to increase sales, she may choose to have a sale. Lowering prices will reduce gross margin. She would have to advertise the sale and hire additional sales help, thus increasing operating expenses. So, although she may be able to achieve the 10 percent sales increase, net profit margin might go down.

Looking at the turnover path, increasing sales without an appreciable change in inventory will increase inventory turnover. Assuming other assets aren't affected, asset turnover will also increase. When she multiplies the lower net profit margin by the higher asset turnover, the resulting return on assets may remain unchanged. Retailing View 6.5 looks at the very different strategic profit model of a service retailer.

We'll look at another method of evaluating strategic options in this chapter's appendix on activity-based costing. First, however, let's see how financial performance objectives are set in retailing organizations.

REFACT

The Target store chain has become such a cash cow for its parent company (about 80 percent of sales) that in 2000 the parent, formerly Dayton Hudson, renamed itself Target Corporation.[12]

SETTING PERFORMANCE OBJECTIVES

Setting performance objectives is a necessary component of any firm's strategic planning process. How would a retailer know how it has performed if it doesn't have specific objectives in mind to compare actual performance against? Performance objectives should include (1) the performance sought, including a numerical index against which progress may be measured, (2) a time frame within which the goal is to be achieved, and (3) the resources needed to achieve the objective. For example, "earning reasonable profits" isn't a good objective. It doesn't provide specific goals that can be used to evaluate performance. What's reasonable? When do you want to realize the profits? A better objective would be "earning $100,000 in profit during calendar year 2005 on $500,000 investment in inventory and building."

Top-down planning means that goals are set at the top of the organization and filter down through the operating levels.

Top-Down versus Bottom-Up Process

Setting objectives in large retail organizations entails a combination of the top-down and bottom-up approaches to planning. **Top-down planning** means that goals are set at the top of the organization and filter down through the operating levels.

In a retailing organization, top-down planning involves corporate officers developing an overall retail strategy and assessing broad economic, competitive, and consumer trends. Armed with this information, they develop performance objectives for the corporation. This overall objective is then broken down into specific objectives for each merchandise category and each region or store.

The overall strategy determines the merchandise variety, assortment, and product availability plus store size, location, and level of customer service. Then the merchandise vice presidents decide which types of merchandise are expected to grow, stay the same, or shrink. Next performance goals are established for each category

RETAILING VIEW The Strategic Profit Model of a Service Retailer: Bally Total Fitness

6.5

Chicago-based Bally Total Fitness is the largest, and only nationwide, commercial operator of fitness centers in the United States. With approximately 4 million members, Bally's membership is more than the estimated total for its six biggest competitors combined. On any given day, more than 350,000 health-and weight-conscious adults visit one of Bally's over 400 facilities, located in 28 states and Canada. Management's primary goals are to open more fitness clubs, make the basic club operations more profitable, and begin selling more ancillary services and products.

As a service retailer, Bally's strategic profit model has some differences from those of the merchandise retailers we've looked at in this chapter. We can see some of these differences in the profit path. Bally's operating expenses as a percentage of sales is 30.6 percent. This is comparable to Tiffany's 39.4 percent but is nearly double the 16.5 percent of Wal-Mart. One would expect Bally to have higher operating profit than a firm like Wal-Mart. After all, Bally is a service business, and a good percentage of those expenses are tied up in personnel—administrators, personal trainers, and maintenance people. Bally's net profit margin is 7.8 percent, compared to 3.1 percent at Wal-Mart and 10.9 percent at Tiffany. Since most of Bally's sales are in service contracts to customers, rather than merchandise, its cost of goods sold is relatively minor. As a result, its net profit margin can compare favorably to Wal-Mart.

There are also differences in the turnover path. One of Bally's primary current assets is accounts receivable—the fees paid for monthly membership dues. Bally's receivables account for 18.3 percent of its total assets, compared to 6.0 percent at Tiffany and 2.4 percent at Wal-Mart. Therefore, customer retention is a significant concern. In an attempt to lower its accounts receivables, and at the same time increase customer retention, Bally is focusing on increasing down payments on financed membership plans and on obtaining installment payment through direct withdrawals or credit cards.

Bally's facilities, a fixed asset, is a sizable portion of its total assets. Bally's property and facilities comprise 63.7 percent of its total assets, compared to 66.2 percent at Wal-Mart and 41.4 percent at Tiffany. To adapt to the changing needs of its members, Bally is continually acquiring or building new facilities and upgrading existing ones. For example, new clubs and renovated clubs have eliminated pools, Jacuzzis, and courts for racquet sports and replaced them with weightlifting and aerobic facilities, which are used by more members. The costs of acquiring, opening and upgrading its health clubs are steep, and, unfortunately, Bally's spending on upgrades and expansion has been rising faster than sales. As a result, the com-

Bally Fitness Centers now have retail stores in the majority of their centers. How does adding this inventory impact their strategic profit model?

pany's asset turnover was only 0.65 times in 2000, compared to Wal-Mart's 2.6 and Tiffany's 0.99.

In 2000, Bally's return on assets was just over 5 percent, compared to 8.2 percent at Wal-Mart and 10.7 percent at Tiffany. The company's low asset turnover combined with a relatively low profit margin adversely affected its return on assets. One should not infer from these financial results that all service providers do not achieve high returns compared to merchandise retailers. We can see, however, why some of the strategic profit model's component ratios are different.

To increase profitability in light of its low returns, Bally has developed a number of new business initiatives in an effort to become a "total fitness provider." In 2000, Bally boosted the number of centers that have in-club retail stores by 54 percent. These initiatives will move Bally from a pure service retailer to one that also sells merchandise like apparel and proprietary nutritional supplements. The move will impact the strategic profit model in two ways. First, there will be an increase in inventory—a current asset. As inventory becomes a more significant portion of the firm's balance sheet, inventory turnover will become an important financial ratio. At the same time, the gross margin ratio will become more important. After all, since pure service providers don't have a cost of goods sold in the sense that they don't have inventory, gross margin is not a useful financial ratio.

Sources: www.ballytotalfitness.com; www.freeedgar.com; "Bally Expands in the Upscale Market," *Mergers and Acquisitions,* December 2001; Elizabeth MacDonald, "Ballyhoo," *Forbes,* November 26, 2001; and Harlan S. Byrne, "Pumped Up," *Barron's,* November 29, 1999.

manager or buyer. A category manager, discussed in Chapter 12, is like a "super-buyer" primarily in the grocery industry.

The director of stores works on the performance objectives with each regional store manager. Next these regional managers develop objectives with their store managers. The process then trickles down to department managers in the stores.

This top-down planning is complemented by a **bottom-up planning** approach. Buyers and store managers are also estimating what they can achieve. Their estimates are transmitted up the organization to the corporate planners. Frequently there are disagreements between the goals that have trickled down from the top and those set by lower-level employees of the organization. For example, a store manager may not be able to achieve the 10 percent sales growth set for the region because a major employer in the area has announced plans to lay off 2,000 employees.

These differences between bottom-up and top-down plans must be resolved through a negotiation process involving corporate planners and operating managers. If the operating managers aren't involved in the objective-setting process, they won't accept the objectives and thus will be less motivated to achieve them.

Accountability

At each level of the retail organization, the business unit and its manager should be held accountable only for revenues and expenses it directly controls. Thus, expenses that benefit several levels of the organization (such as the labor and capital expenses incurred in operating a corporate headquarters) shouldn't be arbitrarily assigned to lower levels. In the case of a store, for example, it may be appropriate to set performance objectives based on sales and employee productivity. If the buyer lowers prices to get rid of merchandise and therefore profits suffer, then it's not fair to assess a store manager's performance based on the store's profit. (Activity-based costing, discussed in this chapter's appendix, provides a vehicle for allocating costs.)

Performance measures should only be used to pinpoint problem areas. Reasons why performance is above or below planned levels must be examined. Perhaps the people involved in setting the objectives aren't very good at making predictions. If so, they may need to be trained in forecasting. Also, a manager may misrepresent a business unit's ability to contribute to the firm's financial goals in order to get a larger inventory budget than is warranted. In either case, funds could be misallocated.

Actual performance may be different than the plan due to circumstances beyond the manager's control. For example, there may have been a recession. Assuming the recession wasn't predicted, or was more severe or lasted longer than anticipated, there are several relevant questions: How quickly were plans adjusted? How rapidly and appropriately were pricing and promotional policies modified? In short, did the manager react to salvage an adverse situation or did those reactions worsen the situation?

Performance Measures

Many factors contribute to a retailer's overall performance. Thus, it's hard to find one single measure to evaluate performance. For instance, sales is a global measure of how much activity is going on in the store. However, a store manager could easily increase sales by lowering prices, but the profit realized on the

EXHIBIT 6–12 Examples of Performance Measures Used by Retailers

Level of Organization	Output	Input	Productivity (output/input)
Corporate (measures of entire corporation)	Net sales Net profits Growth is sales, profits	Square feet of store space Number of employees Inventory Advertising expenditures	Return on assets Asset turnover Sales per employee Sales per square foot
Merchandise management (measures for a merchandise category)	Net sales Gross margin Growth in sales	Inventory level Markdowns Advertising expenses Cost of merchandise	Gross margin return on investment (GMROI) Inventory turnover Advertising as a percentage of sales* Markdown as a percentage of sales*
Store operations (measures for a store or department within a store)	Net sales Gross margin Growth in sales	Square feet of selling areas Expenses for utilities Number of sales associates	Net sales per square foot Net sales per sales associate or per selling hour Utility expenses as a percentage of sales*

*These productivity measures are commonly expressed as an input/output.

merchandise (gross margin) would suffer as a result. Clearly, an attempt to maximize one measure may lower another. Managers must therefore understand how their actions affect multiple performance measures. It's usually unwise to use only one measure since it rarely tells the whole story.

The measures used to evaluate retail operations vary depending on (1) the level of the organization where the decision is made and (2) the resources the manager controls. For example, the principal resources controlled by store managers are space and money for operating expenses (such as wages for sales associates and utility payments to light and heat the store). Store managers focus on performance measures like sales per square foot and employee costs.

Types of Measures   Exhibit 6–12 breaks down a variety of retailers' performance measures into three types: output measures, input measures, and productivity measures. **Input measures** assess the amount of resources or money used by the retailer to achieve outputs. These inputs are used by the retailer to generate sales and profits. **Output measures** assess the results of a retailer's investment decisions. For example, sales revenue results from decisions on how many stores to build, how much inventory to have in the stores, and how much to spend on advertising. A **productivity measure** (the ratio of an output to an input) determines how effectively a retailer uses a resource.

Exhibit 6–13 shows productivity measures used at different levels of a retailing organization. This chapter has concentrated on productivity measures used at the corporate level since they are most closely tied to a retailer's overall strategy. Productivity measures used to evaluate merchandise are discussed in Chapters 12 and 13, whereas we look at productivity measures for evaluating the space in stores in Chapter 18.

In general, since productivity measures are a ratio of outputs to inputs, they can be used to compare different business units. Suppose Kelly Bradford's two stores are different sizes: One has 5,000 square feet and the other has 10,000 square feet. It's hard to compare stores' performances using just output or input measures. The larger store will probably generate more sales and have

Illustrative Productivity Measures Used by Retailing Organizations | **EXHIBIT 6–13**

Level of Organization	Output	Input	Productivity (output/input)
Corporate (chief executive officer)	Net profit	Owners' equity	Net profit/owners' equity = return on owners' equity
Merchandising (merchandise manager and buyer)	Gross margin	Inventory*	Gross margin/inventory* = GMROI
Store operations (director of stores, store manager)	Net sales	Square foot	Net sales/square foot

*Inventory = Average inventory at cost

higher expenses. But if the larger store generates $210 net sales per square foot and the smaller store generates $350 per square foot, Kelly knows that the smaller store is operating more efficiently even though it's generating lower sales.

SUMMARY

This chapter explains some basic elements of retailing financial strategy and examines how retailing strategy affects the financial performance of a firm. We used the strategic profit model as a vehicle for understanding the complex interrelations between financial ratios and retailing strategy. We found that different types of retailers have different financial operating characteristics. Specifically, jewelry store chains like Tiffany generally have higher profit margins and lower turnover than discount stores like Wal-Mart. Yet, when margin and turnover are combined into return on assets, we showed that it's possible to achieve similar financial performance.

We also described some financial performance measures used to evaluate different aspects of a retailing organization. Although the return on assets ratio in the strategic profit model is appropriate for evaluating the performance of retail operating managers, other measures are more appropriate for more specific activities. For instance, gross margin return on investment (GMROI) is appropriate for buyers, whereas store managers should be concerned with sales or gross margin per square foot.

The chapter concludes with an appendix describing the use and benefits of activity-based costing. Based on contribution analysis, activity-based costing is a method of allocating the cost of all major activities a retailer performs to products, product lines, SKUs, and the like. Using activity-based costing, retailers can make more informed and profitable decisions, since they have a clear understanding of the costs associated with the different activities involved in making those decisions.

KEY TERMS

accounts payable, *199*
accounts receivable, *195*
accrued liabilities, *199*
activity-based costing (ABC), *214*
assets, *194*

bottom-up planning, *209*
current assets, *194*
current liabilities, *199*
customer returns, *190*
expenses, *191*
fixed assets, *197*

gross margin, *190*
gross profit, *190*
input measure, *210*
liabilities, *194*
long-term liabilities, *199*
net profit, *192*

net sales, *190*

notes payable, *199*

output measure, *210*

owners' equity, *194*

productivity measure, *210*

retained earnings, *200*

stockholders' equity, *200*

top-down planning, *207*

GET OUT & DO IT!

1. INTERNET EXERCISE Go to www.hoovers.com and use the financial information to update the numbers in the profit margin model in Exhibit 6–3 and the asset turnover model in Exhibit 6–6. Use these two models to develop the strategic profit model in Exhibit 6–8 for Wal-Mart and Tiffany. Then repeat the process for Amazon and Bally Total Fitness. Has there been any significant changes in their financial performance? Why are the key financial ratios for these four retailers so different?

The following links take you to financial information of each company.

Wal-Mart: www.hoovers.com/quarterlies/0/0,2167,11600,00.html

Tiffany: www.hoovers.com/quarterlies/1/0,2167,11481,00.html

Amazon: www.hoovers.com/quarterlies/3/0,2167,51493,00.html

Bally Total Fitness Holding Corporation: www.hoovers.com/annuals/5/0,2168,47485,00.html

2. GO SHOPPING Go to your favorite store and interview the manager. Determine how the retailer sets its performance objectives. Evaluate its procedures relative to the procedures presented in the text.

3. INTERNET EXERCISE/GO SHOP- **PING** Get balance sheet and income statement information for your favorite publicly traded retailer by going to www.hoovers.com or by visiting the store and interviewing the owner/manager. Construct a strategic profit model and evaluate its financial performance. Explain why you believe its ratios are or are not consistent with its strategy.

4. CD-ROM EXERCISE Insert the CD that accompanies *Retailing Management* and go to the Strategic Profit Model (SPM). The SPM tutorial was designed to provide a refresher for the basic financial ratios leading to return on assets. The tutorial walks you through it step-by-step. A "calculation page" is also included that will calculate all the ratios. You can type in the numbers from a firm's balance sheet and income statement to see the financial results that are produced with the current financial figures. You can also access an Excel spreadsheet for doing SPM calculations. The calculation page or the Excel spreadsheet can be used for Case 11: Neiman Marcus and Family Dollar: Comparing Strategic Profit Models, page XXX.

DISCUSSION QUESTIONS AND PROBLEMS

1. Why must a retailer use multiple performance measures to evaluate its performance?

2. Describe how a multiple-store retailer would set its annual performance objectives.

3. Buyers' performance is often measured by their gross margin. Why is this figure more appropriate than net profit or loss?

4. How does the strategic profit model (SPM) assist retailers in planning and evaluating marketing and financial strategies?

5. Nordstrom Department Stores (a chain of high-service department stores) and Price/Costco (a chain of warehouse clubs) target different groups of customers. Which

should have the higher asset turnover, net profit margin, and return on assets? Why?

6. Given the following information, construct an income statement for the Neiman Marcus Group, Inc., and determine if there was a profit or loss in 2001. (Figures are in $000.)

Sales	$3,015,534
Cost of goods sold	2,020,954
Operating expenses	193,628
Interest expense	15,188
Taxes	67,807

7. Using the following information taken from Sharper Image Corporation's 2001 balance sheet, determine the asset turnover. (Figures are in $000.)

Net sales	$383,222
Total assets	162,338
Total liabilities	67,595

8. Using the following information taken from the 2001 balance sheet and 2001 income statement for Lands' End, Inc., develop a strategic profit model. (Figures are in $000.)

Sales	$1,448,230
Cost of goods sold	758,792
Operating expenses	575,662

Interest expenses	(1,350)
Inventory	227,220
Accounts receivable	13,297
Other current assets	162,067
Accounts payable	83,363
Notes payable	0
Other current liabilities	102,201
Fixed assets	196,536
Long-term liabilities	0

9. Assume Sears is planning a special promotion for the upcoming holiday season. It has purchased 2.5 million Santa Bears, a stuffed teddy bear dressed like Santa Claus, from a vendor in Taiwan. The GMROI for the bears is expected to be 144 percent (gross margin = 24 percent and sales-to-stock ratio = 6), about average for a seasonal promotion. Besides the invoice cost of the bears, Sears will incur import fees, transportation costs from Taiwan to distribution centers and then to stores, and distribution center and store costs such as marking and handling. Since the bears arrived early in April, additional storage facilities are needed until they are shipped to the stores the first week of October. Is GMROI an adequate measure for evaluating the performance of Santa Bears? Explain your answer.

SUGGESTED READINGS

Daly, John L. *Pricing for Profitability: Activity-Based Pricing for Competitive Advantage*. New York: John Wiley & Sons, October 2001.

"Hows and Whys of High Performance Retailing." *Chain Store Age* 76, no 11 (November 2000), p. 68.

Keys, David E., and Robert J. Lefevre. "Why Is 'Integrated' ABC Better?" *Journal of Corporate Accounting & Finance* 13, no. 3 (March–April 2002), pp. 45–53.

Nair, Mohan. "Helping Ensure Successful Implementations of Activity-Based Management." *Journal of Corporate Accounting & Finance* 13, no. 2 (January–February 2002), pp. 73–86.

Salanie, Bernard. *The Microeconomics of Market Failures*. Boston: MIT Press, November 2000.

Scheumann, Jon. "Defining Productivity." *Cost Management Update*, no. 126 (April 2002), p. 1.

Sutton, Gary. *The Six-Month Fix: Adventures in Rescuing Failing Companies*. New York: John Wiley & Sons, November 2001.

Swamy, Ramesh. "Strategic Performance Measurement in the New Millennium." *CMA Management* 76, no. 3 (May 2002), pp. 44–47.

Vida, Irena; Lames Reardon; and Ann Fairhurst. "Determinants of International Retail Involvement: The Case of Large U.S. Retail Chains." *Journal of International Marketing* 8, no. 4 (2000), pp. 37–60.

Weeks, Andrea; Dorothy A. Metcalfe; Veronica Miller-Mordaunt; and Madelyn Perenchio. *Effective Marketing Management: Using Merchandising and Financial Strategies for Retail Success*. 3rd ed. New York: Fairchild Books, 1998.

APPENDIX 6A   Activity-Based Costing*

Activity-based costing (ABC) is a financial management tool that has been recently adopted by many retail companies.[13] This accounting method is superior to traditional methods in that it enables retailers to better understand costs and profitability. Retailers that adopt ABC gain an information-based means of improving financial analysis and performance.

In activity-based costing, all major activities within a cost center are identified and the costs of performing each are calculated. The resulting costs are then charged to cost objects, such as stores, product categories, product lines, specific products, customers, and suppliers. Using ABC to plan and evaluate merchandising performance provides an alternative to the standard gross margin and inventory turnover measures. As discussed in this chapter, maximizing these traditional measures may produce less than optimal results.

Although ABC uses general ledger data, it differs from other costing methods in that it assigns all expenses—all sales, marketing, administrative, financing, and operating costs. The process of assigning all these costs is difficult because they are typically not easily identified.

Retailers have focused on improving costing analyses for some time. For example, the direct product profit (DPP) accounting system was developed and used by food and general merchandise retailers beginning in the mid-1970s to permit the calculation of product profitability. Activity-based costing represents a more comprehensive approach because, unlike DPP, it recognizes overhead and administrative expenses as well as direct product costs.

IMPLEMENTATION OF ACTIVITY-BASED COSTING

The five-step process used to conduct activity-based costing is as follows:

1. *Summarize the resources.* Organize costs by grouping those that are related. For example, people-related costs could be grouped as wages and benefits.

2. *Define the activities.* Identify the activities performed in the key departments or cost centers that represent significant work.

3. *Define the resource drivers.* Convert general ledger costs into activity costs by quantifying the relationship between resources and activities.

4. *Specify the cost objects.* Identify the focus of the profitability assessment. For example, the cost object could be a product category such as paper goods, health and beauty aids, or gourmet foods.

5. *Identify the activity drivers.* Measure the amount of activity performed in servicing the cost object. These drivers are aspects of the activity that are highly correlated with the activity cost.

AN ILLUSTRATION OF ABC

Consider the following hypothetical example illustrated in Exhibit 6–14. Safeway is considering reducing the amount of shelf space dedicated to Pepperidge Farm's line of premium cookies in order to expand Safeway's own private-label cookie line. The company is performing an ABC analysis to evaluate the profitability of the two lines. Based on past experience, Safeway believes

EXHIBIT 6–14

Activity-Based Costing Profitability Statement for Pepperidge Farm and Private-Label Cookies at Safeway

	Pepperidge Farm	Private-Label Cookies
Retail price per case	$31.20	$27.00
Cost per case	24.00	18.00
Gross margin	7.20	9.00
Other relevant costs	1.50	5.00
Operating margin	5.70	4.00

*This appendix was written by Professor Kathleen Seiders, Babson College.

that, in general, private-label, (store-brand) items offer higher profits.

Suppose Safeway's cost is $2 per unit ($24 per case of 12) for each variety of Pepperidge Farm cookies. The retail selling price is $2.60 ($31.20 per case), so the gross margin (per case) is $7.20, or 23 percent. Safeway pays $1.50 per unit ($18 per case of 12) for its private-label cookies, which retail for $2.25 ($27 per case). The gross margin per case is $9, or 33.33 percent.

The traditional gross margin measure of profitability suggests that the private-label cookies are Safeway's most attractive option. However, the "real" profit picture may be obscured because all relevant costs have not been applied directly to the products.

The cost of handling the private-label cookies must be considered because there are no distribution costs related to the Pepperidge Farm cookies, which are delivered directly to each Safeway store by the vendor (a direct-store-delivery [DSD] approach). Pepperidge Farm allows 30 days for payment and gives immediate credit for any damaged merchandise. The private-label cookies are shipped to a Safeway distribution center, stored, and then shipped to individual stores. The private-label vendor demands payment in 10 days, rather than 30, and is not responsive to damaged-goods claims. Safeway's ABC analysis, which followed the steps outlined above, included an examination of the warehouse costs related to the company's private-label cookies.

1. *Summarize the resources.* The accounts identified for this analysis included warehouse expenses related to (1) wages and benefits, (2) equipment depreciation, and (3) occupancy (depreciation and utilities).

2. *Define the activities.* The key warehouse activities identified were receiving, storing, shipping, and quality control.

3. *Define the resource drivers.* Wages were assigned based on the number of workers performing the activity. Depreciation was allocated based on each activity's use of the equipment. Occupancy costs were assigned based on square footage used by the activity.

4. *Specify the cost objects.* The cost objects in this case were initially specified as Safeway's private-label cookie line and Pepperidge Farm's cookie line.

5. *Identify the activity drivers.* Receiving was based on number of receipt transactions; storing on number of pallet positions; shipping on number of cases shipped; and inspection on a complexity factor.

The total costs (classified as operating expenses) of receiving, inspection, storage, and shipping Safeway's private-label cookie line were calculated to be $5 per case. The cost for Pepperidge Farm (primarily for receiving) was calculated at $1.50 per case. Operating margins are $5.70 per case (or 18.3 percent) for Pepperidge Farm and $4 per case (14.8 percent) for Safeway private label. The ABC analysis, unlike the traditional gross margin analysis, suggests that it would not be optimal for Safeway to expand its private-label cookie line by reducing Pepperidge Farm's shelf space.

Retail Locations

7

"In addition to our Florida-based department stores, we operate over 500 Beall's Outlet and Burke's Outlet stores in Sunbelt states from South Carolina to California. Our strategy is to sell to price-sensitive customers, value-priced apparel in 12,000 to 15,000 square foot stores. To service these customers, we need to keep our prices and costs down. In 2000, we eliminated all advertising. That decision had a very positive impact on our costs and profits. However, our "no-ad" strategy increased the importance of attracting customers by locating our stores in heavily trafficked intersections or strip shopping centers. Some experts say you can't pay too much for a good location, but the results show that in our business, controlling rent cost is critical to profitability.

We use a geodemographic service to identify and evaluate potential markets. We know the clusters that our customers are in and our goal is to locate our stores where those clusters are overrepresented. Once we identify a community that meets our criteria, the next step is to find a specific location in the area. Our best locations are in strip shopping centers with a cotenant like Wal-Mart, Target, or a grocer that attracts a lot of shoppers.

Bankruptcies, store closings, and strategy of the drug store chains to move from in-line to stand-alone stores, have opened up a number of economical location opportunities for us. Sometimes we find an appealing site that is 30,000 to 40,000 square feet—far too big for us. To take advantage of these opportunities, we sometimes partner with a complementary retailer, like Big Lots (an off-price, hard-lines retailer) and approach the property owner together."

QUESTIONS

- What types of locations are available to retailers?

- Why do certain types of retailers typically locate in one type of location, while others locate in other location types?

- What are the relative advantages of each location type?

- Which types of locations are growing in popularity with retailers?

- Which types of locations have become less desirable for retailers in recent years?

One of our competitors is taking an interesting approach in smaller, more rural markets where there is no vacant shopping center space available. They are putting up low-cost, metal buildings with concrete-block fronts on stand-alone sites. The stores are finished on the inside such that the interior is indistinguisable from a regular store. While the traffic patterns aren't the same as those expected in shopping centers, this approach has promise as a cost-effective way to break into a new market, particularly if the location is on an out-parcel of a good center or a heavily trafficked street."

For several reasons, store location is often the most important decision made by a retailer. First, location is typically the prime consideration in a customer's store choice. For instance, when choosing where you're going to have your car washed, you usually pick the location closest to your home or work. Second, location decisions have strategic importance because they can be used to develop a sustainable competitive advantage. As stated in Chapter 5, retailers can change their pricing, service, and merchandise assortments in a relatively short time. However, location decisions are harder to change because retailers frequently have to either make substantial investments to buy and develop real estate or commit to long-term leases with developers. It's not unusual, for instance, for a national chain store to sign a lease for 7 to 10 years. If that location is the best in a particular mall or central business district, the retailer then has a strategic advantage competitors can't easily copy, because they are precluded from locating there.

Location decisions have become even more important in recent years. First, there are more retailers (particularly national chains like Target, Kohl's, and Starbucks) opening new locations, making the better locations harder to obtain. This problem is made more complex by a slowdown in both population growth and new shopping center construction. A retailer may find a suitable location, but high rent, complicated leases, and expensive fixturing and remodeling can make it very costly. Many experts believe that there is too much retail space in the United States and that the best retail locations are already taken. This problem is more severe in Western Europe and Japan, where available locations are often older and government regulations regarding development are more restrictive.

This chapter describes the types of locations available to retailers and the relative advantages of each. We then examine factors that retailers should consider when choosing a particular location type. In the next chapter, the topic of location continues. Chapter 8 examines issues in selecting areas of the country in which to locate stores and how to evaluate specific locations.

Many types of locations are available for retail stores—each with its own strengths and weaknesses. Choosing a particular location type involves evaluating a series of trade-offs. These trade-offs generally concern the cost of the location versus its value to customers. For instance, the best location for a 7-Eleven convenience store isn't necessarily, or usually, the best location for a Saks Fifth Avenue specialty store.

Retailers have three basic types of locations to choose from: a shopping center, a city or town location, or a freestanding location. Retailers can also locate in a nontraditional location like an airport or within another store. The following sections describe each type of location and present criteria for choosing a particular location type.

SHOPPING CENTERS

From the 1950s through the 1980s, suburban shopping centers grew as populations shifted to the suburbs. Life in the suburbs has created a need for stores a short drive from home. Large shopping centers provide huge assortments for consumers. Combining many stores under one roof creates a synergy that attracts more customers than if the stores had separate locations. It's not uncommon, for instance, for one department store's sales to increase after a competing store enters a shopping center.

The term *shopping center* has been evolving since the early 1950s. A **shopping center** is a group of retail and other commercial establishments that is planned, developed, owned, and managed as a single property. The two main configurations of shopping centers are strip centers and enclosed malls. **Strip centers** are shopping centers that usually have parking directly in front of the stores. Open canopies may connect the store fronts, but a strip center does not have enclosed walkways linking the stores. **Malls,** on the other hand, are shopping centers in which customers park in outlying areas and walk to the stores. Traditional malls are enclosed, with a climate-controlled walkway between two facing strips of stores. The main shopping center types are defined in Exhibit 7–1.

Strip Shopping Centers

The primary advantages of strip centers are that they offer customers convenient locations and easy parking and they entail relatively low rents for retailers. The primary disadvantages are that there is no protection from the weather, and they offer less assortment and entertainment options for customers than malls. As a result, strip centers do not attract as many customers as larger shopping centers.

Type	Concept	Square Footage	Number of Anchors	Type of Anchors	Trade Area*
Strip Centers					
Traditional	General merchandise; convenience	30,000–350,000	One or more	Discount; supermarket; drug; home improvement; large specialty discount apparel	3–7 miles
Power	Category-dominant anchors; few small tenants	250,000–600,000	Three or more	Category specialist; home improvement; discount; warehouse club; off-price	5–10 miles
Shopping Malls					
Regional	General merchandise; fashion (typically enclosed)	400,000–800,000	Two or more	Department; discount; fashion apparel, other specialty stores	5–15 miles
Superregional	Similar to regional but has more variety and assortment	800,000+	Three or more	Department; discount; fashion apparel; other specialty stores	5–25 miles
Lifestyle	Higher-end, fashion-oriented	Variable	N/A	Higher-end specialty stores and restaurants	5–15 miles
Fashion/specialty	Higher-end, fashion-oriented	80,000–250,000	N/A	Higher-end fashion and other specialty stores	5–15 miles
Outlet	Manufacturers' outlet stores	50,000–400,000	N/A	Manufacturers' outlet stores	25–75 miles
Theme/festival	Leisure; tourist oriented	80,000–250,000	N/A	Restaurants; entertainment; fashion and other specialty stores	N/A

*The area from which 60 to 80 percent of the center's sales originate.

There are two types of strip shopping centers: a traditional strip center and a power center.

Traditional Strip Centers A **traditional strip center** is a shopping center that is designed to provide convenient shopping for the day-to-day needs of consumers in their immediate neighborhood. Smaller strip centers are typically anchored by a supermarket or a drugstore; the larger strips are anchored by discount stores, off-price stores, or category killers selling such items as apparel, home improvement/furnishings, toys, shoes, pet supplies, electronics, and sporting goods. These anchors are supported by stores offering sundries, food, and a variety of personal services such as barber shops and dry cleaners.

The traditional strip centers of today have fewer mom-and-pop stores than in the past. Instead, there are more national tenants like the Children's Place, Gap Kids, Kay Bee Toys, Blockbuster Video, and Walgreens. National chains like these are able to compete effectively in strip centers against their rival stores in malls. They can offer lower prices, partly because of the lower rents, plus their customers can drive right up to the door. Strip centers have started to take on nontraditional service-oriented tenants (see Retailing View 7.1).

REFACT

Kohl's Department Stores likes to locate in strip centers beside a grocery store. Once Kohl's is in the center, it attracts retailers such as Bath and Body Works.[2]

The traditional strip centers of today have fewer mom-and-pop stores than in the past. Instead, there are more national tenants like the Children's Place, Gap Kids, Kay Bee Toys, Blockbuster Video, and Walgreens.

Power Centers   A **power center** is a shopping center that is dominated by several large anchors, including discount stores (Target), off-price stores (Marshalls), warehouse clubs (Costco), or category specialists such as Home Depot, Office Depot, Circuit City, Sports Authority, Best Buy, and Toys "R" Us. Unlike traditional strip centers, power centers often include several freestanding (unconnected) anchors and only a minimum number of small specialty tenants. They are typically unenclosed in a strip center configuration, or they can be arranged in a "village" cluster. Many power centers are located near an enclosed shopping mall.

Power centers were virtually unknown before the 1990s, but they have steadily grown in number. Many are now larger than some regional malls. Why have they become so popular? First and foremost, their tenants have experienced tremendous growth and prosperity. A power center is a natural location for these large tenants. They don't want to pay the high rents of regional shopping malls, and they benefit from the synergy of being with other big-box stores. Also, shoppers are seeking value alternatives to the stores found in shopping malls.

Shopping Malls

Shopping malls have several advantages over alternative locations. First, because of the many different types of stores, the merchandise assortments available within those stores, and the opportunity to combine shopping with entertainment, shopping malls have become the Main Street for today's shoppers. Teenagers hang out and meet friends, older citizens in Nikes get their exercise by walking the malls, and families make trips to the mall an inexpensive form of entertainment (as long as they don't buy anything). To enhance the total shopping experience, many malls incorporate food and entertainment.

The second major advantage of locating in a shopping mall is that the tenant mix can be planned. Shopping mall owners control the number of different types of retailers so that customers can have a one-stop shopping experience with a well-balanced assortment of merchandise. For instance, it's important to have several women's clothing stores in a major mall to draw in customers. Yet, too many such stores could jeopardize any one store's success. Mall managers also attempt to create a complementary tenant mix. They like to have all stores that appeal to certain target markets (such as all upscale specialty clothing stores) located together. Thus, customers know what types of merchandise they can expect to find in a particular mall or location within a mall. Managers also strive for a good mix between shopping and specialty goods stores. A strong core of shopping goods stores, like shoe stores, brings people to the mall. Specialty stores, like computer software stores, also bring shoppers to the mall. While specialty store customers are in the mall, they'll likely be attracted to other stores.

The third advantage of shopping malls is that the retailers and their customers don't have to worry about their external environment. The mall's management takes care of maintenance of common areas. Mall tenants can look forward to a strong level of homogeneity with the other stores. For instance, most major malls enforce uniform hours of operation. Many malls even control the external signage used for window displays and sales. Since most shopping malls are enclosed, customers are protected from the weather.

Although shopping centers are an excellent site option for many retailers, they have some disadvantages. First, mall rents are higher than those of some strip centers, freestanding sites, and many central business districts. As a result, retailers that require large stores, such as home improvement centers, typically seek other options. Second, some tenants may not like mall managers' control of their operations. Managers can, for instance, dictate store hours and window displays. Finally, competition within shopping centers can be intense. It may be hard for small specialty stores to compete directly with large department stores. In the past few years, some shopping centers have had a particularly hard time keeping their space rented.

Shopping malls are facing several challenges. First, there is increasing competition from other types of retail location alternatives, such as power and lifestyle centers, catalogs, and the Internet. Second, many of today's shoppers are looking for value alternatives to stores found in shopping malls. Also, the apparel business, which makes up a large percentage of mall tenants, has continued to be weak, causing some specialty store chains to close. Finally, having been built after World War II, many malls are getting old and are therefore less appealing to customers than they once were. The result is lots of empty space in America's shopping malls.

REFACT

At least 300 older malls, each with one or two anchor stores, have shut down since the mid-1990s.[4]

The Service Side of Strips   RETAILING VIEW

7.1

The innovative tenant moving into space formerly occupied by Laneco Department Store in the Trexler Mall Allentown, Pennsylvania, is not a multiscreen theater or bookstore that serves cups of caffe latte with its literature. Rather, the new tenant in this supermarket-anchored strip center will be the Wellness Place, a 50,000-square-foot medical facility with outpatient services provided by a local hospital. The Wellness Place is not just another medical building. It will also contain retail and food shops.

Medical and other service tenants are hardly as sexy as entertainment retail, which gets most of the credit for breathing new life into today's shopping centers. But service should not be overlooked. Many strip developers say nontraditional tenants are quickly and quietly becoming a greater part of a strip's landscape.

The increase in these types of tenants, particularly health care and financial services, can be traced to changes in their respective industries as well as to retail trends affecting unenclosed shopping centers. Category specialists such as Staples are expanding to larger prototypes, and supermarkets are opening more boutique shops within their stores. Thus, there is less room, and less need, for small specialty shops. That leaves holes for nontraditional retailers such as check-cashing stores.

Strip center developers also report doing more deals with chains of orthodontics practices. One prominent company is Orthodontics Centers of America. Because 80 percent of its patients are children, it looks to locate in strip centers or professional buildings near retailers with a complementary consumer base, such as Toy "R" Us and Home Depot.

Another trend bringing more health care facilities to shopping centers is the aging population. By 2000, people 50 years and older will account for about 29 percent of the population, according to the U.S. Bureau of the Census. This market not only needs medical attention but wants it close to home. As a result, it seems only natural to revamp unused retail space in community centers to house medical practices that cater to this powerful demographic.

On another front, hospitals needing more convenient and cost-effective ways to reach out and treat people are opening more outpatient, satellite facilities in locations like community shopping centers, where space and parking already exist. By locating away from a medical campus, hospitals can cut overhead costs, increase visibility, and improve access.

Sources: Michael Fickes, "Retrenchment or Renewal?" *National Real Estate Investor*, May 1, 2001, p. 50; Joanne Gordon, "The Service Side of Strips," *Chain Store Age*, February 1998, pp. 136–38; and "Renovation Case Study: Spruced Up by Office Space," *Shopping Center World*, May 30, 1999.

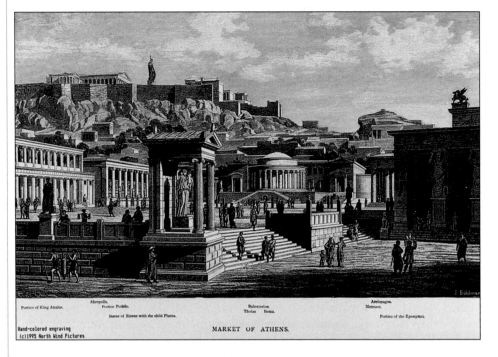

Portion of King Attalos.   Akropolis.   Portico Poikile.   Buleuterion.   Areiopagos.
Statue of Eirene with the child Plutos.   Tholus.   Bema.   Metroon.
                    Portico of the Eponymoi.

Hand-colored engraving
(c)1995 North Wind Pictures   MARKET OF ATHENS.

The first shopping center, a marketplace with retail stores, was the Agora at the foot of the Parthenon in Athens in 600 B.C. It was the center of all commerce, politics, and entertainment in ancient Greece.
Source: John Fleischman, "In Classic Athens, a Market Trading in Currency of Ideas," *Smithsonian* 24 (July 1993), pp. 38–47.

What are they doing about their problem? Some mall owners are turning their centers into traditional town squares with lots of entertainment opportunities.[5] They believe if they can encourage people to spend more time in the mall, people will spend more money there. The owners are renting to nontraditional mall tenants like dry cleaners, doctors' offices, and even chapels—everything that you would have found in a town square in the 1950s. Others are forging links to their communities by opening wellness centers, libraries, city halls, and children's play areas.

Some malls view their new role as a family entertainment center. For example, the Circle Center mall in Indianapolis has no shops on the fourth floor. Instead, people can play virtual reality games like throwing virtual grenades at their friends wearing space age wraparound goggles. If they don't want to play games, they can go to a movie, theme restaurant, or bar.

To help keep their parents shopping, some malls provide entertainment for their kids.

But some industry professionals warn that not enough thought is given to the costs and sometimes less desirable impact of entertainment tenants. Some don't consider, for instance, how existing customers and tenants will be affected. Some entertainment formats, after all, can be teen magnets, and these sometimes do not coexist with older apparel customers, who have always been the industry's bread and butter. Careful attention also must be paid to where entertainment is placed to make sure it helps, rather than hinders, existing tenants.

A more extreme approach to revitalizing a mall is known as demalling.[6] **Demalling** usually involves demolishing a mall's small shops, scrapping its common space and food courts, enlarging the sites once occupied by department stores, and adding more entrances onto the parking lot. For example, Anaheim Plaza was one of the first enclosed malls in Orange County, California, near Disneyland. During the 1980s, it had lost most of its original glamour. Its owner bulldozed most of the mall and built in its place a string of stores, opening onto a parking lot. The new tenants include a Wal-Mart, CompUSA, Old Navy, Radio Shack, Petco, and Payless Shoes.

Regional Centers   A **regional center** is a shopping mall that provides general merchandise (a large percentage of which is apparel) and services in full depth and variety. Its main attractions are its anchors, department and discount stores, or fashion specialty stores. A typical regional center is usually enclosed with an inward orientation of the stores connected by a common walkway, with parking surrounding the outside perimeter.

Superregional Centers   A **superregional center** is a shopping center that is similar to a regional center, but because of its larger size, it has more anchors and a deeper selection of merchandise, and it draws from a larger population base. As with regional centers, the typical configuration is an enclosed mall, frequently with multilevels. Exhibit 7–2 lists the biggest shopping centers in the world.

According to the *Guiness Book of Records*, the world's largest shopping, amusement, and recreation center is the West Edmonton Mall in Alberta, Canada. It has nearly 5.2 million square feet of covered space, 3.8 million square feet of selling space, more than 800 stores and services, and 110 restaurants. But the mall has more than shopping to attract millions of people a year. It also sports the Galaxyland Amusement park, a seven-acre waterpark, an NHL-size ice arena, submarines, an exact replica of the Santa Maria ship, a dolphin lagoon, aquarium facilities, Fantasyland Hotel, a miniature golf course, 26 movie theaters and IMAX, and a casino. Don't worry about parking. It is also the largest capacity in the world, enough for 20,000 vehicles.

REFACT

People are shopping less in malls and more online. About 6.3 million people in the United States spent over 50 percent of their holiday shopping budget online during the 2000 holiday season.[7]

REFACT

On any given day, Mall of America near Minneapolis, Minnesota, the largest mall in the United States, has enough people in it to qualify as the third-largest city in the state. It has more than 42 million visitors each year—more than Disney World, the Grand Canyon, and Graceland combined.[8]

Name	Location	Gross Leasable Space (in Square Feet)
West Edmonton Mall	Alberta, Canada	5,200,000
Mall of Asia	Manila, Philippines	5,000,000
Mall of America	Blooomington, MN	4,200,000
SM Prime's Megamall	Manila, Philippines	3,500,000
Del Amo Fashion Center	Torrance, CA	3,000,000
South Coast Plaza	Costa Meso, CA	2,700,000
Seacon Square	Thailand	2,700,000
Plaza/Crystal Court Woodfield Mall	Schaumburg, IL	2,700,000
The Plaza and the Court at King of Prussia	King of Prussia, PA	2,500,000
Sawgrass Mills	Sunrise, FL	2,300,000

EXHIBIT 7–2
The World's Largest Shopping Malls

Sources: Susan Thorn, "Megamalls Gaining Favor in Asia," *Shopping Centers Today*, April 1, 1997, p. 1; Susan Thorn, "Recovery Slow in Thailand, Malaysia, Philippines," *Shopping Centers Today*, May 2000; and "100 Largest Shopping Centers in the U.S.," ICSC Library.

According to the *Guiness Book of Records,* the world's largest shopping, amusement, and recreation center is the West Edmonton Mall in Alberta, Canada with over 5.2 million square feet of covered space.

REFACT

The average income of lifestyle center customers is about double that of mall shoppers: They visit 2.5 times more often, and they spend 50 percent more per visit.[10]

Lifestyle Centers   A **lifestyle center** is an outdoor traditional streetscape layout with sit-down restaurants and a conglomeration of retailers such as Williams-Sonoma, Pottery Barn, and Eddie Bauer. But there are no self-service discount stores like Best Buy or Target.[9]

The centers offer shoppers convenience, safety, an optimum tenant mix, and a pleasant atmosphere. Like "Main Street" locations, shoppers go because it's an attractive, energetic place to meet their friends and have fun. Some lifestyle centers consist only of stores and restaurants; some have cinemas and entertainment; and others still mingle retail with homes and offices. Nearly all of them are located in high-income areas. They have gone into posh neighborhoods where they depend on a market radius far smaller, but a lot richer, than malls.

Many of the projects are designed to look as though they've been there for decades. As a result, they are expensive to build. The centers now number between 30 and 50 and include the Deer Park Town Center in Deer Park, Illinois; the Grove at Shrewsbury, in Shrewsbury, New Jersey; and the Avenue of the Peninsula, in Rolling Hills Estates, California. Retailing View 7.2 explains how one lifestyle center took root in an old farm pasture.

Fashion/Specialty Centers   A **fashion/specialty center** is a shopping center that is composed mainly of upscale apparel shops, boutiques, and gift shops carrying selected fashions or unique merchandise of high quality and price. These centers need not be anchored, although sometimes gourmet restaurants, drinking establishments, and theaters can function as anchors. The physical design of these centers is very sophisticated, emphasizing a rich decor and high-quality landscaping.

Fashion/specialty centers are similar to lifestyle centers in terms of the clientele and the types of stores they attract. The difference is that these centers are typically enclosed and are larger than most lifestyle centers.

Fashion/specialty centers usually are found in trade areas having high income levels, in tourist areas, or in some central business districts. These centers' trade areas may be large because of the specialty nature of the tenants and their products. Customers are more likely to travel great distances to shop for specialty products sold at nationally known shops such as Neiman Marcus and Ralph Lauren/Polo than for other types of goods.

A great example of a fashion/specialty center is the newly renovated Sommerset Collection in the wealthy Detroit, Michigan, suburb of Troy. Although the mall is over 25 years old, it has recently become the fashion focus of Michigan and western Ontario. The owners believed that their upscale customers were traveling to trendy shops in New York and Chicago, so they expanded the mall and brought in anchor stores like Neiman Marcus, Hudson's, Nordstrom, and

Saks Fifth Avenue as well as specialty shops like F.A.O. Schwarz, Crate & Barrel, and Rand McNally. Mall management offers customers a variety of services, including free valet parking and car washes, as well as complimentary beverages from a café in the mall.

Outlet Centers   **Outlet centers** are shopping centers that consist mostly of manufacturers' outlet stores selling their own brands, supposedly at a discount.[11] These centers also sometimes include off-price retailers such as T.J. Maxx and Burlington Coat Factory or retailer clearance centers like Neiman Marcus' Last Call or Saks Fifth Avenue's Off Fifth. As a result of the shifting tenant mix in some of these centers, various industry experts now refer to outlet centers as value centers or value megamalls. Similar to power centers, a strip configuration is most common, although some are enclosed malls, and others can be arranged in a "village" cluster.

Deer Park Town Center in Deer Park, Ill. is one of a new breed of Lifestyle Centers.

Outlet center tenants view this location option as an opportunity to get rid of excess or distressed merchandise, sell more merchandise, and, to a lesser extent, test new merchandise ideas. Yet the number of outlet stores has declined in recent years, a trend that will continue over the coming years. For instance, Ralph Lauren/Polo announced that it will not expand its chain of outlet stores so that it can concentrate on its core businesses. Other outlet store operators, such as JCPenney, Coldwater Creek, and Lands' End, have found that their Internet outlet sites are a more efficient way to get rid of excess merchandise.

Farm Takes on New Life as a Lifestyle Center   RETAILING VIEW

7.2

The tension between development and preservation plays out in many unpredictable ways. In heritage-conscious Denville, New Jersey, the interplay has resulted in plans for a shopping center that takes its design inspiration from some nearby and well-loved barns. Clothing stores, including The Gap, Ann Taylor Loft, and Talbots; a couple of restaurants; a high-toned stationery store; and other specialty shops are to occupy 88,000 square feet of space featuring detailed barn facades.

After years of debate and adjustment, a revised plan for the Shoppes at Union Hill was unanimously approved by the township's authorities. A lifestyle center has been built on an 18-acre parcel that was previously part of the town's Ayres-Knuth historic farm. The developers installed a white three-board horse fence along the highway. The design incorporates such materials as fieldstone, manufactured stone, and brick. Peaked and domed roofs with wood shakes top the buildings. Still, the Shoppes don't re-

ally look much like the barns on the historic farm. For one thing, the old farm structures appear as if they might blow over in a stiff wind. For another, the Shoppes are actually in one long strip of a building—not barns scattered in a field. But town planners and interested neighbors of the farm and the Shoppes wanted a design that would acknowledge local character.

The center's typical shopper is a 45-year-old woman with a busy life and a couple of kids who wants to pop in to shop at a particular store; she may then get interested in looking in Eastern Mountain Sports for something for her son's camping trip, or stop for a quick bite or a cup of coffee if she gets hungry. Within a five-mile radius of the center there are 151,000 people, with a median family income of $87,000 per year.

Source: Antoinette Martin, "New Jersey: Strip Mall in Denville Looks to Barns for Its Design," *New York Times*, December 2, 2001.

Consumer demand for stores in outlet centers has also diminished in recent years. Although customers can shop an extensive assortment within individual brands and buy below full retail prices everyday, they have to deal with broken assortments, distressed or damaged goods, and less convenient locations. Additionally, traditional retailing has become more price competitive.

Outlet centers have progressed from no-frills warehouses to well-designed buildings with landscaping, gardens, and food courts that make them hard to distinguish from more traditional shopping centers. The newest outlet centers have a strong entertainment component, including movie theaters and theme restaurants, comprising about 15 to 20 percent of the leasable area.[12] Mall developers believe that these entertainment concepts help keep people on the premises longer. Outlet center tenants have also upgraded their offerings by adding credit, dressing rooms, and high-quality fixtures and lighting.

Outlet centers are often located some distance from regional shopping centers so outlet tenants don't compete directly for department and specialty store customers, although manufacturer outlets have learned to peacefully coexist with their department and specialty store customers by editing assortments in their outlet stores to minimize overlap. Outlet centers can be located in strong tourist areas. For instance, since shopping is a favorite vacation pastime, and Niagara Falls attracts 15 million tourists per year, the 1.2 million–square-foot Factory Outlet Mega Mall in Niagara Falls, New York, is a natural location for an outlet center. Some center developers actually organize bus tours to bring people hundreds of miles to their malls. As a result, the primary trade area for some outlet centers is 50 miles or more.

 While there may be a downturn in outlet centers in the United States, their popularity is beginning to take off in other areas like Japan (see Retailing View 7.3) and Europe. Japan is particularly attractive given its large population, love for American brands, and growing consumer enthusiasm for value retailing concepts. European growth is more problematic, however, given Western Europe's more restrictive planning environment, strong opposition by High Street (downtown) retailers,[14] and overall lower levels of enthusiasm for American brands. Germany has perhaps the most restrictive policies in Europe: Seasonal sales can be held only during certain times and apply to only certain products, and discounts are limited.[15] Compared to American outlet centers, the existing European centers are smaller, have fewer entertainment options, and have fewer well-known manufacturer outlets of European brands due to high levels of concern about channel conflict.

Theme/Festival Centers **Theme/Festival centers** are shopping centers that typically employ a unifying theme that is carried out by the individual shops in their architectural design and, to an extent, in their merchandise. The biggest appeal of these centers is to tourists. These centers typically contain tenants similar to those in the specialty centers, except that there are usually no large specialty stores or department stores. They can be anchored by restaurants and entertainment facilities. Because they lack traditional anchor stores and are often perceived as being trendy, these centers are viewed by some industry experts as being risky, unstable investments.

A theme/festival center can be located in a place of historical interest such as Faneuil Hall in Boston or Ghirardelli Square in San Francisco. Alternatively, they can attempt to replicate a historical place (such as the Old Mill Center in

Mountain View, California) or create a unique shopping environment (like MCA's CityWalk in Los Angeles).

Merchandise Kiosks Although not a type of shopping mall, merchandise kiosks are found in shopping malls of all types and are a popular location alternative for retailers with small space needs. Merchandise **kiosks** are small selling spaces offering a limited merchandise assortment. These selling spaces are typically between 40 and 500 square feet and can be in prime mall locations. They're relatively inexpensive compared to a regular store. They usually have short-term leases, shielding tenants from the liability of having to pay long-term rent in case the business fails. Some merchandise kiosks operate seasonally, for instance, selling polar fleece in winter and baseball hats in summer. Of course, vendors also can be evicted on short notice. These alternatives to regular stores are often a great way for small retailers to begin or expand.

Mall operators see these alternative selling spaces as an opportunity to generate rental income in otherwise vacant space. Some of the nation's biggest mall developers are installing merchandise kiosks in every available space. These

Merchandise kiosks, like this one in the Galleria at Roseville in Roseville, California, are found in shopping malls of all types and are a popular location alternative for retailers with small space needs.

Once-Proud Japanese Discover Outlet Malls RETAILING VIEW

7.3

On any given Saturday more than 20,000 people venture into an industrial district of the port city of Yokohama, Japan, and converge on a fake New England fishing village named Sawtucket.

Sawtucket has a clock tower, quaint storefronts, and windmills. But the big lure isn't ersatz Americana. It's shopping. Within the Sawtucket complex, which opened in September 1998, is Yokohama Bayside Marina Shops and Restaurants, a factory outlet mall offering famous brands—J. Crew, Eddie Bauer, Reebok, and the like—at bargain prices. Crowds of yen-pinching consumers are heeding the call.

A familiar retail format in the United States, the outlet mall is a revolutionary retailing concept in Japan. For decades, Japanese retailers had assumed, with considerable reason, that consumers wanted only the newest versions of products. And manufacturers avoided selling leftovers openly, often destroying inventory so as not to risk hurting their brand images or annoying department stores that sold at list price.

Then came national economic distress, overturning the assumptions of retailers and altering the attitudes of consumers, who increasingly patronized secondhand stores and discounters. Today, factory outlet malls can be found in or near Japan's big cities and are increasingly popular with shoppers.

In the past, Japanese tourists by the busload descended on American outlet malls armed with the floor plans of stores and Japanese translations of important English phrases like "Buy one, get one free." The mall developers wanted to have consumers experience an American outlet mall without ever getting on an airplane. So they courted 50 outlet tenants, including U.S. outlet regulars such as Nike, Levi's, Guess, and Coach. It was much harder attracting Japanese tenants, many of whom worried about backlash from the department stores.

Some Japanese companies that agreed to open a store in the Yokohama mall are still reluctant to describe just what they're doing. Some insist that its products are ones that were on regular store shelves just a few weeks ago and aren't the season's leftovers. In many stores, big banners on the walls assure customers that the discounted products are legitimate. Products marked "second-class," one banner explains, are items that are slightly damaged and thus can't be sold in regular stores.

Sources: "Chelsea Osaka Outlet to Add 40 Stores, Become Japan's Largest," *Jiji Press English News Service,* February 6, 2002, p. 1; George Wehrfritz, "Destination Shoppers; They Come from All over Japan to Reach This Factory Outlet," *Newsweek,* international ed., November 13, 2000, p. 44; and Yumiko Ono, "Once-Proud Japanese Discover Outlet Malls," *The Wall Street Journal,* December 30, 1998, p. B1.

kiosks sell everything from concert tickets to gift certificates. They also can generate excitement, leading to additional sales for the entire mall. For instance, Woodbridge Center in Woodbridge, New Jersey, typically has several kiosks selling ethnic merchandise such as clothing and art made by Africans and Native Americans. Mall operators must be sensitive to their regular mall tenants' needs, however. These kiosks can block a store, be incompatible with its image, or actually compete with similar merchandise.

CITY OR TOWN LOCATIONS

Although shopping centers are also located in cities or towns, the locations that are discussed in this section are typically unplanned, have multiple owners, and have access from the street. In particular, we will examine central business districts, inner-city locations, "Main Streets," and the redevelopment efforts being undertaken in these locations.

Central Business Districts

The **central business district (CBD)** is the traditional downtown business area in a city or town. Due to its business activity, it draws many people into the area during business hours. Also, people must go to the area for work. The CBD is also the hub for public transportation, and there is a high level of pedestrian traffic. Finally, the most successful CBDs for retail trade are those with a large number of residents living in the area.

But many central business district locations in the United States have been declining in popularity with retailers and their customers for years. Retailers can be concerned about CBDs because high security may be required, shoplifting can be especially common, and parking is often limited. High crime rates, urban decay, and no control over the weather can discourage shoppers from the suburbs. Shopping in the evening and on weekends can be particularly slow in many CBDs. Also, unlike modern shopping centers, CBDs tend to suffer from a lack of planning. One block may contain upscale boutiques, while the next may be populated with low-income housing, so consumers may not have enough interesting retailers that they can visit on a shopping trip.

Inner-City Locations   Another city or town location alternative is the inner city. The **inner city** is typically a high-density urban area consisting of apartment buildings populated primarily by ethnic groups: African Americans, Hispanics, and Asians. There are about 8 million households in America's inner cities. Conservatively, inner-city consumers constitute $85 billion in annual retail buying power—far more than the entire country of Mexico. Unmet demand tops 25 percent in many inner-city markets, and reaches 60 percent in others.[18] Importantly, these customers desire to buy branded merchandise from nationally recognized retailers in the neighborhoods where they live.[19] Although income levels are lower in inner cities than in other neighborhoods in a particular region, most inner-city retailers achieve a higher sales volume and often higher margins, resulting in higher profits.

Successful operations in inner cities, however, require special attention.[20] Senior management must be committed to inner-city initiatives. Retailers must do their marketing research and real estate homework before entering these markets. The best, most experienced, and culturally sensitive managers should be used in these locations. The stores, their managers, and employees should be integrally involved in the community. Finally, assortments must be customized to the specific needs of the trade area. Retailing View 7.4 describes how former basketball star "Magic" Johnson is investing in urban retailing.

Main Street Locations   **Main Street** is the CBD located in the traditional shopping area of smaller towns, or a secondary business district in a suburb or within a larger city. Main Streets share most of the characteristics of the primary CBD. But their occupancy costs are generally lower than that of the primary CBD. They do not draw as many people as the primary CBD because fewer people work in the area, and fewer stores generally mean a smaller overall selection. Finally, Main Streets typically don't offer the entertainment and recreational activities available in the more successful primary CBDs.

Main Street isn't new to national retailers.[22] Woolworth, Kresges, and McCrory's were Main Street mainstays in the past. Today, however, Main Street locations across the United States have The Gap, Crate & Barrel, J. Crew, The Limited, Sunglass Hut, and garden emporium Smith & Hawken interspersed with local, independent merchants as tenants. Even General Cinema Theaters, normally found in malls, are returning to Main Street. Saks Fifth Avenue is opening small stores in several Main Street locations. These Saks stores carry an edited stock selection from full-line Saks stores, with an emphasis on frequently purchased categories such as cosmetics, shoes, and intimate apparel. Why does Saks find Main Street so appealing? Because that's where its core customers—affluent women and men between 35 and 45 years old—live and shop there already.

Some drawbacks of CBD and Main Street locations in the United States are not found in cities and towns in other industrialized countries, particularly in Europe. Retailing View 7.5 examines how Main Street locations in Europe are fighting to maintain their traditional advantage over the encroachment of large retailers.

Redevelopment Efforts in City and Town Locations

Some city and town locations have become very attractive location alternatives to shopping centers. Why is this happening?

Inner-city locations are profitable for retailers. Why? Inner-city consumers constitute $85 billion in annual retail buying power—far more than the entire country of Mexico.

REFACT

Inner-city groceries in Boston charge as much as 40 percent more for basic groceries than their suburban counterparts. This pricing difference is attributable mainly to the low supply of larger grocery stores compared to convenience stores.[21]

- Some of these locations have undergone a process of **gentrification,** which is the renewal and rebuilding of offices, housing, and retailers in deteriorating areas, coupled with the influx of more affluent people that often displaces earlier, usually poorer residents. Retailers are simply locating where their customers are.

- Developers aren't building as many malls as before, and it's often hard to find a good location in a successful mall.

- These same chains are finding that occupancy costs in city and town locations compare favorably to malls.

- City and town locations often offer retailers incredible expansion opportunities because of a stable and mature customer base and relatively low competition.

- Cities often provide significant incentives to locate in urban centers. Not only do these retailers bring needed goods and services to the area, but they also bring jobs. If, for instance, a major retailer hires 500 people, there would be

---

RETAILING VIEW   "Magic" Johnson Brings Retailing to Inner Cities

7.4

In 13 unparalleled years in the National Basketball Association, Earvin "Magic" Johnson rewrote the record books and dazzled fans with his no-look passes and gorgeous perimeter jumpshots. He also led the Los Angeles Lakers to five championships. After he announced to the world in 1991 that he had contracted HIV, many thought that was the end. Instead, for Johnson, that was just the beginning. "People thought I was going to go away," he says. "But I never planned on going anywhere."

Rather, he took his game to a different arena, one where the obstacles are higher and the challenges greater. His new career began with a relatively modest partnership with Loews Cineplex Entertainment, formerly Sony Retail Entertainment. After doing some research, Magic and his partners realized that minorities make up approximately 32 to 35 percent of the movie audience, but there are generally few theaters in minority neighborhoods. They were driving 30 to 40 minutes to get to a theater. So it seemed natural to build movie theaters in urban neighborhoods across the country.

With the theaters in place, the next step was finding other businesses that would complement the theme. Johnson and his partners didn't have to look far. They built theaters and waited for quality sit-down casual restaurants to follow. What they found was an industry that was very much like the theater industry. Either through the franchise holders or the companies in charge, eateries weren't willing to commit to urban locations. They had customers coming in saying they loved the theaters, but they had to

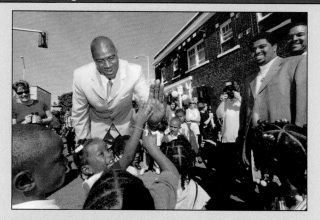

No longer on the basketball court, Magic Johnson now spends much of his time investing in urban retailing.

go all the way across town if they wanted to get something to eat. So next Magic collaborated with Starbucks and TGI Fridays. He also owns fitness clubs and a bank. He is also developing shopping centers and malls in African American neighborhoods around the country.

Sources: "Magic Johnson," *Jet* 101, no. 3 (January 7, 2002), pp. 54–59; David Bloom, "He's Got That Magic Touch," *Variety* 385, no. 7 (January 13, 2002), pp. 11, 32; and Alan Cohen, "Your Next Business," *Fortune Small Business* 12, no. 1 (February 2002), pp. 32–39.

more than 100 additional new jobs created to satisfy the retailing needs of that retailer's employees.

- Young professionals and retired empty-nesters are moving to urban centers to enjoy the convenience of shopping, restaurants, and entertainment.

Successful national chain stores like Staples, The Limited, and Starbucks need these locations to fuel their expansion. Even big-box stores like Home Depot and Wal-Mart are opening up city and town locations. Dubbed "Home Depot Lite," a new store in Brooklyn is only a third of the size of a typical Home Depot.[23] Wal-Mart solved the space problem associated with urban locations by opening a three-level store in Los Angeles.[24]

Main Street Europe: The Fate of Mom-and-Pop Stores   RETAILING VIEW

7.5

During the 1990s, European retailing changed at the expense of the traditional mom-and-pop retail stores. In the past, mom-and-pop stores were the town or village meeting place. The locals would shop at these stores for convenience and service and because the owner was their neighbor.

Yet in most of Europe, the number of small and medium-size stores has fallen over the past several years. In the U.K., for example, shopping centers are growing twice as fast as retail sales as a whole. Less than a third of consumers describe the CBD (or High Street as it is known in the U.K.) as their preferred shopping location. Downtown and corner stores are threatened with extinction as suburban hypermarkets, like French-based Carrefour, selling everything under one roof—from food and cosmetics to clothing and electronics—have become more popular. The two countries experiencing the largest expansion of superstores are Germany (in particular, what was East Germany) and the Commonwealth of Independent States (formerly the USSR).

In countries where this change has been occurring steadily over the past few years, local governments have tried to restrain superstores' growth by limiting their size, thus helping local entrepreneurs compete. For instance, in metropolitan Norwich, England, a horse trots down a dirt lane. It may sound sleepy and pastoral, but this is all happening only three miles from the center of this county capital of 250,000. The nearby downtown has more than 500 shops and 200 restaurants, an open-air market, and a new mall that lures a quarter of a million shoppers into the city center each week.

Were this an American city of similar size, the dirt lane no doubt would be replaced by a highway, the plowed field by a Wal-Mart, and the meadows by a multiplex cinema. European cities such as Norwich like to do things differently, partly because they have less space and partly because they take great pride in their heritage. Strict planning and greenbelt laws force a sharp division between town and country. Suburbs are few. There is no place for the urban area to sprawl.

The efforts help Main Streets thrive and protect the underdeveloped countryside. The London-based Association of Town Center Management says 80 percent of U.K. retail sales are still conducted in towns, despite a crusade by food superstores, mall developers, and other big retailers that want to locate outside downtown. In the United States, only 4 percent of the retail market is still downtown, according to the International Downtown Association in Washington, DC.

But preservation comes at a cost for Europe. The limits on out-of-town retailing reduce competition and retailing efficiency, causing higher prices. Looking for a Trivial Pursuit game? It will cost about $55 in downtown Norwich. A short-sleeve Polo shirt from Ralph Lauren? $90. What's more, the protection of town centers may also be a culprit behind Europe's chronic unemployment woes. A McKinsey & Co. study said policies such as strict zoning laws "represent the most obvious and easily correctable barriers to increased employment" in retail.

Sources: Sally Patten, "Pressure on High Street 'Set to Grow,'" *Financial Times*, February 26, 2001; Sarah Ellison and Christopher Rhoads, "Already Hurting, European Retailers Hold Their Breath—Confidence and Consumption Were Already Weakening," *The Wall Street Journal*, September 24, 2001, p. 25; Jonathan Reynolds, "Who Will Dominate European E-Commerce? Threats and Opportunities for European Retailers," *International Journal of Retail & Distribution Management* 28, no. 1 (2000), p. 9; and Dana Milbank, "Guarded by Greenbelts, Europe's Town Centers Thrive," *The Wall Street Journal*, May 3, 1995, pp. B1, B9.

232

FREESTANDING SITES

Although most retailers locate in strip centers or planned shopping malls, a frequent option for large retailers is a freestanding site. A **freestanding site** is a retail location that's not connected to other retailers, although many are located adjacent to malls. Retailers with large space requirements, such as warehouse clubs and hypermarkets, are often freestanding. Category specialists such as Toys "R" Us also utilize freestanding sites. Advantages of freestanding locations are greater visibility, lower rents, ample parking, no direct competition, greater convenience for customers, fewer restrictions on signs, hours, or merchandise (which might be imposed in a shopping center), and ease of expansion. The most serious disadvantage is the lack of synergy with other stores. A retailer in a freestanding location must be a primary destination point for customers. It must offer customers something special in merchandise, price, promotion, or services to get them into the store.

Many retailers (e.g., Sports Authority and Walgreens) report freestanding stores perform better than stores in malls. Specifically, the 70-plus Walgreens stores that have moved to freestanding sites attract 10 percent more customers and achieve 30 percent higher revenues than they did in their previous strip center locations.[25] Walgreens and other drugstore chains have shifted their emphasis to freestanding locations because they wanted drive-through windows for prescriptions and more space for the front-end merchandise.

OTHER RETAIL LOCATION OPPORTUNITIES

Mixed-use developments, airports, resorts, hospitals, and stores within a store are interesting, if not unusual, location alternatives for many retailers.

Mixed-Use Developments (MXDs) **Mixed-use developments (MXDs)** combine several different uses in one complex, including shopping centers, office towers, hotels, residential complexes, civic centers, and convention centers. MXDs are popular with retailers because they bring additional shoppers to their stores. Developers like MXDs because they use space productively. For instance, land costs the same whether a developer builds a shopping mall by itself or builds an office tower over the mall or parking structure.

A good example of an MXD is found in Kansas City, Missouri's Country Club Plaza. Originally developed in the 1920s, "the Plaza" is home to many of Kansas City's toniest stores and restaurants. Surrounded by offices and apartments, the Plaza draws tourists and residents to stores like Saks Fifth Avenue, Restoration Hardware, and Tommy Bahama, and restaurants like Cheesecake Factory, Ruth's Chris Steakhouse, and Capital Grille.[26]

Airports One important high-pedestrian area that has become popular with national retail chains is airports. After all, what better way to spend waiting time than to have a Starbucks coffee or stop into Victoria's Secret? Sales per square foot at airport malls are often three to four times as high as at regular mall

REFACT

About 25 percent of air traffic is delayed. There are 670 million U.S. air passengers per year, and the 20 busiest airports have 55 percent of all air traffic. That is a lot of potential shoppers![28]

stores.[27] However, rents are at least 20 percent higher than at malls. Also, costs can be higher—hours are longer, and since the location is often inconvenient for workers, the businesses have to pay higher wages. The best airport locations tend to be ones where there are many layovers (Pittsburgh) and international flights (Miami). The best-selling products are those that make good gifts, necessities, and easy-to-pack items.

A smaller-format Fox Sports Sky Box sportsbar and restaurant was created for several airports and features a video control center that resembles Fox's NFL anchor desk.

Resorts Who needs anchor stores to bring in customers when there are mountains or a beach to attract people? Retailers view resorts as prime location opportunities. There is a captive audience of well-to-do customers with lots of time on their hands. As noted earlier, outlet malls are popular in tourist areas. In fact, some outlet malls, such as Sawgrass Mills in Sunrise, Florida, or Silver Sands Factory Stores of Destin, Florida, actually draw tourists to the area. Resort retailing also attracts small unique local retailers and premium national brands like Starbucks or Polo. Resorts like Beaver Creek in Colorado can support dozens of art galleries and fashion retailers with high-end designers. After all, it isn't unusual for visitors at such places to have a net worth of several million dollars.[29]

Hospitals Hospitals are an increasingly popular location alternative. Both patients and their guests often have time to shop. Necessities are important for patients since they can't readily leave. Gift-giving opportunities abound. At the University Pointe hospital in West Chester, Ohio, there is 75,000 square feet of retail space filled with restaurants serving healthy fare and a host of health-related stores and services, such as a day spa.[30]

Retailers are experimenting with nontraditional locations, such as this **PNC Bank** in an **A&P supermarket.**

Store within a Store Another nontraditional location for retailers is within other, larger stores. Retailers, particularly department stores, have traditionally leased space to other retailers such as sellers of fine jewelry or furs. Grocery stores have been experimenting with the store-within-a-store concept for years with service providers like banks, film processors, and video outlets. Wal-Mart had been putting McDonald's and independently owned coffee shops in some of its new stores. Radio Shack has put stores inside Blockbuster Video stores. A variation on the store-within-a-store concept is the kiosk within a store that OfficeMax is partnering with Hewlett-Packard, through which customers can configure computers to order. The in-store kiosks are examined in Chapter 18.

LOCATION AND RETAIL STRATEGY

Now that we've examined the types of locations available to retailers, let's see why some retailers choose the locations they do. Exhibit 7–3 reviews relative advantages of the major retail locations. In this section, we'll examine the location strategies of department stores, specialty apparel stores, category specialists, grocery stores, and an independent optical boutique.

Department Stores

Department stores—like those owned by May Department Stores Company (Foley's) or Federated Department Stores (Bloomingdale's)—are usually located in central business districts and regional or superregional shopping centers. Department stores have historically been the backbone of CBDs. Since the 1950s, they have become the anchors for most regional and superregional shopping centers.

CBDs and shopping centers are natural locations for department stores. These locations draw a large number of people due to their large size and merchandise selection. Of course, a department store creates its own traffic for a CBD or mall. CBDs have the advantage of having potential customers working in the area. Most malls and some CBDs are a source of entertainment and recreation. Some cities in the United States and around the world have CBDs where residents can enjoy a leisurely stroll. In Italy, for instance, it is customary to take a walk through the shopping district every night before dinner between 6 and 8 P.M. As we noted earlier, malls have become America's Main Street where people gather, walk, and simply hang out.

It is not difficult to understand why regional and superregional shopping centers are locations of choice for department stores. Since they're enclosed, they protect shoppers against the weather. Most people would rather stroll around the climate-controlled malls during Minnesota's winters than venture out to the

EXHIBIT 7–3
Relative Advantages of
Major Retail Locations

Location Issues	CBD	Main Street	Strip Center	Shopping Mall	Freestanding
Large size draws people to area	+	–	–	+	–
People working/living in area provide source of customers	+	+	+	–	–
Source of entertainment/recreation	?	–	–	+	–
Protection against weather	–	–	–	+	–
Security	–	–	–	+	–
Long, uniform hours of operation	–	–	+	+	+
Planned shopping area/balanced tenant mix	–	–	–	+	–
Parking	–	–	+	?	+
Occupancy costs (e.g., rent)	?	+	+	–	+
Pedestrian traffic	+	+	–	+	–
Landlord control	+	+	+	–	+
Strong competition	+	+	+	–	+
Tax incentives	?	?	?	?	?

CBDs. Malls also afford customers the feeling of a secure environment. Department stores appreciate malls' uniform and long hours of operation. Also, better malls design their tenant mix so that stores appealing to certain target markets are located together. For instance, upscale specialty stores will tend to be clustered near Neiman Marcus or Nordstrom, while more moderately priced stores will be near Sears.

Specialty Apparel Stores

Specialty apparel stores like The Limited or The Gap thrive in central business districts, Main Street locations, and most types of malls, including regional and superregional shopping centers, lifestyle centers, fashion/specialty centers, and theme/festival centers. These locations appeal to these specialty stores for the same reasons that they are popular with department stores: They are all capable of drawing large numbers of people, and they provide entertainment and recreational opportunities for their customers. Shopping centers also provide security, uniform and long hours of operation, protection against weather, and a balanced tenant mix that is consistent with their target market.

Specialty apparel stores carry **shopping goods**—products for which consumers spend time comparing alternatives. It's not uncommon, for instance, for a woman to go from The Limited to The Gap and on to other apparel stores during one shopping trip. Malls and to some extent CBDs facilitate this type of shopping behavior by having several stores with the same types of merchandise so that customers can compare across stores.

Category Specialists

Category specialists like Home Depot, Sports Authority, and Staples are likely to be found in power centers or in freestanding locations. Category specialists have different locational needs than department stores or specialty apparel stores. They choose power centers or freestanding locations for several reasons. First, such stores typically compete on price, and these locations cost less than CBDs or malls. Second, easy access to parking is important to customers of category specialists since purchases are often large and difficult to carry. Finally, category specialists are destination stores. A **destination store** is one in which the merchandise, selection, presentation, pricing, or other unique features act as a magnet for customers. As such, it is not as important for these stores to be located adjacent to stores selling similar merchandise or in areas that have a natural customer draw. People in the market for a kitchen faucet or a child's birthday present will seek out Home Depot or Toys "R" Us, irrespective of the store's location.

Grocery Stores

Grocery stores are typically located in strip centers. Like category specialists, grocery stores are price competitive, and strip centers have relatively inexpensive rent. These centers' readily accessible parking is also important to grocery store customers. People generally aren't willing to travel long distances to shop for groceries. Grocery stores carry convenience goods—products consumers aren't willing to spend effort to evaluate prior to purchase, such as milk and bread. The location factor that is critical to the success of stores carrying convenience goods is being readily accessible to customers. Strip centers meet this criterion.

REFACT

Malls in southern Europe are typically anchored with supermarkets instead of department stores because people in that region spend half their income on food compared to one-third in the U.K. and United States.[31]

Wholesale clubs, like Sam's Club and Costco, are stores that carry food, but they aren't located in strip centers. Like other category specialists, these stores are very price competitive. Their customers are willing to give up some of the convenience of shopping at their neighborhood grocery store for lower prices. So wholesale clubs are typically located in freestanding sites.

Optical Boutique

Let's examine the location options for Edward Beiner Optical, a South Miami, Florida, store specializing in upper-end, high-fashion eyewear. Edward Beiner's has chosen a Main Street location. Although a Main Street location does not draw from a trade area as large as a CBD or a shopping center, it serves the people working and living in the area.

The retailers in this Main Street location recognize that their location lacks the entertainment and recreation found in shopping centers, so they sponsor art and music festivals to bring people to the area. On Halloween, each store provides candy to its future customers and their parents.

Edward Beiner Optical recognizes other issues that make the South Miami Main Street location less than perfect. There's no protection against the heavy rains that characterize the area's subtropical climate. Security also could be an issue, but most stores are closed at night (when most of their customers have the time to shop). Although most of the stores cater to upscale customers living in surrounding neighborhoods, the tenant mix isn't always balanced. For instance, Edward Beiner's shares its block with a secondhand clothing store and an inexpensive diner. Finally, parking is often a problem.

Edward Beiner Optical, a store in a South Miami, Florida neighborhood, specializes in upper-end, high-fashion eyewear.

In general, though, Edward Beiner's finds this Main Street location attractive. The rent is much less expensive than it would be in a shopping mall. There is usually good pedestrian traffic. Since the properties in the Main Street location are owned by several individuals, the landlords have less control over the tenants than they would in a shopping mall. Finally, although there are other optical stores in the area, the competition is not intense due to the exclusive lines Edward Beiner's carries.

SUMMARY

Decisions about where to locate a store are critical to any retailer's success. A clear, coherent strategy should specify location goals. A location decision is particularly important because of its high cost and long-term commitment. A location mistake is clearly more devastating to a retailer than a buying mistake, for instance.

Retailers have a plethora of types of sites from which to choose. Many central business districts, inner-city, and Main Street locations have become a more viable option than in the past due to gentrification of the areas and lack of suburban mall opportunities. Retailers also have many types of shopping centers from which to choose. They can locate in a strip or power center, or they can go into a mall. We examined the relative advantages of several types of malls, including regional and superregional centers, lifestyle, fashion/specialty centers, theme/festival centers, and outlet centers. We also examined the viability of kiosks, freestanding sites, mixed-use developments, and other nontraditional locations.

Retailers have a hard time finding a perfect site. Each site has its own set of advantages and disadvantages. In assessing the viability of a particular site, a retailer must make sure the store's target markets will patronize that location. The location analyst's job isn't finished until terms of occupancy and other legal issues are considered. (See this chapter's appendix.)

Chapter 8 continues the discussion of how to locate a retail store by examining the issues used to determine which region, trade areas, and sites are best and how to obtain and analyze data for making these decisions.

KEY TERMS

central business district (CBD), *228*
demalling, *222*
destination store, *235*
fashion/specialty center, *224*
freestanding site, *232*
gentrification, *230*
inner city, *228*

kiosk, *227*
lifestyle center, *224*
Main Street, *229*
mall, *218*
mixed-use development (MXD), *232*
outlet centers, *225*
power center, *220*

regional center, *223*
shopping center, *218*
shopping goods, *235*
strip center, *218*
superregional center, *223*
theme/festival centers, *226*
traditional strip center, *219*

GET OUT AND DO IT!

1. **INTERNET EXERCISE** The largest mall in the world is the West Edmonton Mall in Alberta, Canada. Go to www.westedmontonmall.com/ videotour/videotour.html and take a video tour. Do you think the attractions overshadow the shopping?

2. **INTERNET EXERCISE** The Mills Corporation (www.millscorp.com) and Prime Retail (www.primeretail.com) are the largest developers of outlet malls in the United States. Visit their websites and evaluate how their strategies are different. In which company would you want to invest?

3. **INTERNET EXERCISE** Go to www.faneuil hallmarketplace.com and www.coco walk.com. What kind of centers are these? What are their similarities and differences?

4. **GO SHOPPING** Go to your favorite shopping center and analyze the tenant mix. Do the tenants appear to complement each other? What changes would you make in the tenant mix to increase the overall health of the center?

5. **GO SHOPPING** Go to a theme/festival center, a lifestyle center, and a fashion/specialty center either in your area or, if that is not possible, on the Internet. Explain why you believe your chosen locations deserve the designation you have given them. How are they different or similar?

DISCUSSION QUESTIONS AND PROBLEMS

1. Why have location decisions become more important in recent years?

2. Pick your favorite store. Explain why you believe it is (or isn't) in the best location, given its target market.

3. Home Depot, a rapidly growing chain of large home improvement centers, typically locates in either a power center or a freestanding site. What are the strengths of each location for a store like Home Depot?

4. As a consultant to 7-Eleven convenience stores, American Eagle Outfitters, and Porsche of America, what would you say is the single most important factor in choosing a site for these three very different types of stores?

5. Retailers have a tradition of developing shopping centers and freestanding locations in neighborhoods or central business districts that have suffered decay. Some people have questioned the ethical and social ramifications of this process, which is known as gentrification. What are the benefits and problems associated with gentrification?

6. Staples and Office Depot both have strong multichannel strategies. How does the Internet affect their strategies for locating stores?

7. In many malls, fast-food retailers are located together in an area known as a food court. What are this arrangement's advantages and disadvantages to the fast-food retailer?

8. Why would a Payless ShoeSource store locate in a neighborhood shopping center instead of a regional shopping mall?

9. Why would a company like Coach, manufacturer of high-quality leather goods, open outlet stores? What are the disadvantages to such a strategy?

SUGGESTED READINGS

Beyard, Michael D., and W. Paul O'Mara. *Shopping Center Development Handbook*. 3rd ed., Urban Land Institute, 1998.

Buckner, Robert W. *Site Selection: New Advancements in Methods and Technology*. 2d ed. New York: Lebhar-Friedman Books, 1998.

Davies, R.L., and D.S. Rogers, eds. *Store Location and Store Assessment Research*. New York: John Wiley & Sons, 1984.

Howard, Elizabeth. "The Management of Shopping Centres: Conflict or Collaboration?" *International Review of Retail, Distribution and Consumer Research* 7, no. 3 (1997), pp. 143–56.

ICSC Research Quarterly. New York: International Council of Shopping Centers.

Lowry, James R. "The Life Cycle of Shopping Centers," *Business Horizons*, January–February 1997, pp. 77–86.

Miron, John R. "Loschian Spatial Competition in an Emerging Retail Industry," 34, no. 1, Geographical Analysis January 2002, p. 34–61.

O'Kelly, M.E. "Retail Market Share and Saturation." *Journal of Retailing and Consumer Services* 8, no. 1 (2001), pp. 37–45.

Salvaneschi, Luigi, and Camille Akin eds. *Location, Location, Location: How to Select the Best Site for Your Business*. PSI Research/The Oasis Press, 1996.

Tayman, Jeff, and Louis Pol. "Retail Site Selection and Geographic Information Systems." *Journal of Applied Business Research* 11, no. 2 (Spring 1995), pp. 46–54.

Wakefield, Kirk L., and Julie Baker. "Excitement at the Mall: Determinants and Effects on Shopping Response." *Journal of Retailing* 74, no. 4 (Fall 1998), pp. 515–39.

White, John Robert, and Kevin D. Gray. *Shopping Centers and Other Retail Properties: Their Investment, Development and Financing*. Urban Land Institute, John Wiley & Sons, 1995.

APPENDIX 7A   Terms of Occupancy and Location Legal Issues

TERMS OF OCCUPANCY

Once a particular site is chosen, retailers still face a multitude of decisions, including types of leases and terms of the lease.

Types of Leases

Most retailers lease store sites. Although there are advantages to owning a store site (such as stable mortgage payments and freedom from lease covenants), most retailers don't wish to tie up their capital by owning real estate. Also, most of the best locations—such as in shopping malls—are only available by leasing.

There are two basic types of leases: percentage and fixed-rate leases.

Percentage Leases   Although there are many combinations within each type of lease, the most common form is a percentage lease, in which rent is based on a percentage of sales. In addition to the percentage of sales, retailers also typically pay a maintenance fee based on a percentage of their square footage of leased space. Most malls use some form of percentage lease. Since retail leases typically run from 5 to 10 years, it appears to be equitable to both parties if rents go up (or down) with sales and inflation.

A percentage lease with a specified maximum is a lease that pays the lessor, or landlord, a percentage of sales up to a maximum amount. This type of lease rewards good retailer performance by allowing the retailer to hold rent constant above a certain level of sales. A similar variation, the percentage lease with a specified minimum, specifies that the retailer must pay a minimum rent no matter how low sales are.

Another type of percentage lease uses a sliding scale in which the percentage of sales paid as rent decreases as sales go up. For instance, a retailer may pay 4 percent on the first $200,000 in sales, and 3 percent on sales greater than $200,000. Like the percentage lease with a specified maximum, the sliding scale rewards high-performing retailers.

Fixed-Rate Leases   The second basic type of lease is a fixed-rate lease. These leases are most commonly used by community and neighborhood centers. Here a retailer pays a fixed amount per month over the life of the lease. With a fixed-rate lease the retailer and landlord know exactly how much will be paid in rent, but, as noted earlier, this type doesn't appear to be as popular as the various forms of percentage leases.

A variation of the fixed-rate lease is the graduated lease. Here rent increases by a fixed amount over a specified period of time. For instance, rent may be $1,000 per month for the first three years and $1,250 for the next five years.

A maintenance-increase–recoupment lease can be used with either a percentage or fixed-rate lease. This type of lease allows the landlord to increase the rent if insurance, property taxes, or utility bills increase beyond a certain point.

Finally, a net lease is a popular leasing arrangement. In a net lease, the retailer is responsible for all maintenance and utilities. Thus, the landlord is freed from these responsibilities. A net lease can also be used with either a fixed-rate or percentage lease.

Terms of the Lease

Although leases are formal contracts, they can be changed to reflect the relative power and specific needs of the retailer. Recognize that since the basic format of most leases is developed by the lessor (the property's owner), the lease's terms may be slanted in favor of the lessor. It's up to the lessee (the party signing the lease, in this case the retailer) to be certain that the lease reflects the lessee's needs. Let's look at some clauses retailers may wish to include in a lease.

Prohibited Use Clause   A prohibited use clause limits the landlord from leasing to certain kinds of tenants. Many retailers don't want the landlord to lease space to establishments that take up parking spaces and don't bring in shoppers—for example, a bowling alley, skating rink, meeting hall, dentist, or real estate office. Retailers may also wish to restrict the use of space to those establishments that

could harm the shopping center's wholesome image. Prohibited use clauses often specify that bars, pool halls, game parlors, off-track betting establishments, massage parlors, and pornography retailers are unacceptable.

Exclusive Use Clause   An exclusive use clause prohibits the landlord from leasing to retailers selling competing products. For example, a discount store's lease may specify that the landlord can't lease to other discount stores, variety stores, dollar stores, or discount clothing outlet stores.

Some retailers are particular about how the storefront appears. For instance, a women's specialty store may specify that the storefront must have floor-to-ceiling glass to maximize window displays to improve customers' ability to see into the store. Other retailers believe it's important that nothing blocks the view of the store from the street, so they specify that the landlord can't place any outparcels in the parking lot. An outparcel is a building (like a bank or McDonald's) or kiosk (like an automatic teller machine) that's in the parking lot of a shopping center but isn't physically attached to the shopping center.

It's crucial to some retailers that they be in shopping centers with specific types of tenants. For instance, a chain of moderately priced women's apparel shops benefits from the traffic flow of Kmart and Wal-Mart stores. It therefore specifies in its leases that if the major retailer leaves the shopping center, it has the option of canceling its lease or paying a reduced rent.

Escape Clause   An interesting feature that any retailer would want to have in a lease, if it could get away with it, is an escape clause. An escape clause allows the retailer to terminate its lease if sales don't reach a certain level after a specified number of years, or if a specific cotenant in the center terminates its lease.

Finally, retailers must attempt to protect themselves from legal actions by citizens or government agencies that result from a landlord's action or inaction. Clauses may be inserted into leases that protect retailers from these legal problems. The next section looks at some of these legal issues.

LEGAL CONSIDERATIONS

Laws regarding how land is used have become so important that they should be a retailer's first consideration in a site search. Legal issues that affect the site decision include environmental issues, zoning, building codes, signs, and licensing requirements.

Environmental Issues

The Environmental Protection Agency plus state and local agencies have become increasingly involved with issues that could affect retail stores.[32] Two environmental issues have received particular attention in recent years. First is above-ground risks such as asbestos-containing materials or lead pipes used in construction. These materials can be removed relatively easily.

The second issue is hazardous materials that have been stored in the ground. This can be particularly important for a dry cleaner because of the chemicals used, or an auto repair shop because of disposal of used motor oil and battery fluid. The costs of cleaning up hazardous materials can range from $10,000 to over $6 million.

Real estate transactions almost always require an environmental impact statement on the property. But relying on past public filings of buried tanks and other potential hazards can be unreliable and not a protection in court. Retailers have two remedies to protect themselves from these environmental hazards. The best option is to stipulate in the lease that the lessor is responsible for removal and disposal of this material if it's found. Alternatively, the retailer can buy insurance that specifically protects it from these risks.

Zoning and Building Codes

Zoning determines how a particular site can be used. For instance, some parts of a city are zoned for residential use only; others are zoned for light industrial and retail uses. Building codes are similar legal restrictions determining the type of building, signs, size and type of parking lot, and so forth that can be used at a particular location. Some building codes require a certain size parking lot or architectural design. In Santa Fe, New Mexico, for instance, building codes require buildings to keep the traditional mud stucco (adobe) style.

Signs

Restrictions on the use of signs can also impact a particular site's desirability. Size and style may be restricted by building codes, zoning ordinances, or even the shopping center management. At the Bal Harbour Shops in North Miami Beach, for example, all signs (even sale signs) must be approved by the shopping center management.

Licensing Requirements

Licensing requirements may vary in different parts of a region. For instance, some Dallas neighborhoods are dry, meaning no alcoholic beverages can be sold; in other areas, only wine and beer can be sold. Such restrictions can affect retailers other than restaurants and bars. For instance, a theme/festival shopping center that restricts the use of alcoholic beverages may have limited clientele at night.

Legal issues such as those mentioned here can discourage a retailer from pursuing a particular site. These restrictions aren't always permanent, however. Although difficult, time-consuming, and possibly expensive, lobbying efforts and court battles can change these legal restrictions.

Site Selection

CHAPTER

EXECUTIVE BRIEFING | Scott Jennerich, Director of Real Estate, Northeast, Famous Footwear

"Our location strategy has changed to support the changes in our retail strategy. When we were focusing on 4,000-to-5,000-square-foot stores, we located our stores in neighborhood centers typically anchored by supermarkets and regional malls. With the shift in our emphasis to larger, category killer stores, with a 10,000-square-foot format, our preferred locations are power centers. These centers are typically anchored by a discount department store and a home improvement store [Lowe's or Home Depot]. We look for centers that also have major soft goods anchors such as TJ Maxx, Marshall's, Old Navy, Ross, Bed Bath & Beyond, and Linens-N-Things because these stores attract customers also interested in buying shoes.

"Typically, to fully develop a market, we will have one store per 50,000 households that meet our customer profile. Our bottom line is profitable market optimization. To select the trading area, we use a variety of data to analyze potential sites, including GIS data, the brand development index, the population index, Prism clusters, comparable store analysis, and the Famous Footwear customer profile. We evaluate the population density, household income levels, education levels, household size, households with children, median age, lifestyle interests, and numerous other variables to determine whether a trade area meets our criteria. Co-tenacity is critical for us. Our ideal location is between a Target or Kohl's and a TJ Maxx, Ross, or Old Navy store. But site selection is really a combination of science and art. Even with all of the analysis, sometimes you have to draw upon your own past experience when the data may contradict what your gut tells you!

QUESTIONS

● What issues should be considered when determining in which region or trade area to locate a store?

● What is a trade area, and why should a retailer choose one over another?

● What factors should retailers consider when deciding on a particular site?

● How can retailers forecast sales for new store locations?

"After graduating college with a finance degree, I went to work for a developer for three years. Then I took a position at McDonald's. Before coming to Famous Footwear, I had been promoted to regional real estate manager responsible for new store development, relocations, remodels, and asset management for the New Jersey, New York City, and Hartford districts. Real estate decisions are a long-term commitment by our company and have a tremendous impact on our resources, sales, profits, and shareholder value. I understand the magnitude of these decisions and enjoy my role in the complex analysis in making these decisions."

Chapter 7 examined different types of locations available to retailers and why certain types of retailers gravitate toward particular types of locations. In this chapter, we take a closer look at how retailers choose specific sites.

Retail site selection is a very strategic decision. Once a location is chosen, a retailer must live with it for many years. The difference between moving into a superior trade area and one that isn't can mean the difference between a successful store and a failure. Further, even if a retailer finds the "right" neighborhood, the wrong site can spell disaster. Consider, for instance, the location of a new doughnut shop. The retailer has the option to locate in two sites, one across the street from the other. One might think that it should simply choose the cheaper site. But one site has easier access and its signs are highly visible to motorists passing by. More important, that same site is on the way into the central business district, whereas the other is on the way to the suburbs. Chronic doughnut eaters know that it tastes best on the way to work with a big cup of coffee. Without careful analysis of trade areas and specific sites, multimillion dollar mistakes can be easily made. Fortunately, sophisticated analyses, described in this chapter, can be accomplished relatively easily and inexpensively.

Exhibit 8–1 breaks the location decision into three levels: region, trade area, and specific site. The **region** refers to the country, part of the country, a particular city, or **Metropolitan**

EXHIBIT 8–1 | Three Levels of Spatial Analysis

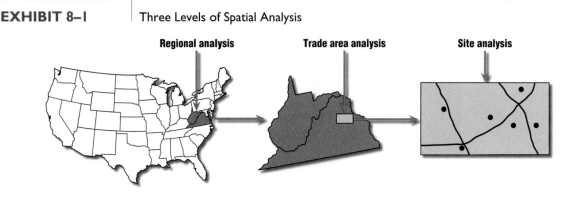

Statistical Area (MSA). An MSA is a city with 50,000 or more inhabitants or an urbanized area of at least 50,000 inhabitants and a total MSA population of at least 100,000 (75,000 in New England). A **trade area** is a contiguous geographic area that accounts for the majority of a store's sales and customers. A trade area may be part of a city, or it can extend beyond the city's boundaries, depending on the type of store and the density of potential customers surrounding it. For instance, a video rental store's trade area may be only a few city blocks within a major metropolitan area. On the other hand, a Wal-Mart Supercenter's trade area in the rural South may encompass 1,000 square miles.

In making store location decisions, retailers must examine all three levels simultaneously. For instance, suppose Taco Bell is expanding operations in the Pacific Northwest and has plans to open several stores simultaneously. Its research indicates that competition in the Tacoma, Washington, market is relatively weak, making it an attractive region. But maybe it can't find enough suitable sites in Tacoma, so it must temporarily postpone locating there.

The remainder of the chapter examines these three location decisions sequentially. First, we look at the factors that affect the attractiveness of a particular region and trade area. Then we examine what retailers look for in choosing a particular site. Of course, the most important factor in choosing a site is the amount of sales it can generate. Thus, we will examine several methods of predicting the amount of sales.

FACTORS AFFECTING THE DEMAND FOR A REGION OR TRADE AREA

The best regions and trade areas are those that generate the highest demand or sales for a retailer. Although the regional analysis is distinct from the trade area analysis, the factors that make them attractive are the same. To assess overall demand in a particular region/market or trade area, the retail location analyst considers economies of scale versus cannibalization, the population's demographic and lifestyle characteristics, the business climate, competition from other retailers in the area, and the retailer's propensity to manage multiple stores (see Exhibit 8–2). Locating in a trade area outside a retailer's home country requires the

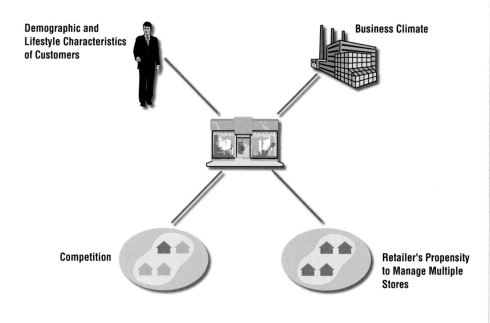

Demographic and Lifestyle Characteristics of Customers

Business Climate

Competition

Retailer's Propensity to Manage Multiple Stores

EXHIBIT 8–2
Factors Affecting the Demand for a Region or Trade Area

analyst to examine all these factors, plus additional issues such as differences in the legal, political, and cultural environment.

Economies of Scale versus Cannibalization

At first glance, you would expect that a retailer should choose the one best location in a given trade area. But most chains plan to go into an area with a network of stores. After all, promotion and distribution economies of scale can be achieved with multiple locations. The total cost is the same to run a newspaper ad for a retailer with 20 stores in an area as it is if the retailer has only one store. Likewise, chains like Wal-Mart expand into areas only where they have a distribution center designed to support the stores.

The question is, What is the best number of stores to have in an area? The answer depends on who owns the stores. For company-owned stores, the objective is to maximize profits for the entire chain. In this case, the retailer would continue to open stores as long as the marginal revenues achieved by opening a new store are greater than the marginal costs. Home Depot subscribes to this fundamental axiom of site selection: It is better to have two stores producing $75 million each than one store producing $100 million. The company believes that a store can do too much business. The store might be overcrowded, offer poor service, have a hard time staying in stock, and actually be underperforming. Home Depot believes that the solution to an underperforming store is to build another store in the same trade area. Although this strategy may sound illogical at first glance, it works for Home Depot.

Home Depot believes that if a store is underperforming, then it may be overcrowded. So they build another store in the same trade area.

For franchise operations, however, each individual franchise owner wants to maximize his or her profits. Some **franchisors** (owners of the franchise) grant their **franchisees** (owners of the individual stores) an exclusive geographic territory so that other stores under the same franchise do not compete directly with them. In other franchise operations, the franchisees have not been afforded this protection and often have been involved in very antagonistic negotiations with the franchisors in an attempt to protect their investment.

Demographic and Lifestyle Characteristics

In most cases, areas where the general population is growing are preferable to those with declining populations. Some retailers, such as Subway Sandwich & Salad Shops, often go into new strip shopping centers in anticipation that the surrounding suburban area will eventually be built up enough to support demand. Yet population growth alone doesn't tell the whole story. Edward Beiner Optical (discussed in Chapter 7 and later in this chapter), for example, is in a Main Street location in a mature neighborhood with a stable population. A reason for the success of this store and similar independently owned retailers in the area is that household income in the trade area is relatively high.

Size and composition of households in an area can also be important success determinants. For instance, Ann Taylor (a chain specializing in traditional and business apparel for women) generally locates in areas with high-income, dual-career families and in tourist areas; household size, however, isn't a particularly critical issue. Toys "R" Us, on the other hand, is interested in locations with heavy concentrations of families with young children.

Finally, lifestyle characteristics of the population may be relevant, depending on the target market(s) a particular retailer is pursuing. Many college students, for instance, have relatively low incomes. However, they may come from well-to-do families, and, by the fact that they are in college, they're relatively educated. Their lifestyles more closely resemble those of recent college graduates in professional jobs making a good income than they do people with similar incomes working odd jobs on a ranch in a rural area. Thus, the way people spend their money is often as important as how much money people make.

Some retailers, such as Subway Sandwich Shops, often go into new strip shopping centers in anticipation that the surrounding suburban area will eventually be built up enough to support demand.

Business Climate

It's important to examine a market's employment trends because a high level of employment usually means high purchasing power. Also, it's useful to determine which areas are growing quickly and why. For instance, the east side of Seattle, Washington, has become a desirable retail location because of its proximity to Microsoft's corporate headquarters. Retail location analysts must determine how long such growth will continue and how it will affect demand for their merchandise. For instance, the economies of some Rust Belt cities like Flint, Michigan, experience greater peaks and valleys due to their dependence on specific industries such as automobiles.

Employment growth in and of itself isn't enough to ensure a strong retail environment in the future. If growth isn't diversified in a number of industries, the area may suffer from adverse cyclical trends. For instance, many areas that have been traditionally dependent on agriculture have attempted to bring in new industries, either manufacturing or high-tech, to help diversify their economies.

Competition

The level of competition in an area also affects demand for a retailer's merchandise. The level of competition can be defined as saturated, understored, or overstored. A **saturated trade area** offers customers a good selection of goods and services, while allowing competing retailers to make good profits. Since customers are drawn to these areas because of the great selections, retailers who believe they can offer customers a superior retail format in terms of merchandise, pricing, or service may find these areas attractive. Some restaurants such as Burger King seek locations where their major competition—McDonald's—has a strong presence. They believe that it's important to go head-to-head with their strongest competitors so that they can develop methods and systems that will allow them to successfully compete with them. They contend that locating in areas with weak competition allows them to become complacent. The strongest competitor will eventually enter the trade area. By then, however, it will have lost its competitive edge.[2]

Another strategy is to locate in an **understored trade area**—an area that has too few stores selling a specific good or service to satisfy the needs of the population. Wal-Mart's early success was based on a location strategy of opening stores in small towns that were relatively understored. Now these stores experience high market share in their towns and draw from surrounding communities.

In effect, these areas have gone from being understored before Wal-Mart arrived to being an **overstored trade area**—having so many stores selling a specific good or service that some stores will fail. Unable to compete head-to-head with Wal-Mart on price or breadth of selection, many family-owned retailers in those towns have had to either reposition their merchandising or service strategies or else go out of business.

Span of Managerial Control

Some retailers focus on certain geographic regions or trade areas. For instance, Davenport, Iowa–based Von Maur (www.vonmaur.com) is a family-owned regional department store chain with 20 stores. Although it can compete with larger, national chains on several dimensions, one of its advantages stems from its regional orientation. It can maintain a loyal customer base by remaining a regional chain. It has excellent visibility and is well known throughout the area. Second, its merchandising, pricing, and promotional strategies specifically target the needs of a regional market rather than a national market. For instance, Von Maur knows that merchandise that's popular in Davenport will also sell in Des Moines. Finally, the management team can have greater locus of control over a regional market. Managers can easily visit the stores and assess competitive situations.

Global Location Issues

Many of the issues and procedures used for making global location decisions are the same as we have discussed throughout this and the previous chapter.[4] The retailer needs to decide on a region, a trade area within that region, and a specific site. The retailer still needs to examine competition, the population characteristics, traffic patterns, and the like. What makes global location decisions more difficult and potentially interesting is that those in charge of making these decisions are typically not as familiar with the nuances of the foreign location issues as they are with the same issues in their home country. Further, national chains in the United States typically have close working relationships with a handful of major developers. Developers work with retailers on a strategic level while the malls are still on the drawing board.

While similar developer–retailer relationships are growing worldwide, often retailers must deal with landlords directly—and cope with a confusing world of site requirements, red tape, and restrictions. For example, a retailer may be surprised to learn that the local government requires a $1 million key payment upfront. A landlord may demand a 25-year lease. And if there's to be construction, it's likely to be a slow, politically charged process.

Real estate selection is where many grand global designs ultimately succeed or fail. A retailer may devote months to targeting a region—Latin America, for instance—before choosing a country to enter. From that point, a city must be chosen.

But when it comes to picking an exact site within that city—a decision that often demands knowing local **traffic flows,** the most desirable side of a street, or urban development patterns—the decision is sometimes rushed and made without the right knowledge. As with many locations in the United States, particularly congested urban areas, if the retailer chooses the wrong side of the street, it may fail.

Costs can also be troublesome. Compared to U.S. locations, occupancy costs in cities like London, Paris, or Tokyo are extremely high. Retailers have to be extremely high-volume to survive. Real estate rental costs are 30 percent more in the U.K. than they are in Germany, which are 30 percent more than they are in the United States, which are 30 percent more than they are in Canada.

Real estate restrictions also complicate international location decisions. For instance, tough European laws make it difficult for big-box retailers to open large stores that have historically required a large piece of property. Solutions occasionally demand a little ingenuity and flexibility. Costco Wholesale's solution, for example, has been to modify store formats in some overseas markets—most notably, the adoption of two-level operations in Korea and Taiwan.

FACTORS AFFECTING THE ATTRACTIVENESS OF A SITE

Now let's look at the issues that make a particular site attractive. Specifically, we'll examine the site's accessibility and locational advantages within the center.

Accessibility

The **accessibility** of a site is the ease with which a customer may get into and out of it. The accessibility analysis has two stages: a macro analysis and then a micro analysis.

Macro Analysis   The macro analysis considers the primary trade area, such as the area two to three miles around the site in the case of a supermarket or drugstore. To assess a site's accessibility on a macro level, the retailer simultaneously evaluates several factors, such as road patterns, road conditions, and barriers.

In the macro analysis, the analyst should consider the **road pattern.** The primary trade area needs major arteries or freeways so customers can travel easily to the site. A related factor is the **road condition,** including the age, number of lanes, number of stoplights, congestion, and general state of repair of roads in the primary trade area. For instance, a location on an old, narrow, congested secondary road in disrepair with too many stoplights wouldn't be a particularly good site for a retail store.

Natural barriers, such as rivers or mountains, and **artificial barriers,** such as railroad tracks, major highways, or parks, may also affect accessibility. These barriers' impact on a particular site primarily depends on whether the merchandise or services are available on both sides of the barrier. If, for instance, only one supermarket serves both sides of a highway, people on the opposite side must cross to shop.

Micro Analysis   The micro analysis concentrates on issues in the immediate vicinity of the site, such as visibility, traffic flow, parking, congestion, and ingress/egress.

Visibility refers to customers' ability to see the store and enter the parking lot safely. Good visibility is less important for stores with established and loyal customers and for stores with limited market areas because customers know where the store is. Nonetheless, large national retailers like Kmart insist that there be no impediments to a direct, undisturbed view of their store. In an area with a highly transient population, such as a tourist center or large city, good visibility from the road is particularly important.

The success of a site with a good traffic flow is a question of balance. The site should have a substantial number of cars per day but not so many that congestion impedes access to the store. To assess the level of vehicular traffic, the analyst can usually obtain data from the regional planning commission, county engineer, or state highway department. But the data may have to be adjusted for special situations. As a result, it's sometimes easier and more accurate to do the analysis in-house. For instance, the analyst must consider that the presence of large places of employment, schools, or big trucks may lessen a site's desirability. Also, areas congested during rush hours may have a good traffic flow during the rest of the day when most shopping takes place. Finally, some retailers might wish to adjust the raw traffic counts by excluding out-of-state license plates or counting only homeward-bound traffic.

When doing a microanalysis of a potential site, retailers look at many factors. At the Gurnee Mills Mall in Gurnee, Illinois, there is plenty of parking available. Using an aerial view, analysts can judge traffic flow, level of congestion, and ingress/egress.

The **amount and quality of parking facilities** are critical to a shopping center's overall accessibility. If there aren't enough spaces or if they're too far from the stores, customers will be discouraged from entering the area. On the other hand, if there are too many open spaces, the shopping center may be seen as a failure or as having unpopular stores. It's hard to assess how many parking spaces are enough, although location analysts use parking ratios as a starting point. A standard rule of thumb is 5.5:1,000 (five and a half spaces per thousand square feet of retail store space).[5] Nevertheless, there's no good substitute for observing the shopping center at various times of the day, week, and season. The analyst must also assess the availability of employee parking, the proportion of shoppers using cars, parking by nonshoppers, and the typical length of a shopping trip.

An issue that's closely related to the amount of available parking facilities, but extends into the shopping center itself, is the relative congestion of the area. **Congestion** can refer to the amount of crowding of either cars or people. There's some optimal range of comfortable congestion for customers. Too much congestion can make shopping slow, irritate customers, and generally discourage sales. On the other hand, a relatively high level of activity in a shopping center creates excitement and can stimulate sales.[6]

The last factor to consider in the accessibility analysis is **ingress/egress**—the ease of entering and exiting the site's parking lot. Often, medians or one-way streets make entering or exiting difficult from one or more directions, limiting accessibility.

Locational Advantages within a Center

Once the center's accessibility is evaluated, the analyst must evaluate the locations within it. Since the better locations cost more, retailers must consider their importance. For instance, in a strip shopping center, the more expensive locations are closest to the supermarket. A liquor store or a flower shop that may attract impulse buyers should thus be close to the supermarket. But a shoe repair store, which shouldn't expect impulse customers, could be in an inferior location because customers in need of this service will seek out the store.

The same arguments hold for regional multilevel shopping centers. It's advantageous for shopping goods stores like American Eagle Outfitters or Wet Seal to be clustered in the more expensive locations near a department store in a mall. Women shopping for clothing may start at the department store and naturally gravitate to stores near it. Yet a store such as Foot Locker, another destination store, needn't be in the most expensive location, since many of its customers know they're in the market for this type of product before they even get to the center.

Another consideration is to locate stores that appeal to similar target markets close together. In essence, customers want to shop where they'll find a good assortment of merchandise. This is based on the principle of **cumulative attraction** in which a cluster of similar and complementary retailing activities will generally have greater drawing power than isolated stores that engage in the same retailing activities. This is why antique shops, car dealers, and shoe and clothing stores all seem to do better if they're close to one another. Of course, an area can become overstored when it has too many competing stores to profitably satisfy demand.

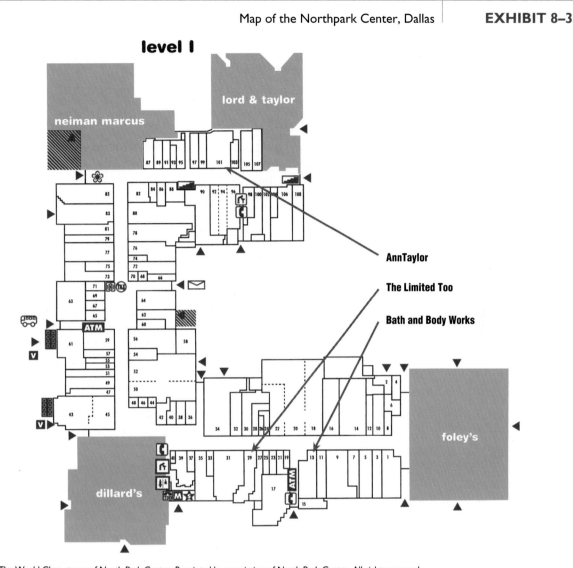

Source: The World Class stores of North Park Center. Reprinted by permission of North Park Center. All rights reserved.

The principle of cumulative attraction applies to both stores that sell complementary merchandise and those that compete directly with one another. Consider Exhibit 8–3, a map of the Northpark Center in Dallas. The more fashion-forward, higher-income customers will find stores like Ann Taylor and other exclusive boutiques between Neiman Marcus and Lord & Taylor. Some stores sell exactly the same merchandise categories, while others sell complementary products, such as perfumes in one store and lingerie in another. A similarly healthy tenant mix is found in the more moderately priced wing between Dillard's and Foley's. Customers can buy accessories at Foley's or at Bath and Body Works store. At the same time they can find a skirt at Dillard's and tank tops for teens at The Limited Too. Thus a good location is one whose tenant mix provides (1) a good selection of merchandise that competes with itself and (2) complementary merchandise.

ESTIMATING DEMAND FOR A NEW LOCATION

Retailers estimate the demand for a new location by defining its trade area and then estimating how much people within the trade area will spend. In this section, we will take a close look at how retailers delimit their trade areas and the factors they consider when defining trade area boundaries. Then we describe the types of information and techniques retailers use to estimate demand.

Trade Area

A trade area is a contiguous geographic area that accounts for the majority of a store's sales and customers. Trade areas can be divided into two or three zones, as depicted by the concentric polygons in Exhibit 8–4. Such trade areas are called **polygons** because their boundaries conform to streets and other map features. The zones' exact definitions should be flexible to account for particular areas' nuances.

The **primary zone** is the geographic area from which the store or shopping center derives 60 to 65 percent of its customers. The **secondary zone** is the geographic area of secondary importance in terms of customer sales, generating

EXHIBIT 8–4

Trade Area for Edward Beiner Optical

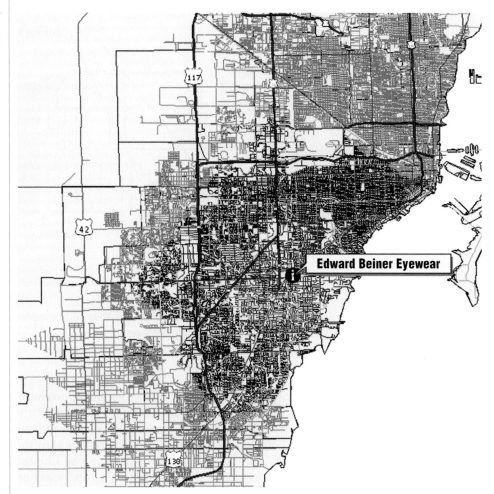

Edward Beiner Eyewear

Source: ESRI. Reprinted by permission.

about 20 percent of a store's sales. The **tertiary zone** (the outermost ring) includes customers who occasionally shop at the store or shopping center. There are several reasons for the tertiary zone. First, these customers may lack adequate retail facilities closer to home. Second, there are excellent highway systems to the store or center so customers can get there easily. Third, customers may drive near the store or center on the way to or from work. Finally, customers are drawn to the store or center because it is in or near a tourist area.

Factors Defining Trade Areas   The actual boundaries of a trade area are determined by the store's accessibility, natural and physical barriers, type of shopping area, type of store, and competition. Exhibit 8–4 illustrates the trade area for Edward Beiner Optical, a store in South Miami, Florida, specializing in upper-end, high-fashion eyewear. The map, generated by ESRI's ArcView GIS system, is based on drive times: 5 minutes for the primary trade area (red), 10 minutes for the secondary trade area (blue), and 20 minutes for the tertiary trade area (green). Driving time is a useful criterion for defining trade areas because the time it takes to get to a particular shopping area is more important to the potential customer than distance.

The trade area for Edward Beiner Optical in South Miami, Florida is limited on the East by Biscayne Bay, but is extended North and South by highway U.S. 1.

Note that the trade area boundaries are oblong. This is because the major highways, especially U.S. 1, run north and south. Not only do the north–south highways bring traffic to the area, but heavy traffic often makes them difficult to cross. Biscayne Bay also limits the trade area on the east. Other barriers, such as a river, mountain range, or high-crime area, may also influence the shape and size of a trade area.

Trade area size is also influenced by the type of store or shopping area. A 7-Eleven convenience store's trade area, for example, may extend less than one mile, whereas a category specialist like Toys "R" Us may draw customers from 20 miles away. The difference is due to the nature of the merchandise sold and the total size of the assortment offered. Convenience stores succeed because customers can buy products like milk and bread quickly and easily. If customers must drive great distances, the store is no longer convenient. Category specialists offer a large choice of shopping and specialty products for which customers are willing to put forth additional effort to shop. Thus, customers will generally drive some

A 7-Eleven convenience store's trade area is small, possibly only a mile, compared to a Sears store that may draw customers from 10 miles away.

This dry cleaning shop is in a strip mall in Grayslake, Illinois. A Walgreens drug store anchors the center. Which is the parasite and which is the destination store?

distance to shop at a category specialist. Edward Beiner Optical is located in a Main Street location rather than a major shopping center. Thus, its trade area is smaller than it would be if it were located in a regional shopping center.

Another way of looking at how the type of store influences the size of a trade area is whether it's a destination or a parasite store. A **destination store** is one in which the merchandise, selection, presentation, pricing, or other unique features act as a magnet for customers. In general, destination stores have larger trade areas than parasite stores—people are willing to drive farther to shop there. Edward Beiner Optical would qualify as a destination store due to the exclusive nature of its merchandise. Other examples of destination stores are anchor stores in shopping centers, such as grocery stores or department stores; certain specialty stores such as Radio Shack, Cartier, and Polo/Ralph Lauren; category killers such as Staples and Office Depot; and some service providers such as movie theaters.

A **parasite store** is one that does not create its own traffic and whose trade area is determined by the dominant retailer in the shopping center or retail area. A dry cleaner would qualify as a parasite store to a Wal-Mart store. People tend to stop at this cleaner on the way to or from Wal-Mart and other stores. Its business is thus derived from Wal-Mart and other businesses in the area. Some retail experts have noted that Wal-Mart can be a destructive force to competition in a trade area because it's so fiercely competitive. Yet some parasite stores and stores that have learned to provide product/service offerings that complement, rather than compete with, Wal-Mart actually benefit from its presence. Other examples of parasite stores are food court restaurants and kiosks in a mall. Retailing View 8.1 examines the strategy of a retailer that actually seeks out locations near Wal-Mart and Target.

The level of competition also affects the size and shape of a trade area for a particular store. If two convenience food stores are too close together, their respective trade areas will shrink since they offer the same merchandise. On the other hand, Edward Beiner Optical is one of several optical shops in this business

RETAILING VIEW   Party City Likes to Locate Next to Wal-Mart and Target

8.1

How many retailers go out of their way to put up stores anywhere near Wal-Mart or Target? Not many—and particularly not stores selling some of the same merchandise that Wal-Mart and Target also carry. A more typical scenario is that the smaller store ends up closing or moving because it can't compete with the discount giants' prices or selection.

Party City, America's largest party-goods chain store, has 200 company-owned outlets and 244 franchised stores in 35 states. They offer a wide selection of merchandise for celebratory occasions, such as birthdays and anniversaries, as well as for seasonal events, such as Halloween and Thanksgiving holidays. The party-goods market is estimated at $12 billion, including crossover categories, such as candy and sweets.

Party City is always on the lookout for locations close to Wal-Mart and Target for three reasons. First, it carries a wider selection of party stuff than Wal-Mart or Target. Second, the giant discount stores bring customers to the shopping center. Finally, the discount stores attract customers who buy lots of party merchandise.

Source: Gene Marcial, "Having a Ball with Party City," *Business-Week Online*, April 16, 2002. Reprinted by special permission of the McGraw-Hill Companies.

district. Having similar shopping goods stores in the same vicinity generally expands the trade area boundaries; more people are drawn to the area to shop because of its expanded selection. Additionally, Edward Beiner Optical's trade area is limited on the south by a large regional shopping center that has several stores carrying similar merchandise.

Sources of Information

Three types of information are required to define a trade area. First, retailers must determine how many people are in the trade area and where they live. For this, retailers use a technique known as customer spotting. Second, retailers use the *Decennial Census of the United States* published by the U.S. Department of Commerce, demographic and GIS (geographic information systems) data, to describe their potential customers in an attempt to assess how much they will buy in the proposed trade area. Finally, retailers use the Internet and other published sources to assess their competition. In strongly competitive trade areas, a retailer can expect to achieve a smaller piece of the total market potential for a particular type of merchandise or store.

Customer Spotting   The purpose of the customer spotting technique is to spot, or locate, the residences of customers for a store or shopping center.[7] Data specific to a retailer's customers are usually obtained from information from credit card or check purchases or from customer loyalty programs (described in Chapter 11). Retailers can also collect this information manually as part of the checkout process.

Another method is by collecting automobile license plates in the parking lot and tracing them to the owner by purchasing the information from state governments or private research companies. A word of caution, however: This method is not thought to be very accurate and is illegal in some states. Experts believe that at least 500 plates are necessary to provide a good sample. R.L. Polk and Co. (www.polk.com) can match the plates against its national vehicle registration database and summarize where the vehicles originate. This approach may, however, be the easiest way to understand the trade area of competitors.

The data collected from customer spotting can be processed in two ways: by manually plotting the location of each customer on a map or by using a GIS system like those described later in this chapter.

Once the customers are spotted, the retailer can delineate a trade area like the one in Exhibit 8–4. This process involves a lot of subjectivity, so the guidelines presented earlier in this chapter are helpful.

Decennial Census of the United States   The *Decennial Census of the United States* is a complete source of information for making location decisions. But as the name implies, it's taken only once every 10 years, so it's often out of date and requires supplementary reports and updates by government agencies and private firms. In the census, each household in the country is counted to determine the number of persons per household, household relationships, sex, race, age, and marital status. Additionally, a report on each building identifies the number of housing units at the address, the status of plumbing facilities, the number of rooms, whether the dwelling is owned or rented, whether the dwelling is owner-occupied, the housing value, the rent, and the vacancy status.

Additional information is obtained for approximately one-sixth of U.S. households.

The decennial census data is available in many formats. Data can be obtained for areas as small as a city block or as large as the entire country. One of the most useful designations for regional evaluations is the Metropolitan Statistical Area. **Census tracts** are subdivisions of an MSA with an average population of 4,000. Because of their smaller size, they are more useful than MSAs for doing trade area or site analyses.

Not only is the census taken only once a decade, but also the information is not totally published for up to three years after the census has been conducted. Fortunately, the Bureau of the Census does release preliminary reports in the interim. It also publishes a variety of supplementary reports that the analyst can use as an update even after the census is published. The census, supplementary reports, and maps are usually available in public libraries, from state data centers that operate in conjunction with the Bureau of the Census; from the U.S. Government Printing Office in Washington, DC.; or at the census website, www.census.gov.

Demographic Data and GIS Vendors   There are hundreds of private companies specializing in providing retailers with information that will help them make better store location decisions. Some, known as demographic data vendors, such as Claritas (www.claritas.com, discussed in Chapter 4), specialize in repackaging and updating census-type data in a format that's easy to understand, easy and quick to obtain, and relatively inexpensive. Since the data from the census can be dated, these firms construct computer models to generate estimates of current and future population and demographic characteristics.

Other firms, such as ESRI, Inc. (www.esri.com), specialize in geographic information systems. A **geographic information system (GIS)** is a computerized system that enables analysts to visualize information about their customers' demographics, buying behavior, and other data in a map format.[8] In many ways it resembles a database program because it analyzes and relates information stored as records. Additionally, however, each record contains information used to draw a geometric shape—usually a point, a line, or a polygon—and represents a unique place on earth to which the data corresponds. As such, GIS is a spatial database, a database that stores the location and shape of information. Using GIS, analysts can identify the boundaries of a trade area and isolate target customer groups. Data for GIS are collected at the point of sale and stored in data warehouses and combined with the type of information that is available from the demographic data vendors.

GIS firms like ESRI offer a wide range of tools that are useful for assessing consumer demand in an area. They utilize data from consumer surveys from private marketing research companies; the Consumer Expenditure Surveys (CEX) developed by the Bureau of Labor Statistics, which is based on interview and consumer diary surveys; and U.S. Census data. The manipulated data produces the ACORN® lifestyle clustering system, a market potential index (MPI), and a spending potential index (SPI).

ACORN (A Classification of Residential Neighborhoods) is a market segmentation system that classifies neighborhoods in the United States into distinctive consumer groups, or market segments. A statistical technique known as cluster analysis is used to develop the classification. Neighbor-

REFACT

The worldwide market for GIS software, hardware, and services is greater than $6 billion.[9]

hoods with the most similar characteristics are grouped together, while neighborhoods showing divergent characteristics are separated.

Several similar and competing systems are currently commercially available, including PRIZM (Potential Rating Index for Zip Markets), which was developed by Claritas and is described in Chapter 4. Each is based on the old adage "birds of a feather flock together." Specifically, people like to live in neighborhoods with their peers, and people in a neighborhood tend to have similar consumer behavior patterns.

The ACORN system starts with blocks and aggregates them into neighborhoods, each with an average of about 400 households. ACORN assigns over 226,000 neighborhoods into one of 43 market segments. Each block group is analyzed and sorted by over 60 characteristics, including income, home value, occupation, education, household type, age, and other key determinants of consumer behavior. An example of how ACORN is used to help assess potential retail sites is described later in this chapter.

Which **ACORN** cluster do you think these people best represent: "High Rise Renters" or "Wealthy Seaboard Suburbs"?

The **market potential index (MPI)** measures the likely demand for a product or service in a county, zip code, or other trade area. An MPI compares the demand for a specific product or service in a trade area with the demand for that product or service nationally. An MPI index of 100 means that the demand for the product or service in that area is equal to the average in the United States. A value of more than 100 represents higher than average demand, and a value of less than 100 represents lower demand. For instance, an MPI index of 120 for sausages in Minneapolis implies that demand for sausages in that city is likely to be 20 percent higher than average in the United States—people eat a lot of sausages there!

The **spending potential index (SPI)** compares the average expenditure in a particular area for a product to the amount spent on that product nationally. Similar to the MPI, an average expenditure compared to the rest of the United States is 100. So an SPI of 80 for new automobiles in Lexington, Kentucky, for instance, means that people spend 20 percent less for cars in that city than the average for the rest of the United States.

Care should be taken before making conclusions regarding the MPI and the SPI. People may eat a lot of sausages in Minneapolis because there are a lot of sausage restaurants, or because people really like sausages. Further, an 80 SPI in Lexington may either imply that there is less demand for new cars, that people buy less expensive cars, or there are not enough dealers to satisfy demand in Lexington. Without knowing the level of competition in these areas, it is impossible to determine whether demand for sausages in Minneapolis or new cars in Lexington can sustain more competition. So let's look at how one measures competition.

Like most industries, these data providers have their own niche specialties. However, the major players now offer a full-service array of information in both table and map formats. A retailer can obtain this information on an annual licensing basis for as little as $1,000; here the retailer is equipped with annually updated computer disks or CD-ROMs, or given data on a site-by-site basis for as little as $100 per report, based on requests by retailers. An analyst can choose

REFACT

There are approximately 78 million baby boomers, born between 1946 and 1965, representing the 800-pound gorilla of demographic market segments. The metropolitan counties with the largest share of boomers include Falls Church County, Virginia; suburban Washington, DC; Marin County, California; suburban San Francisco; and Putnam County, New York.[10]

EXHIBIT 8–6

Income Distribution

	1990 Census		2001 Estimates		2006 Projections	
Population	85,979		92,385		97,160	
In group quarters	4,252		3,764		N/A	
Per capita income	$26,021		$29,114		$33,888	
Aggregate income ($mil)	2,230		2,674		3,275	
Households by income	32,450		33,848		35,346	
Less than $5,000	1,588	4.9%	698	2.1%	724	2.0%
$5,000–$9,999	1,638	5.0	1,474	4.4	1,168	3.3
.						
.						
$40,000–49,999	2,951	9.1	3,609	10.7	3,511	9.9
$50,000–59,999	2,432	7.5	3,114	9.2	2,923	8.3
$60,000–74,999	2,678	8.3	3,583	10.6	3,154	8.9
$75,000–149,999	5,977	18.4	8,127	24.0	9,765	27.6
$150,000+	2,963	9.1	3,655	10.8	4,844	13.7
Median household income	41,967		54,511		60,348	
Average household income	68,729		79,002		92,653	

Source: ESRI.

1930s. A more formalized statistical version of the analog approach uses regression analysis. A third approach, known as Huff's gravity model, is based on Newton's law of gravity. We discuss these location analysis methods below.

The Analog Approach   The analog approach could just as easily be called the *similar store approach.* Suppose Edward Beiner Optical wants to open a new location. Since its present location in South Miami has been very successful, it would like to find a location whose trade area has similar characteristics. It would estimate the size and customer demographic characteristics of its current trade area and then attempt to match those characteristics to new potential locations. Thus, knowledge of customer demographics, the competition, and sales of currently operating stores can be used to predict the size and sales potential of a new location.

The analog approach is divided into three steps.[12]

1. The current trade area is determined by using the customer spotting technique described earlier in the chapter.

2. Based on the density of customers from the store, the primary, secondary, and tertiary trade area zones are defined.

3. The characteristics of the current store are matched with the potential new stores' locations to determine the best site.

Steps 1 and 2: Define Current Trade Area   Based on customer spotting data generated from its data warehouse of current customers, Exhibits 8–6, 8–7, and 8–8 describe the primary trade area (three-mile ring) for Edward Beiner Optical in South Miami, Florida.[13] ESRI's income distribution report (Exhibit 8–6) contains detailed household income figures as well as growth projections. With the

	1990 Census		2001 Estimate		2006 Projection	
Population	85,979		92,385		97,160	
Households	32,186		33,848		35,346	
Average household size	2.54		2.62		2.64	
Race						
White	74,733	86.9%	79,944	86.5%	83,063	85.5%
Black	5,501	6.4	5,389	5.8	5,835	6.0
Asian/Pacific Islander	2,303	2.7	2,774	3.0	3,029	3.1
American Indian	109	0.1	133	0.1	163	0.2
Multirace/other	3,333	3.9	4,145	4.5	5,070	5.2
Hispanic	28,536	33.2	43,161	46.7	51,576	53.1
Median age	35.0		37.4		38.7	
Males	41,690		44,015		46,498	
0–19	10,596	25.4	12,075	27.4	12,292	26.4
20–44	17,887	42.9	16,258	36.9	16,104	34.6
45–64	8,780	21.1	10,720	24.4	12,491	26.9
65–84	4,152	10.0	4,593	10.4	5,145	11.1
85+	274	0.7	368	0.8	466	1.0
Females	44,289		48,371		50,662	
0–19	9,784	22.1	11,945	24.7	12,044	23.8
20–44	18,332	41.4	17,373	35.9	17,160	33.9
45–64	9,744	22.0	12,037	24.9	13,851	27.3
65–84	5,762	13.0	6,051	12.5	6,512	12.9
85+	668	1.5	965	2.0	1,095	2.2
Males 45+	13,206	15.4	15,681	17.0	18,102	18.6
Females 45+	16,174	18.8	19,053	20.6	21,458	22.1
Total population 45+	29,380	34.2	34,734	37.6	39,560	40.7

EXHIBIT 8–7
Demographic Trends

Source: ESRI.

estimated year 2006 average household income at $92,653 and 27.6 percent of the households with incomes between $75,000 and $149,000 and 13.7 percent with incomes over $150,000, the three-mile ring surrounding Edward Beiner Optical is very affluent.

ESRI's demographic trends report (Exhibit 8–7) includes data on population, households by number of persons, race, ethnic origin, and age by sex. An interesting characteristic of the area surrounding Edward Beiner Optical is that an estimated 53.1 percent of the population will be of Hispanic descent by 2006.

As we said earlier in this chapter, it is just as important to look at consumer lifestyles or psychographics as it is to examine their demographics. We know that Edward Beiner's trade area is generally affluent, but are the residents the kind of people who would appreciate its upscale fashion eyewear?

Exhibit 8–8 summarizes the most prominent ACORN lifestyle report for the three-mile ring surrounding Edward Beiner Optical. These segments, described in Exhibit 8–9, indicate an interesting mix of potential customers. Top One Percent and Wealthy Seaboard Suburbs both represent affluent, older groups—perfect for Edward Beiner Optical. High-Rise Renters and Thriving

EXHIBIT 8–8
ACORN
Neighborhood Lifestyle
Clusters for Three-
Mile Ring Surrounding
Edward Beiner Optical

Acorn Cluster Classification	Population Count in Three-Mile Ring	Percent of Population in Each ACORN Classification
High-Rise Renters	9,129	26.00%
Thriving Immigrants	5,175	14.90
Top One Percent	4,257	12.30
Wealthy Seaboard Suburbs	4,211	12.10

Immigrants will also be drawn to Edward Beiner's high-fashion product lines. Generally, the ACORN reports mirror the income and demographic trends reports—the area is affluent and is therefore ideal for selling exclusive and expensive eyewear.

Step 3: Match Characteristics of Current Store with Potential New Store's Location to Determine the Best Site   Now that the trade area for Edward Beiner's existing store is defined, the information can be used to choose a new store location. The trick is to find a location whose market area is similar or analogous to its existing store.

On the basis of the factors affecting demand described earlier in the chapter, it can be concluded that the five factors that contribute most to the success of Edward Beiner's current location are high income, predominantly white-collar occupations, relatively large percentage of older residents, upscale ACORN profile, and relatively low competition for expensive, high-fashion eyewear. Exhibit 8–10

EXHIBIT 8–9
Descriptions of Largest
ACORN Clusters
Surrounding Edward
Beiner Optical

High-Rise Renters	Thriving Immigrants
These single professionals are well educated and working; their growing incomes support their affluent tastes. They join health clubs and environmental groups, go dancing at clubs, and attend the theater or museums. They also jog, bike, and play racquet sports. They use credit cards to buy expensive clothing.	This diverse segment has married couples with either very young or adult children. Most work; unemployment is low. Despite their relative affluence, they don't invest or save, and few take out loans. Their home values or rents are unusually high because of location; most live in urban areas of California. They travel overseas, make long-distance phone calls, and enjoy going to theme parks.
Top One Percent	**Wealthy Seaboard Suburbs**
These are the wealthiest U.S. neighborhoods. They receive their income from salaries, interest, dividends, owning rental properties, or self-employment. Their single-family homes in older suburbs are valued at more than four times the national average. These residents are older married couples with sophisticated tastes. They purchase luxury items and enjoy visiting museums and other cultural events. They frequently order clothing via phone or mail, drive expensive cars, vacation in the United States and overseas, play racquet sports, and read newspapers.	This segment is found along the East Coast and California. These middle-aged, married professionals are at the peak of their earning years. They don't have young children, but many are empty-nester wannabes whose adult children still live at home. Their income sources include salaries, dividends, interest, and owning rental properties. Some receive pensions or retirement income. Their single-family homes built in the 50s or 60s are valued at more than twice the national average. They keep physically fit by working out at the gym, playing racquet sports and golf, and taking vitamins. When not vacationing overseas and in the United States, they purchase home furnishings and contract for home improvements.

compares Edward Beiner's current location with four potential locations on these five factors. These locations are pictured in Exhibit 8-11.

Although the potential customers of site A typically have white-collar occupations, they have relatively low incomes and are comparatively young. Young Immigrant Families also tend to have young families, so expensive eyewear may not be a priority purchase. Finally, there's a medium level of competition in the area.

The Gray Power residents surrounding site B have moderate incomes and are mostly retired. Even though competition would be low and most residents need glasses, these customers are more interested in value than in fashion.

Site C has strong potential since the Twentysomethings residents in the area are young and have a strong interest in fashion. Although working, they are busy furnishing their first homes and apartments and paying off college loans. Although they would appreciate Edward Beiner's fashionable assortment, they won't appreciate the high prices. Also, other high-end optical stores are entrenched in the area.

Site D is the best location for Edward Beiner. The residents are older professionals, or early retirees with high incomes. Upper-Income Empty-Nesters are sophisticated consumers of adult luxuries like high-fashion eyewear. Importantly, this ACORN cluster is similar to Top One Percent and Wealthy Seaboard Suburbs.

Unfortunately, finding analogous situations isn't always as easy as in this example. The weaker the analogy, the more difficult the location decision will be. When a retailer has a relatively small number of outlets (say, 20 or fewer), the analog approach is often best. Even retailers with just one outlet like Edward Beiner Optical can use the analog approach. As the number of stores increases, it becomes more difficult for the analyst to organize the data in a meaningful way. More analytical approaches such as regression analysis are necessary.

The best location for Edward Beiner Optical should contain many older professionals with high incomes.

Descriptions of Edward Beiner Optical and Four Potential Locations' Trade Areas | **EXHIBIT 8–10**

Store Location	Average Household Income	White-Collar Occupations	Percentage Residents Age 45 and Over	Predominant ACORN Profile	Level of Competition
Edward Beiner					
Optical	$XXX	High	37%	Top One Percent	Low
Site A	60,000	High	25	Young Immigrant Families	Medium
Site B	70,000	Low	80	Retirement Communities	Low
Site C	100,000	High	30	Young Literate	High
Site D	120,000	High	50	Upper-Income Empty-Nesters	Medium

Average household income is taken from the year 2006 projections in Exhibit 8–6. Level of white-collar occupations is estimated from ACORN data in Exhibit 8–8. Percentage of residents 45 years old and over is estimated from Exhibit 8–7. Level of competition was subjectively determined.

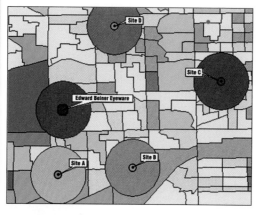

Source: ESRI.

Regression Analysis Regression analysis is a common method of defining retail trade area potential for retail chains with greater than 20 stores.[14] Although multiple regression analysis uses logic similar to that of the analog approach, it uses statistics rather than judgment to predict sales for a new store.

The initial steps in regression analysis are the same as those in the analog approach. First, the current trade areas are determined by using the customer spotting technique. Second, the primary, secondary, and tertiary zones are determined by plotting customers on a map. But then the regression procedure begins to differ from the analog approach. Instead of matching characteristics of trade areas for existing stores with a potential new store by using the location analyst's subjective experience, a mathematical equation is derived.

Using "canned" statistical packages, three steps are followed to develop the multiple regression equation:

1. Select appropriate measures of performance, such as per capita sales or market share.

2. Select a set of variables that may be useful in predicting performance.

3. Solve the regression equation and use it to project performance for future sites.

Steps 1 and 2: Select Store Performance Measure and Variables Used to Predict Performance Sales or per capita sales is the store performance measure most often used in location regression analyses.

Potential variables used to predict performance include demographic and lifestyle composition of the individual store trading areas; business climate; specific information on the location; image of the store; strength of each potential competitor; and site-related real estate variables such as visibility, access, or other types of tenants at the site. The predictor variables should differ, depending on the type of store being analyzed. For instance, household income may be an important variable when predicting sales of a new Peoples Jewelry store, whereas the number of school-age children per household would be appropriate for predicting sales of a McDonald's restaurant.

Step 3: Solve the Regression Equation and Use It to Project Performance for Future Sites Data for each store's performance measure and predictor variables are entered into a computerized regression program. The end result of the regression analysis is an equation that can be used to predict sales of a new store, given data on the predictor variables for that store. A simple example illustrates how the regression procedure works.[15] Exhibit 8–12 provides data for 10 hypothetical home improvement centers. (The example has been simplified considerably; simple regression should not be performed without at least 30 stores. Also, only one predictor variable is used: population within a three-mile radius of the store. Normally, the analyst would utilize several predictor variables.)

Exhibit 8–13 plots yearly sales and population data from Exhibit 8–12. A regression line has been drawn on the plot that best describes the relationship between sales and population. Specifically, the regression line is statistically defined as that which minimizes the squared distances from the points to the line. (The exact form of this line can be determined by any statistical package designed for personal computers as well as some handheld calculators.) The closer the points are to the line, the better the fit and, therefore, the better the sales forecast. As indicated by the line, as population increases, so do sales. Assume a proposed site had a zero-to-three–mile radius population of 40,000. To estimate sales, extend a vertical line from the 40 mark on the horizontal axis of the graph to the regression line, and then extend it horizontally to the vertical axis. (See the dotted line in Exhibit 8–13.) Sales would be approximately $366,000.

Store	Yearly Sales ($000)	Zero-to-Three-Mile Radius Population
1	$402	54,000
2	367	29,500
3	429	49,000
4	252	22,400
5	185	18,600
6	505	61,100
7	510	49,000
8	330	33,200
9	210	26,400
10	655	83,200

Source: Reprinted by permission of *Site Selection*, 1982. Copyright Lebhar-Friedman, Inc. 425 Park Avenue, New York, NY 10022.

EXHIBIT 8–12
Yearly Sales, Population, and Income for 10 Home Improvement Centers

EXHIBIT 8–13
Regression of Population on Sales

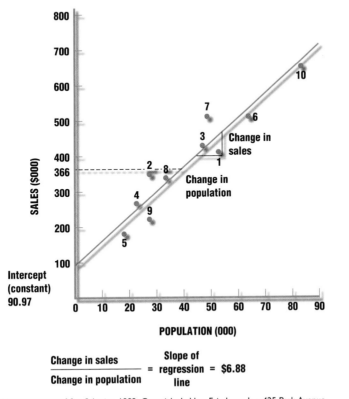

Source: Reprinted by permission of *Site Selection*, 1982. Copyright Lebhar-Friedman, Inc. 425 Park Avenue, New York, NY 10022.

Note: Each number on the graph corresponds to the store number on Exhibit 8–11.

The regression line is derived from the equation

$$\text{Sales} = a + b_1 x_1$$

where

a = A constant derived by the regression program; a also defines where the regression line in Exhibit 8–13 intercepts the y-axis and is therefore also known as the y-intercept.

b_1 = A number derived by the regression program that defines the relationship between sales and the predictor variable(s); it is also the slope of the regression line.

x_1 = The predictor variable (zero-to-three–mile population).

Continuing with the example,

$$\text{Sales} = \$91,000 + (\$6.88 \times 40,000)$$
$$= \$366,200$$

In this case, the regression-derived b indicates that sales will increase positively at a rate of $6.88 for every person in the zero-to-three–mile population. Since the zero-to-three–mile population is 40,000 people, and a is derived as $91,000, the sales total is forecast as $366,200. Note that the mathematical and graphic approaches give the same answer (within one's ability to read the graph). This simplified illustration used only one predictor variable. Assume that other predictor variables were tested and that average family income was also shown to have a strong and statistically significant relationship to sales. (The number of predictor variables is limited to two in this example for simplification purposes.) The new regression equation is

$$\text{Sales} = a + b_1 x_1 + b_2 x_2$$

where

a, b_1, and x_1 are as previously defined.

b_2 = A number derived by the regression program that defines the relationship between sales and average family income.

x_2 = The predictor variable (average family income).

Assume the new store has a zero-to-three–mile radius population of 55,000, and average family income is $28,000. After solving the regression equation,

a = –144,146
b_1 = 6.937
b_2 = 10.132

Substituting these values into the equation, the new sales forecast is derived:

$$\text{Sales} = -144,146 + (6.937 \times 55,000) + (10.132 \times 28,000)$$
$$= \$521,085$$

Using the regression method, then, a retailer can predict sales of a new store if variables that have been successfully used to predict sales in other stores are known. Regression analysis does have limitations, however. First, to be reliable, a large database is required. Second, the analyst must be properly trained and must adhere to strict statistical procedures. Finally, since regression is an averaging technique, it seldom identifies extremely good or extremely poor potential locations.

Huff's Gravity Model   Huff's model,[16] loosely based on Newton's law of gravity, is built on the premise that the probability that a given customer will shop in a particular store or shopping center becomes larger as the size of the store or center grows and the distance or travel time from customers to the store or center shrinks. Huff's model is derived from earlier research by Reilly, Converse, and Christaller dating back to the early 1930s.[17]

The objective of Huff's model is to determine the probability that a customer residing in a particular area will shop at a particular store or shopping center. To forecast sales, the location analyst multiplies the probability that the customer will shop at a particular place by an estimate of the customer's expenditures. Then, all the estimated expenditures in an area are aggregated to estimate sales from the area. To begin the process of estimating sales using the Huff method, the general model is defined as follows:

$$P_{ij} = \frac{S_j \div T_{ij}^{\ b}}{\displaystyle\sum_{j=1}^{n} S_j \div T_{ij}^{\ b}}$$

where

P_{ij} = Probability of a customer at a given point of origin i traveling to a particular shopping center j.

S_j = Size of shopping center j.

T_{ij} = Travel time or distance from customer's starting point to shopping center.

b = An exponent to T_{ij} that reflects the effect of travel time on different kinds of shopping trips.

The model indicates that the larger the size (S_j) of the shopping center compared to competing shopping centers' sizes, the larger the probability that a customer will shop at the center. A larger size is generally better in the customer's eye because it means more assortment and variety. Travel time or distance (T_{ij}) has the opposite effect on the probability that a customer will shop at a given shopping center. The greater the travel time or distance from the customer compared to competing shopping centers, the smaller the probability that the customer will shop at the center. Generally, customers would rather shop at a close center than a distant one.

The exponent $T_{ij}^{\ b}$ reflects travel time's effect on different kinds of shopping trips. The larger the value of b, the larger the effect of travel time or distance (T_{ij}) on the probability that a customer will shop at a given center. Travel time or distance is generally more important with convenience goods than with shopping goods—people are less willing to travel a great distance for a quart of milk than for a new pair of shoes. Thus, a larger value for b is assigned if the store or shopping center being studied specializes in convenience goods rather than shopping goods. The value b is usually determined through surveys of shopping patterns or from previous experience.

The Huff model is currently being used by retailers to define their trade areas and forecast sales. To see the use of Huff's model, examine Exhibit 8-14. Assume a local shoe store is thinking of opening a new store at the University Park Center shopping center. Two major shopping centers—The Falls and Old Town—provide competition for women's shoes.

The following four steps are repeated for each area surrounding the shopping center. Since University Park Center will draw heavily from a nearby university, the process for determining a sales forecast from the university students is described.

Shopping Center	Size (000 sq. ft.)	Distance from University (mi.)
University Park Center	1,000	3
The Falls	500	5
Old Town	100	1

(The exponent *b* is assumed to be 2.)

1. Determine the probability that a student at this university will shop at University Park Center. Using the formula for Huff's model and data for the centers,

$$P_{ij} = \frac{1,000 \div 3^2}{(1,000 \div 3^2) + (500 \div 5^2) + (100 \div 1^2)}$$

Probability = .48

2. Determine the number of students who will buy their shoes at University Park Center. The probability is multiplied by the number of students:

.48 × 12,000 students = 5,760 customers

3. Determine the sales forecast. Assuming each customer will spend an average of $150 on shoes, the forecasted sales will be

5,760 customers × $150 = $864,000

4. Estimate sales for the entire trade area. The university population represents only one geographic sector of the trade area for University Park Center. There are four other geographic sectors that comprise the entire trade area for University Park Center. To estimate sales for the entire trade area, repeat steps 1 to 3 for the remaining four areas and then sum them.

Choosing the Best Method(s)   In any decision, the more information that's available, the better the outcome is likely to be. This is true for research in general and location analysis in particular. Therefore, if a combination of the techniques is applied and the same conclusion is reached, the retailer should have more confidence in the decision.

Some methods used for analyzing trade areas are better in certain situations, however. The analog and Huff approaches are best when the number of stores with obtainable data is small, usually fewer than 30. These approaches can also be used by small retailers. The regression approach, on the other hand, is best when there are multiple variables expected to explain sales, since it's hard to keep track of multiple predictor variables when using a manual system like the analog approach. Also, the Huff gravity model explicitly considers the attractiveness of competition and customers' distance or travel time to the store or shopping center in question. Finally, since Huff's gravity model usually does not utilize demographic variables, it's particularly important to use it in conjunction with the analog or regression methods.

There are three trends that will shape site selection research in the next few decades.[18] First, it will be easier to collect and store data on customers in data warehouses. (This topic will be explored in Chapter 11.) Second, advanced statistical modeling techniques, such as CHAID (chi square automatic interaction detection) and spatial allocation models, will become more popular. Finally, GIS will become more sophisticated and at the same time more accessible to users.

SUMMARY

Retailers consider several issues when assessing the attractiveness of a particular region, market, or trade area. They want to know about the people living in the area. What are their lifestyles? How wealthy and large are the households? Is the area growing or declining? Does it have a favorable business climate? Importantly, what is the level of competition? Retailers should only locate in areas with heavy competition if they believe their retailing format is superior to that of their competitors. A safer strategy is to locate in an area with little competition. Of course, in today's overbuilt retail environment, such areas are nearly impossible to find. Does a retailer have the ability to manage multiple stores in an area or in multiple areas? What is the most profitable number of stores to operate in a particular area?

Retailers have a hard time finding a perfect site. Each site has its own set of advantages and disadvantages. In assessing the viability of a particular site, a retailer must consider the location's accessibility as well as locational advantages within the center.

Trade areas are typically divided into primary, secondary, and tertiary zones. The boundaries of a trade area are determined by how accessible it is to customers, the natural and physical barriers that exist in the area, the type of shopping area in which the store is located, the type of store, and the level of competition.

Retailers have three types of information at their disposal to help them define a trade area. First, they use a customer spotting technique to determine how many people are in their trade area and where they live. Second, they use demographic data and GIS firms and the U.S. Census. Finally, to assess their competition they use the Internet, other sources of secondary information, and a good old-fashioned walk through the neighborhood.

Once retailers have the data that describes their trade areas, they use several analytical techniques to estimate demand. The analog approach—one of the easiest to use—can be particularly useful for smaller retailers. Using this method, the retailer makes predictions about the sales of a new store based on sales in stores in similar areas. Regression analysis uses the same logic as the analog approach but is statistically based and requires more objective data. Finally, we showed how Huff's model is used to predict the probability that a customer will frequent a particular store in a trade area. It is based on the premise that customers are more likely to shop at a given store or shopping center if it's conveniently located and offers a large selection.

KEY TERMS

accessibility, *248*
ACORN (A Classification of Residential Neighborhoods) , *256*

amount and quality of parking facilities, *250*
artificial barrier, *249*

census tracts, *256*
congestion, *250*
cumulative attraction, *250*

destination store, *254*
franchisee, *246*
franchisor, *246*
geographic information system (GIS) , *256*
ingress/egress, *250*
market potential index (MPI), *257*
Metropolitan Statistical Area (MSA) , *243*

natural barrier, *249*
overstored trade area, *247*
parasite store, *254*
polygon, *252*
primary zone, *252*
region, *243*
road condition, *249*
road pattern, *249*
saturated trade area, *247*

secondary zone, *252*
spending potential index (SPI) , *257*
tertiary zone, *253*
trade area, *243*
traffic flow, *248*
understored trade area, *247*
visibility, *249*

GET OUT AND DO IT!

1. **INTERNET EXERCISE** ESRI and Claritas both provide the types of information and maps described in this section. Go to their websites at www.esri.com and www.claritas.com and compare their product/service offerings. Which company would you call first?

2. **INTERNET EXERCISE** See if birds of a feather really do flock together. Go to www.esribis.com/free_samples/zip_code_searches.htm. Type in your zip code. Does the information you get accurately describe you?

3. **INTERNET EXERCISE** Do a competitive trade area analysis for a store of your choice by going to competitors' Internet corporate websites and determining the probability that they will be entering a particular trade area.

4. **GO SHOPPING** Go to two stores owned by the same chain. Define and evaluate their trade area. Which store do you think is the most successful?

5. **GO SHOPPING** Go to a shopping mall. Get or draw a map of the stores. Analyze whether or not the stores are clustered appropriately. For instance, are all the high-end stores together? Is there a good mix of shopping goods stores adjacent to each other?

DISCUSSION QUESTIONS AND PROBLEMS

1. What are the shape and size of the trade area zones of a shopping center near your school?

2. When measuring trade areas, why is the analog approach not a good choice for a retailer with several hundred outlets?

3. True Value Hardware plans to open a new store. Two sites are available, both in middle-income neighborhood centers. One neighborhood is 20 years old and has been well maintained. The other was recently built in a newly planned community. Which site is preferable for True Value? Why?

4. Trade areas are often described as concentric circles emanating from the store or shopping center. Why is this practice used? Suggest an alternative method. Which would you use if you owned a store in need of a trade area analysis?

5. Marisol Perez is a graduate student at Florida State University. She is supporting herself by working at a mental hospital. Mary Petrey also lives in Tallahassee, Florida, but never went to college and works in a factory. Both make $20,000 per year and are single and 21 years old. Would they be in the same ACORN cluster? How do you think they spend their disposable income?

6. Under what circumstances would a retailer use the analog approach for estimating demand for a new store? What about regression?

7. Burdines (a division of Federated Department Stores, Inc.) has made a strategic decision to operate stores only in Florida. In fact, it's known as "the Florida store." Evaluate this strategy.

8. Some specialty stores prefer to locate next to or close to an anchor store. But Little Caesars, a takeout pizza retailer typically found in strip centers, wants to be at the end of the center away from the supermarket anchor. Why?

9. Retailers have a choice of locating on a mall's main floor or second or third level. Typically, the main floor offers the best, but most expensive, locations. Why would specialty stores such as Radio Shack and Foot Locker choose the second or third floor?

10. A drugstore is considering opening a new location at shopping center A, with hopes of capturing sales from a new neighborhood under construction. Two nearby shopping centers, C and E, will provide competition. Using the following information and Huff's probability model, determine the probability that residents of the new neighborhood will shop at shopping center A:

Shopping Center	Size (000 sq. ft.)	Distance from New Neighborhood (Miles)
A	3,500	4
C	1,500	5
E	300	3

Assume that $b = 2$.

SUGGESTED READINGS

Birkin, M.; G.P. Clarke; M. Clarke; and A. Wilson. "Intelligent GIS: Location Decisions and Strategic Planning." *Journal of Retailing and Consumer Services* 5, no. 4 (June 1998).

Buckner, Robert W. *Site Selection: New Advancements in Methods and Technology.* 2d ed. New York: Lebhar-Friedman Books, 1998.

Harder, Christian. *GIS Means Business.* Redlands, CA: Environmental Systems Research Institute, Inc., 1997.

Jones, Ken, and Michael Pearce. "The Geography of Markets: Spatial Analysis for Retailers." *Ivey Business Journal* 63, no. 3 (March–April 1999), pp. 66–70.

Kaufmann, Patrick J.; Naveen Donthu; and Charles M. Brooks. "Multi-Unit Retail Site Selection Processes: Incorporating Opening Delays and Unidentified Competition." *Journal of Retailing* 76, no. 1 (Spring 2000), pp. 113–27.

Miron, John R. "Loschian Spatial Competition in an Emerging Retail Industry." *Geographical Analysis* 34, no. 1. (January 2002).

Napoleon, Eileen, ed. *Getting to Know ArcView GIS: The Geographic Information System (GIS) for Everyone.* Environmental Research Systems Institute, Incorporated, 1999.

O'Kelly, Morton E. "Retail Market Share and Saturation." *Journal of Retailing and Consumer Services* 8, no. 1 (2001), pp. 37–45.

———. "Trade Area Models and Choice Based Samples." *Environment and Planning A* 31, no. 4 (1999), pp. 613–27.

Salvaneschi, Luigi, and Camille Akin, eds. *Location, Location, Location: How to Select the Best Site for Your Business.* Psi Successful Business Library, 1996.

Serra, Daniel and ReVelle Charles. "Competitive Location and Pricing on Networks." *Geographical Analysis* April 31, no. 2 (1999).

Weiss, Michael J. *The Clustered World: How We Live, What We Buy, and What It All Means about Who We Are.* Little Brown and Company, 1999.

Human Resource Management

CHAPTER

Teresa Marme, Director of Corporate Human Resources, Champs Sports

"Since I joined the Champs Sports HR department in early 1992, the roles and responsibilities of the human resources function have changed dramatically. As the HR assistant, I was part of a two-person personnel department focused primarily on payroll and benefits administration, organizing company events, and so forth. Ten years later, our HR department has evolved to include specialists in the areas of fair employment and labor law in the United States and Canada, training and development, field and corporate recruiting, and more. Although each member of the HR department has a specific area of expertise, our cohesiveness as a team is vital in providing resources to support the entire Champs organization (more than 7,000 associates in the stores and corporate office).

"The athletic retail environment is challenging, highly competitive, and subject to constant change. As corporate HR director, I often serve as a change agent to communicate and manage changes that have a direct effect on our associates and the company. Effective and timely communication through-

out the company is key to helping our associates understand and adapt quickly to change and adversity pertaining to our day-to-day business.

"My biggest accomplishment with Champs has been increasing diversity within the company. In

QUESTIONS

● Why does the management of human resources play a vital role in a retailer's performance?

● How do retailers build a sustainable competitive advantage by developing and managing their human resources?

● What activities do retail employees undertake, and how are they typically organized?

● How does a retailer coordinate employees' activities and motivate them to work toward the retailer's goals?

● What are the human resource management programs for building a committed workforce?

● How and why do retailers manage diversity among their employees?

years past, it was traditional to fill all new and open positions internally with Champs or Foot Locker associates who were predominantly male. While promoting from within is truly positive, it was easy to develop tunnel vision and lose our creative edge. It was rewarding and exciting to recruit highly qualified external individuals who brought diversity and other true life experience, and delivered new ideas and insight to the table. It was just as fulfilling to watch the company re-energize as new partnerships were formed and our business grew.

"Over the past 10 years, the Champs human resources function has evolved to keep pace with a very competitive athletic retail industry. Today, a diverse team of HR specialists is dedicated to providing resources to balance the needs of our business in order to achieve the company's organizational objectives. It's clear to me that the HR department plays an important role in sustaining Champs' competitive edge in the marketplace."

Retailers achieve their financial objectives by effectively managing their five critical assets: their locations, merchandise inventory, stores, employees, and customers. This chapter focuses on the organization and management of employees—the retailer's human resources. Howard Schultz, chairman and chief global strategist of Starbucks, emphasizes that "the relationship that we have with our people and the culture of our company is our most sustainable competitive advantage."[1]

Human resource management is particularly important in retailing because employees play a major role in performing critical business functions. In manufacturing firms, capital equipment (machinery, computer systems, robotics) often is used to perform jobs employees once did. But retailing and other service businesses remain labor-intensive. Retailers still rely on people to perform the basic retailing activities such as buying, displaying merchandise, and providing service to customers.

Two chapters in this text are devoted to human resource management because it's such an important issue in the performance of retail firms. This chapter focuses on the broad strategic issues involving organization structure, the general approaches used for motivating and coordinating employee activities, and management practices for building an effective, committed workforce and reducing turnover. The activities undertaken to implement the retailer's human resource strategy, including recruiting, selecting, training, supervising, evaluating, and compensating sales associates, are typically undertaken by store management. We discuss these operational issues in more detail in Chapter 17 in the Store Management section of the textbook.

GAINING COMPETITIVE ADVANTAGE THROUGH HUMAN RESOURCE MANAGEMENT

Human resource management can be the basis of a sustainable competitive advantage for three reasons. First, labor costs account for a significant percentage of a retailer's total expenses. Thus, the effective management of employees can produce a cost advantage. Second, the experience that most customers have with a retailer is determined by the activities of employees who select merchandise, provide information and assistance, and stock displays and shelves. Thus, employees can play a major role in differentiating a retailer's offering from its competitor's offering. Finally, these potential advantages are difficult for competitors to duplicate. For example, every department store executive knows that Nordstrom's employees provide outstanding customer service; however, they are not able to develop the same customer-oriented culture in their firms. Retailing View 9.1 describes how Men's Wearhouse built a competitive advantage through effective human resource management.

Objectives of Human Resource Management

The strategic objective of human resource management is to align the capabilities and behaviors of employees with the short-term and long-term goals of the retail firm.[3] One human resource management performance measure is **employee productivity**—the retailer's sales or profit divided by the number of employees. Employee productivity can be improved by increasing the sales generated by employees or reducing the number of employees, or both.

While employee productivity is directly related to the retailer's short-term profits, employee attitudes such as job satisfaction and commitment have important effects on customer satisfaction and subsequent long-term performance of the retailer. In addition to employee survey measures of these attitudes, a behavioral measure of these attitudes is employee turnover. **Employee turnover** is

$$\frac{100 \times \text{number of people in a set of positions during a year}}{\text{Number of positions}} - 100$$

A failure to consider both long- and short-term objectives can result in mismanagement of human resources and a downward performance spiral as shown in Exhibit 9–1. Often, when retailers' sales and profits decline due to increased competition, they respond by decreasing labor costs. They reduce the number of sales associates in stores, hire more part-timers, and spend less on training. Although these actions may increase short-term productivity and profits, they have an adverse effect on long-term performance because employee morale and customer service decrease.[5]

The Men's Wearhouse: Using HR to Succeed in a Declining Industry   RETAILING VIEW

Specialty retailing of men's tailoring apparel was not an attractive business when George Zimmer, at the age of 24, opened his first Men's Wearhouse store in Houston in 1973, and it continues to be an unattractive business. The sale of men's tailored clothing has declined over the last 30 years, and this trend looks to continue with the shift to business casual dress codes. Department stores have decreased the space devoted to men's clothing. Specialty chains such C & R Clothiers, Today's Man, Barney's, Hart, Shaffner and Marx, and Anderson Little have experienced financial problems over the last 10 years. During this bleak period, Men's Wearhouse's sales have increased by more than 400 percent as it has expanded to 600 stores in the United States and Canada.

The core of the company's strategy is to offer superior customer service, delivered by knowledgeable, caring salespeople, called wardrobe consultants. The phrase *wardrobe consultant* was chosen intentionally. Charlie Bresler, executive vice president for human development, commented: "We talked about clerks, consultant, and slammer. A clerk is somebody who will meet your initial request. A slammer is somebody who'll sell anything regardless of what your interests are, for their benefit. And a consultant is like a physician or an attorney, a professional."

George Zimmer believes in a win–win–win philosophy, where the customer, the wardrobe consultant, and the company all do well. Because the company believes that its job is to develop the untapped human potential in its employees, it devotes considerable attention to training and will not necessarily fire people for the first instance of stealing from the company. Charlie Bresler emphasizes, "George has seen people who have never been treated particularly well, and that when you treat them well and give them a second and sometimes a third chance, even when they've ripped off a pair of socks, even when they've taken a deposit and put it in their pocket and not returned it for several days. . . you try to re-educate the person. . . . We want to help ourselves and other people get better than most of the world thought we could ever be."

An important part of the company's philosophy is teamwork and helping others. The company emphasizes "team selling" and provides incentives for consultants both on their individual performance and the store's performance. Incentives are based on number of sales made rather sales dollars so that consultants are not motivated

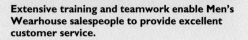

Extensive training and teamwork enable Men's Wearhouse salespeople to provide excellent customer service.

to sell customers more than what they want. In a training session for wardrobe consultants at Suits University, Bresler told the group: "[As] a wardrobe consultant, you are expected to define your success in part as only achieved when your teammates . . . are also successful . . . and that you will, over time, define your success not only in terms of your own goals, but also the goals and aspirations of the other people in your store. And that you will really come to care about them as human beings." The culture promotes teamwork, all of which emphasizes the responsibility of every person to help his or her peers develop their potential. George Zimmer reflected, "When I hand out certain awards at the Christmas parties, I always say the same thing: 'I love the fact that we are a company in which somebody writes a thousand dollar sale and somebody else comes over and gives them a 'high five'; that we celebrate each other's successes.' "

Sources: Jean E. Palmeri and Dan Burrows, "Men's Wearhouse to Focus Again on Suits," *WWD*, March 4, 2002, p. 4; Men's Wearhouse 2000 annual report; and Charles A. O'Reilly III and Jeffrey Pfeffer, *Hidden Value: How Great Companies Achieve Extraordinary Results with Ordinary People* (Boston: Harvard Business Press, 2000).

EXHIBIT 9–1
Downward
Performance Spiral

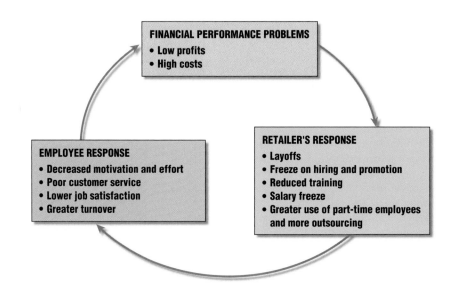

The Human Resource Triad

Retailers such as Home Depot, Men's Wearhouse, and the Container Store believe that human resources are too important to be left to the HR department.[6] The full potential of a retailer's human resources is realized when three elements of the human resource triad work together—HR professionals, store managers, and employees.

HR professionals typically working out of the corporate office, have specialized knowledge of HR practices and labor laws. They are responsible for establishing HR policies that reinforce the retailer's strategy and provide the tools and training used by line managers and employees to implement the policies. The line managers, who primarily work in the stores, are responsible for bringing the policies to life through their daily management of employees working for them. The issues confronting HR professionals are discussed in this chapter; and Chapter 17, in the Store Management section of this book, reviews the responsibilities of the line managers. Finally, the employees also share in the management of human resources. They can play an active role in providing feedback on the policies, managing their own careers, defining their job function, and evaluating the performance of their managers and co-workers. These three elements of the HR triad are illustrated in Exhibit 9–2.

EXHIBIT 9–2
Human Resource Triad

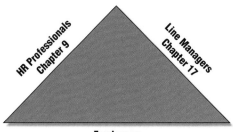

Special HR Conditions Facing Retailers

Human resource management in retailing is very challenging due to (1) the need to use part-time employees, (2) the emphasis on expense control, and (3) the changing demographics of the workforce. Retailers operating in international markets face additional challenges.

Part-Time Employees   Most retailers are open long hours and weekends to respond to the needs of family shoppers and working people. In addition, peak shopping periods occur during lunch hours, at night, and during sales. To deal with these peak periods and long hours, retailers have to complement their one or two shifts of full-time (40-hours-per-week) store employees with part-time workers. Part-time workers can be more difficult to manage than full-time employees. They often are less committed to the company and their jobs, and they're more likely to quit than full-time employees.

Expense Control   Retailers often operate on thin margins and must control expenses. Thus, they are cautious about paying high wages to hourly employees who perform low-skill jobs. To control costs, retailers often hire people with little or no experience to work as sales associates, bank tellers, and waiters. High turnover, absenteeism, and poor performance often result from the use of inexperienced, low-wage employees.

The lack of experience and motivation among many retail employees is particularly troublesome because these employees are often in direct contact with customers. Unlike manufacturing workers on an assembly line, the lowest-paid retail employees work in areas that are highly visible to customers. Poor appearance, manners, and attitudes can have a negative effect on sales and customer loyalty.

Employee Demographics   The changing demographic pattern will result in a chronic shortage of qualified sales associates. Annual percent growth in U.S. labor market in 1980 was 14 percent. In 2010, it is forecasted to be only 4 percent and then drop to 2 percent in 2020. Thus, retailers need to explore approaches for operating effectively in a tight labor market—approaches that increase retention; recruit, train, and manage minorities, handicapped, and mature workers; and use incentive and technology to increase productivity.

To satisfy their human resource needs, retailers are increasing the diversity of their workforces, employing more minorities, handicapped people, and the elderly. The work values of young employees are quite different than those of their baby boomer supervisors. Many older managers feel that younger employees have poor work ethics. Younger employees respond by saying "Get a life," as they strive to balance their personal and professional lives. Managing this growing diversity and changing values in the retail workforce creates opportunities and problems for human resource managers.[9]

 International Human Resource Issues   Finally, the management of employees working for an international retailer is especially challenging because differences in work values, economic systems, and labor laws mean that human resource practices effective in one country might not be effective in another. For example, U.S. retailers rely heavily on individual performance appraisals and rewards tied to individual performance—a practice consistent with the individualistic U.S. culture. However, in countries with a collectivist culture such as China and Japan, employees downplay individual desires and focus on the needs of the group. Thus, group-based evaluations and incentives are more effective in those countries.

The legal-political system in countries often dictates the human resource management practices that retailers can use. For example, the United States has led the world in eliminating workplace discrimination. However, in Singapore it is perfectly legal to place an employment ad specifying that candidates must be male, between the ages of 25 and 40, and ethnic Chinese. In the Netherlands, a retailer can make a substantial reduction in its workforce only if it demonstrates to the government that the cutback is absolutely necessary. In addition, a Dutch retailer must develop a plan for the cutback, which must then be approved by unions and other involved parties.[10]

Finally, the staffing of management positions in foreign countries raises a wide set of issues. Should management be local or should expatriates be used? How should the local managers or expatriates be selected, trained, and compensated? Cole Peterson, vice president of the People Division of Wal-Mart, says its biggest problem with international expansion is its lack of "human capital." Wal-Mart makes every effort to replace expatriates with locals, and in every overseas country team except China, its operations are now led by a non-American. Yet it is expanding faster than it can train people internally and has lost high-quality local managers to rivals.[11]

The following sections of this chapter examine three important strategic issues facing retail HR professionals: (1) the design of the organization structure for assigning responsibility and authority for doing tasks to people and business units, (2) the approaches used to coordinate the activities of the firm's departments and employees and to motivate employees to work toward achieving company goals, and (3) the programs used to build employee commitment and retain valuable human resources.

DESIGNING THE ORGANIZATION STRUCTURE FOR A RETAIL FIRM

The **organization structure** identifies the activities to be performed by specific employees and determines the lines of authority and responsibility in the firm. The first step in developing an organization structure is to determine the tasks that must be performed. Exhibit 9–3 shows tasks typically performed in a retail firm.

These tasks are divided into four major categories: strategic management, administrative management (operations), merchandise management, and store management. The organization of this textbook is based on these tasks and managers who perform them.

Section II of the text focuses on the strategic and administrative tasks. The strategic market and finance decisions (discussed in Chapters 5 and 6) are undertaken primarily by senior management: the CEO, COO, vice presidents, and the board of directors representing shareholders in publicly held firms. Administrative tasks (discussed in Chapters 7 through 11) are performed by corporate staff employees who have specialized skills in human resource management, finance,

Tasks Performed in a Retail Firm | **EXHIBIT 9–3**

STRATEGIC MANAGEMENT	MERCHANDISE MANAGEMENT	STORE MANAGEMENT	ADMINISTRATIVE MANAGEMENT (OPERATIONS)

• **Develop a retail strategy**
• **Identify the target market**
• **Determine the retail format**
• **Design organizational structure**
• **Select locations**
	• **Buy merchandise**
	  Locate vendors
	  Evaluate vendors
	  Negotiate with vendors
	  Place orders
	• **Control merchandise inventory**
	  Develop merchandise budget plans
	  Allocate merchandise to stores
	  Review open-to-buy and stock position
	• **Price merchandise**
	  Set initial prices
	  Adjust prices
		• **Recruit, hire, train store personnel**
		• **Plan work schedules**
		• **Evaluate performance of store personnel**
		• **Maintain store facilities**
		• **Locate and display merchandise**
		• **Sell merchandise to customers**
		• **Repair and alter merchandise**
		• **Provide services such as gift wrapping and delivery**
		• **Handle customer complaints**
		• **Take physical inventory**
		• **Prevent inventory shrinkage**
			• **Promote the firm, its merchandise, and services**
			  Plan communication programs
			  Develop communication budget
			  Select media
			  Plan special promotions
			  Design special displays
			  Manage public relations
			• **Manage human resources**
			  Develop policies for managing store personnel
			  Recruit, hire, train managers
			  Plan career paths
			  Keep employee records
			• **Distribute merchandise**
			  Locate warehouses
			  Receive merchandise
			  Mark and label merchandise
			  Store merchandise
			  Ship merchandise to stores
			  Return merchandise to vendors
			• **Establish financial control**
			  Provide timely information on financial performance
			  Forecast sales, cash flow, profits
			  Raise capital from investors
			  Bill customers
			  Provide credit

accounting, real estate, distribution, and management information systems. People in these administrative functions develop plans, procedures, and information to assist operating managers in implementing the retailer's strategy.

In retail firms, the primary operating or line managers are involved in merchandise management (Section III) and store management (Section IV). These operating managers implement the strategic plans with the assistance of administrative personnel. They make the day-to-day decisions that directly affect the retailer's performance.

To illustrate the connection between the tasks performed and the organization structure, the tasks are color coded. Brown is used to represent the strategic tasks, gold for the merchandise management, green for the store management, and blue for the administrative management tasks.

Organization Design Considerations

Once the tasks have been identified, the retailer groups them into jobs to be assigned to specific individuals and determines the reporting relationships.[12]

Strategic decisions, discussed in Chapters 5 and 6, are undertaken primarily by senior management in a retail firm.

Specialization Rather than performing all the tasks shown in Exhibit 9–3, individual employees are typically responsible for only one or two tasks. **Specialization,** focusing employees on a limited set of activities, enables employees to develop expertise and increase productivity. For example, a real estate manager can concentrate on becoming expert at selecting retail sites, while a benefit manager can focus on becoming expert in developing creative and cost-effective employee benefits. Through specialization, employees work only on tasks for which they were trained and have unique skills.

But employees may become bored if they're assigned a narrow set of tasks, such as putting price tags on merchandise all day long, every day. Also, extreme specialization may increase labor costs. For example, salespeople often don't have many customers when the store first opens, mid-afternoon, or at closing. Rather than hiring a specialist for stocking shelves and arranging merchandise, many retailers have salespeople perform these tasks during slow selling periods.

Responsibility and Authority Productivity increases when employees have the proper amount of authority to effectively undertake the responsibilities assigned to them. For example, buyers who are responsible for the profitability of a merchandise category need to have the authority to make decisions that will enable them to fulfill this responsibility. They should have the authority to select and price merchandise for their category and determine how the merchandise is displayed and sold.

Sometimes the benefits of matching responsibility and authority conflict with benefits of specialization. For example, buyers rarely have authority over how their merchandise is sold in the stores or through the Internet. Other employees, such as store managers who specialize in management of salespeople or designers who specialize in constructing websites, have this authority.

Reporting Relationships After assigning tasks to employees, the final step in designing the organization structure is determining the reporting relationships. Productivity can decrease when too many or too few employees report to a supervisor. The effectiveness of supervisors decreases when they have too many employees reporting to them. On the other hand, if managers are supervising very few employees, the number of managers increases and costs go up.

The appropriate number of subordinates ranges from 4 to 12, depending on the nature of their tasks, skills, and location. The number of subordinates is greater when they perform simple standardized tasks, when they're well trained and competent, and when they perform tasks at the same location as the supervisor. Under these conditions, supervision isn't as difficult, and the supervisor can effectively manage more people.

Matching Organization Structure to Retail Strategy The design of the organization structure needs to match the firm's retail strategy. For example, category specialists and warehouse clubs such as Best Buy and Costco target price-sensitive customers and thus are very concerned about building a competitive advantage based on low cost. They minimize the number of employees by having decisions made by a few people at corporate headquarters. These centralized organization structures are very effective when there are limited regional or local differences in customer needs.

On the other hand, high-fashion clothing customers often aren't very price-sensitive, and tastes vary across the country. Retailers targeting these segments tend to have more managers and decision making at the local store level. By having more decisions made at the local store level, human resource costs are higher, but sales also increase since merchandise and services are tailored to meet the needs of local markets. Retailing View 9.2 illustrates how all of the elements of the human resource strategy, including the organization structure, are used to reinforce PETsMART's strategy.

PETsMART's HR Practices Support Its Retail Strategy RETAILING VIEW 9.2

When PETsMART launched its concept for a pet supply category killer in 1988, it followed the lead of other category killers and emphasized its low prices, broad product assortment, limited customer service, and warehouse atmosphere. But it discovered that pet owners wanted more. They viewed their pets as part of the family, not just an animal that they needed to feed. They want to be good "pet parents" and deal with a company that is as concerned about their pets' health and well-being as they were. Thus, PETsMART undertook a strategy to reposition its brand from category killer to a caring and trusted source of products and service for pets.

To implement this new positioning, PETsMART started to provide some new services in the stores such as pet styling, veterinary services, and training classes. Rather than hire veterinarians, PETsMART made arrangements to have the clinics operated by Banfield, The Pet Hospital, a trusted source of "human" quality medical care for pets. PETsMART also decided to provide facilities and space for shelters to make homeless pets available rather than sell dogs and cats. The company also changed its marketing communications to be less price-oriented and more service-driven, with all messages highlighting the fact that pets are welcomed in the store as much as the rest of their family. Promotional tie-ins with major animal shelters and pet rescue services became major focal points nationally and at store level.

PETsMART also recognized that its employees would play a crucial role in the development of a new brand image. Its front-line employees in the stores have to understand and accept the brand's values and the promise the brand is making to its customers. To develop these values in its employees, PETsMART changed the criteria it used for selecting sales associates. The company no longer looked for people who could just stock the shelves. It now hires people who have a deep love for dogs or cats or tropical fish. The groomers in its styling salons love making a pet look beautiful. To develop its employees, PETsMART provides extensive training so that the store employees would be even more knowledgeable about the pets they work with.

Source: Ken Banks, former senior vice president of marketing and branding for PETsMART, and co-founder of Totalbrand Integration.®

RETAIL ORGANIZATION STRUCTURES

Retail organization structures differ according to the type of retailer and the size of the firm. For example, a retailer with a single store will have an organization structure quite different from a national chain.

Organization of a Single-Store Retailer

Owner-managers of a single store may be the entire organization. When they go to lunch or go home, the store closes. As sales grow, the owner-manager hires employees. Coordinating and controlling employee activities is easier in a small store than in a large chain of stores. The owner-manager simply assigns tasks to each employee and watches to see that these tasks are performed properly. Since the number of employees is limited, single-store retailers have little specialization. Each employee must perform a wide range of activities, and the owner-manager is responsible for all management tasks.

As sales increase, specialization in management may occur when the owner-manager hires additional management employees. Exhibit 9–4 illustrates the common division of management responsibilities into merchandise and store management. The owner-manager continues to perform strategic management tasks. The store manager may be responsible for administrative tasks associated with receiving and shipping merchandising and managing the employees. The merchandise manager or buyer may handle the advertising and promotion tasks as well as the merchandise tasks. Often the owner-manager contracts with an accounting firm to perform financial control tasks for a fee.

Organization of a Regional Department Store

In contrast to the management of a single store, retail chain management is complex. Managers must supervise units that are geographically distant from each other. In this section, we use Rich's/Lazarus/Goldsmith's (a regional department store chain headquartered in Atlanta, Georgia, and owned by Federated Depart-

---

EXHIBIT 9–4 | Organization of a Small Retailer

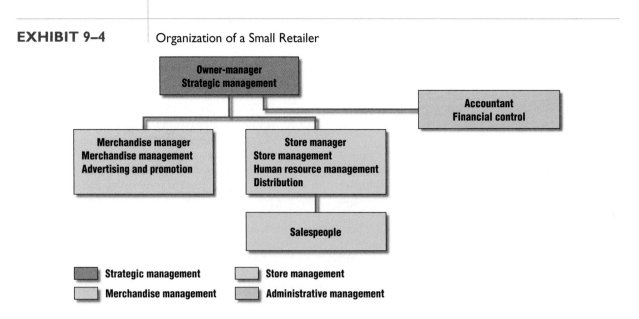

ment Stores) to illustrate the organization of a large, multi-unit retailer. The Rich's/Lazarus/Goldsmith's division was formed in 1995 when Federated Department Stores merged three regional department store chains. While the stores in each region continue to carry the name of the regional chains, there's only one headquarters office. Rather than using the full name of the division, we'll refer to it as Rich's in the following discussion.

Traditionally, department stores were family-owned and -managed. Organization of these firms was governed by family circumstances. Executive positions were designed to accommodate family members involved in the business. Then, in 1927, Paul Mazur proposed a functional organization plan that has been adopted by most retailers.[16] The organization structures of retail chains, including Rich's, continue to reflect principles of the Mazur plan, such as separating buying and store management tasks into separate divisions.

Exhibit 9–5 shows Rich's organization. Most retail chains such as The Gap, Home Depot, and T. J. Maxx have similar organization structures. Vice presidents responsible for administrative tasks (blue), specific merchandise categories (gold), stores (green), report to the chairperson and president.

In most retail firms, the two senior executives, typically called the CEO and COO, work closely together in managing the firm. They are frequently referred to as principals or partners. One member of the partnership is primarily responsible for the merchandising activities of the firm—the merchandise and marketing divisions. The other partner is primarily responsible for the operating divisions—stores, human resources, distribution, information systems, and finance divisions. In Rich's, the CEO is responsible for merchandising and the COO is responsible for operations. However, these responsibilities might be switched in other retail firms.

Most managers and employees in the stores division work in stores located throughout the geographic region. Merchandise, planning, marketing, finance, visual merchandising, and human resource managers and employees work at corporate headquarters.

Merchandise Division   The merchandise division is responsible for procuring the merchandise sold in the stores and ensuring that the quality, fashionability, assortment, and pricing of merchandise are consistent with the firm's strategy. Chapters 12 through 15 discuss major activities performed in the merchandise division.

Exhibit 9–6 shows a detailed organization structure of Rich's merchandise division. This exhibit is simply a more detailed view of the gold boxes on the left side of Exhibit 9–5. Each senior vice president/general merchandise manager (GMM) is responsible for specific categories of merchandise. GMMs report directly to the chairperson and CEO, the partner in charge of the merchandising activities.

Buyers   **Buyers** are responsible for procuring merchandise, setting prices and markdowns, and managing inventories for specific merchandise categories. They attend trade and fashion shows and negotiate with vendors on prices, quantities, assortments, delivery dates, and payment terms. In addition, they might specify private-label merchandise or request modifications to tailor the merchandise to the retailer's target market and differentiate it from competitive offerings.

REFACT

Rich's/Lazarus/Goldsmith's employs 17,200 people in 76 stores located in nine midwestern and southeastern states; it has annual sales of $2.2 billion.[15]

EXHIBIT 9–5 Organization of a Regional Department Store: Rich's

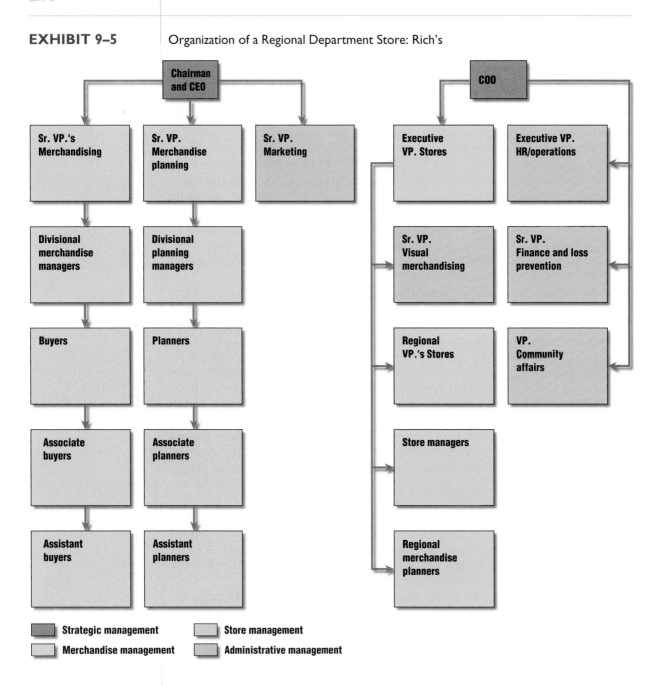

Although buyers are given considerable autonomy to "run their own business," they must adhere to an inventory budget that will vary from season to season. The budget is the result of a negotiation between the buyers and their superiors, divisional merchandise managers. The issues involved in managing the inventory budget are discussed in Chapters 12 and 13, and the merchandise buying activities are reviewed in Chapter 14.

In recent years, the buyer's role in supermarket chain has evolved into a category manager. Traditional supermarket buyers were vendor focused. For exam-

Merchandise Division Organization: Rich's   **EXHIBIT 9–6**

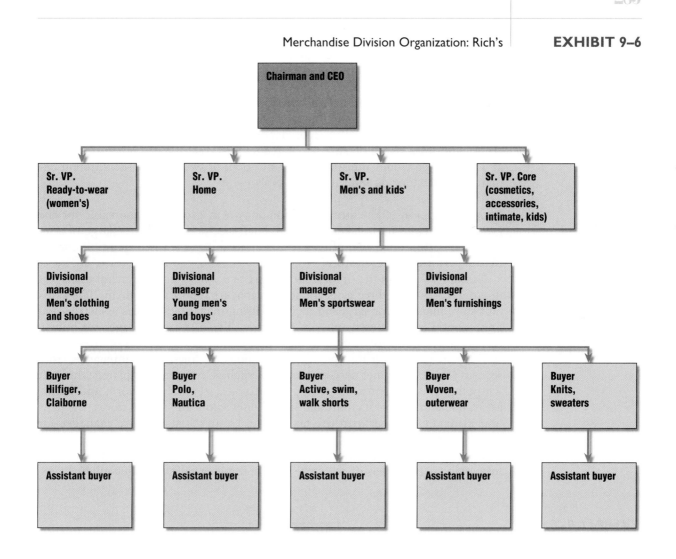

ple, they would just be responsible for buying merchandise from a vendor such as Campbell or Kraft. They developed close relationships with vendors and were more concerned with maintaining these vendor relationships than selling products to customers. This focus was partially caused by evaluation systems that rewarded supermarket buyers more for securing price discounts rather than sales, gross margins, and inventory turns.

Category managers are responsible for a set of products that are viewed as substitutes by customers. For example, a category manager might be in charge of all pastas—fresh, frozen, packaged, or canned. Category managers are evaluated on the profitability of their category and thus are motivated to eliminate "me too" products and keep essential niche products. Note that buyers in most other types of retail firms have always been responsible for merchandise categories. Thus, the term *category manager* is used primarily by supermarket retailers.

Planners   Traditionally, buyers or category managers were also responsible for determining the assortment stocked in each store, allocating merchandise to the stores, monitoring sales, and placing reorders. Giving this responsibility to buyers meant that the merchandise strategy within a store might not be coordinated. For example, some buyers might allocate more expensive merchandise to a store in high-income areas, but others wouldn't make this adjustment.

To address these problems, most retail chains created merchandise planners, with a senior VP of planning and distribution, who are at the same level as the merchandise managers in the buying organization. Each **merchandising planner** is responsible for allocating merchandise and tailoring the assortment in several categories for specific stores in a geographic area. For example, the planner at The Limited would alter the basic assortment of sweaters for the different climates in south Florida and the Pacific Northwest.

Stores Division   The stores division shown in green is responsible for the group of activities undertaken in stores. Each vice president is in charge of a set of stores. A store manager, often called a general manager, is responsible for activities performed in each store.

Exhibit 9–7 shows the organization chart of a Rich's store. General managers in large stores have three assistant store managers reporting to them. The assistant store manager for sales and merchandising manages the sales associates and presentation of the merchandise in the store. The assistant manager for human resources is responsible for selecting, training, and evaluating employees. The assistant store manager for operations is responsible for store maintenance; store security; some customer service activities, such as returns, complaints, and gift wrapping; the receiving, shipping, and storage areas of the store; and leased areas, including the restaurant and hair-styling salon. In smaller stores, the general manager may perform the tasks done by an assistant store manager for merchandise.

Group sales managers, sales managers, and the salespeople work with customers in specific areas of the store. For example, a sales manager might be re-

EXHIBIT 9–7
Store Organizations: Rich's

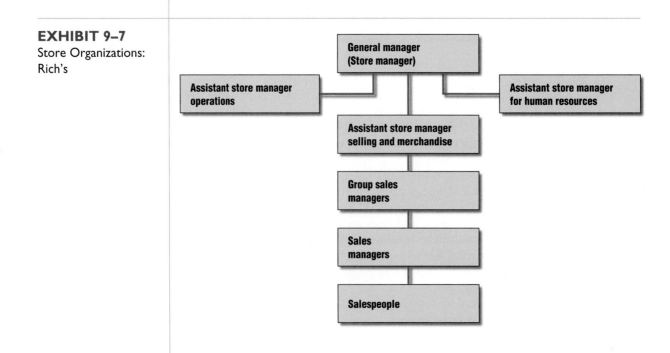

sponsible for the entire area in which kitchen appliances, gifts, china, silver, and tableware are sold, while a group sales manager might be responsible for an entire floor of the store.

Corporate Organization of a Regional Department Store Chain

As mentioned in Chapter 2, many regional chains such as Rich's are owned by retail corporations. Exhibit 9–8 shows the organization chart of Federated's corporate headquarters in Cincinnati, Ohio. Retailing View 9.3 reviews the evolution of Federated Department Stores into one of the world's largest department store chains.

The decisions made at the corporate office involve activities that set strategic directions and increase productivity by coordinating the regional chains' activities. For example, having one corporate management information system and one private-brand merchandise program is much more efficient and effective than having separate systems and programs in each regional chain.

Corporate Organization of Federated Department Stores **EXHIBIT 9–8**

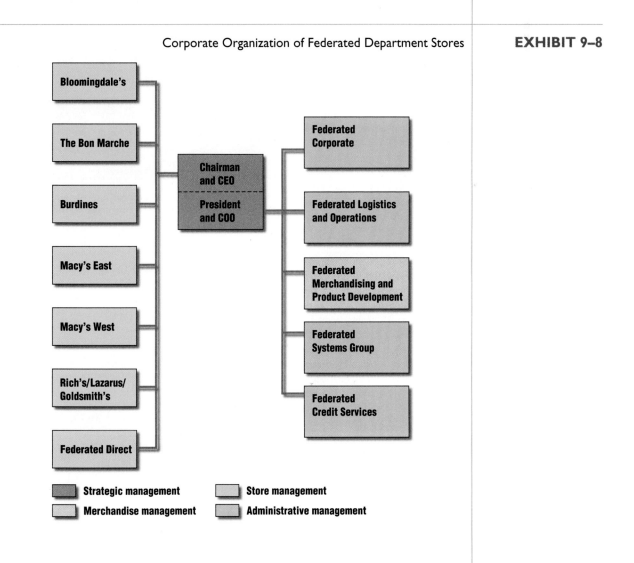

Corporate Functions Activities performed at the Federated corporate office, rather than at the regional chain level, include

- *Corporate* (Cincinnati, Ohio): Support services cover tax, audit, accounting, cash management and finance, internal audit, planning, insurance, economic forecasting, law, corporate communications, purchasing, store design/construction, and real estate.

- *Merchandising and Product Development* (New York): This function develops merchandising strategies, coordinates relationships with vendors, designs and sources private-label merchandise, and manages marketing programs for private-brand merchandise. Among Federated's private brands are Charter

RETAILING VIEW | The History of Federated Department Store Chain

9.3

Federated Department Stores was founded in 1929 as a holding company by several family-owned, regional department store chains, including Shillito's, founded in 1830 in Cincinnati, Ohio; Bloomingdale's, founded in 1885 in New York; Jordan Marsh, founded in 1841 in Boston; F&R Lazarus, founded in 1851 in Columbus, Ohio; and Abraham & Straus, founded in 1865 in New York. Over the next 30 years, Bon Marche (Seattle), Rike's (Dayton, Ohio), Goldsmith's (Memphis), Burdines (Miami), and Rich's (Atlanta) joined Federated. In addition, the company started Filene's Basement (an off-price retailer) and Gold Circle (a full-line discounter) and acquired Ralph's (a West Coast supermarket chain). Each of these chains was operated as an independent division with its own buying office, distribution center, corporate offices, and human resource policies. While the divisions were profitable, the stock price was low.

In 1986, Robert Campeau, a successful Canadian real estate developer, felt that the stock for retail conglomerate companies like Federated was low and he bought Allied, a similar holding company, for $3.5 billion. In April 1988, he bought Federated for $6.6 billion. To finance these acquisitions, he sold off over 25 chains owned by the two holding companies (including Brooks Brothers, Ann Taylor, Ralph's, Filene's, Joske's, Miller's, Bonwit Teller, and Gold Circle) and attempted to cut operating costs. However, most of the acquisition was financed by issuing bonds and taking out loans. On January 15, 1990, the retail subsidiaries could not pay the interest on the debt and filed for bankruptcy, the largest bankruptcy in U.S. history at that time.

Under the protection of the bankruptcy court, Federated's new management team closed unprofitable stores, sold divisions unrelated to its core department store activities, and reduced operating costs dramatically by developing information, distribution, and buying systems used by most of the department store divisions. In 1992, Feder-

Macy's was acquired by Federated and the stores in three regional divisions were converted to the Macy's name plate.

ated emerged from bankruptcy as one of the largest and best managed retail chains. The company has since acquired four department store chains—Macy's, Horne's (Pittsburgh), The Broadway (Los Angeles), and Liberty House (Hawaii)—and Fingerhut, an Internet and catalog retailer, but it maintains its focus on developing synergies among its department store divisions. Federated appears to have a long-term strategy of operating two national retail chains (Bloomingdale's and Macy's) positioned at different points on the price/quality continuum. The Bullock's and Broadway stores in southern California and the Jordan Marsh stores in New England were converted to the Macy's nameplate in 1995 and 1996, and the Liberty House stores were converted in 2001.

Sources: *Reflections: 2001 Fact Book* (Cincinnati, OH: Federated Department Stores, 2000); and personal communications with Carol Sanger, vice president, Corporate Affairs, Federated Department Stores.

Club, I.N.C. International Concepts, Arnold Palmer, Club Room, Tools of the Trade, Badge, Style & Co., and Alfani.

- *Financial, Administrative, and Credit Services Group* (Mason, Ohio): This group provides proprietary credit cards and services for each regional department store chain. Federated has over 58 million credit card holders. The group also is responsible for payroll and benefits processing.
- *Federated Systems Group* (Norcross, Georgia): This division designs, installs, and manages the information system used by all divisions.
- *Federated Logistics and Operations* (Secaucus, New Jersey): Logistics coordinates and manages the logistics and distribution functions as well as accounts payable, purchasing, store planning, vendor technology, and energy management and expense control.[17]

Organization Structures of Other Types of Retailers

Most retail chains have an organization structure very similar to Rich's structure shown in Exhibit 9–5, with people in charge of the merchandising, store management, and administrative tasks reporting to the CEO and COO. Only corporations that operate several different chains, such as Target, The Limited, and The Gap, have the overarching corporate structure shown in Exhibit 9–8. Large supermarket chains such as Safeway and Kroger are often organized geographically, like Federated Department Stores, with each region operating as a semi-independent unit having its own merchandise and store management staff.

The primary difference between the organization structure of a department store and other retail formats is the numbers of people and management levels in the merchandising and store management areas. Many national retailers such as The Gap, Kohl's, and Circuit City centralize merchandise management activities at corporate headquarters and have fewer buyers and management levels in the merchandise group. On the other hand, these national retailers have many more stores than a regional department store chain like Rich's; thus, they have more managers and management levels in the stores division. For example, one person is responsible for stores and operations at The Gap, in contrast to the five regional chain and one national chain (Bloomingdale's) executives for stores and operations in the decentralized Federated Stores organization. But The Gap, with over 1,000 stores, needs more levels of store management (14 zone vice presidents, 18 regional managers, and 195 district managers) than Rich's, which only has 76 stores.

RETAIL ORGANIZATION DESIGN ISSUES

Two important issues in the design of a retail organization are (1) the degree to which decision making is centralized or decentralized and (2) approaches used to coordinate merchandise and store management. In the context of Federated Department Stores, the first issue translates into whether the decisions concerning activities such as merchandise management, information and distributions systems, and human resource management are made by the regional department stores or the corporate headquarters. The second issue arises because retailers divide the merchandise and store management activities into different organizations within the firm. Thus, they need to develop ways for coordinating these interdependent activities.

Centralization versus Decentralization

Centralization is when authority for retailing decisions is delegated to corporate managers rather than to geographically dispersed regional, district, and store managers; whereas **decentralization** is when authority for retail decisions is assigned to lower levels in the organization. Federated Department Stores, Inc., is an example of a retail corporation with a geographically decentralized organization structure. Many retailing decisions are made by the regional department store chains, not by corporate managers.

Retailers reduce costs when decision making is centralized in corporate management. First, overhead falls because fewer managers are required to make the merchandise, human resource, marketing, and financial decisions. For example, Federated has both regional women's blouse buyers and corporate buyers coordinating the regional chains and buying private-label blouses. The Gap has one buyer for women's blouses at the corporate headquarters. With annual sales of about $2.2 billion, Rich's has over 90 people in its buying organization. The Gap has about twice those annual sales and only half as many buyers. Centralized retail organizations can similarly reduce personnel in administrative functions such as marketing and human resources.

Second, by coordinating buying across geographically dispersed stores, the company achieves lower prices from suppliers. The retailer can negotiate better purchasing terms by placing one large order rather than a number of smaller orders.

Third, centralization provides an opportunity to have the best people make decisions for the entire corporation. For example, in a centralized organization, people with the greatest expertise in areas such as MIS, buying, store design, and visual merchandise can have all stores benefit from their skills.

Finally, centralization increases efficiency. Standard operating policies are used for store and personnel management; these policies limit the decisions made by store managers. For example, corporate merchandisers do considerable research to determine the best method for presenting merchandise. They provide detailed guides for displaying merchandise to each store manager so that all stores look the same throughout the country. Because they offer the same core merchandise in all stores, centralized retailers can achieve economies of scale by advertising through national media rather than more costly local media.[18]

While centralization has advantages in reducing costs, the disadvantage of centralization is that it makes it more difficult for a retailer to adapt to local market conditions. For example, Gainesville is located in central Florida and thus the manager in charge of the fishing category at Sports Authority corporate office might think that the Gainesville store customers primarily engage in freshwater fishing. But the local store manager knows that most of his customers drive 90 miles to go saltwater fishing in either the Gulf of Mexico or the Atlantic Ocean.

In addition to problems with tailoring merchandise to local needs, the centralized retailer also may have difficulty responding to local competition and labor markets. Since pricing is established centrally, individual stores may not be able to respond quickly to competition in their market. Finally, centralized personnel policies can make it hard for local managers to pay competitive wages in their area or to hire appropriate types of salespeople.

However, centralized retailers are relying more on their information systems to react to local market conditions. For example, American Drug Stores buyers at the division's headquarters use data collected by point-of-sale terminals to understand local conditions. Most drugstore chains are cutting back on the space devoted to automotive supplies. But American Drug sales data indicated that people in the inner city are more likely to change their own oil, so it maintains its automotive supply offering in these stores. By looking at buying patterns across a large number of stores, the centralized buyer might uncover opportunities that local managers would not see.

Large retailers are using their information systems to make more and more merchandise and operations decisions at corporate headquarters. For example, the corporate staff at Federated is taking responsibility for operational activities such as distribution, information systems, private-brand merchandise, and human resource management policies that were formerly made in the regional divisions. However, each Federated division is still responsible for the management of merchandise.

Coordinating Merchandise and Store Management

Small independent retailers have little difficulty coordinating their stores' buying and selling activities. Owner-managers typically buy the merchandise and work with their salespeople to sell it. Being in close contact with customers, the owner-managers know what their customers want.

On the other hand, large retail firms organize the buying and selling functions into separate divisions. Buyers specialize in buying merchandise and have limited contact with the store management responsible for selling it. While this specialization increases buyers' skills and expertise, it makes it harder for them to understand customers' needs. Four approaches large retailers use to coordinate buying and selling are (1) improving buyers' appreciation for store environment, (2) making store visits, (3) assigning employees to coordinating roles, and (4) involving store managers in the buying decisions.

Improving Appreciation for Store Environment Fashion-oriented retailers use several methods to increase buyers' contact with customers and to improve informal communication between buyers and store personnel who sell the merchandise they buy. Management trainees, who eventually become buyers, are required by most retailers to work in the stores before they enter the buying office. During this 6-to-10-month training period, prospective buyers gain appreciation for the activities performed in the stores, the problems salespeople and department managers encounter, and the needs of customers.

Making Store Visits Another approach to increasing customer contact and communication is to have buyers visit the stores and work with the departments they buy for. At Wal-Mart, all managers (not just the buyers) are required to visit stores frequently and practice the company philosophy of CBWA (coaching by wandering around). Managers leave corporate headquarters in

This store owner does not have a problem coordinating employee activities because she has daily face-to-face contact with her employees and customers.

Bentonville, Arkansas, Sunday night and return to share their experiences at the traditional Saturday morning meetings.[19] This face-to-face communication provides managers with a richer view of store and customer needs than they can get from impersonal sales reports from the company's management information system. Spending time in the stores improves buyers' understanding of customer needs, but this system is costly because it reduces the time the buyer has to review sales patterns, plan promotions, manage inventory, and locate new sources of merchandise.

Assigning Employees to Coordinating Roles Some retailers, like Rich's, have people in the merchandise division (the planners who work with buyers) and the stores (the managers of sales and merchandise who work for the store managers) who are responsible for coordinating buying and selling activities. Many national retail chains have regional and even district staff personnel to coordinate buying and selling activities. For example, Target's regional merchandise managers in Chicago work with stores in the north-central region to translate plans developed by corporate buyers into programs that meet the regional needs of consumers.

Involving Store Management in Buying Decisions Another way to improve coordination between buying and selling activities is to increase store employees' involvement in the buying process. Some retailers such as Belks, Home Depot, Nordstrom, and JCPenney have had a tradition of decentralized store management. For example, management in each JCPenney store determined what merchandise that store would sell. Each season, buyers at corporate headquarters in Dallas selected merchandise and presented it to managers in all Penney stores using CDs and closed-circuit TVs. Store managers were given an order-planning form with retail prices, margins, and suggested quantities and assortments for their store size. Store merchandise managers then placed their orders for the merchandise presented through computer terminals linked to the Penney management information system. However, even these retailers with a tradition of decentralization are shifting to more centralization of decision making. Store managers at JCPenney are no longer involved in determining the merchandise stocked in their stores.[20]

Besides developing an organization structure, human resource management undertakes a number of activities to improve employee performance, build commitment in employees, and reduce turnover. In the following two sections of this chapter, we examine these human resource management activities.

MOTIVATING RETAIL EMPLOYEES

A critical task of human resource management is to motivate employees to work toward achieving the firm's goals and implementing its strategy. The task is often difficult because employees' goals may differ from those of the firm. For example, a sales associate might find it more personally rewarding to creatively arrange a display than to help a customer. Retailers generally use three methods to motivate their employees' activities: (1) written policies and supervision, (2) incentives, and (3) organization culture.[21]

Policies and Supervision

Perhaps the most fundamental method of coordination is to (1) prepare written policies that indicate what employees should do and (2) have supervisors enforce these policies. For example, retailers may set policies on when and how merchandise can be returned by customers. If employees use the written policies to make these decisions, their actions will be consistent with the retailer's strategy.

But strict reliance on written policies can reduce employee motivation. Employees might have little opportunity to use their own initiative to improve performance of their areas of responsibility. As a result, they eventually might find their jobs uninteresting.

Relying on rules as a method of coordination leads to a lot of red tape. Situations will arise that aren't covered by a rule. Then employees will need to talk to a supervisor or wait for a new policy before they can deal with a new situation.

Incentives

The second method of motivating and coordinating employees uses incentives to motivate them to perform activities consistent with the retailer's objectives. For example, buyers will be motivated to focus on the firm's profits if they receive a bonus based on the profitability of the merchandise they buy.

Types of Incentive Compensation   Two types of incentives are commissions and bonuses. A commission is compensation based on a fixed formula such as 2 percent of sales. For example, many retail salespeople's compensation is based on a fixed percentage of the merchandise they sell. A bonus is additional compensation awarded periodically based on an evaluation of the employee's performance. For example, store managers often receive bonuses at the end of the year based on their store's performance relative to its budgeted sales and profits. Chapter 17 details advantages and disadvantages of compensation plans with other nonfinancial incentives like recognition and promotions.

Besides incentives based on individual performance, retail managers often receive additional income based on their firm's performance. These profit-sharing arrangements can be offered as a cash bonus based on the firm's profits or as a grant of stock options that link additional income to performance of the firm's stock.

A number of retailers such as Wal-Mart and Home Depot use stock incentives to motivate and reward all employees, including sales associates. Employees are encouraged to buy shares in their companies at discounted prices through payroll deduction plans. These stock incentives align employees' interests with those of the company and can be very rewarding when the company does well. However, if growth in the company's stock price declines, employee morale declines too, corporate culture is threatened, and demands for higher wages and more benefits develop.[24]

Drawbacks of Incentives   Incentives are very effective in motivating employees to perform the activities on which the incentives are based. But incentives may cause employees to ignore other activities. For example, salespeople whose compensation is based entirely on their sales may be reluctant to spend time restocking the fixtures and shelves. Excessive use of incentives to motivate employees also can reduce employee commitment. Company loyalty falls because

REFACT

The late Mary Kay Ash, founder of Mary Kay Cosmetics, was fond of saying, "There are two things that people want more than sex and money—recognition and praise."[22]

REFACT

Until recently, Japanese companies were not permitted to issue their stock as compensation.[23]

REFACT

An employee who paid $1,650 for 100 shares of Wal-Mart stock when the company went public in 1970 would now have stock worth over $5 million.

employees feel that the firm hasn't made a commitment to them (since it's un-willing to guarantee their compensation). Thus, if a competitor offers to pay a higher commission rate, they'll feel free to leave.[25]

Organization Culture

The final method for motivating and coordinating employees is to develop a strong organization culture. An **organization culture** is the set of values, traditions, and customs in a firm that guides employee behavior. These guidelines aren't written in a set of policies and procedures; they are traditions passed along by experienced employees to new employees.[26]

RETAILING VIEW Partners in JCPenney

9.4

One hundred years ago, Thomas Callahan and William Guy Johnson opened a new store in Kemmerer, Wyoming. When they invited James Cash Penney to manage the store and become a one-third partner, a retailing tradition was launched. Mr. Penney has said that this simple act was the key to his success. Becoming a partner fired his ambition to succeed, and he made it a cornerstone in the company he built.

Presently, all JCPenney managers who've been promoted to profit-sharing status and have worked for the firm for five years are inducted into the partnership program. Entering the partnership program is a milestone in a Penney manager's career. In October 2001, over 1,000 new partners were inducted.

Mr. Penney made the following comment about the significance of being a partner at the 1942 induction meeting. "When the JCPenney Company is faced with the opportunity of choosing partners . . . I say partners because we believe that all our associates work together as partners . . . we make our selection of partners according to the character qualities that best fit into our business, that build rapidly into the principles of our business: Honor, Confidence, Service, and Cooperation [HCSC]."

At the first induction meeting in 1913 in Salt Lake City, the following HCSC company motto was outlined:

- Honor is the fundamental ingredient of character. It confers respect and esteem, because it is a constant guide to what is right and true. Our sense of honor will continue to ensure our customers' respect for us. May your every thought and your every act be prompted by that which is honorable.

- Confidence is important. We must have confidence in ourselves and confidence in others in order to inspire confidence. May your conduct and your influence be such that you inspire confidence at all times in yourself and in this company.

JCPenney's profit-sharing program has its roots in James Cash Penney's (above) concept of partnership developed 100 years ago when he opened the first JCPenney store.

- Service is the keynote of success; it attracts customers. Service is the art of making ourselves useful to our jobs, to our associates, and to our communities.

- Cooperation is the fourth essential of the Penney partnership. The goals toward which we all strive can be reached only through cooperation with each other and with all those with whom we deal.

Source: Company documents.

Many retail firms have strong organization cultures that give employees a sense of what they ought to do on their jobs and how they should behave to be consistent with the firm's strategy. For example, Nordstrom's strong organization culture emphasizes customer service, while Wal-Mart's organization culture focuses on reducing costs so the firm can provide low prices to its customers.

An organization culture often has a much stronger effect on employees' actions than rewards offered in compensation plans, directions provided by supervisors, or written company policies. Retailing View 9.4 describes how JCPenney's partnership program reinforces the values of the company when its managers qualify for profit sharing.

Nordstrom emphasizes the strength of organization culture in the policy manual given to new employees. The manual has one rule: Use your best judgment to do anything you can to provide service to our customers. Lack of written rules doesn't mean that Nordstrom employees have no guidelines or restrictions on their behavior. Its organization culture guides employees' behavior. New salespeople learn from other employees that they should always wear clothes sold at Nordstrom, that they should park their cars at the outskirts of the parking lot so customers can park in more convenient locations, that they should approach customers who enter their department, that they should accept any merchandise returned by a customer even if the merchandise wasn't purchased at a Nordstrom store, and that they should offer to carry packages to the customer's car.

Developing and Maintaining a Culture   Organization cultures are developed and maintained through stories and symbols.[27] Values in an organization culture are often explained to new employees and reinforced to present employees through stories. For example, Nordstrom's service culture is emphasized by stories describing the "heroic" service undertaken by its salespeople. Salespeople will relate how a fellow salesperson went across the mall and bought a green, extra-large Ralph Lauren/Polo shirt for a customer who was upset because Nordstrom didn't have the shirt in his size. Department sales managers encourage storytelling by holding contests in which the salesperson with the best hero story for the week wins a prize.

The Container Store emphasizes the importance of add-on sales using the "man in the desert" story. A man crawling through the desert, gasping for water, is offered water by a retailer at the oasis. But if a Container Store was at the oasis, the salesperson would have said, "Here's some water but how about some food? I see you're wearing a wedding ring. Can we call your family to let them know you are here?"[28]

Using symbols is another technique for managing organization culture and conveying its underlying values. Symbols are an effective means of communicating with employees because the values they represent can be remembered easily. Wal-Mart makes extensive use of symbols and symbolic behavior to reinforce its emphasis on controlling costs and keeping in contact with its customers. Photocopy machines at corporate headquarters have cups on them for employees to use to pay for any personal copying. At a traditional Saturday morning executive meeting, employees present

Sam Walton, founder of Wal-Mart, symbolized Wal-Mart's corporate culture emphasizing cost control.

information on cost-control measures they've recently undertaken. Managers who've been traveling in the field report on what they've seen, unique programs undertaken in the stores, and promising merchandise. Headquarters are spartan. Founder Sam Walton, one of the world's wealthiest people before he died, lived in a modest house and drove a pickup truck to work.

Disney strengthens its organization culture through the labels it uses for its employees and by steeping employees in the culture during the selection process. Management and employees view themselves as part of a team whose job is to produce a very large show. Applicants are trying out for a role in the cast rather than being hired for a job. For hourly jobs, the casting director (the person in charge of recruiting) interviews applicants to determine if they can adapt to the company's strong organizational culture. Do they understand and accept the fact that Disney has strict grooming requirements (no facial hair for men, little makeup for women)? Is the applicant willing to work on holidays? After the initial screening, the remaining applicants are judged on how well they might fit in with the show. Current employees participate in the entire process—they assess the applicant's behaviors and attitudes while also providing firsthand information on their role in the "production."

Finally, the CEO's philosophies and actions play a major role in establishing corporate culture. Herbert Kelleher, former CEO of Southwest Airlines, the world's fastest-growing and most profitable airline, built his company's corporate culture on two principles: (1) people are important—each person makes a difference—and (2) work should be fun. Humor plays an important role at Southwest because it encourages the frank expression of ideas and feelings without making people uncomfortable. Kelleher hires people with a sense of humor—people who don't take themselves too seriously but don't use humor to make others uncomfortable.

The importance of people at Southwest is expressed through its altruistic values. The airline emphasizes that its employees must be motivated to help others. Southwest employees treat each other as family. When a Midland, Texas, agent's son was dying of leukemia, 3,000 Southwest employees (60 percent of its employees at the time) sent cards to him on their own.[29]

BUILDING EMPLOYEE COMMITMENT

As mentioned previously, an important challenge in retailing is to reduce turnover.[30] High turnover reduces sales and increases costs. Sales are lost because inexperienced employees lack the skills and knowledge about company policies and merchandise to effectively interact with customers. Costs increase due to the need to continually recruit and train new employees.

Consider what happens when Bob Roberts, meat department manager in a supermarket chain, leaves the company. His employer promotes a meat manager from a smaller store to take Bob's position, then promotes an assistant department manager to the position in the smaller store, promotes a meat department trainee to assistant manager's position, and hires a new trainee. Now the supermarket chain needs to train two meat department managers and one assistant manager and hire and train one trainee. The estimated cost for replacing Bob Roberts is almost $10,000.

To reduce turnover, retailers need to build an atmosphere of mutual commitment in their firms. When a retailer demonstrates its commitment, employees respond by developing loyalty to the company. Employees improve their skills and work hard for the company when they feel the company is committed to them over the long run, through thick and thin. Some approaches that retailers take to build mutual commitment are (1) developing employee skills through selection and training, (2) empowering employees, and (3) creating a partnering relationship with employees.[32] Research indicates that engaging in these human resource management practices increases the firm's financial performance.[33]

Developing Skills

Two activities that retailers undertake to develop knowledge, skills, and abilities in their human resources are selection and training. Retailers that build a competitive advantage through their human resources are very selective in hiring people and make significant investment in training.

 Selective Hiring   The first step in building a committed workforce is recruiting the right people. Singapore Airlines, one of Asia's most admired companies, is consistently ranked among the top airlines in terms of service quality. Since its flight attendants are the critical point of contact with its customers, senior management is personally involved in their selection. Only 10 percent of the applicants make the initial screen and 2 percent are eventually hired.[34]

The job requirements and firm strategy dictate the type of people hired. Simply seeking the best and the brightest often is not the best approach. For example, at Recreational Equipment Inc., a category killer in outdoor gear, the motto is "You live what you sell." Outdoor enthusiasts are hired as sales associates so they can help customers and serve as a resource for the buying staff. Borders Books and Music wants avid readers in its workforce.[35]

Training   Training is particularly important in retailing because more than 60 percent of retail employees have direct contact with customers. They are responsible for helping customers satisfy their needs and resolve their problems. A key to the success of the Men's Wearhouse is how it treats its employees and its emphasis on training. All wardrobe consultants and store management go through a five-day training program at "Suits University," the company's 35,000-square-foot training center in Fremont, California. The training program emphasizes "clienteling," a process designed to foster a strong relationship between the wardrobe consultants and their customers. Periodically, experienced store personnel come back to the training center for three- and four-day retraining. The employee commitment Men's Wearhouse builds through its training investment is reflected in its low inventory shrinkage rate. Its employees watch out for the company. They don't steal, and they stop others from shoplifting.[36]

Investing in developing employee skills tells employees that the firm considers them important. In response to the difficulty in finding qualified service workers, Marriott has made a considerable investment in recruiting and training entry-level workers. The training goes beyond the basics of doing the job to include grooming habits and basic business etiquette like calling when you can't come to work.

Employees involved in this program have a strong commitment to Marriott. For example, Sara Redwell started working at Marriott as a housekeeper after emigrating from Mexico. She's now a housekeeping manager supervising

REFACT

Averaging only seven hours per employee over a year, the retail industry spends less time on training than all other industries.[37]

20 employees and mentoring other Mexican immigrants. "What Marriott gave to me, I want to give to others," she says. Tom Lee, a bartender at the Seattle Marriott, proudly proclaims, "Every day I put on this uniform just like an NBA player."[38] Walgreen's, Wal-Mart, and T. J. Maxx also have active programs for hiring people who do not possess entry-level skills. Retailing View 9.5 illustrates how Starbucks creates strong commitment in its employees.

Empowering Employees

Empowerment is the process of managers sharing power and decision-making authority with employees. When employees have the authority to make decisions, they are more confident in their abilities, have greater opportunity to provide service to customers, and are more committed to the firm's success.

RETAILING VIEW Starbucks' Baristas Are Committed to Providing the Perfect Cup of Coffee

9.5

Starbucks develops a passion for coffee in its customers by providing the perfect cup in an entertaining atmosphere. Recognizing that its front-line employees are critical to providing the perfect cup, the company has built an organization culture based on two principles: (1) strict standards for how coffee should be prepared and delivered to customers and (2) a laid-back, supportive, empowering attitude toward employees.

All new hires go through a 24-hour training program that instills a sense of purpose, commitment, and enthusiasm. The new staff are treated with dignity and respect that goes along with their title as *baristas* (Italian for bartender). To emphasize their responsibility for pleasing customers, they're presented with a scenario in which a customer complains that a pound of beans was ground incorrectly. The preferred response is to replace the beans on the spot without checking with the manager or someone with greater authority.

So the firm can hold on to these motivated, well-trained employees, all employees, both full-time and part-time, are eligible for health benefits and a stock option plan called "Bean Stock." Baristas know about and are encouraged to apply for promotion to store management positions. Due to the training, empowerment, benefits, and opportunities, Starbucks' turnover is only 60 percent of its store employees, considerably less than 300 percent average turnover experienced by similar food service firms.

Starbucks' human resource practices have facilitated its entry into foreign markets. For example, its joint venture partner Mei Da Coffee Company faced a challenge hiring local managers for its first four restaurants in Beijing. Even though the demand for good managers was far greater than the supply, Starbucks was viewed as an attractive em-

Starbucks' organizational culture supports this barista's role in providing customers with a satisfying experience.

ployer because of its corporate culture and opportunities for career development and advancement. Candidates were impressed with the casual atmosphere and respect employees show for one another. One recruit stated, "People are looking for a good working environment where they can learn, and they are looking for dignity." The new recruits were trained in Seattle so they could experience the corporate culture and learn how to make the different coffee drinks.

Sources: Ira Berkow, "Sonics' New Owner Is out to Revive Passion," *New York Times*, April 24 2001, p. D2; Craig S. Smith, "Globalization Puts a Starbucks into the Forbidden City in Beijing," *New York Times*, November 25, 2000, p. B1; and Naomi Weiss, "How Starbucks Impassioned Workers to Drive Growth," *Workforce*, August 1998, pp. 60–65.

The first step in empowering employees is to review employee activities that require a manager's approval. For example, Parisian, a regional department store chain owned by Saks, changed its check authorization policy, empowering sales associates to accept personal checks of up to $1,000 without a manager's approval. Under the old policy, a customer often had to wait more than 10 minutes for the sales associate to locate a manager. Then the busy manager simply signed the check without reviewing the customer's identification. When the sales associates were empowered to make approvals, service improved and the number of bad checks decreased because the sales associates felt personally responsible and checked the identification carefully.

Each store in the Whole Foods chain is a profit center with the store employees organized in 10 self-managed teams. The teams are responsible and accountable for the store's performance. For example, the store manager recommends new hires. It takes a two-third vote of the team to actually hire the candidate. The team members pool their ideas and come up with creative solutions to problems. Empowerment of retail employees transfers authority and responsibility for making decisions to lower levels in the organization. These employees are close to the retailer's customers and in a good position to know what it takes to satisfy customers. For empowerment to work, managers must have an attitude of respect and trust, not control and distrust.[39]

Creating Partnering Relationships

Three human resource management activities that build commitment through developing partnering relationships with employees are (1) reducing status differences, (2) promoting from within, and (3) enabling employees to balance their careers and families.

Reducing Status Differences Many retailers attempt to reduce status differences among employees. With limited status differences, employees feel that they play an important role in the firm's achieving its goals and that their contributions are valued.

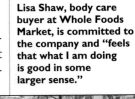

Lisa Shaw, body care buyer at Whole Foods Market, is committed to the company and "feels that what I am doing is good in some larger sense."

Status differences can be reduced symbolically through the use of language and cut substantively by lowering wage differences and increasing communications between managers at different levels in the company. For example, hourly workers at JCPenney are referred to as associates and managers are called partners, a practice that Sam Walton adopted when he started Wal-Mart.

Whole Foods has a policy of limiting executive compensation to less than eight times the compensation of the average full-time salaried employee. When Herb Kelleher was CEO of Southwest Airlines, he negotiated a five-year wage freeze for his employees in exchange for stock options. He also agreed to freeze his base salary at $380,000. Sam Walton was typically on lists of the most underpaid CEOs.

All Home Depot senior executives spend time in the stores, wearing the orange apron, talking with

customers and employees. This "management by walking around" makes employees feel that their inputs are valued by the company and reinforces the customer service culture at Home Depot.[41]

Promotion from Within **Promotion from within** is a staffing policy that involves hiring new employees only for positions at the lowest level in the job hierarchy and then promoting employees for openings at higher levels in the hierarchy. Nordstrom, Home Depot, JCPenney, and Wal-Mart have had promotion-from-within policies, whereas others frequently hire people from competitors when management positions open up.

Promotion-from-within policies establish a sense of fairness. When employees do an outstanding job and then outsiders are brought in over them, employees feel that the company doesn't care about them. Promotion-from-within policies also commit the retailer to develop its employees.[42]

Balancing Careers and Families The increasing number of two-income and single-parent families makes it difficult for employees to effectively do their jobs and manage their households. Retailers build employee commitment by offering services like job sharing, child care, and employee assistance programs to help their employees manage these problems.

Flextime is a job scheduling system that enables employees to choose the times they work. With **job sharing,** two employees voluntarily are responsible for a job that was previously held by one person. Both programs let employees accommodate their work schedules to other demands in their life such as being home when children return from school.[43]

Many retailers offer child care assistance. Sears corporate headquarters near Chicago has a 20,000-square-foot day care center. At Eddie Bauer, a catalog retailer in Seattle, the corporate headquarters cafeteria stays open late and prepares takeout meals for time-pressed employees. Some companies will even arrange for a person to be at an employee's home waiting for the cable guy to come or to pick up and drop off dry cleaning.[44]

TRENDS IN RETAIL HUMAN RESOURCE MANAGEMENT

In this final section we discuss three trends in human resource management: (1) the increasing importance of having a diverse workforce, (2) the growth in legal restrictions on HR practices, and (3) use of technology to increase employee productivity.

Managing Diversity

Managing diversity is a human resource management activity designed to realize the benefits of a diverse workforce. Today, diversity means more than differences in skin color, nationality, and gender. Managing a diverse workforce isn't a new issue for retailers. In the late 1800s and early 1900s, waves of immigrants entering America went to work in retail stores. The traditional approach for dealing with these diverse groups was to blend them into the "melting pot." Minority employees were encouraged to adopt the values of the majority, white, male-oriented culture. To keep their jobs and get promoted, employees abandoned their ethnic or racial distinctiveness.

But times have changed. Minority groups now embrace their differences and want employers to accept them for what they are. The appropriate metaphor now is a salad bowl, not a melting pot. Each ingredient in the salad is distinctive, preserving its own identity, but the mixture of ingredients improves the combined taste of the individual elements.[45]

Some legal restrictions promote diversity in the workplace by preventing retailers from practicing discrimination based on non–performance-related employee characteristics. But retailers now recognize that promoting employee diversity can improve financial performance. By encouraging diversity in their work-force, retailers can better understand and respond to the needs of their customers and deal with the shrinking labor market.

Retailers are increasing the diversity of their workforce to match the diversity of their customers.

Retail customers' racial and ethnic backgrounds are increasingly diverse. To compete in this changing marketplace, retailers need management staffs that match the diversity of their target markets. For example, 85 percent of the men's clothing sold in department stores is bought by women, and over 50 percent of Home Depot's sales are made to women. To better understand customer needs, department store and home improvement retailers feel that they must have women in senior management positions—people who really understand their female customers' needs. Besides gaining greater insight into customer needs, retailers must deal with the reality that their employees will become more diverse in the future. Many retailers have found that these emerging groups are more productive than their traditional employees.

After renovating its national reservation center to accommodate workers with disabilities, Days Inn found that turnover among disabled workers was only 1 percent annually compared with 30 percent for its entire staff. Lowe's, a home improvement center chain, changed floor employees' responsibilities so they wouldn't have to lift heavy merchandise. By assigning these tasks to the night crew, the firm was able to shift its floor personnel from male teenagers to older employees who provided better customer service and had personal experience with do-it-yourself projects. Effectively managing a diverse workforce isn't just morally correct, it's necessary for business success.[46]

The fundamental principle of managing diversity is the recognition that employees have different needs and require different approaches for accommodating those needs. Managing diversity goes beyond meeting equal employment opportunity laws. It means accepting and valuing differences. Some programs that retailers use to manage diversity involve offering diversity training, providing support groups and mentoring, and managing career development and promotions.[47]

Diversity Training   Diversity training typically consists of two components: developing cultural awareness and building competencies. The cultural awareness component teaches people about how their own culture differs from the culture of other employees and how stereotypes they hold influence the way they treat people often in subtle ways they might not realize. Then role-playing is used to help employees develop better interpersonal skills, including showing respect and treating people as equals.

Support Groups and Mentoring   **Mentoring programs** assign higher-level managers to help lower-level managers learn the firm's values and meet other senior executives.[48] Many retailers help form minority networks to exchange information and provide emotional and career support for members who traditionally haven't been included in the majority's networks. In addition, mentors are often assigned to minority managers. At Giant Foods, a Maryland-based supermarket chain, the mentoring program has reduced turnover of minorities by making them more aware of the resources available to them and giving them practical advice for solving problems that arise on their jobs.

Career Development and Promotions   Although laws provide entry-level opportunities for women and minority groups, these employees often encounter a glass ceiling as they move through the corporation. A **glass ceiling** is an invisible barrier that makes it difficult for minorities and women to be promoted beyond a certain level. To break through this glass ceiling, JCPenney monitors high-potential minorities and women employees and makes sure they have opportunities for store and merchandise management positions that are critical for eventual promotion to senior management.

Similarly, women in the supermarket business have traditionally been assigned to peripheral departments like bakery and deli, while men were assigned to the critical departments in the store: meat and grocery. Even in the supermarket chain corporate office, women traditionally have been in staff-support areas like human resource management, finance, and accounting, while men are more involved in store operations and buying. To make sure that more women have an opportunity to break through the glass ceiling in the supermarket industry, firms are placing them in positions critical to the firm's success.[50]

Legal and Regulatory Issue in Human Resource Management

The proliferation of laws and regulations affecting employment practices in the 1960s was a major reason for the emergence of human resource management as an important organization function. Managing in this complex regulatory environment required an expertise in labor laws and skills in helping other managers comply with these laws. The major legal and regulatory issues involving the management of retail employees are (1) equal employment opportunity, (2) compensation, (3) labor relations, (4) sexual harassment, and (5) employee privacy.

Retailing View 9.6 describes how Denny's responded to legal pressure about its discriminatory practices resulted in a stronger company.

Equal Employment Opportunity   The basic goal of equal employment opportunity regulations is to protect employees from unfair discrimination in the workplace. **Illegal discrimination** is the actions of a company or its managers that result in members of a protected class being treated unfairly and differently than others. A protected class is all of the individuals who share a common characteristic defined by the law. Companies can not treat employees differently simply based on their race, color, religion, sex, national origin, age, or disability status. There are a very limited set of circumstances when employees can be treated differently. For example, it is even illegal for a restaurant to hire young, attractive servers because that is what its customers prefer. Such discrimination must be absolutely necessary, not simply preferred.

In addition, it is illegal to engage in a practice that disproportionately excludes a protected group even though it might seem to be nondiscriminatory. For example, suppose that a retailer uses scores on a test to make hiring decisions. If a protected group systematically performs worse on the test, the retailer is illegally discriminating even if there was no intention to discriminate.

Compensation Laws relating to compensation define the 40-hour workweek, the pay rate for working overtime, and the minimum wage, and they protect employee investments in their pensions. In addition, they require that firms provide the same pay for men and women who are doing equal work.

Labor Relations Labor relations laws describe the process by which unions can be formed and the ways in which companies must deal with the unions. They precisely indicate how negotiations with unions must take place and what the parties can and cannot do.

Employee Safety and Health The basic premise of these laws is that the employer is obligated to provide each employee with an environment that is free from hazards that are likely to cause death or serious injury. Compliance officers from the Department of Labor routinely conduct inspections to assure that employers are providing such an environment for their workers.[51]

Sexual Harassment Sexual harassment includes unwelcome sexual advances, requests for sexual favors, and other verbal and physical conduct. Harassment isn't confined to requests for sexual favors in exchange for job considerations such as a raise or promotion. Simply creating a hostile work environment can be considered sexual harassment. For example, actions that are considered sexual harassment include lewd comments, joking, and graffiti, as well as showing obscene photographs, staring at a co-worker in a sexual manner, alleging that an

Denny's Transition from Sinner to Saint in Diversity | RETAILING VIEW

9.6

In the early 1990s, Denny's restaurant chain was synonymous with racism in terms of how it treated both customers and employees. Even Jay Leno singled out the chain for ridicule. ("They are serving something new at Denny's this year. . . African American customers.") It was no laughing matter, however, when in 1992, Denny's paid out over $45 million to settle a class action suit filed by customers. In addition to the cash payment, Denny's agreed to increase minority-owned franchises, purchase goods and services from minority-owned businesses, and increase the number of minority employees.

While the agreement dealt with some of the discriminatory practices, the appointment of a new management headed by CEO James Adamson changed the chain's culture. The team includes several women and minorities. Previously, the Denny's executive group had been almost exclusively white males.

Adamson sent a clear message for employees, managers, and franchises: "If you discriminate, you're history!" A mandatory diversity training program was developed for managers, and a portion of their bonus is based on results in reducing customer complaints, including those relating to discrimination.

Six years later, Denny's was selected as one of the 50 best companies for African Americans and Hispanics. *Fortune* also reported that the 50 best companies for African Americans and Hispanics outperformed the *Fortune* 500 by 12 percent over the previous three years and by 17 percent over the previous five years.

Sources: Tannette Johnson-Elie, "Denny's Turnabout Means Fair Play for Minority Employees," *Milwaukee Journal Sentinel*, October 31, 2000, p. 1D; and A. Faircloth, "Guess Who's Coming to Denny's?" *Fortune*, August 3, 1998, pp. 1C8–C10.

employee got rewards by engaging in sexual acts, and commenting on an employee's moral reputation.

Customers can engage in sexual harassment as well as supervisors and co-workers. For example, female pharmacists find that some male customers demand lengthy discussions when they buy condoms. Pharmacists have difficulty dealing with these situations because they want to keep the person as a customer and also protect themselves from abuse.

Employee Privacy Employees' privacy protection is very limited. For example, employers can monitor e-mail and telephone communications, search an employee's work space and handbag, and require drug testing. However, employers can not discriminate among employees when undertaking these activities unless they have a strong suspicion that employees are acting inappropriately.

Developing Policies The human resource department is responsible for developing programs and policies to make sure that managers and employees are aware of these restrictions and know how to deal with potential violations. These legal and regulatory requirements are basically designed to treat people fairly. Employees want to be treated fairly and companies want to be perceived as treating their employees fairly. The perception of fairness encourages people to join a company and leads to trust and commitment of employees to a firm. When employees believe they are not being treated fairly, they can either complain, stay and accept the situation, stay but engage in negative behavior, quit, or complain to an external authority and even sue the employer.

 Perceptions of fairness are based on two factors: the perceptions of (1) distributive justice and (2) procedural justice. **Distributive justice** arises when outcomes received are viewed as fair with respect to outcomes received by others. However, the perception of distributive justice can differ across cultures. For example, in the individualistic culture of the United States, merit-based pay is perceived as fair, whereas in collectivist cultures such as China and Japan, equal pay is viewed as fair. **Procedural justice** is based on fairness of the process used to determine the outcome. U.S. workers consider formal processes as fair whereas group decisions are considered fairer in collectivist cultures.[52] Some illustrations of policies on procedural justice are presented in Chapter 17.

Use of Technology

Retail chains are using intranets to automate and streamline human resource operations. For example, Penney's 150,000 employees use kiosks in the 1,200 Penney stores to make changes in their personnel records, request time off, register for training classes, review the company's policies and procedures manual, and request services such as direct-deposit of their paychecks. These self-service kiosks are also used by job applicants to review open positions, submit applications, and take prescreening tests. The use of these kiosks, connected through an intranet to a centralized database, dramatically reduces the time human resources administrators spend on paperwork.[53]

REFACT

It costs a retailer $20 to $30 to process a paper HR form, but processing the form over an intranet only costs $.05 to $.10.[54]

SUMMARY

Human resource management plays a vital role in supporting a retailing strategy. The organization structure defines supervisory relationships and employees' responsibilities. The four primary groups of tasks performed by retailers are strategic decisions by the corporate officers, administrative tasks by the corporate staff, merchandise management by the buying organization, and store management.

In developing an organization structure, retailers must make trade-offs between the cost savings gained through centralized decision making and the benefits of tailoring the merchandise offering to local markets—benefits that arise when decisions are made in a decentralized manner.

Two critical human resource management issues are the development of a committed workforce and the effective management of a diverse workforce. Building a committed workforce is critical in retailing because high turnover has a major impact on profitability. A key factor in reducing turnover is developing an atmosphere of mutual commitment.

Managing diversity is important in retailing because customers are becoming more diverse and new entrants into the retail workforce will come largely from the ranks of women and minorities. Programs for managing diversity include diversity training, support groups and mentors, and promotion management.

The human resource department is also responsible for making sure that its firm complies with the laws and regulations that prevent discriminatory practices against employees and ensure that they have a safe and harassment-free work environment.

KEY TERMS

buyer, *283*
category manager, *285*
centralization, *290*
decentralization, *290*
distributive justice, *304*
employee productivity, *274*
employee turnover, *274*

empowerment, *298*
flextime, *300*
glass ceiling, *302*
illegal discrimination, *302*
job sharing, *300*
managing diversity, *300*
mentoring program, *301*

merchandising planner, *286*
organization culture, *294*
organization structure, *278*
procedural justice, *304*
promotion from within, *300*
specialization, *280*

GET OUT & DO IT!

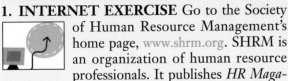

1. INTERNET EXERCISE Go to the Society of Human Resource Management's home page, www.shrm.org. SHRM is an organization of human resource professionals. It publishes *HR Magazine* with articles available online at www.workforceonline.com. Find and summarize the conclusions of articles addressing the HR challenges that retailers are facing, such as the management of a diverse workforce, international expansion, and the use of technology to increase productivity.

2. INTERNET EXERCISE The Fair Measures Law Consulting Group provides training and legal services for employers. Go to its website, www.fairmeasures.com, and choose one of the legal areas to investigate (sexual harassment, wrongful termination, and so forth). Another source of information about legal issues regarding employees is www.law.cornell.edu/topics/employment.html. Read the most recent court opinions and articles about the issue, and summarize the implications for human resource management in retailing.

3. **GO SHOPPING** Meet with the manager of a store and ask him or her about the store's policies concerning the legal and regulatory issues discussed in the chapter. Does the retailer have written policies that enable the manager to deal effectively with situations that arise? Have situations arisen that were not covered by the policies? How was the situation dealt with?

4. **GO SHOPPING** Talk with a salesperson in a store. Ask him or her how committed he or she is to working for the retailer. Why does the salesperson feel that way? What could the retailer do to build a great sense of commitment?

DISCUSSION QUESTIONS AND PROBLEMS

1. Why is human resource management more important in retailing than in manufacturing firms?

2. Describe the similarities and differences between the organization of small and large retail companies. Why do these similarities and differences exist?

3. Some retailers have specific employees (merchandise assistants) assigned to restocking the shelves and maintaining the appearance of the store. Other retailers have sales associates perform these tasks. What are the advantages and disadvantages of each approach?

4. How can national retailers like Best Buy and Victoria's Secret, which both use a centralized buying system, make sure that their buyers are aware of the local differences in consumer needs?

5. What are the positive and negative aspects of employee turnover? How can a retailer reduce the turnover in its sales associates?

6. To motivate employees, several major department stores are experimenting with incentive compensation plans. Frequently, compensation plans with a lot of incentives don't promote good customer service. How can retailers motivate employees to aggressively sell merchandise and at the same time not jeopardize customer service?

7. Assume that you're starting a new restaurant catering to college students and plan to use college students as waiters and waitresses. What human resource management problems would you expect to have? How could you build a strong organization culture in your restaurant to provide outstanding customer service?

8. Three approaches for motivating and coordinating employee activities are policies and supervision, incentives, and organization culture. What are the advantages and disadvantages of each?

9. Why should retailers be concerned about the needs of their employees? What can retailers do to satisfy the needs of employees?

10. You've been promoted to manage a general merchandise discount store. Your assistant managers are an African-American male, a Hispanic male, a white female, and a female who has worked for the company for 35 years. What are the strengths of your management group, and what problems do you see arising?

SUGGESTED READINGS

Breuer, Nancy L. "Shelf Life: Retaining Employees in the Retail Trade." *Workforce,* August 2000, pp. 8, 28.

Colin, Mitchell. "Selling the Brand Inside." *Harvard Business Review,* January 2002, pp. 99–105.

Chang, Myong-Hun, and Joseph E. Harrington Jr. "Centralization vs. Decentralization in a Multi-Unit Organization: A Computational Model of a Retail Chain as a Multi-Agent Adaptive System." *Management Science* 46 (November 2000), pp. 1427–43.

Duane, Michael J. *Policies and Practices in Global Human Resource Systems.* Westport, CT: Quorum Books, 2001.

Jackson, Susan, and Randall Schuler. *Managing Human Resources Through Strategic Relationships.* 8th ed. Mason, OH: Southwestern, 2003.

Kabachnick, Terri. "Retailers Need to Be Aware of the Trends Transforming Today's Workforce." *WWD,* Chicago Supplement, May 1999, p. 28.

Kraut, Allen, and Abraham Korman, eds. *Evolving Practices in Human Resource Management: Responses to a Changing World of Work.* San Francisco: Jossey-Bass Publishers, 1999.

Noe, Raymond; John Hollenbeck; Barry Gerhart; and Patrick Wright. *Human Resource Management.* 4th ed. Burr Ridge, IL: McGraw-Hill Irwin, 2003.

Reichheld, Frederick F. "Lead for Loyalty." *Harvard Business Review,* July 2001, pp. 76–84.

"The 100 Best Companies to Work For." *Fortune,* January 8, 2002, pp. 148–68.

Walker, Alfred J., ed. *Web-Based Human Resources.* New York: McGraw-Hill, 2001.

Information Systems and Supply Chain Management

10

CHAPTER

EXECUTIVE BRIEFING | Jeff Perdick, Inventory Business Analyst, Electronic Boutique

"Our inventory and distribution systems play an important role in Electronic Boutique's success. When a new game is released, we want to be the first store in the market to have it available for sale. On the other hand, we need to actively manage our inventory to make sure we are getting as good a return on it as possible and still meet the needs of our customers."

Electronics Boutique (EB) is the leading specialty retailer of computer software, accessories, and video games. Its annual sales in 2002 were over $1 billion through 937 stores in the United States, Australia, Canada, Denmark, Germany, Italy, New Zealand, Norway, South Korea, and Sweden and its website, www.ebgames.com. Each store stocks and displays over 2,000 different programs plus a wide variety of brand-name and private-label accessories.

Jeff Perdick became interested in a retailing career after his summer internship with Electronic Boutique. After graduating with a BSBA from the University of Florida, he took a position with EB as a store manager. In 1990, his store in Columbia, Maryland, won the Flagship

Sales Award for the highest percent sales increase in the mall. Two years later he was promoted to area manager of three stores. Soon after, he was again promoted to the corporate office as a product distribution analyst and proceeded to be promoted to positions of increasing responsibility in the Inventory Planning Department.

"In my present position, I produce a number of reports used by the buyers and planners that analyze inventory levels and make recommendations. For example, one report I produce each month is a recommendation for products we should discontinue. I feel

QUESTIONS

- How do merchandise and information flow from vendor to retailer to consumer and back?
- What advanced information technology developments are facilitating vendor–retailer communications?
- What are quick response delivery systems?
- Why does getting merchandise faster translate to stronger retailer profits?

like I am in the command and control center for our company. I can see what is really going on and get a great sense of accomplishment when I see the results of my recommendations." Data are utilized on a daily basis to make business decisions. An example of this is determining which stores will no longer carry declining categories, such as N64 and Dreamcast.

"Managing the business on a global basis is really a challenge because the popularity of items varies from country to country. Currently, every SKU in foreign markets is different from those in our domestic stores. This increases the complexity of SKU maintenance and the need for separate merchandising divisions. We need to continue making major investments in our systems if we want to maintain the 25 percent annual growth rate in sales we have had over the last five years."

When you walk into a Target store to buy a Black & Decker toaster, your transaction triggers a series of information flows that result in merchandise replenishment. Your toaster is scanned at the point of sale (POS). The information on the black-and-white bar code (UPC, or Universal Product Code) goes directly to a computer at Target's regional distribution center and, importantly, to Black & Decker's computer as well.

When a specified number of toasters are sold, a replenishment order is automatically generated from the POS data and sent electronically to Target's distribution center. There is a loading dock assigned at a specified time waiting for the truck from Black & Decker to arrive. The Black & Decker merchandise is unloaded, combined with merchandise from other vendors, and immediately loaded onto a Target truck going to the store that is running out of toasters. As a result of this immediate access to information, both Target and Black & Decker know exactly what, where, and when something is being sold. Additionally, Target stores collect information on customers to be used to plan promotions and to merchandise their stores. By sharing this information, Target and Black & Decker have become partners in this supply chain. Everyone benefits. Black & Decker can plan its production and distribution activities, and Target has better merchandise availability because it works together with Black & Decker to get merchandise to stores.

In this penultimate chapter of the Retailing Strategy section, we describe how retailers can gain a strategic advantage through supply chain management. We then examine supply chain information flows, with an emphasis on how retailers communicate with their vendors over the Internet. This is followed by a discussion of merchandise flows from the point of sale at the store, to distribution centers, and on to vendors. Examine Retailing View 10.1 to see how information systems and technology gave Wal-Mart a sustainable competitive advantage.

STRATEGIC ADVANTAGES GAINED THROUGH SUPPLY CHAIN MANAGEMENT

Supply chain management is the integration of business processes from end user through original suppliers that provides products, services, and information that add value for customers.[1]

Retailers may be the most important link in the supply chain. They connect customers with the vendors who provide the merchandise. It is the retailers' responsibility to gauge customers' wants and needs and work with the other members of the supply chain—wholesalers, manufacturers, transportation companies, and so on—to make sure the merchandise customers want is available when they want it. A simplified supply chain is illustrated in Exhibit 10–1. Manufacturers ship merchandise either to a distribution center operated by a retailer (as is the case for manufacturers M_1 and M_3), or they ship directly to stores (as is the case for manufacturer M_2). The relative advantages of shipping directly to stores versus to distribution centers are discussed later in the chapter.

RETAILING VIEW   Information Systems Technology: The Wal-Mart Effect

10.1

Retail may be the last place you would expect to find a productivity miracle. More than half of the productivity acceleration in the retailing of general merchandise can be explained by only two syllables: Wal-Mart. In 1987, Wal-Mart had a market share of just 9 percent but was 40 percent more productive than its competitors as measured by real sales per employee. A variety of Wal-Mart innovations, both large and small, are now industry standards. Wal-Mart created the large-scale, or big-box, format; everyday low prices; electronic data interchange (EDI) with suppliers; and the strategy of expanding around central distribution centers. These innovations allowed the company to pass its savings on to customers. By 1995, it commanded a market share of 27 percent and had widened its productivity edge to 48 percent.

Information technology (IT) was a necessary if not a sufficient part of Wal-Mart's success. The company invested in most of the waves of retail IT systems earlier and more aggressively than did its competitors: It was among the first retailers to use computers to track inventory (1969), just as it was one of the first to adopt bar codes (1980), EDI for better coordination with suppliers (1985), and wireless scanning guns (late 1980s). These investments, which allowed Wal-Mart to reduce its inventory significantly and to reap savings, boosted its capital productivity and labor productivity.

Wal-Mart's secret was to focus its IT investments on applications that directly enhanced its core value proposition of low prices. The company's later IT investments—such as the Retail Link program, which captures sales data and gives vendors real-time stock and flow information—are aimed more at increasing sales through micromerchandising and cutting the incidence of stockouts, though Wal-Mart also hopes to gain further reductions in inventory. Whether this new wave of IT investments will be as fruitful as its predecessors remains to be seen.

Source: Bradford C. Johnson, "Retail, The Wal-Mart Effect," *The McKinsey Quarterly*, no. 1 (2002). Reprinted by permission.

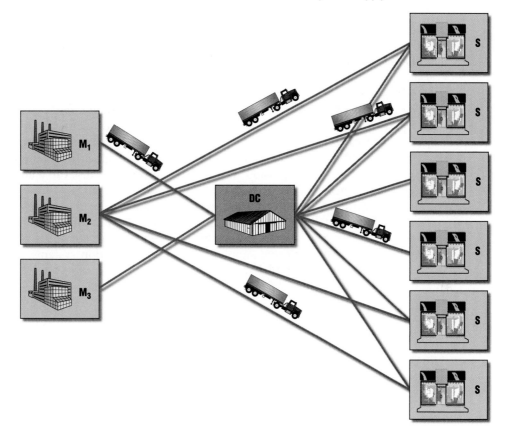

Retailers have increasingly taken a leadership position in their respective supply chains. Clearly this is not always the case. Small, family-owned retailers continue to thrive even though they are often at the mercy of their larger suppliers. But over the past 30 years, chains such as Wal-Mart, Carrefour (France), 7-Eleven (Japan), Home Depot, Zara (Spain), and Kroger have grown to dominate and control their supply chains. Not only does size generate power, but knowledge about their customers plays a vital role as well. As a result of their position in the supply chain, retailers are in the unique position to collect purchase information customer by customer, transaction by transaction. This information can be shared with suppliers to plan production, promotions, deliveries, assortments, and inventory levels.

Improved Product Availability

An efficient supply chain has two benefits for customers: (1) fewer stockouts and (2) assortments of merchandise that customers want, where they want it. These benefits translate into greater sales, higher inventory turns, and lower markdowns for retailers.

Giao Nguyen recently went to her local department store on a Saturday afternoon when she saw an ad for silk blouses. Unfortunately, the store was out of her size in all the colors she liked. The store gave her a rain check so she could come back and still pay the sale price when it received a new shipment. Nguyen wasn't impressed. She had fought the traffic, waited in line, and generally wasted her afternoon. In the end, Nguyen never returned to the store, and she told all of her friends about her problems there. The problem could have been avoided since the merchandise was available in the distribution center, but it hadn't been delivered to the store on time.

To meet the specific needs of a wide variety of customers, retailers are carrying more stock keeping units (SKUs). For instance, only a few years ago a bath department in a discount store consisted of three sizes of towels in five colors. Now there are twice as many SKUs in towels, plus rugs, shower curtains, wastebaskets, toothbrush holders, and other accessories—all in matching colors and patterns. This SKU explosion means that the retailer must carry additional inventory that needs to be carefully managed and distributed.

The challenge is national, and even international, in scope for many chain stores. Bath and Body Works, for instance, has 1,600 stores.[2] Although many items are carried at all stores, some are tailored to meet the needs of local markets. Without sophisticated supply chain and information systems, it would be impossible for the chain to stay in stock.

Improved Return on Investment

One measure of retailing performance is the ability to generate a target return on investment (ROI) (see Chapter 6). Consider the commonly used return on investment measure, return on assets:

$$\text{Return on assets} = \text{Net profit margin} \times \text{Asset turnover}$$

$$\frac{\text{Net profit}}{\text{Total assets}} = \frac{\text{Net profit}}{\text{Net sales}} \times \frac{\text{Net sales}}{\text{Total assets}}$$

An efficient supply chain and information system can increase net profit and net sales, while at the same time reducing total assets. Net sales can increase by providing customers with better assortments. Consider the silk blouse that Nguyen was trying to purchase. Another retailer with a strong consumer database would have information about the group of customers who like silk blouses, including their color and style preferences. That retailer would not only try to stay in stock on these items, but it would entice this group into the store with promotions designed for them and announcements sent directly to them. It would merchandise the silk blouses with other items it knows Nguyen and customers like to purchase.

Net profit can increase by either raising gross margin or lowering expenses. An information system coordinating the buying staffs and vendors could allow the retailer to take advantage of special buying opportunities and obtain the silk blouses at a low cost, thus improving the gross margin. This same retailer can lower operating expenses by coordinating deliveries, thus cutting transportation expenses. The retailer's distribution center is so efficient that merchandise can be received, prepared for sale, and shipped to stores with minimum handling.

Its inventory management system, which is directly linked to the vendor's computer, is so sophisticated that the retailer needs to carry relatively little backup inventory to stay in stock. Thus, since inventory investment is low, the total assets are also low, and inventory turns are high. In sum, there's untapped

EXHIBIT 10–2
Information and
Merchandise Flows

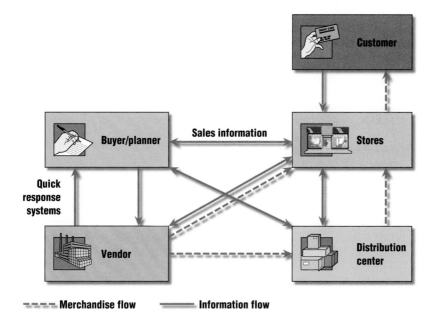

----- Merchandise flow ——— Information flow

opportunity for many retailers to improve their performance through better supply chain management.

Exhibit 10–2 shows the complexities of the merchandise and information flows in a typical multistore chain. Although information and merchandise flows are intertwined, in the following sections we describe how information on customer demand is captured at the store and then triggers a series of responses from the buyer, distribution center, and vendor that are designed to ensure that merchandise is available at the store when the customer wants it.

THE FLOW OF INFORMATION

The flow of information is complex in a retail environment. Although Giao Nguyen is disappointed that the store is out of the silk blouse that she wants, she's successful in purchasing a new pair of Guess? jeans. This purchase triggers a series of information messages throughout the system (depicted in Exhibit 10–3).

1. The sales associate scans the UPC tag on the jeans. A sales receipt is created for Nguyen.

2. The purchase information is recorded in the POS terminal and sent to the buyer/planner. The buyer/planner uses this information to plan additional purchases (Chapters 12 and 13) and make markdown decisions (Chapter 15).

3. The purchase information is typically aggregated by the retailer, and an order is created and sent to the vendor using a system called electronic data interchange (EDI)—the computer-to-computer exchange of business documents from retailer to vendor, and back. Issues surrounding EDI are also discussed later in this section. In situations where the merchandise is

EXHIBIT 10–3
Information Flows

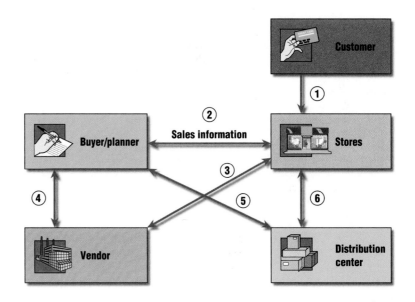

reordered frequently, the ordering process can be automatic and virtually bypass the buyer. In other cases, such as for newer or more fashion-oriented items, buyers input is required prior to sending the order.

4. The buyer/planner communicates with the vendor regarding the purchase order for the merchandise. At this point they often negotiate shipping dates and terms of purchase (Chapter 14).

5. The buyer/planner communicates with the distribution center to coordinate deliveries from the vendor and to the stores, check inventory status, and so on.

6. Store managers also communicate with the distribution center to coordinate deliveries and check inventory status.

In the next sections of this chapter, we will explore how retailers store information in data warehouses and how the information is transmitted to vendors through EDI. Retailing View 10.2 examines how information is used in the Prada store in New York's SoHo district.

Data Warehousing

Purchase data collected at the point of sale goes into a huge database known as a data warehouse. (See flow number 2 in Exhibit 10–3.) A **data warehouse** is the coordinated and periodic copying of data from various sources, both inside and outside the enterprise, into an environment ready for analytical and informational processing.[3] The information stored in the data warehouse is accessible on several dimensions and levels, depicted in the data cube in Exhibit 10–4. As shown on the horizontal axis, data can be accessed by level of merchandise aggregation—SKU (item), vendor, category (dresses), department (women's apparel), or all merchandise. Along the vertical axis, data can be accessed by level of the company—store, division, or the total company. Finally, along the third dimension, data can be accessed by point in time—day, season, or year. Thus, a CEO interested in how the corporation is generally doing could look at the data by all merchandise, by division or total corporation, and by year. A buyer may be more interested in a particular vendor in a certain store, on a particular day.

Analysts from various levels of the retail operation extract information from the data warehouse for making a plethora of marketing decisions about developing and replenishing merchandise assortments. Data warehouses also contain detailed information about customers, which is used to target promotions and group products together in stores. These applications are discussed in Chapter 11.

Now let's take a look at how information flows back and forth from retailer to vendor (flow numbers 3 and 4 in Exhibit 10–3).

Electronic Data Interchange

Electronic data interchange (EDI) is the computer-to-computer exchange of business documents from retailer to vendor, and back. In addition to sales data, purchase orders, invoices, and data about returned merchandise are transmitted from retailer to vendor.

Many retailers now require vendors to provide notification of deliveries before they take place. An **advanced shipping notice (ASN)** is an electronic document received by the retailer's computer from a supplier in advance of a shipment. It tells the retailer exactly what to expect in the shipment. If accurate, the retailer can dispense with opening cartons and checking in merchandise. Information about on-hand inventory status, vendor promotions, and cost changes can be transmitted from vendor to retailer too, or in the case of vendor-affixed price

---

Prada Knows Its Customers and Its Inventory   RETAILING VIEW

10.2

Sales associates at the new Prada store in the fashionable SoHo section of New York City carry a wireless handheld device with a keypad and a color display screen that provides up-to-date information about inventory and customers. The device also controls video displays throughout the store, including clips of fashion shows, advertising, or pictures of specific garments or shoes.

This radio frequency identification (RFID) technology also plays a role in the dressing room and postsale. Once a garment is placed in the dressing room, the "RFID Closet" automatically reads the tag and accesses Prada's database for product information and imagery. A flat-screen display in the dressing room shows garment information, related runway clips, and inventory availability. Interacting with the closet screen, a customer can elect to save that print and visual content to her personal online profile. The customer can access the profile online, review saved selections, and send messages to her personal shopper.

Upon returning to the store, the customer can use her Prada Customer Card to give a new sales associate access to her profile and preferences, allowing the associate to better serve her needs. This both builds loyalty with customers as well as capturing important history data.

Once a garmet is placed in a dressing room, an electronic device reads the price/identification tag and accesses Prada's database. A flat screen display in the dressing room shows garment information, related runway clips, and inventory availability.

Source: Todd Sowers, " Prada Looks to Iconmedialab to Develop Retail Solutions Using Texas Instruments RFID Technology," Iconmedialab, New York, February 14, 2002. Reprinted by permission.

EXHIBIT 10–4 | Retail Data Warehouse

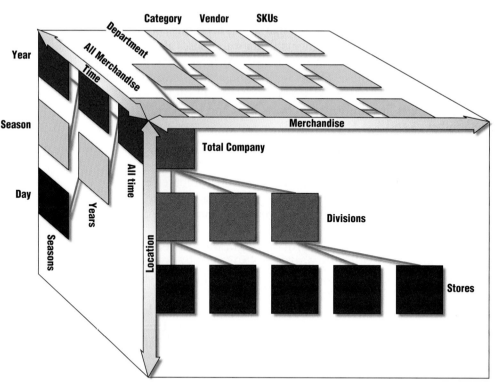

SOURCE: Marketmax.

tickets from retailer to vendor as well. It's also possible to exchange information about purchase order changes, order status, retail prices, and transportation routings by EDI.

There are a variety of ways in which EDI data can be transmitted: proprietary systems and web-based systems, which include intranets and extranets.

Proprietary EDI Systems **Proprietary EDI systems** are data exchange systems that are developed primarily by large retailers for the purpose of exchanging data with their vendors. Wal-Mart, for instance, has spent millions of dollars and several years developing one of the most advanced EDI systems in retailing. It has worked with its vendors to develop systems compatible with theirs. Due to strategic advantages, virtual elimination of manual intervention—no paper—via automated exchange of data, Wal-Mart mandates the use of EDI to their supplier community.

Intranets Also available over the Internet are **intranets,** which are secure communication systems that take place within one company. For instance, in Exhibit 10–3, communications from store to buyer (flow 2), buyer to distribution center (flow 5), and distribution center to store (flow 6) could all be accomplished through intranets. Using intranets, buyers can communicate and coordinate with store and distribution center personnel.

Extranets Increasingly, EDI data are transmitted over the Internet through extranets. An **extranet** is a collaborative network that uses Internet technology to link businesses with their suppliers, customers, or other businesses. Extranets are typically private and secure in that they can be accessed only by certain parties. An extranet is generally an extension of a company's intranet, modified to allow access by specified external users. While the largest retailers and their vendors have embraced EDI through proprietary networks for some time, the Internet empowers smaller concerns—particularly international vendors—that could not afford to implement their own systems to participate in a secure system and take advantage of EDI.

Target Corporation, the parent company of Target, Mervyn's, Dayton's, Hudson's, and Marshall Field's, has extended its traditional EDI program to an extranet system called Partners Online.[4] The company has made some time-sensitive procedures, confidential information, and general supplier information such as shipping requirements and prerequisites for packing cartons available via the extranet.

Retailing View 10.3 examines Harry Rosen's EDI extranet and intranet application.

Advanced EDI Applications EDIs, especially those through extranets, have gone beyond the mere communication of order and shipping information. The Internet enables suppliers to describe and show pictures of their products. Buyers can issue requests for proposals, and then the two parties can electronically negotiate an order and specify product development.

Popular in the grocery and drug industries, **collaboration, planning, forecasting, and replenishment (CPFR)** is an inventory management system using EDI in which a retailer will send information to a manufacturer and the manufacturer will use the data to construct a computer-generated replenishment forecast that will be shared back with the retailer before it's executed. Using CPFR, the manufacturer and retailer jointly decide on replenishment issues. CPFR is discussed in Chapter 12. Retailing View 10.4 Describes how Costco and Kimberly-Clark manage their supply chain together.

REFACT

According to supply chain specialists, $200 billion to $300 billion in excess inventory and missed sales in the United States could be eliminated through closer collaboration between retailers and their suppliers.[5]

Harry Rosen Embraces EDI | RETAILING VIEW 10.3

Harry Rosen Inc. is one of Canada's premiere menswear retailers. Founded in 1954, Harry Rosen Inc. has grown from a single 500-square-foot store in Toronto to 18 stores from Vancouver to Montreal as well as nine Hugo Boss boutiques across the United States. The stores offer the finest menswear labels: Hugo Boss, Ermenegildo Zegna, Giorgio Armani Le Collezioni, Canali, Brioni, and Versace Classic.

Their new management information system replaces the bulky printed weekly buyers' reports with data that are instantaneously accessible from laptops. Sales, inventory, and forecast information is available to the buyer at the item (SKU) level, or at a more aggregated level for top management.

The system coordinates purchase and receipt of merchandise from suppliers. This function lets the retailer and vendors communicate one to one via electronic data interchange. The EDI technology lets Harry Rosen send instantaneous electronic purchase orders to its suppliers, and in return, the suppliers send electronic advance shipping notices and invoices to Harry Rosen. The EDI function extends to the store, enabling stores to accurately communicate receipt of merchandise.

Sources: Andree Conrad, "Harry Rosen Unveils IT Refit," *DNR* 31, no. 5 (January 2001), p. 10; and "Harry Rosen: The Company," March 25, 2002, www.harryrosen.com/company/e_index.html.

These buyers are communicating with a vendor using EDI technology.

Security

Successful multichannel retailers must build security into their business processes so that their customers will be assured that their personal information will be private and secure. The Internet has heightened security problems. Multichannel retailers are now open to the world all the time—$24 \times 7 \times 365$.

Some of the potential implications of security failures besides the most obvious and devastating one, loss of revenue from customers, are the loss of business data essential to conducting business; disputes with partners, suppliers, distributors, customers; loss of public confidence; and bad publicity.

Security has become a more intense challenge in recent years because, as a result of electronic retailing, suppliers, customers, and prospective new clients all need some form of access. Also, the control of retail information is slipping from a centralized information technology orientation to the functional areas of the business, such as buying and distribution.

To help control this changing information environment, retailers need to develop a corporate security policy. A **security policy** is a set of rules that apply to activities in the computer and communications resources that belong to an organization. Although security policies cover theft and the security of individuals and property, we will limit our discussion here to network security. It is not enough, however, to

---

RETAILING VIEW | Kimberly-Clark Manages Costco's Huggies

10.4

One morning, a Costco store in Los Angeles began running low on Huggies. Crisis loomed. So what did Costco managers do? Nothing. They didn't have to, thanks to a special arrangement with Kimberly-Clark Corp., the company that makes the diapers.

Under this deal, responsibility for replenishing stock falls on the manufacturer, not Costco. In return, the big retailer shares detailed information about individual stores' sales. So, long before babies in Los Angeles would ever notice it, diaper dearth was averted by a Kimberly-Clark data analyst working at a computer hundreds of miles away.

Just a few years ago, the sharing of such data between a major retailer and a key supplier would have been unthinkable. But the arrangement between Costco and Kimberly-Clark underscores a sweeping change in American retailing. Across the country, powerful retailers—from Wal-Mart to Target to JC Penney—are pressuring their suppliers to take a more active role in shepherding products from the factory to store shelves.

In some cases, that means requiring suppliers to shoulder the costs of warehousing excess merchandise. In others, it means pushing suppliers to change product or package sizes. In the case of Costco and Kimberly-Clark, whose coordinated plan is officially called "vendor-managed inventory," Kimberly-Clark oversees and pays

for everything involved with managing Costco's inventory except the actual shelf-stockers in store aisles.

Whatever the arrangement and the terminology, the major focus for these big retailers is the same: cutting costs along the supply chain. The assumption is that suppliers themselves are in the best position to spot inefficiencies and fix them.

For Costco, the benefits of such close operation with a major supplier are clear: Costco saves money not only on staffing in its inventory department, but also on storage. Before Kimberly-Clark began managing Costco's inventory, in late 1997, the retailer would keep an average of a month's supply of Kimberly-Clark products in its warehouses. Now, because Kimberly-Clark has proven it can replenish supplies more efficiently, Costco needs to keep only a two-week supply.

What's more, Costco says its shelves are less likely to go empty under the new system. That's important for both retailer and supplier, because consumer studies indicate that a majority of customers will walk out of a store empty-handed if they can't find a particular item they need.

Source: Emily Nelson and Ann Zimmerman, "Minding the Store: Kimberly-Clark Keeps Costco in Diapers, Absorbing Costs Itself," *The Wall Street Journal,* September 7, 2000, pp. A11–A12. Copyright 2000 by Dow Jones & Co., Inc. Reprinted with permission of Dow Jones & Co., Inc. via Copyright Clearance Center.

have a security policy; retailers must train employees and add the necessary software and hardware to enforce the rules.

The security policy should meet the following objectives:

- *Authentication.* The system should be able to assure or verify that the person or computer at the other end of the session really is what it claims to be.

- *Authorization.* The system should be able to assure that the person or computer at the other end of the session has permission to carry out the request.

- *Integrity.* The system should be able to assure that the arriving information is the same as that sent. This means that the data are protected from unauthorized changes or tampering (data integrity).

THE PHYSICAL FLOW OF MERCHANDISE—LOGISTICS

Logistics is that part of the supply chain process that plans, implements, and controls the efficient, effective flow and storage of goods, services, and related information from the point of origin to the point of consumption in order to meet customers' requirements.[6] Supply chain management includes logistics, but it is a more comprehensive and strategic concept that includes customer relationship management (Chapter 11), inventory management (Chapters 12 and 13), and vendor relations (Chapter 14).[7] For instance, supply chain management would be involved in new-product development because logistics considerations may affect the profitability of a new product. When Ford Motor Company's engineers design a new component for its cars, for example, they attempt to get all divisions, including Jaguar and Mazda, involved. The entire supply chain would be more efficient if newly designed parts could be manufactured at one or several strategically located plants and then shipped globally. In this section, however, we will concentrate on issues limited to the physical flow of merchandise.

Exhibit 10–5 illustrates the different merchandise flows.

1. Merchandise flows from vendor to distribution center.

2. Merchandise then goes from distribution center to stores.

3. Alternatively, merchandise can also go from vendor directly to stores.

Sometimes merchandise is temporarily stored at the distribution center; other times it's immediately prepared to be shipped to individual stores. This preparation may include breaking shipping cartons into smaller quantities that can be more readily utilized by the individual stores (breaking bulk), as well as tagging merchandise with price tags or stickers, UPC codes, and the store's label. A **UPC code**—the black-and-white bar code printed on the package of most products—is illustrated in the cartoon on page 321. UPC stands for universal product code. Later in this chapter, we'll discuss why some retailers use distribution centers, and others have vendors ship directly to stores.

Logistics has presented new challenges and opportunities for multichannel retailers. Retailing View 10.5 describes how Home Depot and Sam's Club have risen to the challenge.

The Distribution Center

To fully understand the logistics function within a retailing organization, consider a shipment of Haggar pants arriving at a Sears distribution center. The

EXHIBIT 10–5
Merchandise Flows

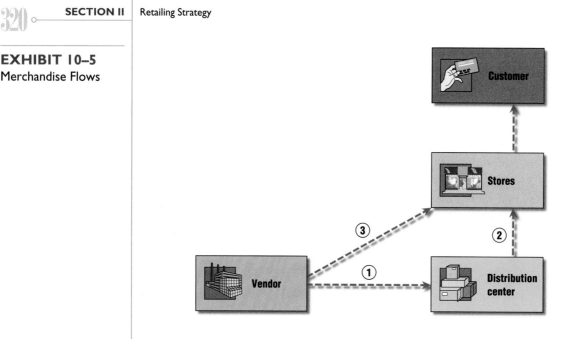

distribution center performs several functions for Sears: coordinating inbound transportation, receiving, checking, storing and crossdocking, getting merchandise "floor-ready," filling orders, and coordinating outbound transportation.

Management of Inbound Transportation   Examine flow number 1 in Exhibit 10–5. Merchandise flows from vendor to distribution center. Buyers have

---

RETAILING VIEW | Multichannel Logistics

10.5

Matching merchandise supply with specific consumer demand is one of the most important activities a retailer performs. This is especially critical in a multichannel world where fulfillment forms such a key part of the consumer value proposition. As a result, much greater flexibility in fulfillment and delivery models is required in the multichannel environment.

Simply stated, the goal of fulfillment is to get the right products to the right place at the right time. While store and nonstore inventories are managed separately for most multichannel retailers, a growing number are using the Web to provide real-time information to customers on the inventory status of merchandise in local stores. By allowing consumers to place orders online and pick up the merchandise at stores, retailers are able to obtain more value from locations that already carry the costs of receiving, storing, and merchandising goods. Using the Internet to increase foot traffic also helps ease the objections of store retailers who say that websites steal their business. Consider the multichannel logistics fulfillment strategies of Home Depot and Sam's Club.

- **Home Depot.** By electronically integrating with each store's merchandising system, Home Depot plans to

localize its online offerings based on on-hand, store-level inventory. Any time a new item is added or deleted from the store's assortment, it will be instantly reflected on the website for shoppers in the local market.

As a result, Home Depot can guarantee next-day delivery. Products ordered online at Home Depot can be picked up at one of its stores, delivered by Home Depot to a job site or other location, or shipped via UPS.

- **Sam's Club.** Sam's Club has linked the order fulfillment systems of its e-commerce and bricks-and-mortar operations down to the local level. Consumers nationwide can order online for pickup within 24 hours at a local Sam's Club store. Called "Click'n'Pull," the service requires a $250 minimum purchase. Members log in, choose a location, and shop from more than 2,500 items from a local club's real-time inventory. An e-mail informs members when the order is ready for pickup.

Source: Linda Hyde, "Critical Issues: Multi-Channel Integration—The New Retail Battleground," March 2001, Retail Forward, Inc., www.retailforward.com, pp. 33–34. Reprinted by permission.

- Distribution centers enable the retailer to carry less merchandise in the individual stores, resulting in a lower inventory investment systemwide. If the stores get frequent deliveries from the distribution center, they need to carry relatively little extra merchandise as backup stock.

- It's easier to avoid running out of stock or having too much stock in any particular store since merchandise is ordered from the distribution center as needed.

- Retail space is typically much more expensive than space at a distribution center, and distribution centers are better equipped than stores to prepare merchandise for sale. As a result, many retailers find it cost-effective to store merchandise and get it ready for sale at a distribution center rather than in individual stores.

But distribution centers aren't viable for all retailers. If a retailer has only a few outlets, then the expense of a distribution center is probably unwarranted. Also, if many outlets are concentrated in metropolitan areas, then merchandise can be consolidated and delivered by the vendor to all the stores in one area. In some cases, it's quicker to get merchandise to stores by avoiding the extra step of shipping to a distribution center. This is particularly important for perishable goods (meat and produce), high-fashion items, or fads since shelf life is limited.

What type of retailer should use a distribution center?

- Retailers with wildly fluctuating demand for specific items at the store level, like CDs, since more accurate sales forecasts are possible when demand from many stores is aggregated at distribution centers.

- Stores that require frequent replenishment, like grocery stores, because a direct store delivery system would require stores to spend too much time receiving and processing orders from many vendors. There wouldn't be enough hours in the day to process that many trucks.

- Stores that carry a relatively large number of items that are shipped to stores in less than full-case quantities.

- Retailers with a large number of outlets that aren't geographically concentrated within a metropolitan area but are within 150 to 200 miles of a distribution center.

Retailing View 10.7 explains how Amazon.com has increased warehouse efficiency to be able to ship 200,000 items on a busy day by running two 10-hour shifts.

Management of Outbound Transportation

The management of outbound transportation from distribution center to stores (flow number 2 in Exhibit 10–5) has become increasingly complex as chain stores expand. The Sears distribution center runs almost 100 truck routes in one day. To handle its complex transportation problem, the center uses a sophisticated routing and scheduling computer system. This system considers the rate of sales in the store, road conditions, and transportation operating constraints to develop the most efficient routes possible. As a result, stores are provided with an accurate estimated time of arrival and vehicle utilization is maximized.

REFACT

One trend in the grocery industry is to lay out the warehouse like the stores. That way, orders are picked in the DC in the same order that they are placed on the shelves in the stores. Although it slightly increases labor costs in the DC, there are significant labor savings in the store.[10]

Reverse Logistics   **Reverse logistics** is a flow back of merchandise through the channel, from the customer to the store, distribution center, and vendor, for customer returns. Although not shown in Exhibits 10–2 or 10–5, sometimes merchandise has to flow back through the channel. Reverse logistics can be a serious problem. For instance, returns for apparel bought from catalogs range from 12 to 35 percent, depending on the product's style and how fashion-forward it is.[11] The more fashion-forward the item, the more likely it is to be returned.

Reverse logistics systems have never been simple or inexpensive. The items may be damaged, and without the original shipping carton, thus causing special handling needs. Transportation costs can be high because items are shipped back in small quantities. Retailers and their vendors usually wish returns to vendors would just disappear.

Some retailers are following a strategy used by Sears, which is moving a portion of its returned merchandise to online auctions.[13] Sears has sold thousands of items at auction on eBay.com and has recovered an average two to three times more than it would have using other liquidation channels. A third-party distribution facilitator, Genco Distribution Systems, collects the merchandise to be auctioned from Sears, inspects it, and, following criteria set by Sears, lists the items on eBay without identifying the Sears brand name. After the auction, Genco packs and ships the merchandise to the consumer.

Now we will look at some additional logistics issues facing retailers today. First, probably the most important development in supply chain management is the advent of quick response delivery systems. Second, traditional bricks-and-

REFACT

Returns cost retailers from .2 percent to 25 percent of their sales.[12]

RETAILING VIEW   Amazon.com Ships 200,000 Items a Day

10.7

Ever since it built five vast warehouses, Amazon.com has boasted of the wonders of the machinery inside them—10 miles of conveyer belts and myriad other gadgets. Amazon is focused on filling orders accurately.

One big goal had been to reduce errors that occur in keeping track of the several million items continually being placed onto and pulled off of hundreds of thousands of bins on metal shelves. To reduce errors, Amazon wrote new software to take better advantage of the gizmo that each warehouse worker was already carrying—a shoe-horn-size device that combines a bar-code scanner, a display screen, and a two-way data transmitter. The new software checks their work by forcing them to scan each item every time they put it on or take it off a shelf.

Amazon also built a special sorting machine. The machine reads the bar code on each item and routes it into one of 2,100 chutes, each chute representing an order for a single customer. When all the items in an order are in the chute, a light flashes, and a worker rushes to put them in a box. They are then sent on other conveyers to machines that print packing slips, seal the boxes, and send them off to shippers' trucks.

Source: Saul Hansell, "Amazon Ships to Sorting Machine Beat," *New York Times,* NYTimes.com January 21, 2002. Reprinted by permission.

At Amazon.com, an Internet order is filled using sophisticated material handling equipment.

mortar retailers are finding that distribution to Internet customers requires a different logistics system than they are used to. Finally, retailers are outsourcing many functions. **Outsourcing** is obtaining a service from outside the company that had previously been done by the firm itself.

Quick Response Delivery Systems

There are only two groups of retail businesses today: the quick and the dead.[15]

Quick response (QR) delivery systems are inventory management systems designed to reduce the retailer's lead time for receiving merchandise, thereby lowering inventory investment, improving customer service levels, and reducing logistics expenses. QR is the integrating link between the information and the merchandise flows depicted in Exhibit 10–2 earlier in this chapter.

Many of the concepts that comprise QR systems have been previously discussed in this chapter. In this section, however, we describe how they all work together. The origins of the present QR systems were derived from just-in-time (JIT) initiatives undertaken by manufacturers and adapted for retailing. QR is part of the efficient consumer response (ECR) initiatives undertaken by packaged goods manufacturers and food and drugstore retailers.[16] The systems used for coordinating sales forecasts between retailer and vendors are referred to as CPFR (introduced earlier in the chapter and described further in Chapter 12). EDI facilitates the exchange of data between retailer and vendors.

Originally, quick response delivery systems seemed better suited to basic items, such as underwear, paper towels, or toothpaste, than to high fashion. By its nature, fashion dictates being able to quickly adjust to the changing seasons as well as to new colors and styles. Thus, quick response is as important in managing fashion inventories as in managing basic-item inventories. Fashion retailers need to determine what's selling (so it can be reordered quickly) and what isn't selling (so it can be marked down).

To illustrate a QR system, consider how the system works at Zara.[17] Zara, located in Galicia, Spain, is now the third-largest clothing retailer in the world, with profits growing at 30 percent per year. It operates over 500 stores in 31 countries, including several in New York City.

The process starts with the store managers, who are equipped with handheld devices linked directly to the company's design rooms in Spain. They report daily on what customers are buying, scorning, and asking for but not finding. For instance, when buyers found that customers were requesting a purple shirt that was similar to one they were selling in pink, they passed this information onto the designers in Spain. Fabrics are cut and dyed by robots in the company's 23 highly automated factories in Spain. The final assembly is entrusted to a network of 300 or so small shops that are located near the factories in Galicia and northern Portugal.

Because Zara controls the entire production and design process, it can make products in very small lots. By so doing, it can see how the

Instead of shipping new products once a season like many fashion retailers, Zara makes deliveries to each of its stores every few days. Small shipments more often is the key to QR systems.

first few hundred items are selling before making more. Instead of shipping new products once a season like many fashion retailers, Zara makes deliveries to each of its stores every few days. The purple shirts were in stores in two weeks—compared to the several months it would take for most department stores and other specialty apparel stores to accomplish the same feat. Small shipments more often is the key to QR systems.

Benefits of a QR System   The benefits of a QR system are reduced lead time, increased product availability, lower inventory investment, and reduced logistics expenses.

Reduces Lead Time   By eliminating the need for paper transactions using the mail, overnight deliveries, or even fax, EDI in the QR system reduces lead time. **Lead time** is the amount of time between the recognition that an order needs to be placed and its arrival in the store, ready for sale. Since the vendor's computer acquires the data electronically, no manual data entry is required on the recipient's end. As a result, lead time is reduced even more, and vendor recording errors are eliminated. Thus, use of EDI in the QR system can cut lead time by a week or more. Shorter lead times further reduce the need for inventory because the shorter the lead time, the easier it is to forecast demand; therefore, the retailer needs less inventory.

Zara successfully reduces lead time by communicating electronically with the factory, by using automated equipment, by using assemblers who are in close proximity to the factory, and by using premium transportation such as air freight to get merchandise to the stores.

Increases Product Availability and Lowers Inventory Investment   In general, as a retailer's ability to satisfy customer demand by being in stock increases, so does its inventory investment. (This concept is explored in Chapter 12.) Yet with QR, the ability to satisfy demand can actually increase while inventory decreases! Since the retailer can make purchase commitments or produce merchandise closer to the time of sale, its inventory investment is reduced. Stores need less inventory because they're getting less merchandise on each order, but they receive shipments more often. Inventory is further reduced because the retailer isn't forecasting sales so far into the future. For instance, fashion retailers that don't use QR make purchase commitments as much as six months in advance and receive merchandise far in advance of actual sales. QR systems align deliveries more closely with sales.

The ability to satisfy customer demand by being in stock also increases in QR systems as a result of the more frequent shipments. For instance, if a Zara store is running low on a medium kelly-green sweater, its QR system will ensure a shorter lead time than that of more traditional retailers. As a result, it's less likely that the Zara store will be out of stock before the next sweater shipment arrives.

Reduces Logistics Expenses   QR systems also have the potential to significantly reduce logistics expenses. Many retailers receive merchandise in their distribution centers, store it, consolidate shipments from multiple vendors, attach price labels and theft prevention devices, and then reship the merchandise to stores. Retailers have two options for reducing these logistics expenses using QR systems. They can either use a crossdocking warehouse system or they can negotiate a direct store delivery system. Crossdocking eliminates storage and some handling costs. Direct store delivery eliminates all distribution center costs and transportation costs from the DC to stores. If the merchandise is floor-ready, there's no need to devote expensive retail space for receiving and processing merchandise in the store, and sales associates can devote all of their attention on their customers.

Costs of a QR System   Although retailers achieve great benefits from a QR system, it's not without costs. The logistics function has become much more complicated with more frequent deliveries. With greater order frequency come smaller orders, which are more expensive to transport. The greater order frequency also makes deliveries and transportation more difficult to coordinate.

QR systems also require a strong commitment by the retailer and its vendors to cooperate, share data, and develop systems like EDI and CPFR. Successful QR systems not only require financial support from top management but also a psychological commitment to become partners with their vendors. Large retailers often apply their power to get their vendors to absorb many of these expensive logistics costs.

The Logistics of Electronic Retailing

Fulfilling Internet orders from customers is very different than distributing merchandise to stores. Retailers with stores are concerned with moving a large amount of merchandise from distribution centers to individual stores. These distribution centers typically have automated material-handling equipment and warehouse-management software linked to store POS terminals. Internet retailers, on the other hand, have outbound shipments averaging 1.8 items per order that are shipped to addresses all over the world.[18]

How do traditional retailers with a successful Web presence handle these two disparate distribution tasks? Some, like Staples, have a fully integrated information system, whereby distribution to stores and to customers ordering through a website or catalog is handled by the same information system. Yet they use different DCs to service stores and Internet and catalog customers. Staples makes deliveries by trucks or UPS. Sharper Image, which started as a catalog merchant, now operates almost 100 stores in the United States and has a fast-growing website. One distribution center serves all three retail formats. Catalog and Web orders are treated identically but are separated from the store-based distribution system. Toys "R" Us is partnering with Internet retailers like Amazon.com to assist it in online fulfillment needs.

Outsourcing

To streamline their operations and make more productive use of their assets and personnel, retailers are constantly looking to outsource logistical functions if those functions can be performed better or less expensively by **third-party logistics companies.**

Third-Party Logistics Companies   These are firms that facilitate the movement of merchandise from manufacturer to retailer but are independently owned. Specifically, they provide transportation, warehousing, consolidation of orders, and documentation.

Transportation Retailers must choose their shippers carefully and demand reliable, customized services. After all, to a large extent, the retailer's lead time and the variation in lead time are determined by the chosen transportation company. Also, many retailers are finding that it is worth the added cost of airfreight to get merchandise into stores quicker. It is also easier for independent transportation companies to contract for full trucks on the return trip (backhaul) than it is for the retailer. By arranging a productive round-trip, they can offer their services at a lower cost than most retailers can do it themselves. Some retailers mix modes of transportation to reduce overall cost and time delays. For example, many Japanese shippers send Europe-bound cargo by ship to the U.S. West Coast. From there, the cargo is flown to its final destination in Europe. By combining the two modes of transport, sea–air, the entire trip takes about two weeks, as opposed to four or five weeks with an all-water route, and the cost is about half of an all-air route.

Warehousing To meet the increasingly stringent demands retailers are placing on their vendors to meet specific delivery times for floor-ready merchandise, many vendors must store merchandise close to their retail customers. Rather than owning these warehouses themselves, vendors typically use **public warehouses** that are owned and operated by a third party. By using public warehouses, vendors can provide their retailers with the level of service demanded without having to invest in warehousing facilities.

Freight Forwarders **Freight forwarders** are companies that purchase transport services. They then consolidate small shipments from a number of shippers into large shipments that move at a lower freight rate. These companies offer shippers lower rates than the shippers could obtain directly from transportation companies because small shipments generally cost more per pound to transport than large shipments.[19]

One of the most daunting tasks for a retailer involved in importing merchandise to the United States is government bureaucracy. International freight forwarders not only purchase transportation services but also prepare and expedite all documentation, such as government-required export declarations and consular and shipping documents.

Integrated Third-Party Logistics Services Traditional definitions distinguishing between transportation, warehousing, and freight forwarding have become blurred in recent years. Some of the best transportation firms, for example, now provide public warehousing and freight forwarding. The same diversification strategy is being used by the other types of third-party logistics providers. Retailers are finding this one-stop shopping quite useful.

SUMMARY

Supply chain management and information systems have become important tools for achieving a sustainable competitive advantage. Customers are demanding better product availability and broader assortments than in the past. There are simply more retail outlets for chains to service. Many retailers can no longer count on double-digit annual sales increases to sustain growth in profits. Developing more efficient methods of distributing merchandise creates an opportunity to reduce expenses and improve customer service levels in an era of slow growth, or even no growth, in sales.

The systems used to control the flow of information to buyers and onto vendors have become quite sophisticated. Retailers have developed data warehouses that provide them with intimate knowledge of who their customers are and what they like to buy. These data warehouses are being used to strengthen the relationship with their customers and improve the productivity of their marketing and inventory management efforts. Electronic data interchange enables retailers to communicate electronically with their vendors. The Internet has accelerated the adoption of EDI, especially among smaller, less sophisticated vendors. Information security has become such an important issue in the world of multichannel retailing that retailers are advised to adopt a stringent security policy.

Retailers are reacting to today's environmental opportunities and threats by changing the way they distribute merchandise. Quick response delivery systems represent the nexus of information systems and logistics management. QR systems reduce lead time, increase product availability, lower inventory investment, and reduce overall logistics expenses. Some retailers are using distribution centers for crossdocking instead of for storing merchandise. Others are forcing their vendors to supply them with floor-ready merchandise and adhere to strict delivery schedules as part of their quick response delivery system. Other retailers are having vendors deliver merchandise directly to their stores and are using pull logistics strategies that base inventory policy on consumer demand. Retailers are outsourcing many of these logistics functions to third-party logistics companies.

KEY TERMS

advanced shipping notice (ASN), *315*

checking, *321*

collaboration, planning, forecasting, and replenishment (CPFR), *317*

crossdocking distribution center, *321*

data warehouse, *314*

dispatcher, *321*

electronic data interchange (EDI), *315*

extranet, *317*

floor-ready merchandise, *322*

freight forwarders, *330*

intranet, *316*

lead time, *328*

logistics, *319*

outsourcing, *327*

proprietary EDI systems, *316*

pick ticket, *324*

public warehouse, *330*

pull logistics strategy, *324*

push logistics strategy, *324*

quick response (QR) delivery system, *327*

receiving, *321*

reverse logistics, *326*

security policy, *318*

supply chain management, *310*

third-party logistics companies, *329*

ticketing and marking, *322*

traditional distribution center, *321*

UPC code, *319*

GET OUT & DO IT!

1. INTERNET EXERCISE Oracle Corporation is the world's second-largest independent software company and the information management company of choice for 70 percent of the *Fortune* 500 and 64 percent of the *Fortune* 100. Oracle uses Internet technology to help businesses manage information so that it is reliable, secure, and accessible to the right people, at the right time. Go to www.oracle.com/seetrybuy and see how it can help manage retailers' information flow.

2. INTERNET EXERCISE SAP, a German firm, specializes in integrated software solutions. Go to www.sap.com/products/industry/retail/index.htm and see what it's doing to help retailers.

3. INTERNET EXERCISE Go to Slingshot Solutions (www.slingshotsolutions.com) and its partner Genco Distribution Systems (www.genco.com) to learn more about how they are helping firms like Sears liquidate returned, overstock, or damaged merchandise.

4. INTERNET EXERCISE The Council of Logistics Management is the premier industry organization in the logistics area. Go to its website (www.clm1.org) and find out about new trends in logistics.

DISCUSSION QUESTIONS AND PROBLEMS

1. Retail system acronyms include QR, EDI, POS, and UPC. How are these terms related to each other?

2. What is the future of proprietary EDI systems?

3. Explain how QR systems can increase a retailer's level of product availability and decrease its inventory investment.

4. Design a logistics system for a national retailer that is embarking on a multichannel strategy.

5. This chapter has presented trends in logistics and information systems that benefit retailers. How do vendors benefit from these trends?

6. Evaluate the options retailers have for dealing with return merchandise?

7. What would you include in the ideal retailing data warehouse? Why would you include it?

8. Why haven't more fashion retailers adopted a quick response system similar to Zara's?

9. Explain the differences between pull and push logistics strategies.

10. Why is global logistics much more complicated than domestic logistics?

SUGGESTED READINGS

Bowersox, Donald J.; M. Bixby Cooper; and David J. Closs. *Supply Chain Logistics Management.* New York: McGraw-Hill, January 2002.

Coyle, John Joseph; Edward J. Bardi; and C. John Langley. *Management of Business Logistics: A Supply Chain Perspective.* Thomson Learning, January 2002.

Kahn, Barbara E., and Leigh McAlister. *Grocery Revolution: The New Focus on the Consumer.* Reading, MA: Longman, Addison-Wesley, 1997.

Knolmayer, Gerhard; Alexander Zeier; and Peter Mertens. *Supply Chain Management Based on Sap Systems.* New York: Springer-Verlag, 2002.

Nelson, David; Jonathan Stegner; and Patricia E. Moody. *The Purchasing Machine: How the Top Ten Companies Use Best Practices to Manage Their Supply Chains.* New York: Free Press, 2001.

Niraj, Rakesh; Mehendra Gupta; and Chakravarthi Narasimhan. "Customer Profitability in a Supply Chain." *Journal of Marketing* 65, no.3 (July 2001), pp. 1–33.

"The New Dynamics of Returns." ReturnBuy.com/business, December 2000.

Rutner, Stephen M., and C. John Langley, Jr. "Logistics Value: Definition, Process, and Measurement." *International Journal of Logistics Management* 11, no. 2 (2000), pp. 73–81.

Sawabini, Stuart. "EDI and the Internet." *Journal of Business Strategy* 22, no. 1 (January 2001), p. 41.

Stock, James R., and Douglas Lambert. *Strategic Logistics Management.* 4th ed. New York: McGraw-Hill, 2000.

Sullivan, Pauline, and Jikyeong Kang. "Quick Response Adoption in the Apparel Manufacturing Industry: Competitive Advantage of Innovation." *Journal of Small Business Management*, January 1999, pp. 1–24.

Customer Relationship Management

11

EXECUTIVE BRIEFING | Torbjörn Norberg, CRM Manager, ICA Handlarnas AB, Sweden

"It is becoming more and more difficult to get your customers' attention. For us at ICA Handlarnas AB, CRM is a means to cut through the clutter, talk directly to our customers, and cater specifically to our best customers. ICA Handlarnas AB is part of the ICA Ahold group in Scandinavia. We have 1,900 independent retailers operating ICA stores in five different store formats, ranging from large superstores to small neighborhood stores.

"Today about half of Sweden's 4.3 million households have an ICA card. Every month we send out 2.2 million copies of our *Buffé* food magazine, in which we provide our customers with tantalizing recipes, helpful hints, and of course, special offers. Each of our independent retailers also sends out a monthly letter that includes special offers to their target customers.

"Based on data collected at POS terminals, we provide store specific data analysis to identify differ-ent customer segments. Most of our independent retailers elect to target their very best customers who spend a lot in the store, as well as good customers that they would like to see more often in their store. We have developed campaigns that target customers who currently spend less in the store, but could be persuaded to become regular customers. We have also begun to tailor offers on the customer level based on their purchase history. This is more efficient for us, and better for our cus-

QUESTIONS

- What is customer relationship management?
- Why do retailers want to treat customers differently?
- How do retailers determine who their best customers are?
- How can retailers build customer loyalty?
- What can retailers do to increase their share of wallet?
- What can retailers do to alleviate the privacy concerns of their customers?

tomers since they will get offers that truly match their preferences.

"My vision when it comes to the future of CRM is really going back to the way stores were run before the introduction of the self-service supermarket. The old-fashioned grocer would know every customer's name, what she usually bought, which brands she preferred, and so forth. He could easily keep a dialogue with his customers and tailor his offerings to every customer, thereby being able to run his store more efficiently. We're not there yet, but with the advances in information technology, the next 10 to 15 years will bring us much closer to that ideal."

The business press and companies are talking a lot about the importance of managing customer relationships. Companies are spending billions of dollars on computer systems to help them collect and analyze data about their customers. With all of this buzz, you'd think that the customer is a popular new kid in the neighborhood. However, the customer is more like an old friend who's been taken for granted—until now.

Consider the following example. Shari Ast is on her third business trip this month. She takes a cab from Boston Logan airport to the Ritz-Carlton, her favorite hotel. As the door man opens the car door for her, he greets her, "Welcome back to the Ritz-Carlton, Ms. Ast." When she goes to the registration desk, the receptionist gives her the room key and asks if she would like to have her stay charged to her American Express card. Then she goes to her room and finds just what she prefers—a room with a view of the Boston Commons, a single queen-size bed, an extra pillow and blanket, a fax machine connected to her telephone, and a basket with her favorite fruits and snacks.

Shari Ast's experience is an example of the Ritz-Carlton's customer relationship management program. **Customer relationship management (CRM)** is a business philosophy and set of strategies, programs, and systems that focuses on identifying and building loyalty with a retailer's most valued customers. CRM is based on the philosophy that retailers can increase their profitability by building relationships with their better customers. Effectively managing merchandise inventory and the stores provides value and supports the primary objective of building customer loyalty. The goal is to develop a base of loyal customers who patronize the retailer frequently. In the following sections of this chapter, we discuss in more depth the objective of CRM programs and the elements in the CRM process.

THE CRM PROCESS

Traditionally, retailers have focused their attention on encouraging customers to visit their stores, look through their catalogs, and visit their websites. To accomplish this objective, they have traditionally used mass media advertising and price promotions, treating all of their customers the same. Now retailers are beginning to concentrate on providing more value to their best customers using targeted promotions and services to increase their **share of wallet**—the percentage of the customers' purchases made from the retailer—with these customers. This change in perspective is supported by research indicating that it costs over six times more to sell products and services to new customers than existing customers and that small increases in customer retention can lead to dramatic increases in profits.[1]

What Is Loyalty?

Customer loyalty, the objective of CRM, is more than having customers make repeat visits to a retailer and being satisfied with their experiences and the merchandise they purchased. **Customer loyalty** to a retailer means that customers are committed to purchasing merchandise and services from the retailer and will resist the activities of competitors attempting to attract their patronage. They have a bond with the retailer, and the bond is based on more that a positive feeling about the retailer.[2] Retailing View 11.1 describes how Neiman Marcus builds loyalty with its best customers.

Loyal customers have an emotional connection with the retailer. Their reasons for continuing to patronize a retailer go beyond the convenience of the retailer's store or the low prices and specific brands offered by the retailer. They feel such goodwill toward the retailer that they will encourage their friends and family to buy from it.

Programs that encourage repeat buying by simply offering price discounts can be easily copied by competitors. In addition, these types of price promotion programs encourage customers to be always looking for the best deal rather than developing a relationship with one retailer. However, when a retailer develops an emotional connection with a customer, it is difficult for a competitor to attract the customer.[3]

Emotional connections develop when customers receive personal attention. For example, many small, independent restaurants build loyalty by functioning as neighborhood cafés,

By providing good value, Wal-Mart increases its share of its customers' wallets.

where waiters and waitresses recognize customers by name and know their preferences. At Deleece in Chicago, for example, regulars find their favorite cocktail waiting when they arrive. It is not surprising that 80 percent of Deleece's customers are regulars.[4]

Unusual positive experiences also build emotional connections. For example, Peter Nordstrom, president of Nordstrom, related the story about a woman on a business trip who called the local store at 8:50 P.M. after discovering that she had forgotten to pack her dress shoes for a meeting the first thing the next morning. The sales associate in the shoe department located a similar pair of shoes in the woman's size and brought them over to the hotel for her. This customer was so impressed with the personalized service that she related the experience to her business colleague the next day, who then started buying most of his apparel at Nordstrom, even though there was not a Nordstrom store in his home town.[5] Providing such memorable experiences is an important avenue for building customer loyalty.[6]

CRM at Neiman Marcus   RETAILING VIEW

11.1

One of the best examples of a CRM activity designed to build customer loyalty is Neiman Marcus' InCircle program. Customers spending more than $3,000 annually are enrolled in the program and get special gifts, awards, and services. Customers at higher spending levels such as "Passport" and "Platinum" generate additional rewards and services.

Customers earn one point for each dollar charged on a Neiman Marcus credit card. The points can be redeemed for everything from bottles of Dom Perignon to new, fully loaded Jaguars or Caribbean cruises for two. Reward options are refined and expanded annually, but the options are designed to enhance Neiman's exclusive image and reputation for uniqueness.

InCircle members receive frequent communications from Neiman Marcus throughout the year, including the quarterly InCircle newsletter and the semiannual InCircle *Entrée* magazine, a quality publication produced by the creators of *Southern Living* and *Southern Accents*.

Customer relationships are also nurtured at the store level. Neiman's sales associates can tap into information about customers' purchases and shopping behaviors and are encouraged to contact these customers personally. Sales associates have the freedom to be creative in helping InCircle customers shop in multiple departments and use the various services Neiman's offers, from gift wrapping to travel services. Store managers invite InCircle members to free luncheons on their birthdays.

Recognizing the value of these preferred customers, Neiman's invites InCircle members to sit on a board that

Neiman Marcus uses a number of different methods for stimulating the interest in and promoting the benefits of its frequent shopper program.

provides feedback and suggestions as to how Neiman's can improve its customers' shopping experience and enhance and broaden its role in the community. These board meetings help Neiman's maintain genuine, ongoing dialogue with its best customers and make these customers feel the company respects them and their opinions. Due in part to this program, the 160,000 InCircle members account for over $1.6 billion in annual sales for Neiman Marcus.

Sources: Mark Albright, "Peddling Prestige," *St. Petersburg Times*, August 27, 2001, p. 8E; and "Mining the Store," *Chain Store Age*, January 2000, pp. 4A–5A

store-based retailers use to overcome this problem are (1) asking customers for the identifying information, (2) offering a frequent shopper cards, and (3) linking checking account numbers and third-party credit cards to customer names.

Asking for Identifying Information Some retailers such as Radio Shack, Nine West, and the Container Store have their sales associates ask customers for identifying information such as their phone number or name and address when

RETAILING VIEW   Chico's Uses Customer Data to Reconnect with Its Customers

11.2

Several years ago, specialty apparel retailer Chico's FAS Inc. fell into a fashion trap. The chain with over 350 stores targets females between the ages of 35 and 55 who like loose, comfortable clothes. But it was lured by the newest fashions to stock more trendy merchandise in smaller sizes oriented for a younger market. "We weren't talking directly to [our core customer] anymore, and by not doing that, we lost focus," said Bari Horton, director of direct marketing for Chico's, in Fort Myers, Florida. "Had we had the [CRM] data at the time, we never would have strayed."

In the early 1990's, Chico's tried to connect with its core customers through its Passport loyalty program that offered customers a 5 percent discount if they spent more than $500 annually. While customers were pleased with the program, the structure of the data file didn't allow Chico's to analyze the data in depth and learn about the specific items bought by individual customers and at spe-

cific locations. Chico's let the original Passport program die in the mid-90s.

In 1998, Chico's relaunched its Passport loyalty program as part of a CRM program. Members are entitled to a 5 percent discount on all purchases and free shipping, in addition to receiving notice of members-only sales and promotions. The over 500,000 members who have reached the $500 level account for 80 percent of the company's sales.

The information on its 2.5 million customers is collected from all customer touchpoints with the company—from call centers, its website, responses to its catalogs, and in-store transactions. With this information, Chico's segments its customer base to find its best clients; identifies buying trends among them to create cross-selling opportunities; and uses direct-marketing campaigns via e-mail.

Chico's also uses the database to run targeted promotional campaigns designed to increase the buying frequency of its best customers as well as to motivate customers close to Passport status and new prospects to shop more. Horton illustrates this application of the database: "If the system says a woman hasn't been in the store in over eight months, we ask why? Perhaps she moved away from a store and is now shopping online, or the offer no longer entices her, or we changed the styles or colors. Based on the reasons, we can choose to focus on her differently, such as using e-mail offers instead of mail."

Sources: Beth Stackpole, "Chico's Fashions a New Plan—Retailer Uses CRM to Reconnect with Customers," *EWeek*, May 28, 2001, pp. 51–53; and Mark Franco and Sherry Chiger, "Customer Care Loyalty," *Catalog Age*, May 2001, pp. 23–25.

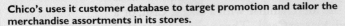
Chico's uses it customer database to target promotion and tailor the merchandise assortments in its stores.

they ring up a sale.[10] This information is then used to create the transaction database for the customer. However, this approach has two limitations. First, some customers may be reluctant to provide the information and feel that the sales associates are violating their privacy. Second, sales associates might forget to ask for the information or decide not to spend the time getting and recording it during a busy period.

Offering a Frequent Shopper Card **Frequent shopper programs,** also called **loyalty programs,** are programs that identify and provide rewards for customers who patronize a retailer. When customers enroll in one of these programs, they provide some descriptive information about themselves or their household and are issued a card with an identifying number. The customers then are offered an incentive to show the card when they make purchases from the retailer. For example, a supermarket might offer frequent shoppers a point for every dollar spent in the store. The points can be redeemed for items in a gift catalog.

From the retailer's perspective, frequent shopper programs offer two benefits: (1) customers provide demographic and other information when they sign up for the program and then are motivated to identify themselves at each transaction, and (2) customers are motivated by the rewards offered to increase the number of visits to the retailer and the amount purchased on each visit. We will discuss the second retailer benefit, building share of wallet, later in the chapter.

The major problems with using frequent shopper cards for identification are that the card is often squeezed out of the customer's wallet by other cards, the customer might forget to bring it to the store when shopping, or the customer might decide not to show it if he or she is in a hurry. Retailers have developed innovative approaches for overcoming these problems. For example, Berdorf Goodman of New York, an upscale apparel retailer, allows its customers to register all of their credit cards and receive rewards when any of them are used to purchase merchandise.

Other retailers are experimenting with cardless ways of identifying customers. For example, Von's, a southern California supermarket chain, allows customers to enter their phone numbers on a keypad if they forget to bring their card. Kroger, another supermarket chain, is using fingerprint scanners in its Texas stores to identify customers and validate them for check cashing and well as link their purchases with their data file.[13]

Linking Checking Account Numbers and Third-Party Credit Cards Rather than asking for identifying information or requiring a frequent shopper card, some retailers unobtrusively collect enough information about the customer to link transactions to the individual. For example, Kmart gets enough information from the credit card and check account numbers used by a customer to link the transactions to that person.[14]

REFACT

In 1984, Neiman Marcus launched the first frequent shopper program sponsored by a retailer.[11]

REFACT

Customers enrolled in a frequent shopper program only use the card for 67 percent of their purchases.[12]

Frequent shoppers cards are becoming so common that consumers cannot carry the cards they have easily.

Privacy and CRM Programs

While detailed information about individual customers helps retailers provide more benefits to their better customers, consumers are concerned about retailers violating their privacy when they collect this information. In September 2000, Amazon.com e-mailed its customers to say it was changing its privacy rules. The new rules indicated that Amazon would no longer allow its customers to preclude Amazon from sharing the information about the customers' purchases with third parties. The adverse public reaction spurred on by two online privacy organizations—Junkbusters (www.junkbusters.com) and the Electronic Privacy Information Center (www.epic.org)—created such an uproar that Amazon altered its policy. Similarly, many well-known firms have been criticized for disrespecting consumer privacy: America Online for attempting to sell subscribers' telephone numbers; Intel for developing a new Pentium chip that identifies users; and Microsoft for incorporating a personal identifier in Windows software.

Privacy Concerns The degree to which consumers feel their privacy has been violated depends on

- Their control over their personal information when engaging in marketplace transactions. Do they feel they can decide on the amount and type of information collected by the retailer?

- Their knowledge of the collection and use of personal information. Do they know what information is being collected and how the retailer will be using it? Will the retailer be sharing the information with other parties?[15]

These concerns are particularly acute for customers using an electronic channel because many of them do not realize the extensive amount of information that can be collected without their knowledge. In addition to collecting transaction data, electronic retailers can collect information by placing cookies on visitor's hard drives. **Cookies** are text files that identify visitors when they return to a website. Due to the data in the cookies, customers do not have to identify themselves and use passwords every time they visit a site. However, the cookies also collect information about other sites the person has visited and what pages they have downloaded.[16]

Protecting Customer Privacy What is personal information? The definition of personal information is debatable. Some people define personal information as all information that is not publicly available; others include both public (i.e., driver's license, mortgage data) and private (hobbies, income) information in the definition of personal information.

Who is responsible for ensuring consumer privacy? In the United States, legal protection for individual privacy is limited.[17] Existing legislation is limited to the protection of information in a few specific contexts, including government functions and practices in credit reporting, video rentals, and banking. However, the European Union (EU) is much more aggressive in protecting consumer privacy. Some of the provisions of the EU directive on consumer privacy are

- Businesses can collect consumer information only if they have clearly defined the purpose such as completing the transaction.

- The purpose must be disclosed to the consumer from whom the information is being collected.

- The information can only be used for that specific purpose.

- The business can only keep the information for the stated purpose. If the business wants to use the information for another purpose, it must initiate a new collection process.

- Businesses operating in Europe can only export information from the 15 EU countries to importing countries with similar privacy policy. Thus, U.S. retailers, hotel chains, airlines, and banks can not transfer information from Europe to the United States because the United States does not have similar privacy policies.

Basically, the EU perspective is that consumers own their personal information. Retailers must get consumers to explicitly agree to share this personal information. This is referred to as **opt in.** On the other hand, personal information in the United States is generally viewed as being in the public domain, and retailers can use it in any way they desire. U.S. consumers must explicitly tell retailers not to use their personal information—they must **opt out.**[18]

The EU has delayed enforcement of its directive. The United States is currently negotiating a safe harbor program that would enable U.S. companies abiding by the EU directives to export information. However, due to the increasing concern about consumer privacy, Congress is considering new legislation on consumer privacy. The Federal Trade Commission has developed the following set of principles for fair information practices:

- *Notice and awareness*—covers the disclosure of information practices, including a comprehensive statement of information use such as information storage, manipulation, and dissemination.

- *Choice/consent*—includes both opt out and opt in options, and allows consumers the opportunity to trade information for benefits.

- *Access/participation*—allows for the confirmation of information accuracy by consumers.

- *Integrity/security*—controls for the theft of and tampering with personal information.

- *Enforcement/redress*—provides a mechanism to ensure compliance by participating companies.

In summary, there is growing consensus that personal information must be fairly collected, the collection must be purposeful, and the data should be relevant, maintained as accurate, essential to the business, subject to the rights of the owning individual, kept reasonably secure, and transferred only with the permission of the consumer. To address these concerns, many retailers that collect customer information have privacy policies. The Electronic Privacy Information Center (www.epic.org) recommends that privacy policies clearly state what information is collected from each visitor and how it will be used, give consumers a choice as to whether they give information, and allow them to view and correct any personal information held by an online retail site. Retailers using an electronic channel should also ensure that consumer information is held securely and is not passed on to other companies without the permission of the customer.[19]

344

The Gap provides a detailed description of its privacy policy on its website.

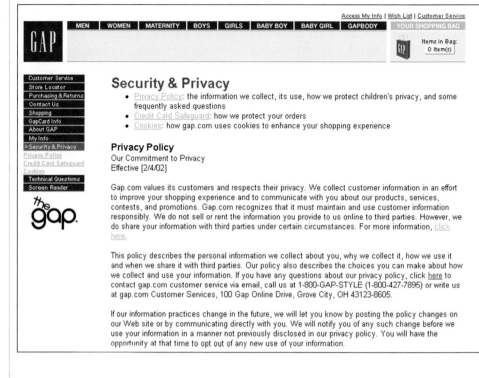

ANALYZING CUSTOMER DATA AND IDENTIFYING TARGET CUSTOMERS

The next step in the CRM process is analyzing the customer database and converting the data into information that will help retailers develop programs for building customer loyalty. Data mining is one approach commonly used to develop this information. **Data mining** is a technique used to identify patterns in data, typically patterns that the analyst is unaware of prior to searching through the data. For example, an electronic retailer in London discovered that customers who had bought portable DVD players typically commuted to work by train. Using this information, the retailer experienced a 43 percent increase in portable DVD player sales when it redirected most of its communication budget from daytime television commercials to newspapers and billboards along the train tracks.[20]

Market basket analysis is a specific type of data analysis that focuses on the composition of the basket, or bundle, of products purchased by a household during a single shopping occasion. This analysis is often useful for suggesting where to place merchandise in a store. For example, based on market basket analyses, Wal-Mart changed the traditional location of several items:

- Since bananas are the most common item in America's grocery carts, Wal-Mart Supercenters sell bananas next to the corn flakes as well as in the produce section.

- Kleenex tissues are in the paper-goods aisle and also mixed in with cold medicine.

- Measuring spoons are in housewares and also hanging next to Crisco shortening.
- Flashlights are in the hardware aisle and also with the Halloween costumes.
- Little Debbie snack cakes are next to the coffee.
- Bug spray is merchandised with the hunting gear.

Identifying Market Segments

Traditionally, customer data analysis has focused on identifying market segments—groups of customers who have similar needs, purchase similar merchandise, and respond in a similar manner to marketing activities. For example, when Eddie Bauer analyzed its customer database, it discovered two types of shoppers. One group it calls "professional shoppers"—people who love fashion and value good customer service. The other group it calls "too busy to shop people"—people who want the shopping experience over as quickly as possible. The professional shoppers tended to use the alteration service, call the customer service desk, and seek out the same salesperson when they made purchases in the stores. On the other hand, the people too busy to shop typically shop from the catalog and website. Eddie Bauer uses this information for developing unique advertising programs targeting each of these segments.

Eddie Bauer also discovered that morning shoppers are more price-sensitive and like to buy products on sale more than evening shoppers. Evening shoppers tended to be in the professional shopper segment. Using this information, Eddie Bauer installed electronic window posters in some test stores that allowed different images to be displayed at different times of the day. In the morning, the displays featured lower-priced merchandise and items on sale, while, in the evening, the more expensive and fashionable merchandise was displayed.[22]

Identifying Best Customers

Using information in the customer database, retailers can develop a score or number indicating how valuable they are to the firm. This score can then be used to determine which customers to target.

Lifetime Value A commonly used measure to score each customer is called lifetime customer value. **Lifetime customer value (LTV)** is the expected contribution from the customer to the retailer's profits over his or her entire relationship with the retailer.

LTV is estimated by using past behaviors to forecast the future purchases, gross margin from these purchases, and costs associated with servicing the customers. Some of the costs associated with a customer are the cost of advertising and promotions used to acquire the customer and the cost of processing merchandise that the customer has returned. Thus, a customer who purchases $200 on groceries from a supermarket every other month would have a lower LTV for the supermarket than a customer who buys $30 on each visit and shops at the store three times a week. Similarly, a customer who buys apparel only when it's

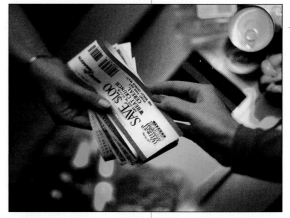

Using market basket analysis and its customer data base, supermarkets generate personalized coupons to encourage customers to patronize the store for additional merchandise categories.

on sale in a department store would have a lower LTV than a customer who typically pays full price and buys the same amount of merchandise.

These assessments of LTV are based on the assumption that the customer's future purchase behaviors will be the same as they have been in the past. Sophisticated statistical methods are typically used to estimate the future contributions from past purchases. For example, these methods might consider how recent purchases have been made. The expected LTV of a customer who purchased $600 on one visit six months ago is probably less than the LTV of a customer who has been purchasing $100 of merchandise every month for the last six months.

Customer Pyramid   Most retailers realize that their customers differ in terms of their profitability or LTV. In particular, they know that a relatively small number of customers account for the majority of their profits. This realization is often called the **80-20 rule**—80 percent of the sales or profits come from 20 percent of the customers. Thus, retailers could group their customers into two groups based on the LTV scores. One group would be the 20 percent of the customers with the highest LTV scores, and the other group would be the rest. However, this two-segment scheme, "best" and "rest," does not consider important differences between the 80 percent of the customers in the "rest" segment.[24]

A commonly used segmentation scheme divides customers into four segments, illustrated in Exhibit 11–2. This scheme allows retailers to develop more appropriate strategies for each of the segments. Each of the four segments is described below.

- *Platinum segment*—This segment is composed of the retailer's customers with the top 25 percent LTVs. Typically, these are the most loyal customers who are not overly concerned about merchandise price and place more value on customer service.

EXHIBIT 11–2
The Customer Pyramid

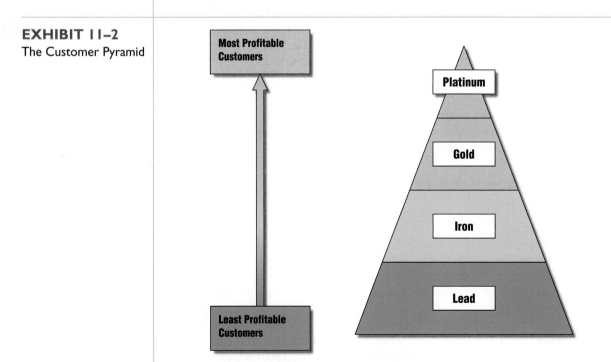

SOURCE: Valerie Zeithaml, Roland Rust, and Katherine Lemon, "The Customer Pyramid: Creating and Serving Profitable Customers," *California Management Review* 43 (Summer 2001), p. 125. Reprinted by permission.

selling more products and services to existing customers and increasing the retailer's share of wallet with these customers. For example, Tesco, the U.K. supermarket chain, added a second tier to its frequent shopper program to increase share of wallet.

The first tier has a traditional design to gather customer data. The second tier, targeted at its better customers, is more innovative. Customers earn a "key" when they spend $38 or more in a single transaction. Fifty keys make the customer a "keyholder," 100 keys a "premium keyholder." When customers achieve these higher levels, they get discounts on popular entertainment events, theater tickets, sporting events, and hotel vacations. The key program seeks to convert iron and gold customers into platinum customers. In the four years since starting the key program, Tesco has raised its market share from 13 percent to more than 17 percent.

The retailer's customer database reveals opportunities for cross selling and add-on selling. **Cross selling** is selling a complementary product or service in a specific transaction, such as selling a customer a printer when he or she has decided to buy a computer. For example, Fresh Farm, a Norfolk, Virginia–based supermarket chain, has a frequent shopper program, called the Gold Card program, for its best customers. When Gold Card member Debra Onsager enters the store, she "swipes" her card at a kiosk, and a high-speed printer provides a

Building a Community of Boaters | RETAILING VIEW

11.3

MarineMax, the world's largest recreational boat retailer based in Clearwater, Florida, offers a number of programs so that its customers won't accept the cliché that the two best days in boating are the day you buy your boat and the day you sell it. The company organizes hundreds of "Getaways" annually that give their customers an opportunity to take trips with other boaters. The trips range from weekend runs to two-week voyages to the Bahamas. Each of the Getaways is led by a MarineMax pilot. Thus, the boat owners can feel comfortable in doing something more adventuresome than they might normally do. In addition to providing an exciting boating experience, boaters can meet and share experiences with others on the trip.

In addition to sponsoring the Getaways, MarineMax provides other services that ensure that its customers have good boating experiences and are motivated to trade up to larger and more expensive crafts. For example, the retailer provides hands-on training for all new "Captains," including fundamentals of boat operations, safety, and docking, right down to tying to the cleat.

MarineMax takes on all other aspects of the boating life including financing, insurance, and operating a brokerage for used boats when someone decides to sell or upgrade. "Our focus is on the boating experience, not just selling boats," says Dawna Stone, chief marketing officer. "When we get a customer, we tend to keep that customer for as long as they're in boating." Moreover, she

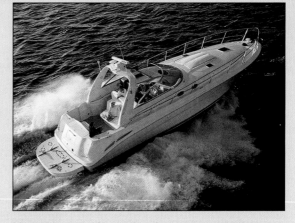

MarineMax provides services for its customers that enhance their boating experience and increase the likelihood that they will buy an even larger craft in the future.

adds, "One of our most powerful selling tools is word-of-mouth. We count our existing customers among our best salespeople."

Sources: Don Peppers, "Building Relationships across the Product Lifecycle," *Inside 1to1*, March 11, 2002, p. 2; and Gene G. Marcial, "A Stiff Breeze behind MarineMax," *Business Week*, April 24, 2000, p. 199.

Amazon uses its customer data base to cross sell complementary books.

personalized shopping list with up to 25 deals. The deals offered are based on Debra's purchase history. If Debra's history shows she frequently purchases corn chips but does not buy dip. She'll get a deal on bean dip printed on her shopping list to encourage her to try a new product. If she passes up the deal this time in the market, the next time the value of the bean dip coupon will be automatically increased.

Add-on selling is selling additional new products and services to existing customers, such as a bank encouraging a customer with a checking account to also apply for a home improvement loan from the bank. Vons, a southern California division of Safeway U.S., explored the opportunity to offer dry cleaning services in its supermarkets. To determine the stores and customers that would find this new service appealing, it looked through its customer database for households with two-income professionals, 25 to 35 years old, who sought one-stop shopping as indicated by purchases of cosmetics, hosiery, and prepared meals.[34] Retailing View 11.4 illustrates how Oprah Winfrey builds add-on sales for her offerings.

Dealing with Unprofitable Customers

In many cases, the bottom tier of customers actually have negative LTV. Retailers actually lose money on every sale they make to these customers. For example, catalog retailers have customers who repeatedly buy three or four items and return all but one of them. The cost of processing two or three returned items is much greater than the profits coming from the one item that the customer kept. The process of no longer selling to these unprofitable customers can be referred to as "getting the lead out," in terms of the customer pyramid.[35]

Two approaches for getting the lead out are (1) offering less costly approaches for satisfying the needs of lead customers, and (2) charging the customers for the services they are abusing. Fidelity Investments has about 550,000 website visits a day and more than 700,000 daily calls, about three-quarters of which go to automated systems that cost the company less than a $1.00 each. The remaining calls are handled by call center agents, who cost $13 per call. Fidelity contacted 25,000 lower tiered customers who place a lot of calls to agents and told them they must use the website for automated calls for simple account and price information. Each name was flagged and routed to a special representative who would direct callers back to automated services and tell them how to use it. "If all our customers chose to go through live reps, it would be cost-prohibitive," said a Fidelity spokeswoman.[36]

IMPLEMENTING CRM PROGRAMS

Increasing sales and profits from the CRM programs is a challenge. For example, according to a study, 52 percent of the retailers surveyed indicated that they were engaged in some type of data mining, but 76 percent of those retailers undertaking data mining indicated that the activity had made no contribution to the bottom line.[37]

This experience of retailers emphasizes that effective CRM requires more than appointing a manager of CRM, installing a computer systems to manage and analyze a customer database, and making speeches about the importance of customers. The effective implementation of CRM programs requires the close coordination of activities by different functions in a retailer's organization. The

Oprah and Add-On Selling | RETAILING VIEW

11.4

Oprah Winfrey is a master of add-on selling. She has capitalized on her popularity to build on her daytime television show (*The Oprah Show*) to sell and promote books, movies, and television specials (Harpo Productions), a cable channel (Oxygen Media), a website (www.oprah.com), and widely read magazine (*O*) to her target audience—woman interested in self-improvement and empowerment. For viewers of the television show, each of these products provides additional value. For example, when a respected celebrity appears on her television show, an article with more detailed information about the celebrity will be published in *O*. The magazine also provides much more intimate information about Oprah's likes and dislikes, joys and fears than revealed to viewers of *The Oprah Show*. Since Oprah often performs in the movies and television specials she produces, her audience gets a chance to see her in a role other than talk-show host.

Oprah develops a strong emotional bond with her target market by revealing personal aspects of her life. She shares with her audience her experiences as a poor, African American child growing up in Mississippi, her survival of child abuse, and her battle with obesity. Sharing this intimate information builds loyalty and enables her to successfully develop and sell add-on products. Customers are confident that each new product she endorses will be of high quality and tailored to satisfying their needs for self-improvement and empowerment.

Oprah also engages in community building. She uses her television show and magazine to encourage her customers to exchange experiences with her and others through her website. For example, a customer reading an article on volunteering with nonprofit organization can go online and share her interests and experiences with other interested in volunteering.

Sources: Robert C. Blattberg, Gary Getz, and Jacquelyn S. Thomas, *Customer Equity: Building and Managing Relationships as Valuable Assets* (Boston: Harvard Business School Press, 2001), pp. 112–15; and "Oprah on Oprah Perfectionist," *Newsweek International,* January 8, 2001, pp. 33–35.

Oprah Winfrey provides a number of different offerings of interest to her loyal following.

MIS department needs to collect, analyze, and make the relevant information readily accessible for employees implementing the programs—the front-line service providers and sales associates and the marketers responsible for communicating with customers through impersonal channels (mass advertising, direct mail, and e-mail). Store operations and human resource management needs to hire, train, and motivate the employees who will be using the information to deliver personalized services.

Most retailers are product-centric, not customer-centric. As shown in Chapter 9, buyers in a retailer firm are organized by type of product. Typically, there is no area of a retail firm organized by customer type—responsible for delivering products and services to types of customers. Perhaps in the future, retailers will have market managers to perform this coordinating function.

SUMMARY

To develop a strategic advantage, retailers need to effectively manage their critical resources—their finances (Chapter 6), human resources (Chapter 9), real estate and locations (Chapters 7 and 8), inventory and information (Chapter 10), and customers (Chapter 11). This chapter focuses on activities that retailers are undertaking now and will undertake in the future to increase the sales and profits they get from their better customers.

Customer relationship management is a business philosophy and set of strategies, programs, and systems that focuses on identifying and building loyalty with a retailer's most valued customers. Loyal customers are committed to patronizing a retailer and are not prone to switch to a competitor. In addition to building loyalty, CRM programs are also designed to increase the share of wallet from the retailer's best customers.

CRM is an iterative process that turns customer data into customer loyalty through four activities: (1) collecting customer data, (2) analyzing the customer data and identifying target customers, (3) developing CRM programs, and (4) implementing CRM programs. The first step of the process is to collect and store data about customers. One of the challenges in collecting customer data is identifying the customer with each transaction and contact. Retailers use a variety of approaches to overcome this challenge.

The second step is analyzing the data to identify the most profitable customers. Two approaches used to rank customers according to their profitability are calculating the customer's lifetime value and categorizing customers on the basis of characteristics of their buying behavior—recency, frequency, and monetary value.

Using this information about customers, retailers can develop programs to build loyalty in their best customers, increase their share of wallet with better customer (converting gold customers into platinum customers), and deal with unprofitable customers (getting the lead out). Four approaches that retailers use to build loyalty and retain their best customers are (1) launching frequent shopper programs, (2) offering special customer service, (3) personalizing the services they provide, and (4) building a sense of community. Retailers increase share of wallet through cross selling and add-on selling. Unprofitable customers are dealt with by developing lower-cost approaches for servicing these customers. Effectively implementing CRM programs is difficult because it requires coordinating a number of different areas in a retailer's organization.

KEY TERMS

add-on selling, *354*

cookies, *342*

cross selling, *353*

customer database, *338*

customer data warehouse *338*

customer loyalty, *336*

customer relationship
management (CRM) *335*

data mining, *344*

decile analysis, *347*

80–20 rule, *346*

frequent shopper
program, *341*

lifetime customer value
(LTV), *345*

loyalty program, *341*

market basket analysis, *344*

1-to-1 retailing, *351*

opt in, *343*

opt out, *343*

RFM analysis, *347*

share of wallet, *336*

GET OUT & DO IT!

1. **GO SHOPPING** Go to a local retailer that offers a frequent shopper program. Talk to the manager of the store and ask him or her how effective the program is in terms of increasing the store's sales and profits? Find out why the manager has these views and what could be done to increase the effectiveness of the program.

2. **INTERNET EXERCISE** CRM Forum. Com (www.crm-forum.com) is a site containing information about CRM programs. Based on the information on the site, what are the major CRM issues confronting retailing?

3. **INTERNET EXERCISE** Go to some of the retail sites that you frequent and compare their privacy policies. Which policies make you less concerned about violations of your pri-

vacy? Why? Which policies, or lack of, raises your concern? Why?

4. **SHOPPING** Talk to customers in a store that has a frequent shopper program. Ask them why they are members or not members. Find out how membership in the program affects their shopping behavior and loyalty toward the retailer.

5. **INTERNET EXERCISE** Go to the website for the Electronic Privacy Information Center (www.epic.org) and review the issues raised by the organization. What does this watchdog organization feel are the most important issues? How will these issues affect retailers and their customers?

DISCUSSION QUESTIONS AND PROBLEMS

1. What is CRM?

2. Why do retailers want to determine the lifetime value of their customers?

3. Why do customers have privacy concerns about frequent shopper programs that supermarkets have, and what can supermarkets do to minimize these concerns?

4. What are examples of opportunities for add-on selling that might be pursued by (a) travel agents, (b) jewelry stores, and (c) dry cleaners?

5. How would you suggest that a dry cleaner build greater loyalty and retention with its best customers?

6. Which of the following types of retailers do you think would benefit most from instituting CRM: (a) supermarkets, (b) banks, (c) automobile dealers, or (d) consumer electronic retailers? Why?

7. Develop a CRM program for a local store that sells apparel with your college or university's logo. What type of information would you collect about your customers, and how would you use this information to increase the sales and profits of the store?

8. How can a real estate agent deal with people who are just looking and not ready to buy? What are the potential benefits to and the risks for the agent in undertaking these actions?

9. What are the different approaches retailers can use to identify customers with their transactions? What are the advantages and disadvantages of each approach?

10. A CRM program focuses on building relationships with a retailer's better customers. Some customers who do not receive the same benefits as the retailer's best customers may be upset because they are treated different. What can retailers do to minimize this negative reaction?

SUGGESTED READINGS

Blattberg, Robert C.; Gary Getz; and Jacquelyn S. Thomas. *Customer Equity: Building and Managing Relationships as Valuable Assets.* Boston: Harvard Business School Press, 2001.

Bolton, Ruth; P. K. Kannan; and Matthew D. Bramlett. "Implications of Loyalty Program Membership and Service Experiences for Customer Retention and Value." *Journal of the Academy of Marketing Science* 28, no.1 (Winter 2000), pp. 95–108.

"Data Mining/CRM: Searching For an ROI." *Chain Store Age*, October 1, 2001, pp. 24–25.

Dyche, Jill. *The CRM Handbook.* Upper Saddle River, NJ.: Addison-Wesley, 2002.

Johnson, Lauren Keller. "The Real Value of Customer Loyalty: Customer-Lifetime Value Is More than a Metric; It's a Way of Thinking and of Doing Business." *Sloan Management Review* 43 (Winter 2002, pp. 14–16.

Kelly, E., and H. Rowland. "Ethical and Online Privacy Issues in Electronic Commerce." *Business Horizons* 45 (May–June 2002), pp. 3–12.

Rigby, Darrell; Fredrick Reichheld; and Phil Schefter. "Avoiding the Four Perils of CRM." *Harvard Business Review*, February 2002, pp. 5–11.

Russell, Gary, and Ann Petersen. "Analysis of Cross Category Dependence in Market Basket Selection." *Journal of Retailing* 76 (Fall 2000), pp. 367–391.

Rust, Roland; Valerie Zeithaml; and Katherine Lemon. *Driving Customer Equity.* New York: Free Press, 2002.

Winer, Russell. "A Framework for Customer Relationship Management." *California Management Review* 43 (Summer 2001), pp. 89–109.

Zeithaml, Valerie; Roland Rust; and Katherine Lemon. "The Customer Pyramid: Creating and Servicing Profitable Customers." *California Management Review* 43 (Summer 2001), pp. 118–143.

● CHAPTERS 5 AND 6 ("Retail Market Strategy" and "Financial Strategy") provided an overall framework for making the tactical decisions that will be examined more closely in Section III. In Sections III and IV, we offer tactical solutions to the strategic problems posed in Section II.

● Section III provides an in-depth discussion of the activities involved in the basic functions of merchandise management.

Chapter 12 discusses how retailers develop profitable assortments and forecast sales.

Chapter 13 examines the buying systems used to make these decisions.

MERCHANDISE MANAGEMENT

Introduction to the World of Retailing

Retailing Strategy

Merchandise Management

Store Management

CHAPTER TWELVE
PLANNING MERCHANDISE ASSORTMENTS

CHAPTER THIRTEEN
BUYING SYSTEMS

CHAPTER FOURTEEN
BUYING MERCHANDISE

CHAPTER FIFTEEN
PRICING

CHAPTER SIXTEEN
RETAIL COMMUNICATION MIX

Chapter 14 explores branding options, sourcing internationally, and establishing and maintaining a competitive advantage by developing long-term relationships with vendors.

Chapter 15 addresses the important question of how to set and adjust retail prices.

Chapter 16 looks at the relative advantages of various promotional vehicles available to retailers. In addition, it considers how promotion affects the consumer decision-making process. The chapter also describes how to develop a promotion program and how to set a budget.

Planning Merchandise Assortments

CHAPTER

"One of the exciting challenges in my job is trying to figure out what merchandise customers are going to buy. The big swimwear markets for us are Miami in July and Surf Expo in September. So we need to place our bet nine months before most of the merchandise arrives in the stores.

Ron Jon Surf Shop is known worldwide for its extensive selection of active lifestyle apparel, board sports equipment, and dive apparatus. Our 52,000 square-foot Coco Beach, Florida store is open 24 hours a day, 365 days a year—just like the beach. We also have stores in Ft. Lauderdale, Orange, California, and Long Beach Island, New Jersey.

To keep on top of the fashion trends, our buyers read the trade publications like *WWD* and *DNR,* look through teen magazines, surf magazines, and watch MTV. But the best source of information is looking at what our customers are wearing. We find that the fashion trends typically start on the West Coast and move East. However, these

fashion waves are spreading a lot faster due to the Internet and MTV.

Even though we have to place our orders months before the season, we negotiate with our vendors to reduce the risk of making a bad choice. With our longtime vendors, we are able to reduce the size of an order if the merchandise is not selling or switch our commitment to better-selling items. We have relationships with these vendors and we can generally work out problems. Dealing with the new vendors with hot merchandise is more problematic. Their merchandise is in demand and they are not very flexible.

The key to buying is staying on top of things. If we have merchandise that isn't selling, we mark it down to get rid of it so we can get faster-selling merchandise in the stores. I really feel a sense of accomplishment when we can get all aspects of the business—sportswear, shoes, hardgoods, swimwear, and accessories—to do well at the same time."

The primary goal of most retailers is to sell merchandise and services. Nothing is more central to the strategic thrust of the retailing firm. Thus, deciding what to buy and how much is a vital task for any retailer.

This is the first of five chapters that deal with merchandise management. **Merchandise management** is the process by which a retailer attempts to offer the right quantity of the right merchandise in the right place at the right time while meeting the company's financial goals. This chapter examines strategic and planning issues that lay the foundation for the merchandise management process shown in the top portion of Exhibit 12–1. The issues examined in this chapter are used as input into the buying systems described in Chapter 13, as shown in the bottom portion of Exhibit 12–1. As such, Chapters 12 and 13 are integrally related and can be studied together.

Small and large retailers are required to make decisions about thousands of individual items from hundreds of vendors. If the buying process is not organized in a systematic, orderly way, chaos will result. Thus, in the first section we describe how and why merchandise is organized by categories for buying purposes.

As in any business, a retailer's ultimate objective is to achieve an adequate return on the investment to the owners. In Chapter 6 we looked at how retailers set and evaluate their financial

EXHIBIT 12–1
Merchandise
Management Issues

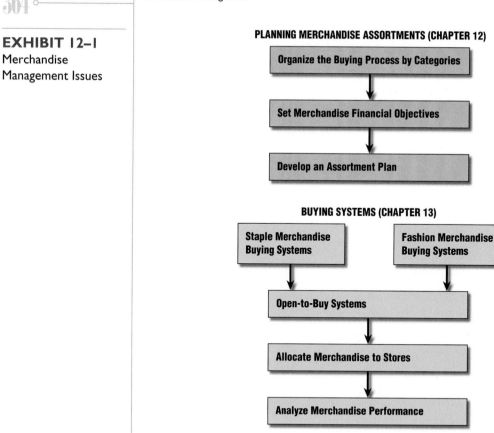

EXHIBIT 12–1
Merchandise
Management Issues

objectives. In this chapter, we show how these financial objectives trickle down the merchandising organization, and how these objectives are used to make buying decisions. Specifically, we look at how gross margin and inventory turnover merge together into a merchandise-specific return on investment measure called gross margin return on investment (GMROI). We also describe how retailers forecast sales.

Once the financial objectives are set, the retailer starts the task of determining what to buy. Superficially, one would think this would be easy. If the store is a women's clothing store, then the retailer would purchase women's clothing. Unfortunately, it isn't that simple. Retailers are limited by the amount of money available for merchandise and the space in the store. They must decide whether to carry a large variety of different types of clothing (categories)—for example, dresses, blouses, and jeans—or carry fewer categories but a larger assortment of more styles and colors within each category. To complicate the situation, they need to decide how much backup stock to carry for each item. The more backup stock, the less likely they are to run out of a particular item. On the other hand, if they decide to carry a lot of backup stock, they will have less money available to invest in a deeper assortment or in more categories. The process of trading off variety, assortment, and backup stock is called **assortment planning.**

The culmination of planning the financial and merchandising objectives for a particular merchandise category is the assortment plan. An **assortment plan** is a list of merchandise that indicates in general terms what the retailer wants to carry in a particular merchandise category. For instance, an assortment plan for girls' jeans would include the average number and percentage of each style/fabric/color/size combination that the retailer would have in inventory. From the assortment plan, we move to the more formal buying systems described in Chapter 13.

ORGANIZING THE BUYING PROCESS BY CATEGORIES

The category is the basic unit of analysis for making merchandising decisions. In this section, we define the category, examine the process of category management, explain the role of a category captain, and describe where the category fits into the buying organization.

The Category

It would be virtually impossible to keep the buying process straight without grouping items into categories. In general, a **category** is an assortment of items that the customer sees as reasonable substitutes for each other. Girls' apparel, boys' apparel, and infants' apparel are categories. Each of these categories has similar characteristics. For instance, girls' jeans are purchased from a set of vendors that are similar to each other. Also, the merchandise is priced and promoted to appeal to a similar target market. The price promotions are timed to occur at the same times of the year, such as back-to-school in August.

Retailers and their vendors might begin with different definitions of a category. A vendor might assign shampoos and conditioners, for example, to different categories, on the basis of significant differences in product attributes. The category manager for a grocery store, however, might put them and other combination shampoo–conditioner products into a single category on the basis of common consumers and buying behavior. Paper towels could be assigned to a "paper products" category or combined with detergent, paper tissues, and napkins in a "cleaning products" category.

Some retailers such as department stores may define categories in terms of brands. For example, Tommy Hilfiger might be one category and Estée Lauder and Polo/Ralph Lauren another. Why? Because a "Tommy" customer buys Tommy and not Ralph. Also, it is easier for the buyer to purchase merchandise and plan distribution and promotions if the entire line is coordinated. No matter how the category is defined, supply chain members must agree on the category definition, and it must be based on what is logical to the consumer.

Category Management

Category management is the process of managing a retail business with the objective of maximizing the sales and profits of a category. This sounds simple. As indicated previously, many retailers organize their merchandising activities around brands or vendors. For instance, in a grocery store chain there might be three buyers for breakfast cereal: Kellogg's, General Mills, and General Foods. If all three buyers have merchandise on the same shelves, they will be, in essence, competing with one another. Further, the salespeople for the three vendors will each be vying for the same shelf space.

The category management approach to managing breakfast cereals would be to have one buyer or category manager who oversees every aspect of the merchandising function.[1] Although a category manager is more than a buyer in the traditional sense, we will interchange the terms. For instance, the buyer is responsible for developing the assortment plan for the entire category, working with vendors, selecting merchandise, pricing merchandise, and coordinating promotions with the advertising department and stores.

An important reason for adopting category management is that one person, the category manager, is ultimately responsible for the success or failure of a category. It's harder to identify the source of a problem and solve it without category management. Suppose, for instance, an ad is placed in a newspaper for a Memorial Day sale, but the store doesn't receive the merchandise. Who caused the problem? Was it because the buyer didn't order the merchandise in time? Did the advertising manager fail to inform the buyer or the logistics manager that the ad was going to run? Did the distribution center fail to get the merchandise to the stores? Importantly, without the emphasis on category management, the buyer doesn't have the power to solve the problem. By using category management, all of the activities and responsibilities just mentioned come under the control of the buyer's staff.

The second reason for using category management is that it is easier to manage to maximize profits. For example, the breakfast cereal category manager has a choice of purchasing corn flakes from Kellogg's, General Mills, General Foods, a private-label vendor, and a popular locally produced brand. The category manager cannot purchase every size box from each of these vendors or there wouldn't be any room for any other cereal type in the cereal section. By the same token, the category manager needs some representation for each brand. An analysis indicates that there is relatively little demand for the giant-size box of corn flakes, when aggregated across all brands. It also indicates that although the locally produced brand is not a top seller, it has a strong following. If the store drops the local brand, it may lose some very good customers. Managing by category can help assure that the store's assortment is represented by the "best" combination of sizes and vendors, that is, the one that will get the most profit from the allocated space.

The Category Captain

The importance of establishing strategic relationships with vendors has been emphasized throughout *Retailing Management* (see especially Chapters 5, 10, and 14). Since retailers and their vendors share the same goals—to sell merchandise and make profits—it's only natural for them to share the information that will help them achieve those goals. Since vendors can develop systems for collecting information for all of the areas that they service, they can provide buyers with valuable information. Later in this chapter we discuss CPFR, a system some retailers use with their vendors to share sales data to better manage inventories.

Some retailers turn to one favored vendor to help them manage a particular category. Known as the **category captain,** this supplier forms an alliance with a retailer to help gain consumer insight, satisfy consumer needs, and improve the performance and profit potential across the entire category.

Kraft acts as a category captain by working with key retailers to help balance assortments.[2] Since it spends $850 million a year on promotion and advertising,

Kraft has a lot of influence in the grocery industry. As category captain, grocery chains give Kraft access to all market and store information, including costs and sales of its competitors. In return, the captain works with the category manager/buyer to make decisions about product placement on shelves, promotions, and pricing for all of the brands in the category. Before category management, these decisions were often made by whichever vendor was able to make the best argument to the store manager. Shelf space allocation, for instance, could change daily, depending on which vendor's salesperson was in the store that day.

A potential problem with establishing a category captain, however, is that vendors could take advantage of their position. It is somewhat like letting the fox into the henhouse. Suppose, for example, that Kraft chose to maximize its own sales at the expense of its competition. There are also serious antitrust considerations.[3] The captain could collude with the retailers to fix prices. It could also block other brands, particularly smaller brands, from access to shelf space.

Appointing a category captain can be enticing for a retailer. It makes the category manager's job easier and brings the promise of higher profits. But retailers should not turn over important decisions to their vendors. Working with their vendors and carefully evaluating their suggestions is a much more prudent approach.

Category captains must temper their zeal for control over retailers as well. What should a category captain do to avoid potential problems with the Justice Department?[4]

- Divulge all information obtained from the retailer to the other brands in the category.

- Appoint another large brand as a "category adviser" to oversee the captain's decisions.

- To circumvent potential collusion in price setting, don't serve as captain for two retailers in the same market.

The Buying Organization

Now that the category and category management have been defined, it is important to understand where in the buying organization the category fits. Although each retailer has its own system of categorizing merchandise, we have chosen the standard merchandise classification scheme used by the National Retail Federation (NRF) for illustrative purposes. Exhibit 12–2 shows how the NRF scheme is used at major department store chains like Federated Stores, Inc. (Bloomingdale's, Lazarus, and others). In Exhibit 12–2, we have concentrated on the buyer. Recall from Chapter 9, there is a merchandise planning group that works with the buying organization (see Exhibits 9–5 and 9–6). Similar schemes are used by other types of stores such as specialty chain stores (The Gap), category specialists (Toys "R" Us), and discount stores (Wal-Mart).

Merchandise Group   Recall from Chapter 9 that the largest classification level is the merchandise group. The **merchandise group** is managed by the senior vice presidents of merchandise, also called general merchandise managers, or GMMs (Exhibit 12–2). These merchandise managers are responsible for several departments. For instance, the second senior vice president on the chart in the exhibit is responsible for men's, children's, and intimate apparel.

EXHIBIT 12–2 Standard Merchandise Classification Scheme and Organizational Chart

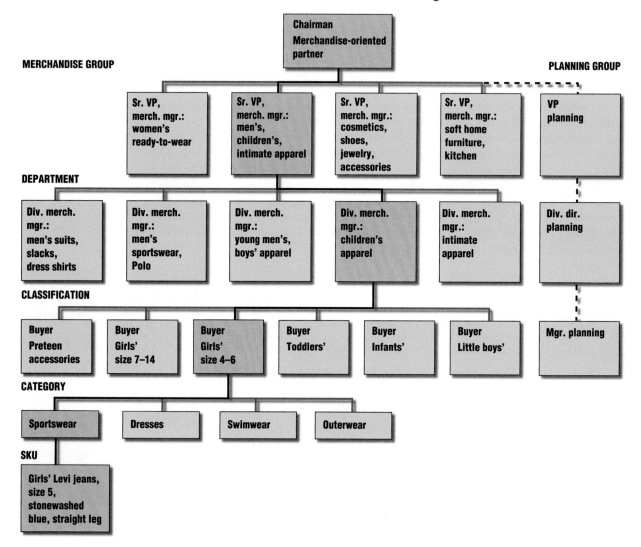

Department The second division in the classification scheme in the exhibit is the department. These **departments** are managed by divisional merchandise managers who report to the vice presidents. For example, the vice president of merchandising for men's, children's, and intimate apparel has responsibility for five divisional merchandise managers. Each divisional merchandise manager is responsible for a department. For example, the divisional merchandise manager highlighted in Exhibit 12–2 is responsible for children's apparel.

Classification The classification is the third level in the exhibit's classification scheme. Each divisional merchandise manager is responsible for a number of buyers or category managers. The children's apparel divisional merchandise manager here is responsible for six buyers. Each buyer purchases a

classification—a group of items or SKUs for the same type of merchandise (such as men's pants as opposed to men's jackets or suits) supplied by different vendors. The exhibit highlights the one buyer responsible for girls' apparel sizes 4 to 6. In some cases, a buyer is responsible for several classifications.

As we discussed in Chapter 9, many retail organizations divide responsibility for buying merchandise between a buyer or category manager and a merchandise planner. Since the merchandise planning function is a relatively new concept, it's handled in various ways by different retailers. In some organizations, the category manager or buyer supervises the planners; in others, they're equal partners.

The planners' role is more analytical. They are responsible for buying the correct quantities of each item, allocating those items to stores, monitoring sales, and suggesting markdowns. In effect, they implement the assortment plan developed by the buyer. Together, the buyer and planner are the merchandising team. This team attempts to maximize the sales and profits of the entire classification, not just a particular category or brand.

Categories   Categories are the next level in the classification scheme. Each buyer purchases a number of categories. So the men's pants buyer might buy jeans, khakis, and dress slacks. The girls' size 4 to 6 buyer in Exhibit 12–2 purchases several categories, such as sportswear, dresses, swimwear, and outerwear. A category like swimwear may be made up of merchandise from one or several manufacturers.

Stock Keeping Unit   A **stock keeping unit (SKU)** is the smallest unit available for keeping inventory control. In soft goods merchandise, for instance, a SKU usually means size, color, and style. For example, a pair of girls' size 5, stonewashed blue, straight-legged Levis is one SKU.

Now that we've examined how and why retailers manage their merchandise by categories, the following sections will examine three critical aspects of merchandise planning: (1) the objectives of the plan, (2) sales forecasting, and (3) the assortment plan.

How many SKUs are there in this picture?

SETTING OBJECTIVES FOR THE MERCHANDISE PLAN

Retailers cannot hope to be financially successful unless they preplan the financial implications of their merchandising activities. Financial plans start at the top of the retail organization and are broken down into categories, while buyers and merchandise planners develop their own plans and negotiate up the organization. Top management looks at the overall merchandising strategy. They set the merchandising direction for the company by (1) defining the target market, (2) establishing performance goals, and (3) deciding, on the basis of general trends in the marketplace, which merchandise classifications deserve more or less emphasis. Buyers and merchandise planners, on the other hand, take a more micro approach. They study their categories' past performance, look at trends in the market, and try to project the assortments for their merchandise categories for the coming seasons.

The financial planning process is similar for smaller retailers. Although there aren't as many layers of management involved in planning and negotiations, they still start with the firm's overall financial goals and break them down into categories.

The resulting merchandise plan is a financial buying blueprint for each category. It considers the firm's financial objectives along with sales projections and merchandise flows. The merchandise plan tells the buyer and planner how much money to spend on a particular category of merchandise in each month so that the sales forecast and other financial objectives are met. Once the merchandise plan is set, the buyers and planners develop the assortment plan. The buyers work with vendors choosing merchandise, negotiating prices, and developing promotions. The merchandise planners break down the overall financial plan into how many of each item to purchase and how they should be allocated to stores. In Chapter 13 we'll describe specific systems used for merchandise and assortment planning.

As you can imagine, there's a great deal of negotiating at each step. Merchandise managers and buyers compete with each other over the size of their merchandise budgets. If they increase their sales forecasts, they will get more money to spend on merchandise. Buyers and merchandise managers have to plan elaborate presentations to convince their superiors to increase their merchandise budgets. Of course, they must be accurate in their projections. If they succeed in having a larger sales forecast approved, and the merchandise doesn't sell, their profitability—and their performance evaluation—will suffer and future forecasts will be questioned.

The next section examines the performance measure on which the merchandise plan is evaluated. This measure, GMROI, is composed to two ratios: inventory turnover and gross margin percentage. The section concludes with a discussion of how retailers forecast sales.

Putting Margin, Sales, and Turnover Together: GMROI

At the corporate level, return on assets is used to plan and evaluate performance of overall retail operations (see Chapter 6).

$$\text{Return on assets} = \text{Net profit margin} \times \text{Asset turnover}$$
$$= \frac{\text{Net profit}}{\text{Net sales}} \times \frac{\text{Net sales}}{\text{Total assets}}$$
$$= \frac{\text{Net profit}}{\text{Total assets}}$$

With the strategic profit model, one can use return on assets to plan and compare the performance of executives since they are responsible for managing all of the retailer's assets and realizing a return based on these assets.

But merchandise managers have control over only the merchandise they buy and manage. Buyers generally have control over gross margin but not expenses involved with the operation of the stores and the management of the retailer's human resources, locations, and systems. As a result, the financial ratio that is useful for planning and measuring merchandising performance is a return on investment measure called gross margin return on inventory investment, or GMROI.[5] It measures how many gross margin dollars are earned on every dollar of inventory investment.

GMROI is a similar concept to return on assets, only its components are under the control of the buyer rather than other managers. Instead of combining net profit margin and asset turnover, GMROI uses gross margin percentage and the sales-to-stock ratio, which is similar to inventory turnover.

$$\text{GMROI} = \text{Gross margin percentage} \times \text{Sales-to-stock ratio}$$
$$= \frac{\text{Gross margin}}{\text{Net sales}} \times \frac{\text{Net sales}}{\text{Average inventory}}$$
$$= \frac{\text{Gross margin}}{\text{Average inventory}}$$

Average inventory in GMROI is measured at cost, because a retailer's investment in inventory is the cost of the inventory, not its retail value.

Like return on assets, GMROI combines the effects of both profits and turnover. It's important to use a measure that considers both of these factors so that departments with different margin/turnover profiles can be compared and evaluated. For instance, within a supermarket, some departments (such as wine) are high margin/low turnover, whereas other departments (such as dairy products) are low margin/high turnover. If the wine department's performance is compared to that of dairy products using inventory turnover alone, the contribution of wine to the supermarket's performance will be undervalued. On the other hand, if only gross margin is used, wine's contribution will be overvalued.

Consider the situation in Exhibit 12–3. Here a supermarket manager wants to evaluate performance of two classifications: bread and ready-to-eat prepared foods. If evaluated on gross margin percentage or sales alone, prepared foods is certainly the winner with a 50 percent gross margin and sales of $300,000 compared to bread's gross margin of 1.333 percent and sales of $150,000. Yet prepared foods turns (sales-to-stock ratio) only four times a year, whereas bread turns 150 times a year. Using GMROI, both classifications achieve a GMROI of 200 percent and so are equal performers from a return on investment perspective.

			Bread	Prepared Foods		
		Gross margin	$2,000	$150,000		
		Sales	$150,000	$300,000		
		Average inventory	$1,000	$75,000		
	GMROI =	$\dfrac{\text{Gross margin}}{\text{Net sales}}$	×	$\dfrac{\text{Net sales}}{\text{Average inventory}}$	=	$\dfrac{\text{Gross margin}}{\text{Average inventory}}$
Bread	GMROI =	$\dfrac{\$2,000}{\$150,000}$	×	$\dfrac{\$150,000}{\$1,000}$	=	$\dfrac{\$2,000}{\$1,000}$
	=	1.333%	×	150 times	=	200%
Prepared Foods	GMROI =	$\dfrac{\$150,000}{\$300,000}$	×	$\dfrac{\$300,000}{\$75,000}$	=	$\dfrac{\$150,000}{\$75,000}$
	=	50%	×	4	=	200%

EXHIBIT 12–3
Illustration of GMROI

The GMROI for low margin/high turnover products like bread can be the same as high margin/low turnover products like prepared foods.

GMROI is used as a return on investment profitability measure to evaluate departments, merchandise classifications, vendor lines, and items. It's also useful for management in evaluating buyers' performance since it can be related to the retailer's overall return on investment. As we just demonstrated, merchandise with different margin/turnover characteristics can be compared. Exhibit 12–4 shows GMROI percentages for selected departments from discount stores. The range is from 235 (for apparel) to 90 (for furniture). It's no wonder that many discount stores are placing so much emphasis on apparel and that some have discontinued furniture. They continue to carry consumer electronics and health and beauty products—both with low GMROIs—because they have traditionally brought customers into the store. The retailers hope that while there, customers will purchase higher-GMROI items.

The gross margin component of GMROI is affected by pricing decisions, which we discuss in Chapter 15. The following section explains how inventory turnover is measured and the advantages and disadvantages of a rapid rate of inventory turnover.

Measuring Inventory Turnover

The notion of inventory turnover was introduced in Chapter 6 as "merchandise in motion." Jeans are delivered to the store through the loading dock in the back, spend some time in the store on the racks, and then are sold and go out the front door. The faster this process takes place, the higher the inventory turnover will be. We thus can think of inventory turnover as how many times, on average, the jeans cycle through the store during a specific period of time, usually one year. It's a measure of the productivity of inventory—that is, how many sales dollars can be generated from a dollar invested in jeans.

EXHIBIT 12–4

Gross Margin Percentage, Inventory Turnover, and GMROI for Selected Departments in Discount Stores

Category	Gross Margin (%)	Inventory Turnover	GMROI
Apparel	37	4	235
Housewares	35	3	162
Food	20	7	175
Jewelry	38	2	123
Furniture	31	2	90
Health and beauty	22	4	113
Consumer electronics	21	4	106

Inventory turnover is defined as follows:

$$\text{Inventory turnover} = \frac{\text{Net sales}}{\text{Average inventory at retail}}$$

or

$$\text{Inventory turnover} = \frac{\text{Cost of goods sold}}{\text{Average inventory at cost}}$$

Since most retailers tend to think of their inventory at retail, the first definition is preferable. Arithmetically there's no difference between these two definitions, and they yield the same result.[6] Be careful, however; since both the numerator and denominator must be at retail or at cost, it is different than the sales-to-stock ratio where the inventory is always expressed at cost. To illustrate:

$$\text{Sales-to-stock ratio} = \frac{\text{Net sales}}{\text{Average cost inventory}}$$

So if

Sales $= \$100,000$

and

Average cost inventory $= \$33,333$

then

$$\text{Sales-to-stock ratio} = \frac{\$100,000}{\$33,333} = 3$$

Thus,

Inventory turnover $= \text{Sales-to-stock ratio} \times (100\% - \text{Gross margin }\%)$[7]

Continuing the example, if

Gross margin $= 40$ percent

then

Inventory turnover $= 3 \times (100\% - 40\%) = 1.8$

Retailers normally express inventory turnover rates on an annual basis rather than for parts of a year. Suppose the net sales used in an inventory turnover calculation are for a three-month season. If turnover for a quarter is calculated as 2.3 turns, then annual turnover will be four times that number (9.2). Thus, to convert an inventory turnover calculation based on part of a year to an annual figure, multiply it by the number of such time periods in the year.

Exhibit 12–4 shows inventory turnover ratios for selected departments from discount stores. The range is from 7 (for food) to 2 (jewelry and furniture). There are no real surprises in this data. One would expect food to have the highest turnover. Food is either sold quickly or it spoils. It is perishable. By the same token, being a luxury item, jewelry turns relatively slowly. Furniture achieves a low turnover because a relatively large assortment of expensive items is needed to support the sales level.

Calculating Average Inventory   Average inventory is calculated by dividing the sum of the inventory for each of several months by the number of months:

$$\text{Average inventory} = \frac{\text{Month}_1 + \text{Month}_2 + \text{Month}_3 + \ldots}{\text{Number of months}}$$

But how many months should be used? How could we determine the inventory for the month? One approach is to take the end-of-month (EOM) inventories for several months and divide by the number of months available. For example,

Month	Retail Value of Inventory
EOM January	$22,000
EOM February	$33,000
EOM March	$38,000
Total inventory	$93,000
Average inventory = $93,000 ÷ 3 = $31,000	

This approach is adequate only if the end-of-month figure doesn't differ in any appreciable or systematic way from any other day. For instance, January's end-of-month inventory is significantly lower than the other two since it represents the inventory position at the end of the winter clearance sale and before the spring buildup.

Most retailers no longer need to use physical counts to determine average inventory. Point-of-sale terminals capture daily sales and automatically subtract them from on-hand inventory. Retailers with POS systems can get accurate average inventory estimates by averaging the inventory on hand for each day in the year. Retailers do typically take occasional physical inventories, usually twice a year, to determine the amount of inventory shrinkage due to theft of paperwork/ entry mistakes.

Advantages of High Inventory Turnover

Retailers want rapid inventory turnover—but not too rapid, as we'll soon see. Advantages of rapid inventory turnover include increased sales volume, less risk of obsolescence and markdowns, improved salesperson morale, more money for market opportunities, decreased operating expenses, and increased asset turnover.[8]

Increased Sales Volume   A rapid inventory turnover increases sales volume since fresh merchandise is available to customers, and fresh merchandise sells better and faster than old, shopworn merchandise. Fresh merchandise encourages customers to visit the store more frequently because they see new things. Also, notice the produce next time you're in a less-than-successful supermarket. Brown bananas! Since turnover is slow, the produce is old, which makes it even harder to sell.

Recall from Chapter 10 that quick response delivery systems are inventory management systems designed to reduce retailers' lead time for receiving mer-

A rapid rate of inventory turnover ensures fresh merchandise. Since fresh merchandise is easier to sell, sales increase and so does employee morale.

chandise. Retailers order less merchandise, more often, so merchandise supply is more closely aligned with demand. As a result, inventory turnover rises since inventory investment falls, and sales climb since the retailer is out of stock less often.

Less Risk of Obsolescence and Markdowns   The value of fashion and other perishable merchandise is said to start declining as soon as it's placed on display. When inventory is selling quickly, merchandise isn't in the store long enough to become obsolete. As a result, markdowns are reduced and gross margins increase.

Improved Salesperson Morale   With rapid inventory turnover and the fresh merchandise that results, salesperson morale stays high. No one likes to sell yesterday's merchandise. Salespeople are excited over new merchandise, the assortment of sizes is still complete, and the merchandise isn't shopworn. When salespeople's morale is high, they try harder so sales increase—increasing inventory turnover even further.

More Money for Market Opportunities   When inventory turnover is high, money previously tied up in inventory is freed to buy more merchandise. Having money available to buy merchandise late in a fashion season can open tremendous profit opportunities. Suppose Levi Strauss overestimates demand for its seasonal products. It has two choices: (1) holding the inventory until next season and (2) selling it to retailers at a lower-than-normal price. If retailers have money available because of rapid turnover, they can take advantage of this special price. Retailers can pocket the additional markup or choose to maintain their high-turnover strategy by offering the special merchandise at a reduced cost to the consumer. In either case, sales and gross margin increase.

Decreased Operating Expenses   An increase in turnover may mean that a lower level of inventory is supporting the same level of sales. And lower inventory means lower inventory carrying costs, which is an operating expense. For instance, if a retailer has one million dollars in inventory and the cost to carry the inventory—including money borrowed from a bank, insurance, and taxes—is 20 percent a year, the inventory carrying cost is $200,000. Lowering inventory can therefore represent a significant savings.

Increased Asset Turnover   Finally, since inventory is a current asset, and if assets decrease and sales stay the same or increase, then asset turnover increases. This directly affects return on assets, the key performance measure for top management.

Disadvantages of Too High an Inventory Turnover

Retailers should strike a balance in their rate of inventory turnover. An excessively rapid inventory turnover can hurt the firm due to a lower sales volume, an increase in the cost of goods sold, and an increase in operating expenses.

Lowered Sales Volume   One way to increase turnover is to limit the number of merchandise categories or the number of SKUs within a category. But if customers can't find the size or color they seek—or even worse, if they can't find the product line at all—a sale is lost. Customers who are disappointed on a regular basis will shop elsewhere and will possibly urge their friends to do the same. In this case, not only is a sale lost, but so are the customers and their friends.

Increased Cost of Goods Sold   To achieve rapid turnover, merchandise must be bought more often and in smaller quantities, which reduces average inventory without reducing sales. But by buying smaller quantities, the buyer can't take advantage of quantity discounts and transportation economies of scale. It may be possible, for instance, to buy a year's supply of Levi's at a quantity discount that offsets the high costs of carrying a large inventory.

Retailers who pay transportation costs must consider that the more merchandise shipped and the slower the mode of transportation, the smaller the per-unit transportation expense. For instance, to ship a 10–pound package of jeans from Dallas to Denver, overnight delivery, would cost about $50 ($5 per pound). If the retailer could order 50 pounds of jeans at the same time and could wait 5 to 10 days for delivery, the cost would be only about $30 (60 cents per pound). In this example, it costs over eight times more to ship small packages quickly.

Increased Operating Expenses   Economies of scale can also be gained when a retailer purchases large quantities. A buyer spends about the same amount of time meeting with vendors and writing orders whether the order is large or small. It also takes about the same amount of time, for both large and small orders, to print invoices, receive merchandise, and pay invoices—all factors that increase merchandise's cost.

In summary, rapid inventory turnover is generally preferred to slow turnover. But the turnover rate can be pushed to the point of diminishing returns, a key concern for merchandise managers in all retail sectors.

SALES FORECASTING

An integral component of any merchandising plan is the sales forecast. A retailer needs to forecast sales to determine how much to buy. We begin the sales forecasting section by discussing category life cycles. We then develop a forecast for a merchandise category based on historical sales data and other sources. Following that, we examine the importance and complexities of forecasting sales by store and SKU. We conclude with an examination of how retailers are collaborating with their vendors to develop forecasts using CPFR. Retailing View 12.1 discusses how to become a better sales forecaster.

Category Life Cycles

When developing a sales forecast, a retailer must be able to predict how well product categories will sell over time. Product categories typically follow a predictable sales pattern—sales start off low, increase, plateau, and then ultimately decline. (This phenomenon is discussed in the Chapter 4 appendix.) Yet the shape of that pattern varies considerably from category to category and will help buyers forecast sales. This section describes the most fundamental form of sales pattern, the category life cycle. Using the category life cycle as a basis, we'll examine some commonly found variations on it: fad, fashion, staple, and seasonal.

Use the SCAN Technique to Become a Better Trendspotter | RETAILING VIEW 12.1

Retailers spend millions of dollars every year on marketing research—surveys, focus groups, data mining, and so forth. But to really find out what customers are going to want in the future, retailers have to immerse themselves in the customers' world: go into Internet chat rooms, look in their closets, attend soccer games and concerts. How do you start being your own trend spotter? Use the SCAN method: Shop, Converse, Act, and Notice.

- *Shop* the store website and catalog as an actual customer. Don't use the traditional upper-management "walk-through" when your employees know you are coming and are on their best behavior. Surprise them: Watch how your staff interacts with shoppers. Pretend to be a customer. The key is open your eyes to things that are new and different.

- *Converse* with consumers, sales clerks, neighbors, your children. Ask them, What are your favorite bands? Why did you buy a $20 Gap T-shirt to wear with a $500 suit? What TV and radio shows are you tuning into? What do you do in your spare time? Talk to vendors and other people who are close to consumers such as beauticians and real estate agents.

- *Act* like your customer. Remember the movie *Trading Places?* For one weekend, become your customer and see your product or store through the eyes of the

consumer. Is the target customer a member of Generation Y? Buy yourself a pair of cargo shorts, Skecher shoes, and a vintage-inspired T-shirt. Spend the day in a mall, pick up a copy of *Teen People,* listen to Britney Spears, go to a trendy nightclub (the ones that get going at midnight or later). Check out online teen websites such as Bolt.com's Coolhunting polls to see how teens feel about the WWF, toe rings, and inflatable furniture. At the end of the weekend, review your notes. Do you understand your customer better, now that you've traded places?

- *Notice,* notice, notice. Become a cultural sleuth by noticing the things that make you uncomfortable or seem strange and different. What movies are hits at the box office? Who is going to see them? What books and albums are on the top 10 lists? What magazines are consumers purchasing? Become an information junkie and read voraciously. Are there themes that keep popping up? All of these clues are cultural trendposts that can become an on ramp into the mainstream.

Source: Suzanne Barry Osborn, "Stop, Look and Listen," *Chain Store Age,* May 2000, p. 40. Copyright Lebhar-Friedman, Inc. 425 Park Avenue, New York, NY 10022. Reprinted by permission.

EXHIBIT 12–5
The Category Product
Life Cycle

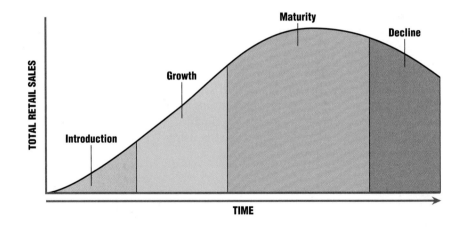

The **category life cycle** describes a merchandise category's sales pattern over time. The category life cycle (Exhibit 12–5) is divided into four stages: introduction, growth, maturity, and decline. Knowing where a category, or specific item within a category, is in its life cycle is important in developing a sales forecast and merchandising strategy.

When personal digital assistants (PDAs) were first introduced in 1996, the target market was businesspeople who were high-tech aficionados, people who wanted to be first in adopting an innovation and were willing to pay for the convenience of having a very small computer.[9] PDAs were very expensive compared to paper address and appointment books, and they weren't available at all stores that normally sell office supplies or computers. PDAs were next marketed to doctors, stockbrokers, and business executives, who use them for access to medical databases, stock markets, and e-mail. As categories reach the growth and maturity stages, they usually appeal to broader, mass-market customers who patronize discount store and category specialists.

Knowing where a category is in its life cycle is useful for predicting sales. However, the shape of the life cycle can be affected by the activities undertaken by retailers and vendors. For instance, a vendor might set a low introductory price for a new product to increase the adoption rate of the product, or set a high price to increase profits even though sales might not grow as fast. Care must be taken, however, that use of the category life cycle as a predictive tool does not adversely affect sales. If a product is classified as being in decline, it's likely that retailers will stock less variety and limit promotions. Naturally, sales will go down. Thus, the decline classification may actually become a self-fulfilling prophesy. Many products have been successfully maintained at the maturity stage because their buyers have maintained innovative strategies that are consistent with a mature product. For instance, Kellogg's Corn Flakes has been the best-selling ready-to-eat cereal over many decades because it has innovative advertising and competitive pricing.

Variations on the Category Life Cycle Most categories follow the basic form of the category life cycle: sales increase, peak, and then decline. Variations on the category life cycle—fad, fashion, staple, and seasonal—are shown in Exhibit 12–6. The distinguishing characteristics between them are whether the cat-

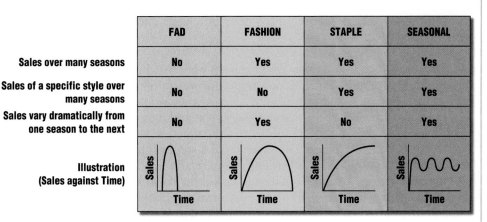

	FAD	**FASHION**	**STAPLE**	**SEASONAL**
Sales over many seasons	No	Yes	Yes	Yes
Sales of a specific style over many seasons	No	No	Yes	Yes
Sales vary dramatically from one season to the next	No	Yes	No	Yes
Illustration (Sales against Time)				

EXHIBIT 12–6
Variations on the Category Life Cycle

egory lasts for many seasons, whether a specific style sells for many seasons, and whether sales vary dramatically from one season to the next.

A **fad** is a merchandise category that generates a lot of sales for a relatively short time—often less than a season. Examples are Pogs, Furbys, Pokémon, butterfly hair clips, and some licensed characters like Star Wars action figures. More mainstream examples are certain computer games, new electronic equipment, and some apparel, such as cropped and flared jeans. Fads are primarily the providence of children and teens.

Fads are often illogical and unpredictable. The art of managing a fad comes in recognizing the fad in its earliest stages and immediately locking up distribution rights for merchandise to stores nationwide before the competition does. Marketing fads is one of the riskiest ventures in retailing because even if the company properly identifies a fad, it must still have the sixth sense to recognize the peak so it can bail out before it's stuck with a warehouse full of merchandise.

Retailing View 12.2 poses four questions for determining whether a new item or category will be a fad or a fashion.

Unlike a fad, a **fashion** is a category of merchandise that typically lasts several seasons, and sales can vary dramatically from one season to the next. A fashion is similar to a fad in that a specific style or SKU sells for one season or less. A fashion's life span depends on the type of category and the target market. For instance, double-breasted suits for men or certain colors are fashions whose life may last several years. On the other hand, fashions like see-through track shoes may last only a season or two.

Retailing View 12.3 provides a glimpse of how one of the world's hottest fashion retailers, H&M, operates.

Items within the **staple merchandise**, also called **basic merchandise**, category are in continuous demand over an extended period of time. Even certain brands of basic merchandise, however, ultimately go into decline. Most merchandise in grocery stores, as well as housewares, hosiery, basic blue jeans, and women's intimate apparel, are considered to be staple merchandise.

Seasonal merchandise is inventory whose sales fluctuate dramatically according to the time of the year. Both fashion and staple merchandise usually have seasonal influences. For instance, wool sweaters sell better in fall and winter, whereas staples like lawn mowers and garden tools are more popular in spring and summer. Retailers carefully plan their purchases and deliveries to coincide with seasonal demand.

Fad, Fashion, or Staple? When DVD players were first introduced, no one knew if they would be a fad, a fashion, or a staple. Buyers purchased the category carefully at first, buying small quantities to see how they would sell. As they began to sell, the buyers reordered throughout the season and into the next. Had the merchandise sold briskly for a few months and then died, it would have been considered a fad. Now DVD players are considered a staple. They've become available with a large variety of features through many retail outlets at competitive prices. Ultimately, however, with today's technological breakthroughs, DVD players will eventually go the way of other staples like rotary phones and vinyl-disc record players—they'll be readily available only at your local secondhand store.

The forecasting and inventory management systems used for fads and fashion merchandise are very different from those used for staples. Managing fashion merchandise can be tricky. Since there is little or no history for specific SKUs, buyers forecast sales by category rather than by item. Then skill, experience, and creativity enable the buyer to select quantities for specific SKUs.

RETAILING VIEW | Is It a Fad or a Fashion?

12.2

To determine whether an item will be a fad or a more enduring fashion, retailers must ask the following questions:

- *Is it compatible with a change in consumer lifestyles?* Innovations that are consistent with lifestyles will endure. For example, denim jeans is an enduring fashion because they are comfortable to wear and can be worn on multiple occasions. Leather pants, on the other hand, can be hot, heavy, and are typically worn in the evening. They are fads.

- *Does the innovation provide real benefits?* The switch from poultry and fish from beef is not a fad because it provides real benefits to a health-conscious society.

- *Is the innovation compatible with other changes in the marketplace?* For example, shorter skirts resulted in a greater emphasis on women's hosiery. Now the sales of hosiery are declining due to the growing emphasis on casual apparel.

- *Who adopted the trend?* If it is not adopted by large, growing segments like working mothers, baby boomers, Generation Y, or the elderly, it is not likely to endure.

Source: Martin Letscher, "How to Tell Fads from Trends," *American Demographics,* December 1994, pp. 38–45. Reprinted by permission.

These Japanese teenagers have the latest fashions. Or are they fads? Is Harry Potter a fashion or a fad?

Disposable Chic at H&M | RETAILING VIEW

12.3

It's 11:30 A.M. on a cold, rainy day in Manhattan. What's going on in the store with the loud music, the wide-open doors, and the people streaming in and out? The one with lines already 12 deep waiting to get into the fitting rooms and pay at the checkout? The one whose windows are filled with hip fashions at rock-bottom prices?

Welcome to retail's new fashion import—H&M (short for Hennes & Mauritz). A retail powerhouse in Europe, the $3.9 billion Swedish chain dropped anchor in the United States. The stores are crammed with the hottest looks of the moment. The setting is stark and contemporary with theatrical lighting, pulsating music, and dramatic photo images that extend up through the space. There is little decor to speak of. The merchandise is the story here.

Value-priced, cutting-edge fashion is H&M's calling card. With prices similar to those of Old Navy, and a hip, international fashion sensibility akin to Club Monaco or Zara, the Stockholm-based chain ignited a feeding frenzy with its initial Manhattan outing. Checkout lines snaked around the store the weekend after it opened as eager shoppers scooped up $9 peasant print skirts, $13 suede fringe handbags, $29 racerback slipdresses, $17 leather bikinis, and $4.50 sequined cuff bracelets.

The majority of the merchandise at H&M is priced well below $100, with some exceptions (mostly suede and leather items). But such affordable price points are a double-edged sword: Anyone looking for fine fabrics or superb detailing should probably shop elsewhere. The chain puts most of its energy into churning out cutting-edge clothing at a price the masses not only can afford, but also can afford to throw out when the fashion tides turn.

H&M's high-fashion, low-price concept distinguishes it from Gap Inc., with its all-basics-at-all-price-points philosophy, and chains such as Bebe and Club Monaco, whose fashions are of the moment but by no means inexpensive. It offers an alternative for consumers who may be bored

with chinos and cargo pants but not able or willing to trade up for more fashion. H&M has seized on the fact that what's in today will not be in tomorrow. H&M is introducing the concept of disposable cheap chic to an older consumer, from the twenties on up.

Even shoppers who can afford the real thing when it comes to hip fashion, who don't blink at shelling out big bucks for Prada, Helmut Lang, or Chloe, are seen as potential H&M customers. These days, no one turns up their noses at a good bargain. Affluent consumers are just as likely to shop at Target or an outlet center as they are at upscale Barneys of New York or a pricey boutique.

Part of H&M's appeal lies in its breadth of product. It features more than 20 different collections (each with its own label), including a plus-sized line, maternity wear, intimate apparel, children's wear, baby clothes, and cosmetics—shoes are the only apparel-related area it has not ventured into. Fashion basics are marketed under the L.O.G.G. line.

H&M is a vertical retailer. Clothing is designed by a team of 70 in-house designers who keep a close watch on trends across the globe, from fashion runways to urban street scenes, interpreting them through the chain's unique filter. The company works with 1,600 suppliers throughout Europe and Asia. Its capabilities are such that it can jump on a particularly hot item and get it into its stores around the globe within a few weeks.

Goods move fast at H&M. Merchandise is delivered to stores in daily shipments. A truck pulls up each morning to the Manhattan store as associates wait on the street with empty garment racks. The scene is repeated throughout the day. Items that don't sell out quickly are marked down to make room for the next round.

Source: Marianne Wilson, "Disposable Chic at H&M," *Chain Store Age,* May 2000, pp. 64–66. Copyright Lebhar-Friedman, Inc. 425 Park Avenue, New York, NY 10022. Reprinted by permission.

Fashion is so "hot" at H & M, people wait outside for the store to open.

On the other hand, forecasting staple merchandise is fairly straightforward. Since there's a rich sales history for each SKU, SKU-based inventory management systems are readily available that forecast future sales using information from the past. Chapter 13 examines these systems.

Armed with information about where an item or a category is in its life cycle, retailers develop their sales forecast.

REFACT

Men in New York get inspired to buy a winter coat when the temperature drops to 51 degrees Fahrenheit. But in Chicago, it has to drop to 41![10]

Developing a Sales Forecast

A simple way to develop a sales forecast for a merchandise category is to adjust the past sales to make projections into the future. This type of sales forecasting technique is done at the category, rather than SKU, level and is used primarily for fashion merchandise. Forecasting sales of staple merchandise is typically done at the SKU level. These sales forecasting techniques for staple merchandise are examined later in this section and in Chapter 13. In the remaining portion of this section, we review the sources of information for forecasting fashions and fads.

Sources of Information for Category-Level Forecasts Buyers utilize a variety of sources in making these decisions. Discussed in the following sections, these include examining previous sales volume, reading published sources, analyzing customer information, shopping at the competition, and utilizing vendors and buying offices. More Information 12.1 discusses the special sales forecasting challenges for service retailers.

Previous Sales Volume Exhibit 12–7 shows Levi's sales by season over a 10-year period. Sales have been increasing by about 25 percent per season for several years. The exhibit illustrates a strong seasonality pattern. Typically, 40 percent of the annual sales occur in fall, 30 percent in winter, and 15 percent each in spring and summer. In the eighth year, the fall season was unusually strong due to early cold weather, whereas spring sales were particularly weak because of a temporary turndown in the local economy.

MORE INFORMATION ABOUT . . . Sales Forecasting for Service Retailers

12.1

Due to the perishable nature of services, service retailers can't stockpile as merchandise retailers can. Instead they must have extra equipment (e.g., ski lifts) or additional service providers (telephone repair people) to meet surges in demand. Of course, having idle equipment and service providers is a waste of resources. So service retailers have devised strategies for handling surges in demand.

Many service retailers attempt to match customers with service providers by taking reservations or making appointments. Physicians are notorious for making their patients wait, but patients are fighting back—they walk out and don't come back. Other service retailers use different strategies for lessening the impact of having to wait for service. Sticking a television in front of customers is a simple, inexpensive method used by service providers from airlines to barbershops. Distracting customers by allowing them to watch the service being performed is a strategy used by car washes, photo finishers, and restaurants.

The most innovative service retailers, however, actually devise methods to perform the service better. United Parcel Services of America, Inc. (UPS) and Federal Express (FedEx) now guarantee overnight delivery of packages and letters by 8 A.M. This service isn't inexpensive, however. Delivery of a letter, for instance, costs $43 for UPS and $40.50 for FedEx, almost three times the price of a letter delivered at 10:30.* Finally, some retailers have devised innovative pricing strategies that entice customers to utilize service during off-peak times (see Chapter 15).

*Prices based on Boston to New York delivery.

For fashion merchandise, where styles change from year to year, sales figures older than three years probably aren't very useful. When forecasting sales, retailers must identify real trends (either up or down) and try to isolate a real change in demand from random occurrences. Thus, the unusually high and low sales in the eighth year should be ignored when trying to forecast sales for the current season.

More Information 12.2 shows a simple method of forecasting sales, using the data from Exhibit 12–7. Chapter 13 covers more sophisticated methods to forecast sales of staples at the SKU level. Retailing View 12.4 describes how retailers should take weather into consideration when forecasting sales.

Published Sources Adjustments to sales trends are based on economic trends in the geographic area for which the forecast is developed. For example, a buyer for The Gap would consider national economic indicators such as the gross national product (GNP), interest rates, and employment rates, whereas an independent local clothing store would primarily consider local conditions. Even if national unemployment rates are low, they may be significantly higher where a particular retailer has a store. If so, people may spend less money on fashion in this region than in other areas.

Data on a monthly basis are obtainable from the *Monthly Retail Trade Report* published by the U.S. Department of Commerce (www.census.gov/mrts/ www/mrts.html). This information source covers general trends, but it may not be particularly helpful for a buyer forecasting sales for a particular merchandise category.

Retailers and their vendors can also buy data from private firms like InfoScan (www.infores.com). InfoScan buys information from individual supermarkets on price and promotion activity that has been scanned through their POS terminals

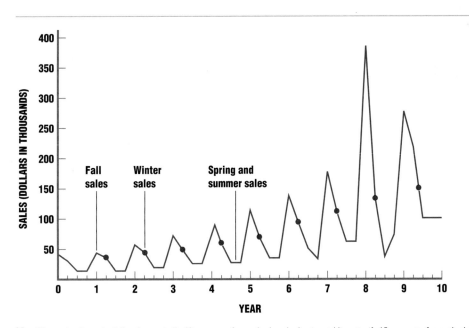

EXHIBIT 12–7
Sales for Levi's Jeans at Trendsetters Department Store

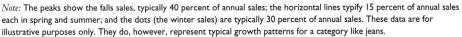

Note: The peaks show the falls sales, typically 40 percent of annual sales; the horizontal lines typify 15 percent of annual sales each in spring and summer; and the dots (the winter sales) are typically 30 percent of annual sales. These data are for illustrative purposes only. They do, however, represent typical growth patterns for a category like jeans.

and aggregates the data by region, chain, or market area. Information on customer demographics and psychographics as well as competitive information is available from firms like ESRI (www.esri.com). (Chapter 8 gives details.) Finally, general retail trade publications such as *Stores*, *WWD*, *Chain Store Age*, and *Discount Store News* analyze general retail trends.

Customer Information   Customer information can be obtained either by measuring customer reactions to merchandise through sales, by asking customers about the merchandise, or by observing customers and trendsetters. Knowing what customers want today is very helpful in predicting what should be purchased in the future.

Obtaining market information about the merchandise directly from the customer is probably the easiest yet most underused method. For example, a cashier at a restaurant may ask how a customer liked a meal but not record the answer in any systematic way. Another excellent source of customer information is retail

---

● MORE INFORMATION ABOUT . . .   Forecasting Sales for Levi's Jeans

12.2

The procedure for forecasting sales by season is accomplished in two steps. First, the retailer determines a sales forecast for the entire year. Then it considers seasonal sales patterns for each season.

The accompanying exhibit summarizes sales by reason for Levi's jeans for years 6 through 9 from Exhibit 12–7. For instance, during the fall season of year 6, the store sold $152,587 in jeans, which represents 41.9 percent of the total sales for year 6 ($152,587 ÷ $364,247 = 41.9 percent). The last column indicates the percentages of the increases for the previous three years: 30.1, 48.5, and 5 percent. The 30.1 percent increase from year 6 to year 7 was calculated as follows: ($364,247 − $476,835) ÷ $364,247. Unfortunately, the data don't show a consistent pattern due to unusually high sales in year 8. The buyer should probably discount the impact of year 8 sales on the forecast and examine sales increases from earlier years as well

as more qualitative factors. The average sales increase over the previous nine years has been 25 percent, general economic indicators in the area are strong, and top management sees an opportunity to grow this classification, so the buyer estimates the sales increase for year 10 to be 30 percent. Thus, the sales forecast for year 10 is [($745,056 × .3) + $745,056] or $968,573.

The second step is to apply the seasonal sales pattern to the annual sales forecast to determine sales for each season. The percentage of annual sales occurring in each season has been fairly stable except in year 8. Thus, the buyer decides to apply the same percentages as those in years 7 and 9. To forecast sales for each season, the buyer multiplies the annual sales by each of the seasonal sales percentages. For instance, fall sales for year 10 should equal ($968,573 × .4) or $387,429.

Year	SEASON				Total	Percentage Increase
	Fall	Winter	Spring	Summer		
6	$152,587	$114,440	$57,220	$40,000	$364,247	
	41.9%	31.4%	15.7%	11.0%	100%	
7	190,734	143,051	71,525	71,525	476,835	30.1%
	40.0%	30.0%	15.0%	15.0%	100%	
8	400,000	178,813	40,000	89,406	708,219	48.5%
	56.5%	25.3%	5.6%	12.6%	100%	
9	298,023	223,517	111,758	111,758	745,056	5.0%
	40.5%	30.0%	15.0%	15.0%	100%	
6–9 (total)	1,041,344	659,821	280,503	312,689	2,294,357	
	45.4%	28.2%	12.2%	13.6%	100%	
10 (forecast)	387,429	290,572	145,286	145,286	968,573	

salespeople. They have the direct contact with the customer necessary to determine customer attitudes in depth. Unless the store is owner-operated, however, this information doesn't filter in to the buyer automatically. Salespeople require both training and incentives to pass customer information on to buyers. Some retailers maintain a **want book** in which salespeople record out-of-stock or requested merchandise. This information is collected by buyers for making purchasing decisions.

Customer information can be collected through traditional forms of marketing research like depth interviews and focus groups. The **depth interview** is an unstructured personal interview in which the interviewer uses extensive probing to get individual respondents to talk in detail about a subject. For example, one

---

PETsMART Can Now Predict the Flea Season   RETAILING VIEW

12.4

Weather, not past sales or economic conditions, drives the flea season. Also Ohio may have a bad flea season one year, while Vermont is flea-less the same year. Fortunately for PETsMART and many other major retailers, Planalytics (www.planalytics.com) can help by predicting seasonal weather factors that can impact sales.

For all this talk about the weather, as the old saying goes, Nobody does anything about it. Certainly in the world of retailing, the traditional tendency has been to regard weather, when it's regarded at all, as a great unknown factor. Merchandise allocation plans tend to be based on the previous year's sales, which means they assume that the previous year's weather conditions will be repeated.

But according to Frederick D. Fox, president and CEO of Planalytics, weather repeats itself from year to year only about 35 percent of the time. Thus, retailers that assume a repeat of the previous year's weather will be wrong two seasons out of three.

The result can be devastating. For example, prior to PETsMART's getting sales forecasting help from Planalytics, consumers coming into the retailer's stores in the south looking for flea powder and collars may have been disappointed if the previous year had been dry, even though PETsMART stores in Michigan were fully stocked.

In 1993, Planalytics began advising the retail industry on how to apply future weather to decisions in receipt timing, merchandise allocation and distribution, advertising, promotions, and markdowns. Today, some of the biggest names in retailing—7-Eleven, Bloomingdale's, Carson Pirie Scott, Charming Shoppes, Lowe's, Ross Stores, Sears, The Children's Place, Home Depot, and Wal-Mart—routinely factor the effects of future weather into their plans in order to increase sales and profits.

Sources: "PETsMART Selects Planalytics' Impact LR to Support Flea and Tick Product Allocation and Marketing," January 23, 2002, (www.planalytics.com/app/corp/start.jsp?j=newsarticle&id=468); Rebecca Winters, "Weathering the Business Climate," *Time*, February 21, 2000, pp. B18–B19; and Jennifer Goldblatt, "Winter Clothing Is Scarce as Retailers Think Spring," *Virginian-Pilot*, January 27, 2000.

FORECAST WEATHER IMPACT Compared to LY in %

better				worse		
60%	30 to 60%	10 to 30%	± 10%	10 to 30%	30 to 60%	60%

▶ Show Zone Numbers

Planalytics forecasts the weather impact on consumer demand for women's shorts compared to last year. It looks like retailers in the southeastern portion of the United States should stock up.

grocery store chain goes through the personal checks received each day and selects all customers with large purchases of groceries and several with small purchases. Representatives from the chain call these customers and interview them to find out what they like and don't like about the store.

A more informal method of interviewing customers is to require buyers to spend some time on the selling floor waiting on customers. In most national retail chains, buyers are physically isolated from their customers. For example, buying offices for Target and The Gap are both in northern California, yet their stores are throughout America. It has become increasingly hard for buyers in large chains to keep a pulse on local customer demand. Frequent store visits help the situation. Some retailers require their buyers to spend a specified period of time, like a day a week, in a store.

A **focus group** is a small group of respondents interviewed by a moderator using a loosely structured format. Participants are encouraged to express their views and to comment on the views of others in the group. To keep abreast on the teen market, for instance, some stores have teen boards comprised of opinion leaders that meet to discuss merchandising and other store issues.[11]

One of the most useful methods of spotting new fashion trends is to observe trendsetters. Where in the past, designers dictated fashions, today's fashions are often discovered by observing cool city kids. By definition, fashion is fickle. Yet retailers and their vendors need time, usually several months, to bring new fashions to market. Unless they can spot these trends in advance of the typical mall shopper, their opportunity will have passed. So they hire research firms, like Triple Dot Communications, that specialize in spotting fashion trends. See Retailing View 12.5.

Shop Competition   Buyers need to observe their competition. They need to remain humble and keep in mind that, no matter how good they are, their competition and similar stores in other markets may be even better. Shopping at local competition helps buyers gauge the immediate competitive situation. For instance, a Macy's buyer shopping at a Nordstrom store may determine that Macy's prices on a particular line of handbags are too high.

With the popularity of the Internet, the local competition may not be the most important competition to shop. Retailers must therefore be constantly aware of all of their competitive venues. Shopping markets in buying centers such as New York, Milan, London, and Paris provides information on trends.

Vendors and Resident Buying Office   Buyers must seek information from vendors and resident buying offices. **Resident buying offices** either are independent organizations or are directly associated with particular retailers that offer a number of services associated with the procurement of merchandise. (Chapter 14 gives details.) Vendors and resident buying offices are excellent sources of market information. They know what's selling in markets around the world. Buyers, vendors, and buying offices must share such information if all are to succeed. Now that we have set the financial and sales goals for a merchandise category, we can begin to look at what type of merchandise to buy.

Store-Level Forecasting[12]

As retailers respond to increased competition, oversaturated markets, and shoppers who want more of everything for less, it is becoming increasingly important for retailers to become more efficient and quickly tailor merchandise offerings to meet the needs and desires of smaller and smaller market segments. To do this requires the merchandise planner to predict sales at the store SKU level. The forecasting method described in the previous sections was performed by buyers at more aggregate levels, like a region or a distribution center servicing many stores, and it was done by category, not by SKU. The problem with forecasting at more aggregate levels is that store-level variability gets averaged or summed out of the data. This, for example, happens when one store sells more single-serving-sized food products and a different store sells more family-sized products. Combining results from the two stores results in demand data that report evenly distributed sales.

Although sophisticated systems infrastructure and computational power enable the move to store-level forecasting, traditional approaches are not designed to

Coolhunters Hunt Cool   RETAILING VIEW

12.5

Tru Pettigrew just might have the coolest job in town. He isn't an undercover cop or a talent scout. He's a "cool-hunter," someone who prowls skate parks, basketball courts, movie theaters, and bowling alleys, watching people for clues. These sites are ground zero: He tracks down what's hot and appealing to people under 25, before those trends hit the mainstream. By traveling around the country, Pettigrew has become an expert on youth culture. "My friends think I just get paid to have fun," he says. But what he's doing is gathering information for the corporate clients of his employer, marketing and public relations firm Triple Dot Communications.

Being a coolhunter isn't easy. For one thing, he says, you have to be cool or trendsetters won't talk to you. Most adults would get shrugs, sullen stares, and the silent treatment if they asked a teenager his or her opinion about clothing or a new sneaker.

His job might look like fun, says Pettigrew, but he takes it very seriously. "I don't just collect lists of what's hot and what's not." He leads a team of six people in their 20s who research the Generation Y market (12- to 24-year-olds) nationwide for corporate clients. The team's work is threefold. It conducts general information-gathering sessions with kids (What's the hot store to shop? What's your favorite website?). It conducts client-specific sessions (If Jansport launched a backpack with wheels, would you use it? Since camouflage is in, do you expect it on your Reeboks?).

Team members people-watch at hot spots around the country. The team travels three weeks out of a month to major cities such as San Francisco, New York, Chicago, and Atlanta. Using a network of teachers, community-center directors, and athletic coaches, team members arrange to meet with multiple groups of about eight kids at a time in high school cafeterias, recreation centers, restaurants, and even private homes of students they've

How cool would it be to be a coolhunter?

met before. The students and the adult coordinators are paid for their time, generally $25 to $100 in cash or gift certificates. Free products samples or pizza are sometimes offered, too.

The profession of cool-hunting is fairly new. With the Internet's ability to quickly move trends around the globe, however, traditional research tools are often too slow to be helpful. As Pettigrew notes, "To keep your finger on the pulse, you have to interact with teens in their environment. You have to step out of your world and into theirs." Moreover, as the youth population grows, more companies are aiming for a share of the $84 the average teen spends weekly. There were an estimated 20 million 15- to 19-year-olds in the United States last year, up from 18 million in 1990, according to the U.S. Census Bureau.

Sources: Suzanne C. Ryan, "Cool Aide," *Boston Globe,* May 15, 2001, pp. D1, D4; and Jody Scott, "Life at the Cutting Edge of Culture and the Queen of Coolhunters," *The Times of London,* January 23, 2000, p. 27.

address the complexity and operational issues related to store-level data in a timely manner. To predict store-level demand, forecasting systems need to be able to measure simultaneously the impact of many factors on unit sales. These factors include promotion, price, placement of merchandise in the store, substitution, competition, location, and others. These factors are described in Exhibit 12–8.

Observing the impact of, say, adding another SKU to a supermarket shelf or of making a 2 percent price increase when weekly sales are fluctuating by 30 percent presents a daunting task, especially since most routine merchandising changes are made in response to manufacturer price increases or other incentives or seasonal trends and therefore affect competition as well. When multiple changes occur simultaneously, it is difficult to determine how much of the change should be attributed to each independent change. Traditional forecasting techniques such as exponential smoothing (described in Chapter 13) that are found in spreadsheets or standard statistical packages cannot pick up the subtle differences at the store level.

Today, most large retailers have implemented sophisticated systems that can track and archive weekly sales at the store and SKU level. With the advent of low-cost data storage and computing, it is now economically feasible to implement sales forecasting solutions that require massive computational power, such as advanced planning systems that are commercially available to retailers.

EXHIBIT 12–8 | Factors Impacting Sales Forecasts

Price The amount of unit sales of an item obviously depends on the price at which it is offered. Generally, with a few exceptions, raising the price causes unit sales to decrease, and vice versa. The question is, by how much? The answer can be found by determining the item's elasticity—the percentage change in unit sales resulting from a given percentage change in price. Thus, items that have a high elasticity are price-sensitive, and items with a low elasticity are insensitive to price.

Promotion The degree and type of promotion is also critical in determining the unit sales of an item. Promotional techniques include weekly circulars, store signage, end-caps and other special product displays, and manufacturer coupons and rebates. These promotions are examined in Chapter 16.

Store Location There can be large variances in demand depending on store location. Snow shovels obviously have a much higher demand in Minnesota than in Florida. Even in the same metropolitan area, the same item could have a different demand depending on whether the store is in an inner-city location or a suburban or rural location. Customer demographics plays a role, as the buying patterns in a store adjacent to a retirement community will be different from those in a store located in a residential neighborhood with many young families.

Product Placement The amount of shelf space afforded an item, as well as its location on the shelf, can have a large impact on sales. A diagram that shows how and where specific products should be placed on the shelves, called a planogram, is created to help maximize sales. The use of planograms are examined in Chapter 18.

Seasonality Some categories, most notably apparel, are highly seasonal in nature. In the extreme case, all of the sales of a particular merchandise category will occur during a single season. Seasonality also refers to increased sales associated with Christmas, Thanksgiving, Fourth of July, Mother's Day, and others.

Other Factors There are many other factors that impact sales, usually to a lesser degree, but sometimes significantly. Among these are

- *Product life cycle*—knowledge of whether product demand is growing, stable, or in decline, is important.

- *Product availability*—the degree to which the merchandise is, or is not, on the shelves ready for sale impacts sales.

- *Competitor price and promotional activity*—these also affect a retailer's sales.

- *Business cycles*—sales may be higher at the beginning of the month due to payroll cycles; also, sales are higher on weekends than on weekdays.

- *Weather*—late or early arrival of hot or cold weather can have a significant impact on sales of seasonal items.

- *Unusual events*—a new highway, an unexpected or severe storm, and other natural disasters can have a large local impact.

- *Cannibalization*—for example, decreasing the price of Apple Jacks would increase sales, but perhaps to the detriment of the sales of Fruit Loops.

- *Complementary products*—putting hot dogs on sale will also cause an increase in sales of hot dog buns.

SOURCE: KhiMetrics.

CPFR

CPFR—short for collaboration, planning, forecasting, and replenishment—is a natural outgrowth of the EDI technology that was discussed in Chapter 10. CPFR is a collaborative inventory management system in which a retailer shares information with vendors. CPFR software uses the data to construct a computer-generated replenishment forecast that is shared by the retailer and vendor before it's executed. CPFR generates exception reports that spit out unusual sales patterns. Then, when authorized by both the retailer and vendor, the computer makes automatic changes in the amount of merchandise going to the stores or distribution center based on the changes in the forecasting plan. The data in a CPFR system can be concentrated into a common pool that can be accessed by multiple vendors, as well as by multiple users within the retail chain, including the retailer's transportation specialists, buyers, merchandisers, logistics specialists, and store operations people.

CPFR benefits both retailers and their vendors. Because parties are working together with sophisticated forecasting and inventory management software, sales and gross margin increase and in-store inventory levels decrease, resulting in a higher GMROI. What are the dynamics behind a successful CPFR system? Because the forecast is more accurate, the **fill rate** (the percentage of an order that is shipped by the vendor) increases. A high fill rate means that in-store merchandise availability increases, resulting in fewer out-of-stocks. The more accurate forecast also causes inventory investment to decrease because there is need for less backup stock. Thus, the goal of CPFR is to increase on-shelf availability while lowering inventory throughout the supply chain.

The CPFR methodology (www.cpfr.org) was developed by Voluntary Interindustry Commerce Standards, or VICS (www.vics.org), a U.S. organization, and adopted by ECR Europe (www.ecrnet.org).[14] This methodology comprises a nine-step process designed for planning, forecasting, and replenishment of retail inventory by enhancing coordination of all trading parties in a supply chain. It centers on the sharing of the following data: business plans, promotion plans, new-product plans, inventory data, POS data, production and capacity plans, and lead-time information.

CPFR has only been recently adopted, and the verdict is still out. However, case studies in the United States support its potential. Kimberly Clark and Kmart, Nabisco and Wegman's, and Procter & Gamble with Target, Kroger, and Wal-Mart, Federated Department Stores with Liz Claiborne, Pillowtex and several intimate apparel resources, and others report benefits such as reduced out-of-stocks, higher order-fill, improved forecast accuracy, higher inventory turns, and higher category turnover. In Europe, 19 trials are underway, among others with Sainsbury's Tesco, Metro, Procter & Gamble, Kraft, Unilever, and Kimberly Clark.

CPFR isn't just for large retailers and suppliers. Since it is Internet-based, the data is more easily and inexpensively accessible from all parties than in the past when EDI systems were primarily operated by large retailers. Further, retail exchanges such as WorldWide Retail Exchange (www.worldwideretailexchange.org) and Global NetXchange (www.gnx.com) now offer CPFR software to their members. Retailing View 12.6 describes how some well-known retailers are experimenting with CPFR.

THE ASSORTMENT PLANNING PROCESS

All retailers face the fundamental strategic question of what type of retail format to maintain to achieve a sustainable competitive advantage (see Chapter 5). A critical component of this decision is determining what merchandise assortment will be carried. Merchandise decisions are constrained by the amount of money available to invest in inventory and the amount of space available in the store. Based on the financial objectives that have been set at the top and have trickled through the retail organization, decisions regarding variety, assortment, and product availability must be made.

In this section, we first define variety, assortment, and product availability. Then we examine the strategic trade-offs between them and the special issues faced by e-retailers. In the next section, we zero in on the assortment plan itself.

Variety

Variety is the number of different merchandising categories within a store or department. Stores with a large variety are said to have good breadth—the terms *variety* and **breadth** are often used interchangeably. Some stores, like Banana Republic, carry a large variety of categories of sportswear to meet all the needs of their target customers. Banana Republic carries updated slacks, sweaters, shirts, outerwear, and other categories for both men and women. Levi Strauss & Co. stores, on the other hand, carry a much more limited number of categories (variety): jeans and related apparel. Retailing View 12.7 considers Costco's unusual approach to achieving variety.

RETAILING VIEW CPFR in Action with Large and Small Retailers

12.6

It all started with Wal-Mart and Procter & Gamble in 1987 when they forged a groundbreaking partnership to cooperate more fully on everything from sharing sales data to planning promotions. The partnership required trust and commitment, instead of the traditional adversarial price negotiation process between retailers and their suppliers, so experts were skeptical. But the partnership program improved product availability and decreased inventory. Wal-Mart passed on the savings to its customers, and the rest is history.

Consider Ace Hardware the U.S.-based dealer-owned cooperative that supplies 5,100 stores in the United States and 62 countries. Manufacturers, both large and small, can dial into Ace's computer system to collaborate on sales forecasts and promotions. The 23 manufacturers that use Ace's Web-based program include giants like Master Lock, but also many small businesses. They plan to introduce software that will automatically feed forecasts directly into manufacturers' production schedules.

The Home Depot, the largest home improvement retailer in the United States, also shares information with suppliers over the Internet, such as inventory tracking, placing orders, and internal-office functions like personnel management.

Office Depot, which orders 7 billion to 8 billion items annually, uses an extranet to communicate with suppliers. It is implementing a CPFR system to do collaborative forecasting with suppliers and provide more comprehensive information, such as product descriptions and pictures.

Even the smallest retailers are trying to set up Web-based systems to deal with suppliers. RedEnvelope, the privately held Web and catalog gift retailer aims to build such a site as soon as possible to make communicating with its mostly small suppliers more efficient.

Source: Amy Tsao, "Where Retailers Shop for Savings," *Business-Week Online*, www.businessweek.com, April 15, 2002. Reprinted by special permission of the McGraw-Hill Companies.

Assortment

Assortment is the number of SKUs within a category. Stores with large assortments are said to have good depth—the terms *assortment* and **depth** are also used interchangeably. Levi Strauss & Co. stores, for instance, carry a large assortment of jeans and accessories, such as shirts and belts, that complement jeans. Banana Republic, on the other hand, has a narrow assortment of jeans because it appeals to a more narrowly defined target market and doesn't have the space to devote to jeans due to its emphasis on variety.

Product Availability

Product availability defines the percentage of demand for a particular SKU that is satisfied. For instance, if 100 people go into a Levi Strauss & Co. store to purchase a pair of tan jeans in size 33–34, and it sells only 90 pairs before it runs out of stock, its product availability is 90 percent. Product availability is also referred to as the **level of support** or **service level**.

Assortment Planning for Service Retailers

Consider health clubs. Some offer a large variety of activities and equipment from exercise machines to swimming, wellness programs, and New Age lectures. Others, like Gold's Gym, don't offer much variety but have an excellent assortment of body-building equipment and programs. Some hospitals, such as big municipal hospitals found in most urban areas, offer a large variety of medical

Costco Goes for Variety, or Does It? RETAILING VIEW

12.7

Costco keeps customers on their toes by offering a wide variety of merchandise. Don't try to guess what you will find there on any particular day, because you might be surprised. Costco is the place where individual and business customers, paying $35 to $100 per year for "membership," buy 24 rolls of toilet paper or none at all. This is where laundry detergent and Italian olive oil come in drums big enough to dunk a toddler, and where a 1,000-piece lot of Ralph Lauren golf jackets, selling 75 percent below retail at $19.99 each, will vanish in an afternoon. In its three-acre stores, you can also splurge on $20,000 engagement rings, or Dom Perignon champagne, which it sells for about $94 a bottle.

All these disparate categories provide an illusion of expansive variety. A Wal-Mart Supercenter carries as many as 125,000 items; a grocery store stocks roughly 40,000. Not so at Costco, where you'll find just 3,600 carefully chosen products. This makes it easier for the company to manage inventory and to obsessively monitor prices. Three-quarters of the merchandise is "basic," like tuna fish and paper towels; the other items are discretionary, often with high-end names such as Godiva chocolates and Waterford crystal. The store's periphery offers a variety of services:

film developing, a pharmacy, and a tire shop. Crazy product juxtapositions—face creams next to crackers—are all part of a selling formula that hones in on the middle-class tastes for cross-shopping and impulse purchases.

Does its assortment strategy work? In the United States, Costco's approximately 229 stores had average annual revenue of $114.3 million in 2000, while Sam's Wholesale Club's 439 stores averaged only $61.1 million. Sam's is fighting back. It has added brand names such as Maytag appliances and Ralph Lauren bedding and clothes and is beefing up its fresh-foods department with steamed shrimp and bagels. In 2001, Sam's unveiled a revamped jewelry division that offers a wider assortment and higher grade of diamonds (up to $1 million), pearls, and other gems, plus watches by Ebel, Concord, and TechnoMarine that sell for little more than half of department-store prices.

Sources: Ann Zimmerman, "Wal-Mart's Warehouse Club Attempts to Poach Costco's Upscale Customers," *The Wall Street Journal*, August 9, 2001, online.www.wsj.com. Shelly Branch, "Inside the Cult of Costco," *Fortune*, September 6, 1999, pp. 184–90.

The Chippery in Vancouver rates high on assortment and low on variety. It is THE place to get fresh potato (or beet, or yam) chips, a selection of gourmet dips and fruit smoothies. That is it!

services. Smaller private hospitals often specialize in physical rehabilitation or psychiatry. For service retailers, the level of product availability is a sales forecasting issue. (See More Information 12.1 on page (382)

Trade-Offs between Variety, Assortment, and Product Availability

How do retailers make the trade-off between variety, assortment, and product availability? It depends on their particular marketing strategy. Recall from Chapter 5 that a retail strategy identifies (1) the target market toward which a retailer plans to commit its resources, (2) the nature of the retail offering that the retailer plans to use to satisfy the target market's needs, and (3) the bases upon which the retailer will attempt to build a sustainable competitive advantage.

As a specialty store, Banana Republic tries to be the one-stop shopping alternative for its target markets. It carries a large variety of merchandise categories for both men and women. As a result, it can't physically or financially carry either gigantic assortments within each category or sufficiently high backup stock so as never to be out of stock. Alternatively, Levi Strauss & Co. stores have developed a marketing strategy around a target market of people who are particularly interested in buying jeans. As a result, they provide a large assortment of a limited number of categories. At Levi stores, product availability is high; they don't want to miss a sale because they don't have the right size. If any of these three elements—variety, assortment, or product availability—aren't what the customer expects or needs, a retailer will likely lose the sale and possibly the customer.

The trade-offs between variety, assortment, and product availability are strategic issues. Of the three issues, variety is the most strategic. Variety is most important in defining the retailer in the customer's eyes. For instance, is the retailer perceived to be a category specialist like Toys "R" Us or a generalist like a department store? Variety also defines the retailer's vendor structure. Does it purchase from many different types of manufacturers or just a few? Finally, decisions regarding variety are typically made less often and at higher levels in the organization than decisions regarding assortment or product availability. Top managers, for instance, make decisions about whether to delete categories or even departments from the store. Since these decisions have important ramifications, they're made only after serious consideration.

Determining Variety and Assortment

In attempting to determine the variety and assortment for a category like jeans, the buyer would consider the following factors: profitability of the merchandise mix, the corporate philosophy toward the assortment, physical characteristics of the store, layout of the Internet site, balance between too much versus too little assortment, and the degree to which categories of merchandise complement each other.

Banana Republic (left) tries to be the one-stop shop for its target market. It carries a large variety of merchandise categories. Levi Strauss & Co (right) stores don't have a large variety, but the assortment of jeans and related items are fantastic!

Profitability of Merchandise Mix   Since retailers are constrained by the amount of money they have to invest in merchandise and space to put the merchandise in, they're always trying to find the most profitable mix of products. Thus, for a chain of stores like Levi Strauss & Co. to add a category like shoes to the assortment, a reduction must be made elsewhere. It would attempt to take the inventory investment that it's been making in a less profitable merchandise category (flannel shirts in which it's invested $1 million to generate $2 million in sales) and shift it to shoes, which it hopes will generate $2.5 million.

Corporate Strategy and Positioning toward the Assortment   The corporate strategy toward the assortment helps the buyer determine the number of styles and colors to purchase. To illustrate, let's again consider the hypothetically different philosophies of Levi Strauss stores and Banana Republic. Both chains have a merchandise budget of $150,000 to spend on jeans that retail for $50. Thus, both stores can purchase 3,000 pairs. The Levi Strauss stores purchase 30 different style/color combinations (100 units per combination); Banana Republic purchases 10 (300 per combination). Similar to a portfolio of stocks, the Levi Strauss stores with 30 styles and colors are more diversified than Banana Republic.

As with stocks, the more diversified the portfolio, the less risk of large losses. With Levi Strauss stores, since there are so many style/color combinations, on average the category will perform adequately even if a few don't sell. But by spreading the 3,000 pairs across so many style/color combinations, the buyer runs the additional risk of **breaking sizes,** which means running out of stock on particular sizes. Typically, retailers take markdowns on assortments with broken sizes since they become harder to sell. Additionally, a large assortment of styles and colors won't enable the buyer to maximize profits by investing a large portion of the budget on the big winners.

Another issue is whether top management wants to grow or shrink a particular merchandise category. Some department stores, for instance, have dropped furniture and major appliances altogether because of low turnover, low profit marin the coming season. For instance, if a particular style, such as boot-cut jeans, is expected to be especially popular in the coming season, the merchandise planner will use more of the merchandise budget for that style and cut back on traditional jeans.

Exhibit 12–11 shows an abbreviated assortment plan for girls' jeans. This assortment plan identifies general styles (traditional five-pocket, straight-leg jeans, and boot-cut jeans), general price levels ($20, $35, and $45 for traditional jeans; $25 and $40 for boot-cut jeans), composition of fabric (regular denim and stonewashed), and colors (light blue, indigo, and black).

Assortment plans for apparel and shoes also typically include a size distribution. To illustrate, Exhibit 12–12 breaks down size and length for the 429 units for girls' traditional $20 denim jeans in light blue. Thus, the store wants to have nine units of size 1–short, which represent 2 percent of the 429 total. Note that the size distribution approximates a normal distribution or bell-shaped curve. The buyer buys less of the small and large sizes, and more of the middle sizes. The process of applying the size distribution is repeated for each style/color combination for each store.

EXHIBIT 12–11 | Assortment Plan for Girls' Jeans

Styles	Traditional	Traditional	Traditional	Traditional	Traditional	Traditional
Price levels	$20	$20	$35	$35	$45	$45
Fabric composition	Regular denim	Stonewashed	Regular denim	Stonewashed	Regular denim	Stonewashed
Colors	Light blue	Light blue	Light blue	Light blue	Light blue	Light blue
	Indigo	Indigo	Indigo	Indigo	Indigo	Indigo
	Black	Black	Black	Black	Black	Black

Styles	Boot-Cut	Boot-Cut	Boot-Cut	Boot-Cut
Price levels	$25	$25	$40	$40
Fabric composition	Regular denim	Stonewashed	Regular denim	Stonewashed
Colors	Light blue	Light blue	Light blue	Light blue
	Indigo	Indigo	Indigo	Indigo
	Black	Black	Black	Black

EXHIBIT 12–12
Size Distribution for Traditional $20 Denim Jeans in Light Blue for a Large Store

		SIZE									
LENGTH		1	2	4	5	6	8	10	12	14	
Short		2	4	7	6	8	5	7	4	2	%
		9	17	30	26	34	21	30	17	9	units
Medium		2	4	7	6	8	5	7	4	2	%
		9	17	30	26	34	21	30	17	9	units
Long		0	2	2	2	3	2	2	1	0	%
		0	9	9	9	12	9	9	4	0	units
									Total		100%
											429 units

The development of an assortment plan can be complicated. In an actual multistore chain, the process is even more complex than in our example. A good assortment plan requires a good forecast for sales, GMROI, and inventory turnover along with a mix of subjective and experienced judgment. A good inventory management system that combines these elements is also critical to successful merchandise management. These systems are described in the next chapter.

SUMMARY

This chapter was the first of five on merchandise management. As such, it examined basic strategic issues and planning tools for managing merchandise. First, merchandise must be broken down into categories for planning purposes. Buyers and their partners, merchandise planners, control these categories, often with the help of their major vendors. Without a method of categorizing merchandise like the one described here, retailers could never purchase merchandise in any rational way.

Tools to develop a merchandising plan include GMROI, inventory turnover, and sales forecasting. GMROI is used to plan and evaluate merchandise performance. The GMROI planned for a particular merchandise category is derived from the firm's overall financial goals broken down to the category level. Gross margin percentage and inventory turnover work together to form this useful merchandise management tool.

Calculating inventory turnover and determining inventory turnover goals are important. Retailers strive for a balanced inventory turnover. Rapid inventory turnover is imperative for the firm's financial success. But if the retailer attempts to push inventory turnover to its limit, severe stockouts and increased costs may result.

When developing a sales forecast, retailers must know what stage of the life cycle a particular category is in and whether the product is a fad, fashion, or staple so they can plan their merchandising activities accordingly. Creating a sales forecast involves such sources of information as previous sales volume, published sources, customer information, and shopping at the competition as well as utilizing vendors and buying offices.

The trade-off between variety, assortment, and product availability is a crucial issue in determining merchandising strategy. Examining this trade-off helps retailers answer the important question of what type of store to be: a specialist or generalist.

The culmination of planning the GMROI, inventory turnover, sales forecast, and assortment planning process is the assortment plan. The assortment plan supplies the merchandise planner with a general outline of what should be carried in a particular merchandise category. Yet the merchandise planner's repertoire of tools is still incomplete. In the next chapter, we show how GMROI, inventory turnover, and the sales forecast are integral components to (1) the merchandise budget plan used for fashion merchandise and (2) inventory management systems used for staple products.

KEY TERMS

assortment, *391*

assortment plan, *364*

assortment planning, *364*

backup stock, *396*

base stock, *396*

basic merchandise, *379*

breadth, *390*

breaking sizes, *393*

buffer stock, *396*

category, *365*

category captain, *366*

category life cycle, *378*

category management, *365*

classification, *369*

cycle stock, *396*

department, *368*

depth, *391*

depth interview, *385*

fad, *379*

fashion, *379*

fill rate, *389*

focus group, *386*

lead time, *397*

level of support, *391*

merchandise group, *367*

merchandise
management, *363*

product availability, *391*

resident buying office, *386*

safety stock, *396*

seasonal merchandise, *379*

service level, *391*

staple merchandise, *379*

stock keeping unit
(SKU), *369*

variety, *390*

want book, *385*

GET OUT & DO IT!

1. **INTERNET EXERCISE** Go to www.bad

   fads.com. Choose some fads. Ask the four questions presented in Retailing View 12.2. Based on the answers, did these fads deserve a sudden and quick death?

2. **INTERNET EXERCISE** InfoScan's website is located at www.infores.com. Go to its site and describe the services it offers retailers.

3. **INTERNET EXERCISE** Go to www.macys.com and www.JCPenney.com. Which seems to have the largest variety? Choose a merchandise category and determine which retailer contains the largest assortment.

4. **INTERNET EXERCISE** Go to World-Wide Retail Exchange (www.world wideretailexchange.org) and Global NetXchange (www.gnx.com). Compare their CPFR programs for retailers. Which would you choose?

5. **GO SHOPPING** Go to your favorite apparel specialty store and your favorite

   department store. Do an audit of the variety and assortment at the specialty store. (Tabulate how many merchandise categories it carries and how many SKUs within each category.) Compare the variety and assortment for the same type of merchandise in the department store.

DISCUSSION QUESTIONS AND PROBLEMS

1. What are the differences between a fashion, fad, and staple? How should a merchandise planner manage these types of merchandise differently?

2. How and why would you expect variety and assortment to differ between a traditional bricks-and-mortar store and its Internet counterpart?

3. Simply speaking, increasing inventory turnover is an important goal for a retail manager. What are the consequences of turnover that's too slow?

4. Assume you are the grocery buyer for canned fruits and vegetables at a five-store supermarket chain. Del Monte has told you and your boss that it would be responsible for making all inventory decisions for those merchandise categories. It would determine how much to order and when shipments should be made. It promises a 10 percent increase in gross margin dollars in the coming year. Would you take Del Monte up on its offer? Justify your answer.

5. An assortment plan indicates that a buyer can purchase 1,000 units of fashion wristwatches. The buyer must choose between buying 20 styles of 50 units each or 5 styles of 200 units each. In terms of the store's philosophy toward risk and space utilization, how does the buyer make this decision?

6. A buyer has had a number of customer complaints that he has been out of stock on a certain category of merchandise. The buyer subsequently decides to increase this category's product availability from 80 percent to 90 percent. What will be the impact on backup stock and inventory turnover? Will your answer be the same if the buyer is implementing a quick response inventory system?

7. Variety, assortment, and product availability are the cornerstones of the assortment planning process. Provide examples of retailers that have done an outstanding job of positioning their stores on the basis of one or more of these issues.

8. The fine jewelry department in a department store has the same GMROI as the small appliances department even though characteristics of the merchandise are quite different. Explain this situation.

9. Calculate GMROI and inventory turnover given

Annual sales	$20,000
Average inventory (at cost)	$75,000
Gross margin	45%

10. Calculate GMROI and inventory turnover given

Annual sales	$12,000
Average inventory (at cost)	$4,000
Gross margin	35%

SUGGESTED READINGS

"A Vision and Case Example for Transforming the Retail Industry Using Optimization Technologies." www.retailoptimizationcouncil.com/html_folder/resources.html

Basuroy, Suman; Murali K. Mantrala; and Rockney G. Walters. "The Impact of Category Management on Retailer Prices and Performance: Theory and Evidence." *Journal of Marketing* 65, no. 4 (October 2001), pp. 16–32.

Boatwright, Peter, and Joseph C. Nunes. "Reducing Assortment: An Attribute-Based Approach." *Journal of Marketing*, July 2001, pp. 50–63.

Crocker, Paul. *Focus Group Research for Marketers: What Marketers Need to Know About this Popular Research Technique to Use it Safely, Effectively and Wisely:* Xlibris Corporation, 2001

Crosby, John V. *Cycles, Trends, and Turning Points: Practical Marketing and Sales Forecasting Techniques.*: NTC Publishing Group, 1999.

Dhar, Sanjay K.; Stephen J. Hoch; and Nanda Kumar. "Effective Category Management Depends on the Role of the Category." *Journal of Retailing*, Summer 2001, pp. 165–184.

Dussart, C. "Category Management: Strengths, Limits and Developments." *European Management Journal* 16, no. 1, (1998), pp. 50–62.

Gruen, Thomas W., and Reshma H. Shah. "Determinants and Outcomes of Plan Objectivity and Implementation in Category Management Relationships." *Journal of Retailing*, 76, no. 4 (Winter 2000), pp. 483–511.

Mentzer, John T., and Carol C. Bienstock. *Sales Forecasting Management.* Sage Publications, June 1998.

Rosenau, Jeremy A., and David Wilson. *Apparel Merchandising.* Fairchild Books, 2000.

Seifert, Dirk. *Collaborative Planning Forecasting and Replenishment: How to Create a Supply Chain Advantage.* Galileo Press, 2002.

"Turning Your Store-SKU Data into Gold Using Retail Revenue Management." www.khimetrics.com/Downloads/KhiSpeaks4_DataIntoGold.pdf

Buying Systems

13

EXECUTIVE BRIEFING | Ramin Mozafarim, VP, Merchandise Manager, Decorative Home, Burdines

"You may find this strange, but I look forward to reviewing daily financial results, the report cards that track the sales generated by my departments. It is a very satisfying experience to see the merchandise we bought selling well, and the strategies we implemented being so successful. And even when sales are below expectations, I am excited about the interesting challenge ahead on our hands."

"Some of the factors we need to consider when buying merchandise are trends in customer needs and wants: price of the merchandise, financial constraints, store presentation, marketing plans and competitive issues in the market. Burdines is the Florida Store and we are focused on Florida Friendly products. Our focus on Florida is a competitive advantage. For example, in home products, we concentrate on palm, bamboo, banana leaves and the Florida casual lifestyle. Our competitors with national territories and markets are unable to focus on the Florida lifestyle in a meaningful manner and offer the depth of assortment in Florida Friendly merchandise."

"If you are interested in retail buying, you need to be very careful in selecting the first company you join with. Not every company is great at training, coaching, and mentoring entry-level associates. If you

QUESTIONS

- What are a merchandise budget plan and open-to-buy system, and how are they prepared?
- How does a staple merchandise buying system operate?
- How do multistore retailers allocate merchandise to stores?
- How do retailers evaluate their merchandising performance?

do not initially have good support and training, it will be difficult to be successful. One way to determine if a company is great at training is to check track records of entry-level associates and where they have ended up over the years."

Mr. Mozafarim started his retail career at the May Department Stores in Los Angeles as a part-time associate. He joined the Broadway Department Stores management program. After several store management positions in operations, sales, and merchandising, he joined the planning division and subsequently became a director of merchandise planning and allocation. He joined Burdines in 1996 as a director of planning for women's apparel and shortly after was promoted to vice president of planning and allocation. He has recently joined the buying team at Burdines as vice president, merchandise manager for decorative home areas.

Selling generates revenue, but buying right generates profit.

In Chapter 12, we examined the issues in forecasting sales and developing assortment plans, which indicates in very general terms what and how much should be carried in a particular merchandise category. As Exhibit 13–1 shows, this chapter examines the merchandise management process in more depth by showing how retailers utilize various tools in formal buying systems. While the assortment plan provides a general outline of what types of merchandise should be carried, it doesn't tell you how much to buy.

Specifically, these systems and tools help buyers and merchandise planners determine how much to buy. Retailers use two distinct types of buying systems: (1) a staple merchandise buying system for basics and (2) a merchandise budget for fashion merchandise. Forecasting demand is much more straightforward for staples than for fashion merchandise. Since there's an established sales history for each staple SKU, standard statistical techniques are used to forecast sales. Since there is no sales history for specific fashion SKUs, buyers forecast sales at the category level. Buyers must determine the quantity of specific SKUs to purchase on the basis of many of the issues described in Chapter 12.

The open-to-buy system keeps track of the merchandise flows while they are occurring so

EXHIBIT 13–1
Merchandise
Management Issues

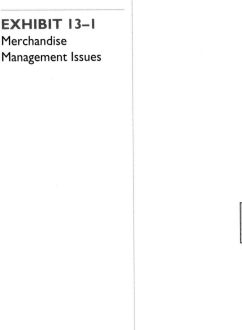

PLANNING MERCHANDISE ASSORTMENTS (CHAPTER 12)

Organize the Buying Process by Categories

Set Merchandise Financial Objectives

Develop an Assortment Plan

BUYING SYSTEMS (CHAPTER 13)

Staple Merchandise Buying Systems

Fashion Merchandise Buying Systems

Open-to-Buy Systems

Allocate Merchandise to Stores

Analyze Merchandise Performance

buyers don't spend too much or too little. Once the merchandise is purchased, it is allocated to stores. In the end, the merchandise and buyer's performance are evaluated.

The chapter begins with a look at buying systems for staple merchandise. Buying systems for fashion merchandise are examined next, followed by a look at open-to-buy systems. The chapter then discusses how multistore retailers allocate merchandise among stores and how buying performance is evaluated. At the end of this chapter, Appendix 13A describes the retail inventory method (RIM).

STAPLE MERCHANDISE BUYING SYSTEMS

Staple merchandise buying systems are used for merchandise that follows a predictable order-receipt-order cycle. Most merchandise fits this criterion. These systems don't work well with fashion merchandise, however, because they use past history to predict sales for the future—and fashion merchandise has no history from previous seasons on specific SKUs. These systems are used for buying most of the merchandise found in food and discount stores in addition to some categories in specialty and department stores like underwear, socks, and housewares.

Numerous inventory management systems for staple merchandise are currently available for both micro- and mainframe computers for retailers of all sizes. Let's explore the basics of these systems using Marketmax's system. Retailing View 13.1 describes how Retek improved the inventory system at South Africa's Edcon.

What the Staple Merchandise Buying System Does

Staple merchandise buying systems contain a number of program modules that show how much to order and when. These systems assist buyers by performing three functions:

- Monitoring and measuring average current demand for items at the SKU level.

- Forecasting future SKU demand with allowances made for seasonal variations and changes in trend.

- Developing ordering decision rules for optimum restocking.

The inventory management report, discussed in the next section, provides the information for performing these functions.

Most merchandise at home improvement centers like Home Depot and Lowe's are staples.

Edgars Consolidated Stores Improves Replenishment and Pricing with Retek   RETAILING VIEW

13.1

Edgars Consolidated Stores (Edcon) is South Africa's leading group of fashion retailers. It focuses on clothing, footwear, accessories, mobile phones, and home textiles with six chains: Edgars department stores, Jet, Smileys and Sales House value apparel stores, and ABC and Cuthberts specialty shoe stores. The various Edcon operations serve different segments of the South African market. For example, Edgars is an upscale department store concept, whereas Jet, Sales House, and Cuthberts are discount, volume-oriented operations. With over 700 stores across all chains, Edcon needs inventory management systems to manage both fashion and staple merchandise.

Edcon uses supply chain, merchandising, and logistics systems from Retek Inc. (Minneapolis, Minnesota) to manage inventory and stay responsive to the changing needs of its customers. Retek Demand Forecast and the Retek Merchandising System enable Edcon to accurately forecast at the store level which stores will sell the greatest number of core items, like jeans, cosmetics, and underwear, by color and size. The forecasting system uses sophisticated mathematical algorithms to analyze large amounts of SKU/store data from which it generates accurate forecasts.

Together with this information, and Retek's automated replenishment functions, Edcon has improved in stock positions on some lines by as much as 20 percent, without carrying additional inventory. This has enabled Edcon to improve sales and reduce costs. With the implementation of the Retek systems, Edcon has also improved the pricing of its merchandise, particularly in the area of managing markdowns. Using a price management system, Edcon was able to reduce the time it took to run its markdown process down from six days to two. By compressing the markdown process and leveraging technology, Edcon has been able to execute pricing changes faster to stay more in tune with local demand factors.

Source: Retek.

The Inventory Management Report

The inventory management report provides information on sales velocity, inventory availability, the amount on order, inventory turnover, sales forecast, and most important, the quantity to order for each SKU. Take a look at Exhibit 13–2, which shows an actual inventory management report for Rubbermaid, a large manufacturer of household plastic products. Note the last number of each row for each SKU. This is the suggested order quantity for each SKU—the end product of the inventory management process.

The retailer will have a prespecified schedule for each vendor. The schedule is determined by weighing the cost of carrying inventory versus the cost of buying and handling the inventory. The more the retailer purchases at one time, the higher the carrying costs, but the lower the buying and handling costs.

Although each line has a prespecified schedule for ordering, each vendor's inventory status is checked daily. For instance, even though Rubbermaid items may be scheduled to be purchased every five days, occasionally increased demand may dictate that several items need replenishment sooner. The combination of having a prespecified schedule based on the trade-off between inventory carrying and ordering costs, and the flexibility to react to demand fluctuations, helps to ensure a profitable ordering strategy.

Basic Stock List The first four columns of Exhibit 13–2 represent what many retailers call the basic stock list. The **basic stock list** describes each SKU and summarizes the inventory position. Specifically, it contains the stock number and description of the item, how many items are on hand and on order, and sales for the past 12 and 4 weeks. The basic stock list differs from the assortment plan used in fashion-based systems in that it defines each SKU in precise rather than general terms. Examine the first item: stock number 4050, a Rubbermaid bath mat in avocado green. There are 6 on hand and 120 on order. Thus, the quantity available is 126. (Quantity on hand + quantity on order = quantity available.) Sales for the past 12 and 4 weeks were 215 and 72 units, respectively.

The basic stock list is a necessary component of any inventory management system, yet many retailers go beyond the basic record-keeping function. The last eight columns of Exhibit 13–2 are needed too. Using this information, the inven-

EXHIBIT 13–2 | Marketmax Inventory Management Report for Rubbermaid

Marketmax - Performance Analysis - Worksheet: Inventory Management Report : Admin (Business View: 'Inventory Management Report : Admin')

Worksheet   Performance Analysis

Plan Edit View Tools Help

Loc - 01
Time - Spring 2002

	Quantity On Hand	Quantity On Order	Sales Last 12 Wks	Sales Last 4 Wks	Turnover Actual	Turnover Plan	Product Availability	Backup Stock	Forecast Current 4 Wks	Forecast Next 8 Wks	Order Point	Order Quantity
RMBath - RM Bath												
4050 - RM Bath Mat avocado	6	120	215	72	9	12	96	20	94	117	167	42
4051 - RM Bath Mat Blue	0	96	139	56	5	9	100	17	58	113	110	96
4052 - RM Bath Mat Gold	1	60	234	117	9	12	95	27	42	196	200	144
4053 - TM Bath Mat Pink	2		41	31	5	9	95	10	41	131	58	60

tory management part of the system manipulates the numbers in the basic stock list to arrive at sales forecasts and suggested order quantities. Now let's talk about the remaining entries in Exhibit 13–2 and how they fit into the system.

Inventory Turnover   The planned inventory turnover is based on overall financial goals and drives the inventory management system. The buyer achieves an actual inventory turnover of 9 for the avocado bath mat, but the planned turnover was 12.

Product Availability   In the avocado bath mat example, on average, out of every 100 customers wanting the item, 96 found it in stock. Determining the appropriate planned level of product availability for staple merchandise can be difficult and requires considerable managerial judgment.

Backup Stock   Backup stock, also known as safety stock or buffer stock, is inventory used to guard against going out of stock when demand exceeds forecasts or when merchandise is delayed (see Chapter 12). Backup stock for the avocado bath mat is 20 units.

Forecast   Sales forecasts for staple items are fairly straightforward and mechanical compared to those for fashion merchandise. With fashion merchandise, past trends and other issues that help determine the future are examined. Forecasting sales of staple items entails extending sales trends from the past into the future.

Exponential smoothing is a forecasting technique in which sales in previous time periods are weighted to forecast future periods. To understand exponential smoothing, again consider the Rubbermaid avocado bath mat, whose average sales forecast over the past few four-week periods is 100 units (not shown in Exhibit 13–2). But the sales total for the past four-week period was 72 units. To forecast the next four-week period, the buyer wants to be responsive to the decrease in sales from 100 to 72, but doesn't want to overreact by ignoring the historical average since the decrease could be a random occurrence. The following formula takes into account the two sales forecasting objectives of being responsive and ignoring random occurrences:

New forecast = Old forecast + α (Actual demand – Old forecast)

The Greek letter alpha (α) is a constant between 0 and 1 that determines the influence of actual demand on the new forecast. When demand is increasing or decreasing sharply, high values of alpha, such as .5, cause the forecast to react quickly. Low values of alpha, such as .1, are appropriate when demand is changing very slowly. Let's continue the forecast for the bath mat using high and low alphas:

New forecast = Old forecast + α (Actual demand – Old forecast)

94	=	96	+ .1	(72 – 96)
84	=	96	+ .5	(72 – 96)

Alpha in Exhibit 13–2 is .1, indicating a forecast for the next four-week period of 94. Determining what alpha to use requires experimentation. If the buyer believes the last period's decrease in demand represents a real shift rather than a random occurrence, the .5 alpha is more appropriate since it yields the much lower forecast of 84 bath mats. In general, if alpha is too high, an unstable forecasting process results because the forecast overreacts to random changes in demand. If alpha is too low, the forecast will always lag behind or ahead of the trend. Once the system is forecasting properly, the software will automatically adjust alpha when necessary.

Even staple items like bath mats have some seasonality—typically, demand rises slightly around spring-cleaning time. The new forecast, which the buyer calculated using exponential smoothing, is called the deseasonalized demand. **Deseasonalized demand** is forecast demand without the influence of seasonality. The season's influence is removed before making the calculations. To obtain the actual forecast of demand including the influence of seasonality, the inventory management system multiplies deseasonalized demand times a seasonality index in the same way that it will be done in the first two lines in the merchandise budget plan in Exhibit 13–3. In the bath mat case, there was no seasonality for the example month.

Order Point The **order point** is the amount of inventory below which the quantity available shouldn't go or the item will be out of stock before the next order arrives. The order point in the periodic system is defined as

Order point = [(Demand/Day) (Lead time + Review time)] + (Backup stock)

The lead time is the amount of time between recognition that an order needs to be placed and when it arrives in the store and is ready for sale. Assume demand per day is 1 and lead time is zero days. (This may be the case in a pharmacy receiving shipments from its wholesaler more than once a day.) Here the order point would be zero. The buyer would wait until stock ran out and then order and replenish the merchandise almost instantaneously.

With lead time of two weeks, there's some point below which the buyer shouldn't deplete the inventory without ordering, or the retailer would start selling the backup stock before the next order arrived. Further, the buyer only reviews the line once a week, and 20 units of backup stock are necessary to maintain a high service level. In this case, if demand is 7 units per day, then

Order point = [(7 units) × (14 + 7 days)] + (20 units) = 167 units

Here the buyer orders if quantity available falls to 167 units or fewer.

Order Quantity The question remains, How much should the buyer order when the quantity available is less than the order point? He or she should order enough so the cycle stock isn't depleted and sales dip into backup stock before the next order arrives—this is the difference between the quantity available and the order point. Using the avocado bath mats in Exhibit 13–2, since quantity available is 126, the buyer orders 41 units, because the order point is 167 (i.e., 167 − 126 = 41). The actual suggested order quantity is 42 since the bath mats are packed 6 to a carton, and the computer rounds up to the next whole carton.

Now that we've see how inventory management systems work for staple merchandise, let's look at a system designed for fashion merchandise.

MERCHANDISE BUDGET PLAN
FOR FASHION MERCHANDISE

The merchandise budget plan specifies the inventory investment in a category over time. It isn't a complete buying plan since it doesn't indicate the specific assortment to buy or the quantities. The plan just specifies how much money should be spent each month to support sales and achieve turnover and GMROI objectives.

Exhibit 13–3 shows a six-month merchandise budget plan for men's tailored suits at a national specialty store chain. For a category like this, the buyer is probably doing the plan in the summer for the following spring. The buyer needs to plan how much merchandise should be delivered in each month to achieve the financial goals for the period.

Actual sales might differ from the sales forecasted in the merchandise budget plan. Even with this uncertainty, the plan is used to coordinate the supply and demand for merchandise and to ensure that the financial goals are realized. In addition, the plan coordinates the activities of buyers for different merchandise categories, so that there is not too much merchandise in some categories and not enough in others. From a global perspective, the merchandise variety could become off balanced and be less appealing to customers.

Take a close look at line 8, "Monthly Additions to Stock," in Exhibit 13–3. In the next few pages, we will systematically work through Exhibit 13–3 on our way to this last line. "Monthly Additions to Stock" tells the buyer how much money to spend in each month, given the category's sales forecast, GMROI, inventory turnover, and monthly fluctuations in sales. As such, the merchandise budget plan coordinates purchases to coincide with the category's financial goals.

Even relatively small stores now use advanced computer technologies like this one to plan merchandise budgets. Retailing View 13.2 shows how a similar system developed by Retex is being used by Gap Inc.

In the remaining portion of this section, we will examine each line in the merchandise budget plan. The merchandise planning system illustrated here was developed by Marketmax.

Marketmax Six-Month Merchandise Budget Plan for Men's Tailored Suits | **EXHIBIT 13–3**

Loc - 01 Merch - Mens	Spring 2002	April 2002	May 2002	June 2002	July 2002	August 2002	September 2002
1. Sales % Distribution to Season	100.00%	21.00%	12.00%	12.00%	19.00%	21.00%	15.00%
2. Monthly Sales	$130,000	$27,300	$15,600	$15,600	$24,700	$27,300	$19,500
3. Reduc.% Distribution to Season	100.00%	40.00%	14.00%	16.00%	12.00%	10.00%	8.00%
4. Monthly Reductions	$16,500	$6,600	$2,310	$2,640	$1,980	$1,650	$1,320
5. BOM Stock to Sales Ratio	4.00	3.60	4.40	4.40	4.00	3.60	4.00
6. BOM Inventory	$98,280	$98,280	$68,640	$68,640	$98,800	$98,280	$78,000
7. EOM Inventory	$65,600	$68,640	$68,640	$275,080	$98,280	$78,000	$65,600
8. Monthly Additions to Stock	$113,820	$4,260	$17,910	$48,400	$26,160	$8,670	$8,420

Monthly Sales Percent Distribution to Season (Line 1)

Line 1 of the plan projects what percentage of the total sales is expected to be sold in each month. Thus, in Exhibit 13–3, 21 percent of the six-month sales is expected to occur in April.

1. Sales % Distribution to Season	100.00%	21.00%	12.00%	12.00%	19.00%	21.00%	15.00%

The starting point for determining the percent distribution of sales by month is historical records. The percentage of total sales that occurs in a particular month doesn't vary appreciably from year to year. Even so, it's helpful to examine each month's percentage over a few years to check for any significant changes. For instance, the buyer realizes that the autumn selling season for men's tailored suits continues to be pushed further back into summer. Over time, this general shift toward earlier purchasing will affect the percent distribution of sales by month. The distribution may also vary due to changes made by the buyer or the competitors' marketing strategies. The buyer must include special sales that did not occur in the past, for instance, in the percent distribution of sales by month in the same way that they're built into the overall sales forecast.

Monthly Sales (Line 2)

Monthly sales equal the forecast total sales for the six-month period (first column = $130,000) multiplied by each sales percentage by month (line 1). We discussed methods of determining the sales forecast in Chapter 12. In Exhibit 13–3, monthly sales for April = $130,000 × 21% = $27,300.

2. Monthly Sales	$130,000	$27,300	$15,600	$15,600	$24,700	$27,300	$19,500

RETAILING VIEW | **Gap Inc. Uses Merchandise Planning to Manage Fast-Moving Fashions**

13.2

As a leading apparel retailer, Gap Inc.'s goal is to bring great style and value to customers year-round. To accomplish this, The Gap, Banana Republic, and Old Navy deliver new styles and new products multiple times a year. One of the company's challenges is to accurately plan and forecast the optimal quantities, distribution, and pricing strategies for these new products. With significant volumes from more than 4,300 stores, and constantly changing styles, this merchandise planning process is very complex, requiring industrial-strength technology support.

Recently, Gap Inc. upgraded its technology by selecting and implementing the planning and forecasting software applications from Retek Inc. (Minneapolis, Minnesota). The planning process consists of a top-down and bottom-up approach, incorporating disciplines for reconciling budgets with key item plans. Leveraging integrated software, Gap Inc.'s planners now more easily reconcile their plans within a single framework. The planning and forecasting applications also incorporate mathematical modeling into the process, which enhances accuracy and simplifies use.

The Retek application software enables Gap Inc. to have a more consistent, streamlined, and efficient planning process. With integrated forecasting, optimization engines, and the ability to reconcile and approve plans quickly and efficiently, Gap Inc. can make better, faster, and more accurate decisions for forecasting sales and making price and markdown optimization decisions. This supports Gap Inc.'s goal of providing the right merchandise to the right store at the right time and price, providing great style and value to customers.

Source: Gap Inc.

Monthly Reductions Percent
Distribution to Season (Line 3)

To have enough merchandise every month to support the monthly sales forecast, the buyer must consider factors that reduce the inventory level. Although sales are the primary reduction, the value of the inventory is also reduced by markdowns, shrinkage, and discounts to employees. The merchandise budget planning process builds in these additional reductions into the planned purchases. Otherwise, the retailer would always be understocked. Note that in Exhibit 13–3, 40 percent of the season's total reductions occur in April as a result of end-of-season sales.

3. Reduc. % Distribution to Season	100.00%	40.00%	14.00%	16.00%	12.00%	10.00%	8.00%

Markdowns can be forecast fairly accurately from historical records. Of course, changes in markdown strategies—or changes in the environment, such as competition or general economic activity—must be taken into consideration when forecasting markdowns. (Chapter 15 discusses markdowns.)

Discounts to employees are like markdowns, except that they're given to employees rather than to customers. Cost of the employee discount is tied fairly closely to the sales level and number of employees. Thus, its percentage of sales and dollar amount can be forecast fairly accurately from historical records.

Shrinkage is an inventory reduction that is caused by shoplifting by employees or customers, by merchandise being misplaced or damaged, or by poor bookkeeping. The buyer measures shrinkage by taking the difference between (1) the inventory's recorded value based on merchandise bought and received and (2) the physical inventory in stores and distribution centers. (Physical inventories are

In the seven days before Christmas, retailers have marked peaks in their sales that can amount to as much as 40% of their December sales figures.

typically taken semiannually.) Shrinkage varies by department and season. Typically, shrinkage also varies directly with sales. So if sales of men's tailored suits rise 10 percent, then the buyer can expect a 10 percent increase in shrinkage. Chapter 17 provides details on how retailers reduce inventory losses.

Monthly Reductions (Line 4)

The buyer calculates the monthly reductions in the same way as the monthly sales. The total reductions are multiplied by each percentage in line 3. In Exhibit 13–3,

$$\text{April reductions} = \$16,500 \times 40\% = \$6,600$$

4. Monthly Reductions	$16,500	$6,600	$2,310	$2,640	$1,980	$1,650	$1,320

BOM (Beginning-of-Month) Stock-to-Sales Ratio (Line 5)

The **stock-to-sales ratio** specifies the amount of inventory that should be on hand at the beginning of the month to support the sales forecast and maintain the inventory turnover objective. The numerator is BOM inventory (specified at retail), and the denominator is the forecasted sales for the month. Thus, a stock-to-sales ratio of 2 means that we plan to have twice as much inventory on hand at the beginning of the month as we plan to sell for that month.

5. BOM Stock to Sales Ratio	4.00	3.60	4.40	4.40	4.00	3.60	4.00

To reduce losses from internal theft, this sophisticated security device enables security personnel to monitor checkout lanes and sales transactions simultaneously.

The stock-to-sales ratio is equivalent to the amount of **months of supply** on hand at the beginning of the month. A stock-to-sales ratio of 2 means we have two months of inventory, or approximately 60 days, on hand at the beginning of the month. A stock-to-sales ratio of 1/2 represents a half month's supply of merchandise, or approximately 15 days, and so on. Many retailers prefer to express this relationship as weeks of supply instead of stock to sales or months of supply because of its conceptual simplicity. **Weeks of supply** is simply the months of supply times four weeks. So a stock-to-sales ratio and months of supply of 2 is equivalent to 8 weeks of supply.

As you will see in the next few paragraphs, there is a direct relationship between GMROI, the sales-to-stock ratio, inventory turnover, and the stock-to-sales ratio. Importantly, if inventory turnover is six times per year, on average you have a two-month supply of inventory, or an eight-week supply, and a BOM stock-to-sales ratio of 2. Likewise, a 24 inventory turn represents only a half month's supply (2 weeks), or 15-day supply, that is, a BOM stock-to-sales ratio of 1/2.

The stock-to-sales ratios are calculated in four steps.

Step 1: Calculate Sales-to-Stock Ratio   Recall from Chapter 12 that GMROI is equal to the gross margin percentage times the sale-to-stock ratio, where the sales-to-stock ratio is conceptually similar to inventory turnover except the inventory is expressed at cost instead of at retail. The GMROI is based on overall corporate financial objectives, and broken down into the gross margin and sales-to-stock ratio.

$$\text{GMROI} = \text{Gross margin \% } \times \text{ Sales-to-stock ratio}$$
$$122.72\% = \qquad 45\% \times \qquad 2.727$$

Note that since we are doing a six-month rather than an annual plan, the sales-to-stock ratio is based on six-month, rather than annual sales. So for this six-month period, we forecast 2.727 times as much sales as we have invested in cost inventory.

Step 2: Convert the Sales-to-Stock Ratio to Inventory Turnover   As stated in Chapter 12,

$$\text{Inventory turnover} = \text{Sales-to-stock ratio} \times (100\% - \text{Gross margin \%,}$$
$$\text{expressed as a decimal})$$
$$1.5 \qquad\qquad = \qquad 2.727 \quad \times \qquad .55$$

This adjustment is necessary since the sales-to-stock ratio defines sales at retail and inventory at cost, whereas inventory turnover defines both sales and inventory either at retail or at cost. Like the sales-to-stock ratio, this inventory turnover is based on a six-month period.

Step 3: Calculate Average Stock-to-Sales Ratio

$$\text{Average stock-to-sales ratio} = 6 \text{ months} \div \text{Inventory turnover}$$
$$4 \qquad\qquad = 6 \quad \div \qquad 1.5$$

(If preparing a 12-month plan, the buyer must divide 12 into the annual inventory turnover.) As with inventory turnover, both the numerator and denominator can be either at cost or at retail. Since the merchandise budget plan in Exhibit 13–1 is based on retail, it's easiest to think of the numerator as BOM retail inventory and the denominator as sales for that month. Thus, to achieve a six-month inventory turnover of 1.5, on average, the buyer must plan to have a BOM inventory that's four times the amount of sales for a given month. This is equivalent to four months of supply or 16 weeks of supply.

Even a buyer must be careful when thinking about the average stock-to-sales ratio. It can be easily confused with the sales-to-stock ratio. One isn't the inverse of the other, however. Sales are the same in both ratios. But stock in the sales-to-stock ratio is the average inventory at cost over all days in the period, whereas stock in the average stock-to-sales ratio is the average BOM inventory at retail. Also, the BOM stock-to-sales ratio is an average for all months. Adjustments are made to this average in line 5 to account for seasonal variation in sales.

Step 4: Calculate Monthly Stock-to-Sales Ratios   The monthly stock-to-sales ratios in line 5 must average the BOM stock-to-sales ratio calculated above to achieve the planned inventory turnover. Generally, monthly stock-to-sales ratios vary in the opposite direction of sales. That is, in months when sales are larger, stock-to-sales ratios are smaller, and vice versa.

The merchandise buyer must consider the seasonal pattern for men's tailored suits in determining the monthly stock-to-sales ratios. In the ideal situation, men's tailored suits arrive in the store the same day and in the same quantity that customers demand them. Unfortunately, the real-life retailing world isn't this simple. Note in Exhibit 13–3 (line 8) that men's tailored suits for the spring season start arriving slowly in April, yet demand lags behind these arrivals until the weather starts getting warmer. Monthly sales then jump from 12 percent of annual sales in May and June to 19 percent in July (line 1). But the stock-to-sales ratio (line 5) decreased from 4.4 in May and June to 4.0 in July. Thus, in months when sales increase (e.g., July), beginning-of-month inventory also increases (line 6) but at a slower rate. This causes stock-to-sales ratios to decrease. Likewise, in months when sales decrease dramatically, like in May (line 1), inventory also decreases (line 6), again at a slower rate, causing stock-to-sales ratios to increase (line 5).

How, then, should specific monthly stock-to-sales ratios be determined? When doing a merchandise budget plan for a classification that has accumulated history (like men's tailored suits), the buyer examines previous stock-to-sales ratios. To judge how adequate these past ratios were, the buyer determines if inventory levels were exceedingly high or low in any months. Then the buyer makes minor corrections to adjust for a previous imbalance in inventory levels.

We must also make adjustments for changes in the current environment. For instance, assume the buyer is planning a promotion for Memorial Day. Since this promotion has never been done before, the stock-to-sales ratio for that May should be adjusted downward to allow for the expected increase in sales. Caution: Monthly stock-to-sales ratios don't change by the same percentage as the percent distribution of sales by month is changing. In months when sales increase, stock-to-sales ratios decrease, but at a slower rate. Since there's no exact method of making these adjustments, the buyer must make some subjective judgments.

BOM Stock (Line 6)

The amount of inventory planned for the beginning of the month (BOM) equals

Monthly sales (line 2) × BOM stock-to-sales ratio (line 5)

When doing this multiplication, sales drops out of the equation, leaving BOM stock. In Exhibit 13–3,

BOM stock for April = $27,300 × 3.6 = $98,280

6. BOM Inventory	$98,280	$98,280	$68,640	$68,640	$98,800	$98,280	$78,000

EOM (End-of-Month) Stock (Line 7)

The BOM stock from the current month is the same as the EOM (end-of-month) stock in the previous month. So to derive line 7, the buyer simply moves the BOM stock in line 6 down one box and to the left.

In Exhibit 13–3, the EOM stock for April is the same as the BOM stock for May, $68,640. We must forecast ending inventory for the last month in the plan.

7. EOM Inventory	$65,600	$68,640	$68,640	$275,080	$98,280	$78,000	$65,600

Monthly Additions to Stock (Line 8)

The monthly additions to stock is the amount to be ordered for delivery in each month, given turnover and sales objectives.

Additions to stock = Sales (line 2) + Reductions (line 4) +
EOM inventory (line 7) – BOM inventory (line 6)

In Exhibit 13–3,

Additions to stock for April = $27,300 + 6,600 + 68,640 – 98,280 = $4,260

8. Monthly Additions to Stock	$113,820	$4,260	$17,910	$48,400	$26,160	$8,670	$8,420

This formula isn't particularly enlightening, so consider the following explanation. At the beginning of the month, the inventory level equals BOM stock. During the month, merchandise is sold and various reductions, such as markdowns, occur. So BOM stock minus monthly sales minus reductions equals EOM stock if nothing is purchased. But something must be purchased to get back up to the forecast EOM stock. The difference between EOM stock if nothing is purchased (BOM stock – sales – reductions) and the forecast EOM stock is the additions to stock.

Evaluating the Merchandise Budget Plan

GMROI, inventory turnover, and the sales forecast are used for both planning and control. The previous sections have described how they all fit together in planning the merchandise budget. A buyer negotiates a GMROI, inventory turnover, and sales forecast goal based on the top-down/bottom-up planning process described in Chapter 6. This plan is used to purchase men's tailored suits for the upcoming season. Well in advance of the season, the buyer purchases the amount of merchandise found in the last line of the merchandise budget plan to be delivered in those specific months—the monthly additions to stock.

After the selling season, the buyer must determine how the category actually performed compared to the plan for control purposes. If the actual GMROI, turnover, and forecast are greater than those in the plan, then performance is better than expected. No performance evaluation should be based on any one of these measures, however. Several additional questions must be answered to evaluate the buyer's performance: Why did the performance exceed or fall short of the plan? Was the deviation from the plan due to something under the buyer's control? (For instance, was too much merchandise purchased? Did the buyer react quickly to changes in demand by either purchasing more or having a sale? Was the deviation due to some external factor, such as a change in competitive level or economic activity?) Every attempt should be made to discover answers to these questions. Later in this chapter, we'll examine several additional tools used to evaluate merchandise performance.

OPEN-TO-BUY

The open-to-buy system starts after the merchandise is purchased using the merchandise budget plan or staple merchandise system. That is, these systems provide the buyer with a plan for purchasing merchandise. The **open-to-buy** system is one that keeps track of merchandise flows while they're occurring. Specifically, open-to-buy systems record how much is spent each month, and therefore how much is left to spend.

Even if everything in the buyer's merchandise budget for men's tailored suits goes according to plan, without careful attention to the record keeping performed in the open-to-buy system, the buyer will fail. Also, although the Rubbermaid buyer is purchasing merchandise that should be in the store year around, the buyer still needs to keep track of how much is purchased, compared to how much there is to spend in the budget.

In the same way that you must keep track of the checks you write, the buyer must keep careful records of the merchandise purchased and when it's to be delivered. Otherwise the buyer would buy too much or too little. Merchandise would be delivered when it wasn't needed, and it would be unavailable when it was needed. Sales and inventory turnover would suffer, rendering the merchandise budget plan and staple goods system useless. Thus, the open-to-buy system presented here is a critical component of the merchandise management process.

For simplicity, we will continue this example with the merchandise budget plan, although the open-to-buy system is also applicable to staple goods systems. For the merchandise budget plan to be successful (i.e., meet the sales, inventory turnover, and GMROI goals for a category), the buyer attempts to buy merchandise in quantities and with delivery dates such that the actual EOM stock for a month will be the same as the projected or forecasted EOM stock. For example, at the end of September, which is the end of the spring/summer season, the buyer would like to be completely out of spring/summer men's tailored suits so there will be room for the fall collection. Thus, the buyer would want the projected EOM stock and the actual EOM stock to both equal zero.

Using the Marketmax planning system, Exhibit 13–4 presents the six-month open-to-buy for the same category of men's suits discussed in the mer-

EXHIBIT 13–4 | Six-Month Open-to-Buy

Merch - Aged Soft	April	May	June	July	August	September
EOM Stock Plan	$68,640	$68,640	$98,800	$98,280	$78,000	$65,600
EOM Actuals	$59,500					
BOM Stock Plan	$98,280	$68,640	$68,640	$98,800	$98,280	$78,000
BOM Stock Actual	$95,000	$59,500				
Monthly Additions Plan	$4,260	$17,910	$48,400	$26,160	$8,670	$8,420
Monthly Additions Actuals	$3,500	$7,000				
OnOrder	$45,000	$18,000	$48,400			
Sales Plan	$27,300	$15,600	$15,600	$24,700	$27,300	$19,500
Sales Actuals	$26,900					
Monthly Reductions Plan	$6,600	$2,310	$2,640	$1,980	$1,650	$1,320
Monthly Reductions Actuals	$1,650					
Projected EOM Stock Plan	$59,500	$66,590	$96,750	$70,070	$41,120	$20,300
Projected BOM Stock Plan	$24,570	$59,500	$66,500	$96,750	$70,070	$41,120
OTB	$0.00	$2,050	$2,050	$28,210	$36,880	$45,300

Marketmax - In-Season Planning - Worksheet: Mens department (Business View: 'OTB : Global')
Worksheet — In-Season Management
Plan Edit View Tools Help
Skip To Month
Loc - 10 — Spring

chandise planning section earlier in the chapter. So, for instance, in April our EOM stock was planned to be $68,640, but it was actually $59,500. Note also that most of the row entries also appear in the merchandise budget plan: EOM stock, BOM stock, monthly additions to stock, monthly sales, and monthly reductions.

Calculating Open-to-Buy for Past Periods

The way we view open-to-buy and how it is calculated vary depending on whether we're looking at a past period or at the current period. Let's start with a past period. We're now in the middle of May—April is over. Notice that there's an entry for actual April EOM stock ($59,500), but not one for February. The calculation of open-to-buy at the end of a period is easy. Since the month is over, we know that the actual EOM stock is equal to the projected EOM stock. Open-to-buy is zeroed out because there's no point in buying merchandise for a month that's already over. Thus,

$$\text{Projected EOM stock plan} = \text{EOM actuals}$$
$$\$59,500 = \$59,500$$
$$\text{Open-to-buy} = 0$$

Calculating Open-to-Buy for the Current Period

Now let's look at May, the current month. Notice that there is a BOM stock actual of $59,500, but there is no EOM stock actual because the month has started but it hasn't finished. When calculating the open-to-buy for the current month, the projected EOM stock plan comes into play. Think of the projected EOM stock plan as a new and improved estimate of the planned EOM stock from the merchandise budget plan. This new and improved version takes information into account that wasn't available when the merchandise budget plan was made. The formula for projected EOM stock plan is

Actual BOM stock	59,500
+ Monthly additions actual (what merchandise was actually received)	+ 7,000
+ On order (what is on order for the month)	+ 18,000
– Sales plan	– 15,600
– Monthly reductions plan	– 2,310
Projected EOM stock plan	= $66,590

Although this formula may seem complicated, think of it this way: The projected EOM stock is equal to the inventory we have at the beginning of the month plus what we buy minus what we get rid of through sales or other inventory reductions.

The open-to-buy formula used during the current month is simply the difference between what you originally planned to end with from the merchandise budget plan (EOM stock plan) and what you think you will end with based on information collected during the month (projected EOM stock plan):

$$\text{Open-to-buy plan} = \text{EOM stock planned} - \text{Projected EOM stock}$$
$$\$2,050 = \$68,640 - \$66,590$$

This means that we have $2,050 left to spend in February if we want to reach our planned EOM stock of $68,640. If the open-to-buy was negative, we would have overspent our budget.

As this section's example shows, the assortment planning process can be complicated. In an actual multistore chain, the process is even more complex than in our example. A good assortment plan requires a fine mix of subjective and experienced judgments, a good information system, and a systematic method of keeping historical records. Now let's look at how multistore retailers allocate merchandise to stores.

ALLOCATING MERCHANDISE TO STORES

Once the buyer has purchased either fashion or staple merchandise, it is typically allocated to stores by the merchandise planner. Retailers utilize historical sales information, but they pay close attention to current supply and demand situations to determine the proper inventory allocation. For instance, if a retailer is having difficulty meeting demand because a vendor is unable to deliver, or if actual sales are lagging behind the forecast, the retailer will have to adjust the historically derived allocation downward.

Exhibit 13–5 illustrates a traditional percent contribution method through which a planner allocates additions to stock of $150,000 among 15 stores to girls' traditional $35 denim jeans in light blue.

EXHIBIT 13–5
Breakdown by Store of Traditional $35 Denim Jeans in Light Blue

(1) Type of Store	(2) Number of Stores	(3) Percentage of Total Sales, Each Store	(4) Sales per Store (total sales × col. 3)	(5) Sales per Store Type (col. 2 × col. 4)	(6) Unit Sales per Store (col. 4/$35)
A	4	10.0%	$15,000	$60,000	429
B	3	6.7	10,000	30,000	286
C	8	5.0	7,500	60,000	214
Total sales $150,000					

Chain stores traditionally classify their stores as A, B, or C stores based on their potential sales volume (column 1). This chain has four A stores, each of which is expected to sell 10 percent of the total, equaling $15,000 per store; three B stores, each expected to sell 6.7 percent, equaling $10,000 per store; and eight C stores, each expected to sell 5 percent, equaling $7,500 per store (columns 2, 3, and 4). The percentage breakdown (column 3) is based on historical records for similar merchandise for that chain.

Every chain's allocation of merchandise to stores is different. A **core assortment** is a relatively large proportion of the total assortment that is carried by each store in the chain, regardless of size. The core assortment is necessary to maintain the image of the chain. If the chain were to cut back the assortment too far in smaller stores, customers would perceive the smaller stores as having an inferior assortment. Hence, smaller stores require a higher-than-average stock-to-sales ratio. The opposite is true for stores with larger-than-average sales. For instance, one major department store chain allocates merchandise to stores as follows:[2]

	Fewer Sales, More Inventory						More Sales, Less Inventory	
Percentage of total sales	1	1.5	2.5	3.5	4	6	8	12
Percentage of total inventory	1.5	2	3	4	4	4	6	10

This means that if a store generates 4 percent of the sales of a classification for the chain, it should also receive 4 percent of the inventory. Note that stores with sales below 4 percent require proportionally more inventory. For instance, the smallest store, which generates only 1 percent of sales, requires 1.5 percent of the total inventory—inventory equals 1.5 times the level of sales.

Even though this store has low sales, it still needs to stock an adequate assortment and backup stock. Customers must not feel that just because the store is small or has relatively low sales that it isn't well stocked.

At the other extreme, stores with sales greater than 4 percent require proportionally less inventory. The largest store, with sales of 12 percent, requires only 10 percent of the inventory allocation for the classification—here inventory equals 83 percent of sales. This store can boost inventory turnover by receiving more frequent shipments. Also, thanks to high sales, the largest store can present an aesthetically pleasing, well-stocked look with less inventory.

Sales per store (column 4 of Exhibit 13–5) is total sales multiplied by the percentage of total sales for each store. Thus, the four A stores are each expected to generate sales of $15,000.

Sales per store type (column 5) is the number of stores (column 2) times sales per store (column 4). Thus, combined sales for the four A stores is $60,000. The jeans are expected to sell for $35. Therefore, unit sales per store is dollar sales per store (column 4) divided by $35. Thus, each A store is expected to sell 429 units.

The process of allocating merchandise to stores that we just described is useful for fashion merchandise and new staple items. As merchandise sells, it must be replenished, either by the vendor or through distribution centers. As discussed in Chapter 10, retailers use either a pull or a push distribution strategy to replenish merchandise. With a pull distribution strategy, orders for merchandise are generated at the store level on the basis of demand data captured by point-of-sale terminals. With a push distribution strategy, merchandise is allocated to the stores on the basis of historical demand, the inventory position at the distribution center, and the needs of the stores. As Chapter 10 noted, a pull strategy is used by more sophisticated retailers because it's more responsive to customer demand.

ANALYZING MERCHANDISE PERFORMANCE

As part of the ongoing merchandise planning process, retailers should continually ask when to add or delete SKUs, vendors, classifications, or departments. Here we examine three procedures for analyzing merchandise performance. The first, known as ABC analysis, is a method of rank-ordering merchandise to make inventory stocking decisions. The second procedure, a sell-through analysis, compares actual and planned sales to determine whether early markdowns are required or whether more merchandise is needed to satisfy demand. The third approach is a method for evaluating vendors using the multiattribute model.

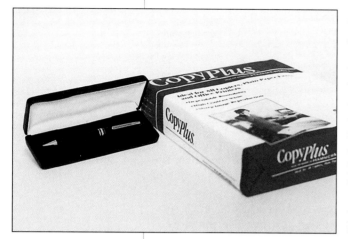

At Office Depot, copier paper is an "A" item, while a Mont Blanc pen is a "B" item. What could be a "C" item at Office Depot?

ABC Analysis

ABC analysis rank-orders merchandise by some performance measure to determine which items should never be out of stock, which items should be allowed to be out of stock occasionally, and which items should be deleted from the stock selection.[3] An ABC analysis can be done at any level of merchandise classification, from the SKU to the department. The SKU is the level of analysis discussed in this section.

ABC analysis utilizes the general 80–20 principle that implies that approximately 80 percent of a retailer's sales or profits come from 20 percent of the products. This means that retailers should concentrate on products that provide the biggest bang for their buck.

The first step in the ABC analysis is to rank-order SKUs using one or more criteria. The most important performance measure for this type of analysis is contribution margin:

Contribution margin = Net sales – Cost of goods sold – Other variable expenses

An example of an "other variable expense" in retailing is sales commissions. It's important to do ABC analyses using multiple performance measures since different measures give the planner different information. Other measures commonly used in ABC analysis are sales dollars, sales in units, gross margin, and GMROI.

Some less profitable items, like portable appliances, may be high in sales dollars or units. Such items are often important because they draw people into the store. It may also be important to carry some low-profit/high-volume merchandise because such merchandise complements other items in the store. For instance, batteries may sell at a low price, but they're necessary to sell cameras, radios, and flashlights.

Sales or gross margin per square foot measures are also useful in ABC analyses. For instance, a line of sunglasses may not appear particularly profitable in comparison to other items on the basis of contribution margin, sales, or units. But the display also takes relatively little space. Thus, performance of the merchandise on a square-foot basis may be very high.

The next step is to determine how items with different levels of profit or volume should be treated differently. Consider the dress shirts for a chain of men's stores in Exhibit 13–6. Even though the exact distribution varies across products, the general shape of the curve is the same for most types of products due to the 80–20 principle. Here the planner has defined the A, B, C, and D SKUs by rank-ordering each SKU by sales volume and examining the distribution of those sales.

The planner defines A items as those that account for 5 percent of items and represent 70 percent of sales. These items should never be out of stock. A items can be expensive to carry because they generally require high levels of backup stock to buffer against variations in demand and lead times. They include most sizes of long- and short-sleeve white and blue dress shirts.

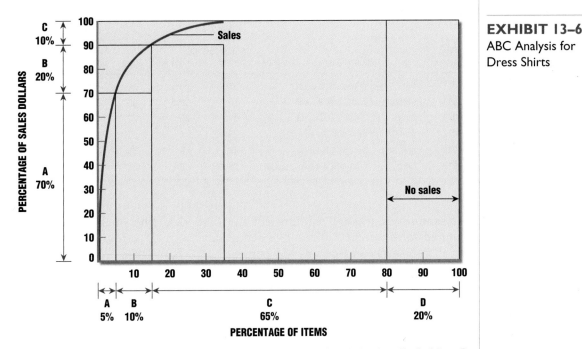

EXHIBIT 13–6
ABC Analysis for
Dress Shirts

SOURCE: Reprinted with permission of The Free Press, a Division of Simon & Schuster, from the *Distribution Handbook,* James F. Robeson and Robert G. House, eds. Copyright © by The Free Press.

B items represent 10 percent of the SKUs and an additional 20 percent of sales. The store should pay close attention to the B items, which include some of the other better-selling colors and patterned shirts. Occasionally, however, it will run out of some SKUs in the B category because it's not carrying the same amount of backup stock as for A items.

C items account for 65 percent of SKUs but contribute only 10 percent of sales. The planner may plan to carry C items only in certain odd sizes (very small or very large), with special orders used to solve out-of-stock conditions.

Although the analysis is called ABC, there are also D items. D items, the remaining 20 percent of SKUs, had no sales whatsoever during the past season, having become out of date or shopworn. Not only is excess merchandise an unproductive investment, but it also distracts from the rest of the inventory and clutters the store. Most retailers with excess merchandise should have a simple decision strategy: Mark it down or give it away, but get rid of it. Retailing View 13.3 looks at the tough decisions that Victoria's Secret has to deal with in evaluating its assortment of bras.

Sell-Through Analysis

A **sell-through analysis** is a comparison between actual and planned sales to determine whether early markdowns are required or whether more merchandise is needed to satisfy demand. Exhibit 13–7 shows a sell-through analysis for blouses for the first two weeks of the season. Because the blouses are very high fashion items, the buyer believes that, if necessary, corrective action should be made to the buying plan after only two weeks.

EXHIBIT 13–7
Sell-Through Analysis for Blouses

Stock Number	Description		WEEK 1 Plan	WEEK 1 Actual-to-Plan Actual	WEEK 1 Actual-to-Plan Percentage	WEEK 2 Plan	WEEK 2 Actual-to-Plan Actual	WEEK 2 Actual-to-Plan Percentage
1011	Small	White silk V-neck	20	15	−25%	20	10	−50%
1011	Medium	White silk V-neck	30	25	−16.6	30	20	−33
1011	Large	White silk V-neck	20	16	−20	20	16	−20
1012	Small	Blue silk V-neck	25	26	4	25	27	8
1012	Medium	Blue silk V-neck	35	45	29	35	40	14
1012	Large	Blue silk V-neck	25	25	0	25	30	20

Examine the week 1 columns for the first SKU, the small white blouse. Planned sales were 20 units. The actual sales were 15 units. Therefore, the actual-to-plan percentage was −25 percent [(15 − 20) ÷ 20 = −25 percent]. This means that actual sales were 25 percent less than the planned sales. In fact, the actual-to-plan percentage is negative for all of the white blouses and positive for all of the blue blouses.

RETAILING VIEW   Evaluating Bra Assortment at Victoria's Secret

13.3

In a busy Victoria's Secret store in New York's SoHo district, Amanda White, 27, picks up a matching set of leopard-print bra and undies, a black negligee, a turquoise lace bra, and three simple cotton bras, in pale blue, white, and yellow. After about a half-hour in the fitting rooms, she walks out of the store carrying three items: the simple cotton bras. "My boyfriend won't love these, but I need something I can wear everyday," she says.

Victoria's Secret has more bad news for Ms. White's boyfriend. The chain, which built its image as a sexy-lingerie retailer with expensive ad campaigns featuring famous models, wants to include more basic, less-expensive styles of lingerie. American women seem to prefer them. The move carries risks but has a clear business logic: A large majority of the bras sold at Victoria's Secret fall into the so-called glamour category with lace or push-up features. But between 70 to 80 percent of the total bra market in the United States still consists of what some women call "workhorse" bras—simple styles that are comfortable and durable—analysts say.

Victoria's Secret, a unit of Limited Inc., Columbus, Ohio, wants a larger "share of drawer" in its customers' dressers and hopes to grab a good chunk of the everyday market currently dominated by other lingerie players and from retailers such as Gap Inc. and J. Crew, which have their own lingerie lines.

Adjusting an assortment from sexy to practical is a tricky business. So far, however, the strategy is working: When the company launched its "Body by Victoria" collection in 1999, a simple line of bras in nylon and spandex that promised its wearers, "all you see is curves," it quickly became a best-seller. Victoria's Secret is considering expanding its line of cotton lingerie.

The move to plainer styles is perilous because the company could smudge its image as a purveyor of fancy lingerie. Its brand says "sexy," but being too sexy has given the company problems in the past, such as when Victoria's Secret made a misstep in its sleepwear range for the 2000 holiday. It offered a lot of see-through negligees and too few flannel pajamas. Sales fell. In 2002, the stores were full of linen and cotton pajamas for spring.

Also, if it is going to continue to grow, the company must expand its market. Although its image is still "26 and sexy," not every Victoria's Secret client fits that image anymore. To broaden its appeal, instead of featuring models in black lace, thigh-high stockings on the cover, one recent catalog touted, "NEW! SEXY SUPPORT." Underneath, in smaller print, is written, "Sizes 34B–40DD."

Source: Sarah Ellison, "Is Less Risqué Risky for Victoria's Secret?" *The Wall Street Journal,* May 20, 2002, p. B1. Copyright 2002 by Dow Jones & Co. Inc. Reproduced with permission of Dow Jones & Co. Inc. via Copyright Clearance Center.

What should the buyer do? There's no exact rule for determining when a markdown is necessary or when more merchandise should be ordered. The decision depends on experience with the merchandise in the past, whether the merchandise is scheduled to be featured in advertising, whether the vendor can reduce the buyer's risk by providing markdown money (funds a vendor gives a retailer to cover lost gross margin dollars that result from markdowns), and other merchandising issues. In this case, however, it appears that the white blouses are selling significantly less than planned. Therefore, early markdowns are probably justified to ensure that the merchandise isn't left unsold at the end of the season.

The decision regarding the blue blouses isn't so clear, though. The small blue blouses are selling slightly ahead of the plan. The medium blue blouses are selling briskly. The large blue blouses are selling ahead of plan only in the second week. In this case, the buyer may need to wait another week or two before a distinct sales pattern emerges. If actual sales stay significantly ahead of planned sales, a reorder should be made.

Multiattribute Method

The multiattribute method for evaluating vendors uses a weighted average score for each vendor. This score is based on the importance of various issues and the vendor's performance on those issues. This method is identical to the multiattribute approach that can be used to understand how customers evaluate stores and merchandise (discussed in Chapter 4).

To illustrate the multiattribute method for evaluating vendors, either current or proposed, consider the example in Exhibit 13–8 for a vendor of men's tailored suits. A buyer can evaluate vendors by using the following five steps:

1. Develop a list of issues to consider in the decision (column 1).[4] A balance should be made between having too short or too comprehensive a list of issues. Too short a list will ignore some relevant issues. Too long a list will be hard to use. Also, the list should be balanced so that one dimension of vendor performance doesn't receive too much attention. For instance, if there are three issues dealing with different aspects of a vendor's promotional package and only one with product characteristics, promotional considerations will receive too much attention in the overall evaluation.

2. Importance weights for each issue in column 1 should be determined by the buyer/planner in conjunction with the merchandise manager (column 2). Here we used a scale of 1 to 10, where 1 equals not important and 10 equals very important. In developing these importance scores, be sure that all issues don't receive high (or low) ratings. For instance, the buyer and the merchandise manager might believe that vendor reputation should receive a 9 since it's very important. Merchandise quality could receive a 5 since it's moderately important. Finally, a vendor's selling history is less important, so it could be rated 3.

3. Make judgments about each individual brand's performance on each issue (the remaining columns). This procedure should also be a joint decision between the category and merchandise managers. Note that some brands have high ratings on some issues but not on others.

4. We can't evaluate the overall performance of the vendors without combining the importance and performance scores. We do this by multiplying the importance for each issue by the performance for each brand or its vendor. For instance, vendor reputation importance (9) multiplied by the performance rating (5) for brand A is 45. Vendor promotional assistance importance (4) multiplied

EXHIBIT 13–8
Evaluating a Vendor:
A Weighted Average
Approach

Issues (1)	Importance Evaluation of Issues *(I)* (2)	PERFORMANCE EVALUATIONS OF INDIVIDUAL BRAND ACROSS ISSUES			
		Brand A (P_a) (3)	Brand B (P_b) (4)	Brand C (P_c) (5)	Brand D (P_d) (6)
Vendor reputation	9	5	9	4	8
Service	8	6	6	4	6
Meets delivery dates	6	5	7	4	4
Merchandise quality	5	5	4	6	5
Markup opportunity	5	5	4	4	5
Country of origin	6	5	3	3	8
Product fashionability	7	6	6	3	8
Selling history	3	5	5	5	5
Promotional assistance	4	5	3	4	7
Overall evaluation $\sum_{i=1}^{n} I_j * P_{ij}$		290	298	212	341

$\sum_{i=1}^{n}$ = Sum of the expression

I_j = Importance weight assigned to the *i*/th dimension

P_{ij} = Performance evaluation for *j*/th brand alternative on the *i*/th issue

1   = Not important

10 = Very important

by the performance rating (7) for vendor D is 28. This type of analysis illustrates an important point: It doesn't pay to perform well on issues that customers don't believe are very important. Although vendor D performed well on promotional assistance, the buyer didn't rate this issue highly on importance so the resulting score was still low.

5. To determine a vendor's overall rating, sum the product for each brand for all issues. In Exhibit 13–8, brand D has the highest overall rating (341) so D is the preferred vendor.

SUMMARY

This chapter (the second to deal with merchandise management) built on basic concepts and tools of assortment planning described in Chapter 12. Buying systems for staple merchandise are very different than for fashion merchandise. Since information is available on past sales for each SKU, it is relatively straightforward to forecast future merchandise needs.

The sales forecast and inventory turnover described in Chapter 12 work together to drive the merchandise budget plan for fashion merchandise. The sales forecast is broken down by month, based on historical seasonality patterns. It's necessary to

purchase more in months when sales are forecast to be higher than average. Planned inventory turnover is converted to stock-to-sales ratios and used in the merchandise budget plan to determine the inventory level necessary to support sales. Monthly stock-to-sales ratios are then adjusted to reflect seasonal sales patterns. The end product of the merchandise budget planning process is the dollar amount of merchandise a buyer should purchase each month for a category if the sales forecast and inventory turnover goals are to be met.

The open-to-buy system begins where the merchandise budget plan and staple goods inventory management systems leave off. It tracks how much merchandise is purchased for delivery in each month. Using an open-to-buy system, buyers know exactly how much money they've spent compared to how much they plan to spend.

Once the merchandise is purchased, merchandise buyers in multistore chains must allocate the merchandise to stores. Not only must the buyers look at the differences in sales potential among stores, they also must consider the differences in the characteristics of the customer base.

In the end, the performance of buyers, vendors, and individual SKUs must be determined. We examined three different approaches to evaluating merchandise performance. In ABC analysis, merchandise is rank-ordered from highest to lowest. The merchandising team uses this information to set inventory management policy. For example, the most productive SKUs should carry sufficient backup stock so as to never be out of stock. The second evaluation technique, sell-through analysis, is more useful for examining the performance of individual SKUs. The buyer compares actual-to-planned sales to determine whether more merchandise needs to be ordered or whether the merchandise should be put on sale. Finally, the multiattribute method is most useful for evaluating vendors' performance. The chapter concludes with Appendix 13A, in which we examine the retail inventory method.

KEY TERMS

ABC analysis, *420*
basic stock list, *406*
core assortment, *418*
deseasonalized demand, *408*

months of supply, *412*
open-to-buy, *415*
order point, *408*
shrinkage, *411*

sell-through analysis, *421*
stock-to-sales ratio, *412*
weeks of supply, *412*

GET OUT & DO IT!

1. INTERNET EXERCISE Go to www. retex.com. How are Retex products being used by retailers today? Which retailers are using Retex products?

2. INTERNET EXERCISE Go to www.mar ketmax.com. How are their products different than Retex? Which retailers are using marketmax products? Who would you hire, Retex or Marketmax?

3. CD-ROM EXERCISE The merchandise budget plan determines how much merchandise should be purchased in each month of a fashion buying season (in dollars), given the sales and reduction forecast, inventory turnover goals, and the seasonal monthly fluctuations in sales.

Go to the student CD accompanying *Retailing Management*, and click on Merchandise Budget Plan. The merchandise budget plan generally covers one fashion season for one merchandise category. This application presents both a one-month and a six-month example. In addition, practice calculations are presented for the one-month example. So have your calculator ready. Finally, in the calculation section you have access to an Excel-based six-month merchandise budget plan that can be used for doing Case number 20 in the text.

4. CD EXERCISE The Vendor Evaluation Model utilizes the multiattribute method for evaluating vendors described in the chapter.

Go to the student CD that accompanies *Retailing Management*, and click on Vendor Evaluation Model. There are two spreadsheets. Open the first spreadsheet, vendor evaluation 1.xls. This spreadsheet is the same as Exhibit 13–8. If you were selling Brand A to the retailer, which numbers would change? Change the numbers in the matrix and see the effect of the numbers you might change on the overall evaluation.

Go to the second spreadsheet, labeled evaluation 2.xls. This spreadsheet can be used to evaluate brands or merchandise you might stock in your store. Assume you own a bicycle shop. List the brands you might consider stocking and the issues you would consider in selecting brands to stock. Fill in the importance of the issues (10 = very important, 1 = not very important) and the evaluation of each brand on each characteristic (10 = excellent, 1 = poor). Determine which is the best brand for your store.

DISCUSSION QUESTIONS AND PROBLEMS

1. Inventory shrinkage can be a problem for many retailers. How does the merchandise budget planning process account for inventory shrinkage?

2. Using the following information, calculate additions to stock:

Sales	$24,000
EOM stock	$90,000
BOM stock	$80,000

3. Using the following information, calculate the average beginning-of-month stock-to-sales ratio for a six-month merchandise budget plan:

GMROI	150%
Gross margin	40%

4. Today is July 19. The buyer is attempting to assess his current open-to-buy given the following information:

Actual BOM stock	$50,000
Monthly additions actual	25,000
Merchandise on order to be delivered	10,000
Planned monthly sales	30,000
Planned reductions	5,000
Planned EOM stock	65,000

   What is the open-to-buy on July 19? What does this number mean to you?

5. Now it is July 31 and we need to calculate the open-to-buy for August given the following information:

Planned monthly sales	$20,000
Monthly additions actual	40,000
Planned markdowns	5,000
Projected BOM stock	50,000
Projected EOM stock	30,000

   Calculate open-to-buy and explain what the number means to you.

6. Typically, August school supplies sales are relatively low. In September, sales increase tremendously. How does the September stock-to-sales ratio differ from the August ratio?

7. Using the 80–20 principle, how can a retailer make certain that there's enough inventory of fast-selling merchandise and a minimal amount of slow-selling merchandise?

8. What's the order point and how many units should be reordered if a food retailer has an item with a 7-day lead time, 10-day review time, and daily demand of 8 units? Say 65 units are on hand and the retailer must maintain a backup stock of 20 units to maintain a 95 percent service level.

9. A buyer at a sporting goods store in Denver receives a shipment of 400 ski parkas on October 1 and expects to sell out by January 31. On

November 1, the buyer still has 375 parkas left. What issues should the buyer consider in evaluating the selling season's progress?

10. If you have a stock-to-sales ratio of 2, how many months of supply do you have? How many weeks of supply?

11. A buyer is trying to decide from which vendor to buy a certain item. The item can be purchased as either a manufacturer brand or private-label brand. Using the following information, determine which vendor the buyer should use.

	PERFORMANCE EVALUATIONS OF BRANDS		
Issues	**Importance Weight**	**Manufacturer Brand**	**Private-Label Brand**
Vendor reputation	8	5	5
Service	7	6	7
Meets delivery dates	9	7	5
Perceived merchandise quality	7	8	4
Markup opportunity	6	4	8
Demand-generating ability	5	7	5
Promotional assistance	3	6	8

SUGGESTED READINGS

Bauer, Michael J.; Charles C. Poirier, Lawrence Lapide; and John Bermudez. *E-Business: The Strategic Impact on Supply Chain and Logistics.* Chicago: Council of Logistics Management, 2001.

Beninati, Marie. "A Blueprint for Local Assortment Management." *Chain Store Age Executive with Shopping Center Age*, February 1997, pp. 27, 28.

Bohlinger, Maryanne Smith. *Merchandise Buying.* 5th ed. New York: Fairchild Books, 2001.

Campo, Katia; Els Gijsbrechts; and Patricia Nisol. "Towards Understanding Consumer Response to Stock-Outs." *Journal of Retailing*, 76, no. 2 (Summer 2000), pp. 219–42.

Grewal, Dhruv; Michael Levy; Anuj Mehrotra; and Arun Sharma. "Planning Merchandising Decisions to Account for Regional and Product Assortment Differences." *Journal of Retailing* 75, no. 3 (Fall 1999), pp. 405–24.

Kunz, Grace I. *Merchandising: Theory, Principles, and Practice.* New York: Fairchild Books, 1998.

Lawrence, F. Barry; Brian E. Reynolds; and Daniel F. Reynolds. *E-Distribution*, Cincinnati: South-Western Thomson Learning, 2002.

Powers, James T. *The Retail Inventory Method Made Practical.* New York: National Retail Federation, 1971.

Russell, Gary J., and Ann Peterson. "Analysis of Cross Category Dependence in Market Basket Selection." *Journal of Retailing* 76, no. 3 (Fall 2000), pp. 367–92.

Tepper, Bette K. *Mathematics for Retail Buying.* 5th ed., 2002. Fairchild Books.

APPENDIX 13A   Retail Inventory Method

Like firms in most industries, retailers can value their inventory at cost—and in fact, some retailers do so. Yet many retailers find significant advantages to the retail inventory method (RIM).[5] RIM has two objectives:

1. To maintain a perpetual or book inventory in terms of retail dollar amounts.

2. To maintain records that make it possible to determine the cost value of the inventory at any time without taking a physical inventory.

THE PROBLEM

Retailers generally think of their inventory at retail price levels rather than at cost. They take their initial markups, markdowns, and so forth as percentages of retail. (These terms are thoroughly defined in Chapter 15 and the Glossary.) When retailers compare their prices to competitors', they compare their retail prices. The problem is that when retailers design their financial plans, evaluate performance, and prepare financial statements, they need to know the cost value of their inventory. One way to keep abreast of their inventory cost is to take physical inventories. Anyone who has worked in retailing knows that this process is time-consuming, costly, and not much fun. So retailers usually only take physical inventories once or twice a year. By the time management receives the results of these physical inventories, it's often too late to make any changes.

Many retailers use POS terminals that easily keep track of every item sold, its original cost, and its final selling price. The rest of the retail world faces the problem of not knowing the cost value of its inventory at any one time. RIM can be used by retailers with either computerized or manual systems.

ADVANTAGES OF RIM

RIM has five advantages over a system of evaluating inventory at cost.

- The retailer doesn't have to "cost" each time. For retailers with many SKUs, keeping track of each item at cost is expensive and time-consuming, and it increases the cost of errors. It's easier to determine the value of inventory with the retail prices marked on the merchandise than with unmarked or coded cost prices.

- RIM follows the accepted accounting practice of valuing assets at cost or market, whichever is lower. The system lowers the value of inventory when markdowns are taken but doesn't allow inventory's value to increase with additional markups.

- As a by-product of RIM, the amounts and percentages of initial markups, additional markups, markdowns, and shrinkage can be identified. This information can then be compared with historical records or industry norms.

- RIM is useful for determining shrinkage. The difference between the book inventory and the physical inventory can be attributed to shrinkage.

- The book inventory determined by RIM can be used in an insurance claim in case of a loss (e.g., due to fire).

DISADVANTAGES OF RIM

RIM is a system that uses average markup. When markup percentages change substantially during a period, or when the inventory on hand at a particular time isn't representative of the total goods handled in terms of markup, the resulting cost figure may be distorted. As with inventory turnover, merchandise budget planning, and open-to-buy, RIM should be applied on a category basis to avoid this problem.

The record-keeping process involved in RIM is burdensome. Buyers must take care so that changes made to the cost and retail inventories are properly recorded.

STEPS IN RIM

Exhibit 13–9 is an example of RIM in action. The following discussion, which outlines the steps in RIM, is based on this exhibit.

Calculate Total Goods Handled at Cost and Retail

To determine the total goods handled at cost and retail:

1. *Record beginning inventory at cost* ($60,000) *and at retail* ($84,000). The initial markup is reflected in the retail inventory.

Total Goods Handled	Cost		Retail	
Beginning Inventory		$60,000		$84,000
Purchases	$50,000		$70,000	
– Return to vendor	(11,000)		(15,400)	
Net purchases		39,000		54,600
Additional markups			4,000	
– Markup cancellations			(2,000)	
Net markups				2,000
Additional transportation		1,000		
Transfers in	1,428		2,000	
– Transfers out	(714)		(1,000)	
Net transfers		714		1,000
Total goods handled		$100,714		$141,600

Reductions	Retail	
Gross sales	$82,000	
– Customer returns and allowances	(4,000)	
Net sales		$78,000
Markdowns	6,000	
– Markdown cancellations	(3,000)	
Net markdowns		3,000
Employee discounts		3,000
Discounts to customers		500
Estimated shrinkage		1,500
Total reductions		$86,000

EXHIBIT 13–9

Retail Inventory Method Example

2. *Calculate net purchases* ($39,000 at cost and $54,600 at retail) by recording gross purchases ($50,000 at cost and $70,000 at retail) and adjusting for merchandise returned to vendor ($11,000 at cost and $15,400 at retail).

3. *Calculate net additional markups* ($2,000) by adjusting gross additional markups ($4,000) by any additional markup cancelations ($2,000). *Note:* These are recorded only at retail because markups affect only the retail value of inventory.

4. *Record transportation expenses* ($1,000). Here transportation is recorded at cost because it affects only the cost of the inventory.

5. *Calculate net transfers* ($714 at cost and $1,000 at retail) by recording the amount of transfers in and out. A transfer can be from one department to another or from store to store. Transfers are generally made to help adjust inventory to fit demand. For instance, a sweater may be selling well at one store but not at another. A transfer is,

in effect, just like a purchase (transfer in) or a return (transfer out). Thus, it's recorded at both cost and retail.

6. *The sum is the total good handled* ($100,714 at cost and $141,600 at retail).

Calculate Retail Reductions Reductions are the transactions that reduce the value of inventory at retail (except additional markup cancelations, which were included as part of the total goods handled). Reductions are calculated as follows:

1. *Record net sales.* The largest reduction in inventory is sales. Gross sales ($82,000) are reduced to net sales ($78,000) by deducting customer returns and allowances ($4,000).

2. *Calculate markdowns.* Net markdowns ($3,000) are derived by subtracting any markdown cancellations ($3,000) from gross markdowns ($6,000).

3. *Record discounts to employees ($3,000) and customers ($500).*

4. *Record estimated shrinkage ($1,500).* Estimated shrinkage is used to determine the ending book inventory if the buyer is preparing an interim financial statement. The estimate is based on historical records and is presented as a percentage of sales. Estimated shrinkage wouldn't be included, however, if a physical inventory was taken at the time the statement was being prepared. In this case, the difference between physical inventory and book inventory would be the amount of shrinkage due to loss, shoplifting, and so forth.

5. *The sum is the total reductions ($86,000).*

Calculate the Cumulative Markup and Cost Multiplier The cumulative markup is the average percentage markup for the period. It's calculated the same way the markup for an item is calculated:

$$\text{Cumulative markup} = \frac{\text{Total retail} - \text{Total cost}}{\text{Total retail}}$$

$$28.87\% = \frac{\$141,600 - \$100,714}{\$141,600}$$

The cumulative markup can be used as a comparison against the planned initial markup. If the cumulative markup is higher than the planned initial markup, then the category is doing better than planned.

The cost multiplier is similar to the cost complement.

$$\text{Cost multiplier} = (\$100\% - \text{Cumulative markup \%})$$

$$71.13\% = 100\% - 28.87\%$$

or

$$\frac{\text{Total cost}}{\text{Total retail}} = \frac{\$100,714}{\$141,600} = 71.13\%$$

The cost multiplier is used in the next step to determine the ending book inventory at retail.

Determine Ending Book Inventory at Cost and Retail

$$\begin{aligned}\text{Ending book} \\ \text{inventory at retail}\end{aligned} = \begin{aligned}\text{Total goods handled at retail} \\ - \text{Total reductions}\end{aligned}$$

$$\$55,600 = \$141,600 - \$86,000$$

The ending book inventory at cost is determined in the same way that retail has been changed to cost in other situations—multiply the retail times (100% – gross margin percentage). In this case,

$$\begin{aligned}\text{Ending book} \\ \text{inventory} \\ \text{at cost}\end{aligned} = \begin{aligned}\text{Ending book inventory at retail} \\ \times \text{Cost multiplier}\end{aligned}$$

$$\$39,548 = \$55,600 \times 71.13\%$$

Buying Merchandise

CHAPTER

EXECUTIVE BRIEFING | Stephanie Calhoun, Senior Assistant Buyer, JCPenney Company

"Growing up, I was interested in the fashion industry and the retail arena. My passion for fashion triggered my drive to pursue a career in fashion merchandising. My primary focus was the buying side of the business. At this point in my career, I have served on both sides of the business, stores and buying. I must say that I have enjoyed them both."

Stephanie started her career as a merchandise management trainee in the JCPenney store in Hurst, Texas. She quickly advanced to increasing levels of responsibility in various positions: senior merchandise manager, district staff, and college relations manager. "When I was college relations manager, I really found it rewarding and satisfying to tell aspiring business students about the wonderful benefits the retail industry could offer."

Still, her childhood dreams of becoming a buyer were never forgotten. In May 2001, an opportunity presented itself: Stephanie was promoted to a senior assistant buyer in Special Occasion Dresses.

In this position, "I am responsible for providing input to the buyer in building detailed assortment plans. I am also responsible for confirming the delivery schedule and quantity of the products chosen and communicating this information to the vendors. In order to maintain a competitive advantage over other leading department stores, it's imperative that we have good vendor relationships. Communication and trust are critical in these relationships. You have to be honest in sharing any information about the merchandise.

"Finally, the buying process is really a numbers game. I spend a lot of time analyzing and interpreting sales data. I need to know what's selling profitably and what's not. The numbers tell us what merchandise we need to reorder. All these numbers may make buying seem a little monotonous, but it is really a thrill to see how your merchandise is performing.

"Overall, I have enjoyed a wonderful and exciting career with the JCPenney Company and I look forward to more rewarding challenges in the future."

In the preceding two chapters, we discussed the process that buyers go through to determine what and how much merchandise to buy. But the process of buying merchandise is not all analytical. There are lots of subjective issues that buyers and their merchandise managers must deal with strategically and on a day-to-day basis.

Specifically, retailers must determine their branding strategy. Should they buy well-known national brands, or should they develop private brands with their own name on it? The issue of branding goes hand in hand with international sourcing decisions, particularly for those retailers purchasing private-label merchandise. How should retailers determine whether they should buy merchandise made in other countries or from their home country?

Retailers also must determine how and where they will meet and communicate with their vendors. Will it be face to face or over the Internet? Negotiations occur when communicating with vendors on purchasing. There are many issues, such as price and delivery times, that need to be negotiated. Retailers need to plan ahead for these negotiations and leave as little as possible to chance. A good negotiator can easily make his or her yearly salary in one good negotiating session.

Many retailers have developed strategic partnerships with some of their vendors. In this chapter, we examine why these relationships can be important and what it takes to solidify a strategic partnership.

This chapter concludes with two appendixes. The first examines the ethical and legal issues surrounding purchasing merchandise. The second describes the terms under which merchandise is purchased from vendors. The various types of discount and payment date combinations that vendors offer are illustrated.

BRANDING STRATEGIES

Buyers have lots of branding choices. They can buy manufacturer brands like Levi's, Kellogg's, or Black & Decker. Or they can develop their own private labels like Gap jeans, America's Choice cookies from A&P, or Craftsman tools from Sears. Some use a mix of the two. In this section, we examine the relative advantages of these branding decisions, which are summarized in Exhibit 14–1.

Manufacturer Brands

Manufacturer brands, also known as **national brands,** are products designed, produced, and marketed by a vendor. The manufacturer is responsible for developing the merchandise and establishing an image for the brand. In some cases, the manufacturer will use an umbrella or family-branding strategy in which its name appears as part of the brand name for a specific product, such as Kellogg's Corn Flakes. However, some manufacturers, such as Philip Morris—owner of Kraft Foods, Miller Brewing Company, as well as Philip Morris (tobacco products)—don't associate their name with the brand. Exhibit 14–2 shows some of the most recognizable apparel and accessories brands.

Some retailers organize some of their categories around their most important national brands. For instance, buyers in department stores are responsible for brands, such as Clinique or Estée Lauder, rather than for products, such as lipstick and fragrances. Clothing is also often organized by manufacturer brand (e.g., Polo/Ralph Lauren, Levi's, Liz Claiborne, or DKNY). These brands often have their own boutique within stores. Managing a category by national brand, rather than a more traditional classification scheme, is useful so that merchandise can be purchased in a coordinated manner around a central theme. However, as we indicated in Chapter 12 there are problems with managing merchandise at a brand rather than category level.

EXHIBIT 14–1

Relative Advantages of Manufacturer versus Private Brands

Impact on Store	TYPE OF VENDOR	
	Manufacturer Brands	**Private-Label Brands**
Store loyalty	?	+
Store image	+	+
Traffic flow	+	+
Selling and promotional expenses	+	−
Restrictions	−	+
Differential advantages	−	+
Margins	?	?

+ advantage to the retailer, − disadvantage to the retailer, ? depends on circumstances.

EXHIBIT 14–2
Most Recognized
Apparel and Accessory
Brands

Rank	Brand	Product
1	L'eggs	Leg wear
2	Hanes	Hosiery, innerwear
3	Hanes Her Way	Underwear, daywear, bras, at-home wear, body wear, baby wear, kids' wear, casual wear, socks, casual shoes
4	Levi Strauss	Jeans wear, licensing
5	Nike	Active wear, athletic foot wear, accessories, sporting goods
6	Liz Claiborne	Sportwear, dresses, licenses
7	Lee	Jeans wear
8	No-nonsense	Leg wear
9	London Fog	Outerwear, rain wear
10	Playtex	Bras, shape wear
Private-Label Brands		
13	Victoria's Secret	Bras, day wear, hosiery, robes, sleepwear, swimwear, casual wear, ready-to-wear, beauty, bath, and body products
15	The Gap	Jeans and sportswear
27	Eddie Bauer	Outerwear, sportswear
28	Land's End	Sportswear, outerwear, accessories
36	Anne Klein	Sportswear, licensing
45	Jaclyn Smith	Sportswear, accessories, hosiery, intimate apparel
46	Esprit	Sportswear, shoes, children's wear, accessories, retail
51	Arizona	Denim items and casual sportswear
68	Frederick of Hollywood	Bras, panties, day wear, sleepwear, robes, ready-to-wear, bath and body products
74	Kathie Lee Collection	Dresses and sportswear for Wal-Mart
83	Tiffany	Fine jewelry, watches, tabletop, accessories
90	Cartier	Fine jewelry, watches, luxury products

Source: "The Fairchild 100," *Women's Wear Daily*, January 2000, www.wwd.com. Courtesy of Fairchild Publications.

Liz Claiborne (cotton top), Nike (Pegasus running shoes), and Levi's jeans are among the most recognized national brands in the U.S.

Buying from vendors of manufacturer brands can help store image, traffic flow, and selling/promotional expenses (see Exhibit 14–1). Retailers buy from vendors of manufacturer brands because they have a customer following—people go into the store and ask for them by name. Loyal customers of manufacturer brands generally know what to expect from the products and feel comfortable with them.

Manufacturers devote considerable resources to creating demand for their products. As a result, relatively less money is required by the retailer for selling and promotional expenses for manufacturer brands. For instance, Guess? Inc., manufacturer of jeans and other casual clothing, attempts to communicate a constant and focused message to the consumer by coordinating advertising with in-store promotions and displays.

Manufacturer brands typically have lower realized gross margins than private-label brands. These lower

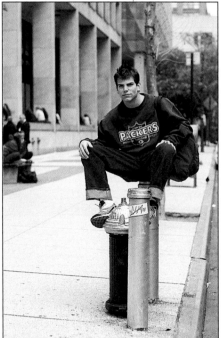

The use of the Green Bay Packer logo is licensed to the manufacturer of this sweatshirt by the Green Bay Packers football team.

REFACT

Macy's was among the first department stores to pioneer the concept of private brands for fashion goods. In the 1890s, its "Macy's" and "Red Star" brands were the rage in New York.[2]

gross margins are due to the manufacturer assuming the cost of promoting the brand and increased competition among retailers selling these brands. Typically, many retailers offer the same manufacturer brands in a market so customers compare prices for these brands across stores. Retailers often offer significant discounts on some manufacturer brands to attract customers to their stores.

Stocking national brands may increase or decrease store loyalty. If the manufacturer brand is available through a limited number of retail outlets (e.g., Lancôme cosmetics or Diesel jeans), customers loyal to the manufacturer brand will also become loyal to the limited number of stores selling the brand. If, on the other hand, manufacturer brands are readily available from many retailers in a market, customer loyalty may decrease because the retailer can't differentiate itself from competition.

Another problem with manufacturer brands is that they can limit a retailer's flexibility. Vendors of strong brands can dictate how their products are displayed, advertised, and priced. Jockey underwear, for instance, tells retailers exactly when and how its products should be advertised.

Licensed Brands   A special type of manufacturer brand is a **licensed brand,** in which the owner of a well-known brand name (licensor) enters a contract with a licensee to develop, produce, and sell the branded merchandise. The licensee may be either (1) the retailer that contracts with a manufacturer to produce the licensed product or (2) a third party that contracts to have the merchandise produced and then sells it to the retailer.

Licensed brands' market share has grown increasingly large in recent years. Owners of trade names not typically associated with manufacturing have also gotten into the licensing business. For instance, the manufacturer of the sweatshirt or baseball cap emblazoned with your university's logo pays your school a licensing fee. If it didn't, it would be infringing on the university's logo (a trademark) and therefore be involved in counterfeiting. (Counterfeiting is discussed in Appendix 14A of this chapter.) Retailing View 14.1 describes how the Olsen twins have introduced their licensed private-label clothing to the U.K.

Private-Label Brands

Private-label brands, also called **store brands,** are products developed by a retailer and available for sale only from that retailer. Refer back to Exhibit 14–2, which lists the most recognizable private-label brands. Note that only Victoria's Secret and The Gap are in the top 20 private-label brands. Exhibit 14–3 gives examples of more private-label brands. Typically, retail buyers or category managers develop specifications for the merchandise and then contract with a vendor to manufacture it. But the retailer, not the manufacturer, is responsible for promoting the brand.

Retailers' use of private labels was relatively small in the past for several reasons. First, national brands had been heavily advertised on TV and other media for decades, creating a strong consumer franchise. Second, it had been hard for retailers to gain the economies of scale in design and production necessary to compete against manufacturer brands. Third, many retailers weren't sophisticated enough to aggressively compete against manufacturer brands. Finally, private labels had a reputation of being inferior to manufacturer brands.

In recent years, as the size of retail firms has increased through consolidation, private labels have assumed a new level of significance by establishing distinctive identities among retailers. Some retailers, such as The Gap and The Limited, sell their own labels exclusively as an integral element of their distinctiveness. Other retailers, such as JCPenney and Sears, successfully mix manufacturer brands with their own retailer brands to project their unique image statement.

Private-branded products now account for an average of 25 percent of the purchases in the United States and roughly 45 percent in Europe.[3] Private-label dollar volume in supermarkets, drug chains, and mass merchandisers is increasing twice as fast as national brands.

Mary-Kate and Ashley Olsen Private Label Comes to U.K. RETAILING VIEW 14.1

Mary-Kate and Ashley are America's favorite teenagers. Superstars from birth, the typical southern Californian beauties are pretty and blonde and have perfect teeth. They may be only 15, but they have already starred in two sitcoms, sold 35 million copies of their videos, released 17 pop albums, launched clothing lines in Wal-Mart, and have written a shelf full of teen novels. They have their own magazine and website (www.marykateandashley.com) and are idolized by millions of teenage girls. America loves them so much that theirs is the most profitable teen brand in the country.

The phenomenon has come to Britain: 191 Asda stores have launched the Mary-Kate and Ashley range of clothing and accessories and are experiencing Olsenmania firsthand as British teenage girls lap them up. Paving the way for the clothes is their latest sitcom, *So Little Time.* Another sitcom, *Two of a Kind,* has been shown, and their books and videos are being introduced too. The girls have been in Britain to promote the clothing range.

The Asda private label, designed for girls aged 6 to 13, is typically American, with plenty of denim pieces, including shorts, jackets, and jeans decorated with stars and stripes motifs and matching jersey tops and T-shirts.

The sisters claim they started producing clothes because they couldn't find anything to wear. "We could never find anything that was stylish and affordable, so we ended up wearing adult clothes that had been altered," says Mary-Kate. "We thought maybe other kids were in the same boat, so we started the label."

Closely involved with the clothing label is executive designer Judy Swartz, who travels regularly to Europe in search of inspiration and presents trends to the central design team. Mary-Kate and Ashley pick a few trends they

Is the U.K. ready for Mary-Kate and Ashley Olsen?

like, and Swartz creates the drawings and styles, while the sisters choose fabrics and shapes. "We won't go with styles that we wouldn't like or wear," adds Mary-Kate.

Source: Molly Gunn, "Golden Girl Twins Set for Supermarket Sweep," March 28, 2002, www.fahion.telegraph.co.uk. Reprinted by permission.

EXHIBIT 14–3
Examples of Private-Label Brands

Industry	Store	Brand
Grocery stores	Safeway	Safeway Select
	Sobey's	Our Complements, Smartchoice
	A&P	Master Choice, American Choice
	Loblaw	President's Choice
	Wegman's	Wkids, Italian Classics
Chain stores	Kmart	Sesame Street, Martha Stewart, Benchtop
	Target	Merona, Sonia Kashuk, Honors, Michael Graves, Durabilt
	Wal-Mart	Sam's Choice, Popular Mechanics, Kathie Lee
	Sears	Kenmore, Diehard, Craftsman
	JCPenney	Arizona, St. John's Bay, Stafford, USA Olympic, Hunt Club, JCPenney Home Collection, Worthington, Jaqueline Ferrar
Department stores	May	Valerie Stevens, Karen Scott, Clairbrooke, Brandini
	Macy's	Charter Club
	Dillard's	Roundtree & York
	Nordstrom	Classiques Entier, Previews, Essentials, Premier, E-wear
Specialty stores	Neiman Marcus	Calerow, Will Swilly, Shelly Burton
	The Limited, Express	The Limited, Express
	Lowe's	Kobalt
	Home Depot	Husky

REFACT

Private labels are big business in Europe: Aldi's private brands account for 95 percent of its sales; Lidl, 80 percent; Sainsburys, 60 percent; Tesco's, 40 percent; Wal-Mart in Europe, 40 percent; and Carrefour, 33 percent.[5]

Offering private labels provides a number of benefits to retailers, as Exhibit 14–1 shows. First, the exclusivity of strong private labels boosts store loyalty. For instance, fashion designer Todd Oldham's line of home furnishings in Target stores, described in Retailing View 14.2, won't be found at JCPenney stores. A second advantage of buying from private-label vendors is that they can enhance store image if the brands are of high quality and fashionable. Third, like manufacturer brands, successful private-label brands can draw customers to the store. They can be a good deal—10 to 18 percent less expensive than national brands in the United States and as much as 25 percent cheaper in Europe.[4] Fourth, retailers that purchase private-label brands don't have the same restrictions on display, promotion, or price that often encumber their strategy with manufacturer brands. Retailers purchasing private brands also have more control over manufacturing, quality control, and distribution of the merchandise. Talbot's, for instance, can contract with any vendor to manufacture its private-label sweaters. Finally, gross margin opportunities may be greater.

But there are drawbacks to using private-label brands. Although gross margins may be higher for private-label brands than for manufacturer brands, there are other expenses that aren't readily apparent. Retailers must make significant investments to design merchandise, create customer awareness, and develop a favorable image for their private-label brands. When private-label vendors are located outside the United States, the complications become even more significant, as we'll see in the next section. Sales associates may need additional training to help them sell private-label brands against better-known brands. If the private-label merchandise doesn't sell, the retailer can't return the merchandise to the vendor. These problems are most severe for high-fashion merchandise.

Private-Label Options[6]   Retail branding strategies have run the gamut from closely imitating manufacturer-brand packaging and products to distinct brand images, from low product quality and prices to premium positioning, and from nonexistent promotion and merchandising to intense activity. We group private brands into four broad categories: copycat, bargain, premium, and parallel.

Bargain branding targets a price-sensitive segment by offering a no-frills product at a discount price. Known as **generic** or **house brands,** such unbranded, unadvertised merchandise is found mainly in drug, grocery, and discount stores. The bargain brand, frequently referred to as the house brand, generally is perceived by the consumer to be of lower quality, and its packaging identifies it as a brand of the retailer.

In the context of differentiating the retailer, bargain branding is primarily defensive. Its value comes from neutralizing competitors who may gain an advantage from discount pricing and by serving a secondary market segment whose patronage potentially leads to collateral sales.

Premium branding offers the consumer a private label at a comparable manufacturer-brand quality, usually with modest price savings. Safeway's Select

Target's Private Labels Have Cachet   RETAILING VIEW

14.2

Target is crafting a savvy strategy to gain cachet. In a bid to further distance itself from rivals, lure shoppers from other retailers, and capture higher profits, Target is stepping up its partnerships with designers. Target announced a deal with fashion designer Todd Oldham, who'll design a line of home furnishings that will appear in Target stores.

Target has long sought a position as a slightly higher-end discounter than Wal-Mart or Kmart, with cleaner and better-lighted stores. Target's strategy involves a whole range of designers. Target partnered with Mossimo Gian-nulli, a youth designer whose star had faded but then came back through his exclusive association with Target. It has also introduced a line of beauty products from makeup artist Sonia Kashuk.

The retailer has done a better job than Kmart of integrating all its designer brands through marketing and store layout so that they add to Target's cachet. Target's more upscale marketing and product message appeals to shoppers at a time when they're more willing to trade down to save money. Target's more upscale image helps attract higher-income shoppers.

Target is also aiming its designer strategy at the youth market. With the weak economy, teens, too, are more inclined to shop at a discounter. By positioning itself as a trendier retailer and offering designer goods other sellers don't have, Target differentiates itself from its toughest rival, Wal-Mart. Having more unique merchandise to attract shoppers allows Target to evade this trap and price everyday items at a price that's three to five percentage points higher. Target's cachet as a style-conscious discounter gives it an advantage in teaming up with higher-end designers, who might not want to be associated with Wal-Mart.

Target has partnered with fashion designers like Mossimo to create an unrivaled cachet among discount stores.

Source: Robert Berner, "Target's Aim: The Designer's Edge," *Business Week,* February 27, 2002. Reprinted by special permission of the McGraw-Hill Companies.

brand in grocery products and JCPenney's Worthington brand in women's clothing are two examples. The premium brand attempts to match or exceed the product quality standard of the prototypical manufacturer brand in its category. There is no intention to duplicate the packaging or to trade off the brand equity of a particular manufacturer brand. However, consumers frequently perceive the retailer premium labels as competing manufacturer brands.

Retailer premium brands, with the appearance of comparability, compete directly with manufacturer national brands. To succeed, the retailer must commit the resources in market research, product development, quality control, and promotion in its market area commensurate with its manufacturer-brand competitors. Consequently, development of a premium branding program precludes many retailers that have few resources from diverting to this strategy.

Copycat branding imitates the manufacturer brand in appearance and packaging, generally is perceived to be of lower quality, and is offered at a lower price. For example, copycat brands abound in the fragrance market. By not drawing attention to the brand's origin, the copycat can confuse the consumer about the source of the product. Copycat branding is a risky private-branding alternative because close copies can violate packaging and patent laws. Poor copies are ineffective.

Parallel branding represents private labels that closely imitate the packaging and product attributes of leading manufacturer brands but with a clearly articulated "invitation to compare" in its merchandising approach and on its product label. This invitation to compare on the product label was the basis for a recent legal action. Like copycat branding, parallel branding seeks to benefit from the brand equity of the manufacturer brand by closely imitating the national brand's packaging and product qualities. However, the invitation to compare leaves little doubt that different manufacturers produce the two products. Consequently, the imitative packaging does not constitute a trademark infringement. Nevertheless, patent considerations can be an issue if appropriate discretion is not used.

Parallel branding is a leveraging strategy used to bolster a retailer's private-brand sales. The closer two products are in form, logo, labeling, and packaging, the more they are perceived as substitutes. Parallel brands attempt to produce a product and packaging so similar to the manufacturer brand that the only noticeable difference between the two is price. This promotes the view that the parallel brand provides better value for the consumer. Manufacturer brands produce store traffic, and the parallel brand leverages this traffic into parallel brand sales through similar packaging and aggressive store signage, displays, and shelf location.

A Brand or a Store?

The distinction between a store and a brand has become blurred in recent years. Some large retailers have developed strong private-label merchandise. Other retailers, such as The Gap and its sister store Banana Republic, have such a strong brand name that the average consumer cannot make a distinction between store and brand. The Gap has capitalized on its strong name recognition by widening the variety of merchandise offered at its stores. It now sells personal care products like perfume, lotion, and lip gloss. Brooks Brothers (the traditional clothing retailer) and Crate & Barrel (the upscale soft home store chain) carry only merchandise with their names on it.

A natural extension of the retailer's brand strategy is to exploit a strong retail name recognition by selling its products through channels other than its own stores. For instance, Tiffany's, the upscale jewelry store with its flagship store in Manhattan and other outlets around the country, now sells its products to other jewelry stores. Starbucks staged one of the most aggressive moves by a retailer to broaden its customer base. The coffee shop retailer that brought middle America the "short, skinny, decaf latte" has teamed up with PepsiCo to market Frappuccino, a coffee-and-milk blend sold through traditional grocery channels. Starbucks also is engaged in a joint venture with Dreyer's Grand Ice Cream to distribute Starbucks coffee-flavored ice cream. Starbucks has entered into a long-term licensing agreement with Kraft Foods, Inc., to accelerate the growth of the Starbucks brand into the grocery channel in the United States. Kraft handles all distribution, marketing, advertising, and promotions for Starbucks whole-bean and ground coffee in grocery, warehouse club, and mass-merchandise stores.[7]

On the other side of the distribution spectrum, several firms that have traditionally been exclusively manufacturers have become retailers. Examples are Guess?, Calvin Klein, Ralph Lauren, Georgio Armani, Levi's, Harley-Davidson, Sony, and Nike. Why have these manufacturers chosen to become retailers? First, by becoming retailers they have total control over the way their merchandise is presented to the public. They can price, promote, and merchandise their line with a unified strategy. They don't have to worry about retailers cherry-picking certain items or discounting the price, for instance. Second, they can use these stores to test new merchandise and merchandising concepts. Based on these tests' results, they can better advise other retailers what to buy and how to merchandise their stores. Third, these manufacturers/retailers use their stores to showcase their merchandise to the public as well. The Sony and Nike stores, Ralph Lauren's flagship store in Manhattan, and Levi's flagship store in San Francisco have atmospheres that enhance the manufacturer's image as well as help to sell merchandise. Finally, although these stores often compete with stores that carry the same merchandise, some would argue that having a stronger retail presence creates a name recognition and synergy between the manufacturer and retailer that benefit both parties.

INTERNATIONAL SOURCING DECISIONS

 A decision that's closely associated with branding decisions, which we discussed in the previous section, is to determine where the merchandise is made. Retailers involved in private branding are faced with all of the issues that we'll examine in this section. Although retailers buying manufacturer brands usually aren't responsible for determining where the merchandise is made, a product's country of origin is often used as a signal of quality. Certain items are strongly associated with specific countries, and products from those countries, such as gold jewelry from Italy or cars from Japan, often benefit from those linkages.

In this section, we'll first examine the cost implications of international sourcing decisions. Superficially, it often looks like retailers can get merchandise from foreign suppliers cheaper than from domestic sources. Unfortunately, there are a lot of hidden costs, including managerial issues, associated with sourcing globally

REFACT

Apparel imports have risen from 5 percent of U.S. domestic consumption in 1970, to 25 percent in 1988, to over 50 percent by 1997.[8]

that make this decision more complicated. We then examine the trend toward sourcing closer to home or actually reversing the trend toward international sourcing by buying "made in America." This section concludes by exploring ethical issues associated with retailers who buy from vendors engaged in human rights and child-labor violations.

Costs Associated with Global Sourcing Decisions

A demonstrable reason for sourcing globally rather than domestically is to save money. Retailers must examine several cost issues when making these decisions. The cost issues discussed in this chapter are country-of-origin effects, foreign currency fluctuations, tariffs, free trade zones, inventory carrying costs, and transportation costs.

Country-of-Origin Effects   The next time you're buying a shirt made in Western Europe (e.g., Italy, France, or Germany), notice that it's probably more expensive than a comparable shirt made in a developing country like Hungary, Ecuador, or Cambodia. These Western European countries have a reputation for high fashion and quality. Unfortunately for the U.S. consumer, however, the amount of goods and services that can be purchased from those countries with U.S. dollars is significantly less than the amount of merchandise that can be purchased from developing countries for the same amount of money. When making international sourcing decisions, therefore, retailers must weigh the savings associated with buying from developing countries with the panache associated with buying merchandise from a country that has a reputation for fashion and quality.

Other countries might have a technological advantage in the production of certain types of merchandise and can therefore provide their products to the world market at a relatively low price. For example, Japan has always been a leader in the development of consumer electronics. Although these products often enter the market at a high price, the price soon drops as manufacturers learn to produce the merchandise more efficiently.

Foreign Currency Fluctuations   An important consideration when making global sourcing decisions is fluctuations in the currency of the exporting firm. Unless currencies are closely linked, for example, between the United States and Canada, changes in the exchange rate will increase or reduce the cost of the merchandise.

Suppose, for instance, that Best Buy is purchasing watches from Swatch in Switzerland for $100,000, which is equivalent to 150,000 Swiss francs (SFr) since the exchange rate is 1.5 SFr for each U.S. dollar. If the dollar falls to, say, 1.1 SFr before the firm has to pay for the watches, it would end up paying $136,364 (or 150,000 SFr ÷ 1.1). The euro has all but eliminated this problem between the participating European countries.

When making global sourcing decisions, retailers must consider country-of-origin effects. Switzerland is known for its quality watches, while Japan is known for high-quality reliable automobiles.

PATEK PHILIPPE
GENÈVE

Jamais vous ne
posséderez complètement une Patek Philippe.
Vous en serez
juste le gardien, pour les générations futures.

Tariffs   A **tariff,** also known as a **duty,** is a tax placed by a government on imports.[10] Import tariffs have been used to shield domestic manufacturers from foreign competition and to raise money for the government. In general, since tariffs raise the cost of imported merchandise, retailers have always had a strong incentive to reduce them. The General Agreement on Tariffs and Trade (GATT), the North American Free Trade Agreement (NAFTA), and foreign trade zones all reduce tariffs.

World Trade Organization   The World Trade Organization (WTO) replaced GATT in 1996. With 144 member-countries, the WTO has become the global watchdog for free trade. As a result of the WTO and its predecessor GATT, worldwide tariffs have been reduced from 40 percent in 1947 to an estimated 4 percent in 2000.[11] The WTO will continue to push for tariff reductions on manufactured goods as well as liberalization of trade in agriculture and services.

North American Free Trade Agreement   The ratification of NAFTA on January 1, 1994, created a tariff-free market with 364 million consumers. NAFTA members are currently the United States, Canada, and Mexico. NAFTA is expected to strengthen North America's position when negotiating with the European Union.

U.S. retailers stand to gain from NAFTA for two reasons. First, Mexican labor is relatively low-cost and abundant. Thus, retailers can either search for low-cost suppliers in Mexico or begin manufacturing merchandise there themselves. **Maquiladoras**—plants in Mexico that make goods and parts or process food for export to the United States—are plentiful, have lower costs than their U.S. counterparts, and are located throughout Mexico, particularly in border towns such as Nogales and Tijuana. Second, with the growing importance of quick response inventory systems, the time it takes to get merchandise into stores becomes ever more critical. Transit times are shorter and managerial control problems are reduced when sourcing from Mexico, compared to the Far East or Europe.

Retailing View 14.3 describes how Wal-Mart has benefited from NAFTA.

Free Trade Zones   Retailers involved in foreign sourcing of merchandise can lower import tariffs by using free trade zones. A **free trade zone** is a special area within a country that can be used for warehousing, packaging, inspection, labeling, exhibition, assembly, fabrication, or transshipment of imports without being subject to that country's tariffs.

To illustrate how a free trade zone can benefit retailers, consider how German cars are imported to a foreign trade zone in Guatemala for distribution throughout Central America. The duty for passenger vehicles is 100 percent of the landed cost of the vehicle. The duty for commercial vehicles, however, is only 10 percent. The German manufacturer imported

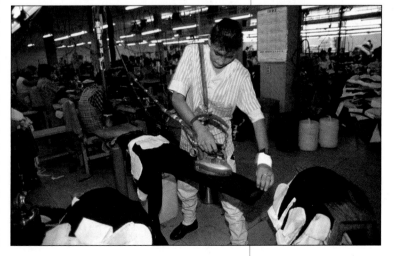

Maquiladoras are manufacturing plants in Mexico that make goods and parts or process food for export to the United States. They are very popular because their costs are lower than those of their U.S. counterparts.

commercial vans with no seats or carpeting, and with panels instead of windows. After paying the 10 percent import duty, it converted the vans to passenger station wagons in the free trade zone in Guatemala and sold them throughout Latin America.

Inventory Carrying Cost   The cost of carrying inventory is likely to be higher when purchasing from suppliers outside the United States than from domestic suppliers.

$$\text{Cost of carrying inventory} = \text{Average inventory value (at cost)} \\ \times \text{Opportunity cost of capital}$$

The **opportunity cost of capital** is the rate available on the next best use of the capital invested in the project at hand. It would include the cost of borrowing money for a similar investment, plus insurance and taxes.

There are several reasons for the higher inventory carrying costs. Consider The Spoke bicycle store in Aspen, Colorado, which is buying Moots bicycles manufactured in Steamboat Springs, Colorado. The Spoke knows that the **lead time**—the amount of time between recognition that an order needs to be placed

---

RETAILING VIEW | How NAFTA Helped Wal-Mart Reshape the Mexican Market

14.3

Shopkeeper Carlos Huerta recently walked into a Sam's Club warehouse store in Mexico City and bought $6,000 of Act II brand microwave popcorn. Then he trundled across the street to resell it at his stall in Latin America's biggest wholesale market.

Huerta used to buy the U.S.-made popcorn direct from the manufacturer's distributor here. But with the U.S.-Mexican border growing increasingly porous, Wal-Mart Stores Inc. now can deliver Act II to its Mexican Sam's Club outlets for only a few cents more than to its U.S. stores, undercutting the product's Mexican distributor.

"I've lost a lot of business," says Huerta, who sells mostly to small corner grocers. "Now, a lot of people just go directly to Sam's."

Squeezing out middlemen such as Huerta is just one of the ways in which Wal-Mart is changing the way Mexico does business. By seizing upon the new opportunities offered by free trade and exploiting its massive buying power and distribution network, Wal-Mart is replicating its U.S. success south of the Rio Grande. Barely a decade after it entered Mexico in anticipation of the North American Free Trade Agreement, Wal-Mart dominates this country's retail sector.

Wal-Mart's success here owes to more than just opening cavernous discount stores. It also stems from NAFTA, which has turned the United States, Mexico, and Canada into a single trading zone. After NAFTA took effect in 1994, tariffs tumbled, unleashing pent-up Mexican demand

for U.S.-made goods. The trade treaty helped eliminate some of the transportation headaches and government red tape that had kept Wal-Mart from fully realizing its competitive advantages here. And it sent European and Asian manufacturers racing to build new plants in the NAFTA zone, giving Wal-Mart cheaper access to more foreign brands.

Consider Sony Corp.'s Wega line of flat-screen television sets. In 1998, Ricardo Perera, Sam's Club's electronics buyer in Mexico City, imported a handful of Wegas from Japan. Wal-Mart offered the 29-inch Wegas for sale at about $1,600. The high price reflected a 23 percent import duty and the cost of shipping the sets across the Pacific. That year, Mexican Sam's Clubs sold just five of the TVs.

The following year, Sony built a giant Wega factory in the border town of Mexicali in order to take advantage of NAFTA. Locating the plant in Mexico allowed Sony to ship the plant's TVs anywhere in the NAFTA zone duty-free. Though Sony's primary target was the U.S. market, Perera spotted an opportunity.

The Mexican-made sets saved Sam's Club a bundle in shipping costs, and it passed those savings on to consumers. Today, Sam's Club sells the 29-inch Wega sets in Mexico for about $600, roughly what they fetch in the United States.

Source: David Luhnow, "How NAFTA Helped Wal-Mart Reshape the Mexican Market," *The Wall Street Journal*, August 31, 2001, pp. A1, A2. Copyright 2001 by Dow Jones & Co. Inc. Reproduced with permission of Dow Jones & Co. Inc. via Copyright Clearance Center.

and the point at which the merchandise arrives in the store and is ready for sale—is usually two weeks, plus or minus three days. But if The Spoke is ordering bikes from Italy, the lead time might be three months, plus or minus three weeks. Since lead times are longer, retailers must maintain larger inventories to ensure that merchandise is available when the customer wants it. Larger inventories mean larger inventory carrying costs.

It's also more difficult to predict exactly how long the lead time will be when sourcing globally. When the bicycle goes from Steamboat Springs to Aspen, the worst that could happen is getting caught in a snowstorm for a day or two. On the other hand, the bicycle from Italy might be significantly delayed because of multiple handlings at sea or airports, customs, strikes of carriers, poor weather, or bureaucratic problems. Similar to long lead times, inconsistent lead times require the retailer to maintain high levels of backup stock.

Transportation Costs   In general, the farther merchandise has to travel, the higher the transportation cost will be for any particular mode of transportation. For instance, the cost of shipping a container of merchandise by ship from China to New York is significantly higher than the cost from Panama to New York.

Managerial Issues Associated with Global Sourcing Decisions

In the previous section, we examined the specific costs associated with global sourcing decisions. In most cases, retailers can obtain hard cost information that will help them make their global sourcing decisions. The managerial issues discussed in this section—quality control and developing strategic partnerships—are not as easily evaluated.

Quality Control   When sourcing globally, it's harder to maintain and measure quality standards than when sourcing domestically. Typically, these problems are more pronounced in countries that are far away and underdeveloped. For instance, it's easier to address a quality problem if it occurs on a shipment of dresses from Costa Rica to the United States than if the dresses were shipped from Singapore because Costa Rica is much closer.

There are both direct and indirect ramifications for retailers if merchandise is delayed because it has to be remade due to poor quality. Suppose Banana Republic is having pants made in Haiti. Before the pants leave the factory, Banana Republic representatives find that the workmanship is so poor that the pants need to be remade. This delay reverberates throughout the system. Banana Republic could have extra backup stock to carry it through until the pants can be remade. More likely, however, it won't have advance warning of the problem, so the stores will be out of stock.

A more serious problem occurs if the pants are delivered to the stores without the problem having been detected. This could happen if the defect is subtle, such as inaccurate sizing. Customers can become irritated and question merchandise quality. Also, markdowns ensue because inventories become unbalanced and shopworn.

Building Strategic Partnerships   The importance of building strategic partnerships is examined later in this chapter. It is typically harder to build these alliances when sourcing globally, particularly when the suppliers are far away and in underdeveloped countries. Communications are more difficult. There is often a language barrier, and there are almost always cultural differences. Business practices—everything from terms of payment to the mores of trade practices such as commercial bribery—are different in a global setting. The most important element in building a strategic alliance—maintaining the supplier's trust—is more arduous in an international environment.

Source Close to Home or Buy "Made in America"?

Why are many U.S. retailers buying more merchandise "Made in America?" It may be less expensive. It is consistent with Quick Response inventory systems. Their customers prefer it. There are concerns about abuses of human rights and child labor in factories in other countries.

Some U.S. retailers are shifting suppliers from Asia and Europe to nearby Central American and Caribbean countries, or they're seeking products made in America. There are four reasons for this shift. First, it may be more profitable for all of the reasons that we detailed above.

Second, quick response delivery systems described in Chapter 10 and sourcing globally are inherently incompatible. Yet both are important and growing trends in retailing. Quick response systems are based on short and consistent lead times. Vendors provide frequent deliveries with smaller quantities. There's no room for defective merchandise. For a quick response system to work properly, there needs to be a strong alliance between vendor and retailer that is based on trust

and a sharing of information through electronic data interchange (EDI) and collaborative planning, forecasting, and replenishment (CPFR). In the preceding section we argued that each of these activities is more difficult to perform globally than domestically. Further, the level of difficulty increases with distance and the vendor's sophistication. Catalog and Internet retailer Coldwater Creek (www.coldwatercreek.com), for instance, sources about 75 percent of its merchandise from North America so it can purchase relatively small orders and receive quick delivery.[14]

The third reason why retailers are taking a close look at domestic sources of supply is that some of their customers prefer products that are made in America. Retailers are simply reacting to their customers' quality perceptions.

The fourth reason for sourcing closer to home is that it's easier to police potential violations of human rights and child labor. Sears, Wal-Mart, Ralph Lauren, The Gap, Nordstrom, J. Crew, The Limited, and others have had to publicly deflect allegations about human rights, child labor, or other abuses involving factories and countries where their goods are made.[15]

In China, for instance, many desperate for work have endured torture in sweatshops, where thousands of factories churn out goods for Western companies.[16] One former worker described the working condition as a life of fines and beating. Managers demanded long

In response to the U.S. anti-sweatshop movement, high-profile companies like Reebok, Nike, and Liz Claiborne Inc. are publishing reports about audits undertaken in their factories.

REFACT

American territories overseas are an attractive site for garment factories producing for consumers in the United States. Minimum wage is lower than on the mainland—$3.05 an hour in Saipan—and products can come in without import quotas or tariffs and bear a Made in America label. In Saipan, 30 factories make clothes for dozens of American brands like The Gap, Dayton Hudson, and The Limited.[17]

hours of their workers and sometimes hit them. Workers were locked in the walled factory compound for all but a total of 60 minutes a day for meals. Guards regularly punched and hit workers for talking back to managers or even for walking too fast. They were fined up to $1 for infractions such as taking too long in the bathroom, when their wage, on an average is only half cent an hour.

Wal-Mart, Payless, and other U.S. companies assure American consumers that their goods aren't produced under sweatshop conditions. In the early '90s, Wal-Mart required its suppliers to sign a code of basic labor standards. After exposés in the mid-1990s of abuses in factories making Kathie Lee products, which the chain carries, Wal-Mart and Kathie Lee both began hiring outside auditing firms to inspect supplier factories to ensure their compliance with the code. Many other companies that produce or sell goods made in low-wage countries do similar self-policing, from Toys "R" Us to Nike and The Gap. While no company suggests that its auditing systems are perfect, most say they catch major abuses and either force suppliers to fix them or yank production. Self-policing allows companies to avoid painful public revelations about them.

REFACT

Human rights advocates estimate that as many as one in 10 diamonds sold today is a "conflict" stone, meaning it came from a country—say, Sierra Leone, Angola, or the Congo—where the diamond trade uses slave labor and funds warlords who routinely kill innocent civilians.[18]

CONNECTING WITH VENDORS

Now that we've examined the different branding decisions available to retailers and the issues surrounding global sourcing, we will concentrate on how and where retailers connect with their vendors. Retailers "go to market" to see the variety of available merchandise and to buy. A **market,** from the retail buyer's perspective, is a concentration of vendors within a specific geographic location, perhaps even under one roof or over the Internet. These markets may be Internet exchanges, permanent wholesale market centers, or temporary trade fairs. Retailers may also buy on their own turf, either in stores or at corporate headquarters. Finally, buyers can use resident buying offices that prearrange opportunities for buyers to visit vendors in major market centers in the United States and abroad.

Internet Exchanges

As we have seen in previous chapters, especially Chapter 3, retailers are exploring many strategies that provide consumers with the tools they need to purchase merchandise and services from them. Retailers also use the Internet for doing research for buying merchandise or services.

One of the most innovative and potentially useful developments stemming from retailers' growing level of sophistication with the Internet is retail exchanges. **Retail exchanges** are electronic marketplace operated by organizations that facilitate the buying and selling of merchandise using the Internet. They provide an opportunity for vendors and retailers to interact electronically rather than meet face to face in a physical market. Retail exchanges can increase the efficiency of the buying process by integrating several of the systems we discussed in previous chapters, such as EDI (Chapter 10), with the ability to view merchandise and negotiate prices online. Although exchanges will never replace going to markets and interacting with vendors, they now make it possible for buyers to access any type of merchandise information with a mouse click.

In this section, we will describe what exchanges do and the types of exchanges that are currently in operation.

Functions of Exchanges   Retail exchanges are still evolving. As such, we still do not know which functions or activities will become the most valuable to retailers. Some of the more prominent exchange functions are directory, selection, pricing, collaboration, and content.

Directory   No longer do buyers have to wander trade shows or showrooms. Retail exchanges enable them to search for merchandise by vendor or type of product electronically.

Selection   Buyers can then narrow the search to a particular vendor. Much of what used to be accomplished in the vendor's showroom can now be done online. Buyers can view individual SKUs. With technology improving all the time, they can be increasingly confident in the online catalog's picture quality and color. To help determine order quantities, buyers can obtain sales history from prior seasons for specific SKUs or for complementary products. Rather than traveling to Paris or Milan, buyers can replay runway fashion shows and obtain 360-degree views of merchandise from the comfort of their offices.

Pricing   Retail exchanges utilize several pricing methods. In fact, the same exchange may use more than one pricing method depending on the situation. Merchandise can be offered at a fixed price where everyone pays the same amount. The price of merchandise can be negotiated. In this case, the exchange acts as a broker between vendors and retailers. Finally, merchandise can be auctioned.

In traditional auctions like those conducted by eBay, there is one seller and many buyers. Auctions conducted by retailer buyers are called **reverse auctions** because there is one buyer and many potential sellers. In reverse auctions, retail buyers provide a specification for what they want to a group of potential vendors. The competing vendors then bid down the price at which they are willing to sell until the buyer accepts a bid.[19] However, the retailer is not required to place an order with the lowest bidder. The retailer can chose to place the order at the price of vendor that the retailer feels will provide the merchandise in timely manner at the specified quality. For example, Bashas', a privately held supermarket chain based in Chandler, Arizona, uses reverse auctions to purchase about 70 percent of its meat. Twice weekly, seven competing suppliers bid for the business.[20]

Reverse auctions have not been very popular with vendors. Few want to be anonymous contestants in bidding wars where price alone, not service or quality, is the sole basis for winning the business. Strategic relationships are also difficult to nurture when the primary interactions with vendors are through electronic auctions.[21]

The most common applications for reverse auctions are to buy products and services used in retail operations rather than merchandise for resale. For example, a number of retailers worked together to develop a specification for POS terminal paper tape and then pooled their buying power to run a reverse auction and find a low-cost supplier that would meet all of their needs. Other operating materials that are frequently bought on reverse auctions are store carpeting, fixtures, and supplies. Reverse auctions can also be used by retailers to procure private-label merchandise, commodities (like the meat example above), and in and out seasonal merchandise like lawn furniture.

Collaboration   Collaboration with vendors on every phase of the production and distribution process may become the most important benefit of retail exchanges. We discussed EDI and quick response inventory systems in Chapter 10 and CPFR in Chapter 12. These systems are integral components of retail exchanges.

The fashion world, where a short time period from idea conception to store shelf is a key success factor, stands to benefit significantly from retail exchanges. Although retailers have always provided design input to their vendors, it is the speed and clarity with which collaboration is facilitated with exchanges that is important. Suppose a buyer spots a potentially hot item on the street or in a movie. She snaps a digital picture and concurrently sends it to a designer in Hong Kong and a fabric supplier in Thailand. The designer works out the specifications for the item, while the supplier sends both parties electronic versions of the fabric. All three parties collaborate on fine-tuning the design and product specifications. Not only does this collaborative effort shorten the lead time to market, but it minimizes the potential for errors.

Collaboration with other retailers for sourcing merchandise also has potential, but it may be difficult to achieve. Competing retailers aren't used to talking to each other. In fact, antitrust legislation may prohibit them from so doing. One senior executive of a major U.S. department store chain noted that it took six months to agree on the type of paper that should be purchased for giving receipts at point-of-sale terminals. He would not speculate about how long and what it would take for competing retailers to agree on a merchandise purchase.[22]

Content   Exchanges can even be an excellent source of general information. Many provide the latest industry news, trends, and fashions.

Types of Exchanges   There are three basic types of exchanges: consortium, private, and independent. These types of exchanges are defined in terms of who owns and operates the exchange.

Consortium Exchanges   A **consortium exchange** is a retail exchange that is owned by several firms within one industry. A firm must be a member of the consortium to participate in the exchange. The three primary consortium exchanges are Transora (www.transora.com), the WorldWide Retail Exchange (www.wwre.org), and GlobalNetXchange (www.gnx.com)

- Transora is a consortium of 50 leading food, beverage, and consumer products companies, including Heinz, Gillette, Coca-Cola, Kraft Foods, Procter & Gamble, Sara Lee, Unilever, NV, and the Grocery Manufacturers of America (the leading trade organization in the grocery industry).

- Unlike Transora, the WorldWide Retail Exchange is a consortium composed of 61 retailers (not manufacturers), including Ahold (the Netherlands), Albertson's, Best Buy, The Boots Company (U.K.), CVS, The Gap, JCPenney, Target, and Safeway.

- GlobalNetXchange is also a consortium composed of retailers. They include Carrefour (France), Kroger, Metro AG (Germany), J. Sainsbury Plc (U.K), Coles Myer (Australia), Pinault-Printemps-Redoute SA (Europe), and Sears.

WorldWideRetailExchange.org (WWRE.org), is a consortia exchange owned by retailers and used to facilitate the purchase of goods and services.

The potential advantage of these exchanges is that retailers can pool their buying power to get better prices and the fixed cost of developing the software and administering the exchange is shared across member-firms. However, coordinating the activities of different firms, and in some cases competing firms, has been difficult. There are often conflicting agendas between the founding members. Although not all members are in competition with one another, some are, making communication and goal setting complicated.[23] Also, since these exchanges are in competition with one another, companies are hesitant to back one for fear that it will be the wrong one. Finally, several major players have opted out of these consortia: Wal-Mart, Costco, Home Depot, Aldi, Office Depot, and Staples, just to name a few.

Private Exchanges   **Private exchanges** are exchanges that are operated for the exclusive use of a

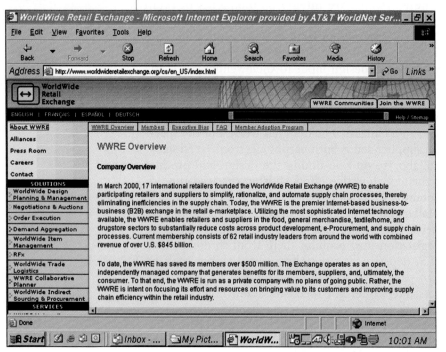

single firm. Although currently relatively small in number, they represent large players like Wal-Mart and Dell Computer. These larger companies have the size and scale to develop and operate their own exchanges. For example, Wal-Mart moved its existing information system, Retail Link, to the Internet.[24] Retail Link was built during the 1990s at an estimated cost of $1 billion. Wal-Mart's private network enables its 10,000 suppliers to get information about sales and inventory levels in every store. Its plans are to use its private exchange to consolidate purchasing worldwide, create global collaboration with its vendors, and bring suppliers online to compete for contracts. Although this and other exchanges are clearly designed to benefit the operator/owner, the vendors benefit from the strategic relationship and immediate access to sales and inventory data for planning purposes, such as CPFR.

Independent Exchanges   An **independent exchange** is a retail exchange owned by a third party that provides the electronic platform to perform the exchange functions. For example, a retailer is interested in running a reverse auction for an air-conditioning system. It contacts an independent exchange like FreeMarkets (www.freemarkets.com). In the previous weeks, the retailer's purchasing agent and prospective suppliers prepare for the auction with the help of FreeMarkets. Now, the purchasing agent and the 12 suppliers log on to a FreeMarket's secure private network, and the bidding begins. Within minutes, the purchasing agent has saved thousands of dollars from its historic spending level. New bids come in every couple of minutes, driving the unit price lower and lower. In the ensuing hours, more than 250 interactive bids are received, saving the retailer more than $400,000—a 16 percent savings below its historic spending level of $2.5 million.[25]

Wholesale Market Centers

For many types of merchandise, retailers can do much of their buying in established market centers. Wholesale market centers have permanent vendor sales offices retailers can visit throughout the year. Probably the world's most significant wholesale market center for many merchandise categories is in New York City. The Fashion Center, also known as the Garment District, is located from Fifth to Ninth Avenues and from 35th to 41st Streets. An estimated 22,000 apparel buyers visit every year for five market weeks and 65 annual related trade shows. The Garment District has 5,100 showrooms and 4,500 factories.[26]

The United States also has a number of regional wholesale market centers. The Dallas Market Center, the world's largest, is a 6.9-million-square-foot complex of six buildings.[27] Over 26,000 manufacturers and importers display their international products in its 2,200 permanent showrooms and 460,000 square feet of temporary spaces. Some regional centers have developed into national markets for specific merchandise categories (for example, the Miami Merchandise Mart for swimwear).

Trade Shows

Many wholesale market centers host **trade shows,** also known as **merchandise shows** or **market weeks.** Permanent tenants of the wholesale market centers and vendors leasing temporary space participate. Here retailers place orders and get a concentrated view of what's available in the marketplace. The Dallas Market Center conducts 50 markets annually, attended by more than 130,000 buyers for products ranging from floor coverings to toys, apparel, jewelry, and gifts. Trade shows are also staged by convention centers not associated with wholesale market centers. McCormick Place in Chicago (the nation's largest convention complex, with more than 2.2 million square feet) hosts over 65 meetings and trade shows per year, including the National Hardware Show, National House-wares Manufacturers Association International Exposition, and National Sporting Goods Association Market.[29]

Buying on Their Own Turf

Although buyers go to wholesale market centers and trade shows to search for new merchandise, place orders, and meet with vendors, vendors also work with buyers in their offices. Most buying activity in buyers' offices is for basic merchandise or rebuys on fashion merchandise.

Resident Buying Offices

Resident buying offices are organizations located in major buying centers that provide services to help retailers buy merchandise. Doneger Group and Associated Merchandising Corporation (owned by Target Corp.[30]) are the two primary buying offices in the United States. As retailers have become larger and more sophisticated, the third-party resident buying offices have become less important in recent years. Retailers simply perform the services formerly provided by these buying offices themselves.

To illustrate how buying offices operate, consider how David Smith of Pockets Men's Store in Dallas utilizes his resident buying offices when he goes to market in Milan. Smith meets with market representative Alain Bordat of the Doneger Group. Bordat, an English-speaking Italian, knows Smith's store and his upscale customers, so in advance of Smith's visit he sets up appointments with Italian vendors he believes would fit Pockets' image.

When Smith is in Italy, Bordat accompanies him to the appointments and acts as translator, negotiator, and accountant. Bordat informs Smith of the cost of importing the merchandise into the United States, taking into account duty, freight, insurance, processing costs, and so forth.

Once the orders are placed, Bordat writes the contracts and follows up on delivery and quality control. The Doneger Group also acts as a home base for buyers like Smith, providing office space and services, travel advisers, and emergency aid. Bordat and his association continue to keep Smith abreast of what's happening on the Italian fashion scene through reports and constant communication. Without the help of a resident buying office, it would be difficult, if not impossible, for Smith to penetrate the Italian wholesale market.

NEGOTIATING WITH VENDORS

Negotiations are as basic to human nature as eating or sleeping. A negotiation takes place any time two parties confer with each other to settle some matter. Negotiations take place between parents and their children about issues like allowances. People negotiate with their friends about what to do on the weekend.

Business negotiations occur almost daily. People negotiate for higher salaries, better offices, and bigger budgets. Negotiations are crucial in buyers' discussions with vendors.

No one should go into a negotiation without intensive planning. We first provide guidelines for planning negotiations with vendors. Then we discuss some tips for conducting the negotiation face to face.

Guidelines for Planning Negotiations with Vendors

As a vehicle for describing how a buyer should prepare for and conduct a negotiation with a vendor, consider the hypothetical situation in which Carolyn Swigler, men's designer shirt buyer at Lord & Taylor, is preparing to meet with Dario Carnevale, the salesman from Tommy Hilfiger, in her office in New York. Swigler is ready to buy Tommy Hilfiger's spring line, but she has some merchandising problems that have yet to be resolved from last season. Let's go over seven general guidelines for planning a negotiation session and seven for conducting a face-to-face negotiation session, all described in terms of Swigler's hypothetical situation.

KNOWLEDGE IS POWER! The more the buyer knows about the vendor, the better his negotiating strategy will be.

Consider History   Buyers need a sense of what has occurred between the retailer and vendor in the past. Though Swigler and Carnevale have only met a few times in the past, their companies have had a long, profitable relationship. A sense of trust and mutual respect has been established, which may work to Swigler's advantage in the upcoming meeting. An established vendor may be more likely to take care of old problems and accept new demands if a long-term, profitable relationship already exists.

Assess Where Things Are Today   Although Tommy Hilfiger shirts have been profitable for Lord & Taylor in the past, three patterns sold poorly last season. Some vendors believe that once they've sold merchandise to the retailer, their responsibility ends. This is a short-term perspective, however. If the merchandise doesn't sell, a good vendor, like Tommy Hilfiger, will arrange to share the risk of loss. Swigler will ask Carnevale to let her return some merchandise. Or Carnevale may provide markdown money—funds a vendor gives a retailer to cover lost gross margin dollars due to markdowns and other merchandising issues—usually in the form of a credit to the Lord & Taylor account.

Set Goals   Besides taking care of last season's leftover merchandise, the buyer Swigler has set goals in six areas for the upcoming meeting: additional markup opportunities, terms of purchase, transportation, delivery and exclusivity, communications, and advertising allowances.

Additional Markup Opportunities   Vendors may have excess stock (manufacturers' overruns) due to order cancelations, returned merchandise from retailers, or simply an overly optimistic sales forecast. To move this merchandise, vendors offer it to retailers at lower than normal prices. Retailers can then make a higher than normal gross margin or pass the savings on to the customer. Since Lord & Taylor is noted as a fashion leader, it probably isn't interested in any excess inventory that Tommy Hilfiger has to offer. Off-price retailers such as T. J. Maxx and Marshalls (both owned by TJX) or Internet retailer Bluefly.com specialize in purchasing manufacturers' overruns. Another opportunity for additional markups is with private-label merchandise, which we discussed earlier in this chapter.

Terms of Purchase   It's advantageous for buyers to negotiate for a long time period in which to pay for merchandise. Long terms of payment improve the firm's cash flow position, lower its liabilities (accounts payable), and can cut its interest expense if it's borrowing money from financial institutions to pay for its inventory. According to the Robinson-Patman Act, however, a vendor can't offer different terms of purchase or prices to different retailers unless the difference can be cost-justified. But buyers would be remiss if they didn't ask for the best terms of purchase available. (Terms of purchase are detailed in Appendix 14B to this chapter.)

Transportation   Transportation costs can be substantial, though this doesn't pose a big problem with the Tommy Hilfiger shirts due to their high unit cost and small size. Nonetheless, the question of who pays for shipping merchandise from vendor to retailer can be a significant negotiating point. (Transportation issues are part of the terms of purchase discussed in this chapter's Appendix 14B.)

Delivery and Exclusivity   In retailing in general, and in fashion in particular, timely delivery is essential. Being the only retailer in a market to carry certain products helps a retailer hold a fashion lead and achieve a differential advantage. Swigler wants to be certain that her shipment of the new spring line arrives as early in the season as possible, and that some shirt patterns won't be sold to competing retailers.

Communications   Vendors and their representatives are excellent sources of market information. They generally know what is and isn't selling. Providing good, timely information about the market is an indispensable and inexpensive marketing research tool, so Swigler plans to spend at least part of the meeting talking to Carnevale about market trends.

Advertising Allowances   Retailers have the choice of advertising any product in the store. They can sometimes share the cost of advertising through a cooperative arrangement with vendors known as co-op advertising—a program undertaken by a vendor in which the vendor agrees to pay all or part of a pricing promotion. By giving retailers advertising money based on a percentage of purchases, vendors can better represent their product to consumers. (Chapter 16 describes cooperative advertising.) Under the Robinson-Patman Act, vendors are allowed to give advertising allowances on an equal basis—the same percentage to everyone—usually based on a percentage of the invoice cost. As a fashion leader, Lord & Taylor advertises heavily. Swigler would like Tommy Hilfiger to support a number of catalogs with a generous ad allowance.

Know the Vendor's Goals and Constraints   Negotiation can't succeed in the long run unless both parties believe they've won. By understanding what's important to Carnevale and Tommy Hilfiger, Swigler can plan for a successful negotiating session. Generally, vendors are interested in providing a continuous relationship, testing new items, facilitating good communications, and providing a showcase to feature their merchandise.

A Continuous Relationship   Vendors want to make a long-term investment in their retailers. For seasonal merchandise like men's designer shirts, they have to plan their production in advance so it's important to Tommy Hilfiger that certain key retailers like Lord & Taylor will continue their support. Swigler plans to spend some time at the beginning of the meeting reviewing their mutually profitable past and assuring Carnevale that Lord & Taylor hopes to continue their relationship.

Testing New Items   There's no better way to test how well a new product will sell than to put it in a store. Retailers are often cautious with new items due to the risk of markdowns and the opportunity cost of not purchasing other, more successful merchandise. Yet vendors need their retailers to provide sales feedback for new items. Lord & Taylor has always been receptive to some of Tommy Hilfiger's more avant-garde styles. If these styles do well in certain Lord & Taylor stores, they'll likely succeed in similar stores around the country.

Communication   Just as Carnevale can provide market information to Swigler, she can provide sales information to him. Also, Swigler travels the world market. On one buying trip to England, she found an attractive scarf. She bought the scarf and gave it to Carnevale, who had it copied for a shirt. It was a big success!

Showcase   In certain urban centers—notably New York, Los Angeles, Dallas, London, Milan, and Paris—vendors use large stores to showcase their merchandise. For instance, many U.S. buyers go to market in New York. Most stop at Lord & Taylor to see what's new, what's selling, and how it's displayed. Thus, Carnevale wants to make sure that Tommy Hilfiger is well represented at Lord & Taylor.

A good understanding of the legal, managerial, and financial issues that constrain a vendor will facilitate a productive negotiating session. For instance, Swigler should recognize from past experience that Tommy Hilfiger normally doesn't allow merchandise to be returned, but does provide markdown money. If Carnevale initially says that giving markdown money is against company policy, Swigler will have strong objective ammunition for her position.

Plan to Have at Least as Many Negotiators as the Vendor   There's power in numbers. Even if the vendor is more powerful, aggressive, or important in the marketplace, the retailer will have a psychological advantage at the negotiating table if the vendor is outnumbered. At the very least, the negotiating teams should be of equal number. Swigler plans to invite her merchandise manager into the discussion if Carnevale comes with his sales manager.

Choose a Good Place to Negotiate   Swigler may have an advantage in the upcoming meeting since it will be in her office. She'll have everything at her fingertips, such as information plus secretarial and supervisory assistance. From a psychological perspective, people generally feel more comfortable and confident in familiar surroundings. On the other hand, if the negotiation were to be in Carnevale's office Swigler would be able to learn a lot about Carnevale and his company. Further, Swigler might get more out of the negotiation if Carnevale feels comfortable. In the end, the preferable location for a negotiation is a personal choice.

Be Aware of Real Deadlines   To illustrate the importance of deadlines, consider when labor strikes are settled. An agreement is often reached one minute before everyone walks out. There's always pressure to settle a negotiation at the last minute. Swigler recognizes that Carnevale must go back to his office with an order in hand since he has a quota to meet by the end of the month. She also knows that she must get markdown money or permission to return the unsold shirts by the end of the week or she won't have sufficient open-to-buy to cover the orders she wishes to place. Recognizing these deadlines will help Swigler come to a decisive closure in the upcoming negotiation.

Guidelines for Face-to-Face Negotiations

The most thoughtful plans can go astray if the negotiators fail to follow some important guidelines in the meeting. Here are seven tips for successful negotiations, including separating people from the problem, insisting on objective criteria, and inventing options for mutual gain.[31]

Separate People from the Problem   Suppose Swigler starts the meeting with "Carnevale, you know we've been friends for a long time. I have a personal favor to ask. Would you mind taking back $10,000 in shirts?" This personal plea puts Carnevale in an uncomfortable situation. Swigler's personal relationship with Carnevale isn't the issue here and shouldn't become part of the negotiation.

An equally detrimental scenario would be for Swigler to say, "Carnevale, your line is terrible. I can hardly give the stuff away. I want you to take back $10,000 in shirts. After all, you're dealing with Lord & Taylor. If you don't take this junk back, you can forget about ever doing business with us again." This approach serves as a personal attack on Carnevale. Even if he had nothing to do with the shirts' design, Swigler is attacking his company. Reminding Carnevale that he's dealing with a larger concern like Lord & Taylor is threatening and would probably further alienate him. Finally, threats usually don't work in negotiations; they put the other party on the defensive. Threats may actually cause negotiations to break down, in which case no one wins.

Conversely, if Carnevale takes a personal, aggressive, or threatening stance in the negotiations, what should Swigler do? Let him talk. If Swigler allows Carnevale to work through his aggression or anger, it will probably dissipate like a tropical storm going out to sea. Listen. Swigler may find that Carnevale's problem can be easily resolved. Finally, apologize if necessary. Even if Swigler doesn't believe she or Lord & Taylor did anything to cause Carnevale's anger, an apology that doesn't admit to any personal or corporate responsibility will probably calm him down.

Insist on Objective Criteria   The best way to separate people from the problem is to insist on objective criteria. Swigler must know exactly how many shirts need to be returned to Tommy Hilfiger or how much markdown money is necessary to maintain her gross margin.

If Carnevale argues from an emotional perspective, Swigler should stick to the numbers. For instance, suppose that after Swigler presents her position,

Carnevale says that he'll get into trouble if he takes back the merchandise or provides markdown money. With the knowledge that Tommy Hilfiger has provided relief in similar situations in the past, Swigler should ask what Tommy Hilfiger's policy is regarding customer overstock problems. She should also show Carnevale a summary of Lord & Taylor's buying activity with Tommy Hilfiger over the past few seasons. Using this approach, Carnevale is forced to acknowledge that providing assistance on this overstock situation—especially if it has been done in the past—is a small price to pay for a long-term profitable relationship.

Invent Options for Mutual Gain   Inventing multiple options is part of the planning process, but knowing when and how much to give, or give up, requires quick thinking at the bargaining table.

Consider Swigler's overstock problem. Her objective is to get the merchandise out of her inventory without significantly hurting her gross margin. Carnevale's objective is to maintain a healthy yet profitable relationship with Lord & Taylor. Thus, Swigler must invent options that could satisfy both parties. Her options are

- Sell the shirts to an off-price retailer at 10 cents on the retail dollar.

- Have Carnevale take back the shirts.

- Get Tommy Hilfiger to provide markdown money and put the shirts on sale.

- Return some of the shirts and get markdown money for the rest.

Clearly, selling the shirts to an off-price retailer would cause Swigler to take a loss. But from Carnevale's perspective, taking back the merchandise may be unacceptable because the styles are from last season and some shirts may be shopworn. Swigler could, however, present this option first with the knowledge that it will probably be rejected. Then she could ask for markdown money. Carnevale would believe he got off easy, and Swigler would have her problem solved.

In developing her plan for the meeting, Swigler followed some important rules of negotiation. She identified viable options for both parties. Then she determined which options would satisfy both parties' objectives. When presenting the options, she held back the one she believed would be most acceptable to Carnevale so he would think he was a winner.

Let Them Do the Talking   There's a natural tendency for one person to continue to talk if the other person involved in the conversation doesn't respond. If used properly, this phenomenon can work to the negotiator's advantage. Suppose Swigler asks Carnevale for special financial support on Lord & Taylor's Christmas catalog. Carnevale begins with a qualified no and cites all the reasons why he can't cooperate. But Swigler doesn't say a word. Although Carnevale appears nervous, he continues to talk. Eventually, he comes around to a yes. In negotiations, those who break the silence first, lose!

Know How Far to Go   There's a fine line between negotiating too hard and walking away from the table with less than necessary. If Swigler overnegotiates by getting the markdown money, better terms of purchase, and a strong advertising allowance, the management of Tommy Hilfiger may decide that other retailers are more worthy of early deliveries and the best styles. Carnevale may not be afraid to say no if Swigler is pushing him beyond a legal, moral, profitable relationship.

Don't Burn Bridges   Even if Swigler gets few additional concessions from Carnevale, she shouldn't be abusive or resort to threats. Professionally, Lord & Taylor may not wish to stop doing business with Tommy Hilfiger on the basis of this one encounter. From a personal perspective, the world of retailing is relatively small. Swigler and Carnevale may meet at the negotiating table again—both working for different companies. Neither can afford to be known in the trade as being unfair, rude, or worse.

Don't Assume   Many issues are raised and resolved in any negotiating session. To be certain there are no misunderstandings, participants should orally review the outcomes at the end of the session. Swigler and Carnevale should both summarize the session in writing as soon as possible after the meeting.

ESTABLISHING AND MAINTAINING STRATEGIC RELATIONSHIPS WITH VENDORS

As we discussed in Chapter 5, maintaining strong vendor relationships is an important method of developing a sustainable competitive advantage. In Chapter 10, we discussed some of the ways partnering relations can improve information, exchange, planning, and the management of supply chains. For example, electronic data interchange could not be accomplished without the vendor and retailer making a commitment to work together and have a trusting relationship. In the same way, category management using category captains and CPFR used in sales forecasting and discussed in Chapter 12 would be impossible without partnering relationships. In this section, we examine how retailers can develop strategic relationships and the characteristics of a successful long-term relationship.

Defining Strategic Relationships

Relationships between retailers and vendors are often based on arguing over splitting up a profit pie.[32] This is basically a win–lose relationship because when one party gets a larger portion of the pie, the other party gets a smaller portion. Both parties are interested exclusively in their own profits and are unconcerned about the other party's welfare. These relationships are common when the products are commodities and have no major impact on the retailers' performance. Thus, there is no benefit to the retailer to enter into a strategic relationship.

A **strategic relationship,** also called a **partnering relationship,** is when a retailer and vendor are committed to maintaining the relationship over the long term and investing in opportunities that are mutually beneficial to the parties. In these relationships, it's important for the partners to put their money where their mouth is. They've taken risks to expand the pie—to give the relationship a strategic advantage over other companies.

Thus, a strategic relationship is a win–win relationship. Both parties benefit because the size of the pie has increased—both the retailer and vendor increase their sales and profits. Strategic relationships are created explicitly to uncover and exploit joint opportunities. Members in strategic relationships depend on and trust each other heavily; they share goals and agree on how to accomplish those goals; and they're willing to take risks, share confidential information, and make significant investments for the sake of the relationship.

A strategic relationship is like a marriage. When businesses enter strategic relationships, they're wedded to their partners for better or worse. For example, UK's Marks & Spencer had jointly developed a kitchen product with a vendor.[33] Four months after the product's introduction, the manufacturer realized that it had miscalculated the product's cost and, as a result, had underpriced the product and was losing money on the deal. It was a big hit at Marks & Spencer because it was underpriced. Marks & Spencer decided not to raise the price because the product was already listed in its catalog. Instead, it helped the vendor reengineer the product at a lower cost, cut its own gross margin, and gave that money to the manufacturer. It took a profit hit to maintain the relationship.

Retailing View 14.4 examines how two big, tough companies, Wal-Mart and Procter & Gamble, have learned to work together. Now let's look at characteristics that are necessary to maintain strategic relationships.

Maintaining Strategic Relationships

The four foundations of successful strategic relationships are mutual trust, open communication, common goals, and credible commitments.

Mutual Trust   The glue in strategic relationship is trust. **Trust** is a belief that a partner is honest (reliable, stands by its word, sincere, fulfills obligations) and is benevolent (concerned about the other party's welfare).[35] When vendors and buyers trust each other, they're more willing to share relevant ideas, clarify goals and problems, and communicate efficiently. Information shared between the parties becomes increasingly comprehensive, accurate, and timely. There's less need for the vendor and buyer to constantly monitor and check up on each other's actions because each believes the other won't take advantage, given the opportunity.[36]

REFACT

The population of Bentonville, Arkansas, the corporate headquarters for Wal-Mart, is 17,000, with 7,000 of these people working for Wal-Mart. Another 7,000 people representing vendors call on Wal-Mart every month. More than 100 companies that are suppliers to Wal-Mart have opened offices in Bentonville, including Hewlett-Packard, Clorox, Nabisco, and Procter & Gamble.[34]

Two Tough Companies Learn to Dance Together | RETAILING VIEW 14.4

Historically, Procter & Gamble (P&G) used its enormous market power to dominate its retailers. After all, everyone needs to carry Crest toothpaste, Folgers coffee, Pepto-Bismol, Pampers, and so forth, right? That is, everyone except the world's largest retailer, Wal-Mart. Wal-Mart is known for demanding the lowest prices and the best service from its vendors.

What happens when an unstoppable force meets an immovable object? Things either blow up or get worked out. Today the companies have a relationship that is emulated thoughout the industry. But it wasn't always that way. In the bad old days, there was no sharing of information, no joint planning, and no systems coordination. In the mid-1980s, Sam Walton went on a canoe trip with Lou Pritchett, P&G's vice president for sales. On this trip they started a process of examining how the two firms could mutually profit by working together. Today they use a sophisticated EDI system coupled with CPFR that enables P&G to work with Wal-Mart to establish sales forecasts and replenishment goals for products like Crest. P&G receives continual data on sales, inventory, and

prices for its products at individual Wal-Mart stores. This information allows P&G to anticipate Crest sales and automatically ship orders. Electronic invoicing and electronic transfer of funds complete the transaction cycle.

This relationship benefits all parties. Customers get lower prices and high product availability. P&G has reduced order processing costs, including lessening the need for salespeople store visits. P&G produces according to demand, thereby lowering the need for backup stock. Wal-Mart needs less inventory as well. By working together, the two have turned what used to be a sometimes adversarial relationship into a win–win proposition.

Sources: Thomas W. Gruen, Daniel S. Corsten, and Sundar Bharadwaj, "Retail out of Stocks: A Worldwide Examination of Extent, Causes, and Consumer Responses," unpublished working paper, May 7, 2002; Nirmalya Kumar, "The Power of Trust in Manufacturer–Retailer Relationships," *Harvard Business Review,* November–December 1996, pp. 92–106; and Mark E. Parry and Yoshinobu Sato, "Procter & Gamble: The Wal-Mart Partnership," University of Virginia case #M-0452, 1996.

Strategic relationships and trust are often developed initially between the leaders of organizations. For example, when Wal-Mart started to work with Procter & Gamble to coordinate its buying activities, Sam Walton got together with P&G's vice president of sales on a canoeing trip. (See Retailing View 14.4.) They discussed the mutual benefits of cooperating and the potential risks associated with altering their normal business practices. In the end, they must have concluded that the potential long-term gains were worth the additional risks and short-term setbacks that would probably occur as they developed the new systems.

Open Communication In order to share information, develop sales forecasts together, and coordinate deliveries, Wal-Mart and P&G have to have open and honest communication. This may sound easy in principle, but most businesses don't like to share information with their business partners. They believe it is none of the other's business. But open, honest communication is a key to developing successful relationships. Buyers and vendors in a relationship need to understand what's driving each other's business, their roles in the relationship, each firm's strategies, and any problems that arise over the course of the relationship.

Common Goals Vendors and buyers must have common goals for a successful relationship to develop. Shared goals give both members of the relationship incentive to pool their strengths and abilities and to exploit potential opportunities between them. There's also assurance that the other partner won't do anything to hinder goal achievement within the relationship.

For example, Wal-Mart and P&G recognized that it was in their common interest to remain business partners—they needed each other—and to do so, both had to be allowed to make profitable transactions. Wal-Mart can't demand prices so low that P&G can't make money, and P&G must be flexible enough to accommodate the needs of its biggest customer. With a common goal, both firms have incentive to cooperate because they know that by doing so, each can boost sales.

Common goals also help to sustain the relationship when expected benefit flows aren't realized. If one P&G shipment fails to reach a Wal-Mart store on time due to an uncontrollable event like misrouting by a trucking firm, Wal-Mart won't suddenly call off the whole arrangement. Instead, Wal-Mart is likely to view the incident as a simple mistake and will remain in the relationship. This is because Wal-Mart knows it and P&G are committed to the same goals in the long run.

Credible Commitments Successful relationships develop because both parties make credible commitments to the relationship. Credible commitments are tangible investments in the relationship. They go beyond just making the hollow statement "I want to be a partner." Credible commitments involve spending money to improve the supplier's products or services provided to the customer.[37] For example, one of the strengths of the Wal-Mart/P&G partnership is the obvious and significant investments both parties have made in EDI systems, CPFR forecasting systems, and material handling equipment.

Building Partnering Relationships

Although not all retailer–vendor relationships should or do become strategic partnerships, the development of strategic partnerships tends to go through a series of phases characterized by increasing levels of commitment: (1) awareness, (2) exploration, (3) expansion, and (4) commitment.

In the awarenss stage, no transactions have taken place. This phase might begin with the buyer seeing some interesting merchandise at a retail market or an ad in a trade magazine. Reputation and image of the vendor can play an important role in determining if the buyer moves to the next stage.

During the exploration phase, the buyer and vendor begin to explore the potential benefits and costs. At this point, the buyer may make a small purchase and try to test the demand for the merchandise in several stores. In addition, the buyer will get information about how easy it is to work with the vendor.

Eventually, the buyer has collected enough information about the vendor to consider developing a longer-term relationship. The buyer and the vendor determine that there is a potential for a win–win relationship. They begin to work on joint promotional programs, and the amount of merchandise sold increases.

If both parties continue to find the relationship mutually beneficial, it moves to the commitment stage and becomes a strategic relationship. The buyer and vendor make significant investments in the relationship and develop a long-term perspective toward it.

It is difficult for retailer–vendor relationships to be as committed as some supplier–manufacturer relationships. Manufacturers can enter into monogamous (sole source) relationships with other manufacturers. However, an important function of retailers is to provide an assortment of merchandise for their customers. Thus, they must always deal with multiple, sometimes competing suppliers.

SUMMARY

This chapter examined issues surrounding vendor relations and purchasing merchandise. Simply put, retailers can't succeed without their vendors. To survive, they must be able to count on a predictable supply of merchandise at competitive prices and with sufficient promotional support.

Retailers can purchase either manufacturers' brands or private-label brands. Each type has its own relative advantages. Choosing brands and a branding strategy is an integral component of a firm's merchandise and assortment planning process.

A large percentage of the merchandise we buy is manufactured outside of the United States. The decision to buy from domestic manufacturers or source internationally is a complicated one. The cost, managerial, and ethical issues surrounding global sourcing decisions were discussed. Buyers and their merchandise managers have several opportunities to meet with vendors, view new merchandise, and place orders. They can utilize Internet exchanges or visit their vendors at wholesale market centers such as New York, Paris, or Milan. Virtually every merchandise category has at least one annual trade show at which retailers and ven-

dors meet. Buyers often meet with vendors on their own turf—in the retail store or corporate offices. Finally, meetings with vendors are facilitated by resident buying offices. Market representatives of these resident buying offices facilitate merchandising purchases in foreign markets.

Retailers should prepare for and conduct negotiations with vendors. Successful vendor relationships depend on planning for and being adept at negotiations.

Retailers that can successfully team up with their vendors can achieve a sustainable competitive advantage. There needs to be more than just a promise to buy and sell on a regular basis. Strategic relationships require trust, shared goals, strong communications, and a financial commitment.

With thousands of annual transactions taking place between retailers and their vendors, there's plenty of room for ethical and legal problems. The issues of charging vendors for shelf space or taking bribes are discussed in Appendix 14A. There are also problems associated with counterfeit and gray-market merchandise and issues that vendors face when selling to retailers, such as exclusive territories and tying contracts. Care should be taken when making restrictions on which retailers they will sell to, what merchandise, how much, and at what price.

Appendix 14B reviews the purchase and payment terms given to retailers. Retailers face a plethora of discount/payment date combinations. A working knowledge of these terms of purchase is essential for any person involved in merchandising. More important, the most advantageous application of the terms can make a significant impact on corporate profits.

KEY TERMS

alternative dispute resolution, *464*

arbitration, *464*

bargain branding, *439*

buyback, *465*

chargeback, *464*

commercial bribery, *464*

consortium exchange, *450*

copycat branding, *440*

copyright, *466*

counterfeit merchandise, *466*

diverted merchandise, *467*

duty, *443*

exclusive dealing agreements, *469*

exclusive geographic territory, *469*

free trade zone, *443*

generic brand, *439*

gray-market good, *467*

house brand, *439*

independent exchanges, *451*

intellectual property, *466*

lead time, *444*

licensed brand, *436*

lift-out, *465*

manufacturer brands, *434*

maquiladoras, *443*

market, *447*

market weeks, *451*

med-arb, *464*

mediation, *464*

merchandise shows, *451*

national brands, *434*

opportunity cost of capital, *444*

parallel branding, *440*

partnering relationship, *458*

premium branding, *439*

private-label brands, *436*

private exchanges, *450*

resident buying offices, *452*

retail exchanges, *448*

reverse auctions, *448*

slotting allowance, *465*

slotting fee, *465*

stocklift, *465*

store brands, *436*

strategic relationship, *458*

tariff, *443*

trade show, *451*

trademark, *466*

trust, *459*

tying contract, *469*

GET OUT & DO IT!

1. INTERNET EXERCISE Go to www.Doneger.com and click on "Guests" to learn more about this resident buying office.

2. GO SHOPPING Go to your favorite department or discount store. Perform an audit of national and private brands. Interview a manager to determine whether the percentage of private brands has increased or decreased over the last five years. Ask the manager to comment on the store's philosophy toward national versus private brands. On the basis of what you see and hear, assess its branding strategy.

3. INTERNET EXERCISE Go to the WorldWide Retail Exchange (www.wwre.org) and GlobalNetXchange.com (www.gnx.com). Compare their offerings. Write a recommendation to a retailer of your choice regarding which of these exchanges it should join. You can also recommend that it doesn't join either exchange.

4. GO SHOPPING See if you can find some counterfeit, gray-market or diverted merchandise. Compare it with the real thing. (Refer to Appendix 14A.)

DISCUSSION QUESTIONS AND PROBLEMS

1. Do retailers take advantage of their power positions by charging slotting fees, buybacks, and chargebacks (see Appendix 14A)?

2. Assume you have been hired to consult with The Gap on sourcing decisions for sportswear. What issues would you consider when deciding whether you should buy from Mexico or China, or find a source in the United States?

3. How would the decision to source outside the United States affect a retailer's need to carry backup stock?

4. What kinds of social courtesies or gifts (lunches, theater tickets, etc.) are appropriate for buyers to accept from vendors (see Appendix 14A)?

5. Does your favorite clothing store have a strong private-brand strategy? Should it?

6. When setting goals for a negotiation session with a vendor, what issues should a buyer consider?

7. A $500 invoice is dated October 1, the merchandise arrives October 15, and the terms are 3/30, n/60 ROG (see Appendix 14B).
   a. How many days does the retailer have to take advantage of the discount?
   b What is the percentage of discount?
   c. How much is due November 10?
   d. What's the final date the retailer can pay the invoice without being considered late?

8. What do you think will be the future of retail exchanges?

9. What factors should a buyer consider when deciding which vendors to develop a close relationship with?

SUGGESTED READINGS

Bloom, Paul N.; Gregory T. Gundlach; and Joseph P. Cannon. "Slotting Allowances and Fees: Schools of Thought and the Views of Practicing Managers." *Journal of Marketing* 64, no. 2 (April 2000), pp. 92–108

Desiraju, Ramarao. "New Product Introductions, Slotting Allowances, and Retailer Discretion." *Journal of Retailing* 77, no. 3 (Fall 2001), p. 335–358.

Fisher, Roger, and William Ury. *Getting to Yes.* New York: Penguin, 1981.

Greenhalgh, Leonard. *Managing Strategic Relationships: The Key to Business Success.* New York: Free Press, 2001.

Harvey, Michael. "The Trade Dress Controversy: A Case of Strategic Cross-Brand Cannibalization." *Journal of Marketing Theory and Practice* 6, no. 2 (Spring 1998), pp. 1–15.

Jap, Sandy. "Online Reverse Auctions: Issues, Themes, and Prospects for the Future." *Journal of the Academy of Marketing Science* 30, no. 4 (Fall 2002), Forthcoming.

Li, Zhan G., and Rajiv P. Dant. "An Exploratory Study of Exclusive Dealing in Channel Relationships." *Journal of the Academy of Marketing Science* 25, no. 3 (1997), pp. 201–13.

Lowson, Robert H. "Offshore Sourcing: An Optimal Operational Strategy?" *Business Horizons*, 44, no. 6 (November–December 2001), pp. 61–66.

Sculley, Arthur B., and William W. Woods. *B2B Exchanges: The Killer Application in the Business-to-Business Internet Revolution.* HarperInformation, 2001.

Skrovan, Sandra J., and Elaine Pollack. "Creative Partnerships: Key Asset of the New Competition." Retail Forward, Inc., 2000.

Watkins, Michael. *Breakthrough Business Negotiation: A Toolbox for Managers.* New York: John Wiley & Sons, 2002.

APPENDIX 14A   Ethical and Legal Issues in Purchasing Merchandise*

As you can imagine, given the thousands of relationships and millions of transactions between retailers and their vendors, unethical or illegal situations may arise. In this section, we'll view ethical and legal issues from both retailers' and vendors' perspectives. The most fundamental question is whether a retailer and vendor have a binding contract for a particular transaction. If they do, the next question is how to resolve disputes under that contract. In addition, retailers should not take advantage of their position of power in the marketing channel. In this regard, we'll examine chargebacks, commercial bribery, slotting allowances, buybacks, and category management.

To protect their customers' interests and their own reputation, retailers must be cognizant of whether the merchandise is counterfeit or from the diverted market (the gray market). Vendors aren't likely to become legally entangled with their retailers so long as they sell to whomever wants to buy, sell whatever they want, and sell at the same price to all. But since most vendors don't want to be this free with their merchandise, we'll look at exclusive territories, exclusive dealing agreements, tying contracts, and refusals to deal.

CONTRACT DISPUTES

Contract formation in the retail context is usually straightforward. The retailer places an order with a vendor that in most cases the vendor accepts. This creates a binding mutual obligation for the vendor to deliver the promised goods in exchange for the retailer agreeing to pay the specified price. Disputes arise when one party does not perform or when the parties disagree about details of the transaction such as the precise specifications of the goods.

Most retailers and vendors are more interested in continuing sales relationships than expensive litigation over legal rights. For this reason, many disputes are simply settled by negotiation and agreement between the two parties. It is common to include **alternative dispute resolution** provisions in contracts. Such provisions can include

*This section was developed with the assistance of Professor Ross Petty, Babson College.

methods of settling the dispute that the parties agree upon, such as mediation, arbitration, or med-arb. **Mediation** involves selecting a neutral mediator to assist the parties in reaching a mutually agreeable settlement. **Arbitration** involves the appointment of an arbitrator who considers the arguments of both sides and then makes a decision that is usually agreed upon in advance as binding. **Med-arb** involves an initial attempt at mediation followed by binding arbitration if the mediation is unsuccessful. Overworked courts routinely enforce alternative dispute resolution contract provisions in the United States.

CHARGEBACKS

A **chargeback** is a practice used by retailers in which they deduct money from the amount they owe a vendor. There are two reasons for a chargeback. The first is when the retailer deducts money from an invoice because merchandise isn't selling. The second reason is vendor mistakes such as shoddy labeling, lost billings, wrong-size boxes or hangers, missing items, and late shipments. Although often legitimate contract disputes, chargebacks are frequently viewed as being unjustified by vendors. Retailers can use chargebacks as a profit center. For instance, one senior executive at a large department store chain was told to collect $50 million in chargebacks.[38] What makes chargebacks especially difficult for vendors is that once the money is deducted from an invoice, and the invoiced is "paid," it is difficult to get the missing amount back, and negotiations or threats of litigation often appear to fall on deaf ears.

COMMERCIAL BRIBERY

Commercial bribery occurs in retailing when a vendor or its agent offers to privately give or pay a retail buyer "something of value" to influence purchasing decisions. Say a sweater manufacturer takes a department store buyer to lunch at a fancy private club and then proposes a ski weekend in Vail. The buyer enjoys the lunch but graciously turns down the ski trip. These gifts could be construed as bribes or kickbacks, which are illegal unless the buyer's manager is informed of them (and

there are multiple retail outlets within a chain, a manufacturer's sales staff may expend more effort when selling to retailers than to wholesalers. The manufacturer may also incur larger transportation expenses due to multiple delivery points and smaller shipments to retailers.

In recent years, however, most large retailers have convinced some vendors to give them the lowest prices offered. These retailers argue that they perform all the functions that would otherwise be performed by an independent wholesaler, such as transportation from distribution centers to stores, price marking, and inventory management. Thus, they say, they should receive the lowest price.

Another question is, why would the manufacturer discount a suggested retail price rather than simply quoting a net cost? It's because retailers generally think of their merchandise in terms of retail rather than cost. By quoting prices as discounted suggested retail prices, the manufacturer's practice remains consistent with retailing thought. Further, by providing suggested retail prices, the manufacturer has some subtle influence on the retail price. Note, however, that manufacturers can influence retailers to maintain suggested retail prices only under certain circumstances. (See "Vertical Price Fixing" in Chapter 15.)

CHAIN DISCOUNTS

In some lines of trade—such as housewares and hardware—chain discounts are used. A chain discount is a number of different discounts taken sequentially from the suggested retail price. An example is 50–10–5 (spoken "fifty, ten, and five"). Using the previous example, if the TV set has a suggested retail price of $100, then the price is calculated as follows:

1. A 50 percent reduction is taken:

   $100 × .5 = $50

2. An additional 10 percent reduction from the remaining $50 is taken:

   $50 – ($50 × .1) = $50 – $5 = $45

3. A 5 percent discount from the remaining $45 is taken:

   $45 – ($45 × .05) = $45 – $2.25 = $42.75.

So, with a 50–10–5 chain discount on a $100 suggested retail item, the retailer pays $42.75. But note that the discounts can't be added. A 50–10–5 discount isn't the same as a 65 percent discount: $100 – (100 × .65) = $35.

Why do vendors and retailers use such an awkward pricing scheme? Simply because it's traditional. In the precalculator era, it was easier for people to calculate chain discount prices in their heads without having to resort to tedious computations.

QUANTITY DISCOUNTS

Quantity discounts are of two types: cumulative and noncumulative. Retailers earn cumulative quantity by purchasing certain quantities over a specified period of time. For instance, a vendor may grant an additional discount to a retailer that purchases $100,000 worth of merchandise in one year. These discounts have the same effect as a year-end rebate. Vendors grant cumulative quantity discounts as an incentive to buy more merchandise and to encourage retailer loyalty. Under the Robinson-Patman Act, however, it's hard for a vendor to justify lower costs for higher quantities on a cumulative basis.[56] To justify cumulative quantity discounts, a vendor could show that having retailers commit to certain levels of purchases in advance allows the vendor to plan production more efficiently and thus cut costs. Cumulative quantity discounts could be easily justified in the garment industry, for instance, since garment manufacturers must commit to their cloth suppliers months in advance.

Noncumulative quantity discounts are offered to retailers as an incentive to purchase more merchandise on a single order. Larger, less frequent orders may save vendors order processing, sales, and transportation expenses. These expenses are often found in retailing and are more easily cost-justified than cumulative quantity discounts.[57]

Exhibit 14–4 presents a sample price list that combines trade/functional, chain, and noncumulative quantity discounts for an appliance manufacturer. The headings "Price to Wholesaler" and "Price to Retailer" illustrate trade/functional discounts. The "40–5%," "50–10," and "50–10–5" under the "Price to Wholesaler, Discount" represent different chain discounts. Finally, the first column, "Quantity per Order," illustrates noncumulative quantity discounts.

Examine the columns under "Price to Retailer." At which price should the retailer buy? At first

EXHIBIT 14–4
A Sample Price List

Quantity per Order	PRICE TO WHOLESALER		PRICE TO RETAILER	
	Discount	Price	Discount	Price
1–10	40–5%	$57*	30%	$70
11–25	50–10	45	40	60
26+	50–10–5	42.75	40–10	54

*Based on a $100 suggested retail price.

glance, the lowest price appears to be $54. But the lowest price isn't always the most profitable. If the dealer purchases 26 or more TV sets all at once, it may have more than a year's supply. Inventory turnover and the cost of carrying the inventory would be unsatisfactory. The merchandise may become shopworn, and the large quantity might even require more space than is available.[58]

SEASONAL DISCOUNTS

A seasonal discount is an additional discount offered as an incentive to retailers to order merchandise in advance of the normal buying season. For instance, Black & Decker garden tools may be offered to retailers at a special price in January. Black & Decker can more easily plan its production schedules and lower its finished goods inventory if it can ship early in the season. Retailers, on the other hand, must consider the benefits of a larger gross margin from the discount versus the additional cost of carrying the inventory for a longer period of time.[59]

CASH DISCOUNTS

A cash discount is a reduction in the invoice cost for paying the invoice prior to the end of the discount period. It's applied after the functional/trade, chain, quantity, and seasonal discounts. An example is 1/30, n/60 (spoken as "one, thirty, net sixty"). This means the retailer can take a 1 percent discount if it pays on or before the 30th day after the date of invoice. Or the full invoice amount is due 60 days after the date of invoice.

Thus there are three components of a cash discount: the percentage of the discount, the number of days in which the discount can be taken, and the net credit period (when the full amount of the invoice is due). For example, a typical cash discount is 1/30, n/60. This means that if the invoice is dated on November 1, the retailer has 30 days (until December 1) to take the 1 percent discount. The full amount is due 60 days after the invoice date, on January 1. (If retailers really counted days, the full amount would be due on December 31 since there are 31 days in December. But retailers usually don't pay that much attention to the number of days in a month for the purpose of taking cash discounts.)

1/30, N/60		
Nov. 1	Dec. 1	Jan. 1
Date of invoice	30 days	60 days
	1% discount	Full amount due

There are a number of variations on the basic cash discount format known as dating. The term *dating* refers to the dates on which discounts can be taken and full amounts are due in a cash discount pricing policy. Here are four examples of common forms of dating.

Receipt of Goods (ROG) Dating

Using ROG dating, the cash discount period starts on the day the merchandise is received. If the merchandise is shipped and invoiced on November 1, but doesn't arrive until November 15, using dating of 1/30, n/60, ROG, the cash discount can be taken until December 15, and the full amount is due January 15.

ROG DATING			
Nov. 1	Nov. 15	Dec. 15	Jan. 15
Date of invoice	Merchandise arrives	30 days ROG 1% discount	60 days ROG Full amount due

End-of-Month (EOM) Dating

In EOM dating, the discount period starts at the end of the month in which the invoice is dated (except when the invoice is dated the 25th or later—as we'll discuss shortly). As in the previous example, if merchandise is invoiced on November 1, using dating of 1/30, n/60, EOM, the cash discount can be taken until January 1, and the full amount is due February 1. The retailer can pay 30 days later than the same terms without the EOM designation.

EOM DATING			
Nov. 1	Dec. 1	Jan. 1	Feb. 1
Date of invoice	30-days discount period begins	30 days EOM 1% discount	60 days EOM Full amount due

EOM Dating, Grace Period

A grace period is often given when an invoice with EOM dating is dated after the 25th of the month. The vendor starts counting on the first of the next month. If the merchandise is invoiced on October 25, using the same dating of 1/30, n/60, EOM, the cash discount can still be taken until January 1, and the full amount is due February 1. This time the retailer gets 36 days longer to pay than without the EOM designation. So if the retailer

wanted to maximize the length of time to pay for the merchandise and still take the cash discount, the merchandise would be ordered so that it would be invoiced as close to the 25th of the month as possible.

EOM DATING, GRACE PERIOD				
Oct. 25	Nov. 1	Dec. 1	Jan. 1	Feb. 1
Date of invoice		30 days discount period begins	30 days EOM 1% discount	60 days EOM Full amount due

Extra Dating

With extra dating, the retailer receives an extra amount of time to pay the invoice and still take the cash discount. Assume again that the merchandise is invoiced on November 1. Using dating of 1/30, n/60, EOM, 60 days extra (also written 60X or 60 ex.), the cash discount could be taken until March 1, with the net amount due April 1. That is, the discount period starts December 1, due to the EOM designation. The buyer gets 30 days for the regular discount period, plus an additional 60 days.

The rationale for offering extra dating is similar to that for the seasonal discount. The vendor may need to give the retailer an additional incentive to purchase risky or seasonal merchandise. Instead of giving the retailer a lower price (as is the case with the seasonal discount), the vendor grants the retailer a longer time in which to pay.

ANTICIPATION DISCOUNTS

Under the previously discussed dating policies, a retailer has no incentive to pay earlier than the last day of the discount period. An anticipation

EXTRA DATING						
Nov. 1	Dec. 1	Jan. 1	Feb. 1	Mar. 1		Aug. 1
Date of invoice	30-day discount period begins	60-day Extra discount period begins		60-day Extra 1% discount		Full amount due

EXHIBIT 14–5
Alternative Shipping Terms and Conditions

	Pays Freight Charges	Owns Merchandise in Transit and Files Claims (If Any)
FOB origin, freight collect	Retailer	Retailer
FOB origin, freight prepaid	Supplier	Retailer
FOB destination, freight collect	Retailer	Supplier
FOB destination, freight prepaid	Supplier	Supplier

discount provides this incentive. It's a discount offered in addition to the cash discount or dating if an invoice is paid before the end of the cash discount period. Let's say the dating is 1/30, n/60, EOM, with anticipation of 18 percent per year, and the invoice is dated November 1, the 30-day discount period ends at the end of December, but the retailer pays on December 1, 30 days earlier. Let's calculate the net cost on a $100 item.

Cash discount = $100 × .01 = $1
Invoice less discount = $100 – $1 = $99

Since the anticipation is 18 percent a year, but the retailer is paying 30 days early, we calculate the anticipation as

Anticipation = $99 × .18 × (30 days early ÷ 360 days per year) = $1.49
Net amount = $99.00 – $1.49 = $97.51

The retailer can earn an extra $2.49 (or $100 – $97.51) by paying early, taking the cash discount, and taking the anticipation.

SHIPPING TERMS AND CONDITIONS

The last question in any terms of purchase policy is who (the retailer or the vendor) has responsibility for the different aspects of shipping the merchandise. Two basic issues must be agreed upon when designating the shipping terms and conditions: Who pays the freight charges, and who owns the merchandise while it's in transit?

Transportation costs for shipping merchandise from vendor to retailer can be substantial. If the retailer incurs this expense, it increases the cost of the merchandise.

The party owning the merchandise in transit is responsible for filing a claim with the transportation company in case of lost or damaged merchandise. This is a time-consuming, potentially expensive process. The party filing the claim may have to wait months before it's reimbursed for the loss or damage. Also, the party owning the merchandise while in transit may be responsible for paying insurance that might be needed above the liability of the transportation company to cover merchandise lost or damaged in transit.

Many forms of shipping terms and conditions are used. Exhibit 14–5 outlines the most common ones. The designation *freight prepaid* means freight is paid by the vendor; *freight collect* means the retailer pays the freight. The term *FOB (free on board) origin* means ownership of the merchandise changes hands at the location where the shipment originates. When the ownership changes hands, so does responsibility for filing claims and insurance in case of lost or damaged merchandise. Thus FOB origin is beneficial to the vendor. The term *origin* is often substituted for plant or factory. *FOB destination* means ownership of the merchandise changes hands at the store. So the term *destination* is often substituted for *store* or *retailer*.

Pricing

15

| Bruce Peterson, Senior Vice President, GMM
of Perishables, Wal-Mart Supercenters

"The pricing of perishable goods plays a major role in our supercenter strategy. It supports the overall image of the store. For example, bananas are one of the most popular items in our supercenters. When bananas are at a great price, our customers will realize that other products in the store, like blenders and Vanilla Wafers, are also at great prices. Offering products at low prices benefits both Wal-Mart and its customers.

"Because Wal-Mart's strategy is to sell products at the lowest prices, we need to keep our produce prices low. But if we set our prices too low, then we will not meet our gross margin goals. We are able to offer lower prices and still make money because we work closely with our produce vendors. We set up contracts specifying the prices we will pay based on the time of year, availability of products, and the competition in different markets. To reduce inventory levels and make sure we have the freshest produce, we work closely with our vendors on collaborative planning, forecasting, and replenishment (CPFR).

"My interest in retail, specifically produce, started early when I was working at a grocery store as a bag boy in high school. At first I worked there to save up to buy a car, but as I got older, my part-time job turned into a career. Most of my experience in

QUESTIONS

- Why do some retailers have frequent sales while others attempt to maintain an everyday low price strategy?
- How do retailers set retail prices?
- What pricing strategies can retailers use to influence consumer purchases?
- How is the Internet changing the way retailers price their merchandise?
- Under what circumstances can retailers' pricing practices get them into legal difficulties?

produce and retail was acquired when I worked as a buyer at an independent grocery store. I would go to a produce terminal (located in Detroit) and negotiate deals with vendors. Instead of just selling produce to me, they taught be about the business, such as when certain produce come into season and what to sell them for.

"I left the company and started my own produce wholesale company. Owning my own company prepared me for the position I hold today because working for Wal-Mart is like running your own business within a business. You're in charge of your department, making sure others are doing their job and, most important, sales goals are being reached.

"It is really a thrill when you make a great buy. One year I negotiated a great deal on apples from New Zealand. We were able to sell them for 69 cents a pound compared to $1.29 the previous year. Our sales increased from 4,000 boxes to 100,000 boxes. Not only did we have a huge increase in sales in the following year but we also helped our customers make a big saving."

The importance of pricing decisions is growing because today's customers are looking for good value when they buy merchandise and services. **Value** is the relationship of what the customer gets (goods/services) to what he or she has to pay for it. To some people, a good value means always getting a low price. Many types of consumers have become price-sensitive. Others are willing to pay extra as long as they believe they're getting their money's worth in terms of product quality or service.

Retailers have responded to their customers' needs with retail formats that emphasize low prices as a means of creating a differential advantage. National discount store chains that offer everyday low prices, such as Wal-Mart, dominate many markets in many product categories. A close competitor in the price-oriented market is the membership-only warehouse club, such as Sam's Warehouse Club and Costco. Another retail format is the off-price retailer (e.g., T. J. Maxx, Marshalls, and Bluefly.com), which purchases closeout and end-of-season merchandise at lower-than-normal prices and passes the savings on to the customer. (Chapter 2 describes these stores.)

Some of the more mature retailing institutions, like department stores and supermarkets, have come to grips with these forms of price competition by adapting a more aggressive pricing strategy with a significant amount of their merchandise being sold below the manufacturers' suggested price through a strong promotion orientation. Finally, many retailers such as Nordstrom and Banana Republic have successfully maintained their market appeal by providing good value by offering customers high-quality merchandise and service without attempting to offer the lowest prices on a particular product category.

In the middle of this price competition among national giants are the smaller retailers. Typically unable to purchase in large quantities to receive lower prices like their larger competitors, mom-and-pop retailers have either learned to use other strategies to compete or have gone out of business. For instance, to compete with Wal-Mart's low prices, small retailers have developed niche strategies by providing a broader assortment of merchandise within a given product category and better service.

Pricing decisions are also being affected by the development of electronic channels. Using shopping bots like mysimon.com, consumers can easily compare the prices for branded products sold by different retailers. However, as we discussed in Chapter 3, the Internet also makes it easier for consumers to compare product attributes in addition to price. Due to the targeting capabilities of the electronic channel, retailers have the opportunity of charging different prices to customers on the basis of their price sensitivity.

The Internet has facilitated the use of an auction pricing mechanism. People have used auctions to facilitate trade for centuries. As eBay has demonstrated, no longer do auction participants have to be located at a same place.

This chapter begins by comparing everyday low pricing with high/low pricing. Then we explore three complementary methods of setting retail prices: cost-oriented, competition-oriented, and demand-oriented approaches. In addition, we describe the various methods retailers use to adjust the retail price and stimulate store sales. The appendix of this chapter discusses important legal issues involved in making price decisions.

PRICING STRATEGIES

In today's retail market, two opposing pricing strategies prevail: everyday low pricing and high/low pricing.[2] We will describe these two strategies and the conditions under which each are used.

Everyday Low Pricing

Many retailers have adopted an **everyday low pricing (EDLP)** strategy. This strategy emphasizes continuity of retail prices at a level somewhere between the regular nonsale price and the deep-discount sale price of the retailer's competitors. The term *everyday low pricing* is therefore somewhat of a misnomer. Low doesn't necessarily mean lowest. Although retailers using EDLP strive for low prices, they aren't always the lowest price in the market. At any given time, a sale price at a competing store or a special purchase at a wholesale club store may be the lowest price. A more accurate description of this strategy is therefore everyday *same* prices because the prices don't have significant fluctuations.

Several of the biggest U.S. retailers—Home Depot, Wal-Mart, and Staples—have adopted EDLP. In supermarket retailing, Albertson's (California), Omni (Illinois), and Cub (Illinois) are positioned as EDLP stores.[3] Although these retailers embrace EDLP as their strategy, they do occasionally have sales. They are just not as frequent as their high-low competitors.

Since it is difficult to always have the lowest prices, some retailers, such as Circuit City, have adopted a **low price guarantee policy** in which they guarantee that they will have the lowest possible price for a product or a group of products. The guarantee usually promises to match or better any lower price found in the local market. The promise normally includes a provision to refund the difference between the seller's offer price and the lower price.

High/Low Pricing

In a **high/low pricing** strategy, retailers offer prices that are sometimes above their competition's EDLP, but they use advertising to promote frequent sales. The sales undertaken by retailers using high/low strategies have become more intense in recent years. In the past, fashion retailers would mark down merchandise at the end of a season; grocery and drugstores would have sales only when their vendors offered them special prices or when they were overstocked. Today, many retailers respond to increased competition and a more value-conscious customer by promoting more frequent sales.

Wal-Mart's Everyday Low Pricing (EDLP) strategy has helped make them the market leader in every market they enter, and the largest retailer in the world.

Deciding Which Strategy Is Best

An EDLP has three relative benefits in relation to high/low:

- *Reduced price wars.* Many customers are skeptical about initial retail prices. They have become conditioned to buying only on sale—the main characteristic of a high/low pricing strategy. A successful EDLP strategy enables retailers to withdraw from highly competitive price wars with competitors. Once customers realize that prices are fair, they'll buy more each time and buy more frequently.

- *Reduced advertising.* The stable prices caused by EDLP limit the need for weekly sale advertising used in the high/low strategy. Instead, retailers can focus on more image-oriented messages. Also, catalogs don't become obsolete as quickly since prices don't change as often.

Retailers using a high/low pricing strategy start with a high price and use advertising to promote frequent sales.

- *Reduced stockouts and improved inventory management.* An EDLP reduces the large variations in demand caused by frequent sales with large markdowns. As a result, retailers can manage their inventory with more certainty. Fewer stockouts mean more satisfied customers, higher sales, and fewer rain checks. (**Rain checks** are given to customers when merchandise is out of stock; they're written promises to sell customers merchandise at the sale price when the merchandise arrives.) In addition, a more predictable customer demand pattern enables the retailer to improve inventory turnover by reducing the average inventory needed for special promotions and backup stock.

But EDLP policy isn't for every retailer. A high/low strategy has several strengths too:

- *The same merchandise appeals to multiple markets.* High/low strategy allows retailers to charge higher prices to customers who are not price-sensitive and lower prices to price-sensitive customers. When fashion merchandise first hits the store, it's offered at its highest price. Fashion leaders, those who are less sensitive to price, and hard-to-fit customers often buy as soon as the merchandise is available. As the season progresses and markdowns are taken, more price-sensitive customers enter the market and pay a lower price for the same merchandise. Finally, hard-core bargain hunters enter the market for the end-of-season deep-discount sales like the Neiman Marcus Last Call Sale at the end of each season—25 percent off merchandise that has already been marked down 33 to 50 percent.

  Grocery and drugstore customers react to high/low prices in a similar manner. Some customers pay little attention to the prices they pay; others will wait for merchandise to go on sale and stockpile for future use.

- *Sales create excitement.* A "get them while they last" atmosphere often occurs during a sale. Sales draw crowds, and crowds create excitement. Some retailers augment low prices and advertising with special in-store activities like product demonstrations, giveaways, and celebrity appearances.

- *Sales move merchandise.* All merchandise will eventually sell—the question is, at what price? Frequent sales enable retailers to move the merchandise, even though profits erode. The reasons retailers put certain merchandise on sale are discussed later in this chapter.

- *Emphasis is on quality.* A high initial price sends a signal to customers that the merchandise is high quality. When merchandise goes on sale, customers still use the original, or reference, price to gauge quality. An EDLP policy may send the wrong signal to customers. They may assume that since prices are low, quality or services may suffer.

Retailing View 15.1 tells how Dollar General has elevated EDLP to a higher plane.

APPROACHES FOR SETTING PRICES

After selecting an overall pricing strategy, retailers still need to set the prices for each item. Retailers want to set prices to maximize long-term profits. To do this, they need to consider the following: (1) cost, because they want to make a profit, (2) demand, because this is what customers will pay for the merchandise, and (3) competition, because customers shop around and compare prices. The following sections examine three approaches for setting retail prices—cost-oriented, demand-oriented, and competition-oriented—and describe how retailers determine how much they need to sell to break even.

Under the **cost-oriented method,** the retail price is determined by adding a fixed percentage to the cost of the merchandise. For instance, Primrose Fashions, a family-owned women's specialty store in Dallas, uses the **keystone method** of setting prices, in which it simply doubles the cost of the merchandise to obtain the original retail selling price. If a dress costs Primrose $50, the original selling price is $100.

With the **demand-oriented method,** prices are based on what customers expect or are willing to pay. In this case, Primrose may have found a particularly good value at $50 but believes that the profit-maximizing price is $115. With the **competition-oriented method,** prices are based on competitors' prices.

Which method is best? The answer is all three! The cost-oriented method's strength is that it is quick, mechanical, and relatively simple to use. Retailers use it because they are making thousands of pricing decisions each week and cannot take the time to thoroughly analyze and determine the best price for each product.

As indicated by economic theory, the demand-oriented method's strength is that it allows retailers to determine which price will give them the greatest profit. But demand-oriented pricing is hard to implement, especially in a retailing environment with thousands of SKUs that require individual pricing decisions.

The competition-oriented method should be considered because it is always important to keep in mind what competition is doing—after all, the customer does. The degree to which a retailer sets the market price or follows the market leader is, however, a complicated issue.

Retailers need to consider costs, demand, and competition in setting prices. The cost-oriented method would be the starting point for setting a price. The competition-oriented method provides an outside check on the marketplace. The demand-oriented method is then used for fine-tuning the strategy. Retailers would start with a price based on costs and their profit goals, consider competition, and then perform tests to determine if it's the most profitable price.

Service retailers face unique challenges that aren't as important to merchandise retailers. See More Information About 15.1 for details.

Dollar General: Referential Treatment of EDLP | RETAILING VIEW

15.1

The success of Dollar General, according to CEO Cal Turner Jr., grandson of the founder, is simple. Reflecting his strong religious values, Turner believes that people want to be a part of an organization that makes a difference and that values them. "There's a real ministry when you're dedicated to selling toilet paper and bleach cheaper than anybody in the business," Turner said.

Dollar General shares its profits with associates at all levels and goes beyond offering financially strapped consumers value-priced products. Efforts such as Dollar General's literacy referral program and learning center work programs at inner-city stores have made a real difference in customers' lives.

The predecessor to the first Dollar General store opened in 1939. Today there are over 5,500 stores in 27 states, with sales in fiscal 2001 of $4.55 billion. Opening stores at an average rate of two per day, Dollar General is surpassed only by Radio Shack in number of stores. Stores are located in small communities of less than 20,000 population and in urban areas with low-income demographics.

Understanding the needs of Dollar General's core customer is key to comprehending what makes the concept work. Its core customers fall into two distinct groups—mothers ages 25 to 40 with household income of under $25,000, and retired seniors living on fixed incomes. Therefore, supplying consumables and apparel basics at low prices is paramount.

In 1998, Dollar General shifted its assortment to roughly 18 percent soft lines and 82 percent hard lines. It changed its apparel offerings to what Turner calls "consumable basics" (such as khakis, jeans, T-shirts, socks, and underwear) and culled more fashion-oriented items.

Pricing is also simple. "We'll clothe you from the waist up for 5 bucks and from the waist down for 10 bucks," he said. Core merchandise price points range from four items for $1 up to $20. Noncore items go as high as $35. The average transaction is $8.

Sources: Hoovers Online, 2002, www.hoovers.com; Debbie Howell, "Dollar General Hits Milestone," *DSN Retailing Today* 40, no. 2 (February 19, 2001), p. 1; Debbie Howell, "The Right Reverend of EDLP," *Discount Store News*, May 24, 1999, p. xxx; and Jennifer Negley, "Taking Value to the Extreme," *Discount Store News*, April 19, 1999. Reprinted by permission from *Discount Store News*, April and May 1999. Copyright Lebhar-Friedman, Inc. 425 Park Avenue, New York, NY 10022.

The Cost-Oriented Method of Setting Retail Prices

This section explains how retail prices are set on the basis of merchandise cost. Unfortunately, the process isn't always as simple as doubling the cost, which we described earlier. For instance, the retail price at which the product is originally sold may not be the same as the final retail selling price due to markdowns. So retailers have devised methods of keeping track of changes in the retail price so they can achieve their overall financial goals, as we discussed in Chapter 6.

Recall that the retailer's financial goals are set by top management in terms of a target return on assets. In the strategic profit model, return on assets is calculated as net profit margin multiplied by asset turnover. Pricing goals are determined primarily from net profit margin.

● MORE INFORMATION ABOUT . . . Pricing Retail Services

15.1

The pricing of services can be more complicated than the pricing of goods for three reasons: inability of customers to match supply and demand, to determine an accurate reference price, and to judge quality.

First, it is more difficult to match supply and demand for services than it is for products. When buying a product like shoes, for example, the store keeps an inventory of shoes available for when the customer comes in. Supply may not exactly match demand in that there are more shoes in the store than the retailer is able to sell in one day. But at least the shoes are available.

This is not necessarily the case, however, for a service like a haircut or a movie theater. The hair-cutting boutique is constrained by the number of hair stylists, and the movie theater is constrained by the number of seats. If more people want to get their hair cut or go to the movies on Saturday than on Monday, the demand for and supply of these services become out of alignment. Service retailers can use some of the same strategies applied by merchandise retailers to better align supply with demand. For instance, both can offer discounts or coupon incentives to get more people to go to the movies or get their hair cut on Monday. They could bundle services—get a haircut and a manicure for a 20 percent discount, or go to the movie and get a box of popcorn free. Finally, these service retailers can use multiunit pricing—one haircut, or movie admission, at full price and the second one at half price. These pricing strategies are explored in more depth later in this chapter.

Second, it is more difficult for consumers to obtain accurate reference prices for services. A **reference price** is a price point in memory for a good or a service and can consist of the price last paid, the price most frequently paid, or the average of all prices customers have paid for similar offerings.[5] Consumers get information to form their reference prices from the experience of buying similar merchandise, information obtained from peer groups, or from advertising. Second, customers use price as an indicator of service quality more than they do the quality of goods.

Because services are intangible and are not created on a factory assembly

When in need of an attorney, do you look for the cheapest one in town?

For pricing decisions, the key component of net profit margin is gross profit margin percentage (gross margin ÷ net sales). Retailers set initial prices high enough so that after markdowns and other adjustments (known as reductions) are made, they'll end up with a gross margin consistent with their overall profit goals. We'll now describe how retailers determine their initial selling price based on their gross margin goal.

Determining the Initial Markup from Maintained Markup and Gross Margin   The performance measure usually used to evaluate pricing decisions is gross margin. Exhibit 15–1 summarizes its components. In Chapter 6, we used the traditional accounting definition of gross margin: net sales minus cost of goods sold. But retailers use an additional term called *maintained markup* that is

---

line, service retailers have greater flexibility in the configurations of services they offer than do retailers of goods. As a result, it is difficult for customers to discern the reference price. Service retailers can conceivably offer an infinite variety of combinations and permutations, leading to complex and complicated pricing structures. As an example, consider how difficult it is to get comparable price quotes when buying life insurance. With the multitude of types (e.g., whole life versus term), features (different deductibles), and variations associated with customers (age, health risk, smoking or nonsmoking), few insurance companies offer exactly the same features and the same prices. Only an expert customer, one who knows enough about insurance to completely specify the options across providers, is likely to find prices that are directly comparable.

Another factor that results in the inaccuracy of reference prices is that individual customer needs vary. Some hair stylists' service prices vary across customers on the basis of length of hair, type of haircut, and whether a conditioning treatment and style are included. Therefore, if you were to ask a friend what a cut costs from a particular stylist, chances are that your cut from the same stylist may be a different price. In a similar vein, a service as simple as a hotel room will have prices that vary greatly: by size of room, time of year, type of room availability, and individual versus group rate.

Still another reason customers lack accurate reference prices for services is that they feel overwhelmed with the information they need to gather. With most goods, retail stores display the products by category to allow customers to compare and contrast the prices of different brands and sizes. Rarely is there a similar display of services in a single outlet. If customers want to compare prices, for example, for dry cleaning, they must drive to or call individual outlets.

The third difference between pricing services and merchandise is that buyers are likely to use price as an indicator of both service costs and service quality.[6] Customers' use of price as an indicator of quality depends on several factors, one of which is the other information available to them. When service cues to quality are readily accessible, when brand names provide evidence of a company's reputation, or when level of advertising communicates the company's belief in the brand, customers may prefer to use those cues instead of price. In other situations, however, such as when quality is hard to detect or when quality or price varies a great deal within a class of services, consumers may believe that price is the best indicator of quality. Many of these conditions typify situations that face consumers when purchasing services.[7]

Another factor that increases the dependence on price as a quality indicator is the risk associated with the service purchase. In high-risk situations, many of which involve credence services such as medical treatment or management consulting, the customer will look to price as a surrogate for quality.

Because customers depend on price as a cue to quality and because price sets expectations of quality, service prices must be determined carefully. In addition to being chosen to cover costs or match competitors, prices must be chosen to convey the appropriate quality signal. Pricing too low can lead to inaccurate inferences about the quality of the service. Pricing too high can set expectations that may be difficult to match in service delivery.

Source: Valarie A. Zeithaml and Mary Jo Bitner, *Services Marketing: Integrating Customer Focus across the Firm*, 3rd ed., (New York: McGraw-Hill Higher Education, 2002).

484

EXHIBIT 15–1
Sample Income
Statement Showing
Gross Margin

Net Sales	$120,000
–Cost of goods sold	58,000
= Maintained markup	62,000
–Alteration costs + Cash discounts	3,000
= Gross margin	$ 59,000

similar to gross margin, but it considers two additional costs. The relationship can be expressed as:

$$\text{Maintained markup percentage} = \frac{\text{Net sales} - \text{Costs of goods sold}}{\text{Net sales}}$$

$$\frac{\text{Gross margin}}{\text{percentage}} = \frac{\text{Maintained markup} - \text{Workroom costs} + \text{Cash discounts}}{\text{Net sales}}$$

Thus, the only difference between the two terms is the workroom costs (such as alterations to a suit or the cost of putting a table together) and cash discounts (given to the store by the vendor for paying invoices early). Why do retailers make this distinction between maintained markup and gross margin? In many retail organizations, these workroom costs aren't controlled by the person who makes the pricing decision. For instance, the furniture buyer doesn't have control over costs associated with assembling a dining room table. In the same way, a buyer typically has no control over whether the accounting department takes the cash discounts offered to the company from its vendors for paying invoices early. But remember that, conceptually, maintained markup and gross margin are similar.

The term *maintained markup* is very descriptive. It's the amount of profit (markup) a retailer plans to maintain on a particular category of merchandise. For example, in Exhibit 15–1, planned maintained markup is $62,000 on sales of $120,000, or 51.67 percent ($62,000 ÷ $120,000). In other words, to meet its profit goals, this retailer must obtain a 51.67 percent maintained markup.

A retailer's life would be relatively simple if the amount of markup it wanted to maintain (maintained markup) were the same as the initial markup.

Initial markup = Retail selling price initially placed on the merchandise –
                Cost of goods sold

whereas,

Maintained markup = The actual sales that you get for the merchandise –
                   Cost of goods sold

Why is there a difference? A number of reductions to the value of retail inventory occur between the time the merchandise is originally priced (initial markup) and the time it's sold (maintained markup). **Reductions** include markdowns, discounts to employees and customers, and inventory shrinkage (due to shoplifting, breakage, or loss). Initial markup must be high enough so that after reductions are taken out, the maintained markup is left.

A few retail customers might feel slightly guilty when buying a product that has been drastically marked down. They shouldn't, however. Retailers that successfully plan their sales and markdowns also build the markdown into the initial price. Even though a customer may receive a very good price on a particular purchase, other people paid the premarkdown price. So, on average, the markup was maintained.

Retailers expect shrinkage and include this loss in the price customers pay. To illustrate, consider a TV campaign that ran a few years ago showing someone shoplifting. The message was "When you shoplift, you are ripping off your neighbor." If two retailers plan to achieve the same maintained markup, but one has a high percentage of shrinkage due to shoplifting, that store needs a higher initial markup if all other factors are held constant.

The relationship between initial markup and maintained markup is

$$\text{Initial markup} = \frac{\text{Maintained markup} + \text{Reductions}}{\text{Net sales} + \text{Reductions}}$$

or

$$\text{Initial markup} = \frac{\begin{array}{c}\text{Maintained markup (as a \% of net sales)} \\ + \text{Reductions (as a \% of net sales)}\end{array}}{100\% + \text{Reductions (as a \% of net sales)}}$$

Using the information in Exhibit 15–1 and assuming that reductions of $14,400 here equal 12 percent of net sales,

$$\text{Initial markup} = \frac{\$62,000 + \$14,400}{\$120,000 + \$14,400} = 56.85\%$$

or

$$\text{Initial markup} = \frac{51.67\% + 12\%}{100\% + 12\%} = 56.85\%$$

Note that the same answer is obtained using both formulas. Also, initial markup is always greater than maintained markup so long as there are any reductions. Finally, initial markup is expressed either in dollars or as a percentage of retail price. This is because retailers using the retail inventory method (RIM) of inventory accounting (described in Appendix 13A) think of their inventory in "retail" rather than "cost" terms. Also, expressing initial markup as a percentage of retail price closely resembles the other accounting conventions of expressing net profit, gross margin, and maintained markup as percentages of net sales, which are, of course, at retail.

Determining the Initial Retail Price under Cost-Oriented Pricing

Continuing the preceding example, with the initial markup of 56.85 percent, assume that the suggested retail price of a certain item is $100. What is the dollar markup and the merchandise cost?

Retail = Cost + Markup
$100 = Cost + (56.85% × Retail)
$100 = Cost + $56.85
$100 = $43.15 + $56.85

The dollar markup is $56.85 and the merchandise cost is $43.15.

Here's another example. A salesperson comes into a buyer's office with a great new product that will cost $100. What will be the retail price if the initial markup is still 56.85 percent?

There are three ways to solve this problem. First, the buyer can convert the initial markup as a percentage of retail to initial markup as a percentage of cost using the formula[8]

$$\text{Initial markup as a \% of cost} = \frac{\text{Initial markup as a \% of retail}}{100\% - \text{Initial markup as a \% of retail}}$$

$$131.75\% = \frac{56.85\%}{100\% - 56.85\%}$$

Then the problem can be set up as before:

Retail = Cost + Markup
Retail = $100 + (131.75% × Cost)
$231.75 = $100 + $131.75

The second way to solve this problem uses algebra. Let's say that R stands for the retail price.

Retail = Cost + Markup
Retail = $100 + (56.85% × Retail)
R = $100 + .5685   × R

By subtracting $.5685 \times R$ from both sides of the equation, the resulting initial retail price can be figured as follows:

$.4315 \times R = \$100$
$R = \$231.75$

The third way to solve this problem uses the formula

$$\text{Retail} = \frac{\text{Cost}}{1 - \text{Markup}}$$

$$\$231.75 = \frac{\$100}{1 - .5685}$$

The Demand-Oriented Method of Setting Retail Prices

Demand-oriented pricing should be used in conjunction with the cost-oriented method to determine retail prices. Using this method, retailers not only consider their profit structure but also pay close attention to the effect that price changes have on sales. For instance, if customers are extremely sensitive to price, then a price cut can increase demand so much that profits actually increase. Alternatively, if customers are insensitive to price, raising the price also can boost profits, since sales likely won't decrease. Demand-oriented pricing seeks to determine the price that maximizes profits.

To illustrate how an initial retail price is set using the demand-oriented method, we will use a hypothetical situation of The Gap's new ribbed sleeveless T-shirt for women. Assume that the fixed cost of developing the product is $300,000 and the variable cost is $5 each. One benefit of private-label merchan-

Market	(1) Unit Price	(2) Market Demand at Price (in units)	(3) Total Revenue (col. 1 × col. 2)	(4) Total Cost of Units Sold ($300,000 fixed cost + $5 variable cost)	(5) Total Profits (col. 3 – col.4)
1	$ 8	200,000	$1,600,000	$1,300,000	$300,000
2	10	150,000	1,500,000	1,050,000	450,000
3	12	100,000	1,200,000	800,000	400,000
4	14	50,000	700,000	550,000	150,000

EXHIBIT 15–2
Results of Pricing Test

dise is the flexibility of being able to set any retail price. The Gap decides to test the T-shirt in four markets at different prices. Exhibit 15–2 shows the pricing test's results. It's clear (from column 5) that a unit price of $10 is by far the most profitable ($450,000).

While determining the optimal price based on a demand analysis is simple for one product, most retailers carry so many products that these tests become a very expensive proposition. Also, a retailer must have multiple outlets to be able to manipulate prices in this manner.

A more sophisticated method of determining the most profitable price is a pricing experiment. In a pricing experiment, a retailer actually changes the price in a systematic manner to observe changes in purchases or purchase intentions. Exhibit 15–3 shows an example of a simple experiment—a classic before/after experiment with control group design. Two stores are similar in size and customer characteristics. Their weekly sales for a compact microwave oven are almost identical (10 and 12 units per week), and the ovens are selling at the same price, $100. Price at the first store is changed to $80, but the second store's price is left at $100. Thus, the second store is used as a control to make sure that any change in sales is due to the price change rather than to some outside force such as competition or weather. Now sales at the first store jump to 21 units per week, while sales at the control store hit 13 units. Barring any circumstances unknown to the retailer, the change in sales is due to the price cut. And, by the way, the $100 price is more profitable than the $80 price in the second store! Since product cost is $50, the $100 retail price provides a $650 gross margin [($100 – $50) × 13 units], whereas the $80 price provides a $630 gross margin [($80 – $50) × 21 units].

In the past, these pricing experiments weren't regularly applied because of the time and expense of administering them. But now any retailer with point-of-sale terminals can run large-scale experiments. Retailers can utilize the data warehouses derived from their loyalty programs in conjunction with sales and price data to run experiments. (See Chapter 11 for information on how these loyalty programs work.) These records cover what customers have purchased, prices

	Before	After
Store 1	10 units @ $100 Gross margin = $500	21 unit @ $80 Gross margin = $630
Store 2 (Control)	12 units @ $100 Gross margin = $600	13 units @ $100 Gross margin = $650

EXHIBIT 15–3
A Pricing Experiment

paid, and conditions of sale (such as coupon usage and price specials). Various demographic information on customers makes it possible to correlate price sensitivity with customer profiles.

Retailers and their vendors can also buy from private firms like Information Resources, Inc. (www.infores.com). For one of its many products, InfoScan, the company purchases information from individual supermarket chains on price and promotion activity that has been scanned through their POS terminals; it then aggregates data by region, chain, or market area.

The Competition-Oriented Method of Setting Retail Prices

As the name implies, when retailers use competition-oriented pricing, they set their prices on the basis of their competition rather than cost or demand considerations. Retailers can price either above, below, or at parity with the competition. The chosen strategy must be consistent with the retailer's overall strategy and its relative market position. Consider, for instance, Wal-Mart and Tiffany and Co. as we did in Chapter 6. Wal-Mart's overall strategy is to be the low-cost provider of any market basket of goods in every market in which it competes. It tries to price below competition. Tiffany and Co., on the other hand, has significant brand equity, which connotes high quality, unique merchandise, impeccable service, and elegant locations. Those little blue boxes and wonderful trinkets stamped Tiffany & co. can command more than market price.

Market leaders cannot, however, ignore their small competitors. Suppose that a sporting goods store in Norman, Oklahoma, consistently underprices Wal-Mart on fishing gear. Wal-Mart will adjust its prices to meet or even beat the competitor in that market.

What should small competitors do to compete with market leaders? A jewelry store could price at parity or below Tiffany & Co. Additionally, it could strive for competitive advantages in assortment or service. A more difficult question is how a western wear store can compete against Wal-Mart's prices. It cannot compete head to head with Wal-Mart on every item. To do so would probably put it out of business because it cannot achieve the buying quantities of scale of Wal-Mart. Instead, it should pick items that are very visible to customers and generate margin on items that customers cannot readily compare. If Wal-Mart is advertising Lee jeans at $19.99, then the western store should either carry another brand of jeans or bite the bullet and price with or below Wal-Mart.

Collecting and Using Competitive Price Data[9]   Retailers work to provide a consistent shopping experience, and part of that requires consistency between a retailer's market strategy and its pricing position within a market. To ensure consistency, most large retailers routinely collect competitive price data from top competitors to see where they have room to raise margins and also where margins need to be lowered to maintain a desired market position.

From the price comparison in Exhibit 15–4 you can see three pricing strategies at work. CVS, the national drug store chain, is priced above the other channels of trade, but not on everything. Pricing for shampoo, toothpaste, and shaving gel is very competitive. Similarly, Winn-Dixie, a grocery chain with high/low pricing, is moderately priced with low everyday prices on select items, like baby food. Wal-Mart, which uses an EDLP strategy, is generally priced below the market and does not stock a full range of products.

SKU	CVS	Winn-Dixie	Wal-Mart
Centrum Vitamins (130 tablets)	$9.49	$9.99	$8.26
Tylenol Liquid	6.49	4.69	5.47
Emfamil Liquid Baby Food	3.29	2.99	3.13
VO5 Shampoo	0.99	1.19	0.97
Pedialyte (1 liter)	5.79	5.29	
Colgate Toothpaste (6 oz.)	2.99	2.99	2.84
Duracell AA Batteries (4 pack)	4.79	3.49	3.24
9 Lives Canned Cat Food	1.49	1.29	0.98
Advil (50 caps)	5.99	5.59	
Edge Shaving Gel (7 oz.)	2.39	2.39	2.14
Competitive Price Index*	100%	91%	85%

EXHIBIT 15–4
Competitive Price Data

*Only common items are indexed.
SOURCE: Reprinted by permission of Comparative Prices International CPI.

Competitive price data are typically collected using store personnel, third-party providers, and vendor representatives (whose interests often bias the data). Costing between $0.15 and $2.00 per price point to collect, competitive price comparisons are typically still performed using pen and paper and sometimes without the consent of the competitor. Because of the costs associated with collecting and then managing the data is significant, retailers need to be very strategic when structuring competitive price projects.

How Retailers Reduce Price Competition   Retailers have two fundamental strategies available to them for reducing price competition. First, they can adopt an EDLP strategy as described at the beginning of this chapter. Conditioning customers to expect a fair and relatively low price on a typical market basket of merchandise enables a retailer to charge slightly higher prices on some individual items. Second, they can utilize some of the branding strategies described in Chapter 14. For instance, they can develop lines of premium private-label merchandise. Since competition doesn't have such merchandise, there is no external way to develop a reference price from a competitor.

Profit Impact of Setting a Retail Price: The Use of Break-Even Analysis

Now that we've examined how retailers set prices on the bases on the cost-, demand-, and competition-oriented methods, let's look at how retailers determine the volume of sales necessary for them to make a profit. A useful analytical tool is **break-even analysis,** which analyzes the relationship between total revenue and total cost to determine how much merchandise is required to be sold to achieve a break-even (zero) profit at various sales levels. Break-even analysis has many applications in retailing. Just to name a few:

- Break-even volume and dollars of a new product, product line, department, store, and so on.
- Break-even sales change needed to cover a price change.
- Break-even sales to cover a target profit.
- Change in profit based on change in sales volume.

Let's look more closely at the first two: the break-even volume of a new private-label product and the break-even sales change needed to cover a price change.

Calculating Break-Even for a New Product Let's return to the example discussed earlier of The Gap's new private-label product—a ribbed sleeveless T-shirt for women. Cost of developing this shirt is about $300,000, including executives' and designers' salaries, rent on the design team's buildings, and warehousing. Since these costs are stable and don't change with the quantity of product that's produced and sold, they're known as **fixed costs.** Management plans to sell the T-shirt for $12—the unit price. Cost of the shirt is $5. In economic terms, this is known as the **variable cost**—the sum of the firm's expenses that vary directly with the quantity of product produced and sold. Variable costs often include direct labor and materials used in producing the product. But in this case, The Gap is purchasing the shirt from a third party. Thus, the only variable cost is the shirt's cost. The **break-even point (BEP)** is the quantity at which total revenue equals total cost, and beyond which profit occurs.

$$\text{BEP quantity} = \frac{\text{Fixed cost}}{\text{Unit price} - \text{Unit variable cost}}$$

In this example,

$$\text{BEP quantity} = \frac{\$300,000}{\$12 - \$5} = 42,857 \text{ units}$$

This means The Gap must sell 42,857 T-shirts to break even. If it sold only one less T-shirt—42,856—it would lose money on this buy! To make things interesting, let's assume The Gap wishes to make a $100,000 profit. The break-even quantity now becomes

$$\text{BEP quantity} = \frac{\$300,000 + \$100,000}{\$12 - \$5} = 57,143 \text{ units}$$

If it decides to reduce the selling price to $10, we calculate the break-even quantity again:

$$\text{BEP quantity} = \frac{\$300,000 + \$100,000}{\$10 - \$5} = 80,000 \text{ units}$$

To convert the break-even quantity to break-even sales dollars, simply multiply the BEP quantity by the selling price: 80,000 units $\times$ $10 = $800,000.

Calculating Break-Even Sales A closely related issue to the calculation of a break-even point is determining how much sales would have to increase to profit from a price cut, or how much sales would have to decline to make a price increase unprofitable.[10] Continuing with The Gap example, assume the break-even quantity is 57,143 units (based on the $300,000 fixed cost, the $100,000 profit, a selling price of $12, and a cost of $5). How many units must The Gap sell to break even if it lowers its selling price by 16.6 percent to $10? Using the formula,

$$\% \text{ break-even sales change} = \frac{-\% \text{ price change}}{\%\text{CM} + \% \text{ price change}} \times 100$$

where %CM stands for percent contribution margin. **Contribution margin** is gross margin less any expense that can be directly assigned to the merchandise. In this example, since there are no variable costs besides the cost of the shirt, the contribution margin is the same as the gross margin. Also, don't forget the minus sign in the formula's numerator.

CM   = Selling price – Variable costs
CM   = \$12 – \$5 = \$7
%CM = (CM ÷ Selling price) × 100
%CM = (\$7 ÷ \$12) × 100 = 58.33%

Substituting the %CM into the formula, we can calculate the break-even sales change:

$$\% \text{ break-even sales change} = \frac{-(-16.6)}{58.33 + (-16.6)} \times 100 = 39.78\%$$

Unit break-even sales change = 39.78% × 57,143 units = 22,731 units

Thus, if The Gap reduces its price to \$10, it must sell an additional 22,731 units to break even. It should come as no surprise that when we add the break-even quantity at \$12 to the break-even sales change to \$10, we get 79,874 units (57,143 + 22,731)—almost the same break-even point of 80,000 units that we obtained using the first formula. (The difference is due to rounding.) The same formula can be used to determine the sales change necessary to break even with a price increase.

PRICE ADJUSTMENTS

In the United States, retailers are relatively free to promote adjustments to the initial retail price with the hope of generating sales. In this section we will examine markdowns, coupons, rebates, price bundling, multiple-unit pricing, variable pricing, and some special Internet pricing issues. Retailers in other parts of the world, however, are not so lucky. Retailing View 15.2 describes the pricing restrictions that until recently were imposed on German retailers.

Markdowns

Markdowns are reductions in the initial retail price. Markdowns are a type of second-degree price discrimination because the lower price induces price-sensitive customers to buy more merchandise. Let's examine why retailers take markdowns, how to optimize markdown decisions, how to reduce the amount of markdowns by working with vendors, how to liquidate markdown merchandise, and the mechanics of taking markdowns.

Reasons for Taking Markdowns

Retailers' many reasons to take markdowns can be classified as either clearance (to get rid of merchandise) or promotional (to generate sales).

Many retailers think of markdowns as mistakes. When merchandise is slow-moving, obsolete, at the end of its selling season, or priced higher than competitors' goods, it generally gets marked down for clearance purposes. This merchandise can become an eyesore and impair a store's image. Further, even if the merchandise can be sold in the following season, it may become shopworn or out of style. Also, the cost of carrying inventory is significant. If a buyer has to carry $10,000 of unwanted inventory at cost for a year with an annual inventory carrying cost of 35 percent, the cost would be $3,500 (or $10,000 × .35)—not a trivial amount!

Markdowns are part of the cost of doing business. As we've said, retailers plan their markdowns. They set an initial markup high enough so that after markdowns and other reductions are taken, the planned maintained markup is achieved. Thus, a retailer's objective shouldn't necessarily be to minimize markdowns. If markdowns are too low, the retailer is probably pricing the merchandise too low, not purchasing enough merchandise, or not taking enough risks with the merchandise being purchased.

Using a high/low pricing strategy described earlier in this chapter, retailers employ markdowns to promote merchandise to increase sales. A buyer may decide to mark down some merchandise to make room for something new. An additional benefit is that the markdown sale generates cash flow to pay for new merchandise. Markdowns are also taken to increase customers' traffic flow. Retailers plan promotions in which they take markdowns for holidays, for special events, and as part of their overall promotional program. (Chapter 16 gives details.) In fact, small portable appliances (such as toasters) are called *traffic appliances* because they're often in a leader pricing program and sold at reduced prices to generate in-store traffic. Retailers hope that customers will purchase other

REFACT

Marked-down goods, which accounted for just 8 percent of department-store sales three decades ago, have climbed to around 20 percent, according to the National Retail Federation.[11]

RETAILING VIEW   Pricing Restrictions Ending in Germany

15.2

In the 1930s, Nazis in Germany enacted laws that sharply restricted coupons, rebates, discounts, free items with purchase, and other promotional tools that American retailers take for granted. They are still on the books, and enforced.

Giving customers something for nothing violates the Free Gift Act, and almost any price discount or small trinket is prohibited. When a German drugstore tried to give away 75-cent shopping bags in honor of its birthday, a court stepped in to block the giveaway. Half-price happy-hour drinks also are forbidden, because the discount is ruled to be too large. (Generally, discounts of more than 3 percent of list are prohibited.) Lands' End cannot advertise its unconditional guarantee return policy, even though it can offer it if a customer asks about a return. Quelle AG, a large retailer, was forbidden to advertise that it would contribute a small amount to fight AIDS for each Visa card transaction. This violates the act because a retailer may only advertise its products, not attempt to exploit customer emotions. Clearance sales are limited to

twice a year and the anniversaries of the founding of the retailer.

But Germany is repealing these regulations for two reasons: The Internet and globalization. First, the EU decided that the Internet rules of commerce should be based on the home of the retailer, not the consumer. This would free French, British, and other retailers to offer discounts and frequent buyer plans to German customers that German retailers are prohibited from offering. Some considerations may be incorporated for small retailers, but the promotional tactics would be largely liberalized.

Companies from McDonald's to Procter & Gamble are ready to drop coupons. Banks and other services are planning to launch their frequent flier plans on their credit cards. In 2001, only 4 of 2,700 German banks offer frequent flier miles on Visa.

Sources: David Wessel, "German Shoppers Get Coupons," *The Wall Street Journal*, April 5, 2001, p. A1; and Neal E. Boudette, "Germany's Competition Center Fights Ultimate Consumer Scourge: Bargains," *The Wall Street Journal*, January 23, 2002, www.wsj.com.

products at regular prices while they're in the store. Another opportunity created by markdowns is to increase the sale of complementary products. For example, a supermarket's markdown on hot dog buns may be offset by increased demand for hot dogs, mustard, and relish—all sold at regular prices.

Optimizing Markdown Decisions   Retailers have traditionally created a set of arbitrary rules for taking markdowns.[12] One retailer, for instance, flags markdown candidates when their weekly sell-through percentages fall below a certain value. Another retailer cuts prices on the basis of how long the merchandise has been in the store—marking products down by 20 percent after eight weeks, then by 30 percent after 12 weeks, and finally by 50 percent after 16 weeks.

Such a rules-based approach, however, is limited in several ways. First, it assumes that all the items within a category exhibit the same, consistent behavior. So it treats a cashmere sweater the same way it treats a wool one. Second, a rules-based approach follows a fixed schedule; it's not sophisticated enough to determine how shifts in sales trends or other factors such as promotions or holidays will affect demand. And third, this approach fails to take gross margin into consideration; its only goal is to clear inventory.

Instead of relying on rules developed from averages, a retailer can benefit significantly from merchandising optimization software. **Merchandising optimization software** is a set of algorithms that monitors merchandise sales, promotions, competitors' actions, and other factors to determine the optimal (most profitable) price and timing for merchandising activities, especially markdowns. This software is currently being used by a growing number of major retailers, including Gymboree, JCPenney, KB Toys, and ShopKo, and is commercially available from a number of specialty firms such as ProfitLogic, KhiMetrics, and Spotlight Solutions Inc. as well as part of comprehensive merchandise management systems such as Retek, Marketmax, JDA, and SAP.

The optimization software works by constantly refining its pricing forecasts on the basis of actual sales throughout the season. For example, the software recognizes that in early November, a winter item's sales are better than expected, so it delays taking a markdown that had been planned. Each week, as fresh sales data become available, it readjusts the forecasts to include the latest information. It computes literally thousands of scenarios for each item—a process that is too complicated and time-consuming for retailers to do on their own. It then evaluates the outcomes based on expected profits and other factors and selects the action that produces the best results.

Making good markdown decisions isn't all about relying on sophisticated computer software. Retailers must also work closely with their vendor partners to coordinate deliveries and help share the financial burden of taking markdowns.

Reducing the Amount of Markdowns by Working with Vendors   Retailers can reduce the amount of markdowns by working closely with their vendors to time deliveries with demand. Merchandise that arrives ahead of when it is needed takes up valuable selling space and can get shopworn or damaged. On the other hand, when merchandise arrives too late, retailers may have trouble selling it without extensive markdowns. Quick response inventory systems (Chapter 10) reduce the lead time for receiving merchandise so that retailers can more closely monitor changes in trends and customer demand, thus reducing markdowns.

Vendors have a vested interest in retailers' success. Vendors that are knowledgeable of the market and competition can help with stock selections. Of course, a retailer must also trust its own taste and intuition; otherwise, its store will have the same merchandise as all other stores. Retail buyers can often obtain **markdown money**—funds a vendor gives the retailer to cover lost gross margin dollars that result from markdowns and other merchandising issues. For instance, assume a retailer has $1,000 worth of ties at retail that are given a 25 percent markdown. Thus, when the ties are sold, the retailer receives only $750. But if the vendor provides $250 in markdown money, the maintained markup is maintained. In this way, the vendor helps share the risk. According to the Robinson-Patman Act, markdown money should be provided to all retailers on a proportionally equal basis, typically as a percentage of purchases. (Markdown money falls under the umbrella of potentially illegal price discrimination discussed in this chapter's appendix.)

Liquidating Markdown Merchandise   No matter what markdown strategy a retailer uses, some merchandise may still remain unsold. A retailer can use one of five strategies to liquidate this merchandise:

1. "Job-out" the remaining merchandise to another retailer.

2. Consolidate the marked-down merchandise.

3. Place the remaining merchandise on an Internet auction site like eBay, or have a special clearance location on its own website.

4. Give the merchandise to charity.

5. Carry the merchandise over to the next season.

Selling the remaining marked-down merchandise to another retailer has been very popular among retailers. For instance, TJX Corporation (owners of T. J. Maxx and Marshalls) and Bluefly.com purchase end-of-season merchandise from other retailers and sell it at deep discounts (see Chapter 2 for details). This strategy enables the retailer to have a relatively short markdown period, provides space for new merchandise, and at the same time eliminates the often unappealing sale atmosphere. The problem with this strategy is that the retailer can only recoup a small percentage of the merchandise's cost—often a mere 10 percent.

Marked-down merchandise can be consolidated in a number of ways. First, the consolidation can be made into one or a few of the retailer's regular locations. Second, marked-down merchandise can be consolidated into another retail chain or an outlet store under the same ownership. Saks Fifth Avenue (Off Fifth) and Neiman Marcus (Last Call Clearance Center) use this strategy. Finally, marked-down merchandise can be shipped to a distribution center or a rented space such as a convention center (Barney's of New York and J. Crew) for final sale. Retailers that use these strategies condition customers to anticipate out-of-stock situations at locations that don't participate in the consolidation sales, since the merchandise is only at those loca-

Neiman Marcus' Last Call Clearance Center is the last stop for merchandise that hasn't sold at sale prices at regular Neiman Marcus' or Bergdorf Goodman's stores.

tions for a relatively short time. This practice encourages a successful yet relatively short markdown period. Further, customers who shop during the consolidation sale enjoy a better selection than they'd find in the individual stores. But consolidation sales can be complex and expensive due to the extra transportation and record keeping involved.

The Internet is expected to be increasingly useful for liquidating marked-down merchandise. For example, an electronics store is partnering with eBay to sell goods it has received from trade-ins (see Chapter 10). J. Crew and many others have separate areas of their websites for clearance merchandise.

Giving clearance merchandise to charities is an increasingly popular practice. Charitable giving is always a good corporate practice. It is a way of giving back to the community and has strong public relations benefits. Also, the cost value of the merchandise can be deducted from income.

The final liquidation strategy—to carry merchandise over to the next season—is used with relatively high priced nonfashion merchandise, such as traditional men's clothing and furniture. Generally, however, it's not worth carrying over merchandise because of excessive inventory carrying costs.

Markdowns and Price Discrimination   Ideally, retailers would like to have the opportunity to charge customers as much as they would be willing to pay. This practice is called **first-degree price discrimination.** For instance, if a wealthy customer wants to buy something, the retailer charges more. If a price-sensitive customer comes in, the retailer charges less. Although this practice is legal and is widely used in some retail sectors, such as by automobile and antique dealers (see this chapter's appendix), it is impractical in a retail store with 20,000 SKUs and prices that are displayed for everyone to see. Recently, however, customers are initiating first-degree price discrimination by haggling. See Retailing View 15.3.

Markdowns and the other widely used retail adjustment practices described in the next section are known as **second-degree price discrimination**—charging

Retailers Try Haggling   RETAILING VIEW

15.3

Out shopping a few weeks ago, Regina Ranonis was trying to decide between trendy low-heeled boots or a more conservative style. Then the salesman spoke up: If she would spring for both pairs, he would knock $270 off the total price.

Does this sound like the local flea market? It wasn't. An array of retailers are hoping to reel in sales by allowing haggling, or some form of it. While the practice isn't entirely new—and officially denied by most companies—good consumers say they're getting deals everywhere from Sunglass Hut to trendy boutique Kenneth Cole. Big-name stores like Saks and Macy's say savvy shoppers who can cite competitors' prices may also find some wiggle room.

Many of the country's biggest retailers, from The Gap to Pottery Barn, say they're sticking to firm no-haggling policies. Many department stores use cash registers that won't accept unauthorized discount prices without manager approval. Some even have video cameras not only to watch shoppers but also to make sure the staff isn't cutting sweetheart deals.

Some of the best negotiating territory is at franchises, where owners have the flexibility to operate more like mom-and-pop shops. But even at major department stores and small chains, a growing number of managers are now authorized to lower a price to meet the competition, or throw in free alterations and delivery. Many stores take pains to insist that haggling is off limits, even as customers and sales associates say it goes on all the time. The policy is "try not to come down in price too much, but don't let the business walk out."

Source: Teri Agins and Sarah Collins, "Retailers Hoping to Lift Holiday Sales Begin to Allow Customers to Haggle," *The Wall Street Journal*, November 16, 2001, www.wsj.com. Copyright 2001 by Dow Jones & Co. Inc. Reproduced with permission of Dow Jones & Co. Inc. via Copyright Clearance Center.

different prices to different people on the basis of the nature of the offering. We'll now examine the following second-degree price discrimination strategies: coupons, rebates, price bundling, multiple-unit pricing, variable pricing, and some Internet pricing practices.

Coupons

Coupons offer a discount on the price of specific items when they're purchased at a store. Coupons are also considered to be a second-degree price discrimination because they provide an incentive to price-sensitive customers to purchase more merchandise. Coupons are issued by manufacturers and retailers in newspapers, on products, on the shelf, at the cash register, over the Internet, and through the mail. Coupons are used because they are thought to induce customers to try products for the first time, convert those first-time users to regular users, encourage large purchases, increase usage, and protect market share against competition.

The evidence on couponing's overall profitability is mixed, depending on the product category.[13] Since coupons have the seemingly positive effect of encouraging larger purchases than without coupons, the coupon promotion may be stealing sales from a future period without any net increase in sales. For instance, if a supermarket runs a coupon promotion on sugar, households may buy a large quantity of sugar and stockpile it for future use. Thus, unless the coupon is used mostly by new buyers, the net impact on sales will be negligible, and there will be a negative impact on profits by the amount of the redeemed coupons and cost of the coupon redemption procedures. Unfortunately, it's very hard to isolate a market for new users without allowing current users to take advantage of the coupon promotion. If, on the other hand, the coupon is for a CD or other product whose demand is not controlled by the degree of everyday usage, it might increase overall consumption.

Some believe that coupons annoy, alienate, and confuse consumers and therefore do little to increase store loyalty.[14] Consider the following ad for a supermarket. The headline reads "Double Coupons," meaning the customer gets twice the face value of the coupon. Sounds good so far, but it's followed by these eight caveats:

1. No minimum purchase required.

2. Manufacturers' paper coupons only. Coupons with a face value over $1.00 will be redeemed at face value.

3. If doubled coupon value is greater than price of the product, you get it FREE!

4. The value of the double coupon is not to exceed the retail value of the product.

5. Tobacco, milk, pharmacy, and other coupons excluded by law will not be doubled.

6. Coupons identified as "ShopRite Super Coupon" or "Valuable ShopRite Coupon" in any ShopRite advertisement will not be doubled.

7. Check-out coupons and Act Media coupons will not be doubled.

8. The offer applies to manufacturers' paper coupons only (from newspapers, magazines, etc.). It does not include clipless coupons.

Rebates

A **rebate** is a portion of the purchase price returned to the buyer. Generally, the customer sends a proof of purchase to the manufacturer or a rebate clearinghouse that processes rebates for the manufacturer, and the customer is sent the rebate. Rebates are most useful when the dollar amount is relatively large. Otherwise, it's not worth the customer's time and postage to redeem the rebate. For instance, rebates are often offered on cars, major and portable appliances, computers, and electronic products.

From the retailer's perspective, rebates are more advantageous than coupons since they increase demand in the same way coupons may, but the retailer has no handling costs.

Manufacturers like rebates because many consumers never bother to redeem them, allowing manufacturers to offer, in effect, phantom discounts.[15] Many advertisements prominently proclaim low prices, noting the requirement to send in for rebates in microscopic letters. Consumers are drawn to the store and purchase the product, but only 5 to 10 percent claim the rebate. As a result, consumer advocates hate rebates.

Manufacturers also like rebates because they let them offer price cuts to consumers directly. With a traditional price cut, retailers can keep the price on the shelf the same and pocket the difference. Rebates can also be rolled out and shut off quickly. That allows manufacturers to fine-tune inventories or respond quickly to competitors without actually cutting prices. Finally, because buyers are required to fill out forms with names, addresses, and other data, rebates become a great way to build a customer data warehouse.

Price Bundling

Price bundling is the practice of offering two or more different products or services for sale at one price. For instance, Friendly's, a chain of restaurants in New England, has tied ice cream to food purchases and bundles a "free" hot fudge sundae into the price of certain meals. Another form of second-degree price discrimination, price bundling is used to increase both unit and dollar sales by bringing traffic into the store. The practice allowed Friendly's to increase the average check in 2001 by $ 1, to $ 6.50, and lifted overall sales.[16] The strategy can also be used to move less desirable merchandise, such as a chicken dinner, by including it in a package with merchandise in high demand, like the sundae.

Multiple-Unit Pricing

Multiple-unit pricing is similar to price bundling in that the lower total merchandise price increases sales, but the products or services are similar rather than different.[17] For example, a convenience store may sell three liters of soda for $2.39 when the price per unit is 99 cents—a savings of 58 cents. Like price bundling, this strategy is used to increase sales volume. Depending on the type of product, however, customers may stockpile for use at a later time. For example, although a person typically purchases and consumes one liter of soda a week, he may purchase several if he perceives a substantial cost savings. If customers stockpile, demand is shifted back in time with no long-term effect on sales.

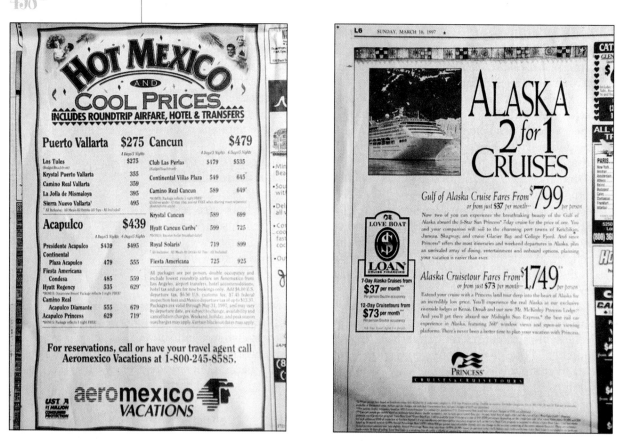

Which ad is using price bundling and which is using multiple-unit pricing?

Variable Pricing[18]

Variable pricing (or **zone pricing**) means charging different prices in different stores, markets, or zones. Retailers generally use variable pricing to address different competitive situations in their various markets. For example, Barnes & Noble.com, Virgin, and others have discounted prices on the Internet compared to their bricks-and-mortar stores to compete with Amazon.com and others.[19] While this may be necessary in the short run because of these highly competitive commodity-type products, it may cause ill will among customers who become accustomed to shopping in multiple channels. Staples and other national multichannel retailers utilize variable **pricing.** Customers are required to enter their zip code before they are quoted a price.

For instance, food retailers often have up to four or five pricing zones in a single city. They'll have one zone if they're next to a Wal-Mart, and another zone if they're next to a less price-competitive regional chain. Prices can vary as much as 10 percent depending on the competition and the economic health of the neighborhood.[20] Drugstores frequently charge higher prices in poor urban areas and in neighborhoods populated by elderly retirees, because customers in those areas tend to be relatively insensitive to price.[21]

Variable pricing is easier in the food and drug retail sectors than for other stores because many do not **item price**—put a price tag on each item. It is easy to have different prices in various stores because it is so easy to change them. They just scan the bar code on the shelf tag, change the price in the store's price database, and replace the shelf tag with a new label.

Variable pricing also doesn't conflict with their promotional strategy because many newspapers print different editions or can use different freestanding inserts (FSI), which are ads printed at the retailer's expense and distributed as an insert in the newspaper. Even if the newspaper doesn't use zones, a store might carry 40,000 SKUs, advertise 1,000, and still have 39,000 left for variable pricing.

There are two problems associated with variable pricing in traditional stores. First, as for multichannel retailers, if customers shop in more than one price zone, they will tend to be confused and possibly get irritated. Also, from a managerial perspective, it is difficult to keep track of different prices for the same item in different stores.

Pricing on the Internet

In the mid-1990s, when e-retailing was in its infancy, Internet retailers used low prices to attract customers and make them loyal.[23] Others offered free shipping and lots of coupons.[24] Clearly, price or other strategies that have the effect of lowering the total cost have made companies that use them vulnerable. Many start-up e-retail firms invested millions in this low-margin pricing strategy, never making a profit and ultimately going out of business.

Although Internet pricing is not all about low prices, there are some interesting strategies being pursued that are different than those found in traditional retailing. No longer the domain of wealthy collectors of art and other luxury goods, Internet auctions have gone from nowhere in the mid-1990s to big business today.[25] Auctions are particularly good for merchandise whose value is unclear, such as collectables, antiques, damaged and returned merchandise, and fashions that are old or out of season. Auctions enable sellers to locate and sell to the highest bidder. The auction site eBay has revolutionized the way many Web surfers spend their time and money. As we said in Chapter 10, retailers like Sears are using eBay to auction their overstocked, returned, and out-of-season merchandise. Moreover, eBay has created a worldwide market for small retailers of specialized or collectable merchandise.

Priceline.com provides a different bidding mechanism. Consumers post the price they want to pay for, say, an airline ticket from Los Angeles to Denver. Priceline then attempts to find a seller that will fulfill the request. The airline would rather sell the seat at a low price than have it go empty. So it may take the offer. Nothing is without its price, however. Priceline customers give up the flexibility of being able to travel exactly when they want. They also may have a layover or change of planes. Priceline.com also offers hotels and other travel packages, automobiles, and home mortgages.

The Internet is a great tool for comparison shoppers who can click around looking for great prices; or shoppers can let shopper.com, mysimon.com,

REFACT

State and local governments lost $13.3 billion in tax revenue in 2001 because Internet and catalog retailers do not pay taxes on merchandise sold out of their states of operation.[28]

bottomdollar.com, or shopping.yahoo.com find the lowest price for a specific item. Even though customers say they shop around for low prices, many customers visit one, perhaps two sites.[27] A McKinsey study found that 89 percent of online book buyers purchase from the first site they visit. Similarly, 81 percent of online music buyers, 84 percent of online toy buyers, and 76 percent of online electronics buyers visited only one site when making a purchase. In a separate study, fewer than 10 percent could be categorized as aggressive bargain hunters. The rest seemed to find favorite sites to return to time after time. Clearly, Internet retailing is no longer all about low prices. As we said in Chapter 3, multichannel retailers are experimenting with many strategies that make shopping easier and more convenient for shoppers.

Retailers using an electronic channel currently do not have to charge sales tax except in states in which they have a bricks-and-mortar store. National retailers don't think it is fair that they have to collect sales tax while e-retailers located in only one state have to collect tax only on sales in that state. See Retailing View 15.4 for more details.

RETAILING VIEW | Should You Have to Pay Taxes on Internet Purchases?

15.4

In 1997, Congress passed a three-year moratorium on Internet taxation and created an Advisory Commission on Electronic Commerce to come up with recommendations on handling tax issues associated with electronic commerce. The commission failed to reach a consensus on whether e-retailing should be taxed and, if so, how. As a result, the moratorium has been extended until November 2003, but experts predict it will not be extended again.

Several states concerned over the loss of taxes resulting from Internet and catalog sales have formed the Streamlined Sales Tax Project to simplify the difficulty of collecting taxes for out-of-state retailers and also to lobby Congress to require that all out-of-state retailers pay sales taxes when selling to residents of the 46 taxing states. This would eliminate any tax advantage of pure Internet or catalog e-tailers over multichannel retailers such as JCPenney that must collect taxes for every Internet sale because they have stores located in every state.[29]

Arguments against Internet sales taxes, however, abound. First, some say that it would be unfair to treat Internet firms differently from mail-order firms that don't charge sales tax unless the company has a physical presence in a state. If a customer in Florida buys something from a catalog store in Maine, then the consumer generally doesn't have to pay taxes on the purchase. It now seems likely that any sales tax intiative will cover all distance sales.

Second, requiring Internet purchases to be taxed in the area where the purchaser resides would force all e-retailers to be concerned with the requirements of at least 46 state taxing authorities and possibly thousands of localities as well. Small Internet businesses and mom-and-pop sales sites would be particularly affected by schemes of taxation that would require them to track transactions, ascertain the appropriate jurisdiction for each transaction, sift through thousands of pages of mind-boggling tax codes, and make innumerable tax filings with the various authorities. Such complexities would seriously hamper all but the largest firms from participating and flourishing in e-retailing.

Finally, there is a concern about Internet privacy. Specifically, Internet taxation may violate consumers' privacy because some states and local jurisdictions may force e-retailers or third-party providers like credit card companies to disclose personal information for tax liability and collection purposes.

Congress and the states definitely have their hands full as they attempt to make this decision.

Sources: This Retailing View was prepared by Professor Ross Petty, Babson College. David Cowling and Gregg Perry, "The E-Tax Man Cometh," *E-Business Law Bulletin,* April 2002, p. 1; Frances B. Smith, "Internet Taxation Schemes Threaten Consumers' Privacy," *Consumers' Research Magazine,* October 1, 1999, p. 34; and McGregor McCance, "Internet Tax Commission Finds Bit of Harmony," *KRTBN Knight-Ridder Tribune Business News: Richmond Times-Dispatch-Virginia,* December 15, 1999.

USING PRICE TO STIMULATE RETAIL SALES

The price adjustments described in the previous section have the effect of increasing sales. In this section, we examine three strategies designed to increase sales without using price discrimination. Each of these strategies—leader pricing, price lining, and odd pricing—makes the processing of price information easier for consumers and therefore facilitates sales.

Leader Pricing

In **leader pricing,** certain items are priced lower than normal to increase customers' traffic flow or to boost sales of complementary products. Reasons for using leader pricing are similar to those for coupons. The difference is that with leader pricing, merchandise has a low price to begin with, so customers, retailers, and vendors don't have to handle coupons.

Some retailers call these products *loss leaders*. In a strict sense, loss leaders are sold below cost. But a product doesn't have to be sold below cost for the retailer to be using a leader-pricing strategy. The best items for leader pricing are frequently purchased products like white bread, milk, and eggs or well-known brand names like Coke used as loss leaders. Customers take note of ads for these products because they're purchased weekly. The retailer hopes consumers will also purchase their weekly groceries while buying loss leaders. Toys "R" Us has successfully used a leader-pricing strategy for disposable diapers. New parents get in the habit of shopping at Toys "R" Us when their children are infants and become loyal customers throughout their parenting period.

Price Lining

In **price lining,** retailers offer a limited number of predetermined price points within a classification. For instance, a tire store may offer tires only at $29.99, $49.99, and $79.99. Both customers and retailers can benefit from such a strategy for several reasons:

- Confusion that often arises from multiple price choices is essentially eliminated. The customer can choose the tire with either the low, medium, or high price. (There need not be three price lines; the strategy can use more or fewer than three.)

- From the retailer's perspective, the merchandising task is simplified. That is, all products within a certain price line are merchandised together. Further, when going to market, the firm's buyers can select their purchases with the predetermined price lines in mind.

- Price lining can also give buyers greater flexibility. If a strict formula is used to establish the initial retail price (initial markup), there could be numerous price points. But with a price-lining strategy, some merchandise may be bought a little below or above the expected cost for a price line. Of course, price lining can also limit retail buyers' flexibility. They may be forced to pass up potentially profitable merchandise because it doesn't fit into a price line.

- Although many manufacturers and retailers are simplifying their product offerings to save distribution and inventory costs and to make the choice simpler for consumers, price lining can be used to get customers to "trade up"

REFACT

Under proposed European Union legislation, supermarkets could be forced to charge customers at least their cost, putting an end to loss leaders. This could undermine the strategy of several UK retailers, notably Wal-Mart's Asda, Tesco, and Iceland, which have pursued a strategy of everyday low prices.

to a more expensive model. Research indicates a tendency for people to choose the product in the middle of a price line. So, for example, if a camera store starts carrying a "super deluxe" model, customers will be more likely to purchase the model that was previously the most expensive. Retailers must decide whether it's more profitable to sell more expensive merchandise or save money by paring down their stock selection.[30]

Odd Pricing

Odd pricing refers to the practice of using a price that ends in an odd number, typically a nine.[31] Odd pricing has a long history in retailing. In the nineteenth and early twentieth centuries, odd pricing was used to reduce losses due to employee theft. Because merchandise had an odd price, salespeople typically had to go to the cash register to give the customer change and record the sale. This reduced salespeople's chances to take money for an item from a customer, keep the money, and never record the sale. Odd pricing was also used to keep track of how many times an item had been marked down. After an initial price of $20, the first markdown would be $17.99, the second markdown $15.98, and so on.

Although results of empirical studies in this area are mixed,[32] many retailers believe that odd pricing can increase profits. Assume that shoppers in a grocery store don't notice the last digit of a price, so the retailer is free to round a price up to the nearest nine. So, if the price would normally be $2.90, the retailers would round up to $2.99. This tactic would increase sales by three percent, more than most grocery store's entire profit margin, with no increase in costs (increase in sales: $2.99 − $2.90 = $0.090 or $0.090 ÷ $2.99 = 3% of sales).

For products that are believed to be sensitive to price, many retailers will round the price down to the nearest nine to create a positive price image. If, for example, the price would normally be $3.09, many retailers will lower the price to $2.99. This practice is so prevalent that when planning new-product introductions, many manufacturers plan their cost to retailers such that the retail price will be rounded to a nine or a ninety-nine. Some of the more sophisticated price optimization systems (discussed earlier in this chapter) are capable of taking these factors into account, using ending numbers to optimize profits and price image.

SUMMARY

In this chapter, we've answered several questions. First, what fundamental pricing strategies are retailers adopting? Retailers lie on a continuum from using pure everyday low pricing to pure high low strategies, where prices start high but decrease with the frequent sales. However, most EDLP retailers must resort to occasional sales, and most high low pricers are attempting to create an image of providing customers good value.

Second, how do retailers set retail prices? There are three primary approaches for establish-

ing prices: the cost-, demand-, and competition-oriented methods. Each method has its merits, but a mix of the methods is best. In making pricing decisions, retailers also use break-even analyses to determine the volume of sales necessary for them to make a profit.

Third, since the initial retail price isn't necessarily the price at which the merchandise is finally sold, how do retailers adjust the initial retail price and how do these adjustments affect profits? Retailers have several tactics available, including markdowns coupons, rebates, bundling, multiunit pricing, variable pricing, and special Internet pricing.

Finally, how do retailers use price to stimulate sales without resorting to price discrimination? Three strategies are prevalent: price lining, leader pricing, and odd pricing.

Legal issues that impact pricing decisions come from two sides. Those that affect the buy-ing of merchandise include price discrimination and vertical price-fixing. The legal pricing issues that affect consumers are horizontal price-fixing, predatory pricing, comparative price advertising, bait-and-switch, and scanned versus posted prices. These issues are considered in Appendix 15A.

KEY TERMS

bait-and-switch, *510*

break-even analysis, *489*

break-even point (BEP), *490*

comparative price advertising, *509*

competition-oriented method, *481*

contribution margin, *491*

cost-oriented method, *480*

coupons, *496*

demand-oriented method, *481*

everyday low pricing (EDLP), *478*

fair trade laws, *508*

first-degree price discrimination, *495*

fixed cost, *490*

functional discount, *506*

high/low pricing, *479*

horizontal price-fixing, *509*

initial markup, *484*

item price, *499*

keystone method, *480*

leader pricing, *501*

low-price guarantee policy, *479*

maintained markup, *484*

markdowns, *491*

markdown money, *494*

merchandising optimization software, *493*

multiple-unit pricing, *497*

odd pricing, *502*

predatory pricing, *507*

price bundling, *497*

price discrimination, *506*

price lining, *501*

quantity discount, *506*

rain check, *479*

rebate, *497*

reductions, *484*

reference price, *509*

resale price maintenance laws, *508*

second-degree price discrimination, *495*

trade discount, *506*

value, *477*

variable cost, *490*

variable pricing, *498*

vertical price-fixing, *508*

zone pricing, *498*

GET OUT & DO IT!

1. INTERNET EXERCISE AND GO SHOPPING Go to the websites for Bloomingdale's (www.bloomingdales.com) and Dillard's Department Stores (www.dillards.com) and to a local department store. Which department store chains are using an everyday low pricing strategy and which are using a high/low strategy? How can you tell?

2. INTERNET EXERCISE Go to www.ebay.com, www.priceline.com, www.expedia.com, and www.ual.com (United Airlines) and shop for an airline ticket. Where did you get the best deal? Which was the easiest site to navigate? Which company do you think will have the strongest market position in five years?

3. INTERNET EXERCISE Price bundling is very common in the travel and vacation industry. Go to the website for Sandals (www.sandals.com) and see what you can get—all for one price.

4. GO SHOPPING Go to a supermarket that uses shelf pricing labels instead of labels on each item. Note each shelf label price. Buy 20 items. How many items were priced correctly? How many were under- and overpriced?

5. GO SHOPPING Go to five different types of stores and try to bargain your way down from the tagged price. Explain your experience. Was there any difference in your success rate as a result of type of store or type of merchandise? Did you have better luck when you spoke to a manager?

6. GO SHOPPING Go to five different types of stores and ask the manager of each how he or she determines when to take markdowns and how much the markdown should be. What rule-based approaches are they using? Are any using merchandising optimization software?

7. CD-ROM EXERCISE ProfitLogic has provided you with the opportunity to play buyer and test your analytical abilities for taking markdowns. You will be given the opportunity to make markdown decisions for several products over several weeks. You can either play this simulation game on your own or against your classmates.

DISCUSSION QUESTIONS AND PROBLEMS

1. How does merchandising optimization software help buyers make better markdown decisions?

2. Simple examination of markdowns could lead us to believe that they should be taken only when a retailer wants to get rid of merchandise that's not selling. What other reasons could a retailer have to take markdowns?

3. Do you know any retailers that have violated any of the legal issues discussed in the appendix to this chapter? Explain your answer.

4. Which of the pricing strategies discussed in this chapter are used by your favorite retailer? Do you think they're used effectively? Can you suggest a more effective strategy?

5. A department's maintained markup is 38 percent, reductions are $560, and net sales are $28,000. What's the initial markup percentage? You can use your Student CD to answer this question.

6. Maintained markup is 39 percent, net sales are $52,000, alterations are $1,700, shrinkage is $500, markdowns are $5,000, employee discounts are $2,000, and cash discounts are 2 percent. What are gross margin in dollars and initial markup as a percentage? Explain why initial markup is greater than maintained markup. You can use your Student CD to answer this question.

7. Cost of a product is $150, markup is 50 percent, and markdown is 30 percent. What's the final selling price? You can use your Student CD to answer this question.

8. Manny Perez bought a tie for $9 and priced it to sell for $15. What was his markup on the tie? You can use your Student CD to answer this question.

9. What is the difference in the pricing strategies of ebay.com, priceline.com, and staples.com?

Which firm do you think will be the strongest in 10 years? Why?

10. You can use your Student CD to answer the following:

(a) The Limited is planning a new line of leather jean jackets for fall. It plans to retail the jackets for $100. It is having the jackets produced in the Dominican Republic. Although The Limited does not own the factory, its product development and design costs are $400,000. The total cost of the jacket, including transportation to the stores, is $45. For this line to be successful, The Limited needs to make $900,000 profit. What is its break-even point in units and dollars?

(b) The buyer has just found out that The Gap, one of The Limited's major competitors, is bringing out a similar jacket that will retail for $90. If The Limited wishes to match The Gap's price, how many units will it have to sell?

SUGGESTED READINGS

Ackerman, David, and Gerald Tellis. "Can Culture Affect Prices? A Cross-Cultural Study of Shopping and Retail Prices." *Journal of Retailing* 77 (Spring 2001), pp. 57–82.

Ailawadi, Kusum L.; Donald R. Lehmann; and Scott A. Neslin. "Market Response to a Major Policy Change in the Marketing Mix: Learning from Procter & Gamble's Value Pricing Strategy." *Journal of Marketing* 65 (January 2001), pp. 44–61.

Baker, Julie; A. Parasuraman; Dhruv Grewal; and Glenn B. Voss. "The Influence of Multiple Store Environment Cues on Perceived Merchandise Value and Patronage Intentions." *Journal of Marketing* 66, no. 2 (April 2002), pp. 120–41.

Baker, Walter; Mike Marn; and Craig Zawada. "Price Smarter on the Net." *Harvard Business Review*, February 2001, pp. 122–27.

Cohen, Adam. *The Perfect Store: Inside e-Bay.* Little, Brown & Co., 2001.

Friend, Scott C., and Patricia H. Walker. "Welcome to the New World of Merchandising." *Harvard Business Review*, November 2001, pp. 133–41.

Gedenk, Karen, and Henrik Sattler. "The Impact of Price Thresholds on Profit Contribution—Should Retailers Set 9-Ending Prices?" *Journal of Retailing* 75, no. 1 (1999), pp. 33–57.

Grewal, Dhruv; Kent B. Monroe; and R. Krishnan. "The Effects of Price Comparison Advertising on Buyers' Perceptions of Acquisition Value and Transaction Value." *Journal of Marketing* 137, no. 3 (April 1998), pp. 16–59.

Han, Sangman; Sunil Gupta; and Donald R. Lehmann. "Consumer Price Sensitivity and Price Thresholds." *Journal of Retailing* 77 (Winter 2001), pp. 435–56.

Manning, Kenneth C.; William O. Bearden; and Randall L. Rose. "Development of a Theory of Retailer Response to Manufacturers' Everyday Low Cost Programs." *Journal of Retailing* 74, no. 1 (March 1998), pp. 107–137

Nagle, Thomas T., and Reed K. Holden. *The Strategy and Tactics of Pricing: A Guide to Profitable Decision Making.* Prentice Hall, 2002.

Shugan, Steven M., and Ramarao Desiraju. "Retail Product-Line Pricing Strategy When Costs and Products Change." *Journal of Retailing* 77 (Spring 2001), pp. 17–38.

Tang, Christopher S.; David R. Bell; and Teck-Hua Ho. "Store Choice and Shopping Behavior: How Price Format Works." *California Management Review* 43, no. 2 (Winter 2001), pp. 56–74

Tsay, Andy A. "Managing Retail Channel Overstock: Markdown Money and Return Policies." *Journal of Retailing* 77 (Winter 2001), pp. 457–92.

APPENDIX 15A   Legal Issues in Retail Pricing*

The legal environment surrounding retail pricing is complex. Let's examine legal issues surrounding the buying of merchandise (price discrimination and vertical price fixing) and legal issues affecting the customer (horizontal price-fixing, predatory pricing, comparative price advertising, bait-and-switch tactics, and scanned versus posted prices).

PRICE DISCRIMINATION

Price discrimination occurs when a vendor sells identical products to two or more customers at different prices. Although the Supreme Court has held that price discrimination can occur between a national brand and an identical private-label product, the Fifth Circuit Court of Appeals has ruled that the normal price difference between these two types of products does not lessen competition, so the price discrimination is not illegal.[33] Price discrimination can occur between vendors and retailers, or between retailers and their customers, although the legal ramifications are different in the two situations. We will first examine price discrimination between vendors and retailers and then between retailers and their customers.

Although price discrimination between vendors and their retailers is generally illegal if it lessens competition (i.e., if the favored and disfavored retailers compete with each other), there are three situations where it's acceptable. First, different retailers can be charged different prices when justified by differences in the cost of manufacture, sale, or delivery resulting from the differing methods or quantities in which such commodities are sold or delivered. Under what conditions may these differences exist?

It's often less expensive per unit to manufacture, sell, or deliver large quantities than small quantities. Manufacturers can achieve economies of scale through the longer production runs achieved with large quantities. Cost of selling to a customer also decreases as the quantity of goods ordered increases because it costs almost the same for a salesperson to write a small order as a large order. Finally, delivery or transportation expenses decrease on a per unit basis as quantities of goods ordered increase. These exceptions give rise to **quantity discounts,** the practice of lowering prices to retailers that buy in high quantities (see Chapter 14, Appendix 14B).

The differences in methods of sale that allow for differing prices refer specifically to the practice of granting **functional discounts,** also known as **trade discounts.** Functional discounts are different prices, or percentages off suggested retail prices, granted to customers in different lines of trade (e.g., wholesalers and retailers). Wholesalers often receive a lower price than retailers for the same quantity purchased. This is legal as long as wholesalers perform more functions in the distribution process than do retailers. For instance, wholesalers store and transport merchandise, and they use salespeople for writing orders and taking care of problems in the stores. Essentially, manufacturers "pay" wholesalers for servicing retailers by giving the wholesalers a lower price.

With the growth of large chain retailers like Home Depot and Wal-Mart, functional discounts become more difficult to justify. Wal-Mart performs virtually all the functions an independent wholesaler provides. Therefore, Wal-Mart demands and should receive the same low prices as wholesalers. These lower prices make it hard for smaller retailers to compete.

The second exception to the no-price-discrimination rule is when the price differential is in response to changing conditions affecting the market for or the marketability of the goods concerned, such as selling last year's fashions at a lower price today than last month when they were still this year's fashions.

The third exception is when the differing price is made in good faith to meet a competitor's equally low price. Suppose, for example, that Ben & Jerry's ice cream is experiencing severe price competition with a locally produced ice cream in Wisconsin. Ben & Jerry's is allowed to lower its price in this market below its price in other markets to meet the low price of local competition. In this case, market conditions have changed and Ben & Jerry's has reacted by meeting the competition's price.

*This appendix was prepared with the assistance of Professor Ross Petty, Babson College.

Large retailers often benefit from subtle forms of price discrimination. For instance, 25 bookstores across the country have filed an antitrust lawsuit against their large competitors, Barnes & Noble and Borders Group, Inc. They charge that the nation's largest book retailers are in violation of the Robinson-Patman Act because they illegally use their buying clout with publishers to get special discounts and benefits not available to smaller rivals.[34]

Unless a particular situation comes within one of the exceptions just discussed, retailers should never ask a vendor for or accept a net price (after all discounts, allowances, returns, and promotional allowances) that they know, or experience tells them, won't be offered to their competitors on a proportional basis for similar merchandise to be purchased at about the same time.

Price discrimination between retailers and their customers is not illegal under federal law. Different customers typically receive different prices after negotiating for such items as cars, jewelry, or collectibles. Price discrimination becomes illegal in some states, when different groups of people, such as men and women, systematically receive different prices. See Retailing View 15.5.

Predatory Pricing

Predatory pricing is a particular form of price discrimination where a market-dominating firm charges below-cost prices for some goods or in some areas in order to drive out or discipline one or more rival firms. Eventually, the predator hopes to raise prices and earn back enough profits to compensate for the losses during the period of predation. The firm challenging prices as being predatory bears the burden of proving three things: (1) the predator has significant market power; (2) the predator prices some goods at least below its total costs, including an allocation for overhead costs for a significant period (some courts require prices to be below variable costs, which for retailers would

Why Do Women Pay More? RETAILING VIEW

15.5

It's well known that women often earn less than men in similar jobs, even when they have similar education and experience. It's also true that they pay more for products and services ranging from haircuts to cars. For the most part, trying to explain gender-differentiated prices is like trying to justify racial discrimination—it just doesn't cut it.

Why do women's haircuts cost more than men's? The traditional response is that it takes longer and more skill to cut more hair. But a survey in Pennsylvania found that 90 of 130 hair salons charged women more than men even though a state law prohibits price discrimination based on gender.

For years, dry cleaners have cited the same reasons for pricing women's services higher. They have argued that it's harder to press a woman's shirt with equipment designed for men's shirts. However, the Massachusetts Attorney General's office did a study and found this not to be the case.

Clothing merchants usually have different staff altering men's and women's clothing, so it's hard to make true comparisons based on job difficulty. However, the fact remains that many stores still offer most alterations free to men, but not to women.

Unlike alterations, dry cleaning, and haircuts, where the actual service provided to men and women may vary slightly, there is no comparable explanation why women pay more for cars. In some cases, salespeople simply don't offer women the same deals they offer men because they think they can get away with it. But women are less likely than men to bargain on car prices, partly because in the past they have been less knowledgeable about the process. Salespeople perceive that women are not comfortable about dickering on prices, and they take advantage of the situation. Gender-based price discrimination should decrease as more women educate themselves with Internet services such as Kelley Blue Book (www.kbb.com).

In many businesses, however, the price women pay is not seriously challenged or addressed. Until women get fed up with paying more, they will continue to be taken to the cleaners.

Sources: Dianna Marder, "Study Finds Gender Bias in Philadelphia Merchants Pricing," *Philadelphia Inquirer*, March 5, 1999; and Gerry Myers, "Why Women Pay More," *American Demographics*, April 1996, pp. 40–41. For more details about gender and pricing, see Frances Cerra Whittelsey, *Why Women Pay More* (Washington, DC: Center for Study of Responsive Law).

probably be the cost of merchandise without any allocation of overhead); and (3) there is a reasonable likelihood that the predator will be able to recoup its predatory losses.

Some states have old statutes that declare it illegal to sell merchandise at unreasonably low prices, usually below their cost. However, a retailer generally may sell merchandise at any price so long as the motive isn't to destroy competition. For instance, independent retailers in small towns have long accused Wal-Mart of selling goods below cost to drive them out of business and then boosting prices after seizing control of the local market. Wal-Mart maintains that it hasn't violated the law because it didn't intend to hurt competitors. But it admits it has sold some products below cost, as do other retailers. These loss-leader products are intended to attract customers into the store where it is hoped, they will then buy other products that are priced to be profitable. Wal-Mart claims its loss leaders are part of its everyday low price strategy. More competition leads to lower prices, while less competition leads to higher prices. Wal-Mart's so-called predatory pricing strategy has been tested in the courts. After an early conviction in a lower court, the Arkansas Supreme Court ruled that the chain had no intent to destroy competition through its practice of selling a revolving selection of prescription and nonprescription drugs at less than cost.[36] In essence, the Arkansas Supreme Court distinguished loss-leader pricing, even by a firm with market power, as a legitimate competitive tactic from predatory pricing.

VERTICAL PRICE-FIXING

Vertical price-fixing involves agreements to fix prices between parties at different levels of the same marketing channel (e.g., retailers and vendors). The agreements are usually to set prices at the manufacturer's suggested retail price (MSRP). So pricing either above or below MSRP is often a source of conflict.

Resale price maintenance laws, or **fair trade laws,** were enacted in the early 1900s to promote vertical price-fixing and have had a mixed history ever since. Initially, resale price maintenance laws were primarily designed to help protect small retailers by prohibiting retailers to sell below MSRP.

Congress believed that these small, often family-owned, stores couldn't compete with large chain stores like Sears or Woolworth, which could buy in larger quantities and sell at discount prices. By requiring retailers to maintain manufacturers' suggested retail prices, however, prices to the consumer may have been higher than they would have been in a freely competitive environment.

Due to strong consumer activism, the Consumer Goods Pricing Act (1975) repealed all resale price maintenance laws and enabled retailers to sell products below suggested retail prices. Congress's attitude was to protect customers' right to buy at the lowest possible free market price—even though some small retailers wouldn't be able to compete. For instance, in a 2000 settlement, Nine West, the women's shoe marketer, agreed with the Federal Trade Commission (FTC) not to fix the price at which dealers may "advertise, promote, offer of sale or sell any product." The firm also agreed to pay $34 million to state attorneys general. The money is being used to fund women's health, educational, vocational, and safety programs.[37]

Unfortunately, some vendors coerce retailers into maintaining the MSRP by delaying or canceling shipments.[38] A less risky tactic from a legal perspective is for a vendor to simply announce it will only sell to full-price retailers. If any of its re-

Is it legal to sell Harley-Davidson motorcycles above MSRP?

tailers violate that policy, the vendor can terminate the discounters without discussion or negotiation. In this way, the vendor exercises its right to choose with whom it will deal but avoids forming an illegal agreement with its dealers to vertically fix prices.

Some retailers, on the other hand, want to be able to price above MSRP. For instance, Harley-Davidson motorcycles are so popular that some dealers have sold them over the manufacturer's suggested retail price. Large manufacturers and franchise companies are generally against pricing above MSRP. They argue that their brand's image can be damaged if retailers price above MSRP. Retailers like the extra profit potential and argue that competitive conditions may vary by locality. The Supreme Court ruled in 1997 that price ceilings would not necessarily violate federal antitrust laws. This was the first time the Court had carved an exception to the general ban on vertical price-fixing. From now on, each case will be judged on whether it restricts competition.[39]

HORIZONTAL-PRICE FIXING

Horizontal price-fixing involves agreements between retailers that are in direct competition with each other to have the same prices. As a general rule of thumb, retailers should refrain from discussing prices or terms or conditions of sale with competitors. Terms or conditions of sale may include charges for alterations, delivery, or gift wrapping, or the store's exchange policies. If a buyer or store manager needs to know a competitor's price on a particular item, he or she can check advertisements or the Internet or send an assistant to the store to check the price. But the buyer or manager shouldn't call the competitor to get the information or personally visit the store for fear that this information would be used against him or her in a price-fixing case. Further, retailers shouldn't respond to any competitor's request to verify those prices. The only exception to the general rule is when a geographically oriented merchants association, such as a downtown area or a shopping center, is planning a special coordinated event. In this situation, a retailer may announce to other merchants that merchandise will be specially priced during the event, but the spe-

cific merchandise and prices shouldn't be identified except in advertising or through in-store labeling and promotion.

COMPARATIVE PRICE ADVERTISING

A department store in Denver was selling two cutlery sets on "sale," reduced from "original" or "regular" prices of $40 and $50. The true regular prices were $19.99 and $29.99. The store sold few at the "original" price for two years. This common retailing practice, known as **comparative price advertising,** compares the price of merchandise offered for sale with a higher "regular" price or a manufacturer's list price. Consumers use the higher price, known as the *reference price*, as a benchmark for what they believe the "real" price of the merchandise should be.

This practice may be a good strategy, since it gives customers a price comparison point and makes the merchandise appear to be a good deal. Retailers, like the one in Denver, may use comparative price

If these vests sold for $9.94 for a short time before being reduced to $7.00, the higher price would be a deceptive reference price.

advertising to deceive the consumer, however. To avoid legal problems, particularly with state governments that have been actively prosecuting violators, retailers should check for local rules and guidelines. Generally,

- The retailer should have the reference price in effect at least one-third of the time the merchandise is on sale.
- The retailer should disclose both how sale prices are set and how long they will be offered and how the reference price was determined.
- The retailer should be careful when using a manufacturer's suggested list price. Don't use it as the reference price unless it is the store's regular price, or is clearly identified only as the manufacturer's suggested price.
- If the retailer advertises that it has the lowest prices in town or that it will meet or beat any competitor's price, it should have proof that its prices are, in fact, the lowest in town before the ad is placed.
- If the retailer advertises that it will meet or beat any competitor's prices, it must have a company policy that enables it to adjust prices to preserve the accuracy of its advertising claims.[40]

BAIT-AND-SWITCH TACTICS

Bait-and-switch is an unlawful deceptive practice that lures customers into a store by advertising a product at a lower-than-usual price (the bait) and then induces the customer to switch to a higher-priced model (the switch). Bait-and-switch can occur in two ways. Suppose customer Smith is in the market for a new refrigerator. Smith checks the ads in the newspaper and finds a particularly attractively priced unit. At the store, however, Smith finds that the retailer has significantly underestimated demand for the advertised product and no longer has any available for sale. The person begins pushing a higher-priced model that's heavily stocked.

In the second bait-and-switch method, the retailer has the advertised model in stock but disparages its quality while highlighting the advantages of a higher-priced model. In both cases, the retailer has intentionally misled the customer.

To avoid disappointing customers and risking problems with the FTC, the retailer should have sufficient quantities of advertised items. If it runs out of stock on these items, it should offer customers a rain check. Finally, it should caution salespeople that while trying to "trade up" customers to a higher-priced model is legal, they must sell the low-priced item if that is what the customer wants.

SCANNED VERSUS POSTED PRICES

Advertising one price but charging another is obviously illegal. Many states and localities have specific laws regarding accurate pricing. FTC-led studies of the accuracy of price scanning versus posted or advertised prices have generally found a high level of accuracy, but mistakes are made in about one out of 30 scans.[41] In many cases, retailers lose money because the scanned price is below the recommended price.

Experts recommend that retailers adopt specific practices to ensure accurate pricing. Most basic is the adoption of written procedures for all forms of pricing activity in the store. Adopting procedures for immediate correction of pricing errors is important to reduce exposure to possible law enforcement action and to ensure customer satisfaction. On-going training of employees, with an emphasis on the store's commitment to pricing accuracy, ensures that the procedures are properly implemented. Designating one person as the pricing coordinator, with overall responsibility for pricing accuracy, also is important. An essential component of good pricing practices is periodic price audits. Price audits of a random sample, perhaps 50 items, can be done on a daily basis. Regular price audits of the entire store can be done several times a year. Procedures for regularly checking and replacing damaged or missing shelf tags and signs helps ensure that consumers can get the correct price.

In summary, retailers, wholesalers, and manufacturers should be aware that whenever they decide to sell the same merchandise for different prices at different locations, or to sell merchandise at extraordinarily low prices to attract customers, they may be susceptible to federal and state prosecution and to lawsuits from competitors. But as a practical matter, the length of time and the expense of acquiring sufficient data and legal assistance to prove injury by a competitor may be so great that the injured party may still lose its business.

Retail Communication Mix

16

"Some of Sears' most valuable assets are its brands, including the Sears name and our private-label brands—Craftsman Professional, Kenmore, Kenmore Elite, DieHard, Whole Home, and our new apparel brands like Covington. We have a lot of customers who are loyal to these brands, and they can only get them in our stores or from our website and catalogs. Now we have added another strong brand to our portfolio with the acquisition of Lands' End.

"Developing great brands starts with having great products. Our private-label program is designed to insure that our merchandise meets and exceeds our customer's expectations in terms of performance, quality, and reliability. We build on the performance of our products using an integrated marketing communications program. We make sure that we communicate the same message about each of our brands at all of the touch points we have with customers. Our advertising and public relations activities are designed to present a consistent image of our brands. For example, we sponsor the NASCAR Craftsman Truck Series, which offers some of the toughest and most rugged racing and competitors in all of motor sports. It consists of 24 events at 23 different tracks in 18 states from coast to coast. These events emphasize a key association we want to make with our tools—tough truck, tough tools. In addition, we work with sales associates and service providers to make sure that they reinforce this image.

"We have had our ups and downs at Sears in recent years, but the strength of our brands has con-

QUESTIONS

- How can retailers build brand equity for their stores and their private-label merchandise?

- What are the strengths and weaknesses of the different methods for communicating with customers?

- Why do retailers need to have an integrated marketing communication program?

- What steps are involved in developing a communication program?

- How do retailers establish a communication budget?

- How can retailers use the different elements in a communication mix to alter customers' decision-making processes?

tinued to provide a solid foundation. They differentiate us from our competitors. Only Sears sells Kenmore appliances and Craftsman tools—brands with the greatest awareness and highest sales in their categories."

The preceding chapters described how retailers develop a merchandise budget plan and then buy and price merchandise. The next step in the retail management decision-making process is developing and implementing a communication program to build appealing brand images, attract customers to stores and Internet sites, and encourage them to buy merchandise. The communication program informs customers about the retailer as well as the merchandise and services it offers and plays a role in developing repeat visits and customer loyalty.

Communication programs can have both long-term and short-term effects on a retailer's business. From a long-term perspective, communications programs can be used to create and maintain a strong, differentiated image of the retailer and its store brands. This image develops customer loyalty and creates a strategic advantage. Thus, brand image building communication programs complement the objective of a retailer's CRM program discussed in Chapter 11.

On the other hand, retailers frequently use communication programs to realize the short-term objective of increasing sales during a specified time period. For example, retailers often have sales during which some or all merchandise is priced at a discount for a short time. Grocery stores usually place weekly ads with coupons that can be used to save money on purchases made during the week.

Retail advertising can be used to achieve long-term objectives such as building a brand image or short-term sales. The Fashion Bug ad (left) supports a long-term objective by reinforcing the retailer's fashionable image. The Payless ShoeSource ad (right) generates short-term sales through a special promotion.

In the first part of this chapter, we will discuss the role of communications programs in building brand images. The second part of the chapter will focus on developing and implementing communication programs. The appendix to this chapter includes more detailed material related to the implementation of advertising programs, including the development of the ad message and selection of media for distributing the message.

USING COMMUNICATION PROGRAMS TO DEVELOP BRANDS AND BUILD CUSTOMER LOYALTY

A **brand** is a distinguishing name or symbol, such as a logo, that identifies the products or services offered by a seller and differentiates those products and services from the offerings of competitors.[1] In a retailing context, the name of the retailer is a brand that indicates to consumers the type of merchandise and services offered by the retailer. As discussed in Chapter 14, some retailers develop private-label or store brands that are exclusively sold through their channels. In some cases, this private-label merchandise bears the retailer's name, such as Walgreens aspirins and Victoria's Secret lingerie. In other cases, special brand names are used, such as Federated Department Stores' I.N.C apparel and JCPenney's Arizona jeans.

Value of Brand Image

Brands provide value to both customers and retailers. Brands convey information to consumers about the nature of the shopping experience—the retailer's mix—they will encounter when patronizing a retailer. They also affect the customers' confidence in decisions made to buy merchandise from a retailer. Finally, brands can enhance the customers' satisfaction with the merchandise and services they buy. Consumers feel different when wearing jewelry bought from Tiffany than from Zales or lingerie from Victoria's Secret than from Kmart.

The value that brand image offers retailers is referred to as **brand equity.** Strong brand names can affect the customer's decision-making process, motivate repeat visits and purchases, and build loyalty. In addition, strong brand names enable retailers to charge higher prices and lower their marketing costs.

Customer loyalty to brands arises from heightened awareness of the brand and the emotional ties toward it. For example, in Chapter 4, we discussed the need for retailers to be in a customer's consideration set. Some brands such as Wal-Mart and Sears are so well known by consumers that they are typically in a consumer's consideration set. In addition, customers identify and have strong emotional relationships with some brands. For example, Target has an image of offering fashionable merchandise at bargain prices. As one retail consultant says, "Going to Target is a cool experience, and everybody now considers it cool to save money. On the other hand, is it cool to save at Kmart, at Wal-Mart? I don't think so. You walk into Wal-Mart, and there are these big boxes of corn flakes. How ugly! How totally uncool!" Customers affectionately use the faux French pronunciation of "Tar-zhay" when referring to Target.[4] High brand awareness and strong emotional connnections reduce the incentive of customers to switch to competing retailers.

A strong brand image enables retailers to increase their margins. When retailers have high customer loyalty, they can engage in premium pricing and reduce their reliance on price promotions to attract customers. Brands with weaker images are forced to offer low prices and frequent sales to maintain their market share.

Finally, retailers with strong brand names can leverage their brand to successfully introduce new retail concepts with only a limited amount of marketing effort. For example, The Gap has efficiently extended its brand to GapKids and babyGap and The Limited extended its brand name to Limited Too.

As we discussed in Chapter 5, a strong brand name creates a strategic advantage that is very difficult for competitors to duplicate. Just think how hard it would be for Kmart to change its image to that of Wal-Mart or Target, the more successful discount store chains.

Building Brand Equity

The activities that a retailer needs to undertake to build the brand equity for its firm or its private-label merchandise are (1) create a high level of brand awareness, (2) develop favorable associations with the brand name, and (3) consistently reinforce the image of the brand.

Target uses advertising to build its image of offering fashionable merchandise at low prices.

Brand Awareness   **Brand awareness** is the ability of a potential customer to recognize or recall that the brand name is a type of retailer or product/service. Thus, brand awareness is the strength of the link between the brand name and type of merchandise or service in the minds of customers. There is a range of awareness from aided recall to top-of-mind awareness. **Aided recall** is when consumers indicate they know the brand when the name is presented to them. **Top-of-mind awareness,** the highest level of awareness, arises when consumers mention a brand name first when they are asked about the type of retailer, a merchandise category, or a type of service. For example, Best Buy has top-of-mind awareness if a consumer responds "Best Buy" when asked about retailers that sell consumer electronics. High top-of-mind awareness means that a retailer typically will be in the consideration set when customers decide to shop for a type of product or service.

Retailers build top-of-mind awareness by having memorable names; repeatedly exposing their name to customers through advertising, locations, and sponsorships; and using memorable symbols. Some brand names are easy to remember. For example, the name Home Depot, because "Home" is in its brand name, probably is more memorable and closely associated with home improvements than the name Lowe's.[5]

Starbucks does very little advertising but has high awareness because of the large number of stores it has. Customers walk and drive by the stores to and from work. The sheer number of stores provides substantial exposure to its brand.

Symbols involve visual images that typically are more easily recalled than words or phrases and thus are useful for building brand awareness. For example, the image of Colonel Sanders and the Golden Arches enhances the ability of customers to recall the names KFC and McDonald's.

Sponsorships of well-publicized events can provide considerable exposure to a retailer's name and increase awareness. For example, watching the Macy's Thanksgiving Parade in New York City has become a holiday tradition. The Macy's brand name is now exposed to tens of millions of television viewers for several hours. In addition, newspaper articles are devoted to previewing the parade and describing it afterward.

Associations   Building awareness is the first step in developing brand equity, but the value of the brand is largely based on the associations that customers make with the brand name. **Brand associations** are anything linked to or connected with the brand name in a consumer's memory. For example, some of the associations that consumers might have with McDonald's are golden arches, fast food, clean stores, hamburgers, French fries, Big Mac, and Ronald McDonald. In the case of McDonald's, these links are so strong that when a consumer thinks of fast food, hamburgers, or French fries, they also think of McDonald's. These strong associations influence consumer buying behavior. For example, when consumers think about camping, REI might immediately come to mind, stimulating a visit to an REI store or the REI website.

Some common associations that retailers develop with their brand name are

1. *Merchandise category.* The most common association is to link the retailer to a category of merchandise. For example, Office Depot would like to have consumers associate its name with office supplies. Then when a need for office supplies arises, consumers immediately think of Office Depot.

2. *Price/quality.* Some retailers, such as Neiman Marcus, want to be associated with offering high prices and unique, high fashion merchandise. Other retailers, such as Wal-Mart, want associations with offering low prices and good value.

3. *Specific attribute or benefit.* A retailer can link its stores to attributes such as convenience (7-Eleven) or service (Nordstrom).

4. *Lifestyle or activity.* Some retailers associate their name with a specific lifestyle or activity. For example, The Nature Company, a retailer offering books and equipment to study nature, is linked to a lifestyle of interacting with the environment. Electronic Boutique is associated with home use of computer game software.

The **brand image** is a set of associations that are usually organized around some meaningful themes. Thus, the associations that a consumer might have about McDonald's might be organized into groups such as kids, service, and type of food. Retailing View 16.1 illustrates how L. L. Bean nurtures its brand image of selling high-quality, functional products and providing helpful service for outdoor living.

L. L. Bean—Celebrating the Outdoors | RETAILING VIEW

16.1

Leon Leonard Bean, an outdoorsman living in Freeport, Maine, founded L. L. Bean in 1912. The first product he sold through the mail was boots (The Maine Hunting Shoe) with waterproof rubber bottoms and lightweight leather tops. The boots provided significant benefits over wearing heavyweight, all-leather boots in wet weather. However, the first pairs he sold had a stitching problem. Bean decided to refund each customer's money, which led to L. L. Bean's legendary "Guarantee of 100% Satisfaction."

Some of the associations that L. L. Bean reinforces through its advertising and website as well as other elements in its retail mix are

1. *Friendly*—L. L. Bean is comfortable and familiar, easy to approach.

2. *Honesty*—L. L. Bean is straightforward and honest. It would never mislead its customers. It provides factual information about its products.

3. *Expertise*—L. L. Bean's employees are experts about their products and the outdoors. They'll do anything they can to help customers chose which product is best for them or even help them find the best place to camp out.

4. *Practical and economical*—Bulding on its Yankee New England roots, L. L. Bean offers products that are functional, with no-nonsense features at fair prices. As Bean said, "I attribute our success to the fact that, to the best of my judgment, every article we offer for sale is practical for the purpose for which we recommend it."

These associations that L. L. Bean promotes might also result in the development of less favorable set of impressions. For example, the association with its New England heritage may associate L. L. Bean, in some customers' minds, with old-fashion and out-of-date merchandise and way of doing business. The brand might also be viewed as being very male-oriented and not appealing to women or families.

Sources: David Aaker and Erich Joachimsthaler. *Brand Leadership* (New York: Frees Press, 2000), pp. 68–71; and www.llbean.com

L. L. Bean uses its website to reinforce its image of having expertise in providing practical and economical outdoor merchandise.

Consistent Reinforcement   The retailer's brand image is developed and maintained through the retailer's communication program as well as other elements of the communication mix, such as merchandise assortment and pricing, the design of its stores and website, and the customer service it offers. To develop a strong set of associations and a clearly defined brand image, retailers need to be consistent in portraying the same message to customers over time and across all of the elements of its retail mix.

Rather than creating unique communication programs for sales associates, retailers need to develop an **integrated marketing communication program**—a program that integrates all of the communication elements to deliver a comprehensive, consistent message. Without this coordination, the communication methods might work at cross-purposes. For example, the retailer's TV advertising campaign might attempt to build an image of exceptional customer service, but the firm's sales promotions might all emphasize low prices. If communication methods aren't used consistently, customers may become confused about the retailer's image and therefore may not patronize the store.

For example, Abercrombie & Fitch uses an integrated marketing communication program to reinforce its brand image associated with fun-loving, independent, and uninhibited teenagers and young adults. To stay on top of its target market's taste and find ideas for new merchandise, A&F has employees go to college campuses each month to chat with students about what they play, wear, listen to, and read.

The stores have comfortable armchairs, designed to be gathering places for its customers. They are staffed by high-energy "brand reps" recruited from local campuses who dress in A&F clothes. Selling skills are not required. The brand reps just need to fit the company's brand image, wear its apparel, and have fun inside the store.

A&F's main promotional tool has been its controversial "magalog," a quarterly magazine-catalog crammed with product information, sexual imagery, and provocative articles, such as "Condoms in ample supply" and "Drinking 101." (A **magalog** is a combination of a magazine and catalog.) Large blowups of enticing photographs from the magalog appear in store displays.[7]

Toys "R" Us is using a similar approach to target teenagers. It has created RZone boutiques within its stores, which offer video games. The visual merchandising in the boutiques is designed to appeal to teenagers. To build its image of the RZone brand with teenagers, Toys "R" Us launched *RZone Magazine.* The glossy magazine has cutting-edge graphics and content desired by teen pop-culture junkies who listen to hybrid rap and rock music, watch MTV's "Total Request," and drink Code Red. It reinforces the image and visual merchandising in the boutiques that

Abercrombie & Fitch uses webcasts as part of an integrated marketing communication program to reinforce its image associated with fun-loving, independent teenagers and young adults.

associate the RZone brand with what is hot in the worlds of entertainment, sports, and gaming.[8]

Extending the Brand Name

Retailers can leverage their brand names to support the growth strategies discussed in Chapter 5. For example, IKEA used its strong brand image to successfully enter the U.S. home furnishing retail market; Talbots introduced a Talbots Woman collection for women wearing sizes 12 to 18; and the Pottery Barn launched its Pottery Barn Kids catalog to target children. In other cases, retailers have pursued growth opportunities using a new and unrelated brand name. For example, The Gap used the brand name Old Navy for its off-the-mall, value concept, and Sears named its new home store concept The Great Indoors.

There are pluses and minuses to extending a brand name to a new concept. An important benefit of extending the brand name is that minimal communication expenses are needed to create awareness and a brand image for the new concept. Customers will quickly transfer the original brand's awareness and associations to the new concept. However, in some cases, the retailer might not want to have the original brand's associations connected with the new concept. For example, The Limited decided to invest in building a new and different brand image for Victoria's Secret rather than branding the new concept with a name like Limited Secret.

 These issues also arise as a retailer expands internationally. Associations with the retailer's brands that are valued in one country may not be valued in another. For example, French consumers prefer to shop at supermarkets that offer good service and high-quality grocery products, whereas German shoppers prefer supermarkets that offer low prices and good value. Thus, a French supermarket retailer with a brand image of quality and service might not be able to leverage its image if it decides to enter the German market.[9]

Retailers communicate with customers through five vehicles: advertising, sales promotion, publicity, store atmosphere and visual merchandising, and personal selling. This chapter focuses on the first three of these vehicles in the communication mix. In large retail firms, these three elements of the communication mix are managed by the firm's marketing or advertising department and the buying organization. The other elements, store atmosphere and salespeople, are managed by store personnel and are thus discussed in Section IV. In the following sections, we discuss the methods that retailers use to communicate with their customers and how they plan and implement communication programs to build brand equity as well as short-term sales.

METHODS OF COMMUNICATING WITH CUSTOMERS

Exhibit 16–1 classifies communication methods used by retailers. The classification is based on whether the methods are impersonal or personal and paid or unpaid.

Paid Impersonal Communications

Advertising, sales promotions, store atmosphere, and websites are examples of paid impersonal communications.

EXHIBIT 16–1
Communications
Methods

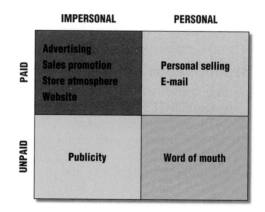

	IMPERSONAL	PERSONAL
PAID	Advertising Sales promotion Store atmosphere Website	Personal selling E-mail
UNPAID	Publicity	Word of mouth

Albertson's holds special promotions in its store like the Shrimp Fest that are tied to neighborhood activities. These promotions increase store traffic.

Advertising   **Advertising** is a form of paid communication to customers using impersonal mass media such as newspapers, TV, radio, direct mail, and the Internet.

Sales Promotions   **Sales promotions** offer extra value and incentives to customers to visit a store or purchase merchandise during a specific period of time. For example, Winkler's Diamonds, Kansas City, Kansas, has a "repair promotion" twice a year. It sends out mailers to its customers offering free jewelry checkups and special discounts on repairs. "Once people are in the store, we show them things they haven't seen before or that complement something they have," says a spokesperson. "Many come in for a repair and walk out with a diamond bracelet."[10] The most common sales promotion is a sale. Other sales promotions involve special events, in-store demonstrations, coupons, and contests.

Some retailers use in-store demonstrations and offer free samples of merchandise to build excitement in the store and stimulate purchases. In department stores, fashion shows and cooking demonstrations draw customers to the store and encourage impulse purchases.[12]

Contests are promotional games of chance. They differ from price-off sales in that (1) only a few customers receive rewards and (2) winners are determined by luck. For example, fast-food restaurants frequently have contests associated with major films (such as *Men in Black II*) or sports events (such as the Super Bowl).

Coupons offer a discount on the price of specific items when they're purchased at a store. Coupons are the most common promotional tool used by supermarkets. Retailers distribute them in their newspaper ads and in direct-mail programs. For example, Publix, a Florida-based supermarket chain, targets promotions at affluent customers using a direct-mail piece that includes recipes for a gourmet meal with coupons to purchase the products needed to prepare it.

Manufacturers also distribute coupons for their products that can be used at retailers that stock the products. To attract customers, some supermarkets accept coupons distributed by competing retailers. Another technique is for a retailer to offer double or triple the value of coupons distributed by manufacturers.

Although sales promotions are effective at generating short-term interest among customers, they aren't very useful for building long-term loyalty. Customers who participate in the promotion might learn more about a store and return to it, but typically customers attracted by sales promotions are interested in the promoted merchandise, not the retailer. Unfortunately, when a specific promotion is effective for a retailer, competing retailers learn about it quickly and offer the same promotion, which prevents the innovating retailer from gaining any long-term advantage.

Store Atmosphere   The retail store itself provides paid, impersonal communications to its customers. **Store atmosphere** is the combination of the store's physical characteristics, such as architecture, layout, signs and displays, colors, lighting, temperature, sounds, and smells, which together create an image in the customer's mind. The atmosphere communicates information about the store's service, its pricing, and the fashionability of its merchandise.[15] Chapter 18 discusses elements of store atmosphere.

Website   Finally, retailers are increasing their emphasis on communicating with customers through their websites. Retailers use their websites to build their brand image; inform customers of store locations, special events, and the availability of merchandise in local stores; and sell merchandise and services. For example, in addition to selling merchandise, Office Depot's website has a business center with forms and worksheets used by businesses to comply with the Occupational Safety and Health Act (OSHA) requirements, check job applicant records, estimate cash flow, and develop a sexual harassment policy; "how-to" tutorials for running a business; and local and national business news. By providing this information on its website, Office Depot reinforces its image as the essential source of products, services, and information for small businesses.

Office Depot uses its website to develop relationships with small business customers by offering information on best business practices.

Paid Personal Communications

Retail salespeople are the primary vehicle for providing paid personal communications to customers. **Personal selling** is a communication process in which salespeople assist customers in satisfying their needs through face-to-face exchanges of information.

than other paid communication methods. Retailers have very little control over the content or timing of publicity and word-of-mouth communications. Since unpaid communications are designed and delivered by people not employed by the retailer, they can communicate unfavorable as well as favorable information. For example, news coverage of food poisoning at a restaurant or racial discrimination at a hotel can result in significant declines in sales.

Flexibility   Personal selling is the most flexible communication method, because salespeople can talk with each customer, discover their specific needs, and develop unique presentations for them. E-mails are also very flexible because they can be personalized to specific customer interests. Other communication methods are less flexible. For example, ads deliver the same message to all customers. However, websites can be tailored to individual visitors.

Credibility   Because publicity and word of mouth are communicated by independent sources, their information is usually more credible than the information in paid communication sources. For example, customers see their friends and family as highly credible sources of information. Customers tend to doubt claims made by salespeople and in ads since they know retailers are trying to promote their merchandise.

Circuit City's sponsorship for a NASCAR racing team generates publicity and builds brand awareness. However, this publicity could be unfavorable if its NASCAR team engaged in unsanctioned activities.

Cost   Publicity and word of mouth are classified as unpaid communication methods, but retailers do incur costs to stimulate them. For example, Staples spends $5 million a year to name the Staples Center in Los Angeles, home of the NBA's Los Angeles Lakers. However, the local and national exposure offered by this sponsorship helped Staples successfully enter the California market and become a national office supply retailer.[21]

Paid impersonal communications often are economical. For example, a full-page ad in the *Los Angeles Times* costs about two cents per person to deliver the message in the ad. In contrast, personal selling, because of its flexibility, is more effective than advertising; but it is more costly. A 10-minute presentation by a retail salesperson paid $12 per hour costs the retailer $2—100 times more than exposing a customer to a newspaper, radio, or TV ad. While maintaining a website on a server is relatively inexpensive, it is costly to design, continuously update the site, and promote the site to attract visitors; however, e-mails can be sent to customers at low cost.

E-mail communications like Macy's Back to School promotion are very cost effective in targeting messages to specific customers.

Due to the differences just described, communication methods differ in their effectiveness in performing communication tasks and their effectiveness in different stages of the customer's decision-making process (see Chapter 4). Typically, advertising in mass media advertising is most effective at building awareness. Websites, direct mail, and newspaper advertising are effective for conveying information about a retailer's offerings and prices. Personal selling and sales promotion are most effective at persuading customers to purchase merchandise. Mass media and magazine advertising, publicity, websites, and store atmosphere are most cost-effective at building the retailer's brand image and encouraging repeat purchases and store loyalty.

PLANNING THE RETAIL COMMUNICATION PROCESS

Exhibit 16–3 illustrates the four steps in developing and implementing a retail communication program: setting objectives, determining a budget, allocating the budget, and implementing and evaluating the mix. The following sections detail each of these steps.

REFACT

In 2001, Sears spent over $1.5 billion on advertising and was the twelfth largest advertiser in the United States. McDonald's was eighteenth and JCPenney was twenty-third.[22]

Setting Objectives

Retailers establish objectives for communication programs to provide (1) direction for people implementing the program and (2) a basis for evaluating its effectiveness. Some communication programs have a long-term objective, such as creating or altering a retailer's brand image. Other communication programs focus on improving short-term performance, such as increasing store traffic on weekends.

Communication Objectives   While retailers' overall objective is to generate long- and short-term sales and profits, they often use communications objectives rather than sales objectives to plan and evaluate their communication programs. **Communication objectives** are specific goals related to the retail communication mix's effect on the customer's decision-making process.

Exhibit 16–4 shows hypothetical information about customers in the target market for a Safeway supermarket. This information illustrates goals related to stages in the consumer decision-making process outlined in Chapter 4. Note that 95 percent of the customers are aware of the store (the first stage in the decision-making process) and 85 percent know the type of merchandise it sells. But only 45 percent of the customers in the target market have a favorable attitude toward the store. Thirty-two percent intend to visit the store during the next few weeks; 25 percent actually visit the store during the next two weeks; and 18 percent regularly shop at the store.

In this hypothetical example, most people know about the store and its offering. The major problem confronting the Safeway supermarket is the big drop between knowledge and favorable attitude. Thus, the store should develop a communication program with the objective of increasing the percentage of customers with a favorable attitude toward it.

To effectively implement and evaluate a communication program, objectives must be clearly stated in quantitative terms. The target audience for the communication mix needs to be defined along with the degree of change expected and the time period over which the change will be realized.

Steps in Developing a Retail Communications Program   **EXHIBIT 16–3**

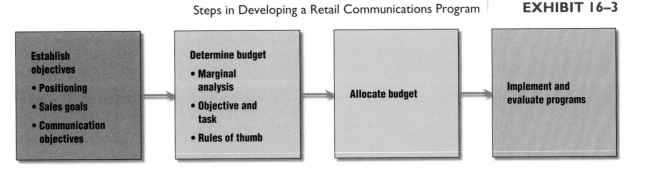

EXHIBIT 16–4
EXHIBIT 16–4
Communication
Objectives and Stages
in Consumers'
Decision-Making
Process

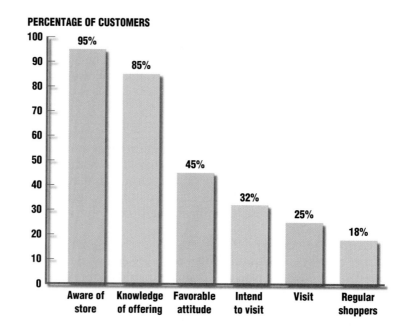

PERCENTAGE OF CUSTOMERS

Stage	Percentage
Aware of store	95%
Knowledge of offering	85%
Favorable attitude	45%
Intend to visit	32%
Visit	25%
Regular shoppers	18%

For example, a communication objective for a Safeway program might be to increase from 45 percent to 55 percent within three months the percentage of customers within a five-mile radius of the store who have a favorable attitude toward the store. This objective is clear and measurable. It indicates the task the program should address. The people who implement the program know what they're supposed to accomplish.

The communication objectives and approaches used by vendors and retailers differ and these differences can lead to conflicts. Some of these points of conflict are:

- **LONG-TERM VERSUS SHORT-TERM GOALS**

  Most communications done by vendors (manufacturers) are directed toward building a long-term image of their products. On the other hand, most retailer communications are typically used to announce promotions and special sales that generate short-term revenues.

- **PRODUCT VERSUS LOCATION**

  When vendors advertise their branded products, they don't care where the customer buys them. On the other hand, retailers don't care what brands customers buy as long as they buy them in their store.

- **GEOGRAPHIC COVERAGE**

  Since people tend to shop at stores near their homes or workplaces, most retailers use local newspapers, TV, and radio to target their communications. On the other hand, most vendors sell their brands nationally and thus tend to use national TV and magazines.

- **BREADTH OF MERCHANDISE OFFERED**

  Typically, vendors have a relatively small number of products to advertise. They can devote a lot of attention to developing consistent communication programs for each brand they make. Retailers offer a much broader set of products and often focus on building short-term sales.

Marginal Analysis for Setting Diane West's Communication Budget | **EXHIBIT 16–5**

Level	Communication Expenses (1)	Sales (2)	Gross Margin Realized (3)	Rental Expense (4)	Personnel Expense (5)	Contribution before Communication Expenses (6) = (3)–(4)–(5)	Profit after Communication Expenses (7) = (6) – (1)	
1	$0	$240,000	$96,000	$44,000	$52,200	$ (200)	$ (200)	
2	5,000	280,000	112,000	48,000	53,400	10,600	5,600	
3	10,000	330,000	132,000	53,000	54,900	24,100	14,100	
4	15,000	380,000	152,000	58,000	56,400	37,600	22,600	
5	20,000	420,000	168,000	62,000	57,600	48,400	28,400	
6	25,000	460,000	184,000	66,000	58,800	59,200	34,200	
7	30,000	500,000	200,000	70,000	60,000	70,000	40,000	Last year
8	35,000	540,000	216,000	74,000	61,200	80,800	45,800	
9	40,000	570,000	228,000	77,000	62,100	88,900	48,900	
10	45,000	600,000	240,000	80,000	63,000	97,000	52,000	
11	50,000	625,000	250,000	82,500	63,750	103,750	53,750	
12	55,000	650,000	260,000	85,000	64,500	110,500	55,500	
13	60,000	670,000	268,000	87,000	65,100	115,900	55,900	
14	65,000	690,000	276,000	89,000	65,700	121,300	56,300	Best profit
15	70,000	705,000	282,000	90,500	66,150	125,350	55,350	
16	75,000	715,000	286,000	91,500	66,450	128,050	53,050	
17	80,000	725,000	290,000	92,500	66,750	130,750	50,750	
18	85,000	735,000	294,000	93,500	67,050	133,450	48,450	
19	90,000	745,000	298,000	94,500	67,350	136,150	46,150	
20	95,000	750,000	300,000	95,000	67,500	137,500	42,500	
21	100,000	750,000	300,000	95,000	67,500	137,500	37,500	

Setting the Communication Budget

The second step in developing a retail communication program is determining a budget (see Exhibit 16–3). The economically correct method for setting the communication budget is marginal analysis. Even though retailers usually don't have enough information to perform a complete marginal analysis, the method shows how managers should approach budget-setting programs.

The marginal analysis method for setting a communication budget is the approach retailers should use when making all of their resource allocation decisions, including the number of locations in a geographic area (Chapter 8), the staffing of stores (Chapter 17), and the floor and shelf space devoted to merchandise categories (Chapter 18).

Marginal Analysis Method   **Marginal analysis** is based on the economic principle that firms should increase communication expenditures so long as each additional dollar spent generates more than a dollar of additional contribution. To illustrate marginal analysis, consider Diane West, owner-manager of a specialty store selling women's business clothing. Exhibit 16–5 shows her analysis to determine how much she should spend next year on her communication program.[23]

For 21 different communication expense levels (column 1), she estimates store sales (column 2), gross margin (column 3), and other expenses (columns 4 and 5). Then she calculates the contribution excluding expenses on communications (column 6) and the profit when the communication expenses are considered (column 7). To estimate the sales generated by different levels of communications, West can simply rely on her judgment and experience, or she might analyze past data to determine the relationship between communication expenses and sales. Historical data also provide information about the gross margin and other expenses as a percentage of sales.

Notice that at low levels of communication expenses, an additional $5,000 in communication expenses generates more than a $5,000 incremental contribution. For example, increasing the communication expense from $15,000 to $20,000 increases contribution by $10,800 (or $48,400 − $37,600). When the communication expense reaches $65,000, further increases of $5,000 generate less than $5,000 in additional contributions. For example, increasing the budget from $65,000 to $70,000 generates only an additional $4,050 in contribution ($125,350 − $121,300).

In this example, West determines that the maximum profit would be generated with a communication expense budget of $65,000. But she notices that expense levels between $55,000 and $70,000 all result in about the same level of profit. Thus, West makes a conservative decision and establishes a $55,000 budget for communication expenses.

In most cases, it's very hard to do a marginal analysis because managers don't know the relationship between communication expenses and sales. Note that the numbers in Exhibit 16–5 are simply West's estimates; they may not be accurate.

Sometimes retailers do experiments to get a better idea of the relationship between communication expenses and sales. Say, for example, a catalog retailer selects several geographic areas in the United States with the same sales potential. The retailer then distributes 100,000 catalogs in the first area, 200,000 in the second area, and 300,000 in the third area. Using the sales and costs for each distribution level, it could go through an analysis like the one in Exhibit 16–5 to determine the most profitable distribution level. (Chapter 15 described the use of experiments to determine the relationship between price and sales.)

Some other methods that retailers use to set communication budgets are the objective-and-task method and rules of thumb, such as the affordable, percentage-of-sales, and competitive parity methods. These methods are less sophisticated than marginal analysis but easier to use.

Objective-and-Task Method   The **objective-and-task method** determines the budget required to undertake specific tasks for accomplishing communication objectives. To use this method, the retailer first establishes a set of communication objectives. Then the necessary tasks and their costs are determined. The sum total of all costs incurred to undertake the tasks is the communication budget.

Exhibit 16–6 illustrates how Diane West uses the objective-and-task method to complement her marginal analysis. West establishes three objectives: to increase the awareness of her store, to create a greater preference for her store among customers in her target market, and to promote the sale of merchandise remaining at the end of each season. The total communication budget she requires to achieve these objectives is $55,300.

Objective: Increase the percentage of target market (working women living or working within 10 miles of our store) who know of our store's location and that it sells women's business attire from 25 percent to 50 percent over the next 12 months.	
Task: 480, 30–second radio spots during peak commuting hours (7:00 to 8:00 A.M. and 5:00 to 6:00 P.M.).	$12,300
Task: Sign with store name near entrance to mall.	4,500
Task: Display ad in the Yellow Pages.	500
Objective: Increase the percentage of target market who indicate that our store is their preferred store for buying their business wardrobe from 5 percent to 15 percent in 12 months.	
Task: Develop TV campaign to improve image and run 50, 30–second commercials.	$24,000
Task: Hold four "Dress for Success" seminars followed by a wine-and-cheese social.	8,000
Objective: Selling merchandise remaining at end of season.	
Task: Special event.	$6,000
Total budget	**$55,300**

EXHIBIT 16–6
Illustration of Objective-and-Task Method for Setting a Communication Budget

Besides defining the objectives and tasks, West also rechecks the financial implications of the communication mix by projecting the income statement for next year using the communication budget (see Exhibit 16–7). This income statement includes an increase of $25,300 in communication expenses over last year. But West feels that this increase in the communication budget will boost annual sales from $500,000 to $650,000. Based on West's projections, the increase in communication expenses will raise store profits. The results of the marginal analysis and the objective-and-task methods suggest a communication budget between $55,000 and $65,000.

Rule-of-Thumb Methods In the previous two methods, the communication budget is set by estimating communication activities' effects on the firm's future sales or communication objectives. The **rule-of-thumb methods** discussed in this section use the opposite logic. These methods use past sales and communication activity to determine the present communication budget.[24]

Affordable Method When using the **affordable budgeting method,** retailers first forecast their sales and expenses excluding communication expenses during the budgeting period. The difference between the forecast sales and expenses plus desired profit is then budgeted for the communication mix. In other words, the affordable method sets the communication budget by determining what money is available after operating costs and profits are budgeted.

	Last Year	Next Year
Sales	$500,000	$650,000
Gross margin (realized)	200,000	260,000
Rental, maintenance, etc.	70,000	85,000
Personnel	60,000	64,500
Communications	30,000	55,300
Profit	$ 40,000	$ 55,200

EXHIBIT 16–7
Financial Implications of Increasing the Communication Budget

The major problem with the affordable method is that it assumes that the communication expenses don't stimulate sales and profit. Communication expenses are just a cost of business, like the cost of merchandise. When retailers use the affordable method, they typically cut "unnecessary" communication expenses if sales fall below the forecast rather than increase communication expenses to increase sales.

Percentage-of-Sales Method

The **percentage-of-sales method** sets the communication budget as a fixed percentage of forecast sales. Retailers use this method to determine the communication budget by forecasting sales during the budget period and using a predetermined percentage to set the budget. The percentage may be the retailer's historical percentage or the average percentage used by similar retailers.

The problem with the percentage-of-sales method is that it assumes the same percentage used in the past, or by competitors, is still appropriate for the retailer. Consider a retailer that hasn't opened new stores in the past but plans to open many new stores in the current year. It must create customer awareness for these new stores, so the communication budget should be much larger in the current year than in the past.

Using the same percentage as competitors also may be inappropriate. For example, a retailer might have better locations than its competitors. Due to these locations, customers may already have a high awareness of the retailer's stores. Thus, the retailer may not need to spend as much on communications as competitors with poorer locations spend.

One advantage of both the percentage-of-sales method and the affordable method for determining a communication budget is that the retailer won't spend beyond its means. Since the level of spending is determined by sales, the budget will only go up when sales go up and the retailer generates more sales to pay for the additional communication expenses. When times are good, these methods work well because they allow the retailer to communicate more aggressively with customers. But when sales fall, communication expenses are cut, which may accelerate the sales decline.

Competitive Parity Method

Under the **competitive parity method,** the communication budget is set so that the retailer's share of communication expenses equals its share of the market. For example, consider a sporting goods store in a small town. To use the competitive parity method, the owner-manager would first estimate the total amount spent on communications by all of the sporting goods retailers in town. Then the owner-manager would estimate his or her store's market share for sporting goods and multiply that market share percentage by the sporting goods stores' total advertising expenses to set its budget. Assume that the owner-manager's estimate of advertising for sporting goods by all stores was $5,000 and the estimate of his or her store's market share was 45 percent. On the basis of these estimates, the owner-manager would set the store's communication budget at $2,250 to maintain competitive parity.

Like the other rule-of-thumb methods, the competitive parity method doesn't allow retailers to exploit the unique opportunities or problems they confront in a market. If all competitors used this method to set communication budgets, their market shares would stay about the same over time (assuming that the retailers develop equally effective campaigns).

Allocation of the Promotional Budget

After determining the size of the communication budget, the third step in the communication planning process is allocating the budget (see Exhibit 16–3). In this step, the retailer decides how much of its budget to allocate to specific communication elements, merchandise categories, geographic regions, or long- and short-term objectives. For example, Dillard's must decide how much of its communication budget to spend in each area where it has stores: Arkansas, Texas, Florida, North Carolina, Arizona, and Ohio. Sears decides how much to allocate to appliances, hardware, and apparel. The sporting goods store owner-manager must decide how much of the store's $2,250 communication budget to spend on promoting the store's image versus generating sales during the year and how much to spend on advertising and special promotions.

Research indicates that allocation decisions are more important than the decision on the amount spent on communications.[26] In other words, retailers often can realize the same objectives by reducing the size of the communication budget but allocating the budget more effectively. Retailing View 16.3 illustrates how T. J. Maxx cut its advertising budget and increased sales.

An easy way to make such allocation decisions is just to spend about the same in each geographic region or for each merchandise category. But this allocation rule probably won't maximize profits because it ignores the possibility that communication programs might be more effective for some merchandise categories or for some regions than for others. Another approach is to use rules of thumb such as basing allocations on the sales level or contribution for the merchandise category.

Allocation decisions, like budget-setting decisions, should use the principles of marginal analysis. The retailer should allocate the budget to areas that will yield the greatest return. This approach for allocating a budget is sometimes referred to as the **high-assay principle.** Consider a miner who can spend his time digging on two claims. The value of the gold on one claim is assayed at $20,000 per ton, while the assay value on the other claim is $10,000 per ton. Should the miner spend 2/3 of his time at the first mine and 1/3 third of his time at the other mine? Of course not! The miner should spend all of his time mining the first claim until the assay value of the ore mined drops to $10,000 a ton, at which time he can divide his time equally between the claims.

Similarly, a retailer may find that its customers have a high awareness and very favorable attitude toward its women's clothing but may not know much about the store's men's clothing. In this situation, a dollar spent on advertising men's clothing might generate more sales than a dollar spent on women's clothing even though the sales of women's clothing is greater than the sales of men's clothing.

Planning, Implementing, and Evaluating Communication Programs—Three Illustrations

The final stage in developing a retail communication program is implementation and evaluation (see Exhibit 16–3). In this chapter's appendix, we discuss some specific issues in implementing advertising programs, including developing the message, selecting the media used for delivering the message, and determining the timing and frequency for presenting the message. In this final section of the chapter, we illustrate the planning and evaluation process for three communication programs—an advertising campaign by a small specialty retailer, a sales promotion opportunity confronting a supermarket chain, and a communication program emphasizing direct marketing undertaken by a large retail chain.

Advertising Campaign   South Gate West is one of several specialty import home furnishing stores competing for upscale shoppers in Charleston, South Carolina. The store has the appearance of both a fine antique store and a traditional home furnishing shop, but most of its merchandise is new Asian imports.[27]

Harry Owens, the owner, realized his communication budget was considerably less than the budget of the local Pier 1 store. (Pier 1 is a large national import home furnishings chain.) He decided to concentrate his limited budget on a specific segment and use highly distinctive copy and art in his advertising. His target market was experienced, sophisticated consumers of housewares and home decorative items. His experience indicated the importance of personal selling for more seasoned shoppers because they (1) make large purchases and

---

RETAILING VIEW

T. J. Maxx Finds That Advertising Does Not Always Increase Profits

16.3

When TJX, the corporation that owns T. J. Maxx, bought Marshalls, another off-price retail chain, the firm reduced Marshalls' ad budget by $28 million and eliminated Marshalls' "buy one, get one free" promotion program—and sales actually increased. Prior to the acquisition by TJX, Marshalls' advertising frequently featured new shipments of clothing and products. An ad would say, "We just got in a boatload of Armani suits. Please come down and see us," or it would highlight prices of specific items, emphasizing the size of the discount off-list price. Shoppers were attracted to the stores by these ads, but they just cherry picked the advertised items. (**Cherry picking** involves customers visiting a store and buying only merchandise sold at big discounts.)

The T. J. Maxx executives believed that advertising is different for off-price retailers than for other retailers. Visiting an off-price retailer is like going on a treasure hunt. Shoppers can find apparel, glassware, and jewelry at 30 to 60 percent below department store prices. The chance of finding a real bargain keeps customers going through the merchandise until they find something to buy. But Marshalls' advertising told customers what was new and what were the good buys, thus eliminating the adventure in the off-price shopping experience.

The T. J. Maxx ads now feature "Taylor," a sophisticated 30–something blonde in an upscale apartment, sharing her shopping secrets ("Come on, it's T. J. Maxx. There are things you need to know!"), then reels off a list of dos and don'ts: "Never take a friend who wears your size. You've got to take the big car. When you get there, get a cart because you're going to need it!"

Sources: Vincent Coppola and David Gianatasio, "Mullen/LHC Continues to Tell 'Maxximum Stories' Second Phase of Agency's T. J. Maxx Campaign Makes Its Debut," *ADWEEK*, June 4, 2001, p. 3; and Joseph Pereira, "TJX Slashes Ad Budget to Revitalize Unit," *The Wall Street Journal*, October 8, 1996, p. B4.

TJMaxx's advertising uses Taylor to promote the excitement of shopping in its stores.

(2) seek considerable information before making a decision. Thus, Owens spent part of his communication budget on training his sales associates.

The advertising program Owens developed emphasized his store's distinctive image. He used the newspaper as his major vehicle. Competitive ads contained line drawings of furniture with prices. His ads emphasized the imagery associated with Asian furniture by featuring off-the-beaten-path scenes of Asian countries with unusual art objects. This theme was also reflected in the store's atmosphere.

To evaluate his communication program, Owens needed to compare the results of his program with the objectives he developed during the first part of the planning process. To measure his campaign's effectiveness, he conducted an inexpensive tracking study. Telephone interviews were performed periodically with a representative sample of furniture customers in his store's trading area. Communication objectives were assessed using the following questions:

Communication Objective	Question
Awareness	What stores sell East Asian furniture?
Knowledge	Which stores would you rate outstanding on the following characteristics?
Attitude	On your next shopping trip for East Asian furniture, which store would you visit first?
Visit	Which of the following stores have you been to?

Here are the survey results for one year:

	Before Campaign	Six Months After	One Year After
Awareness (% mentioning store)	38%	46%	52%
Knowledge (% giving outstanding rating for sales assistance)	9	17	24
Attitude (% first choice)	13	15	19
Visit (% visited store)	8	15	19

The results show a steady increase in awareness, knowledge of the store, and choice of the store as a primary source of East Asian furniture. This research provides evidence that the advertising was conveying the intended message to the target audience.

Sales Promotion Opportunity   Many sales promotion opportunities undertaken by retailers are initiated by vendors. For example, Colgate-Palmolive might offer the following special promotion to Kroger: During a one-week period, Kroger can order Fab laundry detergent in the 48-ounce size at 15 cents below the standard wholesale price. However, if Kroger elects to buy Fab at the discounted price, the grocery chain must feature the 48-ounce container of Fab in its Thursday newspaper ad at $1.59 (20 cents off the typical retail price). In addition, Kroger must have an end-aisle display of Fab.

Before Kroger decides whether to accept such a trade promotion and then promote Fab to its customers, it needs to assess the promotion's impact on its profitability. Such a promotion may be effective for the vendor but not for the retailer.

To evaluate a trade promotion, the retailer considers

- The realized margin from the promotion.
- The cost of the additional inventory carried due to buying more than the normal amount.
- The potential increase in sales from the promoted merchandise.
- The potential loss suffered when customers switch to the promoted merchandise from more profitable private-label brands.
- The additional sales made to customers attracted to the store by the promotion.[28]

This end-aisle display of Fab is part of a special Colgate-Palmolive promotion in which the supermarket chain participated.

When Fab's price is reduced to $1.59, Kroger will sell more Fab than it normally would. But Kroger's margin on the Fab will be less because the required retail discount of 20 cents isn't offset by the wholesale discount of 15 cents. In addition, Kroger might suffer losses because the promotion encourages customers to buy Fab, which has a lower margin than Kroger's private-label detergent customers might have bought. In fact, customers may stockpile Fab, buying several boxes, which will reduce sales of Kroger's private-label detergent for some time after the special promotion ends. On the other hand, the promotion may attract customers who don't normally shop at Kroger but who will visit to buy Fab at the discounted price. These customers might buy additional merchandise, providing a sales gain to the store that it wouldn't have realized if it hadn't promoted Fab.

Special Promotion Using a CRM/Campaign Management Tool   A national retailer with 1,600 store locations used its Matrix Technology Group CRM/campaign management system to plan, design, evaluate, and implement a special Easter promotion.[29] The diagram of the system is shown in Exhibit 16–8. The retailer has a customer database with purchase information complemented with additional customer information acquired through external sources (Exhibit 16–8).

After an initial planning meeting, the retailer decided to use both direct-mail and e-mail communication channels with supporting in-store promotions and existing advertising. Customers would need to bring in a coupon to take advantage of the special promotion. The goal of the campaign was to generate a 10 percent increase in sales during the holiday period.

Using the campaign management tool in the system, the retailer examined a number of what-if scenarios enabling the team to chart out all of the tasks, costs, and related deadlines, to determine projected ROI. Initially, they wanted to target customers who had visited the stores and made a purchase within the last nine months. During the target market segmentation evaluation process,

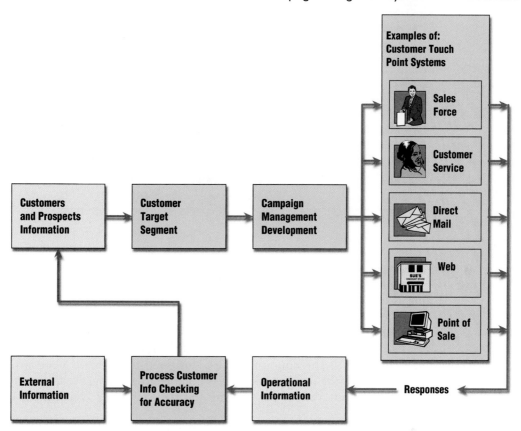

they determined that the counts were too low and increased the target criteria to customer purchases within the last 12 months. Using this criterion, the communication program would be directed to 2.6 million customers. A review of past holiday promotion programs suggested at response rate of 2.5 percent.

Based on the 2.5 percent response rate for 2.6 million customers, the number of people projected to visit the stores was 65,000. The special promotion was a $49 item, but the average sale once people were in the store was $99. On the basis of this information, the holiday event special promotion was targeted to generate gross sales between $3.1 million and $6.4 million.

The cost for the direct-mail piece was $.65/piece and the e-mail piece was $.03/e-mail. To mail and e-mail 2.6 million customers, the cost was $1,768,000. In determining the product costs on the special promotion item, a 75 percent markup was used. The campaign profitability margin was projected to be between $600,000 and $3.1 million. The financial analysis developed by the planning tool is shown in Exhibit 16–9.

Once the what-if analysis was completed, and the campaign plan was built with all of the details and responsibilities of each department, it was set into action. The action plan includes all the required steps in the campaign process,

CAMPAIGN PLANNING FINANCIALS			
Target Market Count		**Campaign Costs**	
Records in 12-month period	2.6 million	Direct mail ($.65/piece)	$1,690,000
2.5% response rate		E-mail ($.03/e-mail)	$ 78,000
Project response count	65,000	Total cost	$1,768,000
Gross Revenue		**Net Revenue (less product cost of 25%)**	
Special promotion $49/each	$3,185,000	$2,388,750	
Average sale $99/each	$6,435,000	$4,826,250	
Campaign Profitability			
	Special promotion	$620,750	
	Average sale	$3,058,250	

along with the costs, responsibilities, and deadlines on the marketing production schedule. By putting the plan into production, all of the tasks are sent to the people responsible for completing them, so that deadlines and costs are tracked. Each department would receive a series of tasks specific to that department's deliverables.

The Creative Department was assigned the responsibility to design the direct-mail piece with the coupon. It also designed the e-mail piece with a print coupon. Once the design process was completed and approved, the artwork was sent to the Print Vendor for printing and the Marketing Department for e-mail distribution.

The Database Marketing Department was responsible for sending the list of customers in the target market analysis (the customers who had visited a store and made a purchase in the last 12 months) to the Mail Vendor. Each record in the customer database had a unique identifier so that the results of the campaign would be properly tracked and analyzed.

The Store Promotions Department received its responsibilities to make sure that the in-store promotional materials were consistent with the message in the campaign. Media Services also received a task to verify consistency in all media with the campaign message.

During the entire campaign process, a management view of the financial information and campaign deliverables/deadline information was available. As the stores reported their customer sales, management's reports were automatically generated, and the response ROI was analyzed to determine if the marketing campaign was successful.

The information from all of the customer touch points was collected, processed, and added to the customer database. The successful campaign was then templated for future use that would save time in the planning phase for the next holiday campaign. The matrix solution allowed management to optimize resources and manage deadlines and deliverables, thus increasing productivity, efficiency, and ROI.

SUMMARY

The communication program can be designed to achieve a variety of objectives for the retailer. Objectives include building a brand image of the retailer in the customer's mind, increasing sales and store traffic, providing information about the retailer's location and offering, and announcing special activities.

Retailers communicate with customers through advertising, sales promotions, websites, store atmosphere, publicity, personal selling, e-mail, and word of mouth. These elements in the communication mix must be coordinated so customers will have a clear, distinct image of the retailer and won't be confused by conflicting information.

Many retailers use rules of thumb to determine the size of the promotion budget. Marginal analysis (the most appropriate method for determining how much must be spent to accomplish the retailer's objectives) should be used to determine whether the level of spending maximizes the profits that could be generated by the communications mix.

The largest portion of a retailer's communication budget is typically spent on advertising and sales promotions. A wide array of media can be used for advertising. Each medium has its pros and cons. Newspaper advertising is effective for announcing sales, whereas TV ads are useful for developing an image. Sales promotions are typically used to achieve short-term objectives, such as increasing store traffic over a weekend. Most sales promotions are supported in part by promotions offered to the retailer by its vendors. Publicity and word of mouth are typically low-cost communications, but they are very difficult for retailers to control.

KEY TERMS

advertising, *520*

affordable budgeting method, *529*

aided recall, *516*

brand, *514*

brand associations, *516*

brand awareness, *516*

brand equity, *515*

brand image, *517*

cherry picking, *532*

communication objectives, *525*

competitive parity method, *530*

contests, *520*

cooperative (co-op) advertising, *540*

cost per thousand (CPM), *545*

coupons, *520*

coverage, *545*

cumulative reach, *545*

e-mail, *522*

free-standing insert (FSI), *542*

frequency, *546*

high assay principle, *531*

impact, *546*

integrated marketing communication program, *518*

magalog, *518*

marginal analysis, *527*

objective-and-task method, *528*

percentage-of-sales method, *530*

personal selling, *521*

preprint, *542*

publicity, *522*

reach, *545*

rule-of-thumb methods, *529*

sales promotion, *520*

shelf talker, *541*

shopping guides, *544*

spot, *543*

store atmosphere, *521*

top-of-mind awareness, *516*

word of mouth, *523*

GET OUT & DO IT!

1. GO SHOPPING Go to a retail store and make a list of all of the specific elements and information in the store that communicate the store's image and the merchandise it is offering to customers.

2. GO SHOPPING Look though the free-standing inserts in your Sunday newspaper. Evaluate the general use of FSIs, and select the FSIs that you think are most effective. Why are these FSIs more effective than the other ones?

3. INTERNET EXERCISE Retailers and manufacturers now deliver coupons through the Internet rather than by mail or in free-standing inserts. Go to www.coolsavings.com or www.supercoups.com for coupons offered over the Internet. How does this coupon distribution system compare to more traditional distribution systems? Which system is more effective from the retailers' perspective and from the consumers' perspective?

4. INTERNET EXERCISE Trader Joe's has an interesting retail concept: it's an off-price retailer selling gourmet food and wine. Go to www.traderjoes.com and see how the firm uses its Internet site to promote its retail offering. How effective do you think the site is in promoting the store and building its image?

5. INTERNET EXERCISE You can find more information about the use of radio as an advertising media at the Radio Advertising Bureau site, www.rab.com. Based on this information, what types of retail messages can be delivered most effectively by radio compared to other media?

DISCUSSION QUESTIONS AND PROBLEMS

1. How do brands benefit consumers? Retailers?

2. How can advertising, personal selling, and promotion complement each other in an integrated marketing communications program?

3. As a means of communicating with customers, how does advertising differ from publicity?

4. Why is the newspaper the favorite medium used by retailers for advertising? What are the advantages and disadvantages of newspaper advertising? Why is the use of newspaper decreasing and use of direct mail increasing?

5. For which of the following growth opportunities do you think the retailer should use its brand name when pursuing the opportunity? Why?

   (a) McDonald's starts a new chain of restaurants to sell seafood in a sit-down environment competing with Red Lobster.

   (b) Sears starts a chain of stand-alone stores that sell just home appliances.

   (c) Blockbuster starts a chain of stores selling consumer electronics.

6. What factors should be considered in dividing up the budget among a store's different merchandise areas? Which of the following should receive the highest advertising budget: fashionable women's clothing, men's underwear, women's hosiery, or kitchen appliances? Why?

7. Outline some elements in a communcation program to achieve the following objectives:

   (a) Increase store loyalty by 20 percent.

   (b) Build awareness of the store by 10 percent.

   (c) Develop an image as a low-price retailer.

   How would you determine whether the communication program met the objective?

8. Retailers use TV to build a brand image. TV advertisers have identified many types of markets based on the day, time, and type of show during which their ads may appear. During which days, times, and types of shows should

retailers advertise fresh produce and meat, power drills, beer, and health club memberships? Why?

9. Some retailers direct their advertising efforts toward reaching as wide an audience as possible. Others try to expose the audience to an advertisement as many times as possible. When should a retailer concentrate on reach? When should a retailer concentrate on frequency?

10. A retailer plans to open a new store near a university. It will specialize in collegiate merchandise such as T-shirts, fraternity/sorority accessories, and sweatshirts. Develop an integrated communication program for the retailer. What specific advertising media should the new store use to capture the university market?

11. Cooperative (co-op) advertising is a good way for a retailer to extend an ad budget. Why isn't it always in a retailer's best interests to rely extensively on co-op advertising?

SUGGESTED READINGS

Aaker, David, and Erich Joachimsthaler. *Brand Leadership: Building Assets in an Information Economy.* New York: Free Press, 2000.

Belch, George, and Michael Belch. *Advertising and Promotion : An Integrated Marketing Communications Perspective.* 5th ed. Burr Ridge, IL: Irwin/McGraw-Hill, 2001.

Corstjens, Marcel, and Rajiv Lal. "Building Store Loyalty through Store Brands." *Journal of Marketing Research* 37 (August 2000), pp. 281–302.

Henderson, Terilyn, and Elizabeth Mihas. "Building Retail Brands." *McKinsey Quarterly,* Summer 2000, pp. 110–115

Jones, John Philip. *The Ultimate Secrets of Advertising.* Thousand Oaks, CA: Sage Publications, 2002.

Moreaua, Page; Aradhna Krishna; and Bari Harlam. "The Manufacturer-Retailer-Consumer Triad: Differing Perceptions Regarding Price Promotions." *Journal of Retailing* 77 (Winter 2001), pp. 547–70.

Shimp, Terence. *Advertising, Promotion and Supplemental Aspects of Integrated Marketing Communications.* 5th ed. Fort Worth: Dryden Press, 2000.

Tisch, Carol. "Branding and Retail." *HFN,* January 17, 2000, pp. 4–10

"What's in Store? Consumer Desires, Branding Concerns and Service Industries Shape Store-Design Trends." *Chain Store Age,* May 2002, pp. 114–17.

Yadin, Daniel. *Creative Marketing Communications: A Practical Guide to Planning, Skills and Techniques.* 3rd ed. London: Kogan Page Ltd. 2001

Zhang, Z. John; Aradhna Krishna; and Sanjay K. Dhar. "The Optimal Choice of Promotional Vehicles: Front-Loaded or Rear-Loaded Incentives?" *Management Science* 46 (March 2000), pp. 348–67.

APPENDIX 16A   Implementing Retail Advertising Programs

Implementing an ad program involves developing the message, choosing the specific media to convey the message, and determining the frequency and timing of the message. Let's look at each of these decisions.

DEVELOPING THE ADVERTISING MESSAGE

Most retail advertising messages have a short life and are designed to have an immediate impact. This immediacy calls for a copywriting style that grabs the reader's attention. Exhibit 16–10 outlines specific suggestions for developing local newspaper ads.[30]

REFACT

The average consumer sees over 2,000 advertising messages per week.[31]

Assistance in Advertising

Retailers get assistance in developing advertising campaigns from vendors through their co-op

EXHIBIT 16–10   Suggestions for Developing Local Ads

Have a dominant headline	The first question a consumer asks is, What's in it for me? Thus, retailers need to feature the principal benefit being offered in the headline along with a reason why the consumer should act immediately. The benefit can be expanded on in a subhead.
Use a dominant element	Ads should include a large picture or headline. Typically, photographs of real people attract more attention than drawings. Action photographs are effective in getting readers' attention.
Stick to a simple layout	The ad's layout should lead the reader's eye through the message from the headline to the illustration and then to the explanatory copy, price, and retailer's name and location. Complex elements, decorative borders, and many different typefaces distract the reader's attention from the retailer's message.
Provide a specific, complete presentation	Ad readers are looking for information that will help them decide whether to visit the store. The ad must contain all of the information pertinent to this decision, including the type of merchandise, brands, prices, sizes, and colors. Consumers are unlikely to make a special trip to the store on the basis of vague information. Broadcast ads, particularly radio ads, tend to be very creative but often leave the consumer thinking, Gee, that was a clever ad, but what was it advertising?
Use easily recognizable, distinct visuals	Consumers see countless ads each day. Thus, to get the consumers' attention, retailers must make their ads distinct from those of the competition. Ads with distinctive art, layout, design elements, or typeface generate higher readership.
Give the store's name and address	The store's name and location are the two most important aspects of a retail ad. If consumers don't know where to go to buy the advertised merchandise, the retailer won't make a sale. The retailer's name and location must be prominently displayed in print ads and repeated several times in broadcast ads.

This ad incorporates many of the features of an effective ad—dominant headline and elements, specific and complete presentation, easily recognized visuals, and the name and address of the retailer.

programs, advertising agencies, and media companies.

Co-op Programs   **Cooperative (co-op) advertising** is a program undertaken by a vendor. The vendor pays for part of the retailer's advertising. But the vendor dictates some conditions for the advertising. For example, Sony may have a co-op program that pays for half of a consumer electronics retailer's ads for Sony digital TVs.

Co-op advertising enables a retailer to increase its advertising budget. In the previous example, Best Buy only pays for half of its expenses (for ads including Sony digital TVs). In addition to lowering costs, co-op advertising enables a small retailer to associate its name with well-known national brands and use attractive artwork created by the national brand.

Co-op advertising programs are often used to support a vendor's effort to discourage retailers from discounting the vendor's products. For example, Estée Lauder might give its department store retailers 7 percent of sales for co-op advertising only if the retailers agree not to advertise a price below its suggested retail price.

> **REFACT**
>
> Co-op advertising accounts for approximately 50 percent of all department store and 75 percent of all grocery store advertising.[32]

Co-op advertising has other drawbacks. First, vendors want the ads to feature their products, while retailers are more interested in featuring their store's name, location, and assortment of merchandise and services offered. This conflict in goals can reduce the effectiveness of co-op advertising from the retailer's perspective. In addition, ads developed by the vendor often are used by several competing retailers and may list the names and locations of all retailers offering their brands. Thus, co-op ads tend to blur any distinctions between retailers. Finally, restrictions the vendor places on the ads may further reduce their effectiveness for the retailer. For example, the vendor may restrict advertising to a period of time when the vendor's sales are depressed, but the retailer might not normally be advertising during this time frame.

In addition to co-op programs, retailers and vendors can work together as partners on a co-marketing program. An example of a co-marketing program undertaken by Wal-Mart and Coppertone is described in Retailing View 16.4.

Agencies Most large retailers have a department that creates advertising for sales and special events. Advertising agencies are often used by large retailers to develop ads for store image campaigns. Many small retailers use local agencies to plan and create their advertising. These local agencies are often more skilled in planning and executing advertising than the retailer's employees are. Agencies also work on other aspects of the communication programs, such as contests, direct mail, and special promotions.

Media Companies Besides selling newspaper space and broadcast time, the advertising media offer services to local retailers ranging from planning an ad program to actually designing the ads.

Wal-Mart and Coppertone Partner to Sell Sunscreen | RETAILING VIEW

16.4

Coppertone is the market leader in the sun care category. It has a very high brand awareness that it has leveraged through the use of its well-known icon "Little Miss Coppertone," a blond, pigtailed little girl with a dog tugging at her bathing suit. This icon was featured in the company's first co-marketing program with a retailer, Wal-Mart.

The promotional program was based on Little Miss Coppertone's losing her dog in a Wal-Mart store. For three months prior to the event, the program was promoted to sales associates over Wal-Mart's internal communication channels, including its satelite TV broadcasts, headquarters meeting, and sell sheets distributed to sales associates. On the day of the event, a scavanger hunt, Wal-Mart greeters wore "Spot the Dog" buttons and distributed game pieces to children and their parents. The game pieces described the scavanger hunt and encouraged customers to find clues located in different areas of the store—sun care, lawn and garden, and pet food. The pieces also promoted Coppertone's innovative rub-free sprays and had a $2 Wal-Mart coupon for the products. **Shelf talkers**—signs on the shelf providing information about the merchandise and its price—in each area provided the answer to the clues. When all three answers were filled in, the customer turned in the game pieces for a free beach ball at the "Scavenger Hunt Center" in the store.

The co-marketing promotion benefited both Wal-Mart and Coppertone. It built sun care customers' loyalty for

The "Spot the Dog" scavenger hunt was a co-marketing program developed by Wal-Mart and Coppertone. The program increased Wal-Mart's and Coppertone's sales.

Wal-Mart and Coppertone, kept customers in the Wal-Mart store longer and encouraged them to visit different areas of the store, and increased sunscreen sales for Wal-Mart and Coppertone. Almost 2,500 stores participated in the one-day event. Over 1.2 million prizes were delivered. Wal-Mart's sales of Coppertone sunscreen increased by 6 percent, and the sales in other categories also increased.

Source: George Belch and Michael Belch, *Advertising and Promotion,* 5th Ed. (New York: McGraw-Hill, 2001), p. 531. Copyright © 2001 by the McGraw-Hill Companies. Reprinted by permission of the McGraw-Hill Companies.

Media companies also do market research on their audiences and can provide information about shopping patterns in the local area.

CHOOSING THE MOST EFFECTIVE MEDIA

After developing the message, the next step is deciding what medium to use to communicate the message. The media used for retail advertising are newspapers, magazines, direct mail, radio, TV, outdoor billboards, the Internet, shopping guides, and the Yellow Pages. Exhibit 16–11 summarizes their characteristics.

Newspapers

Retailing and newspaper advertising grew up together over the past century. But the growth in retail newspaper advertising has slowed recently as retailers have begun using other media. Still, 16 of the nation's 25 largest newspaper advertisers are retailers.[33]

In addition to displaying ads with their editorial content, newspapers distribute free-standing inserts. A **free-standing insert (FSI),** also called a **preprint,** is an ad printed at the retailer's expense and distributed as an insert in the newspaper.

Since newspapers are distributed in a well-defined local market area, they're effective at targeting retail advertising. Often the local market covered by a newspaper is similar to the market served by the retailer. Newspapers offer opportunities for small retailers to target their advertising by developing editions for different areas of a city. For example, the *Los Angeles Times* has 11 special editions for regions of southern California, including editions for Ventura County, the desert cities, and San Diego County.

Newspapers also offer quick response. There's only a short time between the deadline for receiving the ad and the time that the ad will appear. Thus, newspapers are useful for delivering messages on short notice.

Newspapers, like all print media, effectively convey a lot of detailed information. Readers can go through an ad at their own pace and refer back to part of the ad when they want to. In addition, consumers can save the ad and take it to the store with them. This makes newspaper ads effective at conveying information about the prices of sale items. But newspaper ads aren't effective for showing merchandise, particularly when it's important to illustrate colors, because of the poor reproduction quality.

While newspapers are improving their printing facilities to provide better reproductions and color in ads, retailers continue to rely on preprints to get good reproduction quality. JCPenney uses FSIs extensively, distributing them to over 50 million newspaper readers weekly. However, FSIs are so popular that the insert from one retailer can be lost among the large number of inserts in the newspaper. Walgreens has reduced its FSIs from two to one a week because of the clutter and be-

EXHIBIT 16–11
Media Capability

Media	Targeting	Timeliness	Information Presentation Capacity	Life	Cost
Newspapers	Good	Good	Modest	Short	Modest
Magazines	Modest	Poor	Modest	Modest	High
Direct mail	Excellent	Modest	High	Short	Modest
Television	Modest	Modest	Low	Short	Modest
Radio	Modest	Good	Low	Short	Low
Internet					
Banner	Excellent	Excellent	Low	Modest	High
Website	Excellent	Excellent	High	Long	Modest
E-mail	Excellent	Excellent	Modest	Short	Low
Outdoor billboards	Modest	Poor	Very low	Long	Modest
Shopping guides	Modest	Modest	Low	Modest	Low
Yellow Pages	Modest	Poor	Low	Long	Low

There are so many FSIs in local newspapers, that it is difficult for a retailer to gets its FSIs read.

cause it has found that young people don't read newspapers as much as their parents. However, Walgreens is trying to increase the effectiveness of its FSIs by streamlining the message and using a better grade of paper.[34]

The life of a newspaper ad is short because the newspaper is usually discarded after it's read. In contrast, magazine advertising has a longer life since consumers tend to save magazines and read them several times during a week or month.

Finally, the cost of developing newspaper ads is very low. Newspaper ads can be developed by less experienced people and don't require expensive color photography or typesetting. However, the cost of delivering the message may be high if the newspaper's circulation is broader than the retailer's target market, thus requiring the retailer to pay for exposures that won't generate sales.

Magazines

Retail magazine advertising is mostly done by national retailers such as Target and The Gap. But magazine advertising is increasing with the growth of local magazines and regional editions of national magazines. Retailers tend to use this medium for image advertising because the repro-

duction quality is high.[36] Due to the lead time—the time between submitting the ad and publication—a major disadvantage is that the timing of a magazine ad is difficult to coordinate with special events and sales.

Direct Mail

Retailers frequently use data collected at POS terminals to target their advertising and sales promotions to specific customers using direct mail (see Chapter 11). For example, Neiman Marcus keeps a database of all purchases made by its credit card customers. With information on each customer's purchases, Neiman Marcus can target direct mail on a new perfume to customers with a history of purchasing such merchandise.

Retailers also can purchase a wide variety of lists for targeting consumers with specific demographics, interests, and lifestyles. For example, a home furnishings store could buy a list of subscribers to *Architectural Digest* in its trading area and then mail information about home furnishings to those upscale consumers. Finally, many retailers encourage their salespeople to maintain a preferred customer list and use it to mail personalized invitations and notes. While direct mail can be very effective due to the ability to personalize the message, it's also costly. Many consumers ignore direct-mail advertising and treat it as junk mail.

Television

TV commercials can be placed on a national network or a local station. A local television commercial is called a **spot.** Retailers typically use TV for image advertising.[37] They take advantage of the high reproduction quality and the opportunity to communicate through both visual images and sound. TV ads can also demonstrate product usage. For example, Eckerd Drug's TV ad program is built around the theme "It's Right at Eckerd." The ads summarize the advantages of shopping at Eckerd on many levels: convenient location, available parking, broad assortment, and fast, easy checkout. Lifestyle ads connect Eckerd as a vital link to an active, healthy, reduced-stress lifestyle. On the other hand, Walgreens' advertising campaign emphasizes its position as the leading national drugstore via the theme "The Pharmacy America Trusts."[38]

Besides high production costs, broadcast time for national TV advertising is expensive. Spots have relatively small audiences, but they may be economical for local retailers. To offset the high production costs, many vendors provide modular commercials, in which the retailer can insert its name or a "tag" after information about the vendor's merchandise.

Radio

Many retailers use radio advertising because messages can be targeted to a specific segment of the market.[40] Some radio stations' audiences are highly loyal to their announcers. When these announcers promote a retailer, listeners are impressed. The cost of developing and broadcasting radio commercials is quite low.

One disadvantage of radio advertising is that listeners generally treat the radio broadcast as background, which limits the attention they give the message. As with all broadcast media, consumers must get the information from a radio commercial when it's broadcast. They can't refer back to the ad for information they didn't hear or remember.

Internet

Three uses of the Internet by retailers to communicate with customers are (1) banner ads and affiliate programs to generate awareness, (2) websites to provide information about merchandise and special events, and (3) e-mails to target messages.[41] Banner ads and affiliate programs are very effective for targeting communication, but they are not cost-effective for building awareness. Using information from a visitor's navigation and purchase behavior and IP address, banner ads can be targeted to specific individuals. For example, Sportsline.com visitors who look at the box scores for Kansas City Royals baseball games are shown ads for Royals logo apparel and hats. DoubleClick, an Internet ad agency, downloads different banner ads from its server to host websites based on information it has on the specific visitor. However, Internet advertising is not cost-effective for building awareness because the large number of websites reduces the number of customers visiting a site and seeing a particular ad.

While the Internet is not effective for building awareness, it is an excellent vehicle for conveying information to customers. In addition to selling merchandise for a website, retailers can provide a wide array of information ranging from the store locations to the availability and pricing of merchandise in specific stores. The interactivity of the Internet gives customers the opportunity to quickly sift through a vast amount of information. For example, visitors to the Circuit City website can find detailed information on specific digital camera models and generate a table comparing a select group of cameras on features of importance to the customer.

Finally, retailers can use the Internet to send e-mails to customers informing them of special events and new merchandise.

Outdoor Billboards

Billboards and other forms of outdoor advertising are effective vehicles for creating awareness and providing a very limited amount of information to a narrow audience. Thus, outdoor advertising has limited usefulness in providing information about sales. Outdoor advertising is typically used to remind customers about the retailer or to inform people in cars of nearby retail outlets.[42]

Shopping Guides

Shopping guides are free papers delivered to all residents in a specific area. This medium is particularly useful for retailers that want to saturate a specific trading area. Shopping guides are cost-effective and assure the local retailer of 100 percent coverage in a specific area. In contrast, subscription newspapers typically offer only 30 to 50 percent coverage. An extension of the shopping guide concept is the coupon book or magazine. These media contain coupons offered by retailers for discounts. Shopping guides and coupon books make no pretense about providing news to consumers. They're simply delivery vehicles for ads and coupons.

HOW TO BUILD A TROPHY CASE

The Sports Authority uses billboards to create awareness and remind customers to consider The Sports Authority when they need sports equipment.

Yellow Pages

The Yellow Pages are useful for retailers because they have a long life. The Yellow Pages are used as a reference by consumers who are definitely interested in making a purchase and seeking information.

Factors in Selecting Media

To convey their message with the most impact to the most consumers in the target market at the lowest cost, retailers need to evaluate media in terms of coverage, reach, cost, and impact of the advertising messages delivered through the medium.

Coverage **Coverage** refers to the number of potential customers in the retailer's target market that could be exposed to an ad in a given medium. For example, assume that the size of the target market is 100,000 customers. The local newspaper is distributed to 60 percent of the customers in the target market, 90 percent of the potential customers have a TV set that picks up the local station's signal, and 5 percent of the potential customers drive past a billboard. Thus, the coverage for newspaper advertising would be 60,000; for TV advertising, 90,000; and for the specific billboard, 5,000.

Reach In contrast to coverage, **reach** is the actual number of customers in the target market exposed to an advertising medium. If on any given day, 60 percent of the potential customers who receive the newspaper actually read it, then the newspaper's reach would be 36,000 (or 60 percent of 60,000). Retailers often run an ad several times, in which case they calculate the **cumulative reach** for the sequence of ads. For example, if 60 percent of the potential customers receiving a newspaper read it each

day, 93.6 percent (or 1 minus the probability of not reading the paper three times in a row [.40 × .40 × .40]) of the potential customers will read the newspaper at least one day over the three-day period in which the ad appears in the paper. Thus, the cumulative reach for running a newspaper ad for three days is 56,160 (or 93.6 percent × 60,000), which almost equals the newspaper's coverage.

When evaluating Internet advertising opportunities, the measure used to assess reach is the number of unique visitors—the number of different people who access the web page on which the ad is located.

Cost The **cost per thousand (CPM)** measure is often used to compare media. Typically, CPM is calculated by dividing an ad's cost by its reach. Another approach for determining CPM is to divide the cost of several ads in a campaign by their cumulative reach. If, for instance, in the previous example, one newspaper ad costs $500 and three ads cost $1,300, the CPM using simple reach is $13.89, or $500/(36,000/1,000). Using cumulative reach, the CPM is $23.15, or $1,300/(56,160/1,000). Note that the CPM might be higher using cumulative reach rather than simple reach, but the overall reach is also higher, and many potential customers will see the ad two or three times.

CPM is a good method for comparing similar-size ads in similar media, such as full-page ads in the *Los Angeles Times* and the *Orange County Register*. But CPM can be misleading when comparing the cost-effectiveness of ads in different types of media, such as newspaper and TV. A TV ad may have a lower CPM than a newspaper ad, but the newspaper ad may be much more effective at achieving the ad's communication objectives, such as giving information about a sale.

EXHIBIT 16–12   Effectiveness of Media on Communication Objectives

Communication Task	Newspapers	Magazine	Direct Mail	TV	Radio	Websites	E-Mail	Outdoor
Getting attention	Low	Medium	Medium	Medium	Low	Low	High	Medium
Identifying name	Medium	High	Low	Low	Low	Low	Medium	High
Announcing events	High	Low	High	High	Medium	Low	High	Low
Demonstrating merchandise	Low	Medium	High	High	Low	Highest	Low	Low
Providing information	Low	High	High	Low	Low	Highest	Medium	Lowest
Changing attitudes	High	Medium	High	High	Medium	High	Low	Low
Building brand image	Low	Medium	High	High	Low	High	Low	Low

Impact Impact is an ad's effect on the audience. Due to their unique characteristics, different media are particularly effective at accomplishing different communication tasks. Exhibit 16–12 shows the effectiveness of various media for different communication tasks. TV is particularly effective at getting an audience's attention, demonstrating merchandise, changing attitudes, and announcing events. Magazines are particularly appropriate for emphasizing the quality and prestige of a store and its offering and for providing detailed information to support quality claims. Newspapers are useful for providing price information and announcing events. Websites are particularly effective for demonstrating merchandise and providing information. Outdoor advertising is most effective at promoting a retailer's name and location.

DETERMINING AD FREQUENCY AND TIMING

The frequency and timing of ads determine how often and when customers will see the retailer's message.

Frequency

Frequency is how many times the potential customer is exposed to an ad. When assessing frequency for Internet advertising, it is typically as-sessed by measuring the number of times a web page with the ad is downloaded during a visit to the site.

The appropriate frequency depends on the ad's objective. Typically, several exposures to an ad are required to influence a customer's buying behavior. Thus, campaigns directed toward changing purchase behavior rather than creating awareness emphasize frequency over reach. Ads announcing a sale are often seen and remembered after one exposure. Thus, sale ad campaigns emphasize reach over frequency.

Timing

Typically, an ad should appear on, or slightly precede, the days consumers are most likely to purchase merchandise. For example, if most consumers buy groceries Thursday through Sunday, then supermarkets should advertise on Thursday and Friday. Similarly, consumers often go shopping after they receive their paychecks at the middle and the end of the month. Thus, advertising should be concentrated at these times.

IV Section IV focuses on implementation issues associated with store management, including managing store employees and controlling costs (Chapter 17), presenting merchandise (Chapter 18), and providing customer service (Chapter 19).

Traditionally, the issues concerning merchandise management were considered the most important retail implementation decisions, and buying was considered the best career path for achieving senior retail management positions.

Developing a strategic advantage through merchandise management is becoming more and more difficult. Competing stores often have similar assortments of branded merchandise.

STORE MANAGEMENT

Since customers can find the same assortments in a number of conveniently located retail outlets and through the Internet, store management issues have become a critical basis for developing strategic advantage.

Retailers are increasing their emphasis on differentiating their offering from competitive offerings based on the experience that customers have in the stores—the service they get from store employees and quality of the shopping environment.

Managing the Store

CHAPTER

"My job is anything but boring. Everyday is different. Some days I work with the corporate office, other days I have one-on-one sessions with sales associates and customers. I interact with a lot of different people and each one has specific problems that must be dealt with. These situations range from customer service problems to various technical and equipment changes. One thing I have learned is that when a problem arises you need to deal with it in a fast and timely fashion."

"My goal as an assistant district manager is to reach and satisfy the needs of our target market—value-conscious consumers who value their time and money. At the beginning of the day, I go through the sales numbers to see how the stores are doing compared to their budgeted expectations. Then I visit selected stores to look over the overall operation. My goal is to 'make car care easier for our customer' and to fix it right the first time. During the course of a day, some of our busier stores will work with 70 to 80 customers. We listen to find out each customer's needs and suggest the best products or services for their car and driving lifestyle.

"An important aspect of my job is selecting and hiring associates. No matter what the job is, I look for someone who is outgoing and personable—people who have a natural tendency to smile. This is an important quality that can't be taught and is really critical when dealing with customers. At Bridgestone/

QUESTIONS

● What are the responsibilities of store managers?

● How should store managers recruit, select, motivate, train, and evaluate their employees?

● How should store managers compensate their salespeople?

● What legal and ethical issues must store managers consider in managing their employees?

● What can store managers do to increase productivity and reduce costs?

● How can store managers reduce inventory losses due to employee theft and shoplifting?

Firestone, the customer is number one, and Bridgestone/Firestone searches for those people who will treat customers the right way."

After graduating from the University of Alabama at Birmingham, James McClain started as a manager trainee for Toys "R" Us. He then accepted a sales associate position with Bridgestone/Firestone. Through his hard work and dedication, he worked his way up to his present position. He feels that the major factor in staying with Bridgestone/Firestone for eight years is the company rewards. Firestone acknowledges employees' hard work through promotions, rather than focusing promotions on the seniority of an employee.

Store managers are responsible for increasing the productivity of two of the retailer's most important assets: the firm's investments in its employees and real estate. Store managers are on the firing line in retailing. Due to their daily contact with customers, they have the best knowledge of customer needs and competitive activity. From this unique vantage point, store managers play an important role in formulating and executing retail strategy. Buyers can develop exciting merchandise assortments and procure them at low cost, but the retailer only realizes the benefits of the buyer's effort when the merchandise is sold. Good merchandise doesn't sell itself. Store managers must make sure that the merchandise is presented effectively and offer services that stimulate and facilitate customer buying decisions.

Even in national chains, store managers are treated as relatively independent managers of a business within the corporation. Some department store managers are responsible for $150 million in annual sales and manage over 1,000 employees. For example, James Nordstrom (former CEO of Nordstrom) told store managers, "This is your business. Do your own thing. Don't listen to us in Seattle, listen to your customers. We give you permission to take care of your customers."[1]

STORE MANAGEMENT RESPONSIBILITIES

REFACT

For supermarket retailers, which are largely self-service, wages account for 51.3 percent of operating expenses.[2]

The responsibilities of store managers are shown in Exhibit 17–1. These functions are divided into four major categories: managing employees, controlling costs, managing merchandise, and providing customer service. Issues concerning managing store employees and controlling costs are discussed in this chapter. The following chapters examine the store manager's responsibilities for presenting and managing merchandise and providing customer service.

While an important objective of store managers is increasing the revenues generated by employees, managers also increase their stores' profits by reducing costs. The major costs are the compensation and benefits of employees. But store managers also need to control maintenance and energy costs and inventory loss due to shoplifting and employee theft. These cost control issues are discussed at the end of the chapter.

The first portion of this chapter, focusing on the management of store employees, complements the strategic human resource management issues discussed in Chapter 9. Chapter 9 examined the organization of the tasks performed by the retailers and the general approaches for motivating retail employees and building their commitment to the firm. In this chapter, we discuss how store managers implement the retailer's human resource strategy. Even though most of this chapter focuses on managing store employees, Retailing View 17.1 describes how retailers are using technology to reduce costs and increase store productivity.

Exhibit 17–2 outlines the steps in the employee management process that affect store employees' productivity. These steps, discussed in the following sections, are (1) recruiting and selecting effective people, (2) improving their skills through socialization and training, (3) motivating them to perform at higher levels, and then (4) evaluating and rewarding them. Store managers also need to develop employees who can assume more responsibility and be promoted to

EXHIBIT 17–1

Responsibilities of Store Managers

MANAGING STORE EMPLOYEES (Chapter 17)

Recruiting and selecting
Socializing and training
Motivating
Evaluating and providing constructive feedback
Rewarding and compensating

CONTROLLING COSTS (Chapter 17)

Increasing labor productivity
Reducing maintenance and energy costs
Reducing inventory losses

MANAGING MERCHANDISE

Displaying merchandise and maintaining visual standards (Chapter 18)
Working with buyers
   Suggesting new merchandise
   Buying merchandise
   Planning and managing special events
   Marking down merchandise

PROVIDING CUSTOMER SERVICE (Chapter 19)

higher-level management positions. By developing subordinates, managers help both their firm and themselves. The firm benefits from having more effective managers, and the manager benefits because the firm has a qualified replacement when the manager is promoted.[3]

RECRUITING AND SELECTING STORE EMPLOYEES

The first step in the employee management process is recruiting and selecting employees. To effectively recruit employees, store managers need to undertake a job analysis, prepare a job description, find potential applicants with the desired capabilities, and screen the best candidates to interview.[4] (Appendix 1A to Chapter 1 describes the recruiting and selection process from the perspective of

Retail Stores Are Becoming High Tech | RETAILING VIEW

Men's Wearhouse has installed touch-screen POS terminals that enable sales associates to quickly respond to customer requests. If the store is out of stock for a particular sports jacket size, there's no need for the sales associate to call around—the Internet-enabled terminal provides instant access to the inventory at every one of the chain's 600 stores. If a customer needs directions to another store, the associate can immediately link to Mapquest on the Internet. The most unusual time-saving feature of the new terminals is a fingerprint scanner that lets associates make returns and exchanges more swiftly because the computer instantly recognizes them. With the old system, employees had to go through several screens and passwords to handle returns. The fingerprint scanners also help the chain cut down on inventory losses from employee theft. Now an associate cannot use another person's ID number when making a fraudulent transaction.

Many supermarket retailers are installing self-checkout lanes. This technology offers benefits to both retailers and their customers. Ninety percent of the cost of maintaining a checkout line is the cashier. Thus, eliminating the cashier can save costs and enable the store to open more checkout lanes. The retailers are using a number of techniques to limit potential theft in the self-checkout lanes. Some of these deterrents are psychological, such as showing the customer on a video screen as he or she scans the merchandise. In addition, there is an electronic scale beneath the shopping bags that knows what's just been scanned and how much it's supposed to weigh. So if a shopper scans a candy bar while slipping a rib roast in the shopping bag, the system beeps and asks that the item be entered again.

Federated Department Stores nationally spends up to $250,000 a month changing hundreds of thousands of signs when it prepares for sales and other special promotions. Some of the signs are changed incorrectly, which upsets customers, who end up arguing with cashiers when scanned prices are different than those shown on signs. Macy's East, a division of Federated, is testing electronic signs controlled through a wireless radio connection from a central store computer. The system will dramatically reduce the cost of preparing for sales.

Stores are using technology to reduce employee workload and increase customer convenience. This customer is paying for her merchandise by simply scanning the merchandise and touching the screen. Her fingerprint is recognized and linked to her credit card information in the retailer's customer database.

Sources: Suzanne Smalley, "Next Frontiers," *Newsweek*, April 29, 2002, p. 40; and William Bulkeley, "Retail Stores Are Bringing the Net into the World of Bricks and Mortar," *The Wall Street Journal*, September 6, 2001, p. B1.

17.1

EXHIBIT 17–2 | Steps in the Employee Management Process

1. Recruit and select employees

2. Socialize and train new employees

3. Motivate and manage employees to achieve store performance goals

4. Evaluate employee performance and provide feedback

5. Compensate and reward employees

people interested in pursuing retail careers and applying for management trainee positions.)

Job Analysis

The **job analysis** identifies essential activities and is used to determine the qualifications of potential employees. For example, retail salespeople's responsibilities vary from company to company and from department to department within a store. Apparel salespeople work on an open floor and need to approach customers. Jewelry salespeople work behind a counter, so their customers approach them. Due to these differences, effective open-floor selling requires more aggressive behavior than counter selling.

Managers can obtain the information needed for a job analysis by observing employees presently doing the job and by determining the characteristics of exceptional performers. Exhibit 17–3 lists some questions that managers should consider in a job analysis for sales associates. Information collected in the job analysis then is used to prepare a job description.

EXHIBIT 17–3
Questions for Undertaking a Job Analysis

- How many salespeople will be working in the department at the same time?
- Do the salespeople have to work together in dealing with customers?
- How many customers will the salesperson have to work with at one time?
- Will the salesperson be selling on an open floor or working behind the counter?
- How much and what type of product knowledge does the salesperson need?
- Does the salesperson need to sell the merchandise or just ring up the orders and provide information?
- Is the salesperson required to make appointments with customers and develop a loyal customer base?
- Does the salesperson have the authority to negotiate price or terms of the sale?
- Does the salesperson need to demonstrate the merchandise?
- Will the salesperson be expected to make add-on sales?
- Is the salesperson's appearance important? How should an effective salesperson look?
- Will the salesperson be required to perform merchandising activities such as stocking shelves and setting up displays?
- Who will the salesperson report to?
- What compensation plan will the salesperson be working under?

Job Description

A **job description** includes (1) activities the employee needs to perform and (2) the performance expectations expressed in quantitative terms. The job description is a guideline for recruiting, selecting, training, and eventually evaluating employees.

Locating Prospective Employees

Staffing stores is becoming a critical problem because changing demographics are reducing the size of the labor pool.[5] Here are some suggestions for recruiting employees in this tight labor market:

- *Look beyond the retail industry.* For example, a jewelry store owner recruited a waitress from a deli she frequented who was "unflappable and was paid next to nothing." Another jeweler hired a dance instructor whose artistic eye and charisma made her a very effective jewelry salesperson.[6]

- *Use your employees as talent scouts.* Ask employees if they know someone you could hire or if they have recently encountered a particularly good salesperson when purchasing any item.

- *Provide incentives for employee referrals.* For example, some retailers offer a referral bonus to its employees. Employees get $100 after a recommended recruit is on the job for 30 days, another $100 on the recruit's six-month anniversary, and $500 if the recruit works for the company for a year.

- *Recruit from minority and immigrant communities.* Retailers that aggressively pursue the growing number of immigrants print application forms in English and Spanish. Prospective employees can bring a family member or friend to act as an interpreter during the interview. Training programs are developed for people who aren't familiar with U.S. business practices. For example, many foreign-born workers don't understand benefits like life insurance and are reluctant to report job-related injuries for fear of being fired.

- *Use your storefront creatively.* Don't just post a "Help Wanted" sign. Print one reading, "Thank you! Business is great. Because things are so good, we're hiring additional staff. Please stop in to discuss career opportunities."

Retailers are using the Internet to locate prospective employees. For example, the Olive Garden posts job openings on sites as www.restaurantmanagers.com, www.restaurantjobsnetwork.com, and www.restaurantrecruit.com. It has found that applicants coming from these sites are better prepared for today's retail environment. Andy Snitz, director of employment at the Olive Garden, comments, "Fifteen years ago, if someone wrote 'computers and electronics,' under 'special interests,' we would have thought, 'What a nerd.' Today you can't survive in business unless you have computer skills. [These people] aren't going to be challenged by our point-of-sale systems or running a back office program."[7]

T. J. Maxx uses this ad to interest prospective employees in its entry-level positions as assistant store managers.

Screening Applicants to Interview

Retailers often use web-based terminals to pre-screen potential employees.

The screening process matches applicants' qualifications with the job description. Many retailers use automated prescreening programs as a low-cost method for identifying qualified candidates. Applicants either interact with a web-enabled store kiosk or call a toll-free telephone number, and a computer program asks some basic questions that the applicants answer using the keyboard or telephone buttons.

The questions are tailored to the retailer's specific needs and environment. For example, Hot Topics, a mall-based chain selling music-themed merchandise, asks, "Would you work in an environment where loud, alternative music is played?" The response time for answering the questions is monitored and follow-up questions are asked when the answers are unusually slow. When applicants pass this automated prescreen, additional information is collected using application forms, reference checks, and tests.[8] The unusual screening criteria used by Enterprise Rent-A-Car are described in Retailing View 17.2.

RETAILING VIEW   Good Grades Make It Tough to Get a Job at Enterprise

17.2

Jack Taylor started Enterprise in St. Louis in 1957. Taylor had a unique strategy in mind for Enterprise, and that strategy has been remarkably successful from the firm's earliest days. Most car-rental firms like Hertz and Avis are located in or near airports. Their customers are business travelers and people who fly for vacation and then need transportation when they arrive. But Enterprise goes after a different customer. Specifically, the firm seeks to rent cars to individuals whose own cars are being repaired, who are driving on vacation, or who for some other reason simply need an extra car for a few days. Enterprise Rent-A-Car is now both the largest and the most profitable business in the U.S. car-rental industry.

One key to Enterprise's success has been its human resource strategy. The firm carefully targets a certain kind of individual to hire: its preferred new employee is a college graduate from the *bottom* half of the graduating class, and preferably one who was an athlete or actively involved in campus social activities. The rationale for this unusual academic standard is actually quite simple. Managers do not believe that especially high levels of academic achievement are necessary to perform well in the car-rental industry, but having a college degree nevertheless demonstrates intelligence and motivation. In addition, because interpersonal relations are important to its business, Enterprise wants people who were social directors

or high-ranking officers of social organizations such as fraternities or sororities. Athletes are also desirable because of their competitiveness.

Once hired, these new employees at Enterprise are often shocked at the performance expectations placed on them by the firm's higher-level managers. New employees generally work long, grueling hours for what many see as relatively low pay. And all Enterprise managers are expected to jump in and help wash or vacuum cars when the agency gets backed up.

What are the advantages to signing on with Enterprise? For one thing, it's an unfortunate fact of life that many college graduates with low grades often struggle to find work. Thus, a job at Enterprise is still better than no job at all! Moreover, the firm does not hire outsiders for jobs other than those at entry level—every position is filled by promoting someone already inside the company. Thus, Enterprise employees know that if they work hard and do their best, they may very well succeed in moving up the corporate ladder at a growing and successful firm.

Sources: Repps Hudson, "New Hire at Enterprise Rent-A-Car Went from Web to Working in Just Days," *St. Louis Post-Dispatch*, March 24, 2001, p. 12; Ron Lieber, "First Jobs Aren't Child's Play," *Fast Company*, June 1999, pp. 154–71 and "Enterprise Takes New Direction," *USA Today*, October 28, 1999, p. 3B.

Application Forms   **Job application forms** contain information about the applicant's employment history, previous compensation, reasons for leaving previous employment, education and training, personal health, and references. This information enables the manager to determine whether the applicant has the minimum qualifications and also provides information for interviewing the applicant.[9]

References   A good way to verify the information given on an application form is to contact the applicant's references. Contacting references is also helpful for collecting additional information from people who've worked with the applicant. In addition, store managers should check with former supervisors not listed as references. Due to potential legal problems, however, many companies have a policy of not commenting on past employees.[11]

Store managers generally expect to hear favorable comments from an applicant's references or even from previous supervisors who may not have thought highly of the applicant. One approach for reducing the positive bias is to ask the reference to rank the applicant relative to others in the same position. For example, the manager might ask, "How would you rate Pat's customer service skill in relation to other retail sales associates you have worked with?" Another approach is to use a positively toned scale ranging from "somewhat effective" to "extremely effective."

Testing   Intelligence, ability, personality, and interest tests can provide insights about potential employees. For example, intelligence tests yield data about the applicant's innate abilities and can be used to match applicants with job openings and to develop training programs. However, tests must be scientifically and legally valid. They can only be used when the scores have been shown to be related to job performance. It is illegal to use tests assessing factors that are not job-related or that discriminate against specific groups.

Due to potential losses from theft, many retailers such as Wal-Mart and Home Depot require applicants to take drug tests. Some retailers use tests to assess applicants' honesty and ethics. Paper-and-pencil honesty tests include questions to find out if an applicant has ever thought about stealing and if he believes other people steal ("What percentage of people take more than $1 from their employer?").[14]

The use of lie detectors in testing employees is prohibited. Retailers and other employers have been discouraged from HIV testing for prospective employees. But testing for illegal drug use isn't prohibited because drug users are violating the law.[16]

Realistic Job Preview   Turnover is reduced when the applicants understand both the attractive and unattractive aspects of the job. For example, PETsMART, a pet supply category specialist, has each applicant view a 10-minute video that begins with the advantages of being a company employee and then shows scenes of employees dealing with irate customers and cleaning up animal droppings. This type of job preview typically screens out 15 percent of the applicants who would most likely quit within three months if they were hired.[17]

Selecting Applicants

After screening applications, the selection process typically involves a personal interview. Since the interview is usually the critical factor in the hiring decision,

REFACT

Wal-Mart receives over 4 million applicants a year and many of them are customers.[10]

REFACT

In the United States, 50 percent of employers check for criminal records of applicants but in the Netherlands, only 20 percent check for criminal records.[12]

REFACT

Seventy-two percent of retailers check references as part of the selection process; 43 percent do drug screening; and 28 percent use paper-and-pencil honesty tests.[13]

REFACT

A retailer incurs an additional $7,000 to $10,000 of expenses in medical costs, absences, turnover, and lost productivity when it hires a drug user.[15]

the store manager needs to be well prepared and to have complete control over the interview.

Preparation for the Interview   The objective of the interview is to gather relevant information, not simply to ask a lot of question. The most widely used interview technique, called the *behavioral interview*, asks candidates how they handled actual situations they have encountered in the past—situations requiring skills outlined in the job description. For example, applicants applying for a job requiring them to handle customer complaints would be asked to describe a situation in which they were confronted by someone who was angry with something they had done. Candidates are asked to describe the situation, what they did, and what were the outcomes of their actions. These situations also can be used to interview references for the applicants.[18]

An effective approach to interviewing involves some planning by the managers but also allows some flexibility in selecting questions. Managers should develop objectives for what they want to learn about the candidate. Each topic area covered in the interview starts with a broad question, such as "Tell me about your last job," designed to elicit a lengthy response. The broad opening question is followed by a sequence of more specific questions, such as "What did you learn from that job?" or "How many subordinates did you have?" Finally, managers need to avoid asking questions that are discriminatory.[19]

Managing the Interview   Exhibit 17–4 shows questions the manager might ask. Here are some suggestions for questioning the applicant during the interview:

- Encourage long responses by asking questions like "What do you know about our company?" rather than "How familiar are you with our company?"
- Avoid asking questions that have multiple parts.
- Avoid asking leading questions like "Are you prepared to provide good customer service?"
- Be an active listener. Evaluate the information that is being presented and sort out the important comments from the unimportant ones. Some techniques for active listening are repeating or rephrasing information, summarizing the conversation, and tolerating silences.[20]

Some managers interview candidates while giving a candidate a tour through the store. When the manager sees a display that's out of order, he might say, "While we're talking, would you help me straighten this out?" Some candidates will stand back; others will jump right in and help out. (*Hint:* You want to hire candidates from the second group.)

Legal Considerations in Selecting and Hiring Store Employees

Heightened social awareness and government regulations emphasize the need to avoid discriminating against hiring the handicapped, women, minorities, and older workers. Title VII of the Civil Rights Act prohibits discrimination on the basis of race, national origin, sex, or religion in company personnel practices. Discrimination is specifically prohibited in the following human resource decisions: recruitment, hiring, discharge, layoff, discipline, promotion, compensation, and access to training. In 1972, the act was expanded by the **Equal Em-**

EDUCATION

What were your most favorite and least favorite subjects in college? Why?

What types of extracurricular activities did you participate in? Why did you select those activities?

If you had the opportunity to attend school all over again what, if anything, would you do differently? Why?

How did you spend the summers during college?

Did you have any part-time jobs? Which of your part-time jobs did you find most interesting? What did you find most difficult about working and attending college at the same time? What advice would you give to someone who wanted to work and attend college at the same time?

What accomplishments were you most proud of?

PREVIOUS EXPERIENCE

What's your description of the ideal manager? Subordinate? Co-worker?

What did you like most/least about your last job?

What kind of people do you find it difficult/easy to work with? Why?

What has been your greatest accomplishment during your career to date?

Describe a situation at your last job involving pressure. How did you handle it?

What were some duties on your last job that you found difficult?

Of all the jobs you've had, which did you find the most/least rewarding?

What is the most frustrating situation you've encountered in your career?

Why do you want to leave your present job?

What would you do if . . . ?

How would you handle . . . ?

What would you like to avoid in future jobs?

What do you consider your greatest strength/weakness?

What are your responsibilities in your present job?

Tell me about the people you hired on your last job. How did they work out? What about the people you fired?

What risks did you take in your last job and what were the results of those risks?

Where do you see yourself in three years?

What kind of references will your previous employer give?

What do you do when you have trouble solving a problem?

QUESTIONS THAT SHOULD NOT BE ASKED PER EQUAL EMPLOYMENT OPPORTUNITY GUIDELINES

Do you have plans for having children/a family? What are your marriage plans? What does your husband/wife do? What happens if your husband/wife gets transferred or needs to relocate? Who will take care of your children while you're at work? (Asked of men) How would you feel about working for a woman?

How old are you? What is your date of birth? How would you feel working for a person younger than you? Where were you born? Where were your parents born?

Do you have any handicaps? As a handicapped person, what help are you going to need to do your work? How severe is your handicap?

What's your religion? What church do you attend? Do you hold religious beliefs that would prevent you from working on certain days of the week?

Do you feel that your race/color will be a problem in your performing the job? Are you of _____ heritage/race?

---

ployment Opportunity Commission (EEOC) to allow employees to sue employers that violate the law. Several major retailers have been successfully sued because they discriminated in hiring and promoting minorities and women.

Discrimination arises when a member of a protected class (women, minorities, etc.) is treated differently from nonmembers of that class **(disparate treatment)** or when an apparently neutral rule has an unjustified discriminatory effect **(disparate impact).** An example of disparate treatment is if a qualified woman does not receive a promotion given to a lesser qualified man. Disparate impact occurs when a retailer requires high school graduation for all its employees, thereby excluding a larger proportion of disadvantaged minorities, when at least some of the jobs (e.g., custodian) could be performed just as well by people who did not graduate from high school. In such cases, the retailer is required to prove the imposed qualification is actually needed to be able to perform the job.

The **Age Discrimination and Employment Act** makes it illegal to discriminate in hiring and termination decisions concerning people over the age of 40. Finally, the **Americans with Disabilities Act (ADA)** opens up job opportunities for the disabled by requiring employees to provide accommodating work environments. A **disability** is defined as any physical or mental impairment that substantially limits one or more of an individual's major life activities or any condition that is regarded as being such an impairment. Although merely being HIV positive does not limit any life activities, it may be perceived as doing so and is therefore protected as a disability. Similarly, extreme obesity may either be actually limiting or perceived as such and also be protected as long as the obese person can perform the duties of the job.

SOCIALIZING AND TRAINING NEW STORE EMPLOYEES

REFACT

The U.S. Department of Labor estimates that it costs a company one-third of a new hire's annual compensation to replace an employee.[22]

After hiring employees, the next step in developing effective employees (as Exhibit 17–2 shows) is introducing them to the firm and its policies. Retailers want the people they hire to become involved, committed contributors to the firm's successful performance. On the other hand, newly hired employees want to learn about their job responsibilities and the company they've decided to join. **Socialization** is the set of steps taken to transform new employees into effective, committed members of the firm. Socialization goes beyond simply orienting new employees to the firm. A principal objective of socialization is to develop a long-term relationship with new employees to increase productivity and reduce turnover costs.[21]

A key factor in socializing new employees is to create a training and work environment that articulates the retailer's culture and strategy. For example, at Target the phrase "Fast, Fun, and Friendly" is used to explain its customer-service philosophy to its employees. Karen Grabow, Target's human resources VP, emphasizes that "Everything must work around the culture; check everything against 'Fast, Fun, and Friendly.' You have to reiterate it with mind-numbing repetition, but more importantly you have to walk the talk."[23]

Orientation Programs

Orientation programs are critical in overcoming entry shock and socializing new employees.[24] Even the most knowledgeable and mature new employees encounter some surprises. College students who accept management trainee positions often are quite surprised by the differences between student and employee roles. Retailing View 17.3 describes some of these differences.

Orientation programs can last from a few hours to several weeks. The orientation and training program for new salespeople might be limited to several hours during which the new salesperson learns the retailer's policies and procedures and how to use the POS terminal. On the other hand, the orientation program for management trainees might take several weeks. For example, Burdines hires approximately 150 college students each year into its management training program. New trainees typically report to work at corporate headquarters in Miami. They're housed in a hotel for a four-week orientation during which they attend classes, meet company executives, and work on projects. After completing the orientation program, they begin their initial assignment as a department manager in a store or an assistant buyer.

Effective orientation programs need to avoid information overload and one-way communication. When new hires are confronted with a stack of forms and company policies, they get the impression the company is very bureaucratic. Large quantities of information are hard to absorb in a short period of time. New employees learn information best when it's parceled out in small doses.

Store managers need to foster two-way communication when orienting new employees. Rather than just presenting information about their firm, managers need to give newly hired employees a chance to have their questions and concerns addressed. Disney overhauled its orientation program to emphasize emotion rather than company policies and procedures. The new program begins with current employees, referred to as cast members, discussing their earliest memories of Disney, their visions of great service, and their understanding of teamwork. Then trainers relate "magic moments" they have witnessed to emphasize that insignificant actions can have a big impact on a guest. For example, a four-year-old trips and falls, spilling his box of popcorn. The boy cries, the mother is concerned, and a costumed cast member, barely breaking stride, picks up the empty box, takes it to the popcorn stand for a refill, presents it to the child, and goes on his way.

The orientation program is just one element in the overall training program. It needs to be accompanied by a systematic follow-up to ensure that any problems and concerns arising after the initial period are considered.

Training Store Employees

Effective training for new store employees includes both structured and on-the-job learning experiences.

The Transition from Student to Management Trainee   **RETAILING VIEW**

17.3

Many students have some difficulty adjusting to the demands of their first full-time job, because student life and professional life are very different. Students typically "report" to three or four supervisors (professors). A student selects new "supervisors" every four months. On the other hand, management trainees have limited involvement, if any, in selecting the one supervisor they'll report to often for several years.

Student life has fixed time cycles, one to two-hour classes with a well-defined beginning and end. Retail managers are involved in a variety of activities with varied time horizons, ranging from a five-minute interaction with a customer to developing and implementing a merchandise budget over a season.

The decisions students encounter differ dramatically from the decisions retail managers encounter. For example, business students might make several major decisions a day when they discuss cases in class. These decisions are made and implemented in one class period, and then a new set of decisions is made and implemented in the next class. In a retail environment, strategic decisions evolve over a long time period. Most decisions, such as those regarding merchandise buying and pricing, are made with incomplete information. The buyers in real life often lack the extensive information provided in many business cases studied in class. Finally, there are long periods of time when retail managers undertake mundane tasks associated with implementing decisions and no major issues are being considered. Students typically don't have these mundane tasks to perform.

Source: Professor Daniel Feldman, University of South Carolina.

The new Men's Wearhouse's salespeople are learning about the merchandise they will be selling in a structured program.

Structured Program   During the structured program, new employees are taught the basic skills and knowledge they'll need to do their job. For example, salespeople learn what the company policies are, how to use the point-of-sale terminal, and how to perform basic selling skills; stockroom employees learn procedures for receiving merchandise. This initial training might include lectures, audiovisual presentations, manuals, and correspondence distributed to the new employees. In large firms, structured training may be done at a central location (such as the corporate headquarters or district office) under the human resources department's direction.

The initial structured program should be relatively short so new employees don't feel they are simply back in school. Effective training programs bring new recruits up to speed as quickly as possible and then get them involved in doing the job for which they've been hired.

On-the-Job Training   The next training phase emphasizes on-the-job training. New employees are assigned a job, given responsibilities, and coached by their supervisor. The best way to learn is to practice what is being taught. New employees learn by doing activities, making mistakes, and then learning how not to make those mistakes again. Information learned through classroom lectures tends to be forgotten quickly unless it's used soon after the lecture.[25]

For example, students can learn about developing a merchandise budget plan by reading Chapter 13 of this text or by listening to a lecture. But they typically don't acquire all the necessary information or remember the information from these sources. The actual hands-on experience of making a plan and getting feedback provides more complete and lasting knowledge.

Analyzing Successes and Failures   Every new employee makes mistakes. Store managers should provide an atmosphere in which salespeople try out different approaches for providing customer service and selling merchandise. Store managers must recognize that some of these new approaches are going to fail, and when they do, managers shouldn't criticize the individual salesperson. Instead, they should talk about the situation, analyze why the approach didn't work, and discuss how the salesperson could avoid the problem in the future.

Similarly, managers should work with employees to help them understand and learn from their successes. For example, salespeople shouldn't just consider a large multiple-item sale to be simply due to luck. They should be encouraged to reflect on the sale, identify their key behaviors that facilitated the sale, and then remember these sales behaviors for future use.

It's important to help salespeople assign the right kinds of reasons for their performance. For example, some salespeople take credit for successes and blame the company, the buyers, or the merchandise for their failures. This tendency to avoid taking responsibility for failures doesn't encourage learning. When salespeople adopt this reasoning pattern, they aren't motivated to change their sales behavior because they don't take personal responsibility for losing a sale.

Managers can help salespeople to constructively analyze their successes and failures by asking salespeople "why" questions that force them to analyze the reasons for effective and ineffective performance. To encourage learning, managers should get salespeople to recognize that they could have satisfied the customer if they had used a different approach or been more persistent. When salespeople accept such responsibility, they'll be motivated to search for ways to improve their sales skills.

The on-the-job training provided by the Hallmark manager gives new employees an opportunity to make decisions and get constructive feedback.

MOTIVATING AND MANAGING STORE EMPLOYEES

After employees have received their initial training, managers must work with them to help them meet their performance goals by being an effective leader and providing the appropriate motivation (refer to Exhibit 17–2).

Leadership

Leadership is the process by which one person attempts to influence another to accomplish some goal or goals. Store managers are leaders of their group of employees. Managers use a variety of motivational techniques to increase productivity by helping employees achieve personal goals consistent with their firm's objectives.[26]

Leader Behaviors   Leaders engage in task performance and group maintenance behaviors. **Task performance behaviors** are the store manager's efforts at planning, organizing, motivating, evaluating, and coordinating store employees' activities.

Group maintenance behaviors are activities store managers undertake to make sure that employees are satisfied and work well together. These activities include considering employees' needs, showing concern for their well-being, and creating a pleasant work environment.

Leader Decision Making   Store managers vary in how much they involve employees in making decisions. **Autocratic leaders** make all decisions on their own and then announce them to employees. They use the authority of their position to tell employees what to do. For example, an autocratic store manager determines who will work in each area of the store, when they'll take breaks, and what days they'll have off. On the other hand, a **democratic leader** seeks information and opinions from employees and bases decisions on this information.

Democratic store managers share their power and information with their employees. The democratic store manager asks employees where and when they want to work and makes schedule to accommodate employee desires.

Leadership Styles   Store managers tend to develop a specific leadership style. They emphasize either task performance or group maintenance behaviors. They range from autocratic to democratic in their decision-making style.

Which leadership style is best for store managers? After 60 years of research, psychologists have concluded there's no one best style. Effective managers use all styles, selecting the style most appropriate for each situation. For example, a store manager might be autocratic and relations-oriented with an insecure new trainee, but be democratic and task-oriented with an effective, experienced employee.

Effective store managers must consider both their firm's objectives and their employees' needs. They must recognize that employees aren't all the same. For some employees, promotions are crucial. Others want

Tim O'Donnell (right rear), the manager of the Sandy Hill, Utah, Shopko store, is a democratic leader who holds meetings to keep employees informed about company and store activities. He encourages suggestions for improving store performance.

more compensation, and some simply want to be recognized for doing a good job. Some employees need to be motivated to work harder; others need to be taught how to do their jobs effectively. Thus, effective leaders use different approaches or styles for managing each employee.

Transformational Leaders   The previous discussion and most of this chapter describe specific behaviors, activities, and programs store managers use to influence their employees. But the greatest leaders and store managers go beyond influencing employee behaviors to changing the beliefs, values, and needs of their employees. **Transformational leaders** get people to transcend their personal needs for the sake of the group or organization. They generate excitement and revitalize organizations.

Transformational store managers create this enthusiasm in their employees through their personal charisma. They're self-confident, have a clear vision that grabs employee attention, and communicate this vision through words and symbols. Finally, transformational leaders delegate challenging work to subordinates, have free and open communication with them, and provide personal mentoring to develop subordinates.[27]

Motivating Employees

Motivating employees to perform up to their potential may be store managers' most important and frustrating task. The following hypothetical situation illustrates issues concerning employee motivation and evaluation.

After getting an associates degree at a local community college, Jim Taylor was hired for a sales position at the Foley's store in Denver's Cherry Creek Mall. The position offers firsthand knowledge of the firm's customers, managers, and policies. Taylor was told that if he did well in this assignment, he could become a management trainee.

His performance as a sales associate was average. After observing Taylor on the sales floor, his manager, Jennifer Chen, felt he was effective only when working with customers like himself: young, career-oriented men and women. To encourage Taylor to sell to other types of customers, Chen reduced his salary and increased his commission rate. She also reviewed Taylor's performance goals with him.

Taylor now feels a lot of pressure to increase his sales level. He's beginning to dread coming to work in the morning and is thinking about getting out of retailing and working for a bank.

In this hypothetical situation, Chen focused on increasing Taylor's motivation by providing more incentive compensation. In discussing this illustration, we'll examine the appropriateness of this approach versus other approaches for improving Taylor's performance.

Sears builds morale and motivates its sales associates by holding "ready meetings" in each department before the store opens. At this meeting, the department manager discusses approaches for providing better customer service.

Setting Goals or Quotas   Employee performance improves when employees feel that (1) their efforts will enable them to achieve the goals set for them by their managers and (2) they'll receive rewards they value if they achieve their goals. Thus, managers can motivate employees by setting realistic goals and offering rewards employees want.[28]

For example, Jennifer Chen set specific selling goals for Jim Taylor when he started to work in her department. Taylor, like all Foley's sales associates, had goals in five selling areas: sales per hour, average size of each sale, number of multiple-item (add-on) sales, number of preferred clients, and number of appointments made with preferred clients. (**Preferred clients** are customers whom salespeople communicate with regularly, send notes to about new merchandise and sales in the department, and make appointments with for special presentations of merchandise—the upper-tier customer discussed in Chapter 11.) Besides the selling goals, salespeople are evaluated on the overall department shrinkage due to stolen merchandise, the errors they make in using the point-of-sale terminal, and their contribution to maintaining the department's appearance.

Chen also designed a program for Taylor's development as a sales associate. The activities she outlined over the next six months required Taylor to attend classes to improve his selling skills. Chen needs to be careful in setting goals for Taylor. If she sets goals too high, he might become discouraged, feel the goals are unattainable, and thus not be motivated to work harder. On the other hand, if she sets goals too low, Taylor can achieve them easily and won't be motivated to work to his full potential.

Rather than setting specific goals for each salesperson, Foley's uses the average performance for all salespeople as its goal. However, goals are most effective at motivating employees when they're based on the employee's experience and confidence. Experienced salespeople have confidence in their abilities and should have "stretch" goals (high goals that will make them work hard). New salespeople need lower goals that they have a good chance of achieving. The initial good experience in achieving and surpassing goals builds new salespeople's confidence and motivates them to improve their skills.[29] Later in the chapter we'll look at the use of rewards to motivate employees.

Maintaining Morale

Store morale is important in motivating employees. Typically, morale goes up when things are going well and employees are highly motivated. But when sales aren't going well, morale tends to decrease and employee motivation declines. Here are some suggestions for building morale:

- Have storewide or department meetings prior to the store opening. Pass along information about new merchandise and programs and solicit opinions and suggestions from employees.

- Educate employees about the firm's finances, set achievable goals, and throw a pizza party when the goals are met.

- Divide the charity budget by the number of employees and invite the employees to suggest how their "share" should be used.

- Print stickers that tell customers that this sandwich was "wrapped by Roger" or this dress was "dry cleaned by Sarah."

- Give every employee a business card with the company mission printed on its back.[30]

Paula Hankins, a store manager for Pier 1 Imports, uses real-time sales data collected in her firm's information system (see Chapter 10) to build excitement among her employees. On the first day of the Christmas season, she wrote $3,159 on a blackboard in the store. That was the store's sales during the first day of the Christmas season last year. She tells her sales associates that beating that number is not enough. She wants a 36 percent increase, the same sales increase the store achieved in the prior Christmas season.

By setting financial objectives and keeping sales associates informed of the up-to-the-minute results, an eight-hour shift of clock watchers is converted into an excited team of racers. All day, as customers come and go, sales associates take turns consulting the backroom computer recording sales from the store's POS terminals. David Self, Hankins' regional manager, emphasizes, "The more information you give the associates, the more ownership they feel in the store's performance."[32]

Sexual Harassment

Sexual harassment is an important issue in productivity of the work environment. Managers must avoid and make sure that store employees avoid actions that are, or can be interpreted as, sexual harassment. Otherwise, the retailer and the manager may be held liable for the harassment. EEOC guidelines define **sexual harassment** as a form of gender discrimination:

> Unwelcome sexual advances, requests for sexual favors, and other verbal or physical conduct of a sexual nature constitutes

Store managers must avoid behaviors that employees might interpret as sexual harassment.

EXHIBIT 17–5
Procedure for Sexual
Harassment Allegations

Step 1: Establish and post an anti-sexual harassment policy, including a complaint procedure outside the normal supervisory channels. Supervisors are often accused of sexual harassment.

Step 2: If a complaint is made to you, always treat it seriously.

Step 3: Get information from the alleged victim. Ask questions like

- **Tell me what happened. Who was involved?**
- **What did the harasser do and say?**
- **When did this happen? If this wasn't the first time, when has it happened before?**
- **Where did it happen?**
- **Were there any witnesses?**
- **Have you told anyone else about this or these instances?**
- **Has anyone else been the object of harassment?**
- **How did you react to the harasser's behavior?**
- **Would you care to speak with someone else: another member of management, the personnel department, or the company employment assistance plan person?**

Step 4: Document your meeting with the alleged victim.

Step 5: Inform your human resource department or the next higher level of company management of the complaint and your meeting with the alleged victim.

Sources: Professor Ross Petty, Babson College, and John Farr, "Sexual Harassment: Handling the 'He–Said–She–Said' Hot Potato," *Chain Store Age*, April 1998, pp. 56–59. Copyright Lebhar-Friedman, Inc. 425 Park Avenue, New York, NY 10022. Reprinted by permission.

sexual harassment when . . . submission to or rejection of such conduct by an individual is used as a basis for employment decisions affecting such individual, or . . . such conduct has the purpose or effect of unreasonably interfering with an individual's work performance or creating an intimidating, hostile, or offensive working environment.

An appropriate procedure for dealing with a sexual harassment allegation is outlined in Exhibit 17–5.

EVALUATING STORE EMPLOYEES AND PROVIDING FEEDBACK

The fourth step in the management process (Exhibit 17–2) is evaluating and providing feedback to employees. The objective of the evaluation process is to identify employees who are performing well and those who aren't. On the basis of the evaluation, high-performing employees should be rewarded and considered for positions of great responsibility. Plans need to be developed to increase the productivity of employees performing below expectations. Should poor performers be terminated? Do they need additional training? What kind of training do they need?

Who Should Do the Evaluation?

In large retail firms, the evaluation system is usually designed by the human resources department. But the evaluation itself should be done by the employee's immediate supervisor—the manager who works most closely with the employee. For example, in a discount store, the department manager is in the best position to observe a salesperson in action and understand the reasons for the salesperson's performance. The department manager also oversees the recommendations that come out of the evaluation process. Inexperienced supervisors are often assisted by a senior manager in evaluating employees.

REFACT

Among retail workers, 92 percent say their employers do not identify or deal with poor performers.[33]

How Often Should Evaluations Be Made?

Most retailers evaluate employees annually or semiannually. Feedback from evaluations is the most effective method for improving employee skills. Thus, evaluations should be done more frequently when managers are developing inexperienced employees' skills. However, frequent formal evaluations are time-consuming for managers and may not give employees enough time to respond to suggestions. Managers should supplement these formal evaluations with frequent informal ones. For example, Jennifer Chen should work with Jim Taylor informally and not wait for the formal six-month evaluation. The best time for Chen to provide this informal feedback is immediately after she has obtained, through observations or reports, positive or negative information about Taylor's performance.

Format for Evaluations

Evaluations are only meaningful if employees know what they're required to do, what level of performance is expected, and how they'll be evaluated. Exhibit 17–6 shows The Gap's criteria for evaluating sales associates.

The Gap employee's overall evaluation is based on subjective evaluations made by the store manager and assistant managers. It places equal weight on individual sales/customer relations activities and activities associated with overall store per-

EXHIBIT 17–6 | Factors Used to Evaluate Sales Associates at The Gap

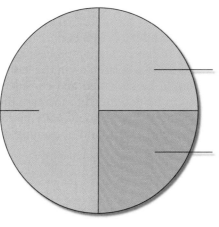

25%
OPERATIONS

1. Store appearance. Demonstrates an eye for detail (color and finesse) in the areas of display, coordination of merchandise on tables, floor fixtures, and wall faceouts. Takes initiative in maintaining store presentation standards.

2. Loss prevention. Actively follows all loss prevention procedures.

3. Merchandise control and handling. Consistently achieves established requirements in price change activity, shipment processing, and inventory control.

4. Cash/wrap procedures. Accurately and efficiently follows all register policies and cash/wrap procedures.

50%
SALES/CUSTOMER RELATIONS

1. Greeting. Approaches customers within 1 to 2 minutes with a smile and friendly manner. Uses open-ended questions.

2. Product knowledge. Demonstrates knowledge of product, fit, shrinkage, and price and can relay this information to the customer.

3. Suggests additional merchandise. Approaches customers at fitting room and cash/wrap areas.

4. Asks customers to buy and reinforces decisions. Lets customers know they've made a wise choice and thanks them.

25%
COMPLIANCE

1. Dress code and appearance. Complies with dress code. Appears neat and well groomed. Projects current fashionable Gap image.

2. Flexibility. Able to switch from one assignment to another, open to schedule adjustments. Shows initiative, awareness of store priorities and needs.

3. Working relations. Cooperates with other employees, willingly accepts direction and guidance from management. Communicates to management.

formance. By emphasizing overall store operations and performance, The Gap's assessment criteria motivate sales associates to work together as a team.

The criteria used at Foley's to evaluate Jim Taylor are objective sales measures based on point-of-sale data rather than the subjective measures used by The Gap. Exhibit 17–7 summarizes Taylor's formal six-month evaluation. The evaluation form lists results for various factors in terms of (1) what's considered average performance for company salespeople and (2) Taylor's actual performance. His department has done better than average on shrinkage control, and he has done well on system errors and merchandise presentation. However, his sales performance is below average even though he made more than the average number of presentations to preferred customers. These results suggest that Taylor's effort is good but his selling skills may need improvement.

Evaluation Errors

Managers can make evaluation errors by first forming an overall opinion of the employee's performance and then allowing this opinion to influence the ratings of each performance factor (haloing). For example, a store manager might feel a salesperson's overall performance is below average and then rate the salesperson below average on selling skills, punctuality, appearance, and stocking. When an overall evaluation casts such a halo on specific aspects of a salesperson's performance, the evaluation is no longer useful for identifying specific areas that need improvement.

In making evaluations, managers are often unduly influenced by recent events (recency) and by their evaluations of other salespeople (contrast). For example, a manager might remember a salesperson's poor performance with a customer the day before and forget the salesperson's outstanding performance over the past three months. Similarly, a manager might be unduly harsh in evaluating an average salesperson just after completing an evaluation of an outstanding salesperson.

Finally, managers have a natural tendency to attribute performance (particularly, poor performance) to the salesperson and not to the environment the salesperson is working in. When making evaluations, managers tend to underemphasize effects of external factors such as merchandise in the department and competitors' actions.

The Foley's evaluation of sales associates (Exhibit 17–7) avoids many of these potential biases because most ratings are based on objective data. In contrast, The Gap evaluation (Exhibit 17–6) considers a wider range of activities but uses

	Average Performance for Sales Associates in Department	Actual Performance for Jim Taylor
Sales per hour	$75	$65
Average amount per transaction	$45	$35
Percent multiple transactions	55%	55%
Number of preferred customers	115	125
Number of preferred customer appointments	95	120
Departmental shrinkage	2.00%	1.80%
Systems errors	10	2
Merchandise presentation (10-point scale)	5	8

EXHIBIT 17–7
Summary of Jim Taylor's Six-Month Evaluation

more subjective measures of performance. Since subjective information about specific skills, attitudes about the store and customers, interactions with co-workers, enthusiasm, and appearance aren't used in the Foley's evaluation, performance on these factors may not be explicitly communicated to Jim Taylor. The subjective characteristics in The Gap evaluation are more prone to bias, but they also might be more helpful to salespeople as they try to improve their performance. To avoid bias when making subjective ratings, managers should observe performance regularly, record their observations, avoid evaluating many salespeople at one time, and remain conscious of the various potential biases.

COMPENSATING AND REWARDING STORE EMPLOYEES

The fifth and final step in improving employee productivity in Exhibit 17–2 is compensating and rewarding employees. Store employees receive two types of rewards from their work: extrinsic and intrinsic. **Extrinsic rewards** are rewards provided by either the employee's manager or the firm—such as compensation, promotion, and recognition. **Intrinsic rewards** are rewards employees get personally from doing their job well. For example, salespeople often like to sell because they think it's challenging and fun. Of course, they want to be paid, but they also find it rewarding to help customers and make sales.[34]

Public recognition programs make employees feel they are appreciated and motivate them to improve their performance. Marshalls' stores that deliver exceptional customer service are recognized by the "All-Star Award," which includes a plaque to hang in the store.

Extrinsic Rewards

Managers can offer a variety of extrinsic rewards to motivate employees. However, store employees don't all seek the same rewards. For example, some salespeople want more compensation; others strive for a promotion in the company or public recognition of their performance. Jim Taylor wants a favorable evaluation from his manager so he can enter the management training program. Part-time salespeople often take a sales job to get out of the house and meet people. Their primary work objective isn't to make money.

Because of these different needs, managers may not be able to use the same rewards to motivate all employees. Large retailers, however, find it hard to develop unique reward programs for each individual. One approach is to offer **à la carte plans** that give effective employees a choice of rewards for good performance. For example, salespeople who achieve their goals could choose a cash bonus, extra days off, or a better discount on merchandise sold in the store. This type of compensation plan enables employees to select the rewards they want. Recognition is an important nonmonetary extrinsic reward for many employees. (Compensation and financial rewards are discussed later.) Telling employees they've done a job well is appreciated. However, it's typically more rewarding when good performance is recognized publicly. In addition, public recognition can motivate all store employees, not just the star performers, because it demonstrates management's interest in rewarding employees.

Most managers focus on extrinsic rewards to motivate employees. For example, a store manager might provide additional compensation if a salesperson achieves a sales goal. However, an emphasis on extrinsic rewards can make employees lose sight of their job's intrinsic rewards. Employees can begin to feel that their only reason for working is to earn money and that the job isn't fun.

Retailing View 17.4 discusses how the differences between the goals and rewards sought by boomer managers and Generation X employees (ages 26 to 37 years old) can cause problems.

Intrinsic Rewards

Note that Jennifer Chen tried to motivate Jim Taylor by using extrinsic rewards when she linked his compensation to how much he sold. This increased emphasis on financial rewards may be one reason Taylor now dreads to come to work in the morning. He might not think his job is fun anymore.

When employees find their jobs intrinsically rewarding, they're motivated to learn how to do them better. They act like a person playing a video game. The game itself is so interesting that the player gets rewards from just trying to master it. Charlene Rogers, manager of a Hot Topic store in Brea, California, described how the involvement of her employees is intrinsically rewarding: "Hot Topic buyers rely on my associates for input on trends that change quickly. The company encourages all of us to call the buyers after we come back from a club or a concert to fill them in on what people are wearing. Store associates feel appreciated. They crave responsibility."[35]

Another approach to making work fun is to hold contests with relatively small prizes. Contests are most effective when everyone has a chance to win. Contests in which the best salespeople always win aren't exciting and may even be demoralizing. For example, consider a contest in which a playing card is given to salespeople for each men's suit they sell during a two-week period. At the end of two weeks, the best poker hand wins. This contest motivates all salespeople during

---

Generational Tension   RETAILING VIEW

17.4

Some of the problems of dissatisfied employees and high turnover in retail are due to the generation gap between boomer store managers and Generation Xers who have entered the workforce a few years ago. "A lot has been made of Generation Xers not having a strong work ethic," retail consultant Terri Kabachnick notes. "I don't agree; it's just that it is a lot different. Boomers feel they have to work a lot of hours, while GenXer's ask, 'Why? Who are you trying to impress?'" Boomers emphasize that you need to work long and hard to get ahead, paying your dues before you get more responsibility and higher pay. The younger employee responds with "Get a life. I don't mind working hard, but what about my family, my happiness?"

Rather than getting regular performance reviews, Generation Xers want a pat on the back and recognition when they have accomplished something. They want flexibility in their work schedules and time for themselves, their interests, and their priorities.

"They don't want time off to be sick; they want time off to be well," says Kabachnick. To address this need for flexibility, retailers are experimenting with sabbaticals—weeks or months off to think about how to do your job better—and time banks, where sick days, overtime, or vacation time can be deposited for use at some time in the future with no questions asked.

Retailers also should consider personal needs by having pet and child care centers, on-site fitness centers, personnel to run personal errands such as dropping off and picking up laundry, and "relaxation rooms" where employees can go to sit, think, or nap. One company even provides back rubs at desks and workstations.

Sources: Pamela Paul, "Meet the Parents," *American Demographics*, January 2002, pp. 25–30; and David Schulz, "Generational Tensions Add to 'Quiet Rebellion' in Retail Workforce," *Stores*, March 11, 1999, pp. 61–62.

the entire period of the contest. A salesperson who sells only four suits can win with four aces. Contests should be used to create excitement and make selling challenging for everyone, not to pay the best salespeople more money.

Experienced employees often lose interest in their jobs. They no longer find them exciting and challenging. Extrinsic rewards, such as pay or promotion, might not be so attractive to them. They might be satisfied with their present income and job responsibilities.

More experienced employees can be motivated by providing intrinsic rewards through job enrichment. **Job enrichment** is the redesign of a job to include a greater range of tasks and responsibilities. For example, an experienced sales associate who has lost some interest in his or her job could be given responsibility for merchandising a particular area, training new salespeople, or planning and managing a special event.

Compensation Programs

The objectives of a compensation program are to attract and keep good employees, motivate them to undertake activities consistent with the retailer's objectives, and reward them for their effort. In developing a compensation program, the store manager must strike a balance between controlling labor costs and providing enough compensation to keep high-quality employees.[36]

A compensation plan is most effective for motivating and retaining employees when the employees feel the plan is fair and when their compensation is related to their efforts. In general, simple plans are preferred to complex plans. Simple plans are easier to administer and employees have no trouble understanding them.

Types of Compensation Plans
Retail firms typically use one or more of the following compensation plans: straight salary, straight commission, salary plus commission, and quota–bonus.

With **straight salary compensation,** salespeople or managers receive a fixed amount of compensation for each hour or week they work. For example, a salesperson might be paid $8 per hour, or a department manager $800 per week. This plan is easy for the employee to understand and for the store to administer.

Under a straight salary plan, the retailer has flexibility in assigning salespeople to different activities and sales areas. For example, salaried salespeople will undertake nonselling activities, such as stocking shelves, and won't be upset if they're transferred from a high–sales-volume department to a low–sales-volume department.

The major disadvantage of the straight salary plan is employees' lack of immediate incentives to improve their productivity. They know their compensation won't change, in the short run, whether they work hard or slack off. Another disadvantage for the retailer is that straight salary becomes a fixed cost the firm incurs even if sales decline.

Incentive compensation plans reward employees on the basis of their productivity. Many retailers now use incentives to motivate greater sales productivity. Under some incentive plans, a salesperson's income is based entirely on commission—called a **straight commission.** For example, a salesperson might be paid a commission based on a percentage of sales made minus merchandise returned. Normally, the percentage is the same for all merchandise sold (such as

7 percent). But some retailers use different percentages for different categories of merchandise (such as 4 percent for low-margin items and 10 percent for high-margin items). By using different percentages, the retailer provides additional incentives for its salespeople to sell specific items. Typically, the compensation of salespeople selling high-priced items such as men's suits, appliances, and consumer electronics is based largely on their commissions.

Incentive plans may include a fixed salary plus a commission on total sales or a commission on sales over quota. For example, a salesperson might receive a salary of $200 per week plus a commission of 2 percent on all sales over a quota of $50 per hour.

Incentive compensation plans are a powerful motivator for salespeople to sell merchandise, but they have a number of disadvantages. For example, it's hard to get salespeople who are compensated totally by commission to perform non-selling activities. Understandably, they're reluctant to spend time stocking shelves when they could be making money by selling. Also, salespeople will concentrate on the more expensive, fast-moving merchandise and neglect other merchandise. Incentives can also discourage salespeople from providing services to customers. Finally, salespeople compensated primarily by incentives don't develop loyalty to their employer. Since the employer doesn't guarantee them an income, they feel no obligation to the firm. Retailing View 17.5 illustrates the adverse effects of placing too much of a store manager's incentives on controlling costs.

Under a straight commission plan, salespeople's incomes can fluctuate from week to week, depending on their sales. Since retail sales are seasonal, salespeople might earn most of their income during the Christmas season and much less during the summer months. To provide a more steady income for salespeople under high-incentive plans, some retailers offer a **drawing account.** With a drawing account, salespeople receive a weekly check based on their estimated

Wal-Mart's Incentives for Store Managers Cause Problems | RETAILING VIEW

17.5

After finishing her 10 P.M. to 8 A.M. shift, Verette Richardson clocked out and was heading to her car when a Wal-Mart manager ordered her to turn around and straighten up the store's apparel department. She spent the next hour working unpaid, tidying racks of slacks and blouses and picking up hangers and clothes that had fallen to the floor. Other times after clocking out, she was ordered to round up shopping carts in the parking lot or rush to a cash register and start ringing up purchases, without clocking in. Sometimes, she said, she worked for three hours before clocking in.

She and 40 other current and former Wal-Mart workers interviewed say Wal-Mart forced or pressured employees to work hours that were not recorded or paid. Federal and state laws bar employers from making hourly employees work unpaid hours. Many current and former workers and managers said an intense focus on cost cutting had created an unofficial policy that encouraged managers to request or require off-the-clock work and avoid paying overtime. These practices have helped Wal-Mart control its cost, offer lower prices, and become the world's largest retailer.

In response, a Wal-Mart spokesperson said, "Off-the-clock work is an infrequent and isolated problem that is corrected whenever we become aware of it. It is Wal-Mart's policy to pay its employees properly for the hours they work." Managers who required or requested off-the-clock work were subject to disciplinary action, including dismissal.

Although company policy prohibits off-the-clock work, Wal-Mart has created a system of rewards and punishments that gives managers strong incentives to squeeze down labor costs by pegging annual bonuses to the profits of individual stores. Many store managers have a base salary of $52,000, with bonuses often running $70,000 to $150,000.

Source: Steven Greenhouse, "Suits Say Wal-Mart Forces Workers to Toil off the Clock," *New York Times,* June 25, 2002, pp. B16. Reprinted by permission.

annual income. Then commissions earned are credited against the weekly payments. Periodically, the weekly draw is compared to the commission earned. If the draw exceeds earned commissions, the salespeople return the excess money they've been paid, and their weekly draw is reduced. If commissions earned exceed the draw, salespeople are paid the difference.

Quotas are often used with compensation plans. A **quota** is a target level used to motivate and evaluate performance. Examples are sales per hour for salespeople and maintained margin and inventory turnover for buyers. For department store salespeople, selling quotas vary across departments due to differences in sales productivity.

A **quota–bonus plan** provides sales associates with a bonus when their performance exceeds their quota. A quota–bonus plan's effectiveness depends on setting reasonable, fair quotas. Setting effective quotas can be hard. Usually, quotas are set at the same level for everyone in a department. But salespeople in the same department may have different abilities and face different selling environments. For example, in the men's department, salespeople in the suit area have much greater sales potential than salespeople in the accessories area. Newly hired salespeople might have a harder time achieving a quota than more experienced salespeople. Thus, a quota based on average productivity may be too high to motivate the new salesperson and too low to effectively motivate the experienced salesperson. Quotas should be developed for each salesperson based on his or her experience and the nature of the store area where he or she works.[37]

Group Incentives To encourage employees in a department or store to work together, some retailers provide additional incentives based on the performance of the department or store as a whole. For example, salespeople might be paid a commission based on their individual sales and then receive additional compensation based on the amount of sales over plan or quota generated by all salespeople in the store. The group incentive encourages salespeople to work together on nonselling activities and handling customers so the department sales target will be achieved.[38]

Designing the Compensation Program A compensation program's two elements are the amount of compensation and the percentage of compensation based on incentives. Typically, market conditions determine the amount of compensation. When economic conditions are good and labor is scarce, retailers pay higher wages. Retailers that hire inexperienced salespeople pay lower wages than those that recruit experienced salespeople with good skills and abilities.

Incentive compensation is most effective when a salesperson's performance can be measured easily and precisely. It's difficult to measure individual performance when salespeople work in teams or when they must perform a lot of nonselling activities. Retailers can easily measure a salesperson's actual sales, but it's hard to measure their customer service or merchandising performance.

When the salesperson's activities have a great impact on sales, incentives can provide additional motivation. For example, salespeople who are simply cashiers have little effect on sales and thus shouldn't be compensated with incentives. However, incentives are appropriate for salespeople who provide a lot of information and assistance about complex products such as designer dresses or stereo systems. Incentives are less effective with inexperienced salespeople because they inhibit learning. Inexperienced salespeople are less confident in their skills, and incentives can cause excessive stress.

Finally, compensation plans with too much of the incentives based on sales may not promote good customer service. Salespeople on commission become interested in selling anything they can to customers. They aren't willing to spend time helping customers buy the merchandise they need. They tend to stay close to the cash register or the dressing room exits so they can ring up a sale for a customer who's ready to buy.

Setting the Commission Percentage   Assume that a specialty store manager wants to hire experienced salespeople. To get the type of person she wants, she feels she must pay $12 per hour. Her selling costs are budgeted at 8 percent of sales. With compensation of $12 per hour, salespeople need to sell $150 worth of merchandise per hour ($12 divided by 8 percent) for the store to keep within its sales cost budget. The manager believes the best compensation would be one-third salary and two-thirds commission, so she decides to offer a compensation plan of $4 per hour salary (33 percent or $12) and a 5.33 percent commission on sales. If salespeople sell $150 worth of merchandise per hour, they'll earn $12 per hour ($4 per hour in salary plus $150 multiplied by 5.33 percent, which equals $8 per hour in commission).

Legal Issues in Compensation

The **Fair Labor Standards Act** of 1938 set minimum wages, maximum hours, child labor standards, and overtime pay provisions. Enforcement of this law is particularly important to retailers because they hire many low-wage employees and teenagers and have their employees work long hours.

The **Equal Pay Act,** now enforced by the EEOC, prohibits unequal pay for men and women who perform equal work or work of comparable worth. Equal work means that the jobs require the same skills, effort, and responsibility and are performed in same working environment. Comparable worth implies that men and women who perform different jobs of equal worth should be compensated the same. Differences in compensation are legal when compensation is determined by a seniority system, an incentive compensation plan, or market demand.

CONTROLLING COSTS

Labor scheduling, store maintenance, and energy management offer three opportunities for reducing store operating expenses. Retailing View 17.6 describes how a convenience store chain reengineered its operations to reduce cost and increase customer service.

Labor Scheduling

Using store employees efficiently is an important and challenging problem. While store employees provide important customer service and merchandising functions that can increase sales, they also are the store's largest operating expense. **Labor scheduling** (determining the number of employees assigned to each area of the store) is difficult because of the multiple-shift and part-time workers needed to staff stores 12 hours a day, seven days a week. In addition,

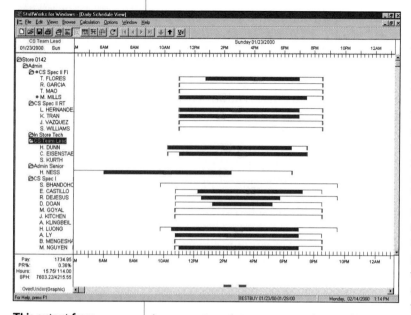

This output from Campbell Software labor scheduling system helps store managers improve their labor efficiency.

customer traffic varies greatly during the day and the week. Bad weather, holidays, and sales can dramatically alter normal shopping patterns and staffing needs.

Managers can spot obvious inefficiencies like long checkout lines and sales associates with nothing to do. But some inefficiencies are more subtle. For example, if 6 percent of a store's sales volume and 9 percent of the total labor hours occur between 2 and 3 P.M. the store might be overstaffed during this time period. Many stores use specially designed computer software to deal with the complexities of labor scheduling. Labor schedulers can reduce store payroll costs between 2 and 5 percent without affecting store sales.[39]

Efficient labor scheduling requires more than POS sales data by day and time of day. The manager also needs to know the traffic patterns and the impact of store employees on sales. For example, one store manager saw a downturn in sales during the hour before the store closed, so she considered reducing the level of staffing. However, when traffic counters were installed, the manager discovered that the number of customers in the store did not decline during the last

---

RETAILING VIEW   Sheetz Increases Operating Efficiency

17.6

Sheetz, a 270-store convenience store chain based in Altoona, Pennsylvania, started a series of detailed studies to determine how store-level tasks could be performed more efficiently. Charlie Campbell, a former store manager and now director of organizational efficiency, says, "We looked at everything from how the store manager closed out the day to how the staff emptied the trash." Two years after the company implemented the recommendations from the study, it saved $5.1 million in payroll costs alone.

Sheetz found that store managers were taking three to four hours to close out their sales day. Each day, they had to fill out 40 computer screens of information and would spend an hour looking for a $5 error. The time spent on closing was affecting customer service. Managers would do this paperwork during the morning of the following day, the busiest traffic time, when they should have been out in the stores managing. When Sheetz reexamined these practices, it eliminated over 160,000 hours annually of time the store managers were spending on nonproductive administrative tasks.

Sheetz also found that a lot of the information being sent to store managers was of questionable value. Campbell noted, "There were too many redundant reports. Two hundred and four reports were available on the store managers' computers. We've gotten that number down to 23."

Sheetz saved 55 employee-hours per week per store by reexamining its labor scheduling. Prior to the study, staffing for stores was based on sales. This approach did not consider that some stores generate a lot of sales from labor-intensive activities such as food service, while others derive sales from labor-free pay-at-the-pump transactions (called *outside sales* by convenience store operators). Some tasks performed in the store were eliminated. The company stopped tracking newspapers at the SKU level. On some papers, Sheetz only makes a two-cent margin. If store employees spend time receiving and tracking them by SKU, the firm loses money on each paper it sells.

Sources: "Sheetz: Customer-Friendly, Technologically Superior," *Beverage Aisle*, March 15, 2002, p. 38; and "Rap Sheetz," *Chain Store Age*, June 1999, pp. 78–82.

open hour. The manager then realized that employees were forsaking customer service and spending time preparing to close the store. Rather than reducing the staff, the manager extended the work hours so sales associates would realize the sales potential during the last hour.

 Labor scheduling is even more difficult in some European countries. For example, in France, a store manager works only 35 hours a week, rarely at night or on weekends, and has six weeks of annual paid vacation. A store manager in the United States with similar responsibilities works 44 hours a week, including evening and weekend shifts; frequently brings work home at night; and spends some off-time shopping the competitors. Workers in France are guaranteed five weeks paid vacation by law, and stores often are not open more than one night a week and only a half-day on Saturday.

Keeping work hours short is an obsession in France and a goal of the country's powerful labor unions. When France introduced Thursday night and Sunday shopping, retail workers went on strike. French store managers still find it difficult to staff the extra hours. In contrast, many American retail employees work a second job to send their children through college or save money for a house.

REFACT

In France, the average number of hours worked annually is 1,568, compared to 1,976 in the United States. French workers have 253 paid hours off, compared to 160 hours for U.S. workers.[40]

Store Maintenance

Store maintenance entails the activities involved with managing the exterior and interior physical facilities associated with the store. The exterior facilities include the parking lot, the entrances to the store, and signs on the outside of the store. The interior facilities include the walls, flooring, ceiling, and displays and signs.

Store maintenance affects both the sales generated in the store and the cost of running the store. A store's cleanliness and neatness affect consumer perceptions of the quality of its merchandise. Maintenance is costly. Floor maintenance for a 40,000-square-foot home center is about $10,000 a year. Poor maintenance shortens the useful life of air conditioning units, floors, and fixtures.

Energy Management

Energy management, the management of expenses on lighting, heating, and cooling, is a major issue in store operations, especially in stores with special refrigeration needs such as supermarkets and restaurants.[41] Wal-Mart has been very innovative in designing an energy-efficient store located in Commerce, California. Rather than using individual energy-efficient systems for heating, air conditioning, and lighting, the store uses a systems approach that results in an annual energy savings of $75,000. To use more daylight, the store has 180 skylights. Photo sensors continuously monitor the light levels so that as the amount of daylight increases, the artificial lighting in the store is reduced automatically, reducing the heat generated by the artificial lighting and the need for air conditioning. Electronic sensors on faucets and toilets reduce water consumption in the store. Solar panels in the store's atrium provide 15 percent of the energy used in the store.[42]

REDUCING INVENTORY LOSS

An important issue facing store management is reducing inventory losses due to employee theft, shoplifting, mistakes and inaccurate records, and vendor errors. Examples of employee mistakes are failing to ring up an item when it's sold and miscounting merchandise when it's received or when physical inventories are taken. Inventory shrinkage due to vendor mistakes arises when vendor shipments contain less than the amount indicated on the packing slip.

Although shoplifting receives most of the publicity, employee theft accounts for more inventory loss. A recent survey attributes 46 percent of inventory shrinkage to employee theft, 31 percent to shoplifting, 17 percent to mistakes and inaccurate records, and 6 percent to vendor errors.[43]

In developing a loss prevention program, retailers confront a trade-off between providing shopping convenience and a pleasant work environment and, on the other hand, preventing losses due to shoplifting and employee theft. The key to an effective loss prevention program is determining the most effective way to protect merchandise while preserving an open, attractive store atmosphere and a feeling among employees that they are trusted. Loss prevention requires coordination between store management, visual merchandising, and store design.

Calculating Shrinkage

Shrinkage is the difference between the recorded value of inventory (at retail prices) based on merchandise bought and received and the value of the actual inventory (at retail prices) in stores and distribution centers divided by retail sales during the period. For example, if accounting records indicate inventory should be $1,500,000, the actual count of the inventory reveals $1,236,000, and sales were $4,225,000, the shrinkage is 6.7 percent [($1,500,000 − $1,236,000) ÷ $4,225,000]. Reducing shrinkage is an important store management issue. Retailers' annual loss from shrinkage is between 1 and 5 percent of sales. Every dollar of inventory shrinkage translates into a dollar of lost profit.

Detecting and Preventing Shoplifting

Losses due to shoplifting can be reduced by store design, employee training, and special security measures.

Store Design   Security issues need to be considered when placing merchandise near store entrances, delivery areas, and dressing rooms. For example, easily stolen merchandise such as jewelry and other small, expensive items should never be displayed near an entrance. By reducing the height of fixtures and having open sight lines to entrances and exits, store employees can see customers in the store and watch for shoplifters while providing better service. Dressing room entrances should be visible to store employees so they can easily observe customers entering and exiting with merchandise. Since cash wraps are always staffed, they should be near areas that theft is likely to occur. (**Cash wraps** are the places in a store where customer can buy purchase and have it "wrapped"—placed in a bag.)[45]

Employee Training   Store employees can be the retailer's most effective tools against shoplifting. They should be trained to be aware, visible, and alert to potential shoplifting situations. Exhibit 17–8 outlines rules for spotting shoplifters. Perhaps the best deterrent to shoplifting is an alert employee who is very visible.

Security Measures   Exhibit 17–9 describes retailers' use of security measures. Department stores often chain expensive merchandise to fixtures. Another approach for deterring shoplifting is to embed dye capsules in the merchandise. If

REFACT

Retailers lose more than $33 billion annually due to shrinkage.[44]

DON'T ASSUME THAT ALL SHOPLIFTERS ARE POORLY DRESSED

To avoid detection, professional shoplifters dress in the same manner as customers patronizing the store. Over 90 percent of all amateur shoplifters arrested have either the cash, checks, or credit to purchase the merchandise they stole.

SPOT LOITERERS

Amateur shoplifters frequently loiter in areas as they build up the nerve to steal something. Professionals also spend time waiting for the right opportunity, but less conspicuously than amateurs.

LOOK FOR GROUPS

Teenagers planning to shoplift often travel in groups. Some members of the group divert employees' attention while others take the merchandise. Professional shoplifters often work in pairs. One person takes the merchandise and passes it to a partner in the store's restroom, phone booths, or restaurant.

LOOK FOR PEOPLE WITH LOOSE CLOTHING

Shoplifters frequently hide stolen merchandise under loose-fitting clothing or in large shopping bags. People wearing a winter coat in the summer or a raincoat on a sunny day may be potential shoplifters.

WATCH THE EYES, HANDS, AND BODY

Professional shoplifters avoid looking at merchandise and concentrate on searching for store employees who might observe their activities. Shoplifters' movements might be unusual as they try to conceal merchandise.

EXHIBIT 17–8
Spotting Shoplifters

the capsules aren't removed properly by a store employee, the capsules break and damage the merchandise.

By placing convex mirrors at key locations, employees can observe a wide area of the store. Closed-circuit TV cameras can be monitored from a central location, but purchasing the equipment and hiring people to monitor the system can be expensive. Some retailers install nonoperating equipment that looks like a TV camera to provide a psychological deterrent to shoplifters.

While these security measures reduce shoplifting, they can also make the shopping experience more unpleasant for honest customers. The atmosphere of

Live closed-circuit TV	74%
Check approval screening systems	68
Cables, locks, and chains	46
EAS tags	43
Mystery and honesty shoppers	42
Observation mirrors	41
Secured displays	46
Uniformed guards	37
Simulated closed-circuit TV	31
Plain-clothes detectives	29
Ink/dye tags	28
Fitting room attendants	13
Observation booths	11

EXHIBIT 17–9
Use of Security
Measures by Retailers

Source: Richard Hollinger and Jason Davis, *2001 National Retail Security Survey* (Gainesville, FL: University of Florida, 2001), p. 11, web.soc.ufl.edu/SRP/NRSS_2001.pdf. Reprinted by permission.

Retailers use EAS tags to reduce shoplifting. The tags (left and right) contain a device that is part of the price tag. If the tags are not deactivated when the merchandise is purchased, the stolen merchandise will be detected when the shopper passes through the sensor gates (center) at the store exit.

a fashionable department store is diminished when guards, mirrors, and TV cameras are highly visible. Customers may find it hard to try on clothing secured with a lock-and-chain or an electronic tag. They can also be uncomfortable trying on clothing if they think they're secretly being watched via a surveillance monitor. Thus, when evaluating security measures, retailers need to balance the benefits of reducing shoplifting with the potential losses in sales.

Electronic article surveillance is a promising approach for reducing shrinkage with little effect on shopping behavior. In **electronic article surveillance (EAS) systems,** special tags are placed on merchandise. When the merchandise is purchased, the tags are deactivated by the POS scanner. If a shoplifter tries to steal the merchandise, the active tags are sensed when the shoplifter passes a detection device at the store exit and an alarm is triggered.[46]

EAS tags do not affect shopping behavior because customers do not realize they're on the merchandise. Due to the effectiveness of tags in reducing shoplifting, retailers can increase sales by displaying theft-prone, expensive merchandise openly rather than behind a counter or in a locked enclosure.

Some large national retailers insist that vendors install EAS tags during the manufacturing process because the vendors can install the tags at a lower cost than the retailers. In addition, retail-installed tags can be removed more easily by shoplifters. Vendors are reluctant to get involved with installing EAS tags because industry standards have not been adopted. Without these standards, a vendor would have to develop unique tags and merchandise for each retailer.[47]

Prosecution   Many retailers have a policy of prosecuting all shoplifters. They feel a strictly enforced prosecution policy deters shoplifters. Some retailers also sue shoplifters in civil proceedings for restitution of the stolen merchandise and the time spent in the prosecution.

Reducing Employee Theft

The most effective approach for reducing employee theft and shoplifting is to create a trusting, supportive work environment. When employees feel they're respected members of a team, they identify their goals with the retailer's goals. Stealing from their employer becomes equivalent to stealing from themselves or their family, and they go out of their way to prevent others from stealing from the "family." Thus, retailers with a highly committed workforce and low turnover typically have low inventory shrinkage. Additional approaches for reducing employee theft are carefully screening employees, creating an atmosphere that encourages honesty and integrity, using security personnel, and establishing security policies and control systems.

Redner's Warehouse Markets, a chain in Reading, Pennsylvania, has one of the industry's lowest inventory shrinkages, 0.16 percent of retail sales. Redner's achieves this low shrinkage by educating its employees about the causes and effects of shrinkage on the business. Then it backs this message with incentives. It annually budgets 0.50 percent for shrinkage. If a store improves on this budgeted level, the difference is paid back to its employees. Employees earned $590,000 in annual bonuses for beating the budgeted shrinkage level.[49]

Screening Prospective Employees   As mentioned previously, many retailers use paper-and-pencil honesty tests and make extensive reference checks to screen out potential employee theft problems. A major problem related to employee theft is drug use. Some retailers now require prospective employees to submit to drug tests as a condition of employment. Employees with documented performance problems, an unusual number of accidents, or erratic time and attendance records are also tested. Unless they're involved in selling drugs, employees who test positive are often offered an opportunity to complete a company-paid drug program, submit to random testing in the future, and remain with the firm.

Using Security Personnel   In addition to uniformed guards, retailers use undercover shoppers to discourage and detect employee theft. These undercover security people pose as shoppers. They make sure salespeople ring up transactions accurately.

Establishing Security Policies and Control Systems   To control employee theft, retailers need to adopt policies relating to certain activities that may facilitate theft. Some of the most prevalent policies are

- Randomly search containers such as trash bins where stolen merchandise can be stored.
- Require store employees to enter and leave the store through designated entrances.
- Assign salespeople to specific POS terminals and require all transactions to be handled through those terminals.
- Restrict employee purchases to working hours.
- Provide customer receipts for all transactions.
- Have all refunds, returns, and discounts cosigned by a department or store manager.
- Change locks periodically and issue keys to authorized personnel only.
- Have a locker room where all employee handbags, purses, packages, and coats must be checked.

In addition, computer software is available to detect unusual activity at POS terminals. For example, a POS terminal where shortages are frequently reported

REFACT

A dishonest employee typically takes over $1,000 worth of goods and cash, while the average customer shoplifter takes $128 in merchandise.[48]

or return activity is unusually high can be located and then employees using the terminal can be monitored. Transactions can also be analyzed to identify employees who ring up a lot of no-receipt returns or void other employees' returns.

SUMMARY

Effective store management can have a significant impact on a retail firm's financial performance. Store managers increase profits by increasing labor productivity, decreasing costs through labor deployment decisions, and reducing inventory loss by developing a dedicated workforce.

Increasing store employees' productivity is challenging because of the difficulties in recruiting, selecting, and motivating store employees. Employees typically have a range of skills and seek a spectrum of rewards. Effective store managers need to motivate their employees to work hard and to develop skills so they improve their productivity. To motivate employees, store managers need to understand what rewards each employee is seeking and then provide an opportunity to realize those rewards. Store managers must establish realistic goals for employees that are consistent with the store's goals and must motivate each employee to achieve them.

Store managers also must control inventory losses due to employee theft, shoplifting, and clerical errors. Managers use a wide variety of methods in developing loss prevention programs, including security devices and employee screening during the selection process. However, the critical element of any loss prevention program is building employee loyalty to reduce employee interest in stealing and increase attention to shoplifting.

KEY TERMS

Americans with Disabilities Act (ADA), *560*

Age Discrimination and Employment Act, *560*

à la carte plan, *570*

autocratic leader, *563*

cash wraps, *578*

democratic leader, *563*

disability, *560*

discrimination, *559*

disparate impact, *559*

disparate treatment, *559*

drawing account, *573*

Equal Employment Opportunity Commission (EEOC), *558*

electronic article surveillance (EAS) system, *580*

energy management, *577*

Equal Pay Act, *575*

extrinsic reward, *570*

Fair Labor Standards Act, *575*

group maintenance behavior, *563*

incentive compensation plan, *572*

intrinsic reward, *570*

job analysis, *554*

job application form, *557*

job description, *555*

job enrichment, *572*

labor scheduling, *575*

leadership, *563*

preferred clients, *565*

quota, *574*

quota–bonus plan, *574*

sexual harassment, *566*

shrinkage, *578*

socialization, *560*

store maintenance, *577*

straight commission, *572*

straight salary compensation, *572*

task performance behavior, *563*

transformational leader, *564*

GET OUT & DO IT!

1. GO SHOPPING Go to a store and meet with the person responsible for personnel scheduling. Report on the following:

- Who is responsible for employee scheduling?
- How far in advance is the schedule made?
- How are breaks and lunch periods planned?
- How are overtime hours determined?
- What are the total number of budgeted employee hours for each department based on?
- How is flexibility introduced into the schedule?
- How are special requests for days off handled?
- How are peak periods (hourly, days, or seasons) planned for?
- What happens when an employee calls in sick at the last minute?

2. GO SHOPPING Go to a store and talk to the person responsible for human resource management to find out how salespeople are compensated and evaluated for job performance.

- What are the criteria for evaluation?
- How often are they evaluated?
- How much importance does the store attach to a buyer's or manager's merchandising skill versus his or her ability to work with people?
- For an associate, what action is taken if the person does not meet sales goals? Can goals be adjusted? Can associates be moved to another area or type of function?
- Do salespeople have quotas? If they do, how are they set?
- Can sales associates make a commission? If yes, how does the commission system work? What are the advantages of a commission system? What are the disadvantages?
- If no commission system, are any incentive programs offered? Give an example of a specific program or project used by the store to boost employee morale and productivity.

3. GO SHOPPING Go to a store, observe the security measures in the store, and talk with the person about the store's loss prevention program.

- Are there surveillance cameras? Where are they located?
- What is the store's policy against shoplifters?
- What are the procedures for approaching a suspected shoplifter?
- How are shoplifters handled?
- How are sales associates and executives involved in the security programs?
- Is employee theft a problem? Elaborate.
- How is employee theft prevented in the store?
- How is shrinkage prevented in the store?
- How is customer service related to loss prevention in the store?

4. INTERNET EXERCISE Go to www.astd. org, the website for the American Society for Training and Development, and read one of the articles from the latest issue of *Training and Development*, a magazine published by the society. How would you suggest that a retailer use the information in this article to increase the effectiveness of its employees?

5. INTERNET EXERCISE Bunyar Malenfant International (www.bmi.ca) sells systems that enable retailers to assess potential sales by counting the customers entering the stores and passing through areas. Campbell Software (www.campbellsoft.com), a division of SAP, is a leader in developing software for labor scheduling. Visit the home pages of these companies. What products and services are they selling? By looking at the comments in the discussion groups, decide what issues are of concern to retailers.

DISCUSSION QUESTIONS AND PROBLEMS

1. How do on-the-job training and classroom training differ? What are the benefits and limitations of each approach?

2. Give examples of a situation in which a manager of a McDonald's fast-food restaurant must utilize different leadership styles.

3. Job descriptions should be in writing so employees clearly understand what's expected of them. But what are the dangers of relying too heavily on written job descriptions?

4. Name some laws and regulations that affect the employee management process. Which do you believe are the easiest for retailers to adhere to? Which are violated the most?

5. What's the difference between extrinsic rewards and intrinsic rewards? What are the effects of these rewards on the behavior of retail employees? Under what conditions would you recommend that a retailer emphasize intrinsic rewards over extrinsic rewards?

6. Many large department stores such as JC Penney, Sears, and Macy's are changing their salespeople's reward system from a traditional salary to a commission-based system. What problems can incentive compensation systems cause? How can department managers avoid these problems?

7. When evaluating retail employees, some stores use a quantitative approach that relies on checklists and numerical scores similar to the form in Exhibit 17–7. Other stores use a more qualitative approach whereby less time is spent checking and adding and more time is devoted to discussing strengths and weaknesses in written form. Which is the best evaluation approach? Why?

8. What are the different methods for compensating employees? Discuss which methods you think would be best for compensating a sales associate, store manager, and buyer.

9. Is training more important for a small independent retailer or a large national chain? Why? How does training differ between these two types of retailers?

10. Discuss how retailers can reduce shrinkage from shoplifting and employee theft.

SUGGESTED READINGS

Cooper, Cary, and Ivan Robertson. *Personnel Psychology and Human Resource Management: A Reader for Students and Practitioners.* New York: John Wiley & Sons, 2001.

Devine, Mary-Lou. *The Practical Guide to Employment Law.* Gaithersburg, MD: Aspen Publishers, 2000.

"Front Lines." *Chain Store Age*, September 1, 2001, pp. 35–40.

Greco, Susan. "Sales: What Works Now." *Inc.*, February 2002, pp. 52–55.

Hacker, Carol. *The Costs of Bad Hiring Decisions and How to Avoid Them.* 2d ed. Boca Raton, FL: St. Lucie Press. 1999.

Hollinger, Richard, and Jason Davis. *2001 National Retail Security Survey.* Gainesville, FL: University of Florida, 2001.
web.soc.ufl.edu/SRP/NRSS_2001.pdf.

Klinvex, Kevin; Matthew O'Connell; and Christopher Klinvex. *Hiring Great People.* New York: McGraw-Hill, 1999.

Lawler, Edward. *Rewarding Excellence: Pay Strategies for the New Economy.* New York: Jossey-Bass, 1999.

"Leadership Style Profiles of Retail Managers: Personal, Organizational and Managerial Characteristics." *International Journal of Retail and Distribution Management* 30 (2002), pp. 186–202.

McAfee, R. Bruce. "Workplace Harassment: Employees vs. Customers." *Business Horizons* 42 (March–April 1999), pp. 79–85.

Store Layout, Design, and Visual Merchandising

18

"Creating an appealing environment in our video stores is really a challenge. Our merchandise all looks alike—5 × 7 inch boxes with movie graphics, which are then arranged basically, in alphabetical order. We have experimented with merchandising the stores in a variety of ways. As a result, we've found we need to appeal to two basic customer types, browsers and transactors. Browsers want to spend more time in the store shopping, while transactors want to get in and out fast. Our newest store designs and philosophies break the merchandising and communications down so that transactors can find what they want quickly and browsers can shop at a leisurely pace.

"Another interesting planning challenge is that our prime real estate in the store is the back wall, which is opposite most traditional retailers. Many of our customers go directly to the new releases, which are merchandised on the back wall. One of my design objectives is to encourage traffic to move through the center of the store as well, in order to expose our entire inventory. Our latest merchandising challenge is to increase awareness of our huge movies for sale category. By designing new fixtures and graphics, the store environment takes the lead in communicating to our consumers that we are the best place to buy as well as rent.

"I have always been attracted to retailing. I was a mall rat when I was a teenager. After college, I took a job at Diamonds department store and was in-

QUESTIONS

- What are the critical issues in designing a store?
- What are the alternative methods of store layout?
- How is space assigned to merchandise and departments?
- What are the best techniques for merchandise presentation?

trigued with the way merchandising of a department can affect sales. The exciting part of retailing is the constant change. It seems like everyday there is a new challenge.

"While retailing is exciting, there is an extra layer added by working for Blockbuster. I am not just designing our stores to increase sales and rentals, I am merchandising movie stars."

A good store design should be like a good story.[1] Every story has a beginning, middle, and end, usually in that order. The entrance sets up the story. It creates expectations and contains promises. As for the first impression, the storefront says, "I'm cheap" or "I'm sophisticated" or "I'm cool." Too often, stores launch right into "Here's what we've got to sell. Don't you love it?" A good entrance should entice, hint, and tease. There should be mystery.

Inside the store comes the middle of the story. It should start off slow. Customers need a few seconds to orient themselves after the entrance. A single message has a far greater chance of sticking than do a dozen products cluttering the way.

Customers need to be led on a journey throughout the store. Using light, motion, and visuals, take customers down a path of discovery. There should, for instance, be visual destinations at the end of a long aisle. Exciting stores should be like Paris. Sighting down the Champs-Elysées, you are enticed by the Arc de Triomphe as a powerful destination. Finally, the cash wrap or checkout counter is the story's climactic finale. It's where retailers can convey subtle messaging without hard-selling.

This chapter is part of the store management section. We start with the objectives of store design. Then we examine the big picture—How should the overall store be laid out? Next we look at how retailers plan and evaluate the location of departments and then merchandise within departments. Finally, we explore specific methods of altering a store's atmosphere.

OBJECTIVES OF A GOOD STORE DESIGN

When designing or redesigning a store, managers must meet five objectives.

Design Should Be Consistent with Image and Strategy

To meet the first objective, retail managers must define the target customer and then design a store that complements customers' needs.[2] For instance, warehouse clubs, like Sam's or Costco, have high ceilings with metal grids and concrete floors instead of tile—all of those things are perceived to mean low prices. Actually, they are more expensive than some alternatives, but they are used to maintain an image.[3] Customers would find it hard to accurately judge value if the physical environment were inconsistent with the merchandise or prices. Throughout this chapter, keep in mind the relationships between the overall retail strategy and the store's image as it's portrayed by the physical aspects of the store. REI is a master of matching its target customer with store design. See Retailing View 18.1.

RETAILING VIEW | Peak Experience

18.1

Recreational Equipment Inc. (REI) has transformed a decaying 99-year-old historic landmark building in Denver into a modern retail adventure. The 94,000-square-foot, three-level store raises the bar on interactive retailing, taking the try-it-before-you-buy-it concept to new heights.

Among the new attractions: a large, steel-encased freezer-like fixture where shoppers can test winter parkas and sleeping bags. The temperatures inside can drop to as low as −30° F. Simulated wind chills can make it seem even colder. Mountain bikes can be tested on a rugged 318-foot trail that runs through the store's landscaped outdoor courtyard. Inside, shoppers can try out hiking boots on a footwear test track, compare bike lights and reflectors in an illuminator room, and test water purifiers in a ministream.

The centerpiece of the store is a 45-foot sculptured indoor rock-climbing pinnacle. It offers a variety of climbing terrains, including routes specifically geared for children. Weary shoppers can take a break at the on-premise Starbucks.

REI is in an industry where people love to get the product in their hands and test it. Letting them do so makes for a happier and better-informed customer—one who enters into the purchase with a much better feel as to how the product is supposed to perform.

Source: Marianne Wilson, "Peak Experience," *Chain Store Age*, June 2000, pp. 144–45. Copyright Lebhar-Friedman, Inc. 425 Park Avenue, New York, NY 10022. Reprinted by permission.

REI is more than just a place to buy outdoor apparel and equipment. This store in Denver features a 45-foot rock-climbing pinnacle

Design Should Positively Influence Consumer Behavior

To meet the second design objective of influencing customer buying decisions, retailers concentrate on store layout and space-planning issues. Imagine a grocery store laid out like a women's specialty store, or an art gallery that looked like a tire store. Grocery stores are organized to facilitate an orderly shopping trip and to display as much merchandise as possible. Yet boutiques are laid out in a free-form design that allows customers to browse.

Customers' purchasing behavior is also influenced, both positively and negatively, by the store's atmosphere.[4] Signs are designed to attract attention. On a more subtle level, Mrs. Fields stores attract customers because of the smell of chocolate chip cookies. This chapter explores the methods retailers use to positively influence consumers' purchase behavior.

Design Should Consider Costs versus Value

Consistent with any retail decision, the third design objective is to consider the costs associated with each store design element versus the value received in terms of higher sales and profits. For instance, the free-form design found in many boutiques is much more costly than rows of gondolas in a discount store. (A *gondola* is an island type of self-service counter with tiers of shelves, bins, or pegs. See Exhibit 18–4D on page 609.) Also, the best locations within a store are "worth" the most, so they're reserved for certain types of merchandise. For instance, many grocery stores place their produce near the store's entrance because it has a higher margin than other merchandise categories and it creates a nice atmosphere. Retailers develop maps called *planograms* that prescribe the location of merchandise based on profitability and other factors. Finally, when considering atmospheric issues of store design, retailers must weigh the costs along with the strategy and customer attraction issues. For instance, certain types of lighting used to highlight expensive jewelry and crystal cost more than rows of bare fluorescent bulbs.

Design Should Be Flexibile

As merchandise changes, so must a store's image. Thus, store planners attempt to design stores with maximum flexibility. Flexibility can take two forms: the ability to physically move store components, and the ease with which components can be modified.

Most retailers have learned from the mistakes made by their predecessors following World War II. Stores during this period were often more like monuments, with inflexible wall-to-wall fixtures. The role of merchandise was almost an afterthought. Unfortunately, most of these architectural cathedrals quickly became outdated as tastes, attitudes, and the merchandise itself changed. Although they've long since closed for business, some still stand vacant as a sad tribute to what they once were, and others have been demolished. A few stores, like the Marshall Field's flagship store in Chicago, have been restored to their original splendor at a cost of millions of dollars.

Today, however, most stores are designed with flexibility in mind. For instance, Wallace's Bookstores, one of the nation's largest operators of college bookstores, is rolling out an innovative new concept with built-in merchandising and design flexibility[5] (see the photo on page 590). Called *flexsmart*, the format allows the store to expand or contract its space to accommodate the seasonal flux

Wallace's Bookstores are designed with flexibility in mind. Metal frames on endcaps swing open and shut, allowing the store to expand or contract its space as needed.

inherent in the college-bookstore business. The rush for textbooks at the beginning of each semester and the slower in-between periods make for extreme peaks and valleys in sales.

Stores with the new design can respond to seasonal changes and renew themselves from an image perspective without the need of large-scale renovations. During busy times, as much as 30 percent more retail space can be provided for books or apparel in various departments. The key to Wallace's new flexibility lies in an innovative fixturing and wall system that is used to portion off the textbook area. On the front end of each textbook aisle there is a panel with an end-cap display that can swing open or closed as needed.

Design Should Recognize the Needs of the Disabled—The Americans with Disabilities Act

A critical consideration in any store design or redesign decision is the 1990 Americans with Disabilities Act (ADA).[6] This landmark federal civil rights law protects people with disabilities from discrimination in employment, transportation, public accommodations, telecommunications, and the activities of state and local government.

Besides providing for a nondiscriminatory work environment for the disabled, it calls for "reasonable access" to merchandise and services in a retail store that was built before 1993. Stores built after 1993 must be fully accessible. Although seemingly straightforward, it is not. As it applies to store layout and design, reasonable access generally means that a person in a wheelchair or one using a walker or a motorized cart should have unencumbered access to merchandise through adequately wide pathways. Does this mean access to all sides of all fixtures, to a 32- or 36-inch space, at all times of the year including sales and Christmas, at all times the store is open, and so forth? The answers are not clear or easy; as a result, they are being considered on a case-by-case basis in federal courts around the United States.

What makes the decisions even more difficult is that the accessibility issues must be weighed in conjunction with the rights of the retailers, which the act protects from an undue burden in compliance. This generally means that if achieving accessibility means that the store has to change its fundamental business model, then it is an undue burden. For instance, Macy's West, a division of Federated Department Stores, Inc., unsuccessfully argued in federal court that it should not have to provide a fixed yardstick of 32- or 36-inch accessibility because to do so would change the fundamental way it does business as a highly promotion-oriented, high/low department store. In this case, the court disagreed and found for the disabled plaintiffs.[7] Many similar cases are currently underway.

Case after case reported in the popular press appears to document actual accommodations, when a closer look indicates that the accommodations are forced, claims and complaints are necessary, and compliance is generally after the fact. Thus, in many cases the ADA is working as a coercive law, not as a signal to build access to public environments.[8]

To complicate matters, the requirements for compliance with the ADA are different depending on whether it's an existing facility, a newly built facility, or a facility undergoing remodeling. It's easiest to comply in an existing facility. In essence, barriers must be removed if doing so doesn't involve much difficulty or expense. The ADA insists on higher standards for larger facilities. For most stores and shopping centers, the ADA requires adding adequate spacing between merchandise fixtures, building ramps, adding grab bars, rearranging restroom stall dividers, adding a handrail to stairs, providing braille elevator buttons, and other measures.

STORE LAYOUT

To develop a good store layout, store designers must balance many objectives—objectives that often conflict. For example, the store layout should entice customers to move around the store to purchase more merchandise than they may have originally planned. However, if the layout is too complex, customers may find it difficult to locate the merchandise they are looking for and decide not to patronize the store.

The trade-off between ease of finding merchandise and providing a varied and interesting layout is determined by the needs of the customers shopping at the store. For example, supermarket shoppers typically have specific things they want to buy, so these retailers need to place an emphasis on the ease of locating merchandise. On the other hand, department store shoppers are not as goal-oriented and are therefore more willing to explore the store for new merchandise. Thus, department store retailers can place more emphasis on exploration rather than ease of finding merchandise.

One method of encouraging customer merchandise exploration is to present to them a layout that facilitates a specific traffic pattern. Customers can be enticed to follow what amounts to a yellow brick road, as in *The Wizard of Oz*. For instance, Toys "R" Us uses a layout that almost forces customers to move through sections of inexpensive impulse-purchase products to get to larger, more expensive goods. It takes a strong-willed parent to navigate through the balloons and party favors without making a purchase.

Another method of helping customers move through the store is to provide interesting design elements. For example, antique stores have little nooks and crannies that entice shoppers to wander around. Off-price retailers intentionally create some degree of messiness so that people will be encouraged to look through the racks for bargains. A second objective of a good layout is to provide a balance between giving customers adequate space in which to shop and productively using this expensive, often scarce resource for merchandise. For example, some customers may be attracted to stores with wide aisles and fixtures whose primary purpose is to display rather than to hold the merchandise. However, this type of design reduces the amount of merchandise that can be shown to the customer, which may also reduce the customer's chances of finding what he or she is looking for. Also, a store with lots of people creates a sense of excitement and, it is hoped, increases buying. But too many racks and displays in a store can cause customers to get confused or even lost. The issue of overcrowding display fixtures and merchandise is particularly important as retailers consider the special needs of the disabled.

To meet their objectives, retailers must decide which design type to use and how to generate traffic through feature areas.

Types of Design

Today's modern retailers use three general types of store layout design: grid, racetrack, and free-form.

Grid   The **grid layout** is best illustrated by most grocery and drugstore operations. It contains long gondolas of merchandise and aisles in a repetitive pattern (Exhibit 18–1). The grid isn't the most aesthetically pleasing arrangement, but it's very good for shopping trips in which customers need to move throughout the entire store and easily locate products they want to buy. For instance, when customers do their weekly grocery shopping, they weave in and out of the specific aisles easily picking up similar products every week. Since they know where everything is, they can minimize the time spent on a task that many don't especially enjoy. The grid layout is also cost-efficient.

There's less wasted space with the grid design than with others because the aisles are all the same width and are designed to be just wide enough to accommodate shoppers and their carts. Since the grid design is used with long gondolas that have multiple shelf levels, the amount of merchandise on the floor can be significantly more than with other layouts. Thus, space productivity is enhanced.

EXHIBIT 18–1
Grid Store Layout

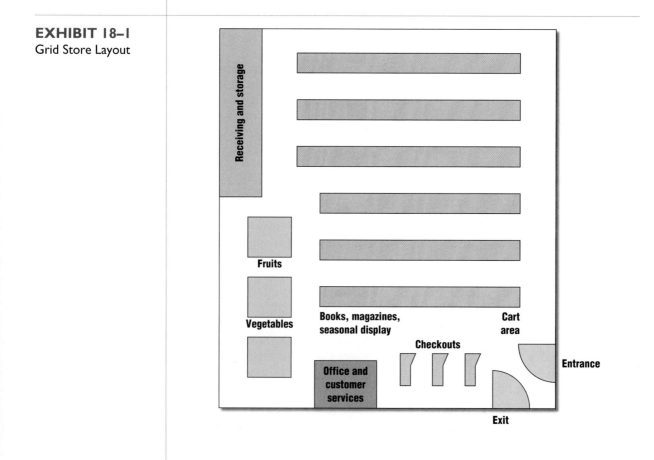

(Space productivity is discussed later in this chapter.) Finally, since the fixtures are generally standardized and repetitive, the fixturing cost is reduced.

Racetrack   One problem with the grid design is that customers aren't exposed to all of the merchandise in the store. This isn't an issue in grocery stores, where most customers have a good notion of what they're going to purchase before they enter the store. But how can a design pull customers through stores that want to encourage them to explore and seek out new and interesting merchandise?

The racetrack layout facilitates the goal of getting customers to visit multiple departments. The **racetrack layout,** also known as a **loop,** is a type of store design that provides a major aisle to facilitate customer traffic, with access to the store's multiple entrances. This aisle loops through the store, providing access to all the departments. The racetrack design encourages impulse purchasing. As customers go around the racetrack, their eyes are forced to take different viewing angles rather than looking down one aisle as in the grid design.

Exhibit 18–2 shows the layout of the JCPenney store in the upscale North-Park Center in Dallas, Texas. Since the store has multiple entrances, the loop design tends to place all departments on the main aisle by drawing customers through the store in a series of major and minor loops. To entice customers

JCPenney Racetrack Layout at NorthPark Center in Dallas   **EXHIBIT 18–2**

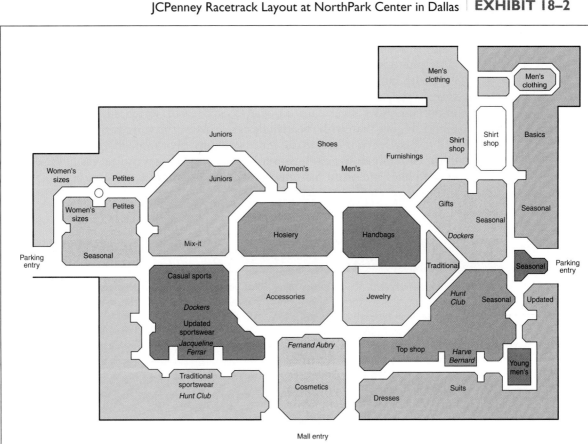

This racetrack layout at a Goody's store draws customers through the store and encourages impulse purchasing.

through the various departments, the design has placed some of the more important departments, like juniors, toward the rear of the store. The newest items are featured on the aisles to draw customers into departments and around the loop. To direct customers through the store, the aisles must be defined by a change in surface or color. For instance, the aisle flooring is of marble-like tile, while the departments vary in material, texture, and color, depending on the desired ambiance. Retailing View 18.2 describes the racetrack design at Kohl's Department Stores.

Free-Form   A **free-form layout,** also known as **boutique layout,** arranges fixtures and aisles asymmetrically (Exhibit 18–3). It's successfully used primarily in small specialty stores or within the departments of large stores. In this relaxed environment, customers feel like they're at someone's home, which facilitates shopping and browsing. A pleasant atmosphere isn't inexpensive, however. For one thing, the fixtures are likely to be expensive custom units. Since the customers aren't naturally drawn around the store as they are in the grid and racetrack layouts, personal selling becomes more important. Also, since sales associates can't easily watch adjacent departments, theft is higher than with the grid design. Finally, the store sacrifices some storage and display space to create the more spacious environment. If the free-form layout is carefully designed, however, the increased costs can be easily offset by increased sales and profit margins because the customer feels at home.

RETAILING VIEW   Kohl's Racetrack

18.2

With an average 86,000 square feet, a Kohl's store is about half the size of most department stores. Although management's objective is to help busy shoppers get in and out quickly, there appears to be ample room to roam from department to department. The wide aisle that forms the track provides room for shoppers with carts or families with children in tow. A middle aisle divides the track, serving as a shortcut for shoppers who don't need to finish a whole lap. During clearance periods, Kohl's lines the track with markdown merchandise to get shoppers' attention. Cash register stations mark the start and finish point of the track. A shopper walks roughly a quarter of a mile on the track and its main aisles in order to cover the whole store.

Conventional retail wisdom says store layouts ought to keep people shopping longer, but Kohl's management believes that their customers want the convenience of easy access. So they actually try to shorten the shopping trip.

Source: Calmetta Coleman, "Kohl's Retail Racetrack," *The Wall Street Journal,* March 1, 2001, pp. B1, B6. Copyright 2001 by Dow Jones & Co. Inc. Reproduced with permission of Dow Jones & Co. Inc. via Copyright Clearance Center.

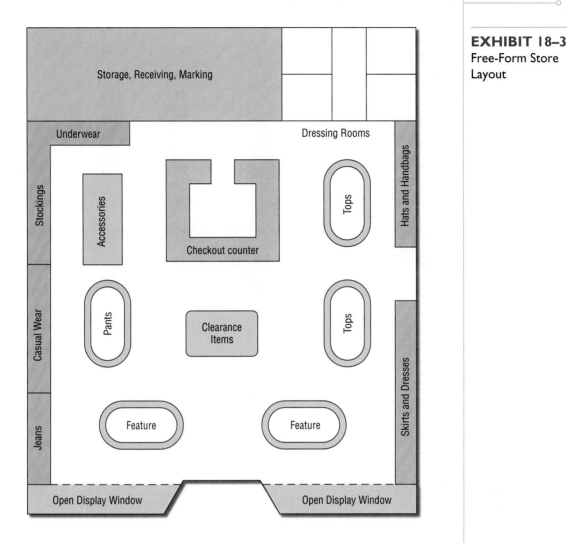

EXHIBIT 18–3
Free-Form Store
Layout

To illustrate a free-form boutique within a racetrack layout, consider the Bloomingdale's I.C.B. boutique in the picture on page 596. The designers' objective was to create a simple, clear space that draws customers into the area. Fixtures with the latest garments are placed along the perimeter of the boutique. Yet the flooring and lighting clearly delineate the area from adjacent departments and the walkway.[9]

One would think that the issues to be considered when designing a bricks-and-mortar store would be very different than the design issues surrounding an Internet store. Think again, and see More Information About 18.1 on page 597.

Feature Areas

Besides the area where most of the merchandise is displayed and stored, there are **feature areas**—areas within a store designed to get the customer's attention. They include end caps, promotional aisles or areas, freestanding fixtures and

In this I.C.B. department at Bloomingdale's, fixtures with the latest garments are placed along the perimeter of the boutique to draw customers into the area. Flooring and lighting clearly delineate the area from adjacent departments and the walkway.

mannequins that introduce a soft goods department, windows, point-of-sale or cash-wrap areas, and walls.

End Caps

End caps are displays located at the end of an aisle. For instance, a Kroger food store's large end-cap display of Coca-Cola is designed to catch consumers' attention. The Coca-Cola is located near the rest of the soft drinks, but it is on sale. It's not always necessary to use end caps for sales, however. Due to their high visibility, end caps can also be used to feature special promotional items, like beer and potato chips before the Fourth of July.

Promotional Aisle or Area

A **promotional aisle** or **area** is an aisle or area used to display merchandise that is being promoted. Walgreens, for instance, uses a promotional aisle to sell seasonal merchandise, such as lawn and garden in the summer and Christmas decorations in the fall. Apparel stores, like The Gap, often place their sale merchandise in the back of the store so customers must wander through the full-price merchandise to get to the sale merchandise.

Freestanding Fixtures and Mannequins

Freestanding fixtures and mannequins located on aisles are designed primarily to get customers' attention and bring them into a department. These fixtures often display and store the newest, most exciting merchandise in the department. (Reexamine the Bloomingdale's I.C.B. boutique in the picture on this page.)

Windows

Although windows are clearly external to the store, they can be an important component of the store layout. Properly used, window displays can help draw customers into the store. They provide a visual message about the type of merchandise for sale in the store and the type of image the store wishes to

MORE INFORMATION ABOUT . . . Designing a Website: Lessons from Store Design

18.1

Superficially, nothing could be more different.[10] A website is virtual, and a store is physical. In many but not all cases, good design components appear to transcend the physical world to the virtual world. In other cases, the Web requires a different approach. Consider the following examples:

Simplicity matters. A good store design allows shoppers to move freely, unencumbered by clutter. There is a fine line between providing customers with a good assortment and confusing them with too much merchandise.

Similarly in a website, it is not necessary to mention all the merchandise available at a site on each page. It is better to present a limited selection tailored to the customer's needs and then provide a few links to related merchandise and alternative assortments. It is also important to have a search feature on each page in case a customer gets lost. Note, the search feature in the virtual world is similar to having sales associates readily available in the physical world. Also, less is more. Having a small number of standard links on every page makes it more likely that users will learn the navigation scheme for the site.

Getting around. When a store is properly designed, customers should be able to easily find what they are looking for. The products that customers purchase together are merchandised together—umbrellas are with raincoats, soft drinks are with snack foods.

One way to help customers get around a website is by using *local links*—links that are internal to a website. When establishing local links, websites should link

- Products that are close in price, both higher and lower. If you link only to higher-priced merchandise, you might lose customer trust.

- Complementary products.

- Products that differ from the current product in some important dimension (for example, link to a color printer if the user is looking at a black-and-white printer).

- Different versions of the current product (for example, the same blouse in yellow).

Let them see it. Stores are designed so customers can easily view the merchandise and read the signs. But in a store, if the lighting isn't good or a sign is too small to read, the customer can always move around to get a better view. Customers don't have this flexibility on the Internet. Web designers should assume that all potential viewers don't have perfect vision. They should strive for realistic colors and sharpness. Some retailers who use the Internet channel have developed interesting ways of viewing merchandise in multiple dimensions (see, for instance, www.landsend.com).

Blend the website with the store. It is important to visually reassure customers that they're going to have the same satisfactory experience on the website that they have in stores. So even if the electronic store is designed for navigation efficiency, there should still be some design elements that are common to both channels. For instance, although very different store types, www.tiffany.com and www.officedepot.com have a similar look and feel to their stores.

Prioritize. Stores become annoying if everything jumps out at you as if to say, "buy me, no buy me." Other stores are so bland that the merchandise appears boring.

Setting priorities for merchandise displays and locations is just as important on the website as it is in a physical store. A common mistake on many Internet sites is that everything is too prominent: overuse of colors, animation, blinking, and graphics. If everything is equally prominent, then *nothing* is prominent. Being too bland is equally troublesome.

The site should be designed to advise the customers and guide them to the most important or most promising choices, while at the same time ensuring their freedom to go anywhere they please. Like a newspaper, the most important items or categories should be given the bigger headlines and more prominent placement.

Type of layout. Some stores are laid out to be functional like supermarkets and discount stores. They use a grid design to make it easy to locate merchandise. Other stores, like department stores or bookstores, use a more relaxed layout to encourage browsing. The trick is to pick the appropriate layout that matches the typical motives of the shopper.

Here is where store layout and website layout differ. Although many higher-end multiple-channel retailers experimented with fancy and complex designs in their early years on the Internet, most have become much more simple and utilitarian than their bricks-and-mortar counterparts (see, for instance, www.polo.com, www.neimanmarcus.com, and www.bloomingdales.com). When shopping on the Web, customers are interested in speed, convenience, and ease of navigation—not necessarily fancy graphics.

Store designers also strive to make their stores different, to stand out in the crowd. A website, on the other hand, must strive for the balance between keeping the customers' interest and providing them with a comfort level based on convention. Users spend most of their time on *other* sites, so that's where they form their expectations for how most sites work. So when trying to make a decision about website design, good designers look at the most-visited sites on the Internet to see how they do it. If 90 percent or more of the big sites do things in a single way, then this is the de facto standard.

Source: Jakob Nielsen's *Alertbox*, www.useit.com; and "Communicating with Your Customers on the Web," *Harvard Management Communication Letter,* article reprint no. COOO8A, 2000.

portray. Window displays should be tied to the merchandise and other displays in the store. For instance, if beach towels are displayed in a Bed, Bath & Beyond store, they should also be prominently displayed inside. Otherwise, the drawing power of the window display is lost. Finally, windows can be used to set the shopping mood for a season or holiday like Christmas or Valentine's Day.

Point of Sale Areas **Point-of-sale areas,** also known as **point-of-purchase, POP, checkout,** or **cash-wrap areas,** are places in the store where customers can purchase merchandise. These areas can be the most valuable piece of real estate in the store, because the customers often wait there for the transactions to be completed. While waiting in a long checkout line at a grocery store, notice how people pick up things like batteries, candy, razors, and magazines. Did they need these items? Not really, but the wait bored them, so they spent the extra time shopping.

Several department store chains are experimenting with centralized checkout stations.[11] Discount and value-priced retailers, such as Wal-Mart, Target, and Kohl's, have long used centralized checkouts at the front of their stores. But department stores have traditionally placed cash registers deep within each department. By centralizing the checkout areas, these department stores hope to reduce staff and customer complaints arising from slow or poor checkout service. For instance, JCPenney is testing a plan to place checkout stations at its entrances and move others close to aisles.[12] The Bon Marche, division of Federated Department Stores, Inc., and Sears are also experimenting with centralized checkouts.

Walls Since retail space is often scarce and expensive, many retailers have successfully increased their ability to store extra stock, display merchandise, and creatively present a message by utilizing wall space. Merchandise can be stored on shelving and racks. The merchandise can be coordinated with displays, photographs, or graphics featuring the merchandise. At Nike Town, for instance, a lot of merchandise is displayed relatively high on the wall. Not only does this allow the merchandise to "tell a story," but customers feel more comfortable because they aren't crowded by racks or other people, and they can get a perspective of the merchandise by viewing it from a distance.

SPACE PLANNING

Allocation of space to departments, categories, and finally items is one of store planners' and buyers' most complicated and difficult decisions. They must answer four questions:

1. What items, vendors, categories, and departments should be carried?

2. How much of each item should be carried?

3. How much space should the merchandise take?

4. Where should the merchandise be located?

Chapter 12's discussion of assortment planning gave procedures for answering the first two questions. Now let's examine the last two.

Store planners in conjunction with buyers typically start by allocating space based on sales productivity. For instance, if knit shirts represent 15 percent of the total expected sales for the men's furnishings department, they will initially get

15 percent of the space. Store planners must then adjust the initial estimate on the basis of the following five factors.

1. *How profitable is the merchandise?* The marginal analysis approach for allocating promotional expenditures to merchandise (as Chapter 16 related) also works for allocating space. In this situation, a retailer allocates space to SKUs to maximize the merchandise category's profitability. Similar analyses can be performed for departments. Consider, for instance, allocating space for beer in a supermarket. At first glance, you might think that since Bud Light is the most profitable brand, it should get all the space. But if the store took this approach, it would lose sales on less profitable brands—and it might even lose customers who are loyal to other brands. Thus, the store should experiment with different shelf space allocations until it finds a combination that maximizes profits for the category. Optimal space allocation systems are part of the planogramming programs discussed later in this section.

2. *How will the planned inventory turnover and the resulting stock-to-sales ratio affect how many SKUs will normally be carried in stock?* Recognize that (as in the merchandise budget plan) monthly inventory levels vary according to seasonal demands, holidays, and so on. Buyers and store planners must allocate space on the basis of these seasonal needs rather than yearly averages. They must also estimate the proportion of merchandise kept on display versus backup stock. Merchandise kept as backup stock in a storage area takes much less room.

3. *How will the merchandise be displayed?* Merchandise and fixtures go hand in hand. Store planners design fixtures to go with the merchandise. But once the fixtures are in the store, buyers must consider the fixtures' physical limitations when assigning space to merchandise. Will the shirts be displayed on hangers or folded on tables? Customers can more easily examine merchandise on hangers, but this display method takes more space.

4. *Will the location of certain merchandise draw the customer through the store, thus facilitating purchases?* Notice, for instance, the way the mannequins and fixtures are placed on the perimeter of the department in the Bloomingdale's I.C.B. boutique in the picture on page 596. Throughout this section, we examine how retailers locate departments and specific merchandise to facilitate purchases of impulse and complementary products.

5. *What items does the retailer wish to emphasize?* Suppose that a buyer has decided that this season will be particularly strong in knit shirts rather than woven shirts. The buyer purchases accordingly and plans additional advertising. As a result, knit shirts must also receive additional selling and display space. Retailing View 18.3 examines how some department stores have cut back on their space to designers like Tommy Hilfiger so they can make room for other merchandise.

We've discussed in general terms how store planners and buyers plan the space requirements for a category like knit shirts or beer. Similar decisions are made for larger groups of merchandise like classifications, departments, and even merchandise groups. Now let's examine how retailers decide where to locate departments and where to locate merchandise within departments.

Location of Departments

Sandy Williams recently went to Nordstrom for a haircut. On the way in, she stopped at the cosmetics counter to buy makeup. Then on the escalator, she spotted a red dress to examine on her way out. Before leaving the store, she stopped by the lingerie department to browse.

Did she simply take a random walk through the store? Probably not. The departments she shopped, like all Nordstrom departments, are strategically located to maximize the entire store's profits. The profit-generating abilities of various locations within a store aren't equal. (Remember the retail site selection techniques in Chapter 8?) The more traffic through a department, the better the location will be. Unfortunately, every department can't be situated in the best location. Retailers must consider additional demand-generating factors and the interrelations between departments when determining their locations.

Relative Location Advantages   The best locations within the store depend on the floor location, the position within a floor, and its location relative to traffic aisles, entrances, escalators, and so on. In general, in a multilevel store, a space's value decreases the farther it is from the entry-level floor. Since men aren't generally as avid shoppers for clothing as women, many large stores locate the men's department on the entry-level floor to make shopping as easy as possible.

The position within a floor is also important when assigning locations to departments. The best locations are those closest to the store's entrances, main aisles, escalators, and elevators. Williams spotted the red dress because she could see it from the escalator. Multilevel stores often place escalators so customers must walk around the sales floor to get to the next level. Also, most customers turn right when entering a store or floor, so the right side will be especially desirable space. Finally, most customers won't get all the way to the center of the store, so many stores use the racetrack design to induce people to move into the store's interior.

Impulse Products   **Impulse products** are products that are purchased without prior plans, like fragrances and cosmetics in department stores and magazines in supermarkets. They are almost always located near the front of the store, where they're seen by everyone and may actually draw people into the store.

RETAILING VIEW   Bloomingdale's Wrestles Tommy for Space

18.3

The Tommy Hilfiger men's section once sprawled 2,400 square feet in the center of Bloomingdale's flagship store in Manhattan. Surrounded by racks stuffed with khakis and plaid button-downs, interactive computer kiosks dispensed fashion tips. A wall of television screens flashed shots of Hilfiger models strutting along runways to the thump of loud rock music. That was 1998.

Building a solid shop inside a store offers a designer several advantages. It helps build consumer awareness. It also carves out a set area of floor space at the department store to insulate the designer from a lousy season. From the retailers' perspective, a designer shop helps attract customers into the store, makes a statement about the store's image, and often reduces design and construction costs since some designers pick up at least part of the tab.

Everyone seems like a winner until the brand begins to fade. Today, the same Tommy department comprises about 1,500 square feet in a cramped, lower-profile section next to an escalator. The video screens are gone. In their place: sedate, ivory-colored walls and standard-issue, easy-listening music piped in from above. It's a scene playing out in department stores across the country. Over the last decade, designers took over much of the stores' prime space—with the stores footing a lot of the bill.

Now those same boutiques are struggling as shoppers bypass them for specialty retailers such as Club Monaco and Banana Republic as well as big discounters such as Wal-Mart. And the department stores, convinced they ceded too much, are trying to wrest back control from their designer tenants.

Source: Rebecca Quick, "Department Stores and Designer Tenants Jockey over Real Estate," *The Wall Street Journal*, October 2000, pp. A1, A10. Copyright 2001 by Dow Jones & Co. Inc. Reproduced with permission of Dow Jones & Co. Inc. via Copyright Clearance Center.

Williams didn't plan her makeup purchase, for example, but decided she wanted some once she saw the displays.

Demand/Destination Areas   Children's, expensive specialty goods, and furniture departments as well as customer-service areas like beauty salons, credit offices, and photography studios are usually located off the beaten path—in corners and on upper floors. Due to the exclusive nature of Steuben glass, for instance, the department is typically located in a low-traffic area of high-end stores like Neiman Marcus. A purchase of one of these unique, expensive pieces requires thought and concentration. Customers would probably become distracted if the department were adjacent to a high-traffic area. Besides, customers looking for these items will find them no matter where they're located in the store. These departments are known as **demand/destination areas** because *demand* for their products or services is created before customers get to their *destination*. Thus, they don't need prime locations.

Why are cosmetics counters typically located near the front of the store?

Seasonal Needs   Some departments need to be more flexible than others. For instance, it's helpful to locate winter coats near sportswear. Extra space in the coat department can be absorbed by sportswear or swimwear in the spring when the bulk of the winter coats have been sold.

Physical Characteristics of Merchandise   Departments that require large amounts of floor space, like furniture, are often located in the less desirable locations. Some departments, like curtains, need significant wall space, while others, like shoes, require accessible storage.

Adjacent Departments   After trying on the red dress, Williams found a complementary scarf and stockings nearby. Retailers often cluster complementary products together to facilitate multiple purchases.

Some stores are now combining traditionally separate departments or categories to facilitate multiple purchases using market-basket analysis. Stores are laid out according to the way customers purchase merchandise rather than traditional categories or departments (see Chapter 11 for details).

The Special Case of Grocery Stores   Now consider some of the special departmental location issues in grocery stores. As a customer walks in, there is typically a barricade—checkout stands and grocery carts—that pushes the customer to the right. The items almost everyone buys—milk, eggs, butter, and bread—are in the back left-hand corner. To get to them, a shopper tending to turn right must travel half the store's perimeter and go past every aisle.

Most supermarkets steer shoppers immediately into the produce section because they can see and feel and smell the food there. The smell of fresh fruits and vegetables gets a shopper's mouth watering, and the best grocery store customer is a hungry one.

The first produce item the customer sees is apples, and that's no accident either. Apples are by far the most popular item in produce, almost twice as popular as oranges, bananas, lettuce, and potatoes, the runners-up.

Supermarkets place private-label brands and other higher margin items to the right of national brands. Most languages are read from left to right. So a customer will see the higher-priced national brand first and then see and purchase the lower-priced private-label item on the right.

Evaluating a Departmental Layout Envirosell, a consulting firm in New York, has made a science out of determining the best ways to lay out a department or a store.[13] Although the firm utilizes lots of hidden video cameras and other high-tech equipment, its most important research tool is a piece of paper called a *track sheet* in the hands of individuals called *trackers*. Trackers follow shoppers and note everything they do. They also make inferences on consumer behavior based on what they've observed. Here are just a few of the things they have learned:

- *Avoid the butt-brush effect.* The butt-brush effect was discovered at New York City's Bloomingdale's. The researchers taped shoppers attempting to reach the tie rack while negotiating an entrance during busy times. They noticed that after being bumped once or twice, most shoppers abandoned their search for neckwear. The conclusion: Shoppers don't like to shop when their personal space is invaded.
- *Place merchandise where customers can readily access it.* This sounds easy and obvious. But until little kids and old ladies were observed having difficulty reaching treats for their pets in a supermarket, they were typically stocked near the top of the shelf.
- *Allow a transition zone.* The first product encountered in a department isn't always going to have an advantage. Sometimes, just the opposite will happen. Allowing some space between the entrance of a store and a product gives it more time in the shopper's eye as he or she approaches it. For instance, cosmetics firms don't usually want to occupy the first counter inside the entrance of a department store because they know that women want a little privacy.

Location of Merchandise within Departments: The Use of Planograms

To determine where merchandise should be located within a department, retailers of all types generate maps known as planograms. A **planogram** is a diagram created from photographs, computer output, or artists' renderings that illustrate exactly where every SKU should be placed (see planogram on page 604). Planograms should be visually appealing, represent the manner in which a consumer shops (or the manner in which the retailer would like the consumer to shop), and embody the strategic objectives of the corporation. There is an art and a science to planogramming. The art is in ensuring that the proper visual impact and presentation is maintained; the science is in the financial analysis portion. A planogrammer must be able to balance these two elements in creating a planogram that is best for the store. Technology for computer-generated planograms can be somewhat sophisticated, lending to advanced analysis, or it can be fairly simple.[14]

Electronic planogramming requires the user to input model numbers or UPC codes, product margins, turnover, sizes of product packaging or actual pictures of the packaging, and other pertinent information into the program. The computer plots the planogram based on the retailer's priorities. For instance, if the retailer wants prime shelf space given to products that produce the highest turns, the computer will locate those products in the best locations. If margins are more important, the computer will determine the shelf space priority and the optimal number of SKUs to stock in that space. Adjustments to the initial planogram can be made to see how additional space or different fixtures would affect the productivity measures.

Planograms are also useful for merchandise that doesn't fit nicely on gondolas in a grocery or discount store. The Gap and Banana Republic, for instance, provide their managers with photographs and diagrams of how merchandise should be displayed.

Recent advances in computer graphics and three-dimensional modeling allow planograms to be designed, tested with consumers, and changed, all in a "virtual" shopping environment.[15] A consumer can view merchandise on a computer screen that looks like a real store. The shopper can "pick up" a package by touching its image on the monitor. She can turn the package so it can be examined from all sides. If she wants, she can "purchase" the product. In the meantime, the computer tracks the time spent shopping for and examining a particular product and the quantity purchased. Armed with this information, the retailer can test the effectiveness of different planograms.

Recall from Chapter 6 that a productivity measure (the ratio of an output to an input) determines how effectively a retailer uses a resource. Most retailers measure the productivity of space using **sales per square foot,** since rent and land purchases are assessed on a per-square-foot basis. But sometimes it's more efficient to measure profitability using **sales per linear foot.** For instance, in a grocery store, most merchandise is displayed on multiple shelves on long gondolas. Since the shelves have approximately the same width, only the length, or linear dimension, is relevant. Sales per cubic foot may be most appropriate for stores like wholesale clubs that use multiple layers of merchandise.

When allocating space to merchandise or a department, a retail manager must consider the profit impact on all departments. Remember, the objective is to maximize the profitability of the store, not just a particular department. Since the cosmetics department has a relatively high gross margin per square foot, should management give it more or less space? The answer depends on whether profitability of the entire store would increase if more space were allotted to this department. A department may be achieving its high productivity ratio because it's too small and has only a limited assortment. Conversely, a department may actually be too large—if so, almost as much profit could be generated with a smaller space. The buyer could buy smaller quantities more often, thereby making more productive use of a smaller space. If management decides to shrink the cosmetics department more space would be available for, say, female apparel. If the store's overall profitability would be increased by making this move, then the retailer should do it.

Retailing View 18.4 describes how Marketmax's planogramming system automated Marks & Spencer's food business.

Leveraging Space: In-Store Kiosks

In-store kiosks are spaces located within stores containing a computer connected to the store's central offices or to the Internet. In-store kiosks can be used by customers or salespeople to order merchandise through a retailer's electronic channel, check on product availability at distribution centers or other stores, get more information about the merchandise, and scan bar codes to check the prices.

RETAILING VIEW | Marks & Spencer Automates Planograms

18.4

Marks & Spencer is a large retailer of clothing, home goods, and high-quality food products. Its food business, specializing in high-quality convenience fresh foods such as sandwiches and home dinners, occupies a prominent position in the UK food retailing sector.

The retailer is continuously updating its product range with new products developed in conjunction with leading manufacturers of short-life food products. Until recently, this has been a labor-intensive process. For example, the adjustment of 50 displays in 50 stores requires 2,500 new individual planograms, unless some stores are exactly the same, which is not likely. It would take between 80 and 100 full-time planogrammers to implement weekly changes in their 310 stores.

Seeking to turn its food supply chain from a push to a pull system, the $4.2 billion retailer began looking for a planogramming system for its fresh-food products. Store-specific space plans were necessary to reflect each store's individual needs.

Working with Massachusetts-based Marketmax, the 310-unit retailer was able to develop an automated planogramming system that could optimize weekly fresh-

food assortments to individual stores, as well as improve product layout and customer satisfaction.

The Marks & Spencer/Marketmax system calculates an optimal layout by determining how many shelf-facings are needed for each SKU in each store. At the same time, the system maintains a consistent look but considers specific fixtures and store layouts.

By implementing automated space planning, Marks & Spencer has greatly increased the productivity of its centralized space planning team and gained control over store layout and product presentation. It can now do weekly plans with 20 planogrammers—and it does a much better job. Product placement is now more efficient and uniform throughout the chain, and customers can more easily find specific products. This is of particular importance to Marks & Spencer as many of its customers shop in more than one of its stores, particularly in clusters of high density (e.g., six stores within a two-mile radius).

Sources: "A New Approach to Merchandise Planning, Distribution and Logistics," March 2002, www.groceryheadquarters.com; and RetailSystems Alert, www.retailsystems.com, February 1, 2002.

Marks & Spencer in the U.K. utilizes a sophisticated planogram system by Marketmax to help layout and evaluate the productivity of their food business.

Retailers are interested in installing these kiosks because they create a synergy between the store and the Internet site (see Chapter 3). Kiosks provide additional assortment choices that aren't available in stores. For instance, Radio Shack makes slower-moving electronic accessories available at its kiosks so it doesn't have to carry them in the stores.[16] The typical Staples store has 9,000 SKUs, compared to 100,000 offered via in-store kiosks.[17]

Kiosks can encourage customers to stay in the store longer and, it is hoped to spend more money. For instance, allowing customers to check their e-mail is an added service that will endear customers to the store. Sears and Starbucks are examining programs to deliver more or less conventional Internet access in their respective stores.[18]

Do kiosks cannibalize store sales? Yes, but only initially. Shoppers who purchase in stores and online from an in-store kiosk tend to buy more. When REI installed in-store kiosks, it found that customers who shop both online and in the store spend 22 percent more than those who buy only from traditional stores.[19] Staples provided an incentive to store managers to push the use of kiosks. Online sales are credited to the stores from which they're placed.[20]

There are downsides to making investments in these kiosks, however. First, they can be expensive—anywhere from $3,000 to $25,000 per kiosk.[21] Second, once the investment is made, there is no guarantee that customers will use them. Gap Inc. abandoned its program because shoppers didn't use them enough.[22] Finally, there are significant costs in maintaining the kiosks—making sure they are working properly.

This kiosk is in the Dickson Cyber Mall in the Kowloon Station (transit/subway station) in Hong Kong. This couple is ordering clothing at their "dress me up interactive kiosk."

REFACT

Eighty percent of all major retailers plan to install kiosks in their stores.[23]

MERCHANDISE PRESENTATION TECHNIQUES

Many methods are available to retailers for effectively presenting merchandise to the customer. To decide which is best for a particular situation, store planners must consider the following four issues.

First, and probably most important, merchandise should be displayed in a manner consistent with the store's image. For instance, some traditional men's stores display dress shirts by size so all size 15 1/2–34 shirts are together. Thus, the customer can easily determine what's available in his size. This is consistent with a no-nonsense image of the store. Other stores keep all color/style combinations together. This presentation evokes a more fashion-forward image and is more aesthetically pleasing, but it forces the customer to search in each stack for his size.

Second, store planners must consider the nature of the product. Basic jeans can easily be displayed in stacks, but skirts must be hung so the customer can more easily examine the design and style.

Third, packaging often dictates how the product is displayed. Discount stores sell small packages of nuts and bolts, for example, but some hardware stores still sell individual nuts and bolts. Although the per-unit cost is significantly higher for the packages, self-service operations don't have adequate personnel to weigh and bag these small items.

Finally, products' profit potential influences display decisions. For example, low-profit/high-turnover items like back-to-school supplies don't require the same elaborate, expensive displays as Mont Blanc fountain pens.

In this section, we'll examine some specific presentation techniques. Then we'll describe the fixtures used in these merchandise presentations. First, however, consider how Diesel stores seem to break all the store design rules (Retailing View 18.5).

Idea-Oriented Presentation

Some retailers successfully use an **idea-oriented presentation**—a method of presenting merchandise based on a specific idea or the image of the store. Women's fashions, for instance, are often displayed to present an overall image

---

RETAILING VIEW   **Diesel Breaks Store Design Rules**

18.5

Diesel jeans stores are so confusing that it begs a question: Are they the worst run stores in America, or is something sneaky going on? The answer: something sneaky.

Walking into a Diesel jeans store feels a lot like stumbling into a rave. Techno music pounds at a mind-rattling level. A television plays a videotape of a Japanese boxing match, inexplicably. There are no helpful signs pointing to men's or women's departments and no obvious staff members in sight.

Customers who are industrious, or simply brave enough to reach the "denim bar"—Diesel's name for the counter separating shoppers from the wall of jeans at the back of the store—find themselves confronted by 35 different types of blue jeans costing $115 to $210 a pair. A placard intending to explain the various options looks like an organizational chart for a decent-size federal agency.

The company, which was founded in Italy in 1978 and last year had its sales climb 40 percent from 2000, reaching $500 million, is one of the brands most successfully exploiting young men's new fashion interest—expensive denim.

While large clothing retailers like Banana Republic and The Gap have standardized and simplified the layout of their stores in an effort to put customers at ease, Diesel's approach is based on the unconventional premise that the best customer is a disoriented one. They intentionally designed an intimidating, user-unfriendly environment so that customers have to interact with the sales staff.

Indeed, it is at just the moment when a potential Diesel customer reaches a kind of shopping vertigo that members of the company's intimidatingly with-it staff make their move. Acting as salespeople-in-shining-armor, they rescue—or prey upon, depending on one's point of view—wayward shoppers.

Source: Warren St. John, "A Store Lures Guys Who Are Graduating from Chinos," *New York Times*, July 14, 2002, www.nytimes.com. Reprinted by permission.

Diesel's approach to merchandising is based on the unconventional premise that the best customer is a disoriented one. They intentionally designed an intimidating, user-unfriendly environment so that customers have to interact with the sales staff.

or idea. Also, furniture is combined in room settings to give customers an idea of how it would look in their homes. Individual items are grouped to show customers how the items could be used and combined. This approach encourages the customer to make multiple complementary purchases.

Manufacturers with strong consumer demand are often merchandised together in the boutique layout described earlier in this chapter. This technique is similar to the idea-oriented presentation in that merchandise made by the same vendor will tend to be coordinated. Some apparel manufacturers like Liz Claiborne and Jaeger coordinate both style and color to influence multiple purchases within the line and enhance the line's overall image.

Style/Item Presentation

Probably the most common technique of organizing stock is by style or item. Discount stores, grocery stores, hardware stores, and drugstores employ this method for nearly every category of merchandise. Also, many apparel retailers use this technique. When customers look for a particular type of merchandise, such as sweaters, they expect to find all items in the same location.

Arranging items by size is a common method of organizing many types of merchandise, from nuts and bolts to apparel. Since the customer usually knows the desired size, it's easy to locate items organized in this manner.

Color Presentation

A bold merchandising technique is by color. For instance, in winter months women's apparel stores may display all white cruisewear together to let customers know that store is "the place" to purchase clothing for their winter vacation.

Price Lining

Organizing merchandise in price categories, or *price lining* (when retailers offer a limited number of predetermined price points within a classification), was discussed in Chapter 15. This strategy helps customers easily find merchandise at the price they wish to pay. For instance, men's dress shirts may be organized into three groups selling for $30, $45, and $60.

Vertical Merchandising

Another common way of organizing merchandise is **vertical merchandising.** Here merchandise is presented vertically using walls and high gondolas. Customers shop much as they read a newspaper—from left to right, going down each column, top to bottom. Stores can effectively organize merchandise to follow the eye's natural movement. Retailers take advantage of this tendency in several ways. Many grocery stores put national brands at eye level and store brands on lower shelves because customers scan from eye level down. Finally, retailers often display merchandise in bold vertical bands of an item. For instance, you'll see vertical columns of towels of the same color displayed in a department store or a vertical band of yellow-and-orange boxes of Tide detergent followed by a band of blue Cheer boxes in a supermarket.

Tonnage Merchandising

As the name implies, **tonnage merchandising** is a display technique in which large quantities of merchandise are displayed together. Customers have come to equate tonnage with low price, following the retail adage "stock it high and let it fly." Tonnage merchandising is therefore used to enhance and reinforce a store's price image. Using this display concept, the merchandise itself is the display. The retailer hopes customers will notice the merchandise and be drawn to it. For instance, before many holidays, grocery stores use an entire end of a gondola (i.e., an end cap) to display six-packs of Pepsi.

Frontage Presentation

Often, it's not possible to create effective displays and efficiently store items at the same time. But it's important to show as much of the merchandise as possible. One solution to this dilemma is the **frontal presentation,** a method of displaying merchandise in which the retailer exposes as much of the product as possible to catch the customer's eye. Book manufacturers, for instance, make great efforts to create eye-catching covers. But bookstores usually display books exposing only the spine. To create an effective display and break the monotony, book retailers often face the cover out like a billboard to catch the customer's attention. A similar frontal presentation is achieved on a rack of apparel by simply turning one item out to show the merchandise.

Fixtures

The primary purposes of fixtures are to efficiently hold and display merchandise. At the same time, they must help define areas of a store and encourage traffic flow. Fixtures must be in concert with the other physical aspects of the store, such as floor coverings and lighting, as well as the overall image of the store. For instance, in stores designed to convey a sense of tradition or history, customers automatically expect to see lots of wood rather than plastic or metal fixtures. Wood mixed with metal, acrylic, or stone changes the traditional orientation. The rule of thumb is that the more unexpected the combination of textures, the more contemporary the fixture.

Fixtures come in an infinite variety of styles, colors, sizes, and textures, but only a few basic types are commonly used. For apparel, retailers utilize the straight rack, rounder, and four-way. The mainstay fixture for most other merchandise is the gondola.

The **straight rack** consists of a long pipe suspended with supports going to the floor or attached to a wall (Exhibit 18–4A). Although the straight rack can hold a lot of apparel, it's hard to feature specific styles or colors. All the customer can see is a sleeve or a pant leg. As a result, straight racks are often found in discount and off-price apparel stores.

A **rounder,** also known as a **bulk fixture** or **capacity fixture,** is a round fixture that sits on a pedestal (Exhibit 18–4B). Although smaller than the straight rack, it's designed to hold a maximum amount of merchandise. Since they're easy to move and they efficiently store apparel, rounders are found in most types of apparel stores. But as with the straight rack, customers can't get a frontal view of the merchandise.

A **four-way fixture,** also known as a **feature fixture,** has two crossbars that sit perpendicular to each other on a pedestal (Exhibit 18–4C). This fixture holds a large amount of merchandise and allows the customer to view the entire garment. The four-way is harder to properly maintain than the rounder or straight rack, however. All merchandise on an arm must be of a similar style and color, or the customer may become confused. Due to their superior display properties, four-way fixtures are commonly utilized by fashion-oriented apparel retailers.

EXHIBIT 18–4
Four Fixture Types

(A) Straight rack

(B) Rounder

(C) Four-way

(D) Gondola

Gondolas are extremely versatile (Exhibit 18–4D). They're used extensively, but not exclusively, in grocery and discount stores to display everything from canned foods to baseball gloves. Gondolas are also found displaying towels, sheets, and housewares in department stores. Folded apparel too can be efficiently displayed on gondolas, but because the items are folded, it's even harder for customers to view apparel on gondolas than on straight racks.

ATMOSPHERICS

Atmospherics refers to the design of an environment via visual communications, lighting, colors, music, and scent to stimulate customers' perceptual and emotional responses and ultimately to affect their purchase behavior.[25] Many retailers have discovered the subtle benefits of developing atmospherics that complement other aspects of the store design and the merchandise. Research has shown that it is important for these atmospheric elements to work together, for example, the right music with the right scent.[26] Now let's explore some basic principles of good atmospheric design and examine a few new, exciting, and somewhat controversial trends.

Visual Communications

Visual communications—comprising graphics, signs, and theatrical effects, both in the store and in windows—help boost sales by providing information on products and suggesting items or special purchases. Signs and graphics also help customers find a department or merchandise. Graphics, such as photo panels, can add personality, beauty, and romance to the store's image.

Retailers should consider the following seven issues when designing visual communications strategies for their stores.

Coordinate Signs and Graphics with the Store's Image Signs and graphics should act as a bridge between the merchandise and the target markets. The colors and tone of the signs and graphics should complement the merchandise. Colors that aren't pleasing to the overall presentation will visually destroy a good display and detract from the merchandise. For example, a pastel pink sign in a store selling nautical supplies would not be as appropriate as bold red, white, and blue. Also, a formally worded black-and-white rectangular sign doesn't relate to a children's display as well as a red-and-yellow circus tent design does. Color combinations should appeal to specific target customers or highlight specific merchandise—primary colors for kids, hot vivid colors for teens, pastels for lingerie, brights for sportswear, and so forth. At the Athlete's Foot for Her, for instance, sliding graphic panels highlight the lifestyles of the target market while at the same time display product and conceal inventory (see photo on this page).

At Athlete's Foot for Her, sliding graphic panels highlight the target market's lifestyles.

Inform the Customer Informative signs and graphics make merchandise more desirable. For instance, Athlete's Foot uses a series of freestanding prints to explain its five-step fitting process.[27] The process begins with a foot scanner, which ensures a perfect fit for each customer. Then after analyzing customers' activity levels, in-store personnel help them choose the right shoes and determine the best way to tie shoes to fit their feet.

Use Signs and Graphics as Props Using signs or graphics that masquerade as props, or vice versa, is a great way to unify a theme and merchandise for an appealing overall presentation. For instance, Alphabet Soup, a small Iowa-based chain of educational toy stores, uses lively graphics and props in a unifying theme that is consistent with the store's image.

Keep Signs and Graphics Fresh Signs and graphics should be relevant to the items displayed and shouldn't be left in the store or in windows after displays are removed. Forgotten, faded, and fraught with water spots, such signs do more to disparage a store's image than sell merchandise. Also, new signs imply new merchandise.

Limit the Copy of Signs   Since a sign's main purpose is to catch attention and inform customers, the copy is important to its overall success. As a general rule, signs with too much copy won't be read. Customers must be able to quickly grasp the information on the sign as they walk through the store.

Use Appropriate Typefaces on Signs   Using the appropriate typeface is critical to a sign's success. Different typefaces impart different messages and moods. For instance, carefully done calligraphy in an Old English script provides a very different message than a hastily written price-reduction sign.

Create Theatrical Effects   Part of any theatrical set are special effects that transcend yet coordinate the other elements. To heighten store excitement and enhance store image, retailers have borrowed from the theater. Theatrical effects may be simple extensions of more functional elements, like signs using colored fabric to identify a department. Or bold graphic posters or photographs can be hung from ceilings and walls to decorate, provide information, or camouflage less aesthetic areas, such as the ceiling structure.

Lighting

Good lighting in a store involves more than simply illuminating space. Lighting is used to highlight merchandise, sculpt space, and capture a mood or feeling that enhances the store's image. Lighting can also be used to downplay less attractive features that can't be changed. Having the appropriate lighting has been shown to positively influence customer shopping behavior.[28]

Galleri Orrefors Kosta Boda on Manhattan's Madison Avenue uses special lighting to make their limited and one-of-a kind glass sculptures POP.

Highlight Merchandise   A good lighting system helps create a sense of excitement in the store. At the same time, lighting must provide an accurate color rendition of the merchandise. A green silk tie should look the same color in the store as at the office. Similarly, lighting should compliment the customer. A department store's cosmetics area, for instance, requires more expensive lighting than the bare fluorescent lighting found in most grocery stores because it has to compliment the customer and make her skin look natural.

Another key use of lighting is called **popping the merchandise**—focusing spotlights on special feature areas and items. Using lighting to focus on strategic pockets of merchandise trains shoppers' eyes on the merchandise and draws customers strategically through the store. At Galleri Orrefors Kosta Boda on Manhattan's Madison Avenue, for example, limited and one-of-a-kind glass sculptures are highlighted with special lighting (see the picture on this page).

To downplay an unsightly ceiling, Sentry Foods in Madison, Wisconsin, intentionally kept the ceiling in dark contrast to the rest of the store.

Capture a Mood and Maintain an Image   Traditionally, U.S. specialty and department stores have employed incandescent lighting sources to promote a warm and cozy ambience.[29] Overall lighting sources were reduced and accent lighting was pronounced to call attention to merchandise and displays. It was meant to feel like someone's home—dim lighting overall, with artwork and other areas of interest highlighted.

The European method of lighting can now be found in the most exclusive specialty stores of Rodeo Drive and Bal Harbour and even some department stores like Bloomingdale's.[30] European stores have long favored high light levels, cool colors, and little contrast or accent lighting. European lighting design has been more bold, stark, and minimal than in the United States, creating a very different mood and image than the softer incandescent lighting.

Downplay Features   Lighting can hide errors and outmoded store designs. At Sentry Foods in Madison, Wisconsin, product lighting is very high compared to the rest of the store. The ceiling was intentionally kept dark to downplay an unsightly concrete ceiling. (See the picture on this page.)

Color

The creative use of color can enhance a retailer's image and help create a mood. Research has shown that warm colors (red and yellow) produce opposite physiological and psychological effects from cool colors (blue and green), which are opposite on the color spectrum.[31] For example, red and other warm colors have been found to increase blood pressure, respiratory rate, and other physiological responses. As we translate these findings to a retail store environment, warm colors are thought to attract customers and gain attention, yet they can be distracting and even unpleasant. Fast-food restaurants often use warm colors to facilitate rapid turnover.

In contrast, research has shown that cool colors, like blue or green, are relaxing, peaceful, calm, and pleasant. Thus, cool colors may be most effective for retailers selling anxiety-causing products, such as expensive shopping goods, or services like those provided at a dentist's office.

Music

Like color and lighting, music can either add or detract from a retailer's total atmospheric package. Unlike other atmospheric elements, however, music can be easily changed. Several companies, such as AEI (www.aeimusic.com) are now using Internet-based technologies to individualize stores' musical repertoires with the daily ebbs and flows of customer demographics.[32] Let's say a retailer with 1,000 stores across the United States wants to play jazzy music in the morning and adult contemporary in the afternoon, but just for stores on the East Coast. After all, most of its morning shoppers are older, whereas the afternoon shoppers are more in the 35–40 range. For its West Coast stores, it wants modern rock in the morning and Caribbean beats in the afternoon. And in Texas, it's country music all day, every day.

Other retailers use volume and tempo for crowd control. For instance, Dick Clark's American Bandstand Grills play faster and louder songs at times of the day when the restaurant wants to turn more tables.[33] Although research in grocery stores indicates that music's tempo and volume don't significantly influence patrons' shopping time or purchase amount,[34] other research has shown that the presence of music positively affects customers' attitudes toward the store.[35]

Retailers can also use music to affect customers' behavior. Music can control the pace of store traffic, create an image, and attract or direct consumers' attention. For instance, Limited Too, a division of Limited Group, has created a signature sound to appeal to its target market—8- to 14-year-old girls. It is a mix of hip hop, R&B, pop, and swing featuring artists such as Brandy, Fastball, and Brian Setzer Orchestra.[36] The Disney Stores pipe in soundtracks from famous Disney movies that are tied directly to the merchandise.

Like variations in lighting, fixtures, and other store design elements, changing music in different parts of a store can help alter a mood or appeal to different markets. The Joslins department store in Englewood, Colorado, has an environmental sound system with 10 different sound zones aimed at emotionally connecting with customers.[37] As customers move from one department to another, the sounds quickly change from modern jazz in men's contemporary to big band in men's suiting, hip hop and rock in juniors, and classical in fragrance. Activewear brings the outdoors in with wind and bird sounds. The home area features campy 1930s and 40s music conjuring up mom, the smells of the kitchen, and home. Each zone is treated to its own specialty store ambience of sound.

Scent

Many buying decisions are based on emotions, and smell has a large impact on our emotions. "Smell, more than any other sense, is a straight line to feelings of happiness, hunger, disgust, and nostalgia—the same feelings marketers want to tap."[38] Research has shown that scent, in conjunction with music, has a positive impact on impulse buying behavior and customer satisfaction.[39] Another study reported that although the presence or absence of a scent affects consumers' evaluations and behaviors about a store, the nature of the scent itself appears to be less important.[40] That is, scents that are neutral were found to produce better perceptions of the store than no scent. But it didn't matter much which scent was used. Similarly, the intensity of the scent, within a reasonable range so as not to become offensive, did not dramatically affect the results. Importantly, the research found that customers in the scented store perceived that they had spent less time in the store than subjects in the no-scent store. And subjects in the no-scent store perceived having spent significantly more time in the store than they actually did; subjects in the scented condition did not show this discrepancy. This study suggests that stores using scents may improve customers' subjective shopping experience by making them feel that they are spending less time examining merchandise or waiting for sales help or to check out.

Although the research in this area is not definitive,[41] retailers from Federated Department Stores to The Limited are experimenting with scents in their stores. Most of the proof is anecdotal. Consider, for instance, that in the Aventura Shoe Store in Chicago's Watertower Place, sales tripled after it introduced an aroma that combined leather, citrus, and baby powder.

Retailers must carefully plan the scents that they use, depending on their target market. Gender of the target customer should be taken into account in deciding on the intensity of the fragrance in a store. Research has shown that women have a better ability to smell than men. Age and ethnic background are also factors. As people get older, their sense of smell decreases. Half of all people over 65 and three-quarters over 80 have almost no smell at all.[42]

How are these scents introduced into the store? Retailers can use time-release atomizers available through janitorial supply vendors, or computerized heating and air-conditioning systems. But polymer pellets soaked in a fragrance and placed in ordinary light fixtures, where the lamp's heat activates the scent, are the most economical way to disperse fragrance.

SUMMARY

This chapter examined issues facing store designers, buyers, and merchandise planners. A good store layout helps customers find and purchase merchandise. Several types of layouts are commonly used by retailers. The grid design is best for stores in which customers are expected to explore the entire store, such as grocery stores and drugstores. Racetrack designs are more common in large upscale stores like department stores. Free-form designs are usually found in small specialty stores and within large stores' departments. Store planners also must carefully delineate different areas of the store. Feature areas, bulk of stock, and walls each have their own unique purpose but must also be coordinated to create a unifying theme.

There's more to assigning space to merchandise and departments than just determining where they'll fit. Departments' locations should be determined by the overall profitability and inventory turnover goals of the assortment, type of product, consumer buying behavior, the relationship with merchandise in other departments, and the physical characteristics of the merchandise. Planograms, both manual and computer-generated, are used to experiment with various space allocation configurations to determine the most productive use of space. When evaluating the productivity of retail space, retailers generally use sales per square foot. In-store kiosks are leveraging retail space by connecting customers to the Internet.

Several tricks of the trade can help retailers present merchandise to facilitate sales. Retailers must attempt to empathize with the shopping experience and answer the following questions: How does the customer expect to find the merchandise? Is it easier to view, understand, and ultimately purchase merchandise when it's presented as a total concept or presented by manufacturer, style, size, color, or price? Ultimately, retailers must decide on the appropriate type of fixture to use for a particular purpose.

Retailers utilize various forms of atmospherics—graphics, signs, and theatrical effects—to facilitate sales. Strategies involve lighting, colors, music, and scent.

KEY TERMS

atmospherics, *609*
boutique layout, *594*
bulk fixture, *608*
capacity fixture, *608*
cash-wrap areas, *598*
checkout area, *598*
demand/destination area, *601*
end cap, *596*
feature area, *595*
feature fixture, *608*
four-way fixture, *608*
free-form layout, *594*

freestanding fixture, *596*
frontal presentation, *608*
gondola, *609*
grid layout, *592*
idea-oriented presentation, *606*
impulse product, *600*
in-store kiosks, *604*
loop, *593*
planogram, *602*
point-of-purchase (POP) area, *598*

point-of-sale area, *598*
popping the merchandise, *611*
promotional aisle or area, *596*
racetrack layout, *593*
rounder, *608*
sales per linear foot, *603*
sales per square foot, *603*
straight rack, *608*
tonnage merchandising, *607*
vertical merchandising, *607*

GET OUT & DO IT!

1. INTERNET EXERCISE Go to your favorite multichannel retailer's Internet site. Evaluate its degree of simplicity, its ease of navigation, its readability and use of color, and its consistency with the image of its bricks-and-mortar store.

2. INTERNET EXERCISE: Go to www.marketmax.com; www.metirimensus.com (Apollo), www.wellingtoninc.com (Pegman), and www.acnielsen.com (Spaceman). Evaluate their planogram programs. Which one would you choose?

3. GO SHOPPING: Go into a store of your choice and evaluate the store layout, design, and visual merchandising techniques employed. Explain your answers to the following questions:

(*a.*) In general, are the store layout, design and visual merchandising techniques used consistent with the exterior of the store and location?

(*b.*) Is the store's ambience consistent with the merchandise presented and the customer's expectations?

(*c.*) Does the store look like it needs to be redesigned? Do you think it needs a face lift, update, remodel, or renovation?

(*d.*) To what extent are the store's layout, design, and merchandising techniques flexible?

(*e.*) Notice the lighting. Does it do a good job in highlighting merchandise, structuring space, capturing a mood, and downplaying unwanted features?

(f.) Are the fixtures consistent with the merchandise and the overall ambience of the store? Are they flexible?

(g.) Evaluate the store's signage. Does it do an effective job in selling merchandise?

(h.) Has the retailer used any theatrical effects to help sell merchandise?

(i.) Does the store layout help draw people through the store?

(j.) Evaluate the retailer's use of empty space.

(k.) Has the retailer taken advantage of the opportunity to sell merchandise in feature areas?

(l.) Does the store make creative use of wall space?

(m.) What type of layout does the store use? Is it appropriate for the type of store? Would another type of layout be better?

(n.) Ask the store manager how the profitability of space is evaluated; for example, profit per square foot. Is there a better approach?

(o.) Ask the store manager how space is assigned to merchandise. Critically evaluate the answer.

(p.) Ask the store manager if planograms are used. If so, try to determine what factors are considered when putting together a planogram.

(q.) Has the retailer employed any techniques for achieving greater space productivity, such as using the cube, downsizing gondolas and racks, and minimizing nonselling space?

(r.) Are departments in the most appropriate locations? Would you move any departments?

(s.) What method(s) has the retailer used for organizing merchandise? Is this the best way? Suggest appropriate changes.

DISCUSSION QUESTIONS AND PROBLEMS

1. One of the fastest growing sectors of the population is the over-60 age group. But these customers may have limitations in their vision, hearing, and movement. How can retailers develop store designs with the older population's needs in mind?

2. Assume you have been hired as a consultant to assess a local discount store's space productivity. What analytical tools would you use to assess the situation? What suggestions would you make to improve the store's space productivity?

3. What are the different types of design that can be used in a store layout? Why are some stores more suited for a particular type of layout than others?

4. Generally speaking, departments located near entrances, on major aisles, and on the main level of multilevel stores have the best profit-generating potential. What additional factors help to determine the location of departments? Give examples of each factor.

5. A department store is building an addition. The merchandise manager for furniture is trying to convince the vice president to allot this new space to the furniture department. The merchandise manager for men's clothing is also trying to gain the space. What points should each manager use when presenting his or her rationale?

6. As a manager for a large department store, you are responsible for ADA compliance. But your performance evaluation is based on bottom-line profitability. How would you make sure your store is accessible to people in wheelchairs and at the same time not lose any sales?

7. Describe the ways in which designing a website is similar to and different from designing a store.

8. Which retailers are particularly good at presenting their store as theater? Why?

9. Lighting in a store has been said to be similar to makeup on a model. Why?

10. Why do supermarkets put candy, gum, and magazines at the front of the store?

SUGGESTED READINGS

Baker, Julie; A. Parasuraman; Dhruv Grewal; and Glen Voss. "The Influence of Multiple Store Environment Cues on Perceived Merchandise Value and Patronage Intentions." *Journal of Marketing* 66 (April 2002), pp. 120–41.

Barr, Vilma, and Katherine Field. *Stores: Retail Display and Design.* PBC International, 1999.

Bell, Judith, and Kat Ternus. *Silent Selling: Practices and Effective Strategies for Visual Merchandising.* 2nd ed. New York: Fairchild Books, November 2000.

Bone, Paula Fitzgerald, and Pam Scholder Ellen. "Scent in the Marketplace: Explaining a Fraction of Olfaction." *Journal of Retailing* 75, no. 2 (Summer 1999), pp. 243–62.

Greely, Dave, and Joe Cataudella. *Creating Stores on the Web.* Peachpit Press, December 1999.

Green, William R. *Retail Store: Design and Construction.* Universe, Incorporated, 2000.

Huant, Jeffrey. "Future Space: A New Blueprint for Business Architecture." *Harvard Business Review*, April 2001, reprint R0104L.

Hui, Michael E.; Laurette Dube; and Jean-Charles Chebat. "The Impact on Consumers' Reactions to Waiting for Services." *Journal of Retailing* 73, no. 1 (1997), pp. 87–104.

Kaufman-Scarborough, Carol. "Reasonable Access for Mobility-Disabled Persons Is More than Widening the Door." *Journal of Retailing* 75, no. 4 (Winter 1999), pp. 479–508.

Mattila, Anna S., and Jochen Wirtz. "Congruency of Scent and Music as a Driver of In-Store Evaluations and Behavior." *Journal of Retailing* 77, no. 2 (Summer 2001), pp. 273–90.

Spangenberg, Eric R.; Ayn E. Crowley; and Pamela W. Henderson. "Improving the Store Environment: Do Olfactory Cues Affect Evaluations and Behaviors?" *Journal of Marketing* 60, no. 2 (Spring 1996), pp. 67–80.

Underhill, Paco. *Why We Buy: The Science of Shopping.* New York: Simon & Schuster, 2000.

Customer Service

19

CHAPTER

EXECUTIVE BRIEFING | Philip Wee, General Manager, IKEA Singapore

"As a general manager in IKEA Singapore, I try to encourage a strong service culture within a self-help concept. We believe that superior service is not just confined to the customer service department but requires the input of every single employee at every level. Each employee in IKEA is empowered to make decisions on the spot so as to give the customer a superior experience. I believe that a positive service attitude starts with the president of any business. When top management is service-oriented, everyone in the company is service-oriented and the company can distinguish itself from the rest of the pack.

"I was first exposed to the benefits of great customer service on my first job in Ship Operations in Singapore. Due to its high level of service, Singapore is recognized as the best port in the world. After working for nine years in Ship Operations, I relocated to London. I was so impressed with the merchandise, creative displays, and general level of excitement in the Oxford Street stores that I wanted to be part of it. So I decided to pursue a career in retailing. My first job in retailing was at Selfridges of London. The company believes in developing its employees, and I learned a lot about buying, displaying, and selling merchandise.

"My most memorable lesson in service quality came when Roy Stevens, then CEO and managing director of Selfridges, said to me: 'Our customers judge us and the quality of our merchandise by the state of our fitting rooms.' His successor, Tim Daniels, taught me the value of nurturing young trainees, as they are the successors and the future.

QUESTIONS

- What services do retailers offer customers?
- How can customer service build competitive advantage?
- How do customers evaluate a retailer's service?
- What activities does a retailer have to undertake to provide high-quality customer service?
- How can retailers recover from a service failure?

"When I returned to Singapore in 1983, I started managing department stores and specialty stores such as Mothercare and Habitat. My seven years with Robinsons on Orchard Road Singapore were full of excitement and satisfaction. Robinsons leads the retail scene in Singapore with superior customer care, and it was exciting and rewarding to get public recognition and industry awards.

"Looking back, retailing has been very rewarding and satisfying for me. I started as a porter and am today the general manager. Retailing in Asia is in a very exciting stage of growth and change. There is no better time than now for good people to enter into this profession."

Suppose you are surfing the Internet for a digital camera. At www.realcheapcameras.com, a hypothetical site, you are asked to type in the name of a specific brand and model number you want. Then a price with shipping charges is quoted and you are asked for your credit card number and a shipping address. In contrast, when you go to www.circuitcity.com, you can buy a specific digital camera or review the specifications for different cameras or look through the reviews of different cameras. You can then go to a store to see the cameras, get additional information about the cameras from a sales associate, and look at accessories, such a carrying case and additional memory units. Circuit City is providing some valuable services to its customers—services customers can not get from RealCheapCameras.com.

Customer service is the set of activities and programs undertaken by retailers to make the shopping experience more rewarding for their customers. These activities increase the value customers receive from the merchandise and services they purchase. All employees of a retail firm and all elements of the retailing mix provide services that increase the value of merchandise. For example, employees in the distribution center contribute to customer service by making sure that the merchandise is in stock. The employees responsible for store location and design contribute by increasing the customer's convenience in getting to the store and finding merchandise in the store.

EXHIBIT 19–1
Services Offered by
Retailers

Acceptance of credit cards	Parking
Alterations of merchandise	Personal assistance in selecting
Assembly of merchandise	merchandise
ATM terminals	Personal shoppers
Bridal registry	Play areas for children
Check cashing	Presentations on how to use
Child care facilities	merchandise
Credit	Provisions for customers with
Delivery to home or work	special needs (wheelchairs,
Demonstrations of merchandise	translators)
Display of merchandise	Repair services
Dressing rooms	Rest rooms
Extended store hours	Return privileges
Signage to locate and identity merchandise	Rooms for checking coats and
Facilities for shoppers with special needs	packages
(physically handicapped)	Shopping carts
Layaway plans	Special orders
Gift wrapping	Warranties

REFACT

Seventy-three percent
of consumers attribute
their best customer
service experience to
store employees.
Conversely, 81 percent
of consumers attribute
their worst customer
service experience to
employees.[1]

Exhibit 19–1 lists some of the services provided by retailers. Most of these services furnish information about the retailer's offering and make it easier for customers to locate and buy products and services. Services, such as alterations and the assembly of merchandise, actually change merchandise to fit the needs of a specific customer. Some of these services are derived from the retailer's store design or website or from policies established by the retailer. However, this chapter focuses on some of the most important personalized services provided by sales associates interacting directly with customers.

In the next section, we discuss retailers' opportunities to develop strategic advantage through customer service. Then we examine how retailers can take advantage of this opportunity by providing high-quality service.

STRATEGIC ADVANTAGE THROUGH CUSTOMER SERVICE

REFACT

The word *service* is
from the Latin term
servus, meaning "slave."[3]

REFACT

Nearly one out of four
shoppers who have a
bad service experience
will either tell their
friends about their
experience and urge
them not to shop there
or will stop shopping at
the store.[4]

Nordstrom, Disney World, McDonald's, Amazon.com, and Marriott differentiate their retail offerings, build customer loyalty, and develop a sustainable competitive advantage by providing excellent customer service (see Chapter 5). Good service keeps customers returning to a retailer and generates positive word-of-mouth communication, which attracts new customers.[2]

Providing high-quality service is difficult for retailers. Automated manufacturing makes the quality of most merchandise consistent from item to item. For example, all Super Twist Skil electric screwdrivers look alike and typically perform alike. But the quality of retail service can vary dramatically from store to store and from salesperson to salesperson within a store. It's hard for retailers to control the performance of employees who provide the service. A sales associate may provide good service to one customer and poor service to the next customer.

In addition, most services provided by retailers are intangible—customers can't see or feel them. Clothing can be held and examined, but the assistance provided by a sales associate or an electronic agent can't. Intangibility makes it hard to provide and maintain high-quality service because retailers can't count, measure, or check service before it's delivered to customers.

The challenges of providing consistent high-quality service provides an opportunity for a retailer to develop a sustainable competitive advantage. For example, Nordstrom devotes much time and effort to developing an organizational culture that stimulates and supports excellent customer service. Competing department stores would like to offer the same level of service but find it hard to match Nordstrom's performance.[5]

Customer Service Strategies

Customization and standardization are two approaches retailers use to develop a sustainable customer service advantage. Successful implementation of the customized approach relies on the performance of sales associates or the degree to which customer interactions can be customized using an electronic channel. The standardization approach relies more on policy, procedures, and store and website design and layout.[6]

Customization Approach   The **customization approach** encourages service providers to tailor the service to meet each customer's personal needs.[7] For example, sales associates in specialty stores help individual customers locate appropriate apparel and accessories.

Some retailers are introducing a human element into their electronic channel. At Lands' End, customers can simply click on a button and chat—referred to as *instant messaging*—with a service provider. Lands' End was one of the first retailers to offer live chats with service represents on its website. Sales representatives respond within 20 seconds when a customer clicks the Help button. Over 200 of Lands' End's 2,500 service representatives are dedicated to providing the service. Lands' End has found that the average order increases 8 percent when customers use the instant messaging service.[8]

Lands' End customizes the service it offers by providing the opportunity for live chats with a service representative.

Inspired by the Disney approach to customer service, Target launched its Guest Service program. Customers are treated as guests, with store employees as their hosts. Stock clerks are taught that helping guests isn't an intrusion on their work. Several employees called *guest ambassadors* roam the store looking for customers who need assistance. Employees are also empowered to make sure that guests have a satisfying experience in the store. If the shelf price isn't on an item, checkout clerks can take the customer's word for prices up to $20. The guest doesn't have to wait for the clerk to check the price with someone on the floor. When customers return merchandise without a receipt, employees at the Guest Service counter simply ask them how much they paid for the merchandise and give a refund.[9]

The customized approach typically results in most customers' receiving superior service. But the service might be inconsistent because service delivery

The office supply category killer on the left uses its signage as part of a standarization approach for providing customer service, while Target's (right) sales associate uses a customized approach tailoring service to match the needs of individual customers.

depends on the judgment and capabilities of the service providers. Some service providers are better than others, and even the best service providers can have a bad day. In addition, providing the customized service is costly since it requires more well-trained service providers or complex computer software.

Standardization Approach The **standardization approach** is based on establishing a set of rules and procedures and being sure that they are implemented consistently. By strict enforcement of these procedures, inconsistencies in the service are minimized. Through standardization, customers receive the same food and service at McDonald's restaurants across the globe. The food may not be exactly what customers want, but it's consistent and served in a timely manner at a low cost.

Store or website design and layout also play an important role in the standardization approach. In many situations, customers don't need the services employees provide. They know what they want to buy, and their objective is to find it in the store and buy it quickly. In these situations, retailers offer good service by providing a layout and signs that enable customers to locate merchandise easily, by having relevant information in displays, and by minimizing the time required to make a purchase.[11]

Retailing View 19.1 shows how IKEA uses a standardized service approach with some unique elements to attract customers expecting the traditional customized approach employed in furniture retailing.

Cost of Customer Service As indicated previously, providing high-quality service, particularly customized service, can be very costly. For over 100 years, the Savoy Hotel in London maintained a special place in the hearts of the world's elite. Maids switch off vacuum cleaners when greeting guests entering the hallway in the morning. Each floor has it own waiter on duty from 7 A.M. to 3 P.M. Guests can get cotton sheets instead of the standard Irish linen sheets if they wish. Preferred fruits are added to the complimentary fruit bowl in each room. Rooms are personally furnished for customers who regularly have extended stays at the hotel. At times, the hotel staff moves the customers' furniture, including personal pictures, from storage into their rooms when they arrive.

But this high level of personal attention is very costly to provide. The Savoy employed about three people for each of its 200 rooms, about double the average for a London hotel. These services resulted in annual losses, and the hotel was eventually sold to a corporation that eliminated some of the services.

In many cases, however, good customer service can actually reduce costs and increase profits. A study by Andersen Consulting estimates that it costs 5 to 15 times more to acquire a new customer than to generate repeat business from present customers, and a 5 percent increase in customer retention can increase profits by 25 to 40 percent.[12] Thus, it costs a business much less to keep its existing customers satisfied and sell more merchandise to them than it does to sell to people who aren't buying from the business now.

Retailers need to consider the costs and benefits of service policies. For example, many retailers are reconsidering their "no questions asked" return policy. Home Depot's policy was to take back all merchandise and give cash back. Now, if customers don't have a receipt, they can only get store credit. If they have a receipt, they can get cash back. Target now requires that customers have a receipt and return the merchandise in 90 days to get a credit. In addition, for some consumer electronics products customers must pay a 15 percent restocking charge. Retailers are seeing too many big-screen TVs coming back the day after the Super Bowl and too many prom dresses coming back the day after prom night.[13]

In the next section, we examine how customers evaluate service quality.

REFACT

About 6 percent of all merchandise purchased in stores is returned.[14]

IKEA Offers a Different Type of Service than Traditional Furniture Stores   RETAILING VIEW

19.1

IKEA is a global furniture retailer based in Sweden. Its concept of service differs from the traditional furniture store. The typical furniture store has a showroom displaying some of the merchandise sold in the store. Complementing the inventory are books of fabric swatches, veneers, and alternative styles customers can order. Salespeople assist customers in going through the books. When the customer makes a selection, an order is placed with the factory, and the furniture is delivered to the customer's home in six to eight weeks. This system maximizes customization, but the costs are high.

In contrast, IKEA uses a self-service model based on extensive in-store displays. At information desks in the store, shoppers can pick up a map of the store plus a pencil, order form, clipboard, and tape measure. After studying the catalog and displays, customers proceed to a self-service store and locate their selections using codes copied from the sales tags. Every product available is displayed in over 70 roomlike settings throughout the 150,000-square-foot warehouse store. Thus, customers don't need a decorator to help them picture how the furniture will go together. Adjacent to the display room is a warehouse with ready-to-assemble furniture in boxes that customers can pick up when they leave the store.

Although IKEA uses a "customers do it themselves" approach, it does offer some services that traditional furniture stores do not, such as in-store child care centers and information on the quality of the furniture. Toddlers can be left in a supervised ballroom filled with 50,000 brightly colored plastic balls. There are changing rooms in each store complete with bottle warmers and disposable diaper dispensers. Displays cover quality of products in terms of design features and materials, with demonstration of testing procedures.

Sources: "IKEA Remains King in the Hearts and Purses," *Cabinet Maker*, February 22, 2002, pp. 17–21; and "Then and Now: IKEA," *Chain Store Age*, March 1, 1998, p. 114.

CUSTOMER EVALUATION OF SERVICE QUALITY

When customers evaluate retail service, they compare their perceptions of the service they receive with their expectations. Customers are satisfied when the perceived service meets or exceeds their expectations. They're dissatisfied when they feel the service falls below their expectations.[15]

Role of Expectations

Customer expectations are based on a customer's knowledge and experiences.[16] For example, customers do not expect to get an immediate response to a letter or even a telephone call, but they expect to get a response to an e-mail the next time they turn on their computer.

Technology is dramatically changing the ways in which customers and firms interact. Customers now can interact with companies through automated voice response systems and place orders and check on delivery through the Internet. But customers still expect dependable outcomes, easy access, responsive systems, flexibility, apologies, and compensation when things go wrong. In other words, they still want good service. Now they just expect this level of service even when people are not involved.[18]

Expectations vary depending on the type of store. Customers expect a supermarket to provide convenient parking, to be open from early morning to late evening, to have a wide variety of fresh and packaged food that can be located easily, to display products, and to offer fast checkout. They don't expect the supermarket to have store employees stationed in the aisle to offer information about groceries or how to prepare meals. On the other hand, when these same customers shop in a specialty store, they do expect the store to have knowledgeable salespeople who can provide information and assistance.

Since expectations aren't the same for all types of retailers, a customer may be satisfied with low levels of actual service in one store and dissatisfied with high service levels in another store. For example, customers have low service expectations for self-service retailers such as discount stores and supermarkets. Wal-Mart provides an unusual service for a discount store: An employee stands at the entrance to each store, greeting customers and answering questions. Because this service is unexpected in a discount store, customers evaluate Wal-Mart's service positively, even though the actual level of service is far below that provided by a typical specialty store.

Department stores have many more salespeople available to answer questions and provide information than Wal-Mart does. But customer service expectations are also higher for department stores. If department store customers can't locate a salesperson quickly when they have questions or want to make a purchase, they're dissatisfied.

When retailers provide unexpected services, they build a high level of customer satisfaction, referred to as *customer delight*.[19] Some examples of unexpected positive service experiences are

1. A restaurant that sends customers who have had too much to drink home in a taxi and then delivers their cars in the morning.

The Wal-Mart employee greets customers when they enter the store and answers their questions. Since this service is unexpected in a discount store, it creates a favorable perception of Wal-Mart's customer service.

2. A men's store that sews numbered tags on each garment so the customer will know what goes together.

3. A gift store that keeps track of important customer dates and suggests appropriate gifts.

 Customer service expectations vary around the world. Although Germany's manufacturing capability is world renowned, its poor customer service is also well known. People wait years to have telephone service installed. Many restaurants do not accept credit cards, and customers who walk into stores near closing time often receive rude stares. Customers typically have to bag merchandise they buy themselves. Because Germans are unaccustomed to good service, they don't demand it. But as retailing becomes global and new foreign competitors enter, German retailers are becoming more concerned.

On the other hand, the Japanese expect excellent customer service. In the United States, it's said that "the customer is always right." In Japan the equivalent expression is *okyakusama ha kamisama desu*, "the customer is God." When a customer comes back to a store to return merchandise, he or she is dealt with even more cordially than when the original purchase was made. Customer satisfaction isn't negotiable. The customer is never wrong. Even if the customer misused the product, retailers feel they were responsible for not telling the customer how to use it properly. The first person in the store who hears about the problem must take full responsibility for dealing with the customer, even if the problem involved another department.

This salesperson at the Kelo Department Store is providing the excellent personalized service that Japanese customers expect. The computer system scans the customer's feet and suggests shoes that will provide a good fit.

Perceived Service

Customers base their evaluations of store service on their perceptions. While these perceptions are affected by the actual service provided, service due to its intangibility is often hard to evaluate accurately. Five customer service characteristics that customers use to evaluate service quality are reliability, assurance, tangibility, empathy, and responsiveness.[20] Some cues that customers use to assess these service characteristics are shown below:

- Reliability: Accuracy of billing, meeting promised delivery dates.
- Assurance (trust): Guarantees and warranties, return policy.
- Tangibility: Appearance of store, salespeople.
- Empathy: Personalized service, receipts of notes and e-mails, recognition by name.
- Responsiveness: Returning calls and e-mails, giving prompt service.

Retailing View 19.2 describes how the Broadmoor Hotel maintains its five-star rating by focusing on the five service characteristics listed above.

As Retailing View 19.2 indicates, employees can play an important role in customer perceptions of service quality.[21] Customer evaluations of service quality are often based on the manner in which store employees provide the service, not just the outcome. Consider the following situation: A customer goes to a store to return an electric toothbrush that isn't working properly. In one case, company policy requires the employee to ask the customer for a receipt, check to see if the receipt shows the toothbrush was bought at the store, examine the toothbrush to see if it really doesn't work properly, ask a manager if a refund can be provided, complete some paperwork, and finally give the customer the amount paid for the toothbrush in cash. In a second case, the store employee simply asks the customer how much he paid and gives him a cash refund. The two cases have the same outcome: The customer gets a cash refund. But the customer might be dissatisfied in the first case because the employee appeared not to trust the customer and took so much time providing the refund. In most situations, employees have a great effect on the process of providing services and, thus, on the customer's eventual satisfaction with the services.

RETAILING VIEW   The Broadmoor Manages Service Quality for Five-Star Rating

19.2

The Broadmoor Hotel and Spa in Colorado Springs, Colorado, has a record of 41 consecutive years of five-star ratings from the *Mobil Travel Guide*. Perry Goodbar, vice president of marketing for the Broadmoor emphasizes, "It's the people who truly make this place special. Exceptional service quality begins with exceptional people."

Reliability. Every new Broadmoor employee, before ever encountering a customer, attends a two-and-a-half day orientation session and receives an employee handbook. Making and keeping promises to customers is a central part of this orientation. Employees are trained to always give an estimated time for service, whether it be room service, laundry service, or simply estimating how long it will take to be seated at one of the restaurants. When an employee makes a promise, he or she keeps the promise. Employees are trained to never guess if they don't know the answer to a question. Inaccurate information only frustrates customers. When an employee is unable to answer a question accurately, he or she immediately contacts someone who can.

Assurance. The Broadmoor conveys trust by empowering its employees. An example of an employee empowerment policy is the service recovery program. If a guest problem arises, employees are given discretionary resources to rectify the problem or present the customer with something special to help mollify them. For example, if a meal is delivered and there's a mistake in the order or how it was prepared, a waiter can offer the guest a free item such as a dessert or, if the service was well below expectations, simply take care of the bill. Managers then review expenses in order to understand the nature of the problem and to help prevent it from occurring again.

Tangibility. One of the greatest challenges for the Broadmoor in recent years has been updating rooms built in the early part of the twentieth century to meet the needs of twenty-first century visitors. To accomplish this, it spent $200 million between 1992 and 2002 in improvements renovating rooms and adding a new outdoor pool complex.

Empathy. One approach used to demonstrate empathy is by personalizing communications. Employees are instructed to always address a guest by name, if possible. To accomplish this, employees are trained to listen and observe carefully to determine a guest's name. Subtle sources for this information include convention name tags, luggage ID tags, credit cards, or checks. In addition, all phones within the Broadmoor display a guest's room number and name on a screen.

Responsiveness. Every employee is instructed to follow the HEART model of taking care of problems. First, an employees must "Hear what a guest has to say." Next, they must "Empathize with them," and then, "Apologize for the situation." Finally, they must "Respond to the guest's needs" by "Taking action and following up."

Source: Andrew J. Czaplewski, Eric M. Olson, and Stanley F. Slater, "Applying the RATER Model for Service Success: Five Service Attributes Can Help Maintain Five-Star Ratings," *Marketing Management,* January–February 2002, pp. 14–20. Reprinted by permission.

THE GAPS MODEL FOR IMPROVING RETAIL SERVICE QUALITY

The Gaps Model (Exhibit 19–2) indicates what retailers need to do to provide high-quality customer service.[22] When customers' expectations are greater than their perceptions of the delivered service, customers are dissatisfied and feel the quality of the retailer's service is poor. Thus, retailers need to reduce the **service gap** (the difference between customers' expectations and perceptions of customer service) to improve customers' satisfaction with their service.

Four factors affect the service gap:

1. **Knowledge gap:** The difference between customer expectations and the retailer's perception of customer expectations.

2. **Standards gap:** The difference between the retailer's perceptions of customers' expectations and the customer service standards it sets.

3. **Delivery gap:** The difference between the retailer's service standards and the actual service provided to customers.

4. **Communication gap:** The difference between the actual service provided to customers and the service promised in the retailer's promotion program.

Gaps Model for Improving Retail Service Quality | **EXHIBIT 19–2**

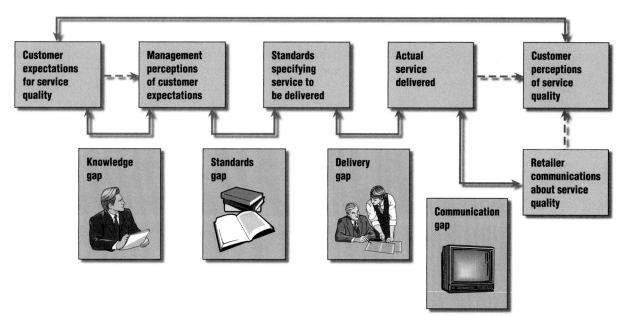

628

These four gaps add up to the service gap. The retailer's objective is to reduce the service gap by reducing each of the four gaps. Thus, the key to improving service quality is to (1) understand the level of service customers expect, (2) set standards for providing customer service, (3) implement programs for delivering service that meets the standards, and (4) undertake communication programs to accurately inform customers about the service offered by the retailer. The following sections describe these gaps and methods for reducing them.

KNOWING WHAT CUSTOMERS WANT: THE KNOWLEDGE GAP

The most critical step in providing good service is to know what the customer wants. Retailers often lack accurate information about what customers need and expect. This lack of information can result in poor decisions. For example, a supermarket might hire extra people to make sure the shelves are stocked so customers will always find what they want, but it may fail to realize that customers are most concerned about waiting at the checkout line. From the customer's perspective, the supermarket's service would improve if the extra employees were used to open more checkout lines rather than to stock shelves.

Retailers can reduce the knowledge gap and develop a better understanding of customer expectations by undertaking customer research, increasing interactions between retail managers and customers, and improving communication between managers and employees who provide customer service.

Researching Customer Expectations and Perceptions

Market research can be used to better understand customers' expectations and the quality of service provided by a retailer. Methods for obtaining this information range from comprehensive surveys to simply asking some customers about the store's service.

Comprehensive Studies   Some retailers have established programs for assessing customers' expectations and service perceptions. For example, every year JCPenney sales associates pass out questionnaires to shoppers in each store and its mall. Shoppers are asked about the service and merchandise offered by Penney and by competing department stores in the mall. Over 50,000 completed questionnaires are collected and analyzed. Since the same questionnaire is used each year, Penney can track service performance, determine whether it's improving or declining, and identify opportunities for improving service quality. The annual customer service profile is so important to Penney that it is used as part of store managers' performance evaluation.

Gauging Satisfaction with Individual Transactions
Another method for doing customer research is to survey customers immediately after a retail transaction has oc-

The first step in providing good customer service is understanding customer expectations. This sales associate is conducting a survey in a mall to assess customer expectations.

curred. For example, Sears employees who deliver and assemble furniture in homes ask customers to complete a short survey describing how helpful, friendly, and professional the employees were. Airlines periodically ask passengers during a flight to evaluate the ticket-buying process, flight attendants, in-flight service, and gate agents.

Customer research on individual transactions provides up-to-date information about customers' expectations and perceptions. The research also indicates the retailer's interest in providing good service. Since the responses can be linked to a specific encounter, the research provides a method for rewarding employees who provide good service and correcting those who exhibit poor performance.

Customer Panels and Interviews Rather than surveying many customers, retailers can use panels of 10 to 15 customers to gain insights into expectations and perceptions. For example, some store managers might meet once a month for an hour with a select group of customers who are asked to provide information about their experiences in the stores and to offer suggestions for improving service.

To reduce the knowledge gap, some supermarket managers go through the personal checks they receive each day and select customers who've made large and small purchases. They call these customers and ask them what they liked and didn't like about the store. With small purchasers, they probe to find out why the customers didn't buy more. Could they find everything they wanted? Did they get the assistance they expected from store employees?

Some retailers have consumer advisory boards composed of a cross section of their preferred customers. Members of the board complete questionnaires three to four times a year on subjects like holiday shopping problems, in-store signage, and service quality. In exchange for their inputs, members receive gift certificates.

Interacting with Customers Owner-managers of small retail firms typically have daily contact with their customers and thus have accurate firsthand information about them. In large retail firms, managers often learn about customers through reports so they miss the rich information provided by direct contact with customers.

Stanley Marcus, founder of Neiman Marcus, felt managers can become addicted to numbers and neglect the merchandise and customers. He uses suspenders as an example of how buyers can make poor decisions by only looking at the numbers. Originally, suspenders came in two sizes: short and long. By analyzing the numbers, buyers realized they could increase turnover by stocking one-size-only suspenders. The numbers looked good, but the store had a lot of dissatisfied customers. With only one size, short men's pants fell down, and the fit was uncomfortable for tall men. "It comes back to the fact that the day is still only 24 hours long, and if you're a retailer, you've still got to spend some of those 24 hours with your customers and your products. You can't allow the computer to crowd them out as crucial sources of information."[24]

Customer Complaints Complaints allow retailers to interact with their customers and acquire detailed information about their service and merchandise. Handling complaints is an inexpensive means to isolate and correct service problems.[25]

Catalog/electronic retailer L. L. Bean keeps track of all complaints and reasons for returned merchandise. These complaints and returns are summarized daily and given to customer service representatives so they can improve service. For example, a customer who returns a sweater might indicate the sweater was too large or the color tone differed from the picture in the catalog. With this information, customer service representatives can inform other customers who place an order for the sweater that it tends to be large and has a slightly different color than shown in the catalog. The information can also be used by buyers to improve vendor merchandise.

Although customer complaints can provide useful information, retailers can't rely solely on this source of market information. Typically, dissatisfied customers don't complain. To provide better information on customer service, retailers need to encourage complaints and make it easy for customers to provide feedback about their problems. For example, some retailers set up a complaint desk in a convenient location where customers can get their problems heard and solved quickly.

Feedback from Store Employees Salespeople and other employees in regular contact with customers often have a good understanding of customer service expectations and problems. This information will improve service quality only if the employees are encouraged to communicate their experiences to high-level managers who can act on it.

Some retailers regularly survey their employees, asking questions like

1. What is the biggest problem you face in delivering high-quality service to your customers?

2. If you could make one change in the company to improve customer service, what would it be?

Using Customer Research

Collecting information about customer expectations and perceptions isn't enough. The service gap is reduced only when retailers use this information to improve service. For example, store managers should review the suggestions and comments made by customers daily, summarize the information, and distribute it to store employees and managers.

Feedback on service performance needs to be provided to employees in a timely manner. Reporting the July service performance in December makes it hard for employees to reflect on the reason for the reported performance.

Finally, feedback must be prominently presented so service providers are aware of their performance. For example, at Marriott, front desk personnel's performance feedback is displayed behind the front desk, while restaurant personnel's performance feedback is displayed behind the door to the kitchen.

SETTING SERVICE STANDARDS: THE STANDARDS GAP

After retailers gather information about customer service expectations and perceptions, the next step is to use this information to set standards and develop systems for delivering high-quality service. Service standards should be based on customers' perceptions rather than internal operations. For example, a supermarket chain might set an operations standard of a warehouse delivery every day to each store. But frequent warehouse deliveries may not result in more merchandise on the shelves or improve customers' impressions of shopping convenience.

To close the standards gap, retailers need to (1) commit their firms to providing high-quality service, (2) develop innovative solutions to service problems, (3) define the role of service providers, (4) set service goals, and (5) measure service performance.

Commitment to Service Quality

Service excellence occurs only when top management provides leadership and demonstrates commitment. Top management must be willing to accept the temporary difficulties and even the increased costs associated with improving service quality. This commitment needs to be demonstrated to the employees charged with providing the service. For example, a Lands' End poster prominently displays the following inscription for employees who process customer orders:

> What is a Customer? A Customer is the most important person in this office . . . in person or by mail. A Customer is not dependent on us . . . we are dependent on her. A customer is not an interruption in our work . . . she is the purpose of it. We are not doing her a favor by serving her . . . she is doing us a favor by giving us an opportunity to do so. A Customer is not someone to argue or match wits with.[27]

Top management's commitment sets service quality standards, but store managers are the key to achieving those standards. Store managers must see that their efforts to provide service quality are noticed and rewarded. Providing incentives based on service quality makes service an important personal goal. Rather than basing bonuses only on store sales and profit, part of store managers' bonuses should be determined by the level of service provided. For example, some retailers use results of customer satisfaction studies to determine bonuses.

Lands' End emphasizes its commitment to high-quality service by providing an unconditional guarantee and setting high standards for employees.

Developing Solutions to Service Problems

Frequently, retailers don't set high service standards because they feel service improvements are either too costly or not achievable with available employees. This reflects an unwillingness to think creatively and to explore new approaches for improving service.

Innovative Approaches Finding ways to overcome service problems can improve customer satisfaction and, in some cases, reduce costs. For example, when customers complained about the long wait to check out, many hotels felt they couldn't do anything about the problem. Marriott, however, thought of a creative approach to address this service problem. It invented Express Checkout, a system in which a bill is left under the customer's door the morning before checkout

The Container Store uses the cartoon character Gumby to remind its employees that they need to be flexible and do whatever needs to be done to assist customers and fellow employees.

and, if the bill is accurate, the customer can check out by simply using the TV remote or calling the front desk and have the bill charged automatically to his or her credit card.

The Container Store emphasizes the importance of flexibility, teamwork, and empowerment using the cartoon character known as Gumby. A six-foot Gumby character is prominently displayed at the entrance to the corporate headquarters, and small versions are on managers' desks. The frequent use of the phrase "We have to be Gumby-like" reinforces the corporate standard of doing whatever needs to be done to provide service for customers and to help fellow employees complete tasks.[28] The Gumby cartoon character reinforces this point because it is so flexible, it can bend over backwards, in much the same way as Container Store employees bend over backwards to solve customer problems.

Using Technology Many retailers are installing kiosks with broadband Internet access in the stores. In addition to offering customers the opportunity to order merchandise not available in the store, kiosks can provide routine customer service, freeing employees to deal with more demanding customer requests and problems. For example, customers can use kiosks to locate merchandise in the store and to indicate whether specific products, brands, and sizes are available in the store. Kiosks can also be used to automate existing store services such as gift registry management, rain checks, film drop-off, and credit applications, and preorder service for bakeries and delicatessens.

Customers can use a kiosk to find out more information about products and how they are used. For example, a Home Depot customer can go to a kiosk to find out how to install a garbage disposal and to get a list of all of the tools and parts that are needed for the installation. A Best Buy customer can use a kiosk to provide side-by-side comparisons of two VCRs and to find more detailed information than is available from the shelf tag or from a sales associate. The customer can also access evaluations of the models as reported by *Consumer Reports.* The information provided by the kiosk could be tailored to specific customers by accessing the retailer's customer database. For example, a customer who is considering a new set of speakers might not remember the preamplifier purchased previously from Best Buy. This customer might not know whether the speakers are compatible with the preamplifier or what cables are needed to connect the new speakers. These concerns could be addressed by accessing the retailer's customer database through the kiosk.

Kiosks can also be used to provide customized solutions. For example, a customer, perhaps with the assistance of a salesperson, wants to design a home entertainment system. A kiosk could allow the customer to see what the system would look like after setup. Music store customers could use a kiosk to review and select tracks and make a custom compact disc. Finally, customers could use a kiosk to see how different color cosmetics would look on them without having to apply the cosmetics. These types of applications could complement the efforts of salespeople and improve the service they can offer to customers.[29]

Defining the Role of Service Providers

Managers can tell service providers that they need to provide excellent service, but not clearly indicate what excellent service means. Without a clear definition of the retailer's expectations, service providers are directionless.

The Ritz-Carlton Hotel Company, winner of the Malcolm Baldrige National Quality Award, has its "Gold Standards" printed on a wallet-size card carried by all employees. The card contains the hotel's motto ("We Are Ladies and Gentlemen Serving Ladies and Gentlemen"), the three steps for high-quality service (warm and sincere greeting, anticipation and compliance with guests' needs, and fond farewell), and 20 basic rules for Ritz-Carlton employees, including

Retailers are using technology to assist sales associates in providing customer service. This salesperson at Sam Dell Dodge reviews the cars in stock with a customer.

1. Any employee who receives a complaint "owns" the complaint.
2. Instant guest gratification will be ensured by all. React quickly to correct problems immediately.
3. "Smile. We are on stage." Always maintain positive eye contact.
4. Escort guests rather than giving directions to another area of the hotel.[30]

Setting Service Goals

To deliver consistent, high-quality service, retailers need to establish goals or standards to guide employees. Retailers often develop service goals based on their beliefs about the proper operation of the business rather than the customers' needs and expectations. For example, a retailer might set a goal that all monthly bills are to be mailed five days before the end of the month. This goal reduces the retailer's accounts receivable but offers no benefit to customers. Research undertaken by American Express showed customer evaluations of its service were based on perceptions of timeliness, accuracy, and responsiveness. Management then established goals (such as responding to all questions about bills within 24 hours) related to these customer-based criteria.

Employees are motivated to achieve service goals when the goals are specific, measurable, and participatory in the sense that they participated in setting them. Vague goals—such as "Approach customers when they enter the selling area" or "Respond to e-mails as soon as possible"—don't fully specify what employees should do, nor do such goals offer an opportunity to assess employee performance. Better goals would be "All customers should be approached by a salesperson within 30 seconds after entering a selling area" or "All e-mails should be responded to within three hours." These goals are both specific and measurable.

Employee participation in setting service standards leads to better understanding and greater acceptance of the goals. Store employees resent and resist goals arbitrarily imposed on them by management. Chapter 17 says more on goal setting.

Measuring Service Performance

Retailers need to continuously assess service quality to ensure that goals will be achieved.[31] Many retailers do periodic customer surveys to assess service quality. Retailers also use mystery shoppers to assess their service quality. **Mystery shoppers** are professional shoppers who "shop" a store to assess the service provided by store employees and the presentation of merchandise in the store. Some retailers use their own employees as mystery shoppers, but most contract with a firm to provide the assessment. Information typically reported by the mystery shoppers includes (1) How long before a sales associate greeted you? (2) Did the sales associate act as if he wanted your business? and (3) Was the sales associate knowledgeable about the merchandise?

Retailers typically inform salespeople that they have "been shopped" and provide feedback from the mystery shopper's report. Some retailers offer rewards to sales associates who receive high marks and schedule follow-up visits to sales associates who get low evaluations.[32]

MEETING AND EXCEEDING SERVICE STANDARDS: THE DELIVERY GAP

To reduce the delivery gap and provide service that exceeds standards, retailers must give service providers the necessary knowledge and skills, provide instrumental and emotional support, improve internal communications and reduce conflicts, and empower employees to act in the customers' and firm's best interests.[33] Retailing View 19.3 describes how chat rooms offered through an electronic channel enable customers to help the retailer to provide services to others.

Giving Information and Training

Store employees need to know about the merchandise they offer as well as their customers' needs. With this information, employees can answer customers' questions and suggest products. This also instills confidence and a sense of competence, which are needed to overcome service problems.

In addition, store employees need training in interpersonal skills. Dealing with customers is hard—particularly when they're upset or angry. All store employees, even those who work for retailers that provide excellent service, will encounter dissatisfied customers. Through training, employees can learn to provide better service and to cope with the stress caused by disgruntled customers.

Specific retail employees (salespeople and customer service representatives) are typically designated to interact with and provide service to customers. However, all retail employees should be prepared to deal with customers. For example, Walt Disney World provides four days of training for its maintenance workers, even though people can learn how to pick up trash and sweep streets in much less time. Disney has found that its customers are more likely to direct questions to maintenance people than to the clean-cut assistants wearing ASK ME, I'M IN GUEST RELATIONS buttons. Thus, Disney trains maintenance people to confidently handle the myriad of questions they'll be asked rather than responding, "Gee, I dunno. Ask her."[34]

Toys "R" Us assesses customer satisfaction with checkout service by counting the number of abandoned shopping carts with merchandise left in the store because customers became impatient with the time required to make a purchase. After the firm noticed an alarming increase in abandoned carts, it developed a unique program to reduce customers' time in line waiting to pay. Cashiers' motions while ringing up and bagging merchandise were studied. Based on this research, a training program was developed to show cashiers how to use their right

Retailers Use Customers to Deliver Services   RETAILING VIEW

19.3

Retailers use message boards and chat rooms on their websites to provide a valuable service by enabling customers to communicate with each other. **Message boards** are locations in an Internet site at which customers can post comments; **chat rooms** are locations at which customers can engage in interactive, real-time, text-based discussions. For example, Tomboy Tools (www.tomboytools.com) sells tools and provides home improvement information to women. Its website has bulletin boards, called Tool Talk, on which customers can post home improvement questions to which other customers offer solutions.

Authors and visitors to Amazon.com post comments and book reviews. Visitors to electronic travel retail sites frequently post messages inquiring about hotels, restaurants, and tourist attractions at places they will be visiting. Other customers who are familiar with the places respond to these inquiries with their suggestions.

Many electronic retailers offer public chat rooms. At The Knot site (www.theknot.com) people can enter a public chat room and have a real-time discussion about their experiences planning their weddings, seven days a week, 24 hours a day. In addition to the public chat room, The Knot also offers moderated chat rooms in which a staff member or a well-known expert on an issue leads an electronic discussion at specific times during the day.

| ONLINE STORE | TOOL PARTIES | TOMBOY TIPS | TOOL TALK | IN THE NEWS | THE TEAM |

Home   About Us   Contact Us   Trainer Login

TOOL TALK

VIEW CART 🛒

Paint and Wallpaper - Need a new look? Tell us all about it.

Karen

We are painting our very weathered exterior siding. We would like to thin the first coat because of getting into the cracks etc. better. Someone suggested that we could use vinegar for a thinning agent...I am a little hesitant of that. Would water be better?

Liz

I recently purchased a home that has wooden beams in the ceilings of the living room, the dining room and my bedroom. I would like to paint the lr and dr, but need much help! First, is there a way to lighten the dark stain on these beams? Second, if I paint the walls one color, should the panels between the beams be the same color. I want to go for an Oriental look – something like a gold color. Any suggestions appreciated!

Carrie

Does anytbody have a good tip for getting candle wax off of a painted wall??

Sources: Lorrie Grant, "Tomboy Tools Caters to Handy Women," *USA Today*, June 13, 2002, p. D3; Mary C. Hickey, "Click, Click, and a Way!" *Business Week*, March 29, 1999, p. 188; and Rochelle Rafter, "Can We Talk?" *The Industry Standard*, February 8, 1999, pp. 12–13.

636

REFACT

Two-thirds of the customers who put merchandise into an electronic shopping cart at a website do not complete the transaction.[35]

hand to record purchases on the POS terminal and their left hand to push merchandise along the counter. Counters were redesigned to have a slot lined with shopping bags in the middle of the counter. As the cashier pushes the merchandise along the counter, it drops into a bag. After the customer pays for the merchandise, the cashier simply lifts the bag from the slot and hands it to the customer, and a new bag pops into place.

To motivate cashiers to use the new system effectively, Toys "R" Us holds competitions in each store, district, and region to select the fastest cashiers. Regional winners receive a free vacation in New York City and participate in a competition at corporate headquarters to select a national champion.

Providing Instrumental and Emotional Support

Service providers need to have the **instrumental support** (the appropriate systems and equipment) to deliver the service desired by customers. For example, a hotel chain installed a computer system to speed up the checkout process. A study of the new system's effectiveness revealed that checkout time was not reduced because clerks had to wait to use the one stapler available to staple the customer's credit card and hotel bill receipts.

In addition to instrumental support, service providers need emotional support from their co-workers and supervisors. **Emotional support** involves demonstrating a concern for the well-being of others. Dealing with customer problems and maintaining a smile in difficult situations are psychologically demanding. Service providers need to be in a supportive, understanding atmosphere to deal with these demands effectively.[36] Retailing View 19.4 describes how Wing Zone reduces the emotional labor experienced by its service providers.

Improving Internal Communications and Providing Support

When providing customer service, store employees must often manage the conflict between customers' needs and the retail firms' needs.[37] For example, many retailers have a no-questions-asked return policy. Under such a policy, the retailer will provide a refund at the customer's request even if the merchandise wasn't purchased at the store or was clearly used improperly. When JCPenney inaugurated this policy, some employees refused to provide refunds on merchandise that had been worn or damaged by the customer. They were loyal Penney employees and didn't want customers to take advantage of their firm.

Retailers can reduce such conflicts by having clear guidelines and policies concerning service and by explaining the rationale for these policies. Once Penney employees recognized that the goodwill created by the no-questions-asked policy generated more sales than the losses due to customers' abusing the policy, they implemented the policy enthusiastically.

Conflicts can also arise when retailers set goals inconsistent with the other behaviors expected from store employees. For example, if salespeople are expected to provide customer service, they should be evaluated on the service they provide, not just on the sales they make.

Finally, conflicts can also arise between different areas of the firm. An auto dealer with an excellent customer service reputation devotes considerable effort to reducing conflict by improving communication between its employees. The dealership holds a town hall meeting in which employees feel free to bring up service problems. For example, the receptionist discussed her frustration when she couldn't locate a sales rep for whom a customer had called. The customer finally said, "Well, I'll just take my business elsewhere." She used this example to emphasize that sales reps should tell her when they slip out to run an errand. Now no one forgets that the front desk is the nerve center for the dealership.

Empowering Store Employees

Empowerment means allowing employees at the firm's lowest level to make important decisions concerning how service is provided to customers. When the employees responsible for providing service are authorized to make important decisions, service quality improves.[38] Retailing View 19.5 shows how an ice cream parlor empowers employees to be creative.

Nordstrom provides an overall objective—satisfy customer needs—and then encourages employees to do whatever's necessary to carry out the objective. For example, a Nordstrom department manager bought 12 dozen pairs of hosiery from a competitor in the mall when her stock was depleted because the new shipment was delayed. Even though Nordstrom lost money on this hosiery, management applauded her actions to make sure customers found hosiery when they came to the store looking for it. Empowering service providers with only a rule like "Use your best judgment" can cause chaos. At Nordstrom, department managers avoid abuses by coaching and training salespeople. They help salespeople understand what "Use your best judgment" means.

However, empowering service providers can be difficult. Some employees prefer to have the appropriate behaviors clearly defined for them. They don't want to spend the time learning how to make decisions or assume the risks of

> **REFACT**
>
> Trader Joe's, a gourmet supermarket chain, found that a change in their service policy that empowered employees to solve customer problems was accompanied by an increase in annual sales growth from 15 percent to 26 percent.[39]

Reducing the Emotional Labor of Service Providers | RETAILING VIEW

19.4

Robert Girau, a corporate manager for Atlanta-based fast-food chain Wing Zone, just spent 30 minutes on the phone with an irate customer who hadn't received her order. "She said I was a liar," Girau says. She also threatened him. But Girau knew he had to keep his cool and try to solve the problem. "It was frustrating," he says. "No matter what the customer is saying, you [have to] try not to take it personally."

This experience describes the emotional labor that service providers experience when they have to manage their emotions on the job. While "the customer is always right" is a business mantra, employees on the receiving end of a service interaction gone wrong face incredible pressure to simply grin and bear it. Retailers need to be aware of how these stressful customer interactions affect the morale and performance of their service providers.

Matt Friedman, 29, CEO and co-founder of Wing Zone, understands the stress that angry customers can cause in his employees, who take the majority of the company's food orders over the phone. Friedman says his entry-level employees, who are mostly college students,

just don't have the experience needed to handle these customers. Therefore, they've been trained to hand off overly demanding customers to the nearest manager right away. Wing Zone's managers then put the complaints back on the customers, asking them how they'd like the company to handle the problem. When both parties can't find some middle ground, managers refer the customer to the corporate office's toll-free number and website to file a formal complaint.

Girau, the point person at corporate headquarters for complaints that escalate, thinks the company's strategy works because the service providers know how to handle angry customers, managers understand what they can offer and are empowered to solve problems, and complaints with no easy solution can be routed up the organization. Having procedures to follow at the store level, Girau says, has made life easier for everyone.

Source: Chris Penttila, "Touch Customer: Managing Abusive Customers," *Entrepreneur*, May 2001, pp. 5, 95. Reprinted by permission.

information can increase customer satisfaction even when customers must wait longer than desired.[41]

Sometimes service problems are caused by customers. Customers may use an invalid credit card to pay for merchandise, may not take time to try on a suit and have it altered properly, or may use a product incorrectly because they failed to read the instructions. Communication programs also can inform customers about their role and responsibility in getting good service and can give tips on how to get better service, such as the best times of the day to shop and the retailer's policies and procedures for handling problems.

SERVICE RECOVERY

As we said, delivery of customer service is inherently inconsistent, so service failures are bound to arise. Rather than dwelling on negative aspects of customer problems, retailers should focus on the positive opportunities they generate. Service problems and complaints are an excellent source of information about the retailer's offering (its merchandise and service). Armed with this information, retailers can make changes to increase customer satisfaction.

Service problems also enable a retailer to demonstrate its commitment to providing high-quality customer service. By encouraging complaints and handling problems, a retailer has an opportunity to strengthen its relationship with its customers. Effective service recovery efforts significantly increase customer satisfaction, purchase intentions, and positive word of mouth. However, postrecovery satisfaction is less than that satisfaction prior to the service failure.[42]

Most retailers have standard policies for handling problems. If a correctable problem is identified, such as defective merchandise, many retailers will make restitution on the spot and apologize for inconveniencing the customer. The retailer will either offer replacement merchandise, a credit toward future purchases, or a cash refund.

In many cases, the cause of the problem may be hard to identify (did the salesperson really insult the customer?), uncorrectable (the store had to close due to bad weather), or a result of the customer's unusual expectations (the customer didn't like his haircut). In this case, service recovery might be more difficult. The steps in effective service recovery are (1) listen to the customer, (2) provide a fair solution, and (3) resolve the problem quickly.[43]

Listening to Customers

Customers can become very emotional over their real or imaginary problems with a retailer. Often this emotional reaction can be reduced by simply giving customers a chance to get their complaints off their chests.

Store employees should allow customers to air their complaints without interruption. Interruptions can further irritate customers who may already be emotionally upset. It's very hard to reason with or satisfy an angry customer.

Customers want a sympathetic response to their complaints. Thus, store employees need to make it clear they're happy that the problem has been brought to their attention. Satisfactory solutions rarely arise when store employees have an antagonistic attitude or assume that the customer is trying to cheat the store.

Employees also need to listen carefully to determine what the customer perceives to be a fair solution. For example, a hotel employee might assume that a customer who's irritated about a long wait to check in will be satisfied with an apology. But the customer might be expecting to receive a free drink as compensation for the wait. A supermarket employee may brusquely offer a refund for spoiled fruit, when the customer is also seeking an apology for the inconvenience of having to return to the store. Store employees shouldn't assume they know what the customer is complaining about or what solution the customer is seeking.[44]

Providing a Fair Solution

When confronted with a complaint, store employees need to focus on how they can get the customer back, not simply how they can solve the problem. Favorable impressions arise when customers feel they've been dealt with fairly. When evaluating the resolution of their problems, customers compare how they were treated in relation to others with similar problems or how they were treated in similar situations by other retail service providers. This comparison is based on observation of other customers with problems or on information about complaint handling learned from reading books and talking with others. Customers' evaluations of complaints' resolutions are based on distributive fairness and procedural fairness.[45]

Distributive Fairness   **Distributive fairness** is a customer's perception of the benefits received compared to their costs (inconvenience or loss). Customers want to get what they paid for. The customer's needs can affect the perceived correspondence between benefits and costs. For example, one customer might be satisfied with a rain check for a food processor that was advertised at a discounted price but was sold out. This customer feels the low price for the food processor offsets the inconvenience of returning to the store. But another customer may need the food processor immediately. A rain check won't be adequate compensation for him. To satisfy this customer, the salesperson must locate a store that has the food processor and have it delivered to the customer's house.

Customers typically prefer tangible rather than intangible resolutions to their complaints. Customers may want to let off steam, but they also want to feel the retailer was responsive to their complaint. A low-cost reward, a free soft drink, or a $1 discount, communicates more concern to the customer than a verbal apology.

If providing tangible restitution isn't possible, the next best alternative is to let customers see that their complaints will have an effect in the future. This can be done by making a note, in front of the customer, to a manager about the problem or writing to the customer about actions taken to prevent similar problems in the future.

Procedural Fairness   **Procedural fairness** is the perceived fairness of the process used to resolve complaints. Customers consider three questions when evaluating procedural fairness:

1. Did the employee collect information about the situation?

2. Was this information used to resolve the complaint?

3. Did the customer have some influence over the outcome?

This customer service representative is empowered to resolve the problems the customer has with a windbreaker purchased at the store.

Discontent with the procedures used to handle a complaint can overshadow the benefits of a positive outcome. For example, customers might be less satisfied with their refund for a clerk's mistake in ringing up groceries if they get no chance to talk about their other problems with the clerk.

Customers typically feel they're dealt with fairly when store employees follow company guidelines. Guidelines reduce variability in handling complaints and lead customers to believe they're being treated like everyone else. But rigid adherence to guidelines can have negative effects. Store employees need some flexibility in resolving complaints, or customers may feel they had no influence in the resolution.

Resolving Problems Quickly

Customer satisfaction is affected by the time it takes to get an issue resolved. To respond to customers quickly, Smith & Hawken, a garden-supply mail-order company, uses the telephone instead of the mail. The company feels that sending a letter is too time-consuming and impersonal. Resolving complaints by phone can take minutes, whereas sending letters can take weeks.

Retailers can minimize the time to resolve complaints by reducing the number of people the customer must contact, providing clear instructions, and speaking in the customer's language.

As a general rule, store employees who deal with customers should be made as self-sufficient as possible to handle problems. Customers are more satisfied when the first person they contact can resolve a problem. When customers are referred to several different employees, they waste a lot of time repeating their story. Also, the chance of conflicting responses by store employees increases.

Giving Clear Instructions Customers should be told clearly and precisely what they need to do to resolve a problem. When American Express cardholders ask to have an unused airline ticket removed from their bill, they're told immediately that they must return the ticket to the airline or travel agency before a credit can be issued. Fast service often depends on providing clear instructions.

Speaking the Customer's Language Customers can become annoyed when store employees use company jargon to describe a situation. To communicate clearly, store employees should use terms familiar to the customer. For example, a customer would be frustrated if a salesperson told her the slacks in her size were located on a rounder to the right of the four-way.

Resolving customer complaints increases satisfaction. But when complaints are resolved too abruptly, customers might feel dissatisfied because they haven't received personal attention. Retailers must recognize the trade-off between resolving the problem quickly and taking time to listen to and show concern for the customer.

SUMMARY

Due to the inherent intangibility and inconsistency of service, providing high-quality customer service is challenging. However, customer service also provides an opportunity for retailers to develop a strategic advantage. Retailers use two basic approaches for providing customer service: customization and standardization approaches. The customized approach relies primarily on sales associates. The standardized approach places more emphasis on developing appropriate rules and procedures and the store design.

Customers evaluate customer service by comparing their perceptions of the service delivered with their expectations. Thus, to improve service, retailers need to close the gaps between the service delivered and the customer's expectations. This gap is reduced by knowing what customers expect, setting standards to provide the expected service, providing support so store employees can meet the standards, and realistically communicating the service they offer to customers.

Due to inherent inconsistency, service failures are bound to arise. These lapses in service provide an opportunity for retailers to build even stronger relationships with their customers.

KEY TERMS

chat rooms, *635*
communication gap, *627*
customer service, *619*
customization approach, *621*
delivery gap, *627*
distributive fairness, *641*

emotional support, *636*
empowerment, *637*
instrumental support, *636*
knowledge gap, *627*
message boards, *635*

mystery shoppers, *634*
procedural fairness, *641*
service gap, *627*
standardization approach, *622*
standards gap, *627*

GO OUT & DO IT!

1. INTERNET EXERCISE Bizrate (www.bizrate.com) is a company that collects information about consumer shopping experiences with electronic retailers. Go to Bizrate's site and review the evaluations of different retailers selling products electronically. How useful is this information to you? What could Bizrate do to make the information more useful?

2. INTERNET EXERCISE Visit the Lands' End website (www.landsend.com) and look for a shirt. How does the website help you locate the shirt that you might be interested in buying? How does customer service offered at the website compare to the service you would get at a specialty store like The Gap? A department store?

3. GO SHOPPING Go to a local store and ask the store manager if you can talk to some customers in the store about the service they received. Choose customers who have made a purchase, customers who have not made a purchase, and customers with a problem (refund, exchange, or complaint). Talk with them about their experience, write a report describing the conversations, and make suggestions for improving the store's customer service.

4. GO SHOPPING Go to a discount store such as Wal-Mart, a department store, and a specialty store to buy a pair of jeans. Compare and contrast the customer service you receive in the stores. Which store made it easiest to find the pair of jeans you would be interested in buying? Why?

DISCUSSION QUESTIONS AND PROBLEMS

1. For each of these services, give an example of a retailer for which providing the service is critical to its success. Then give an example of a retailer for which providing the service is not critical: (*a*) personal shoppers, (*b*) home delivery, (*c*) money-back guarantees, (*d*) credit.

2. Nordstrom and McDonald's are noted for their high-quality customer service. But their approaches to providing this quality service are different. Describe this difference. Why have the retailers elected to use these different approaches?

3. Is customer service more important for store-based retailers or electronic retailers? Why?

4. Providing customer service can be very expensive for retailers. When are the costs for providing high-quality services justified? What types of retailers find it financially advantageous to provide high-quality customer service? What retailers can't justify providing high-quality service?

5. Assume you're the department manager for menswear in a local department store that emphasizes empowering its managers. A customer returns a dress shirt that's no longer in the package it was sold in. The customer has no receipt, says that when he opened the package he found that the shirt was torn, and wants cash for the price the shirt is being sold at now. The shirt was on sale last week when the customer claims to have bought it. What would you do?

6. Citibank found that chat rooms were not an important service for customers of its electronic banking offering. However, the Wedding Channel, an electronic retailer targeting couples about to get married, found that chat rooms are an important service for attracting customers. Why did these retailers have different experiences with the use of chat rooms?

7. Gaps analysis provides a systematic method of examining a customer service program's effectiveness. Top management has told an information systems manager that customers are complaining about the long wait to pay for merchandise at the checkout station. How can the systems manager use gaps analysis to analyze this problem and suggest approaches for reducing this time?

8. How could an effective customer service strategy cut a retailer's costs?

9. Employees play a critical role in customer perceptions of quality service. If you were hiring salespeople, what characteristics would you look for to assess their ability to provide good customer service?

SUGGESTED READINGS

Berry, Leonard. *Discovering the Soul of Service.* New York: Free Press, 1999.

"Enhancing the Shopping Experience." *Discount Store News*, July 12, 1999, pp. 13, 15.

Grönroos, Christian. *Service Management and Marketing: A Customer Relationship Management Approach.* 2nd ed. New York: Wiley, 2000.

Henderson, Timothy. "Despite Service Advances, Many Question Technology's Impact on the Shopping Experience." *Stores*, January 2001, pp. 54–60.

Iacobucci, Dawn. "Services Marketing and Customer Service." In *Kellogg on Marketing*, ed. Dawn Iacobucci. New York: Wiley, 2001.

Karr, Albert. "A Hot New Job Is Chief of Customer Service for Internet Retailers." *The Wall Street Journal*, June 1, 1999, pp. A1, A8.

Korczynski, Marek. *Human Resource Management in Service Work.* New York: Palgrave, 2002.

Smith, Amy; Ruth Bolton; and Janet Wagner. "A Model of Customer Satisfaction with Service Encounters Involving Failure and Recovery." *Journal of Marketing Research*, August 1999, pp. 356–72.

Spector, Robert, and Patrick D. McCarthy. *The Nordstrom Way: The Inside Story of America's #1 Customer Service Company.* 2nd ed. New York: John Wiley, 2000.

"10 Commandments of Customer Service." *Stores*, January 2001, p. 48.

Zemke, Ron, and John Woods. *Best Practices in Customer Service.* New York: AMACOM, 1999.

CASES

Case	1	2	3	4	5	6	7	8	9	10	11	12	13	14	15	16	17	18	19	C
CHAPTER																				
1 Rainforest Café	P	S					S											S		
2 Build-A-Bear	P	P																		
3 Gadzooks	P	S	S		S											S				
4 Sears	P	S	S		P		S													
5 Toys "R" Us Online			P																	
6 WeddingChannel.com		S	P	S																
7 Chen Family Buys Bicycles				P																
8 Value Retailers	S	S			P															
9 Ahold					P															
10 A&F/American Eagle	S	S			P												P			
11 Neiman/Family Dollar						P														
12 Stephanie's Boutique							P													
13 Hutch								P												
14 Home Depot					S					P										
15 Avon			S		S					P										
16 Lawson Sportswear											P									
17 SaksFirst												P							S	
18 Nolan's Finest Foods													P	S						
19 Hughe's													P	P						
20 McFadden's Department Store													S	P						
21 eBay		S	S		S										P					
22 Enterprise					S				P								P		S	
23 Borders Bookstore																	P			
24 Promoting a Sale															P					
25 Best Display																		P		
26 Sephora			S		S													P	S	
27 Discmart																	S		P	
28 Nordstrom					S				S		P								P	
29 GoodLife Fitness Clubs										S							S		S	P
30 Lindy's Bridal Shoppe					S		S						S			S				P
31 Starbucks						S										S				P

P Primary Use
S Secondary Use
C Comprehensive

CASE I   Rainforest Café: A Wild Place to Shop and Eat

Steve Schussler opened the first Rainforest Café in the Mall of America, the largest enclosed mall in the world, in 1994. Before opening this unique retail store and theme restaurant, Schussler tested the concept for 12 years, eventually building a prototype in his Minneapolis home. It was not easy sharing a house with parrots, butterflies, tortoises, and tropical fish, but Schussler's creativity resulted in a highly profitable and fast-growing chain.

In 1996, the Rainforest Cafés (www.rainforest.com), located in Chicago, Washington, DC, Fort Lauderdale, and Disney World in Orlando, Florida, in addition to the Mall of America in Minneapolis, Minnesota, generated $48.7 million in sales and $5.9 million in profits. They offer a unique and exciting atmosphere, recreating a tropical rain forest in 20,000 to 30,000 square feet. The cafés are divided into a restaurant seating 300 to 600 people and a retail store stocking 3,000 SKUs of unique merchandise.

Retail merchandise accounts for 30 percent of the revenues generated by the cafés. Most theme restaurants stock fewer than 20 SKUs. The merchandise emphasizes eight proprietary jungle animals featured as animated characters in the restaurant. They include Bamba the gorilla, Cha Cha the tree frog, and Ozzie the orangutan. In addition to stuffed animals and toys, the characters are utilized on clothing and gifts and in animated films and children's books.

The cafés provide an environmentally conscious family adventure. The menu features dishes such as Rasta Pasta, Seafood Galapagos, Jamaica Me Crazy, and Eye of the Ocelot (meatloaf topped with sautéed mushrooms on a bed of caramelized onions). The restaurants have live tropical birds and fish plus animated crocodiles and monkeys, trumpeting elephants, gorillas beating their chests, cascading waterfalls surrounded by cool mist, simulated thunder and lightning, continuous tropical rain storms, and huge mushroom canapés. As Schussler said, "Our cafés feature the sophistication of a Warner Brothers store with the animation of Disney."

Rainforest Cafés contribute to the local community through an outreach program. Over 300,000 schoolchildren visit the cafés each year to hear curators talk about the vanishing rain forests and endangered species. All coins dropped into the Wishing Pond and Parking Meter in the cafés are donated to causes involving endangered species and tropical deforestation.

Technology is used in the Rainforest Cafés to increase efficiency and profits. When a party enters the restaurant, the host (called a tour guide) enters the party's name in a computer, which prints a "passport" indicating the party's name, size, and estimated seating time. The party can then go shopping or sightseeing, knowing it will be ushered into the dining room within 5 to 10 minutes of the assigned seating time. When the party returns, the computer tells the "safari guide" the table at which the party will be seated. Tour and safari guides communicate with each other using headsets. This technology enables the Rainforest Cafés to turn tables five to six times a day compared to two to three turns in the typical restaurant.

The company expanded rapidly. By 2000, it had annual sales of $200 million but earned only $8 million in profits from 28 locations. Many of the locations were in regional malls rather than high-traffic entertainment centers at which the restaurants were initially located.

After a protracted negotiation, Rainforest Café was acquired by Landry's Restaurant Inc. Landry's is an $800 million company that operates 200 restaurants primarily under the names of Joe's Crab Shack and Landry's Seafood House. Tilman Fertitta, the founder and CEO of Landry's, explains his strategy for operating restaurants: "Our approach has always been simple. Put good concepts in good locations. Rainforest is a strong concept. The problem wasn't with sales. The worst stores do $5 million a year. That's very different from other eatertainment chains like Planet Hollywood and Hard Rock Café. The major problem was poor locations in shopping centers with high lease costs." Following the acquisition, Landry's closed a number of Rainforest's mall locations but opened up new locations in London's Piccadilly Circus, Euro Disney outside Paris, Niagara Falls, MGM Grand Hotel and Casino in Las Vegas, and Fisherman's Wharf in San Francisco.

● DISCUSSION QUESTIONS

1. What is Rainforest Café's retail offering and target market?

2. Were malls good locations for Rainforest Cafés? Why or why not? What would be the best locations?

3. Many retailers have tried to make their stores more entertaining. In a number of cases, these efforts have failed. What are the pros and cons of providing a lot of entertainment in a retail store or restaurant?

Source: This case was written by Barton Weitz, University of Florida.

CASE 2   Retail Entertainment at Build-A-Bear Workshop

Today's consumers want good value, low prices, and convenience, but they also are attracted to a great shopping experience. Build-A-Bear Workshop, a chain with over 100 stores generating $100 million in annual sales, is a teddy-bear-themed entertainment retailer whose stores are playgrounds for children.

The stores are exactly what the name says: Customers choose an unstuffed animal and, working with the retailer's staff, move through eight "creation stations" to build their own bear. At the first station, the Stuffiteria, children can pick fluff from bins marked "Love," "Hugs and Kisses," "Friendship," and "Kindness." The stuffing is sent through a long, clear tube and into this machine. A sales associate holds the bear to a small tube while the builder pumps a foot peddle. In seconds, the bear takes its form. Before the stitching, builders must insert a heart. The builders follow the sales associate's instructions and rub the heart between their hands to make it warm. They then close their eyes, make a wish, and kiss the heart before putting it inside the bear. After selecting a name and having it stitched on the bear, builders take their bears to the Fluff Me station, where they brush their bears on a "bathtub" that features spigots blowing air. Finally they move to a computer station to create a birth certificate for their bear.

Bears are sent home in Club Condo boxes, which act as minihouses complete with windows and doors. Besides adding value as playhouses, the boxes advertise Build-A-Bear to the child's friends. "[You] could buy a bear anywhere" says Maxine Clark, founder and Chief Executive Bear. "It's the experience that customers are looking for." The experience is depicted on the retailer's website, www.buildabear.com.

Customers pay about $25 for the basic bear, but they can also buy sound, clothing, and accessories for their bear. To keep the experience fresh, Build-A-Bear regularly introduces new and limited-edition animals. Clothes and accessories are also updated to reflect current trends. There are also in-store birthday parties and an official CD. To make sure that customers have a great experience everytime they visit, all sales associates attend a three-week training program at "Bear University" and the firm offers incentive programs and bonuses.

The inventory in the stores changes frequently, with different bear styles arriving weekly. To commemorate the 100th anniversary of the teddy bear in 2003, Build-A-Bear has a limited edition Collectibear for every year. Build-A-Bear stores also feature seasonal merchandise such as a black cat with an orange nose for Halloween and a penguin for Christmas.

REFACT

The origin of the teddy bear was a 1903 incident in which President Teddy Roosevelt refused to shoot a cub while bear hunting. The spared animal was thereafter referred to as the Teddy Bear.

DISCUSSION QUESTIONS

1. Is the Build-A-Bear concept a fad, or does it have staying power?

2. What can Build-A-Bear do to generate repeat visits to the store?

Source: This case was written by Barton Weitz, University of Florida.

CASE 3   Gadzooks Targets the Teen Market

Gadzooks, along with American Eagle, Wet Seal, Abercrombie & Fitch, PacSun, and Hot Topics, target the teen market. The U.S. teen population is growing about a third faster than the overall population in the United States. By 2005, teenagers will number about 34 million in the United States, and their spending power will be more than $160 billion. It is estimated that almost 40 percent, or $64 billion, of teen expenditures will be on clothing and accessories alone.

Gadzooks differentiates its retail offering through its unique image, positioning, and vision. Its image is very closely linked to its "casual yet energetic store environment." All of its stores have dynamic atmospheres featuring the latest music videos and movie clips, and they often hold in-store promotions and contests to create an excitement and enthusiasm that other retailers cannot match. Gadzooks wants its customers to have a pleasurable yet productive shopping experience every time they visit its stores.

Rather than selling only private-brand merchandise like most of its competitors, Gadzooks' assortment consists of well-known brand names. CEO Gerry Szczepanski emphasizes, "We have never used Gadzooks as a brand name. It's dangerous to make Gadzooks a brand because if that brand were ever to be tarnished, we would be really hurting. We survive by changing brands as the kids change brands. We deal in the brands teenagers want: Puma, Mudd, Candies, Hot Kiss, and Led." Gadzooks offers some private labels in its stores using the brand names of Decibel, Epidemic, Verbal Assault, Misdemeanor, and Bad Kitty; but the private-label merchandise accounts for only 20 percent of retail sales.

Teenagers' tastes change just as fast as the fads, so it is up to Gadzooks to make certain that its stores stock merchandise that is trendy, fashionable, and tasteful. The merchandising mix contains clothing, shoes, and accessories for both young men and women that are ever changing with the style and attitude of their customers.

Gadzooks advertises nationally in popular teen periodicals such as *Seventeen, Teen People, Spin,* and *Rolling Stone.* This advertising builds awareness and the brand image with the company's target audience. The firm also jointly promotes events with some of its vendors. For example, Gadzooks and Puma teamed up to offer consumers a chance to win a trip to view the filming of MTV's "The Real World" and "Road Rule Challenge."

Gadzooks has a highly interactive website that features current fashion trends, monthly calendar of events, and promotional contests. Furthermore, it includes interactive features such as online music videos and daily horoscopes. The site is intended to provide customers with "a more personalized experience that meets their lifestyle needs." The site also host live chats with performers in popular bands.

In 2001, Gadzooks developed and launched a new retail concept, Orchid. Orchid stores target female teenagers, but they offer a combination of branded and private-label innerwear, sleepwear, fragrances, and bath/body products in a shopping environment carefully designed to provide an inviting and comforting shopping experience for young women. Roughly 80 percent of the items are sold under the Orchid private label, including the fragrance line with price points 25 percent lower on average than Victoria's Secret. "With the help of focus groups, we identified a real niche in the market," says Paula Masters, president and chief merchandising officer of Gadzooks. She explains, "A lot of girls like Victoria's Secret, but they are not totally comfortable shopping in that environment. For one thing, it's where their mothers shop."

●DISCUSSION QUESTIONS

1. Go to the website of Gadzooks (www.gadzooks.com), American Eagle (www.ae.com), Abercrombie & Fitch (www.abercrombie.com), Wet Seal (www.wetseal.com), Pacific Sunwear (www.pacsun.com) and Hot Topics (www.hottopic.com). All of these retailers target teenagers. On the basis of their websites, discuss if they are targeting different teen segments. Are their images different? How?

2. What are some of the things that you associate with Gadzooks stores? Do they need to be repositioned in the market?

3. Pretend that you are a market analyst. How do you project that the Gadzooks spin-off store Orchid will perform in our economy?

4. Why does Orchid carry so much private-label merchandise while the CEO strongly feels that Gadzooks should carry national brands?

Source: This case was written by Kristina Pacca, University of Florida.

CASE 4   Sears Looks for a New Direction

COMPANY HISTORY

Sears, Roebuck and Co. traces its history to 1886, when Richard W. Sears began selling watches in Minneapolis. By 1895, the business was publishing a 532-page catalog that included clothing, furniture, patent medicines, and many other items. In 1925, Sears opened its first store, which was immediately successful, and by 1941, Sears had expanded to 600 stores. After World War II, the company continued to expand, opening new stores in suburban areas and shopping malls. Sears was the largest retailer in the United States for most of the twentieth century. In the 1960s, its revenues exceeded those of its four largest competitors combined, and its semiannual catalog with over 1,000 pages was a fixture in many U.S. homes.

However, Sears' market share began declining in the 1970s due to the growth of discounters such as Kmart and Wal-Mart and various specialty retailers. In 1990, Wal-Mart overtook Sears to become the largest retailer in the country. Over the last 10 years, the company faced the challenge of regaining its position of leadership and prominence in American retailing.

THE COMPETITION

Sears, JCPenney, Montgomery Ward, and Kohl's are mid-tier retailers, with product quality, service, and selling prices between those of discount stores and high-end department stores. Throughout the 1990s, the mid-tier lost market share to discount stores and specialty retailers such as Home Depot, Circuit City, and Bed, Bath & Beyond. Sears and JCPenney both struggled to maintain sales and profits. In December 2000, Montgomery Ward filed for bankruptcy and began closing its 250 stores.

Department Stores

In the mid-tier, only Kohl's is thriving. Kohl's is a much smaller retailer than Sears, with annual sales of about $6 billion, operating 320 stores in 26 states. It is the fastest-growing department store in the United States, pursuing an aggressive expansion policy. Kohl's stores, mostly in off-mall locations, carry apparel, home furnishings, and home products at competitive prices. Kohl's emphasizes convenience through its off-mall locations, centralized cash wraps, and store layouts that make it easy for customers to locate merchandise they want.

JCPenney is one of the largest retailers in the United States, with more than 1,140 stores. The company sells apparel, accessories, and home furnishings, having eliminated hard lines more than a decade ago. Like Sears, the majority of its retailing space is found in malls. Also like Sears, Penney is struggling to maintain relevance in today's retailing environment. Penney acquired the Eckerd drugstore chain, hoping to increase its revenues and profits.

Target Corporation traces its history to 1902, with the opening of the Goodfellows store in Minneapolis. In 1962, it entered discount merchandising, establishing its first Target store. In 1978, the company acquired Mervyn's. In the 1990s, the corporation made a number of acquisitions, including Marshall Field's. Target Corporation is the fourth-largest general retailer in the United States, serving consumers through multiple retail formats ranging from upscale discount through full-service department stores. Most of the corporation's revenues come from Target stores, which are more attractive than Sears or Penney to shoppers who are looking for fashionable merchandise at value prices.

Category Killers

Home Depot and Lowe's are category killers specializing in home improvement products that compete against Sears's hard lines. Home Depot is the world's largest home improvement retailer with more than 1,000 stores. Home Depot serves the do-it-yourself market as well as professional builders, selling appliances, flooring, lawn and garden supplies, paint, tools, lumber, and related products. During the 1990s, Home Depot's sales grew rapidly, primarily due to construction of new stores. In 1999, Sears was removed from the Dow Jones Industrial Average, and Home Depot was added, indicating that stores like Home Depot are perceived as the future of retailing, and Sears is not.

Lowe's Corporation is the fourteenth-largest retailer in the United States, with more than 700 stores in 40 states. Lowe's has the largest superstores in the industry, stores with more than 150,000 square feet of selling space. The stores serve the do-it-yourself market, offering more than 40,000 home improvement items. Lowe's also grew rapidly during the 1990s, building new stores and increasing its sales and income.

Discount Retailers

Wal-Mart is the world's largest retailer, with sales that are double the combined sales of Sears, Penney, and Kmart. In 2003, Wal-Mart's sales revenue exceeded $250 billion, and Wal-Mart was number two on the *Fortune* 500. Wal-Mart has over 4,500 retail stores, including discount stores, supercenters (discount and grocery stores), and Sam's Club stores (members-only stores). Wal-Mart's growth has been a dominant force in the retailing industry for the last 15 years. Much of its growth has come from taking market share from mid-tier retailers. Wal-Mart is among the most innovative retailers in its use of technology. Its logistics systems, management information systems, and collaboration with suppliers allow the company to cut costs and pass savings on to their customers.

Kmart is the second-largest discount retailer behind Wal-Mart, operating more than 2,100 stores. It operates discount stores and more than 100 superstores. While Kmart emerged as a discounter before Wal-Mart did, it has had difficulty competing with Wal-Mart for the last 10 years. Kmart has incurred substantial charges to income in its efforts to revamp stores and gain momentum against Wal-Mart. It has experienced slow sales growth for several years, incurred significant losses, and declared bankruptcy in 2002.

SEARS' STRATEGY IN THE 1990S

Sears, Roebuck and Company, an American institution, was on the verge of bankruptcy in 1992. Profits were only 0.7 percent on $31 billion in revenues. The company was experiencing significant cash flow problems. To avert disaster, then-CEO Ed Brennan decided to make a change.

Arthur Martinez was hired from Saks Fifth Avenue as the head of merchandising. In 1995, he was named CEO upon Brennan's retirement. Martinez came to Sears with a mission to turn around the failing retailer. He took an aggressive position and began by cutting over 50,000 jobs, closing 113 stores, and eliminating the Sears Big Book, its 97-year-old catalog. Some thought these dramatic changes would be the demise of Sears.

Sears has some of the most recognized brand names in hard goods: Kenmore appliances and Craftsman tools. Both brands ranked in the top 10 of 500 brands evaluated by consumers in a recent study. After touring stores, Martinez was struck by the store layout in which women purchasing lingerie would be next to men buying power tools. Martinez decided to place more emphasis on apparel, particularly women's apparel, in the mall-based department stores.

Some other changes instituted by Martinez were the launch of an advertising campaign, "The Softer Side of Sears," announcing this new direction in 1993; the addition of cosmetics departments to over 200 stores; and the remodeling of stores to add more floor space for apparel. Private-label merchandise played an important role in Sears' new positioning. Circle of Beauty, an in-house brand of cosmetics, was expected to produce $500 million in revenues in 1996. Canyon River Blues, the new private-label brand of jeans and casual wear, reached $100 million in revenues only seven months after its introduction in 1995.

While Martinez initially was reluctant to build an electronic channel for Sears, the company launched Sears.com in 1998. The site initially focused on promoting Craftsman tools and has since expanded its offering to include all of Sears hardline product categories, including Kenmore appliances.

While the emphasis on soft goods resulted in a temporary growth in sales and profits, near the end of the 1990s Sears once again faced a decline in sales and profits. Martinez retired and Alan Lacy assumed the CEO position.

THE FUTURE OF SEARS

Alan Lacy became Sears CEO and president on October 1, 2000. At 46, he had served as the company's senior vice president of finance, chief financial officer, and president of services. He had also been responsible for Sears' online business and credit operations.

In 2003, Sears was more than just department stores. The company had four Great Indoors home decorating stores and had targeted this chain for expansion, identifying it as an opportunity for growth. Sears also had a chain of hardware stores, 822 Sears Auto Centers, and 229 tire and battery stores. There were also 790 locally owned dealer stores, which sold hardware, lawn and garden, and automotive lines. The company had one of the most successful online operations among conventional bricks-and-mortar retailers. However, Sears' 863 full-line department stores were still the cornerstone of the business.

Lacy identified improving profitability of Sears' retailing as a top priority. Retailing has accounted for 75 percent of the company's overall revenues, but in recent years credit operations had provided most of the profits. Lacy saw increasing competition from Kohl's and Target Stores as key challenges, along with overcoming a poor image with consumers.

Hard goods are Sears' strong suit, bringing in 60 percent of sales at its mall stores. The company has three of the best-selling names in retailing: Craftsman, DieHard, and Kenmore. Sears is the number one appliance retailer in the United States, with appliance sales accounting for more than 10 percent of the company's total business. The company has a 38 percent market share, and its private-label, Kenmore, is the top-selling appliance brand in the country. However, Home Depot is expanding its appliance offerings and Wal-Mart is test marketing a home appliance department. Competition in appliance sales is increasing, and Sears has the most to lose.

Sears is the country's largest seller of tires and auto batteries, featuring its DieHard brand. The Craftsman brand has made Sears a leader in tool sales with a 25 to 40 percent market share; in some categories, Sears is the sales leader. Home centers have more space for tools than Sears, so Sears is developing an expanded hardware department, Tool Territory, in its mall stores. Sears is the only retailer selling traditional tools and hardware at most shopping malls.

As Sears has discovered, succeeding in both hard and soft lines is difficult—for example, customers do not buy tools and apparel on the same visit to the store. Apparel sales were $5.7 billion in 1992 and had grown to $9.3 billion in 1999. Sears stocks everything from suits to socks, seeking to be a one-stop destination for clothing. Most successful apparel retailers offer a more limited line targeting specific customer groups. Leslie Mann, Sears' senior vice president of soft lines, said that the company doesn't have a brand personality in apparel—"we have no personality." An article in *Forbes* recommended Sears get out of apparel altogether. But apparel is about 20 percent of Sears' overall business—could the company afford to give up billions of dollars in sales? Late in 2000, the company decided to reduce the selling space devoted to soft lines and increase space for tools and other hard goods.

Sears is primarily a mall-based retailer in a time when the mall is becoming less attractive. Most shoppers go to the mall less often than they did 15 years ago. Few new malls are being built, reducing opportunities for growth for mall-based enterprises. Sears itself may be something of a misfit in malls: most retailers in malls specialize in apparel and related items, and Sears is scaling back its apparel and expanding hard lines. Sears is a general merchandise retailer in a time when general merchandise retailing may be losing its relevance.

Lacy leads an organization struggling to find its identity and regain the prominence it once had in American business. Lacy has said that the key for Sears is to do "fewer things better." He must find the right things for Sears to do, if he is to restore Sears' relevance to today's consumers and build on the company's century of tradition.

In 2002, Sears acquired Lands' End, a successful catalog retailer with a strong apparel brand name. Sears' purchase of Lands' End offers an opportunity to improve its apparel image and sales. Lands' End merchandise is now being sold in Sears stores. It represents the "best" selection in Lacy's stated "good, better, best" apparel strategy. The "better" component consists of the company's new private-label line called Covington. The plans are for Lands' End to continue to run its catalog and Internet businesses. In addition, Lands' End management will assume responsibility for Sears.com. Eventually, Sears expects to offer products like Lands' End camping equipment and other outdoor goods.

Source: This case was written by Professors Sue Cullers and Stephen Vitucci, Tarleton State University.

CASE 5   Toys "R" Us Online

"How do I explain to my son that Santa is giving him a gift a week late?" said Michele Read on December 24, 1999, as she worried that the Leap Frog Learning toy she had ordered from Toysrus.com for her four-year-old son Tyler was not going to be under the Christmas tree the next day.

"This does nothing to appease a child on Christmas morning when he doesn't find his present," said Kevin Davitt, a customer who was still waiting for an order from Toysrus.com on December 23, 1999. "A six-year-old doesn't want a gift certificate, he wants his Nintendo or his Pokemon," said Davitt, a publicist from Glen Rock, New Jersey, who had ordered two video games for his six-year-old son on December 13, 1999, and agreed to pay $19.90 for express shipping so that the gift would arrive within five days.

Michael Kinney, a customer from South Pasadena, California, who is the manager of a local taxi service, ordered a Chickaboom game for his son and was promised delivery within two weeks. After seven weeks, Kinney declared, "I'll never shop Toysrus.com again."

During Christmas 1999, Toysrus.com employees faced a real siege. The company's "Black Sunday" came on Sunday, November 6, 1999, as 62 million advertising circulars were placed in local newspapers around the United States offering free shipping on Christmas toy orders placed over the Internet. When Toysrus.com was unable to fulfill orders in time for Christmas, the firm received numerous consumer complaints and negative publicity from newspaper and magazine articles and TV news reports about the firm's problems. Toys "R" Us had the toys available in its warehouses, but was unable to pick, pack, and ship customer orders in a timely manner. Many employees worked for 49 straight days to fill orders, with some employees pulling sleeping bags out from under their desks to rest during the round-the-clock operation. Despite the heroic efforts, customers were still displeased. "I have never been exposed to fouler language," explained Joel Anderson, a Toysrus.com vice president, as he described the angry e-mails from unhappy customers.

In January 2000, John Eyler became the fourth CEO of the 53-year-old Toys "R" Us toy chain and parent of Toysrus.com. He came from being president of much smaller FAO Schwarz toy chain and entered on the heels of the 18-month tenure of the previous CEO. He was immediately faced with the aftermath of the Christmas 1999 crisis and had less than 12 months to fix things for Christmas 2000.

TOYS "R" US TODAY

Toys "R" Us, Inc., headquartered in Paramus, New Jersey, is one of the largest retailers in the world, with 2002 sales over $12 billion. The corporation consists of five businesses: (1) Toys "R" Us U.S., operating 701 toy stores, (2) Kids "R" Us, with 184 children's clothing stores, (3) Babies "R" Us, consisting of 165 infant-toddler stores, (4) Imaginarium, 42 educational specialty stores, and (5) Toys "R" Us, International, which operates, licenses, or franchises 507 toy stores in 28 countries outside the United States. In addition, the firm sells merchandise through Internet sites at www.toysrus.com, www.babiesrus.com, and www.imaginarium.com.

Toys "R" Us stores carry everything from Crazy Bones at $1.99 to Sony PlayStation at $129.99. The merchandise mix includes both children's and adult's toys and games, bicycles, sporting goods, small pools, infant and juvenile furniture, infant and toddler apparel, and children's books. An electronics section features video games, electronic handheld toys, videotapes, audio CDs, and computer software, along with a smattering of small TVs, shelf stereos, and radios.

Most Toys "R" Us stores conform to a traditional big-box format, with stores averaging about 46,000 square feet. Stores in smaller markets range between 20,000 and 30,000 square feet. In 1999, the company began converting stores to a new layout named the C3 (customer-driven, cost-effective concept) format store intended to make the Toys "R" Us stores easier to shop with wider aisles, more feature opportunities and end caps, more shops, and logical category layouts.

THE TOY INDUSTRY

Bricks and Mortar   The $30 billion traditional toy industry has undergone significant changes during the last 10 years. Over this time period, the market share of general merchandise discount stores (Wal-Mart, Kmart, and Target) increased from 22 to 33.6 percent, while Toys "R" Us' market share decreased from 19.1 to 16.5 percent. In 1998, Wal-Mart overcame Toys "R" Us to become the top toy retailer in the United States.

Online   Between 1999 and 2002, the share of the toy market purchased over the Internet increased significantly but still was less than 5 percent of total toy sales. In March 2001, with annual sales over $200 million eToys filed for bankruptcy. It was noted for its excellent customer service and user-friendly website. But its fixed costs were so high, that its break-even sales volume escalated to $750 million in annual sales.

THE NEW TOYS "R" US STRATEGY

Customers complained that the stores were ugly and untidy, that shopping was difficult, and that there were not enough sales personnel. To help regain its number one place from Wal-Mart, Toys "R" Us developed a new corporate strategy and marketing plan. It hired a new marketing VP, Warren Kornblum, who immediately overhauled the company's whole marketing operation. In the past, Toys "R" Us had joined in small vendor promotions and managed scattered marketing efforts. Kornblum changed that around, deciding to do fewer but bigger promotions. The company teamed with Major League Baseball as a sponsor for a youth skill competition. It also did a promotional deal with Fox Kids Network and Walt Disney for the feature film *Toy Story 2*. As a result of these marketing efforts, sales increased from $11.2 billion in 1998 to $11.9 billion in 1999. For 2000–01, the company restructured its budget to allocate more money toward marketing. It planned to continue with sports and movie entertainment themes for promotions.

Warren Kornblum's strategy seemed to work. He set up a "Scan and Win" promotion where shoppers held up UPC game pieces to scanners to see if they had won a prize. More than a million consumers were scanned in with this promotion, making this one of the company's most successful store traffic improvement programs. The mountains of sweepstakes entries and packed venues, however, began causing inventory shortages in the all-important holiday period. Inventory mishaps were the main reason fourth-quarter 1999 sales stayed at a flat $5 billion.

When John Eyler came in as the new CEO of Toys "R" Us in January 2000, he slashed expenses across the board, started efforts to provide better customer service, increased the number of employees in stores, and expanded store operating hours. All of the marketing activities were aimed at bringing customers into the chain's new store design and layout concept, C3. This easier-to-shop C3 format was installed in 75 percent of the stores by the end of 2000. Toys "R" Us hoped this new strategy would take market share back from Wal-Mart, KMart, Target, and KB Toys.

In addition to changing the layout of the stores, Toys "R" Us is opening boutique areas within the stores. For example, the Imaginarium area features educational toys and games, and the R Zone areas offers video games targeting teenagers.

TOYSRUS.COM

Toys "R" Us arrived late to the e-business world with Toysrus.com in 1998, losing critical early battles to eToys.com and ceding some of the market to Amazon.com and KBkids.com. The development, launch, and operation of Toysrus.com turned out to be both a corporate and public relations headache for almost a year. Things fell apart just as quickly as they came together. The investment deal with Benchmark Capital to fund the venture crumbled a few months after it was made as neither party could agree to the shares they would have. Bob Moog, who was hired to run Toysrus.com, backed out of his employment deal in July 1999 three months after agreeing to come on board. With Christmas 1999 approaching, Toys "R" Us scrambled to put its Internet venture together. Hasbro executive John Barbour was hired as the new president for Toysrus.com in August 1999. He quickly developed a new plan, redesigned the site, and prepared for a holiday traffic onslaught.

The company began promoting online offers in its offline marketing efforts, the most ambitious of which dangled a $10 discount for online purchases in the nationally distributed Toys "R" Us "holiday big book" coupon circulars. Toysrus.com also offered free shipping for the holiday season. The free shipping and "big book" coupon strategy worked, but a little too well for the logistics department of the company. Traffic exploded, and the site was buried in an avalanche of orders "beyond our most optimistic forecasts," said Barbour. The company was finally forced to announce that 5 percent of all online orders would not be fulfilled in time for Christmas. Embarrassed, Toys "R" Us issued a formal apology and issued $100 gift certificates to customers whose orders didn't make it under the tree. Toysrus.com declared revenues of $49 million in 1999, $39 million of which came during the holiday season.

Partnership with Amazon.com

Learning from the fiasco of Christmas 1999 where it failed to deliver goods in time, the company decided to go into a partnership with Amazon.com in 2000. Amazon.com took over the Toys "R" Us site operations, customer service, and fulfillment, while Toys "R" Us selected and bought the merchandise that it inventoried in Amazon warehouses. Through this arrangement, Toysrus.com has realized a 40 percent reduction in operating costs, largely by outsourcing fulfillment activities. Its conversion rate, the percentage of site visitors who make purchases, doubled since the deal took effect in August 2000. In the critical 2000 holiday season, Toysrus.com boasted 99 percent on-time delivery amid a huge volume of orders, and sales volume more than tripled from the previous year, to $124 million.

DISCUSSION QUESTIONS

1. Why were the general merchandise stores able to take market share away from Toys "R" Us while they have not been as competitive with the consumer electronics category killers such as Circuit City and Best Buy?

2. How can Toys "R" Us regain its position as the number one toy retailer?

3. How do Amazon.com and Toys "R" Us each benefit from their partnership?

4. What are the pros and cons of this relationship with Amazon.com from Toys "R" Us' perspective?

Source: This case was written by Professors Alan B. Eisner, Lubin School of Business, Pace University; Jerome C. Kuperman, Minnesota State University, Moorhead Department of Business Administration; Robert F. Dennehy, Lubin School of Business, Pace University; and John P. Dory, Lubin School of Business, Pace University. A full-length version of this case is forthcoming in the *Journal of Behavioral and Applied Management*. Special thanks to Margaret Ann deSouza-Lawrence for research assistance on this project. © 2002 Alan B. Eisner.

CASE 6   WeddingChannel.com

Anne is sitting at her desk eating her lunch and surfing the Internet. For a few months, she has been preparing for her wedding, which will be in less than a month. She found many helpful articles that gave her some good ideas. These articles helped her face reality and change her childhood dreams of a white carriage pulled by a team of horses to a stretch limo. She gave up the Snow White wedding gown with a 15-foot train and has now settled on a sleek sheath gown.

In planning her big day, Anne used the help of WeddingChannel.com to make up a checklist of what she needs to do. The website helped her organize a guest list, design and buy her invitations, set up a gift registry, and post some information for her friends about how she and Steven met. They met in college and are from different cities, therefore they decided to have their wedding somewhere in between where their friends and family could meet. She used the resources provided on WeddingChannel.com to book the chapel and restaurant where the reception would be held.

Every year, $70 billion is spent on weddings. The average wedding ceremony costs $20,000. The average age of brides is 26, while the average groom is 28. With these statistics, it is no wonder that WeddingChannel.com has become so popular. Its target market is 18 to 35 years. Approximately 48 percent of engaged couples plan to use the

Internet to help plan their wedding. WeddingChannel.com's goal is to help couples make their special day become easier to plan as well as save time finding up-to-date information.

WeddingChannel.com began on July 15, 1997. It is privately owned by Federated Department Stores Inc., Neiman Marcus Group, Tiffany & Company, Crate & Barrel, Williams-Sonoma, and venture capital companies.

The venture has helped not only brides-to-be but also the retailers. Over $19 billion was spent purchasing gifts in the past year, and over a million couples registered in 2001. With so many couples registered with this site, WeddingChannel.com has an attractive market. "Consistently, our targeted marketing tactics have resulted in five times the average Internet response rate, providing the most effective platform for companies to build their brand messages during a significant life stage when brand loyalties are being developed," said Adam Berger, president and CEO of WeddingChannel.com. About 89 percent of all gift purchasers buy wedding gifts from a registry.

WeddingChannel.com is not only the largest bridal registry online, but it also provides a comprehensive site that couples can use to plan their wedding. WeddingChannel.com is a virtual community that provides services for couples who have many questions. Where do brides start first? Most start with finding the perfect dress. Wedding Channel.com offers over 20,000 styles of wedding gowns. It has a large selection of designer brands as well as less expensive brands. It also provides a great way of sorting through the many different styles by choosing a different button to select sleeve length, silhouette, length, and neckline. It even has a virtual model so the bride-to-be can see how she would look in a particular style of gown.

The site also provides many interactive tools that help couples to make a budget, calendar, guest list, wedding page, and registry. There are also many articles that range from how to budget the wedding to what kind of pantyhose to buy.

WeddingChannel.com is unique because it allows for couples to make an Internet page containing how they met, how they became engaged, who is in their wedding party, as well as the theme/colors. Guests can go online and shop at the well-known stores associated with Wedding Channel.com. Some of the companies are Federated Department Stores, Inc., Tiffany & Co., Crate & Barrel, Neiman Marcus, Williams-Sonoma, Restoration Hardware, REI, and Gumps. A disadvantage of the online registry is there are only select stores that the bride can register for items online. An advantage is her guests can purchase from any of the stores online. They can get exactly what the couple wants without the hassle of making a trip, gift-wrapping, or shipping.

● DISCUSSION QUESTIONS

1. What are the keys to making the WeddingChannel.com a success from the perspective of the companies investing in it?

2. Why would a retailer want to invest in a virtual community like the WeddingChannel.com?

3. Can you think of other retailers that might benefit from developing a virtual community?

Source: This case was written by Teresa Scott, University of Florida.

CASE 7   The Chen Family Buys Bicycles

The Chens live in Riverside, California, west of Los Angeles. Terry is a physics professor at the University of California, Riverside. His wife Cheryl is a volunteer, working 10 hours a week at the Crisis Center. They have two children: Judy, age 10, and Mark, age 8.

In February, Cheryl's parents sent her $100 to buy a bicycle for Judy's birthday. They bought Judy her first bike when she was five. Now they wanted to buy her a full-size bike for her eleventh birthday. Even though Cheryl's parents felt every child should have a bike, Cheryl didn't think Judy really wanted one. Judy and most of her friends didn't ride their bikes often, and she was afraid to ride to school because of traffic. So Cheryl decided to buy her the cheapest full-size bicycle she could find.

Since most of Judy's friends didn't have full-size bikes, she didn't know much about them and had no preferences for a brand or type. To learn more about the types available and their prices, Cheryl and Judy checked the JCPenney catalog. After looking through the catalog, Judy said the only thing she cared about was the color. She wanted a blue bike, blue being her favorite color.

Using the Yellow Pages, Cheryl called several local retail outlets selling bikes. To her surprise, she found that a local hardware store actually had the best price for a 26-inch bicycle, even lower than Toys "R" Us and Wal-Mart.

Cheryl drove to the hardware store, went straight to the toy department, and selected a blue bicycle before a salesperson approached her. She took the bike to the cash register and paid for it. After making the purchase, the Chens found out that the bike was cheap in all senses. The chrome plating on the wheels was very thin and rusted away in six months. Both tires split and had to be replaced.

A year later, Cheryl's grandparents sent another $100 for a bike for Mark. From their experience with Judy's bike, the Chens realized that the lowest-priced bike might not be the least expensive option in the long run. Mark is very active and somewhat careless, so the Chens wanted to buy a sturdy bike. Mark said he wanted a red, 10-speed, lightweight imported bike with lots of accessories: headlights, special foot pedals, and so forth. The Chens were concerned that Mark wouldn't maintain an expensive bike with all these accessories.

When they saw an ad for a bicycle sale at Kmart, Cheryl and Terry went to the store with Mark. A salesperson approached them at an outdoor display of bikes and directed them to the sporting goods department inside the store. There they found row after row of red three-speed bikes with minimal accessories—the type of bike Cheryl and Terry felt was ideal for Mark.

A salesperson approached them and tried to interest them in a more expensive bike. Terry dislikes salespeople trying to push something on him and interrupted her in midsentence. He said he wanted to look at the bikes on his own. With a little suggestion, Mark decided he wanted one of these bikes. His desire for accessories was satisfied when they bought a wire basket for the bike. After buying a bike for Mark, Terry decided he'd like a bike for himself to ride on weekends. Terry had ridden bikes since he was five. In graduate school, before he was married, he'd owned a 10-speed. He frequently took 50-mile rides with friends. But he hadn't owned a bike since moving to Riverside 15 years ago.

Terry didn't know much about current types of touring bicycles. He bought a copy of *Touring* at a newsstand to see what was available. He also went to the library to read *Consumer Reports*' evaluation of touring bikes. Based on this information, he decided he wanted a Serrato. It had all the features he wanted: lightweight, durable construction, and flexible setup. When Terry called the discount stores and bicycle shops, he found they didn't carry Serrato. He then decided he might not really need a bike. After all, he'd been without one for 15 years.

One day, after lunch, he was walking back to his office and saw a small bicycle shop. The shop was run down with bicycle parts scattered across the floor. The owner, a young man in grease-covered shorts, was fixing a bike. As Terry was looking around, the owner approached him and asked him if he liked to bicycle. Terry said he used to but had given it up when he moved to Riverside. The owner said that was a shame because there were a lot of nice places to tour around Riverside.

As their conversation continued, Terry mentioned his interest in a Serrato and his disappointment in not finding a store in Riverside that sold them. The owner said that he could order a Serrato for Terry but that they weren't very reliable. He suggested a Ross and showed Terry one he had in stock. Terry thought the $400 price was too high, but the owner convinced him to try it next weekend. They would ride together in the country. The owner and some of his friends took a 60-mile tour with Terry. Terry enjoyed the experience, recalling his college days. After the tour, Terry bought the Ross.

DISCUSSION QUESTIONS

1. Outline the decision-making process for each of the Chens' bicycle purchases.

2. Compare the different purchase processes for the three bikes. What stimulated each of them? What factors were considered in making the store choice decisions and purchase decisions?

3. Using the multiattribute module on the CD accompanying the text, construct a multiattribute model for each purchase decision. How do the attributes considered and importance weights vary for each decision?

Source: This case was written by Barton Weitz, University of Florida.

CASE 8   Dollar General and Family Dollar Buy Low and Sell Low

Dollar General, headquartered in Goodlettsville, Tennessee, and Family Dollar, based in Mathews, North Carolina, are the leading retailers in the fastest-growing segment of the industry, referred to as value retailing. In 2002, Dollar General had over 5,700 stores with sales surpassing $5 billion. Its annual growth in sales has been above 20 percent for the last six years. Family Dollar, with 4,100 stores, generated over $4 billion in sales in 2002. Both retailers are opening new stores at rates exceeding a store a day.

The value retail format has become increasing popular among a variety of customers, including rural shoppers, low- to middle-income young families, ethnic groups, and older customers with fixed incomes. Consumers have come to trust both of these retailers to provide good-quality merchandise at low prices without the hassle of crowds and lines. The breakdown by geographic segments is 25 percent rural, 33 percent urban, and 44 percent suburban.

This distribution is about the same as the sales distribution for Wal-Mart and Kmart stores. About 25 percent of the U.S. households shop at a value retailer once a month.

Sometimes these firms are grouped under the category of dollar retailers—retailers that sell merchandise priced under one dollar. While Dollar General and Family Dollar keep their prices typically under $15, most of their merchandise is priced over a dollar. Family Dollar has multiple price points, whereas Dollar General prices its merchandise at even-dollar price points.

About 50 percent of the merchandise sold in the stores is consumables (pet supplies, food, paper, household cleaning, and personal care products), with the remaining sales equally divided between basic clothing, hardware and seasonal merchandise, and home products. The percentage of consumable sales has been increasing over the last five years. The basic stock is supplemented with opportunistic buys of closeout/liquidation and impulse merchandise that gives the impression of a changing merchandise mix in the stores.

Vendors are developing new products and packaging to meet the needs of these value retailers. For example, Fruit of the Loom typically sells men's underwear in a nine pack, but it offers small packs to value retailers. Procter & Gamble and Johnson Products also sell smaller sizes of hair care products with lower retail prices to value retail chains.

Most of their locations are in the Southeast where the companies are headquartered. The stores are small, 6,000 to 8,000 square feet, primarily located in small towns with populations under 40,000 and suburban strip shopping centers. Since the stores are relatively small, it is easy to find good locations in almost any market the retailers choose to enter.

Initially, these value retailers focused on low-income communities that were too small to support a large Wal-Mart or Kmart discount store. Residents of these towns appreciate the convenience of buying merchandise close to their homes rather than driving 30 minutes to a discount store in a larger town. Many of their customers walk to the stores. Not only are the stores closer to customers, but shoppers are able to park closer to the stores in uncrowded parking lots and avoid long checkout lines. With a small store, customers can get in easily, find what they are looking for, and get out in a few minutes. The average transaction is between $8 and $9. To maximize operating efficiencies, the retailers typically open a cluster of stores in a geographic area before entering a new area. Dollar General and Family Dollar are now opening stores in suburban strip shopping centers, using space that has been abandoned by drugstores that moved to stand-alone locations.

At one time, these value retailers advertised sales using circulars. But both Dollar General and Family Dollar reduced their advertising expenses when they converted to an everyday low pricing strategy. This cost saving allowed the retailers to pass even more savings to their customers.

The Family Dollar 2001 annual report stated, "Supply chain efficiencies are vital to the success of any retailer, particularly one growing as fast as Family Dollar." Thus, Family Dollar and Dollar General are making significant investments in point-of-sale terminals, store-level inventory tracking systems, automated distribution centers, space allocation software, and replenishment systems to reduce stockouts and increase inventory turnover.

> ### DISCUSSION QUESTIONS
>
> 1. What is the target market for value retailers like Dollar General and Family Dollar?
>
> 2. Why are customers increasingly patronizing these value retailer stores?
>
> 3. How do value retailers make a profit when their prices and average transactions are so low?
>
> 4. Can value retailers defend themselves against general merchandise discount retailers like Wal-Mart, or will Wal-Mart eventually drive them out of business? Why or why not?

Source: This case was written by Valerie Bryan, University of Florida.

CASE 9   Ahold: The Biggest Supermarket Retailer You Have Never Heard Of

 In 1887, 22-year-old Albert Heijn took over his father's small grocery store near Zaandam, West Holland. His strategy for growing the family business was to offer quality products with excellent customer service at the lowest prices. Now, 115 yesrs later, Ahold (an abbreviation of Albert Heijn Holding) is the world's second-largest food retailer. It operates 9,000 stores in 27 countries, with 2002 sales greater than $60 billion. But its name is not on a single store it owns.

Ahold operates under 26 different names in Europe, America, Asia, and Latin America. In addition, it owns two food-service companies and Peapod, an online grocer, in the United States. It uses 10 different formats for its stores, ranging from tiny gas station outlets in the Netherlands to 150,000-square-foot hypermarkets in northern Brazil. The company refers to its strategy as "multilocal, multiformat, multichannel." "Our culture is first and foremost the culture of the local operating company," says Cees van der Hoeven, Ahold's 54-year-old CEO. "What makes Ahold unique is that we're perceived by our customers as the local guy." Very few customers at a Bruno's supermarket in Alabama or a Disco store in Argentina realize that their store is part of global retail giant headquartered in the Netherlands.

Wal-Mart and Carrefour, the first- and third-largest food retailers, use a different approach. From Paris to Shanghai, all Carrefour stores look the same and have identical layouts (to reach the deli counter, for example, you always turn left at the entrance). Wal-Mart also uses its name on most of its stores across the world. Three years ago, it acquired the Asada chain in the U.K. and still operates the stores under the Asada name. But when it bought the Wertkauf chain and some Spar stores in Germany, it converted the stores to Wal-Marts. Their British and German stores are expected to conform to the cost conscious, customer-oriented Wal-Mart culture.

Ahold is a food retailer. Food sales account for 90 percent of its revenues. Recognizing the lifestyle trend toward more out-of-home food consumption, Ahold is attempting to increase its share of the stomach through its acquisition of food-service companies. In contrast, Wal-Mart and Carrefour focus on operating larger supercenters or hypermarkets that offer general merchandise as well as food.

Another difference between Ahold and its major international competitors is its growth strategy. Although Wal-Mart has made some acquisitions, most of its international growth, and all of Carrefour's, has been internally generated. On the other hand, Ahold has grown primarily through acquisitions. More than 50 percent of Ahold's revenue now comes from the U.S. supermarket chains it acquired. Its first acquisition in the United States, in 1977, was BI-LO, a South Carolina–based grocery store chain operating about 450 stores in South Carolina, Georgia, Tennessee, Florida, and Alabama. Then it acquired Stop & Shop, with 320 stores stretching from Massachusetts to eastern New Jersey; Giant Landover of Maryland in Maryland, Washington, DC, Delaware, southern New Jersey, and northern Virginia; Giant Carlisle in Pennsylvania; Tops in New York; and Bruno in Alabama, the Florida Panhandle, and Mississippi. With 1,400 stores in the United States, Ahold is the largest food retailer in the eastern part of the country and the fourth biggest in the whole country, after Wal-Mart, Kroger, Safeway, and Albertson's.

In 1999, the company bought U.S. Foodservice, America's second-largest supplier of ready-made meals, prepared foods, and ingredients to restaurants, hotels, and other institutions. Finally, Ahold rescued Peapod, one of the first Internet grocers, from bankruptcy in 2000 by taking a majority stake in the company. Peapod now operates out of Stop & Shop and Giant stores in the Boston, New York, and Washington, DC, areas, as well as on its own in its home base of Chicago.

No other European retailer has been as successful in entering the U.S. market as Ahold. For example, Carrefour opened two stores in suburban Philadelphia in the late 80s but gave up quickly when it faced labor problems and the loyalty customers had to their local supermarket chains. The profit margin for Ahold's U.S. division are 5.7 percent, while the profit margin for the European division are only 3.9 percent of sales.

Van der Hoeven has a vision of a future in which Ahold's stores in Guatemala would offer tips on pricing to their colleagues in the United States and the flooring for every Ahold supermarket from Boston to São Paulo would be ordered from the same supplier. The payoff from this networked global juggernaut would be the ability to leverage its size to get rock-bottom prices from its vendors on every thing from corn flakes to oranges. Meanwhile, Ahold's companies in Europe, America, Asia, and Latin America would lower their costs by using the same trucks, sharing the same accountants, and exchanging ideas over the corporate intranet. But this global network would be invisible to the 40 million customers who pass through Ahold stores every week.

Ahold has yet to realize this vision. While Ahold has now centralized the procurement of fresh and chilled products across its six U.S. chains, only 5 percent of all merchandise in Ahold's stores is ordered on a cross-continental basis, about the same as Wal-Mart and Carrefour. Ahold's U.S. managers are just beginning to exchange best practices with their counterparts overseas. For example, Stop & Shop and Peapod are trying to improve their fulfillment accuracy by learning how Ahold's Scandinavian Internet home-delivery service has achieve its successes in performing these activities. However, Ahold's goal is to bring the same supply chain efficiencies achieved by Wal-Mart and Carrefour in general merchandise distribution to food distribution.

● DISCUSSION QUESTIONS

1. What are the advantages and disadvantages of the growth strategies pursued by Ahold and Carrefour and Wal-Mart?

2. Should Ahold use its name on all of its stores like Wal-Mart and Carrefour? Why or why not?

3. What are the advantages and disadvantages of Wal-Mart and Carrefour's more centralized decision making compared to Ahold's decentralized decision making?

Source: This case was written by Barton Weitz, University of Florida.

CASE 10 American Eagle and Abercrombie & Fitch Battle for the Teen/College Market

Jennifer Shaffer, a 17-year-old living in Newton, Massachusetts, used to shop at Abercrombie & Fitch (A&F) once a month. She thought the prices were high, but the brand name and image appealed to her. She says, "It's like I really had to have Abercrombie." Then an American Eagle store opened about 15 minutes from her home. Now she shops at the American Eagle store about twice a month and rarely goes to the Abercrombie store. "They look the same, and they're both really cute," she says. "But American Eagle's prices are a little cheaper."

Both Abercrombie & Fitch and American Eagle are still growing into their present strategy of selling casual apparel to the teen/college market. A&F was established as an outdoor sporting goods retailer over 100 years ago. It sold the highest-quality hunting, fishing, and camping goods. A&F outfitted some of the greatest explorations in the early part of the twentieth century, including Robert Perry's expedition to the North Pole and Theodore Roosevelt's trips to the Amazon and Africa.

Over time, its tweedy image became less attractive to consumers. The chain experienced a significant decline in sales and profits, and, in 1977, it was forced to declare bankruptcy. The company, initially acquired by Oshman's Sporting Goods, did not experience a turnaround until The Limited Inc. acquired it in 1988. Initially, The Limited positioned A&F as a tailored clothing store for men. In 1995, The Limited repositioned A&F to target both males and females in the teen and college market with an emphasis on casual American style and youth.

In 1999, The Limited sold A&F, which now operates as a separate company. Currently, the company has over 500 Abercrombie & Fitch stores in the United States; 150 "abercrombie" stores for children; and a new, lower-priced chain of 32 stores called Hollister, targeted at high school students.

American Eagle, while not having the rich tradition of A&F, initially also was positioned as outfitter when it started in 1977. Initially offering apparel only for men, American Eagle shifted its focus to teens and college students in 1995. In 2000, it acquired two Canadian specialty retail chains—Bluenotes/Thriftys and Braemar. The Braemar locations were converted to American Eagle stores. The Thriftys stores are being converted into Bluenotes stores, specialty stores that target a slightly younger, more urban teen demographic and that carry more denim merchandise. Today, American Eagle has over 600 stores in the United States and Canada.

Even though A&F and American Eagle have evolved from their roots, there is still an outdoor, rugged aspect in their apparel. Both retail chains carry similar assortments of cargoes, tech pants, T-shirts, and sweaters, all private-label. A lot of the merchandise is athletically inspired.

The rivalry between A&F and American Eagle is intense. A&F even filed a lawsuit, in 1998 in federal court accusing American Eagle of copying its clothing styles and catalog. The courts found that while the designs were similar, there was nothing inherently distinctive in Abercrombie's clothing designs that could be protected by a trademark. But the courts have ruled that Abercrombie's catalog design and image are worthy of trade dress protection. However, they also felt that American Eagle's catalog had a different image that did not infringe upon the image of the A&F catalog.

A&F's catalog, the *A&F Quarterly* (www.abercrombie. com/anf/lifestyles/html/afquarterly.html), plays an important role in developing the company's brand image. The photographs in the catalog are sexually suggestive, featuring college-age girls and guys, sometimes partially nude. The chain's marketing has historically been controversial, particularly when it printed drink recipes in the *Quarterly*. Some people felt the recipes promoted binge drinking on college campuses.

But it is the *Quarterly* that first drew Jennifer to an A&F store a couple of years ago. She recalls going through the catalog with some girlfriends and looking at the muscular young men featured. "The guys in the magazine— that's what made us all go," she says. This young and sexy image is enhanced by store signage featuring scantily clad lacrosse players and young beachgoers. Abercrombie & Fitch has exploited this image by introducing a line of intimate apparel in 2001. Intimate apparel is now one of the best-selling merchandise categories in the stores.

The image of American Eagle (www.ae.com) is more homecoming rather than hot tub. American Eagle provides the wardrobe for the stars of "Dawson's Creek," and it also has its apparel featured in various movies. While its commercials are less suggestive than those of A&F, its "Get Together" commercials features college- and high-school-age teens dancing and then coming together and kissing.

Even though A&F devotes its advertising and marketing resources toward reaching college-age consumers, many teenagers also patronize its stores. The company is concerned that the image of its stores will be negatively affected if they become a place for teenagers to hang out. The development of the Hollister chain is one of the approaches that A&F has taken to preserve the A&F image while catering to the growing teenage market

The Hollister stores are unique. Their target market consists of consumers aged 14 to 18. The merchandise in the stores is 20 to 30 percent less than A&F's merchandise.

The styling of the merchandise is also different. It has brighter colors and larger logos. However, many teenagers fail to recognize the subtle differences. They contend that it is essentially the same merchandise except at lower prices.

Furthermore, Hollister stores are roughly 2,000 square feet smaller than A&F stores, and the store design is completely distinct. While A&F stores still convey an outdoor ruggedness in their décor, Hollister stores present a California beach-inspired theme. They want their customers to feel as though they are part of a beach party. This casual atmosphere provides young consumers with a more enjoyable shopping experience. The décor in the stores inspires and evokes memories of hot summer days at any time of the year.

DISCUSSION QUESTIONS

1. What, if any, are the differences in A&F's and American Eagle's retail strategy?

2. What are the brand images of A&F and American Eagle? What words and phrases are associated with each retailer's brand name?

3. Which retailer is in a stronger competitive position? Why?

4. Would you take a risk like A&F and pursue Hollister as a growth strategy? Why or why not?

Source: This case was written by Kristina Pacca, University of Florida.

CASE 11   Neiman Marcus and Family Dollar: Comparing Strategic Profit Models

Janis Lockwood works in the finance department of Family Dollar, a value retailer with 4,000 stores in the southeast U.S. Family Dollar targets middle- to low-income consumers and offers a limited assortment of consumables, clothing, and personal care products in 6,000-square-foot stores. Most of the stores are located in rural areas or suburban strip shopping centers. Her new boss, Sam Popkin, was hired from Neiman Marcus to be the chief financial officer. Neiman Marcus operates upscale department stores located in 35 malls across the United States, including in Arkansas, Tennessee, Texas, New Mexico, Oklahoma, Missouri, Nebraska, Kansas, Louisiana, Nevada, Arizona, Illinois, Alabama, Ohio, North Carolina, South Carolina, Mississippi, Iowa, Utah, Florida, and Kentucky.

Popkin is concerned and somewhat confused about why the key financial ratios for Family Dollar are so different from those of Neiman Marcus. Specifically, executives at Neiman Marcus always emphasized the importance of net profit margin, and Neiman's net profit margin percentage is significantly higher than Family Dollar's.

You can do the strategic profit models by hand by using the form accompanying this case or you can prepare the plan using the strategic profit model module on the CD accompanying the text.

DISCUSSION QUESTIONS

1. Using Exhibit 3, construct strategic profit models for Family Dollar and Neiman Marcus using data from the abbreviated income statements and balance sheets in Exhibits 1 and 2.

2. Explain, from a marketing perspective, why you would expect the gross margin percentage,

expenses-to-sales ratio, net profit margin, inventory turnover, and asset turnover to be different for Neiman Marcus and Family Dollar.

3. Assess which chain has better overall financial performance. Why?

Source: This case was written by Barton Weitz, University of Florida.

EXHIBIT 1

Income Statements for Family Dollar and Neiman Marcus, 2001

	Family Dollar ($000)	Neiman Marcus ($000)
Net sales and other income	$ 3,665	$ 3,016
Less: Cost of goods sold	2,439	2,021
Gross margin	1,226	995
Less: Operating expenses	928	791
Less: Interest expenses	0	15
Total expenses	928	806
Net profit, pretax	298	189
Less: Taxes	109	68
Net profit, after taxes	189	121

Source: SEC 10K filings at www.sec.gov/edaux/searches.htm.

EXHIBIT 2
Balance Sheet Information for Family Dollar
and Neiman Marcus

	Family Dollar ($000)	Neiman Marcus ($000)
Current Assets		
Cash	$ 22	$ 97
Accounts receivable	0	242
Merchandise inventory	721	649
Other current assets	50	76
Total current assets	793	1,064
Fixed assets		
Property and equipment	581	586

Source: SEC 10K filings at www.sec.gov/edaux/searches.htm.

EXHIBIT 3   Strategic Profit Model

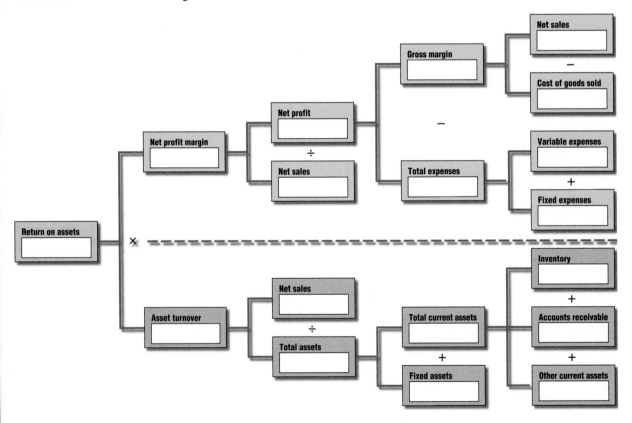

CASE 12   Stephanie's Boutique: Selecting a Store Location

Stephanie Wilson must decide where to open a ready-to-wear boutique she's been contemplating for several years. Now in her late 30s, she's been working in municipal government ever since leaving college, where she majored in fine arts. She's divorced with two children (ages five and eight) and wants her own business, at least partly to be able to spend more time with her children. She loves fashion, feels she has a flair for it, and has taken evening courses in fashion design and retail management. Recently, she heard about a plan to rehabilitate an old arcade building in the downtown section of her midwestern city. This news crystallized her resolve to move now. She's considering three locations.

THE DOWNTOWN ARCADE

The city's central business district has been ailing for some time. The proposed arcade renovation is part of a master redevelopment plan, with a new department store and several office buildings already operating. Completion of the entire master plan is expected to take another six years.

Dating from 1912, the arcade building was once the center of downtown trade, but it's been vacant for the past 15 years. The proposed renovation includes a three-level shopping facility, low-rate garage with validated parking, and convention center complex. Forty shops are planned for the first (ground) floor, 28 more on the second, and a series of restaurants on the third.

The location Stephanie is considering is 30 feet square and situated near the main ground floor entrance. Rent is $20 per square foot, for an annual total of $18,000. If sales exceed $225,000, rent will be calculated at 8 percent of sales. She'll have to sign a three-year lease.

TENDERLOIN VILLAGE

The gentrified urban area of the city where Stephanie lives is nicknamed Tenderloin Village because of its lurid past. Today, however, the neat, well-kept brownstones and comfortable neighborhood make it feel like a yuppie enclave. Many residents have done the remodeling work themselves and take great pride in their neighborhood.

About 20 small retailers are now in an area of the Village adjacent to the convention center complex. Most of them are "ferns-and-quiche" restaurants. There are also three small women's clothing stores.

The site available to Stephanie is on the Village's main street on the ground floor of an old house. Its space is also about 900 square feet. Rent is $15,000 annually with no coverage clause. The landlord knows Stephanie and will require a two-year lease.

APPLETREE MALL

This suburban mall has been open for eight years. A successful regional center, it has three department stores and 100 smaller shops just off a major interstate highway about eight miles from downtown. Of its nine women's clothing retailers, three are in a price category considerably higher than what Stephanie has in mind.

Appletree has captured the retail business in the city's southwest quadrant, though growth in that sector has slowed in the past year. Nevertheless, mall sales are still running 12 percent ahead of the previous year. Stephanie learned of plans to develop a second shopping center east of town, which would be about the same size and character as Appletree Mall. But groundbreaking is still 18 months away, and no renting agent has begun to enlist tenants.

The store available to Stephanie in Appletree is two doors from the local department store chain's mall outlet. At 1,200 square feet, it's slightly larger than the other two possibilities. But it's long and narrow—24 feet in front by 50 feet deep. Rent is $24 per square foot ($28,800 annually). In addition, on sales that exceed $411,500, rent is 7 percent of sales. There's an additional charge of 1 percent of sales to cover common-area maintenance and mall promotions. The mall's five-year lease includes an escape clause if sales don't reach $411,500 after two years.

> ● **DISCUSSION QUESTIONS**
>
> 1. Give the pluses and minuses of each location.
> 2. What type of store would be most appropriate for each location?
> 3. If you were Stephanie, which location would you choose? Why?

Source: This case was prepared by Professor David Ehrlich, Marymount University.

CASE 13 Hutch: Locating a New Store

In June, after returning from a trip to the Bahamas, Dale Abell, vice president of new business development for the Hutch Corporation, began a search for a good location to open a new store. After a preliminary search, Abell narrowed the choice to two locations, both in Georgia. He now faces the difficult task of thoroughly analyzing each location and determining which will be the site of the next store.

COMPANY BACKGROUND

The Hutch store chain was founded in 1952 by John Henry Hutchison, a musician and an extremely successful insurance salesman. Hutchison established the headquarters in Richmond, Virginia, where both the executive offices and one of two warehouse distribution centers are located. Hutch currently operates 350 popularly priced women's clothing stores throughout the Southeast and Midwest. Manufacturers ship all goods to these distribution centers. They are delivered floor-ready in that the vendor has attached price labels, UPC identifying codes, and source tags for security purposes and has placed appropriate merchandise on hangers. Once at the distribution centers, the merchandise is consolidated for reshipment to the stores. Some staple merchandise, such as hosiery, is stored at these distribution centers. All Hutch stores are located within 400 miles of a distribution center. This way, as Abell explains, "A truck driver can deliver to every location in two days."

Hutch Fashions

Hutch Fashions is considered one of the leading popular-priced women's fashion apparel chains in the Southeast. The stores carry trendy apparel selections in juniors', misses', and women's sizes, all at popular prices. The chain offers a complementary array of accessories in addition to its main features of dresses, coats, and sportswear. Located mainly in strip centers and malls, these shops typically require 4,000 to 5,000 square feet.

Hutch Extra

Hutch Extra stores are primarily located in strip centers and malls. They bear a strong resemblance to Hutch Fashions. The difference is that Hutch Extra stores require less space (from 2,000 to 3,000 square feet) and cater to women requiring large and half-size apparel. (Women who wear half-sizes require a larger size but are not tall enough to wear a standard large size. In other words, a size 18 1/2 is the same as size 18 except that it is cut for a shorter woman.)

Hutch Fashions* Hutch Extra

Although Hutch Fashions and Hutch Extra stores selectively appear as separate entries, the corporate goal is to position both as a single entity. The combination store emerged in 1986 and is now used for all new stores.

The Hutch Fashions* Hutch Extra combination occupies a combined space of 6,000 to 7,000 square feet, with separate entrances for each entity. A partial wall separates the two frontal areas of the store but allows a combined checkout/customer service area in the rear. The new stores are primarily located in strip centers and can occasionally be found in malls (Exhibit 1 shows a typical layout).

MARKETING STRATEGY

Customers

Hutch's target market is women between the ages of 18 and 40 who are in the lower-middle to middle-income range. Abell explains, "We don't cater to any specific ethnic group, only to women who like to wear the latest fashions."

EXHIBIT I
Layout of a Hutch Fashions* Hutch Extra Store

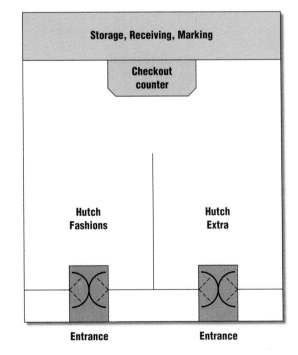

Product/Price

Hutch positions merchandise and price levels between the mass merchandisers and the department stores. You won't find any bluelight specials or designer boutiques in a Hutch store. By avoiding direct competition for customers with the large discounters (Kmart and Wal-Mart) and the high-fashion department stores and specialty shops, Hutch has secured a comfortable niche for itself. "Our products must be priced at a level where our customers perceive our products to be elegant and fashionable but not too expensive," notes Abell.

Location

Hutch stores are located throughout the Southeast and Midwest and must be within a 400-mile radius of a Hutch distribution center. Within this geographic area, Hutch stores are located in communities with a population range of 10,000 to 50,000 and a trade area of 50,000 to 150,000. These locations are characterized by a large concentration of people in the low- to middle-income brackets who work in agriculture and industry.

Hutch stores are primarily located in strip malls or strip centers—generally ones anchored by either a regional or national mass merchandiser (Wal-Mart or Kmart). In addition, these centers contain a mix of several nationally recognized and popular local tenants. Hutch stores are primarily located adjacent to the center's anchor. Mall locations must be on the main corridor as close to "center court," as economics (rent) will allow. Abell remarked, "We don't care if it's the only center in the region. If the only space available is at the end of the mall, we won't go in there. Our plan is to be a complement to the anchor and to feed off the traffic coming to it. We may have a reputation for being picky and having one of the toughest lease agreements in the business, but it's one of the main reasons for our continued success."

DATA SOURCES

Abell is using several reports generated by Claritas/UDS Data Service to help him decide which location to choose for the next Hutch store. He has chosen reports that describe the 10-mile ring around each of the proposed locations.

Exhibits 2 and 3 summarize these reports. They contain detailed population, household, race, income, education, and employment data plus figures on retail sales and number of establishments. The reports also provide information about women's apparel sales and give a market index that estimates the annual per-person spending potential for the trade area divided by the national average (see Exhibit 3). Dalton's 99 index means that the spending potential for women's clothing is slightly lower than the national average of 100.

Finally, Abell is using Claritas/UDS's PRIZM lifestyle reports. These reports contain numeric figures and percentages on the population, households, families, sex, age, household size, and ownership of housing. An excerpt from the report is given in Exhibit 4. Some of the cluster group names are described in Exhibit 5.

THE POTENTIAL LOCATIONS

Dalton

Dalton produces most of the carpeting in the United States. Consequently, the carpet mills are the major employers in Dalton. Stain Master carpeting has been putting a strain on the city's water supply. Stain Master is said to require seven times the amount of water as regular carpeting and is rapidly becoming the largest proportion of carpeting produced. Expressing concern over market viability, Abell said, "If the Dalton area were ever to experience a severe drought, the carpet mills would be forced to drastically reduce production. The ensuing layoffs could put half the population on unemployment."

The proposed site for the new store is the Whitfield Square shopping center located off the main highway approximately two miles from the center of town (see Exhibit 6). After meeting with the developer, Abell was pleased with several aspects of the strip center. He learned that the center has good visibility from the highway, will be anchored by both Wal-Mart and Kroger (a large grocery chain), and has ample parking. Abell is also reasonably pleased with the available location within the center, which is one spot away from Wal-Mart. However, he was displeased with the presence of two large outparcels in front of the center that would reduce the number of parking spaces and direct visibility of the center. (An outparcel is a freestanding structure at the front of a mall, commonly a fast-food outlet, a bank, or a gas station.) Other tenants in the center include a nationally recognized shoe store, a beauty salon, two popular restaurants (Chinese and Mexican), and McSpeedy's Pizza at the end of the center, and a Century 21 real estate training school in the middle.

Hinesville

Like Dalton, Hinesville has one major employer, the Fort Stuart army base. Abell recalls that popular-priced stores generally do very well in military towns. Additionally, Fort Stuart is a rapid-deployment force base. Since the United States currently is involved in a number of international activities, Abell is concerned with a comment by a Hinesville native, "If these guys have to ship out, this place will be a ghost town."

The location under consideration is the Kmart Plaza at the junction of State Route 119 and U.S. Highway 82 (see Exhibit 7). The center is anchored by Kmart and a grocery

EXHIBIT 2

Population and Competitive Profile, 10-Mile Ring from Center of Dalton and Hinesville, Georgia

		Dalton	Hinesville
Population	2005 projection	93,182	64,195
	1999 estimate	87,293	57,945
	1990 Census	79,420	49,853
	1980 Census	71,373	34,125
	% change, 1990–96	9.9%	16.2%
	% change, 1980–90	11.3%	46.1%
	In group quarters (military base) 1996	.9%	11.2%
Household	2005 projection	35,570	20,010
	1999 estimate	33,140	17,541
	1990 Census	29,340	14,061
	1980 Census	24,302	8,557
	% change, 1990–96	12.9%	24.7%
	% change, 1980–90	20.7%	64.3%
Families	1996 estimate	24,347	14,277
Race, 1999	White	92.0%	54.1%
	Black	4.9%	38.3%
	American Indian	0.2%	0.5%
	Asian or Pacific Islander	0.6%	3.1%
	Other	2.3%	4.0%
Age, 1999	0–20	31.2%	40.2%
	21–44	37.1%	47.0%
	45–64	21.7%	9.2%
	65+	9.9%	3.4%
	Median age, 1996	33.7	23.9
	Male	32.5	23.6
	Female	35.0	24.6
Household size, 1999	1 person	21.0%	15.2%
	2 persons	32.3%	26.6%
	3–4 persons	38.1%	45.7%
	5+ persons	8.7%	12.6%
Income, 1999	Median household income	$30,516	$23,686
	Average household income	$40,397	$28,677
Sex (% male)		49.1%	55.8%
Education, 1999	Population age 25+	49,298	22,455
	No high school diploma	41.0%	15.5%
	High school only	28.6%	41.2%
	College, 1–3 years	19.1%	29.7%
	College, 4+ years	11.3%	13.5%
Industry	Manufacturing: nondurable goods	42.3%	7.2%
	Retail trade	12.6%	23.3%
	Professional and related services	13.3%	21.4%
	Public administration	2.2%	20.0%
Retail sales (000)	Total	$706,209	$172,802
	General merchandise stores		
	Apparel stores	$26,634	$9,339
Retail establishments	General merchandise stores	12	3
	Women's apparel stores	21	8

EXHIBIT 3
Sales Potential Index
for Women's Apparel

	Area Sales ($ mil.)	Area Sales per Capita	U.S. Sales per Capita	Index (area sales ÷ U.S. sales)
Dalton	$18.01	$206.26	$207.65	99
Hinesville	$8.97	$154.74	$207.65	75

PRIZM Neighborhood Clusters **EXHIBIT 4**

Prizm Cluster	Population, 1999	Percentage of Population	Prizm Cluster	Population, 1999	Percentage of Population
Dalton			Mines & mills	7,694	8.8
Big fish, small pond	4,727	5.4%	Back country folks	4,293	4.9
New homesteaders	6,030	6.9	Hinesville		
Red, white, & blues	31,123	35.7	Military quarters	45,127	77.9
Shotguns & pickups	8,881	10.2	Scrub pine flats	3,476	6.0
Rural industrial	12,757	14.6			

PRIZM Lifestyle Clusters **EXHIBIT 5**

Big Fish, Small Pond

Small-town executive families; upper-middle incomes; age groups 35–44, 45–54; predominantly white. This group is married, family-oriented, and conservative. Their neighborhoods are older. Best described as captains of local industry, they invest in their homes and clubs, and vacation by car in the United States.

Rural Industrial

Low-income, blue-collar families; lower-middle incomes; age groups <24, 25–34, predominantly white, high Hispanic. Nonunion labor found in this cluster, which is comprised of hundreds of blue-collar mill towns on American's rural backroads.

Mines & Mills

Older families; mine and mill towns; poor; age groups 55–64, 65+; predominantly white. Down the Appalachians, across the Ozarks to Arizona, and up the Missouri, this cluster is exactly as its name implies. This older, mostly single population with a few children lives in the midst of scenic splendor.

Shotguns and Pickups

Rural blue-collar workers and families; middle income; age groups 35–44, 45–54; predominantly white. This cluster is found in the Northeast, the Southeast, and in the Great Lakes and Piedmont industrial regions. They are in blue-collar jobs; most are married with school-age kids. They are churchgoers who also enjoy bowling, hunting, sewing, and attending car races.

Back Country Folks

Older African-American farm families; lower-middle income; age groups 55–64, 65+; predominantly white. This cluster is centered in the eastern uplands along a wide path from the Pennsylvania Poconos to the Arkansas Ozarks. Anyone who visits their playground in Branson, Missouri, or Gatlinburg, Tennessee, can attest that these are the most blue-collar neighborhoods in America. Centered in the Bible Belt, many back country folks are hooked on Christianity and country music.

Scrub Pine Flats

Older African-American farm families; poor; age groups 55–64, 65+; predominantly black. This cluster is found mainly in the coastal flatlands of the Atlantic and Gulf states from the James to the Mississippi rivers. These humid, sleepy rural communities, with a mix of blacks and whites, live in a seemingly timeless, agrarian rhythm.

New Homesteaders

Young middle-class families; middle income; age groups 35–44, 45–54; predominantly white. This cluster has above-average for college education. Executives and professionals work in local service fields such as administration, communications, health, and retail. Most are married; the young have children, the elders do not. Life is homespun with a focus on crafts, camping, and sports.

Red, White, & Blues

Small-town blue-collar families; middle income; age groups 35–54, 55–64; predominantly white, with skilled workers primarily employed in mining, milling, manufacturing, and construction. Geocentered in the Appalachians, Great Lakes industrial region, and western highlands, these folks love the outdoors.

Military Quarters

GIs and surrounding off-base families; lower-middle income; age groups under 24, 25–34; ethnically diverse. Since this cluster depicts military life with personnel living in group quarters, its demographics are wholly atypical because they are located on or near military bases. Racially integrated, and with the highest index for adults under 35, "Military Quarters" likes fast cars, bars, and action sports.

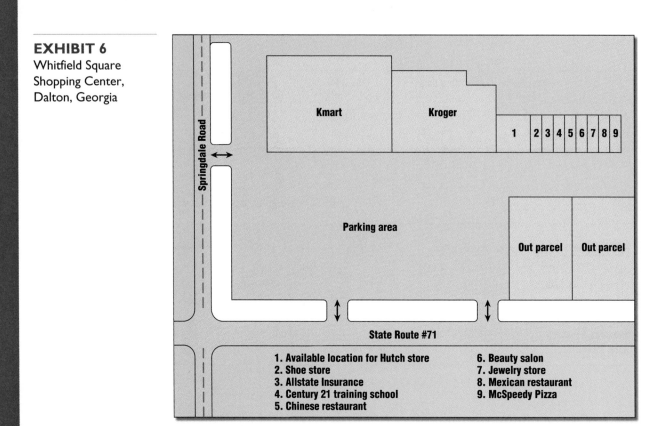

EXHIBIT 6
Whitfield Square
Shopping Center,
Dalton, Georgia

Springdale Road

Kmart

Kroger

1 2 3 4 5 6 7 8 9

Parking area

Out parcel

Out parcel

State Route #71

1. Available location for Hutch store
2. Shoe store
3. Allstate Insurance
4. Century 21 training school
5. Chinese restaurant

6. Beauty salon
7. Jewelry store
8. Mexican restaurant
9. McSpeedy Pizza

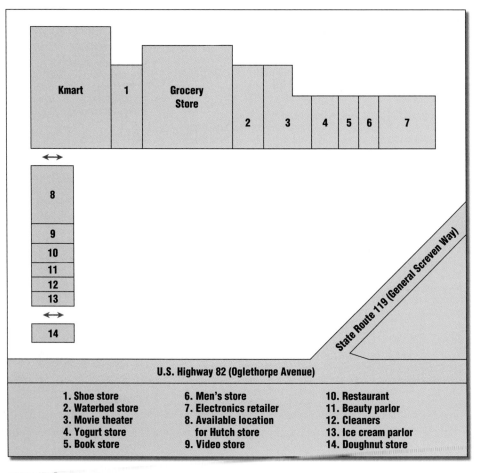

EXHIBIT 7
Kmart Plaza, Hinesville,
Georgia

Kmart

1

Grocery
Store

2 3 4 5 6 7

8

9
10
11
12
13

14

State Route 119 (General Screven Way)

U.S. Highway 82 (Oglethorpe Avenue)

1. Shoe store
2. Waterbed store
3. Movie theater
4. Yogurt store
5. Book store

6. Men's store
7. Electronics retailer
8. Available location
   for Hutch store
9. Video store

10. Restaurant
11. Beauty parlor
12. Cleaners
13. Ice cream parlor
14. Doughnut store

Source: The Ben Tobin Companies.

store that is part of a popular eastern chain. The two anchors are located side by side in the middle of the center. The spot available in the center is a 6,800-square-foot combination of three smaller units immediately adjacent to Kmart. Other tenants in the center include a bookstore, a waterbed store, a shoe store, an electronics retailer, a yogurt store, a video store, and a movie theater.

Source: This case was written by Michael Levy, Babson College.

CASE 14   Home Depot: New Directions

Founded in Atlanta, Georgia, Home Depot has grown into the world's largest home improvement specialty retailer and the second-largest retailer in the United States. Twenty years of consistent growth is quite an achievement for any retailer; however, due to this growth, Home Depot is a much different company than it was when it was founded by Bernard Marcus and Arthur Blank in 1978. Recent changes in the company, put into motion by the new CEO, Bob Nardelli, are shaking up the way Home Depot does business.

HISTORY AND CULTURE OF THE COMPANY

During Home Depot's first 20 years, Bernard Marcus was CEO. In 1997, Arthur Blank succeeded his partner's place at the top of the company. In founding Home Depot, the partnership of Marcus and Blank revolutionized home improvement shopping by creating a different kind of store. Warehouse is a better term for the stores' layout; each location stocks large volumes of goods that enable the company to compete by maintaining low prices. Because Home Depot's primary customer is the individual homeowner or small contractor, the stores also offer knowledgeable customer service to assist those in need of a little direction. In fact, the company took this further by offering how-to clinics and longer four-week courses in its Home Depot University to educate customers about various home improvement projects such as laying tile and caulking bathrooms. Thus, Home Depot effectively combined the strategies of low price and high service, not commonly seen in retailing.

Home Depot's "do-it-yourself" slogan was not just aimed at customers. This philosophy was fostered by the founders and trickled down through the entire company. Home Depot grew, not as a part of a complex plan, but as a result of a good business idea, good people, and some experimentation with new projects such as the Expo home decorating stores. Home Depot's corporate structure was very decentralized; many typical corporate policies were nonexistent in the firm. Each store manager was also a do-it-yourselfer and had a significant amount of control in making decisions pertaining to such areas as merchandising, advertising, and inventory selection for a particular area. Thus, Home Depot stores tended to be less homogeneous in their merchandise offerings than many other national retail chains.

But this decentralization of decision making allows managers to feel a stronger sense of ownership in a store's business. Associates of the company demonstrate a great deal of loyalty and pride in the company. Many store associates are hired with strong background experience in home improvement and are able to pass their knowledge along to customers. By building an enthusiastic staff, Home Depot has been able to deliver its promise of exceptional customer service.

FINDING A NEW LEADER

In 1999, with well over 900 stores, market share of 24 percent, and several growth initiatives, Home Depot exuded success. However, historical success and future success are different concepts. Home Depot's board of directors was becoming increasingly unhappy. The company's performance at the time was faltering with a sharp drop in stock price in October of 2000. After disputes about strategy, stores, and people, Home Depot's directors finally took action and so set out to find a leader capable, in their view, of continuing the firm's growth in sales and profits.

The board found their man in Bob Nardelli. At the time, Nardelli was vying for Jack Welch's position as CEO of GE but lost the battle to Jeff Immelt. Although he was passed up at GE, Bob Nardelli's career has been impressive to say the least. From playing football at Western Illinois University to starting as a manufacturing engineer at GE,

Nardelli's attitude was one of persistence and relentless hard work. Nardelli managed to work up through GE to the position of manufacturing VP, left to join the equipment maker Case as an executive vice president, and then returned to GE to run the Canadian appliance business. He then continued to prove himself at GE as the head of GE Transportation and CEO of GE Power Systems. Throughout his career at GE, Nardelli was recognized for his ability to improve operations and execute, but unfortunately, he was not viewed as a strong strategic leader. Believing he was finally in the right position to succeed Welch, Nardelli was very disappointed at the announcement of Immelt's appointment. Home Depot quickly snatched Nardelli up, placing him as CEO of Home Depot in December of 2000. Nardelli redirected his energy into a mission to develop Home Depot.

CHANGES AT HOME DEPOT

Since Nardelli took the lead at Home Depot, the company has experienced significant changes. Home Depot is shifting toward a more centralized organization, one that can more efficiently handle the operations of a 1,400-store company in Canada, Mexico, and the United States. For example, buying, once handled by nine regional offices, is now located at corporate headquarters in Atlanta. The company as a whole benefits from consolidation; buyers can get larger quantities of goods at lower costs, but how does this affect the do-it-yourself store manager? Nardelli, always a relentless workaholic, expects those around him to have the same attitude by holding frequent meetings and treating weekends like any other day of business.

Although a "can do, will do" atmosphere is necessary to implement Nardelli's plans, the hasty shift from laid back to no-nonsense is creating some anxiety within the organization. In the first 19 months of his office, Nardelli lost 24 of 39 senior officers and has brought on several new faces, many from outside the retail industry. One newcomer, recruited by the new CEO, is Dennis Donovan from GE. Nardelli, believing in Donovan's efficiency, has made him an exceptionally high-paid chief of HR.

Changes are not just affecting Home Depot's associates. In the past, Home Depot's customer return policy was simply to give cash back, no matter what. Although this was fantastic customer service, without receipt restrictions, abuse of the policy was out of control. Home Depot will now save close to $10 million annually with a new return policy of only store credit without a receipt.

Nardelli is applying the GE mind-set, one characterized by strict measurement emphasizing efficiency, to his new company. Home Depot is now using GE's Six Sigma quality control method and is quickly increasing the company's use of the Internet. Another new focus is that of associate training and evaluation. Pre-Nardelli, Home Depot had 157 different associate appraisal forms. All 295,000 associates are now reviewed using just two different forms.

These changes do not mean that the company is less interested in developing its people; in fact, Nardelli is trying to create an environment that will best highlight individual's abilities. At Home Depot's headquarters in Atlanta, the company is forming a leadership institute offering courses on leadership, merchandising, store planning, financial operations, and Six Sigma to executives with high potential. Nardelli wants a "coaching environment" that promotes succession planning and avoids the recent incident of having to hire a CEO from outside the company.

Despite Nardelli's efforts, the market has not been kind to Home Depot. In Nardelli's first six months, the stock price rose from $39 to $53 but then curiously fell 10 percent after a first quarter announcement of 35 percent profits growth. Quarterly earnings continue to grow as in the past, but unfortunately, Home Depot's stock price is not reflecting this trend.

COMPETITION AND GROWTH POTENTIAL

As Home Depot struggles with its own growing pains, the company must also consider the ever-increasing competition from Lowe's. By placing stores in directly competing areas and growing at a faster rate than Home Depot, Lowe's is definitely a factor in future planning. Lowe's best advantage is that its stores are designed with less of a "warehouse" feel, having wider aisles and better lighting. Store appearance may not be a crucial factor, but it is definitely a differentiating feature for a female shopper. And women are increasingly doing a greater percentage of home improvement shopping. Home Depot is trying to address this issue by cleaning up and modernizing its store look with lower shelving and different product mixes.

Extending its already strong business targeted at individual customers, Home Depot is now opening several professional stores for contractors, developers, and superintendent or maintenance people. The firm is also looking to expand through purchases of European home improvement companies.

● DISCUSSION QUESTIONS

1. What is the best way for the Home Depot to continue to grow?

2. Can Home Depot maintain its current market position with its new policies and increasing competition?

3. Will adapting to its size with more efficient operations and increased centralization be effective in streamlining Home Depot's business?

4. How might the shifts in corporate culture affect executives, management, and associates?

Source: This case was written by Cynthia Wongsuwan, University of Florida.

CASE 15   Avon Embraces Diversity

Women have always played an important role at Avon, the largest cosmetics firm in the United States. Mrs. P. F. E. Albee of Winchester, New Hampshire, pioneered the company's now-famous direct-selling method. Women have been selling Avon since 1886—34 years before women in the United States won the right to vote! Today, with sales representatives numbering three and a half million, Avon products are sold in 143 countries around the world.

While most of Avon's employees and customers are women, until recently the company has been run by men. However, a series of poor strategic decisions in the 1980s led the company to aggressively increase the number of women and minorities in its executive ranks. This decision to increase diversity in its managers was a major factor in Avon's improved financial performance.

Now Avon is recognized as a leader in management diversity. It has more women in management positions (86 percent) than any other *Fortune* 500 company. Half of the members of its board of directors are women. The company has undertaken a number of programs to ensure that women and minorities have opportunities for development and advancement. In the United States and elsewhere, Avon has internal networks of associates, including a parents' network, a hispanic network, a black professional association, an Asian network and a gay and lesbian network. The networks act as liaisons between associates and management to bring their voice to critical issues that affect the workplace and the marketplace.

Avon's problems started in the 1970s when its top management team, composed of all men, tried to change the firm's strategy. First the management ignored its own marketing research indicating that more women were entering the workforce and seeking professional careers, that the cosmetic needs would change, and that new approaches for selling products to them were needed. Then sales growth slowed, and the company reacted by seeking growth through unrelated diversifications. Finally, as the firm was on the brink of bankruptcy, a new top management team was brought in. Led by CEO Jim Preston, Avon refocused itself on its roots and began to again market cosmetics to a female, but very different, market.

Preston realized that Avon's customers needed to be represented in senior management. He enacted policies to quickly promote more women into higher-level positions. In addition, Preston shifted the firm's organization culture to be more accommodating of all its employees. For example, the firm dropped its season-ticket purchases to Knicks and Yankees games and replaced them with season tickets for the New York City Ballet and the New York Philharmonic.

Avon has also turned to foreign markets for additional growth. Preston credits several key female executives for championing the international push and for making sure that it was done right. Now many new managers come from international operations.

Preston's vision is reflected in Avon's senior management. Andrea Jung is chairman and CEO, and Susan Kropf is president and COO. Half of the members of the executive committee, the senior management of the firm, are women. Clearly, Avon is a firm that has changed its own culture and that appreciates the power of diversity and multiculturalism.

The new management team has launched a number of growth initiatives building on Avon's strong brand name and distribution channel through its customer representative network. Avon's products fall into three product categories: "Beauty," which consists of cosmetics, fragrance and toiletries; "Beauty Plus," which consists of jewelry, watches, and apparel and accessories; and "Beyond Beauty," which consists of home products, gifts, decorative, and candles. In 2001, Avon, expanded its definition of beauty to include inner health as well as outward appearance and started selling vitamins and nutrition supplements, exercise and fitness items, and a variety of self-care and stress relief products through catalogs.

Additionally, in 2001 Avon launched a line of beauty, health, and wellness products, jewelry, accessories for sales through selected JCPenney department stores. The product line, called "Becoming," is priced significantly higher than the core Avon line but well below prestige brands. In 2003, Avon plans to launch a new product line targeted to teenage girls to win market share in the worldwide youth market.

Finally, Avon is using technology to support the efforts of its 450,000 customer representatives. An electronic ordering system allows the representatives to run their businesses more efficiently and improve order processing accuracy. Now Avon representatives can use the Internet to manage their business electronically. In the United States, Avon representatives use a new online marketing tool called youravon.com. The site helps representatives build their own Avon business by enabling them to sell online through their own personalized web pages, developed in partnership with Avon. Avon e-representatives are able to promote special products, target specific groups of customers, place and track orders online, and capitalize on e-mail to share product information, selling tips, and marketing incentives.

DISCUSSION QUESTIONS

1. Why is Avon so committed to diversity?

2. Why don't more retailers follow Avon's lead?

3. How has increasing diversity been beneficial to Avon as it develops new strategies?

4. Evaluate the new opportunities that Avon is pursuing?

Source: This case was written by Barton Weitz, University of Florida.

CASE 16   Lawson Sportswear

"We need to have vendors who can take this burden off of us," said Clifton Morris, Lawson Sportswear inventory manager. "We have had a sales increase of 20 percent over the last two years and my people can't keep up with it anymore."

Keith Lawson, general manager of Lawson Sportswear, reviewed the colorful chart showing the sales trend and replied, "I never thought I would have to complain about a sales increase, but it is obvious that the sales are well beyond our control. Something has to be done and that is why we are meeting today."

Lawson Sportswear was founded by George Lawson in 1963 in a major southwestern metropolitan area. For five years, Lawson Sportswear has been successful in the sportswear market. In 1995, George Lawson retired, and his son, Keith Lawson, was appointed general manager. From the beginning, Keith Lawson has been a real go-getter. Recently completing his MBA, he has wasted no time in locating new markets for Lawson Sportswear. He immediately contacted the two major universities and gained four-year exclusive contracts for apparel purchases made by the sports teams of their athletic departments. Soon

after, Lawson's sportswear became popular among students. This growing demand for the company's products motivated Lawson to open two more retail stores. During the fall of 2002, the sales had increased beyond expectations. Although the company achieved a successful reputation in the marketplace, sales growth has generated major problems.

In the beginning, operations were fairly smooth and the company's inventory control department updated most of its procedures. Morris emphasized the crucial role of routinization in the overall inventory maintenance process to keep up with the increasing turnover. The sales increase was 20 percent, opposed to 12 percent that had been forecast for 2002. It was this increase that initiated a series of problems in the inventory control department. To temporarily alleviate the backlog, Lawson authorized Morris to lease an additional warehouse (see the replenishment level for July 2002 in Exhibit 1). It was decided that the maximum 16 percent of the total inventory carrying costs were going to be dedicated to the off-premise inventory.

Worrying about not being able to meet demand on time, Morris met with suppliers and asked them to provide

EXHIBIT I
Sales for Lawson
Sportswear in 2002

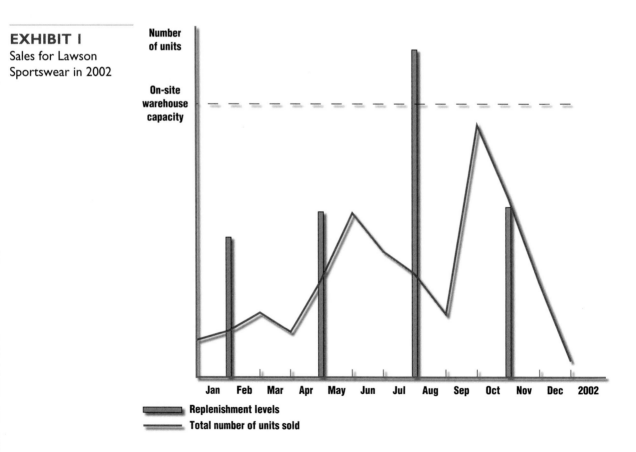

more timely delivery schedules to Lawson Sportswear. When he stated that the company was not going to tolerate any reasons for future delays, two major suppliers expressed their concerns about his lack of flexibility and requested price concessions. They simply indicated that Morris's demand had to be supported by providing cash or reducing quantity discounts. Morris ignored these comments and indicated how serious he really was by stating that Lawson Sportswear could always find new suppliers. By the end of a long discussion, arguments were beyond the manageable point and the two large suppliers decided to quit dealing with the company.

After the meeting, Morris received a memo from Lawson. Lawson was very concerned about the potential reactions of the rest of the vendors. He stated in his memo that since Lawson Sportswear was continuously growing, it was expected to present a more supportive attitude to its suppliers. He expressed his belief that the company needed a cohesive atmosphere with the rest of the channel members, especially with its vendors.

During the next six months, Morris had limited success in locating one or more large suppliers that would be able to deliver the products to Lawson Sportswear on a timely basis. Faced with growing demand from the surrounding high schools, he had to accumulate excess stock to avoid possible shortages. At the end of the six-month period, a memo from the accounting department of the company indicated the financial significance of the problem. In his memo, accounting manager Roger Noles simply addressed the high costs of inventory maintenance/security functions (for details, see Exhibit 2). He advised finding a substitute inventory policy to lower these cost figures. Specifically, he stated that the rental cost for the additional warehouse had leveled off at 16 percent, well beyond the maximum.

Keith Lawson immediately scheduled a meeting and asked the top managers to come up with the alternative plans to eliminate this problem.

"I should have never let those suppliers quit," said Morris. "It had a negative effect on our image, and now we all see the results."

	2003 (forecast)	2002	2001
Net sales	$165,000	$120,000	$100,000
Cost of sales			
Beginning inventory	7,000	6,000	4,000
Purchases (net)	140,000	92,000	62,000
	147,000	98,000	66,000
Ending inventory	9,000	7,000	6,000
	138,000	91,000	61,000
Gross profit	27,000	29,000	39,000
Expenses			
Stock maintenance	7,500	5,250	750
Rent	2,500	1,250	250
Insurance	4,500	3,500	1,500
Interest	4,500	2,500	1,000
Selling	3,500	2,500	2,000
Promotion	7,500	5,500	4,000
Supplies	2,750	1,500	250
Miscellaneous	2,250	1,500	250
	35,000	23,500	10,000
Net profit from operations	(8,000)	5,500	29,000
Other income			
Dividends	925	750	450
Interest	825	600	350
Miscellaneous	650	400	200
	2,400	1,750	1,000
Net profit before taxes	(5,600)	7,250	130,000
Provision for income taxes	1,008	1,305	8,100
Net profit after taxes	(4,592)	5,945	21,900

EXHIBIT 2

Comparative Statement of Profit and Loss for Years Ended December 31

"It's too late to worry about that," admonished Lawson. "Instead, we have to come up with a strategy to meet the demand effectively without increasing our costs to the detriment of profits. You realize that the university contracts will expire at the end of the year."

"That's the crucial fact," said Noles. "We simply cannot afford to stock up beyond the current level; it is just too expensive. It is well beyond the funds we have had even from the increased sales."

"In other words, the elimination of the excess inventory is necessary. Who are the vendors that we have at the moment?" asked Lawson.

"There are only three suppliers remaining after the last meeting," replied Morris. "They are fairly small businesses, but we've been dealing with them for quite some time. They have been successful in keeping up with us, and the details of their operations are summarized in their report."

"It seems like we have a good selection here," said Lawson, after looking at the report in front of him. "If they mostly work with us, we should be able to influence the future direction in their operations. In other words, it should not be difficult to convince them that they need to upgrade their deliveries in such a way that we can eliminate our excess inventory."

"That would cut down the rental costs that we incur from the additional warehouse," said Noles.

"Obviously!" Lawson replied impatiently. "We will probably need to provide those vendors with a comprehensive support program. If we can convert the floor space of the warehouse from storage to sales, we will have additional funds in retail operations. We can invest a portion of these funds in supporting our vendors and improve our image by forming a cohesive network with them. Of course, there will be a limit to this support. After all, it will be expensive for us to make the transition, too. Therefore, I would like you to come up with an analysis of converting the existing system to a more efficient one. I would like to know what we can do and how we can do it. To be very honest, gentlemen, I do not want to increase the sales if we do not know how to handle that increase."

DISCUSSION QUESTIONS

1. How might the use of a quick response system affect the financial performance of Lawson?

2. What problems would Lawson have implementing a quick response system with vendors?

Source: This case was prepared by S. Alton Erdem, University of Minnesota–Duluth.

CASE 17   SaksFirst Builds with Customer Relationships

It's Wednesday afternoon and as usual Gwendolyn has a fitting room ready for Mrs. Johnson. She has picked out some of the new items in Mrs. Johnson's size that came in the previous week. She has everything from scarves to jewelry to shoes ready to go along with the outfits.

"Good evening, Mrs. Johnson. So how was your birthday?" Gwen asked.

"It was wonderful. My husband took me to Italy. Thank you for the card."

"I pulled some new items for you to try on," Gwendolyn said.

"Thank you, Gwen. You are the best!" replies Mrs. Johnson. The reason Mrs. Johnson has such a friendly relationship with Gwen is because Mrs. Johnson is a regular and a SaksFirst member.

Saks Fifth Avenue started in the early twentieth century. Saks is considered the epitome of class, style, and luxury. When customers go to Saks, they receive excellent customer service; when they join SaksFirst—started in 1994—they also receive a lot of additional benefits. SaksFirst is a preferred customer program that helps facilitate more personal customer/sales associate relationship.

To become a member, a customer has to have a charge account, and once she or he spends at least $2,000 dollars a year the customer is automatically enrolled. If a customer wants the benefits of a preferred customer and doesn't spend $2,000 a year, she or he can pay a $50 annual fee. For every dollar she or he spends, the customer will receive a point. At the end of the year, the preferred customers receive 2, 4, or 6 percent in rewards based on how much they spent that year to make more purchases at Saks. The newsletters inform the customers of the hottest trends for the next season. The customers can then plan what purchases to make on their next shopping expedition.

The customers receive many exclusive benefits. The tangible benefits include the points, rewards, and discounts. Customers also receive complimentary local delivery, advance notice of sale events, the SaksFirst newsletter, catalogs, promotions and giveaways, double- and triple-point events, and double points on their birthdays. The intangible benefits include recognition and preferential treatment.

For the retailer, the main purpose for the SaksFirst program is to promote customer service. The better the relationship between the customer and the sales associates, the more money their loyal customers will spend. Every year there is a triple-point event in the first week of November. That one day accounts for the highest volume sales day of the year, higher than the day after Thanksgiving or Christmas Eve. Knowing this, the company understands the importance of the preferred program.

The SaksFirst program can also be used by the sales associates as a selling tool. If a customer is uneasy about purchasing large-ticket items, the sales associate can remind the member of the bonus certificate that will return a percentage of the cost. Sales associates are motivated to enroll as many of their customers as they can because they are given incentives such as "lottery tickets," that are redeemed for cash.

● DISCUSSION QUESTIONS

1. How does SaksFirst build loyalty for Saks Fifth Avenue versus other upscale retailers (such as Nordstrom)?

2. How effective is the SaksFirst program in developing customer loyalty?

3. Who should Saks target the SaksFirst program toward?

4. Is the SaksFirst program worth what it spends giving back to customers?

Source: Case prepared by Teresa Scott, University of Florida.

CASE 18 Nolan's Finest Foods: Category Management

Nolan's Finest Foods is a full-service retailer that offers shoppers the convenience of one-stop shopping at its high-end food-and-drug combo stores in the San Francisco Bay area. The chain features a variety of high-quality products at competitive prices but uses promotional pricing as well. Historically, Nolan's has enjoyed great success in its markets and had led the region for several years. However, on this winter morning Roberto Ignacio, the director of strategic planning, had a more immediate concern. The wire services had reported a few weeks ago that the Valumart grocery chain had announced plans for the construction of 10 new food-and-drug combo centers throughout Nolan's markets. After pouring over current research and financial results, a decision had been made to examine category management as a defense against the encroachment of Valumart.

To date, Nolan's did not have any experience with category management. A decision was also made to pilot test category management in some categories before implementing a systemwide rollout. One of the categories chosen for the test was shampoo. Roberto's immediate assignment was to review the product category and report back to management with an initial recommendation. As Roberto looked out of his window at the scenic sunset over the San Francisco Bay, he reviewed the events of the past few weeks and the information that he had obtained on the shampoo category. He had several third-party reports (Exhibits 1, 2, and 3) that provided background information about national trends in the shampoo category and trends in supermarkets. Another report (Exhibit 4) provided him with information on how Nolan's shampoo sales compared to the rest of the market.

However, these reports did not provide Roberto with information on how Nolan's stacked up against the

EXHIBIT 1
Total U.S. Supermarket Dynamics: Shampoo—Aeorsol, Liquid, Lotion, and Powder

52 Weeks	# Active UPCs	% New UPCs	# UPCs Handled	UPC Dollar Velocity
Category	1,974	15%	235	$1.64
Brands	1,714	16	229	1.65
Private label	241	12	5	1.33
Generic	19	—	1	1.00

EXHIBIT 2
Shampoo Dollar Share

Trade Channel	12 Months Last Year	12 Months This Year
Food	51.7%	50.5%
Drug	25.6	25.0
Mass merchant	22.7	24.5

EXHIBIT 3
Shampoo Growth

Trade Channel	Dollar Sales % Change versus a Year Ago
Food	0.9%
Drug	4.2
Mass merchant	8.1

competition in terms of its assortment and pricing. After some checking around, Roberto found that he could order reports from third-party vendors that would provide him with an analysis of Nolan's and the competition on product mix and pricing. He had placed an urgent order for these analyses, which arrived this morning through courier (Exhibits 5, 6, and 7).

EXHIBIT 4
Dollar Sales: Percent Change versus a Year Ago

	MARKET		NOLAN'S FINEST	
	13 Weeks	52 Weeks	13 Weeks	52 Weeks
Total dollar sales	+.1	+1.2	−10.6	−4.5
HBA department	+1.5	+4.2	−8.5	−4.3
Shampoo category	−3.5	+.7	−19.6	−9.7

EXHIBIT 5
Competitive Price Comparison for Shampoo: Counts of Items Showing Differences from the Base Zone (Nolan's Finest Foods)

	Nolan's	Food #1	Mass Merch.	Chain Drug	Food #2
Competition is higher	0	87	0	101	0
Competition is same	103	0	0	0	59
Competition is lower	0	16	103	2	44
Competition does not carry	0	0	0	0	0

Here are explanations of a few terms in the analyses:

UPC	Supermarket terminology for SKU (stockkeeping unit)
UPCs handled	Average number of UPCs stocked by food stores
UPC dollar velocity	Revenue per UPC per store per week
HBA	Health and beauty aids
Market	All food stores
Remaining market	All food stores excluding Nolan's

As Roberto headed for the water cooler, feeling upbeat in the thought that he had a handle on the shampoo category, he ran into Hal Jeffreys, who was a longtime veteran of Nolan's and a vice president of information systems. Knowing that Hal had at one time managed Health and Beauty Aids at Nolan's, Roberto mentioned his review of the shampoo category and the category management initiative. Hal mentioned that for years he had a simple approach for category management. He would begin by generating a list of slow sellers in the category and then try to replace these slow sellers with new products or by increasing the shelf space for existing products. With the new information systems that Nolan's had installed in the past year, generating a slow seller list was very easy. To prove his point Hal walked back with Roberto to his office and, using his PC, generated a slow seller report for the shampoo category (Exhibit 8). "See, technology has made this a real cinch," said Hal and wondered whether the expense and effort of category management would produce net improvements over and above this very simple "knock off the slow seller" approach. "I'll try to come to your presentation tomorrow," said Hal as he left Roberto's office.

As Hal left his office, Roberto sank back into his chair with a knot in his stomach. He felt that he had jumped the gun in thinking that he had a handle on the shampoo cate-

EXHIBIT 6   Brand Importance Report for Shampoo: Nolan's Foods versus Remaining Market for 13 Weeks

Description	Chain Sales	Chain Rank	Rem. Mkt. Rank	Rem. Mkt. Sales	Chain Mkt. Share	Chain Category Impt.	Rem. Mkt. Cat. Impt.
Clean & Soft	$108,826	1	1	$512,345	17.5%	14.5	13.0
1st Impressions	77,672	2	3	370,341	17.3	10.3	9.4
Mane Tame	64,446	3	4	244,160	20.9	8.6	6.2
Bargain Bubbles	56,864	4	2	433,300	11.6	7.6	11.0
Silky Style	43,198	5	6	147,773	22.6	5.8	3.7
Elegance	30,869	6	5	181,075	14.6	4.1	4.6

Product Mix Summary Report: Shampoo Dollar Sales—13 Weeks

EXHIBIT 7

	Clean & Soft	1st Impressions	Mane Tame	Bargain Bubbles	Silky Style	Elegance	Private Label
Items carried							
Nolan's	25	25	15	21	13	5	7
Rem. mkt.	25	39	28	42	20	16	28
Sizes carried							
Nolan's	6	6	6	2	4	1	4
Rem. mkt.	7	10	11	3	5	4	6
Types carried							
Nolan's	6	7	6	19	4	5	6
Rem. mkt.	6	10	8	32	5	7	21

Slow Seller Report: Shampoo for Nolan's Foods, 13 Weeks versus a Year Ago

EXHIBIT 8

Item	Chain Sales	Chain Mkt. Shr.	Chain Subcat Impt.	Rem. Mkt. Growth	Chain Growth	Chain Avg. % Stores Selling
Golden JJB Lq T 3 oz.	$ 3	9.9%	.0	−51.2-	−50.0	0%
1st Imprs. DF ND Lot. 11 oz.	10	.7	.0	−59.4	−99.4	0
Gentle GLD Lq. 11 oz.	11	100.0	.0	−100.0	9.6	0
Golden AV Lq. T 3 oz.	12	22.4	.0	13.2	−69.2	1
Suds PB Lq. 8 oz.	14	6	.0	107.1	2.9	0
Sikly Style X-B Lq. 18 oz.	14	1.6	.0	−65.6	−99.5	0

gory. Things seemed to be more complicated than they had appeared earlier in the day. Roberto wondered whether the shampoo category seemed so difficult because it was the first attempt at category management. In any case, his immediate concern was to prepare for his presentation tomorrow. Since Hal Jeffreys would be in the audience, he knew that he would have to address the "knock out the slow sellers" perspective.

●DISCUSSION QUESTIONS

1. What are the national sales trends in the shampoo category?

2. What are the differences in shampoo sales trends at Nolan's compared to the national trends?

3. What could be causing these differences?

4. Suggest a plan of action.

Source: This case was written by Professor Kirthi Kalyanam, Retail Management Institute, Santa Clara University. © Dr. Kirthi Kalyanam.

CASE 19 Developing a Buying Plan for Hughe's

A well-established, medium-size department store in the Midwest, Hughe's reflects consumers' needs by featuring popular names in fashion for the individual consumer, family, and home. It tries to offer a distinctive wide assortment of quality merchandise with personalized customer service. The many customer services include personal shoppers; credit with in-house charge, American Express, and Visa; and an interior design studio. Hughe's pricing policy permits it to draw customers from several income brackets. Moderate-income consumers seeking value and fashion-predictable soft goods are target customers, as are upscale customers with special interest in fashion.

The department store is implementing new marketing strategies to prepare for continuing growth and expansion. Hughe's merchandising philosophy is to attract the discerning middle-market customer who comprises 70 percent of the population as well as sophisticated fashion-conscious consumers who expect to buy high-quality, brand-name merchandise at competitive prices.

One portion of Hughe's buying staff is responsible for the oriental rug department within home furnishings. The open-to-buy figure for this classification within the home furnishings division will be based on last year's sales history (Exhibit 1).

It has been projected that a 15 percent increase over last year's sales volume can be attained due to oriental rugs' continued popularity. This year's open-to-buy for fall/winter will be $66,200.

The buying staff will be making its purchases for fall/winter in Amritsar, India, a city known for top-quality carpets. Ghuman Export Private, Ltd., of Amritsar, Punjab, India, is the manufacturer the buyers will contact. Exhibit 2 shows information about Ghuman to use in the decision-making process.

EXHIBIT 2
Ghuman's Wholesale Price List

Size	FABRICATION		
	Silk	Wool	Cotton
3 × 5'	$400	$250	—
4 × 6'	700	500	$200
6 × 9'	850	700	275
8 × 10'	1,200	1,000	350
9 × 12'	1,400	1,300	500

Colors: Background colors available are navy, burgundy, black, and cream.

Quantities required for purchase: No minimum orders required.

Payment plan: Payment can be made in American dollars or Indian rupees. Letter of credit needs to be established prior to market trip.

Delivery: Air freight—10 to 14 days delivery time; cost is usually 25 percent of total order.

Ocean freight—39 days plus inland time is necessary; cost is usually 8–10 percent of total order.

Customer loyalty: Loyalty to customers is exceptional. Damaged shipments can be returned. Ghuman's philosophy is to help the retailers obtain a profit on their product lines.

DISCUSSION QUESTION

1. Work up a buying plan to use when buying from Ghuman's. Decide how to distribute the allotted open-to-buy dollars among the available sizes, colors, and fabrications. Since it's an overseas manufacturer, consider additional costs such as duty and shipping, which also need to be covered by the allocated open-to-buy dollars.

This case was prepared by Professor Ann Fairhurst, Indiana University.

EXHIBIT 1
Last Year's Fall/Winter Sales Results for Oriental Rugs

Sales volume	$120,000		
Markup	51.5%		

Size	Percentage of Sales	Fabrication	Percentage of Sales
3' × 5'	20%	Silk	15%
4' × 6'	40	Cotton	25
6' × 9'	15	Wool	60
8' × 10'	10		
9' × 12'	15		

CASE 20 McFadden's Department Store: Preparation of a Merchandise Budget Plan

 McFadden's Department Store has been a profitable family-owned business since its beginning in 1910. Last year's sales volume was $180 million. More recently, however, many of its departments have been losing ground to national stores moving into the area. To complicate this problem, the National Retail Federation (NRF) predicts recession. The NRF estimates a 6.5 percent drop in sales in the coming year for the Pacific Coast, where McFadden's operates.

Department 121 has one of the more profitable departments in the store, maintaining a gross margin of 55 percent. Its basic merchandise is young men's clothing. Last year sales reached $2,780,750 for the July–December season. The highest sales period is the back-to-school period in August, when autumn fashions are supported by strong promotional advertising. Reductions (including markdowns, discounts to employees, and shrinkage) typically run 20 percent of sales. The percentage of reductions are spread throughout the season as follows:

July	August	September	October	November	December
10	20	15	10	10	35

By month, the percentage of annual sales for Department 121 within this six-month period had been distributed as follows:

	July	August	September	October	November	December
1999	3.6	10.1	9.2	6.4	4.8	9.1
2000	3.5	10.3	9.6	6.8	5.3	8.8
2001	3.5	10.5	9.6	6.2	5.5	8.2
2002	3.0	10.3	9.8	6.6	5.5	8.0

A pre-Christmas sale has been planned in an attempt to counterbalance the slackened sales period following the first of the year. The buyer has decided to bring in some new merchandise for the sale to go along with the remaining fall fashion merchandise. The buyer expects that this will increase December's percentage of annual sales to 30 percent above what it would be without the sale. Top management has emphasized that the department achieve a gross margin return on investment (GMROI) of 250 percent. Forecasted ending stock level in December is $758,000.

Additional information is available on the historical stock-to-sales ratio for this type of department. This information is taken from a similar department in another store that happens to have a lower average stock-to-sales ratio.

July	August	September	October	November	December
3.0	1.9	2.1	2.4	2.5	2.2

DISCUSSION QUESTION

1. Your task is to prepare a merchandise budget plan. You may do the plan by hand by using the form in Exhibit 1, or you may prepare the plan using the spreadsheet on the CD accompanying the text. You will have to prepare some intermediate calculations before inputting your answers onto the spreadsheet. After installing the CD, click on the Merchandise Management Module and plug in the numbers from the case. On a separate sheet of paper, explain how you determined the sales forecast, percentage of sales per month, and the monthly stock-to-sales ratios.

Source: This case was prepared by Michael Levy, Babson College, and Harold Koenig, Oregon State University.

EXHIBIT 1   Form for Merchandise Budget Plan

McFadden's Merchandise Budget

Planning Data

SALES FORECAST $ _____

Planned GMROI $= \dfrac{\text{Gross Margin}}{\text{Net Sales}} \times \dfrac{\text{Net Sales}}{\text{Inventory Costs}}$

$\boxed{} = \dfrac{\boxed{\$}}{\boxed{\$}} \times \dfrac{\boxed{\$}}{\boxed{\$}}$

$\dfrac{\text{Sales}}{\text{Inventory Costs}} \times (100\% - GM\%) = \text{Inventory Turnover}$

$\boxed{X} \times \boxed{\%} = \boxed{X}$

$12 + \text{Inventory Turnover} = \text{B.O.M. Stock/Sales}$

$+ \boxed{X} = \boxed{X}$

Forecasted Ending Inventory $\boxed{\$}$

The Plan

Markdowns	$\boxed{\%}$ $\boxed{\$}$
Discounts	$\boxed{\%}$ $\boxed{\$}$
Shortages	$\boxed{\%}$ $\boxed{\$}$
Total Reductions	$\boxed{\%}$ $\boxed{\$}$

		Jan	Feb	Mar	Apr	May	Jun	Jul	Aug	Sept	Oct	Nov	Dec	Total (Average)	Remarks
% Distribution of Sales by Month	1													100.0%	History/Projection
Monthly Sales	2														Step (1) × Net Sales
% Distribution of Reductions/Mo	3													100.0%	History/Projection
Monthly Reductions	4														Step (3) × Net Sales
B.O.M. Stock/Sales Ratios	5														Adjusted by Mo. Sales Fluctuations
B.O.M. Stock ($000)	6													(Forecasted End Inventory)	Step (2) × Step (5)
E.O.M. Stock ($000)	7														EOM Jan = BOM Feb
Monthly Additions to Stock ($000)	8														Steps 2 + 4 + 7−6 Sales + Reductions + EOM−BOM

CASE 21   eBay

The concept for eBay was born during a conversation between Pierre Omidyar and his wife, an avid Pez collector. (She currently has a collection of more than 400 dispensers.) She commented to Pierre how great it would be if she were able to collect Pez dispensers and interact with other collectors over the Internet. As an early Internet enthusiast, Pierre felt that many people like his wife needed a place to buy and sell unique items and to meet other users with similar interests. He started eBay in 1995 to fulfill this need.

Luckily for Pierre Omidyar, he was living in Silicon Valley when he got the idea for eBay. If Omidyar's family had stayed in France, his idea never would have gotten off the ground. It's not a lack of venture capital or Internet audience in France that would have stopped him. It's the law. Under French regulations, only a few certified auctioneers are allowed to operate; so eBay hasn't even opened for business in its founder's homeland, even though it operates auctions in Germany and the U.K. now.

OFFERING TO CUSTOMERS

The company pioneered online person-to-person trading by developing a web-based community in which buyers and sellers are brought together using an efficient and entertaining auction format to buy and sell items. Initially, most of the items auctioned where collectibles such as antiques, coins, stamps, and memorabilia.

Many of the sellers on eBay are small mom and pop businesses that use the site as a sales channel. By 2003, most of the merchandise available on eBay had shifted from collectibles to practical items, such as power drills and computers. Now big businesses such as Disney and Sun Microsystems have discovered eBay. Retailers, manufacturers, and liquidators are using the site to unload returned merchandise, refurbished merchandise, and used products.

The eBay service permits sellers to list items for sale and enables buyers to bid on items of interest. All eBay users can browse through listed items in a fully automated, topically arranged, intuitive, and easy-to-use online service that is available 24 hours a day, seven days a week. However, even with automated bidding features, participating in an online auction requires more effort than buying fixed-price goods, and once the auction is over, most buyers have to send a check or money order and then get the merchandise up to two weeks later.

More than 500 milion items are listed for sale each year. From Civil War to Star Wars items, from baby clothes to automobiles, chances are that you'll find it among eBay's 20,000 categories. "If you can't sell it on eBay, you might as well open up the window and throw it out in the backyard because it ain't worth a damn," says Bob Watts, an antique dealer in Fairfield, Virginia. The website has over 40 million registered users worldwide, with gross merchandise sales over $10 billion. These members spend an average of 130 minutes a month browsing through its listings of more than 2 million items.

The eBay site is one of the stickiest on the Internet, with a large number of loyal users. Users often refer to eBay as a community—a group of people with similar interests. For example, Dr. Michael Levitt by day is a distinguished medical researcher at the Minneapolis Veterans Medical Center, but at night he is an eBay warrior. Levitt is a collector of antique California Perfume Company bottles. Every night he logs on to eBay to see if anything new is being offered. He has purchased hundreds of bottles through eBay simply because it's the most convenient way to connect with sellers.

The website requires that all new sellers have a credit card on file, insurance, authentication, and escrow accounts. Buyers and sellers can check the "reputation" of anyone using eBay. A Feedback Forum is provided through which eBay users can leave comments about their buying and selling experiences. If you're a bidder, you can check your seller's Feedback Profile before you place a bid to learn about the seller's reputation with previous buyers. If you're a seller, do the same with your bidders.

BUSINESS MODEL

Unlike most e-commerce companies, eBay has been profitable from the very beginning. In 2001, its net profits were $90 million on net revenues of $749 million. Most of the company's revenues come from fees and commissions (between 1.25 and 5.0 percent of the sale price) associated with online and traditional offline auction services. Online revenues come from placement and success fees paid by sellers; eBay does not charge fees to buyers. Sellers pay a nominal placement fee, and by paying additional fees, sellers can have items featured in various ways. Sellers also pay a success fee based on the final purchase price. Online advertising on eBay has not made significant contributions to net revenues, and no significant revenue from advertising is expected in the near future. Additional revenues come from auction-related services, including bidder registration fees and appraisal and authentication.

Its online business model is significantly different from electronic retailers. Because individual sellers, rather than eBay, sell the items listed, the company has no procurement, carrying, or shipping costs and no inventory risk. The company's expenses are just personnel, advertising and promotion, and depreciation on site hardware and software.

COMPETITION

Due to the popularity of auctions with consumers, a number of e-businesses have entered the market. Some competing Internet auctions offering a broad range of products are Onsale, UBid.com, and Firstauction. In addition to these multicategory sites, there are vertical auction sites specializing in a single category of merchandise such as stamps or baseball cards.

Perhaps the most significant competitor is Amazon.com, which launched an auction site in 1999. Amazon has a well-known and highly regarded brand name and has substantial traffic on its website. (Amazon is the most widely known e-business, with eBay ranking third in brand awareness.) When Amazon launched its auction site, it offered some unique benefits to customers, including a no-deductible, no-haggle, no third-party moneyback guarantee for purchases up to $250 and a feature called Going, Going, Gone that extends the auction for 10 minutes if a bid is made in the last 10 minutes before closing. On eBay, it is common for items to be picked off in the closing minutes by vigilant consumers who make the last bid.

Amazon is known for the usability of its site. In response to Amazon's entry, eBay took steps to make buying and selling easier. It now offers a Personal Shopper program that searches out specified products and my eBay, which gives user information about their current eBay activities, including bidding, selling, account balances, favorite categories, and recent feedback.

Finally, some Internet businesses have arisen that simply search and display summary information from many auction sites to enable comparison shopping. However, eBay sued one such site and has used technology to block access of another site to prevent them from gathering and displaying eBay auction data.

DISCUSSION QUESTIONS

1. What are the advantages and disadvantages from the buyer's and seller's perspectives of buying merchandise through Internet auctions like eBay?

2. Will a significant amount of retail sales be made through Internet auctions like eBay in the future? Why or why not?

3. What are eBay's competitive advantages? Will it be able to withstand the competition from other auction sites like Yahoo and Amazon's auctions?

Source: This case was written by Barton Weitz, University of Florida.

CASE 22   Enterprise Builds on People

When most people think of car rental firms, they think of Hertz or Avis, but Enterprise is the largest and most profitable U.S. car rental business. In 1957, Jack Taylor started Enterprise with a unique strategy. Most car rental firms targeted business and leisure travel customers who arrived at an airport and needed to rent a car for local transportation. Taylor decided to target a different segment—individuals whose own cars are being repaired, who are driving on vacation, or who for some other reason simply need an extra car for a few days.

The traditional car rental companies have to charge relatively high daily rates because their locations in or near airports are expensive. In addition, their business customers are price-insensitive because the rental expenses are paid for by their companies. While the location airports are convenient for customers, traveling by air, they are inconvenient for people seeking a replacement car while theirs is in the shop or an extra car to drive for a few days. So Enterprise locates its rental offices in downtown and suburban areas, near where many its target market lives and works. The firm provides local pickup and delivery service in most areas.

Enterprise's human resource strategy is a key to its success. The firm hires college graduates for its management trainee positions because it feels that a college degree demonstrates intelligence and motivation. Rather than recruiting the best students, it focuses on hiring people who were athletes or actively involved in campus social activities. Enterprise wants people who were social directors or high-ranking officers of social organizations such as fraternities, sororities, and clubs because they typically have good interpersonal skills needed to effectively deal with Enterprise's customers.

Jack Taylor's growth strategy was based on providing high-quality, personalized service so that customers would return to Enterprise when they need to rent a car again. But operating managers were compensated on the basis of sales growth initially, not customer satisfaction. So service quality declined.

The first step Enterprise took to improve customer service was to develop a customer satisfaction measure. The questionnaire, called the Enterprise Service Quality Index, was developed on the basis of input from the operating managers. Thus, the managers felt ownership of the measurement tool. As the index gained legitimacy, Enterprise made a big deal about it. It posted the scores for each location prominently in its monthly operating reports—right next to the net profit numbers that determined managers' pay. The operating managers were able to track how they were doing, and how all their peers were doing, because all of the locations were ranked.

To increase the motivation of managers to improve the service at their location. Enterprise announced that managers could be promoted only if their customer satisfaction scores were above the company average. Then it demonstrated that it would abide by this policy by failing to promote some star performers who had achieved good growth and profit numbers but had below-average satisfaction scores.

To provide a high level of service, new employees generally work long, grueling hours for what many see as relatively low pay. They, like all Enterprise managers, are expected to jump in and help wash or vacuum cars when the agency gets backed up. But all this hard work can pay off. The firm does not hire outsiders for other than entry-level jobs—every position is filled by promoting someone already inside the company. Thus, Enterprise employees know that if they work hard and do their best, they may very well succeed in moving up the corporate ladder and earn a significant income.

Source: This case was written by Barton Weitz, University of Florida.

CASE 23   Borders Bookstore: A Merchandise Display Problem

Michael Chaim, general manager of the Borders Bookstore in Madison, Wisconsin, was proud of his store. Located in a city that has one of the highest levels of book purchases per capita, Chaim felt Borders' selection, services, and location near the 40,000-student university served the community well. Even with competitive pressure from the newly opened Barnes & Noble on the west side of town, his bookstore/café was often a busy place.

Chaim was taken aback when an article in a widely read alternative newspaper criticized the bookstore's merchandise arrangement as being prejudiced. The store carries a large selection of literature and poetry, but it separates some specialty categories, such as African American literature, gay and lesbian literature, and feminist literature, from the general literature and poetry sections. In part, this arrangement reflects Borders' college town roots in Ann Arbor, Michigan, where specialty collections were established to match course offerings.

The article described this arrangement as "ghettoizing" authors who were not white males, although some female authors were in the general literature and poetry sections. The article and some follow-up letters to the newspaper's editor derided Borders for the few "nontraditional" au-

thors who made it into the general literature collection. They felt that these African American, homosexual, Native American, and other nontraditional writers probably would not have been separated from the general collection had the management known the literature better. While Madison is known as a very liberal community, Chaim thought the accusation was unfair. He strongly believed that he was doing his customers a service in highlighting authors and literary genres that might be overlooked in a large, nondifferentiated collection. More immediately, he knew that he should respond to the article's accusations.

DISCUSSION QUESTIONS

1. What should Michael Chaim do?

2. One option is to duplicate the titles that could be shelved in either the general literature section or in a specialty collection. What are the advantages and disadvantages of this tactic?

Source: This case was prepared by Jan Owens, University of Wisconsin, Parkside.

CASE 24   Promoting a Sale

A consumer electronic chain in the Washington, DC, area is planning a big sale in its suburban Virginia warehouse over the three-day President's Day weekend (Saturday through Monday). On sale will be nearly $2 million worth of consumer electronic products, 50 percent of the merchandise sold in the store. The company hopes to realize at least $900,000 in sales during the three days. In the retailer's past experience,

1. The first day's sales were 50 percent of the total. The second day's were 35 percent, and the last day's, 15 percent.

2. One of every two customers who came made a purchase.

It's known further that large numbers of people always flock to such sales, some driving as far as 50 miles. They come from all economic levels, but all are confirmed bargain hunters. You're the assistant to the general merchandise manager, who has asked you to plan the event's marketing campaign. You have the following information:

1. A full-page *Washington Post* ad costs $10,000; a half-page ad costs $6,000; and a quarter-page ad costs $3,500. To get the maximum value from a newspaper campaign, it's company policy to always run two ads (not necessarily the same size) for such events.

2. The local northern Virginia paper is printed weekly and distributed free to some 15,000 households. It costs $700 for a full page and $400 for a half page.

3. To get adequate TV coverage, at least three channels must be used, with a minimum of eight 30-second spots on each at $500 per spot, spread over three or more days. Producing a TV spot costs $3,000.

4. The store has contracts with three radio stations. One appeals to a broad general audience aged 25 to 34. One is popular with the 18-to-25 group. A classical music station has a small but wealthy audience. Minimum costs for a saturation radio campaign, including production, on the three stations are $8,000, $5,000, and $3,000, respectively.

5. To produce and mail a full-color flyer to the store's 80,000 charge customers costs $10,000. When the company used such a mailing piece before, about 3 percent responded.

DISCUSSION QUESTIONS

1. Knowing that the company wants a mixed-media ad campaign to support this event, prepare an ad plan for the general merchandise manager that costs no more than $40,000.

2. Work out the daily scheduling of all advertising.

3. Work out the dollars to be devoted to each medium.

4. Justify your plan.

Source: This case was prepared by David Ehrlich, Marymount University.

CASE 25   Picking the Best Display

A specialty apparel store realized that its selling fixtures had become outmoded, so it set aside funds to renovate. The fixtures and layout had not been changed appreciably since the store opened in 1992. There were a number of handsome mahogany-paneled counter islands, which had always given the store an aura of tasteful elegance.

Jim Lewis, director of store fixturing, was debating the merits of several possible display systems. The selling departments that would be affected by the renovation were cosmetics; fine and costume jewelry; women's handbags, scarves, and belts; men's shirts, ties, and furnishings; women's sweaters; and gifts.

As Lewis saw it, the two major issues surrounding his decision were incompatible. On the one hand, the store wanted to make merchandise as accessible to customers as possible; on the other hand, experience had indicated that open-selling fixtures inevitably lead to more shoplifting. As an experiment, the store had tried substituting self-service fixtures in its upstairs sweater department a year earlier. Sales jumped 30 percent, but inventory shrinkage in the department had gone from 2 to almost 5 percent.

A further consideration was that the size and quality of the staff on the selling floor had declined dramatically. There were always two salespeople behind every counter, and customers could count on never having to wait for service. However, selling costs had since escalated, and the store's staff was less than half what it had been then. Furthermore, the store had instituted point-of-sale terminals that enabled every salesperson to ring up a sale from any department in the store at any register. Most of the sales associates were minimum-wage individuals who were only working there until something better turned up. Although some were able to provide useful selling information to the public, most could do little more than ring up sales.

The kind of open-selling fixtures Lewis was considering were contemporary and attractive. They allowed the customer to pick up, unfold, or unpackage merchandise; try it on if appropriate; and then return it to the fixture. Such fixtures would unquestionably lead to more sales, especially since the customer could merely look for any salesperson or perhaps go to a central cashier to pay. However, it was equally unquestionable that such easy access to merchandise, especially to small goods, would encourage shoplifting and would increase the need for ongoing stock keeping.

Another disadvantage to the new type of fixturing was that, in addition to being contemporary, it was somewhat trendy, which would lead to the need to replace it in a few years, thereby adding to capital costs.

An alternative system would be to retain the old counter islands, or a portion of them, but to put more goods on the countertops to encourage a measure of self-service. The disadvantage here, of course, would be the blocking of sight lines. Salespeople could not see customers, customers could not see salespeople, and the store security personnel could not see either. There would also need to have more policing by the store's display and merchandising staff to be sure the countertops looked inviting at all times. Manufacturers often contribute countertop displays to stores as part of the merchandise buying, and many of them might not be in harmony with the store's overall appearance.

Lewis recognized that he would have to make some compromises. Every affected department has its own peculiarities, and his job was to minimize those differences rather than allow them to get out of hand. Some merchandise, such as fine jewelry, would obviously have to remain behind glass, but other departments would probably do much better by opening up their stocks to the public.

DISCUSSION QUESTIONS

1. What display system would you recommend? Why?

2. Would you make the same recommendation for each of the affected departments? Why?

Source: This case was prepared by David Ehrlich, Marymount University.

CASE 26   Sephora

Sephora, a division of Moet Hennessy Louis Vuitton (LVMH), is an innovative retail concept from France that is changing the way cosmetics are sold. Sephora dares to be different in its store design and product offerings. In fact, it defines the fashion retail concept to give its customers what they want: "freedom, beauty, and pleasure." Some of Sephora's product offerings include makeup, fragrances, bath and body products, and skin care. There is no doubt that every woman can find the products that she desires at Sephora to pamper herself like a queen.

Sephora takes beauty offerings in a new, exciting direction, allowing the customer to choose her own level of service. The customer may opt for "an individual experience and reflection to detailed expert advice," whether that is in Sephora's store locations or on its highly interactive website. Sephora has been taking the U.S. market by storm ever since it arrived in mid-1998 with its first two store locations opening in New York and Miami. Furthermore, its flagship store that encompasses 21,000 square feet opened in Rockefeller Center in New York City in October 1999. Now, Sephora operates more than 70 stores nationwide, and it continues to expand at a rapid pace.

Most fashion-oriented cosmetics are sold in department stores. The scent and cosmetics area in department stores consists of areas devoted to the products made by each manufacturer. Salespeople specializing in specific line stand behind a counter and assist customers in selecting merchandise.

Sephora represents "the future of beauty," so it is no surprise that its store designs are a reflection of what to expect in the future. It lures customers into its stores with a bright red carpet that immediately induces an excitement and intrigue that cannot be matched. Once the customers enter the store, they are surrounded by what Sephora likes to call "the temple of beauty." An extraordinary assortment of products are arranged alphabetically and by category along the walls of the store. Customers are encouraged to sample the beauty products on their own from self-serve modules. The stores sell a tremendous variety of brands, including new lines, best-sellers, classics, and an exclusive Sephora collection.

Sephora has a strong presence throughout the United States; however, it also has stores located in France, Luxembourg, Spain, Portugal, Poland, Italy, Turkey, and England. It decided to pull out of Japan and Germany because of financial concerns, unable to sell Japanese and German consumers on its unique retail concept.

Sephora is one of the few retailers offering cosmetic products online. There has been much speculation in recent years that beauty products cannot be displayed properly on a two-dimensional web page. Many other retailers have attempted to make the transition, but they have been unsuccessful time and time again. On the other hand, Sephora has managed to set itself apart from other retailers once again by making it work while still yielding a profit. Sephora offers brands that consumers have a difficult time finding in department stores, such as Urban Decay, Hard Candy, Stila, and Dirty Girl. Women have been making purchases on the Sephora website because they cannot find these products in their hometown malls. To many customer's dismay, Sephora stores are not located in every regional mall across the country. For these customers, Sephora.com represents a one-stop shop for all of their beauty needs. They know that they can find the brands they love at a reasonable price with no hassles. What else can a person ask for?

In August 2001, Sephora unveiled its new advertising campaign. These new advertisements feature "close-up photographs that capture the playful application of colorful makeup to various features of the woman's face." These new photographs will be featured in the company's stores, website, and direct-mail campaigns. Sephora believes that this new advertising campaign will capture their philosophy of "freedom, exploration, and discovery." By focusing on a different feature of a woman's face in each ad, Sephora strives to emphasize that its products are not about a particular kind of look or beauty. Also, it is important for a woman to remember that every feature on her face is unique and beautiful. Beauty products only help to emphasize a woman's natural beauty and make her feel more confident about her overall appearance.

Even though Sephora is the world's largest beauty retailer, it still recognizes the importance of giving back to the community. It has joined forces with Operation Smile, which provides reconstructive facial surgery for young children in developing countries and in the United States, to provide kids with a greater sense of confidence so that they can live a more normal life. It committed itself to help improve the lives of children around the world. This joint effort allows children who would not normally be able to afford surgical procedures to get the help that they deserve to feel like a regular kid. The children have no reason to be self-conscious anymore because they are beautiful on the inside and outside. Sephora continues to make a difference by getting involved in the community even through its daily operations. Even though some women do not believe

in the art of makeup, it is essential to recognize that it does allow many other women to feel more confident about their looks on a daily basis, and this contribution, in itself, is truly irreplaceable.

DISCUSSION QUESTIONS

1. What is Sephora's target market? What segment is attracted to its offerings?

2. Why do women prefer the self-service environment of Sephora rather than the service-oriented environment in department store cosmetic areas?

3. Why was Sephora unsuccessful in Japan and Germany when it has been so successful in other foreign countries? Explain.

4. How can a beauty retailer make a successful transition online? What makes Sephora's online site so successful?

Source: This case was written by Kristina Pacca, University of Florida.

CASE 27   A Stockout at Discmart: Will Substitution Lead to Salvation?

Robert Honda, the manager of a Discmart store (a discount retailer similar to Target and Wal-Mart) in Cupertino, California, was surveying the Sunday morning activity at his store. Shoppers were bustling around with carts; some had children in tow. In the front side of the store a steady stream of shoppers were heading through the checkout counters. Almost all the cash registers that he could see from his vantage point were open and active. The line in front of register 7 was longer than the other lines, but other than that things seemed to be going quite smoothly.

The intercom beeped and interrupted his thoughts. A delivery truck had just arrived at the rear of the store. The driver wanted to know which loading dock to use to unload merchandise. Robert decided to inspect the available space before directing the driver to a specific loading dock. As he passed the cash registers on his way to the rear of the store, Robert noticed that the line at register 7 had gotten a little bit longer. The light over the register was flashing, indicating that the customer service associate (CSA) had requested assistance. (At Discmart all front-line personnel who interact with customers are called customer service associates.) As he passed by the register he could not help overhearing the exchange between what seemed to be a somewhat irate customer and the CSA. The customer was

demanding that another item should be substituted for an item that was on sale but currently out of stock, and the CSA was explaining the store policy to the customer. Normally, during a busy time like this, Robert would have tried to help the CSA resolve the situation, but he knew that the truck driver was waiting to unload merchandise that was needed right away on the floor. Hence, he quickly walked to the rear of the store.

After assigning the truck to a docking bay for unloading, Robert headed back toward the front of the store. On the way back, he ducked into the break room to get a Coke and noticed that Sally Johnson, the CSA who was at register 7, was on a break. Sally had been on the Discmart team for about a year and was considered a very capable employee who always kept the store's interests at heart.

Robert: Hi Sally, I noticed that you had quite a line in front of your register earlier today.

Sally: Hi Robert. Yes, I had a very irate customer and it took us a while to resolve the issue.

Robert: Oh really! What was he irate about?

Sally: We are out of stock on the 100–ounce Tide Liquid Detergent that was advertised in our flyer and was on sale at 20 percent off. I offered the customer a rain check or the same discount on the same size of another brand, but he kept insisting that he wanted us to substitute a 200-ounce container of Tide Liquid Detergent at the same discount. Apparently, Joe Chang (the assistant manager) had told the customer that we would substitute the 200-ounce size.

Robert: Did you point out to the customer that our sale prices are valid only while supplies last?

Sally: I did mention this to him but he thought it was strange that we ran out of stock on the morning of the first day of the sale.

Robert: Well, I guess you should have gone ahead and given him what he wanted.

Sally: As you know, our point-of-sale systems allow me to make adjustments only on designated items. Since the 200-ounce sizes were not designated as substitutes, I had to request a supervisor to help me.

Robert: I am glad that you got it resolved.

Sally: Well, the customer got tired of waiting for the supervisor, who was busy helping another customer, so he decided to take a rain check instead. He seemed quite dissatisfied with the whole episode and mentioned that we should stop running these TV ads claiming that we are always in stock and that we guarantee satisfaction.

Robert: I do hate it when they run these ad campaigns and we have to take the heat on the floor,

trying to figure out what those cowboys in marketing promised the customer.

Sally: Well, my break is nearly over. I have to get back.

Robert pondered the encounter that Sally had with the customer. He wondered whether to discuss this issue with Joe Chang. He remembered talking to Joe about inventory policies a couple of days ago. Joe had indicated that their current inventory levels were fairly high and that any further increases would be hard to justify from a financial perspective. He mentioned some market research that had surveyed a random sample of customers who had redeemed rain checks. The results of the survey indicated that customers by and large were satisfied with Discmart's rain check procedures. Based on this finding, Joe had argued that current inventory levels supplemented with a rain check policy would keep customers satisfied.

●DISCUSSION QUESTIONS

1. Why did this service breakdown occur?

2. How was this service gap related to the other gaps (standards, knowledge, delivery, and communications) described in the Gaps model in Chapter 19?

Source: This case was prepared by Dr. Kirthi Kalyanam, Retail Management Institute, Santa Clara University © Dr. Kirthi Kalyanam.

CASE 28 Customer Service and Relationship Management at Nordstrom

Nordstrom's unwavering customer-focused philosophy traces its roots to founder Johan Nordstrom's values. Johan Nordstrom believed in people and realized that consistently exceeding their expectations led to success and a good conscience. He built his organization around a customer-oriented philosophy. The organization focuses on people, and its policies and selections are designed to satisfy people. As simple as this philosophy sounds, few of Nordstrom's competitors have truly been able to grasp it.

A FOCUS ON PEOPLE

Concentrate on people, and profit takes care of itself. Nordstrom employees treat customers like royalty. Employees are instructed to do whatever is in the customer's best interest. Customer delight drives the values of the company. Customers are taken seriously and are at the heart of the business. Customers are even at the top of the Nordstrom's so-called organization chart, which is an inverted pyramid. Following customers from the top of the inverted

pyramid are the salespeople, department managers, and general managers. Finally, at the bottom is the board of directors. All lower levels work toward supporting the salespeople, who in turn, work to serve the customer.

Employee incentives are tied to customer service. Salespeople are given personalized business cards to help them build relationships with customers. Uniquely, salespeople are not tied to their respective departments, but to the customer. Salespeople can travel from department to department within the store to assist their customer, if that is needed. For example, a Nordstrom salesperson assisting a woman shopping for business apparel helps her shop for suits, blouses, shoes, hosiery, and accessories. The salesperson becomes the "personal shopper" of the customer to show her merchandise and provide fashion expertise. This is also conducive to the building of a long-term relationship with the customer, as over time, the salesperson understands the customer's fashion sense and personality. The opportunity to sell across departments enables salespeople to maximize sales and commissions, while providing superior customer service. As noted on a *60 Minutes* segment, "[Nordstrom's service is] not service like it used to be, but service that never was."

Despite the obsession with customer service at Nordstrom, ironically the "customer comes second." Nordstrom understands that customers will be treated well by their employees, only if the employees themselves are treated well by the company. Nordstrom employees are treated almost like the extended Nordstrom family, and employee satisfaction is a closely watched business variable.

Nordstrom is known for promoting employees from within its ranks. The fundamental traits of a successful Nordstrom salesperson (such as a commitment to excellence and customer service) are the same traits emphasized in successful Nordstrom executives.

Nordstrom hires people with a positive attitude, a sense of ownership, initiative, heroism, and the ability to handle high expectations. This sense of ownership is reflected in Nordstrom's low rate of shrinkage. Shrinkage, loss due to theft and record-keeping errors, at Nordstrom is under 1.5 percent of sales, roughly half the industry average. The low shrinkage can be attributed in large part to the diligence of salespeople caring for the merchandise as if it were their own.

Employees at all levels are treated like businesspeople, and empowered to make independent decisions. They are given the latitude to do whatever they believe is the right thing, with the customers' best interests at heart. All employees are given the tools and authority to do whatever is necessary to satisfy customers, and management almost always backs subordinates' decisions.

In summary, Nordstrom's product is its people. The loyal Nordstrom shopper goes to Nordstrom for the service received—not necessarily the products. Of course, Nordstrom does offers quality merchandise, but that is secondary for many customers.

CUSTOMER-FOCUSED POLICIES

One of the most famous examples of Nordstrom's customer service occurred in 1975 when a Nordstrom salesperson gladly took back a set of used automobile tires and gave the customer a refund, even though Nordstrom had never sold tires! The customer had purchased the tires from a Northern Commercial Company store, whose retail space Nordstrom had since acquired. Not wanting the customer to leave the Nordstrom store unhappy, the salesperson refunded the price of the tires.

Nordstrom's policies focus on the concept of the "Lifetime Value of the Customer." Although little money is made on the first sale, when the lifetime value of a customer is calculated, the positive dollar amount of a loyal customer is staggering. The lifetime value of a customer is the sum of all sales generated from that customer, directly or indirectly. To keep its customers for a "lifetime," Nord-

strom employees go to incredible lengths. In a Nordstrom store in Seattle, a customer wanted to buy a pair of brand-name slacks that had gone on sale. The store was out of her size and the salesperson was unable to locate a pair at other Nordstrom stores. Knowing that the same slacks were available at a competitor nearby, the sales clerk went to the rival, purchased the slacks at full price using petty cash from her department, and sold the slacks to the customer at Nordstrom's sale price. Although this sale resulted in an immediate loss for the store, the investment in promoting the loyalty of the happy customer went a long way.

Nordstrom's employees try to "Never Say No" to the customer. Nordstrom has an unconditional return policy. If a customer is not completely satisfied, he or she can return the new and generally even heavily used merchandise at any time for a full refund. Ironically, this is not a company policy, rather it is implemented at the discretion of the salesperson to maximize customer satisfaction. Nordstrom's advice to its employees is simply, "Use good judgment in all situations." Employees are given the freedom, support, and resources to make the best decisions to enhance customer satisfaction. The cost of Nordstrom's high service, such as its return policy, coupled with its competitive pricing would, on the surface, seem to cut into profit margins. This cost, however, is recouped through increased sales from repeat customers, rare markdowns, and, if necessary, the "squeezing" of suppliers.

Nordstrom's up-channel policies also focus on maximizing customer satisfaction. According to former CEO Bruce Nordstrom, "[Vendors] know that we are liberal with our customers. And if you're going to do business with us, then there should be a liberal influence on their return policies. If somebody has worn a shoe and it doesn't wear satisfactorily for them, and we think that person is being honest about it, then we will send it back." Nordstrom realizes some customers will abuse the unconditional return policy, but Nordstrom refuses to impose that abuse back onto their vendors. Here again, the rule of "doing what is right" comes into play.

Nordstrom's merchandising and purchasing policies are also extremely customer-focused. A full selection of merchandise in a wide variety of sizes is seen as a measure of customer service. An average Nordstrom store carries roughly 150,000 pairs of shoes with a variety of sizes, widths, colors, and models. Typical shoe sizes for women range from 2 1/2 to 14, in widths of A to EEE. Nordstrom is fanatical about stocking only high-quality merchandise. Once when the upper parts of some women's shoes were separating from the soles, *every* shoe from that delivery was shipped back to the manufacturer.

Few products are centrally purchased for all stores. Regional buyers, who often manage the department for which they buy, do much of the purchasing. These buyers are close to customers and know what customers like. The salespeople are, in essence, running their own business.

Typically, buyers purchase for a few stores at most, to keep the selection targeted. This also reduces excess inventory caused by poor buying decisions.

DISCUSSION QUESTIONS

1. What steps does Nordstrom take to implement its strategy of providing outstanding customer service?

2. How do these activities enable Nordstrom to reduce the gaps between perceived service and customer expectations as described in Chapter 19?

3. What are the pros and cons of Nordstrom's approach to developing a competitive advantage through customer service?

Source: This case was written by Alicia Lueddemann, the Management Mind Group; and Sunil Erevelles, University of North Carolina, Charlotte. The authors relied substantially on the following references in the preparation of this case: Sunil Erevelles and Alicia Lueddemann, "Why Winners Win," unpublished manuscript, 2002; and Robert Spector and Patrick D. McCarthy, *The Nordstrom Way: The Inside Story of America's #1 Customer Service Company* (New York: John Wiley and Sons, 1995).

CASE 29   GoodLife Fitness Clubs

"These retention rates are poor. I need to do a better job of keeping members," thought Krista Swain, manager of the GoodLife Fitness Club in Kitchener, Ontario, as she reviewed her retention rates for the 2002–2003 fiscal year.

As she was analyzing the report, Jane Riddell, chief operating officer of the chain, entered her office. Krista looked up and said, "Hi Jane. I've just been looking over the retention rates for the clubs. I'm not happy with my numbers."

"Neither is head office," Jane replied, "and that's why I'm here today. You run one of our best clubs, and yet your retention rates are around 60 percent, the average for the 40 GoodLife Clubs. We lose 40 percent of our members each year."

"I agree," said Krista. "We have to figure out how to keep the members enthused and show that the club offers them value."

"That's what I wanted to hear," replied Jane. "As a first step, let's both think about this and meet again next week with some ideas. Then I'd like you to prepare a retention plan that will be the model for all the clubs."

HEAD OFFICE

In March 1979, David Patchell-Evans established GoodLife as a sole proprietorship. Canadian fitness clubs were largely cash and sales oriented with little emphasis on scientific fitness or member retention. By 2003, "Patch" had built this privately owned fitness company to over 40 clubs (10 were franchises, the rest were company-owned) in Ontario and Quebec. GoodLife had the largest group of fitness clubs in Canada, with over 70,000 members.

The head office was located at the Galleria Mall Fitness Club in London, Ontario. Head office personnel numbered approximately 40, led by Patch; Jane Riddell, chief operating officer; and Maureen Hagen, national director of fitness. The head office's main role was to provide leadership and support for the franchisees and company-owned clubs.

One of Jane Riddell's responsibilities was the design and management of GoodLife University, where each month 50 to 60 new associates went through a one-week program. The training included an orientation to GoodLife (basic knowledge of GoodLife and its philosophy), personal training (skills required to assist members as a personal trainer), and computer program training. When club managers hired the associates, they typically spent their first few weeks learning the ropes at the club and then attended the University program. Jane led some of the training sessions and evaluation of the participants, some of whom failed and left GoodLife.

GOODLIFE KITCHENER

In September 1998, the GoodLife Kitchener Club reopened on the second floor of an indoor mall in downtown Kitchener, Ontario. Prior to that it was located two blocks away in a relatively small (12,000 square feet) and poorly designed facility. The new facility was larger (30,000 square feet) and had an open concept design and an extensive range of equipment and programs. Over the next 18 months, membership increased dramatically under Krista Swain's guidance. As of May 2003, the club had 3,500 members, an increase of 2,300 over the original 1,200 members who moved from the old club.

In early 2003, the Kitchener club was signing up over 230 new members per month (Exhibit 1). At the same time, the club was losing about 100 members per month, for a net gain of about 130 members. On an annual basis, the club was losing 40 percent of its members. Overall, the rapid growth in membership had a very positive effect on revenues, which increased by over 60 percent between June 2002 and March 2003 (Exhibit 2).

The Kitchener club's 40 associates (10 full-time, 30 part-time) worked in four groups: sales, customer service, personal training, and service.

- The four sales associates (all full-time) were responsible for getting new members.
- Customer service employees, who were primarily part-time, worked the front desk.
- Personal trainers worked with individual club members on fitness programs.
- Service employees introduced new members to the club and its philosophy through a series of programs on fitness and equipment use.

All employees were involved in selling. Although the sales associates were dedicated to selling new memberships, the personal trainers spent time encouraging members to sign up for personal training. The customer service employees would sell tanning programs and other services to members. Typically, each group or individual had sales targets and earned bonuses and commissions based on meeting those targets.

Most of the employees earned a base salary of $8.00 per hour plus bonuses if they achieved the weekly targets. As an example, a sales associate might have a target of eight new members per week. If he or she achieved or exceeded the target, the associate could earn $1,250 or more every two weeks. Customer service staff could earn up to $25 per week if they met targets, which included phoning members to remind them of upcoming events, encouraging them to use the club, and selling various club products and services such as tanning. Personal trainers could make up to $27.00 per hour for personal training in addition to their base pay of $8.00 per hour. The more members the trainer signed up, the more hours he or she spent in personal training.

Through these incentive programs GoodLife encouraged its staff, particularly the sales associates, to be entrepreneurial. As Krista often said, "The staff have to make things happen; they can't wait for them to happen. Both GoodLife and the staff do better when they make things happen."

EXHIBIT 1   GoodLife Kitchener Club—Membership by Month

Month	Members Lost during Month	Members Gained during Month	Net Members Gained during Month	Members (at end of month)	Retention Rate per Year (%)	Loss Rate per Month (%)
March 2002	—	—	—	1,900	—	—
April 2002	58*	163	105	2,005	63.5**	3.0
May 2002	61	158	97	2,102	64.0	3.0
June 2002	73	156	83	2,185	59.4	3.4
July 2002	75	155	80	2,263	60.9	3.3
August 2002	68	150	82	2,341	65.2	2.9
September 2002	70	168	98	2,423	64.8	2.9
October 2002	108	196	88	2,521	48.5	4.3
November 2002	91	220	129	2,609	57.9	3.5
December 2002	90	223	133	2,738	60.1	3.3
January 2003	103	244	141	2,871	56.4	3.6
February 2003	99	238	139	3,012	60.1	3.3
March 2003	113	234	121	3,151	56.4	3.6
Annual average					59.8†	3.4

*At the beginning of April, the club had 1,900 members. The monthly loss rate for April is 3.0 percent (based on a yearly retention rate for April of 63.5 percent which is a yearly loss rate of 36.5 percent). The club lost 1,900 × .03 = 58 members in April.

**About 63.5 percent of the members as of April 2001 were still members as of April 2002; 36.5 percent were no longer members.

†The average retention rate for the year shown is 59.8 percent; average loss rate per month is 3.4 percent (1 − .598 = .402/12).

Source: GoodLife Fitness Clubs.

As noted, GoodLife had formal training programs for new employees. In addition, Krista spent time with the new employees teaching them the technical side of the job and establishing the norms and culture of the club. By emphasizing what was important to her, Krista hoped they would understand the importance of excellent customer service:

> If I can show the new employees what's important to me, and get them to trust me, they come on board and are part of the team. For example, we hold weekly staff meetings where we discuss a number of issues, including how to improve the club. People don't miss the meetings. Every once in a while, a new associate decides not to come to the meetings. The team lets him or her know that's not acceptable. Those people either become part of the team or decide to leave GoodLife.

Employee turnover at the Kitchener GoodLife Club was slightly better than the average across all the GoodLife clubs. In the past year, Krista had a turnover of about 35 percent, with the rate for full-time slightly lower than for part-time. Part-time turnover was higher, in part, because many of the part-time employees were students who left to go to university or left after completing their degree programs.

Like Jane Riddell, Krista was concerned about employee turnover, but she wasn't sure what actions could improve the situation. She had noticed that some new employees were surprised at the amount of selling involved in their positions. She also felt that some employees were not satisfied with the base salary of $8.00 per hour.

Typically, when an employee left, Krista needed to hire a new associate relatively quickly. She would place an ad in the local paper, the *Record*; get some applications; conduct interviews; and hire the individual she felt was most suited for the position. With full-time employees, Krista was not always happy with the pool of applicants she interviewed; but there was always the pressure of filling the job, which had to be balanced against the quality of the applicants. With the economy improving and a low local unemployment rate, it was sometimes difficult to attract high-quality applicants.

GoodLife Kitchener Club—Selected Revenues and Expenses   EXHIBIT 2

	June 30, 2002 Month	June 30, 2002 YTD (12 months)	March 31, 2003 Month	March 31, 2003 YTD (9 months)
Revenues	(%)	(%)	(%)	(%)
Membership	89.9	88.2	86.9	83.3
Services*	9.3	10.2	11.9	15.5
Other	1.8	1.6	1.2	1.2
Total revenues	100.0	100.0	100.0	100.0
Expenses				
Sales wages and commissions**	10.5	12.1	8.3	8.9
Service wages and commissions†	9.0	7.1	5.3	12.3
Service and other††	19.4	28.6	20.4	17.1
Total direct expenses	38.9	47.8	34.0	38.3
Manager controlled‡	9.2	15.6	4.8	10.4
Administrative‡‡	31.8	31.1	26.3	32.6
Total expenses§	79.9	94.4	65.0	81.3
Members	2,200		3,200	
Total revenue ($)	120,000	1,004,000	195,000	1,177,000

*Includes personal training, specialty programs, tanning, and pro shop.

**Related to new membership sales.

†Includes personal training and member services.

††Includes service staff wages and expenses.

‡Includes utilities, supplies, and services.

‡‡Includes advertising, administrative management, rent, realty taxes, and equipment leasing.

§Not included are depreciation, amortization, interest, and taxes.

THE MEMBERS

Most new members joined the club through referrals. When an individual asked about joining the club, a sales associate would show him or her the club and discuss the benefits of membership and the GoodLife philosophy. If the individual decided to join, the sales associate would ask if he or she had any friends who might also be interested in joining the club; any such referrals would receive a free membership for one week. Typically, the associate tried to get five referrals. The associate would then contact these people, offer the free one-week membership and set up a meeting with them if they accepted. The cycle was repeated with each new member. On average, the sales associates converted between one and two of the five contacts to new members. Referrals generated between 60 percent and 80 percent of all new members.

The price for a new membership varied depending on the promotion option. The two main options were (1) a $199 initiation fee and the first six months free and $40 per four weeks after that, or (2) the initiation fee was waived and the member paid $40 per four weeks. Payments were on a biweekly basis through an automatic payment plan that the member signed. The new member also paid a total of $54 for the membership card ($15) and a processing fee ($39). A new member could also decide to join for a three-month period for $180. Members could also decide to pay once a year and not use the automatic payment plan.

When an individual joined the club, an associate from the service group would take the new member through three programs as an introduction to the club and the GoodLife approach to a healthy lifestyle. The three programs were (1) Fit Fix 1—an introduction to strength training; (2) Cardio—basic information about cardiovascular training principles; and (3) Fit Fix 2—adding exercises to an existing program. Any new member could also have a fitness assessment (resting heart rate, body-fat measurements, an so forth). After six weeks, the new member could also have a second fitness assessment to track his or her progress.

A problem common to most of the GoodLife Clubs was referred to as the "20–20–60 phenomenon." Twenty percent of the club members were hard-core fitness and health people. These members came three or more times a week, were serious about their training, and would tolerate a lot (e.g., uneven service) as long as it didn't interfere with their training. The second 20 percent were the new members. They were enthusiastic and wanted to get fit; and over time they either became committed or not. The largest group, the remaining 60 percent, were those members who came on an irregular basis. The club staff didn't know their names, these members often were not sure about how the equipment worked or what they should be

doing, and they often wouldn't ask for help. Even when they stopped coming, this group kept their membership for a period until they decided to cancel. When one came to cancel, an associate tried to get her or him to stay, usually with little success.

Krista and other associates at GoodLife felt that getting members to feel that they were part of the GoodLife Club was important in retaining them. Krista believed that many of the 60 percent probably never felt they were part of the club as they didn't know many or any of the other members or the staff. Krista remembered that while many of the 1,200 members from the old club liked the new facility (open, spacious, more equipment, and so forth), they felt that the club was more impersonal. In particular, as the membership grew, the "original" members felt less at home. Krista estimated that, within a year, about 50 percent of these members had left the club.

CUSTOMER RETENTION

As Krista prepared for the meeting with Jane, she knew that improved customer retention rates were possible but was uncertain as to what actions would be most effective. She identified three major areas that she could address: employee turnover, a new bonus system, and swipe card technology.

Employee turnover, at over 40 percent, created a lack of stability at the club. Every time a new employee started, he or she didn't know any members and then over time would learn the members' names (often those who visited frequently). If the employee left, so did the knowledge. Krista had always felt that members would have a greater sense of "belonging" to the club if the front-desk staff could greet them by name. Although many of the front-desk staff knew some of the members by name (most of these members were the hard-core regulars who came frequently), most of the front-desk staff were part-time associates or had recently joined GoodLife; therefore, they knew relatively few members by name.

Krista had two ideas for reducing employee turnover, both based on increasing wages. Increasing the hourly base rate from $8.00 to $9.00 for most employees, excluding managers and sales associates, would add about $4,000 per month to wage costs. The problem was that, although she knew that employee turnover would decline, she didn't know by how much, nor did she know the effect on retention rates. A second option was to focus only on the front-desk employees who greeted members. Increasing their rate to $9.00 would increase monthly wage costs by about $1,000.

Next, Krista considered introducing a bonus plan for increasing customer retention. Virtually all the targets and bonuses at GoodLife focused on increasing sales, reflecting, in part, Patch's aggressive growth targets. Although she didn't have a specific plan in mind, Krista felt that an allocation of at least $1,000 to bonuses for increased retention was feasible. Her initial idea was that for every percent increase in retention rates per month (e.g., from 60 percent to 61 percent), staff would receive $200 in bonuses. Where Krista was uncertain was how the target should be set—on an individual or group basis. The front-desk staff had the most contact with members, but potentially all the employees could be involved.

Krista felt that better use of the swipe card information could improve retention. Members swiped their membership card when they visited the club. A valid card allowed a member to go through a turnstile; a nonvalid card (because it had expired) did not release the turnstile. Krista knew that other information (e.g., number of member visits and so on) was available, but no one at the club or head office had developed a software program to track member visits. Krista contacted two software companies, one of which offered a membership management program that would provide interface with swipe scanners and provide reports on members' frequency of visits, along with a host of other member information. The cost ranged from $3,500 for a license for five sites up to $8,500 for unlimited site use.

One of the targets for the front-desk associates was to make "motivation" calls to members each week. Associates would call a specified number of members to reach their target. The associates would begin anywhere on the member list (a binder at the front desk) and begin calling members to encourage them to use the facilities or inform them of special events. After the call, the associate would record the date called and his or her name next to the member's name. Ideally, all members were called once every six weeks, but this didn't always happen.

With the new software system, reports could identify members who had not visited the club for a particular period. Staff could then contact members who had not visited for a specific time period (e.g., three weeks, four weeks, and so forth). Krista felt that this would substantially improve the existing approach and would improve member retention rates.

Krista knew that there were other available approaches or tactics to improve retention rates. In particular, any activities that built a greater sense of community would increase interaction between members and a sense of belonging. But it was difficult to find the time to figure it out. Managing a club with 3,500 members kept her busy making sure everything was running smoothly, and she spent most of her time "doing" not "planning."

A week later, Jane met Krista in her office. Jane started the conversation.

Let me review the situation. As I mentioned last week, if we could improve your club's retention rates from 60 to 65 percent, based on last year's numbers, gross revenues would increase by over $35,000. In this business most of the costs tend to be fixed, probably about 60 percent of revenues, so most of the revenue would be profits. If we could do that for all the clubs, it would be great for business and I think we would have more satisfied members. And just to put this in perspective, on average, we have about 2,000 members per club.

Jane continued,

In the past year, the story has been about the same for most of our clubs. For every 100 new members signed up each month, we have about 40 people who don't renew or cancel their membership. We spend a lot on marketing to get them in the door. Then we spend time with them setting up an exercise or training program. They are enthusiastic to begin with, then they stop coming to classes or exercise. Then they cancel or don't renew when their membership comes up. When they cancel, we ask them why they are leaving. The most common reasons are that they don't have enough time or they can't fit it in to their schedule. I think that about 30 percent of the time they have a good reason for leaving, such as they are moving out of town. I think that 70 percent of the time we could have done something to keep them with the club.

DISCUSSION QUESTIONS

1. Evaluate the strengths and weaknesses of GoodLife's customer acquisition and retention strategies.

2. Calculate the revenues and net profits at GoodLife Kitchener if retention rates were 65 percent and 70 percent versus 60 percent in the past year.

3. What is the average long-term value of a member at GoodLife in terms of total revenue at 60 percent, 70 percent, and 80 percent retention rates?

4. Evaluate the major options considered by Krista, assuming an average GoodLife Club with 2,000 members. What overall plan would you recommend that GoodLife pursue in increasing customer retention rates? Be specific in your recommendations and be prepared to justify them.

Source: This case was written by Dr. Gordon H. G. McDougall, Professor of Marketing in the School of Business and Economics, Wilfrid Laurier University, Waterloo, Ontario, Canada.

CASE 30   Lindy's Bridal Shoppe

Located in Lake City (population 80,000), Lindy's Bridal Shoppe, a small bridal store, sells bridal gowns, prom gowns, accessories, and silk flowers. It also rents men's formal wear and performs various alteration services.

Lindy Armstrong, age 33, has owned the store since its founding in March 1997. She's married to a high school teacher and is the mother of three young children. A former nurse, she found the demands of hospital schedules left too little time for her young family. An energetic, active woman with many interests, she wanted to continue to work but also have time with her children.

The silk flowers market enabled Lindy to combine an in-home career with child rearing. She started Lindy's Silk Flowers with $75 of flower inventory in Vernon, a small town of about 10,000 people 10 miles from Lake City. Working out of her home, she depended on word-of-mouth communication among her customers, mainly brides, to bring in business. As Lindy's Silk Flowers prospered, a room was added onto the house to provide more space for the business. Lindy was still making all the flowers herself. Her flower-making schedule kept her extremely busy. Long hours were the norm.

Lindy was approached by a young photographer named Dan Morgan, who proposed establishing a one-stop bridal shop. In this new business, Dan would provide photography, Lindy would provide silk flowers, and another partner, Karen Ross (who had expertise in the bridal market), would provide gowns and accessories. The new store would be located in Vernon in a rented structure. Shortly before the store was to open, Dan and Karen decided not to become partners and Lindy became the sole owner. She knew nothing about the bridal business. Having no merchandise or equipment, Lindy was drawn to an ad announcing that a bridal store in a major city was going out of business. She immediately called and arranged to meet the owner. Subsequently, she bought all his stock (mannequins, racks, and carpet) for $4,000. The owner also gave her a crash course in the bridal business.

From March 1997 to December 2002, Lindy owned and operated a bridal gown and silk flowers store named Lindy's Bridal Shoppe in Vernon. The location was chosen primarily because it was close to her home. While Vernon is a very small town, Lindy felt that location wasn't a critical factor in her store's success. She maintained that people would travel some distance to make a purchase as important as a bridal gown. Rent was $250 per month plus utilities. Parking was a problem.

During this period, Lindy's Bridal Shoppe grew. Bridal gowns and accessories as well as prom dresses sold well. As the time approached for Lindy to renew her lease, she wondered about the importance of location. A move to Lake City might be advisable.

A much larger town than Vernon, Lake City is the site of a state university. Lindy decided to move.

GENERAL BUSINESS DESCRIPTION

The majority of Lindy's Bridal Shoppe's current sales are made to individuals who order bridal gowns from the rack or from the catalogs of three major suppliers. At the time of the order, the customer pays a deposit, usually half of the purchase price. The balance is due in 30 days. Lindy would like payment in full at the time of ordering regardless of the delivery date. But payment is often delayed until delivery. Once ordered, a gown must be taken and the bill paid when delivered.

No tuxedos are carried in the store so customers must order from catalogs. Fitting jackets and shoes are provided to help patrons size their purchases. Lindy's Bridal Shoppe rents its men's formal wear from suppliers. Payment from the customer is due on delivery.

Certain times of the year see more formal events than others. Many school proms are held during late April and May, and June, July, and August are big months for weddings. Since traditional dates for weddings are followed less and less closely, Lindy believes that the business is becoming less seasonal, though January and February are quite slow.

PROMOTION PRACTICES

Lindy's Bridal Shoppe engages in various promotional activities but is constrained by her limited finances. The firm has no operating budget, which prevents any formal appropriation for advertising expenses.

Newspaper ads constitute the primary promotional medium, though radio is occasionally used. Ads for prom dresses are run only during prom season. These ads usually feature a photograph of a local high school student in a Lindy's Bridal Shoppe gown plus a brief description of the student's activities.

Other promotional activities include bridal shows at a local mall. Lindy feels these have been very successful, though they're a lot of work. A recent prom show in a local high school used students as models. This proved to be an excellent way to stimulate sales. Lindy hopes to go into several other area high schools during the next prom season, though this will demand much planning.

PERSONNEL

Lindy, the sole owner and also the manager of the firm, finds it hard to maintain a capable workforce. A small company, Lindy's Bridal Shoppe can't offer premium salaries for its few positions. There's one full-time salesperson. The part-time staff includes a salesperson, alterations person, bookkeeper, and custodian.

Lindy handles all the paperwork. Her responsibilities include paying bills, ordering merchandise and supplies, hiring and firing personnel, fitting customers, and selling various items. She makes all the major decisions that directly affect the firm's operations. She also makes all the silk flowers herself. It's time consuming, but she isn't satisfied with how anyone else makes them.

MERCHANDISE OFFERINGS

Lindy's Bridal Shoppe's major product lines are new wedding, prom, and party gowns. No used gowns are sold. Discontinued styles or gowns that have been on the rack for a year are sold at reduced prices, primarily because discoloration is a major problem. Gowns tend to yellow after hanging on the racks for a year.

A wide variety of accessories are provided. Lindy believes it's important that her customers not have to go anywhere else for them. These accessories include shoes, veils, headpieces, jewelry, and foundations. Slips may be rented instead of purchased.

One room of Lindy's Bridal Shoppe is used only to prepare silk flowers.

SERVICE OFFERINGS

Lindy's Bridal Shoppe's major service offering is fitting and alteration. Most gowns must be altered, for which there's a nominal charge. Lindy feels that personal attention and personal service set her apart from her competitors. Emphasizing customer satisfaction, she works hard to please each customer. This isn't always easy. Customers can be picky, and it takes time to deal with unhappy people.

LOCATION

Lindy's Bridal Shoppe is located at the end of Lake City's main through street. Initially Lindy didn't think location was important to her bridal store's success, but she's changed her mind. Whereas business was good in Vernon, it's booming in Lake City. Vehicular traffic is high, and there's adequate, if not excess, parking.

Lindy's Bridal Shoppe has a 12-year lease. Rent ($1,800 per month) includes heat and water, but Lindy's Bridal Shoppe must pay for interior decoration. The physical facility is generally attractive, with open and inviting interior display areas. But some areas both inside and outside the store have an unfinished look.

Some storage areas require doors or screens to enhance the interior's appearance. The fitting room ceilings are unfinished, and the carpeting inside the front door may be unsafe. One other interior problem is insufficient space. There seems to be inadequate space for supporting activities such as flower preparation, customer fittings, and merchandise storage, which gives the store a cluttered look.

Several external problems exist. The signs are ineffective, and there's a strong glare on the front windows. This detracts from the effectiveness of the overall appearance and interior window displays. The parking lot needs minor maintenance. Parking lines should be painted and curbs must be repaired. Much should be done to add color and atmosphere through basic landscaping.

COMPETITION

Lindy's Bridal Shoppe is the only bridal shop in Lake City. Lindy believes she has four main competitors. Whitney's Bridal Shoppe is 30 miles from Lake City; Ender's Brides, a new shop with a good operation, is in Spartan City, 50 miles away; Carole's is a large, established bridal shop in Smithtown, 70 miles distant; and Gowns-n-Such is in Andersonville, 75 miles away. A new store in Yorktown (15 miles away) is selling used gowns and discontinued styles at very reduced prices. Lindy watches this new- and used-gown store closely.

Some of her potential customers are buying wedding gowns from electronic retailers such as the Knot (www.the knot.com) and the Wedding Channel (www.wedding channel.com). While these electronic retailers are making significant sales in her trading area now, Lindy is concerned that some of the services offered by these electronic retailers (such as gift registries, e-mail notices, wedding planning, and wedding picture displays) will attract her customers.

FINANCIAL CONSIDERATIONS

Basic financial information includes

1. Markup: 50 percent.

2. 1999 sales: $200,000 (estimated).

3. Average inventory: $70,000.

4. Turnover: 3.0 (approximately).

5. Annual expenses are
   Rent: $19,200.
   Labor: $24,000.
   Utilities: $7,000.
   Supplies: $12,000.
   Equipment: $4,000.
   Miscellaneous: $4,000.

6. Estimated total costs ($200,000 sales): $170,200.

7. Implied profit including owner's salary: $29,800.

8. Capital invested (equipment, $8,000; inventory, $70,000): $78,000.

9. ROI: $5,800/$78,000 = 7.4 percent. (Assume owner salary of $24,000 per year.)

THE FUTURE

Lindy Armstrong is uncertain about the future. She enjoys the business but feels that she's working very hard and not making much money. During all the years of Lindy's Bridal Shoppe's operation, she hasn't taken a salary. She works 60 hours or more a week. Business is excellent and growing, but she's tired. She has even discussed selling the business and returning to nursing.

⬤ DISCUSSION QUESTIONS

1. Could Lindy change the emphasis of her merchandise mix to increase her sales?

2. Which products should have more emphasis? Which should have less?

3. What personnel decisions must Lindy face to improve her business?

4. How could someone like Lindy Armstrong balance the demands of her family and her business?

5. If one of Lindy's competitors were to offer her $150,000 for her business, should she sell?

Source: This case was prepared by Linda F. Felicetti and Joseph P. Grunewald, Clarion University of Pennsylvania.

CASE 31   Starbucks Coffee Company

By 2002, Starbucks was the leading retailer of specialty coffee beverages and beans and related food and merchandise. Its annual sales were $1.68 billion, with a profit of $102 million. Starbucks owned and operated 3,000 retail stores and licensed an additional 300 airport stores in the United States, Thailand, Australia, and Great Britain.

In addition to its direct retailing activities, Starbucks had formed strategic alliances with Dreyer's Grand Ice Cream, Kraft Foods, Barnes & Noble Booksellers, and PepsiCo to expand its product and distribution portfolios. Howard Schultz, chairman and CEO, and his senior management team were focusing on how to sustain their phenomenal growth and maintain their market leadership position.

THE COFFEE MARKET

The commercial market for coffee began in AD 1000 when Arab traders brought the coffee tree from its native Ethiopia to the Middle East. Over the next 200 years, coffee drinking spread through the Arab world and was eventually introduced in Europe in the 1500s by Italian traders. By 1650, coffee houses emerged as popular meeting places in England and France. Well-known public figures would frequent London coffee houses to discuss political and literary issues.

Coffee consumption flourished in the mid-twentieth century, aided by developments in manufacturing and cultivation. By 1940, large coffee processors such as Nestlé (Hills Bros. brand), Kraft General Foods (Maxwell House), and Procter & Gamble (Folgers) developed instant and decaffeinated coffee varieties in addition to their staple regular ground. Supermarkets emerged as the primary distribution channel for traditional coffee sales.

In the late 1980s, per capita coffee consumption fell slowly and steadily as consumers turned to soft drinks, bottled water, juices, and iced teas. The three major manufacturers—Procter & Gamble, Nestlé, and Kraft—fought for market share in a stagnant market. All of the major coffee brands were unprofitable. In an effort to regain profitability, the majors decreased historically high expenditures on image advertising, increased the use of robusta beans (as opposed to the high-quality arabica beans) to further reduce cost, and converted from 16-ounce cans to 13-ounce cans, claiming that the contents produced the same amount of coffee. Coupons and in-store promotions dominated manufacturer marketing plans as price warfare continued.

THE STARBUCKS COFFEE COMPANY: BACKGROUND

Inspiration for the present Starbucks concept came to Howard Schultz when he went to Italy on a buying trip in 1983. While wandering through the ancient piazzas of Milan, Schultz took particular note of the many cheerful espresso bars and cafes he passed. Italians, he felt, had captured the true romance of the beverage. Coffee drinking was an integral part of the Italian culture. Italians started their day at the espresso bar and returned there later on. "There's such a strong sense of community in those coffee bars," he mused. "People come together every single day and in many cases they don't even know each other's names. In Italy, coffee is the conduit to the social experience."

Schultz realized that Americans lacked the opportunity to savor a good cup of coffee while engaging good conversation in a relaxed atmosphere. He returned to the United States convinced that Americans would find the Italian coffee house culture attractive. In 1987, Schultz bought Starbucks.

THE INITIAL YEARS

Retail Offering

Starbucks offers more than a cup of coffee. Scott Bedbury, the VP of marketing, elaborates:

> Our product is not just that which resides in the cup. The product is the store and the service you get in the store. We need to help people appreciate at a higher level why that coffee break feels the way it does, why it's worth the time it takes to prepare a good cup of coffee. I like to think that Starbucks is not so much *food* for thought, but *brewed* for thought. Coffee has for centuries been for thought. I have sometimes thought to myself, "Get out of this chair. You hit the wall." It's that private time for me between 2 and 3 PM when I walk down the Commons area here and make myself an Americano and think something through. I think that's maybe what Starbucks has to offer people: that safe harbor, that place to kind of make sense of the world. In the long run, what distinguishes us from our customers, what is the most enduring competitive advantage we have, is that we are able to give our customers an experience at the store level . . . better than any competitor out there, even the small ones. Starbucks should be a place, an experience, tied up in inspired thought.

While designs vary in any particular store to match the local market, the typical Starbucks store works around a planned mix of organic and manufactured components: light wood tones at the counters and signage areas, brown bags, polished dark marble countertops, glass shelves, thin modern white track lighting, and pure white cups. Even the logo delivers the double organic/modern message: The Starbucks icon is earthy looking, yet rendered in a modern abstract form, in black and white with a band of color around the center only. The colors of the lamps, walls, and tables mimic coffee tones, from green (raw beans) to light and darker browns. Special package and cup designs are coordinated to create livelier, more colorful tones around holidays. Starbucks also keeps its look lively with rotating in-store variations based on timely themes.

Starbucks stores are spacious so that customers can wander around the store, drinking their coffee and considering the purchase of coffee paraphernalia ranging from coffee beans to brushes for cleaning coffee grinders to $1,000 home cappuccino machines. Retail sales are composed of coffee beverages (58 percent), whole bean coffee by the pound (17 percent), food items (16 percent), and coffee-related equipment (9 percent). Although coffee beverages are standardized across outlets, food offerings vary from store to store.

At Starbucks, espresso is brewed precisely 18 to 23 seconds and thrown away if it is not served within 10 seconds of brewing. Coffee beans are donated to charities seven days after coming out of their vacuum-sealed packs. Drip coffee is thrown away if it is not served within an hour of making it. Throughout the store there exists a keen attention to aroma: Employees are not allowed to wear colognes, stores use no scented cleaning products, and smoking is *verboten*.

Human Resource Management

The company, recognizing that its front-line employees are critical to providing "the perfect cup," has built an organizational culture based on two principles: (1) strict standards for how coffee should be prepared and delivered to customers and (2) a laid-back, supportive, and empowering attitude toward its employees.

All new hires, referred to as partners, go through a 24-hour training program that instills a sense of purpose, commitment, and enthusiasm for the job. New employees are treated with the dignity and respect that goes along with their title as *baristas* (Italian for bartender). To emphasize their responsibility in pleasing customers, baristas are presented with scenarios describing customers complaining about beans that were ground incorrectly. The preferred response, baristas learn, is to replace the beans on the spot without checking with the manager or questioning the complaint. Baristas learn to customize each espresso drink and to explain the origins of different coffees and claim to be able to distinguish Sumatran from Ethiopian coffees by the way it "flows over the tongue."

Holding on to their motivated, well-trained employees is important, so all are eligible for health benefits and a stock option plan called "Bean Stock." Each employee is awarded stock options worth 12 percent of his or her annual base pay. (Starbucks now allows options at 14 percent of base pay in light of "good profits.") Employees are also given a free pound of coffee each week and a 30 percent discount on all retail offerings. Baristas know about and are encouraged to apply for promotion to store management positions. Every quarter the company has open meetings at which company news, corporate values, and financial performance data are presented and discussed.

Due to the training, empowerment, benefits, and growth opportunities, Starbucks' turnover is only 60 percent, considerably less the 150 to 200 percent turnover at other firms in the food service business. "We treat our employees like true partners and our customers like stars," comments Schultz.

And stars they are. The average Starbucks customer visits the store 18 times a month; 10 percent visit twice a day. "I don't know of any retailer or restaurant chain that has that kind of loyalty," Schultz says.

Location Strategy

Starbucks' retail expansion strategy was sequential, based on conquering one area of a city or region at a time. Centralized cities served as hubs or regional centers for roll-out expansion into nearby markets (e.g., Chicago as a hub for the Midwest). "Clustering" was also central to the strategy—major markets were saturated with stores before new markets were entered. For example, there were over 100 Starbucks outlets in the Seattle area before the company expanded to a new region. Having several stores in close proximity to each other generally increased overall revenues, though slowed growth in comparable store sales in saturated markets suggested sales were at the expense of some cannibalization of existing businesses.

Traffic was the major determinant in selecting cities and locations. "We want to be in highly visible locations," senior VP of real estate Jim Rubin explains, "with access to customers that value quality and great coffee. You want a store in the path of people's weekly shopping experience, their route to work, their way home from a movie. You want to be America's porch that no longer exists."

PHASE II GROWTH STRATEGY

Product Strategy

Starbucks has introduced a number of new products designed to capitalize on the company's strong brand name. "My plan is to bring the company and consequently the brand closer to consumers and to help unlock a greater potential for the brand while keeping its soul and integrity intact," explains Bedbury.

- *Blue Note Blend.* Blue Note Blend was introduced in conjunction with Capitol Records and its Blue Note label for jazz. "The combination of jazz music and coffees was consistent with the atmosphere of Starbucks," explained Bedbury.

  - *Frappuccino.* The frappuccino beverage is a sweet, cold, creamy drink that combines milk, coffee, and ice. The product was very successful when introduced to cafés in 1995, so Starbucks entered a joint venture with PepsiCo to bottle a ready-to-drink (RTD) version. While canned or bottled coffee beverages had not been marketed in the United States, they were popular in Japan and other parts of the world. Coca-Cola was experimenting with a Nescafe RTD coffee beverage.

- *MAZAGRAN. MAZAGRAN* is a carbonated coffee RTD beverage. The product is manufactured, bottled, and distributed by PepsiCo, but Starbucks shared in the R&D and set flavor standards.

- *Dreyer's Grand Ice Cream.* Dreyer's Grand Ice Cream agreed to produce a line of premium ice cream products flavored with Starbucks coffee. The first products in this line, five coffee-flavored gourmet ice creams, were sold under the Starbucks name and distributed through supermarket outlets. Starbucks ice cream is the leading brand of gourmet coffee ice cream on the market. Chocolate-covered ice cream novelties and Frappuccino ice cream bars were under consideration.

- *Kraft and supermarkets.* Through an agreement with Kraft, the company also sells its branded coffee beans through supermarkets, which still commanded 80 percent of all coffee sales and generate nearly $3 billion in sales annually. The company designed a line of specialty coffees just for supermarkets and opened Starbucks-operated kiosks in selected grocery chains. Kraft manages all distribution, marketing, advertising, and promotions for Starbucks whole bean and ground coffee in grocery and mass-merchandise stores. By the end of fiscal 2001, the company's whole bean and ground coffees were available throughout the United States in approximately 18,000 supermarkets.

Distribution Strategy

Several alternative channels had already been established, including the sale of whole beans through Nordstrom department stores and the sale of coffee by the cup in the cafés of Barnes & Noble bookstores. Additional channels under consideration included distribution through service providers like Holland America Cruise Lines, United Airlines, and Sheraton and Westin Hotels.

In addition to company-operated stores, Starbucks has entered into licensing and joint venture agreements involving 800 stores in North America plus outlets in 15 countries, including Saudi Arabia, Switzerland, Israel, Japan, Taiwan, China, New Zealand, and South Korea.

Communication Strategy

Starbucks historically invested very little in advertising—less than $100 million in its entire history. Explains Bedbury, "Our brand is at its best in the store."

DISCUSSION QUESTIONS

1. What is Starbucks' retail strategy? What is its target market and how does it try to develop an advantage over its competition?

2. Describe Starbucks' retail mix: location, merchandise assortment, pricing, advertising and promotion, store design and visual merchandising, customer service, and personal selling. How does its retail mix support its strategy?

3. What factors in the environment provided the opportunity for Starbucks to develop a new, successful retail chain? What demand and supply conditions prevailed in the U.S. coffee market when Howard Schultz purchased Starbucks in 1987?

What insight did Schultz have that other players in the coffee market did not?

4. What were the principal drivers behind Starbucks' success in the marketplace? What does the Starbucks brand mean to consumers? How have the growth opportunities that Starbuck has pursued affected the value of its brand name?

5. What are the major challenges facing Starbucks as it goes forward? Is the brand advantage sustainable going forward? Can Starbucks defend its position against other specialty coffee retailers?

Source: This case was written by Susan Fournier, Harvard Business School, and Barton Weitz, University of Florida.

GLOSSARY

ABC analysis An analysis that rank orders SKUs by a profitability measure to determine which items should never be out of stock, which should be allowed to be out of stock occasionally, and which should be deleted from the stock selection.

abilities The aptitude and skills of an employee.

accessibility (1) The degree to which customers can easily get into and out of a shopping center; (2) ability of the retailer to deliver the appropriate retail mix to the customers in the segment.

accessories Merchandise in apparel, department, and specialty stores used to complement apparel outfits. Examples include gloves, hosiery, handbags, jewelry, handkerchiefs, and scarves.

accordion theory A cyclical theory of retailer evolution suggesting that changes in retail institutions are explained in terms of depth versus breadth of assortment. Retail institutions cycle from high-depth/low-breadth to low-depth/high-breadth stores and back again.

account opener A premium or special promotion item offered to induce the opening of a new account, especially in financial institutions and stores operating on an installment credit basis.

accounts payable The amount of money owed to vendors, primarily for merchandise inventory.

accounts receivable The amount of money due to the retailer from selling merchandise on credit.

accrued liabilities Liabilities that accumulate daily but are paid only at the end of a period.

ACORN (A Classification of Residential Neighborhood) A market segmentation system that classifies neighborhoods in the United States into distinctive consumer groups, or market segments.

acquisition A strategic growth activity in which one firm acquires another firm, usually resulting in a merger. See also *leveraged buyout.*

actionability Means that the definition of a market segment must clearly indicate what the retailer should do to satisfy its needs.

activity-based costing (ABC) A financial management tool in which all major activities within a cost center are identified, calculated, and then charged to cost objects, such as stores, product categories, product lines, specific products, customers, and suppliers.

adaptive selling An approach to personal selling in which selling behaviors are altered based on information about the customer and the buying situation.

additional markup An increase in retail price after and in addition to original markup.

additional markup cancelation The percentage by which the retail price is lowered after a markup is taken.

additional markup percentage The addition of a further markup to the original markup as a percentage of net sales.

add-on selling Is selling additional new products and services to existing customers, such as a bank encouraging a customer with a checking account to also apply for a home improvement loan from the bank.

administered vertical marketing system A form of vertical marketing system designed to control a line or classification of merchandise as opposed to an entire store's operation. Such systems involve the development of comprehensive programs for specified lines of merchandise. The vertically aligned companies—manufactuer or wholesaler—even though in a nonownership position, may work together to reduce the total systems cost of such activities as advertising, transportation, and data processing. (See also *contractual vertical marketing system* and *corporate vertical marketing system.*)

advanced shipping notice (ASN) An electronic document received by the retailer's computer from a supplier in advance of a shipment.

advertising Paid communications delivered to customers through nonpersonal mass media such as newspapers, television, radio, direct mail, and the Internet.

advertising manager A retail manager who manages advertising activities such as determining the advertising budget, allocating the budget, developing ads, selecting media, and monitoring advertising effectiveness.

advertising reach The percentage of customers in the target market exposed to an ad at least once.

affinity marketing Marketing activities that enable consumers to express their identification with an organization. An example is offering credit cards tied to reference groups like the consumer's university or an NFL team.

affordable budgeting method A budgeting method in which a retailer first sets a budget for every element of the retail mix except promotion and then allocates the leftover funds to a promotional budget.

Age Discrimination and Employment Act A federal act that makes it illegal to discriminate in hiring and termination decisions concerning people between the ages of 40 and 70.

agent (1) A business unit that negotiates purchases, sales, or both but does not take title to the goods in which it deals; (2) a person who represents the principal (who, in the case of retailing, is the store or merchant) and who acts under authority, whether in buying or in bringing the principal into business relations with third parties.

aging The length of time merchandise has been in stock.

aided recall When consumers indicate they know the brand when the name is presented to them.

alteration costs Expenses incurred to change the appearance or fit, to assemble, or to repair merchandise.

alternative dispute resolution A provision included in a contract between retailer and vendor to help avoid litigation in the case of a dispute. Can include methods of settling the dispute that the parties agree upon, such as mediation, arbitration, or med-arb.

Americans with Disabilities Act (ADA) A federal civil rights law that protects people with disabilities from discrimination in employment, transportation, public accommodations, telecommunications, and the activities of state and local government.

analog approach A method of trade area analysis also known as the *similar store* or *mapping* approach. The analysis is divided into four steps: (1) describing the current trade areas through the technique of customer spotting, (2) plotting the customers on a map, (3) defining the primary, secondary, and tertiary area zones, and (4) matching the characteristics of stores in the trade areas with the potential new store to estimate its sales potential.

anchor store A large, well-known retail operation located in a shopping center or Internet mall and serving as an attracting force for consumers to the center.

ancillary services Services such as layaway, gift wrap, and credit that are not directly related to the actual sale of a specific product within the store.

anticipation discount A discount offered by a vendor to a retailer in addition to the cash discount or dating, if the retailer pays the invoice before the end of the cash discount period.

anticompetitive leasing arrangement A lease that limits the type and amount of competition a particular retailer faces within a trading area.

antitrust legislation A set of laws directed at preventing unreasonable restraint of trade or unfair trade practices. Aim is to foster a competitive environment. See also *restraint of trade*.

application form A form used for information on a job applicant's education, employment experience, hobbies, and references.

arbitration Used in the case of a dispute between retailer and vendor that involves the appointment of an neutral party—the arbitrator—who considers the arguments of both sides and then makes a decision that is usually agreed upon in advance as binding.

artificial barriers In site evaluations for accessibility, barriers such as railroad tracks, major highways, or parks.

asset turnover Net sales divided by total assets.

assets Economic resources, such as inventory or store fixtures, owned or controlled by an enterprise as a result of past transactions or events.

assortment The number of SKUs within a merchandise category. Also called *depth of merchandise*.

assortment plan A list of merchandise that indicates in very general terms what should be carried in a particular merchandise category.

atmospherics The design of an environment via visual communications, lighting, colors, music, and scent to stimulate customers' perceptual and emotional responses and ultimately to affect their purchase behavior.

auction A market in which goods are sold to the highest bidder; usually well publicized in advance or held at specific times that are well known in the trade. Auctions are becoming very popular over the Internet.

autocratic leader A manager who makes all decisions on his or her own and then announces them to employees.

automatic reordering system A system for ordering staple merchandise using a predetermined minimum quantity of goods in stock. An automatic reorder can be generated by a computer on the basis of a perpetual inventory system and reorder point calculations.

average BOM stock-to-sales ratio The number of months in the period divided by planned inventory turnover for the period.

average inventory The sum of inventory on hand at several periods in time divided by the number of periods.

baby boomer The generational cohort of people born between 1946 and 1964.

back order A part of an order that the vendor has not filled completely and that the vendor intends to ship as soon as the goods in question are available.

backup stock The inventory used to guard against going out of stock when demand exceeds forecasts or when merchandise is delayed. Also called *safety stock* or *buffer stock*.

backward integration A form of vertical integration in which a retailer owns some or all of its suppliers.

bait-and-switch An unlawful deceptive practice that lures customers into a store by advertising a product at lower than usual prices (the bait), then inducing the customers to switch to a higher-price model (the switch).

balance sheet The summary of a retailer's financial resources and claims against the resources at a particular date; indicates the relationship between assets, liabilities, and owners' equity.

bank card Credit card issued by a bank, such as Visa and MasterCard.

bar code See *Universal Product Code (UPC)*.

bargain branding A branding strategy that targets a price-sensitive segment by offering a no-frills product at a discount price.

bargaining power of vendors A competitive factor that makes markets unattractive when a few vendors control the merchandise sold in it. In these situations, vendors have an opportunity to dictate prices and other terms, reducing retailer's profits.

barriers to entry Conditions in a retail market that make it difficult for firms to enter the market.

base stock See *cycle stock*.

basic merchandise See *staple merchandise*.

basic stock list The descriptive and record-keeping function of an inventory control system; includes the stock number, item description, number of units on hand and on order, and sales for the previous periods.

basic stock method   An inventory management method used to determine the beginning-of-month (BOM) inventory by considering both the forecast sales for the month and the safety stock.

benchmarking   The practice of evaluating performance by comparing one retailer's performance with that of other retailers using a similar retail strategy.

benefit segmentation   A method of segmenting a retail market on the basis of similar benefits sought in merchandise or services.

benefits   The customer's specific needs that are satisfied when the customer buys a product.

black market   The availability of merchandise at a high price when it is difficult or impossible to purchase under normal market circumstances; commonly involves illegal transactions.

blue laws   Laws prohibiting retailers from being open two consecutive days of the weekend—ostensibly to allow employees a day of rest or religious observance. Most states no longer have blue laws.

bonus   Additional compensation awarded periodically, based on a subjective evaluation of the employee's performance.

book inventory system   See *retail inventory method.*

bottom-up planning   When goals are set at the bottom of the organization and filter up through the operating levels.

boutique   (1) Departments in a store designed to resemble small, self-contained stores; (2) a relatively small specialty store.

boutique layout   See *free-form layout.*

brand   A distinguishing name or symbol (such as a logo, design, symbol, or trademark) that identifies the products or services offered by a seller and differentiates those products and services from the offerings of competitors.

brand association   Anything linked to or connected with the brand name in a consumer's memory.

brand awareness   The ability of a potential customer to recognize or recall that a particular brand name belongs to a retailer or product/service.

brand building   The design and implementation of a retail communication program to create an image in the customer's mind of the retailer relative to its competitors. Also called *positioning.*

brand equity   The value that brand image offers retailers.

brand image   Set of associations consumers have about a brand that are usually organized around some meaningful themes.

brand loyalty   An example of habitual decision making that occurs when consumers like and consistently buy a specific brand in a product category.

breadth of merchandise   See *variety.*

break-even analysis   A technique that evaluates the relationship between total revenue and total cost to determine profitability at various sales levels.

break-even point   The quantity at which total revenue equals total cost and beyond which profit occurs.

breaking bulk   A function performed by retailers or wholesalers in which they receive large quantities of merchandise and sell them in smaller quantities.

breaking sizes   Running out of stock on particular sizes.

broker   A middleman that serves as a go-between for the buyer or seller; assumes no title risks, does not usually have physical custody of products, and is not looked upon as a permanent representative of either the buyer or seller.

buffer stock   Merchandise inventory used as a safety cushion for cycle stock so the retailer won't run out of stock if demand exceeds the sales forecast. Also called *safety stock.*

building codes   Legal restrictions describing the size and type of building, signs, type of parking lot, and so on that can be used at a particular location.

bulk fixture   See *rounder.*

buyback   A strategy vendors and retailers use to get products into retail stores, either when a retailer allows a vendor to create space for goods by "buying back" a competitor's inventory and removing it from a retailer's system, or when the retailer forces a vendor to buy back slow-moving merchandise.

buyer   Person in a retailing organization responsible for the purchase and profitability of a merchandise category. Similar to *category manager.*

buyer's market   Market occurring in economic conditions that favor the position of the retail buyer (or merchandiser) rather than the vendor; in other words, economic conditions are such that the retailer can demand and usually get concessions from suppliers in terms of price, delivery, and other market advantages. Opposite of a *seller's market.*

buyer's report   Information on the velocity of sales, availability of inventory, amount of order, inventory turnover, forecast sales, and, most important, the quantity that should be ordered for each SKU.

buying behavior   The activities customers undertake when purchasing a good or service.

buying calendar   A plan of a store buyer's market activities, generally covering a six-month merchandising season based on a selling calendar that indicates planned promotional events.

buying committee   A committee that has the authority for final judgment and decision making on such matters as adding or eliminating new products.

buying power   The customer's financial resources available for making purchases.

buying process   The stages customers go through to purchase merchandise or services.

buying situation segmentation   A method of segmenting a retail market based on customer needs in a specific buying situation such as a fill-in shopping trip versus a weekly shopping trip.

buzz Genuine, street-level excitement about a hot new product.

call system A system of equalizing sales among salespersons—for example, some stores rotate salespeople, giving each an equal opportunity to meet customers.

capacity fixture See *rounder.*

career path The set of positions to which management employees are promoted within a particular organization as their careers progress.

cash Money on hand.

cash discounts Reductions in the invoice cost that the vendor allows the retailer for paying the invoice prior to the end of the discount period.

cash wraps The places in a store where customers can purchase merchandise and have it "wrapped"—placed in a bag.

catalog retailer A nonstore retailer that communicates directly with customers using catalogs sent through the mail.

catalog retailing Nonstore retail format in which the retail offering is communicated to a customer through a catalog.

catalog showroom A type of retailer that uses a showroom to display merchandise combined with an adjacent warehouse; typically specializes in hard goods such as housewares.

category An assortment of items (SKUs) the customer sees as reasonable substitutes for each other.

category captain A supplier that forms an alliance with a retailer to help gain consumer insight, satisfy consumer needs, and improve the performance and profit potential across the entire category.

category killer A discount retailer that offers a complete assortment in a category and thus dominates a category from the customers' perspective. Also called a *category specialist.*

category life cycle A merchandise category's sales pattern over time.

category management The process of managing a retail business with the objective of maximizing the sales and profits of a category.

category manager See *buyer.*

category specialist See *category killer.*

caveat emptor Latin term for "let the buyer beware."

census tracts Subdivisions of a Metropolitan Statistical Area (MSA), with an average population of 4,000.

central business district (CBD) The traditional downtown business area of a city or town.

central market See *market.*

central place A center of retailing activity such as a town or city.

central place theory Christaller's theory of retail location suggesting that retailers tend to locate in a central place. As more retailers locate together, more customers are attracted to the central place. See also *central place.*

centralization The degree to which authority for making retail decisions is delegated to corporate managers rather than to geographically dispersed regional, district, and store management.

centralized buying A situation in which a retailer makes all purchase decisions at one location, typically the firm's headquarters.

chain discount A number of different discounts taken sequentially from the suggested retail price.

chargeback A practice used by retailers in which they deduct money from the amount they owe a vendor.

chat room Location in an Internet site at which customers can engage in interactive, real-time, text-based discussions.

checking The process of going through goods upon receipt to make sure that they arrived undamaged and that the merchandise received matches the merchandise ordered.

cherry picking Customers visiting a store and buying only merchandise sold at big discounts or buying only the best styles or colors.

classic A merchandise category that has both a high level and a long duration of acceptance.

classification A group of items or SKUs for the same type of merchandise, such as pants (as opposed to jackets or suits), supplied by different vendors.

classification dominance An assortment so broad that customers should be able to satisfy all of their consumption needs for a particular category by visiting one retailer.

classification merchandising Divisions of departments into related types of merchandise for reporting and control purposes.

Clayton Act (1914) An act passed as a response to the deficiencies of the Sherman Act; it specifically prohibits price discrimination, tying arrangements, and exclusive dealing contracts that have the effect of limiting free trade, and it provides for damages to parties injured as a result of violations of the act.

clearance sale An end-of-season sale to make room for new goods; also pushing the sale of slow-moving, shopworn, and demonstration model goods.

close-out (1) An offer at a reduced price to sell a group of slow-moving or incomplete stock; (2) an incomplete assortment, the remainder of a line of merchandise that is to be discontinued and so is offered at a low price to ensure immediate sale.

closeout retailer Off-price retailer that sells a broad but inconsistent assortment of general merchandise as well as apparel and soft home goods, obtained through retail liquidations and bankruptcy proceedings.

cocooning A term that describes a behavioral pattern of consumers who increasingly turn to the nice, safe, familiar environment of their homes to spend their limited leisure time.

COD (cash on delivery) Purchase terms in which payment for a product is collected at the time of delivery.

collaboration, planning, forecasting, and replenishment (CPFR) A collaborative inventory management system in which a retailer shares information with vendors. CPFR software uses the data to construct a computer-generated replenishment forecast that is shared by the retailer and vendor before it's executed.

commercial bribery A vendor's offer of money or gifts to a retailer's employee for the purpose of influencing purchasing decisions.

commission Compensation based on a fixed formula, such as percentage of sales.

committee buying The situation whenever the buying decision is made by a group of people rather than by a single buyer. A multiunit operation is usually the type of firm that uses this procedure.

common stock The type of stock most frequently issued by corporations. Owners of common stock usually have voting rights in the retail corporation.

communication gap The difference between the actual service provided to customers and the service promised in the retailer's promotion program. This factor is one of the four factors identified by the Gaps model for improving service quality.

communication objectives Specific goals for a communication program related to the effects of the communication program on the customer's decision-making process.

comparative price advertising A common retailing practice that compares the price of merchandise offered for sale with a higher "regular" price or a manufacturer's list price.

comparison shopping A market research method in which retailers shop at competitive stores, comparing the merchandise, pricing, visual display, and service to their own offering.

compatibility The degree to which the fashion is consistent with existing norms, values, and behaviors.

compensation Monetary payments including salary, commission, and bonuses; also, paid vacations, health and insurance benefits, and a retirement plan.

competition-oriented pricing A pricing method in which a retailer uses competitors' prices, rather than demand or cost considerations, as guides.

competitive parity method An approach for setting a promotion budget so that the retailer's share of promotion expenses is equal to its market share.

competitive rivalry The frequency and intensity of reactions to actions undertaken by competitors.

competitor analysis An examination of the strategic direction that competitors are likely to pursue and their ability to successfully implement their strategy.

complexity Refers to how easy it is to understand and use a new fashion. Consumers have to learn how to incorporate a new fashion into their lifestyle for it to be successful.

composite segmentation A method of segmenting a retail market using multiple variables, including benefits sought, lifestyles, and demographics.

computerized checkout See *point-of-sale (POS) terminal*.

conditional sales agreement An agreement that passes title of goods to the consumer, conditional on full payment.

conditions of sale See *terms of sale*.

conflict of interest A situation in which a decision maker's personal interest influences or has the potential to influence his or her professional decision.

congestion The amount of crowding of either cars or people.

consideration set The set of alternatives the customer evaluates when making a merchandise selection.

consignment goods Items not paid for by the retailer until they are sold. The retailer can return unsold merchandise; however, the retailer does not take title until final sale is made.

consortium exchange A retail exchange that is owned by several firms within one industry.

consumer cooperative Customers own and operate this type of retail establishment. Customers have ownership shares, hire full-time managers, and share in the store's profits through price reductions or dividends.

Consumer Goods Pricing Act (1975) The statute that repealed all resale price maintenance laws and made it possible for retailers to sell products below suggested retail prices.

consumerism The activities of government, business, and independent organizations designed to protect individuals from practices that infringe upon their rights as consumers.

contest Promotional activity in which customers compete for rewards through games of chance. Contests can also be used to motivate retail employees.

contract distribution service company Firm that performs all of the distribution functions for retailers or vendors, including transportation to the contract company's distribution center, merchandise processing, storage, and transportation to retailers.

contractual vertical marketing system A form of vertical marketing system in which independent firms at different levels in the channel operate contractually to obtain the economies and market impacts that could not be obtained by unilateral action. Under this system, the identity of the individual firm and its autonomy of operations remain intact. See also *administered vertical marketing system* and *corporate vertical marketing system*.

contribution margin Gross margin less any expense that can be directly assigned to the merchandise.

convenience center A shopping center that typically includes such stores as a convenience market, a dry cleaner, or a liquor store.

convenience goods Products that the consumer is not willing to spend the effort to evaluate prior to purchase, such as milk or bread.

convenience store A store that provides a limited variety and assortment of merchandise at a convenient location in a 2,000- to 3,000-square-foot store with speedy checkout.

conventional supermarket A self-service food store that offers groceries, meat, and produce with limited sales of nonfood items, such as health and beauty aids and general merchandise.

co-op advertising Enables a retailer to associate its name with well-known national brands and use attractive art work created by the national brand. Also a method a retailer uses of sharing the cost of advertising with a vendor.

cooperative An establishment owned by an association of customers. In general, the distinguishing features of a cooperative are patronage dividends based on the volume of expenditures by the members and a limitation of one vote per member regardless of the amount of stock owned.

cooperative (co-op) advertising A program undertaken by a vendor in which the vendor agrees to pay all or part of a promotion for its products.

cooperative buying When a group of independent retailers work together to make large purchases from a single supplier.

copy The text in an advertisement.

copycat branding A branding strategy that imitates the manufacturer brand in appearance and trade dress but generally is perceived as lower quality and is offered at a lower price.

copyright A regulation that protects original works of authors, painters, sculptors, musicians, and others who produce works of artistic or intellectual merit.

core assortment A relatively large proportion of the total assortment that is carried by each store in the chain, regardless of size.

corporate vertical marketing system A form of vertical marketing system in which all of the functions from production to distribution are at least partially owned and controlled by a single enterprise. Corporate systems typically operate manufacturing plants, warehouse facilities, and retail outlets. See also administered vertical marketing system and contractual vertical marketing system.

corporation A firm that is formally incorporated under state law and that is a different legal entity from stockholders and employees.

cost code The item cost information indicated on price tickets in code. A common method of coding is the use of letters from an easily remembered word or expression with nonrepeating letters corresponding to numerals. For example,

y o u n g b l a d e

1 2 3 4 5 6 7 8 9 0

cost complement The percentage of net sales represented by the cost of goods sold.

cost method of accounting A method in which retailers record the cost of every item on an accounting sheet or include a cost code on the price tag or merchandise container. When a physical inventory is conducted, the cost of each item must be determined, the quantity in stock is counted, and the

total inventory value at cost is calculated. See *retail inventory method.*

cost multiplier The cumulative markup multiplied by 100 percent minus cumulative markup percentage.

cost-oriented method A method for determining the retail price by adding a fixed percentage to the cost of the merchandise; also known as *cost-plus pricing.*

cost per thousand (CPM) A measure that is often used to compare media. CPM is calculated by dividing an ad's cost by its reach.

counterfeit merchandise Goods that are made and sold without permission of the owner of a trademark, a copyright, or a patented invention that is legally protected in the country where it is marketed.

coupons Documents that entitle the holder to a reduced price or X cents off the actual price of a product or service.

courtesy days The days on which stores extend to loyalty club customers the privilege of making purchases at sale prices in advance of public sale.

coverage The theoretical number of potential customers in the retailer's target market that could be exposed to an ad in a given medium.

credit Money placed at a consumer's disposal by a retailer, financial or other institution. For purchases made on credit, payment is due in the future.

credit limit The quantitative limit that indicates the maximum amount of credit that may be allowed to be outstanding on each individual customer account.

crossdocking distribution center A warehouse at which merchandise is delivered to one side of the facility by vendors, is unloaded, and is immediately reloaded onto trucks that deliver merchandise to the stores. With cross-docking, merchandise spends very little time in the warehouse.

cross-selling When sales associates in one department attempt to sell complementary merchandise from other departments to their customers.

cross-shopping A pattern of buying both premium and low-priced merchandise or patronizing expensive, status-oriented retailers and price-oriented retailers.

culture The meaning and values shared by most members of a society.

cumulative attraction The principle that a cluster of similar and complementary retailing activities will generally have greater drawing power than isolated stores that engage in the same retailing activities.

cumulative markup The average percentage markup for the period; the total retail price minus cost divided by retail price.

cumulative quantity discounts Discounts earned by retailers when purchasing certain quantities over a specified period of time.

cumulative reach The cumulative number of potential customers that would see an ad that runs several times.

current assets Cash or any assets that can normally be converted into cash within one year.

current liabilities Debts that are expected to be paid in less than one year.

customer allowance An additional price reduction given to the customer.

customer buying process The stages a customer goes through in purchasing a good or service. Stages include need recognition, information search, evaluation and choice of alternatives, purchase, and postpurchase evaluation.

customer database See *data warehouse.*

customer loyalty Customers' commitment to shopping at a store.

customer relationship management (CRM) A business philosophy and set of strategies, programs, and systems that focuses on identifying and building loyalty with a retailer's most valued customers.

customer returns The value of merchandise that customers return because it is damaged, doesn't fit, and so forth.

customer service The set of retail activities that increase the value customers receive when they shop and purchase merchandise.

customer service department The department in a retail organization that handles customer inquiries and complaints.

customer spotting A technique used in trade area analysis that "spots" (locates) residences of customers for a store or shopping center.

customization approach An approach used by retailers to provide customer service that is tailored to meet each customer's personal needs.

cycle stock Inventory that results from the replenishment process and is required to meet demand when the retailer can predict demand and replenishment times (lead times) perfectly.

cyclical theories Theories of institutional change based on the premise that retail institutions change on the basis of cycles. See also wheel of retailing and accordion theory.

data mining Technique used to identify patterns in data found in data warehouses, typically patterns that the analyst is unaware of prior to searching through the data.

data warehouse The coordinated and periodic copying of data from various sources, both inside and outside the enterprise, into an environment ready for analytical and informational processing. It contains all of the data the firm has collected about its customers and is the foundation for subsequent CRM activities.

databased retailing The development and implementation of retailing programs to build store loyalty utilizing a computerized file (data warehouse) of customer profiles and purchase patterns.

dating A series of options that tells retailers when discounts can be taken from vendors and when the full invoice amount is due.

deal period A limited time period allowed by manufacturers for retailers to purchase merchandise at a special price.

debit card A card that resembles a credit card but allows the retailer to automatically subtract payments from a customer's checking account at the time of sale.

decentralization When authority for retail decisions is made at lower levels in the organization.

deceptive advertising Any advertisement that contains a false statement or misrepresents a product or service.

decile analysis A method of identifying customers in a CRM program that breaks customers into ten deciles based on their LTV (lifetime value). When using decile analysis, the top 10 percent of the customers would be the most-valued group.

deferred billing An arrangement that enables customers to buy merchandise and not pay for it for several months, with no interest charge.

delivery gap The difference between the retailer's service standards and the actual service provided to customers. This factor is one of the four factors identified by the Gaps model for improving service quality.

demalling The activity of revitalizing a mall by demolishing a mall's small shops, scrapping its common space and food courts, enlarging the sites once occupied by department stores, and adding more entrances into the parking lot.

demand/destination area Department or area in a store in which demand for the products or services offered is created before customers get to their destination.

demand-oriented method A method of setting prices based on what the customers would expect or be willing to pay.

democratic leader A store manager who seeks information and opinions from employees and bases decisions on this information.

demographic segmentation A method of segmenting a retail market that groups consumers on the basis of easily measured, objective characteristics such as age, gender, income and education.

demographics Vital statistics about populations such as age, sex, and income.

department A segment of a store with merchandise that represents a group of classifications the consumer views as being complementary.

department store A retailer that carries a wide variety and deep assortment, offers considerable customer services, and is organized into separate departments for displaying merchandise.

departmentalization An organizational design in which employees are grouped into departments that perform specific activities to achieve operating efficiencies through specialization.

depth interview An unstructured personal interview in which the interviewer uses extensive probing to get individual respondents to talk in detail about a subject.

depth of merchandise See *assortment.*

deseasonalized demand The forecast demand without the influence of seasonality.

destination store A retail store in which the merchandise, selection, presentation, pricing, or other unique feature acts as a magnet for customers.

dialectic theory An evolutionary theory based on the premise that retail institutions evolve. The theory suggests that new retail formats emerge by adopting characteristics from other forms of retailers in much the same way that a child is the product of the pooled genes of two very different parents.

direct investment The investment and ownership by a retail firm or a division or subsidiary that builds and operates stores in a foreign country.

direct-mail catalog retailer A retailer offering merchandise or services through catalogs mailed directly to customers.

direct-mail retailer A nonstore retailer that communicates directly with customers using mail brochures and pamphlets to sell a specific product or service to customers at one point in time.

direct marketing A form of nonstore retailing in which customers are exposed to merchandise through print or electronic media and then purchase the merchandise by telephone, mail, or over the Internet.

direct product profitability (DPP) The profit associated with each category or unit of merchandise. DPP is equal to the per-unit gross margin less all variable costs associated with the merchandise such as procurement, distribution, sales, and the cost of carrying the assets.

direct-response advertising Advertisements on TV and radio that describe products and provide an opportunity for customers to order them.

direct retailing See *nonstore retailing*.

direct selling A retail format in which a salesperson, frequently an independent distributor, contacts a customer directly in a convenient location (either at a customer's home or at work) and demonstrates merchandise benefits, takes an order, and delivers the merchandise to the customer.

disability Any physical or mental impairment that substantially limits one or more of an individual's major life activities or any condition that is regarded as being such an impairment.

disclosure of confidential information An unethical situation in which a retail employee discloses proprietary or confidential information about the firm's business to anyone outside the firm.

discount A reduction in the original retail price granted to store employees as a special benefit or to customers under certain circumstances.

discount-oriented center See *promotional center*.

discount store A general merchandise retailer that offers a wide variety of merchandise, limited service, and low prices.

discrimination An illegal action of a company or its managers that results when a member of a protected class (women, minorities, etc.) are treated differently from nonmembers of that class (see *disparate treatment*) or that an apparently neutral rule has an unjustified discriminatory effect (see *disparate impact*).

disintermediation When a manufacturer sells directly to consumers, thus competing directly with its retailers.

disparate impact In the case of discrimination when an apparently neutral rule has an unjustified discriminatory effect, such as if a retailer requires high school graduation for all its employees thereby excluding a larger proportion of disdvantaged minorities, when at least some of the jobs (e.g., custodian) could be performed just as well by people who did not graduate from high school.

disparate treatment In the case of discrimination when members of a protected class is treated differently than nonmembers of that class—if a qualified woman (protected class) does not receive a promotion given to a lesser qualified man.

dispatcher A person who coordinates deliveries from the vendor to the distribution center or stores, or from the distribution center to stores.

display stock Merchandise placed on various display fixtures for customers to examine.

distribution See *logistics*.

distribution center A warehouse that receives merchandise from multiple vendors and distributes it to multiple stores.

distribution channel A set of firms that facilitate the movement of products from the point of production to the point of sale to the ultimate consumer.

distribution intensity The number of retailers carrying a particular category.

distributive fairness Arises when outcomes received are viewed as fair with respect to outcomes received by others.

diversification opportunity A strategic investment opportunity that involves an entirely new retail format directed toward a market segment not presently being served.

diversionary pricing A practice sometimes used by retailers in which low price is stated for one or a few goods or services (emphasized in promotion) to give the illusion that the retailer's prices are all low.

diverted merchandise Merchandise that is diverted from its legitimate channel of distribution similar to gray-market merchandise except there need not be distribution across international boundaries.

diverter A firm that buys diverted merchandise from retailers and manufacturers and then resells the merchandise to other retailers. See *diverted merchandise*.

double-coupon A retail promotion that allows the customer to double the face value of a coupon.

drawing account A method of sales compensation in which salespeople receive a weekly check based on their estimated annual income.

drugstore Specialty retail store that concentrates on pharmaceuticals and health and personal grooming merchandise.

duty See *tariff*.

economic order quantity (EOQ)　The order quantity that minimizes the total cost of processing orders and holding inventory.

80–20 rule　A general management principle where 80 percent of the sales or profits come from 20 percent of the customers.

electronic agent　Computer program that locates and selects alternatives based on some predetermined characteristics.

electronic article surveillance system (EAS)　A loss-prevention system in which special tags placed on merchandise in retail stores are deactivated when the merchandise is purchased. The tags are used to discourage shoplifting.

electronic data interchange (EDI)　The computer-to-computer exchange of business documents from retailer to vendor, and back.

electronic retailing　A retail format in which the retailers communicate with customers and offer products and services for sale over the Internet.

emotional support　Supporting retail service providers with the understanding and positive regard to enable them to deal with the emotional stress created by disgruntled customers.

employee discount　A discount from retail price offered by most retailers to employees.

employee productivity　Output generated by employee activities. One measure of employee productivity is the retailer's sales or profit divided by its employee costs.

employee turnover　The number of employees occupying a set of positions during a period (usually a year) divided by the number of positions.

empowerment　The process of managers sharing power and decision-making authority with employees.

empty nest　A stage in a family life cycle where children have grown up and left home.

empty nester　Household where all children are grown and have left home.

end cap　Display fixture located at the end of an aisle.

end-of-month (EOM) dating　A method of dating in which the discount period starts at the end of the month in which the invoice is dated (except when the invoice is dated the 25th or later).

energy management　The coordination of heating, air conditioning, and lighting to improve efficiencies and reduce energy costs.

environmental apparel　Merchandise produced with few or no harmful effects on the environment.

Equal Employment Opportunity Commission (EEOC)　A federal commission that was established for the purpose of taking legal action against employers that violate Title VII of the Civil Rights Act. Title VII prohibits discrimination in company personnel practices.

Equal Pay Act　A federal act enforced by the Equal Employment Opportunity Commission that prohibits unequal pay for men and women who perform equal work or work of comparable worth.

escape clause　A clause in a lease that allows the retailer to terminate its lease if sales don't reach a certain level after a specified number of years or if a specific co-tenant in the center terminates its lease.

e-tailing　See *electronic retailing*.

ethics　A system or code of conduct based on universal moral duties and obligations that indicate how one should behave.

evaluation of alternatives　The stage in the buying process in which the customer compares the benefits offered by various retailers.

everyday low pricing (EDLP)　A pricing strategy that stresses continuity of retail prices at a level somewhere between the regular nonsale price and the deep-discount sale price of the retailer's competitors.

evolutionary theories　Theories of institutional change based on the premise that retail institutions evolve. See *dialectic theory* and *natural selection*.

exclusive dealing agreement　Restriction a manufacturer or wholesaler places on a retailer to carry only its products and no competing vendors' products.

exclusive geographical territory　A policy in which only one retailer in a certain territory is allowed to sell a particular brand.

exclusive use clause　A clause in a lease that prohibits the landlord from leasing to retailers selling competing products.

executive training program (ETP)　A training program for retail supervisors, managers, and executives.

expenses　Costs incurred in the normal course of doing business to generate revenues.

experiment　A research method in which a variable is manipulated under controlled conditions.

expert system　Computer program that incorporates knowledge of experts in a particular field. Expert systems are used to aid in decision making and problem solving.

exponential smoothing　A sales forecasting technique in which sales in previous time periods are weighted to develop a forecast for future periods.

express warranty　A guarantee supplied by either the retailer or the manufacturer that details the terms of the warranty in simple, easily understood language so customers know what is and what is not covered by the warranty.

extended problem solving　A buying process in which customers spend considerable time at each stage of the decision-making process because the decision is important and they have limited knowledge of alternatives.

external sources of information　Information provided by the media and other people.

extra dating　A discount offered by a vendor in which the retailer receives extra time to pay the invoice and still take the cash discount.

extranet　A collaborative network that uses Internet technology to link businesses with their suppliers, customers, or other businesses.

extrinsic reward   Reward (such as money, promotion, and recognition) given to employees by their manager or the firm.

factoring   A specialized financial function whereby manufacturers, wholesalers, or retailers sell accounts receivable to financial institutions, including factors or banks.

factory outlet   Outlet store owned by a manufacturer.

fad   A merchandise category that generates a lot of sales for a relatively short time—often less than a season.

Fair Labor Standards Act   A federal law, enacted in 1938, that sets minimum wages, maximum hours, child labor standards, and overtime pay provisions.

fair trade laws   See *resale price maintenance laws.*

fashion   Category of merchandise that typically lasts several seasons, and sales can vary dramatically from one season to the next.

fashion/specialty center   A shopping center that is composed mainly of upscale apparel shops, boutiques, and gift shops carrying selected fashions or unique merchandise of high quality and price.

feature area   Area designed to get the customer's attention that includes end caps, promotional aisles or areas, freestanding fixtures and mannequins that introduce a soft goods department, windows, and point-of-sale areas.

feature fixture   See *four-way fixture.*

features   The qualities or characteristics of a product that provide benefits to customers.

Federal Trade Commission Act (1914)   The congressional act that created the Federal Trade Commission (FTC) and gave it the power to enforce federal trade laws.

fill rate   The percentage of an order that is shipped by the vendor.

financial leverage   A financial measure based on the relationship between the retailer's liabilities and owners' equity that indicates financial stability of the firm.

first-degree price discrimination   Charging customers different prices based on their willingness to pay.

fixed assets   Assets that require more than a year to convert to cash.

fixed costs   Costs that are stable and don't change with the quantity of product that's produced and sold.

fixed expenses   Expenses that remain constant for a given period of time regardless of the sales volume.

fixed-rate lease   A lease that requires the retailer to pay a fixed amount per month over the life of the lease.

flattening the organization   A reduction in the number of management levels.

flexible pricing   A pricing strategy that allows consumers to bargain over selling prices.

flextime   A job scheduling system that enables employees to choose the times they work.

floor-ready merchandise   Merchandise received at the store ready to be sold, without the need for any additional preparation by retail employees.

FOB (free-on-board) destination   A term of sale designating that the shipper owns the merchandise until it is delivered to the retailer and is therefore responsible for transportation and any damage claims.

FOB (free-on-board) origin   A term of sale designating that the retailer takes ownership of the merchandise at the point of origin and is therefore responsible for transportation and any damage claims.

focus group   A marketing research technique in which a small group of respondents is interviewed by a moderator using a loosely structured format.

forward buy   An opportunity to purchase at an extra discount more merchandise than the retailer normally needs to fill demand.

forward integration   A form of vertical integration in which a manufacturer owns wholesalers or retailers.

four-way fixture   A fixture with two cross bars that sit perpendicular to each other on a pedestal.

franchisee   The owner of an individual store in a franchise agreement.

franchising   A contractual agreement between a franchisor and a franchisee that allows the franchisee to operate a retail outlet using a name and format developed and supported by the franchisor.

franchisor   The owner of a franchise in a franchise agreement.

free-form layout   A store design, used primarily in small specialty stores or within the boutiques of large stores, that arranges fixtures and aisles asymmetrically. Also called *boutique layout.*

free trade zone   A special area within a country that can be used for warehousing, packaging, inspection, labeling, exhibition, assembly, fabrication, or transshipment of imports without being subject to that country's tariffs.

freestanding fixture   Fixtures and mannequins located on aisles that are designed primarily to get customers' attention and bring them into a department.

freestanding insert (FSI)   An ad printed at a retailer's expense and distributed as a freestanding insert in the newspaper. Also called a *preprint.*

freestanding site   A retail location that is not connected to other retailers.

freight collect   When the retailer pays the freight.

freight forwarders   Companies that purchase transport services. They then consolidate small shipments from a number of shippers into large shipments that move at a lower freight rate.

freight prepaid   When the freight is paid by the vendor.

frequency   The number of times a potential customer is exposed to an ad.

frequent shopper program   A reward and communication program used by a retailer to encourage continued purchases from the retailer's best customers. See *loyalty program.*

fringe trade area   See *tertiary zone.*

frontal presentation A method of displaying merchandise in which the retailer exposes as much of the product as possible to catch the customer's eye.

full warranty A guarantee provided by either the retailer or manufacturer to repair or replace merchandise without charge and within a reasonable amount of time in the event of a defect.

full-line forcing When a supplier requires a retailer to carry the supplier's full line of products if the retailer wants to carry any part of that line.

functional discount See *trade discount.*

functional needs The needs satisfied by a product or service that are directly related to its performance.

functional product grouping Categorizing and displaying merchandise by common end uses.

functional relationships A series of one-time market exchanges linked together over time.

future dating A method of dating that allows the buyer additional time to take advantage of the cash discount or to pay the net amount of the invoice.

Gaps model A conceptual model that indicates what retailers need to do to provide high-quality customer service. When customers' expectations are greater than their perceptions of the delivered service, customers are dissatisfied and feel the quality of the retailer's service is poor. Thus, retailers need to reduce the service gap—the difference between customers' expectations and perceptions of customer service to improve customers' satisfaction with their service.

general merchandise catalog retailers Nonstore retailers that offer a broad variety of merchandise in catalogs that are periodically mailed to their customers.

Generation X The generational cohort of people born between 1965 and 1976.

Generation Y The generational cohort of people born between 1977 and 1995.

generational cohort People within the same generation who have similar purchase behaviors because they have shared experiences and are in the same stage of life.

generic brand Unbranded, unadvertised merchandise found mainly in drug, grocery, and discount stores.

gentrification A process in which old buildings are torn down or are restored to create new offices, housing developments, and retailers.

geodemographic segmentation A market segmentation system that uses both geographic and demographic characteristics to classify consumers.

geographic information system (GIS) A computerized system that enables analysts to visualize information about their customers' demographics, buying behavior, and other data in a map format.

geographic segmentation Segmentation of potential customers by where they live. A retail market can be segmented by countries, states, cities, and neighborhoods.

glass ceiling An invisible barrier that makes it difficult for minorities and women to be promoted beyond a certain level.

gondola An island type of self-service counter with tiers of shelves, bins, or pegs.

graduated lease A lease that requires rent to increase by a fixed amount over a specified period of time.

gray-market goods Merchandise that possesses a valid U.S. registered trademark and is made by a foreign manufacturer but is imported into the United States without permission of the U.S. trademark owner.

green marketing A strategic focus by retailers and their vendors to supply customers with environmentally friendly merchandise.

greeter A retail employee who greets customers as they enter a store and who provides information or assistance.

grid layout A store design, typically used by grocery stores, in which merchandise is displayed on long gondolas in aisles with a repetitive pattern.

gross margin The difference between the price the customer pays for merchandise and the cost of the merchandise (the price the retailer paid the supplier of the merchandise). More specifically, gross margin = net sales – cost of goods sold (= maintained markup) – alteration cost + cash discounts.

gross margin return on investment (GMROI) Gross margin dollars divided by average (cost) inventory.

gross profit See *gross margin.*

gross sales The total dollar revenues received from the sales of merchandise and services.

group maintenance behaviors Activities store managers undertake to make sure that employees are satisfied and work well together.

habitual decision making A purchase decision involving little or no conscious effort.

high-assay principle A method of allocating a communication budget that uses the principles of marginal analysis. The retailer should allocate the budget to areas that will yield the greatest return.

high/low pricing A strategy in which retailers offer prices that are sometimes above their competition's everyday low price, but they use advertising to promote frequent sales.

historical center A shopping center located in a place of historical interest.

home improvement center A category specialist offering equipment and material used by do-it-yourselfers and construction contractors to make home improvements.

horizontal price-fixing An agreement between retailers in direct competition with each other to charge the same prices.

house brand See *generic brand.*

Huff's model A trade area analysis model used to determine the probability that a customer residing in a particular area will shop at a particular store or shopping center.

human resource management Management of a retailer's employees.

hype Artificially generated word of mouth, manufactured by public relations people.

hypermarket Large (100,000 to 300,000 square feet) combination food (60–70 percent) and general merchandise (30–40 percent) retailer.

idea-oriented presentation A method of presenting merchandise based on a specific idea or the image of the store.

identifiability Permits a retailer to determine a market segment's size and with whom the retailer should communicate when promoting its retail offering.

illegal discrimination The actions of a company or its managers that result in members of a protected class being treated unfairly and differently than others.

impact An ad's effect on the audience.

implied warranty of merchantability A guarantee that accompanies all merchandise sold by a retailer, assuring customers that the merchandise is up to standards for the ordinary purposes for which such goods are used.

impulse buying A buying decision made by customers on the spot after seeing the merchandise.

impulse merchandise See *impulse products.*

impulse products Products that are purchased by customers without prior plans. These products are almost always located near the front of the store, where they're seen by everyone and may actually draw people into the store.

impulse purchase An unplanned purchase by a customer.

in-house credit system See *proprietary store credit card system.*

incentive compensation plan A compensation plan that rewards employees on the basis of their productivity.

income statement A summary of the financial performance of a firm for a certain period of time.

independent exchange A retail exchange owned by a third party that provides the electronic platform to perform the exchange functions.

infomercials TV programs, typically 30 minutes long, that mix entertainment with product demonstrations and solicit orders placed by telephone from consumers.

information search The stage in the buying process in which a customer seeks additional information to satisfy a need.

infringement Unauthorized use of a registered trademark.

ingress/egress The means of entering/exiting the parking lot of a retail site.

initial markup The retail selling price initially placed on the merchandise less the cost of goods sold.

inner city Typically a high-density urban area consisting of apartment buildings populated primarily by ethnic groups: African Americans, Hispanics, and Asians.

input measure A performance measure used to assess the amount of resources or money used by the retailer to achieve outputs.

installment credit plan A plan that enables consumers to pay their total purchase price (less down payment) in equal installment payments over a specified time period.

institutional advertisement An advertisement that emphasizes the retailer's name and positioning rather than specific merchandise or prices.

in-store kiosk Spaces located within stores containing a computer connected to the store's central offices or to the Internet.

instrumental support Support for retail service providers such as appropriate systems and equipment to deliver the service desired by customers.

integrated marketing communication program The strategic integration of multiple communication methods to form a comprehensive, consistent message.

intellectual property Property that is intangible and is created by intellectual (mental) effort as opposed to physical effort.

intelligent agent A computer program that locates and selects alternatives based on some predetermined characteristics.

interactive electronic retailing A system in which a retailer transmits data and graphics over cable or telephone lines to a consumer's TV or computer terminal.

interest The amount charged by a financial institution to borrow money.

internal sources of information Information in a customer's memory such as the names, images, and past experiences with different stores.

Internet A worldwide network of computers linked to facilitate communications between individuals, companies, and organizations.

Internet retailing See *electronic retailing.*

intertype competition Competition between retailers that sell similar merchandise using different formats, such as discount and department stores.

intranet A secure communication system that takes place within one company.

intratype competition Competition between the same type of retailers (e.g., Kroger versus Safeway).

intrinsic rewards Nonmonetary rewards employees get from doing their jobs.

inventory Goods or merchandise available for resale.

inventory management The process of acquiring and maintaining a proper assortment of merchandise while keeping ordering, shipping, handling, and other related costs in check.

inventory shrinkage See *shrinkage.*

inventory turnover Net sales divided by average retail inventory; used to evaluate how effectively managers utilize their investment in inventory.

invoice cost The actual amount due for the merchandise after both trade and quantity discounts are taken.

item price The practice of marking prices only on shelves or signs and not on individual items.

job analysis Identifying essential activities and determining the qualifications employees need to perform them effectively.

job application form A form a job applicant completes that contains information about the applicant's employment history, previous compensation, reasons for leaving previous employment, education and training, personal health, and references.

job description A description of the activities the employee needs to perform and the firm's performance expectations.

job enrichment The redesign of a job to include a greater range of tasks and responsibilities.

job sharing When two or more employees voluntarily are responsible for a job that was previously held by one person.

joint venture An entity formed when the entering retailer pools its resources with a local retailer to form a new company in which ownership, control, and profits are shared.

junk bond Bond that offers investors a higher-risk/ higher-yield investment than conventional bonds.

key items The items that are in greatest demand. Also referred to as *best-sellers*.

keystone method A method of setting retail prices in which retailers simply double the cost of the merchandise to obtain the original retail selling price.

kickback Same as *commercial bribery*.

kiosk A small selling space offering a limited merchandise assortment.

knock-off A copy of the latest styles displayed at designer fashion shows and sold in exclusive specialty stores. These copies are sold at lower prices through retailers targeting a broader market.

knowledge gap The difference between customer expectations and the retailer's perception of customer expectations. This factor is one of four factors identified by the gaps model for improving service quality.

labor scheduling The process of determining the number of employees assigned to each area of the store at each hour the store is open.

layaway A method of deferred payment in which merchandise is held by the store for the customer until it is completely paid for.

lead time The amount of time between recognition that an order needs to be placed and the point at which the merchandise arrives in the store and is ready for sale.

leader pricing A pricing strategy in which certain items are priced lower than normal to increase the traffic flow of customers or to increase the sale of complementary products.

leadership The process by which a person attempts to influence another to accomplish some goal or goals.

leased department An area in a retail store leased or rented to an independent company. The leaseholder is typically responsible for all retail mix decisions involved in operating the department and pays the store a percentage of its sales as rent.

less-than-carload (LCL) The transportation rate that applies to less than full carload shipments.

lessee The party signing the lease.

lessor The party owning a property that is for rent.

level of support See *service level.*

leveraged buyout (LBO) A financial transaction in which a buyer (the firm's management or an outside individual or group) acquires a company by borrowing money from a financial institution or by issuing junk bonds using its assets as collateral. See also merger and acquisition.

liabilities Obligations of a retail enterprise to pay cash or other economic resources in return for past, present, or future benefits.

licensed brand Brand for which the licensor (owner of a well-known name) enters a contractual arrangement with a licensee (a retailer or a third party). The licensee either manufactures or contracts with a manufacturer to produce the licensed product and pays a royalty to the licensor.

lifestyle Refers to how people live, how they spend their time and money, what activities they pursue, and their attitudes and opinions about the world they live in.

lifestyle center A shopping center with an outdoor traditional streetscape layout with sit-down restaurants and a conglomeration of specialty retailers.

lifestyle segmentation A method of segmenting a retail market based on how consumers live, how they spend their time and money, what activities they pursue, and their attitudes and opinions about the world they live in.

lifetime customer value (LTV) The expected contribution from the customer to the retailer's profits over his or her entire relationship with the retailer.

lift-out See *buyback.*

limited problem solving A purchase decision process involving a moderate amount of effort and time. Customers engage in this type of buying process when they have some prior experience with the product or service and their risk is moderate.

limited warranty A type of guarantee in which any limitations must be stated conspicuously so that customers are not misled.

local links A way to help customers get around a website on the Internet by using links that are internal to a website.

logistics Part of the supply chain process that plans, implements, and controls the efficient, effective flow and storage of goods, services, and related information from the point of origin to the point of consumption in order to meet customers' requirements.

long-term liabilities Debts that will be paid after one year.

loop layout See *racetrack layout.*

loss leader An item priced near or below cost to attract customer traffic into the store.

low-price guarantee policy A policy that guarantees that the retailer will have the lowest possible price for a product or group of products, and usually promises to match or better any lower price found in the local market.

loyalty program A program set up to reward customers with incentives such as discounts on purchases, free food, gifts, or even cruises or trips in return for their repeated business.

mail-order retailer See *direct-mail catalog retailer*.

Main Street The central business district located in the traditional shopping area of smaller towns, or a secondary business district in a suburb or within a larger city.

maintained markup The amount of markup the retailer wishes to maintain on a particular category of merchandise; net sales minus cost of goods sold.

maintenance-increase-recoupment lease A provision of a lease that can be used with either a percentage or straight lease. This type of lease allows the landlord to increase the rent if insurance, property taxes, or utility bills increase beyond a certain point.

mall A shopping center with a pedestrian focus where customers park in outlying areas and walk to the stores.

management by objectives A popular method for linking the goals of a firm to goals for each employee and providing information to employees about their role.

managing diversity A set of human resource management programs designed to realize the benefits of a diverse workforce.

manufacturer brand A line of products designed, produced, and marketed by a vendor. Also called a *national brand*.

manufacturer's agent An agent who generally operates on an extended contractual basis; often sells within an exclusive territory; handles noncompeting but related lines of goods; and possesses limited authority with regard to prices and terms of sale.

manufacturer's outlet store A discount retail store owned and operated by a manufacturer.

maquiladoras Manufacturing plants in Mexico that make goods and parts or process food for export to the United States.

marginal analysis A method of analysis used in setting a promotional budget or allocating retail space, based on the economic principle that firms should increase expenditures as long as each additional dollar spent generates more than a dollar of additional contribution.

markdown The percentage reduction in the initial retail price.

markdown cancelation The percentage increase in the retail price after a markdown is taken.

markdown money Funds provided by a vendor to a retailer to cover decreased gross margin from markdowns and other merchandising issues.

market A group of vendors in a concentrated geographic location or even under one roof or over the internet; also known as a central market.

market attractiveness/competitive position matrix A method for analyzing opportunities that explicitly considers the capabilities of the retailer and the attractiveness of retail markets.

market basket analysis Specific type of data analysis that focuses on the composition of the basket (or bundle) of products purchased by a household during a single shopping occasion.

market development See *market penetration opportunity*.

market expansion opportunity A strategic investment opportunity that employs the existing retailing format in new market segments.

market penetration opportunity An investment opportunity strategy that focuses on increasing sales to present customers using the present retailing format.

market potential index (MPI) Measures the likely demand for a product or service in a country, zip code, or other trade area.

market research The systematic collection and analysis of information about a retail market.

market share A retailer's sales divided by the sales of all competitors within the same market.

market week See *trade show*.

marketing segmentation The process of dividing a retail market into homogeneous groups. See *retail market segment*.

markup The increase in the retail price of an item after the initial markup percentage has been applied but before the item is placed on the selling floor.

marquee A sign used to display a store's name or logo.

mass customization The production of individually customized products at costs similar to mass-produced products.

mass-market theory A theory of how fashion spreads that suggests that each social class has its own fashion leaders who play a key role in their own social networks. Fashion information trickles across social classes rather than down from the upper classes to the lower classes.

Mazur plan A method of retail organization in which all retail activities fall into four functional areas: merchandising, publicity, store management, and accounting and control.

med-arb Used in the case of a dispute between retailer and vendor that involves an initial attempt at mediation followed by binding arbitration if the mediation is unsuccessful. See *mediation* and *arbitration*.

media coverage The theoretical number of potential customers in a retailer's market who could be exposed to an ad.

mediation Used in the case of a dispute between retailer and vendor that involves selecting a neutral party—the mediator—to assist the parties in reaching a mutually agreeable settlement.

memorandum purchases Items not paid for by a retailer until they are sold. The retailer can return unsold merchandise; however, the retailer takes title on delivery and is responsible for damages. See *consignment goods*.

mentoring program The assigning of higher-level managers to help lower-level managers learn the firm's values and meet other senior executives.

merchandise budget plan A plan used by buyers to determine how much money to spend in each month on a particular fashion merchandise category, given the firm's sales forecast, inventory turnover, and profit goals.

merchandise category   See *category*.

merchandise classification   See *classification*.

merchandise group   A group within an organization managed by the senior vice presidents of merchandise and responsible for several departments.

merchandise management   The process by which a retailer attempts to offer the right quantity of the right merchandise in the right place at the right time while meeting the company's financial goal.

merchandise show   See *trade show*.

merchandising   See *merchandise management*.

merchandising optimization software   Set of algorithms (computer programs) that monitors merchandise sales, promotions, competitors' actions, and other factors to determine the optimal (most profitable) price and timing for merchandising activities, especially markdowns.

merchandising planner   A retail employee responsible for allocating merchandise and tailoring the assortment in several categories for specific stores in a geographic area.

merger   A financial strategy in which one larger firm acquires a smaller firm. This term is used interchangeably with acquisition. See also *leveraged buyout*.

message board   Location in an Internet site at which customers can post comments.

Metropolitan Statistical Area (MSA)   A city with 50,000 or more inhabitants or an urbanized area of at least 50,000 inhabitants and a total MSA population of at least 100,000 (75,000 in New England).

mission statement   A broad description of the scope of activities a business plans to undertake.

mixed-use development (MXD)   Development that combines several uses in one complex—for example, shopping center, office tower, hotel, residential complex, civic center, and convention center.

model stock list   A list of fashion merchandise that indicates in very general terms (product lines, colors, and size distributions) what should be carried in a particular merchandise category; also known as *model stock plan*.

monthly additions to stock   The amount to be ordered for delivery in each month, given the firm's turnover and sales objectives.

months of supply   The amount of inventory on hand at the beginning of the month expressed in terms of the time it will take to sell. A six-month supply means it will take six months for the merchandise to sell.

multiattribute attitude model   A model of customer decision making based on the notion that customers see a retailer or a product as a collection of attributes or characteristics. The model can also be used for evaluating a retailer, product, or vendor. The model uses a weighted average score based on the importance of various issues and the performance on those issues.

multichannel retailer   Retailer that sells merchandise or services through more than one channel.

multilevel direct selling   A form of direct selling in which people sell directly to customers, serve as master distributors, and recruit other people to become distributors in their network. The master distributors either buy merchandise from the firm and resell it to their distributors or receive a commission on all merchandise purchased by the distributors in their network.

multilevel network   A retail format in which people serve as master distributors, recruiting other people to become distributors in their network.

multiple-unit pricing   Practice of offering two or more similar products or services for sale at one price.

mystery shopper   Professional shopper who "shops" a store to assess the service provided by store employees.

national brand   See *manufacturer brand*.

natural barrier   A barrier, such as a river or mountain, that impacts accessibility to a site.

natural selection   A theory of retail evolation that argues that those institutions best able to adapt to changes in customers, technology, competition, and legal environments have the greatest chance for success.

needs   The basic psychological forces that motivate customers to act.

negligence   A product liability suit that occurs if a retailer or a retail employee fails to exercise the care that a prudent person usually would.

negotiation   An interaction between two or more parties to reach an agreement.

neighborhood center   A shopping center that includes a supermarket, drugstore, home improvement center, or variety store. Neighborhood centers often include small stores, such as apparel, shoe, camera, and other shopping goods stores.

net invoice price   The net value of the invoice or the total invoice minus all other discounts.

net lease   A lease that requires all maintenance expenses such as heat, insurance, and interior repairs to be paid by the retailer.

net profit   A measure of the overall performance of a firm; revenues (sales) minus expenses and losses for the period.

net sales   The total number of dollars received by a retailer after all refunds have been paid to customers for returned merchandise.

net worth   See *owners' equity*.

network direct selling   See *multilevel direct selling*.

never-out list   A list of key items or best-sellers that are separately planned and controlled. These items account for large sales volume and are stocked in a manner so they are always available. These are A items in an ABC analysis.

noncumulative quanity discount   Discount offered to retailers as an incentive to purchase more merchandise on a single order.

nondurable Perishable product consumed in one or a few uses.

nonstore retailing A form of retailing to ultimate consumers that is not store-based. Nonstore retailing is conducted through the Internet, vending machines, mail, direct selling, and direct marketing.

NAICS (North American Industry Classification System) Classification of retail firms into a hierarchical set of six-digit codes.

notes payable Current liabilities representing principal and interest the retailer owes to financial institutions (banks) that are due and payable in less than a year.

objective-and-task method A method for setting a promotion budget in which the retailer first establishes a set of communication objectives and then determines the necessary tasks and their costs.

observability Is the degree to which a new fashion is visible and easily communicated to others in a social group.

observation A type of market research in which customer behavior is observed and recorded.

odd pricing The practice of ending prices with an odd number (such as 69 cents) or just under a round number (such as $98 instead of $100).

off-price retailer A retailer that offers an inconsistent assortment of brand-name, fashion-oriented soft goods at low prices.

off-the-job training Training conducted in centralized classrooms away from the employee's work environment.

on-the-job training A decentralized approach in which job training occurs in the work environment where employees perform their jobs.

one hundred percent location The retail site in a major business district or mall that has the greatest exposure to a retail store's target market customers.

one-price policy A policy that, at a given time, all customers pay the same price for any given item of merchandise.

one-price retailer A store that offers all merchandise at a single fixed price.

1-to-1 retailing Developing retail programs for small groups or individual customers.

open-to-buy The plan that keeps track of how much is spent in each month, and how much is left to spend.

opinion leader Person whose attitudes, opinions, preferences, and actions influence those of others.

opportunity cost of capital The rate available on the next-best use of the capital invested in the project at hand. The opportunity cost should be no lower than the rate at which a firm borrows funds, since one alternative is to pay back borrowed money. It can be higher, however, depending on the range of other opportunities available. Typically, the opportunity cost rises with investment risk.

opt in A customer privacy issue prevalent in the European Union. Takes the perspective that consumers "own" their personal information. Retailers must get consumers to explicitly agree to share this personal information.

opt out A customer privacy issue prevalent in the United States. Takes the perspective that personal information is generally viewed as being in the public domain and retailers can use it in any way they desire. Consumers must explicitly tell retailers not to use their personal information.

optical character recognition (OCR) An industrywide classification system for coding information onto merchandise; enables retailers to record information on each SKU when it is sold and to transmit the information to a computer.

option credit account A revolving account that allows partial payments without interest charges if a bill is paid in full when due.

option-term revolving credit A credit arrangement that offers customers two payment options: (1) pay the full amount within a specified number of days and avoid any finance charges, or (2) make a minimum payment and be assessed finance charges on the unpaid balance.

order form When signed by both parties, a legally binding contract specifying the terms and conditions under which a purchase transaction is to be conducted.

order point The amount of inventory below which the quantity available shouldn't go or the item will be out of stock before the next order arrives.

organization chart A graphic that displays the reporting relationships within a firm.

organization culture A firm's set of values traditions, and customs that guide employee behavior.

organization structure A plan that identifies the activities to be performed by specific employees and determines the lines of authority and responsibility in the firm.

outlet center Typically features stores owned by retail chains or manufacturers that sell excess and out-of-season merchandise at reduced prices.

outlet store Off-price retailer owned by a manufacturer or a department or specialty store chain.

outparcel A building or kiosk that is in the parking lot of a shopping center but isn't physically attached to a shopping center.

output measure Measure that assesses the results of retailers' investment decisions.

outshopping Customers shopping in other areas because their needs are not being met locally.

outsourcing Obtaining a service from outside the company that had previously been done by the firm itself.

overstored trade area An area having so many stores selling a specific good or service that some stores will fail.

owners' equity The amount of assets belonging to the owners of the retail firm after all obligations (liabilities) have been met; also known as *net worth* and *stockholders' equity*.

pallet A platform, usually made of wood, that provides stable support for several cartons. Pallets are used to help move and store merchandise.

parallel branding   A branding strategy that represents a private label that closely imitates the trade dress (packaging) and product attributes of leading manufacturer brands but with a clearly articulated "invitation to compare" in its merchandising approach and on its product label.

parasite store   A store that does not create its own traffic and whose trade area is determined by the dominant retailer in the shopping center or retail area.

partnering relationship   See *strategic relationship.*

party plan system   Salespeople encourage people to act as hosts and invite friends or co-workers to a "party" at which the merchandise is demonstrated. The host or hostess receives a gift or commission for arranging the meeting.

patent   A law that gives the owner of a patent control of the right to make, sell, and use a product for a period of 17 years (14 years for a design).

penetration   A low-pricing strategy for newly introduced categories.

percentage lease   A lease in which rent is based on a percentage of sales.

percentage lease with specified maximum   A lease that pays the lessor, or landlord, a percentage of sales up to a maximum amount.

percentage lease with specified minimum   The retailer must pay a minimum rent no matter how low sales are.

percentage-of-sales method   A method for setting a promotion budget based on a fixed percentage of forecast sales.

percentage variation method   An inventory planning method wherein the actual stock on hand during any month varies from average planned monthly stock by only half of the month's variation from average estimated monthly sales.

periodic reordering system   An inventory management system in which the review time is a fixed period (e.g., two weeks), but the order quantity can vary.

perpetual book inventory   See *retail inventory method.*

perpetual ordering system   The stock level is monitored perpetually and a fixed quantity, known as *EOQ (economic order quantity),* is purchased when the inventory available reaches a prescribed level.

personal selling   A communication process in which salespeople assist customers in satisfying their needs through face-to-face exchange of information.

physical inventory   A method of gathering stock information by using an actual physical count and inspection of the merchandise items.

pick ticket   A document that tells the order filler how much of each item to get from the storage area.

pilferage   The stealing of a store's merchandise. See also *shoplifting.*

planogram   A diagram created from photographs, computer output, or artists' renderings that illustrates exactly where every SKU should be placed.

point-of-purchase (POP) area   See *point-of-sale area.*

point-of-sale area   An area where the customer waits at checkout. This area can be the most valuable piece of real estate in the store, because the customer is almost held captive in that spot.

point-of-sale (POS) terminal   A cash register that can electronically scan a UPC code with a laser and electronically record a sale; also known as *computerized checkout.*

polygon   Trade area whose boundaries conform to streets and other map features rather than being concentric circles.

popping the merchandise   Focusing spotlights on special feature areas and items.

population density   The number of people per unit area (usually square mile) who live within a geographic area.

positioning   The design and implementation of a retail mix to create in the customer's mind an image of the retailer relative to its competitors. Also called *brand building.*

postpurchase evaluation   The evaluation of merchandise or services after the customer has purchased and consumed them.

poverty of time   A condition in which greater affluence results in less, rather than more, free time because the alternatives competing for customers' time increase.

power center   Shopping center that is dominated by several large anchors, including discount stores (Target), off-price stores (Marshalls), warehouse clubs (Costco), or category specialists such as Home Depot, Office Depot, Circuit City, Sports Authority, Best Buy, and Toys "R" Us.

power retailer   See *category killer* or *category specialist.*

power shopping center   An open-air shopping center with the majority of space leased to several well-known anchor retail tenants—category specialists.

predatory pricing   A method for establishing merchandise prices for the purpose of driving competition from the marketplace.

preferred client   High-purchasing customers salespeople communicate with regularly, send notes to about new merchandise and sales in the department, and make appointments with for special presentations of merchandise.

premarking   Marking of the price by the manufacturer or other supplier before goods are shipped to a retail store. Also called *prepricing.*

premium branding   A branding strategy that offers the consumer a private label at a comparable manufacturer-brand quality, usually with a modest price savings.

premium merchandise   Offered at a reduced price, or free, as an incentive for a customer to make a purchase.

prepricing   See *premarking.*

preprint   An advertisement printed at the retailer's expense and distributed as a freestanding insert in a newspaper. Also called a *freestanding insert (FSI).*

press conference   A meeting with representatives of the news media that is called by a retailer.

press release   A statement of facts or opinions that the retailer would like to see published by the news media.

prestige pricing A system of pricing based on the assumption that consumers will not buy goods and services at prices they feel are too low.

price bundling The practice of offering two or more different products or services for sale at one price.

price comparison A comparison of the price of merchandise offered for sale with a higher "regular" price or a manufacturer's list price.

price discrimination An illegal practice in which a vendor sells the same product to two or more customers at different prices. See *first-degree price discrimination* and *second-degree price discrimination*.

price elasticity of demand A measure of the effect a price change has on consumer demand; percentage change in demand divided by percentage change in price.

price-fixing An illegal pricing activity in which several marketing channel members establish a fixed retail selling price for a product line within a market area. See *vertical price-fixing* and *horizontal price-fixing*.

price lining A pricing policy in which a retailer offers a limited number of predetermined price points within a classification.

pricing experiment An experiment in which a retailer actually changes the price of an item in a systematic manner to observe changes in customers' purchases or purchase intentions.

primary data Marketing research information collected through surveys, observations, and experiments to address a problem confronting a retailer.

primary trade area The geographic area from which a store or shopping center derives 60 to 65 percent of its customers.

private exchanges Exchanges that are operated for the exclusive use of a single firm.

private-label brands Products developed and marketed by a retailer and only available for sale by that retailer. Also called *store brands.*

private-label store credit card system A system in which credit cards have the store's name on them, but the accounts receivable are sold to a financial institution.

PRIZM (potential rating index for zip markets) A database combining census data, nationwide consumer surveys, and interviews with hundreds of people across the country into a geodemographic segmentation system.

procedural fairness The perceived fairness of the process used to resolve customer complaints.

procedural justice An employee's perception of fairness (how he or she is treated) that is based on the process used to determine the outcome.

product attributes Characteristics of a product that affect customer evaluations.

product availability A measurement of the percentage of demand for a particular SKU that is satisfied.

product liability A tort (or wrong) that occurs when an injury results from the use of a product.

product line A group of related products.

productivity measure The ratio of an output to an input determining how effectively a firm uses a resource.

profit margin Net profit after taxes divided by net sales.

profitability A company's ability to generate revenues in excess of the costs incurred in producing those revenues.

prohibited use clause A clause in a lease that keeps a landlord from leasing to certain kinds of tenants.

promotion Activities undertaken by a retailer to provide consumers with information about a retailer's store and its retail mix.

promotion from within A staffing policy that involves hiring new employees only for positions at the lowest level in the job hierarchy and then promoting employees for openings at higher levels in the hierarchy.

promotion mix A communication program made up of advertising, sales promotions, websites, store atmosphere, publicity, personal selling, and word of mouth.

promotional aisle Area aisle or area of a store designed to get the customer's attention. An example might be a special "trim-the-tree" department that seems to magically appear right after Halloween every year for the Christmas holidays.

promotional allowance An allowance given by vendors to retailers to compensate the latter for money spent in advertising a particular item.

promotional center A type of specialty shopping center that contains one or more discount stores plus smaller retail tenants. Also called *discount-oriented center.*

promotional department store A department store that concentrates on apparel and sells a substantial portion of its merchandise on weekly promotion.

promotional stock A retailer's stock of goods offered at an unusually attractive price in order to obtain sales volume; it often represents special purchases from vendors.

proprietary EDI systems Data exchange systems that are developed primarily by large retailers for the purpose of exchanging data with their vendors.

proprietary store credit card system A system in which credit cards have the store's name on them and the accounts receivable are administered by the retailer; also known as in-house credit system.

providing assortments A function performed by retailers that enables customers to choose from a selection of brands, designs, sizes, and prices at one location.

psychographics Refers to how people live, how they spend their time and money, what activities they pursue, and their attitudes and opinions about the world they live in.

psychological needs Needs associated with the personal gratification that customers get from shopping or from purchasing and owning a product.

public warehouse Warehouse that is owned and operated by a third party.

publicity Communications through significant unpaid presentations about the retailer (usually a news story) in impersonal media.

puffing An advertising or personal selling practice in which a retailer simply exaggerates the benefits or quality of a product in very broad terms.

pull logistics strategy Strategy in which orders for merchandise are generated at the store level on the basis of demand data captured by point-of-sale terminals.

purchase visibility curve A display technique in which the retailer tilts low shelves so more merchandise is in direct view.

push logistics strategy Strategy in which merchandise is allocated to stores based on historical demand, the inventory position at the distribution center, as well as the stores' needs.

push money (PM) An incentive for retail salespeople provided by a vendor to promote, or push, a particular product; also known as *spiff*.

pyramid scheme When the firm and its program are designed to sell merchandise and services to other distributors rather than to end users.

quantity discount The policy of granting lower prices for higher quantities.

quick response (QR) delivery system System designed to reduce the lead time for receiving merchandise, thereby lowering inventory investment, improving customer service levels, and reducing distribution expenses; also known as a *just-in-time inventory management system*.

quota Target level used to motivate and evaluate performance.

quotas–bonus plan Compensation plan that has a performance goal or objective established to evaluate employee performance, such as sales per hour for salespeople and maintained margin and turnover for buyers.

racetrack layout A type of store layout that provides a major aisle to facilitate customer traffic that has access to the store's multiple entrances. Also known as a *loop layout*.

rain check When sale merchandise is out of stock, a written promise to customers to sell them that merchandise at the sale price when it arrives.

reach The actual number of customers in the target market exposed to an advertising medium. See *advertising reach*.

rebate Money returned to the buyer in the form of cash based on a portion of the purchase price.

receipt of goods (ROG) dating A dating policy in which the cash discount period starts on the day the merchandise is received.

receiving The process of filling out paperwork to record the receipt of merchandise that arrives at a store or distribution center.

recruitment Activity performed by a retailer to generate job applicants.

reduction Markdown; discount to employees and customers; and inventory shrinkage due to shoplifting, breakage, or loss.

reference group One or more people whom a person uses as a basis of comparison for his beliefs, feelings, and behaviors.

reference price A price point in the consumer's memory for a good or service that can consist of the price last paid, the price most frequently paid, or the average of all prices customers have paid for similar offerings. A benchmark for what consumers believe the "real" price of the merchandise should be.

refusal to deal A legal issue in which either a vendor or a retailer reserves the right to deal or refuse to deal with anyone it chooses.

region In retail location analysis, refers to the part of the country, a particular city, or Metropolitan Statistical Area (MSA).

regional center Shopping mall that provides general merchandise (a large percentage of which is apparel) and services in full depth and variety.

Reilly's law A model used in trade area analysis to define the relative ability of two cities to attract customers from the area between them.

related diversification opportunity A diversification opportunity strategy in which the retailer's present offering and market share something in common with the market and format being considered.

relational partnership Long-term business relationship in which the buyer and vendor have a close, trusting interpersonal relationship.

remarking The practice of changing the price label or identification tag on merchandise due to price changes, lost or mutilated tickets, or customer returns.

reorder point The stock level at which a new order is placed.

resale price maintenance laws Laws enacted in the early 1900s to curb vertical price-fixing. These laws were designed to help protect small retailers by prohibiting retailers to sell below manufacturer's suggested retail price. Also called *fair trade laws*. In 1975 these laws were repealed by the Consumer Goods Pricing Act.

resident buying office An organization located in a major buying center that provides services to help retailers buy merchandise.

restraint of trade Any contract that tends to eliminate or stifle competition, create a monopoly, artificially maintain prices, or otherwise hamper or obstruct the course of trade and commerce as it would be carried on if left to the control of natural forces; also known as unfair trade practices.

retail audit See *situation audit*.

retail chain A firm that consists of multiple retail units under common ownership and usually has some centralization of decision making in defining and implementing its strategy.

retail exchanges Electronic marketplaces operated by organizations that facilitate the buying and selling of merchandise using the Internet.

retail format The retailers' type of retail mix (nature of merchandise and services offered, pricing policy, advertising and promotion program, approach to store design and visual merchandising, and typical location).

retail format development opportunity An investment opportunity strategy in which a retailer offers a new retail format—a format involving a different retail mix—to the same target market.

retail information system System that provides the information needed by retail managers by collecting, organizing, and storing relevant data continuously and directing the information to the appropriate managers.

retail inventory method (RIM) An accounting procedure whose objectives are to maintain a perpetual or book inventory in retail dollar amounts and to maintain records that make it possible to determine the cost value of the inventory at any time without taking a physical inventory; also known as *book inventory system* or *perpetual book inventory.*

retail market A group of consumers with similar needs (a market segment) and a group of retailers using a similar retail format to satisfy those consumer needs.

retail market segment A group of customers whose needs will be satisfied by the same retail offering because they have similar needs and go through similar buying processes.

retail mix The combination of factors used by a retailer to satisfy customer needs and influence their purchase decisions; includes merchandise and services offered, pricing, advertising and promotions, store design and location, and visual merchandising.

retail-sponsored cooperative An organization owned and operated by small, independent retailers to improve operating efficiency and buying power. Typically, the retail-sponsored cooperative operates a wholesale buying and distribution system and requires its members to concentrate their purchases from the cooperative wholesale operation.

retail strategy A statement that indicates (1) the target market toward which a retailer plans to commit its resources, (2) the nature of the retail offering that the retailer plans to use to satisfy the needs of the target market, and (3) the bases upon which the retailer will attempt to build a sustainable competitive advantage over competitors.

retailer A business that sells products and services to consumers for their personal or family use.

retailing A set of business activities that adds value to the products and services sold to consumers for their personal or family use.

retailing concept A management orientation that holds that the key task of a retailer is to determine the needs and wants of its target markets and to direct the firm toward satisfying those needs and wants more effectively and efficiently than competitors do.

retained earnings The portion of owners' equity that has accumulated over time through profits but has not been paid out in dividends to owners.

return on assets Net profit after taxes divided by total assets.

return on owners' equity Net profit after taxes divided by owners' equity; also known as return on net worth.

reverse auction Auction conducted by retailer buyers. Known as a *reverse auction* because there is one buyer and many potential sellers. In reverse auctions, retail buyers provide a specification for what they want to a group of potential vendors. The competing vendors then bid down the price at which they are willing to sell until the buyer accepts a bid.

reverse logistics A flow back of merchandise through the channel, from the customer to the store, distribution center, and vendor, for customer returns.

review time The period of time between reviews of a line for purchase decisions.

revolving credit A consumer credit plan that combines the convenience of a continuous charge account and the privileges of installment payment.

RFM (recency, frequency, monetary) analysis Often used by catalog retailers and direct marketers, is a scheme for segmenting customers based on how recently they have made a purchase, how frequently they make purchases, and how much they have bought.

ribbon center See *strip center.*

road condition Includes the age, number of lanes, number of stoplights, congestion, and general state of repair of roads in a trade area.

road pattern A consideration used in measuring the accessibility of a retail location via major arteries, freeways, or roads.

Robinson-Patman Act (1946) The Congressional act that revised Section 2 of the Clayton Act and specifically prohibits certain types of price discrimination.

rounder A round fixture that sits on a pedestal. Smaller than the straight rack, it is designed to hold a maximum amount of merchandise. Also known as a *bulk* or *capacity fixture.*

routine decision making See *habitual decision making.*

rule-of-thumb method A type of approach for setting a promotion budget that uses past sales and communication activity to determine the present communications budget.

safety stock See *buffer stock.*

sale-leaseback The practice in which retailers build new stores and sell them to real estate investors who then lease the buildings back to the retailers on a long-term basis.

sales associate The same as a salesperson. The term is used to recognize the importance and professional nature of the sales function and avoids the negative image sometimes linked with the term salesperson.

sales consultant See *sales associate.*

sales per cubic foot A measure of space productivity appropriate for stores such as wholesale clubs that use multiple layers of merchandise.

sales per linear foot A measure of space productivity used when most merchandise is displayed on multiple shelves of long gondolas, such as in grocery stores.

sales per square foot A measure of space productivity used by most retailers since rent and land purchases are assessed on a per-square-foot basis.

sales promotions   Paid impersonal communication activities that offer extra value and incentives to customers to visit a store or purchase merchandise during a specific period of time.

satisfaction   A postconsumption evaluation of the degree to which a store or product meets or exceeds customer expectations.

saturated trade area   A trade area that offers customers a good selection of goods and services, while allowing competing retailers to make good profits.

scale economies   Cost advantages due to the size of a retailer.

scanning   The process in point-of-sale systems wherein the input into the terminal is accomplished by passing a coded ticket over a reader or having a hand-held wand pass over the ticket.

scrambled merchandising   The offering of merchandise not typically associated with the store type, such as clothing in a drugstore.

search engines   Computer programs that simply search for and provide a listing of all Internet sites selling a product category or brand with the price of the merchandise offered. Also called *shopping bots.*

seasonal discount   Discount offered as an incentive to retailers to place orders for merchandise in advance of the normal buying season.

seasonal merchandise   Inventory whose sales fluctuate dramatically according to the time of the year.

second-degree price discrimination   Charging different prices to different people on the basis of the nature of the offering.

secondary data   Market research information previously gathered for purposes other than solving the current problem under investigation.

secondary trade area   The geographic area of secondary importance in terms of customer sales, generating about 20 percent of a store's sales.

security   An operating unit within a retail organization that is responsible for protecting merchandise and other assets from pilferage (internal or external). Those working in security may be employees or outside agency people.

security policy   Set of rules that apply to activities in the computer and communications resources that belong to an organization.

self-analysis   An internally focused examination of a business's strengths and weaknesses.

self-service retailer   A retailer that offers minimal customer service.

sell-through analysis   A comparison of actual and planned sales to determine whether early markdowns are required or whether more merchandise is needed to satisfy demand.

selling agent   An agent who operates on an extended contractual basis; the agent sells all of a specified line of merchandise or the entire output of the principal, and usually has full authority with regard to prices, terms, and other conditions of sale. The agent occasionally renders financial aid to the principal.

selling process   A set of activities that salespeople undertake to facilitate the customer's buying decision.

selling space   The area set aside for displays of merchandise, interactions between sales personnel and customers, demonstrations, and so on.

seniors   The generational cohort of people born before 1946.

service gap   The difference between customers' expectations and perceptions of customer service to improve customers' satisfaction with their service.

service level   A measure used in inventory management to define the level of support or level of product availability; the number of items sold divided by the number of items demanded. Service level should not be confused with customer service. See *customer service.*

services retailer   Organization that offers consumers services rather than merchandise. Examples include banks, hospital, health spas, doctors, legal clinics, entertainment firms, and universities.

sexual harassment   Unwelcome sexual advances, requests for sexual favors, or other verbal or physical conduct with sexual elements.

share of wallet   The percentage of total purchases made by a customer in a store.

Sherman Antitrust Act (1890)   The act protecting small businesses and consumers from large corporations by outlawing any person, corporation, or association from engaging in activities that restrain trade or commerce.

shoplifting   The act of stealing merchandise from a store by customers or people posing as customers.

shopping bots   See *search engines.*

shopping center   A group of retail and other commercial establishments that is planned, developed, owned, and managed as a single property.

shopping goods   Products for which consumers will spend time comparing alternatives.

shopping guide   Free paper delivered to all residents in a specific area.

shopping mall   Generally more planned than a strip center and with more pedestrian activity, it can be either open-air or enclosed.

shortage   See *shrinkage.*

shrinkage   An inventory reduction that is caused by shoplifting by employees or customers, by merchandise being misplaced or damaged, or by poor bookkeeping.

single-price retailer   Close-out stores that sell all their merchandise at a single price, such as $1.

situation audit   An analysis of the opportunities and threats in the retail environment and the strengths and weaknesses of the retail business relative to its competitors.

skimming A high-pricing strategy for newly introduced categories.

SKU See *stock keeping unit.*

sliding scale A part of some leases that stipulates how much the percentage of sales paid as rent will decrease as sales go up.

slotting allowance Fee paid by a vendor for space in a retail store. Also called *slotting fee.*

slotting fee See *slotting allowance.*

socialization The steps taken to transform new employees into effective, committed members of the firm.

sole proprietorship An arrangement in which an unincorporated retail firm is owned by one person.

span of control The number of subordinates reporting to a manager.

specialization The organizational structure in which employees are typically responsible for only one or two tasks rather than performing all tasks. This enables employees to develop expertise and increase productivity.

specialty catalog retailer A nonstore retailer that focuses on specific categories of merchandise, such as fruit (Harry and David), gardening tools (Smith & Hawken), and seeds and plants (Burpee).

specialty department store A store with a department store format that focuses primarily on apparel and soft home goods (such as Neiman Marcus or Saks Fifth Avenue).

specialty product A product for which the customer will expend considerable effort to buy.

specialty store Store concentrating on a limited number of complementary merchandise categories and providing a high level of service in an area typically under 8,000 square feet.

spending potential index (SPI) Compares the average expenditure in a particular area for a product to the amount spent on that product nationally.

spiff See *push money.*

split shipment A vendor ships part of a shipment to a retailer and back orders the remainder because the entire shipment could not be shipped at the same time.

spot A local television commercial.

spot check Used particularly in receiving operations when goods come in for reshipping to branch stores in packing cartons. Certain cartons are opened in the receiving area of the central distribution point and spot-checked for quality and quantity.

spotting technique See *analog approach.*

staging area Area in which merchandise is accumulated from different parts of the distribution center and prepared for shipment to stores.

standardization Involves requiring service providers to follow a set of rules and procedures when providing service.

standardization approach An approach used by retailers to provide customer service by using a set of rules and procedures so that all customers consistently receive the same service.

standards gap The difference between the retailer's perceptions of customers' expectations and the customer service standards it sets. This factor is one of four factors identified by the Gaps model for improving service quality.

staple merchandise Inventory that has continuous demand by customers over an extended period of time. Also known as *basic merchandise.*

stock balance Trade-offs associated with determining variety, assortment, and product availablity.

stock keeping unit (SKU) The smallest unit available for keeping inventory control. In soft goods merchandise, an SKU usually means size, color, and style.

stock overage The amount by which a retail book inventory figure exceeds a physical ending inventory.

stock-to-sales ratio Specifies the amount of inventory that should be on hand at the beginning of the month to support the sales forecast and maintain the inventory turnover objective. The beginning-of-month (BOM) inventory divided by sales for the month. The average stock-to-sales ratio is 12 divided by planned inventory turnover. This ratio is an integral component of the merchandise budget plan.

stockholders' equity See *owners' equity.*

stocklift See *buyback.*

store atmosphere The combination of the store's physical characteristics (such as architecture, layout, signs and displays, colors, lighting, temperature, sounds, and smells), which together create an image in the customers' mind. See *atmospherics.*

store brand See *private-label brand.*

store image The way a store is defined in a shopper's mind. The store image is based on the store's physical characteristics, its retail mix, and a set of psychological attributes.

store loyalty A condition in which customers like and habitually visit the same store to purchase a type of merchandise.

store maintenance The activities involved with managing the exterior and interior physical facilities associated with the store.

straight commission A form of salesperson's compensation in which the amount paid is based on a percentage of sales made minus merchandise returned.

straight lease A type of lease in which the retailer pays a fixed amount per month over the life of the lease.

straight rack A type of fixture that consists of a long pipe suspended with supports going to the floor or attached to a wall.

straight salary compensation A compensation plan in which salespeople or managers receive a fixed amount of compensation for each hour or week they work.

strategic alliance Collaborative relationship between independent firms. For example, a foreign retailer might enter an international market through direct investment but develop an alliance with a local firm to perform logistical and warehousing activities.

strategic profit model (SPM) A tool used for planning a retailer's financial strategy based on both margin management (net profit margin), asset management (asset turnover), and financial leverage management (financial leverage ratio). Using the SPM, a retailer's objective is to achieve a target return on owners' equity.

strategic relationship   Long-term relationship in which partners make significant investments to improve both parties' profitability.

strategic retail planning process   The steps a retailer goes through to develop a strategic retail plan. It describes how retailers select target market segments, determine the appropriate retail format, and build sustainable competitive advantages.

strengths and weaknesses analysis   A critical aspect of the situation audit in which a retailer determines its unique capabilities—its strengths and weaknesses relative to its competition.

strict product liability   A product liability suit in which the injury to the customer may not have been intentional or under the retailer's control.

strip center   A shopping center that usually has parking directly in front of the stores and does not have enclosed walkways linking the stores.

style   The characteristic or distinctive form, outline, or shape of a product.

subculture   A distinctive group of people within a culture. Members of a subculture share some customs and norms with the overall society but also have some unique perspectives.

subculture theory   A theory of how fashion spreads that suggests that subcultures of mostly young and less affluent consumers, such as motorcycle riders and urban rappers, have started fashions for such things as colorful fabrics, T-shirts, sneakers, jeans, black leather jackets, and surplus military clothing.

subjective employee evaluation   Assessment of employee performance based on a supervisor's ratings rather than on objective measures such as sales per hour.

supercenter   Large store (150,000 to 200,000 square feet) combining a discount store with a supermarket.

superregional center   Shopping center that is similar to a regional center; but because of its larger size, it has more anchors and a deeper selection of merchandise, and it draws from a larger population base

superstore   A large supermarket between 20,000 and 50,000 square feet in size.

supply chain management   The integration of business processes from end user through original suppliers that provides products, services, and information that add value for customers.

survey   A method of data collection, using telephone, personal interview, mail, or any combination thereof.

sustainable competitive advantage   A distinct competency of a retailer relative to its competitors that can be maintained over a considerable time period.

sweepstake   A promotion in which customers win prizes based on chance.

target market   The market segment(s) toward which the retailer plans to focus its resources and retail mix.

tariff   A tax placed by a government upon imports.

task performance behaviors   Planning, organizing, motivating, evaluating, and coordinating store employees' activities.

television home shopping   A retail format in which customers watch a TV program demonstrating merchandise and then place orders for the merchandise by phone.

terms of purchase   Conditions in a purchase agreement with a vendor that include the type(s) of discounts available and responsibility for transportation costs.

terms of sale   Conditions in a sales contract with customers including such issues as charges for alterations, delivery, or gift wrapping, or the store's exchange policies.

tertiary trade area   The outermost ring of a trade area; includes customers who occasionally shop at the store or shopping center.

theme center   A shopping center that tries to replicate a historical place and typically contains tenants similar to those in specialty centers, except there usually is no large specialty store or department store as an anchor. See *historical center*.

theme/festival center   A shopping center that typically employs a unifying theme that is carried out by the individual shops in their architectural design and, to an extent, in their merchandise.

third-party logistics company   Firm that facilitates the movement of merchandise from manufacturer to retailer but is independently owned.

thrift store   A retail format offering used merchandise.

ticketing and marking   Procedures for making price labels and placing them on the merchandise.

tie-in   An approach used to attract attention to a store's offering by associating the offering with an event.

tonnage merchandising   A display technique in which large quantities of merchandise are displayed together.

top-down planning   One side of the process of developing an overall retail strategy where goals are set at the top of the organization and filter down through the operating levels.

top-of-mind awareness   The highest level of brand awareness; arises when consumers mention a brand name first when they are asked about a type of retailer, a merchandise category, or a type of service.

trade area   A geographic sector that contains potential customers for a particular retailer or shopping center.

trade discount   Reduction in a retailer's suggested retail price granted to wholesalers and retailers; also known as a *functional discount*.

trade dress   A product's physical appearance, including its size, shape, color, design, and texture. For instance, the shape and color of a Coca-Cola bottle is its trade dress.

trade show   A temporary concentration of vendors that provides retailers opportunities to place orders and view what is available in the marketplace; also known as a *merchandise show* or *market week*.

trademark Any mark, work, picture, or design associated with a particular line of merchandise or product.

traditional distribution center Warehouse in which merchandise is unloaded from trucks and placed on racks or shelves for storage.

traditional strip center A shopping center that is designed to provide convenience shopping for the day-to-day needs of consumers in their immediate neighborhood.

traffic appliance Small portable appliance.

traffic flow The balance between a substantial number of cars and not so many that congestion impedes access to the store.

transformational leader A leader who gets people to transcend their personal needs for the sake of realizing the group goal.

transportation cost The expense a retailer incurs if it pays the cost of shipping merchandise from the vendor to the stores.

travel time contours Used in trade area analysis to define the rings around a particular site based on travel time instead of distances.

trialability The costs and commitment required to initially adopt a fashion.

trickle-down theory A theory of how fashion spreads that suggests that the fashion leaders are consumers with the highest social status—wealthy, well-educated consumers. After they adopt a fashion, the fashion trickles down to consumers in lower social classes. When the fashion is accepted in the lowest social class, it is no longer acceptable to the fashion leaders in the highest social class.

triple-coupon promotion A retail promotion that allows the customer triple the face value of the coupon.

trust A belief that a partner is honest (reliable, stands by its word, sincere, fulfills obligations) and is benevolent (concerned about the other party's welfare).

tying contract An agreement between a vendor and a retailer requiring the retailer to take a product it does not necessarily desire (the tied product) to ensure that it can buy a product it does desire (the tying product).

ultimate consumers Individuals who purchase goods and services for their own personal use or for use by members of their household.

undercover shopper Person hired by or working for a retailer who poses as a customer to observe the activities and performance of employees.

understored trade area An area that has too few stores selling a specific good or service to satisfy the needs of the population.

unit pricing The practice of expressing price in terms of both the total price of an item and the price per unit of measure.

Universal Product Code (UPC) The black-and-white bar code found on most merchandise; used to collect sales information at the point of sale using computer terminals that read the code. This information is transmitted computer to computer to buyers, distribution centers, and then to vendors, who in turn quickly ship replenishment merchandise.

unrelated diversification Diversification in which there is no commonality between the present business and the new business.

UPC code See *Universal Product Code.*

URL (uniform resource locator) The standard for a page on the World Wide Web (e.g., www.nrf.org).

value Relationship of what a customer gets (goods/services) to what he or she has to pay for it.

value added network (VAN) A third-party logistics company that facilitates electronic data interchange (EDI) by making computer systems between vendors and retailers compatible.

value retailers General merchandise discount stores that are found in either low-income urban or rural areas and are much smaller than traditional discount stores, less than 9,000 square feet.

values of lifestyle survey (VALS2) A tool used to categorize customers into eight lifestyle segments. Based on responses to surveys conducted by SRI Consulting Business Intelligence.

variable costs Costs that vary with the level of sales and that can be applied directly to the decision in question.

variable pricing Charging different prices in different stores, markets or zones.

variety The number of different merchandise categories within a store or department.

vending machine retailing A nonstore format in which merchandise or services are stored in a machine and dispensed to customers when they deposit cash or use a credit card.

vendor Any firm from which a retailer obtains merchandise.

vertical integration An example of diversification by retailers involving investments by retailers in wholesaling or manufacturing merchandise.

vertical merchandising A method whereby merchandise is organized to follow the eye's natural up-and-down movement.

vertical price-fixing Agreements to fix prices between parties at different levels of the same marketing channel (for example, retailers and their vendors).

virtual community A network of people who seek information, products, and services and communicate with each other about specific issues.

virtual mall A group of retailers and service providers that can be accessed over the Internet at one location.

visibility The customers' ability to see the store and enter the parking lot safely.

visual communications The act of providing information to customers through graphics, signs, and theatrical effects—both in the store and in windows—to help boost sales by providing information on products and by suggesting items or special purchases.

want book   Information collected by retail salespeople to record out-of-stock or requested merchandise. Similar to a want slip.

warehouse club   A retailer that offers a limited assortment of food and general merchandise with little service and low prices to ultimate consumers and small businesses.

website   A page or series of pages on the Internet, identified by a unique address (URL), that can provide information or facilitate electronic commerce.

weeks of supply   An inventory management method most similar to the stock-to-sales method. The difference is that everything is expressed in weeks rather than months.

wheel of retailing   A cyclical theory of retail evolution whose premise is that retailing institutions evolve from low-price/service to higher-price/service operations.

wholesale-sponsored voluntary cooperative group   An organization operated by a wholesaler offering a merchandising program to small, independent retailers on a voluntary basis.

wholesaler   A merchant establishment operated by a concern that is primarily engaged in buying, taking title to, usually storing, and physically handling goods in large quantities, and reselling the goods (usually in smaller quantities) to retailers or to industrial or business users.

word of mouth   Communications between people about a retailer.

zone pricing   Charging different prices for the same merchandise in different geographic locations to be competitive in local markets.

zoning   The regulation of the construction and use of buildings in certain areas of a municipality.

ENDNOTES

Chapter 1

1. Hau L. Lee and Seungjin Whang, "Demand Chain Excellence: A Tale of Two Retailers," *Supply Chain Management Review*, March 1, 2001, p. 40.
2. Ellen Florian, "Dead and (Mostly) Gone," *Fortune*, December 24, 2001, pp. 46–47.
3. Personal communication, Kenneth Taylor, Mills Corporation, February 2002.
4. For a more detailed discussion of distribution channels, see Louis W. Stern, Adel I. El-Ansary, Erin Anderson, and Anne T. Coughlan, *Marketing Channels* (Englewood Cliffs, NJ: Prentice Hall, 2002).
5. "Estimated Quarterly U.S. Retail Sales," United States Department of Commerce News, November 28, 2001, www.census.gov/mrts/www/current.html.
6. "1997 Economic Census: Company Statistics Series," September 2001, p. 14, www.census.gov/prod/ec97/e97cs–1.pdf.
7. "Global 200 Highlights," *Stores*, January 2002, p. G7.
8. "World's Richest People," *Forbes*, July 9, 2001, www.forbes.com/billionaires.
9. Justin Hibbard, "Amazon.Com v. Wal-Mart: The Inside Story," *Information Week*, February 22, 1999, p. 27.
10. "The Company Is Not the Stock," *Business Week*, April 30, 2001, pp. 94–96.
11. "United Colors of Benetton," 2002, www.ucad.fr/pubgb/virt/mp/benetton/index.html.
12. "Giorgio Armani S.p.A," Hoovers Online, 2002, www.hoovers.com/officers/bio/9/0,3353,54529_5452918,00.html.
13. "Rating the Stores," *Consumer Reports*, November 1994, p. 714.
14. Ann Zimmerman, "Sales Finally Improve at JCPenney Despite Weak Consumer Confidence," *The Wall Street Journal*, November, 7, 2001; Leslie Kaufman, "Can JCPenney Evolve?" *New York Times*, June 26, 1999, pp. B1, B14; and William Davidson, Daniel Sweeney, and Ronald Stampfl, "JCPenney (A): Marketing and Financial Strategy," in *Retail Management*, 6th ed. (New York: Wiley, 1988).
15. Dan Scheraga, "Penney's Net Advantage," *Chain Store Age*, September 2000, pp. 114–18.
16. "Back to the Future," *New York Times Magazine*, April 6, 1997, pp. 48–49.
17. "Whole Foods Market, Inc. Helps Shape USDA's New National Organic Standards," company news release, December 2000, www.wholefoodmarket.com/company/pr_organicstandards.html.
18. "Declaration of Interdependence," company philosophy, www.wholefoodsmarket.com/company/declaration.html.
19. Matt Nannery, "Front Lines," *Chain Store Age*, September 2001, pp. 54–58.
20. Ibid.

Chapter 2

1. www.hoovers.com/premium/profile/6/0,2147,90426,00.html.
2. Sandy J. Skrovan and Tanya J. Erickson, "Drug Channel," (Columbus, OH: Retail Forward, Inc., February 2001.)
3. Ira Kalish, "The World's Leading Food Retailers," *Global Retail Intelligencer*, (Columbus, OH: Retail Forward, Inc., August 2001).
4. "Markets in Motion," in "66th Annual Report of the Grocery Industry," *Progressive Grocer*, April 1999, p. 31.
5. "Retail Industry Factsheet," National Retail Federation, www.nrf.com.
6. www.census.gov/epcd/www/naics.html.
7. *Chain Store Age*, Cap Gemini Ernst & Young U.S. L.L.C, 2001.
8. Ibid., "Monthly Retail and Food Service Sales," 2001.
9. "Food for Thought: Discount Stores Eat into Supermarket, Drug Store Sales," *Chain Store Age*, May 2000, p. 49, reporting a survey by Leo J. Shapiro & Associates, Chicago.
10. Kalish, "The World's Leading Food Retailers," p. 1.
11. www.aholdusa.com.
12. *Language of the Food Industry*, (Washington, DC: Food Marketing Institute, 1998).
13. Greg Jacobson, "Big Year for Food Lion," *MMR*, March 8, 1999, p. 5.
14. "Roaring 20's Ends in Depression," *Chain Store Age Executive*, June 1994, p. 49.
15. "Markets in Motion," p. 9.
16. Ibid.
17. www.mventures.com.
18. Glen A. Beres, "Centers Host Rapid Growth of Grocery Gas," *International Council of Shopping Center*, January 29, 2002, www.icsc.org/cgi2/htsearch. Research by *Oil Price Information Service*.
19. "Food for Thought," forecast by PricewaterhouseCoopers LLP.
20. *Language of the Food Industry*.
21. Personal communication, Bryan Gildenberg, M. Ventures, February 1002.
22. Sandra J. Skrovan, "Industry Brief: Warehouse Clubs," PricewaterhouseCoopers, June 2001, p. 7.
23. Ibid., p. 12.
24. George Strachan, Keith Wills, and Yukihiro Moroe, "Retail Surprises: A Look Back from 2005," Goldman Sachs, December 2000, pp. 9–10.
25. "A Short History of the Convenience Store Industry," at www.cstorecentral.com.
26. www.eatzis.com.

27. "A *Supermarket Business* Survey of Consumers Shows That the More Prepared Foods They Buy, the Bigger the Ring at the Checkout," *Supermarket Business*, July 15, 2001, pp. 37, 40+.

28. Personal communication, Jo Natale, Wegmans, February 2002.

29. www.marks-and-spencer.co.uk.

30. David P. Schulz, "Triversity Top 100 Retailers: The Nation's Biggest Retail Companies," www.stores.org, 2001.

31. Larry Greenberg, "Hudson's Bay Faces Challenge from Southern Rival," *The Wall Street Journal*, May 24, 1996, p. B4.

32. Michael Levy and Dhruv Grewal, "So Long, Kmart Shoppers," *The Wall Street Journal*, January 28, 2000, www.wsj.com.

33. Strachan, Wills, and Moroe, "Retail Surprises," p. 17.

34. Same-store sales provides a comparison of the same group of stores over a period of time. Thus, new stores are not included in the sales comparisons.

35. Amy Merrick, "Tired of Trendiness, Former Shoppers Leave Gap," *The Wall Street Journal*, December 6, 2001. p. B1

36. Carlta Vitzthum, "Just-in-Time Fashion—Spanish Retailer Zara Makes Low-Cost Lines in Weeks by Running Its Own Show," *The Wall Street Journal*, May 18, 2001, p. B1; and Benjamin Jones, "Madrid: Zara Pioneers Fashion on Demand," *Europe*, September 2001. pp. 43–44

37. Marianne Wilson, "Disposable Chic at H&M," *Chain Store Age*, May 2000, pp. 64–66.

38. Schulz, "Triversity Top 100 Retailers."

39. Chad Terhune, "Sears, Home Depot Ratchet Up Battle for Homeowners' Decorating Dollars," *The Wall Street Journal*, September 4, 2001 p. 28; Mike Duff, "Home Depot Debuts New Format," *Discount Store News*, July 12, 1999, pp. 1, 80; Margaret Pressler, "The High End Gets Higher; Home Depot's Luxury Stores Ride a Trend of Rising Expectations—and Spending," *Washington Post*, July 11, 1999, p. H01.

40. "Lowe's Widens Its Growth Focus," *National Home Center News*, September 8, 1997, p. 7.

41. Schulz, "Triversity Top 100 Retailers."

42. David Moin, "Department Stores: The Issues," *WWD Infotracs*, June 1997, pp. 4–6.

43. Amy Merrick, Jeffrey A. Trachtenberg, and Ann Zimmerman, "Department Stores Fight to Save a Model That May Be Outdated," *The Wall Street Journal*, March 12, 2002, p. 1. Research by Chris Ohlinger, chief executive of Service Industry Research Systems Inc. of Highland Heights, KY.

44. Strachan, Wills, and Moroe, "Retail Surprises," pp. 6, 7.

45. Merrick, Trachtenberg, and Zimmerman, "Department Stores Fight to Save a Model That May Be Outdated."

46. www.stores.org/archives/2001topdrugstores.html, October 1, 2001.

47. "Wal-Mart Stores, Inc.," Hoovers Online, 2002, www.hoovers.com.

48. Skrovan and Erickson, "*Drug Channel.*"

49. Tracie Rozhon, "Main Street's Latest Threat," *New York Times*, June 14, 1999, p. A25; "Annual Report of Categories," *Drug Store News*, May 17, 1999; and "Annual Report on Drug Chains," *Drug Store News*, April 26, 1999.

50. Susan Reda, "Redefining Pharmacy's Role," *Stores*, April 1997, pp. 34–36.

51. Ibid.

52. Schulz, "Triversity Top 100 Retailers."

53. "Back to the Future," *New York Times Magazine*, April 6, 1997, pp. 48–49

54. "Company profiles," Hoovers Online, February 2002, www.hoovers.com.

55. Linda Humphers, "State of the Outlet Industry," *Value Retail News*, May 2001.

56. Schulz, "Triversity Top 100 Retailers."

57. Debby Garbato Stankevich, "More Value to a Dollar: With Traditional Discounters Concentrating Market," *Retail Merchandiser*, October 2001, pp. 21–23.

58. "Consumer Direct Channel Will Account for 12% of U.S. Retail Sales by 2010," *Retail Industry*, June 28, 2000, http://retailindustry.about.com/library/bl/bl_net0628.htm?terms=catalogs.

59. Saul Hansell, "Online Grocer Calls It Quits after Running out of Money," *The Wall Street Journal*, July 10, 2001. pp. A1, 8.

60. "Current Population Survey," U.S. Census Bureau, September 2001.

61. Geoff Wissman "Where's the Growth?" *E-Retailing Intelligence Update* (Columbus, OH: Retail Forward, February 2002), p. 6

62. Rachel Ledford "The Connected Customer," *E-Retailing Intelligence Update* (Columbus, OH: Retail Forward, December 2001), p. 4.

63. Rob Gallo and Geoff Wissman "Spinning the Web," *E-Retailing Intelligence Update* (Columbus, OH: Retail Forward, February 2002), p. 3.

64. Ibid., p. 4

65. Joanna Barsh, Blair Crawford, and Chris Grosso, "How E-Retailing Can Rise from the Ashes," *McKinsey Quarterly*, 2000.

66. "Lessons from the Top 25," *Internet Retailer*, January 2002, pp. 3–7.

67. "Catalog and Mail Order Sales," *Retail Industry*, June 4, 2001, http://retailindustry.about.com/library/bl/q2/bl_dma060401a.htm.

68. Sherry Chiger, "Consumer Shopping Survey: Part 2," *Catalog Age*, October 2001.

69. *1999 Statistical Fact Book* (New York: Direct Marketing Association, 1999), pp. 30, 72.

70. Sherry Chiger, "Catalog Age's Exclusive Consumer Shopping Survey," *Catalog Age*, August 1, 2001, http://industryclick.com/magazine.asp?magazineid=153&siteid=2.

71. *1999 Statistical Fact Book.*

72. Richard S. Hodgson, "It's Still the 'Catalog Age,' " *Catalog Age*, June 1, 2001.

73. Mark Del Franco, "Penney Redesigns Its Big Book," *Catalog Age*, January 16, 2002.

74. "Catalog Age Top Ten," *Catalog Age*, June 1, 2001.

75. www.usaa.com/cp-aboutusaa.asp.

76. "Internet Generates 13 Percent of Catalog Sales," *Retail Industry*, January 2002, http://retailindustry.about.com/library/bl/q2/bl_dma060401b.htm.

77. www.dsa.org/research/numbers.htm.

78. "Home Shopping Due for Upgrade," *Electronic Media*, January 29, 2001, pp. 20, 23.

79. "2001 State of the Vending Industry Report" *Automatic Merchandiser*, www.amonline.com/current/industry reports.shtml.

80. Ibid., chap. 2

81. "Japanese Retailing—Marketplace Is Alive and Kicking," *Retail Week*, April 27, 2001, p. 16.

82. www.zoots.com.

83. Valarie Zeithaml, A. Parasuraman, and Leonard Berry, "Problems and Strategies in Services Marketing," *Journal of Marketing* 49 (Spring 1985), pp. 33–46; and Stephen W. Brown and Mary Jo Bitner, "Services Marketing," *AMA Management Handbook*, 3rd ed. (New York: AMACOM Books, 1994), pp. 15-5-15-15.

84. *Dun and Bradstreet Corporate Starts* (New York: Dun and Bradstreet, 1998).

85. Bill Quinn, *How Wal-Mart Is Destroying America (and the World): And What You Can Do about It* (Ten Speed Press, 2000).

86. Stanley Hollander, "Clio Goes Shopping," *Anderson Retailing Issues Letter*, Center for Retailing Studies, Texas A&M University, September 1998.

87. Stephen Brown, "Postmodernism, the Wheel of Retailing, and Will to Power" *The International Review of Retail, Distribution, and Consumer Research*, July 1995, pp. 387–412.

88. Stanley C. Hollander, "Notes on the Retail Accordion," *Journal of Retailing* 42 (Summer 1966), pp. 20–40, 54.

89. Thomas J. Maronick and Bruce J. Walker, "The Dialectic Evolution of Retailing," in *Proceedings: Southern Marketing Association*, ed. Barnett Greenberg (Atlanta: Georgia State University, 1974), p. 147.

90. A. C. R. Dreesmann, "Patterns of Evolution in Retailing," *Journal of Retailing* (Spring 1968) pp. 81–96; and Murray Forester, "Darwinian Theory of Retailing," *Chain Store Age*, August 1995, p. 8.

Chapter 3

1. *Surveying the Digital Future: UCLA Internet Project Report 2001*, UCLA Center for Communication Policy, 2001, p. 38, www.ccp.ucla.edu/pdf/UCLA-Internet-Report-2001.pdf.

2. This section is based on material in Lyda Hyde, "Multi-Channel Integration: The New Retail Battleground,"

PricewaterhouseCoopers, 2001; and Joseph Alba, John Lynch, Barton Weitz, Chris Janiszewski, Richard Lutz, Alan Sawyer, and Stacy Woods, "Interactive Home Shopping: Consumer, Retailer, and Manufacturers Incentives to Participate in Electronic Markets," *Journal of Marketing* 61 (July 1997), pp. 38–53.

3. William Wilkie and Peter R. Dickson, "Consumer Information Search and Shopping Behavior," working paper, Management Science Institute, Cambridge, MA, 1985.

4. "Survey of Retail Payment Systems," *Chain Store Age*, December 1999, p. 4A.

5. David Moin, "Getting Personal," *Women's Wear Daily Internet Supplement*, May 2000, pp. 10–17.

6. Lorrie Grant, "Grocery Chore No More," *USA Today*, July 21, 1999, pp. B1–B2.

7. Reid Claxton, "Customer Safety: Direct Marketing's Undermarketed Advantage," *Journal of Direct Marketing* 9 (Winter 1995), pp. 67–78.

8. Wilkie and Dickson, "Consumer Information Search and Shopping Behavior."

9. Jared Sandberg, "It Isn't Entertainment That Makes the Web Shine: It's Dull Data," *The Wall Street Journal*, July 20, 1998, pp. A1, A6.

10. James Peltier, John Schibrowsky, and John Davis, "Using Attitudinal and Descriptive Database Information to Understand Interactive Buyer–Seller Relationships," *Journal of Interactive Marketing* 12 (Summer 1998), pp. 32–45; and John Eighmey, "Adding Value in the Information Age: Uses and Gratifications of Sales on the World-Wide Web," *Journal of Business Research* 41 (March 1998), pp. 34–45.

11. Phil Patton, "Buy Here, and We'll Teach You What You Like," *New York Times*, Electronic Commerce Special Section, September 22, 1999, p. 5; and Pattie Maes, "Smart Commerce: The Future of Intelligent Agents in Cyberspace," *Journal of Interactive Marketing* 3 (Summer 1999), pp. 66–76.

12. Pui-Wing Tam, "Surfing for Wedding Help," *The Wall Street Journal*, November 12, 2001, p. B1; Eric Wilson, "Bridal Firms Waltz with the Net," *WWD*, August 10, 1999, pp. 10–11; and Ellen Neuborne, "Weddings and the Web: A Marriage Made in Cyber Heaven," *Business Week*, February 15, 1999, p. 45

13. Steve Jarvis, "Community Spirit: Balance Key to Targeting Online Groups," *Marketing News*, December 3, 2001 p. 4; Aleksandra Djukic, "Websites Offer Ideal Opportunity to Communicate with Pregnant Women," *Brand Strategy*, December 2001, p. 17; and "A Guide to Targeting Women—Reaching Women Online," *Media Week*, June 29, 2001, pp. 4–6.

14. "E-tailing Group Reviewed 100 Retail Sites," E-Retailing Group, November 2001, www.e-tailing.com.

15. Geoff Wissman "Where's the Growth?" *E-Retailing Intelligence Update* (Columbus, OH: Retail Forward, February 2002), p. 6.

16. Everett Rogers, *Diffusion of Innovations*, 4th ed. (New York: Free Press, 1995).

17. www.nua.com/surveys/how_many_online/index.html, February 2002.

18. Rachael Ledford, "The Connected Consumer," *E-Retail Intelligence Update* (Columbus, OH: Retail Forward, March 2002), pp. 10–11.

19. "Meeting Generation Y," *NUA*, July 19, 1999; and "Young Consumers Have Internalized the Net" Forrester Research, August 11, 1999.

20. Bob Tedeschi, "Credit Card Companies Go to Great Lengths Online to Develop Products That Will Corral Teenage Consumers," *New York Times*, January 14, 2002, p. C6.

21. Karen Thomas, "Rocketcash Makes Allowances for Kids," *USA Today*, December 10, 2000, p. 3D.

22. Joanne Cleaver, "Surfing for Seniors," *Marketing News*, July 19, 1999, pp. 1, 7; and Justina Gapper, "The Rise of the New Media Greys," *New Media Age*, January 29, 1998, pp. 10–12.

23. Ibid.

24. Warren Caragata, "An Overview of Electronic Commerce," *Prism*, July 12, 1999, pp. 32–38.

25. Valerie Seckler, "E-Tailing Sales: Data Privacy Is Seen as Key," *WWD*, August 25, 1999, p. 5.

26. Rachel Ledford, "The Connected Customer," *E-Retailing Intelligence Update* (Columbus, OH: Retail Forward, December 2001), p. 6.

27. Michael Hartnett, "Not All Items Prosper in On-Line Sales Arena," *Discount Store News*, April 20, 1998, pp. 16–17.

28. Rachel Ledford, "The Connected Customer," *E-Retailing Intelligence Update* (Columbus, OH: Retail Forward, November 2001), p. 3

29. Timothy Mullaney, "Taking in the Travel Sites," *Business Week*, July 26, 1999, p. EB68; "Travel Special Report," *The Industry Standard*, June 14, 1999, pp. 52–74; and "E-Com Fly with Me," *New Media Age*, March 11, 1999, pp. 12–14.

30. Andrew Osterland, "Nothing but Net," *Business Week*, August 2, 1999, p. 72; Bill Orr, "E-Banks or E-Branches?" *ABA Banking Journal*, July 1999, pp. 32–42; Alex Sheshunoff, "The Wait Is Over for Internet Banking," *ABA Banking Journal*, June 1999, pp. 18–20; "Financial Services On-Line," *The Industry Standard*, May 17, 1999, pp. 44–80; and "Banking in Cyberspace," *International Journal of Retail & Distribution Management* 26 (February–March 1998), pp. 128–30.

31. Michelle Rafter, "Cheap, Cheaper, Cheapest," *The Industry Standard*, January 11, 1999, pp. 50–52; and George Anders, "Comparison Shopping Is the Web's Virtue—Unless You're a Seller," *The Wall Street Journal*, July 23, 1998, pp. A1, A8.

32. Rebecca Quick, "Web's Robot Shoppers Don't Roam Free," *The Wall Street Journal*, September 3, 1998, pp. B1, B8.

33. John Lynch Jr. and Daniel Arliey, "Wine Online: Search Costs and Competition on Price, Quality and Distribution," *Marketing Science* 19, no. 1 (xxxx), pp. 83–103.

34. Xing Pan, Brian Ratchford, and Venkatesh Sankar, "Why Aren't the Prices for the Same Items the Same at Me.com and You.com? Drivers of Price Dispersion among E-Tailers," working paper, Robert H. Smith Business School, University of Maryland, 2001; and Erik Brynjolfsson and Michael Smith, "Frictionless Commerce? A Comparison of Internet and Conventional Retailer," *Management Science* 46, no. 4, (April 2000), pp. 563–85.

35. Ellen Neuborne, "Happy Returns: How to Deal with Rejected Web Purchases," *Business Week*, October 8, 2001, p. SB12.

36. 10-K405 report filed with SEC by CDNOW, Inc., on March 16, 1999.

37. Princeton Survey Research Associates for Consumer WebWatch, January 2002.

38. Mark Bergen, Shantanu Dutta, and Steven M. Shugan, "Branded Variants: A Retail Perspective," *Journal of Marketing Research* 33 (February 1996), pp. 9–19.

39. Gerald Lohse and Peter Spiller, "Electronic Shopping," *Communications of the ACM* 41 (July 1998), pp. 81–88; and Donna Hoffman and Thomas Novak, "Marketing in Hypermedia Computer-Mediated Environments: Conceptual Foundations," *Journal of Marketing* 60 (Summer 1996), pp. 50–63.

40. Ginger Koloszyc, "Internet-Only Retailers Struggle to Improve Product Return Process," *Stores*, July 1999, pp. 54–59; and David Schulz, "Growth of Direct-to-Customer Channels Reshapes Retail Distribution," *Stores*, March 1999, pp. 48–51.

41. Rob Gallo and Geoff Wissman "Spinning the Web," *E-Retailing Intelligence Update* (Columbus, OH: Retail Forward, November 2001), p. 4.

42. George Anders, "Virtual Reality: Web Firms Go on Warehouse Building Boom," *The Wall Street Journal*, September 8, 1999, pp. B1, B9.

43. Faye Brookman, "Drugstores Face New Rival," *WWD*, March 5, 1999, p. 16.

44. James Frederick, "Walgreen's Gears for Opening of Its Own Internet Pharmacy," *Drug Store News*, July 19, 1999, pp. CP1–CP4; and "State of the Industry: Drug Stores: Chain Drug Stores Provide Rx for Whole Health," *Chain Store Age*, State of the Industry Supplement, August 1999, pp. A21–A24.

45. Megan Barnett, "Why Macys.com Won't Sell Levi's," *The Industry Standard*, November 30, 1998, p. 22.

46. Keith Regan, "Five E-Commerce Trends to Watch," *E-Commerce Times*, April 3, 2002, p. 4.

47. James Crawford, *Getting the Retail Technology Advantage* (Cambridge, MA: Forrester Research, April 2002), p. 3.

48. Lisa Vincenti, "Retailers Eye Internet, Global Market," *HFN*, January 25 1999, p. 6.

49. Ledford, "The Connected Customer," November 2001, p. 6.

50. Marco Vriens and Michael Grigsby, "Building Profitable Online Customer-Brand Relationships," *Marketing Management*, November–December 2001, pp. 34–36.

51. For more information on approaches for increasing share of wallet, see Tom Osten, *Customer Share Marketing* (Upper Saddle River, NJ: Prentice Hall, 2002).

52. Hyde, "Multi-Channel Integration," p. 21.

53. "Integrating Multiple Channels," *Chain Store Age Executive*, August 2001, p. A24.

54. Bob Tedeschi, "Bricks-and-Mortar Merchants Struggling to Assess Web Sidelines," *New York Times*, September 3, 2001, p. C3.

55. Hyde, "Multi-Channel Integration," pp. 28–35

Chapter 4

1. "Coldwater Creek Rises to the Top," *Chain Store Age*, November 1997, pp. 41–43.

2. For a detailed discussion of customer behavior, see J. Paul Peter and Jerry C. Olson, *Consumer Behavior and Marketing Strategy*, 6th ed. (New York: McGraw-Hill, 2002); and Michael R. Solomon, *Consumer Behavior: Buying, Having, and Being*, 5th ed. (Upper Saddle River, NJ: Prentice Hall, 2002).

3. Based on John Fetto, David Whelan, and Sandra Yin, "Fashion Forward," *American Demographic*, August 2001, p. 64.

4. R. Puri, "Measuring and Modifying Consumer Impulsiveness: A Cost-Benefit Accessibility Framework," *Journal of Consumer Psychology* 5 (1996), pp. 87–113.

5. Sharon Beatty and M. Elizabeth Ferrell, "Impulse Buying: Modeling Its Precursors," *Journal of Retailing* 74 (Summer 1998), pp. 169–91; and John Willman, "Parting a Fool from His Money," *Financial Times*, August 10, 1998, p. 9. See Alison Smith, "A Grab for Impulse Shoppers," *Financial Times*, September 18, 1998, p. 12, for a discussion of how Internet retailers are trying to encourage impulse shopping.

6. Kevin Armata, "Signs That Sell," *Progressive Grocer*, October 1996, p. 21.

7. Joel Urbany, Peter Dickson, and Rosemary Kalapurakai, "Price Search in the Retail Grocery Market," *Journal of Marketing* 60 (April 1996), pp. 91–111; and Peter Dickson and Alan Sawyer, "The Price Knowledge and Search of Supermarket Shoppers," *Journal of Marketing*, July 1991, pp. 49–59.

8. "Consumer Buying Patterns: Beyond Demographics," *Progressive Grocer*, May 1995, p. 136.

9. Pamela Sebastian, " 'Aspirational Wants' Form the Basis of a Modern Retailing Strategy," *The Wall Street Journal*, October 15, 1998, p. A1; and Barry Babin, William Darden, and Mitch Griffin, "Work and/or Fun: Measuring Hedonic and Utilitarian Shopping Value," *Journal of Consumer Research* 20 (March 1994), pp. 644–56.

10. This hierarchical structure of needs is based on Abraham Maslow, *Motivation and Personality* (New York: Harper & Row, 1954).

11. "Why Do You Shop?" *WWD*, July 22, 1997, pp. 44–46; "Shop, Shop, Shop," *Advertising Age*, August 22, 1994, p. 3; and Scott Dawson, Peter Dawson, and Nancy Ridgeway, "Shopping Motives, Emotional States, and Retail Outcomes," *Journal of Retailing* 66 (Winter 1990), pp. 408–27.

12. Scott Dawson, "The Shopping Mall as Consumer Habitat," *Journal of Retailing* 70 (Winter 1994), pp. 23–42.

13. Stephen Grove and Raymond Fisk, "The Impact of Other Customers on Service Experiences: A Critical Incident Examination of Getting Along," *Journal of Retailing* 73 (Spring 1997), pp. 63–86; Dale Duhan, Scott Johnson, James Wilcox, and Gilbert Harrell, "Influence on Consumer Use of Word-of-Mouth Recommendation Sources," *Journal of the Academy of Marketing Science* 25 (Fall 1997), pp. 283–95; Kenneth Evans, Tim Christiansen, and James Gill, "The Impact of Social Influence and Role Expectations on Shopping Center Patronage Intentions," *Journal of the Academy of Marketing Science* 24 (Summer 1996), pp. 208–18; and Yong-Soon Kang and Nancy Ridgeway, "The Importance of Consumer Market Interactions as a Form of Social Support for Elderly Consumers," *Journal of Public Policy & Marketing* 15 (Spring 1996), pp. 108–17.

14. Susan Caminiti, "Ralph Lauren: The Emperor Has Clothes," *Fortune*, November 11, 1996, p. 82.

15. David Mick, Michelle DeMoss, and Ronald Faber, "A Projective Study of Motivations and Meanings of Self-Gift," *Journal of Retailing*, Summer 1992, pp. 112–44.

16. "Crossover Jeans Customers Shop at Macy's Today, Wal-Mart Tomorrow," *DNR*, August 21, 2000, p. 74; Lisa Vincenti, "Fashion-Forward Discounters Score," *HFN*, July 20, 1998, pp. 9, 59; Michelle Morganosky, "Retail Market Structure Change: Implications for Retailers and Consumers," *International Journal of Retail & Distribution Management* 25 (August 1997), pp. 269–84; and "Cross-Shopping," *Women's Wear Daily*, April 26, 1995, section II.

17. Philip Titus and Peter Everett, "The Consumer Retail Search Process: A Conceptual Model and Research Agenda," *Journal of the Academy of Marketing Science* 23 (Spring 1995), pp. 106–19; and Paul Bloom and James Pailin, "Using Information Situations to Guide Marketing Strategy," *Journal of Consumer Marketing* 12 (Spring 1995), pp. 19–28.

18. Sanjay Putrevu and Brian T. Ratchford, "A Model of Search Behavior with an Application to Grocery Shopping," *Journal of Retailing* 73 (Winter 1997), pp. 463–87; Sridhar Moorthy, Brian Ratchford, and Debabrata Talukdar, "Consumer Information Search Revisited: Theory and Empirical Analysis," *Journal of Consumer Research* 23 (March 1997), pp. 263–78; and Jeffrey Schmidt and Richard Prend, "A Proposed Model of Consumer External Information Search," *Journal of the Academy of Marketing Sciences* 24 (Summer 1996), pp. 246–56.

19. Arch Woodside and Eva Thelen, "Accessing Memory and Customer Choice: Benefit-to-Store Retrieval Models

That Predict Purchase," *Marketing & Research Today* 24 (November 1996), pp. 260–88.

20. Adam Finn and Jordan Louviere, "Shopping Center Image, Considerations, and Choice: Anchor Store Contribution," *Journal of Business Research* 35 (1996), pp. 241–51.

21. Patrich Van Kenhove, Walter Van Waterschoot, and Kristoff De Wulf, "The Impact of Task Definition on Store-Attribute Saliences and Store Choice," *Journal of Retailing* 75 (Spring 1999), pp. 125–36.

22. William L. Wilkie and Edgar D. Pessimier, "Issues in Marketing's Use of Multi-Attribute Attitude Models," *Journal of Marketing Research*, November 1973, pp. 428–41; and Richard J. Lutz and James R. Bettman, "Multi-Attribute Models in Marketing: A Bicentennial Review," in *Consumer and Industrial Buying Behavior*, eds. A. G. Woodside, J. N. Sheth, and P. D. Bennett (New York: Elsevier–North Holland, 1977), pp. 13–50.

23. Pat West, P. Brockett, and Linda Golden, "A Comparative Analysis of Neural Networks and Statistical Methods for Predicting Consumer Choice," *Marketing Science*, 16, no. 4, (1997), pp. 370–91.

24. David Bell, Tech-Hua Ho, and Christopher Tang, "Determining Where to Stop: Fixed and Variable Costs of Shopping," *Journal of Marketing Research* 35 (August 1998), pp. 352–70.

25. Richard Brand and Joseph Cronin, "Consumer-Specific Determinants of the Size of Retail Choice Sets: An Empirical Comparison of Physical Good and Service Providers," *Journal of Services Marketing* 11 (January–February 1997), pp. 19–39; and Ronald LeBlanc and L. W. Turley, "Retail Influence on Evoked Set Formation and Final Choice of Shopping Goods," *International Journal of Retail & Distribution Management* 22 (1994), pp. 10–17.

26. Wayne Hoyer and Steven Brown, "Effects of Brand Awareness of Choice for a Common, Repeat-Purchase Product," *Journal of Consumer Research*, September 1990, pp. 141–49.

27. CDNOW, 8K SEC filing, May 18, 1999.

28. Itamar Simonson, "The Effect of Product Assortment on Buyer Preferences," *Journal of Retailing* 75 (Fall 1999), pp. 347–70; and Susan M. Broniarczyk, Wayne D. Hoyer, and Leigh McAlister, "Consumers' Perceptions of the Assortment Offered in a Grocery Category: The Impact of Item Reduction," *Journal of Marketing Research* 35 (May 1998), pp. 166–77.

29. Masaaki Kiotabe, "The Return of 7-Eleven . . . from Japan: The Vanguard Program," *Columbia Journal of World Business* 30 (Winter 1995), pp. 70–81; and Kevin Helliker, "Some 7-Elevens Try Selling a New Image," *The Wall Street Journal*, October 25, 1991, pp. B1–B2.

30. Peter N. Child, Suzanne Heywood, and Michael Kliger, "Do Retail Brands Travel?" *McKinsey Quarterly*, no. 1 (2002), pp. 25–34.

31. Richard J. Lutz, "Changing Brand Attitudes through Modification of Cognitive Structure," *Journal of Consumer Research* 1 (March 1975), pp. 49–59.

32. Roger Bennett, "Queues, Customer Characteristics and Policies for Managing Waiting-Lines in Supermarkets," *International Journal of Retail & Distribution Management* 26 (February 1998), pp. 78–86; M. Kostecki, "Waiting Lines as a Marketing Issue," *European Management Journal* 14, no. 3 (1996), pp. 295–303; M. K. Hui and D. K. Tsi, "What to Tell Consumers in Waits of Different Lengths: An Integrative Model of Service Evaluation," *Journal of Marketing* 60, no. 2 (1996), pp. 81–90; K. L. Katz, B. M. Larson, and R. C. Larson, "Prescriptions for Waiting in Line Blues: Entertain, Enlighten, and Enrage," *Sloan Management Review* 32, no. 4 (1991), pp. 44–53; and S. Taylor, "The Effects of Filled Waiting Time and Service Provider Control over the Delay on Evaluation of Service," *Journal of the Academy of Marketing Science* 23 (1995), pp. 38–48.

33. Mitch Betts, "Turning Browsers into Buyers," *Sloan Management Review* 42 (Winter 2000), p. 8.

34. Josee Bloemer and Ko de Ruyter, "On the Relationship between Store Image, Store Satisfaction and Store," *European Journal of Marketing* 32 (May–June 1998), pp. 499–514; Eugene Anderson, "Customer Satisfaction and Word-of-Mouth," *Journal of Services Research* 1 (August 1998), pp. 13–21; and Richard Oliver, Roland Rust, and Sajeev Varki, "Customer Delight: Foundations, Findings, and Managerial Insights," *Journal of Retailing* 73 (Fall 1997), pp. 311–36.

35. "Let's Play Shopping," *Marketing Week*, November 22, 2001, pp. 45–47; Conway Lachman and John Lanasa, "Family Decision-Making Theory: An Overview and Assessment," *Psychology & Marketing* 10 (March–April 1993), pp. 81–94; and Robert Boutlier, "Pulling the Family Strings," *American Demographics*, August 1993, pp. 44–48.

36. Jean Darian, "Parent–Child Decision Making in Children's Clothing Stores," *International Journal of Retail & Distribution Management* 26 (October 1998), pp. 421–32; Kay Palanand and Robert Wilkes, "Adolescent–Parent Interaction in Family Decision Making," *Journal of Consumer Research* 24 (September 1997), pp. 159–71; Christy Fisher, "Kidding around Makes Sense," *Advertising Age*, June 27, 1994, pp. 34, 37; and Sharon Beatty and Salil Talpade, "Adolescent Influence in Family Decision Making: A Replication with Extension," *Journal of Consumer Research* 31 (September 1994), pp. 332–41.

37. "Bring the Family . . . Bring the Kids," *Travel Agent* Caribbean and Bahamas Supplement, April 7, 1997.

38. Dianne Pogoda, "It's a Matter of Time: Stores Keep Traffic Moving, Cash Flowing," *Women's Wear Daily*, April 9, 1996, pp. 1, 8

39. Hiroshi Tanaka and Miki Iwamura, "Gift Selection Strategy of Japanese Seasonal Gift Purchasers," Association for Consumer Research Conference, Boston, 1994; and Terrence Witkowski and Yoshito Yamamoto, "Omiyage Gift Purchasing by Japanese Travelers to the U.S.," in

Advances in Consumer Research, vol. 18 (Provo, UT: Association of Consumer Research, 1991), pp. 123–28.

40. Soyeon Shim and Mary Ann Eastwick, "The Hierarchical Influence of Personal Values on Mall Shopping Attitudes and Behaviors," *Journal of Retailing* 74 (Spring 1998), pp. 139–60.

41. Cyndee Miller, "Top Marketers Take a Bolder Approach in Targeting Gays," *Marketing News*, July 4, 1994, pp. 1–2.

42. Geng Cui, "The Different Faces of the Chinese Consumer," *China Business Review*, July 1997, pp. 34–42.

43. www.dreyers.com; and Florence Fabricant, "The Geography of Taste," *New York Times Magazine*, March 10, 1996, pp. 40–41.

44. Robert Verdisco, "Gender-Specific Shopping," *Chain Store Age*, February 1999, pp. 26–28; Matthew Klein, "He Shops, She Shops," *American Demographics*, March 1998, pp. 34–40; and Suein Hwang, "From Choices to Checkout, the Genders Behave Very Differently in Supermarkets," *The Wall Street Journal*, March 22, 1994, pp. A1, A4.

45. Michael J. Weiss, *The Clustered World* (Boston: Little, Brown, 2000).

46. VALS1, the original lifestyle survey, assessed general values and lifestyles. The VALS2 survey focuses more on values and lifestyles related to consumer behavior and thus has more commercial applications.

47. "To Your Health," *Chain Store Age*, February 1, 1999, p. 2RSY.

48. For additional information about fashion and the fashion industry, see Giannino Malossi, ed., *The Style Engine: Spectacle, Identity, Design and Business: How the Fashion Industry Uses Style to Create Wealth* (New York: Monacelli Press, 1998); Jeannette Jarnow and Kitty G. Dickerson, *Inside the Fashion Business*, 6th ed. (Upper Saddle River, NJ: Merrill, 1997); and Mike Easey, ed. *Fashion Marketing* (Oxford, England: Blackwell, 1995).

49. "Millennium Timeline: Ideas," *The Wall Street Journal*, January 11, 1999, p. R14.

50. Ibid.

51. Tina Cassidy, "How Fashions That Models Wear in Milan or Paris Find Their Way to a Mall Near You," *Boston Globe*, March 14, 2002, p. D1.

52. Rich Marin and Sarah Van Boven, "The Buzz Machine," *Newsweek*, July 27, 1998, p. 22.

53. "The Fashion Innovators," *WWD*, March 20, 1997, p. 2.

54. J. Freedom du Lac, "Entering the World of Goth," *Sacramento Bee*, March 9, 1999, p. C1; and "Dressed to Express and Impress," *Women's Wear Daily Echo Boomers Supplement*, February 19, 1998, pp. 26–27.

Chapter 5

1. See David Aaker, *Strategic Market Management*, 6th ed. (New York: John Wiley, 2001); and A. Coskun Samli, *Strategic Marketing for Success in Retailing* (Westport, CT: Quorum Books, 1998).

2. Roger Evered, "So What Is Strategy?" *Long Range Planning* 16 (Fall 1983), p. 120.

3. Michael Porter, *On Competition* (Boston: Harvard Business School Press, 1998); and Michael Porter, "What Is Strategy?" *Harvard Business Review*, November–December 1996, pp. 61–78.

4. "Kohl's Corporation—Company Profile," Hoovers Online, 2002, www.hoovers.com/premium/profile/9/0,2147,11339,00.html.

5. Leslie Kaufman, "Kohl's Thrives Despite Gloom in Retailing," *New York Times*, December 28, 2001. www.nytimes.com

6. Mark McMenamin, "Resurrecting Restoration Hardware," Fairchild Publications, February 18, 2002.

7. Amy Merrick, "Restoration Hardware, Pottery Barn Wagers Consumers Want Nostalgia," *The Wall Street Journal*, November 23, 2001. www.wsj.com

8. Kimberly Pfaff, "Chico's Familiarity with Its Customers Keeps It Ahead in Tough Times," International Council of Shopping Centers. www.icsc.org (May 2002).

9. Kevin Keller, "Managing Brands for the Long Run: Effective Brand Reinforcement and Revitalization Strategies," *California Management Review* 41 (March 1999), pp. 102–21.

10. Anthony Boardman and Aidan Vining, "Defining Your Business Using Product-Customer Matrices," *Long Range Planning* 29 (February 1996), pp. 38–48; and R. L. Rothschild, *How to Gain and Maintain Competitive Advantage in Business* (New York: McGraw-Hill, 1984).

11. Cynthia Montgomery, "Creating Corporate Advantage," *Harvard Business Review*, May–June 1998, pp. 71–80; Shelby Hunt and Robert Morgan, "The Comparative Advantage Theory of Competition," *Journal of Marketing* 59 (April 1995), pp. 1–15; Kathleen Conner and C. K. Prahalad, "A Resource-Based Theory of the Firm: Knowledge versus Opportunism," *Organizational Science* 7 (September–October 1996), pp. 477–501; David Collins and Cynthia Montgomery, "Competing on Resources: Strategy for the 1990s," *Harvard Business Review* 73 (July–August 1995), pp. 118–28; William Werther and Jeffrey Kerr, "The Shifting Sands of Competitive Advantage," *Business Horizons* 38 (May–June 1995), pp. 11–17; "10 Quick Wins to Turn Your Supply Chain into a Competitive Advantage," January 2002, http://retailindustry.about.com/library/bl/bl_ksa0112.htm?terms=competitive+advantage; and "Multi-Channel Integration: The New Retail Battleground," Retail Forward, Inc., March 2001, www.pwcris.com.

12. Gerrard Macintosh and Lawrence Lockshin, "Retail Relationships and Store Loyalty: A Multi-Level Perspective," *International Journal of Research in Marketing* 14 (1997), pp. 487–97.

13. Jo Marney, "Bringing Consumers Back for More," *Marketing Magazine*, September 10, 2001, p. 33; Kathleen Seiders and Douglas Tigert, "Impact of Market Entry and Competitive Structure on Store Switching/Store Loyalty," *International Review of Retail, Distribution and*

Consumer Research 7, no. 3 (1997), pp. 234–56; and Niren Sirohi, Edward McLaughlin, and Dick Wittink, "A Model of Consumer Perceptions and Store Loyalty Intentions for a Supermarket Retailer," *Journal of Retailing* 74 (June 1998), pp. 223–47.

14. Richard Czerniawski and Michael Maloney, *Creating Brand Loyalty: The Management of Power Positioning and Really Great Advertising* (New York: AMACOM, 1999); S. Chandrasekhar, Vinod Sawhney, Rafique Malik, S. Ramesh Kumar, and Pranab Dutta, "The Case of Brand Positioning," *Business Today*, June 7, 1999, pp. 131–40; Bernard Schmitt, Alex Simonson, and Joshua Marcus, "Managing Corporate Image and Identity," *Long Range Planning* 28 (October 1995), pp. 82–92; Tim Ambler, "Category Management Is Best Deployed for Brand Positioning," *Marketing*, p. 18 November 29, 2001; and Harriet Marsh, "Why New Look Must Take Stock," *Marketing*, March 29, 2001. p. 17

15. Amy Merrick, "Tired of Trendiness, Former Shoppers Leave Gap, Defect to Competitors," *The Wall Street Journal*, December 6, 2001. p. B-1

16. S. A. Shaw and J. Gibbs, "Procurement Strategies of Small Retailers Faced with Uncertainty: An Analysis of Channel Choice and Behaviour," *International Review of Retail, Distribution and Consumer Research* 9, no. 1 (1999), pp. 61–75.

17. "Global Brands Face Up to International Retailing," *Marketing Week*, October 26, 2000, p. 32.

18. Mary Jo Bitner, "Self-Service Technologies: What Do Customers Expect?" *Marketing Management*, Spring 2001; Mary Jo Bitner, Steven W. Brown, and Matthew L. Meuter, "Technology Infusion in Service Encounters," *Journal of the Academy of Marketing Science*, March 2000; Mary Jo Bitner and Valerie Zeithaml, *Services Marketing*, 2nd ed. (Burr Ridge, IL: McGraw-Hill/Irwin, 1999); Leonard Berry, "Relationship Marketing of Services Growing Interest: Emerging Perspectives," *Journal of the Academy of Marketing Science* 23 (Fall 1995), pp. 236–45; and Mary Jo Bitner, "Building Service Relationships: It's All about Promises," *Journal of the Academy of Marketing Science* 23 (Fall 1995), pp. 246–51.

19. "Speaking the Language of the Consumer," *Chain Store Age*, December 2000, pp. 119–128.

20. Werther and Kerr, "The Shifting Sands of Competitive Advantage."

21. Aaves, *Strategic Market Management*, chap. 12; and Roger Kerin, Vijay Mahajan, and P. Rajan Varadarajan, *Contemporary Perspectives on Strategic Market Planning* (Boston: Allyn & Bacon, 1991), chap. 6. See also Susan Mudambi, "A Topology of Strategic Choice in Retailing," *International Journal of Retail & Distribution Management*, 1994, pp. 22–25.

22. Ian Murphy, "Marketers Ponder P-O-P in Stores of the Future," *Marketing News*, May 26, 1997, p. 2.

23. Erin White, "Abercrombie Seeks to Send Teeny-Boppers Packing," *The Wall Street Journal*, August 30, 2001, pp. B1, B4.

24. Sarah Ellison, "Carrefour Finds It Difficult to Build Single Global Brand," *The Wall Street Journal*, August 30, 2001. www.wsj.com

25. Tara Murphy, "Foot Locker Poised to Perform," March 26, 2002, www.forbes.com.

26. Anita McGahan, "Sustaining Superior Profits: Customer and Supplier Relationships," *Harvard Business Online*, http://harvardbusinessonline.hbsp.harvard.edu March 1, 1999, pp. 1–7; and Randolph Beard, "Regulation, Vertical Integration and Sabotage," *Journal of Industrial Economics* 49, no. 3, (2001), pp. 319–33.

27. Rebecca Mead, "Brooks Brothers a Go-Go," *New Yorker Magazine*, March 22, 1999, p. 88.

28. Geoff Wissman, "Critical Issues: The Top 100 Retailers Worldwide 2000," Retail Forward, Inc., August 2001, p. 16.

29. Bernard Wysocki, Jr., "In Developing Nations, Many Youth Are Big Spenders," *The Wall Street Journal*, June 26, 1997, pp. A1, A11.

30. Elisabeth Rosenthal, "Buicks, Starbucks and Fried Chicken. Still China?" *New York Times*, February 25, 2002. www.NYTimes.com

31. Wissman, "Critical Issues," p. 14.

32. Ibid.; David Woodruff, "For French Retailers, a Weapon against Wal-Mart," *The Wall Street Journal*, September 27, 1999, pp. B1, B4; and David Woodruff, "Carrefour Is Mounting a Push into Japanese Markets," *The Wall Street Journal*, June 15, 1999, p. B7.

33. "Retailers Are Trying to Go Global," *The Economist Newspaper* (U.S. ed.), June 19, 1999, p. 1.

34. "The World Is Not Their Oyster," *Chain Store Age*, May, 2001, p. 60.

35. This section is adapted from, "Winning Moves on a Global Chessboard: Wal-Mart and Costco in a Global Context," Goldman Sachs Investment Research, May 12, 2000.

36. Wissman, "Critical Issues," p. 2.

37. Lisa Penaloza and Mary Gilly, "Marketer Acculturation: The Changer and the Changed," *Journal Of Marketing* 63 (Summer 1999), pp. 84–95.

38. Ellison, "Carrefour Finds It Difficult to Build Single Global Brand." www.wsj.com

39. Erik Gordon, "Taking the Plunge?" *Chain Store Age Supplement*, December 1997, pp. 14–23; and "Shopping the World," *The Economist Newspaper*, June 18, 1999, pp. 1–2.

40. "Handcuffs on High Street," *The Economist*, May 13, 2000, p. 62.

41. Ibid.

42. Ibid.

43. Jean-Pierre Jeannet and H. David Hennessey, *Global Marketing Strategies*, 5th ed., (Boston: Houghton Mifflin, 2000); and "What's the Best Way to Set Up Shop?" *Chain Store Age Global Retailing Supplement*, December 1997, pp. 32–35.

44. Greg Silverman and David Wasserman, "Retailing in Latin America," Global Retail Forward, July 2001, p. 13; Stephanie Shamroski, "Retailing in Turkey," Global Retail Forward, January 2000, p. 6; Ira Kalish and Stephanie Shamroski, "Global Retail Intelligencer," Global Retail Forward, April 2001, p. 2; Philip Walker, "Retailing in India," Global Retail Forward, March 2000, p. 12; Lois Huff and Stephanie Shamroski, "Retailing in the United Kingdom," Global Retail Forward, December 2000, p. 17; and Marianne Wilson, "Thinking Big," Chain Store Age, July 1, 2001, p. 47.

45. "An Opening Door Policy," Chain Store Age, January 2000, pp. 62–63.

46. www.marksandspencer.com.

47. Donald Lehman and Russell Winer, Analysis for Marketing Planning, 5th. ed. (Burr Ridge, IL: McGraw-Hill/Irwin, 2001); and Aaker, Strategic Market Management.

48. Andrew Campbell, "Mission Statements," Long Range Planning 30 (December 1997), pp. 931–33.

49. Alfred Rappaport, Creating Shareholder Value: The New Standard for Business Performance (New York: Wiley, 1988); Robert C. Higgins and Roger A. Kerin, "Managing the Growth-Financial Policy Nexus in Retailing," Journal of Retailing 59, no. 3 (Fall 1983), pp. 19–47; and Kerin, Mahajan, and Varadarajan, Contemporary Perspectives on Strategic Market Planning, chap. 6.

50. See Linda Gatley and David Clutterbuck, "Superdrug Crafts a Mission Statement," International Journal of Retail & Distribution Management 26 (October–November 1998), pp. 10–11, for an interesting example of the process used by a U.K. drugstore chain to develop a mission statement.

51. Aaker, Strategic Market Management.

52. www.catofashions.com.

53. Michael Porter, "Strategy and the Internet," Harvard Business Review, March 2001, pp. 63–78; and Michael Porter, Competitive Strategy (New York: Free Press, 1980).

54. "The Estée Lauder Companies Inc.," Hoovers Online, 2002, www.hoovers.com/premium/profile/8/0,2147,40148,00.html.

55. "L'Oréal SA," Hoovers Online, 2002, www.hoovers.com/premium/profile/2/0,2147,41772,00.html.

56. Terry Clark, P. Rajan Varadarajan, and William M. Pride, "Environmental Management: The Construct and Research Propositions," Journal of Business Research 29, no. 1 (January 1994), pp. 23–39; James Lang, Roger Calantone, and Donald Gudmundson, "Small Firm Information Seeking as a Response to Environmental Threats and Opportunities," Journal of Small Business Management, January 1997, pp. 11–29; and Masoud Yasai-Ardekani and Paul Nystrom, "Designs for Environmental Scanning Systems: Tests of a Contingency Theory," Management Science 42 (February 1996), pp. 187–204.

57. Bill Quinn, How Wal-Mart Is Destroying America (and the World): And What You Can Do about It (Ten Speed Press, 2000).

58. Erin White, "Retail Brand Buys Brooks Brothers from Marks & Spencer for $225 Million," The Wall Street Journal, November 23, 2001 wsj.com; and Andrew Ross Sorkin, "Owner of Casual Corner Chain in Deal for Brooks Brothers," New York Times, November 23, 2001. NYTimes.com

59. Aaker, Strategic Market Management; G. Stalk, "Competing on Capabilities: The New Rules of Corporate Strategy," Harvard Business Review, March–April 1992, pp. 51–69; and Donna Cartwright, Paul Boughton, and Stephen Miller, "Competitive Intelligence Systems: Relationships to Strategic Orientation and Perceived Usefulness," Journal of Managerial Issues 7 (Winter 1995), pp. 420–34.

60. Cindy Guier, "Cosmic Bowling Strikes at Whole New Audience," Amusement Business, May 18, 1998, pp. 20–24.

61. See Aaker, Strategic Market Management, chap. 7; and Kerin, Mahajan, and Varadarajan, Contemporary Perspectives, chap. 3. Another matrix that is often used in strategic planning is the Boston Consulting Group (BCG) market growth/market share matrix. Rather than considering all of the factors that determine market attractiveness and competitive position, the BCG matrix focuses on just two factors: market growth and market share. Research indicates that concentrating on these two factors may result in poor strategic decisions. See Robin Wensley, "Strategic Marketing: Betas, Boxes, and Basics," Journal of Marketing 45 (Summer 1981), pp. 173–82, for a critical analysis of these approaches.

62. "Global Retailing: Asian Assignment," Chain Store Age Executive, January 1995, sect. 2, p. 5.

Chapter 6

1. "Harper's Index," Harpers, February 1994, p. 13.

2. Robert D. Hof and Heather Green, "How Amazon Cleared the Hurdle," Business Week, February 4, 2002.

3. "Top 100 Retailers," 2001, www.stores.org; and www.freeedgar.com.

4. James Surowiecki, "The Most Devasting Retailer in the World," The New Yorker, September 18, 2000, p. 74.

5. Average retail inventory is estimated from the balance sheet inventory. Assume the end-of-year inventory on the balance sheet is average cost inventory. Average retail inventory = Average cost inventory/1 − Gross margin percent (expressed as decimal).

6. Although the use of asset turnover presented here is helpful for gaining appreciation of the performance ratio, capital budgeting or present value analyses are more appropriate for determining long-term return of a fixed asset.

7. Bryan Gildenberg, Mventures, personal communication, February 2002.

8. All categories of stock, including preferred, paid-in capital, and treasury stock, are included with common stock for simplicity.

9. www.edgar-online.com.

10. "A Strong and Useful Light," *Harvard Business Review* 80, no. 5 (May 2002), p. 12.; John D. Sterman and Nelson P. Repenning, "Nobody Ever Gets Credit for Fixing Problems That Never Happened: Creating and Sustaining Process Improvement," *Harvard Business Online*, July 1, 2001; Loren Gary, "The Right Kind of Failure," *Harvard Management*, update article, January 1, 2002; Gary Sutton, *The Six-Month Fix: Adventures in Rescuing Failing Companies* (New York: John Wiley & Sons, November 2001); and Bernard Salanie, *The Microeconomics of Market Failures* (Boston: MIT Press, November 2000).

11. Average retail inventory is estimated from the balance sheet inventory. Assume the end-of-year inventory on the balance sheet is average cost inventory. Average retail inventory = average cost inventory/1 – gross margin percent (expressed as a decimal).

12. www.hoovers.com.

13. John L. Daly, *Pricing for Profitability: Activity-Based Pricing for Competitive Advantage* (New York: John Wiley & Sons, October 2001); Don R. Hansen and Maryanne M. Mowen, *Cost Management: Accounting and Control* (Cincinnati: South-Western College Publishing, March 2002); Reginald Tomas Yu-Lee, *Explicit Cost Dynamics: An Alternative to Activity-Based Costing* (New York: John Wiley & Sons, February 2001); David E. Keys and Robert J. Lefevre, "Why Is 'Integrated' ABC Better?" *Journal of Corporate Accounting & Finance* 13, no. 3 (March–April 2002), pp. 45–53; and Mohan Nair, "Helping Ensure Successful Implementations of Activity-Based Management," *Journal of Corporate Accounting & Finance* 13, no. 2 (January–February 2002), pp. 73–86.

Chapter 7

1. Kelly Green, "Once-Mighty Avondale Closes Its Doors after Losing Battle against Discounters," *The Wall Street Journal*, December 12, 2001; based on research by National Research Bureau of Chicago and the U.S. Census. www.wsj.com

2. Connie Robbins Gentry, "Groceries, Gap and Rave Girl?" *Chain Store Age*, March 2001, pp. 154–56.

3. "Back to the Future," *New York Times Magazine*, April 6, 1997, pp. 48–49.

4. Green, "Once-Mighty Avondale Closes Its Doors"; based on research from Michael Beyard, Urban Land Institute.

5. Eddie Baeb, "A Mall Struggles to Defend Its Glitz," *Crain's Chicago Business* 23, no. 9 (February 29, 2000), p. 3; Elin Schoen Brockman, "As Malls Die, the Next Generation Re-Creates the Past," *New York Times*, August 8, 1999, p. 4; Kevin Kenyon, "Power Moves: New Formats Help Developers Rejuvenate Enclosed Centers," *Shopping Centers Today*, October 8, 1999; and Herb Greenberg, "Dead Mall Walking," *Fortune* 141, no. 9 (May 1, 2000), p. 304.

6. Debra Hazel, "Demalling for Dollars," *Shopping Centers Today*, January 2, 2001; and Suzette Hill, "To De-Mall or E-Mall? Shaping Web Shopping," *Apparel Industry Magazine* 61, no. 2 (February 2000), pp. 36–38.

7. "$11.6 Billion Expected for Online Holiday Shopping—Study," Newsbytes News Network, November 13, 2000; based on a study by Jupiter Research.

8. Kevin Kenyon, "Mall of America turns Trash into Cash," *Shopping Centers Today*, www.icsc.org/srch/sctl. October 1997, pp. 5–6.

9. Edmund Mander, "Defining a Hot Concept Lifestyle Centers Elude Classification," *Shopping Centers Today*, August 2001, pp. 1, 44–45; Dean Starkman, "The Mall, without the Haul," *The Wall Street Journal*, July 25, 2001, pp. B1, B8; and Dan Peter, "Retail Looks toward New Lifestyle, Continues to Prosper," *Midwest Real Estate News*, July 2001.

10. Mander, "Defining a Hot Concept Lifestyle Centers Elude Classification."

11. Lois Huff and Stephanie Shamroski, "Outlet Centers: The Search for Value," Retail Forward, Inc., May 2001.

12. Ray A. Smith, "Outlet Centers in the U.S. Turn Upmarket in Amenities," *The Asian Wall Street Journal*, June 8, 3002, p. 11.

13. "Back to the Future."

14. Barbara Hogan Galvin, "Outlet Center Challenge," *Shopping Centers Today*, June 2001, pp. 25–28.

15. "Handcuffs on High Street," *The Economist*, May 13, 2000, p. 62.

16. Sarah Raper, "Gap's Tour de Force," *WWD*, July 1, 1999, p. 3.

17. "East 57th Street Again Tops Retail List Highest Rents in the World," *New York Times* www.nytimes.com, December 9, 2001.

18. Frank Green, "Core Values; Retailers Moving into Inner-City Areas Find That It's Just Good Business," *San Diego Union-Tribune*, November 18, 2001.

19. Personal communication, Cynthia Cohen, CEO, Strategic Mindshare, April 2002.

20. Ibid.

21. Mark Blaxil and Jean Mixer, "The Business Case for Pursuing Retail Opportunities in the Inner City." The Boston Consulting Group. (June 1998) pp. 1–31

22. Joanne Gordon, "Saks Appeal," *Chain Store Age*, May 1998, pp. 85–90; and Tara Weingarten, "Main Street vs. the Mall: Part II, the Comeback," *Newsweek*, June 8, 1998, p. 12.

23. Dina L. Boghdady, "For Urban Home Depots, Less May Be More," *Washington Post*, March 28, 2001, p. E01.

24. Connie Robbins Gentry, "The Rebirth of City Development," *Chain Store Age*, May 2000, pp. 83–90.

25. Bill Levine, "The Store Stands Alone," *Chain Store Age*, April 1998, pp. 107–8; research attributed to F. W. Dodge/The McGraw-Hill Cos., Lexington, Kentucky.

26. Joe Gose, "Country Club Plaza Rides Again," Reed Business Information, September 2001. www.reedbusiness.com/index.asp?layout=cahnerscom

27. Jennifer Steinhauser, "It's a Mall . . ., It's an Airport," *New York Times*, June 10, 1998, pp. C1, C4.

28. "Airport 2000," *VM & SD*, December 2000, pp. 40, 42, 44; research attributed to Aviation Consumer Action Project.

29. "Resorts Generate Lucrative Retail Revenues," *Chain Store Age*, June 2000, pp. 150–153.

30. Sheila Muto, "A Frappuccino with Your X-Ray? Hospitals Turn to Retail Stores to Lure Staff and Cash," *The Wall Street Journal* www.wsj.com, November 7, 2001.

31. John McCloud, "The World Beckons American Retail," *Shopping Center World*, May 1998, pp. 23–34.

32. Lisa Holton, "Policies Protect Tenants, Developers from Unseen Environmental Risks," Stores, February 1996, p. 64.

Chapter 8

1. Connie Robbins Gentry, "Site Unseen," *Chain Store Age*, October 1, 2000, p. 153.

2. Michael E. Porter, *Competitive Strategy: Techniques for Analyzing Industries and Competitors* (Simon & Schuster Trade, 1998).

3. "Company Profile," Hoovers Online, June 2002, www.hoovers.com.

4. Erik Gordon, "Taking the Plunge?" *Chain Store Age Global Retailing Supplement*, Ernst & Young, December 1997, pp. 14–23.

5. Robert W. Buckner, *Site Selection: New Advancements in Methods and Technology* (New York: Lebhar-Friedman Books, 1998), p. 18.

6. Karen A. Machleit, Sevgin A. Eroglu, and Susan Powell Mantel, "Perceived Retail Crowding and Shopping Satisfaction: What Modifies This Relationship?" *Journal of Consumer Psychology* 9, no. 1 (2000), p. 29.

7. Buckner, *Site Selection*, pp. 31–32.

8. Buckner, *Site Selection*, chap. 15; and Christian Harder, *GIS Means Business* (Redlands, CA: Environmental Systems Research Institute, Inc., 1997).

9. Harder, *GIS Means Business*, p. 1.

10. William H. Frey, "Boomer Havens and Young Adult Magnets," *American Demographics* 23, no. 9 (September 2001), pp. 22–24.

11. Buckner, *Site Selection*.

12. G. L. Drummey, "Traditional Methods of Sales Forecasting," in *Store Location and Store Assessment Research*, eds. R. L. Davies and D. S. Rogers (New York: John Wiley & Sons, 1984), pp. 279–99.

13. We illustrated Edward Beiner's trade area in Exhibit 8–4 by defining the drive times to the store. To simplify this analysis, we've defined its primary trade area as the three-mile circle around the store rather than the drive time polygons described earlier.

14. Buckner, *Site Selection*, chap. 8.

15. John S. Thompson, *Site Selection* (New York: Lebhar-Friedman, 1982), pp. 13–40.

16. David L. Huff, "Defining and Estimating a Trade Area," *Journal of Marketing* 28 (1964), pp. 34–38; and David L. Huff and William Black, "The Huff Model in Retrospect," *Applied Geographic Studies* 1, no. 2 (1997), pp. 22–34.

17. W. J. Reilly, *The Laws of Retail Gravitation* (New York: Knickerbocker Press, 1931); P. D. Converse, "New Laws of Retail Gravitation," *Journal of Marketing* 14 (1949), pp. 379–84; and Walter Christaller, *Central Places in Southern Germany*, 1935, trans. Carlisle W. Baskin (Englewood Cliffs, NJ: Prentice Hall, 1966).

18. Buckner, *Site Selection*, chap. 15.

Chapter 9

1. Susan Jackson and Randall Schuler, *Managing Human Resources Through Strategic Relationships*, 8th ed. (Mason, OH: Southwestern, 2003); p. 5.

2. *Merchandising and Operations Costs Report* (New York: Fairchild Publications, 1999).

3. Michael Bergdal, "Our 'People' Culture Is a Major Competitive Asset," *Stores*, April 1999, pp. 114–15; Raphael Amit, "Human Resources Management Processes: A Value-Creating Source of Competitive Advantage," *European Management Journal*, April 1999, pp. 174–82; Tim Ambler, "Valuing Human Assets," *Business Strategy Review* 10 (Spring 1999), pp. 57–58; Tony Grundy, "How Are Corporate Strategy and Human Resources Strategy Linked?" *Journal of General Management* 23 (Spring 1998), pp. 49–73; and Gerard Farias, "High Performance Work Systems: What We Know and What We Need to Know," *Human Resource Planning* 21 (June 1998), pp. 50–55.

4. Anthony Rucci, Steven Kirn, and Richard T. Quinn, "The Employee–Customer–Profit Chain at Sears," *Harvard Business Review*, January–February 1998, pp. 82–97.

5. Jeffrey Pfeffer, *The Human Equation* (Boston: Harvard Business School Press, 1998), pp. 26–28.

6. D. Roth, "My Job at the Container Store," *Fortune*, January 10, 2000, pp. 74–78.

7. *Retailing: Mirror on America* (Washington, DC: National Retailer Federation, 2002).

8. Jackson and Schuler, *Managing Human Resources*, p. 69.

9. John A. Challenger, "The Changing Workforce," *Vital Speeches*, September 15, 2001, pp. 721–25; and JoAnn Greco, "America's Changing Workforce," *Journal of Business Strategy* 19 (March–April 1998), pp. 43–47.

10. Pawan S. Budhwar and Yaw A. Debrah, eds., *Human Resource Management in Developing Countries* (London & New York: Routledge, 2001); and Christopher Earley and Harbir Singh, eds. *Innovations in International and Cross-Cultural Management* (Thousand Oaks, CA: Sage Publications, 2000).

11. "Wal around the World," *The Economist*, December 8, 2001, p. 8; and "Pooled Assets," *Chain Store Age*, June 1, 2001, p. 50.

12. Michael Gold and Andrew Campbell, "Do You Have a Well-Designed Organization?" *Harvard Business Review,* March 2002, pp. 117–25; and Richard L. Daft, *Essentials of Organization Theory and Design,* 2nd ed. (Cincinnati: South-Western College Publishing, 2000).

13. *Census of Retail Trade* (Washington, DC: U.S. Department of Commerce, Bureau of the Census, 1999), p. 15.

14. "Business Antiquities," *The Wall Street Journal,* November 17, 1999, p. B1.

15. Data for 2000 from www.federated-fds.com/retail/rlg_1_3.asp.

16. Paul M. Mazur, *Principles of Organization Applied to Modern Retailing* (New York: Harper & Brothers, 1927).

17. *2002 Corporate Fact Book* (Cincinnati, OH: Federated Department Stores, 2002).

18. Walter Loeb, "Unbundling or Centralize: What Is the Answer?" *Retailing Issues Letter* (College Station: Center for Retailing Studies, Texas A&M University, May 1992).

19. "Saturday Morning Fever," *The Economist,* December 8, 2001, p. 30.

20. John Caulfield, "Depot Puts Buying Power in the Hands of a Dozen," *National Home Center News,* September 3, 2001, p. 1; and "Retailing's New Trinity: J.C. Penney Co," *DNR,* February 12, 2001, p. 30.

21. Manfred Krafft, "An Empirical Investigation of the Antecedents of Sales Force Control Systems," *Journal of Marketing* 63 (Summer 1999), pp. 120–34; Bernard Jaworski, "Toward a Theory of Marketing Control: Environmental Context, Control Types, and Consequences," *Journal of Marketing* 52 (July 1988), pp. 23–39; and William Ouchi, "A Conceptual Framework for the Design of Organizational Control Mechanisms," *Management Science* 25 (September 1979), pp. 833–49.

22. Jackson and Schuler, *Managing Human Resources,* p. 405.

23. Ibid., p. 525.

24. Patrica Sellers, "Can Home Depot Fix Its Sagging Stock?" *Fortune,* March 4, 1996, pp. 139–45; and Bob Ortega, "What Does Wal-Mart Do if Stock Drop Cuts into Workers' Morale?" *The Wall Street Journal,* January 4, 1995, pp. A1, A5.

25. Jeffrey Pfeffer, "Six Dangerous Myths about Pay," *Harvard Business Review,* May–June 1998, pp. 109–29.

26. William Bliss, "Why Is Corporate Culture Important?" *Workforce* 78 (February 1999), pp. W8–W10; W. Matthew Juechter, "Five Conditions for High-Performance Cultures," *Training & Development* 52 (May 1998), pp. 63–68; and Andrew Chan, "Corporate Culture of a Clan Organization," *Management Decision,* January–February 1997, pp. 94–100.

27. Beverly Kaye and Betsy Jacobson, "True Tales and Tall Tales: The Power of Organizational Storytelling," *Training & Development* (March 1999), pp. 44–51; and Nancy L. Breuer, "The Power of Storytelling," *Workforce* (December 1998); pp. 36–42.

28. Roth, *Fortune,* pp 75.

29. Hal Lancaster, "Herb Kelleher Has One Strategy: Treat Employees Well," *The Wall Street Journal,* August 31, 1999, p. B1; John Huey, "The Jack and Herb Show," *Fortune,* January 11, 1999, pp. 163–64; and Ronald Lieber, "Why Employees Love These Companies," *Fortune,* January 12, 1998, pp. 72–75.

30. This section is based on Chapter 3 in Jeffrey Pfeffer, *The Human Equation* (Boston: Harvard Business School Press, 1998).

31. "Workers Are Seeking Employers of Choice," *Chain Store Age,* October 1998, p. 72.

32. Gary Desller, "How to Earn Your Employees' Commitment," *Academy of Management Executive* 13 (May 1999), pp. 58–59; Deb McCusker, "Loyalty in the Eyes of Employers and Employees," *Workforce,* November 1998, pp. 23–28; and David L. Stum, "Five Ingredients for an Employee Retention Formula," *HR Focus,* September 1998, pp. S9–S11

33. Shari Caudron, "How HR Drives Profits: Academic Research and Real-World Experience Show How HR Practices Affect the Bottom Line," *Workforce,* December 2001, pp. 26–30; and "HR's New Role: Creating Value," *HR Focus,* January 2000, pp. 1–4.

34. Ling Sing Chee, "Singapore Airlines: Strategic Human Resource Initiatives," in *International Human Resource Management: Think Globally and Act Locally,* ed. Derek Torrington (New York: Prentice Hall, 1994), pp. 314–330.

35. "State of the Industry Operational Management," *Chain Store Age,* August 1, 1998, p. 17A.

36. Michael Hartnett, "Men's Wearhouse Tailors Employee Support Programs," *Stores,* August 1996, pp. 46–49.

37. Jackson and Schuler, *Managing Human Resources,* p. 19.

38. Catherine Yang, "Low-Wage Lessons," *Business Week,* November 11, 1996, pp. 108–16.

39. Graham L. Bradley and Beverley A. Sparks, "Customer Reactions to Staff Empowerment: Mediators and Moderators," *Journal of Applied Social Psychology,* May 2000, pp. 991–1003; Martin Beirne, "Managing to Empower? A Healthy Review of Resources and Constraints," *European Management Journal,* April 1999, pp. 218–26; and Mohammed Rafiq, "A Customer-Oriented Framework for Empowering Service Employees," *Journal of Services Marketing* 12 (May–June 1998), pp. 379–97.

40. Jackson and Schuler, *Managing Human Resources,* p. 141.

41. "Why Going Back to the Floor Ensures Execs Stay in Touch," *Retail Week,* November 16, 2001, p. 31.

42. Shankar Ganesan and Barton Weitz, "The Impact of Staffing Policies on Retail Buyer Job Attitudes and Behaviors," *Journal of Retailing,* Spring 1996, pp. 231–45.

43. Janet Wiscombe, "Flex Appeal—Not Just for Moms," *Workforce,* March 2002, p. 18; Leslie Faught, "At Eddie Bauer You Can Work and Have a Life," *Workforce,* April 1997, pp. 83–88; and Davan Maharaj, "A Suitable Schedule: Flextime Gains as Employers Agree There's More to Life than Work," *Los Angeles Times,* July 10, 1998, p. D2.

44. Charles J. Hobson, Linda Delunas, and Dawn Kesic, "Compelling Evidence of the Need for Corporate Work/Life Balance Initiatives: Results from a National Survey of Stressful Life-Events," *Journal of Employment Counseling*, March 2001, pp. 38–42; and Jeffrey Hill, Alan J. Hawkins, Maria Ferris, and Michelle Weitzman, "Finding an Extra Day a Week: The Positive Influence of Perceived Job Flexibility on Work and Family Life Balance," *Family Relations*, January 2001, pp. 49–57.

45. R. Roosevelt Thomas, "From Affirmative Action to Diversity," *Harvard Business Review*, March–April 1990, pp. 107–17.

46. "Diversity Programs Become Valuable Tools for Increased Profitability," *Black Enterprise*, July 1998, pp. 120–21.

47. Kathleen Iverson, "Managing for Effective Workforce Diversity," *Cornell Hotel & Restaurant Administration Quarterly*, April 2000, pp. 2–7; Parshotam Dass, "Strategies for Managing Human Resource Diversity: From Resistance to Learning," *Academy of Management Executive* 13 (May 1999), pp. 68–69; and Philip Rosenzweig, "Strategies for Managing Diversity," *Financial Times*, March 6, 1998, pp 6–9.

48. Audrey J. Murrell, Faye J. Crosby, and Robin J. Ely, eds., *Mentoring Dilemmas: Developmental Relationships within Multicultural Organizations* (Mahwah, NJ: Erlbaum, 1999); Max Messmer, "Mentoring: Building Your Company's Intellectual Capital," *HR Focus*, September 1998, pp. S11–S13; and Erik Van Slyke, "Mentoring: A Results-Oriented Approach," *HR Focus*, February 1998, pp. 14–15.

49. "80 Most Influential People in Sales and Marketing," *Sales & Marketing Management*, October 1998, p. 78.

50. Linda Wirth, *Breaking through the Glass Ceiling: Women in Management* (Washington DC: International Labour Office, 2001); Sheila Wellington, "Cracking the Ceiling," *Time*, December 7, 1998, p. 187; Alison Maitland, "Cracks Appear in Glass Ceiling," *Financial Times*, April 8, 1999, p. 22; and Tammy Reiss, "More Cracks in the Glass Ceiling," *Business Week*, August 10, 1998, p. 6.

51. Ken Clark, "Ready or Not, Here Comes OSHA," *Chain Store Age*, March 1, 2001, p. 94.

52. A. Colquitt, "On the Dimensionality of Organizational Justice: A Construct Validation of a Measure," *Journal of Applied Psychology* 86 (2001), pp. 386–400.

53. Denise Power, "Penney's Human Resources Goes Self-Service," *WWD*, June 23, 1999, p. 13.

54. Mary Wagner, "Don't Call Us," *Internet Retailer*, June 2002, pp. 8–9.

Chapter 10

1. Douglas M. Lambert, Martha C. Cooper, and Janus D. Pagh, "Supply Chain Management: Implementation Issues and Research Opportunities," *International Journal of Logistics Management* 9, no. 2 (1998), p. 1.

2. "Hoovers Company Capsule," Hoovers Online, May 2002, www.hoovers.com.

3. William H. Inmon, *Building the Datawarehouse* (New York: John Wiley & Sons, Inc., 2002).

4. Susan Reda, "Internet-EDI Initiatives Show Potential to Reinvent Supply Chain Management," *Stores*, January 1999, pp. 26–27.

5. Liz Parks, "Transforming the Supply Chain with Technology," *Drug Store News*, July 19, 1999, p. 10.

6. Presented at the annual business meeting, Council of Logistics Management, Anaheim, CA, October 1998. The definition is posted at the CLM's homepage, www.CLM1.org.

7. Martha C. Cooper, Douglas M. Lambert, and Janus D. Pagh, "Supply Chain Management: More Than a New Name for Logistics," *International Journal of Logistics Management* 8, no. 1 (1997), pp. 1–14.

8. Alan Goldstein, "Logistics Goes High-Tech to Figure Demand in Dallas Area," *Knight Ridder Tribune Business News*, April 21, 2002, p. 1.

9. Susan Reda, "Crossdocking: Can Supermarkets Catch Up?" Stores Online, November 9, 2001, www.stores.org.

10. Connie Robbins Gentry, "From Warehouse to Powerhouse," *Chain Store Age*, September 2001, pp. 90–93.

11. Jan Hammond and Kristin Kohler, "In the Virtual Dressing Room Returns Are a Real Problem," HBS Working Knowledge, www.hbsworkingknowledge.hbs.edu, April 15, 2002.

12. "Returns Don't Need to Cost So Much," *Internet Retailer*, www.internetretailer.com May 23, 2002.

13. "Auctioning Returned Goods Online Is Tougher than Anticipated, Genco Says," Internetretailer.com, May 23, 2002; "Sears Nets Greater Return by Moving Surplus Inventory to Online Auctions," Internetretailer.com, March, 2002.

14. Ken Clark, "Coping with Returns," *Chain Store Age*, November 1, 2000, p. 124; based on focus group research conducted by the Reverse Logistics Executive Council and the University of Nevada's Center for Logistics Management.

15. "Flow-Through DC Yields Savings for Fred Meyer," *Chain Store Age*, October 1995, pp. 64–66; quote by Mary Sammons, senior vice president, Fred Meyer.

16. Barbara E. Kahn and Leigh McAlister, *Grocery Revolution: The New Focus on the Consumer* (Reading, MA: Longman, Addison-Wesley, 1997).

17. James Surowiecki, "The Most Devastating Retailer in the World," *The New Yorker*, September 18, 2000, p. 74; and William Echikson, "The Mark of Zara," *Business Week*, May 29, 2000, p. 98.

18. Laurie Joan Aron, "Delivering on E-Commerce," *Chain Store Age*, June 1999, pp. 130–31.

19. James R. Stock and Douglas Lambert, *Strategic Logistics Management*, 4th ed. (New York: McGraw-Hill, 2000).

Chapter 11

1. Fredrick Reichfeld, *The Loyalty Effect* (Cambridge, MA: Harvard Business School Press, 1996).

2. See Stephanie Coyles and Timothy Gokey, "Customer Retention Is Not Enough," *McKinsey Quarterly* 2 (2002), pp. 3–14.

3. Anna S. Mattila, "Emotional Bonding and Restaurant Loyalty," *Cornell Hotel and Restaurant Administration Quarterly*, December 2001, pp. 73–80; and Susan Fournier, Susan Dobscha, and David Glen Mick, "Preventing the Premature Death of Relationship Marketing," *Harvard Business Review*, January–February 1998, pp. 42–50.

4. Dwayne Gremler and Kevin Gwinner, "Customer–Employee Service Relationships," *Journal of Service Research* 3 (February 2000), pp. 82–104; and C. Walkup, "Restaurants Where Everybody Knows Your Name Enjoy Loyalty," *Nation's Restaurant News*, 34 (July 2000), p. 24.

5. Presented at 2002 Retailing Smarter symposium sponsored by the Miller Center for Retailing Education and Research, University of Florida, June 2002, Orlando.

6. B. Joseph Pine and James Gilmore, *Experience Economy: Work Is Theatre and Every Business a Stage* (Boston: Harvard Business Press, 1999).

7. CyberAtlas, January 23, 2002, www.cyberatlas. internet.com.

8. Frank Badillo, *Retail Perspectives on Customer Relationship Management* (Columbus, OH: Retail Forward, February 2001), p. 33.

9. "Cooking Up a Deep-Dish Database," *Business Week*, November 20, 1995, p. 160.

10. Lorie Grant, "Why Cashiers Want Your Digits?" *USA Today*, April 23, 2002, p. B1.

11. Mark Albright, "Peddling Prestige," *St. Petersburg Times*, August 22, 2001, p. 8E.

12. Doris Hajewski, "Small Grocer Keeps Pace by Marketing Loyalty," *Milwaukee Journal Sentinel*, May 1, 2002, p. B1.

13. Badillo, *Retail Perspectives on Customer Relationship Management*, pp. 11–12.

14. Ibid., p. 9

15. George Milne, "Privacy and Ethical Issues in Database/Interactive Marketing and Public Policy: A Research Framework and Overview of the Special Issue," *Journal of Public Policy and Marketing* 19 (Spring 2000), pp. 1–7.

16. Dan Scheraga, "Courting the Customer," *Chain Store Age*, January 2000, p. 88; Ro Panepinto, "Preventative Customer Care," *Response*, October 1999, pp. 46–53; and Steve Larsen, "Personalization without Privacy Won't Sell: Build Trust by Keeping Customers Informed," *Internet Retailer*, November 1999, p. 70.

17. Mary Culnan, "Protecting Privacy Online: Is Self-Regulation Working?" *Journal of Public Policy and Marketing* 19 (Spring 2000), pp. 20–26.

18. H. Jeff Smith, "Information Privacy and Marketing: What the U.S. Should (and Shouldn't) Learn from Europe," *California Management Review* 43, no. 2 (Winter 2001); pp. 8–34.

19. Christopher Robertson and Ravi Sarathy, "Digital Privacy: A Pragmatic Guide for Senior Managers Charged with Developing a Strategic Policy for Handling Privacy Issues," *Business Horizons* 45 (January–February 2002), pp. 2–6.

20. Jill Dyche, *The CRM Handbook* (Upper Saddle River, NJ.:Addison-Wesley, 2002), pp. 134–5.

21. "Data Mining/CRM: Search for an ROI," *Chain Store Age*, October 1, 2001, p. 24.

22. Badillo, *Retail Perspectives in Customer Relationship Management*, p. 25.

23. "Retailers Plan to Invest in CRM in 2002," CyberAtlas, January 23, 2002, www.cyberatlas.internet.com.

24. Valarie Zeithaml, Roland Rust, and Katherine Lemon, "The Customer Pyramid: Creating and Serving Profitable Customers," *California Management Review* 43 (Summer 2001), p. 124.

25. See Werner Reinartz and V. Kumar, "On the Profitability of Long-Life Customers in a Noncontractual Setting: An Empirical Investigation and Implications for Marketing," *Journal of Marketing* 64 (October 2000), pp. 17–33, for an examination of programs designed to develop long-term relationships.

26. James Cigliano, Margaret Georgladis, Darren Pleasance, and Susan Whalley, "The Price of Loyalty," *McKinsey Quarterly* 4 (2000), p. 69.

27. Ibid., p. 73.

28. Ken Gofton, "Pinpointing Loyalty," *Marketing*, January 21, 1999, p. 65.

29. Graham Dowling and Mark Uncles, "Do Customer Loyalty Programs Really Work?" *Sloan Management Review* 38 (Summer 1007), pp. 71–82.

30. Cigliano, Georgladis, Pleasance, and Whalley, "The Price of Loyalty," p. 70.

31. "Loyalty: At What Cost?" *Marketing*, May 16, 2002, pp. 48–50.

32. "Why Service Stinks?" *Business Week Online*, October 23, 2000.

33. Roland Rust, Valarie Zeithaml, and Katherine Lemon, *Driving Customer Equity* (New York: Free Press, 2002), chap. 13.

34. Badillo, *Retail Perspectives on Customer Relationship Management*, pp. 33–34.

35. Rust, Zeithaml, and Lemon, *Driving Customer Equity*. chap. 13.

36. "Why Service Stinks?"

37. "Retail IT 2001," *Chain Store Age*, October 1, 2001, p. 24

Chapter 12

1. The concept of category management began in the grocery business but has spread rapidly to general merchandise, home furnishings, books, and recordings. In fact, the Food Marketing Institute, the primary trade organization in the grocery industry, has published a book on the subject: Robert C. Blattberg and Edward J. Fox, *Category Management* (Washington, DC: Food Marketing

Institute and the Center for Retail Management, North-western University, 1995).

2. Brandon Copple, "Shelf-Determination," Forbes.com, April 15, 2002.

3. Anna Rominger and Subir Bandyopadyay, "Investigating Antitrust Issues in Category Management," presentation made at the 2002 Research Workshop on Marketing Competitive Conduct and Antitrust Policy, University of Notre Dame, May 2–4, 2002.

4. Ibid.

5. Daniel J. Sweeney, "Improving the Profitability of Retail Merchandising Decisions," *Journal of Marketing*, January 1973, pp. 60–68.

6. To illustrate, suppose net sales = $50,000 and average inventory at retail = $10,000; inventory turnover = $50,000 ÷ $10,000 = 5. To convert inventory turnover expressed at retail to turnover at cost, we multiply by the cost complement, which is the percentage of net sales represented by the cost of goods sold. If the gross margin is 40 percent, the cost complement is 60 percent (100% – 40%). By multiplying the numerator and denominator by 60 percent, the result is cost of goods sold ÷ the average inventory at cost. Thus, inventory turnover is 5 whether it is calculated using retail or cost figures.

7. The rationale behind this equation is as follows: The sales-to-stock ratio is expressed with the numerator at retail and the denominator at cost. To get inventory turnover, both numerator and denominator must be at either retail or cost. 100% – gross margin % is the percentage of net sales represented by the cost of goods sold (also known as the cost complement). By multiplying the sales-to-stock ratio by the cost complement we, in essence, convert the numerator (sales) to the cost of goods sold and therefore have numerator and denominator both expressed at cost.

8. This section is adapted from William R. Davidson, Daniel J. Sweeney, and Ronald W. Stampfl, *Retailing Management*, 5th ed. (New York: John Wiley & Sons, 1984).

9. Walter S. Mossberg, "Palm's New Hand-Held Goes Mano a Mano with BlackBerry," *The Wall Street Journal*, January 31, 2002, p. B1.

10. Teri Agins and Kathryn Kranhold, "Coat Peddlers Are Using Forecasters to Beat the Heat," *The Wall Street Journal*, February 18, 1999, pp. B1, B13.

11. Paul Crocker, *Focus Group Research for Marketers: What Marketers Need to Know About this Popular Research Technique to Use it Safely, Effectively and Wisely.* (Xlibris Corporation, 2001); and Richard A. Kreuger, and Mary Anne Casey, *Focus Groups*, 3rd ed. Sage Publications: April 2000).

12. This section was developed with the assitance of KhiMetrics.

13. Susan Reda, "CPFR Takes Off," *Stores Online*, 2001, www.stores.org

14. Thomas W. Gruen, Daniel S. Corsten, and Sundar Bharadwaj, "Retail Out of Stocks: A Worldwide Exami-nation of Extent, Causes, and Consumer Responses," unpublished working paper, May 7, 2002.

15. *Chain Store Age*/Cap Gemini Ernst & Young U.S.L.L.C, 2001.

16. Dan Scheraga, "Penney's Net Advantage," *Chain Store Age*, September 2000, pp. 114–18.

17. David Moin, "Macy's Web Site Gets a Major Apparel Upload," *WWD*, November 19,1998.

18. Peter Boatwright and Joseph C. Nunes, "Reducing Assortment: An Attribute-Based Approach," *Journal of Marketing 65* (July 2001), pp. 50–63. This research was based on a Web-based grocery chain.

Chapter 13

1. "Robbery, Employee Theft, Leading Causes of Supermarket Losses," *Chain Store Age*, August 1998, p. 84; based on the Food Marketing Institute's annual security survey.

2. The department store chain wishes to remain anonymous. The allocation of inventory to stores is based on each store's standard deviation of sales. Larger stores will have a proportionally smaller standard deviation, causing the backup stock to be proportionally smaller.

3. James R. Stock and Douglas Lambert, *Strategic Logistics Management*, 4th ed. (New York: Irwin/McGraw-Hill, 2000); and Lynn E. Gill, "Inventory and Physical Distribution Management," in *The Distribution Handbook*, eds. James F. Robeson and Robert G. House (New York: Free Press, 1988), pp. 664–67.

4. These issues were taken from Janet Wagner, Richard Ettenson, and Jean Parrish, "Vendor Selection among Retail Buyers: An Analysis by Merchandise Division," *Journal of Retailing 65*, no. 1 (Spring 1989), pp. 58–79.

5. For a thorough treatment of the retail inventory method, see James T. Powers, *The Retail Inventory Method Made Practical* (New York: National Retail Merchants Association, 1971).

6. Robert F. Lusch and Patrick Dunne, *Retail Management* (Cincinnati: South-Western, 1990), p. 356.

Chapter 14

1. Stephen B. Shepard, "The Best Global Brands," *Business Week*, August 6, 2001, p. 12.

2. www.federated-fds.com/home.asp.

3. Robin Rusch, "Private Labels: Does Branding Matter?" Brandchannel.com, May 13, 2002; www.brandchannel.com/;features-effect.asp?id=94 based on research by John Stanley of John Stanley Associates.

4. Ibid.

5. John Stanley, "Brands versus Private Labels," *About Retailing Industry Newsletter*, January 2, 2002. retailindustry.about.com

6. Michael Harvey, "The Trade Dress Controversy: A Case of Strategic Cross-Brand Cannibalization," *Journal of Marketing Theory and Practice 6*, no. 2 (Spring 1998), pp. 1–15.

7. Starbucks 2001 Corporate Report, www.starbucks.com.

8. Bruce C Brown, "Wages and Employment in the U.S. Apparel Industry," *Contemporary Economic Policy* 19, no. 4 (October 2001), pp. 454–64.

9. Sherrie E. Zhan, "Made in the USA," *World Trade*, April 1, 1999, pp. 32–46.

10. Export tariffs are used in some less developed countries to generate additional revenue. For instance, the Argentine government may impose an export tariff on wool that is exported. An export tariff actually lowers the competitive ability of domestic manufacturers, rather than protecting them, as is the case with import tariffs.

11. "Border Battles," *The Economist*, October 3, 1998, p. 6.

12. "Moore Pledges to Build on Doha Success in 2000," *WTO News: 2002*, press release, January 2, 2002.

13. "FAS BACKGROUNDER: Benefits of NAFTA" FASonline, July 2001, www.fas.usda.gov.

14. Personal communication, David Gunter, director of corporate communications, Coldwater Creek, July 2002.

15. Steven Greenhouse, "18 Major Retailers and Apparel Makers Are Accused of Using Sweatshops," *New York Times*, January 14, 1999, p. A9.

16. "A Life of Fines and Beating," *Business Week*, October 2000, pp. 122–28.

17. "Sweatshops under the American Flag," *New York Times*, May 10, 2002, p. A34.

18. Stephanie Williams and Noah Rothbaum, "Returns: All That Glitters Isn't Gold—Ten Secrets of the Trade Your Jeweler Will Probably Never Tell You," *Asian Wall Street Journal*, February 22, 2002, p. W2

19. Sandy Jap, "Online Reverse Auctions: Issues, Themes, and Prospects for the Future," *Journal of the Academy of Marketing Science* 30, no. 4 (Fall 2002); forthcoming M. L. Emiliani, "Business-to-Business Online Auctions: Key Issues for Purchasing Process Improvement," *Supply Chain Management: An International Journal* 5, no. 4 (2000), pp. 176–86.

20. Bruce Fox, "Arizona Chain Pioneers Reverse Auctions for Grocery Buying," *Stores*, January 2002, pp. 62–64.

21. Richard Wise and David Morrison, "Beyond the Exchange: The Future of B2B," *Harvard Business Review*, November–December 2000, pp. 86–96.

22. Personal communication, anonymous, June 2001. Jeffrey Arlen, "Can Off-price Turn Mistakes into Gold?" *DSN Retailing Today*, April 3, 2000, pp. A5, A6

23. Tim Laseter, Brian Long, and Chris Capers "B2B Benchmark: The State of Electronic Exchanges," *Strategy and Business*, 4th quarter, 2001. http://www.strategy-business.com/search/archives

24. Ibid.

25. Adapted from, V. Kasturi Rangan, "FreeMarkets Online," Harvard Business School case #9-598-109, February 1999.

26. www.fashioncenter.com.

27. www.dallasmarketcenter.com.

28. Ibid.

29. www.mccormickplace.com.

30. www.hoovers.com/co/capsule.

31. These guidelines are based on Roger Fisher and William Ury, *Getting to Yes* (New York: Penguin, 1981).

32. Barton Weitz and Sandy Jap, "Relationship Marketing and Distribution Channels," *Journal of the Academy of Marketing Sciences* 23 (Fall 1995), pp. 305–20; and F. Robert Dwyer, Paul Shurr, and Sejo Oh, "Developing Buyer-Seller Relationships," *Journal of Marketing* 51 (April 1987), pp. 11–27.

33. Nirmalya Kumar, "The Power of Trust in Manufacturer–Retailer Relationships," *Harvard Business Review*, November–December 1996, pp. 92–106.

34. Jim Yardley, "Vendorville," *New York Times Magazine*, March 8, 1998, p. 62.

35. Erin Anderson and Anne Coughlan, "Structure, Governance, and Relationship Management," in *Handbook of Marketing*, eds. B. Weitz and R. Wensley (London: Sage, 2002).

36. Erin Anderson and Barton Weitz, "The Use of Pledges to Build and Sustain Commitment in Distribution Channels," *Journal of Marketing Research* 29 (February 1992), pp. 18–34.

37. Ibid.

38. Thomas J. Ryan, "Financial Forum: Chargeback Debate Roars on as Practice Remains Fact of Life," *WWD*, June 1, 1998, pp. 14, 16.

39. Similar types of fees charged to vendors are display fees (paid for special merchandising and display of products) and pay-to-stay fees (paid to continue stocking and displaying a product).

40. Ronald W. Davis, "Slotting Allowances and Antitrust," *Antitrust* 15, no. 2, (Spring 2001), pp. 69–76; and FTC Staff Report, *Report on the Federal Trade Commission Workshop on Slotting Allowances and Other Marketing Practices in the Grocery Industry*, February 2001.

41. Ramarao Desiraju, "New Product Introductions, Slotting Allowances, and Retailer Discretion," *Journal of Retailing* 77, no. 3, (Fall 2001), p. 335. Estimate taken from *Advertising Age*, March 13, 2000, p. 75

42. Ibid.

43. Stephanie Thompson, "Wal-Mart Stomps to Top of Supermarket Heap," AdAge.com, April 29, 2002. http://www.adage.com/news.cms?newsid=34573

44. *Conwood Company, LLP v United States Tobacco Co.*, 2002 Fed App/0171P (6th Cir. 2002).

45. Federal Trade Commission, "World's Largest Manufacturer of Spice and Seasoning Products Agrees to Settle Price Discrimination Charges," FTC press release, March 8, 2000.

46. Ken Bensinger, "Can You Spot the Fake?" *The Wall Street Journal*, February 16, 2001, www.wsj.com

47. "Software Piracy," *The Economist*, June 27, 1998, p. 108.

48. This section draws from Michael R. Czinkota and Ilkka A. Ronkainen, *International Marketing*, 6th ed. (Cincinnati: South-Western, 2000).

49. *Kmart Corp. v. Cartier, Inc.*, 486 U.S. 281 (1988).

50. *Sebao Inc. v. GB Unic. SA*, 1999 E.T.M.R. 681.

51. Irvine Clarke III and Margaret Owens, "Trademark Rights in Gray Markets," *International Marketing Review* 17, no. 2/3 (2000), p. 272.

52. Suein L. Hwant, "Tobacco: As Cigarette Prices Soar, a Gray Market Booms," *The Wall Street Journal*, January 28, 1999, p. B1.

53. *United States v. Dentsply Int'l*, 2001 U.S. Dist. LEXIS 9057 (D. Del. 2001).

54. *Southern Card & Novelty v. Lawson Mardon Label*, 138 F.3d 869 (1998).

55. *In re Toys R Us Antitrust Litigation*, 191 F.R.D. 347 (E.D.N.Y. 2000).

56. Itzhak Sharav, "Cost Justification under the Robinson-Patman Act," *Management Accounting*, July 1978, pp. 15–22.

57. For different perspectives on determining a quantity discount pricing policy, see Abel P. Jeuland and Steven M. Shugan, "Managing Channel Profits," *Marketing Science* 2 (Summer 1983), pp. 239–72; Rajiv Lal and Richard Staelin, "An Approach for Developing an Optimal Discount Pricing Policy," *Management Science* 30 (December 1984), pp. 1524–39; Michael Levy, William Cron, and Robert Novack, "A Decision Support System for Determining a Quantity Discount Pricing Policy," *Journal of Business Logistics* 6, no. 2 (1985), pp. 110–41; James Monahan, "A Quantity Discount Pricing Model to Increase Vendor Profits," *Management Science* 30 (June 1984), pp. 720–27; Kent B. Monroe and Albert J. Della Bitta, "Models for Pricing Decisions," *Journal of Marketing Research* 15 (August 1990), pp. 413–28; James B. Wilcox, Roy D. Howell, Paul Kuzdrall, and Robert Britney, "Price Quantity Discounts: Some Implications for Buyers and Sellers," *Journal of Marketing* 51, no. 3 (July 1987), pp. 60–71; and Pinhas Zusman and Michael Etgar, "The Marketing Channel as an Equilibrium Set of Contracts," *Management Science* 27 (March 1981), pp. 284–302.

58. Michael Levy and Michael van Breda, "A Financial Perspective on the Shift of Marketing Functions," *Journal of Retailing* 60, no. 4 (Winter 1984), pp. 23–42.

59. Ibid.

Chapter 15

1. *Chain Store Age*/Cap Gemini Ernst & Young U.S. L.L.C, 2001.

2. Christopher S. Tang, David R. Bell, and Teck-Hua Ho, "Store Choice and Shopping Behavior: How Price Format Works," *California Management Review* 43, no. 2 (Winter 2001), pp. 56–74; and Alan Sawyer and Peter Dickson, "Everyday Low Prices vs. Sale Price," *Retailing Review* 1, no. 2 (1993), pp. 1–2, 8.

3. Tang, Bell, and Ho, "Store Choice and Shopping Behavior."

4. "Survey Reveals Shoppers' Peeves," *Chain Store Age*, May 2000, p. 54.

5. Kent Monroe, "The Pricing of Services," in *Handbook of Services Marketing*, ed. Carole A. Congram and Margaret L. Friedman (New York: AMACOM, 1989), pp. 20–31.

6. Glenn Voss, A. Parasuraman, and Dhruv Grewal, "The Roles of Price, Performance and Expectations in Determining Satisfaction in Service Exchanges," *Journal of Marketing* 62, no. 4 (October 1998), pp. 46–61; and Dhruv Grewal, Jerry Gotlieb, and Howard Marmorstein, "The Moderating Effects of Contextual Cues on the Relationship between Price and Post-Purchase Perceived Quality," *Journal of Business and Psychology* 14, no. 4 (Summer 2000), pp. 579–91.

7. Dhruv Grewal, Kent B. Monroe, and R. Krishnan, "The Effects of Price Comparison Advertising on Buyers' Perceptions of Acquisition Value and Transaction Value," *Journal of Marketing* 137, no. 3 (April 1998), pp. 16–59.

8. In some rare situations, retail price and initial markup as a percentage of cost are known, and the retailer is seeking to determine the cost. In this case the following formula applies:

$$\text{Initial markup as a \% of retail} = \frac{\text{Initial markup as a \% of cost}}{100\% + \text{Initial markup as a \% of cost}}$$

9. This section was developed with the assistance of Khi-Metrics.

10. This section is based on Thomas T. Nagle and Reed K. Holden, *The Strategy and Tactics of Pricing: A Guide to Profitable Decision Making* (Prentice Hall, 2002).

11. Amy Merrick, "Priced to Move: Retailers Try to Get Leg Up on Markdowns with New Software," *The Wall Street Journal*, August 7, 2001, p. A1.

12. Scott C. Friend and Patricia H. Walker, "Welcome to the New World of Merchandising," *Harvard Business Review*, November 2001, pp. 133–41.

13. D. Soman, "Does Holding on to a Product Result in Increased Consumption Rates?" *Advances in Consumer Research* 24 (1997), pp. 33–35; Brian Wansink, "Do We Use More When We Buy More? The Effects of Stockpiling on Product Consumption," *Advances in Consumer Research* 25 (1998), pp. 21–22; and Valerie S. Folkes, Ingrid M. Martin, and Kamal Gupta, "When to Say When: Effects of Supply on Usage," *Journal of Consumer Research* 20, no. 3, (December 1992), pp. 467–77.

14. Tony Lisanti, "The Almighty Coupon, Redux," *Discount Store News*, September 21, 1998, p. 13.

15. William M. Bulkeley, "Rebates' Big Appeal: Many People Neglect to Redeem Them," *The Wall Street Journal*, February 10, 1998, pp. B1–B2.

16. Greg Gatlin, "Friendly's Savors Taste of Success," *Boston Herald*, June 3, 2002, p. 25.

17. Carl Shapiro, Carol Shapiro, and Hal R. Varian, *Information Rules: A Strategic Guide to the Network Economy* (Harvard Business School Publishing, 1998).

18. This section was developed with the assistance of Khi-Metrics.

19. "Critical Issues: Multi-Channel Integration—The New Retail Battleground," March 2001, www.pwcris.com.

20. Dan Scheraga, "One Price Doesn't Fit All," *Chain Store Age*, March 2001, pp. 104–5; taken from research by Mark Husson, who tracks the supermarket sector for Merrill Lynch.

21. Ibid.

22. "80 Most Influential People in Sales and Marketing," *Sales & Marketing Management*, October 1998, p. 78.

23. David P. Hamilton, "The Price Isn't Right," *The Wall Street Journal*, February 2001, pp. R8, R10.

24. Lisa Vickery, "No More Free Lunch," *The Wall Street Journal*, September 24, 2001, www.wsj.com.

25. Adam Cohen, *The Perfect Store: Inside e-Bay*. (Little, Brown & Co., 2001).

26. "Levi Strauss Reacquires a Pair of Jeans, at Markup," *The Wall Street Journal*, May 29, 2001, p. B.13A.

27. Walter Baker, Mike Marn, and Craig Zawada, "Price Smarter on the Net," *Harvard Business Review*, February 2001, pp. 122–27.

28. David Cowling and Gregg Perry, "The E-Tax Man Cometh," *E-Business Law Bulletin*, April 2002, p. 1.

29. In 1992, the Supreme Court required retailers to have a physical nexus in a particular state before the state could require the retailer to collect its sales tax (*Quill Corp. v. North Dakota*, 504 U.S. 298). While states can still require their residents to pay sales taxes on out-of-state mail, telephone, and Internet purchases, no state tries to collect such taxes.

30. Itamar Simonson, "Shoppers Easily Influenced Choices," *New York Times*, November 6, 1994, p. 311; based on research by Itamar Simonson and Amos Tversky, www.nytimes.com

31. This section was developed with the assistance of KhiMetrics.

32. This discussion has been going on for at least 70 years; see Louis Bader and James De. Weinland, "Do Odd Prices Earn Money?" *Journal of Retailing* 8 (1932), pp. 102–4. For recent research in this area, see Karen Gedenk and Henrik Sattler, "The Impact of Price Thresholds on Profit Contribution—Should Retailers Set 9-Ending Prices?" *Journal of Retailing* 75, no. 1 (1999), pp. 33–57; Robert M. Schindler and Patrick N. Kirby, "Patterns of Rightmost Digits Used in Advertised Prices: Implications for Nine-Ending Effects," *Journal of Consumer Research* 24 (September 1997), p. 192–201; and Mark Stiving and Russell S. Winer, "An Empirical Analysis of Price Endings with Scanner Data," *Journal of Consumer Research* 24 (June 1997), pp. 57–67.

33. *Borden Co v. FTC*, 381 F.2d 175 (5th Cir. 1967).

34. "Booksellers Swear Anti-trust," *Discount Store News*, April 6, 1998, p. 8; and John Accola, "Tattered Cover Takes Aim," *Rocky Mountain News*, March 19, 1998, p. B1.

35. Dianna Marder, "Study Finds Gender Bias in Philadelphia Merchants Pricing," *Philadelphia Inquirer*, March 5, 1999.

36. Bob Ortega, "Suit over Wal-Mart's Pricing Practices Goes to Trial Today in Arkansas Court," *The Wall Street Journal*, August 23, 1993, p. A3; and Pete Hisey, "Ark. Supreme Court Rules Wal-Mart's No Predator: Lack of Proof Overturns Price Conviction," *Discount Store News*, February 6, 1995, pp. 3, 89.

37. "Nine West Settles State and Federal Price Fixing Charges," FTC press release, March 6, 2000.

38. Melody Petersen, "Treading a Contentious Line," *New York Times*, January 13, 1999, pp. C1–C2.

39. *State Oil v. Kahn*, 522 U.S. 3 (1997).

40. Larry D. Compeau, Dhruv Grewal, and Diana S. Grewal, "Adjudicating Claims of Deceptive Advertised Reference Prices: The Use of Empirical Evidence," *Journal of Public Policy & Marketing* 14 (Fall 1994); Dhruv Grewal, Diana S. Grewal, and Larry D. Compeau, "States' Crackdown on Deceptive Price Advertising: Retail and Public Policy Implications," *Pricing Strategy & Practice: An International Journal* 1, no. 2 (1993), pp. 33–40; Dhruv Grewal and Larry D. Compeau, "Comparative Price Advertising: Informative or Deceptive?" *Journal of Public Policy & Marketing* 11 (Spring 1992), pp. 52–62; Robert N. Corley and O. Lee Reed, *The Legal Environment*, 7th ed. (New York; McGraw-Hill, 1987); Teri Agins, "Low Prices or Low Practice? Regulators Cast Wary Eye on Retailers' Many Sales," *The Wall Street Journal*, February 13, 1990, pp. B1, B7; and *Do's and Don'ts in Advertising Copy* (Council of Better Business Bureaus, 1987).

41. "Price Check II Shows Scanner Accuracy Has Improved Since 1996," FTC press release, December 16, 1998.

Chapter 16

1. David Aaker, *Managing Brand Equity* (New York: Free Press, 1991), p. 7

2. "Retail's Best Brands: 10 Stores with the Strongest Brand Image," *Display & Design Ideas*, September 15, 2001, p. 10.

3. Linda Hyde and Elaine Pollack, *What's in a Name?* (Columbus, OH: Retail Forward, Inc., June 1999), p. 9.

4. Shelly Branch, "How Target Got Hot: Hip Goods and Hipper Ads Are Luring the MTV and BMW Crowds into the Big Box," *Fortune*, May 24, 1999, pp. 169–70.

5. Debby Garbato Stankevich, "What's in a Name?" *Retail Merchandiser*, April 2001, p. 59.

6. "History in the Making: A Look at 16 Campaigns That Helped Redefine Promotion Marketing," *Promo*, March 2002, p. 23.

7. "The Return of SEX," May 13, 2002, p. 34; Amy Barrett, "To Reach the Unreachable Teen," *Business Week*, September 18, 2000, p. 78; and Terilyn Henderson and Elizabeth Mihas, "Building Retail Brands," *McKinsey Quarterly*, Summer 2000, pp. 110–15

8. Molly Prior, "TRU Launches RZone Magazine for Teen Pop-Culture Enthusiasts," *DSN Retailing Today*, July 8, 2002, p. 4.

9. Peter Childs, Suzanne Heywood, and Michael Kliger, "Do Retail Brands Travel?" *McKinsey Quarterly* 1 (2001), pp. 12–16.

10. William Shuster, "Retailing in Tough Times: The Power of Promotions," *Jewelers Circular Keystone*, April 1, 2002, p. 70.

11. "The Man Who Created Rudolph from an Idea That Almost Didn't Fly," *Chicago Tribune*, December 13, 1990, p. 1C.

12. Sara Owens, "The Price Is Righter; The Rewards of In-Store Sampling Are Greater than You Think," *Promo*, September 2001, p. 10.

13. Gabriella Stern, "With Sampling, There Is Too a Free Lunch," *The Wall Street Journal*, March 11, 1994, p. B1.

14. Ibid.

15. See A. Coskun Samli, "Store Image Definition, Dimensions, Measurement, and Management," in *Retail Market Strategy*, ed. A. Samli (New York: Quorum, 1989).

16. "State of Couponing," *Brandmarketing*, April 2002, p. 8.

17. Joe Dysart, "E-Mail Marketing Grows Up" *Chain Store Age*, June 2001, pp. 91–92

18. W. Glynn Mangold, Fred Miller, and Gary Brockway, "Word-of-Mouth Communication in the Service Marketplace," *Journal of Services Marketing* 13 (January–February 1999), pp. 73–77; "Word of Mouth Still Works," *Discount Store News*, June 22, 1998, p. 17; George Silverman, "How to Harness the Awesome Power of Word of Mouth," *Direct Marketing*, November 1997, pp. 32–38; and Chip Walker, "Word of Mouth," *American Demographics*, July 1995, pp. 38–43.

19. Frederick Reichheld, "Loyalty-Based Management," *Harvard Business Review*, March–April 1993, p. 65.

20. "Whom Do You Trust?" *Chain Store Age*, July 2, 2002, p. 36.

21. Ken Clark, "Play Ball," *Chain Store Age*, July 2002, p. 39.

22. "Top 100 Advertisers," *Advertising Age*, July 2002, June 26, 2002, www.adage.com/page.cms?pageId=913.

23. Stephen Smith, Narendra Agrawal, and Shelby McIntyre, "A Discrete Optimization Model for Seasonal Merchandise Planning," *Journal of Retailing* 74 (Summer 1998), pp. 193–222; Scott Neslin and John Quilt, "Developing Models for Planning Retailer Sales Promotions: An Application to Automobile Dealerships," *Journal of Retailing* 63 (Winter 1987), pp. 333–64; and Arthur Allaway, J. Barry Mason, and Gene Brown, "An Optimal Decision Support Model for Department-Level Promotion Mix Planning," *Journal of Retailing* 63 (Fall 1987), pp. 216–41.

24. Leonard Lodish, *Advertisers and Promotion Challenge: Vaguely Right or Precisely Wrong* (New York: Oxford University Press, 1986).

25. George Belch and Michael Belch, *Advertising and Promotion*, 5th ed. (New York: McGraw-Hill, 2001), pp. 227–28.

26. Murali Mantralla, "Allocating Marketing Resources," in eds. Barton Weitz and Robin Wensely, *Handbook of Marketing* (London: Sage, 2002), pp. 409–435.

27. This example is adapted by William R. Swinyard, professor of business management, Brigham Young University, from the "Overseas Airlines Service" case.

28. Ronald Curhan and Robert Kopp, "Obtaining Retailer Support for Trade Deals: Key Success Factors," *Journal of Advertising Research* 27 (December 1987–January 1988), pp. 51–60.

29. This illustration was provided by Kathy Perry, senior vice president, Matrix Technology Group, Inc., www.mxtg.net.

30. Donald Ziccardi and David Moin, *Master Minding the Store: Advertising, Sales Promotion, and the New Marketing Reality* (New York: Wiley, 1997); John McCann, Ali Tadlaqui, and John Gallagher, "Knowledge Systems in Merchandising: Advertising Design," *Journal of Retailing*, Fall 1990, pp. 257–77; and Meryl Gardner and Michael Houston, "The Effects of Visual and Verbal Components of Retail Communications," *Journal of Retailing*, Summer 1986, pp. 65–78.

31. Gary Witkin, "Effective Use of Retail Data Bases," *Direct Marketing*, December 1995, pp. 32–35.

32. "Top 100 Advertisers," *Advertising Age*, September 17, 1999, p. 16.

33. Ibid., p. 31.

34. James Fredrick and Allene Symons, "Building an Image," *Drug Store News*, November 18, 1996, p. 9.

35. "Top 100 Advertisers," p. 16.

36. Fredrick and Symons, "Building an Image," p. 9.

37. Joe Dysart, "E-Mail Marketing Grows Up" *Chain Store Age*, June 2001, pp. 91–92

38. Fredrick and Symons, "Building an Image," pp. 9–10.

39. Tony Case, "A Rocky Road Predicted for Newspaper Advertising," *Editor and Publisher*, September 23, 1995, p. 27.

40. "Maximizing the Potential of Audio Advertising," *Chain Store Age*, March 1995, p. B13.

41. Susan Reda, "Retailers Use Affiliate Programs to Drive Internet Traffic and Sales," *Stores*, May 1998, pp. 46–49; Greg Notess, "Intricacies of Advertisement Information on the Web," *Online Magazine*, November 1999, pp. 79–81; and "Retooling for Interactivity," *Response*, November 1999, pp. 28–31.

42. Cyndee Miller, "Outdoors Gets a Makeover," *Marketing News*, April, 10, 1995, pp. 1, 26; and Teresa Andreoli, "From Retailers to Consumers: Billboards Drive the Message Home," *Discount Store News*, September 19, 1994, p. 14.

Chapter 17

1. Seth Lubovek. "Don't Listen to the Boss, Listen to the Customers," *Forbes*, December 4, 1995, pp. 45–46.

2. Food Marketing Institute, www.fmi.org/facts_figs/super fact.htm, July 2002.

3. Diane Lewis, "Train to Retain a Corporate Culture Focused on Workers Is Helping Retailer Kohl's Flourish while Rivals Flounder," *Boston Globe*, March 3, 2002, p. H1.

4. Doug Donaldson, "Smart Hiring," *Do-It-Yourself Retailing*, January 1999, pp. 49–55; and Herbert Heneman III, Timothy Judge, and Robert Heneman, *Staffing Organizations*, 3d ed. (Boston: Irwin/McGraw-Hill, 2000).

5. Aaron Bernstein, "Too Many Workers? Not for Long," *Business Week*, May 20, 2002, p. 126.

6. Jessica Diamond, "New Strategies for Finding a High-Powered Staff," *Jewelers' Circular—Keystone*, September 1999, pp. 86–87.

7. "Recruitment: How to Find the Perfect Match," *In-Store Marketing*, September 6, 2001, p. 23: Ron Ruggles, "Internet Seen as an Effective Way to Recruit New Employees," *Nation's Restaurant News*, October 18, 1999, p. 80; and David Schulz, "Internet Emerging as Major Vehicle for Mid-Level Retail Recruiting," *Stores*, June 1999, pp. 70–73.

8. Debby Stankevich, "Retailers Focus on Optimizing Technology," *Retailer Merchandiser*, March 2002, pp. 55–58; Ginger Koloszyc, "Tight Labor Market Spurs High-Tech Employment Screening," *Stores*, July 1998, pp. 77–81; and David Schulz, "Small Retailers Turn to Pre-Employment Screening Services, *Stores*, May 1998, pp. 72–74.

9. Sarah Fister, "Separating Liars from Hires," *Training*, July 1999, pp. 22–24.

10. Susan Jackson and Randall Schuler, *Managing Human Resources: Through Strategic Relationships*, 8th ed. (Mason, OH: South-Western, 2003), p. 328.

11. Jane Bahls, "Available upon Request," *HR Magazine*, January 1999, pp. S2–S7.

12. Jackson and Schuler, *Managing Human Resources*, p. 330.

13. Richard Hollinger and Jason Davis, *2001 National Retail Security Survey* (Gainesville, FL: Security Research Project, Department of Sociology, University of Florida, 1998), p. 8, web.soc.ufl.edu/SRP/NRSS_2001.pdf.

14. John Bernardin and Donna Cooke, "Validity of an Honesty Test in Predicting Theft among Convenience Store Employees," *Academy of Management Journal* 36 (October 1993), pp. 1097–1099.

15. John McKinnon, "Retailers Beware!" *Florida Trend*, June 1996, pp. 20–21.

16. Jane Easter Bahls, "Dealing with Drugs: Keep It Legal," *HR Magazine*, March 1998, pp. 104–11.

17. Kal Lifson, "Turn Down Turnover to Turn Up Profits," *Chain Store Age*, November 1, 1996, pp. 64–66.

18. Paul Taylor, "Providing Structure to Interviews and Reference Checks, *Workforce*, Workforce Tools Supplement, May 1999, pp. S11–S55; and Allen Huffcutt and David Woehr, "Further Analysis of Employment Interview Validity: A Quantitative Evaluation of Interviewer-Related Structuring Methods," *Journal of Organizational Behavior* 20 (July 1999), pp. 549–56.

19. John Bible, "Discrimination in Job Applications and Interviews," *Supervision*, November 1998, pp. 9–12; Laura Williamson, James Campion, Mark Roehling, Stanley Malos, and Michael Campion, "Employment Interview on Trial: Linking Interview Structure with Litigation Outcomes," *Journal of Applied Psychology* 82 (December 1997; pp. 900–13; and Peter Burgess, "How Those 'Innermost Thoughts' Are Revealed," *Grocer*, March 9, 1996, pp. 60–62.

20. Lucette Comer and Tanya Drollinger, "Active Empathetic Listening and Selling Success: A Conceptual Framework," *Journal of Personal Selling and Sales Management* 9 (Winter 1999), pp. 15–29; and C. David Sheppard, Stephen Castleberry, and Rick Ridnour, "Linking Effective Listening with Sales Performance: An Exploratory Investigation," *Journal of Business and Industrial Marketing* 12 (1997), pp. 315–21.

21. Daniel Cable and Charles Parson, "Socialization Tactics and Person-Organization Fit," *Personnel Psychology* 54 (Spring 2001), pp. 1–24; and Cheri Young and Craig Lundberg, "Creating a First Day on the Job," *Cornell Hotel and Restaurant Administration Journal*, December 1996, pp. 26–29.

22. Gerald White, "Employee Turnover: The Hidden Drain on Profits," *HR Focus*, January 1995, pp. 5–8.

23. "Workers Are Seeking Employers of Choice," *Chain Store Age*, October 1998, pp. 72, 74.

24. John Wanous and Arnon Rechers, "New Employee Orientation Program," *Human Resource Management Review* 10 (Winter 2000), pp. 435–52; and Charlotte Garvey, "The Whirland of a New Job," *HR Magazine* 46 (June 2001), pp. 110–16.

25. Bert Versloot, Jan Jong, and Jo Thijssen, "Organisational Context of Structured on-the-Job Training," *International Journal of Training and Development* 5 (March 2001), pp. 2–23.

26. Chris Roebuck, *Effective Leadership* (New York; AMACOM, 1999); and John Kotter, *John Kotter on What Leaders Really Do* (Boston: Harvard Business School Press, 1999).

27. John Sparks, Joseph Schenk, "Explaining the Effects of Transformation Leadership," *Journal of Organizational Behavior* 22 (December 2001), pp. 849–68; and Vicki Goodwin, J. C. Wofford, and J. Lee Whittington, "A Theoretical and Empirical Extension to the Transformational Leadership Construct," *Journal of Organizational Behavior* 22 (November 2001), pp. 759–72.

28. Gerard Seijts, "Setting Goals," *Ivey Business Journal*, January–February 2001, pp. 40–45.

29. Deborah Gibbons and Laurie Weingart, "Can I Do it? Will I Try? Personal Efficacy, Assigned Goals, and Performance Norms as Motivators of Individual Performance," *Journal of Applied Social Psychology* 31 (March 2001), pp. 624–49.

30. Frank Hammed, "Becoming the Employer of Choice," *Supermarket Business*, June 1996, pp. 98–106.

31. "The 100 Best Companies to Work For," *Fortune*, January 8, 2001, pp. 148–68.

32. Kevin Helliker, "Pressure at Pier 1: Beating the Sales Numbers of a Year Earlier Is a Storewide Obsession," *The Wall Street Journal*, December 7, 1995, pp. B1–B2.

33. Mark Albright, "Hiring the Right Person," *St. Petersburg Times*, March 25, 2002, p. 8E.

34. Carol Sansone and Judith M. Harackiewicz, *Intrinsic and Extrinsic Motivation: The Search for Optimal Motivation and Performance* (San Diego, Academic Press, 2000).

35. "Front Lines," *Chain Store Age*, September 1, 2001, p. 38.

36. Ibid.; and Richard McBain, "Pay, Performance, and Motivation," *Journal of General Management*, Autumn 1998, pp. S20–S32.

37. David Good and Charles Schwepker, "Sales Quotas: Critical Interpretations and Implications," *Review of Business* 22 (Spring–Summer 2001), pp. 32–37; and William Liccione, "Effective Goal Setting: A Prerequisite for Compensation Plans with Incentive Value," *Compensation and Benefits Management*, Winter 1997, pp. 19–26.

38. Todd Zenger and C. R. Marshall, "Determinants of Incentive Intensity in Group-Based Rewards," *Academy of Management Journal* 43 (April 2000), pp. 149–63; and Parbudyal Singh, "Organizational Rewards for a Changing Workplace: An Examination of Theory and Practice," *International Journal of Technology Management* 16 (September–October 1998), pp. 225–39.

39. Dan Scheraga, "Handling Manpower by the Hour," *Chain Store Age*, August 1, 2000, p. 66; and Julie Ross, "Changes in Scheduling Software Target Improved Retail Performance," *Stores*, August 1997, pp. 85–88.

40. Lisa Girion, "Working Longer?" *Los Angeles Times*, September 10, 2000, p. G1.

41. "Keeping a Lid on Costs," *Chain Store Age*, December 2000, p. 9C; and "Deregulation Puts Focus on Energy Conservation," *Chain Store Age*, December 1, 2000, p. 6C.

42. Jennifer Pellet, "Wal-Mart's Rush for California Green," *Discount Merchandiser*, February 1996, pp. 62–63.

43. Hollinger and Davis, *2001 National Retail Security Survey*.

44. Ibid., p. 3.

45. Marianne Wilson, "Building in Security," *Chain Store Age*, November 2001, pp. 129–30.

46. "Combating Shrink at the Source," *Chain Store Age*, December 2000, p. 152.

47. Ginger Koloszyc, "Supermarkets Find Growing Payoff in EAS Anti-Shoplifting Systems," *Stores*, February 1999, pp. 28–30; and "Sales Up, Shrink Down with Source Tagging," *Chain Store Age*, August 1998, p. 84.

48. Timothy Henderson, "Loss Prevention Software Aids in Retail Fight against Costly Employee Theft," *Stores*, March 2001, pp. 68–72.

49. Denise Zimmerman, "Theft Deterrents at Work," *Supermarket Business*, January 15, 1996, p. 21.

Chapter 18

1. Mitchell Mauk, "The Store as Story," *VM & SD*, October 2000, pp. 23, 25.

2. M. Joseph Sirgy, Dhruv Grewal, and Tamara Mangleburg, "Retail Environment, Self-Congruity, and Retail Patronage: An Integrative Model and a Research Agenda," *Journal of Business Research* 49, no. 2 (August 2000), pp. 127–38.

3. Kathleen Purvis, "It's Scary: Your Supermarket Shopping Is Done by Design," *Seattle Times*, June 19, 2002, based on research by Kevin Kelly.

4. Julie Baker, A. Parasuraman, Dhruv Grewal, and Glen Voss, "The Influence of Multiple Store Environment Cues on Perceived Merchandise Value and Patronage Intentions," *Journal of Marketing* 66 (April 2002), pp. 120–41; Barry J. Babin and Jill S. Attaway, "Atmospheric Affect as a Tool for Creating Value and Gaining Share of Customer," *Journal of Business Research* 49, no. 2 (August 2000), pp. 91–101; Alain d'Astous, "Irritating Aspects of the Shopping Environment," *Journal of Business Research* 49, no. 2 August 2000, pp. 149–57; Karen A Machleit and Sevgin A. Eroglu, "Describing and Measuring Emotional Response to Shopping Experience," *Journal of Business Research* 49, no. 2 (August 2000), pp. 101–11; Elaine Sherman, Anil Mathur, and Ruth Belk Smith, "Store Environment and Consumer Purchase Behavior: Mediating Role of Consumer Emotions, *Psychology and Marketing*, July 1997, pp. 361–78; and Teresa A. Summers and Paulette R. Hebert, "Shedding some light on store atmospherics: Influence of Illumination on consumer behaviors" *Journal of Business Research* 54, no. 2 (November 2001), pp. 145–150.

5. "College Bookstore Gets Smart," *Chain Store Age*, September 2000, p. 160.

6. Stacey Menzel Baker and Carol Kaufman-Scarborough, "Marketing and Public Accommodation: A Retrospective on Title III of the Americans with Disabilities Act," *Journal of Public Policy and Marketing* 20, no. 2 (Fall 2001), pp. 297–304; Carol Kaufman-Scarborough, "Reasonable Access for Mobility-Disabled Persons is More than Widening the Door," *Journal of Retailing* 75, no. 4 (Winter 1999), pp. 479–508; and Carol Kaufman-Scarborough, "Sharing the Experience of Mobility-Disabled Consumers: Building Understanding through the Use of Ethnographic Research Methods," *Journal of Contemporary Ethnography* 30, no. 4 (August 2001), pp. 430–65.

7. *Lieber v. Macys West, Inc.* 80 F.Supp. 2d (N.D. Cal. 1999).

8. Baker and Kaufman-Scarborough, "Marketing and Public Accommodation," p. 302.

9. "International Interior Store Design Competition," *Visual Merchandising and Store Design*, February 1996, pp. 35–76.

10. Sevgin A. Eroglu, Karen A. Machleit, and Lenita M. Davis, "Atmospheric Qualities of Online Retailing: A Conceptual Model and Implications," *Journal of Business Research* 54, no. 2 (November 2001), pp. 177–84.

11. Lorrie Grant, "Department Stores Ring Up Centralized Checkouts; Cost-Cutting, Success of Kohl's Help Drive Trend," www.plainvanillashell.com, *Retail and Development News*, June 6, 2002; and Eileen Smith, "Retail Giants Change Checkouts," www.courierpostonline.com, June 13, 2002.

12. Debbie Howell, "JC Penney Retrofits Image," *DSN Retailing Today* 41, no. 7 (April 8, 2002,) pp. 5, 83; and "Penney to Remodel Stores, Centralize Checkouts," *Chain Store Age Online*, April 18, 2002.

13. Paco Underhill, *Why We Buy: The Science of Shopping* (New York: Simon & Schuster, 2000).

14. Four of the most popular planogram programs are Marketmax (www.marketmax.com), Apollo (www.metirimensus.com), Pegman (www.wellingtoninc.com), and Spaceman (www.acnielsen.com).

15. Raymond R. Burke, "Virtual Shopping: Breakthrough in Marketing Research," *Harvard Business Review*, March–April 1996, pp. 120–34.

16. Larry Berk, "The Kiosk's Ship Has Come In," *DSN Retailing Today*, February 19, 2001. www.dsnretailingtoday.com

17. "Staples Touts Kiosk, POS Link," *Chain Store Age*, July 2001, p. 66.

18. Berk, "The Kiosk's Ship Has Come In."

19. Ellen Neuborne, "The Box That Rocks," *Business Week e.biz*, June 4, 2001, p. EB6.

20. "Staples Touts Kiosk, POS Link."

21. Berk, "The Kiosk's Ship Has Come In."

22. Neuborne, "The Box That Rocks."

23. Berk, "The Kiosk's Ship Has Come In."

24. "The Need for Speed," *WWD*, November 5, 1998, p. 2.

25. The concept of atmospherics was introduced by Philip Kotler in "Atmosphere as a Marketing Tool," *Journal of Retailing* 49 (Winter 1973), pp. 48–64. The definition is adapted from Richard Yalch and Eric Spangenberg, "Effects of Store Music on Shopping Behavior," *Journal of Service Marketing* 4, no. 1 (Winter 1990), pp. 31–39.

26. Anna S. Mattila and Jochen Wirtz, "Congruency of Scent and Music as a Driver of In-Store Evaluations and Behavior," *Journal of Retailing* 77, no. 2 (Summer 2001), pp. 273–89.

27. "Five Easy Steps," *VM&SD*, June 2000, pp. 42–43.

28. Teresa A. Summers and Paulette R. Hebert, "Shedding Some Light on Store Atmospherics; Influence of Illumination on Consumer Behavior," *Journal of Business Research* 54, no. 2 (November 2001), pp. 145–50.

29. Susan Franke, "Architects, Experts Say Proper Design Can Propel Shoppers into Stores," *Pittsburgh Business Times*, July 12, 2002.

30. Earl Print, "Euro Lighting," *VM&SD*, May 1999, pp. 38, 40.

31. For a review of this research, see Joseph A. Bellizzi and Robert E. Hite, "Environmental Color, Consumer Feelings, and Purchase Likelihood," *Psychology and Marketing* 9, no. 5 (September–October 1992), pp. 347–63.

32. Jenny Schnetzer, "Sound Solution," *VM & SD*, June 2000, pp. 68–69.

33. Andrea Petersen, "Restaurants Bring in da Noice to Keep out da Nerds," *The Wall Street Journal*, December 30, 1997, pp. B1, B2.

34. J. Duncan Herrington and Louis Capella, "Effects of Music in Service Environments: A Field Study," *Journal of Services Marketing* 10, no. 2 (1996), pp. 26–41.

35. Richard F. Yalch and Eric R. Spangenberg, "The Effects of Music in a Retail Setting on Real and Perceived Shopping Times," *Journal of Business Research* 49, no. 2 (August 2000), pp. 139–48; Michael Hui, Laurette Dube, and Jean-Charles Chebat, "The Impact of Music on Consumers' Reactions to Waiting for Services," *Journal of Retailing* 73, no. 1, (1997), pp. 87–104; and Julie Baker, Dhruv Grewal, and Michael Levy, "An Experimental Approach to Making Retail Store Environmental Decisions," *Journal of Retailing* 68 (Winter 1992), pp. 445–60.

36. Jennifer Markley, "Stay (Just a Little Big Longer)," *VM & SD*, November 1998, pp. 22–26.

37. Stacey Witt Toevs, "Three Stories One Mile High," *VM & SD*, November 1997, pp. 30–35.

38. Maxine Wilkie, "Scent of a Market," *American Demographics*, August 1995, pp. 40–49.

39. Anna S. Mattila and Jochen Wirtz, "Congruency of Scent and Music as a Driver of In-Store Evaluations and Behavior," *Journal of Retailing* 77, no. 2 (Summer 2001), pp. 273–90.

40. Eric R. Spangenberg, Ayn E. Crowley, and Pamela W. Henderson, "Improving the Store Environment: Do Olfactory Cues Affect Evaluations and Behaviors?" *Journal of Marketing* 60 (April 1996), pp. 67–80.

41. Paula Fitzgerald Bone and Pam Scholder Ellen, "Scents in the Marketplace: Explaining a Fraction of Olfaction," *Journal of Retailing* 75, no. 2 (Summer 1999), pp. 243–63.

42. Cathleen McCarthy, "Aromatic Merchandising: Leading Customers by the Nose," *Visual Merchandising and Store Design*, April 1992, pp. 85–87.

Chapter 19

1. James Fitzsimmons and Mona Fitzsimmons, *Service Development: Creating Memorable Experiences* (Thousand Oaks, CA.: Sage Publications, 2000); and Suzanne Barry Osborn, "Is Your Customer Being SERVED?" *Chain Store Age*, November 1, 2000, p. 52.

2. Valarie Zeithaml, Leonard Berry, and A. Parasuraman, "The Behavioral Consequences of Service Quality," *Journal of Marketing* 60 (April 1996), pp. 31–46.

3. Murray Raphael, "Tell Me What You Want and the Answer Is Yes," *Direct Marketing*, October 1996, p. 22.

4. "Driving Customers Away," *Chain Store Age*, June 2001, p. 39.

5. Robert Spector and Patrick McCarthy, *The Nordstrom Way: The Inside Story of America's #1 Customer Service Company*, 2nd ed. (New York: John Wiley, 2001).

6. G. Odekerken-Schroder, K. De Wulf, H. Kasper, M. Kleijnen, J. Hoekstra, and H. Commandeur, "The Impact of Quality on Store Loyalty: A Contingency Approach," *Total Quality Management* 12 (May 2001), pp. 307–22; and Benjamin Schneider and David Bowen, *Winning the Service Game* (Boston: Harvard Business School Press, 1995).

7. Banwari Mittal and Walfried Lassar, "The Role of Personalization in Service Encounters," *Journal of Retailing* 72 (Spring 1996), pp. 95–109.

8. Paul Lima, "Instant Gratification," *Profit*, April 2002, p. 56.

9. "Combining Class with Mass," *MMR*, January 8, 2001, p. 12; and "Workers Are Seeking Employers of Choice," *Chain Store Age*, October 1998, pp. 72, 74.

10. "Retailers Join the War Effort," *Chain Store Age*, June 1994, p. 15.

11. Roger Bennett, "Queues, Customer Characteristics and Policies for Managing Waiting-Lines in Supermarkets," *International Journal of Retail and Distribution Management* 26 (February–March 1998), pp. 78–88; and Julie Baker and Michaelle Cameron, "The Effects of the Service Environment on Affect and Consumer Perceptions of Waiting Time: An Integrative Review and Research Propositions," *Journal of the Academy of Marketing Science* 24 (Fall 1996), pp. 338–49.

12. William Parsons, "Give the Lady What She Wants," *Chain Store Age*, November 1995, pp. 86–87.

13. Martha McNeil Hamilton and Dina El Boghdady, "The Spirit of Giving Back; Shoppers Discover Stricter Policies for Returning Gifts," *Washington Post*, December 27, 2001, p. E01; and "Retailers Get Strict on Merchandise Returns," *St. Louis Post-Dispatch*, May 17, 2002, p. C1.

14. "Retailers Get Strict on Merchandise Returns."

15. A. Parsuraman and Valarie Zeithaml, "Understanding and Improving Service Quality: A Literature Review and Research Agenda," in eds. B. Weitz and R. Wensley, *Handbook of Marketing* (London: Sage, 2002); and Praveen Kopalle and Donald Lehmann, "Strategic Management of Expectations: The Role of Disconfirmation Sensitivity and Perfectionism," *Journal of Marketing Research*, August 2001, pp. 386–401.

16. Kenneth Clow, David Kurtz, John Ozment, and Beng Soo Ong, "The Antecedents of Consumer Expectations of Services: An Empirical Study across Four Industries," *Journal of Services Marketing* 11 (May–June 1997), pp. 230–48; and Ann Marie Thompson and Peter Kaminski, "Psychographic and Lifestyle Antecedents of Service Quality Expectations," *Journal of Services Marketing* 7 (1993), pp. 53–61.

17. Susan Stellin, "Online Customer Service Found Lacking," *New York Times*, January 3, 2002, p. C1.

18. Mary Jo Bitner, "Self-Service Technologies: What Do Customers Expect?; In This High-Tech World, Customers Haven't Changed—They Still Want Good Service," *Marketing Management*, Spring 2001, pp. 10–15.

19. Timothy Keiningham and Terry Vavra, *The Customer Delight Principle* (Chicago: American Marketing Association, 2002).

20. Parasuraman and Zeithaml, "Understanding and Improving Service Quality."

21. Michael Hartline and O. C. Ferrell, "The Management of Customer-Contact Service Employees: An Empirical Investigation," *Journal of Marketing* 60 (October 1996), pp. 52–70; and Lois Mohr and Mary Jo Bittner, "The Role of Employee Effort in Satisfaction with Service Transactions," *Journal of Business Research* 32 (March 1995), pp. 239–52.

22. The following discussion of the gaps model and its implications is based on Deon Nel and Leyland Pitt, "Service Quality in a Retail Environment: Closing the Gaps," *Journal of General Management* 18 (Spring 1993), pp. 37–57; Valarie Zeithaml, A. Parasuraman, and Leonard Berry, *Delivering Quality Customer Service* (New York: Free Press, 1990); and Valarie Zeithaml, Leonard Berry, and A. Parasuraman, "Communication and Control Processes in the Delivery of Service Quality," *Journal of Marketing* 52 (April 1988), pp. 35–48.

23. http://retailindustry.about.com, April 4, 2001.

24. "Merchant Prince: Stanley Marcus," *Inc.*, June 1987, pp. 41–44.

25. U. Chapman and George Argyros, "An Investigation into Whether Complaining Can Cause Increased Consumer Satisfaction," *Journal of Consumer Marketing* 17, 2000, pp. 9–19; Tibbett L. Speer, "They Complain Because They Care," *American Demographics*, May 1996, pp. 13–15; and Jagdip Singh and Robert Wilkes, "When Customers Complain: A Path Analysis of Key Antecedents of Customer Complaint Response Analysis," *Journal of the Academy of Marketing Science* 24 (Fall 1996), pp. 350–65.

26. "Driving Customers Away" *Chain Store Age*, June 2001, p. 39.

27. www.llbean.com.

28. Daniel Roth, "My Job at the Container Store," *Fortune*, January 10, 2000, p. 76.

29. Sandra Guy, "Stores Juggle Service with High-Tech Savvy," *Chicago Sun-Times*, July 1, 2002, p. B12; Julie Clark, "The Importance of Kiosks in Retail Has Grown," *Display and Design Ideas*, September 2001, p. 18; and Ken Clark, "Confused about Kiosks," *Chain Store Age*, November 1, 2000, p. 96.

30. Paul Hemp, "My Week as a Room-Service Waiter at the Ritz," *Harvard Business Review*, June 2002, pp. 50–62; and Len Berry, *On Great Customer Service* (New York: Free Press, 1995), pp. 73–74.

31. See Chuck Chakrapani, *How to Measure Service Quality and Customer Satisfaction: The Informal Field Guide for Tools and Techniques* (Chicago: American Marketing Association, 1998).

32. David Lipke, "Mystery Shoppers," *American Demographics*, December 2000, pp. 41–44; and "Mystery Shopping's Lightweight Reputation Undeserved," *International Journal of Retail and Distribution Management* 27 (February–March 1999), pp. 114–17; Rachel Miller, "Undercover Shoppers," *Marketing*, May 28, 1998, pp. 27–30; and Jennifer Steinhauer, "The Undercover Shoppers," *New York Times*, February 4, 1998, p. D1.

33. See Jim Poisant, *Creating and Sustaining a Superior Customer Service Organization: A Book about Taking Care of the People Who Take Care of the Customers* (Westport, CT: Quorum Books, 2002); "People-Focused HR Policies Seen as Vital to Customer Service Improvement," *Store*, January 2001, p. 60; Michael Brady and J. Joseph Cronin, "Customer Orientation: Effects on Customer Service

Perceptions and Outcome Behaviors," *Journal of Service Research*, February 2001, pp. 241–51; and Michael Hartline, James Maxham III, and Daryl McKee, "Corridors of Influence in the Dissemination of Customer-Oriented Strategy to Customer Contact Service Employees," *Journal of Marketing* 64 (April 2000), pp. 25–41.

34. Disney Institute and Michael Eisner, *Be Our Guest: Perfecting the Art of Customer Service* (New York: Disney Editions, 2001).

35. Moria Cotlier, "Adieu to Abandon Carts," *Catalog Age*, October 2001, p. 39.

36. Alicia Grandey and Analea Brauburger, "The Emotion Regulation behind the Customer Service Smile," in *Emotions in the Workplace: Understanding the Structure and Role of Emotions in Organizational Behavior*, eds. R. Lord, R. Klimoski, and R. Kanfer, (San Francisco: Jossey-Bass, 2002); and Mara Adelman and Aaron Ahuvia, "Social Support in the Service Sector: The Antecedents, Processes, and Consequences of Social Support in an Introductory Service," *Journal of Business Research* 32 (March 1995), pp. 273–82

37. Mark Johlke and Dale Duhan, "Supervisor Communication Practices and Service Employee Job Outcomes," *Journal of Service Research*, November 2000, pp. 154–65.

38. Conrad Lashley, *Empowerment: HR Strategies for Service Excellence* (Boston: Butterworth/Heinemann, 2001).

39. Alan Randolph, and Marshall Sashkin, "Can Organizational Empowerment Work in Multinational Settings?" *Academy of Management Executive* 16 (February 2002), pp. 102–16.

40. Ibid.; and Graham Bradley and Beverly Sparks, "Customer Reactions to Staff Empowerment: Mediators and Moderators," *Group and Organization Management*, 26 (March 2001), pp. 53–68.

41. Piyush Kumar, Manohar Kalawani, and Makbool Dada, "The Impact of Waiting Time Guarantees on Customers' Waiting Experiences," *Marketing Science* 16, no. 4 (1999), pp. 676–785.

42. James Maxham, "Service Recovery's Influence on Consumer Satisfaction, Positive Word-of-Mouth, and Purchase Intentions," *Journal of Business Research*, October 2001, pp. 11–24; and Michael McCollough, Leonard Berry, and Manjit Yadav, "An Empirical Investigation of Customer Satisfaction after Service Failure and Recovery," *Journal of Service Research*, November 2000, pp. 121–37.

43. "Correcting Store Blunders Seen as Key Customer Service Opportunity," *Stores*, January 2001, pp. 60–64; Stephen W. Brown, "Practicing Best-in-Class Service Recovery: Forward-Thinking Firms Leverage Service Recovery to Increase Loyalty and Profits," *Marketing Management*, Summer 2000, pp. 8–10; Stephen Tax, Stephen Brown, and Murali Chandrashekaran, "Customer Evaluations of Service Complaint Experience: Implications for Relationship Marketing," *Journal of Marketing* 62 (April 1998), pp. 60–76; Amy Smith and Ruth Bolton, "An Experimental Investigation of Customer Reactions to Service Failures and Recovery Encounters: Paradox or Peril?" *Journal of Services Research* 1 (August 1998), pp. 23–36; and Cynthia Webster and D. S. Sundaram, "Service Consumption Criticallity in Failure Recovery," *Journal of Business Research* 41 (February 1998), pp. 153–59.

44. Ko de Ruyter and Martin Wetsel, "The Impact of Perceived Listening Behavior in Voice-to-Voice Service Encounters," *Journal of Service Research*, February 2000, pp. 276–84.

45. Hooman Estelami, "Competitive and Procedural Determinants of Delight and Disappointment in Consumer Complaint Outcomes," *Journal of Service Research*, February 2000, pp. 285–300.

CREDITS

Chapter 12
360 Courtesy Albertson's Inc.; **362** Courtesy Debbie Harvey; **369** Courtesy Fleming Companies, Inc.; **372** (left) © Peter Langone/Int'l. Stock; (right) Courtesy Wegman's Food Markets, Inc.; **375** © Amy C. Etra/PhotoEdit; **380** (left) © Makoto Ishida, (right) © M. Hruby; **381** Courtesy Hennes & Mauritz; **387** Republished with permission of Globe Newspaper Company, Inc., from the 05/15/01 issue of *The Boston Globe*, © 2001; **392** Courtesy Shikatani Lacroix Design Inc.; **393** (left) James Leynse/SABA; (right) Courtesy Levi Strauss & Co.

Chapter 13
402 Tom Stack & Associates; **405** © Tom Stewart/Corbis; **411** Vic Bider/PhotoEdit; **412** Courtesy Pelco; **420** © M. Hruby; **422** © Kenneth Lambert/AP Wide World Photos.

Chapter 14
432 © Cindy James Photography; **435** © M. Hruby; **436** © Barry Yee; **437** Fashion Wire Daily/AP Wide World; **439** Courtesy Target Corporation; **442** Courtesy Patek Philippe Geneve; **443** 1993 © Lou Dematteis/The Image Works; **446** Ken Hawkins/Sygma; **447** Paula Bronstein/Liaison Agency; **468** © Barbara Norman.

Chapter 15
476 Reprinted by permission from PRODUCE Merchandising. PRODUCE Merchandising does not review or endorse products, services or opinions; **479** (top) © Dennis McDonald/PhotoEdit; (bottom) The Image Works; **482** © Todd Buchanan; **494** Courtesy Neiman-Marcus; **498** (left) © David Young-Wolff/PhotoEdit; (right) © Michael Newman/PhotoEdit; **508** © James Schnepf; **509** © Dennis McDonald/PhotoEdit.

Chapter 16
512 Courtesy Andy Ginger; **514** (left) Courtesy of Fashion Bug; (right) Courtesy Payless ShoeSource; **515** Courtesy of Target Corporation; **516** (top) Courtesy Kentucky Fried Chicken; (bottom) Courtesy Taco Bell; **518** Courtesy of Ambercrombie and Fitch website (Latest Show page). www.abercrombie.com; **520** Courtesy Abertson's Inc;

521 Courtesy of Office Depot website (Business Center homepage). www.officedepot.com; **522** Courtesy Nieman-Marcus Group; Photo: © M. Hruby; **524** (top) Allsport; **532** Courtesy TJ Maxx; **534** Bonnie Kamin/PhotoEdit; **540** Courtesy ABT Electronics; **541** "Coppertone & Wal-Mart 'Spot the Dog' Scavenger Hunt Promotion," DVC, Morristown, NJ; **543** © M. Hruby; **545** © M. Hruby.

Chapter 17
548 Courtesy JGA and The Dickson Cyber Express Group; **550** Courtesy BFS Retail & Commercial Operations, LLC; **553** Ralph Radford/AP Wide World; **555** Courtesy TJ Maxx; **556** Courtesy Mohr Learning; **562** Jay Freis/Image Bank; **563** Michael Newman/PhotoEdit; **564** Courtesy ShopKo Stores, Inc.; **565** Courtesy Sears Roebuck & Co.; **566** Jack Star/PhotoLink; **570** Courtesy TJ Maxx; **580** (all) Courtesy Checkpoint Systems, Inc.

Chapter 18
586 Stewart Cohen; **588** Scott Dressel-Martin, All Rights Reserved; **590** Courtesy JGA, Inc.; Photographer: Lazlo Regos; **594** © T. Whitney Cox; **596** Paul Warchol/Warchol Photography; **601** © Mario Ruiz/TimePix; **604** (left and right) Courtesy Marketmax, Inc.; **605** Courtesy JGA, Inc.; **606** Courtesy Diesel U.S.A., Inc.; **609, (all)** © Sharon Hoogstraten; **610** Courtesy Chain Store Age; **611** © Scott Francis; **612** Courtesy JGA, Inc.; Photographer: Lazlo Regos.

Chapter 19
618 Courtesy Philip Wee; **621** Courtesy of Lands End. www.landsend.com; **622** (left) Miller/Zell; (right), Discount Store News; **624** Will & Deni; **625** Hironori Miyata/Fujifotos/The ImageWorks; **628** Stock Boston; **631** © Rick Armstrong; **632** Courtesy The Container Store; **633** Dick Blume/The Image Works; **635** Courtesy of TomBoyTools.com (Tool Talk chat page). www.tomboytools.com; **642** Bruce Forster/Stone/GettyImages.

Cases
646 Imagebank.™

NAME INDEX

A

Aaker, David, 179, 517, 539, 731, 733, 742
Aaron, Mark, 188
Accola, John, 742
Ackerman, David, 126, 505
Adamson, James, 304
Adelman, Mara, 748
Adib-Yazdi, Bruce, 52
Agins, Teri, 137, 495, 739
Agrawal, Narendra, 743
Ahuvia, Aaron, 126, 748
Aichlamayr, Mary, 323
Ailawadi, Kusum L., 505
Akin, Camille, 239, 271
Alba, Joseph, 727
Albright, Mark, 337, 522, 738, 744
Alexander, Keith L., 159
Alexander, Nicholas, 179
Allaway, Arthur, 743
Ambler, Tim, 732, 735
Amit, Raphael, 735
Anders, George, 728
Anderson, Erin, 725, 740
Anderson, Eugene, 730
Andreoli, Teresa, 743
Applebaum, William, 259
Archer, Jeanne Smalling, 71
Argyros, George, 747
Arlen, Jeffrey, 740
Arliey, Daniel, 728
Armata, Kevin, 729
Arnould, Eric J., 126
Aron, Laurie Joan, 737
Attaway, Jill S., 745

B

Babin, Barry J., 729, 745
Bader, Louis, 742
Badillo, Frank, 350, 738
Baeb, Eddie, 734
Bahls, Jane Easter, 744
Baker, Julie, 239, 505, 617, 745, 746
Baker, Stacey Menzel, 745
Baker, Walter, 505, 742
Bandyopadyay, Subir, 739
Banks, Ken, 281
Bardi, Edward J., 332
Barnett, Megan, 728

Barr, Vilma, 617
Barrs, Jennifer, 522
Barsh, Joanna, 105, 726
Basuroy, Suman, 401
Bauer, Michael J., 427
Beard, Randolph, 732
Bearden, William O., 505
Beatty, Sharon, 729, 730
Beaudry, Laura M., 181
Beiner, Edward, 735
Beirne, David, 93
Beirne, Martin, 736
Belch, George, 539, 541, 743
Belch, Michael, 539, 541, 743
Bell, David R., 505, 730, 741
Bell, Judith, 617
Bellizzi, Joseph A., 746
Belsie, Laurent, 189
Beng Soo Ong, 747
Beninati, Marie, 427
Bennett, P. D., 730
Bennett, Roger, 730, 746
Bensinger, Ken, 468, 740
Beres, Glen A., 725
Berg, Scott, 176
Bergdal, Michael, 735
Bergen, Mark, 728
Berk, Larry, 745
Berkow, Ira, 298
Bernardin, John, 744
Berner, Robert, 439
Bernstein, Aaron, 743
Berry, Leonard, 645, 727, 732, 746, 747, 748
Bettman, James R., 730
Betts, Mitch, 730
Beyard, Michael D., 239
Bezos, MacKenzie, 15
Bharadwaj, Sundar, 459, 739
Bible, John, 744
Bienstock, Carol C., 401
Birkin, M., 271
Birstwistle, Grete, 137
Bitner, Mary Jo, 483, 727, 732, 747
Black, William, 735
Blank, Arthur, 25
Blattberg, Robert C., 348, 355, 358, 738
Blaxil, Mark, 734
Bliss, William, 736

Bloemer, Josee, 730
Bloom, David, 230
Bloom, Paul N., 463, 729
Boardman, Anthony, 731
Boatwright, Peter, 401, 739
Boghdady, Dina L., 734
Bohlinger, Maryanne Smith, 427
Bolton, Ruth, 358, 645, 748
Bond, Ronald L., 71
Bone, Paula Fitzgerald, 617, 746
Boorstein, Jonathan, 117
Bordat, Alain, 452
Borzo, Jeanette, 105
Boudette, Neal E., 492
Boughton, Paul, 733
Boutlier, Robert, 730
Bowen, David, 746
Bowersox, Donald J., 332
Bradley, Graham L., 736, 748
Brady, Michael, 747
Bramlett, Matthew D., 358
Branch, Shelly, 391, 742
Brand, Richard, 730
Brauburger, Analea, 747
Bresler, Charlie, 275
Breuer, Nancy L., 307, 736
Britney, Robert, 741
Brockett, P., 730
Brockman, Elin Schoen, 734
Brockway, Gary, 743
Broniarczyk, Susan M., 730
Bronstein, Kathy, 141
Brookman, Faye, 728
Brooks, Charles M., 271
Brown, Bruce C., 740
Brown, Gene, 743
Brown, Sheldon, 98
Brown, Stephen, 727, 748
Brown, Steven, 730, 732
Bryan, Valerie, 658
Brynjolfsson, Erik, 728
Buckner, Robert W., 239, 271, 735
Budhwar, Pawan S., 735
Bulkeley, William M., 553, 741
Burgess, Peter, 744
Burke, Raymond R., 745
Burrows, Dan, 275
Butscher, Stephan, 350
Byrne, Harlan S., 208

C

Cable, Daniel, 744
Calantone, Roger, 733
Calhoun, Stephanie, 432
Callahan, Thomas, 294
Cameron, Michaelle, 746
Caminiti, Susan, 729
Campbell, Andrew, 733, 736
Campbell, Charlie, 576
Campion, James, 744
Campion, Michael, 744
Campo, Katia, 427
Cannon, Joseph P., 463
Capella, Louis, 746
Capers, Chris, 740
Caragata, Warren, 728
Carlton, Rachel, 125
Cartwright, Donna, 733
Case, Tony, 743
Cassidy, Tina, 731
Castleberry, Stephen, 744
Cataudella, Joe, 617
Caudron, Shari, 736
Caulfield, John, 736
Chabrow, Eric, 5
Chakrapani, Chuck, 747
Challenger, John A., 735
Chan, Andrew, 736
Chandler, Asa, 521
Chandrasekhar, S., 732
Chandrashekaran, Murali, 748
Chang, Ludwig M. K., 137
Chang, Myong-Hun, 307
Chapman, U., 747
Charles, ReVelle, 271
Chebat, Jean-Charles, 617, 746
Chiger, Sherry, 340, 726
Child, Peter N., 730, 742
Christaller, Walter, 735
Christiansen, Tim, 729
Cigliano, James, 738
Clark, Julie, 747
Clark, Ken, 171, 737, 743, 747
Clark, Maxine, 2–3
Clark, Scott, 171
Clark, Terry, 733
Clarke, G. P., 271
Clarke, Ian, 137
Clarke, Irvine, III, 741
Claxton, Reid, 727
Cleaver, Joanne, 728
Closs, David J., 332
Clow, Kenneth, 747
Clutterbuck, David, 733

Coffy, Tim, 125
Cohen, Adam, 505, 742
Cohen, Alan, 230
Cohen, Cynthia, 734
Coleman, Calmetta, 594
Colin, Mitchell, 307
Collins, David, 731
Collins, Sarah, 495
Colquitt, A., 737
Comer, Lucette, 744
Commandeur, H., 746
Conner, Kathleen, 731
Conrad, Andree, 155, 317
Converse, P. D., 735
Cooke, Donna, 744
Cooper, Cary, 584
Cooper, M. Bixby, 332
Cooper, Martha C., 737
Copple, Brandon, 739
Coppola, Vincent, 532
Corsten, Daniel S., 459, 739
Corstjens, Marcel, 539
Cotlier, Moria, 747
Coughlan, Anne, 740
Cowling, David, 500, 742
Cox, Courtney, 139
Coyle, John Joseph, 332
Coyles, Stephanie, 738
Crawford, Blair, 726
Crawford, James, 728
Crocker, Paul, 401, 739
Cron, William, 741
Cronin, J. Joseph, 730, 747
Crosby, Faye J., 737
Crosby, John V., 401
Crowley, Ayn E., 617, 746
Cullers, Sue, 653
Culnan, Mary, 738
Curhan, Ronald, 743
Czaplewski, Andrew J., 626
Czerniawski, Richard, 732
Czinkota, Michael R., 740

D

Dada, Makbool, 748
Daft, Richard L., 736
Daly, John L., 213, 734
Dant, Rajiv P., 463
Darden, William, 729
Darian, Jean, 730
Dass, Parshotam, 737
d'Astous, Alain, 745
Davidson, William R., 725, 739
Davies, Gary, 179

Davies, R. L., 239, 735
Davis, Jason, 579, 584, 744
Davis, John, 727
Davis, Lenita M., 745
Davis, Ronald W., 740
Dawson, John, 105
Dawson, Peter, 729
Dawson, Scott, 729
De Figueiredo, John, 105
de Ruyter, Ko, 730, 748
De Weinland, James, 742
De Wulf, Kristoff, 730, 746
Debrah, Yaw A., 735
Del Franco, Mark, 727
Della Bitta, Albert J., 741
Delunas, Linda, 737
DeMoss, Michelle, 729
Dennehy, Robert F., 655
Desiraju, Ramarao, 463, 505, 740
Dessler, Gary, 736
deSouza-Lawrence, Margaret Ann, 655
Devine, Mary-Lou, 584
Dhar, Sanjay K., 401, 539
Diamond, Jessica, 743
Dickerson, Kitty G., 731
Dickson, Peter R., 727, 729, 741
Dingle, Derek, 9
Djukic, Aleksandra, 727
Dobscha, Susan, 738
Donaldson, Doug, 743
Donthu, Naveen, 271
Dory, John P., 655
Dowling, Graham, 738
Dreesmann, A. C. R., 727
Drolet, Mary C., 125
Drollinger, Tanya, 744
Drummey, G. L., 735
du Lac, J. Freedom, 731
Duane, Michael J., 307
Dube, Laurette, 617, 746
Duff, Mike, 726
Duhan, Dale, 729, 748
Dunne, Patrick, 739
Dussart, C., 401
Dutta, Pranab, 732
Dutta, Shantanu, 728
Dwyer, F. Robert, 740
Dyche, Jill, 358, 738
Dysart, Joe, 743

E

Earley, Christopher, 735
Earley, Terry, 351
Earnest, Leslie, 141

Eastwick, Mary Ann, 731
Echikson, William, 737
Ehrlich, David, 663, 684, 685
Eighmey, John, 727
Eisner, Alan B., 655
El-Ansary, Adel I., 725
El Boghdady, Dina, 747
Ellen, Pam Scholder, 617, 746
Ellison, Sarah, 231, 422, 732
Ely, Robin J., 737
Emiliani, M. L., 740
Erdem, S. Alton, 674
Erickson, Tanya J., 725, 726
Eroglu, Sevgin A., 735, 745
Estelami, Hooman, 748
Etgar, Michael, 741
Ettenson, Richard, 739
Evered, Roger, 731
Everett, Peter, 729

F
Faber, Ronald, 729
Fabricant, Florence, 731
Faircloth, A., 304
Fairhurst, Ann, 213, 678
Farias, Gerard, 735
Farr, John, 567
Faught, Leslie, 736
Feare, Tom, 323
Feldman, Daniel, 561
Felicetti, Linda F., 696
Ferrell, M. Elizabeth, 729
Ferrell, O. C., 747
Ferris, Maria, 737
Fetto, John, 729
Fickes, Michael, 221
Field, Katherine, 617
Finn, Adam, 730
Fisher, Christy, 730
Fisher, Roger, 463, 740
Fisk, Raymond, 729
Fister, Sarah, 744
Fitzgerald, Kate, 188
Fitzsimmons, James, 746
Fitzsimmons, Mona, 746
Fleischman, John, 222
Florian, Ellen, 725
Foley, Mary Jo, 61
Folkes, Valerie S., 741
Forester, Murray, 727
Fournier, Susan, 699, 738
Fox, Bruce, 740
Fox, Edward J., 738
Fox, Frederick D., 385

Franco, Mark, 340
Franke, Susan, 746
Freathy, Paul, 137
Frederick, James, 728, 743
Frey, William H., 735
Friedman, Matt, 637
Friend, Scott C., 505, 741

G
Galeotti, Sergio, 16
Gallagher, John, 743
Gallo, Rob, 726, 728
Galvin, Barbara Hogan, 734
Ganesan, Shankar, 736
Gapper, Justina, 728
Gardner, Meryl, 743
Garino, Jason, 105
Garvey, Charlotte, 744
Gary, Loren, 734
Gatley, Linda, 733
Gatlin, Greg, 741
Gedenk, Karen, 505, 742
Geng Cui, 731
Gentry, Connie Robbins, 734, 737
Georgladis, Margaret, 738
Gerhart, Barry, 307
Getchell, Margaret, 302
Getz, Gary, 355, 358
Gianatasio, David, 532
Giannulli, Mossimo, 439
Gibbons, Deborah, 744
Gibbs, J., 732
Gijsbrechts, Els, 427
Gildenberg, Bryan, 725, 733
Gill, James, 729
Gill, Lynn E., 739
Gilliland, Michael, 24
Gilly, Mary, 732
Gilmore, James, 738
Ginger, Andy, 512
Girau, Robert, 637
Girion, Lisa, 745
Godfrey, Andrea L., 185
Gofton, Ken, 738
Gokey, Timothy, 738
Gold, Michael, 736
Goldblatt, Jennifer, 385
Goldbrick, Peter, 179
Golden, Linda, 730
Goldstein, Alan, 737
Good, David, 744
Goodbar, Perry, 626
Goodwin, Vicki, 744
Gordon, Erik, 732, 735

Gordon, Joanne, 221, 734
Gose, Joe, 735
Gotlieb, Jerry, 741
Grabow, Karen, 560
Grandey, Alicia, 747
Grant, Lorrie, 635, 727, 738, 745
Gray, Kevin D., 239
Greco, JoAnn, 735
Greco, Susan, 584
Greely, Dave, 617
Green, Frank, 734
Green, Heather, 203, 733
Green, Kelly, 734
Green, William R., 617
Greenberg, Barnett, 727
Greenberg, Herb, 734
Greenberg, Larry, 726
Greenhalgh, Leonard, 463
Greenhouse, Steven, 573, 740
Greenman, Catherine, 115
Gremler, Dwayne, 738
Grewal, Dhruv, 105, 138, 189, 427, 505, 726, 741, 745, 746
Griffin, Mitch, 729
Grigsby, Michael, 729
Grönroos, Christian, 645
Grosso, Chris, 726
Grove, Stephen, 729
Gruen, Thomas W., 401, 459, 739
Grundy, Tony, 735
Grunewald, Joseph P., 696
Gudmundson, Donald, 733
Guier, Cindy, 733
Gulati, Ranjay, 105
Gundlach, Gregory T., 463
Gunn, Molly, 437
Gunter, David, 740
Gupta, Kamal, 741
Gupta, Mehendra, 333
Gupta, Sunil, 505
Guy, Sandra, 747
Gwinner, Kevin, 738

H
Hacker, Carol, 584
Hajewski, Doris, 738
Hamilton, David P., 742
Hamilton, Martha McNeil, 747
Hammed, Frank, 744
Hammond, Jan, 737
Han, Sangman, 505
Hankins, Paula, 566
Hansell, Saul, 93, 326, 726
Hansen, Don R., 734

Harackiewicz, Judith M., 744
Harder, Christian, 271, 735
Harlam, Bari, 539
Harrell, Gilbert, 729
Harrington, Joseph E., Jr., 307
Harris, Aaron, 98
Hartline, Michael, 747
Hartnett, Michael, 728, 736
Harvey, Debbie, 362
Harvey, Michael, 463, 739
Hawkins, Alan J., 737
Hazel, Debra, 734
Hebert, Paulette R., 745, 746
Helliker, Kevin, 730, 744
Hemenan, Herbert, III, 743
Hemp, Paul, 747
Henderson, Pamela W., 746
Henderson, Terilyn, 539, 742
Henderson, Timothy, 645, 745
Heneman, Robert, 743
Hennessey, H. David, 732
Herrington, J. Duncan, 746
Heywood, Suzanne, 730, 742
Hibbard, Justin, 725
Hickey, Mary C., 635
Higgins, Robert C., 733
Hill, Jeffrey, 737
Hill, Suzette, 734
Hisey, Pete, 742
Hite, Robert E., 746
Hiu, Alice S. Y., 137
Ho, Teck-Hua, 505
Hobson, Charles J., 737
Hoch, Stephen J., 401
Hodgson, Richard S., 727
Hoekstra, J., 746
Hof, Robert D., 203, 733
Hoffman, Donna, 728
Holden, Reed K., 505, 741
Hollander, Stanley C., 727
Hollenbeck, John, 307
Hollinger, Richard, 579, 584, 744, 745
Holton, Lisa, 735
Horton, Bari, 340
House, Robert G., 421, 739
Houston, Michael, 743
Howard, Elizabeth, 239
Howell, Debbie, 481, 745
Howell, Roy D., 741
Hoyer, Wayne D., 730
Huant, Jeffrey, 617
Hudson, Repps, 556
Huerta, Carlos, 444

Huey, John, 736
Huff, David L., 735
Huff, Lois, 733, 734
Huffcutt, Allen, 744
Hui, Michael, 617, 730, 746
Humphers, Linda, 726
Hunt, Shelby, 731
Hwant, Suein L., 741
Hyde, Linda, 320, 727, 742

I

Iacobucci, Dawn, 645
Inmon, William H., 737
Iverson, Kathleen, 737
Iwamura, Miki, 730
Iyer, Gopalkrishnan, 105

J

Jackson, Susan, 307, 735, 744
Jacobson, Betsy, 736
Jacobson, Greg, 725
Janiszewski, Chris, 727
Janoff, Barry, 35
Jap, Sandy, 463, 740
Jarnow, Jeannette, 731
Jarvis, Steve, 727
Jaworski, Bernard, 736
Jeannet, Jean-Pierre, 732
Jennerich, Scott, 242
Jeuland, Abel P., 741
Jikyeong Kang, 333
Joachimsthaler, Erich, 517, 539
Johlke, Mark, 748
Johnson, Bradford C., 189, 310
Johnson, Jonathan, 9
Johnson, Lauren Keller, 358
Johnson, Scott, 729
Johnson, William Guy, 294
Johnson-Elie, Tannette, 304
Jones, Benjamin, 726
Jones, John Philip, 539
Jones, Ken, 271
Jong, Jan, 744
Judge, Timothy, 743
Juechter, W. Matthew, 736

K

Kabachnick, Terri, 307, 571
Kahn, Barbara E., 25, 332, 737
Kalapurakai, Rosemary, 729
Kalawani, Manohar, 748
Kalish, Ira, 725, 733
Kalyanam, Kirthi, 677, 687
Kaminski, Peter, 747

Kanfer, R., 748
Kannan, P. K., 358
Karr, Albert, 645
Kashuk, Sonia, 439
Kasper, H., 746
Katz, K. L., 730
Kaufman, Leslie, 725, 731
Kaufman-Scarborough, Carol, 617, 745
Kaufmann, Patrick J., 271
Kaye, Beverly, 736
Keiningham, Timothy, 747
Kelleher, Herbert, 296, 299
Keller, Kevin, 731
Kellner, Tomas, 9
Kelly, E., 358
Kenyon, Kevin, 734
Kerber, Ross, 98
Kerin, Roger A., 732, 733
Kerr, Jeffrey, 731, 732
Kesic, Dawn, 737
Keys, David E., 213, 734
Kiotabe, Masaaki, 730
Kirby, Patrick N., 742
Kirn, Steven, 735
Kleijnen, M., 746
Klein, Matthew, 731
Kliger, Michael, 730, 742
Klimoski, R., 748
Klinvex, Kevin, 584
Knolmayer, Gerhard, 332
Koenig, Harold, 679
Kohler, Kristin, 737
Koloszyc, Ginger, 728, 744, 745
Kopalle, Praveen, 747
Kopp, Robert, 743
Korczynski, Marek, 645
Korman, Abraham, 307
Kostecki, M., 730
Kotler, Philip, 746
Kotter, John, 744
Kozarsky, Neil J., 46
Krafft, Manfred, 736
Kranhold, Kathryn, 739
Kraut, Allen, 307
Kreuger, Richard A., 739
Krishna, Aradhna, 539
Krishnan, R., 505, 741
Kullen, King, 42
Kumar, Nanda, 401
Kumar, Nirmalya, 459, 740
Kumar, Piyush, 748
Kumar, S. Ramesh, 732
Kumar, V., 137, 738

Kunz, Grace I., 427
Kuperman, Jerome C., 655
Kurtz, David, 747
Kuzdrall, Paul, 741

L
Lachman, Conway, 730
Lal, Rajiv, 539, 741
Lambert, Douglas M., 333, 737, 739
Lanasa, John, 730
Lancaster, Hal, 736
Lang, Dori Jones, 25
Lang, James, 733
Langley, C. John, Jr., 332, 333
Lapide, Lawrence, 427
Larsen, Steve, 738
Larson, B. M., 730
Larson, R. C., 730
Laseter, Tim, 740
Lashley, Conrad, 748
Lassar, Walfried, 746
Lawler, Edward, 584
Lawrence, F. Barry, 427
Lazarus, Fred, Jr., 17
Learned, Andrea, 106
LeBlanc, Ronald, 730
Ledford, Rachael, 726, 728
Lee, Hau L., 80, 725
Lee, Tom, 298
Lefevre, Robert J., 213, 734
Lehmann, Donald R., 179, 505, 733, 747
Lemon, Katherine, 346, 358, 738
Letscher, Martin, 380
Levine, Bill, 734
Levy, Michael, 105, 189, 427, 669, 679, 726, 741, 746
Lewis, Diane, 743
Li, Zhan G., 463
Liccione, William, 744
Lieber, Ronald, 556, 736
Lifson, Kal, 744
Lima, Paul, 746
Lindstrom, Marty, 105
Ling Sing Chee, 736
Lipke, David, 747
Lisanti, Tony, 741
Litz, Reginald A., 171
Livingstone, Greg, 125
Lockshin, Lawrence, 731
Lodish, Leonard, 743
Loeb, Walter, 736
Loehmann, Frieda, 55
Lohse, Gerald, 728

Long, Brian, 740
Lord, R., 747
Louviere, Jordan, 730
Lowry, James R., 239
Lowson, Robert H., 463
Lubovek, Seth, 743
Lueddemann, Alicia, 689
Luhnow, David, 444
Lundberg, Craig, 744
Lusch, Robert F., 739
Lutz, Richard J., 727, 730
Lynch, John, Jr., 727, 728

M
MacDonald, Elizabeth, 208
Machleit, Karen A., 735, 745
Macintosh, Gerrard, 731
Mackey, John, 23
Maes, Pattie, 727
Mahajan, Vijay, 732, 733
Maharaj, Davan, 736
Maitland, Alison, 737
Malhotra, Naresh, 105
Malik, Rafique, 732
Maloney, Michael, 732
Malos, Stanley, 744
Malossi, Giannino, 731
Mander, Edmund, 734
Mangleburg, Tamara, 745
Mangold, W. Glynn, 743
Manning, Kenneth C., 505
Manson, Marilyn, 141
Mantel, Susan Powell, 735
Mantrala, Murali, 401, 743
Marcial, Gene G., 254, 353
Marcus, Joshua, 732
Marder, Dianna, 507, 742
Marin, Rich, 731
Markley, Jennifer, 746
Marme, Teresa, 272
Marmorstein, Howard, 741
Marn, Mike, 505, 742
Marney, Jo, 731
Maronick, Thomas J., 727
Marsh, Harriet, 732
Marshall, C. R., 744
Martin, Antoinette, 225
Martin, Ingrid M., 741
Maslow, Abraham, 729
Mason, J. Barry, 743
Mathur, Anil, 745
Mathwick, Charla, 105
Mattila, Anna S., 617, 738, 746
Mauk, Mitchell, 745

Maxham, James, III, 747, 748
Mazur, Paul M., 283, 736
Mazze, Edward, 71
McAfee, R. Bruce, 584
McAlister, Leigh, 332, 730, 737
McAllister, Leigh, 25
McBain, Richard, 744
McCance, McGregor, 500
McCann, John, 743
McCarthy, Cathleen, 746
McCarthy, Patrick D., 25, 645, 689, 746
McClain, James, 550, 551
McCloud, John, 735
McCollough, Michael, 748
McCusker, Deb, 736
McDougall, Gordon H. G., 693
McDowell, Edwin, 52
McGahan, Anita, 732
McGrath, Mary Ann, 138
McIntyre, Shelby, 743
McKee, Daryl, 747
McKinnon, John, 744
McLaughlin, Edward, 732
McMenamin, Mark, 731
Mead, Gary, 339
Mead, Rebecca, 732
Mehrotra, Anuj, 427
Mengleburg, Tmara, 138
Mentzer, John T., 401
Merrick, Amy, 726, 731, 732, 741
Mertens, Peter, 332
Messmer, Max, 737
Metcalfe, Dorothy A., 213
Meuter, Matthew L., 732
Michman, Ronald, 71
Mick, David Glen, 729, 738
Mihas, Elizabeth, 539, 742
Milbank, Dana, 231
Miller, Amy, 638
Miller, Cyndee, 731, 743
Miller, Fred, 743
Miller, Rachel, 747
Miller, Stephen, 733
Miller-Mordaunt, Veronica, 213
Milne, George, 738
Miron, John R., 239, 271
Mittal, Banwari, 746
Mixer, Jean, 734
Mohr, Lois, 747
Moin, David, 726, 727, 739, 743
Monahan, James, 741
Monroe, Kent B., 505, 741
Montgomery, Cynthia, 731

Moody, Patricia E., 333
Moore, Ann, 139
Moorthy, Sridhar, 729
Moreaua, Page, 539
Morgan, Robert, 731
Morganosky, Michelle, 729
Moroe, Yukihiro, 725, 726
Morrison, David, 740
Mossberg, Walter S., 739
Mowen, Maryanne M., 734
Mozafarim, Ramin, 402–403
Mudambi, Susan, 732
Murphy, Ian, 732
Murphy, Tara, 732
Murrell, Audrey J., 737
Muto, Sheila, 735
Myers, Gerry, 507

N
Nagle, Thomas T., 505, 741
Nagpal, Anish, 137
Nair, Mohan, 213, 734
Nannery, Matt, 725
Napoleon, Eileen, 271
Narasimhan, Chakravarthi, 333
Natale, Jo, 726
Negley, Jennifer, 481
Nel, Deon, 747
Nelson, Bruce, 78
Nelson, David, 333
Nelson, Emily, 318
Neslin, Scott A., 505, 743
Neuborne, Ellen, 727, 728, 746
Nielsen, Jakob, 597
Niraj, Rakesh, 333
Nisol, Patricia, 427
Noe, Raymond, 307
Norberg, Torbjön, 334
Notess, Greg, 743
Novack, Robert, 741
Novak, Thomas, 728
Nunes, Joseph C., 401, 739
Nystrom, Paul, 733

O
O'Connell, Matthew, 584
Odekerken-Schroder, G., 746
O'Donnell, Tim, 564
Ody, Penelope, 80
Ohlinger, Chris, 726
O'Kelly, Morton E., 239, 271
Oldham, Todd, 438, 439
Oliver, Richard, 730

Olson, Eric M., 626
Olson, Jerry C., 729
O'Mara, W. Paul, 239
Ono, Yumiko, 227
O'Reilly, Charles A., III, 275
Orr, Bill, 728
Ortega, Bob, 736, 742
Osborn, Suzanne Barry, 377, 746
Osten, Tom, 729
Osterland, Andrew, 728
Otnes, Cele, 138
Ouchi, William, 736
Owens, Harry, 532, 533
Owens, Jan, 683
Owens, Margaret, 741
Owens, Sara, 742
Ozment, John, 747

P
Pacca, Kristina, 650, 661, 686
Pagh, Janus D., 737
Pailin, James, 729
Palanand, Kay, 730
Palmeri, Jean E., 275
Panepinto, Ro, 738
Parasuraman, A., 505, 727, 741,
    745, 746, 747
Parks, Liz, 737
Parrish, Jean, 739
Parry, Mark E., 459
Parson, Charles, 744
Parsons, William, 747
Patsuris, Penelope, 93
Patten, Sally, 231
Patton, Phil, 727
Paul, Pamela, 571
Pearce, Michael, 271
Pellet, Jennifer, 61, 745
Peltier, James, 727
Penaloza, Lisa, 732
Pence, Dennis, 107
Penttila, Chris, 637
Peppers, Don, 105, 353
Perdick, Jeff, 308
Pereira, Joseph, 532
Perenchio, Madelyn, 213
Perry, Gregg, 500, 742
Perry, Kathy, 743
Pessimier, Edgar D., 730
Peter, Dan, 734
Peter, J. Paul, 729
Petersen, Andrea, 746
Petersen, Ann, 358, 427
Petersen, Melody, 742

Peterson, Bruce, 476
Peterson, Cole, 278
Pettigrew, Tru, 387
Petty, Ross, 464, 500, 506, 567
Pfaff, Kimberly, 731
Pfeffer, Jeffrey, 275, 735, 736
Pine, B. Joseph, 738
Pitt, Leyland, 747
Pleasance, Darren, 738
Pogoda, Dianne, 730
Poirier, Charles C., 427
Poisant, Jim, 747
Pol, Louis, 239
Pollack, Elaine, 463, 742
Porter, Michael E., 105, 179, 731,
    733, 735
Power, Denise, 737
Powers, James T., 427, 739
Prahalad, C. K., 731
Prend, Richard, 729
Pressler, Margaret, 726
Pride, William M., 733
Print, Earl, 746
Prior, Molly, 203, 742
Pritchett, Lou, 459
Pui-Wing Tam, 727
Puri, R., 729
Purvis, Kathleen, 745
Putrevu, Sanjay, 729

Q
Quick, Rebecca, 600, 728
Quilt, John, 743
Quinn, Bill, 71, 727, 733
Quinn, Richard T., 735

R
Rafiq, Mohammed, 736
Rafter, Michelle, 635, 728
Randolph, Alan, 748
Rangan, V. Kasturi, 740
Raper, Sarah, 734
Raphael, Murray, 746
Rappaport, Alfred, 733
Ratchford, Brian T., 728, 729
Reard, Louis, 139
Reardon, Lames, 213
Rechers, Arnon, 744
Reda, Susan, 726, 737, 739, 743
Redwell, Sara, 297
Regan, Keith, 728
Reichheld, Frederick F., 307, 358,
    737, 743
Reilly, W. J., 735

Reinartz, Werner, 738
Repenning, Nelson P., 734
Reynolds, Brian E., 427
Reynolds, Jonathan, 231
Rhoads, Christopher, 231
Ridgeway, Nancy, 729
Ridnour, Rick, 744
Rigby, Darrell, 358
Rigdon, Edward, 105
Robertson, Christopher, 738
Robertson, Ivan, 584
Robeson, James F., 421, 739
Rodgers, Martha, 105
Roebuck, Chris, 744
Roehling, Mark, 744
Rogers, Charlene, 571
Rogers, D. S., 239, 735
Rogers, Everett, 727
Rominger, Anna, 739
Ronkainen, Ilkka A., 740
Rose, Randall L., 505
Rosenau, Jeremy A., 401
Rosenthal, Elisabeth, 732
Rosenzweig, Philip, 737
Ross, Julie, 745
Roth, D., 735
Roth, Daniel, 747
Rothbaum, Noah, 740
Rothschild, R. L., 731
Roush, Chris, 71
Rowland, H., 358
Rozhon, Tracie, 726
Rucci, Anthony, 735
Ruggles, Ron, 743
Rusch, Robin, 739
Russell, Gary J., 358, 427
Rust, Roland, 358, 730, 738
Rutner, Stephen M., 333
Ryan, Suzanne C., 387
Ryan, Thomas J., 740

S
Salanie, Bernard, 213, 734
Salvaneschi, Luigi, 239, 271
Samli, A. Coskun, 179, 731, 742
Sanchez, Jennifer, 111
Sandberg, Jared, 727
Sankar, Venkatesh, 728
Sansone, Carol, 744
Sarathy, Ravi, 738
Sashkin, Marshall, 748
Sato, Yoshinobu, 459
Sattler, Henrik, 505, 742
Savitt, Ronald, 138

Sawabini, Stuart, 333
Sawhney, Vinod, 732
Sawyer, Alan, 727, 729, 741
Scardino, Emily, 25
Schefter, Phil, 358
Schenk, Joseph, 744
Scheraga, Dan, 725, 738, 739, 742, 745
Scheumann, Jon, 213
Schibrowsky, John, 727
Schindler, Robert M., 742
Schmidt, Jeffrey, 729
Schmitt, Bernard, 732
Schneider, Benjamin, 746
Schnetzer, Jenny, 746
Schuler, Randall, 307, 735, 744
Schultz, Howard, 25, 273
Schulz, David P., 71, 571, 726, 728, 743, 744
Schwepker, Charles, 744
Scott, Jody, 387
Scott, Linda M., 126
Scott, Teresa, 656, 675
Sculley, Arthur B., 463
Sebastian, Pamela, 729
Seckler, Valerie, 728
Seiders, Kathleen, 214, 731
Seifert, Dirk, 401
Seijts, Gerard, 744
Sejo Oh, 740
Self, David, 566
Sellers, Patricia, 736
Serra, Daniel, 271
Shah, Reshma H., 401
Shamroski, Stephanie, 733, 734
Shapiro, Carl, 741
Shapiro, Carol, 741
Sharav, Itzhak, 741
Shaw, Lisa, 299
Shaw, S. A., 732
Shepard, Stephen B., 739
Sheppard, C. David, 744
Sherman, Andrew J., 71
Sherman, Elaine, 745
Sheshunoff, Alex, 728
Sheth, J. N., 730
Shim, Soyeon, 731
Shimp, Terence, 539
Shugan, Steven M., 505, 728, 741
Shurr, Paul, 740
Shuster, William, 742
Siegel, Dave, 125
Silverman, George, 743
Silverman, Greg, 733

Simmons, Mary, 737
Simonson, Alex, 732
Simonson, Itamar, 730, 742
Singh, Harbir, 735
Singh, Jagdip, 747
Singh, Parbudyal, 745
Sirgy, M. Joseph, 138, 745
Sirohi, Niren, 732
Siu, Noel Y. M., 137
Skrovan, Sandra J., 463, 725, 726
Slater, Stanley F., 626
Smalley, Suzanne, 553
Smith, Alison, 729
Smith, Amy, 645, 748
Smith, Craig S., 298
Smith, David, 452
Smith, Eileen, 745
Smith, Frances B., 500
Smith, H. Jeff, 738
Smith, Michael, 728
Smith, Ray A., 734
Smith, Ruth Belk, 745
Smith, Stephen, 743
Snitz, Andy, 555
Solomon, Michael R., 729
Soman, D., 741
Sorkin, Andrew Ross, 733
Sowers, Todd, 315
Spangenberg, Eric R., 617, 746
Sparks, Beverley A., 736, 748
Sparks, John, 744
Spector, Robert, 25, 71, 645, 689, 746
Speer, Tibbett L., 747
Spiller, Peter, 728
St. John, Warren, 606
Stackpole, Beth, 340
Staelin, Richard, 741
Stalk, G., 733
Stampfl, Ronald W., 725, 739
Stankevich, Debby Garbato, 159, 726, 742, 743
Stanley, John, 739
Starkman, Dean, 734
Stegner, Jonathan, 333
Steinart-Threlkeid, Tom, 61
Steinhauser, Jennifer, 735, 747
Stellin, Susan, 747
Stepanek, Marcia, 86
Sterman, John D., 734
Stern, Gabriella, 742
Stern, Louis W., 725
Stern, Neil Z., 25
Sternquist, Brenda, 179

Stewart, Alice C., 171
Stiving, Mark, 742
Stock, James R., 333, 737, 739
Strachan, George, 725, 726
Stum, David L., 736
Suein Hwang, 731
Sullivan, Pauline, 138, 333
Summers, Teresa A., 745, 746
Sundaram, D. S., 748
Surowiecki, James, 733, 737
Sutton, Gary, 213, 734
Swamy, Ramesh, 213
Swartz, Judy, 437
Sweeney, Daniel, 725
Sweeney, Daniel J., 739
Swinyard, William R., 743
Symons, Allene, 743

T
Tadlaqui, Ali, 743
Talpade, Salil, 730
Talukdar, Debabrata, 729
Tanaka, Hiroshi, 730
Tang, Christopher S., 505, 741, 730
Tang, Fang-Fang, 105
Taubes, Gary, 138
Tax, Stephen, 748
Taylor, Don, 71
Taylor, Jack, 556
Taylor, Kenneth, 725
Taylor, Paul, 744
Taylor, S., 730
Tayman, Jeff, 239
Tazaki, Makoto, 80
Tech-Hua Ho, 730, 741
Tedeschi, Bob, 86, 728, 729
Tellis, Gerald, 126, 505
Tepper, Bette K., 427
Terhune, Chad, 726
Ternus, Kat, 617
Thau, Barbara, 189
Thelen, Eva, 729
Thijssen, Jo, 744
Thilmany, Jean, 86
Thomas, Jacquelyn S., 348, 355, 358
Thomas, Karen, 728
Thomas, R. Roosevelt, 737
Thompson, Ann Marie, 747
Thompson, John S., 735
Thompson, Stephanie, 740
Thorn, Susan, 223
Tiernan, Bernadette, 25
Tigert, Douglas, 731

Tisch, Carol, 539
Titus, Philip, 729
Toevs, Stacey Witt, 746
Torrington, Derek, 736
Trachtenberg, Jeffrey A., 726
Trattner, Douglas, 176
Tsao, Amy, 390
Tsay, Andy A., 505
Tsi, D. K., 730
Turley, L. W., 730
Turner, Cal, Jr., 481

U
Uncles, Mark, 738
Underhill, Paco, 82, 138, 617, 745
Urbany, Joel, 729
Ury, William, 463, 740

V
Van Boven, Sarah, 731
van Breda, Michael, 741
Van Kenhove, Patrich, 730
Van Slyke, Erik, 737
Van Waterschoot, Walter, 730
Varadarajan, P. Rajan, 732, 733
Varian, Hal R., 741
Varki, Sajeev, 730
Vavra, Terry, 747
Verdisco, Robert, 731
Versloot, Bert, 744
Vickery, Lisa, 188, 742
Vida, Irena, 213
Vincenti, Lisa, 728, 729
Vining, Aidan, 731
Vitucci, Stephen, 653
Vitzthum, Carlta, 726
Voss, Glenn B., 505, 741, 745
Vriens, Marco, 729

W
Wagner, Janet, 645, 739
Wagner, Mary, 117, 737
Wakefield, Kirk L., 239
Waldrop, Judith, 133
Walker, Alfred J., 307
Walker, Bruce J., 727
Walker, Chip, 743
Walker, Patricia H., 505, 741
Walker, Philip, 733
Walkup, C., 738
Walters, Rockney G., 401
Wang, Charlie C. L., 137
Wanous, John, 744

Wansink, Brian, 741
Ward, Aaron Montgomery, 58
Wasserman, David, 733
Watkins, Michael, 463
Way, Bill, 71
Webster, Cynthia, 748
Wee, Philip, 618
Weeks, Andrea, 213
Wehrfritz, George, 227
Weingart, Laurie, 744
Weingarten, Tara, 734
Weintraub, Arlene, 105
Weiss, Michael J., 132, 271, 731
Weiss, Naomi, 298
Weitz, Barton, 648, 649, 657, 659, 661, 671, 682, 683, 699, 727, 736, 740, 743, 747
Weitzman, Michelle, 737
Wellington, Sheila, 737
Wensley, Robin, 733, 740, 743, 747
Werther, William, 731, 732
Wessel, David, 492
West, Pat, 730
Wetsel, Martin, 748
Whalley, Susan, 738
Whang, Seungjin, 80, 725
Whelan, David, 729
White, Erin, 732, 733
White, Gerald, 744
White, John Robert, 239
Whittelsey, Frances Cerra, 507
Whittington, J. Lee, 744
Wilcox, James, 729
Wilkes, Robert, 730, 747
Wilkie, Maxine, 746
Wilkie, William L., 727, 730
Williams, Stephanie, 740
Williamson, Laura, 744
Willman, John, 729
Wills, Keith, 725, 726
Wilson, A., 271
Wilson, David, 401
Wilson, Eric, 727
Wilson, Marianne, 5, 125, 141, 381, 588, 726, 733, 745
Winer, Russell S., 179, 358, 733, 742
Winfrey, Oprah, 355
Winters, Rebecca, 385
Wirth, Linda, 737
Wirtz, Jochen, 617, 746
Wiscombe, Janet, 736
Wise, Richard, 740
Wissman, Geoff, 726, 727, 728, 732

Witkin, Gary, 743
Witkowski, Terrence, 730
Wittink, Dick, 732
Woehr, David, 744
Wofford, J. C., 744
Wong, Nancy, 126
Wongsuwan, Cynthia, 670
Woodruff, David, 732
Woodruff, Robert, 179
Woods, John, 645
Woods, Stacy, 727
Woods, William W., 463
Woodside, A. G., 730
Woodside, Arch, 729
Wright, Patrick, 307
Wysocki, Bernard, Jr., 732

X
Xing, Xiaolin, 105
Xing Pan, 728

Y
Yadav, Manjit, 748
Yadin, Daniel, 539
Yalch, Richard F., 746
Yamamoto, Yoshito, 730
Yang, Catherine, 736
Yardley, Jim, 740
Yasai-Ardekani, Masoud, 733
Yin, Sandra, 729
Yong-Soon Kang, 729
Young, Cheri, 744
Yu-Lee, Reginald Thomas, 734

Z
Zawada, Craig, 505, 742
Zeier, Alexander, 332
Zeithaml, Valarie A., 346, 358, 483, 727, 732, 738, 746, 747
Zemke, Ron, 645
Zenger, Todd, 744
Zhan, Sherrie E., 740
Zhang, Z. John, 539
Ziccardi, Donald, 743
Zimmer, George, 275
Zimmerman, Ann, 44, 318, 391, 725, 726
Zimmerman, Denise, 745
Zusman, Pinhas, 741

ORGANIZATION INDEX

A

A.T. Stewart, 53
A&P, 3, 438
ABC Distributing, 59
Abercrombie & Fitch Co., 154, 160, 518, 660–661
AC Moore, 51
AC Nielsen, 41
Ace Hardware, 390
Advance Auto, 49
AEI, 613
Aeon, 12
Afterthoughts, 161
Ahold, 11, 157, 165, 658–659. *See also* Royal Ahold
Ahold USA, 35
AIM Mail Centers, 68
Albertson's, 11, 35, 41, 91, 478, 520
Aldi, 450
alg.com, 115
Alloy.com, 113
AM/PM Convenience Stores, 68
Amazon.com, 3, 4, 15, 34, 57, 80, 91, 96, 97, 112, 160, 190, 202, 203, 326, 342, 351, 352, 354, 395, 498, 620, 635, 655
America Online (AOL), 342
American Airlines, 639
American Drug Stores, 290, 291
American Eagle Outfitters, 96, 154, 250, 660
American Express, 167, 633, 642
Amy's Ice Cream, 638
Anderson Little, 275
Ann Taylor, 225
Arby's, 68
Asda, 437, 501
Associated Merchandising Corporation, 452
Athlete's Foot, 610
Athlete's Foot for Her, 610
Auchan, 11, 43
Autobytel, 115
AutoZone, 49
Aventura Shoe Store, 614
Avis, 556
Avon, 6, 13, 60, 61, 190, 671

B

Babies "R" Us, 51
Bal Harbour Shops, 241
Bally Total Fitness, 208
Banana Republic, 154, 390–393, 410, 440, 478, 600, 603, 606
bankrate.com, 115
Barnes & Noble, 37, 51, 100, 101, 112, 149, 160, 171, 202, 390, 507
Barnes & Noble.com, 57, 498
Barney's, 275, 494
Bashas', 449
Bass Pro Shops, 4, 6, 50, 52, 59, 82
Bath and Body Works, 67, 219, 251, 312
BCBG, 86
Bealls, Inc., 216
Beaver Creek, 233
Bed Bath & Beyond, 34, 51, 52
Belks, 292
Ben Franklin, 16
Benetton, 15
Berdorf Goodman, 341
Best Buy, 4, 35, 37, 51, 75, 99, 117, 202, 220, 281, 390, 478, 516
Better Homes Realty Inc., 68
BI-LO, 41
Big Lots, Inc., 56
BJ's Wholesale Club, 35, 44
Blair Corp., 59
Blockbuster Video, 19, 219, 220, 233, 586
Bloomingdale's, 19, 53, 97, 152, 154, 234, 289, 596, 600, 602
Bluefly.com, 86, 96, 454, 477, 494
Bon Marche, The, 19, 598
Boo.com, 57
Bookseller's, 171
Boots, 165
Borders, 15, 51, 93, 297, 507, 683
bottomdollar.com, 500
Bread & Circus, 23
Bridgestone/Firestone, 550–551
Broadmoor Hotel and Spa, 626
Brooks Brothers, 56, 161, 163, 172, 440
Brunswick, 176
Brylane, 59

Build-A-Bear Workshop, 2–3, 649
Burdines, 53, 402–403, 560
Burger King, 161, 247
Burlington Coat Factory, 55, 225
Burpee, 58, 59

C

C & R Clothiers, 275
Cabela's, 59
Calvin Klein, 441
Campbell Soup Company, 7
Capital Grille, 232
Carclub, 115
CarMax, 34
Carrefour, 3, 4, 11, 35, 41, 42, 99, 160, 162, 163, 165, 166, 169, 199, 231, 311, 658–659
CarsDirect, 115
Cartier, 254
Cato, 169
CDNOW, 6, 92
CDW Computer Centers, 59
Centura Banks, 351
Cerruti, 15
Champs Sports, 67, 161, 272
Charming Shoppes, 127, 166
Cheesecake Factory, 232
Chico's FAS Inc., 148, 340
Children's Place, 219, 220, 323
Chippery, 392
Circuit City, 33, 35, 48, 51, 74, 94, 96, 189, 202, 203, 220, 289, 479, 524, 544, 619
Claritas, 130, 256, 257
Classic Creations, 171
Club Libby Lu, 125
Club Monaco, 600
Coach, 227
Coca-Cola, 442
Coldwater Creek, 107, 225, 446
Coldwell Banker Real Estate Corp., 68
Cole National, 49
Colgate-Palmolive, 534
Community Pride Food Stores, 9
CompUSA, 51, 223
Concord, 44
Container Store, 158, 159, 276, 295, 340, 566, 632

Coppertone, 541
Corporate Express, 59
Costco, 11, 35, 44, 73, 164, 202, 220, 236, 248, 281, 318, 391, 450, 477, 588
Crate & Barrel, 52, 225, 229, 440
CSG Information Services, 258
Cub, 478
CVS, 34, 37, 45, 48, 54, 96, 155, 390, 488, 489

D
Dalei, 12
Days Inn, 301
Dayton Hudson, 11, 67, 207, 317
dELiAs, 96, 394, 395
Dell Computer Corp., 7, 59, 192, 451
Denny's Inc., 68, 303
Denstply International, 469
Dick Clark's American Bandstand Grills, 613
Dickson Cyber Mall, 605
Diesel, 606
Dillard's, 438
Dilmah's, 57
Disney. See Walt Disney Company
Disney World, 620, 634
Dollar General, 56, 481, 657–658
Dollar Tree, 56
Dom Perignon, 44
Domino's, 339
Doneger Group, 452
Donna Karan, 86
DoubleClick, 544
DoughNET.com, 87
Dress Barn, 56
Dreyer's Grand Ice Cream, 441
Drugstore.com, 95, 96
Dunkin' Donuts, 68

E
EatZi's, 46, 47
eBay, 34, 57, 96, 190, 326, 448, 495, 499, 680–682
Ebel, 44
Eckerd Drug, 34, 54, 543
Eddie Bauer, 80, 96, 99, 227, 300, 345
Edeka/AVA, 12
Edgars Consolidated Stores, 405
Edmund's, 115
Edward Beiner Optical, 236, 237, 246, 252–255, 258–263

Eleclerc, 12
Electronic Boutique, 308
Electronic Privacy Information Center, 342, 343
Enterprise Rent-A-Car, 556, 682
Envirosell, 602
Ermenegildo Zegna, 155
ESRI, Inc., 256, 384
Estée Lauder, 171
eToys, 4, 57, 92, 121
Expedia, 90
Expo Design, 51
Exxon Mobil, 189

F
F.A.O. Schwarz, 225
Fakegifts.com, 468
Family Dollar Stores, Inc., 56, 202, 657–658, 661–662
Famous Footwear, 242
Fashion Bug, 514
Federal Express, 382
Federated Department Stores, 53, 59, 86, 202, 234, 282–283, 287–290, 389, 514, 553
Ferrari Automobile Company, 469
Filene's, 53
First Bank, 351
Fogdog.com, 37
Foley's, 234
Food Lion, 3, 42
Foot Locker, 49, 67, 161, 162, 250
Ford Motor Company, 319
Fox Sports Sky Box, 233
Fred Meyer, 43
FreeMarkets, 451
Fresh Farm, 353
Fresh Fields, 23
Friday's, 230, 442
Friendly's, 497

G
G.H. Bass, 56
Gadzooks, 649–650
Galleri Orrefors Kosta Boda, 611
Galyan, 82
Gap, Inc., 4, 7, 37, 49, 50, 94, 129, 151, 154, 162, 163, 165, 174, 197, 202, 225, 228, 229, 235, 283, 289, 290, 344, 367, 386, 410, 422, 436, 437, 440, 446, 495, 515, 519, 568, 596, 603, 605, 606

Gap Kids, 219, 220
Gap.com, 100
Garden.com, 4, 57, 92
Gart Sports, 51
Gateway, 80, 97
Genco Distribution Systems, 326
General Cinema Theaters, 229
General Motors, 189
General Nutrition Centers (GNC), 49, 128–129
Georgio Armani, 441
Ghuman Export Private, Ltd., 678
Giant, 41, 165
Giant Foods, 302
Giorgio Armani S.p.A., 16
GM, 189
GNC, 128–129
Gold's Gym, 391
GoodLife Fitness Club, 689–693
Goody's, 594
Green Bay Packers, 436
Greenbacks, 56
Guess?, 227, 435, 441
Gymboree, 493

H
H&M, 4, 50, 165, 381
Häagen-Dazs, 129
Haggar, 319, 321, 322, 323
Hallmark, 96, 563
Hanover Direct, 59
Harley-Davidson, 441, 442, 509
Harpo Productions, 355
Harris Cyclery, 98
Harrod's, 97
Harry and David, 58, 59
Harry Rosen, 155, 317, 351
Hart, Shaffner and Marx, 275
Hastings Entertainment, 49
HEB, 35, 129
Hemingway's Blue Water Café, 52
Hennes & Mauritz (H&M), 165, 381
Hertz, 556
Hewlett-Packard (HP), 6, 233
Hollister, 660–661
Home Depot, 4, 6, 8, 11, 12, 13, 48, 51, 97, 98, 129, 156, 157, 163, 165, 170, 171, 189, 192, 220, 221, 231, 235, 245, 276, 283, 292, 293, 299, 300, 301, 311, 320, 390, 405, 438, 450, 478, 506, 516, 623, 669–670
Home Shopping Network (HSN), 61

Hot Topic, 49, 141, 154, 556, 571
HotHotHot!, 8
HSN (Home Shopping Network), 61
Hudson's, 67, 224, 317
Hudson's Bay Company, 48
Hughe's, 678
Hugo Boss, 155, 351
Hyatt Hotels, 124

I
IBM, 96
ICA Handlarnas AB, 165, 334
IKEA, 4, 35, 124, 126, 165, 519, 618, 623
Independent Grocers Alliance (IGA), 67
Information Resources, Inc., 488
InfoScan, 383, 488
Intel, 342
Intermarche, 11
International Bicycle Centers, 39–40
International Council of Shopping Centers, 258
Intimate Brands, 49, 59, 67
Ito-Yokado, 12
iVillage, 87

J
J. Crew, 95, 140, 227, 229, 422, 446, 494, 495
J. Sainsbury. See Sainsbury
Jaeger, 607
Jaguar, 319
JCPenney, 7, 11, 16, 21–22, 33, 34, 37, 53, 54, 58, 59, 67, 72, 73, 80, 100, 122, 134, 135, 193, 225, 292, 299, 300, 302, 304, 318, 391, 432, 437, 438, 478, 493, 500, 514, 525, 542, 593, 598, 628, 636
JDA, 493
Jos A. Bank, 96
Joslins, 613
Junkbusters, 342

K
K & K True Value Hardware, 171
Kay Bee Toys, 219, 220
KBToys, 96, 493
Kelley Blue Book, 507
Kellogg, 7
Kelo Department Store, 625
KFC, 35, 68, 163, 516
KhiMetrics, 493

Kids Foot Locker, 67, 161
Kids "R" Us, 51
Kimberly-Clark, 318, 389
Kleenex, 344
Kmart, 4, 11, 34, 41, 43, 45, 48, 100, 150, 152, 203, 249, 341, 389, 438
The Knot, 635
Koc Group's Migros, 166
Kohl's Department Stores, 53, 148, 193, 217, 219, 289, 594, 598
Kraft Foods, Inc., 7, 366–367, 441
Kresges, 229
Kroger Company, 11, 35, 41, 43, 202, 259, 289, 341, 389

L
L.L. Bean, 6, 58, 59, 96, 116, 517, 629
Lady Foot Locker, 67, 161
Lady of America, 68
Lands' End, 58, 59, 84, 89, 94, 95, 96, 99, 117, 166, 202, 225, 492, 621, 631, 653
Lane Bryant, 127
Lawson Sportswear, 80, 672–674
Levi Strauss & Co., 96, 227, 390–393, 441, 442, 499
The Limited, 7, 49, 50, 153, 161, 202, 229, 231, 235, 286, 289, 437, 438, 446, 515, 519
Limited Too, 125, 251, 613
Lindy's Bridal Shoppe, 694–696
Little Caesar's, 339
Liz Claiborne, 389, 447, 607
llbean.com, 395
Loblaw, 438
Loews Cineplex Entertainment, 230
Lord and Taylor, 53
L'Oréal, 171
Los Angeles Times, 542
Louis Vuitton-Moet Hennessy, 35
Lowe's, 8, 51, 301, 405, 438
LVMH, 35

M
MacFrugal's Bargains Close-outs, 56
Macy's, 7, 19, 33, 53, 96, 100, 302, 392, 436, 438, 495, 499, 516, 524, 553
Macy's West, 590
Mail Boxes Etc., 68
MarineMax, 353
Marketmax, 604

Marks & Spencer, 46, 163, 167, 459, 604
Marriott, 127, 128, 196, 297, 298, 620, 630, 631
MARS, 34
Marshall Field's, 48, 55, 67, 220, 317, 454, 477, 532, 570, 589
Marubeni, 166
Mary Kay Cosmetics, 6, 293
Mast Industries, 161
Master Lock, 390
MasterCard, 196, 339
Mattel, 59, 470
May Department Stores Company, 53, 54, 202, 234, 438
Mazda, 319
MCA, 227
McCormick, 7
McCrory's, 229
McDonald's, 13, 35, 52, 65, 68, 157, 158, 163, 166, 233, 247, 442, 492, 516, 525, 620, 622, 638
McFadden's Department Store, 679–680
Medicap Pharmacies Inc., 68
Mei Da Coffee Company, 298
Mellerio dits Meller, 282
Menard, 51
Men's Wearhouse, 51, 156, 275, 276, 297, 553, 562
Mervyn's, 67, 317
Metro AG, 11, 162, 166, 389
Mi Amore Pizza & Pasta, 339
Michaels Stores, 51
Microsoft, 246, 342, 469
MicroWarehouse, 59
Mini Maid, 8
Missouri's Country Club Plaza, 232
Monsoon, 166
Montgomery Wards, 4
Mr. CB's Bait & Tackle, 171
Mrs. Fields, 589
Mrs. Gooch's, 23
mysimon.com, 499

N
Nabisco, 389
National Football League, 37
National Grange, 58
Natural Food Markets, 23
The Nature Company, 517

Neiman Marcus, 53, 59, 97, 150, 152, 154, 172, 224, 225, 235, 337, 438, 494, 517, 522, 543, 601, 629, 661–662
Nestlé, 157
NetGrocer, 94
NFL.com, 37
Nike, 161, 227, 441, 447
Niketown, 82, 598
Nine West Outlet, 56, 340, 508
99 Cents Only Stores, 56
Nolan's Finest Foods, 675–677
Nordstrom, 19, 54, 124, 152, 172, 224, 235, 274, 292, 295, 300, 337, 438, 446, 478, 517, 551, 620, 621, 637, 687–689

O
O, 355
Odd Lots, 56
Office Depot, 7, 35, 50–53, 59, 78–79, 96, 165, 170, 220, 254, 390, 395, 420, 450, 516, 521
OfficeMax, 35, 170, 233
Old Navy, 48, 50, 154, 223, 410
Olive Garden, 555
Omni, 478
oprah.com, 355
Orion Food Systems Inc., 68
Orvis, 58, 89, 96
Overstock.com, 96
Oxygen Media, 355

P
P&G, 6, 156, 389, 390, 459, 460, 492
Pacific Sunwear, 49
Parisian, 299
Party City, 254
Patagonia, 6
Payless Car Rental System Inc., 68
Payless ShoeSource, 2, 223, 49, 447, 478, 514
Peapod, 94, 117, 658–659
Pep Boys, 49, 258
PepsiCo, 441
Pet Valu, 51
Petco, 223
Pets.com, 4
PETsMART, 34, 51, 281, 385, 557
Philip Morris, 434, 467
Pic 'N' Save, 56
Pier 1 Imports, 49, 532, 566
Pillowtex, 389
Pizza Hut, 163, 339, 442

PlanetRx, 95
Play It Again Sports, 8
Playmobil, 171
Pockets Men's Store, 452
Polo/Ralph Lauren. See Ralph Lauren
Polo.com, 6
Potomac Mills Outlet Center, 4
Pottery Barn, 495, 519
Prada, 161, 315
PriceGrabber.com, 91
Priceline.com, 34, 57, 499
Primrose Fashions, 480
Procter & Gamble (P&G), 6, 156, 389, 390, 459, 460, 492
ProfitLogic, 493
Publix, 35, 37, 390, 520

Q
QVC, 61

R
R.L. Polk and Co., 255
Radio Shack, 223, 233, 254, 340, 605
Rainforest Café, 648
Ralph Lauren, 44, 96, 113, 161, 224, 225, 233, 254, 441, 446
Rand McNally, 225
Raymond Weil, 44
REACHWomen, 106–107
Recreational Equipment Inc. (REI), 4, 5, 59, 297, 516, 588, 605
Red Envelope, 90, 390
Redner's Warehouse Markets, 581
Reebok, 227, 447
Rent-a-Wreck, 68
Replacements, 96
Restoration Hardware, 59, 148, 149, 232
Results Travel, 68
Retek Inc., 405, 410, 493
Revco, 4
Rewe, 11
Rich's/Lazarus/Goldsmith's (RLG), 146–147, 282, 286, 289, 290, 292
Rite-Aid, 34, 54, 96
Ritz-Carlton Hotel Company, 633
RitzCamera, 96
Riverside Square Mall, 19
RocketCash, 87
Ron Jon Surf Shop, 362
Ross Stores, 55
Royal Ahold, 41, 162, 165, 166. See also Ahold

Rubbermaid, 406
Rue 21 Company Store, 56
Ruth's Chris Steakhouse, 232
RX.com, 92, 95

S
Sabanci Holding, 166
Safeway, 7, 11, 35, 67, 91, 154, 202, 289, 339, 350, 438
Sainsbury, 12, 129, 163, 164, 389
Saks Fifth Avenue, 19, 53, 54, 56, 97, 114, 150, 225, 229, 232, 299, 351, 419, 495, 674
Sam Dell Dodge, 633
Sam's Wholesale Club, 6, 35, 44, 73, 189, 236, 320, 391, 477, 588
Samuelsohn, 155
SAP, 493
Sara Lee, 389
Savoy Hotel, 622–623
Sawgrass Mills, 233
School Specialty, 59
Sears, Roebuck and Co., 11, 22, 53, 72, 73, 96, 129, 157, 193, 196, 202, 235, 253, 274, 319, 320, 322, 323, 326, 419, 437, 438, 446, 499, 508, 512, 519, 525, 565, 605, 629, 650–653
Seattle's Best Coffee, 151
SeniorNet, 88
Sentry Foods, 612
Sephora, 35, 685–686
Service Merchandise, 4
7-Eleven, 3, 46, 68, 121, 197, 253, 311, 517
Sharper Image, 329
Sheetz, 576
ShopKo, 493, 564
shopper.com, 499
shopping.yahoo.com, 500
Silver Sands Factory Stores, 233
Singapore Airlines, 297
Smith & Hawken, 58, 642
Sobey's, 438
Soma.com, 95, 96
Sony, 94, 441
Sotheby's, 15
South Gate West, 532
Southwest Airlines, 156, 296, 299
Spiegel, Inc., 59, 202
The Spoke, 444
Sports Authority, 48, 51, 74, 75, 171, 220, 232, 235, 545
Sportsline.com, 544

Spotlight Solutions Inc., 493
SRI Consulting, 131
Staples, 35, 51, 53, 170, 231, 235, 254, 329, 450, 478, 498, 524, 605
Starbucks, 149, 155, 156, 163, 165, 217, 230, 231, 233, 273, 298, 441, 516, 588, 605, 696–698
Steel of the Night, 57
Stop & Shop, 3, 41, 165, 659
Subway Sandwich & Salad Shops, 45, 68, 246
Sunglass Hut, 229
Superdiplo, 165

T
T.J. Maxx, 55, 153, 225, 283, 298, 454, 477, 532, 555, 594
Taco Bell, 68, 516
Talbots, 100, 225, 519
Target, 11, 34, 41, 43, 45, 48, 50, 67, 73, 129, 154, 200, 203, 207, 217, 220, 254, 289, 292, 317, 318, 386, 389, 438, 439, 515, 598, 621, 622, 623
TechnoMarine, 44
Tengelmann, 12
Tesco, 11, 34, 93, 129, 350, 353, 389, 501
TGI Friday's, 230, 442
ThirdAge, 88
Tiffany & Co., 49, 97, 186, 187, 188, 190–203, 208, 441, 488
Today's Man, 275
Tomboy Tools, 635
Tommy Bahama, 232
Tops Market, 41
Tower Records, 49
Toys "R" Us, 4, 15, 20, 39–41, 51, 74, 171, 203, 220, 221, 232, 235, 246, 253, 329, 367, 392, 470, 501, 518, 551, 591, 635, 636, 653–655
Trader Joe's, 637
Travelocity, 90
Triple Dot Communications, 386

Tru Serv, 67
True Value Hardware, 67
Tuesday Morning, 48, 56

U
UcanBuy.com, 87
Ukrop's Super Markets, Inc., 32–33
Uncommon Goods, 96
Ungaro, 15
Unilever, 389
United Colors of Benetton, 15
United Parcel Service (UPS), 323, 382
University Pointe hospital, 233
UPS, 323, 382
Urban Land Institute, 258
USA Today, 128
USAA, 58

V
Vacuum Bags, 96
ValueVision, 61
Van Heusen, 56
Vanity Fair, 226
Velox Holdings, 166
Venator, 67, 162
Victoria's Secret, 7, 67, 94, 422, 436, 514
Villager's Hardware, 52
Virgin, 498
Visa, 196, 339, 492
Volkswagen, 15
Von Maur, 247
Von's, 341, 354

W
Wal-Mart, 3, 4, 7, 10, 11, 12, 16, 20, 33, 34, 35, 37, 39–41, 42, 44, 45, 48, 54, 67, 73, 94, 98, 100, 117, 150, 156, 162, 163, 165, 166, 171, 172, 186–203, 208, 223, 231, 233, 244, 245, 247, 254, 278, 291, 293, 295, 298, 299, 300, 310, 311, 316, 318, 319, 321, 336, 344, 367, 389, 390, 438, 444, 446, 447, 450, 451, 459, 460, 465, 477, 478,

479, 488, 489, 498, 501, 506, 508, 517, 541, 557, 573, 577, 598, 600, 624, 658–659
Wal-Mart Discount City, 16, 247
Wal-Mart Supercenters, 43, 391, 476
Walgreens, 12, 33, 34, 45, 48, 54, 95, 96, 155, 184, 219, 220, 232, 254, 298, 514, 542, 543
Wall Street Journal, The, 128
Wallace's Bookstores, 589, 590
Walt Disney Company, 165, 296, 442, 561, 613, 621
Walt Disney World, 620, 634
Warner Brothers, 165
Waterford crystal, 44
Webvan, 4, 57, 92, 93, 94
WeddingChannel.com, 86, 655–656
Wegmans Food Markets, 46, 47, 129, 389, 438
Wellness Place, 221
Westport Ltd., 56
Wet Seal, 141, 154, 250
White Barn Candle Co., The, 67
White Hen Pantry, 68
Whole Foods Market, 23–24, 156, 299
Wild Oats, 24
Williams-Sonoma, 51, 96
Wine Spectator, 44
Wine.com, 96
Wing Zone, 637
Winkler's Diamonds, 520
Winn-Dixie Stores, 202, 488, 489
Woolworth, 229, 508

Y
Yogen Fruz Worldwide, 68
Yokohama Bayside Marina Shops and Restaurants, 227

Z
Zale Corporation, 4, 49, 161, 200
Zara, 50, 162, 165, 197, 311, 327, 328
Zegna, 15
Zellers, 48
Zoots, 63

SUBJECT INDEX

A

á la carte plans, 570
ABC analysis, 420–421
Accessibility, 128, 248–250
Accordion theory, 74
Accountability, 209
Accounts payable, 199
Accounts receivable, 195–196
Accrued liabilities, 199
Accurate pricing, 510
Achievers, 133
ACORN (A Classification of
    Residential Neighborhoods),
    256–257
Actionability, 127
Activity-based costing (ABC),
    214–215
Actualizers, 133
ADA, 560, 590–591
Adaptability, 165
Administrative tasks, 278
Advanced shipping notice (ASN), 315
Advertising agencies, 541
Advertising allowances, 454
Advertising campaigns, 539–546
    agencies, 541
    co-op advertising, 540–541
    developing the message, 539–542
    direct mail, 543
    frequency/timing, 546
    Internet, 544
    magazines, 543
    media companies, 541–542
    newspapers, 542–543
    outdoor billboards, 544
    radio, 544
    selecting the media, 545–546
    shopping guides, 544
    TV, 543–544
    Yellow Pages, 545
Advisory Commission on Electronic
    Commerce, 500
Affiliate programs, 544
Affordable budgeting method, 529
Age Discrimination and Employment
    Act, 560
Aided recall, 516
Airport locations, 232–233
Allocating merchandise to stores,
    418–419

Alternative dispute resolution, 464
Americans with Disabilities Act
    (ADA), 560, 590–591
Analog approach, 260–263
Anticipation discounts, 473–474
Antitrust issues, 465–470, 506–510
Arbitration, 464
Artificial barriers, 249
ASN, 315
Asset turnover, 198–199, 206
Assets, 194
Assistant store manager, 286
Assortment, 38–39, 391–395. See also
    Merchandise assortments
Assortment plan, 397–399
Assortment planning, 364
Assortment planning process,
    390–397
Assortments, 7–8
Atmospherics, 609–614
Autocratic leaders, 563
Average inventory, 374

B

Backup stock, 396
Backward integration, 161
Bait-and-switch, 510
Banner ads, 544
Bargain branding, 439
Bargaining power of vendors, 170
Barriers to entry, 170
Base stock, 396
Basic accounting equation, 194
Basic merchandise, 379
Basic stock list, 406
Behavioral interview, 558
Believers, 133
Benefit segmentation, 133–134
BEP, 490
Best customers, 345–348, 352–354
Big-box food retailers, 42–45
Billboards, 544
BOM stock, 414
BOM stock-to-sales ratio, 412–414
Bonus, 293
Bottom-up planning, 209
Boutique layout, 594–595
Bowling, 176
Brand, 514
Brand associations, 516–517

Brand awareness, 516
Brand equity, 515
Brand image, 517
Brand loyalty, 110
Branding strategies, 434–441
Breadth, 390
Breadth of merchandise, 39
Break-even analysis, 489–491
Break-even point (BEP), 490
Breaking bulk, 8
Breaking sizes, 393
Buffer stock, 396
Building codes, 241
Bulk fixture, 608
Business mission, 168–169
Butt-brush effect, 602
Buybacks, 465–466
Buyers, 283–285
Buying merchandise, 432–474
    branding strategies, 434–441
    connecting with vendors,
        447–452
    international sourcing decisions,
        441–447
    legal/ethical issues, 464–470
    negotiating with vendors,
        452–458
    strategic relationships, 458–462
    terms of purchase, 470–474
Buying offices, 452
Buying process, 108, 111. See also
    Customer buying behavior
Buying situation segmentation,
    132–133
Buying situations, 135
Buying systems, 402–430
    ABC analysis, 420–421
    allocating merchandise to stores,
        418–419
    analyzing merchandise
        performance, 419–424
    inventory management report,
        406–408
    merchandise budget plan,
        409–415
    multiattribute method, 423–424
    open-to-buy, 415–418
    sell-through analysis, 421–423
    staple merchandise, 404–408
Buzz, 140

C

Campaign management software, 534
Cannibalization, 245
Capacity fixture, 608
Career opportunities
　corporate staff, 27
　merchandise management, 26
　store management, 26
Cases, 646–699
　Abercrombie & Fitch, 660–661
　Ahold, 658–659
　American Eagle, 660
　Avon, 671
　Borders Bookstore, 683
　Build-A-Bear Workshop, 649
　Chen family buys bicycles,
　　656–657
　Dollar General, 657–658
　eBay, 680–682
　Enterprise, 682
　Family Dollar, 657–658, 661–662
　Gadzooks, 649–650
　Goodlife Fitness Club, 689–693
　Home Depot, 669–670
　Hughe's, 678
　Hutch Corporation, 664–669
　Lawson Sportswear, 672–674
　Lindy's Bridal Shoppe, 694–696
　McFadden's Department Store,
　　679–680
　Neiman Marcus, 661–662
　Nolan's Finest Foods, 675–677
　Nordstrom, 687–689
　overview, 647
　picking the best display, 684–685
　promoting a sale, 683–684
　Rainforest Café, 648
　Sales First, 674–675
　Sears, Roebuck and Co., 650–653
　Sephora, 685–686
　Starbucks, 696–699
　Stephanie's boutique, 663
　stockout, 686–687
　Toys "R" Us, 653–655
　WeddingChannel.com, 655–656
Cash discount, 472
Cash/other current assets, 197
Cash-wrap areas, 598
Cash wraps, 578
Catalog retailing, 58–59
Catalogs, 82
Category, 365, 369
Category captain, 366–367
Category killers, 50

Category life cycle, 378, 379
Category management, 365–366
Category managers, 285
Category specialists, 50–53, 235
CBD, 228, 234
Census tracts, 256
Central business district (CBD),
　228, 234
Centralization, 290
CEO, 283
CEX, 256
CHAID, 269
Chain discounts, 471
Chargeback, 464
Charitable giving, 495
Chat rooms, 635
Checking, 321
Checkout areas, 598
Cherry picking, 532
Chief executive officer (CEO), 283
Chief operating officer (COO), 283
Child care assistance, 300
Chinese shopping behavior, 126
Circle Center mall
　(Indianapolis), 222
Classification, 368–369
Closed-circuit TV cameras, 579
Closeout retailers, 56
Co-marketing program, 541
Co-op advertising, 540–541
Collaboration, planning, forecasting,
　and replenishment (CPFR),
　317, 389
Color, 612–613
Combination stores, 42
Commercial bribery, 464–465
Commission, 293, 572–573, 575
Common stock, 200
Communication budget, 527–531
Communication gap, 627, 639–640
Communication methods, 519–524
Communication objectives, 525–526
Communication programs. See Retail
　communication mix
Comparative price advertising,
　509–510
Comparison shopping, 72–74
Compatibility, 142
Compensation plans, 572–575
Competition-oriented method, 481,
　488–489
Competitive factors, 170–172
Competitive parity method, 530
Competitive rivalry, 171

Competitors, 17–19
Complementary merchandise, 395
Complexity, 142
Composite segmentation, 134–135
Conflicting needs, 113
Congestion, 250
Connecting with vendors, 447–452
Consideration set, 120
Consortium exchange, 450
Consumer expenditure surveys
　(CEX), 256
Consumer Goods Pricing Act, 508
Contests, 520
Contribution margin, 420, 491
Convenience stores, 45, 46
Conventional supermarket, 42
COO, 283
Cookies, 342
Coolhunter, 387
Cooperative (co-op) advertising,
　540–541
Copycat branding, 440
Copyright, 466
Core assortment, 418
Corporate retail chains, 67–68
Corporate staff, 27
Cosmetics counters, 601
Cosmic bowling, 176
Cost justification defense, 470
Cost multiplier, 430
Cost-oriented pricing, 480–486
Cost per thousand (CPM), 545
Counterfeit merchandise, 466
Counterfeiting, 466–468
Country-of-origin effects, 442
Coupons, 496, 520–521
Coverage, 545
CPFR, 317, 389
CPM, 545
CRM. See Customer relationship
　management (CRM)
CRM/campaign management system,
　534
Cross-selling, 159, 353
Cross-shopping, 113
Crossdocking distribution center, 321
Culture, 125–126
Cumulative attraction, 250, 251
Cumulative markup, 430
Cumulative quantity discounts, 471
Cumulative reach, 545
Currency fluctuations, 442
Current assets, 194–197
Current liabilities, 199

Customer alchemy, 352
Customer allowances, 190
Customer buying behavior, 106–142
  buying process, 111
  decision-making processes, 108–110
  evaluation of alternatives, 117–122
  information search, 114–117
  need recognition, 111–114
  postpurchase evaluation, 123
  purchasing the merchandise, 122
  social influences, 123–126
Customer complaints, 629–630
Customer data warehouse, 338
Customer database, 338–339
Customer decision-making processes, 108–110
Customer delight, 624
Customer expectations, 624, 639
Customer loyalty, 151–155, 336–337
Customer panels/interviews, 629
Customer privacy, 342–343
Customer pyramid, 346
Customer relationship management (CRM), 334–358
  analyzing data/identifying target customers, 344–348
  best customers, 345–348, 352–354
  collecting customer data, 338–343
  converting good customers to best customers, 352–354
  customer retention, 349–352
  defined, 335
  implementation, 355–356
  market segments, 345
  overview, 338
  privacy, 342–343
  unprofitable customers, 354–355
Customer research, 628–630
Customer retention, 349–352
Customer returns, 190
Customer service, 157, 618–645
  communications gap, 639–640
  cost of, 622–623
  customer expectations, 624, 639
  customization approach, 621–622
  defined, 619
  delivery gap, 634–639
  fairness, 641–642
  gaps model, 627–628
  knowledge gap, 628–630
  listening to customers, 640–641
  perceived service, 625–626
  problem resolution, 642
  service recovery, 640–642
  standardization approach, 622
  standards gap, 630–634
  strategic advantage, as, 620–623
Customer services, 39–41
Customer spotting, 255
Customers, 19
Customization approach, 621–622
Cycle stock, 396

D
Dallas Market Center complex, 451
Data mining, 344
Data warehouse, 154, 314–315
Dating, 472–473
Decennial Census of the United States, 255–256
Decentralization, 290
Decile analysis, 347
Definitions (glossary), 700–724
Delivery gap, 627, 634–639
Demalling, 222
Demand/destination area, 601
Demand-oriented pricing, 481, 486–488
Democratic leaders, 563
Demographic data vendors, 256
Demographic segmentation, 130
Department, 368
Department stores, 53–54, 234–235, 282–289
Departmental layout, 599–602
Depth, 391
Depth interview, 385
Depth of merchandise, 39
Deseasonalized demand, 408
Destination store, 235, 254
Dialectic theory, 75
Direct investment, 166
Direct mail, 543
Direct-mail retailers, 58
Direct-response advertising, 61
Direct selling, 60
Disability, 560
Discount store, 48
Discrimination, 302–303, 559
Disintermediation, 96
Disparate impact, 559
Disparate treatment, 559
Dispatcher, 321
Distribution channel, 6
Distribution channels around the world, 13–14
Distributive fairness, 641
Distributive justice, 304
Diversification opportunity, 161
Diversity in the workplace, 300–302
Diversity of retail formats, 34
Diversity training, 301
Diverted merchandise, 467
Domestic sources of supply, 446
Drawing account, 573
Drugstores, 54–55
Duty, 443
DVD players, 380

E
E-mail, 522
E-tailing, 57–58
Early adopters, 142
EAS tags, 580
Economies of scale, 170, 245
EDI, 315–317
EDLP, 42, 478–480
EEOC, 559
80-20 rule, 346
Electronic agent, 85
Electronic article surveillance (EAS) systems, 580
Electronic data interchange (EDI), 315–317
Electronic retailing, 57–58
Electronic retailing issues, 83–97
  benefits, 83–87
  costs, 92
  failures, 92
  growth potential, 87–88
  manufacturers, 96–97
  price competition, 90–91
  required capabilities, 92
  required resources, 92–96
  top retail website designs, 96
  type of merchandise sold, 89–90
Emotional support, 636
Employee compensation, 570–575
Employee demographics, 277
Employee morale, 566
Employee motivation, 292–296
Employee privacy, 304
Employee productivity, 274
Employee theft, 580–582
Employee turnover, 274
Employees. *See* Human resource management; Managing the store
Employees safety and health, 303
Employment, 10
Empowerment, 298–299, 637

End caps, 596
End-of-month (EOM) dating, 473
End-of-month (EOM) stock, 414
Energy management, 577
Entrepreneurial opportunities, 15–16
Entry barriers, 170
Entry strategies, 166–167
Environmental issues
    retail locations, 241
    situation audit, 172–173
EOM dating, 473
EOM stock, 414
Equal employment opportunity,
    302–303
Equal Employment Opportunity
    Commission (EEOC), 559
Equal Pay Act, 575
Escape clause, 240
Estimating demand for new location,
    252–269
    analog approach, 260–263
    Huff's model, 267–268
    measuring competition, 258–259
    MPI, 257
    regression analysis, 264–267
    sources of information, 255
    SPI, 257
    trade area, 252–255
European distribution system, 14
Everyday low pricing (EDLP), 42,
    478–480
Exclusive dealing agreements, 469
Exclusive geographic territories, 469
Exclusive use clause, 240
Expenses, 191–192
Experiencers, 133
Extended problem solving, 108–109
External sources of information, 116
Extra dating, 473
Extranet, 317
Extrinsic rewards, 570–571

F
Factory outlets, 56
Fad, 379, 380
Fair information practices, 343
Fair Labor Standards Act, 575
Fair trade laws, 508
Family decision making, 123–124
Fashion, 138–142, 379, 380
Fashion Center (New York), 451
Fashion leaders, 139
Fashion/specialty center, 224–225
Feature areas, 595–598

Feature fixture, 608
Fill rate, 389
Financial strategy, 184–215
    accounts receivable, 195
    asset turnover, 198–199
    cash/other current assets, 197
    current assets, 194–197
    example (Gifts To Go), 202–206
    expenses, 191–192
    fixed assets, 197–198
    gross margin, 190–191
    liabilities, 199–200
    merchandise inventory, 196–197
    net profit, 192–193
    net sales, 190
    owners' equity, 200
    profit path, 188–193
    strategic profit model, 186–188,
        200–202, 206–207
    turnover path, 194–200
First-degree price
    discrimination, 495
Fixed assets, 197–198, 206
Fixed costs, 490
Fixed-rate leases, 240
Fixtures, 608–609
Flexsmart, 589
Flextime, 300
Floor-ready merchandise, 322–323
FOB destination, 474
FOB origin, 474
Focus group, 386
Food retailers, 41–47
Forecasting sales, 377–389. See also
    Sales forecasting
Foreign currency fluctuations, 442
Forward integration, 161
Four-way fixture, 608, 609
Franchise retailers, 68
Franchises, 246
Franchising, 68–69, 167
Franchisors, 246
Free-form layout, 594–595
Free trade zone, 443–444
Freestanding fixtures, 596
Freestanding insert (FSI), 499, 542
Freestanding site, 232, 234
Freight collect, 474
Freight forwarders, 330
Freight prepaid, 474
Frequency, 546
Frequent shopper programs, 341,
    349–350
Frequent shoppers cards, 341

Frontal presentation, 608
FSI, 499, 542
Fulfilleds, 133
Functional discounts, 470–471, 506
Functional needs, 112
Functions performed by retailers, 7–8
Future directions
    shopping, 102–103
    site selection, 269

G
Gaps model, 627–628
Garment District (New York), 451
General Agreement on Tariffs and
    Trade (GATT), 443
General merchandise catalog
    retailers, 58
General merchandise manager
    (GMM), 283, 367
General merchandise retailers, 47–57
Generational tension, 571
Generic brands, 439
Gentrification, 230
Geodemographic segmentation,
    130–131
Geographic information system
    (GIS), 256
Geographic segmentation, 129
Getting the lead out, 354
Glass ceiling, 302
Global culture, 166
Global growth strategies, 162–167
Global retailers, 10–13
Global sourcing decisions, 441–447
Globalization, 35–76. See also
    International issues
Globally sustainable competitive
    advantage, 164–166
GlobalNetXchange, 389, 450
Glossary, 700–724
GMM, 283, 367
GMROI, 371–372
Gondolas, 609
Grace period, 473
Gray collar neighborhoods, 135
Gray-market good, 467
Grid layout, 592
Grocery chains, 46
Grocery stores, 235, 601
Gross margin, 190–191, 204
Gross margin return on inventory
    investments (GMROI),
    371–372
Gross profit, 190

Group incentives, 574
Group maintenance behaviors, 563
Group sales manager, 287
Growth strategies, 158–162. *See also*
    Global growth strategies
Guest ambassadors, 621
Gumby cartoon character, 632

H
Habitual decision making, 110
Haloing, 569
High-assay principle, 531
High/low pricing, 479, 480
High-low pricing strategy, 42
High-rise renters, 262
Hiring, 297
Home improvement center, 50–52
Home shopping, 60–61
Honesty tests, 557
Horizontal price-fixing, 509
Hospital locations, 233
House brands, 439
Huff's gravity model, 267–268
Human resource management,
    272–307
  employee commitment, 296
  empowering employees, 298–299
  hiring, 297
  international issues, 277–278
  legal/regulatory issues, 302–304
  motivating the employees, 292–296
  objectives, 274
  organization structure, 278–292.
      See also Organization structure
  partnering relationships, 299–300
  technology, 304
  training, 297–298
  trends, 299–304
  workplace diversity, 300–302
Human resource triad, 276
Human rights abuses, 446–447
Hype, 140
Hypermarkets, 43–44

I
Idea-oriented presentation, 606–607
Identifiability, 127
Illegal discrimination, 302–303
Impact, 546
Import tariffs, 443
Impulse buying, 109
Impulse products, 600
In-store demonstrations, 520
In-store kiosks, 604–605

Inbound transportation, 320–321
Incentive compensation, 293
Incentive compensation plans,
    572–573
Independent, single-store
    establishments, 66–67
Independent exchange, 451
Industry concentration, 34–35
Infomercials, 60–61
Information flows, 314
Information search, 114–117
Information systems/supply chain
    management, 308–333
  data warehousing, 314–315
  EDI, 315–317
  flow of information, 313–319
  logistics, 319–330. *See also*
      Logistics
  security, 318–319
  supply chain management,
      310–313
Ingress/egress, 250
Initial markup, 484, 485
Inner city, 228–229
Innovators, 139
Input measures, 210
Instant messaging, 621
Instrumental support, 636
Intangibility, 65
Integrated marketing communication
    program, 518
Integrated third-party logistics
    services, 330
Intellectual property, 466
Interest expense, 192
Internal sources of information, 116
International Anti-Counterfeiting
    Coalition, 467
International issues
  global growth opportunities,
      162–167
  global retailers, 10–13
  global sourcing decisions, 441–447
  globalization, 35–36
  human resources, 277–278
International sourcing decisions,
    441–447
Internet
  advertising medium, as, 544
  comparison shopping, 499–500
  kiosks, 80
  liquidating marked-down
      goods, 495
  one-to-one marketing, 127, 351

pricing, 499–500
  retail exchanges, 448
  security problems, 318
  shopping, 83–97. *See also*
      Electronic retailing issues
  websites, 521, 544
  wedding sites, 86
Internet exchanges, 448–451
Internet retailing, 57–58
Internet taxation, 500
Intertype competition, 18
Interviewing questions, 559
Intranet, 304, 316
Intratype competition, 17
Intrinsic rewards, 571–572
Inventory, 196–197
Inventory carrying cost, 444
Inventory loss, 577–582
Inventory management report,
    406–408
Inventory shrinkage, 411–412, 578
Inventory turnover, 196–197, 205,
    372–376
Item price, 499

J
Japanese distribution system, 14
Japanese large scale retail stores
    law, 14
Job analysis, 554
Job application forms, 557
Job description, 555
Job enrichment, 572
Job interview, 29, 558, 559
Job sharing, 300
Jobs (careers), 25–30
Joint venture, 166–167

K
Keystone method, 480
Kiosks
  in-store, 80, 604–605, 632
  merchandise, 227–228
  self-service, 304
Knock-offs, 140
Knowledge gap, 627, 628–630

L
Labor scheduling, 575–577
Lead time, 328, 397, 444
Leader pricing, 501
Leadership, 563–564
Leadership styles, 564
Lease, 239–240

Leased department, 53
Legal issues
    buying merchandise, 464–470
    compensation, 575
    hiring store employees, 558–560
    pricing, 506–510
Level of competition in an area, 247
Level of support, 391
Liabilities, 199–200
Licensed brands, 436
Licensing requirements, 241
Lifestyle, 131
Lifestyle center, 224
Lifestyle characteristics, 246
Lifestyle segmentation, 131–132
Lifetime customer value (LTV),
    345–347
Lift-out, 465
Lighting, 611–612
Limited problem solving, 109
Liquidating markdown
    merchandising, 494–495
Listening to customers, 640–641
Location. See Retail locations; Site
    selection
Logistics, 319–330
    defined, 319
    distribution center, 319–327
    electronic retailing, 329
    floor-ready merchandise, 322–323
    inbound transportation, 320–321
    outbound transportation, 325
    outsourcing, 329–330
    QR delivery systems, 327–329
    receiving/checking, 321
    reverse, 326
    shipping merchandise to stores,
        323–325
    storing/crossdocking, 321–322
Long-term liabilities, 199–200
Loop, 593
Loppi system, 80
Loss leaders, 501
Low price guarantee policy, 479
Loyalty programs, 154–155, 341
LTV, 345–347

M
"Made in America," 446
Magalog, 518
Magazine advertising, 543
Main Street, 229, 231, 234
Main Street Europe, 231
Maintained markup, 484

Makers, 133
Malls, 218, 220–223
Management by walking around,
    299–300
Management opportunities, 14–15
Managing diversity, 300–302
Managing the store, 550–584
    employee compensation, 570–575
    employee theft, 580–582
    energy management, 577
    evaluating employees, 567–570
    generational tension, 571
    inventory loss, 577–582
    job interview, 558, 559
    labor scheduling, 575–577
    leadership, 563–564
    legal issues, 558–560
    morale, 566
    motivating employees, 564–566
    orientation programs, 560–561
    recruiting employees, 553–557
    responsibilities of store
        managers, 552
    security measures, 579–581
    selecting employees, 557
    sexual harassment, 566–567
    shoplifting, 578–580
    store maintenance, 577
    training employees, 561–563
Manufacturer brands, 434–436
Maquiladoras, 443
Marginal analysis, 527
Markdown money, 494
Markdowns, 491–496
Market, 447
Market analysis, 169
Market attractiveness/competitive
    position matrix, 179–182
Market basket analysis, 344
Market expansion opportunity, 160
Market factors, 169–170
Market penetration opportunity, 159
Market potential index (MPI), 257
Market segmentation, 126–135
    benefit segmentation, 133–134
    buying situation segmentation,
        132–133
    composite segmentation
        approaches, 134–135
    criteria for evaluation segments,
        127–129
    demographic segmentation, 130
    geodemographic segmentation,
        130–131

geographic segmentation, 129
    lifestyle segmentation, 131–132
Market weeks, 451
Marketmax inventory management
    report, 406
Marketmax planning system, 416
Marketmax planogramming
    system, 604
Marketmax six-month merchandise
    budget plan, 409
Mass-market theory, 140
McCormick Place (Chicago), 452
Med-arb, 464
Media companies, 541–542
Mediation, 464
Mentoring programs, 301–302
Merchandise assortments, 362–401
    assortment plan, 397–399
    assortment planning process,
        390–397
    categories, 365–367
    GMROI, 371–372
    inventory turnover, 372–376
    merchandise classification scheme,
        367–369
    objectives for merchandise plan,
        369–376
    product availability, 395–397
    sales forecasting, 377–389. See also
        Sales forecasting
    variety/assortment, 390, 391,
        392–395
Merchandise budget plan, 409–415
Merchandise buying. See Buying
    merchandise
Merchandise classification scheme,
    367–369
Merchandise comparisons, 74
Merchandise division, 283–286
Merchandise group, 367
Merchandise inventory, 196–197
Merchandise kiosks, 227–228
Merchandise management
    buying merchandise, 432–474
    buying systems, 402–430
    career opportunities, 26
    defined, 363
    planning merchandise assortments,
        362–401
    pricing, 476–510
    retail communication mix, 512–546
Merchandise planner, 286
Merchandise presentation
    techniques, 605–609

Merchandise/service continuum, 64
Merchandise shows, 451
Merchandising optimization software, 493
Message boards, 635
Metropolitan statistical area (MSA), 244
Microenvironment, 17–19
Minority groups, 301
Mission statement, 168–169
Mixed-use developments (MXDs), 232
Monthly Retail Trade Report, 383
Months of supply, 412
Morale, 566
MPI, 257
MSA, 244
Multi-channel logistics, 320
Multiattribute attitude model, 117
Multiattribute method for evaluating vendors, 423–424
Multichannel retailer, 80
Multichannel retailing, 78–105
  brand image, 100
  catalogs, 82
  Internet shopping. *See* Electronic retailing issues
  merchandise assortment, 100
  pricing, 100–101
  reasons for using, 97–99
  store channel, 81–82
Multilevel network, 60
Multiple-unit pricing, 497
Music, 613
Mutual trust, 459
MXD, 232
Mystery shoppers, 634

N
NAFTA, 443, 444
NAICS, 37–39
National brands, 434–436
Natural barriers, 249
Natural selection, 76
Need recognition, 111–114
Negotiating with vendors, 452–458
Net profit, 192
Net profit margin, 192, 204–205
Net sales, 190
Newspaper advertising, 542–543
Noncumulative quantity discounts, 471
Nonstore retail formats, 57–62

North American Free Trade Agreement (NAFTA), 443, 444
North American Industry Classification System (NAICS), 37–39
Notes payable, 199
NRF merchandise classification scheme, 367–369

O
Objective-and-task method, 528–529
Observability, 142
Odd pricing, 502
Off-price retailers, 55–56
okyakusama ha kamisama desu, 625
On-the-job training, 562
1-to-1 retailing, 351
1/30, n/60, 472
Open-to-buy, 415–418
Operating expenses, 191, 192
Opportunity cost of capital, 444
Opt in, 343
Opt out, 343
Optical boutique, 236–237
Order point, 408
Order quantity, 408
Organization culture, 294–296
Organization design considerations, 280–281
Organization structure, 278–292
  centralization vs. decentralization, 290–291
  coordinating merchandise/store management, 291–292
  defined, 278
  design considerations, 280–281
  regional department store, 282–287
  regional department store chain, 287–289
  single-store retailer, 282
Orientation programs, 560–561
Outbound transportation, 325
Outdoor advertising, 544
Outlet centers, 225–226
Outlet stores, 56
Output measures, 210
Outsourcing, 327, 329–330
Overstored trade area, 247
Owners' equity, 200
Ownership, 66–69

P
Paid impersonal communications, 519–521
Paid personal communications, 521–522
Paper-and-pencil honesty tests, 557
Parallel branding, 440
Parasite store, 254
Parking facilities, 250
Part-time employees, 277
Partnering relationships, 299–309, 458–462
Partners, 283
Party plan system, 60
PDA, 378
Perceived service, 625–626
Percentage leases, 239–240
Percentage-of-sales method, 530
Perception of fairness, 304
Performance beliefs, 121
Performance measures, 209–211
Performance objectives, 207–211
Perishability, 65
Personal digital assistants (PDA), 378
Personal selling, 521
Personalization, 351–352
Personnel. *See* Human resource management
Physical flow of merchandise. *See* Logistics
Pick ticket, 324
Planners, 285–286
Planogram, 602–604
Point-of-purchase (POP) area, 598
Point-of-sale areas, 598
Point-of-sale terminals, 374
Polygons, 252
POP area, 598
Popping the merchandise, 611
POS systems, 374
Positioning, 152–154
Postpurchase evaluation, 123
Power center, 220
Predatory pricing, 507–508
Preferred clients, 565
Premium branding, 439–440
Preprint, 542
Price adjustments, 491–500
Price audits, 510
Price bundling, 497
Price-cost trade-off, 36–37
Price discrimination, 495–496, 506–508
Price lining, 501–502, 607

Pricing decisions, 476–510
  accuracy, 510
  bait-and-switch, 510
  break-even analysis, 489–491
  comparative price advertising,
      509–510
  competition-oriented method,
      488–489
  cost-oriented pricing, 482–486
  coupons, 496
  demand-oriented pricing, 486–488
  EDLP, 478–480
  high/low pricing, 479, 480
  Internet, 499–500
  leader pricing, 501
  legal issues, 506–510
  markdowns, 491–496
  multichannel retailing, 100–101
  multiple-unit pricing, 497
  odd pricing, 502
  predatory pricing, 507–508
  price bundling, 497
  price discrimination, 495–496,
      506–508
  price fixing, 508–509
  price lining, 501–502
  profit, and, 489–491
  rebates, 497
  retail exchanges, 448–449
  scanned vs. posted prices, 510
  services, 482–483
  stimulating retail sales, 501–502
  variable pricing, 498–499
  women, and, 507
Primary zone, 252
Principals, 283
Privacy, 342–343
Private exchanges, 450
Private-label brands, 156, 436–440
PRIZM, 130, 131, 257
Problem resolution, 642
Procedural fairness, 641
Procedural justice, 304
Product availability, 391, 395–397
Productivity measure, 210–211
Profit path, 188–193
Profit-sharing arrangements, 293
Prohibited use clause, 240
Promotional aisle (area), 596
Promotional budget, 527–531
Proprietary EDI systems, 316
Psychographics, 131
Psychological needs, 112
Public warehouses, 330
Publicity, 522–523

Pull logistics strategy, 324
Purchasing merchandise. See Buying
      merchandise
Push logistics strategy, 324
Pyramid scheme, 60

Q
QR delivery systems, 327–329
Quantity discounts, 471–472
Quick response (QR) delivery
      systems, 327–329
Quota, 574
Quota-bonus plan, 574

R
Racetrack layout, 593–594
Radio advertising, 544
Rain checks, 479
Reach, 545
Realistic job preview, 557
Rebate, 497
Receipt of goods (ROG) dating,
      472–473
Receiving, 321
Recency, 569
Reductions, 484
Reference group, 124–125
Reference price, 482, 509
Refusal to deal, 470
Region, 243
Regional center, 223
Regression analysis, 264–267
Related diversification opportunity, 161
Reporting relationships, 280–281
Resale price maintenance laws, 508
Resident buying offices, 386, 452
Resort locations, 233
Retail chain, 67–68
Retail communication mix, 512–546
  advertising, 520, 539–546. See also
      Advertising campaigns
  allocation of budget, 531
  branding, 514–519
  communication budget, 527–531
  communication methods, 519–524
  communication objectives, 525–526
  e-mail, 522
  implementing/evaluating the
      programs, 531–536
  paid impersonal communications,
      519–521
  paid personal communications,
      521–522
  personal selling, 521
  publicity, 522–523

retail communication process,
      525–536
  sales promotions, 520–521
  store atmosphere, 521
  unpaid impersonal
      communications, 522–523
  unpaid personal
      communications, 523
  websites, 521, 544
  word of mouth, 523
Retail communication process,
      525–536
Retail evolution, 72–76
  accordion theory, 74
  dialectic theory, 75
  natural selection, 76
  wheel of retailing, 72–74
Retail exchanges, 448
Retail format, 148
Retail format development
      opportunity, 160
Retail inventory method (RIM),
      428–430
Retail locations, 216–241. See also
      Site selection
  airports, 232–233
  category specialists, 235
  CBD, 228
  city/town locations, 228
  department stores, 234–235
  fashion/specialty center, 224–225
  freestanding sites, 232
  grocery stores, 235
  hospitals, 233
  inner-city locations, 228–229
  leases, 239–240
  legal considerations, 241
  lifestyle centers, 224
  Main Street locations, 229, 231
  merchandise kiosks, 227–228
  MXDs, 232
  optical boutique, 236–237
  outlet centers, 225–226
  power centers, 220
  regional center, 223
  resorts, 233
  shopping centers, 218–228
  shopping malls, 220–223
  specialty apparel stores, 235
  store within a store, 233
  strip shopping centers, 218–220
  superregional center, 223
  terms of occupancy, 239–240
  theme/festival centers, 226
  wholesale clubs, 236

Retail management decision
    process, 18
Retail market, 151
Retail market segment, 127
Retail market strategy, 146–182
    competitive advantage, 151–158.
        See also Sustainable
        competitive advantage
    global growth strategies, 162–167
    growth strategies, 158–162
    retail strategies, 148–149
    strategic retail planning process,
        167–177. *See also* Strategic
        retail planning process
    target market/retail format,
        149–151
Retail mix, 23
Retail sales, 9
Retail strategy, 19, 148–149
Retailer characteristics, 36–41
Retailers
    career advancement, 28
    career opportunities, 26–27
    compensation/benefits, 28
    defined, 6
    functions, 7–8
    services offered, 620
    types, 32–76. *See also* Types of
        retailers
    websites, 521, 544
Retailing
    careers, 25–30
    defined, 6
    economic significance, 9–14
    job locations, 29
    NAICS codes, 37–39
    opportunities, 14–16
    ownership, 66–69
    trends, 34–36
    working conditions, 28–29
Retailing concept, 151
Retailing strategy
    customer relationship
        management, 334–358
    financial strategy, 184–215
    human resource management,
        272–307
    information systems/supply chain
        management, 308–333
    retail locations, 216–241
    retail market strategy, 146–182
    site selection, 242–271
Retained earnings, 200
Return on assets (ROA),
    200–201, 206

Reverse auctions, 448–449
Reverse logistics, 326
RFM analysis, 347–348
RFM target strategies, 348
RIM, 428–430
ROA, 200–201, 206
Road condition, 249
Road pattern, 249
Robinson-Patman Act, 454, 470,
    471, 494
ROG dating, 472–473
Rounder, 608, 609
Rule-of-thumb methods, 529–530
RZone Magazine, 518

S
Safety stock, 396
Sales forecasting, 377–389
    category life cycle, 377–382
    CPFR, 389
    other factors to consider, 388
    price, 388
    product placement, 388
    promotion, 388
    seasonality, 388
    sources of information, 382–386
    store-level forecasting, 386–388
    store location, 388
Sales manager, 286–287
Sales per linear foot, 603
Sales per square foot, 603
Sales promotions, 520–521
Sales-to-stock ratio, 373
Satisfaction, 123
Saturated trade area, 247
Scale economies, 170, 245
SCAN, 377
Scanned vs. posted prices, 510
Scent, 613–614
Scrambled merchandising, 18
Search engines, 91
Seasonal discount, 472
Seasonal merchandise, 379
Second-degree price discrimination,
    495–496
Secondary zone, 252
Security measures, 579–581
Security personnel, 581
Security policy, 318–319
Segmentation. *See* Market
    segmentation
Self-service kiosks, 304
Sell-through analysis, 421–423
Senior executives, 283
Senior management, 278

Service gap, 627, 628
Service goals, 633
Service level, 391
Service recovery, 640–642
Services retailing, 62–66
Sexual harassment, 303–304, 566–567
Share of wallet, 97, 336
Shelf talkers, 541
Shipping merchandise to stores,
    323–325
Shipping terms and conditions, 474
Shop competition, 386
Shoplifting, 578–580
Shopping bots, 91
Shopping centers, 218
Shopping goods, 235
Shopping guides, 544
Shopping malls, 220–223, 234
Showcase, 455
Shrinkage, 411–412, 578
Signs, 241, 610–611
Single-store retailers, 66–67, 282
Site selection, 242–271. *See also* Retail
    locations
    accessibility, 248–250
    business climate, 246–247
    competition, 247
    demographic/lifestyle
        characteristics, 246
    economies of scale/cannibalization,
        245–246
    estimating demand, 252–269. *See
        also* Estimating demand for
        new location
    future directions, 269
    global location issues, 247–248
    locational advantages within a
        center, 250–251
    span of managerial control, 247
Situation audit, 169–174
SKU (stock keeping unit), 38
Slotting allowances, 465
Slotting fees, 465
Socialization, 560
Sommerset Collection, 224
Southern European retailing, 14
Space planning, 598–605
Span of managerial control, 247
Spatial allocation models, 269
Special customer services, 350–351
Specialization, 280
Specialty apparel stores, 235
Specialty catalog retailers, 58
Specialty store, 48–50
Spending potential index (SPI), 257

SPI, 257
Spot, 543
Staffing. *See* Human resource management
Standardization approach, 622
Standards gap, 627, 630–634
Staple merchandise, 379
Staple merchandise buying systems, 404–408
Status differences, 299
Stock incentives, 293
Stock keeping unit (SKU), 38, 369
Stock-to-sales ratio, 412, 413
Stockholders' equity, 200
Stocklift, 465
Store atmosphere, 521
Store brands, 156, 436
Store design, 588–591
Store employees. *See* Managing the store
Store layout, 591–598
Store-level forecasting, 386–388
Store loyalty, 110
Store maintenance, 577
Store management
    career opportunities, 26
    customer service, 618–645
    managing the store, 550–584
    store layout/visual merchandising, 586–617
Store manager, 286
Store morale, 566
Store structure, 586–617
    atmospherics, 609–614
    color, 612–613
    fixtures, 608–609
    in-store kiosks, 604–605
    lighting, 611–612
    location of departments, 599–602
    location of merchandise within departments, 602–603
    merchandise presentation techniques, 605–609
    music, 613
    planograms, 602–604
    scent, 613–614
    signs, 610–611
    space planning, 598–605
    store design, 588–591
    store layout, 591–598
    visual communications, 610–611

Store visits, 291–292
Store within a store, 233
Stores, 81–82
Stores division, 286
Straight commission, 572–573
Straight rack, 608, 609
Straight salary compensation, 572
Strategic alliance, 167
Strategic decision areas, 20–21
Strategic profit model, 186–188, 200–202, 206–207
Strategic profit model (SPM) ratios, 202
Strategic relationship, 458–462
Strategic retail planning process, 167–177
    competitive factors, 170–172
    environment factors, 172–173
    market factors, 169–170
    step 1 (business mission), 168–169
    step 2 (situation audit), 169–174
    step 3 (identify opportunities), 174
    step 4 (evaluate opportunities), 174–175
    step 5 (specific objectives/resource allocation), 175
    step 6 (retail mix to implement strategy), 175
    step 7 (evaluate performance/make adjustments), 175–176
    steps in process, 168
    strengths and weaknesses analysis, 173–174
Strengths and weaknesses analysis, 173–174
Strip centers, 218, 219, 234
Strip shopping centers, 218–220
Strivers, 133
Strugglers, 133
Subculture theory, 141
Subcultures, 126
Supercenters, 43, 44
Supermarkets, 42, 110
Superregional center, 223
Superstores, 42
Supply chain management, 310–313. *See also* Information systems/supply chain management

Sustainable competitive advantage, 148, 151–158
    customer loyalty, 151–155
    customer service, 157
    distribution/information systems, 156
    human resource management, 156
    location, 155–156
    loyalty programs, 154–155
    positioning, 152–154
    strategic opportunities, 162
    unique merchandise, 156–157
    vendor relations, 157

T
Target market, 148
Tariff, 443
Task performance behaviors, 563
Taxes on Internet sales, 500
Teen trend, 141
Television advertising, 543–544
Television home shopping, 60–61
Terms of occupancy, 239–240
Terms of purchase, 470–474
Territorial arrangements, 469
Tertiary zone, 253
Theatrical effects, 611
Theme/festival centers, 226–227
Theories of retail evolution. *See* Retail evolution
Third-party logistics companies, 329–330
Thriving immigrants, 262
Ticketing and marking, 322
Toilet paper, 379
Tonnage merchandising, 607–608
Top-down planning, 207
Top-of-mind awareness, 516
Top one percent, 262
Total expenses/net sales ratio, 192, 204
Track sheet, 602
Trackers, 602
Trade area, 252–255
Trade barriers, 443
Trade discounts, 470–471, 506
Trade publications, 30–31
Trade shows, 451–452
Trademark, 466
Trademark Counterfeiting Act, 466
Traditional distribution center, 321

Traditional strip centers, 219
Traffic appliances, 492
Traffic flow, 248, 249
Training, 297–298
Transformational leaders, 564
Transora, 450
Transportation, 320–321,
    325–330, 474
Trend spotting, 377
Trends in retailing, 34–36
Trialability, 142
Trickle-down theory, 140
Trust, 459
Turnover path, 194–200
TV advertising, 543–544
TV home shopping, 60–61
Tween shoppers, 125
Tying contract, 469
Type of merchandise, 37
Types of retailers
    big-box food retailers, 42–45
    catalog retailing, 58–59
    category specialist, 50–53
    convenience stores, 45, 46
    department stores, 53–54
    direct selling, 60
    discount stores, 48
    drug stores, 54–55
    e-tailing, 57–58
    food retailers, 41–47
    general merchandise retailers,
        47–57
    nonstore retail formats, 57–62
    off-price retailers, 55–56
    services retailing, 62–66
    specialty stores, 48–50
    supermarkets, 42
    TV home shopping, 60–61
    value retailers, 56–57
    vending machine retailing,
        61–62

U
Undercover security people, 581
Understored trade area, 247
Unique merchandise, 156–157
U.S. distribution system, 13
Unpaid impersonal communications,
    522–523
Unpaid personal
    communications, 523
Unprofitable customers, 354–355
Unrelated diversification, 161
UPC code, 319

V
VALS2, 131–133
Value, 477
Value and Lifestyle Survey (VALS2),
    131–133
Value retailers, 56–57
Variable cost, 490
Variable pricing, 498–499
Variety, 17, 38–39, 390, 392
Vending machine retailing, 61–62
Vendor evaluation, 423–424
Vendor negotiations, 452–458
Vendor relations, 157
Vendor-retailer relationship,
    447–462
    antitrust concerns, 465–470
    connecting with vendors, 447–452
    contract disputes, 464
    legal/ethical issues, 464–470
    negotiating with vendors, 452–458
    strategic relationships, 458–462
Vertical integration, 7, 161
Vertical merchandising, 607
Vertical price-fixing, 508–509
Vice president/GMM, 283
Virtual communities, 87
Visibility, 249
Visual communications, 610–611

W
Want book, 385
Warehouse club, 44–45
Warehousing, 330
Wealthy seaboard suburbs, 262
Website (retailer's), 521, 544
Website design, 597
Weekly draw, 573–574
Weeks of supply, 412
West Edmonton Mall (Canada),
    223, 224
Wheel of retailing, 72–74
Wholesale clubs, 236
Wholesale market centers, 451
Wholesale-sponsored voluntary
    cooperative group, 67
Women, 29
    glass ceiling, 302
    prices, 507
    sexual harassment, 303–304,
        566–567
Women's apparel, 150
Word of mouth, 523
World Trade Organization
    (WTO), 443
WorldWide Retail Exchange, 389
WTO, 443

Y
Yellow Pages, 545

Z
Zone pricing, 498
Zoning, 241